FROMMER'S

ITALY

DARWIN PORTER

Assisted by
**Danforth Prince
and Margaret Foresman**

1990

Published by Prentice Hall Trade Division
A Division of Simon & Schuster Inc.
15 Columbus Circle
New York, NY 10023

ISBN 0-13-217357-3
ISSN 1044-2170

Manufactured in the United States of America

*Although every effort was made to ensure the accuracy
of price information appearing in this book,
it should be kept in mind that prices
can and do fluctuate in the course of time.*

CONTENTS

MAPS

FROMMER'S ITALY

1. THE REASON WHY
2. FROMMER'S DOLLARWISE TRAVEL CLUB—HOW TO SAVE MONEY ON ALL YOUR TRAVELS

The subject of this book is Italy. Admittedly, trying to cram that country between the covers of any book—regardless of size—is really an almost impossible task. But, having assumed that its readers will be average visitors with less than a lifetime to spend exploring one nation, I've tried to sample the finest of Italy in a reasonable number of pages.

The "finest" in this sense is interpreted to include not only cities and attractions, but hotels, restaurants, shops, and nightspots as well. Part of the theme of this book is based on the belief that the finest need not be the most expensive. Hence, my ultimate aim—beyond that of familiarizing you with offerings of the boot of Europe—is to stretch your dollar power . . . to reveal to you that you need not always pay scalpers' prices for charm, comfort, and gourmet-level food.

1. The Reason Why

In this guide, I'll devote a great deal of attention to those old tourist meccas, Rome, Florence, and Venice, with both their main and hidden treasures. But those ancient cities are not the full "reason why" of this book. Important as they are, they simply do not fully reflect the widely diverse and complicated country that is Italy.

To seek out the wonders of this often-perplexing land, you must also go to Naples, Sicily, the Dolomites, the Lake District, the Piedmont section, Milan, the Riviera, the Adriatic, and that galaxy of inland art cities—Siena, Pisa, Vicenza, Brescia, Bergamo, to name only a few.

I think I'm fairly safe in saying that no country in Europe was designed—per square foot—to captivate pilgrims as much as Italy was. It was in the grand tour business when the Americans were still using smoke signals as their only means of cross-country communication.

ABOUT THIS BOOK

In brief, this is a guidebook giving specific, practical details (including prices) about Italy's hotels, restaurants, sight-seeing attractions, and nightlife. Establishments in *all* price ranges have been documented and described, from the extravagant chambers of the Grand Hotel in Rome to a clean but basic pensione in Florence which offers a homey environment, where you'll experience the family life of a professor of art in that city.

In all cases, establishments have been judged by the strict yardstick of value. If they "measure up," they were included in this book—regardless of price classification. The uniqueness of the book, I think, lies in the fact that it could be used by a society matron ("we always stay at the Hassler") or a free-wheeling, lira-lean collegian ("there's this great restaurant in Bologna that'll serve you a big spread real cheap").

But the major focus of the book is not centered either on the impecunious whose sole resources jingle in their pockets or the affluent whose gold rests in numbered accounts in Zurich. Rather, my chief concern is the average, middle-income-bracket voyager who'd like to patronize the almost wholly undocumented establishments of Italy—that is, the second-class hotels and the two-fork restaurants.

Frommer guides attempt to lead readers through the maze of major sights, such as the Colosseum in Rome; then introduce them to a number of more esoteric locales, such as the macabre catacombs at Palermo. Most important, the hours of operation and the prices of admission of these attractions have been detailed.

All these specifics are presented against a backdrop of history and culture that has spanned centuries, from the mysterious Etruscans to the baroque "skies of Tiepolo" to the present-day Romans as depicted by novelist Alberto Moravia ("Signora Cecilia was very like some kind of exotic bird with a tiny body and an enormous, fantastic head").

A proper balance has been struck, I think, between serious sightseeing in the Renaissance art cities and fun-time resorts—holiday centers stretching from Rimini on the Adriatic, to Portofino on the Riviera, to the rocky cliffs of Sorrento.

---

2. Frommer's™ Dollarwise® Travel Club—How to Save Money on All Your Travels

In this book we'll be looking at how to get your money's worth in Italy, but there is a "device" for saving money and determining value on *all* your trips. It's the popular, international Frommer's Dollarwise Travel Club, now in its 27th successful year of operation. The club was formed at the urging of numerous readers of the $-A-Day and Frommer Guides, who felt that such an organization could provide continuing travel information and a sense of community to value-minded travelers in all parts of the world. And so it does!

In keeping with the budget concept, the annual membership fee is low and is immediately exceeded by the value of your benefits. Upon receipt of $18 (U.S. residents), or $20 U.S. by check drawn on a U.S. bank or via international postal money order in U.S. funds (Canadian, Mexican, and other foreign residents) to cover one year's membership, we will send all new members the following items:

(1) Any *two* of the following books
Please designate in your letter which two you wish to receive:

Frommer™ $-A-Day® Guides
Europe on $40 a Day
Australia on $30 a Day
Eastern Europe on $25 a Day
England on $50 a Day
Greece on $30 a Day
Hawaii on $60 a Day
India on $25 a Day
Ireland on $30 a Day
Israel on $40 a Day
Mexico (plus Belize and Guatemala) on $30 a Day
New York on $60 a Day
New Zealand on $40 a Day

Scandinavia on $60 a Day
Scotland and Wales on $40 a Day
South America on $30 a Day
Spain and Morocco (plus the Canary Is.) on $40 a Day
Turkey on $30 a Day
Washington, D.C. & Historic Virginia on $40 a Day

($-A-Day Guides document hundreds of budget accommodations and facilities, helping you get the most for your travel dollars.)

Frommer Guides

Alaska
Austria and Hungary
Belgium, Holland & Luxembourg
Bermuda and The Bahamas
Brazil
California and Las Vegas
Canada
Caribbean
Egypt
England and Scotland
Florida
France
Germany
Italy
Japan and Hong Kong
Mid-Atlantic States
New England
New York State
Northwest
Portugal, Madeira, and the Azores
Skiing USA—East
Skiing USA—West
South Pacific
Southern Atlantic States
Southwest
Switzerland and Liechtenstein
Texas
USA

(Frommer Guides discuss accommodations and facilities in all price ranges, with emphasis on the medium-priced.)

Frommer Touring Guides

Australia
Egypt
Florence
London
Paris
Thailand
Venice

(These new, color-illustrated guides include walking tours, cultural and historic sites, and other vital travel information.)

Gault Millau

Chicago
France
Italy

Los Angeles
New England
New York
San Francisco
Washington, D.C.
(Irreverent, savvy, and comprehensive, each of these renowned guides candidly reviews over 1,000 restaurants, hotels, shops, nightspots, museums, and sights.)

Serious Shopper's Guides
Italy
London
Los Angeles
Paris
(Practical and comprehensive, each of these handsomely illustrated guides lists hundreds of stores, selling everything from antiques to wine, conveniently organized alphabetically by category.)

A Shopper's Guide to the Caribbean
(Two experienced Caribbean hands guide you through this shopper's paradise, offering witty insights and helpful tips on the wares and emporia of over 25 islands.)

Beat the High Cost of Travel
(This practical guide details how to save money on absolutely all travel items—accommodations, transportation, dining, sightseeing, shopping, taxes, and more. Includes special budget information for seniors, students, singles, and families.)

Bed & Breakfast—North America
(This guide contains a directory of over 150 organizations that offer bed & breakfast referrals and reservations throughout North America. The scenic attractions, and major schools and universities near the homes of each are also listed.)

Frommer's Belgium
(Arthur Frommer unlocks the treasures of a country overlooked by most travelers to Europe. Discover the medieval charm, modern sophistication, and natural beauty of this quintessentially European country.)

California with Kids
(A must for parents traveling in California, providing key information on selecting the best accommodations, restaurants, and sightseeing attractions for the particular needs of the family, whether the kids are toddlers, school-age, preteens, or teens.)

Caribbean Hideaways
(Ian Keown describes the most alluring places to stay, rating each establishment on romantic ambience, food, sports opportunities, and price.)

Frommer's Cruises
(This complete guide covers all the basics of cruising and describes in detail over 60 or so ships cruising the waters of Alaska, the Caribbean, Mexico, Hawaii, Panama, Canada, and the United States.)

Frommer's Skiing Europe
(Describes top ski resorts in Austria, France, Italy, and Switzerland. Illustrated with maps of each resort area. Includes supplement on Argentinian resorts.)

Guide to Honeymoon Destinations
(A special guide for that most romantic trip of your life, with full details of planning and choosing the destination that will be just right in the U.S. [California, New Eng-

land, Hawaii, Florida, New York, South Carolina, etc.], Canada, Mexico, and the Caribbean.)

Marilyn Wood's Wonderful Weekends
(This very selective guide covers the best mini-vacation destinations within a 200-mile radius of New York City. It describes special country inns and other accommodations, restaurants, picnic spots, sights, and activities—all the information needed for a two- or three-day stay.)

Manhattan's Outdoor Sculpture
(A total guide, fully illustrated with black and white photos, to more than 300 sculptures and monuments that grace Manhattan's plazas, parks, and other public spaces.)

Motorist's Phrase Book
(A practical phrase book in French, German, and Spanish designed specifically for the English-speaking motorist touring abroad.)

Paris Rendez-Vous
(An amusing and *au courant* guide to the best meeting places in Paris, organized for hour-to-hour use: from power breakfasts and fun brunches, through tea at four or cocktails at five, to romantic dinners and dancing 'til dawn.)

Swap and Go—Home Exchanging Made Easy
(Two veteran home exchangers explain in detail all the money-saving benefits of a home exchange, and then describe precisely how to do it. Also includes information on home rentals and many tips on low-cost travel.)

The Candy Apple: New York with Kids
(A spirited guide to the wonders of the Big Apple by a savvy New York grandmother with a kid's-eye view to fun. Indispensable for visitors and residents alike.)

The New World of Travel
(From America's #1 travel expert, Arthur Frommer, an annual sourcebook with the hottest news and latest trends that's guaranteed to change the way you travel—and save you hundreds of dollars. Jam-packed with alternative new modes of travel that will lead you to vacations that cater to the mind, the spirit, and a sense of thrift.)

Travel Diary and Record Book
(A 96-page diary for personal travel notes plus a section for such vital data as passport and traveler's check numbers, itinerary, postcard list, special people and places to visit, and a reference section with temperature and conversion charts, and world maps with distance zones.)

Where to Stay USA
(By the Council on International Educational Exchange, this extraordinary guide is the first to list accommodations in all 50 states that cost anywhere from $3 to $30 per night.)

(2) Any *one* of the Frommer City Guides
Amsterdam
Athens
Atlantic City and Cape May
Boston
Cancún, Cozumel, and the Yucatán

Dublin and Ireland
Hawaii
Las Vegas
Lisbon, Madrid, and Costa del Sol
London
Los Angeles
Mexico City and Acapulco
Minneapolis and St. Paul
Montréal and Québec City
New Orleans
New York
Orlando, Disney World, and EPCOT
Paris
Philadelphia
Rio
Rome
San Francisco
Santa Fe and Taos
Sydney
Washington, D.C.

(Pocket-size guides to hotels, restaurants, nightspots, and sightseeing attractions covering all price ranges.)

(3) A one-year subscription to *The Dollarwise® Traveler*

This quarterly eight-page tabloid newspaper keeps you up to date on fast-breaking developments in low-cost travel in all parts of the world bringing you the latest money-saving information—the kind of information you'd have to pay $25 a year to obtain elsewhere. This consumer-conscious publication also features columns of special interest to readers: **Hospitality Exchange** (members all over the world who are willing to provide hospitality to other members as they pass through their home cities); **Share-a-Trip** (offers and requests from members for travel companions who can share costs and help avoid the burdensome single supplement); and **Readers Ask . . . Readers Reply** (travel questions from members to which other members reply with authentic firsthand information).

(4) Your personal membership card

Membership entitles you to purchase through the club all Frommer publications for a third to a half off their regular retail prices during the term of your membership.

So why not join this hardy band of international budgeteers and participate in its exchange of travel information and hospitality? Simply send your name and address, together with your annual membership fee of $18 (U.S. residents) or $20 U.S. (Canadian, Mexican, and other foreign residents), by check drawn on a U.S. bank or via international postal money order in U.S. funds to: Frommer's Dollarwise Travel Club, Inc., 15 Columbus Circle, New York, NY 10023. And please remember to specify which *two* of the books in section (1) and which *one* in section (2) you wish to receive in your initial package of members' benefits. Or, if you prefer, use the order form at the end of the book.

Once you are a member, there is no obligation to buy additional books. No books will be mailed to you without your specific order.

GETTING TO AND AROUND ITALY

1. FLYING TO ITALY

2. TRAVELING WITHIN ITALY

3. THE GRAND TOUR OF ITALY

4. ALTERNATIVE AND SPECIAL-INTEREST TRAVEL

"**A**ll roads lead to Rome" in ways the emperors never dreamed of—by super-fast autostrada, ships, freighters, and last but certainly not least, by jet plane. In-deed, of all various ways of reaching Italy, the airplane comes off as the best . . . and for the U.S.-to-Italy run, the cheapest.

Getting to Italy is what this chapter is all about. In the first section I'll cover air travel to Italy. In the second section I'll discuss traveling within Italy—by air, train, rental car, etc.—and find the best ways to save lire.

1. Flying to Italy

Many carriers fly the popular route from North America to Italy, including Alitalia (the national carrier), Pan American, and Trans World Airlines. Rome and Milan, of course, have the busiest airports in Italy, receiving hundreds of daily flights from around the world and expediting dozens of takeoffs for domestic air flights within Italy (see Section 2, "Traveling Within Italy," which immediately follows).

In the lifetime of this edition, any actual fare I quote will surely change, proba-bly before we go to press. Most of the major airlines flying to Rome charge approxi-mately the same fare. In any event, if a price war should break out over the Atlantic (and industry sources hint that these are almost always brewing over the most popu-lar air routes), fares could change overnight, usually in the consumer's favor. Specific fares, of course, should be discussed with your travel agent when you eventually make your plans.

If seeking a budget fare is uppermost in your mind, the key to getting one is "advance booking"—a willingness to make your travel plans, and to purchase your tickets, as far ahead as possible. Moreover, since the number of seats allocated to low-cost "advance purchase" fares is severely limited (sometimes to less than 25% of the capacity of a particular plane), it will often be the early bird who obtains not the worm, but the low-cost seat, although this may not always be the case.

If your travel plans can possibly permit it, a large number of discounts are available for passengers who can travel either midweek or midwinter in either direction. Many travelers, depending on their interests, prefer the respite from the summertime crowds, and there's no reason why your itinerary couldn't begin and end, say, on a Tuesday instead of a weekend.

High season on most airlines' routes to Rome usually stretches from June 1 until September 15 (this could vary), and it is both the most expensive and most crowded time to travel. If your schedule will permit it, you should try to plan your departure for the low season, which falls into the period between September and May.

FARE OPTIONS

All the major carriers offer an **APEX ticket,** which is generally their cheapest way to fly over. Usually such a ticket must be purchased 21 days in advance and a stopover in Italy must last at least 7 days but not more than 90. Changing the date of departure from North America within 21 days of departure requires forfeiture of a $50 penalty. Many of the travelers who opt for this method of travel find that sticking to their predetermined dates doesn't present any real hardship.

Another attractive option is called the **excursion fare.** No advance purchase is necessary and an open return is possible, giving many travelers the amount of freedom they feel they need in choosing a return date once they arrive in Italy. It is, however, required that you wait for between 7 and 180 days before using the return half of your ticket. Several stopovers to other cities within Europe are usually allowed with this kind of ticket, for a reasonable surcharge.

Another option, which most casual visitors might want to avoid, is the **regular economy fare.** This offers the same seating and the same services as passengers using an excursion ticket, but is usually used by passengers who are obligated to return to North America before spending their obligatory seven days in Europe, the number required for an excursion ticket.

If comfort is your primary objective, you might want to avail yourself of the more luxurious services offered by all the major carriers. For example, in **business class** you often get seats as wide as in first-class seating. It is ideal for business travelers or long-legged passengers who prefer wide, roomy comfort, free drinks, and savory meals served on fine linen and china. The ultimate relaxing service, of course, is available in **first class,** where the extra-wide seats (which are limited to four across the entire width of the plane) convert into sleepers.

THE CHOICE OF AIRLINE

Since, as mentioned, the major carriers charge approximately the same fares, the choice of airlines often becomes one of scheduling or of particular likes and dislikes. If you live in or near New York City, it's relatively easy, as all the major carriers fly from there. From other parts of North America, connections can be more difficult. But that service has improved in recent years with the increased volume of traffic.

Many travelers prefer to immerse themselves in Italian ambience from the moment they board their aircraft in North America. The best way to do that is with the national airline of Italy, **Alitalia,** whose red, white, and green 747s and DC-10s reflect the colors of the Italian flag. From New York, Alitalia operates at least one nonstop daily flight to Rome and one nonstop daily flight to Milan every day of the year. In summer, planes leave New York twice a week for Palermo as well, although a brief and carefully scheduled stop in Rome is necessary. Alitalia also flies three to four times a week nonstop between Chicago, Los Angeles, Toronto, and Montréal to Milan on aircraft that then, after a brief stopover, continue to Rome. In summer the company flies nonstop twice weekly from Boston to Milan, with service on to Rome.

Alitalia's transatlantic price structure is similar to fares charged on competitive carriers. Currently, the round-trip high-season Super APEX fare (which requires a 30-day advance purchase and a sojourn abroad of between 6 and 21 days) from New York to Rome is $840. Passengers who opt for the slightly more lenient strictures of the regular APEX ticket (which requires a 21-day advance purchase and a stay abroad of between 7 days and 3 months) pay high-season fares of $916 round trip. Naturally, passage in low season is less expensive.

For example, many visitors find the melancholy charm of midwinter Venice to be its most alluring season. In 1989 Alitalia began orchestrated transfers through Milan or Rome to Venice, where waiting time is reduced to a minimum. Although called "Winter in Italy," the seasons when attractively reduced rates are offered extend through to mid-April, making spring in Italy more affordable than ever. If certain restrictions are met, the round-trip passage to Venice from New York costs $599 per person; from Chicago, $699; and from Los Angeles (truly a bargain), $778.

Alitalia's fares are hotly contested by its two competitors, TWA and Pan Am. **TWA** offers high-season daily flights from its hub in New York to both Rome and Milan. In low season, several of these flights might be combined, taking passengers first to one, then another of the cities. Restrictions and fares are roughly comparable to those on Alitalia. Currently, the least-expensive high-season rate (*warning:* these seats are extremely limited in number, so early planning is important) is $890 round trip from New York to either Rome or Milan if passage occurs in both directions on a weekend. Passage in both directions between Monday and Thursday merits a $50 discount. This ticket doesn't allow changes in the itinerary or flight date, requires a 30-day advance purchase, and a predesignated stay abroad of around 2 weeks. Low-season fares from New York and Rome are $564 midweek and $600 on weekends. Remember that there are many ironbound restrictions on these reduced fares.

Pan Am usually struggles to match prices offered. It offers frequent flights to both Rome and Milan from New York's JFK. Residents of such cities as Columbus, Ohio, or Salt Lake City, Utah, might prefer that their total transit occur on the same carrier, since transfers of luggage are difficult. Pan Am offers connections from many cities in North America through New York's JFK.

Each of the airlines mentioned maintains toll-free or local phone numbers that vary according to the region in which you live. Sometimes it's hard to get through to airline personnel directly, and you may prefer the services of a reputable travel agent instead.

CHARTER FLIGHTS

To many travelers, the convenience, flexibility, and dependability provided by scheduled airlines outweigh the cost advantages of charter travel. In recent years, however, there have been changes in the charter concept that may make charter travel more attractive to you. Today many charter flights are offered in conjunction with economical land packages featuring hotel accommodations and tours to popular tourist attractions. Most such packages also include car rentals or railpasses for land transportation. Some charter specialists are **Council Travel,** a division of the Council on International Educational Exchange (CIEE), 205 E. 42nd St., 16th floor, New York, NY 10017 (tel. 212/661-1450); **LTU,** 10 E. 40th St., Suite 3705, New York, NY 10016 (tel. 212/532-0207, or toll free 800/888-0200); and **Access International,** 250 W. 57th St., Suite 511, New York, NY 10107 (tel. 212/333-7280, or toll free 800/825-3633). For additional assistance, check with a travel agent.

FLYING TO ITALY FROM EUROPE

If you're already in Europe, visiting some other capitals such as Paris and London, and then planning to fly on to Rome, you will have relatively little problem making airline connections. Both Rome and Milan are considered lucrative and essential destinations by the dozens of European carriers that service them. For example, Alitalia flies to all the major capitals of Europe, and all the national carriers of the various countries (such as Air France, British Airways, and Lufthansa) fly to Rome or

The only problem is it's expensive to book these fares once you're in Europe... better to have Rome or Milan written into your ticket when you book your ...o Europe from North America. You'll save a lot of money that way.

---

2. Traveling Within Italy

ALITALIA AND ATI DOMESTIC SERVICE

Italy's domestic air network is one of the largest and most complete in Europe. There are some 40 airports serviced regularly from Rome, and most flights are under an hour. Fares vary, but all can be lowered if you are able to take advantage of these discounts: 2 to 12 years old, 50% off on all flights; 12 to 22 years old, 30% off. Everyone else has the option of a 30% reduction by taking domestic flights that depart at night.

CRUISING IN ITALIAN WATERS

Some of Italy's most seasoned travelers recognize that traffic snarls and road congestion often detract from the country's glamour. An obvious answer to this dilemma is a tour of Italy by a mode of transportation that centuries ago made the Mediterranean the cradle of civilization—sea travel. There are several reputable companies plying the touristic waters for business, but the one offering one of the most attractive options is **Ocean Cruise Lines,** 1510 SE 17th St., Fort Lauderdale, FL 33316.

Its Bahamian-registered ocean liner, the *Ocean Islander,* advertises itself as almost an enlarged version of a private yacht. With berths for only 250 passengers (considered intimate by most cruise-ship standards), it is capable of berthing in shallow waters, close to the action of harbor life, where larger vessels cannot go.

Between May and September, the company offers a seven-day transit between Nice, on France's Riviera, and Venice, with stopovers at seven Italian, Greek, and Yugoslav ports in between. The stress of the tour is on observation and immersion in a foreign culture rather than in the predictable array of shipborne activities. Amazingly, the seven-day per-person price, based on double occupancy, with meals and port taxes included, begins at a reasonable $1,145. That is conceivably less than you might have paid for meals, hotels, and transits had you purchased each of the components separately.

For reservations and more information, call toll free in the U.S. 800/556-8850 (800/528-8500 in Florida).

THOMAS COOK'S EUROPEAN RAILROAD TIMETABLE

If you plan to travel heavily on the European and/or British railroads, you will do well to secure the latest copy of the Thomas Cook European Timetable of Railroads. This comprehensive, 500-plus-page timetable details all of Europe's mainline passenger rail services with detail and accuracy. It is available exclusively in North America from **Forsyth Travel Library,** P.O. Box 2975, Shawnee Mission, KS 66201 (tel. toll free 800/FORSYTH), at a cost of $16.95 plus $3 postage priority mail.

EURAILPASS

Many travelers to Europe have for years been taking advantage of one of its greatest travel bargains, the Eurailpass, which permits unlimited first-class rail travel in any country in Western Europe except the British Isles, and also includes Hungary in Eastern Europe. Passes are purchased for periods as short as 15 days or as long as three months.

Here's how it works: The pass is sold only in North America. Vacationers in Europe for 15 days can purchase a Eurailpass for $320; 21 days costs $398; a one-month pass costs $498; two months, $698; and three months, $860. Children under 4 travel free providing they don't occupy a seat (otherwise, they must pay half fare). Children under 12 pay half fare. If you're under 26, you can purchase a **Eurail Youthpass,** entitling you to unlimited second-class travel for one or two months, costing $360 and $470 respectively.

The advantages are tempting. No tickets, no supplements—simply show the pass to the ticket collector, then settle back to enjoy the scenery. Seat reservations are required on some trains. Many of the trains have couchettes (sleeping cars), for which an additional fee is charged. Obviously, the two- or three-month traveler gets the greatest economic advantages; the Eurailpass is ideal for such extensive trips. Passholders can visit all of Italy's major sights, from the Alps to Sicily, then end their vacation in Norway, for example.

Fourteen-day or one-month voyagers have to estimate rail distance before determining if such a pass is to their benefit. To obtain full advantage of the ticket for 15 days or one month, you'd have to spend a great deal of time on the train.

Eurailpass holders are entitled to considerable reductions on certain station buses and ferryboats. For example, you'll get a 10% or 15% reduction for bus trips from Venice to Florence or Rome to Naples. You'll get a 20% reduction on second-class accommodations from certain companies operating ferries between Naples and Palermo, or for crossings to Sardinia and Malta.

Travel agents in all towns, and railway agents in such major cities as New York, Montréal, Los Angeles, or Chicago, sell all these tickets. A Eurailpass is available at the North American offices of CIT Travel Service, the French National Railroads, the German Federal Railroads, and the Swiss Federal Railways.

Eurail Saverpass is a money-saving ticket offering discounted 15-day travel, but only if groups of three people travel constantly and continuously together between April and September, or if two people travel constantly and continuously together between October and March. The price of a Saverpass, valid all over Europe, good for first class only, is $230 for the 15 days.

Eurail Flexipass is a time-flexible ticket that gives travelers 9 days of rail travel that can be used either consecutively or otherwise in 16 countries within any one 21-day period. It costs $340 and assures 9 days of travel of your choice without the feeling you're losing travel days after you have validated your pass, if you elect to stay in one place a little longer.

B.T.L.C. ITALIAN TOURIST-SEASON TICKETS

These are recommendable if you wish to travel a great deal via train only within Italy. Available for first- or second-class travel, these tickets are purchasable in the United States and Canada at CIT offices and international airports, as well as at major train stations in the largest cities in Italy. They allow unlimited travel during the period in which the ticket is valid. They include trips by fast trains (*IC*) without payment of extra charges for both first- and second-class ticket holders, although second-class travelers on the Trans-European Express trains (T.E.E.) will have to pay an additional supplement. The period of validity begins within six months of the issue of the ticket, which must be stamped at stations where they are first used or by the ticket inspector on the train when crossing the Italian frontier. A passport and proof of residence outside Italy are required.

Adult second-class fares are $107 for 8 days, $130 for 15 days, $152 for 21 days, and $186 for 30 days. First-class travel for adults costs $169 for 8 days, $204 for 15 days, $245 for 21 days, and $295 for 30 days.

In addition, the **Kilometric Ticket** is sold, valid for two months on regular

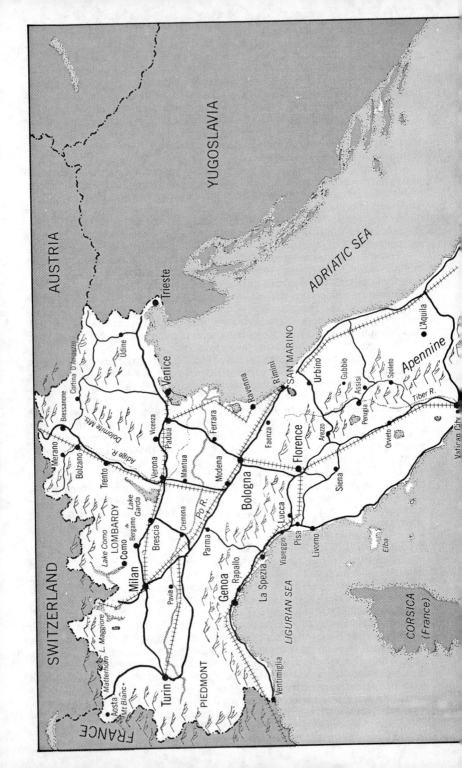

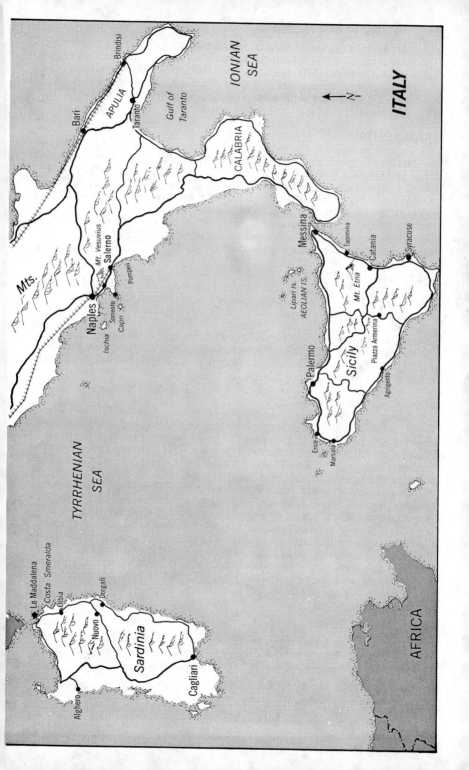

trains. However, it can also be used on special train rides if you pay a supplement. The ticket is valid for 20 trips, providing that your total mileage does not exceed 1,875 miles. The price is $207 in first class, dropping to $116 in second class.

For information about either the Tourist Ticket or the Kilometric Ticket, get in touch with **CIT Italian State Railways,** 666 Fifth Ave., New York, NY 10103 (tel. 212/397-2667).

TRAINS IN ITALY

This can be a medium-priced means of transportation, even if you don't buy the Eurailpass or special Italian Railway tickets. A typical adult fare, *Diretto* between Rome and Florence, would be 31,600 lire ($24) in first class, dropping to 18,600 lire ($14.15) in second class. Between Florence and Venice, the charge is 25,700 lire ($19.55) in first class, 15,100 lire ($11.50) in second. The fare from Rome to Naples is 21,700 lire ($16.50) in first, 12,800 lire ($9.75) in second.

In a land where mamma and bambini are highly valued, families (minimum of four passengers) are granted reductions: adults up to 30%; children 4 to 14, half fare. A family of five or more will get 40% off for adults.

Classification of Trains

IC (Intercity) are fast trains running between main cities. On some IC trains, seats must be reserved in advance, and only first class is offered. **Direttissimo,** long-distance express trains, feature both classes. **Diretto-Express** trains also offer both classes. There is an IC train running nonstop round trip between Milan and Rome, offering first-class service only. Breakfast or dinner is included in the price.

Get in touch with **CIT Italian State Railways,** 666 Fifth Ave., New York, NY 10103 (tel. 212/397-2667). There are also offices in Chicago, Los Angeles, Montréal, and Toronto.

Special Discounts

Senior citizens traveling on Italy's rails get a break. A **Senior Citizen's Silver Card** (Cart ad'Argento) can be bought by women 60 and over and men 65 and over, allowing a 30% discount on the entire Italian rail network. The card can be purchased at any rail station or travel agency in Italy upon presentation of proper identification. Costing 10,000 lire ($7.60), it's good for one year (not valid on Friday, Saturday, and Sunday from late June to late August and during Christmas week).

In addition, **Inter-Rail Youth Pass** is a one-month train pass (second class) available to young people 23 years of age and under. Sold only in Europe, the pass permits the purchase of second-class rail tickets with a 50% reduction on all the railway lines of the country where the pass was issued and free unlimited use in second class of the entire railway network of all other countries that are members of Inter-Rail (some 30 countries belong). Discounts are also available on some of the other transportation services of member countries. In Italy, for example, discounts are granted on the maritime services of the Tirrenia Line. A passport or national identity card must be presented for identification. For around 350,000 lire ($266), you can travel for one month.

Warning

Many irate readers have complained about train service in Italy, finding the railroads dirty and unreliable with little regard for schedules. As you may have heard, strikes plague the country, and you never know as you board a train when it'll reach your destination.

CARS IN ITALY

U.S. driving licenses are valid in Italy if you're driving your own car (the license must be accompanied by a translation). If you're driving a rented car, you'll need an international driver's license. If you don't have an international driver's license, and are asked to produce one, the Automobile Club of Italy (ACI) will issue a declaration upon presentation of a U.S. license. The declaration is obtainable at any ACI frontier or provincial office.

The **ACI** (Automobile Club d'Italia) is the equivalent of the AAA (American Automobile Association). It has offices throughout Italy, including the head office, via Marsala 8, and via C. Colombo 261 in Rome; viale Amendola 36 in Florence; and via Ca' Marcello 67A in Venice.

In case of **car breakdown** and for any tourist information, foreign motorists can call 116 (nationwide telephone service). For **road information,** itineraries, and all sorts of travel assistance, call 06/4212 (ACI's information center). Both services operate 24 hours a day.

Insurance on all vehicles is compulsory in Italy. A *Carta Verde* or "green card" is valid for 15, 30, or 45 days and should be issued to cover your car before your trip to Italy. Beyond 45 days, you must have a regular Italian insurance policy.

Warning: Gasoline is expensive in Italy, as are autostrade tolls. Carry plenty of cash if you're going to do extensive motoring.

Gasoline discount coupons are part of a package of concessions offered to foreign motorists planning to tour Italy. Besides the gasoline coupons, the packages also offer free breakdown service, free motorway toll vouchers, and provision of a replacement car free for up to ten days if the package participant's car is under repair for at least 12 hours. The tourist packages containing these services are of four types, depending on the destination of your trip. They are: 1. Italia Package (Northern Italy); 2. Italia Centro Package (Central Italy); 3. Italia Sud Package (Southern Italy); and 4. Italia Sud Package (Far Southern Italy, Sicily, and Sardinia). The packages must be paid for in foreign currency and may be purchased only outside Italy, at the main European automobile and touring clubs, at the offices of the Italian Government Tourist Office (ENIT) in Europe, and at any ACI or ENIT terrestrial and maritime border offices. These packages are available only to tourists driving their own cars (diesel-fueled vehicles excluded) with a non-Italian registration.

The discounts on gasoline vary according to the type of the package purchased; for example, package one (Northern Italy) provides gasoline coupons worth 180,000 lire ($137), and the discount granted is 27,000 lire ($20.50). Package four (Far Southern Italy, Sicily, and Sardinia) provides gasoline coupons worth 540,000 lire ($410), the discount being 108,000 lire ($82). This information, valid at the time of writing, could change drastically during the lifetime of this edition.

CAR RENTALS

Many lovers of Italy say that the best way to see the country is by car, and I heartily agree with them. Many of the most charming landscapes—the same ones as seen by Leonardo da Vinci—lie away from the main cities, far away from the train stations. And for that, and for the sheer convenience that train travel will never match, you'll find that renting a car is usually the best way to travel if you plan to explore part of the country.

Renting a car is easy. All drivers in Italy must have nerves of steel, a valid driver's license, and a valid passport, and (in most cases) must be between the ages of 21 and 70. Drivers not in possession of a major credit card must pay a minimum deposit of the estimated cost of a rental in advance. The requirement of a cash deposit is waived upon presentation of a major credit card, a notation of which is kept until your eventual return of the vehicle.

All the major international car-rental companies are represented in Italy. For example, Hertz and Avis have kiosks in both Rome and Milan. In Rome the **Hertz** staff is found at via Sallustiana 28 (tel. 463-334), at the Termini station (tel. 474-0389), and at piazza di Spagna 38, c/o American Express (tel. 678-8201). **Avis** is at piazza Esquilino 1 (tel. 470-1216) and at the Termini station (tel. 470-1219).

Maggiore, home-based in Italy, is one of the largest of all the European car-rental companies, with branches and affiliated offices in some 14 countries. Maggiore offices are found in several places in Rome besides the airports, including piazza della Repubblica 57 (tel. 463-715) and at the Terminal Station (tel. 460-049).

I recently sampled the facilities of **Budget Rent a Car** during the course of the update of this guide. The company, which has 44 locations in Italy, is identified in Italy as "Italy by Car," as well as Budget. In Rome, cars can be picked up at each of the major airports and at an inner-city location at via Sistina 24B (tel. 461-905). Cars can also be picked up and dropped off at any of Budget's mainland branches at no extra charge.

If the cost is divided among two or more people, car rentals become a most economical means of touring. Many visitors find that the cheapest rates are priced with unlimited mileage on a weekly rate. To qualify for that, you must reserve your car through a Budget reservations clerk at least two business days before your arrival at the pickup point and keep the car for a minimum of at least five days. Other convenient rates are also available for walk-in clients.

One of the least expensive cars available is a peppy Fiat Panda, with manual transmission and a seating capacity of four people, plus their luggage. This model rents for about $175 per week in summer in high season and slightly less in winter. Mileage, of course, is included. A larger car, seating four or five people in comfort, is the famous Fiat Uno, whose bigger trunk and increased leg room please many North American clients. It costs around $210 per week, with additional days costing an extra $32 each. Automatic-shift cars are also available, and many models are equipped with air conditioning.

The longer in advance that you reserve a car, especially in high season, the more likely you'll be to get the model you want. Budget, like all other car-rental companies in Italy, is required to collect an additional 19% of the final charge as tax. They'll also give you an emergency road service number to call if at any time you should have an accident or a mechanical breakdown.

You can get more information about cars available through Budget by calling their toll-free number during extended business hours throughout the United States. Call toll free 800/472-3325 and ask for the international department.

---

3. The Grand Tour of Italy

I've set out below a tour of only major attractions for those visitors wishing to get the most out of Italy in the shortest possible time. For a list of what to see at these stopovers, refer to the sightseeing commentaries on each city, and for the mileages between cities refer to the mileage chart toward the end of this chapter.

TWO WEEKS—THE MAJOR CITIES

Most visitors fly into Rome or Milan. I've begun this tour in Rome, but it can be reversed if you fly into Milan instead. It takes in the four most visited (by North Americans) cities of Italy—Rome, Florence, Venice, and Milan—with some diversions along the way.

Days 1 to 4: Rome, Rome, and more Rome, and you can't begin to take it all in. The first day will be spent recuperating from jet lag and finding a hotel or else reaching your reserved room through Rome's traffic. The "must-see" sights are outlined in Chapter IV. If you're thinking you've allowed too much time for Rome, remember that it takes a whole day just to see a part of St. Peter's and the treasure-filled Vatican museums. Your final day might be spent visiting Tivoli and Hadrian's Villa in the environs.

Day 5: Drive north to Florence on the autostrada, veering east and inland (the road is marked) to either Assisi or Perugia, where you can spend the night. If there is time, try to visit both towns; otherwise, read the commentaries and make a choice.

Days 6 to 8: From Perugia, drive northwest toward the Tuscan capital, but spend most of the day exploring Siena before heading for Florence, where the average American stays three nights and two days. That will, of course, be shockingly little time to see some of the glories of the Renaissance, but it may be all the time you have.

Day 9: Drive on the autostrada toward Bologna, spending the night in the gastronomic center of Italy. If time is limited, skip a stopover in Bologna and drive directly to Venice.

Days 10 to 12: A minimum of three days is needed just to find your way around the narrow streets and waterways of this once-great maritime republic of the Adriatic. When you leave Venice, you will have seen only a fraction of its attractions in our limited time.

Day 13: Drive west to Verona, city of Romeo and Juliet, where you can spend a busy day sightseeing and can then stay overnight.

Day 14: Continue west to Milan where you may have just enough time to view the Duomo and *The Last Supper* of Leonardo da Vinci before winging your way back home the next day.

SOUTH TO NAPLES AND SICILY—11 DAYS

Leaving Rome and heading south on the autostrada, the wonders of Campagnia open up, as you explore once-buried Roman towns and ancient centers of Magna Graecia.

Days 1 and 2: If you leave Rome early enough, you can be in Naples for lunch and can spend the afternoon sightseeing. The next morning, I'd catch the hydrofoil to Capri and spend the day there, visiting the Blue Grotto and its many attractions, before returning to Naples for the night.

Days 3 and 4: Leave Naples in the morning, heading south to Sorrento or one of the other resorts along the Amalfi Drive, including Amalfi itself or, better yet, Positano. Spend the rest of the day enjoying one of these resorts and get to bed early so you'll be prepared for a strenuous day of sightseeing. Either on your own or via an organized tour, make the traditional visits to the two towns that Vesuvius destroyed, Herculaneum and Pompeii. If time remains in your day, you can even go up to Mount Vesuvius itself to see the crater from which came the violent eruption. Return to Sorrento or one of the other towns for the night.

Day 5: Head down the coast to Paestum to see its three Doric temples before returning to Naples in the early evening to board a boat for Palermo, the capital of Sicily. If you don't have time for Sicily, you can break the tour here, returning to Rome for your flight back home. If you're going on to Sicily, you'll spend the night aboard the boat in a rented cabin, arriving in Palermo in the early hours of morning.

Day 6: Spend the day in Palermo, exploring its monuments and museums, saving time to visit the Church of Monreale in the hills. Overnight in Palermo.

Day 7: Drive west from Palermo, stopping over in either Erice, Trapani, or Marsala for lunch. However, don't linger too long in any place, as your major goal should be the ruins of Selinunte on the southern coast. Arrive in Agrigento for an overnight stop and drive through the "Valley of the Temples" at night (the ruins are floodlit).

Day 8: Leave Agrigento in the morning and drive east to Syracuse where you can spend the rest of the day sightseeing, overnighting there.

Day 9: Leave Syracuse in the morning, driving north to Catania where you can also spend the night, perhaps taking a Jeep tour to Mount Etna in the afternoon unless this active volcano is acting up.

Day 10: The best for last—Taormina, the finest resort in Sicily where you'll want to wind down for at least a night before contemplating the trek back to the mainland.

Day 11: Spend this day getting back to Rome. From Taormina, drive to Messina, which has ferryboat connections to the mainland. Once there, you can get on the autostrada and drive straight to Rome, stopping on the autostrada for lunch. You can arrive in Rome in time to check into a hotel and prepare to fly home the following day.

ESCORTED TOURS

Is this the year for your trip to Italy? Or has the fluctuating currency made you afraid that if you go, you might have to stay in undesirable hotels and search long and hard for inexpensive eating places in order to see the things you want to in this and other European countries?

Don't despair. With the declining dollar value and rising prices for Americans in Europe, one of the few ways to go first class is to take an escorted tour. It's still possible to make an affordable trip to see the highlights of Italy, perhaps in conjunction with travel in other countries, staying in first-class or even deluxe hotels, dining well, and visiting the outstanding attractions. With all the features provided by a good tour group, you can know ahead just what your visit will cost, and you won't be bothered with such matters as having to arrange your own transportation in places where language might be a problem, look after your own luggage, and face other requirements of travel that can make or break your enjoyment of a European journey.

Consult a good travel agent for the latest offerings.

---

4. Alternative and Special-Interest Travel

Mass tourism of the kind that has transported vast numbers of North Americans to the most obscure corners of the map has been a by-product of the affluence, technology, and democratization that only the last half of the 20th century was able to produce.

With the advent of the 1990s, and the changes they promise to bring, some of America's most respected travel visionaries have perceived a change in the needs of many of the world's most experienced (and sometimes jaded) travelers. There has emerged a demand for specialized travel experiences whose goals and objectives are clearly defined well in advance of an actual departure. There is also an increased demand for organizations that can provide like-minded companions to share and participate in increasingly esoteric travel plans.

Caveat: Under no circumstances is the inclusion of an organization in this section to be interpreted as a guarantee either of its credit worthiness or its competency. Information about the organizations coming up is presented only as a preliminary preview, to be followed by your own investigation should you be interested.

INTERNATIONAL UNDERSTANDING

About the only thing the following organizations have in common is reflected in that heading. They not only promote trips to increase international understanding, but they also often encourage and advocate what might be called "intelligent travel."

The Friendship Force, 575 South Tower, 1 CNN Center, Atlanta, GA 30303 (tel. 404/522-9490), is a nonprofit organization existing for the sole purpose of fostering and encouraging friendship among disparate people around the world. Dozens of branch offices lie throughout North America and arrange for en masse visits, usually once a year. Because of group bookings, the price of air transportation to the host country is usually less than what a volunteer would pay if he or she bought an APEX ticket individually. Each participant is required to spend two weeks in the host country (host countries are in Europe and also throughout the world). One stringent requirement is that a participant spend one full week in the home of a family as a guest. Most volunteers spend the second week traveling in the host country.

MILEAGE BETWEEN ITALY'S MAJOR CITIES
Distance in Miles

	Ancona	Bari	Bologna	Bolzano	Florence	Genoa	Milan	Naples	Palermo	Reggio Calabria	Rome	Turin	Trieste	Venice
Ancona		254	130	297	158	306	265	250	766	601	175	337	303	211
Bari	304		432	600	461	609	567	173	493	329	298	640	606	514
Bergamo	269	572	141	141	208	122	31	519	1034	869	386	120	233	151
Bologna	130	432		174	66	177	135	380	894	730	247	208	194	102
Bolzano	297	600	174		240	242	166	547	1061	897	421	255	203	133
Como	291	594	162	171	228	119	27	541	1156	892	407	104	267	185
Florence	158	460	66	240		166	202	326	839	675	181	258	260	169
Genoa	306	609	177	242	166		92	464	978	814	320	103	334	242
Naples	251	173	380	547	326	464	515		518	354	144	567	553	461
Padua	186	489	76	111	143	216	150	436	950	786	324	238	117	25
Palermo	766	493	894	1061	834	978	1029	518		164	658	1081	1068	976
Pisa	209	501	102	265	51	120	180	347	861	697	203	223	296	204
Ravenna	92	394	48	205	81	226	184	342	856	692	235	256	211	120
Rome	175	298	247	421	181	320	380	144	658	494		423	441	350
Siena	157	436	110	283	43	182	242	282	796	632	138	285	304	212
Syracuse	709	358	837	1004	782	921	972	461	203	107	601	1024	1011	919
Taormina	631	640	760	927	705	844	895	384	175	30	524	947	933	841
Turin	337	606	208	255	268	103	89	567	1081	917	423		347	264
Trieste	291	514	194	203	260	334	257	553	1068	903	441	347		102
Venice	211	514	102	133	169	242	175	461	976	812	350	264	102	
Verona	205	507	79	94	146	174	99	454	969	805	327	188	159	77

Servas (translated from the Esperanto, it means "to serve"), 11 John St., New York, NY 10038 (tel. 212/267-0252), is a nonprofit, nongovernment, international, interfaith network of travelers and hosts whose goal is to help build world peace, goodwill, and understanding. They do this by providing opportunities for deeper, more personal contacts among people of diverse cultural and political backgrounds. Servas travelers are invited to share living space with members of communities worldwide, normally staying without charge for visits lasting a maximum of two days. Visitors pay a $45 annual membership fee, fill out an application, and are interviewed for suitability by 1 of more than 200 Servas interviewers throughout the country. They then receive a Servas directory listing the names and addresses of Servas hosts who will allow (and encourage) visitors within their homes.

International Visitors Information Service, 733 15th St. NW, Suite 300, Washington, DC 20005 (tel. 202/783-6540). For $4.95 this organization will mail anyone a booklet listing opportunities for contact with local residents in foreign countries. Europe is heavily featured. For example, if you want to find lodgings with an Italian-speaking family whose members raise grapes and produce wine, this booklet will tell you how. Checks should be made out to Meridian House IVIS.

MEET THE ITALIANS

Italy doesn't have an established "Meet the Italians" program, but cities and most towns have an official tourist office (called either Ente Provinciale per il Turismo or Azienda Autonoma di Soffiorno e Turismo) which might arrange for you to stay with or just meet an Italian family. Such arrangements are usually made for persons staying for several weeks or more in an Italian city, not for brief visits. Requests for such attention should be sent several months before your trip to Italy by writing to the official tourist office of the town.

OPERA TOURS

On a cultural note, **Dailey-Thorp,** 315 W. 57th St., New York, NY 10019 (tel. 212/307-1555), in business since 1971, is probably the best-regarded organizer of music and opera tours operating in America. Because of its "favored" relations with European box offices, it's often able to purchase blocks of otherwise unavailable tickets to such events as the Salzburg Festival, the Vienna, Milan, Paris, and London operas, or the Bayreuth Festival in Germany. Tours range from 7 to 21 days and include first-class or deluxe accommodations and meals in top-rated European restaurants. Dailey-Thorp is also known for its breakthrough visits to operas in Eastern Europe and regional operas of Italy.

SENIOR CITIZEN VACATIONS

One of the most dynamic organizations of post-retirement studies for senior citizens is **Elderhostel,** 80 Boylston St., Boston, MA 02116 (tel. 617/426-7788), established in 1975. Elderhostel maintains an array of programs throughout Europe, including Italy. Most courses last for around three weeks, representing good value, considering that air fare, hotel accommodations in student dormitories or modest inns, all meals, and tuition are included. Courses involve no homework, are ungraded, and are especially interested in liberal arts. In no way is this to be considered a luxury vacation, but rather an academic fulfillment of a type never possible for senior citizens until several years ago. Participants must be more than 60 years of age. However, if a pair of members goes as a couple, only one member needs to be over 60. Anyone interested in participating in one of Elderhostel's programs should write for their free newsletter and a list of upcoming courses and destinations.

One company that has made a reputation exclusively because of its quality tours for senior citizens is **SAGA International Holidays,** 120 Boylston St., Boston, MA 02116 (tel. toll free 800/343-0273). Established in the 1950s as a sensitive and highly appealing outlet for aged (mature) tour participants, they prefer that joiners be at least 60 years of age or older. Insurance and air fare are included in the net price of any of their tours, all of which encompass dozens of locations in Europe and usually last for an average of 17 nights.

A TRAVEL COMPANION

A recent American census showed that 77 million Americans more than 15 years of age are single. However, the travel industry is far better geared for double occupancy of hotel rooms. One company that has made heroic efforts to match single travelers with like-minded companions is now the largest and best-listed company in the United States. Jens Jurgen, the German-born founder, charges $29 to $66 for a six-month listing in his well-publicized records. New applicants desiring a travel companion fill out a form stating their preferences and needs. They then receive a mini-listing of the kinds of potential partners who might be suitable for travel. Companions of the same or opposite sex can be requested. Because of the large number of listings, success is often a reality. For an application and more information, get in touch with Jens Jurgen, **Travel Companion,** P.O. Box P-833, Amityville, NY 11701 (tel. 516/454-0880).

LEARNING THE LANGUAGE

Courses for foreign students are available at several centers covering not only the Italian language and literature but also the country's history, geography, and fine arts. Among these are language courses in Florence at the **Università Centro di Cultura per Stranieri,** via Vittorio Emmanuel 64, 50134 Firenze; **Società Dante Alighieri, Centro Linguistico Italiano,** via de Bardi 12, 50125 Firenze; **Eurocentro,** piazza S. Spirito 9, 50125 Firenze; and **British Institute,** Palazzo Lanfredini, lungarno Guicciardini 9, 50125 Firenze. In Rome, language and literature centers are **Centro Linguistico Italiano,** via B. Marliano 4, 00162 Roma; and **Società Dante Alighieri,** piazza Firenze 27, 00186 Roma.

SETTLING INTO ITALY

1. THE ITALIANS
2. FOOD AND DRINK
3. ITALY FOR CHILDREN
4. THE ABCs OF ITALY

A knowledge of Europe can't begin to be complete without a familiarity with Italy, even for visitors who have only time for a quick overview of the country and its ancient cities, towns, and villages. The long, boot-shaped peninsula jutting out into the Mediterranean has scenery ranging from rugged mountains to fertile valleys to rich coastal plains. The country is topped in the north by snow-covered Alps, and the Appenine Mountains run the length of the boot like a rough spine.

The entire country, if it were cut up and pieced together to form a contiguous land mass, would be about the size of the state of Arizona. The actual formation, however, gives visitors the impression of a much larger area, and the ever-changing sea coast contributes to this feeling, while its large islands, Sicily and Sardinia, give it an even more varied outreach.

Four seas which are part of the Mediterranean bathe the shores of continental Italy. One is the Ligurian Sea, by the port of Genoa and the Italian Riviera on the northwest along the country's curving coast. Southward, still on the west side of the peninsula, is the Tyrrhenian Sea, between southern Italy and Sardinia. Little islands, such as Elba, of the Tuscan archipelago, and the magnificent Bay of Naples with Capri and the steep Sorrento promontory are in the Tyrrhenian coastal waters, which extend all the way to the northern shores of Sicily.

The Ionian Sea laps the east Sicilian coast and the toe, instep, and inner heel of the Italian boot. Dividing the back of the boot from Yugoslavia on the east is the Adriatic, the arm of the Mediterranean that was the highway of the ships which gave Venice, on its northern reaches, a rich and powerful place in history. Along the eastern shores of the Adriatic at the far north, Trieste and its harbor are the only Italian possessions.

Glaciers and volcanoes, together with swift rivers flowing from high in the Appenines and the Alps, have dictated the topography and through it much of the history of Italy. The country today is bordered on the northwest by France, on the north by Switzerland and Austria, and on the east by Yugoslavia—but mainly, it is a sea-girt land.

Two areas that are within the boundaries of Italy but are not under its government are the State of Vatican City and the Most Serene Republic of San Marino.

The 109 acres of Vatican City in Rome, previewed in Chapter IV, were established by a treaty signed by Mussolini in 1929, which also gave the Roman Catholic religion special status in the country. The pope is the sovereign of the State of Vatican City, which has its own legal system and its own post office.

San Marino, previewed in Chapter IX, is also totally surrounded by Italian land, occupying about 24 square miles of land in the Tuscan Apennines. It lies on the slopes and peak of Monte Titano (2,421 feet).

1. The Italians

HISTORY

The checkered past of the country now known as Italy forms a rich and often gory tapestry of history. Parts of the country were inhabited as far back as the Bronze Age, as attested by archeological finds on the mainland as well as in Sicily and Sardinia. The economy and cultures of early inhabitants were influenced by geography, and because of the distinct divisions of physical characteristics of the land, the people of various sections developed in different ways. Many people of Mediterranean stock were changed through communications in earliest times with civilizations across the Adriatic and then through trade with Greece and the Greek maritime colonies around Naples, the entire toe of the Italy boot, and most of Sicily. Also the stock was modified by immigration of people of alpine descent and invaders of Celtic and Teutonic extraction.

The Etruscans

Among early people of Italy, the most talented and the best leaders were the Etruscans—but who were they, actually? No one knows, and the many inscriptions they left behind—mostly on graves—are of no help, since the Etruscan language has never been deciphered by modern scholars. The date of their arrival on the east coast of Umbria has been figured as several centuries before Rome was built, which was around 800 B.C. The religious rites and architecture show an obvious contact with Mesopotamia, and it is thought that the Etruscans may have been refugees from Asia Minor, traveling westward about 1200–1000 B.C. The fact that they came from the Near East is further suggested by some 13th-century B.C. monuments whose inscriptions describe raids on the Nile delta by a warlike people called the "Turuscha." We know that they arrived in Italy in large numbers and within two centuries had subjugated Tuscany and Campania and the Villanova tribes who lived there. They forced the Latin tribes to work the land for them and support them as an aristocratic class of princes. Their sphere of influence eventually extended from south of Rome to as far north as the Arno River on the western side of the Appenines.

While the Etruscans built temples at Tarquinia and Caere (present-day Cerveteri), the few nervous Latin tribes who remained outside their sway consolidated power at Rome, which was then a village in a strategic position in the center of Campania and in command of the Tiber crossing where the ancient Salt Way (via Salaria) turned northeastward toward the Central Appenines. The Latins remained free of the Etruscans until about 600 B.C., thanks mainly to the presence of Greek colonies on the Italian coast, which tended to hold back Carthaginians (Phoenicians) on one side and Etruscans on the other. But the Etruscan advance was as inexorable as that of the later Roman Empire, and by 600 B.C. there was an Etruscan stronghold in the hills above Rome. The frightened tribes concentrated their forces at Rome for a last stand but were swept away by the sophisticated Mesopotamian conquerors. When the new overlords took charge, they not only introduced gold tableware and jewelry, bronze urns and terracotta statuary, and the best of Greek and Asia Minor art and culture, but they made Rome the government seat of all Latium. Roma is an Etruscan name, and the kings of Roma had Etruscan names: Numa, Ancus, Tarquinius, even Romulus.

Under the combined influences of the Greek and Mesopotamian east, Roma grew enormously. A new port was opened at Ostia. The artists from Greece carved statues of Roman gods looking like Greek divinities. The "Servian" army was established, and since soldiers had to provide their own horses and armor, the result was that the richest citizens carried the heaviest burden of protection. It is easy to see how this classification by wealth, which also affected voting and law-making, stemmed from a democratic concept of the army but led to an undemocratic concept of society.

The Roman Republic

Gauls from the alpine regions invaded the northern part of Etruscan territory around 600 B.C., and then the Romans revolted in about 510 B.C., toppling the rulers from their power bases and setting the southern boundary of Etruscan influence at the Tiber. Greeks from Sicily ended Etruscan sea power in 474 B.C. in the battle of Cumae off the coast just north of Naples. By 250 B.C. the Romans and their Campania allies had vanquished the Etruscans, wiping out their language and religion. However, manners and beliefs of the former rulers were respected and maintained by Rome, and Etruscan traces are still believed to exist in modern Tuscany.

Meanwhile, Greeks had been colonizing the Ionian coast and west Sicily from around 730 B.C., following the Greek city-state format and founding Naples and towns in southern Italy. Romans supported the Greeks against the Etruscans, Phoenicians from Carthage, and other warriors. The Sicilians of the time were an aboriginal Mediterranean people who were thought by the Greeks to be of Iberian stock, from Spain. The Phoenicians challenged the Greeks in Sicily and dominated the western part of the island from the latter part of the 6th century to the mid-3rd century B.C.

The Romans increased their powers through conquest of neighboring communities in the highlands and became allied with other Latins of the lowlands, easily becoming the dominant factor. They gave to their Latin allies and then to conquered peoples part or complete Roman citizenship, with the obligation of military service. Citizen colonies were set up as settlements of Roman farmers. Many of the famous cities of Italy today originated as colonies. Later, as seen in the history of Britain and the continent, colonies were established far outside Italy. The colonies were for the most part fortified, and they were linked to Rome by military roads.

The stern Roman republic was characterized by belief in the gods, learning from lessons of the past, strength of the family, education through books and public service, and most important, obedience. R.H. Barrow, in his book *The Romans,* points out that "through obedience comes power," and the Roman dedication to the ideal of a worthy life led to vast empire. The all-powerful Senate presided as Rome grew to become mistress of the Mediterranean, defeating rival powers one after the other. The Punic Wars with Carthage in the 3rd century B.C. cleared away a major obstacle to Rome's growth, although men were to say later that Rome's breaking of the treaty with Carthage (leading to total destruction of that city) put a curse on the Italian city.

The Roman Empire

By 49 B.C. Italy ruled the Mediterranean world either directly or indirectly, but the wealth and possible glory a person might find in Rome lured many there and drained Italian communities of manpower, at the same time that foreign imports, particularly in the field of agriculture, were hurting farmers and landowners. Municipal governments faltered, and civil wars ensued. Public order was restored by the Caesars (planned by Julius but brought to fruition under Augustus). By the time of the death of Julius Caesar, on the eve of the birth of Christ, Rome was a mighty empire whose general had brought the Western world under the sway of Roman law and civilization.

The emperors, whose succession started with Augustus's principate after the death of Julius Caesar, brought Rome to new, almost giddy heights. Augustus transformed the city from brick to marble—much the way Napoléon III transformed Paris centuries later. But success seemed to lead to corruption. What was established as the Roman Empire had been supposed to be a republic, but autocratic power and abuse by the emperors became the custom, and the colorful centuries of the emperors witnessed a steady decay in the ideals and traditions upon which the empire had been founded. The army became a fifth column of barbarian mercenaries; the tax collector became the scourge of the countryside; and for every good emperor (Augustus, Trajan, Vespasian, Hadrian, to name a few), there were three or four incredibly corrupt and debased heads of state (Caligula, Nero, Domitian, Caracalla, and more).

The Roman citizen in the capital either lived on the public dole and spent his days at gladiatorial games and imperial baths, or he was a disillusioned patrician at the mercy of emperors who might murder him for his property. The 3rd century A.D. saw so many emperors that it was common, as H. V. Morton tells us, to hear of the election of an emperor in the provinces together with a report on his assassination. The 4th-century A.D. reforms of Diocletian held the empire together, but at the expense of its inhabitants, who were reduced to tax units. He reinforced imperial power but paradoxically at the same time weakened Roman dominance and prestige by establishing administrative capitals of the empire at such outposts as Milan, Trier in Germany, and elsewhere, a practice followed by Constantine when he built his "New Rome," Constantinople. However, Constantine didn't have this stronghold merely as a subsidiary of the capital of the empire—he moved the administrative functions away from Rome altogether, the menace of possible barbarian attack having increased greatly.

With him to the new capital, Constantine took the best of the artisans, statesmen, and public figures of Rome.

The Empire Falls

The east and west sections of the Roman Empire split in A.D. 395, leaving Italy without the support it could formerly expect from east of the Adriatic. When the Goths moved toward Rome in the early 5th century, citizens in the provinces, who had grown to hate and fear the cruel bureaucracy that had been set up by Diocletian and followed by succeeding emperors, welcomed the invaders. And then the pillage began.

Rome was sacked by Alaric in 410, and after more than 40 troubled years, Attila the Hun laid siege to the once-powerful capital. He was followed in 455 by Gaiseric the Vandal, who engaged in a two-week spree of looting and destruction. The empire of the west lasted for only another 20 years; finally, the sacking and chaos ended it in A.D. 476, and Rome was left to the popes. The empire was terminated by Odovacar, a barbarian chief, who opened areas of Italy to Teutonic settlement. The fortified cities of the country were not much disturbed by this change in the fundamental basis of Italy's government.

Christianity, a new religion creating a new society, was probably founded in Rome around ten years after Christ's crucifixion. It gradually gained strength despite early persecution, moving through the stages of toleration and finally being accepted as the official religion of the empire. To recount the early struggles about and within the Roman Catholic church would be to embark on a mammoth endeavor which space here does not permit. However, by the end of the power of Rome in 476, the popes of Rome were under the nominal auspices of an exarch from Byzantium (Constantinople).

The Holy Roman Empire

After the fall of the Western Empire, the pope took on more and more of the powers of the emperor, although political unity had ended in Italy. Decades of rule by barbarians and then Goths were followed by power takeovers of various areas of the country by various strong warriors, such as Lombards, thus dividing Italy into several spheres of control. It was Pope Gregory II who renounced Rome's dependence on Constantinople in 731, thereby ending the twilight era of the Greek exarch who nominally ruled Rome in the name of the Emperor of Constantinople. Papal Rome turned forever toward Europe and in A.D. 800, a king of the barbarian Franks was crowned Holy Roman Emperor by Pope Leo III. The new emperor's name was Charlemagne. He pledged allegiance to the church and looked to Rome and the papacy as the final word in religious and cultural affairs.

The establishment of the new empire is called the end of the Dark Ages, but it ushered in long and bloody warfare. The Saracens took Sicily, which then was under Muslim control for 2½ centuries. Lombard leaders battled Franks. Magyars from Hungary invaded Lombardy and were in turn defeated by the Venetians. During all this embattled era, the aristocracy of Rome gained control of the papacy, and a series of questionably religious pontiffs let the power of the position become weak, with the selection of popes falling into the hands of the Holy Roman Emperor, a post which came to be filled by German leaders. Aggressive Normans with administrative ability took over control of Sicily in the 11th century, dividing it from Italy completely.

In the 11th century also, the popes shook off the control of the Roman aristocracy and pushed a reform movement in the church, which had the ultimate aim of organizing popes, bishops, and priests in a format modeled on the Roman Empire—a step which put the church on a collision course with the empire.

Rome in the Middle Ages was a quaint, rural town. Narrow lanes with overhanging buildings filled the Campus Martius. Great basilicas were built and embellished with golden-hued mosaics. The forums, stock exchanges, temples, and great theaters of the imperial era slowly collapsed. The decay of ancient Rome was given an assist by periodic earthquakes, centuries of neglect, and especially the growing need for building materials. For a while Rome had receded to provinciality in temporal matters, she was now the seat of the Catholic church, a priest state with constant need for new churches and convents.

The Renaissance

The story of Italy from the dawn of the Renaissance to the Age of Enlightenment in the 17th and 18th centuries is as varied and fascinating as that of the rise and fall of the empire. The papacy soon became essentially a feudal state, and the pope was a medieval (later Renaissance) prince engaged in many of the worldly activities that were to bring criticism upon the church in later centuries. The fall of the Holy Land to the Turks in 1065 catapulted the papacy into the forefront of world politics, primarily because of the Crusades, in which a major part was played by the pope. Until the 14th century, medieval power politics took its toll of the Holy Roman Empire. The turbulence and fighting between powerful families, especially in Rome, was climaxed by the removal of the papacy to Avignon. Until 1377, popes were "protected" in Avignon by the French monarchy from the street battles that raged between opposing Italian families.

The return of the papacy to Rome continued a succession of popes every bit as interesting as that of the Roman emperors. The great families—Barberini, Medici, Borgia—managed to enhance their status and fortunes impressively when a son was elected pope. The age of siege was not yet over either, and in 1527 the worst sack ever was carried out by Charles V. To the horror of Pope Clement VII (a Medici), the entire city was brutally pillaged by the man who was to be crowned Holy Roman Emperor the next year.

During the years of the Renaissance, the Reformation, and the Counter-Reformation, Rome underwent major physical changes. The old centers of culture reverted to pastures and fields, while great churches and palaces were built with the stones of ancient Rome. This building boom, in fact, did far more damage to the temples of the Caesars than did any barbarian sack. Rare marbles were stripped from the imperial baths and used as altarpieces or sent to lime kilns. So enthusiastic was the papal destruction of Imperial Rome that it's a miracle anything is left.

A United Italy

It was the 19th century that witnessed the final collapse of the Renaissance city-states, which had come into being at the end of the 13th century. These units, eventually coming under control of a *signore* (lord), were, in effect, regional states, with mercenary soldiers, civil rights, and assistance for their friendly neighbors. Some had attained formidable power under such signori as the Este family in Ferrara, the Medici in Florence, the Visconti and the Sforza families in Milan, and others. Although the hope, pushed by theocrats, of attaining one empire ruled by the pope and the church, had faded away in the early 14th century, there was still a fight followed by generations of hard feelings when the Papal States, a small principality under the temporal jurisdiction of the pope, were claimed as part of the new kingdom of Italy, which finally came into being in 1861.

There was long turmoil in Italy, through the various wars of succession in Europe, with Napoleon making his temporarily successful bid for power in the peninsular country. After the Congress of Vienna following Napoleon's defeat, dominance was divided in Italy: Austria was given Lombardy and Venetia, while the Papal States were given back to the pope from whom Napoleon's forces had wrestled them. Some duchies were put back in the hands of their own rulers, and southern Italy and Sicily went to a Bourbon dynasty. However, one good move, pointing to eventual unification of Italy, was the assigning of the former republic of Genoa to Sardinia, which was governed by the House of Savoy.

Political unrest continued—in fact, was augmented—during the uncertain state of affairs regarding the affairs of state. Finally, in 1861, the kingdom of Italy was proclaimed and Victor Emmanuel of the House of Savoy, King of Sardinia, was made head of the new kingdom. This did not signal unification of the country, however, since Rome was still under papal control and Venetia was held by Austria. Venetia came into the kingdom after the Seven Weeks' War between Austria and Prussia in 1866, and Rome became the capital of a new country in 1871. The Vatican, however, did not yield, despite guarantees proffered by the Italian government, and relations between the pope and the nation were not finally brought into harmony until 1927, when Mussolini signed a Concordat granting autonomy to Vatican City and making Roman Catholicism the official state religion, a designation which was removed through revision of the Concordat in 1978.

World Wars I and II, the rise of Fascism, and the fall of Mussolini and the Italian monarchy are all now history. The Italian republic was voted in 1946, and the House of Savoy no longer ruled. The political situation in the country today is marked by struggles for power among the leading political parties, and the future of Italy is, in a few words, up for grabs.

LANGUAGE

The official language of Italy, of course, is called Italian, a Romance tongue derived from Latin, although it bears little resemblance to the Latin you may have studied in school. The language spoken today also is based on the Tuscan dialect. Numerous forms of speech were common throughout parts of Italy until establishment of the dialect of Tuscany as the literary language of the country in the 14th century. This was a result of the spread of literary works by such great writers as Dante, Petrarch, and Boccaccio, who lived in the heart section of Italy, Tuscany. Other Latin-based dialects will be heard in various areas, such as a language called Ladin heard in Friuli-Venezia Giulia in the north and in some Dolomite regions. In Sardinia, many people still speak the ancient Romance language called Sardinian. In the Italian Tyrol, German is spoken, and French is the language in the Pennine alpine valley of Aosta.

THE PEOPLE

So far as the appearance of Italian people is concerned, it is impossible to say that one particular type is unquestionably Italian. Because of the geography of the country, which in the prehistoric and even historic eras often discouraged or prevented interaction from section to section of the land, there is often little similarity between one Italian native and another. This is evident when you meet a blond, blue-eyed northern Italian in company with a sloe-eyed, raven-haired native from another part of the country. However, there are persons from Mediterranean stock who are likely to be short of stature and dark of complexion, others who are from Iberian ancestry, hereditary legacies from Greeks, Teutonic races, and even from as far back as Carthaginians.

As the races mixed in various areas, so did the cultures, and you will find in Italy today, especially in rural sections, many interesting customs which have come down from the far reaches of time. Colorful costumes vary from village to village, and handcrafts are turned out as they were by ancestral families. In Sardinia, Sicily, and the interior mountain country of the mainland, shepherds wear the same kind of clothing, tend their flocks in the same way, and exhibit the same independence of spirit as did their forefathers. The custom of having large families and keeping in close touch with relatives still holds, especially in rural Italy.

I have always found the Italian people, whether in small or large towns, to be as friendly and helpful to visitors as the language barrier may allow. Smiles are acceptable in any language.

GOVERNMENT

A democratic government was established in Italy in 1948. The Italian Parliament is composed of the Chamber of Deputies and the Senate of the Republic. The Republic of Italy is divided into 20 regions comprising 94 provinces and more than 8,000 communes. The president of the Republic is elected by the members of both chambers of Parliament, who vote by secret ballot. The average foreign visitor who commits no infraction of the law will not come into contact or have trouble from the authorities (chances are). Italy is a rather free-wheeling land where restrictions are kept to a minimum.

Political parties in Italy are numerous, and party loyalty fluctuates, since it is difficult for any one group to round up sufficient votes for election victory without gathering support from other organizations. The Christian Democrats have been strongest for some time, but they are closely pursued by the Communists, Socialists, Liberals, and Social Democrats, among others.

LITERATURE

The Italian writer most familiar to readers today is probably Umberto Eco, whose fascinating novel, *The Name of the Rose*, was translated in 1983 from the writer's native tongue and became a runaway bestseller in the English version. Eco follows in the train of a long, long line of literary figures of note who use the Tuscan dialect-based Italian language to outstanding effect in literary output.

Since the institution of the Nobel Prize for Literature in 1901, five Italians have been recipients of the coveted prize: Giosuè Carducci, poet and professor of Italian literature at the University of Bologna, in 1906; Grazia Deledda, Sardinia-born writer who used her native island as the subject of her work, in 1926; Luigi Pirandello, Sicily-born dramatist, in 1934; Salvadore Quasimodo, a poet, also a native of Sicily, in 1959; and Eugenio Montale, poet, in 1975.

In the days of Rome's glory—shortly before and after the birth of Christ—mighty men of letters included Cicero, Julius Caesar, Virgil, Horace, Ovid, and Livy. When the thoughts of men turned heavenward, an inevitable trend when the Christian faith became accepted by the majority of the Romans and other Italians, Christian Latin literature became the order of the day. Such writers as St. Augustine, St. Ambrose, and St. Jerome gained repute for their writings and are remembered as among few voices heard during the Dark Ages.

Medieval Italian literature was represented by religious poetry (St. Francis of Assisi), secular lyric poetry (Provençal troubadour musical tributes), and sonnets as produced by the Sicilian school of verse.

Arguably the greatest period in Italian literature was ushered in in the 14th century, with world-acclaimed works that made the Tuscan dialect the literary language of Italy. Dante, Petrarch, Boccaccio—these immortals flourished in this era. The *Divine Comedy* by Dante is called the first masterpiece of the then modern national language. Petrarch is hailed as the forerunner of humanism, and scholars say that Boccaccio, best known for the *Decameron*, did for Italian prose what Dante did for its poetry.

The term "Renaissance man" is applied to those who excelled in many fields of endeavor in that era. Among these, shining examples are Michelangelo, who wrote sonnets in addition to all his other talents; Leonardo da Vinci, writer, inventor, artist, astronomer—whatever; and even Lorenzo de' Medici (Lorenzo the Magnificent), who is credited with establishing the Tuscan dialect as the national speech of Italy. Machiavelli in the 16th century, Goldoni of the 18th century, and D'Annunzio of the early 20th century, are other names to conjure with in connection with Italian literary achievement. I have mentioned a few. You perhaps have other names to remember in the long annals of literature of Rome and Italy.

ART AND ARCHITECTURE

The mysterious Etruscans brought the first impressive art and architecture to the mainland of Italy. Little remains of their architecture, but they built powerful walls, bridges, and aqueducts in Italy, which were similar to Mycenaean architecture. Many of the tombs they left behind can be explored today, especially those that can be visited on a day trip from Rome (see "Ring Around Rome" in Chapter IV). Most of their painting that has survived was discovered in tombs. Likewise, some of their finest sculpture has been discovered on their sarcophagi, many of these coffins now resting in museums. The best collection is at the National Museum of the Villa Giulia in Rome.

As Rome rose to power, it often used Etruscan artists and architects. But, in time, the Romans discovered Greek art and they fell in love with that country's statuary, looting much of it. In Rome, the Hellenistic tradition, launched so bravely in the East, continued in the West. It was in architecture, especially the development of the arch, that Rome was to succeed as monumental buildings were erected, including the Roman Forums, the Colosseum, Trajan's Forum (the greatest of all), the Baths of Caracalla, and the Pantheon, erected during the reign of Hadrian. Of course, it must be pointed out that these achievements on such an immense scale owed their existence to one major resource: slave labor.

The glory that was Rome eventually gave way to early Christian and Byzantine art. In the early Christian art, East met West. No longer concerned with the beauty of the human figure, these artists turned to the supernatural world for their inspiration. It was not an art of the people, but one that served either the court or the church. Churches were lavishly decorated with mosaics and colored marble. Painting concerned itself with the lives of martyrs and saints. Unlike the Etruscans, the Christians saw death as salvation.

The art in the centuries that followed the collapse of Rome became known as early medieval and Romanesque art. Romanesque art, in its many variations, flourished between A.D. 1000 and 1200. Supported by monasteries or churches, it was mainly ecclesiastical art. The motivation of most artists was to "serve God."

In the wake of Romanesque, the Gothic or late medieval period brought to Italy much activity in arts and architecture. The Italians interpreted Gothic in their own particular style, much different from the French. Again the Gothic age, in art and architecture, continued to be profoundly religious, although many secular buildings, such as palaces, were erected. Artists such as Cimabue blazed new trails, bringing emotional realism into his work in a complete break with the Byzantine tradition. The great Giotto removed Byzantium from his art and, by so doing, was a harbinger of the Renaissance.

The Italian Renaissance was born in Florence in the 15th century, where the powerful Medici family became great patrons of the arts. The Renaissance began with great artistic events: Ghiberti beat out Brunelleschi in a contest to design bronze doors for the Baptistery (now in the Duomo Museum). But Brunelleschi was commissioned to design a dome for the cathedral which became "a miracle of design." In Rome, Urbino-born Donato Bramante was to work with others on St. Peter's Basilica, the most significant building of the High Renaissance. (Venice during this period grew prosperous but differed from Florence in steadfastly adhering to Gothic features in architecture.)

Sculpture took on a renewed importance in the Renaissance and many great artists rose out of this period, including Michelangelo, who dazzled the world with his *Pietà* and *David*. Perhaps it was in painting, however, that the Renaissance excelled. Along with Michelangelo, another giant emerged from this period, Leonardo da Vinci, who is considered "the epitome of the Renaissance man," and who gave the world such works as *The Last Supper* and *Mona Lisa*. Urbino-born Raffaello Santi was the third giant of the Renaissance. He went to Rome where he was commissioned to fresco the apartments of Pope Julius II. Michelangelo, on the other hand, was working on the Sistine Chapel, which took four back-breaking years of his life to complete.

The period called the High Renaissance was said to last for only about a quarter of a century, beginning in the early 16th century. For two centuries Italy was the leader in Europe in artistic achievement. It was a great and heady time. The transitional period between the Renaissance and the baroque came to be called "Mannerism." Out of this period emerged such great artists as Tintoretto, whose major work was the cycle of frescoes for the Scuola di San Rocco in Venice (it took 23 years to finish), and Verona-born Paolo Veronese, and perhaps the most sensitive and some say the finest of the Mannerists, Parmigianino, who was born in Parma in 1503.

In the early 17th century and into the 18th century, the baroque (meaning absurd or irregular) movement swept Europe, including Italy. The art of the baroque movement was linked to the Counter-Reformation. Much in architecture was achieved during this period, as some of the great churches and palazzi of Italy testify to this day. Great artists were to emerge, including Bernini, who became renowned both as a sculptor and a painter, and Borromini, one of the great architects of his age. The two painters who best represented the movement were Carracci, who decorated the Roman palace of Cardinal Farnese, and Caravaggio, one of the pioneers of baroque painting. The even more flamboyant rococo grew out of the baroque style.

By the 19th century the great light had gone out of art in Italy, a beacon picked up by France. Neoclassicism swept across the land. The 20th century saw the rise of some major Italian artists whose works once again captured the imagination of the world: De Chirico and Modigliani (the latter's greatest work was in portraiture). The Bolognese painter of bottles and jugs, Morandi, also became known around the world. The greatest Italian sculptor of the 20th century was Medardo Rosso, who died in 1928, and the leading figure in Italian architecture was Pier Luigi Nervi, born in 1891 in Milan. He designed the Palazzo della Sport in Rome for the 1960 Olympics.

OPERA

Italy and opera are linked by marriage, and, in fact, many visitors come to Italy on specially arranged opera tours. Peri's *Dafne,* the first opera, opened in Florence in 1597. But it is Claudio Monteverdi, born in 1567, who is considered the father of modern opera. His masterpiece was *L'Incoronazione di Poppea* (1642). Starting simply in Florence, opera moved to Naples, having been brought there from Venice in the mid-1600s. Thus arose the *bel canto* (beautiful singing) method of the 18th century. Neapolitan opera spread around the world. *Opera buffa,* or comic opera, eventually came into its own with full-fledged comedies.

Just as it seemed opera might have exhausted itself at the end of the 18th century, along came Gioacchino Rossini, born in 1792. Best known for his sparkling, witty *The Barber of Seville,* he constructed brilliant crescendos to express great emotional power.

Romantic opera also came into flower, particularly in the works of Donizetti, best known for his *Lucia di Lammermoor,* which in a much later day was to bring Joan Sutherland fame at the Metropolitan Opera. Bellini's most famous operas are *Norma, I Puritani,* and *La Sonnambula.* Many of his works contain famous showpieces for coloratura sopranos. But it was Giuseppe Verdi, born in 1813, who was to become the greatest Italian operatic composer. In all, he produced 26 operas, which are widely performed today, including *Il Trovatore, La Traviata, Rigoletto,* and *Aïda.*

In 1858, the musical heir of Verdi was born. He was Giacomo Puccini, and he was to become the greatest Italian composer of operas of his day. Influenced by Wagner, his music was melodious and romantic, sometimes exotic, and he was to write such operas as *Madame Butterfly, La Bohème,* and *Tosca.* Caruso became a household name singing Puccini. But since Verdi and Puccini, no Italian composer has entered this exclusive pantheon of the musical greats.

The opera season in Italy begins in early December, lasting to mid-April.

---

2. Food and Drink

Many visitors from North America, at least first-time non-Italian ones, erroneously think of the Italian cuisine as limited. Of course, everybody's heard of minestrone, spaghetti, chicken cacciatore, and spumoni ice cream. But the chefs of Italy hardly confine themselves to such a limited repertoire. Incidentally, except in the south, Italians do not use as much garlic in their food as many foreigners seem to believe. Most Italian dishes, especially those in the north, are butter based. Spaghetti and meatballs, by the way, is not an Italian dish, although certain restaurants throughout the country have taken to serving it "for homesick Americans."

ITALIAN FOOD

Rome might be the best place to introduce yourself to the cookery of Italy, as it has specialty restaurants, representing all the culinary centers such as Bologna and Genoa. Throughout your Roman holiday, you'll encounter such savory viands as *zuppa di pesce* (a soup or stew of various fish, cooked in white wine and herb flavored), *cannelloni* (tube-shaped pasta baked with any number of stuffings), *riso col gamberi* (rice with shrimp, peas, and mushrooms, flavored with white wine and garlic), *scampi alla griglia* (grilled prawns, one of the best-tasting, albeit expensive, dishes in the city), *quaglie col risotto e tartufi* (quail with rice and truffles), *lepre alla cacciatore* (hare flavored with white wine and herbs), *zabaglione* (a cream made with sugar, egg yolks, and marsala), *gnocchi alla romana* (potato-flour dumplings with a sauce made with meat and covered with grated cheese), *abbacchio* (baby spring lamb, often roasted over an open fire), *saltimbocca alla romana* (literally "jump-in-your-mouth"—thin slices of veal with sage, ham, and cheese), *fritto alla romana* (a mixed fry that's likely to include everything from brains to artichokes), *carciofi alla romana* (tender artichokes cooked with such herbs as mint and garlic, and flavored with white wine), *fettuccine all'uovo* (egg noodles served with butter and cheese), *zuppa di cozze* (a hearty bowl of mussels cooked in broth), *fritti di scampi e calamaretti* (baby squid and prawns fast fried), *fragoline* (wild strawberries, in this case from the Alban Hills), and *finocchio* (a celery-like raw vegetable, the flavor of licorice, often eaten as a dessert).

From Rome, it's on to **Florence** and **Siena** where you'll encounter the hearty, rich cuisine of the Tuscan hills (for comments on that cuisine, refer to the introduction to the restaurant section of Chapter V).

The next major city to visit is **Venice,** where the cookery is typical of the Venetia district. It's been called "tasty, straightforward, and homely," by one long-ago food critic, and I concur. The most typical dish is *fegato alla veneziana* (liver and onions), as well as *risi e bisi* (rice and fresh peas). Seafood figures heavily in the Venetian diet, and grilled fish is often served with the bitter red radicchio, a lettuce which comes from Treviso.

In **Lombardy,** of which Milan is the center, the cookery is more refined and tasty, in my opinion. No dish here is more famous than *cotoletta alla milanese* (cutlets of tender veal, dipped in egg and breadcrumbs, and fried in olive oil until it's a golden brown). The Viennese called it wienerschnitzel. *Ossobuco* is the other great dish of Lombardy. This is cooked with the shinbone of veal in a ragoût sauce and served on a bed of rice and peas. *Risotto alla milanese* is also a classic Lombard dish. This is rice which can be dressed in almost any way, depending on the chef's imagination. It's often flavored with saffron and butter, to which chicken giblets have been added. It's always served, seemingly, with heaps of Parmesan cheese. *Polenta,* a cornmeal mush that is "more than mush," is the staff of life in some parts of northeast Italy and is eaten in lieu of pasta.

The cooking in **Piedmont,** of which Turin is the capital, and the Aosta Valley is different from the rest of Italy. Its victuals are said to appeal to strong-hearted men returning from a hard day's work in the mountains. You get such dishes as *bagna cauda,* which is a sauce made with olive oil, garlic, butter, and anchovies in which you dip uncooked fresh vegetables. *Fonduta* is celebrated: it's made with melted Fontina cheese, butter, milk, egg yolks, and, for an elegant touch, white truffles.

In the **Trentino–Alto Adige** area, whose chief towns are Bolzano, Merano, and Trent, the cooking is naturally influenced by the traditions of the Austrian and Germanic kitchens. South Tyrol, of course, used to belong to Austria. Here you get such tasty pastries as strudel.

Liguria, whose chief town is Genoa, turns to the sea for a great deal of its cuisine, as reflected by its version of bouillabaisse, a *buridda* flavored with spices. But its most famous food item is *pesto,* a sauce made with fresh basil, garlic, cheese, and walnuts. It not only dresses pasta or fish, but many dishes such as *gnocchi* (little dumplings).

Emilia-Romagna, with such towns as Modena, Parma, Bologna, Ravenna, and Ferrara, is one of the great gastronomic centers of Italy. Rich in produce, its school of cooking produces many notable pastas, which are now common around Italy. They include *tagliatelle, tortellini,* and *cappelletti* (larger than tortellini and made in the form of "little hats"). Tagliatelle, of course, are long strips of macaroni, and tortellini are little squares of dough that have been stuffed with chopped pork, veal, or whatever. Equally as popular is *lasagne,* which by now nearly everybody has heard of. In Bologna it's often made by adding finely shredded spinach to the dough. The best-known sausage of the area is *mortadella,* and, equally as famous, is a *cotoletta alla bolognese* (veal cutlet fried with a slice of ham or bacon). The distinctive and famous cheese, *parmigiana,* is a product of Parma and also Reggio Emilia. *Zampone* is a specialty of Modena (stuffed pig's foot).

Much of the cookery of **Naples**—spaghetti with clam sauce, pizzas, and so forth—is already familiar to North Americans because so many Neapolitans moved to the New World and opened restaurants there. *Mozzarella* or buffalo cheese is the classic cheese of this area. Mixed fish fries, done a golden brown, are a staple feature of nearly every table.

Sicily has a distinctive cuisine, with good strong flavors and aromatic sauces. For example, a staple of the diet is *maccheroni con le sarde* (spaghetti with pine seeds, fennel, spices, chopped sardines, and olive oil). Fish is good and fresh in Sicily (try swordfish). Among meat dishes, you'll see *involtini siciliani* on the menu (rolled meat with a stuffing of egg, ham, and cheese cooked in breadcrumbs). A *caponata* is a special way of cooking eggplant in a flavor-rich tomato sauce. The desserts and homemade pastries are excellent. The *cannoli* is a cylindrical pastry case stuffed with ricotta and candied fruit (often chocolate). Their ice creams, called *gelati,* are among the best in Italy.

Sardinia is a land unto itself. Game such as wild boar often appears on the Sardinian table, as does *porceddu* (roasted suckling pig prepared using methods a thousand years old). It's cooked in an open-air pit under myrtle branches. *Malloreddus* are little dumplings of corn flour flavored with saffron and served in a spicy sauce (everything sprinkled with goat cheese), and cassola is a highly spiced fish stew.

THE WINES OF ITALY

Italy is the largest wine-producing country in the world, and as far back as 800 B.C. the Etruscans were vintners. It is said that more soil in Italy is used for the cultivation of grapes than for food. Many Italian farmers produce wine just for their own consumption or for their relatives in a big city. However, it wasn't until 1965 that laws were enacted to guarantee regular consistency in winemaking. Wines regulated by the government are labeled DOC (*Denominazione di Origine Controllata*). If you see DOCG on a label (the "G" means *guarantita*), that means even better quality control.

Coming from the volcanic soil of Vesuvius, the wines of **Campania** (Naples) have been extolled for 2,000 years. Homer praised the glory of Falerno, straw yellow in color. With many seafood dishes, Neapolitans are fond of ordering a wine known as Lacrima Christi or "tears of Christ." It comes in amber, red, or pink. With meat dishes, the dark mulberry-colored Gragnano has a faint bouquet of faded violets. Also, the red and white wines of Ischia and Capri are justly renowned.

The heel of the Italian boot, **Apulia** (Puglia), produces more wine than any other part of Italy. Try Castel del Monte, which comes in shades of pink, white, and red.

Latium (Rome) is a major wine-producing region of Italy. Many of the wines from here come from the Castelli Romani, the hill towns around Rome. Horace and Juvenal sang the praises of Latium wines even in imperial times. These wines, experts agree, are best drunk when young, and they are most often white, mellow, and dry (or else "demi-sec"). There are seven different types, including Falerno (yellowish straw in color) and Cecubo (often served with roast meat). Try also Colli Albani (straw yellow with amber tints and served with both fish and meat). The golden-yellow wines of Frascati are famous, produced both in a demi-sec and sweet variety, the latter served with dessert.

The wines of **Tuscany** (Florence and Siena) are famous, ranking with some of the finest reds in France. Chianti is the best known, and it comes in several varieties, some inferior to others. The most highly regarded is Chianti Classico, a lively ruby-red wine mellow in flavor with a bouquet of violets. A good label is Antinori. Lesser known, but a remarkably fine Tuscan wine, is Brunello di Montalcino, a brilliant garnet red which is served with roasts and game. The ruby red, almost purple Vino Nobile di Montepulciano has a rich rugged body—in all, a noble wine which is aged for four years.

The sparkling Lambrusco of **Emilia-Romagna** is by now best known by Americans, but this wine can be of widely varying quality. Most of it is a brilliant ruby red.

Be more experimental and try such wines as the dark ruby-red Sanglovese (with a delicate bouquet) and the golden-yellow Albana, which is somewhat sweet. Trebbiano, generally dry, is best served with fish.

From the **Marches** (capital: Ancona) comes one major wine, Verdicchio dei Castelli di Jesi, amber straw in color, clear and brilliant. Some have said that it's the best wine in Europe "to marry with fish."

From **Venetia** (Venice and Verona) in northeastern Italy, a rich breadbasket of the country, come such world-famous wines as Bardolino (a light ruby-red wine often served with poultry), Valpolicella (produced in "ordinary quality" and "superior dry" and best served with meats), and Soave, so beloved by W. Somerset Maugham, a pale-amber yellow color with a light aroma and a velvety flavor. Try also one of the Cabernets, either the ruby-red Cabernet di Treviso (ideal with roasts and game) or the even deeper ruby-red Cabernet Franc, which has a marked herbal bouquet and is also served with roasts.

The **Friuli–Venetia Giulia** area, whose chief towns are Trieste and Udine, attract those who enjoy a "brut" wine with a trace of flint. From classic grapes comes Merlot, deep ruby in color, and several varieties of Pinot, including Pinot Grigio, whose color ranges from straw yellow to gray pink (good with fish). Also served with fish, the Sauvignon has a straw-yellow color and a delicate bouquet.

The **Trentino–Alto Adige** area, whose chief towns are Bolzano and Trent, produces wine influenced by Austria, to which part of it used to belong. Known for its vineyards, the region has some 20 varieties of wine. The straw-yellow, slightly pale green Riesling is served with fish, as is the pale greenish-yellow Terlano. Santa Maddalena, a cross between a garnet and a ruby in color, is served with wild fowl and red meats, and Traminer, straw yellow in color, has a distinctive aroma and is served with fish. A Pinot Bianco, straw yellow with greenish glints, has a light bouquet, a noble history, and is also served with fish.

The wines of **Lombardy** (Milan) are justly renowned, and if you don't believe me, would you then take the advice of Leonardo da Vinci, Pliny, and Virgil? These great men have sung the praise of this wine-rich region bordered by the Alps to the north and the Po River to the south. To go with the tasty, refined cuisine of the Lombard kitchen, you can sample such wines as Frecciarossa (a pale straw yellow in color with a delicate bouquet; order with fish), Sassella (bright ruby-red in color; order with game, red meat, and roasts), and the amusingly named Inferno (a deep ruby-red in color with a penetrating bouquet; order with meats).

The finest wines in Italy, mostly red, are said to be produced on the vine-clad slopes of the **Piedmont** district (Turin), the word translated literally as "at the foot of the mountain." Of course, Asti Spumante, the color of straw with an abundant champagne-like foam, is considered the prototype of Italian sparkling wines. While traveling through this area of northwestern Italy, you'll want to sample Barbaresco (brilliant ruby-red with a delicate flavor; order with red meats), Barolo (also brilliant ruby-red, best when it mellows into a velvety old age), Cortese (pale straw yellow with green glints; order with fish), and Gattinara (an intense ruby-red beauty in youth that changes with age). Piedmont is also the home of Vermouth, a white wine to which aromatic herbs and spices, among other ingredients, have been added. It's served as an apéritif.

Liguria, which takes in Genoa and the Italian Riviera, doesn't have as many wine-growing regions as other parts of Italy, yet produces dozens of different grapes. These are made into such wines as Dolceacqua (lightish ruby red, served with hearty food) and Vermentino Ligure (a pale yellow in color with a good bouquet; often served with fish).

The wines of **Sardinia** are usually heavy but many find them satisfying. They include Canonau, a light garnet-red color, served with desserts; Vermentino di Gallura, straw yellow in color, produced in both dry and sweet varieties; and one of the several versions of Torbato, classified as extra, passito, and secco.

The wines of **Sicily,** called a "paradise of the grape," were extolled by the ancient poets, including Martial. Caesar himself lavished praise on Mamertine when it was served at a banquet honoring his third consulship. Marsala, of course, an amber-yellow wine served with desserts, is the most famous wine of Sicily. It's velvety and fruity and is sometimes used in cooking, as in veal marsala. The wines made from grapes grown in the volcanic soil of Etna come in both red and white varieties. Try also the Corvo Bianco di Casteldaccia (straw yellow in color, with a distinctive bouquet) and the Corvo Rosso di Casteldaccia (ruby red in color, almost garnet in tone, full-bodied and fruity).

I've only cited a few popular wines. Rest assured that there are hundreds more you may want to discover for yourself.

Other Drinks

Italians drink other libations, not just wine. Perhaps their most world-famous drink is **Campari,** bright red in color and herb flavored, with a quinine bitterness to it. It's customary to serve it with ice cubes and soda.

Beer is also made in Italy and, in general, it is lighter than that served in Germany. If you order beer in a bar or restaurant, chances are it will be an imported beer, for which you will be charged accordingly unless you specify otherwise. Some famous names in European beermaking now operate plants in Italy where the brew has been "adjusted" to Italian taste.

High-proof **Grappa** is made from the "leftovers" after the grapes have been pressed. Many Italians drink this before or after dinner (some put it into their coffee). To an untrained foreign palate, it often appears rough and harsh. Some say it's an acquired taste.

Italy has many **brandies** (according to an agreement with France, it is not supposed to use the word "cognac" in labeling them). A popular one is Vecchia Romagna.

Other popular drinks include several **liqueurs,** to which the Italians are addicted. Try herb-flavored Strega, perhaps an Amaretto tasting of almonds. One of the best known is Maraschino, taking its name from a type of cherry used in its preparation. Galliano is also herb flavored, and Sambucca (anisette) is made of aniseed and is often served with a "fly" (coffee bean) in it. On a hot day, an Italian orders a vermouth, Cinzano, with a twist of lemon, ice cubes, and a squirt of soda water.

---

3. Italy for Children

Italians adore bambini, especially their own, but they are most tolerant of other people's youngsters. Even on shopping expeditions, store owners are fond of giving children candy while you make your purchases. Many cities, such as **Venice,** don't need a special children's section because young ones usually find the canals, the buildings of the city, its narrow humped bridges, and motorboats an experience comparable to visiting an antique Disneyland. So definitely take your children along to Italy, providing you warn them repeatedly to stay out of the way of cars.

In **Florence** children like to go to the top of the Duomo even if it exhausts their parents. Afterward, they can relax at the little zoo by the Cascine (reached by bus 17c or 16a), especially enjoying its swimming pool. A children's playground is found in the botanical gardens, lying on the corner of via XX Settembre and via Vittorio Emanuele (reached by bus 19). Another park suitable for young children is one that lies just on the Arno, past via Amendola (reached by bus 14).

Rome has lots of other amusements for children when they tire of ancient monuments, although they're usually fond of wandering around the Colosseum and the Forum. The Fun Fair (Luna Park) at E.U.R. is one of the largest in Europe. It's known for its "big wheel" at the entrance, and there are such attractions as merry-go-rounds, miniature railways, and shooting galleries.

A children's cabaret gives occasional performances at via Morosini 16 (tel. 06/582-049 for more information). Also in Rome is the Maria Accettella's Marionette Theatre, which stages shows for children. For information, you can reach them at via Tripolitania 195 (tel. 06/832-254). The Puppet Theatre on Pincio Square in the Villa Borghese Gardens has performances nearly every day. While there, you might also like to take your children through the park, the largest public park in Rome (it's closed to traffic). Children enjoy the fountain displays, the lake, and there are many wide spaces in which they can play. Boats can be hired at the Giardino del Lago. A trip to the zoo in Rome is also possible, as it too lies in the Village Borghese, at viale del Giardino Zoologico 20 (tel. 06/870-564). It's open daily all year from 8:30 a.m. to sunset.

You may find that it's worth a detour to visit the tiny town of **Collodi,** 22 miles northeast of Pisa. Collodi was the hometown of the author of the famous Pinocchio story, Carlo Lorenzini. In his memory, the people of the town operate Pinocchio Park, which is "dedicated to the happiness of children everywhere." The park, with many attractions, is dominated by a statue of Pinocchio with the "Blue Fairy."

In the **Naples** area, children delight in wandering through the ruins of Pompeii as much as their parents do. After that, they can enjoy the Aquarium in a city park called Villa Comunale, and the Giardino Zoologico, lying within the Mostra d'Oltremare at the entrance to viale Kennedy. And, to cap it off, take them to the Edenlandia Amusement Park, within the area of Mostra d'Oltremare (entrance on viale Kennedy). It's open all year. Call 081/611-182 for information.

4. The ABCs of Italy

Visitors to Italy are fortunate in that English is understood at most hotels and shops as well as aboard tour buses, trains, and planes. However, Italians are pleased when a foreigner tries to speak their language, even if it's only a few words. You can get some help in the meaning and pronunciation of common terms in the Appendix of this book, and if you combine that information with some of the data below, you should have a pleasant time in this country.

The concierge of your hotel is usually a reliable dispenser of information, offering advice about everything. If he or she fails you, the following summary of helpful facts may be welcome.

BANKING HOURS: Banks in Italy are open Monday through Friday from 8:30 a.m. to 2 p.m.; closed all day Saturday, Sunday, and on national holidays. Traveler's checks can be exchanged for Italian currency at most hotels and at the foreign-exchange offices in main railway stations and at airports.

CAMPING: Italy has more than 1,700 official camping sites, where nominal fees are charged per person on a daily basis. Local tourist boards and provincial tourist offices can be consulted for information on suitable camping sites in their areas. For details on the official sites, get in touch with the Touring Club Italiano, represented in New York by **CIT Travel Service,** 666 Fifth Ave., New York, NY 10103 (tel. 212/397-9300).

CIGARETTES: Seek out stores called *tabacchi.* Some bars also sell cigarettes. For a package of U.S. cigarettes in your familiar brand, you'll pay more than for an Italian variety. However, the taste may be unfamiliar and may require some getting used to. American and British contraband cigarettes are sold freely on the streets for much less than you'll pay in the shops. Although purchasing them is illegal, it seems to be the custom.

CLIMATE: It's warm all over Italy in summer. The high temperatures (measured in degrees Celsius) begin in Rome in May, often lasting until some time in October. Rome experiences its lowest average 24-hour monthly temperatures (Fahrenheit) in January, 49°F; its highest in July, 82°F.

Winters in the north of Italy are cold with rain and snow, but in the south the weather is warm all year, about an average of 50°F in winter (summers tend to be very hot, especially inland).

For the most part, it is drier in Italy than in North America. Scalding temperatures, therefore, don't seem as bad since the humidity is lower. In Rome, Naples, and the south, temperatures can stay in the 90s for days, but nights are most often comfortably cooler.

CLOTHING: Generally speaking, clothing worn in New York can be worn in Italy at the same season. For women, dressy pants suits are suitable almost everywhere, but long-sleeved dresses must be worn for papal audiences, with men wearing jackets and ties. Lightweight clothing is appropriate in summer, lightweight woolens in spring and fall, and warm garb for winter.

For the most part, Italy uses the same clothing sizes as the continent of Europe. The sizes of women's stockings and men's socks are international. However, sizes are not standardized. Always try on if possible.

CRIME: Whenever you're traveling in an unfamiliar city or country, stay alert. Be aware of your immediate surroundings. Wear a moneybelt and don't sling your camera or purse over your shoulder; wear the strap diagonally across your body. This will minimize the possibility of your becoming a victim of crime. Every society has its criminals. It's your responsibility to be aware and be alert even in the most heavily touristed areas.

CURRENCY: There are no restrictions as to how much foreign currency you can bring into Italy, although visitors should declare the amount brought in. This proves to the Italian Customs Office that the currency came from outside the country and therefore the same amount or less can be taken out. Amounts of Italian currency taken into or out of Italy may not exceed 200,000 lire in denominations of 50,000 lire or less.

Here's how your U.S. dollar will translate into local currency. The basic unit of Italian currency is the **lira** (plural: **lire**). The chart below is based on an exchange rate of 1,314.75 lire to the U.S. dollar. The prices in this book were computed on that exchange rate. Because of fluctuations in relative values of world currencies, I suggest that you get in touch with any bank for the latest official exchange rate before going to Italy. For guidelines only, I include the following exchange chart, *which may be invalid at the time of your actual trip.*

Lire	U.S.$	Lire	U.S.$
50	.04	15,000	11.40
100	.08	20,000	15.20
300	.23	25,000	19.00
500	.38	30,000	22.80
700	.53	35,000	26.60
1,000	.76	40,000	30.40
1,500	1.14	45,000	34.20
2,000	1.52	50,000	38.00
3,000	2.28	100,000	76.00
4,000	3.04	125,000	95.00
5,000	3.80	150,000	114.00
6,000	4.56	200,000	152.00
7,500	5.70	250,000	190.00
10,000	7.60	500,000	380.00

CUSTOMS: Most items designed for personal use can be brought duty free into Italy. This includes clothing (new and used), books, camping and household equipment, fishing tackle, a sporting gun and 200 cartridges, a pair of skis, 2 tennis racquets, a portable typewriter, a record player with ten records, a tape recorder or Dictaphone, baby carriage, 2 ordinary hand cameras with 10 rolls of film and 24 slides, 1 movie camera with 10 rolls of film, binoculars, personal jewelry, portable radio set (subject to a small license fee), 400 cigarettes (2 cartons) or a quantity of cigars or pipe tobacco not exceeding 500 grams (1.1 pounds).

A maximum of two bottles of alcoholic beverages per person can be brought in duty free. The bottles must be opened, however. Specifically, overseas tourists arriving in Italy, after having visited other countries, will be allowed to carry with them, without any special formality except a verbal declaration, travel souvenirs purchased in said countries up to a total lire value equivalent of $500 (U.S.), including fine perfumes up to half a liter.

Upon leaving Italy, citizens of the United States who have been outside the country for 48 hours or more are allowed to bring back to their home country $400 worth of merchandise duty free—that is, if they have claimed no similar exemption within the past 30 days. If you make purchases in Italy, it is important to keep your receipts.

DOCUMENTS FOR ENTRY: U.S., Canadian, and British citizens holding a valid passport do not need a visa to enter Italy if they do not expect to stay more than 90 days and do not expect to work there. Those who, after entering Italy, find that they would like to stay more than 90 days, can apply for a permit for an additional stay of 90 days, which as a rule is granted immediately.

ELECTRICAL APPLIANCES: Electric current in Italy varies considerably. The current is usually A.C., the cycles varying from 42 to 50. The voltage can be from 115 to 220. It is recommended that any visitor carrying electrical appliances obtain a transformer either before leaving the U.S. or Canada or in any electrical appliance shop in Italy. Check the exact local current with the hotel where you are staying. Plugs have prongs that are round, not flat; therefore an adapter plug is needed.

EMBASSIES AND CONSULATES: The **American Embassy** in Rome is at via Vittorio Veneto 19A (tel. 06/46-741). **U.S. consulates** are in Florence, lungarno Amerigo Vespucci 46 (tel. 055/298-276); in Genoa, Banca d'America è Italia Building, piazza Portello 6 (tel. 010/282-741); in Milan, piazza della Repubblica 32 (tel. 02/652-841); in Naples, piazza della Repubblica (tel. 081/660-966); and in Palermo, via Vaccarini 1 (tel. 091/291-532).

EMERGENCY SERVICE: Dial 113 for an **ambulance, police,** or **fire.** In case of a **breakdown** on an Italian road, dial 116 at the nearest telephone box. The nearest Automobile Club of Italy (ACI) will be notified to come to your aid.

ETIQUETTE: Women in sleeveless dresses and men with bare chests are not welcome in the best bars and restaurants of Italy and may be refused service. Also, persons so attired are ordered to cover up when they visit museums and churches.

FILM: U.S.-brand film is available in Italy but it's expensive. Take in as much as Customs will allow if you plan to take a lot of pictures. Processing film takes a week or more in Italy, although some of the bigger shops in Rome will return your pictures within four days.

GAMBLING: There are four casinos in Italy: **San Remo,** Italian Riviera, open year round; **Campione,** Lake Lugano, open year round; **Venice,** open October 1 to March 31 at Palazzo-Vendramin and April 1 to September 30 at Venice Lido; and **St. Vincent,** Aosta Valley, open year round.

To be admitted to a casino, persons must be over the age of 18 and must show a passport.

HEALTH SERVICES: First-aid service (Pronto Soccorso) with a doctor on hand is found at airports, ports, railway stations, and in all hospitals. The emergency number in Italy, equivalent to calling 911 at home, is 113.

Italy has no medical program covering U.S. citizens, so you should take out an insurance policy covering possible needs before you leave home. Special coverage for medical emergencies overseas is usually necessary. The American Embassy in Rome has a list of doctors and dentists who speak English (see under "Practical Facts" in Chapter III). You can receive assistance in this regard elsewhere in Italy by getting in touch with the U.S. Consulate General's office (see above).

At every drugstore (Farmacia), there is a list of those that are open at night and on Sundays. This list rotates.

HOLIDAYS AND FESTIVALS: Offices and shops in Italy are closed on the following dates: January 1 (New Year's Day), Easter Monday, April 25 (Liberation Day), May 1 (Labor Day), August 15 (Assumption of the Virgin), November 1 (All Saints Day), December 8 (Day of Immaculate Conception), December 25 (Christmas Day), and December 26 (Santo Stefano).

Closings are also observed in the following cities on feast days honoring their patron saints: Venice, April 25 (St. Mark); Florence, Genoa, and Turin, June 24, (St. John the Baptist); Palermo, July 15 (Santa Rosalia); Naples, September 19 (St. Gennaro); Bologna, October 4 (St. Petronio); Cagliari, October 30 (St. Saturnino); Trieste, November 3 (San Giusto); Bari, December 6 (St. Nicolà); and Milan, December 7 (St. Ambrose).

INFORMATION: Tourist information (town plans, brochures, hotel lists, or particular inquiries) may be obtained by writing direct (in English or Italian) to the provincial or local tourist boards of the places concerned. These provincial tourist boards (known as **Ente Provinciale per il Turismo**) operate in the principal towns of the provinces. The local tourist boards (known as **Azienda Autonoma Soggiorno**) operate in all places of tourist interest, and a list can be obtained from the Italian government tourist offices.

LAUNDRY: All deluxe and first- and second-class hotels have laundry and dry-cleaning facilities. Prices are usually moderate, and a small service charge is added to the actual cost. If a hotel doesn't provide these services, the desk clerk can direct you to the nearest *tintoria* (shop), or you can look in the classified telephone directory under *tintorie* (cleaning and pressing) and *lavanderie* (laundry).

MAIL DELIVERY: At post offices, **general delivery service** is available in Italy. Correspondence can be addressed c/o the post office by adding *Fermo Posta* to the name of the locality. Delivery will be made at the local central post office upon identification of the addressee by passport. In addition to all post offices, you can purchase stamps at little *tabacchi* (tobacco) stores throughout the city.

Mail delivery in Italy is notoriously bad. One letter from a soldier, postmarked in 1945, arrived in his home village in 1982. Letters sent from New York, say, in November, are often delivered (if at all) the following year. If you're writing for hotel reservations, it can cause much confusion on both sides. Many visitors arrive in Italy long before their hotel deposits.

METRIC CONVERSIONS: In Italy, you face a whole new way of measuring.

Even the temperature will be expressed in Celsius. The conversions below will show you how to change kilometers into miles, grams into pounds, meters into yards, and liters into ounces. Once you get the hang of it, it isn't as hard as it first appears.

Length
    1 millimeter = 0.04 inches (*or* less than 1/16 in)
    1 centimeter = 0.39 inches (*or* just under 1/2 in)
    1 meter   = 1.09 yards (*or* about 39 inches)
    1 kilometer = 0.62 mile (*or* about 2/3 mile)

To convert kilometers to miles, take the number of kilometers and multiply by .62 (for example, 25 km × .62 = 15.5 mi).

To convert miles to kilometers, take the number of miles and multiply by 1.61 (for example, 50 mi × 1.61 = 80.5 km).

Capacity
    1 liter = 33.92 ounces
            = 1.06 quarts
            = 0.26 gallons

To convert liters to gallons, take the number of liters and multiply by .26 (for example, 50 l × .26 = 13 gal).

To convert gallons to liters, take the number of gallons and multiply by 3.79 (for example, 10 gal × 3.79 = 37.9 l).

Weight
    1 gram   = 0.04 ounces (*or* about a paperclip's weight)
    1 kilogram = 2.2 pounds

To convert kilograms to pounds, take the number of kilos and multiply by 2.2 (for example, 75 kg × 2.2 = 165 lbs).

To convert pounds to kilograms, take the number of pounds and multiply by .45 (for example, 90 lbs × .45 = 40.5 kg).

Area
    1 hectare (100m²) = 2.47 acres

To convert hectares to acres, take the number of hectares and multiply by 2.47 (for example, 20 ha × 2.47 = 49.4 acres).

To convert acres to hectares, take the number of acres and multiply by .41 (for example, 40 acres × .41 = 16.4 ha).

Temperature

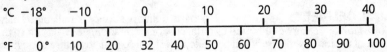

°C	−18°	−10	0	10	20	30	40
°F	0° 10	20	32 40	50	60 70	80	90 100

To convert degrees C to degrees F, multiply degrees C by 9, divide by 5, then add 32 (for example, 9/5 × 20°C + 32 = 68°F).

To convert degrees F to degrees C, subtract 32 from degrees F, then multiply by 5, and divide by 9 (for example, 85°F − 32 × 5/9 = 29°C).

NEWSPAPERS: In major cities, it is possible to find the *International Herald-Tribune* as well as other English-language newspapers and magazines at hotels and news kiosks.

OFFICE HOURS: This varies greatly. However, regular business hours are 9 a.m. (sometimes 9:30 a.m.) to 1 p.m. and 3:30 (sometimes 4) to 7 or 7:30 p.m. In the white heat of an Italian July or August, offices may not open in the afternoon until 4:30 or 5 p.m.

PETS: A veterinarian's certificate of good health is required for dogs and cats, and should be obtained by owners in advance of entering Italy. Dogs must be on a leash or muzzled at all times. Other animals must undergo examination at the border or port of entry. Certificates for parrots or other birds subject to psittacosis must state that the country of origin is free of disease. All documents must be certified first by a notary public, then by the nearest office of the Italian Consulate.

REST ROOMS: All airport and railway stations have rest rooms, often with attendants, who expect to be tipped. Bars, nightclubs, restaurants, cafés, and all hotels have facilities as well. Public toilets are also found near many of the major sights.

SHOPPING HOURS: Most stores are open from 9 a.m. to 1 p.m. year round. Shops in Rome in summer reopen at either 3:30 or 4 p.m., doing business until 7:30 or 8 p.m. Grocery stores are likely to reopen at 5 p.m. This siesta is observed in Rome, Naples, and most cities of southern Italy; however, in Milan and other northern and central cities the siesta is not faithfully observed and has been completely abolished by some merchants. Most shops are closed on Sunday, except for certain barbershops that are open Sunday morning. However, hairdressers are closed on Sunday and Monday. If you're traveling in Italy in summer and the heat is intense, I suggest that you learn the custom of the siesta too.

TAXES: As a member of the European Common Market, Italy imposes a tax on most goods and services. It is a "value-added tax," called I.V.A. in Italy. For example, the tax affecting most visitors is that imposed at hotels, which ranges from 9% in first- and second-class hotels and pensions to 18% in deluxe hotels.

TAXIS: Taxi service is readily available throughout Italy, in all towns and tourist resorts. Generally they wait in special taxi stands at railway stations and main parts of a city, but one can always be called by phone. Meters are provided and fares are displayed. Fares vary considerably from place to place. Find out the starting rate that is legal in the city or town you visit, and be sure that is the amount showing on the meter when you embark, or you might find yourself paying for someone else's ride. Taxi trips outside the town area will have a supplemental charge.

TELEGRAMS: ITALCABLE operates services abroad, transmitting messages by cable or satellite. Both internal and foreign telegrams may be dictated over the phone (dial 186).

TELEPHONES: A public telephone is always near at hand in Italy, especially if you're in the vicinity of a bar. Local calls from public telephones require the use of tokens (*gettone*) or coins. To make your call, deposit a 200-lire (15¢) token in the slot but *do not release it until after the number has been dialed and the party has answered.* Tokens can be purchased at all tobacco shops and bars.

Thanks to ITALCABLE, calls to the U.S. and Canada can be dialed directly. Dial 00 (the international code from Italy), then the country code (1 for the U.S. and Canada), the area code, and the number you are calling. Calls dialed directly are billed on the basis of the call's duration only. A reduced rate is applied from 11 p.m. to 8 a.m. weekdays and all day Sunday.

If you wish to make a collect call or have the call billed to your credit card, dial 170. An ITALCABLE operator will come on and will speak English. If you make a long-distance call from a public telephone, there is no surcharge. However, hotels have been known to double or triple the cost of the call, so be duly warned.

TELEX AND FAX: Chances are your hotel will send or receive one for you.

TIME: In terms of standard time zones, Italy is six hours ahead of Eastern Standard Time in the United States. Daylight Savings Time goes into effect in Italy each year from May 22 to September 24.

TIPPING: This custom is practiced with flair in Italy; in fact, many people depend on tips for their livelihoods.

In **hotels,** the service charge of 15% or 18% is already added to a bill. In addition, it is customary to tip the chambermaid 1,000 lire (75¢) per day; the doorman (for calling a cab), 1,000 lire; and the bellhop or porter, 1,500 lire ($1.15) per bag. A concierge expects 3,000 lire ($2.30) per day, as well as tips for extra services he may perform, which are likely to include long-distance calls, newspapers, or stamps.

In **restaurants,** 15% is added to your bill to cover most charges. An additional tip for good service is almost always expected. Know that it is customary in certain fashionable restaurants in Rome, Florence, Venice, and Milan to leave an additional 10%, which, combined with the assessed service charge, is a very high tip indeed. The sommelier expects 10% of the cost of the wine. **Checkroom attendants** now expect 1,500 lire ($1.15), although in simple places, Italians still hand **washroom attendants** 100 lire (10¢) to 300 lire (25¢), more in deluxe and first-class establishments. Restaurants are required by law to give customers official receipts.

In **cafés** and **bars,** tip 15% of the bill, and give a **theater usher** 1,500 lire ($1.15).

Taxi drivers expect at least 15% of the fare.

ROME

Rome is often called "the Eternal City." If that is true, it is eternal because of its life. The life of Rome is composed mainly of two elements: the Romans and the visitors. Both are virtually inseparable. Paris remains indubitably French, even with its hordes of aliens. But in Rome the visitor and the local people are entwined. The city almost seems at times to exist as a host to its never-ending stream of sightseers. It wines them, dines them, and entertains them.

Rome is also a city of images, beginning at dawn, which, in my view, is best seen from Janiculum Hill if you get up early enough or stay up late enough. With its bell towers and cupolas, the silhouette of Rome comes into view. It is a city of sounds, as the first peal of bells calls the faithful to an early-morning Mass. As the city wakes up, office-workers rush into cafés for their first cappuccinos of the day, often passing by fruit and vegetable stands (the Romans like their produce fresh).

By 10 a.m. the tourists are on the street battling city traffic in their quest for a contact with art and history. Renaissance palaces and baroque façades give way eventually to what is left from the ruins of antiquity, the heritage of a once-great empire.

In the following chapter, I'll take you on seemingly endless treks through ancient monuments and basilicas. But monuments are not the total picture. In Rome, you'll find yourself embracing life with intensity. In other words, "When in Rome. . . ."

1. Orientation

Your feet will probably first touch Roman soil at **Leonardo da Vinci International Airport,** alternatively called Fiumicino in honor of the town whose location is adjacent. It's a big, sparkling glass structure near the mouth of the Tiber River, 18½ miles from downtown Rome. The least expensive way to go into the city is to take the bus that runs from in front of the terminal building (see below). The cost is only a fraction of taxi fare, and you'll be let off in a good part of town to start your hotel hunt.

The drive in is rather uneventful until you pass through the city wall, the **Great Aurelian Wall,** started in A.D. 271 to calm Rome's barbarian jitters and still remarkably intact. Suddenly, ruins of imperial baths loom on one side, great monuments can be seen in the middle of blocks, and you have the shock of recognition that you're really in Rome—not simply looking at pictures. Inside the walls, you'll find a city designed for a population that walked to get where it was going. Parts of Rome actually look and feel more like an oversize village than the former imperial capital of the Western world.

The bus deposits you on via Giolitti, right next to the Stazione Termini, or **Terminal Station.** The station faces a huge piazza, the **piazza dei Cinquecento** (of the 500), which in many ways is an embodiment of the city. It's named after 500 Italians who died heroically in a 19th-century battle in Africa. There are certainly many more attractive sites in Rome, but this piazza has several noteworthy aspects. First, it is flanked by the modern railroad station. Immediately next to the sculptured-cement cantilevered roof of the station façade is a remnant of the **Servian Wall,** built nearly six centuries before the birth of Christ by an ancient Roman king. If that isn't enough, the far side of the piazza is bordered by the ruins of the **Baths of Diocletian,** a former bastion of imperial luxury whose crumbling brick walls were once covered with the rarest of colored marbles and even now enclose marble and bronze statuary.

Most of the old city and its monuments lie on the east side of the **Tiber River** (Fiume Tevere), which meanders through town between 19th-century stone embankments. However, several important monuments are on the other side, to wit: **St. Peter's Basilica** and the **Vatican,** the **Castel Sant' Angelo** (formerly the tomb of the Emperor Hadrian), and the colorful section of town known as **Trastevere.** The bulk of ancient Rome, and Renaissance and baroque Rome too, lies across the Tiber from St. Peter's on the same side as the Terminal Station. The various quarters of the city are linked by large boulevards (large at least in some places) that have mostly been laid out since the late 19th century.

Starting from the **Victor Emmanuel monument,** a highly controversial pile of snow-white Brescian marble whose quarrying and construction must have employed whole cities, there's a street running practically due north to the **piazza del Popolo** and the city wall. This is the **via del Corso,** one of the main streets of Rome, noisy, congested, always crowded with buses and shoppers, called simply "the Corso." Again from the Victor Emmanuel monument, the major artery going west (and ultimately across the Tiber to St. Peter's) is the **corso Vittorio Emanuele.** To go in the other direction toward the Colosseum, you take the **via dei Fori Imperiali,** named for the excavated ruins of the imperial forums that flank this avenue. This road was laid out in the '30s by Mussolini, who was responsible for much of the fine archeological work in Rome, if perhaps for the wrong reasons. Yet another central conduit is the **via Nazionale,** running from the **piazza della Repubblica** (also called the piazza Esedra), ending again right by the Victor Emmanuel monument at the **piazza Venezia,** which lies in front of it.

For the 2½ millennia before these boulevards were built, the citizens had to make their way through narrow byways and curves that defeated all but the best senses of direction. These streets—and they are among the most charming aspects of the city—still exist in large quantities, unspoiled in the main by the advances of modern construction. However, this tangled street plan has one troublesome element: automobiles. The traffic in Rome is awful. When the claustrophobic street plans of the Dark Ages open unexpectedly onto a vast piazza, every driver accelerates full throttle for the distant horizon, while groups of peripatetic tourists and Romans flatten themselves against marble fountains for protection or stride with firm jaws right into the thick of the howling traffic.

The traffic problem in Rome is nothing new. Julius Caesar was so exasperated by it that he banned all vehicular traffic during the daylight hours. Sometimes it's actually faster to walk than to take a bus, especially during any of Rome's four daily rush hours (that's right, *four:* to work, home for lunch/siesta, back to work, home in the evening). The hectic crush of urban Rome is considerably less during the month of August, when many Romans are out of town on holiday. If you visit at any other time of year, however, be prepared for the general frenzy that characterizes your average Roman street.

TRANSPORTATION

The experience for the first-time visitor of plunging madly into the traffic of Rome can be maddening. Your arrival at the airport and transportation to the city must be faced before you check into your hotel room. With this in mind, I have attempted in this section and the "Practical Facts" below to summarize some information that may ease your adjustment into the capital of Italy.

Airlines/Airports

Chances are that your arrival point in Italy will be Rome's **Leonardo da Vinci International Airport** (popularly known as **Fiumicino**), 18½ miles from the center of the capital. Domestic flights arrive at one terminal, international ones at the other. (If you're flying by charter, there is a possibility you might arrive at Ciampino Airport.)

The least expensive way into Rome from Fiumicino is to take one of the many buses leaving every 15 minutes or so. These buses deliver you to the Air Terminal at via Giolitti 36 (tel. 464-613), across from the Terminal Station. The one-way cost is 5,000 lire ($3.80) per passenger. Buses are air-conditioned and have ample room for luggage. I once made the trip in from the airport in half an hour, but you'd better count on more than an hour because of heavy traffic.

Taxis are quite expensive and therefore not recommended for the trip from the airport. From the terminal, however, you can take a taxi to your hotel (or walk, if you're staying in the vicinity of the railway station, providing you don't have too much luggage).

If you arrive at **Ciampino,** you're nearer the city of Rome, which is usually reached in less than half an hour. Because of the shorter distance, you pay the amount shown on the meter if you go by taxi (not double, as some drivers may insist). Suburban buses leaving from the piazza dei Cinquecento (in front of the Terminal Station) also run to Ciampino, and a train leaves Terminal (take the Frascati line).

For air flight information for Fiumicino, telephone 601-541; for Ciampino, 600-251.

Rome is serviced by many international carriers; however, chances are, you'll need to consult one of the following about your return flight: **TWA,** via Barberini 38 (tel. 47-211); **Pan American,** via Bissolati 46 (tel. 47-73); or **British Airways,** via Bissolati 54 (tel. 47-171). The national carrier, **Alitalia,** is at via Bissolati 13 (tel. 46-88).

Buses and Trams

Roman buses are operated by an organization known as **ATAC** (Azienda Tramvie e Autobus del Commune di Roma). Telephone 46-951 for information.

For only 700 lire (55¢), you can ride to most parts of Rome (but not the outlying districts) on quite good bus hookups. At the Terminal Station, you can purchase a special tourist bus pass, costing 2,800 lire ($2.15) for three days or 10,000 lire ($7.60) for a week. This allows you to ride on the ATAC network without bothering to purchase individual tickets. Never, but *never,* ride the trams when the Romans are going to or from work, or you'll be mashed flatter than fettuccine.

Buses and trams stop at areas marked *Fermata,* and in general they are in service from 6 a.m. to midnight. After that and until dawn, service, on mainline stations only, is very marginal. It's best to take a taxi in the wee hours if you can find one.

At the bus transport office in front of the Terminal Station on via Giolitti, you can purchase a directory complete with maps summarizing the particular routes.

Ask there about where to purchase bus tickets, or buy them in a tobacco shop or at a bus terminal. You must have your ticket before boarding the bus, as there are no ticket machines on the vehicles. Also, each transfer requires another ticket.

Subway

This is the fastest means of transportation in Rome, with two underground lines, called the **Metropolitana,** or **Metro** for short. Line A goes from via Ottaviano, near St. Peter's, to piazza di Cinecittà, stopping at piazzale Flaminio (near piazza del Popolo), piazza Vittorio Emanuele, and piazza San Giovanni in Laterano. Line B connects the Terminal Station with via Laurentina, stopping at via Cavour, the Colosseum, Circus Maximus, the Pyramid of C. Cestius, St. Paul's Outside the Walls, the Magliana, and the E.U.R. A big red letter **M** indicates the entrance to the subway. The price anywhere within the walls is 700 lire (55¢), but of course you'll have to pay more to go to the farther reaches of the underground.

Tickets are available from vending machines at all stations. These machines accept 50-lira, 100-lira, and 200-lira coins. Some stations have managers, but they will not make change. Booklets of tickets are available at *tabacchi* (tobacco) shops and in some terminals.

Building an underground system for Rome has not been easy, since every time workers start digging, they discover an old temple or other archeological treasure and heavy earth-moving has to cease for a while.

Taxis

If you're accustomed to hopping a cab in New York or London, then do so in Rome. If not, take less expensive means of transport. I suggest that you avoid paying your fare with large bills. Invariably, taxi drivers don't have change. Also the driver will expect a 10% tip. Don't count on hailing a taxi on the street or even getting one at a stand. If you're going out, have your hotel call one. At a restaurant, ask the waiter or cashier to dial for you. If you want to phone yourself, try one of these numbers: 3875, 3570, 4994, or 8433.

The meter begins at 2,800 lire ($2.15)—subject to change, of course—plus another 700 lire (55¢) for every kilometer. On Sunday, a 1,500-lira ($1.15) supplement is assessed, plus another 2,500-lira ($1.90) supplement from 10 p.m. to 6 a.m. There's yet another 1,000-lira (75¢) supplement for every suitcase. From Fiumicino Airport to town carries still another 5,500-lira ($4.20) supplement in addition to the fare shown on the meter (which I hope is in working order). From Rome to the airport there's a supplement of 1,500 lire ($1.15), plus the fare shown on the meter.

Two-Wheel Vehicles

St. Peter Rent, via Porta Castello 43 (tel. 687-5714), rents bicycles, motorscooters, and motorcycles, and operates an organization for young and active tourists who want to use such vehicles for touring the area. They are open daily from 9 a.m. to 7 p.m. Rates range from 10,000 lire ($7.60) per day for a standard bicycle to 70,000 lire ($53.20) per day for a two-person Suzuki or Honda motorcycle. For the latter, the minimum age for a renter is 21, and a valid driver's license is required.

PRACTICAL FACTS

There are any number of situations that can make or mar your visit to Rome. Although I don't promise to answer all your needs, there is a variety of matters in the city that you need to know about. The **telephone area code** for Rome and its environs is 06. For other telephone information, see "The ABCs of Italy," in Chapter II.

American Express: The lifeline or "pipeline" back to America for many visitors, the Rome offices of American Express, are at piazza di Spagna 38 (tel. 6764). Hours for the travel service are 9 a.m. to 6 p.m. Monday through Friday, to 12:30 p.m. on Saturday. Hours for the financial and mail services are Monday through Friday from 9 a.m. to 5 p.m. and on Saturday from 9 a.m. to noon. The sightseeing counter for the sale of tours is open during the same hours as those for travel services and additionally on Saturday afternoon from 2 to 2:30 p.m. and on Sunday and holidays from 9 to 9:30 a.m. and 2 to 2:30 p.m.

Babysitters: Most hotel desks in Rome will help you secure a babysitter. You should ask for an English-speaking sitter if available. If your hotel doesn't help in this regard, get in touch with **Baby Parking,** via San Prisca 16 (tel. 572-224). If you're traveling in major Italian cities, consult the local newspaper advertisements under "Bambino."

Banks: In general, banks are open Monday through Friday from 9 a.m. to 1 p.m., then after a siesta until 3:30 or 4 p.m., many reopen until 6 p.m. The Rome **American Service Bank** is at piazza Mignanelli 5 (tel. 678-6815). Two other favorite U.S. banks in Rome are **Chase Manhattan,** via M. Mercati 31 (tel. 844-361), and **Citibank,** via Boncompagni 26 (tel. 47-13). Banks are closed on Saturday and Sunday.

Crime in Rome: Purse-snatching is commonplace in Rome. Young men on Vespas or whatever ride through the city looking for victims. To avoid trouble, stay away from the curb and hold tightly to your purse. Likewise, don't lay anything valuable on tables or chairs where it can be grabbed up easily.

Dentists: To secure a dentist who speaks English, call the **American Embassy** in Rome, via Veneto 121 (tel. 46-741 for the switchboard, 46-742, ext. 207, for the Special Consular Services Office of the Consular Section). You may have to call around in order to get an appointment.

Doctors: Likewise, call the **American Embassy** (see above), which provides you with a list of doctors who speak English. Of course, all big hospitals in Rome have a 24-hour first-aid service (go to the emergency room). You'll find English-speaking doctors at the privately run **Salvator Mundi International Hospital,** viale Mura Gianicolensis 67 (tel. 580-041).

Drugstores: In Rome, a pharmacy open 24 hours a day is **Carlo Erba,** via del Corso 125 (tel. 679-0866). Another all-day and all-night one, centrally located, is **Farmacia Internazionale,** piazza Barberini 49 (tel. 462-996). Most other pharmacies are open from 8:30 a.m. to 1 p.m. and 4 to 7:30 p.m. Monday through Saturday.

Embassies: I hope you'll not need such services. But in case of a lost passport or some other emergency, the **U.S. Embassy** in Rome is at via Veneto 121 (tel. 46-741); the **British Embassy** is at via Venti Settembre 80a (tel. 475-5441); and the **Canadian Embassy** is at via G.B. De Rossi 27 (tel. 855-341).

Emergencies: Rome has a police "hot line"—telephone 212-121. Usually, however, dial 113 for the police (the same number to report a fire or summon an ambulance).

Information: Tourist information is available at the **Ente Provinciale per il Turismo,** via Parigi 11, 00185 Roma (tel. 463-748). There's another information bureau at Terminal Station, 00185 Roma (tel. 465-461).

Libraries: Visitors can use the **American Library,** via Veneto 119c (tel. 46-742, ext. 481), open from 1:30 to 5:30 p.m. Monday through Friday (to 7 p.m. on Wednesday). There is also the **British Council Library,** Quattro Fontane 20 (tel. 475-6641), open from 10 a.m. to 1 p.m. and 3 to 6 p.m. Monday through Friday; closed in August.

Newspapers: Most major newsstands in "monumental" Rome, especially those along the via Veneto, carry copies of the *International Herald-Tribune,* as well as certain British newspapers and magazines in English. The English-language daily published in Rome is the *International Daily News,* and in addition to its news coverage (with an emphasis on Europe, of course), it also provides several lists of local events and services that the foreign visitor should find helpful.

Postal Service: In Rome, the **central post office** is at piazza San Silvestro, behind the Rinascente department store on piazza Colonna (tel. 672-225). It's open from 8:30 a.m. to 7:50 p.m. Monday through Friday for mail service, to 1:50 p.m.

for money service. Both are open from 8:30 a.m. to noon on Saturday. Mail addressed to you c/o that central office, with *Fermo Posta* written after the name and address of the post office, will be given to you upon identification by passport. Try to mail your letters and postcards at the Vatican City central post office, as they'll reach home much sooner.

Public Toilets: Facilities are found near many of the major sights of Rome, often with attendants, as are those at bars, nightclubs, restaurants, cafés, and hotels, plus the airports and the railway station. You're expected to leave 200 lire (15¢) or sometimes more for the attendant. If you're not checking into a hotel in Rome but going on by train elsewhere, you can patronize the **Albergo Diurno,** a hotel without beds at the Terminal Station. It has baths, showers, and well-kept toilet facilities.

Religious Services: Catholic churches abound in Rome and throughout Italy. However, there are Catholic churches in Rome that conduct services for English-speaking people, including **San Silvestro,** piazza San Silvestro 1 (tel. 679-7755), and **Santa Susana,** via XX Settembre 14 (tel. 457-1510). The American Episcopal Church is **St. Paul's,** via Napoli 58 at via Nazionale (tel. 463-339). The Jewish temple, **Sinagoga Ebraica,** is at lungotevere dei Cenci (tel. 656-4648).

Shopping Hours: These are governed by the siesta in Rome. Most stores are open from 9 a.m. to 1 p.m. Monday through Saturday year round, reopening at either 3:30 or 4 p.m. and doing business until 7:30 or 8 p.m. Most shops are closed on Sunday except for some barbershops that are open Sunday morning. Hairdressers are closed Sunday and Monday.

Telegrams: See "The ABCs of Italy," in Chapter II. In Rome, you can send telegrams from all post offices during the day and from the telegraph office at the central post office in piazza San Silvestro, off via della Mercede, at night.

THE HOTEL SITUATION

The Italians are never simple. If you aren't aware of that, you soon will be as you find yourself coping with the myriad Italian hotel prices and classifications. A handy computer or a brain-trust accountant would be ideal to carry along with you.

Cardinal rule: If you want to enjoy average, "middle-class" comfort, but keep your wallet fairly intact, patronize the top-rated second-class hotels and their equivalents, the first-class pensiones. Patronage of a second- or even a third-class hotel does not reflect on your social standing. In fact, many of the more cultivated of the world's social, literary, and artistic colony have habitually frequented little unheralded establishments in Rome, not because of financial need but because of the charm and atmosphere they found there.

Italy controls the prices of its hotels, designating a minimum and a maximum rate. The difference between the two may depend either on the season or the location of the room, even its size. Hotels are divided into deluxe, first class, second class, third class, and fourth class. Many second-class hotels stun the visitor with their seeming grandeur. "Why second class?" is an often-asked question. "This is luxury." Government ratings do not depend on sensitivity of decoration or on frescoed ceilings but rather on facilities such as elevators and the like. Many of the finest hostelries in Italy are rated second-class because they do not serve meals other than breakfast (a blessing really, for those seeking to escape the board requirements).

2. Deluxe and First-Class Hotels

LUXURY LEADERS

What follows is a preview of what some critics regard as among the finest hotels in Europe.

Hassler, piazza Trinità dei Monti 6, 00187 Roma (tel. 06/679-2651), the sole deluxe hotel in this old part of Rome, uses the Spanish Steps as its grand entrance. The original Hassler, constructed in 1885 and rebuilt in 1944, was used as headquarters of the American Air Transport Command for the last year of World War II. In 1947 the hotel was finally returned to its original glory, reopening its doors and becoming an immediate success. Through the years its reputation has grown to the point where it is now a legend. In its lifetime, this lush hotel, with its ornate decor, has been favored by such Americans as the Kennedys, Eisenhowers, and Nixons—and by titled Europeans and movie stars. The brightly colored rooms, the lounges with a mixture of modern and traditional furnishings, the bedrooms with their "Italian Park Avenue" trappings, strike a 1930s note. The bedrooms have a personalized look—Oriental rugs, tasteful draperies at the French windows, brocade furnishings, comfortable beds, and (the nicest touch of all) bowls of fresh flowers. A top Paradise Penthouse with a large terrace and the Presidential Suite next to the restaurant have recently been created. The suites, of course, are expensive. A single room with bath and shower costs from 320,000 lire ($243) daily; a double with bath, from 440,000 lire ($334). Taxes are included. Dining at the Hassler is an event, either in the lovely garden in summer or in the roof restaurant with its panoramic view of the city. On Sunday, a lazy brunch is enhanced by the unique view and atmosphere of the Roof Restaurant.

Cavalieri Hilton International, via Cadlolo 101, 00136 Roma (tel. 06/31-511), combines all the advantages of a resort hotel with the convenience of being within a few minutes' drive from the center of town. Overlooking Rome and the Alban Hills from its perch on top of Monte Mario, it is set in 15 acres of trees, flowering shrubs, and stonework. The entrance to the hotel leads into a marble lobby, whose sculpture, 17th-century art, and winding staircases are usually flooded with sunlight from the massive windows. On the premises is an indoor arcade of shops, a garden restaurant and pool veranda in summer—the Trattoria del Cavalieri—serving well-prepared meals of almost any degree of formality, and a constantly changing international clientele that is usually only about 25% American. A 24-hour concierge service is there to provide you with solutions to "whatever your problems," including a free hotel bus that makes frequent runs to the via Veneto and the Spanish Steps.

The 373 guest rooms and suites, many with wonderful views, are designed to fit contemporary standards of comfort, quality, and style. Soft furnishings in pastel colors are paired with Italian furniture in warm-tone woods. Each unit has a keyless electronic lock, independent heating and air conditioning, remote-control color TV featuring in-house movies, direct-dial phone, mini-bar, radio, and bedside control for all electric apparatus in the room, as well as a spacious balcony. The bathrooms, sheathed in Italian marble, are equipped with large mirrors, hairdryer, international electric sockets, vanity mirror, piped-in music, and phone. Singles cost 190,000 lire ($144) to 265,000 lire ($201) daily, and doubles run 280,000 lire ($213) to 380,000 lire ($289). There are tennis courts a few steps away, a jogging path, a sauna with massage facilities, two accommodating bars, and one of the best restaurants in Rome, the Pergola (more about this later).

Eden, via Ludovisi 49, 00187 Roma (tel. 06/474-3551), dates from the 1890s, but you'd never know it because it is so well preserved. It stands at the entrance to the Borghese Gardens and the via Veneto. In the Ludovisi district, it is surrounded by the gardens of Villa Ludovisi, the old Convent of St. Isidoro, and Villa Medici. The hotel is beautifully decorated, and the rooms are generous in size and furnished in a refined, elegant manner. All of the accommodations contain complete baths or showers, with singles renting for 275,000 lire ($209) daily and doubles for 395,000 lire ($300). These tariffs include air conditioning, service, and taxes. The Eden's penthouse restaurant and bar is a stunner, offering a vista that stretches from the Colosseum to the Pincio. At the restaurant, La Terrazza dell'Eden, you can dine well here for 55,000 lire ($41.75) and up per person.

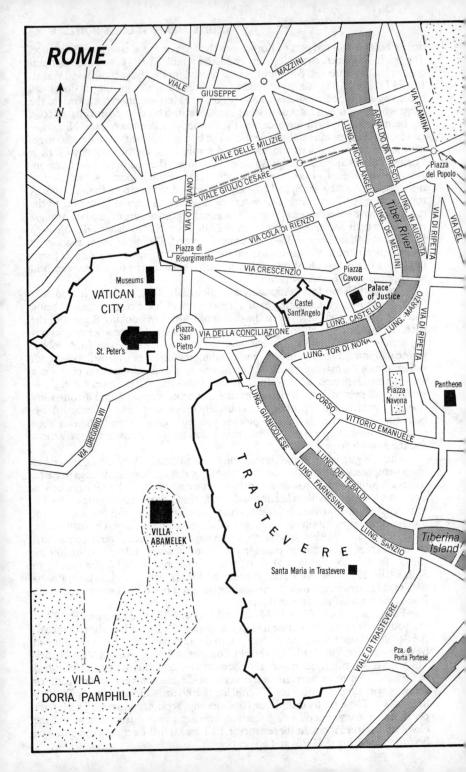

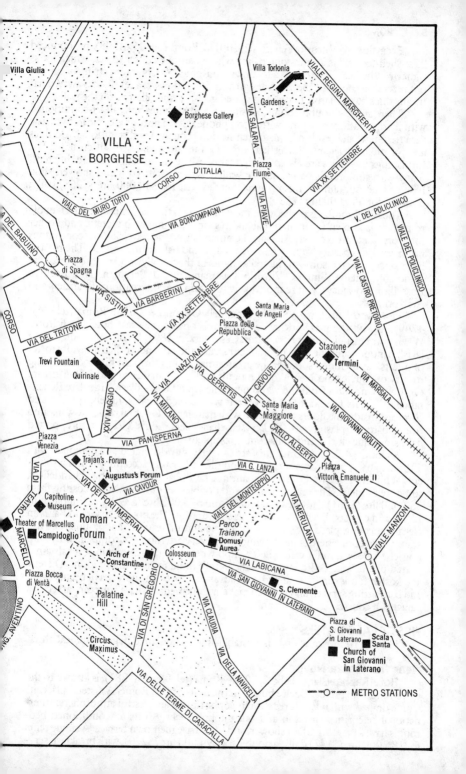

Excelsior, via Vittorio Veneto 125, 00187 Roma (tel. 06/4708), pronounced "Ess-shell-see-or," is a limestone palace whose baroque corner tower, which looks right over the U.S. Embassy, is a landmark in Rome. Guests enter a string of cavernous reception rooms of the same design as the Grand Hotel a few blocks away. That means thick rugs, marble floors, and gilded garlands and pilasters on the walls.

There are 234 double rooms, 96 singles, and 37 suites here, all air-conditioned with thermostatic control and with direct phone lines. The rooms come in two basic varieties: new (the result of a major renovation program) and traditional. Doubles are spacious and elegantly furnished, often with antiques, and with silk curtains. The furnishings in singles are also of high quality. Most of the bedrooms are different, many with sumptuous baths, marble walled with separate bath and shower, sink, bidet, and mountains of fresh towels. Singles rent for 340,000 lire ($258) daily; doubles, for 500,000 lire ($380).

The Excelsior Bar is perhaps the most famous on the via Veneto, and La Cupola restaurant is known for its national and regional cuisine, with dietetic and kosher food prepared on request. Among the amenities at the Excelsior are continuous room service, a beauty salon, a barber, a sauna, and babysitting service. The palatial hotel once attracted some of the stellar lights of the "Hollywood on the Tiber" era —notably Shelly Winters, Vittorio Gassman, Ingrid Bergman, and Roberto Rossellini. Nowadays, you're more likely to bump into international financiers and Arab princesses.

Le Grand Hotel, via Vittorio Emanuele Orlando 3, 00185 Roma (tel. 06/4709), just off the piazza della Repubblica, is one of the great hotels in Europe. When it was inaugurated by its creator, César Ritz, in 1894, Escoffier presided over a lavish banquet, and the note of grandeur struck then has never died away. Its roster of guests has included some of the greatest names in European history, including royalty of course, and New World moguls such as Henry Ford and J. P. Morgan. Only a few minutes from the via Veneto, the Grand looks like a large, late Renaissance palace, its five-floor façade covered with carved loggias, lintels, quoins, and cornices. Inside, the floors are covered with marble and Oriental rugs, the walls are a riot of baroque plasterwork, and crystal chandeliers, Louis XVI furniture, potted palms, antique clocks, and wall sconces complete the picture.

As for the 175 bedrooms, they are often lavishly decorated and equipped with TV, small bar, phone, dressing room, and tile bath. Every accommodation is different. While most are traditional with antique headboards and Venetian chandeliers, some are modern. The regular singles and doubles are quite spacious, costing from 330,000 lire ($251) daily in a single and from 525,000 lire ($399) in a double, plus I.V.A. and city tax. Every guest room is soundproof. The hotel's Le Grand Bar is an elegant meeting place for the elite of Rome and other cities and countries. Also among attractions here is the serving of tea every afternoon, accompanied by harp music. There is a buffet called Le Pavillon where you can enjoy quick meals amid potted plants, and Le Restaurant is the hotel's more formal dining room. Dietetic and kosher foods can be arranged with advance notice. The hotel has a beauty salon and babysitting service, and you can make arrangements to have your car parked in a garage. Of course, service is first rate.

FIRST-CLASS HOTELS

Here's a rundown of first-class establishments presented in geographical order.

Near the Piazza Navona

Hotel Raphaël, largo Febo 2, 00186 Roma (tel. 06/650-881), is known to the discerning who prefer a palace buried in the heart of Old Rome. A tasteful place, its façade draped with ivy, it lures with its sophisticated and restful atmosphere. International celebrities check in and out unobtrusively. All its air-conditioned bedrooms have a private bath or shower, and a few have their own terrace. A single rents for 186,000 lire ($141) daily, a double for 290,000 lire ($220), with breakfast, service, and taxes included. The bedrooms are individually decorated, with wood-grained built-ins. The hotel is air-conditioned. In the lounges are fine antiques, excellent art objects, ornate gilt mirrors, and high-backed chairs. The dining room has a big fireplace, and the bar carries its liquor inside a gilded baroque cabinet. But the special delight is the rooftop terrace, with its many levels. You can have drinks here, enjoying the vista of tile rooftops of nearby buildings.

Near the Railway Station

Hotel Quirinale, via Nazionale 7, 00184 Roma (tel. 06/4707), was originally built a century ago by the same architect who designed Rome's Teatro dell'Opera. The royal family of Vittorio Emmanuel gathered periodically in its soaring lobby for drinks before moving through a private entrance to the opera. Since then, the Quirinale has hosted more opera stars and composers than any other establishment in Rome. Maria Callas was fond of the hotel, and Giuseppe Verdi stayed here on April 13, 1893, during the premiere of *Falstaff*. The hotel is set a few paces from the huge fountains of the piazza della Repubblica.

Its soaring reception area has the predictable forest of marble columns, as well as barrel vaulting painted in imperial tones of gold and terracotta. Units facing the traffic of via Nazionale have soundproof windows. Those fortunate enough to secure a room overlooking the garden can listen to the sound of a splashing fountain or perhaps enjoy a rehearsal of *La Traviata* from the opera across the way. In a setting of trailing vines and ornate statuary, guests can enjoy afternoon coffee in the garden, later patronizing the hotel's restaurant which is of a high international standard.

Depending on the accommodation, singles cost 185,000 lire ($141) to 210,000 lire ($160) daily, and doubles or twins run 242,000 lire ($184) to 290,000 lire ($220), with a buffet breakfast and taxes included. Each of the 200 rooms contains air conditioning, a color TV, a fully accessorized (and often very spacious) bath, a mini-bar, and deeply comfortable, often Empire-inspired furniture. Several of the rooms offer Jacuzzi bathtub, as well as satellite TV reception. Drinks are served amid the antiques and oil paintings of the enormous lounge, but my favorite hideaway is the alcove-style bar decorated with vintage car prints and medallions of leading automobile clubs throughout the world.

Hotel Mediterraneo, via Cavour 15, 00184 Roma (tel. 06/464-051), is one of Rome's most vivid manifestations of Italian art deco styling. Although because of the war it wasn't completed until 1944, its blueprints were executed from 1936 to 1938 in anticipation of the hoped-for World's Fair of 1942. Because its position lay beside what Mussolini planned as his triumphant passageway through Rome, each of the local building codes was deliberately violated, and approval was granted for the creation of an unprecedented ten-floor hotel. Its height, coupled with its position on one of Rome's hills, provides panoramic views from its roof garden and bar, which is especially charming at night.

Mario Loreti, one of Mussolini's favorite architects, was the genius who planned for an interior sheathing of gray marble, the richly allegorical murals of inlaid wood, and the art deco friezes ringing the ceilings of the enormous public rooms. Don't overlook the gracefully curved bar, crafted from illuminated cut crystal, or the ships' figureheads that ring the ceiling of the wood-sheathed breakfast room. The lobby is also decorated with antique busts of Roman emperors, part of the Bettoja family's collection which they proudly display in this, their flagship hotel (they also own four other, less expensive hotels in the neighborhood). Each of the 300 bedrooms is spacious and pleasantly furnished, containing lots of exposed wood, stylish furniture, a private bath, color TV, radio, refrigerator, and phone. Singles cost 190,000 lire ($144) daily and doubles 270,000 lire ($205), with a continental breakfast included.

Hotel Massimo d'Azeglio, via Cavour 18, 00184 Roma (tel. 06/460-646), is the up-to-date hotel near the train station and opera that was established as a small restaurant by one of the founders of an Italian hotel dynasty more than a century ago. In World War II it was a refuge for the king of Serbia and also a favorite with Italian generals. Today this hotel is the "Casa Madre," or Mother House, of the Bettoja chain. Run by Angelo Bettoja and his charming wife, who hails from America's southland, it offers clean and comfortable accommodations in a central part of town. Its façade is one of the most elegant neoclassical structures in the area, and its lobby has been renovated, with light paneling, plus an adjacent bar and a well-trained staff. This oldest member of the Bettoja chain charges 162,000 lire ($123) daily for a single, 235,000 lire ($179) for a double. Each accommodation has a private bath, color TV, mini-bar, and air conditioning, and the rates include a continental breakfast. Its restaurant is covered separately in the dining section.

Near St. Peter's

Hotel Atlante Star, via Vitelleschi 34, 00193 Roma (tel. 06/687-9558), is a first-class hotel a short distance from St. Peter's Basilica and the Vatican. The tastefully renovated lobby is covered with dark marble, chrome trim, and lots of exposed wood, while the upper floors somehow give the impression of being inside a luxuriously appointed ocean liner. This stems partly from the lavish use of curved and lacquered surfaces, walls upholstered in freshly colored printed fabrics, modern bathrooms, and wall-to-wall carpeting. Even the door handles are art deco–inspired brass. These open into small but posh accommodations outfitted with all the modern comforts, such as frigo-bar, phone, color TV, and air conditioning. For 320,000 lire ($243) daily, two people can stay here in a twin or double room, with breakfast, tax, and service included. Singles pay 290,000 lire ($220) per night. The most attractive feature of the hotel is Les Etoiles, its roof-garden restaurant and solarium, with one of the most striking views of St. Peter's of any hotel in Rome. The restaurant has double rows of windows, planting, and terracotta floors along with white-painted garden furniture. A meal here costs from 75,000 lire ($57). If there is no room at this inn, the owner, Benito Mancucci, will try to get you a room at his nearby Atlante Garden.

Hotel Atlante Garden, via Crescenzio 78, 00193 Roma (tel. 06/687-2361), stands on a tree-lined street near the Vatican. More classical in its decor than its sister under the same management (the Hotel Atlante Star), the Atlante Garden offers 19th-century bedrooms that have been freshly papered and painted, and that contain tastefully conservative furniture. The renovated baths are tiled and open into rooms filled with all the modern accessories. Singles cost 260,000 lire ($198) daily, while doubles go for 290,000 lire ($220), breakfast included.

On the Via del Corso

Grand Hotel Plaza, via del Corso 126, 00186 Roma (tel. 06/672-101). The Empress Carlotta of Mexico received Pope Pius IX here in 1866, and in 1933 Pietro Mascagni composed his opera *Nerone* here. Vincent Price always stayed here while making "all those bad movies," and when you see the slightly faded but very grand decor, you'll understand why. The public rooms are vintage 19th century and contain stained-glass skylights, massive crystal chandeliers, potted palms, inlaid marble floors, and a life-size stone lion guarding the entrance to the ornate stairway leading upstairs. The bar seems an interminable distance across the parquet floor of the opulent ballroom. Single rooms cost from 145,000 lire ($110) daily, while doubles begin at 250,000 lire ($190), including a private bath.

West of the Piazza Navona

Cardinal Hotel, via Giulia 62, 00186 Roma (tel. 06/654-2719). Like many of the constructions in this part of town, this particular building has had a long and complicated history. Built by Bramante in the 15th century with stones hauled from the Roman Forum, it was intended as a courthouse but later became the center of the Armenian church in Rome. It stands on the city's most beautiful Renaissance street. Today's clients get a glimpse of the original stonework in the exposed walls of both the bar and the breakfast room, as well as the chiseled inscription of a Sabine tomb built into the red walls of one of the sitting areas. About a block from the Tiber, the hotel includes two inner courtyards dotted with statues, comfortable leather couches, and interior decor almost entirely done in shades of scarlet. The sunny bedrooms are clean and well furnished, and from the upper floors, offer interesting views of Renaissance Rome. Double rooms rent for around 189,000 lire ($144) daily; singles, 114,000 lire ($86.75). Each has a private bath, and a continental breakfast is included.

In the Quartiere Prati

Jolly Leonardo da Vinci, via dei Gracchi 324, 00192 Roma (tel. 06/39-680), stands in the Quartiere Prati, on the Vatican side of the Tiber (across the bridge from the piazza del Popolo). The modern hotel has large public lounges furnished with leather-covered, deep armchairs. Fully redecorated rooms, which come in a wide variety of shapes, are completely equipped with all facilities, including private bath, air conditioning, color TV, phone, mini-bar, and hairdryer. Singles cost from 178,000 lire ($135) daily and doubles begin at 240,000 lire ($182); all tariffs include a buffet breakfast called Buongiorno Jolly. The hotel has an American bar, a restaurant, a grill, and a snackbar. Meals in the restaurant cost from 50,000 lire ($38). Politicians and film and TV stars who live in Rome are regular clients of the outstanding men's hair stylist, Amleto, at this hotel, and there is also a hairdresser for women. You can use the underground garage for your car.

Giulio Cesare, via degli Scipioni 287, 00192 Roma (tel. 06/321-0751), is an elegant villa, the former house of the Countess Paterno Solari, converted into a tasteful hotel in this sedate part of Rome, across the Tiber from the piazza del Popolo. In the guest salon, where the countess once entertained diplomats from all over the globe, the furnishings are antique for the most part, in rose velvet and dusty blue, resting on Oriental carpets. In the public rooms are tapestries, Persian rugs, mirrors, ornate gilt pieces, and crystal chandeliers. In yet a smaller salon, guests gather for drinks in an atmosphere of fruitwood paneling and 18th-century furnishings. The carpeted bedrooms are furnished as in a lovely private home, with a single color theme (of many shades) predominating. Needlepoint chairs are in some of the rooms. With an American breakfast buffet, a single in high season rents for 220,000 lire ($167) daily; a double, 290,000 lire ($220). Other facilities include a garden where breakfast is served, a snackbar, a piano bar, and a garage.

Near the Pantheon

Overlooking this landmark of ancient Rome, an absolute gem of a hotel is the **Albergo del Sole al Pantheon,** piazza della Rotonda 63, 00186 Roma (tel. 06/678-0441). The present-day albergo is one of the oldest hotels in the world; the first records of it as a hostelry appear in 1467. Long known as a retreat for emperors and sorcerers, the hotel has hosted such guests as Frederick III of the Habsburg family. Mascagni celebrated the premiere of *Cavalleria Rusticana* here. In time it was to draw such distinguished company as Jean-Paul Sartre and his companion, Simone de Beauvoir. Today the 26 rooms are exquisitely furnished and decorated with period pieces and stylized reproductions. Singles pay 190,000 lire ($144) nightly; doubles cost from 300,000 lire ($228).

In the Parioli District

Hotel Lord Byron, via G. de Notaris 5, 00197 Roma (tel. 06/361-5404), is an art deco villa set on a residential hilltop in Parioli, an area of embassies and exclusive town houses at the edge of the Villa Borghese. From the curving entrance steps off the staffed parking lot in front, you'll notice design accessories that attract the most sophisticated clientele in Italy. An oval Renaissance urn in chiseled marble fills a niche created for it in the reception area, whose walls are covered with top-quality burled paneling. Flowers are everywhere, the lighting is discreet, and everything is on the kind of cultivated small scale that makes such a place seem more like a well-staffed (and extremely expensive) private home than a hotel. Each of the 40 rooms is different, most often with lots of mirrors, upholstered walls, spacious bathroom with gray marble accessories, big dressing room/closet, and all the amenities needed. Singles cost from 350,000 lire ($266) daily and doubles begin at 420,000 lire ($319), breakfast included. On the premises is one of Rome's best restaurants, covered separately in the dining section.

Near the Spanish Steps

Hotel de la Ville, via Sistina 67-71, 00187 Roma (tel. 06/6733), stands at the top of the Spanish Steps, next door to the deluxe Hassler, on a street lined with boutiques. The severe façade doesn't begin to reveal the beauty of the interior. All its 197 bedrooms and public areas have been completely refurbished in a beautifully classic and yet up-to-date way. Singles with bath cost 269,000 lire ($204) daily; doubles with bath, 356,000 lire ($271). The above rates are inclusive of a continental breakfast, service, taxes, and air conditioning. At the Hotel de la Ville, a multitude of formal lounges and loggias are decked out in a harmonious white, with fruitwoods, reddish browns, and golds. The villa opens onto a rear garden, nestled against the hillside. A large-scale patio is created, surrounded by balconies with flowering plants and vines. The Patio Restaurant on the second floor overlooks the garden and serves both Italian and international cuisine, and there is an American piano bar presided over by a resident pianist. The hotel is housed in a former palace, built in the 19th century on the site of the ancient Lucullus's Gardens. At night, the panoramic view from the roof terrace is inspiring.

Near the Piazza Colonna

Colonna Palace Hotel, piazza Montecitorio 12, 00186 Roma (tel. 06/687-1341), is housed in a stately five-story building within sight of both the Italian Parliament and the newspaper offices of *Il Tempo*. Despite its Renaissance façade, the hotel's busy interior is stylishly modern, with the kind of lobby where politicians and journalists can talk intimately while seated on one of dozens of leather sofas. The keys that open the 110 air-conditioned bedrooms, each well furnished, are attached to brass replicas of the soaring obelisk standing a few steps from the entrance to the hotel. Singles cost 205,000 lire ($156) daily; doubles, 265,000 lire ($201). All accommodations have complete bath, color TV with free in-house movies, radio, refrigerator, and direct-dial phone. The hotel has an American piano bar and an elegant breakfast room.

Albergo Nazionale, piazza Montecitorio 131, 00186 Roma (tel. 06/678-9251), faces one of Rome's most historic squares, the piazza Colonna, with its Column of Marcus Aurelius, the Palazzo di Montecitorio, and the Palazzo Chigi. Because of its location next to the Parliament buildings, the albergo is frequently used by government officials and members of diplomatic staffs. In fact, it maintains the atmosphere of a gentleman's club, although women are welcome too. There are many nooks conducive to conversation in the public lounges. The lobbies are wood-paneled, and many antiques have been used throughout the hotel. Rooms are usually spacious, decorated in a traditional style, either carpeted or floored with marble. A double costs 288,000 lire ($219) daily, and a single is 175,000 lire ($133), including a continental breakfast. Some of the bedrooms contain that thoughtful extra, a small icebox. Air conditioning is available in summer.

Near the Colosseum

Hotel Forum, via Tor dei Conti 25-30, 00184 Roma (tel. 06/679-2446), off the Fori Imperiali, offers an elegance that savors the drama of Old Rome, as well as tasteful, sometimes opulent, accommodations. It's a medium-size gem (90 rooms —all with bath or shower), whose accommodations and dining roof terrace look out upon the sights of the ancient city—the Colosseum or Forum. The hotel is built around a medieval bell tower. The bedrooms are well appointed with antiques, mirrors, marquetry, and Oriental rugs. In high season, the Forum charges an inclusive 330,000 lire ($251) daily for a double and 230,000 lire ($175) for a single. Low-season prices are 240,000 lire ($182) in a double, 170,000 lire ($129) in a single. Reserve in advance. The Forum's lounges are as conservatively conceived as a country estate, with paneled walls, and furnishings that combine Italian and French provincial. Dining is an event—either sitting on tapestry-covered chairs in front of picture windows or on the spacious terrace. During the season, you can enjoy an *aperitivo* at the hotel's bar on the roof, surveying the timeless Roman Forum.

On and Around the Via Veneto

Grand Hotel Flora, via Vittorio Veneto 191, 00187 Roma (tel. 06/497-821), is built in the style of the grand hotel, enjoying one of the most superb locations of any hotel in Rome—right at the top of the via Veneto, at the entrance to the Villa Borghese and the Pincio. Now better than ever, the Flora offers 200 renewed bedrooms, all with bath and shower. There's air conditioning as well. The bedchambers, beautifully maintained, are of generous size, costing 220,000 lire ($167) daily in a single, 320,000 lire ($243) in a double, all with a continental breakfast. The public rooms are tastefully decorated with velvet-upholstered armchairs, Oriental carpets, antiques, and crystal chandeliers.

Jolly Vittorio Veneto, corso d'Italia 1, 00198 Roma (tel. 06/8495), lies between the Villa Borghese gardens and the via Veneto. Totally ignoring the traditional, the hotel's architects opted for modern in metal and concrete, with bronze-tinted windows. Try to get one of the units with a garden view. To register, you descend a grand staircase, arriving at a sunken lobby. The rooms here are bold in concept, compact in space, and contemporary in furnishings. For a room and a buffet breakfast, the single tariff is 200,000 lire ($152) daily, increasing to about 270,000 lire ($205) in a double or twin. These rates include tax and service.

Alexandra, via Vittorio Veneto 18, 00187 Roma (tel. 06/461-943), is a narrow stone building with baroque detail on the windows and a white lobby with carpeting and a scattering of antiques. Fifty rooms are reached via a postage-stamp-size elevator. The accommodations are usually spacious (the biggest are the doubles in the rear), sometimes with views of the action on the via Veneto. Each is equipped with TV, frigo-bar, air conditioning, radio, and phone. Some of the doubles have fine old beds and plaster detail on the ceiling. All are quite comfortable and have private bath or shower. Rates are 115,000 lire ($87.50) daily in a single, 160,000 lire ($122) in a double. Prices include breakfast, taxes, and service.

Victoria Roma, via Campania 41, 00187 Roma (tel. 06/473-931), will fool you. As you sit on wrought-iron chairs on its roof garden, drinking your apéritif in a forest of palms and potted plants—all overlooking the Borghese Gardens—you'll think you're at a country villa. But the via Veneto's just across the way. Even the lounges and living rooms retain that country-house décor, with soft touches, including high-backed chairs, large oil paintings, bowls of freshly cut flowers, provincial tables, and Oriental rugs. The Swiss owner, Alberto H. Wirth, has set unusual requirements of innkeeping (no groups), and has attracted a fine clientele over the years—diplomats, executives, artists. The bedrooms are well furnished and maintained. All the rooms have private bath, color TV, mini-bar, and direct-dial phone. Rates begin at 165,000 lire ($125) daily for a single, 270,000 lire ($205) for a double. Meals can be taken à la carte in the elegant grill room, which serves the best of Italian and French cuisine.

La Residenza, via Emilia 22-24, 00187 Roma (tel. 06/460-789), successfully combines the intimacy of a generously sized town house with the elegant appointments of a well-decorated hotel. The location is superb—in the neighborhood of the via Veneto, the American Embassy, and the Villa Borghese. The converted villa has an ochre-colored façade, an ivy-covered courtyard, a quiet location, and a labyrinthine series of plushly upholstered public rooms. These contain Oriental rugs,

Empire divans, oil portraits, and warmly accommodating groupings of rattan chairs with cushions. Each of the 27 bedrooms has a private bath or shower, plus a mini-bar, TV, and radio, along with a phone. A series of terraces is scattered strategically throughout the hotel, which combines to make this one of my favorite stopovers in the city. Singles cost from 95,000 lire ($72.25) daily and doubles run 155,000 lire ($118) to 180,000 lire ($137), with an American breakfast included, the latter the price of a suite.

Pullman Hotel Boston, via Lombardia 47, 00187 Roma (tel. 06/473-951), just three blocks from the via Veneto and about a five-minute walk from the Spanish Steps, has been entirely renovated and upgraded. Across the street from the Villa Borghese, it is a choice address for conservative-minded readers on a Roman holiday. In all, 121 bedrooms are offered, those on the seventh floor containing private terraces. Singles are rented for 200,000 lire ($152) daily; doubles, 260,000 lire ($198). The private accommodations are most comfortable, the furnishings traditional (much of it reproductions of Victorian pieces). Tariffs include service, taxes, a continental breakfast, and air conditioning. The lobbies are on several levels, and they have a sedate aura with brown marble and velvet-covered pieces. The bar, likewise, continues the theme with its carved wood and smoked mirrors. The hotel also has a good-size restaurant, filled with plush chairs.

Hotel Oxford, via Boncompagni 93, (off the via Veneto), 00187 Roma (tel. 06/475-6852), is centrally located, not only near the smartest street in Rome but also adjacent to Borghese Park. The Oxford has been renovated and is centrally heated and fully carpeted. There is a pleasant lounge and a cozy bar (which serves snacks), plus a dining room offering a good Italian cuisine. The hotel is on the American Embassy's preferred list of moderately priced hotels in Rome that can be confidently recommended to U.S. visitors. In a twin-bedded room the charge is from 170,000 lire ($129) daily, 115,000 lire ($87.50) in a single, including a continental breakfast.

3. Medium-Priced Hotels

NEAR THE COLOSSEUM

Not far from the Santa Maria Maggiore Basilica, the **Colosseum Hotel,** via Sforza 10, 00184 Roma (tel. 06/475-1228), offers baronial living on a miniature scale. Someone with insight and lira notes designed this 50-room hotel (with private baths) in excellent taste, a reflection of the best in Italy's design heritage. The bedrooms are furnished with well-conceived antique reproductions (beds of heavy carved wood, dark-paneled wardrobes, leatherwood chairs)—and all with monk-like white walls. Opened in the summer of 1965, the Colosseum charges an inclusive 130,000 lire ($98.75) daily for a double in season. Singles pay 80,000 lire ($60.75) in season. The drawing room, with its long refectory table, white walls, red tiles, and provincial armchairs, invites lingering. The reception room, with its parquet floors, arched ceilings, and Savonarola chair, makes a good impression.

Hotel Degli Aranci, Barnaba Oriani 11, 00197 Roma (tel. 06/870-202), is a former private villa on a tree-lined residential street, surrounded by similar villas now used, in part, as consulates and ambassadorial town houses. Most of the accommodations have tall windows opening onto city views, and are filled with provincial furnishings or English-style reproductions. The public rooms have memorabilia of ancient Rome scattered about, including bisque-colored medallions of soldiers in profile, old engravings of ruins, and classical vases highlighted against the light-grained paneling. A marble-topped bar in an alcove off the sitting room adds a relaxed touch. Doubles rent for 150,000 lire ($114) daily, and singles, 110,000 lire ($83.50), with a continental breakfast included. All units have private bath and shower. The breakfast room, built at the rear of the house, has walls of glass, opening onto the tops of orange trees.

NEAR THE SPANISH STEPS

The aptly named **Carriage,** via delle Carrozze 36, 00187 Roma (tel. 06/679-5166), caters to the "carriage trade," including many staff members of the British and French embassies, plus an occasional movie star or film director. The 18th-century façade covers some charming, although small, accommodations (if you reserve, ask for one of the two rooftop bedrooms). Antiques have been used tastefully, creating a personal aura, even in the bedrooms, with their matching bedcovers and draperies. All 24 of the accommodations have air conditioning, bath, mini-bar, color TV, phone, and radio. For one of the stylish bedrooms, you pay 140,000 lire ($106) daily in a single, 195,000 lire ($148) in a double, including I.V.A. tax and a continental breakfast. To meet your fellow guests, head for the Renaissance-style salon that is called an American bar or else the roof garden.

Hotel d'Inghilterra, via Bocca di Leone 14, 00187 Roma (tel. 06/672-161), nostalgically holds onto its traditions and heritage, although it has been completely renovated. Considered the most fashionable small hotel in Rome, it's been the favorite of many a discriminating "personage"—Anatole France, Ernest Hemingway, Alec Guinness. (In the 19th century, the king of Portugal met here with the pope.) The bedrooms have mostly old pieces—gilt and much marble, along with mahogany chests and glittery mirrors. Rates quoted include taxes and service charges. Singles cost 275,000 lire ($209) daily; doubles, 355,000 lire ($270). The main salon of the hotel is dominated by an impressive gilt mirror and console, surrounded by Victorian furniture. The preferred bedrooms are higher up, opening onto a tile terrace, with a balustrade and a railing covered with flowering vines and plants. The English-style bar is a favorite gathering spot in the evening, with its paneled walls, tip-top tables, and old lamps casting soft light.

Hotel Gregoriana, via Gregoriana 18, 00187 Roma (tel. 06/679-4269), is a small, elite hotel favored by members of the Italian fashion industry who tend to book rooms here for visiting friends from out of town. The ruling matriarch of an aristocratic family left the building to an order of nuns in the 19th century, but they eventually retreated to other quarters. Today there might be a slightly more elevated spirituality in Room C than in the rest of the hotel, as it used to be a chapel. However, throughout the establishment, the smallish rooms provide comfort and Italian design. The elevator cage is a black-and-gold art deco fantasy, while the door to each accommodation is indicated with a reproduction of an Erté print whose fanciful characters in some way indicate the letter designating that particular room. You'll pay the bill in the tiny, rattan-covered lobby. The rooms, all with air conditioning and private bath, rent for 110,000 lire ($83.50) daily in a single, 175,000 lire ($133) in a double, and 220,000 lire ($167) in a triple, with breakfast included.

Internazionale, via Sistina 79, 00187 Roma (tel. 06/679-30-47), a short walk from the Spanish Steps, is part of the past—built in 1870 and reflecting the traditional ease of life in those days. But some of its rooms go as far back as the 16th century. The hotel has been a popular tourist nesting place since the '20s. The rooms—some with private balconies, ornate furnishings, and all with color TV—go for 146,000 lire ($111) daily in a single, 210,000 lire ($160) in a double, each with private bath. Rates include service, taxes, and air conditioning, as well as continental breakfast.

At the top of the steps, **Scalinata di Spagna,** piazza Trinità dei Monti 17, 00187 Roma (tel. 06/679-3006), was the most famous pensione in Rome before its conversion in 1988 into a three-star hotel. It's directly across the small piazza from the deluxe Hassler. This is a delightful little building—only two floors are visible from the outside—done up in mustard-yellow and burgundy-red paint and nestled between much larger structures. You'll recognize the four relief columns across the façade and the window boxes with their bright blossoms, which look as if they should be out in the country somewhere instead of in the center of Rome. The interior is like an old inn. The public rooms are small, with old clocks and low ceilings. Each of the 14 rooms has a frigo-bar. The decorations vary radically from one room to the next, and some have low, beamed ceilings and ancient-looking wood furniture while others have loftier ceilings and more average appointments. Everything is spotless and pleasing to the eye. In a single with bath the tariff is 107,500 lire ($81.75) daily. A double with shower or bath rents for 165,000 lire ($125). Prices include taxes and a continental breakfast. In season, the morning meal is served on the roof-garden terrace with its sweeping view of the dome of St. Peter's across the Tiber. Reserve well in advance.

Hotel Madrid, via Mario dei Fiori 93, 00187 Roma (tel. 06/679-1243), is a winner for its convenient location near the Spanish Steps in "boutique land." It's a mellow ochre fin-de-siècle building, completely neat and clean. Its furnishings are up-to-date, but utilitarian, with beds set against wood-grained headboards, bedside lights, and phones. The rates are the same all year and include service and taxes. In a double room, prices are 170,000 lire ($129) daily. A few suites, suitable for three persons, go for 190,000 lire ($144), and a double rented as a single costs 130,000 lire ($98.75). These tariffs include a continental breakfast that is often served on the roof garden amid ivy and blossoming plants, with its view of the cupolas of Rome.

King, via Sistina 131, 00187 Roma (tel. 06/474-1515), is a rather regal name for a modestly furnished although comfortable accommodation. However, the location is ideal, right on a boutique-lined narrow street that leads to the Spanish Steps. This sedate older hotel offers many rooms with private bath and shower, plus phone. Many repeat visitors speak of the King as their "oasis in the heart of Rome." The most expensive doubles with bath rent for 150,000 lire ($114) daily, and singles with bath cost 110,000 lire ($83.50). A continental breakfast is the only meal served. On the rooftop is an open terrace with sheltered garden benches, tables, and flower boxes, and from the perch you'll have a sweeping vista of the Eternal City.

NEAR ST. PETER'S

In an impressive 15th-century palace, the **Hotel Columbus,** via della Conciliazione 33, 00193 Roma (tel. 06/686-5245), is within a few minutes' walk of St. Peter's. Once it was the private home of a wealthy cardinal under Julius II, the curse of Michelangelo's life. Its trim, even austere, Renaissance façade belies its rather handsome interior, much overhauled. Some of its dramatic rooms are still intact, with ornate painted ceilings, overscale antique furnishings, and a courtyard with colonnaded arches. Many of the 120 bedrooms have private bath and shower big enough to have housed Pinturicchio and his fellow fresco artists. Some of the bedrooms have a view of the basilica. Rates in rooms with bath at the Columbus, which was built some 12 years before its namesake set off for America, are 90,000 lire ($68.50) to 110,000 lire ($83.50) daily in a single and 150,000 lire ($114) to 170,000 lire ($129) in a double.

NEAR THE PIAZZA VENEZIA

An ancient patrician palace houses **Tiziano,** corso Vittorio Emanuele 110, 00186 Roma (tel. 06/687-5087), renovated and improved in its overall structure. The changes complement the unique style of the Palazzo Pacelli (the family of Pope Pius XII). While making the hotel more comfortable and functional, the atmosphere suggested by the classic architecture has been maintained. Rent is 130,000 lire ($98.75) daily for a single with bath, 165,000 lire ($125) for a double with bath. There is a private garage where customers may park their cars at an extra charge.

IN PARIOLI

A three-star place to stay, the **Hotel delle Muse,** via Tommaso Salvini 18, 00197 Roma (tel. 06/870-095), is not far from the Villa Borghese. It's run by the

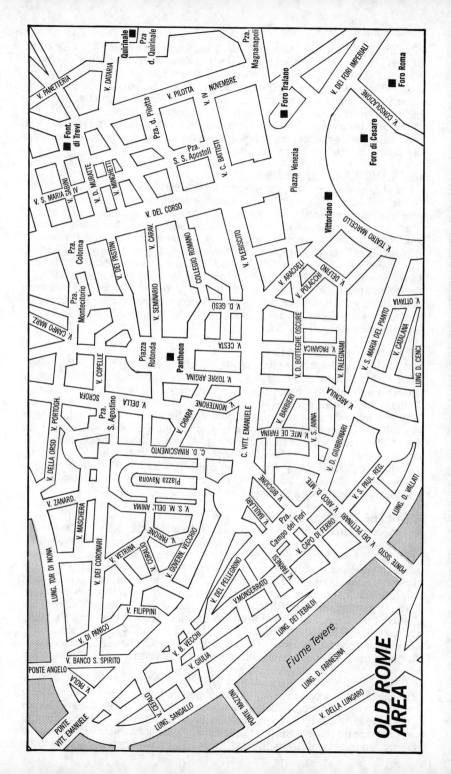

OLD ROME AREA

efficient, English-speaking Giorgio Lazar. Furnishings are modern in a wide range of splashy colors. The 100-bed hotel provides rooms with private baths, direct-dial phones, and color TVs. Singles rent for 74,500 lire ($56.50) daily, doubles go for 116,000 lire ($88.25), and triples cost 160,000 lire ($122). All tariffs include a continental breakfast, taxes, and service. In the summer, Mr. Lazar operates a pleasant restaurant in the garden, where you can obtain a complete meal for 18,000 lire ($13.75). A bar is open 24 hours a day in case you get thirsty at 5 a.m. There's also a TV room, plus a writing room and two dining rooms, along with a garage for your car. Buses that stop nearby run to all parts of the city.

NEAR THE PIAZZA COLONNA

In business since 1787, the **Albergo Cesàri,** via di Pietra 89A, 00186 Roma (tel. 06/679-2886), has long been a favored choice of the literati and political personalities, attracting such names as Stendhal, Garibaldi, and Mazzini. Its interior has been thoroughly overhauled, with many baths installed and a bar drawing a lively social crowd. Today's visitor can be assured of a good accommodation in a history-rich district of Rome. No lunches or dinners are offered—just rooms and breakfast. The charge for singles is 50,500 lire ($38.50) daily without bath, 88,500 lire ($67.25) with bath. Doubles rent for 91,000 lire ($69.25) without bath, 113,500 lire ($86.25) with bath. A triple with bath is offered for 151,500 lire ($115.25). All rates include a continental breakfast, taxes, and service. Prices are reduced from December through February. The Cesàri is handy to the Temple of Neptune and many little antique shops.

NEAR THE QUIRINAL PALACE

Dating from 1900, the **Hotel Bolivar,** via della Cordonata 6, 00187 Roma (tel. 06/679-1614), lies only a few blocks from the presidential palace, but its location on an isolated cul-de-sac makes it seem like something in a rural corner of Tuscany. Designed in the palazzo style of symmetrical windows and overhanging roofs, it was built on a hilltop looking out over the domes of Old Rome. Modernized, the interior still contains the high ceilings of its original design and a staircase wide enough for a Volkswagen. Some of the bedrooms are more stylish than others, but each is clean, relatively spacious, and air-conditioned, with TV and mini-bar. Singles go for 120,000 lire ($91.25) daily, and doubles run 180,000 lire ($137), these rates including breakfast, service, and taxes. On the uppermost floor, the hotel offers a restaurant with a large, sunny terrace.

NEAR THE TERMINAL STATION

A leading selection in its price bracket is the **Hotel Atlantico,** via Cavour 23, 00184 Roma (tel. 06/485-951), founded in 1910 and later rebuilt in 1935. This comfortable hotel has an old-fashioned aura, but it has been considerably modernized and updated, making it one of the finer properties lying within a few blocks of the rail station. This is one of the smaller hotels of the family-run Bettoja chain so, if it is full, one of the polite employees will direct you to one of their nearby hotels. There's a pleasing lobby, and the comfortable, spacious bedrooms are filled with upholstered furniture. Each has a private bath, color TV, and mini-bar. The hotel charges 140,000 lire ($106) daily in a single, 195,000 lire ($148) in a double, with a continental breakfast included. The hotel connects with the Mediterraneo "21" Restaurant and is air-conditioned throughout. It is sensitive to American travel needs.

San Giorgio, via G. Amendola 61, 00185 Roma (tel. 06/475-1341), is a four-star, first-class hotel in the vicinity of the rail station. Built in 1940, it is constantly improved by its founders, the Bettoja family-run hotel chain. In fact, the San Giorgio is connected to the original hotel, Massimo d'Azeglio, so guests of the San Giorgio can patronize that establishment's fine restaurant without having to walk out on the street. Soundproof and air-conditioned, the hotel is ideal for families, as many of its corner rooms can be converted into suites. Each unit has a radio, color TV, and mini-bar, often lying behind wood-veneer doors. In 1950 the hotel became the first one in Rome to be air-conditioned. It charges 140,000 lire ($106) daily in a single, 195,000 lire ($148) in a double, with a continental breakfast included. Breakfast is served in a light and airy room. The staff is most helpful in easing your adjustment into the Roman capital.

Nord Nuova Roma, via G. Amendola 3, 00185 Roma (tel. 06/465-441), is the best bargain in the family-run Bettoja chain. In the vicinity of the rail station, this air-conditioned hotel is a good family choice. Bedrooms are standard and modernized, with air conditioning, color TVs, and mini-bars, all well maintained and comfortable. Singles with bath cost 110,000 lire ($83.50) daily, and twins, also with bath, go for 165,000 lire ($125), including a continental breakfast. The hotel has a small, intimate bar.

Sitea, via Vittorio Emanuele Orlando 90, 00185 Roma (tel. 06/475-4696), is directly across from the Grand Hotel, only three minutes from the railway station plaza. It's family run, and bears the stamp of excellent personal taste and a sense of how to run a good hotel. Perhaps that explains the coterie of painters, writers, and embassy personnel who have been attracted here over the years. All rooms have private bath and air conditioning, and the bedrooms have individual styles—Venetian, provincial, old pieces, or reproductions. In all, there's a happy use of color. Single rooms cost 135,000 lire ($103) daily. Two people pay 220,000 lire ($167) for a room, and all rates include a continental breakfast. There is a large, air-conditioned roof bar, and in one corner of the dining room is a circular fireplace with a raised brick hearth.

Albergo Nizza, via Massimo d'Azeglio 16, 00185 Roma (tel. 06/474-3172), lying within a two-minute walk of the rail station, hides behind the restored dignity of a 19th-century façade. Standing on a quiet street corner in the vicinity of the opera house, it is a breakfast-only hotel, but it's surrounded by low-cost trattorie. It is also convenient to several modes of public transportation. With a continental breakfast included, singles cost 95,000 lire ($72.25) daily; doubles, 135,000 lire ($103). Adjacent to the reception desk is a spacious TV lounge with a stainless-steel bar.

Hotel Marcella, via Flavia 106, 00187 Roma (tel. 06/474-6451), is a most attractive hotel in a residential and commercial neighborhood. After renovations, it won a prize from the Rome Tourist Board. The lattices of its garden-style lobby create a lush decor. Many of the often-stylish bedrooms contain separate sun alcoves raised on a dais, as well as color TV, air conditioning, radio, mini-bar, and a tile bath. Singles cost from 125,000 lire ($95) daily, and doubles start at 190,000 lire ($144), with breakfast included. My favorite area is the flowery rooftop sun terrace, with its well-stocked bar and distant panorama of St. Peter's.

Medici, via Flavia 96, 00187 Roma (tel. 06/475-1319), built in 1906, is a substantial hotel, in a central position for easy access to the railway terminal and the shops along via XX Settembre. Behind its neat chocolate-colored façade are 59 rooms with bath, 10 without bath. All units have phone and frigo-bar. Many of its better rooms overlook an inner patio garden, with Roman columns and benches, posts holding up greenery, and climbing ivy. This miniature refuge is favored by guests for breakfast or afternoon refreshments. The lounge, with its white coved ceiling, has many branches or nooks, all connected by wide white arches. Furnishings are traditional, with lots of antiques. Likewise, the generous-size bedrooms are also attractively furnished, each with a phone and central heating. You'll pay 125,000 lire ($95) daily in a double with private bath; singles cost 75,000 lire ($57). Prices include a continental breakfast, taxes, and service.

Hotel Pavia, via Gaeta 83, 00185 Roma (tel. 06/460-379), is my favorite hotel on this quiet street near the gardens of the Baths of Diocletian and the railway station. You'll pass through a wisteria-covered passageway, which leads to the recently modernized reception area of what used to be a private villa. The public rooms are tastefully covered in light-grained paneling with white lacquer accents and plush carpeting. The staff is attentive. Each room is unusually quiet, often with a good view, and attractively furnished with simple, modern wood furniture and calming colors. Double units, with breakfast included, cost from 149,000 lire ($113) daily; singles begin at 97,000 lire ($73.75). Ask about special weekend rates.

Rex, via Torino 149, 00184 Roma (tel. 06/475-1310), near the opera house, still retains much of the architectural dignity it had when it was the private palazzo of a Spanish duke. You'll still find the marble stairway, the original high coffered ceilings, crystal chandeliers, and a baronial carved-stone fireplace in the living room. However, the former gardens have long ago given way to a modern bedroom annex with up-to-date amenities. The antique accommodations have far greater flair. No matter which wing you're in, a room with bath will cost 70,000 lire ($53.25) daily in a single, 125,000 lire ($95) in a double. There is an American bar where you can order drinks throughout the evening.

Hotel Siviglia, via Gaeta 12, 00185 Roma (tel. 06/404-1195), was built as a private villa late in the 19th century in a Victor Emmanuel style of cream-colored pilasters and neoclassical detailing. Inside is a combination of antique grandeur and modern comfort. Bronze lampbearers ornament the stairs leading to the 41 simply furnished but high-ceilinged bedrooms. A few of these have sun terraces, and each has a private bath. With breakfast included, singles go for 90,000 lire ($68.50) daily; doubles, 135,000 lire ($103). Breakfast is served either in a tavern-like basement dining room or in a small side garden under the shade of a venerable palm.

Fiamma, via Gaeta 61, 00185 Roma (tel. 06/475-0083), is on the far side of the Baths of Diocletian. It's a renovated old building, with five floors of shuttered windows and a ground floor faced with marble and plate-glass windows. The lobby is long and bright, filled to the brim with a varied collection of furnishings, including armchairs, blue enamel railings, and indirect lighting. On the same floor (made of marble, no less) is a small breakfast room. All rooms have private bath. Doubles rent for 133,000 lire ($101) daily; singles, 86,000 lire ($65.25). These prices include a continental breakfast, tax, and service.

Hotel Galileo, via Palestro 33, 00185 Roma (tel. 06/404-1207), renovated in 1985, receives high honors in its category for good value, comfortable accommodations, and a desirable location. Its entrance lies to the side of a buff- and cream-colored 19th-century palace, at the end of a cobblestone passage whose pavement is set into patterns of papyrus leaves. Inside, an intimate bar stands a few steps from the stylishly modern reception area. An elevator leads to 39 often sunny and very clean bedrooms, each a bit larger than you might expect and filled with angular but attractive furniture. Each contains a modern bath and a phone, and a few units offer private terraces. No meals are served other than breakfast, which in inclement weather is offered on a flower garden terrace several floors above street level. With breakfast included, singles cost 83,000 lire ($63) daily; doubles, 127,000 lire ($96.50).

Hotel Centro, via Firenze 12, 00184 Roma (tel. 06/464-142), on a quiet street between the busy via Nazionale and the opera house, offers reasonably priced accommodations and pleasant surroundings. Each of its comfortable 36 rooms contains a private bath, air conditioning, and a radio. With breakfast included, the streamlined bedrooms rent for 115,000 lire ($87.50) daily in a single, 150,000 lire ($114) in a double. The hotel has its own parking garage.

Britannia Hotel, via Napoli 64, 00184 Roma (tel. 06/465-785), takes its name from its location next to an Anglican church on a street right off the via Nazionale, within walking distance of the main rail station. Its elaborately detailed Victor Emmanuel façade is graced with plant-filled upper terraces, each of which adds a note much like that of a private garden. Inside is found one of the neighborhood's most stylish renovations. The bar contains a labyrinth of banquettes, each padded with plush cushions and dramatized with mirrors and lots of plants. Upstairs, the 32 bedrooms are outfitted in monochromatic schemes of gray, blue, or pink, with carpeting and modern paintings. Each unit has a radio, color TV, phone, personal safe, frigo-bar, fire alarm, and a bath with radio, phone, hairdryer, scales, and a sunlamp.

Some of the rooms have wide private terraces. Singles rent for 170,000 lire ($129) daily, and doubles go for 205,000 lire ($156).

NEAR THE VIA VENETO

At the corner of the via Veneto, **Hotel Sicilia,** via Sicilia 24, 00187 Roma (tel. 06/493-841), is a three-star hotel near the American Embassy. The interior of the classic 18th-century building is completely renovated and contains a bar and restaurant as well as 92 well-furnished rooms, all with private bath or shower. A single rents for 87,000 lire ($66) daily; a double goes for 119,000 lire ($90.50). All tariffs include a continental breakfast, service, and taxes. It's important to reserve well in advance if you want to stay here.

NEAR THE BARBERINI PALACE

Favored by Americans is the **Anglo-Americano,** via Quattro Fontane 12, 00184 Roma (tel. 06/472-941). Its location near the piazza Barberini is unbeatable. The hotel has been given a new lease on life, as befits its position next to the Barberini Palace. The interiors of both the public and private rooms are carpeted, and come complete with air conditioning, an automatic switchboard, baths in all the rooms, color TV and radio, even a frigo-bar. Lavish use is made of leather and wood, even fabric on the walls. The rate in a single is 120,000 lire ($91.25) daily, rising to 168,000 lire ($128) in a double. A continental breakfast, included in the rates, is taken on the roof garden.

Hotel Cecil, via Francesco Crispi 55A, 00187 Roma (tel. 06/679-7996), is where Henrik Ibsen lived in the 1860s while preparing *Peer Gynt* and *Brand.* Today it's an attractively streamlined hotel of 32 no-frills bedrooms which, despite their simple furnishings, are clean and comfortable. Many units contain parquet floors and patterned wallpapers, and each has a private bath. With bath and breakfast included, singles cost 80,000 lire ($60.75) daily and doubles run 125,000 lire ($95). The location is not far from the via Sistina, which runs into the top of the Spanish Steps.

4. Budget Lodgings

NEAR THE PIAZZA DEL POPOLO

On a cobblestone street, the **Hotel Margutta,** via Laurina 34, 00187 Roma (tel. 06/679-8440), offers attractively decorated rooms, often in a riot of contrasting fabrics and patterns, and helpful staff. You'll register in a paneled lobby with a black stone floor, off which is a simple breakfast room covered with framed lithographs. The 25 rooms all have private bath and phone. Doubles cost 85,000 lire ($64.50) to 95,000 lire ($72.25) daily, the latter price for one of the three top-floor rooms with a view. There are no singles, but a double can be rented for single occupancy for 70,000 lire ($53.25). All rates include breakfast, service, and taxes.

NEAR THE PIAZZA NAVONA

In the heart of Old Rome, the **Hotel Portoghesi,** via dei Portoghesi 1, 00186 Roma (tel. 06/686-4231), is on a street that intersects via Scrofa between the piazza Navona and the Mausoleum of Augustus. The Portoghesi is in the middle of a perfect tangle of streets that look all the more medieval thanks to the presence of an ancient tower across from the hotel. This was the type of tower into which warring families retreated during the periodic civil chaos that engulfed Rome every time a pope died. Whether the Portoghesi dates from those days is uncertain, but the hotel is much in keeping with the times today. Taking its name from the Portuguese Church of St. Anthony, this pleasant hotel boasts a scattering of antiques along its upper floors and 27 freshly renovated bedrooms. The owner charges 61,000 lire ($46.25) daily in a single with bath, 86,000 lire ($65.25) in a bathless double, and 102,000 lire ($77.50) to 139,000 lire ($106) in a double with bath. Prices include a continental breakfast, service, and taxes.

NEAR THE TERMINAL

Visitors find that the **Hotel Venezia,** via Varese 18, 00185 Roma (tel. 06/445-7101), has three points in its favor: (1) it's convenient to the railway station; (2) it's economical; (3) it's clean and efficiently run. The owner, Mrs. Rosmarie Diletti, is Swiss, and her sophisticated taste is reflected in the decorations. Two sitting rooms, with their 16th-century furniture, are eye-catching. Guests also gather in a stylish bar. You stay here on the breakfast-only plan. The rooms are prettily decorated, simple but comfortable, all with Murano chandeliers and 40 with air conditioning. The rate in a double with bath is 145,000 lire ($110) daily, 100,000 lire ($76) in a bathless double. Singles with bath cost 95,000 lire ($72.25).

Hotel Miami, via Nazionale 230, 00184 Roma (tel. 06/481-7180), is squarely and conveniently situated in the heart of a major shopping artery. This is a fifth-floor pensione done over nicely with warmly tinted marble floors, olive-green wall coverings, and comfortable, low-slung chairs in the conservatively elegant sitting room. From the high-ceilinged street-level lobby, you'll ride an elevator up to the reception area. The spacious and simple bedrooms are filled with lots of sunlight, warm colors, and chrome accents, each with a handsomely tiled bath. This former duchess's palace offers some 20 units for 115,000 lire ($87.50) daily in a double, 90,000 lire ($68.50) in a single, with breakfast included. The quieter rooms get a little less sunlight, as they look out on a courtyard. Air conditioning is available in the rooms for an additional 7,500 lire ($5.70) per person. In winter, a 30% discount is granted on rates. A garage (not connected with the hotel) is conveniently nearby on via Napoli.

Albergo Igea, via Principe Amedeo 97, 00185 Roma (tel. 06/731-1212), is one of the older hotels in the vicinity of the railway station. But it's been renovated and offers fresh and up-to-date accommodations—at reasonable prices. A single room with shower costs 50,000 lire ($38) daily. Doubles run 80,000 lire ($60.75) with shower. Winter heating, service, and taxes are included in the rates quoted. The bedrooms are quite nice, in spite of their severity, softened by white walls and modern walnut beds and night tables.

NEAR SANTA MARIA MAGGIORE

In an offbeat but interesting section of Rome, the **Albergo Amalfi,** via Merulana 278, 00185 Roma (tel. 06/474-4313), lies only a short block from the Corinthian column accenting the piazza in front of the church of Santa Maria Maggiore. It stands behind a narrow and modernized storefront on a busy street. A pleasantly paneled reception area leads to 20 well-scrubbed bedrooms, each with a toilet and phone. About half of them are air-conditioned, but that luxury carries a 20,000-lira ($15.25) supplement. All units have color TV. Standard charges, depending on the season, range from 55,000 lire ($41.75) to 78,000 lire ($59.25) daily in a single, 75,000 lire ($57) to 120,000 lire ($91.25) in a double, with breakfast and taxes included. Mimmo Nigro and his brother, Donato, are the helpful owners. On the premises is a cozy breakfast room and bar.

NEAR THE BATHS OF CARACALLA

Away from the center of the city, the **Hotel Santa Prisca,** largo Manlio Gelsomini 25, 00153 Roma (tel. 06/575-0009), is an unheralded hotel in the

Aventino residential district. It is set aside from the hysterical traffic by the walls sheltering its private garden, whose entrance leads into a square at the bottom of the largo Manlio Gelsomini, at the corner of via Marmorata. A 1960s-style building that is owned by an order of Argentine nuns, it offers basic, quiet, and dignified rooms for visitors to Rome. You won't, I assure you, find a cloistered life here, although the spacious public rooms are occasionally filled with older travelers quietly reading amid the simple modern furniture. All the accommodations have a private bath or shower, as well as a phone. There's also an American-style bar, plus a big outdoor terrace with painted wrought-iron chairs. Singles rent for 61,000 lire ($46.25) daily; doubles, 85,000 lire ($64.50).

5. The Pick of the Pensiones

To judge from the façades, you might think all Roman pensiones can be checked off in Alfred Korzybski fashion (father of general semantics): house$_1$, house$_2$, house$_3$, etc. Not so! Once you enter them, you'll find considerable differences. Most of these "boarding houses" occupy one or two floors of a large apartment building; others, particularly on the outskirts, are housed in private villas.

The *pensione* is generally more intimate and personal than a hotel—in one, the nature and quality of the welcome depend largely on the host, or hostess, who might also be the cook and chief maid. As a general rule, a first-class pensione in Rome is the equivalent of a second-class hotel. A third-class hotel and a second-class pensione are "spiritual sisters." In most of these pensiones, you'll be asked to take half-board arrangements, although not always. I'll first survey my favored recommendations, then follow with even cheaper choices.

NEAR THE SPANISH STEPS

One of the best stopovers in the area is the **Pensione Suisse,** via Gregoriana 56, 00187 Roma (tel. 06/678-3649), which can fulfill one's desire to live inexpensively near the Spanish Steps. This 35-room hotel is owned by Signore Jole Ciucci and stands on the fourth and fifth floors of an ancient elevator building. The decor, if you can call it that, is rather old-fashioned and casual, with parquet or tile floors, occasional throw rugs, and overstuffed armchairs in the lounge. On the roof you can order breakfast. Bedrooms are overscale—unadorned, but comfortable—equipped with "blond" furniture, and occasionally blended with some antiques. More than a dozen have private bath, and the rest offer running water. Bathless singles cost 43,000 lire ($32.75) daily. A bathless double rents for 35,000 lire ($26.50) per person, increasing to 45,000 lire ($34.25) per person with bath. Tariffs include a continental breakfast, service, and I.V.A.

Manfredi Pensione, via Margutta 61, 00187 Roma (tel. 06/679-4735). An Argentina-born family are the highly visible owners of this unpretentious, high-ceilinged pensione. It is found on the third floor of a stately building on a street known for its art galleries. Take a creaking elevator to the narrow lobby, the antique-filled hallway, and the 19 plain bedrooms. With breakfast included, singles cost 90,000 lire ($68.50) daily. Doubles go for 180,000 lire ($137) with shower and toilet.

NEAR THE TERMINAL

Just off via Nazionale, the **Hotel Pensione Elide,** via Firenze 50, 00184 Roma (tel. 06/474-1367), near the opera house, is a simple and attractive 18-room pensione whose entrance is one floor above ground level. It's quiet for an establishment so close to the center of town, with an added calm for rooms facing the inner court-yard. You register in what you might consider a depressingly plain lobby, but then you proceed down papered hallways to clean, well-maintained bedrooms scattered over three floors of the 19th-century building. The rooms without private bath are close to quite adequate facilities a few steps away, and the three floors are connected by a winding marble staircase. Room 18 has what may be the most elaborately gilded ceiling of any pensione in Rome. Its design is repeated in the ceiling of the unpretentious breakfast room, whose workaday furniture provides an amusing contrast to the opulence of another era. Singles without bath rent for 36,000 lire ($27.25) daily, and doubles without bath go for 50,000 lire ($38). Doubles with private bath cost 70,000 lire ($53.25). The owner is Roma Giovanni.

Pensione Nardizzi Americana, via Firenze 38, 00184 Roma (tel. 06/460-368), lies inside a monumental 19th-century building within walking distance of either the via Veneto or the piazza della Repubblica. Take a birdcage-size elevator to the fourth floor and enter the well-organized private world of the Nardizzi family. The building was constructed in 1872 as the Roman headquarters of the American Methodist church. In 1924 Gilberto Nardizzi was born in one of the rooms, and the place has served as his family's hotel ever since. Mr. Nardizzi speaks fluent English, and his wife, Agatha, adds her charming smile to give their guests a warm welcome. They offer about a dozen high-ceilinged and old-fashioned rooms, ten of which contain tile baths. Charges for single or double occupancy, with breakfast included, are 75,000 lire ($57) to 90,000 lire ($68.50) daily. In low season a 10% discount is given on the above rates.

ON OR NEAR THE VIA VENETO

A pleasant hostelry, the **Amati,** via Vittorio Veneto 155, 00187 Roma (tel. 06/493-651), a moderately priced place to stay right in the middle of the via Veneto. It's scattered over two floors of a substantial stone building whose elevator will take you to the second-floor reception area. An adjacent sitting room is outfitted with light-grained oak paneling, carpeting, a baronial staircase, and a comfortable series of overstuffed divans. Many of the attractively simple units face an inner court-yard, which, while not offering a monumental view of the boulevard below, will be a lot quieter. The staff charges 60,000 lire ($45.50) daily in a single and 96,000 lire ($73) in a double, with a continental breakfast included.

NEAR THE PIAZZA DEL POPOLO

A few steps from the piazza is the **Pensione Fiorella,** via Babuino 196, 00187 Roma (tel. 06/361-0597). Antonio Albano and his family are one of the best reasons to visit this unstylish but comfortable pensione. They speak little English, but their humor and warm welcome make a rental of one of their well-scrubbed bed-rooms a lot like visiting a lighthearted relative. A total of eight bedrooms open onto a high-ceilinged hallway. Climb a flight of dingy stairs after entering the street-level vestibule. With a simple breakfast included, the only single costs 25,000 lire ($19) daily; doubles run 43,000 lire ($32.75).

ON THE OUTSKIRTS

With a noncommercial atmosphere, the **Villa del Parco,** via Nomentana 110, 00161 Roma (tel. 06/864-115), is an old Roman villa, set up from the boulevard in the midst of trees and shrubbery. It has a small, tree-shaded front terrace, where guests gather in the late afternoon to chat and sip Campari. The interior suggests a country house on the Mediterranean, with a few antiques intermingled with uphol-stered lounge chairs. The living room has a cozy bar and television area, mellow pho-tographs, and prints of Old Rome. All the rooms have private bath. The bed-and-breakfast charge for a single is 75,000 lire ($57) daily. Doubles pay 150,000 lire ($114). Tariffs include breakfast, service charge, taxes, and air conditioning. The hotel does not offer restaurant service, but there is a snackbar. The bedrooms are well appointed and well kept. To reach the villa, take bus 36, 60, or 62.

6. The Restaurants of Rome

The largest task confronting guidebook writers is to compile a list of best restaurants in such cities as Rome and Paris. For everybody—locals, expatriates, even those who have chalked up only one visit—has favorites ("What . . . you don't know about that little trattoria three doors down from the piazza Navona?").

What follows is not a list of all the best restaurants of Rome, but simply a running commentary on a number of personal favorites. For the most part, I've preferred not to document every deluxe citadel—known to all big spenders. Rather, I've tried to seek out equally fine (or better) establishments often patronized by some of the finest palates in Rome (but not necessarily by the fattest wallets).

Rome's cooking is not subtle, but its kitchen is among the finest in Italy, rivaling anything the chefs of Florence or Venice can turn out. Another feature of Roman restaurants is their skill at borrowing—and sometimes improving upon—the cuisine of other Italian regions. Throughout the capital you'll come across Neapolitan, Bolognese, Florentine, even Sicilian specialties. If you don't like the food, you may enjoy the view—either of the piazza Navona, the Spanish Steps, or the via Veneto.

Some restaurants offer a **tourist menu** at an inclusive price. The tourist menu includes soup (nearly always minestrone) or pasta, followed by a meat dish with vegetables, topped off by dessert (fresh fruit or cheese), as well as a quarter liter of wine or mineral water, along with the bread, cover charge, and service (you'll still be expected to tip something extra).

If you order from the tourist menu, you'll avoid the array of added charges that the restaurateur likes to tack on. You'll not get the choicest cuts of meat, nor will you always be able to order the specialties of the house, but you'll probably get a filling and quite good repast if you pick and choose your restaurants carefully. But be duly warned. Even though a restaurant owner offers such a menu, the staff is often reluctant to serve it, since it is their least profitable item. Often the owner will advertise a tourist menu in the window, but it won't be featured on the menu you're shown by the waiter. You'll have to ask for it in most cases, and you won't win any "most beloved patron" contests when you do.

What about the **prezzo fisso?** A confused picture. A fixed-price meal might even undercut the tourist menu, offering a cheaper meal of the "casa." On the other hand, it might not include wine, service, bread, or cover charge—for which you'll be billed extra. If you're on the most limited of budgets, make sure you understand what the prezzo fisso entails—so as to avoid misunderstandings when you settle the tab.

SOME TOP RESTAURANTS

Upper-bracket dining in Rome is a thoroughly delectable experience, if you can afford it. What follows is a random selection of some of Rome's best restaurants—best from the standpoint of cuisine, ambience, and chic.

Sans Souci, via Sicilia 20, (tel. 493-504), is the most elegant and sophisticated dining choice in Rome, and it also serves some of the finest food. With this unbeatable combination, it's no wonder that it has a chic—and frequently famous—clientele. An additional plus is its location—right off the via Veneto. To begin your evening, you'll enter the dimly lit small lounge/bar to the right at the bottom of the steps. Here, amid tapestries and glittering mirrors, the maître d' will present you with the menu, and you can leisurely make selections while sipping a drink. I've found, in general, that it's best to skip the chef's suggestions of the day and instead order from the imaginative à la carte menu. Recommended is the espadon (an assortment of grilled meat served on a sword flaming with calvados brandy), sole in spumante sauce and strawberries, and veal medallions with black truffles. The house specialty is mazzancolle flambée Danilo—a double treat as the waiters achieve "fireworks" spectaculars with their flambée dishes. I also heartily endorse the cheese soufflé, served only for two persons. Expect a final tab that will range from 75,000 lire ($57) to 100,000 lire ($76) per person. Go for dinner only, from 7:30 p.m. to 1 a.m., and reserve in advance. It is open daily except Monday. You'll be treated to the finest service in the capital.

El Toulà, via della Lupa 29 (tel. 687-3498), offers the quintessence of the Roman haute cuisine with a creative flair. The elegant setting, attracting the international set, is one of vaulted ceilings and large archways dividing the rooms. Guests stop in the charming bar to order a drink while deciding on their food selections from the impressive menu. Main courses include grilled squab with a pungent and well-seasoned sauce of crushed green peppercorns, or a plate of perfectly flavored grilled scampi. I also endorse filet of beef roasted in a bag with fresh Roman artichokes. The selection of sherbets depends on the seasonal availability of fruits, the cantaloupe and fresh strawberry sherbets being celestial concoctions. You can request a mixed plate if you'd like to sample several of them. Expect to spend 75,000 lire ($57) to 100,000 lire ($76) for a meal. Hours are 1 to 3 p.m. and 8 to 11 p.m. It is imperative to make a reservation in the evening, although El Toulà usually isn't crowded at lunchtime. Closed Sunday and in August.

Il Bacaro, via degli Spagnoli 27 (tel. 686-4110), near the Pantheon, is exclusive and chic. The building, constructed in the 1600s, was the locale of a cheap trattoria before a group of devoted chefs took it over in the 1980s. They created a small (six tables) restaurant in a cherry-paneled room evocative of a bistro in France. There they serve dinner only, every night except Sunday from 8:30 to 11:30 p.m., costing from 65,000 lire ($49.50) each. The restaurant prides itself on its selection of more than 100 kinds of wines, and will select and serve a glass of different wine with each course, creating "the perfect drink" with "the perfect food." Dishes include cuisine moderne versions from both the Italian and French kitchens. A consistent house specialty is fresh house-made spaghetti with squid ink, shrimp, and orange segments. Also popular are filet of sole en croûte, and a timbale of sardines and porcini mushrooms in a cream sauce. A delectable version of fish soup is laced with green vegetables. For dessert, try a chestnut mousse or coffee bavaroise with a hot chocolate sauce. Reservations imperative.

Relais Le Jardin, in the Hotel Lord Byron, via dei Notaris 5 (tel. 361-3041), is one of the best places to go in Rome for *la prima cucina*. On the ground floor of one of the most elite small hotels of the capital (see my hotel recommendations), the decor is almost aggressively lighthearted, combining white lattice with cheerful pastel colors. Many of the cooks and service personnel were trained at foreign embassies or diplomatic residences abroad. Classified as a Relais & Châteaux, the establishment serves a frequently changing array of dishes that might include seafood crêpes, noodle pie with salmon and asparagus, or fresh salmon with asparagus. Dessert may be a charlotte kiwi royal or "the chef's fancy." Expect to pay 85,000 lire ($64.50) to 115,000 lire ($87.50) per person for dinner. Reserve in advance. Open from 1 to 3 p.m. and 8 to 10:30 p.m., it is closed on Sunday.

George's, via Marche 7 (tel. 484-575). It's been a favorite of mine ever since Romulus and Remus were being tended by the she-wolf. Right off the via Veneto, it's not run by George, but by Michele Pavia, maître d' there for a quarter of a century before becoming its owner. Many guests drop in for a before-dinner drink, enjoying the music in the piano bar. They then proceed to an elegantly decorated and raised dining room with a tented ceiling. There is a relaxed club-like atmosphere. English is spoken, of course. Oysters are a specialty, and they're served in every form from fritters to "angels on horseback." The kitchen has an uncompromising dedication to quality, as reflected by such dishes as marinated mussels, smoked Scottish salmon, and sole Georges. Many veal and steak dishes are offered, with dinners costing from 85,000 lire ($64.50). From June to October, depending on the weather, the action shifts to the garden, suitably undisturbed because it is in the garden of a papal villa. The restaurant is open from 12:30 to 3 p.m. and 7:30 p.m. to midnight daily except Sunday and in August.

Pergola, in the Cavalieri Hilton International, via Cadlolo 101 (tel. 31-511). You'll enjoy a view of Renaissance and ancient Rome from the panoramic windows of this restaurant set on the uppermost level of a deluxe hotel. You'll be escorted to a table amid window-walls of glass, intimate lighting, modern paintings, and a stylish decor consisting of accents of glittering brass, silver, and black. Clients have included virtually all the political leaders of Italy, as well as film stars such as Marcello Mastroianni and members of the international diplomatic community. The restaurant offers a frequently changing list of seasonal specialties, as well as the popular carpaccio with slivers of parmesan and country salad, risotto with shrimp and filets of chicken, roast rack of lamb in black-pepper sauce, and tenderloin of beef in red wine with bone marrow. Expect to pay 80,000 lire ($60.75) to 100,000 lire ($76) per person for a meal. The Pergola is open daily from 8 p.m. to midnight. Reservations are important.

THE SPECIALTY RESTAURANTS—ALL PRICE RANGES

Rome has many specialty restaurants, representing every major region of the country such as the Abruzzi. The dishes they serve carry such designations as alla genovese, alla milanese, alla napolitana, alla fiorentina, and alla bolognese, to cite only a few.

Massimo d'Azeglio, via Cavour 18 (tel. 460-646), is in a hotel but with a separate entrance. This restaurant has dispensed the Roman cuisine since 1875. Angelo Bettoja runs it today, and it was his great-great-grandfather who founded it. It was built near the Terminal Station, which was considered a fashionable address in the 19th century, attracting the cognoscenti. A set meal costs 35,000 lire ($26.50), while an à la carte dinner may tally from 40,000 lire ($30.50) up. Menu items include an excellent version of penne with vodka, trout Cavour (with pine nuts), grilled swordfish, plus an array of grilled meats. Service is daily, except Sunday, from 12:30 to 3 p.m. and 7 to 11 p.m. Named after a famous Savoy-born statesman who assisted Garibaldi in the unification of Italy, the restaurant is adorned with oil portraits of distinguished Italians.

Girrarrosto Toscano, via Campania 29 (tel. 493-759), faces the walls of the Borghese Gardens. It draws a coterie of guests from via Veneto haunts, which means you may have to wait. Under vaulted ceilings in a cellar setting, some of the finest Tuscan specialties in Rome are served. In the meantime, you can enjoy an enormous selection of antipasti, which the waiters bring around to you: succulent little meatballs, vine-ripened melon with prosciutto, an omelet, mozzarella, and especially delicious Tuscan salami. You're then given a choice of pasta, such as fettuccine in a cream sauce. Priced according to weight, the bistecca alla fiorentina is the best item to order, although it's expensive. This is a grilled steak seasoned with oil, salt, and pepper. Oysters and fresh fish from the Adriatic are served every day. For dessert, I'd recommend what everybody has—an assortment of different flavors of ice cream, called a "gelati misti." A complete meal will cost 50,000 lire ($38) to 65,000 lire ($49.50) per person including wine. Open daily except Wednesday from 12:30 to 3 p.m. and 7:30 p.m. to 12:30 a.m.

La Maiella, piazza Sant' Apollinare 45 (tel. 686-4174), on the corner of a little square between the Tiber and the piazza Navona, specializes in the foods of Abruzzi. From 12:30 to 2:30 p.m. and 7:30 to 11:30 p.m., the restaurant draws the great and near-great, who mingle with tourists, dining outdoors under big umbrellas in summer and in the indoor dining area in winter. Before his elevation to the papal throne, Polish Cardinal Karol Wojtyla, who became Pope John Paul II, liked to come here. Traditional dishes, expertly prepared and served, include such Abruzzi mountain foods as partridge and venison with polenta, suckling pig, and baby lamb. A chef's specialty is green risotto with champagne, but I also like the risotto with zucchini flowers or wild mushrooms. Full meals cost 42,000 lire ($32) to 62,000 lire ($47). The restaurant is closed Sunday and August 10 to August 25.

Il Drappo, vicolo del Malpasso 9 (tel. 687-7365), on a hard-to-find, narrow street off a square near the Tiber, is a Sardinian restaurant operated by an attractive brother-sister team named Paolo and Valentina. The façade is graced with a modernized trompe-l'oeil painting above the stone entrance, which is flanked with potted plants. Inside, you'll have your choice of two tastefully decorated dining rooms festooned with yards of patterned cotton draped from supports on the ceiling. Flowers and candles are everywhere. Dinner, which will be partially selected by the host if you wish his assistance, may include a wafer-thin appetizer called carte di musica (sheet music), which is topped with tomatoes, green peppers, parsley, and olive oil, followed by fresh spring lamb in season, a fish stew made with tuna caviar, or a changing selection of strongly flavored regional specialties that are otherwise difficult to find in Rome. Service is personal, and meals, with wine included, usually cost around 40,000 ($30.50) to 50,000 lire ($38) per person. This restaurant is open from 8 p.m. to 1 a.m. It is closed Sunday and during part of August.

Ambasciata d'Abruzzo, via Pietro Tacchini 26 (tel. 878-256). If you like ambitious portions on an all-you-can-eat basis, a place where the food is well cooked and tasty, and also inexpensive for the value received, then strike out for this little, hard-to-find restaurant in the Parioli district. It's not only superb value, but great fun, providing you are ravenously hungry and enjoy bountiful dining. It accomplishes the seemingly impossible, not skimping on quality or quantity. First, the price is approximately 35,000 lire ($26.50) per person at lunch, 40,000 lire ($30.50) at dinner. The atmosphere is exceedingly informal, and you may have to stand in line if you didn't reserve a table. It's in the true tavern style, with strings of sausages, peppers, and garlic. As soon as you're seated, the culinary parade commences as a basket overflowing with assorted sausages is placed on your table; even a herb-flavored baked ham is presented, resting on a cutting board with a knife. Help yourself—but go easy, as there's more to come. Another wicker basket holds moist, crunchy peasant-style bread, from which you tear off huge hunks. Next a hearty mass of spaghetti vongole (with baby clams) is placed before you. Then you proceed to an overloaded antipasto table, with its selections, including marinated artichokes, salads, whatever. Later those still remaining at the table are served a main dish such as grilled fish. Then comes the large salad bowl, mixed to your liking, followed by an assortment of country cheeses, plus a basket brimming with fresh fruit. You're even given your choice of a dessert. A pitcher of the house wine is at your disposal, and the price not only includes coffee, but an entire bottle of Sambuca is placed on your table. Again, it's help yourself. Open from 12:30 to 4 p.m. and 7 p.m. to midnight daily except Sunday.

Dal Bolognese, piazza del Popolo 1-2 (tel. 361-1426). If *La Dolce Vita* were being filmed now, the director would probably use this restaurant as a backdrop. It is one of those rare dining spots that is not only chic, but noted for its food as well. Young actors, shapely models, artists from the nearby via Margutta, even industrialists on an off-the-record evening on the town, show up here, quickly booking the limited sidewalk tables. To launch you into your repast, I suggest the savory Parma ham or perhaps the melon and prosciutto if you're feeling extravagant (try a little freshly ground pepper on the latter). For your main course, specialties include lasagne verdi, tagliatelle alla bolognese, and a most recommendable cotolette alla bolognese. Expect to spend from 60,000 lire ($45.50) per person for a full meal, including wine. Dal Bolognese, open from 12:45 to 3 p.m. and 8:15 to 11 p.m., is closed for Sunday dinner, on Monday, and from early to mid-August. Instead of lingering in the restaurant, you may want to cap your evening by calling on the Rosati next door (or its competitor, the Canova, across the street), and enjoying one of the tempting pastries. Reservations are essential.

Colline Emiliane, via Avignonesi 22 (tel. 481-7538), is a small restaurant right off the piazza Barberini, serving the *classica cucina bolognese*. It's a family-run place, where everybody helps out. The owner is the cook, and his wife makes the pasta, which, incidentally, is about the best you'll encounter in Rome. The house specialty is tortellini alla panna (cream sauce) with truffles, which is an inspired dish. However, you might prefer one of the less expensive pastas, as all of them are excellent and handmade—maccheroncini al funghetto and tagliatelle alla bolognese. As an opener for your meal, I suggest culatello di Zibello. This delicacy is from a small town in the vicinity of Parma, known for having the finest prosciutto in the world. Main courses include braciola di maiale, boneless rolled pork cutlets which have been stuffed with ham and cheese, breaded, and sautéed. To finish your meal, I'd recommend budino al cioccolato, a chocolate pudding that is baked like flan. Expect to spend from 35,000 lire ($26.50) to 50,000 lire ($38) per person, including service. The restaurant is open from 12:30 to 2:45 p.m. and 7:30 to 10:45 p.m.; closed on Friday and in August.

Ristorante Nino, via Borgognona 11 (tel. 679-5676), off via Condotti, a short walk from the Spanish Steps, is a tavern mecca for writers, artists, and an occasional model from one of the nearby high-fashion houses. Nino's enjoys deserved acclaim for its Tuscan dishes—everything from "devilish done chicken" to "entrails and paw after the Florentine cuisine." The cooking is hearty and completely unpretentious. The restaurant is particularly known for its steaks shipped in from Florence and charcoal broiled—and these are priced according to weight. A plate of cannelloni Nino is one of the chef's specialties. Other good dishes include grilled veal liver, two deviled quail, fagioli cotti al fiasco, baccalà alla livornese, and zampone. For dessert, I suggest the Florentine cake called castagnaccio. Expect to spend from 40,000 lire ($30.50) for a complete meal. Hours are 11:30 a.m. to 3 p.m. and 7:30 to 11 p.m., but "Sunday closed for weekly rest." The annual closing is from late July to September.

Scoglio di Frisio, via Merulana 256 (tel. 734-619), is the choice suprême to introduce yourself to the Neapolitan kitchen. While at it, you might as well get reacquainted with pizza (pizza pie is redundant), abandoning your Yankee concepts and appreciating the genuine article. At night, you can begin with a plate-sized Neapolitan pizza (crunchy, oozy, and excellent) with clams and mussels. After devouring the house specialty, you may then settle for chicken cacciatore, hunter's style, or veal scaloppine. Meals cost 35,000 lire ($26.50) to 45,000 lire ($34.25) up. Scoglio di Frisio also has entertainment—so it makes for an inexpensive "night on the town." All the fun, cornball "O Sole Mio" elements spring forth in the evening—a guitar, mandolin, and a strolling tenor who acts like Mario Lanza reincarnate. The decor's nautical in honor of the top-notch fish dishes—complete with a high-ceilinged grotto with craggy walls, fishermen's nets, crustaceans, and a miniature three-masted schooner hanging overhead. Open only in the evenings from 7:30 to 11 p.m., it's closed Monday from November 1 to April 30, on Sunday from May 1 to October 31. The restaurant is on a broad street, south of the railway station. Take bus 93.

Le Maschere, via Monte della Farina 29 (tel. 68687-9444), near largo Argentina, and within walking distance of the piazza Navona, specializes in the fragrant, often-fiery cookery of Calabria's Costa Viola. That means lots of fresh garlic and wake-up-your-mouth red peppers. The restaurant, decorated in regional artifacts of Calabria, occupies a cellar from the 1600s with small outside tables in summer overlooking one of those tiny little piazzas deep in the heart of Rome. You get going by helping yourself to a selection of antipasti Calabresi. There are many different preparations of eggplant. Others prefer one of the pasta dishes, one made with broccoli, and one flavored with devilish red peppers, garlic, breadcrumbs, and more than a touch of anchovy. The chef also grills meats and also fresh swordfish caught off the Calabrian coast. For dessert, finish with a sheep cheese of Calabria or a fresh-fruit salad. Closed Monday, the restaurant serves from 7:30 p.m. to midnight (no lunch ever). Meals cost from 35,000 lire ($26.50).

MODERATE TO BUDGET DINING

This section links both moderate and budget restaurants in Rome, because the distinction is often blurred. For example, if you order a pasta, a fresh salad, and perhaps a selection of fresh fruit, along with a carafe of the house wine, the restaurant is likely to be a "budget" choice. However, should you prefer a heaping plate of antipasti, a separate pasta course, followed by bottled wine and a Florentine beefsteak, perhaps topped off by dessert, then your bill is likely to be in the more medium-priced category. So it depends a great deal on how much you want to eat. In many places, most vegetable courses are priced separately. The section is further divided according to location. Prices quoted are given with the assumption that you are going to eat a full meal. However, many readers, depending on their appetites, can dine for far less.

Dining in Trastevere

One of the oldest sections of the city, Trastevere is a gold mine of colorful streets and, for our purposes, restaurants with inspired cuisine. Although across the Tiber, it's rather far from St. Peter's. Actually, it's just adjacent to the old ghetto, whose synagogue can be seen across the river between the spires of the island called Tibertina.

Alberto Ciarla, piazza San Cosimato 40 (tel. 581-8668), is one of the best and most expensive restaurants in Trastevere. Some critics consider it one of the finest restaurants in all of Rome. Contained in a building set into an obscure corner of this enormous square, the dinner-only restaurant serves some of the most elegant fish dishes in Rome. From 8:30 p.m. to 12:30 a.m., you'll be greeted at the door with a cordial reception and a lavish display of seafood on ice. A dramatically modern decor plays shades of brilliant light against patches of shadow for a result which a Renaissance artist might have called *chiaroscuro*. Named after its Paris-trained owner and chef, the restaurant offers several set menus, ranging in price from 90,000 lire ($68.50) to 100,000 lire ($76). Specialties include a handful of ancient recipes subtly improved by Signor Ciarla (an example is the soup of pasta and beans with seafood). Original dishes include a delectable salmon Marcel Trompier, and other delicacies feature a well-flavored sushi, spaghetti with clams, ravioli di pesce, and a full array of shellfish. Reservations are important, especially on Friday and Saturday night. The restaurant is closed Sunday.

Le Cabanon, vicolo della Luce 4-5 (tel. 581-8106), is lost on a tiny street in the midst of Trastevere. This brick-lined and vaulted restaurant adds musical entertainment to a cuisine derived from the far edges of the Mediterranean. It is owned by a Tunisian-born Italian, Enzo Rallo, whose cook and staff for the most part enjoy the same origins. The place serves full meals nightly except Sunday from 8:30 p.m. to 2 a.m. Around 10 or 10:30 p.m., a series of singers from around the Mediterranean as well as South America add music to your evening. Full meals cost 50,000 lire ($38) to 60,000 lire ($45.50). Typical dishes might include truffled crêpes, onion soups, and filet of sole stuffed with cream and fresh salmon. North African dishes include couscous, shish kebabs, and spicy Tunisian sausages on a brochette. You face a wide array of Sicilian, Neapolitan, Tunisian, and French desserts. Reservations are important.

Sabatini I, piazza Santa Maria in Trastevere 10 (tel. 582-026), owned by the Sabatini brothers, is one of the most popular dining spots in Rome. At night, piazza Santa Maria—one of the settings used in Fellini's *Roma*—is the center of the liveliest action in Trastevere, and is a favorite with celebrities. In summer, tables are placed outside on this charming square, and you can look across at the floodlit golden mosaics of the church on the piazza. If you can't get a table outside, you may be assigned to a room inside under beamed ceilings, with stenciled walls, lots of paneling, and framed oil paints. So popular is this place that you may have to wait for a table even if you have a reservation. You can choose from a large table of antipasti. Fresh fish and shellfish, especially grilled scampi, may tempt you. The spaghetti with "fruits of the sea" is excellent. My most recent selection was pollo con pepperoni, chicken cooked with red and green peppers, a savory treat. Meals begin at 60,000 lire ($45.50), but can go much higher if you order grilled fish or the Florentine steaks. For wine, if it goes with what you ordered, try a white Frascati or an Antinori chianti in a hand-painted pitcher. The restaurant is open from noon to 3 p.m. and 8 p.m. to midnight; closed Wednesday and for two weeks in August.

If you can't get in at Sabatini I, try **Sabatini II,** vicolo de Santa Maria in Trastevere 18 (tel. 581-8307), just around the corner. It charges the same prices as its sister restaurant above. Hours are noon to 3 p.m. and 8 p.m. to midnight; it is closed Tuesday and for two weeks in August. However, the August closings of the two Sabatinis are staggered so you can dine at one place if you are there at the wrong time for the other. When you're ready to leave either place, ask the waiter to call you a cab. Don't try it yourself, as the Sabatini staff seems to have a special code word to get a taxi to pull up to the door.

Romolo, via Porta Settimiana 7 (tel. 581-8284), is a Trastevere gem established in 1848. You can sit in a Renaissance garden that once belonged to Raphael's mistress, della Fornarina (the baker's daughter), who posed for some of his madonnas. Now it's known and has been patronized by everybody from celluloid heroes (Kirk Douglas) to political personalities and authors (Clare Boothe Luce or Margaret Truman) to collegians. To begin your meal, try the fettuccine with meat sauce, followed by scaloppine al marsala or deviled chicken. A fresh garden salad is extra. For dessert, try a "charlotte"—a sponge cake lathered with whipped cream and topped by a decorative motif. Your final bill should be in the neighborhood of 52,000 lire ($39.50). Even if the garden isn't in use, you'll like the cozy interior, with its bric-a-brac of copper, wood, and silver. The restaurant is closed on Monday and during most of August, but open otherwise from noon to 3:30 p.m. and 7:30 p.m. to midnight.

La Cisterna, via della Cisterna 13 (tel. 582-543), lies deep in the heart of Trastevere—and has for some time. For the last 50 years or so it's been run by the Simmi family, who are genuinely interested in serving only the best as well as providing a good time for all guests. The Cistern in the name comes from an ancient well discovered in the cellar, dating from the heyday of Imperial Rome. When the weather's good, you can dine outside at sidewalk tables, serviced by waiters. If it's rainy or cold, you can select from one of a series of inside rooms decorated with murals, including the *Rape of the Sabine Women.* Roman specialties are featured. In summer you can inspect the antipasto—a mixed selection of hors d'oeuvres—right out on the street before going in. Recommendable are roasted meat dishes, such as veal, and fresh fish. A choice of specialties will mean a final tab in the range of 40,000 lire ($30.50). Hours are 8 p.m. to midnight daily except Sunday.

Trattoria Vincenzo, via della Lungaretta 173 (tel. 589-2876), is surrounded by far more expensive restaurants in the Trastevere district. It has never wasted the cost of an anchovy on fancy trappings; instead, it hauls out some of the best-prepared dishes—particularly seafoods—in this colorful section of the city. And the prices are kind to those on the budget safari. Small, popular (always crowded with flea marketeers at Sunday lunch), the Vincenzo serves a zuppa di pesce, a stew that doesn't need to play second fiddle to the most savory bouillabaisse. Meat items include saltimbocca alla romana (veal with ham and sage). The trattoria doesn't ignore pasta dishes either. Sample the ravioli di ricotta e spinaci (ravioli with cottage cheese and spinach) or the spaghetti alla carbonara. Meals cost from 40,000 lire ($30.50). Hours of food service are noon to 2:45 p.m. and 7:30 to 10:30 p.m. It is closed Sunday night and all day Monday.

Near the Via Veneto

Aurora 10 da Pino il Sommelier, via Aurora 10 (tel. 474-2779). Established in 1981 a few paces from the top of the via Veneto, this restaurant lies within the vaulted interior of what was originally a Maronite convent. Its manager (and namesake) is Pino Salvatore, whose high-energy direction and attentive staff have attracted some of the capital's most influential diplomats and a scattering of film stars. The place is especially noted for its awesome array of more than 250 kinds of wine, collectively representing every province of Italy. Full meals, costing from 40,000 lire ($30.50), are served from noon to 3 p.m. and 7 to 11:15 p.m. daily except Monday. Unusual for Rome, the place features a large soup menu, along with a tempting array of freshly made antipasti. You can begin with a selection of your favorite pasta or risotto, then follow with perhaps a Florentine beefsteak or fondue bourguignonne.

Near St. Peter's
Ristorante Pierdonati, via della Conciliazione 39 (tel. 654-3557), has been serving wayfarers to the Vatican since 1868. In the same building as the Hotel Columbus (see my hotel recommendation), this restaurant was the former home of Cardinal della Rovere. It is today the headquarters of the Cavalry of the Holy Sepulchre of Jerusalem, and the best restaurant in the gastronomic wasteland of the Vatican area. Its severely classical façade is relieved inside by a gargoyle fountain spewing water into a basin. You'll dine beneath a vaulted ceiling from noon to 3 p.m. and 7 to 10:30 p.m. daily except Thursday. Try the calves' liver Venetian style, the stewed veal with tomato sauce, or ravioli bolognese. Meals cost from 30,000 lire ($22.75). It can get rather crowded fast here on days that see thousands upon thousands flocking to St. Peter's.

Taverna Risorgimento, piazza Risorgimento 5 (tel. 317-345), is one of the finest of the family-run trattorie in the area. It stands overlooking the walls of the Vatican on this famous square of Rome which at first appears as though it belongs more to Naples. Nella and Amanda welcome you daily except Monday from noon to 4 p.m. and 7 p.m. to 12:30 a.m. They specialize in many unusual types of pasta such as bucatini (a fat spaghetti) al padellaccio or la mejo pastaciutta der monno. Everything is neat and tidy and you can also enjoy several meat dishes such as grilled beefsteak or fried calves' liver. Full meals are reasonably priced at 22,000 lire ($16.75).

Ristorante Giardinaccio, via Aurelia 53 (tel. 631-367). If you stand facing St. Peter's, turn left and walk around its precincts, which will point you in the right direction to reach this popular restaurant operated by Nicolino Mancini. Unusual for Rome, it offers Molisian specialties (a provincial region of Italy). Its savory cuisine is served daily except Tuesday from noon to 3 p.m. and 7:30 to 11 p.m. At the intersection of two busy streets, it is rustically decorated in the country-tavern style with dark wood and exposed stone. Flaming grills provide succulent versions of perfectly done quail, goat, and other dishes, but perhaps the mutton goulash would be more adventurous. Many versions of pasta are featured, as is risotto. Vegetarians and others will like the large selection of self-service antipasti. Meals cost from 22,000 lire ($16.75).

Il Matriciano, via dei Gracchi 55 (tel. 359-5247), is a family restaurant that enjoys patronage by a devoted set of habitués. Its location near St. Peter's makes it all the more distinguished. The food is good, but it's only country fare—nothing fancy. The decor, likewise, is kept to a minimum. In summer, try to get one of the sidewalk tables behind a green hedge and under a shady canopy. The luncheon clientele seems to linger a long time, perhaps out of reluctance to get back to their offices. For openers, you might prefer a zuppa di verdura or ravioli di ricotta. The preferred choice, however, is tagliolini con tartufi. From many dishes, I recommend scaloppa alla valdostana, abbacchio (baby lamb) al forno, and trippa (tripe) alla romano. From the limited menu, you can compose a complete meal for anywhere from 30,000 lire ($22.75) to 40,000 lire ($30.50). Open from 1 to 2:30 p.m. and 8:30 to 11 p.m., it is closed Wednesday in winter, Saturday in summer.

In the Roman Ghetto
Piperno Monte Cenci, via Monte de' Cenci 9 (tel. 654-0629), is the leading choice in the Eternal City's old Jewish ghetto. However, it's not a kosher restaurant.

Come here to sample a vegetable for which Rome is known in gastronomic circles—carciofi alla giudia, artichokes (a more delicate variety than that of America) sliced crosswise and deep-fried to a golden-brown crispness. Almost equally good is mixed vegetable fry. As you enter the restaurant, a delectable array of antipasto misto awaits your selection. For a main course, I'd recommend filetti di baccalà, (strips of codfish filets batter-fried), Roman tripe, or baked lamb. I also recommend funghi porcini, exquisitely sauced mushrooms, and for dessert, palle di nonno fritte, a flaky pastry (with a stuffing of homemade fruit preserves and rich cream) that has been deep-fried in hot fat. A complete meal runs from 40,000 lire ($30.50) to 62,000 lire ($47). The restaurant, open from 12:30 to 3 p.m. and 8 to 11 p.m., is closed Sunday night, all day Monday, in August, and between Christmas and New Year's.

Da Giggetto, via del Portico d'Ottavia 22 (tel. 686-1105), nestles in the old ghetto of Rome, a short walk from the Theater of Marcellus. Not only does this choice stand side by side with ruins, but old Roman columns extend practically to its doorway. Once you walk into its maze of dining rooms, you'll be entering a bustling trattoria. The Romans flock here for their special traditional dishes. None is more typical than carciofi alla giudia, the baby-tender fried artichokes—thistles to make you whistle with delight. This is a true delicacy. The cheese concoction, mozzarella in carrozza, is another delight. A complete meal will cost 30,000 lire ($22.75) to 50,000 lire ($38). Hours are 12:30 to 2:30 p.m. and 7:30 to 10:30 p.m. Closed Monday and for three weeks in June.

Angelino a Tormargana, piazza Margana 37 (tel. 678-3328), about three blocks from the piazza Venezia, is housed in Goethe's historic inn. In this setting of old palazzi and charmingly ancient cobblestone squares, you can dine al fresco at tables hedged with greenery. At night the colored lanterns are turned on. A somewhat elegant clientele is attracted to the inn, and the atmosphere is sophisticated. The food is very much in the typical Roman trattoria style—not exceptionally imaginative, but good for what it is. Expect a tab of 40,000 lire ($30.50), including a carafe of the house wine. I'd recommend the eggplant parmigiana, followed by chicken with peppers. Open from noon to 3:30 p.m. and 7 p.m. to 12:45 a.m. daily except Sunday.

Vecchia Roma, via della Tribuna di Campitelli 18 (tel. 686-4604), is a charming trattoria, moderately priced, in the heart of the ghetto (a short walk from Michelangelo's Campidoglio). Head in the direction of the Theater of Marcellus, but turn right at the Synagogue. Movie stars have frequented the place, sitting at one of the crowded tables. The room in the back, with its bas-relief, is more popular—but not because of the bas-relief. The owners are known for their "fruits of the sea." Their antipasti marini with fresh sardines and anchovies is exceptional, and you may get tiny octopus, shrimp, mussels, and sea snails. In the Jewish ghetto tradition of Rome, they offer batter-dipped, deep-fried artichokes. If you want meat, try the veal kidneys or veal chop, or perhaps you'd enjoy another specialty, roasted goat. Meals begin at 45,000 lire ($34.25) and are served from 12:30 to 3:30 p.m. and 8 to 11:30 p.m. The restaurant is closed Wednesday and for the first three weeks of August.

Near the Piazza Navona

Passetto, via Giuseppe Zanardelli 14 (tel. 654-0569), is dramatically positioned at the north end of the landmark piazza Navona. Its reputation for excellent Italian food brings people here. The surroundings are stylish—three rooms, one containing frosted-glass cylinder chandeliers, maintaining the tradition of the past. However, one of the outside tables on the big terrace looking out on the piazza Sant'Apollinare is preferred in summer. Formally dressed waiters, crisp white linen, and heavy silverware add a touch of luxury. Pastas are exceptional, including penne alla Norma. One recommendable main dish is orata (sea bass) al cartoccio (baked in a paper bag with tomatoes, mushrooms, capers, and white wine). Another house specialty is rombo passetto (a fish similar to sole) cooked in a cognac and pine-nut sauce. Meals can be accompanied by a selection of fresh varied salads personally chosen from a service trolley. Fresh vegetables are abundant in summer, and a favorite dessert is seasonal fruits, such as lingonberries, raspberries, or blackberries with fresh thick cream. Meals cost 50,000 lire ($38) to 75,000 lire ($57) and are served from 12:30 to 3:30 p.m. and 8 to 11:30 p.m. Closed all day Sunday and Monday at lunchtime.

Alfredo alla Scrofa, via della Scrofa 104 (tel. 686-4519). In both Europe and America you see the word "Alfredo" listed after many dishes in Italian restaurants. When visitors reach Rome, they ask their hotels to direct them to Alfredo's restaurant, some of which even claim to be the original and authentic one. Once, there really was an Alfredo. He was given a gold fork and spoon by two noted travelers to Rome, Mary Pickford and Douglas Fairbanks. That Alfredo crowned himself *Il Re della Fettuccine* (king of noodles), but eventually he sold his business and retired. Since the Pickford-Fairbanks days, there has been much dispute about which Alfredo's owns that gold fork and spoon (as if it really mattered). One of the leading claimants is Alfredo alla Scrofa. Oak panels on the walls contain gold-framed photographs of famous personages who have visited the restaurant. All first-time visitors order the maestose fettuccine al triplo burro. The waiters make choreography out of whipping butter and cheese into this dish. The main-course specialty is filetto di tacchino dorato (breast of turkey, sautéed in batter and covered with thin slices of Piemontese white truffles). You might finish with an Irish coffee. Meals cost 55,000 lire ($41.75) to 75,000 lire ($57) and are served from noon to 3 p.m. and 7:30 to 10 p.m. The restaurant is closed Tuesday.

Pino e Dino, piazza di Montevecchio 22 (tel. 686-1319). You must reserve a table in advance and negotiate the winding streets of one of Rome's most confusing neighborhoods in the vicinity of the piazza Navona. The restaurant lies behind heavy curtains on this Renaissance piazza where both Raphael and Bramante created many of their masterpieces and where Lucrezia Borgia spun many of her intrigues. The entrance opens onto a high-ceilinged, not particularly large room filled with rural mementos and bottles of wine. Your meal might begin with a strudel of fungi porcini (mushrooms) followed with the pasta of the day, invariably good. Then select roebuck with polenta, roast Sardinian goat, or one of several veal dishes (on one occasion, served with salmon mousse). Meals cost from 75,000 lire ($57). The restaurant is open from 1 to 3 p.m. and 7:30 p.m. to midnight daily except Monday and during most of August.

Ristorante Mastrostefano, piazza Navona 94 (tel. 654-2855). The world comes to the door of this restaurant, if not for the food, then for the view of Bernini's *Fountain of the Four Rivers*. With its sidewalk tables, the restaurant offers a ringside view. The restaurant today is considered more desirable than its major competitor, Tre Scalini, across the way. You can order such dishes as smoked or marinated salmon, a fritti di verdure (vegetable fry) in the Roman culinary style, and very fresh fish, followed by a range of tempting ice creams and desserts. Meals cost 50,000 lire ($38) to 75,000 lire ($57), and service is daily except Monday from 12:30 to 3:30 p.m. and 7:30 to 11:30 p.m. The restaurant is closed from mid-August until the first of September.

Il Domiziano, piazza Navona 88 (tel. 687-9647), is a pizzeria and beer cellar, serving all types of antipasti, pasta, meat dishes, and pizzas. It faces a little street called corsa Agonale, leading right into the square where you can admire the statuary in the piazza. The name "Domiziano" commemorates the piazza Navona's former use: a stadium of Emperor Domitian and used for chariot races (note the intact original pillar dating back to Domitian). Reasonably priced and well-prepared antipasti and pizzas are served, and many guests order saltimbocca, grilled lamb, or else chicken. Dining is outside at sidewalk tables, in the main street-level dining room, or in the cellar. Full meals cost from 22,000 lire ($16.75) per person. It's open daily except Thursday from 12:30 to 3 p.m. and 6 p.m. to midnight.

Since you're so near the **Tre Scalini,** piazza Navona 28-32 (tel. 654-1996), you might well stroll across the piazza to its *gelateria* and try its tartufo (bittersweet chocolate-coated ice cream with cherries and whipped cream). If you order two to take out, they'll cost 3,500 lire ($2.65) each. If you eat at one of the sidewalk tables, the charge is 7,000 lire ($5.30) each. Tre Scalini is open from 9 a.m. to 11 p.m. daily except Wednesday.

Near the Trevi Fountain

Quirino, via delle Muratte 84 (tel. 679-4108), is a good place to dine right after you've tossed your coin into the Trevi Fountain. The atmosphere inside is typically Italian, with hanging chianti bottles, a beamed ceiling, and muraled walls. The food is strictly in the "home-cooking" style of Roman trattorie. At times you can enjoy fresh chicory that is perfumed and bitter at the same time. All the ritual dishes of the Roman kitchen are here, including brains in butter. I'm also fond of a mixed fry of tiny shrimp and squid rings which resemble onion rings. For an opening course, I recommend risotto, Milanese style, or spaghetti with clams. For dessert, a basket of fresh fruit will be placed on your table. After a large meal, your final tally will be in the neighborhood of 40,000 lire ($30.50) or more. Hours are 12:15 to 3:15 p.m. and 7:15 to 11:15 p.m. Closed Sunday and from the end of July to August 10.

Near Trajan's Forum

Ristorante Ulpia, piazza del Foro Traiano 2 (tel. 679-6271), sits on a terrace above the sprawling excavations of what used to be Trajan's Market, where the produce of much of ancient Rome was bought and sold. Today you can dine by candle-light on the restaurant's sheltered balcony while reflecting on the fate of faded empires. You might also take a look at the interior, where a statue of Ulpia, goddess of the marketplace, seems to complement the fragments of ancient bas-reliefs, copies of Roman frescoes, Etruscan-style balustrades, and fresh flowers. Your meal might include sole meunière, stewed chicken with peppers, or other straightforward, flavorful dishes. À la carte dinners tally up to 50,000 lire ($38). Hours are noon to 3 p.m. and 7 to 11 p.m. daily except Sunday.

Near the Piazza Ungheria in Parioli

Al Ceppo, via Panama 2 (tel. 844-9696), greets you with a glittering antipasto tray, including such delectable suggestions as stuffed yellow and red peppers, finely minced cold spinach blended with ricotta, and at least two dozen other dishes, many of which taste good either hot or cold. Because of its somewhat hidden location (although it's only two blocks from the Villa Borghese), the clientele is likely to be Roman rather than foreign. "The Log," as its name is in English, features an open fireplace that is fed with wood. On it, the chef does lamb chops, even quail, liver, and bacon, to charcoal perfection. The beefsteak, which hails from Tuscany, is also succulent. Other dishes on the menu include linguine monteconero, a filet of swordfish filled with grapefruit, parmesan cheese, pine nuts, and dry grapes; and a fish carpaccio (raw sea bass) with a green salad, onions, and green pepper. Expect to pay 35,000 lire ($26.50) to 52,000 lire ($39.50) for a filling repast. Al Ceppo is open from 12:30 to 2:30 p.m. and 7:30 to 11 p.m. daily except Monday and in August.

Near the Pantheon

L'Eau Vive, via Monterone 85 (tel. 654-1095), qualifies as an offbeat adventure. It is run by lay missionaries who wear the dress or costumes of their native countries. Dining here is an unusual experience for many people. In this formal atmosphere, the waitresses, at 10 o'clock each evening, chant a religious hymn and recite a prayer. Your gratuity for service will be turned over for religious purposes. Pope John Paul II used to dine here when he was still archbishop of Cracow, and it's a popular place with overseas monsignors on a visit to the Vatican.

Specialties include hors d'oeuvres and frogs' legs. An international dish is featured daily. The restaurant's cellar is well stocked with French wines. Main dishes range anywhere from guinea hen with onions and grapes in a wine sauce to couscous. A smooth finish is the chocolate mousse. Your bill is likely to range from 50,000 lire ($38) to 60,000 lire ($45.50) per person. Under vaulted ceilings, the atmosphere is deliberately kept subdued, and the place settings—with fresh flowers and good glassware—are tasteful. However, some of the most flamboyant members of international society have adopted L'Eau Vive as their favorite spot. On a narrow street in Old Rome, it is hard to find, although it lies near the Pantheon. Closed Sunday and in August, it is open otherwise from noon to 2:30 p.m. and 8 to 9:30 p.m.

Hostaria Angoletto, piazza Rondanini 51 (tel. 686-8019), is on the ground floor of an old palazzo where you dine under umbrellas or awnings. At night it attracts a lively and chic crowd of Romans, drawn to this romantic spot deep in Rome, near the Pantheon. The food is good, especially the fresh fish dishes, available daily. The chef offers both Italian and international menus. A special dessert is crème brulée. The restaurant also boasts an excellent wine list. A complete meal costs 35,000 lire ($26.50) to 40,000 lire ($30.50). The establishment is open from 12:30 to 3 p.m. and 7:30 p.m. to 1 a.m. daily except Monday.

Il Barroccio, via dei Pastini 13-14 (tel. 679-3797), serves generous portions of reasonably priced Roman dishes, attracting a loyal following who crowd into the restaurant, grabbing a table in one of several small salons. The parade of dishes is served against a typical backdrop of horseshoes on the wall, dried corn, wagon-wheel lights, and bronze lanterns. In these busy surroundings, you'll often get haphazard service, but no one seems to mind, especially when itinerant musicians arrive to entertain you and then pass the hat. A la carte items range from a simple but good bean soup to the more elaborate seafood antipasto. At night, pizza is a specialty. Another main-dish specialty is an array of boiled mixed meats, served with an herb-flavored green sauce. A meal of specialties will cost from 32,000 lire ($24.25) up. Open from 6:30 p.m. to 1:30 a.m.; it's closed Monday and in August.

Near the Piazza di Campo dei Fiori

Ristorante de Pancrazio, piazza del Biscione 92 (tel. 686-1246), is a dining oddity. It serenely occupies the ruins of Pompey's ancient theater. The lower section of the theater and the rugged stone-vaulted cellar have been converted into a restaurant that is a national monument, its walls having witnessed 2,000 years of history. A tavern decoration sets the informal mood in several of the dining halls. However, the main room is more dignified, with tall marble columns and a coffered ceiling. An especially good opener for your meal is risotto alla pescatora (with an assortment of fruits of the sea). Main courses include saltimbocca and baked lamb with potatoes. The fish dishes are also good, especially the mixed fish fry and the scampi. For dessert, try torte Saint-Honoré. Meals cost 35,000 ($26.50) to 45,000 lire ($34.25), and are served from noon to 3 p.m. and 7 p.m. to midnight. Closed Wednesday and August 10 to August 20.

Ristorante der Pallaro, largo del Pallaro 15 (tel. 654-1488). The cheerful and kindhearted woman in white who, with clouds of steam, emerges from this establishment's bustling kitchen is the owner, Paola Fazi. With her husband, Mario, she maintains a simple duet of very clean dining rooms where price-conscious Romans go for good food at bargain prices. No à la carte meals are served, but the 19,500-lira ($14.75) fixed-price lunches and dinners have made the place famous. As you sit down, the first of eight courses will appear, one following the other, until you've had more than your fill. You begin with antipasti, then go on to such dishes as the pasta of the day, which might be spaghetti, rigatoni, or pappardelle. The meat courses include roast veal, white meatballs, or (only on Friday) dried cod. Potatoes and eggplant are offered. For your final courses, you're served mozzarella cheese, cake with custard, and fruit in season. The meal also includes bread, a liter of mineral water, and half a liter of the house wine. Food is served from 1 to 3 p.m. and 8 to 11:30 p.m. daily except Monday.

Near the Villa Bonaparte

Taverna Flavia di Mimmo, via Flavia 9 (tel. 474-5214), is a favorite of the visiting movie star, as its famous line-up of celeb photographs will testify—everybody from Frank Sinatra to "Ben Hur." Of course, that was back in those days of Hollywood on the Tiber. The restaurant is still there, serving exactly the same food, and it's a good location for those staying in the general vicinity of the railway station. Specialties include a risotto with scampi and spaghetti al whisky. A different regional dish is featured daily. Perhaps it will be tripe, Roman style. Exceptional dishes include ossobuco with peas, a seafood salad, and fondue with truffles. Expect to spend 50,000 ($38) for a meal here, served daily from 12:45 to 3 p.m. and 7:45 p.m. to midnight.

Near the Terminal Station

Ristorante del Giglio, via Torino 137 (tel. 461-606), is a restaurant and pizzeria that has been offering a savory Roman cuisine longer than anyone cares to remember. An old-fashioned dining room, it lies near the Teatro dell'Opera. English is not a common language around here, but you'll get by fine. You can first select antipasti such as marinated artichokes or Tuscan-style white beans. You might follow with bolliti misti (assorted boiled meats) or Florentine beefsteak. Meals are reasonably priced at 20,000 lire ($15.25) and up, and service is daily except Sunday from 12:30 to 3 p.m. and 6:30 to 10 p.m. Everything tastes better when served with one of the wines of Frascati.

Trattoria Elettra, via Principe Amedeo 74 (tel. 474-5397), bills itself as *"dalla cucina con amore."* But I don't want to mislead; this is not so much a "cuisine for lovers" as the cuisine of a well-run family-style trattoria, offering good food at reasonable prices between the Terminal Station (about three blocks) and the Basilica of Santa Maria Maggiore, quite close to via Manin. The place is bright and cheerfully unpretentious. The pasta is good, like the ravioli stuffed with ricotta, spinach, and salmon. You might also prefer risotto with asparagus in a cream sauce followed by one of the main meat or poultry dishes of the day, including ossobuco. Meals cost from 22,000 lire ($16.75), and are served daily, except Friday evening and all day Saturday, from noon to 2:30 p.m. and 7 to 10 p.m.

Satyricon, via Marsala 56 (tel. 491-824), close to the bustle of the railroad station, does a thriving business at its standup snackbar. There, slices of pizza and sandwiches cost 2,000 lire ($1.50), and must be consumed standing up. Most diners, however, opt for one of the small but immaculate tables where uniformed waiters serve full meals for 15,000 lire ($11.50) and up. These are served daily except Tuesday from noon to 1 a.m. Specialties include lasagne, pennette with a vodka-flavored cream sauce, risotto with scampi, pappardelle with spinach, and a selection of veal, beef, and chicken dishes. In the basement, a trio of dining rooms (usually reserved for groups) is covered with modernized versions of neoclassical frescoes, re-creating the grand old days of Imperial Rome, with recipes from those times.

Monte Arci, via Castelfidardo 33 (tel. 474-4890), is set on a cobblestone street not far from the railway station. Behind a sienna-colored façade also sheltering a stately but faded apartment building, the restaurant features both Roman and Sardinian specialties. Moderate in price for the neighborhood, it charges 25,000 lire ($19) for a complete meal (less, of course, for pizza). Typical dishes include maloreddus (a regional form of gnocchetti), spaghetti with clams, seafood antipasti, grilled fish, and veal dishes. Full meals are served from noon to 2:30 p.m. and 7 to 10 p.m. daily except Wednesday.

Near the Piazza Venezia

Abruzzi, via de Vaccaro 1 (tel. 679-3897), takes its name from a little-explored region known for its haunting beauty and curious superstitions. Its Roman namesake is at one side of the piazza SS. Apostoli, just a short walk from the piazza Venezia, with its memories of Mussolini. For some reason, many young people have selected this restaurant as their enduring favorite—probably because they get good food here at moderate prices. The chef is justly praised for his satisfying assortment of cold antipasti. You can make your own selection from the trolley cart. With your beginning, I suggest a liter of garnet-red wine. Once I had one whose bouquet was suggestive of the wildflowers of Abruzzi. If you'd like a soup as well, you'll find a good stracciatella (made with a thin batter of eggs and grated parmesan cheese poured into a boiling chicken broth). A typical main dish is saltimbocca, the amusing name ("jump-in-the-mouth") for tender slices of veal that have been skewered with slices of ham, sautéed in butter, and seasoned with marsala. An average meal will run 30,000 lire ($22.75) to 40,000 lire ($30.50). The decor is not pretentious. It's open from 12:30 to 3 p.m. and 7:30 to 10:30 p.m.; closed Saturday and for part of August.

Il Canto del Riso, via della Cordonata 21-22 (tel. 678-6227), is chic, sophisticated, and flippantly named ("song of rice" in English). Ring a doorbell to gain entrance to a candle-illuminated interior where Romans gather at a small bar waiting for a table to clear. Dozens of well-framed paintings range from Indian love scenes to Italian moderno. The restaurant enjoys a vogue. Who knows *who* is likely to show up? On my first visit, Boy George and entourage shared the adjoining table. Housed in a stately Renaissance-inspired building on a quiet, almost-hidden square, the restaurant, in honor of its name, offers rice dishes flavored with you name it— asparagus, artichokes, creamed red peppers, apples, or strawberries. You can order a rice dish as an opening course, then follow with one of the main dishes such as straccetti (filet of beef cooked into thin strips), served with either asparagus, artichokes, or spinach. The menu, inked onto a moveable board, also features many vegetarian dishes as well, with meals costing 50,000 lire ($38). Full meals are served daily except Monday from noon to 3:30 p.m. and 7 p.m. to 1 a.m.

In summer the dining room remains open, but business is also funneled to a moored barge in the Tiber where fresh seafood is featured. Meals are also priced at 50,000 lire ($38). The barge is near Ponte Cavour. Head down lungotevere Mellini to the Tiber on the Vatican side of Rome (phone 361-0430 for a table). Service is daily in summer from noon to 3 p.m. and 7 p.m. to 1 a.m.

Near the Piazza Colonna

Er Tartufo, via Vicolo Sciarra 59 (tel. 67-80-226), lies just off the via del Corso, the main street of Rome, which is lined with façades ornamented with covered balconies. While shopping in the area of the piazza Colonna, you may want to escape the roar of traffic along the Corso by dining at this hidden-away "truffle." It is cozy, a neighborhood setting with fast service and just good, mouthwatering food. The decor in the dining room includes a wine keg set in the wall. The restaurateurs, Signori Cesaretti, are most hospitable. A specialty of the house is a plate of truffles, an expensive treat. You might want to try filet of beef with truffles, rosetta di vitello modo nostro (veal "our style"), or spiedino alla siciliana (rolls of veal with ham and cheese inside, onions and bay leaves outside, grilled on a skewer). Dinner will cost from 35,000 lire ($26.50) per person. The place is informal and in a charming location on a crooked street. Open from 12:30 to 3 p.m. and 7 to 11 p.m., it's closed Sunday.

Near the Spanish Steps

Ristorante Ranieri, via Mario de' Fiori 26 (tel. 679-1592), off via Condotti, is well entrenched in its second century (it was founded in 1843). Neapolitan-born Giuseppe Ranieri, for whom the restaurant is named, was the chef to Queen Victoria. Long a favorite dining place of the cognoscenti, Ranieri still maintains its Victorian trappings. Nothing ever seems to change here. Many of the dishes on the good menu reflect the restaurant's ties with royalty: veal cutlet l'Imperiale, mignonettes of veal à la Regina Victoria, and tournedos Enrico IV. Meals cost 50,000 lire ($38) to

65,000 lire ($49.50), and the restaurant is open from 12:30 to 3:15 p.m. and 7:30 to 10:45 p.m. except all day Sunday and Monday at lunchtime.

Il Ristorante 34 (also Al 34), via Mario de' Fiori 34 (tel. 679-5091), is a very good and increasingly popular restaurant close to the most famous shopping district of Rome. Its long and narrow interior is sheathed in scarlet wallpaper, ringed with modern paintings, and capped with a vaulted ceiling. In the rear, stop to admire a display of antipasti proudly exhibited near the entrance to the bustling kitchen. Your meal might include noodles with caviar and salmon, risotto with chunks of lobster, pasta-and-lentil soup, meatballs in a sauce with fat mushrooms, two kinds of entrecôte, or pasta in a pumpkin-flavored cream sauce. The spaghetti with clams is among the best in Rome. Full meals, served from 12:30 to 3 p.m. and 7:30 to 10:30 p.m. every day except Monday, cost from 35,000 lire ($26.50).

Osteria Margutta, via Margutta 82 (tel. 679-8190), is on a street that traditionally has housed the nucleus of Rome's art colony. On Sunday, art shows are staged along the street, and it is the most fun then, although you can visit the galleries and antique shops any day of the week. Should you get hungry during your stroll, drop in at this rustic tavern, given added style by the use of art posters. You'll pass by tables of tempting antipasti, which are priced according to your choice. Dishes include roast beef, lamb with green peppercorns, and various kinds of pasta. A good meal here, served daily except Sunday from 12:45 to 3 p.m. and 8 p.m. to midnight, will cost from 45,000 lire ($34.25).

Da Mario, via della Vite 55-56 (tel. 678-3818), is noted for its game specialties, all moderately priced. Mario also does excellent Florentine dishes, although the typical beefsteak is too costly these days for most budgets. You can dine in air-conditioned comfort on the street level or descend into the cellars. A good beginning is a wide-noodle dish, pappardelle, best when served with a game sauce (caccia). Capretto (kid) is served in the Florentine fashion, although you may prefer two roasted quail with polenta. I heartily recommend the gelato misto, a selection of mixed ice cream. The cost of the average meal ranges from 35,000 lire ($26.50) to 45,000 lire ($34.25). Hours are 7:30 to 11 p.m. Closed Sunday and in August.

Near the Via Veneto

Piccolo Abruzzo, via Sicilia 237 (tel. 486-428). Its imaginative array of antipasti and copious portions make it one of the most popular restaurants in its neighborhood, a good stroll from the via Veneto. Many habitués plan a meal either early or late to avoid the jam, as the place is small but popular. Meals are served daily from 12:30 to 4 p.m. and 7:30 p.m. to midnight. Full meals, costing 35,000 lire ($26.50) to 40,000 lire ($30.50), are priced on what you take from the groaning antipasti buffet. You can follow with a pasta course which might be samples of three different versions, followed by a meat course, then cheese and dessert. All this lively scene takes place in a brick-and-stucco-sheathed room perfumed with hanging cloves of garlic, salt-cured hams, and beribboned bunches of Mediterranean herbs. Closed Saturday at lunch and all day Sunday.

Near the Colosseum

Trattoria l'Albanese, via dei Serpenti 148 (tel. 474-0777). For years visitors always found it difficult to locate a good and inexpensive restaurant while exploring the core of Imperial Rome. However, there is one that is quite fine, although it's small. As compensation for its size, it has a garden in the rear where you can order lunch. A set dinner costs from 22,000 lire ($16.75), and it's very good, or you can order from an à la carte menu. In the evening, pizza is served. The trattoria is open from 12:30 to 3 p.m. and 7 to 11 p.m. daily except Tuesday.

On the Island of Tibertina

Sora Lella, via dei Ponte Quattro Capi 16 (tel. 686-1601), is recommended primarily for its medieval location, on the boat-shaped island of Tibertina, right in the middle of the river. It's housed in a tower at the foot of a bridge, with busy traffic hurrying by. Somewhat of a dining curiosity, it is regionally decorated with hanging lanterns, tavern tables, and a cozy fireplace. Soups are rich and nutritious, and the pasta dishes are homemade, served with savory sauces. Meat courses are also well prepared. A basket of fresh fruit rounds out the repast. The average meal here will cost from 40,000 lire ($30.50), served from 1 to 3 p.m. and 8 to 10:30 p.m. daily except Sunday.

Near the Circus Maximus

Alvaro al Circo Massimo, via dei Cerchi 53 (tel. 678-6112), is as close as Rome comes to having a genuine provincial inn. It's at the edge of the Circus Maximus, with its memories of Ben Hur. Here is all the cornpone decor associated with Italian taverns, including corn on the cob hanging from the ceiling and rolls of fat sausages. You can begin with the antipasti or one of the fine pasta dishes, such as fettuccine. Meat courses are well prepared, and there is an array of fresh fish. A basket of fresh fruit rounds out the repast, along with the "last of the wine." For an average three-course meal, expect to pay 50,000 lire ($38) to 60,000 lire ($45.50). Try to linger longer, making an evening of it—the atmosphere is mellow. Hours are noon to 2:30 p.m. and 8 to 11 p.m. Closed Monday and in August.

The Appian Way

Hostaria l'Archeologia, via Appia Antica 139 (tel. 788-0494), on the historic Appian Way, is only a short walk from the catacombs of St. Sebastian. The family-run restaurant is like an 18th-century village tavern with lots of atmosphere, strings of garlic and corn, oddments of copper hanging from the ceiling, earth-brown beams, and sienna-washed walls. In summer, guests dine in the garden out back, sitting under the spreading wisteria. The kitchen is Roman, and the victuals are first-rate. In the chilly months, two separate dining rooms provide eating space. They are on either side of a gravel walkway. Even the kitchens are visible from behind a partition from the exterior garden parking lot. Many Roman families visit on the weekend, sometimes as many as 30 diners in a group. A joie de vivre permeates the place. Count on spending 35,000 lire ($26.50) to 45,000 lire ($34.25) for a meal. Food is served daily except Thursday from 12:30 to 3:30 p.m. and 7:30 to 11:30 p.m.

Of special interest is the wine cellar, excavated in an ancient Roman tomb. Wines dating back to 1800 are kept there. You go through an iron gate, down some stairs, and into the underground cavern. Along the way, you can still see the holes once occupied by funeral urns.

STATESIDE SNACKS

For a taste of home, **The Cowboy,** via Francesco Crispi 68 (tel. 474-5328), is for the wandering *griglia.* The best corral in Rome for those with a hankering for the vittles of Texas, it offers chili, a southern fried chicken with french fries, and a Texas-burger with cheese. The Italian specialty is cannelloni. For dessert you can order a homemade apple pie with ice cream, followed by American-style coffee. This place is popular with Americans who like the good beer and get a laugh from the satirical western mural inside. Meals cost from 18,000 lire ($13.75), but after midnight prices are raised by 15%. The restaurant is open from noon to 3 p.m. and 7:30 p.m. to 2:30 a.m. Closed Sunday at lunchtime and all day Monday.

TIME OUT FOR TEA

A little bit of England has been preserved at **Babington's Tea Rooms,** piazza di Spagna 23 (tel. 678-6027). Back when Victoria was on the throne in England, an Englishwoman named Amy Mary Babington arrived in Rome and couldn't find a place for "a good cuppa." With stubborn determination, she opened her own tea rooms near the foot of the Spanish Steps. The rooms are still going strong. You can order everything from Scottish scones to a club sandwich to Ceylon tea, even American coffee. Tea will cost from 7,500 lire ($5.70). You can also order a copious brunch for 35,000 lire ($26.50). Hours are 9 a.m. to 8 p.m. daily except Thursday.

FOR VEGETARIANS

One of the few such restaurants in town is **Margutta Vegetariano,** via Margutta 119 (tel. 678-6033). The stone detailing of its maroon façade is known to a circle of friends who ignore the riches of traditional Italian cuisine in favor of a simple list of frequently changing high-fiber items whose names are written on a blackboard. Tables and chairs are about as unpretentious as you'll find in Rome, and at one end of the high-ceilinged room there's a remarkable photographic blowup of green and red peppers in all their colorful detail. When I was there, they had an unfortunate lack of vegetarian pasta dishes, although there's almost always a soup, a mixed salad, a mélange of fried vegetables, a collection of crudités, risotto, and fresh desserts. Expect to spend around 30,000 lire ($22.75) per person. It shuts down on Sunday but on other days serves from 1 to 3 p.m. and 8 to 11 p.m.

DAY AND NIGHT IN ROME

As one of the greatest centers of Western civilization, Rome is thickly studded with ancient monuments that silently evoke its pageantry. In the millennium of the Eternal City's influence, all roads led to Rome with good reason. It became the first cosmopolitan city on earth, importing slaves, gladiators, great art—even citizens—from the far corners of the Empire.

With all its carnage, with all its mismanagement, it left a legacy of law and an uncanny lesson in how to conquer an enemy by absorbing his culture. Rome's pantheon of gods became a galaxy.

But Ancient Rome is only part of the spectacle. Having the papal household in Rome has had an unfathomed effect on making the city a center of world tourism. Although Vatican architects stripped down much of the glory of the past, they created great treasures of the Renaissance, occasionally incorporating the old—as Michelangelo did in turning the Baths of Diocletian into a church.

In the years that followed, Bernini was to adorn the city with the wonders of the baroque—especially fountains. The modern sightseer even owes a debt (as reluctant as one may be to pay it) to Mussolini, who did much to dig out the past, as at the Imperial Forum. Il Duce was a better archeologist, however, than an architect (see "Modern Rome"). Of course, dictators are dangerous business—regardless of their accomplishments—and Mussolini almost got Rome wiped off the map. We can be grateful today that it was spared the wrath of Allied bombers.

Besides being the capital of the Italians, Rome, in a larger sense, belongs to the world. And here are some of its sights.

1. The Top Sights

The sights of Rome are multifarious. To see even the most important ones may make you feel like an elephant of Hannibal's crossing the Alps. For that reason, I've selected a representative sampling of "The Top 12," which will take several days to cover. I hope, however, you'll be in Rome long enough to view at least a dozen more secondary sights, descriptions of which immediately follow the Top 12.

I don't want to bewilder you, but it would be a shame and a loss to strike out for Naples or Florence without having at least visited Hadrian's Villa and the Villa d'Este in the environs—and I haven't even told you of Palestrina and Ostia Antica yet. I'll begin this formidable task with:

(1) ST. PETER'S

As you stand in Bernini's piazza San Pietro (St. Peter's Square), you'll be in the arms of an ellipse. Like a loving mother, the Doric-pillared colonnade reaches out to embrace the faithful. Hugging 300,000 is no problem in this square.

In the center of the square is an Egyptian obelisk, brought from the ancient city of Heliopolis on the Nile Delta—and used to adorn Nero's Circus, which was nearby. Flanking the obelisk are two 17th-century fountains—the one on the right (facing the basilica) by Carlo Maderno, who designed the façade of St. Peter's, was placed there by Bernini himself; the other is by Carlo Fontana.

Inside (open daily from 7 a.m. to 7 p.m. in summer, 7 a.m. to 6 p.m. in winter), the size of the world's largest church is awe-inspiring—although its dimensions are not apparent at first. Guides like to point out to American parties that the basilica is like two football fields joined together. St. Peter's is said to have been built over the tomb of the crucified saint. Originally, it was erected on the order of Constantine, but the present structure is essentially Renaissance and baroque, having employed the talents of some of Italy's greatest artists: Bramante, Raphael, Michelangelo, and Maderno.

In a church of such grandeur—overwhelming in its detail of gilt, marble, and mosaic—you don't expect subtlety. But the basilica is rich in art. The truly devout are prone to kiss the feet of the 13th-century bronze of St. Peter, attributed to Arnolfo di Cambio (at the far reaches of the nave, against a corner pillar on the right). Under Michelangelo's dome is the celebrated "baldacchino" by Bernini, resting over the papal altar. The canopy was created in the 17th century—in part, so it is said, from bronze stripped from the Pantheon. However, analysis of the bronze seems to contradict that.

In the nave on the right (the first chapel) is the best-known piece of sculpture, the *Pietà* that Michelangelo sculpted while still in his early 20s. In one of the most vicious acts of vandalism on record, a madman screaming "I am Jesus Christ" attacked the *Pietà*, battering the Madonna's stone arm, the folded veil, her left eyelid, and nose. Now restored, the *Pietà* is protected by a wall of reinforced glass.

Much farther on, in the right wing of the transept near the Chapel of St. Michael, rests Canova's neoclassic sculptural tribute to Pope Clement XIII.

In addition, you can visit the sacristy and treasury, filled with jewel-studded chalices, reliquaries, and copes. One robe worn by Pius XII casts a simple note in these halls of elegance. It costs 2,000 lire ($1.50) to visit the Historical-Artistic Museum, which is open daily from 9 a.m. to 6 p.m. in summer, 9 a.m. to 5:30 p.m. in winter. Later, you can make an underground visit to the Vatican Grottoes, with their tombs—ancient and modern (Pope John XXIII gets the most adulation). They are open daily from 7 a.m. to 6 p.m. in summer, 7 a.m. to 5 p.m. in winter.

To go even farther down, to the area around St. Peter's own tomb, you must apply several days beforehand by letter to the excavations office (tel. 698-5318). Open daily from 9 a.m. to noon and 2 to 5 p.m., it is reached by passing under the arch to the left of the façade of St. Peter's. For 5,000 lire ($3.80), you are taken on a guided tour of the tombs that were excavated in the 1940s 23 feet beneath the floor of the church.

The grandest sight is yet to come: the climb to Michelangelo's dome, towering about 375 feet high. Although you can scale the steps (2,000 lire or $1.50), I recommend the elevator for as far as it'll carry you. The cost is 3,000 lire ($2.30). The dome is open daily from 8 a.m. to 6:15 p.m. in summer, 8 a.m. to 4:45 p.m. in winter. You can walk along the roof, for which you'll be rewarded with a magnificent view of Rome and the Vatican.

Note: To be admitted to St. Peter's, women are advised to wear longer skirts or pants—anything that covers the knees. Men in shorts are not allowed in. Also, sleeveless tops are a no-no for either gender.

(2) THE VATICAN AND SISTINE CHAPEL

In 1929 the Lateran Treaty between Pope Pius XI and the Italian government created Vatican City, the world's smallest independent state, lying on a man-made island in Rome (tel. 06/6982).

This state may be small, but it contains a gigantic repository of treasures from antiquity and the Renaissance—labyrinthine gallery after gallery, an art that reaches its apex in the Sistine Chapel (save this for last, as everything else will be anticlimactic after seeing Michelangelo's frescoes).

The Vatican museums (a house of museums) comprise a series of lavishly adorned palaces and galleries built over the centuries. The entrance is on viale Vaticano, a long walk around from St. Peter's Square. Take bus 23, 30, 32, 49, 51, 64, 70, 81, 490, 492, 495, 907, 990, 991, or 994; the subway to the Ottaviano station; or a taxi. The museums are open daily except Sunday and religious holidays from 8:45 a.m. to 1:45 p.m., 8:45 a.m. to 4:45 p.m. from July to the end of September and during Easter week. Ticket sales stop one hour before closing time. The admission price may seem high—8,000 lire ($6.10)—but it is reasonable when you see what's inside. Entrance is free on the first Sunday of each month. A cafeteria is open to visitors from 8:45 a.m. to 2:45 p.m. (from 8:45 a.m. to 4:45 p.m. from July to the end of September and during Easter week).

Visitors to the Vatican museums can follow one of four itineraries—A, B, C, or D—according to the time they have at their disposal and their special interests. They can determine their choice by consulting large-size panels placed at the entrance, and they then follow the letter and color of the itinerary chosen. Facilities for disabled visitors are available.

A dozen museums and galleries should be inspected. Obviously, 1, 2, or even 20 trips will not be enough to see the wealth of the Vatican, much less digest it. With that in mind, I've previewed only a representative sampling of masterpieces.

After climbing the spiral stairway, keep to the right which will take you to the:

Pinacoteca (Picture Gallery)

Some of the most enduring works of art from the Byzantine to the baroque are displayed here. But for a break with the Byzantine, see one of the Vatican's finest artworks—the *Stefaneschi Polyptych* (six panels) by Giotto and his assistants. You are introduced to the works of Fra Angelico, the 15th-century Dominican monk who distinguished himself as a miniaturist (his Virgin enthroned with child is justly praised—look for the microscopic eyes of the Madonna).

In the Raphael salon you'll find three paintings by a giant of the Renaissance—including the *Virgin of Foligno* and *The Transfiguration* (completed by assistants following his death). There are also ten tapestries made by Flemish weavers from cartoons by Raphael. Seek out Leonardo da Vinci's masterful—but uncompleted—St. Jerome with the lion, as well as Giovanni Bellini's entombment of Christ. One of Titian's greatest works, the *Virgin of Frari,* is also displayed. Finally, for a view of one of the masterpieces of the baroque period, feast your eyes on Caravaggio's *Deposition from the Cross.*

Egyptian-Gregorian Museum

The sarcophagi, the mummies, statues of goddesses, vases, jewelry, red-granite queens as well as hieroglyphics review the grandeur of the Pharaohs. But even more interesting is another repository—

Etruscan-Gregorian Museum

With its sarcophagi, a chariot, bronzes, urns, jewelry, and terracotta vases, this gallery affords a remarkable insight into a mysterious people. One of the most acclaimed exhibits is the Regolini-Galassi tomb, unearthed at Cerveteri (see "Ring Around Rome") in the 19th century. It shares top honors with the *Mars of Todi,* a bronze sculpture that probably dates from the 5th century B.C.

Pius Clementinus Museum

These rooms are filled with Greek and Roman sculptures, many of them masterpieces that will bring immediate recognition because of the widespread reproductions. In the rotunda is a large gilded bronze of Hercules that dates from somewhere around the time of Christ. Other major works of sculpture are to be seen under porticoes in rooms opening onto the Belvedere courtyard. *Laocoön* and his two sons (1st century B.C.) are locked in their eternal struggle with the serpents (the original statue is broken in parts; the completed version nearby is a copy). The incomparable *Apollo of Belvedere* (Roman reproduction of an authentic Greek work from the 4th century B.C.) has become, of course, the symbol of classic male beauty. The *Torso of Belvedere* is a partially preserved Greek statue from the 1st century B.C. (the rippling muscles and the intricate knowledge of the human body, as revealed in this work, predated Michelangelo by centuries, but equaled his achievements).

Chiaramonti Museum

In these galleries, the array of Roman statuary, plus copies of Greek originals, continue to dazzle us. One of the most remarkable pieces of sculpture from antiquity is displayed, *The Nile,* a magnificent reproduction of a long-lost Hellenistic original. The imposing statue of Augustus presents him as a regal commander.

Vatican Library

So richly decorated and frescoed, the Library detracts from its own treasures—manuscripts under glass. In the Sistine Salon are sketches by Michelangelo, drawings by Botticelli to illustrate the *Divine Comedy,* plus a Greek Bible from the 4th century A.D.

The Stanze of Raphael

While still a young man, Raphael was given one of the greatest assignments of his short life: the decoration of a series of rooms for Pope Julius II, who saw to it that Michelangelo was busy in the Sistine Chapel. In these works Raphael achieves the Renaissance concept of the blending of classic beauty with realism. In the first chamber, the Stanza dell'Incendio, you'll see much of Raphael's pupils, but little of the master—except in the fresco across from the window. The figure of the partially draped man rescuing an older comrade (to the left of the fresco) was executed by Raphael's own hand.

Raphael reigns supreme in the next and most important salon, the Stanza della Segnatura. In this chamber, the majestic *School of Athens,* depicting such figures as Aristotle and Plato (even Raphael himself), is one of the artist's best-known works. Across from it is another well-known masterpiece, the *Disputà* (Disputation). The Stanza d'Eliodoro, also by the master, manages to flatter Raphael's papal patrons (Julius II and Leo X) without compromise to his art. However, one rather fanciful fresco depicts the pope driving Attila from Rome. Finally, the Sala di Constantino was completed by his students after Raphael's death.

THE LOGGIA OF RAPHAEL. This loggia is frescoed with more than 50 scenes from the Bible, designed by Raphael, although the actual work was done by the loyal students who flocked around him.

The Borgia Apartments

Before entering the Sistine Chapel, you may want to visit this apartment frescoed with biblical scenes by Pinturicchio of Umbria, along with his assistants. The apartment was designed for Pope Alexander VI (the famous Borgia pope). The rooms, although generally badly lit, have great splendor and style. At the end of them is the Chapel of Nicholas V, an intimate interlude in a field of museums. The chapel was frescoed by the Dominican monk Fra Angelico, probably the most saintly of all Italian painters.

The Museum of Modern Art

In the Borgia apartments in the Vatican complex, this gallery represents the first invasion of American artists into the Vatican. Until this museum opened in 1973, the church limited its purchases to European art, and usually did not exhibit any works created after the 18th century. But Pope Paul's hobby changed all that. Of the 55 galleries in the new museum complex, at least 12 are devoted solely to American artists. All the works chosen for the museum were judged on the basis of their "spiritual and religious values," but other religious groups outside the church are represented as well. Among the American works is Leonard Baskin's five-foot bronze sculpture of *Isaac*. Modern Italian artists such as de Chirico and Manzù are also displayed, and there's a special room for the paintings of the French artist Georges Rouault.

The Sistine Chapel

The struggle of Michelangelo in the painting of the ceiling of the Sistine Chapel was dramatized by Irving Stone in *The Agony and the Ecstasy,* with Charlton Heston doing the neck-craning in the film version—thus earning a worldwide audience for one of the classic stories of art history. Michelangelo, of course, considered himself a sculptor, not a painter. While in his 30s, he was virtually commanded by Julius II to stop work on the pope's own tomb and to devote his considerable talents to painting frescoes on the ceiling—an art form of which the Florentine master was contemptuous.

Michelangelo, taxing himself physically (he permanently damaged his eyesight), labored for four years over this epic project, and had to contend with the pope's incessant urgings that he hurry up. At one point Julius threatened to topple Michelangelo from the scaffolding—or so Vasari relates.

It is ironic that a project undertaken against the artist's wishes would form his most enduring legend. Glorifying the human body as only a sculptor could, Michelangelo painted nine panels from the pages of Genesis, surrounded by prophets and sibyls. The most notable are the expulsion of Adam and Eve from the Garden of Eden, and the creation of man—with God's outstretched hand imbuing Adam with spirit.

The great Florentine master was in his 60s when he began to paint the masterly *Last Judgement* on the altar wall. Again working against his wishes, Michelangelo presents a more jaundiced view of mankind and his fate, with God sitting in judgment and sinners being plunged into the mouth of hell.

A master of ceremonies under Paul III, Monsignor Biagio, protested to the pope against the "shameless nudes" painted by Michelangelo. Michelangelo showed he wasn't above petty revenge by painting the prude with the ears of a jackass in hell. When Biagio complained to the pope, Paul III maintained he had no jurisdiction in hell. However, Daniele de Volterra was summoned to drape clothing over some of the bare figures—thus earning for himself a dubious distinction as a haberdasher.

On the side walls are frescoes by other Renaissance masters—artists such as Botticelli, Luca Signorelli, Pinturicchio, Cosimo Rosselli, and Ghirlandaio. I hazard a guess that if these paintings had been displayed by themselves in other chapels, they would be the object of special pilgrimages. But having to compete unfairly against the artistry of Michelangelo, they're virtually ignored by the average visitor.

The History Museum

This museum was founded by Pope Paul VI. Exhibiting arms, armor, and uniforms, it was specifically established to tell the history of the Vatican. Some pieces of armor date back to the early days of the Middle Ages. The carriages on display are those used by popes and cardinals in religious processions. Among the showcases of dress uniforms are the colorful outfits worn by the Pontifical Army Corps, which was discontinued by Pope Paul VI.

The Ethnological Museum

The Ethnological Museum is an assemblage of works of art and objects of cultural significance from all over the world. The principal route is a half-mile walk through 25 geographical sections which display thousands of objects covering 3,000 years of world history. The section devoted to China is especially interesting and worthwhile.

The Vatican Gardens

Separating the Vatican on the north and west from the secular world are 58 acres of lush, carefully tended gardens, filled with winding paths, brilliantly colored flowers, groves of massive oaks, ancient fountains and pools. In the midst of this pastoral setting is a small summer house, the Villa Pia, built for Pope Pius IV in 1560 by Pirro Ligorio.

With the exception of Wednesday and Sunday, tours of the Vatican gardens leave daily at 10 a.m. from in front of the Information Office for Pilgrims and Tourists, near the Arco delle Campane, Saint Peter's Square.

Visits to the gardens are exclusively organized by the information office.

(3) THE ROMAN FORUM

When it came to cremating Caesar, raping Sabine women, purchasing a harlot for the night, or sacrificing a naked victim, the Roman Forum was a place where the action was hot. Traversed by the via Sacra, it was built in the marshy land between the Palatine and the Capitoline hills. It flourished as the center of Roman life in the days of the Republic, gradually losing in prestige to the Imperial Forum.

Be duly warned: expect only fragmented monuments, an arch or two, and lots of overturned boulders. That any semblance of the Forum remains today is in itself miraculous, as it was used, like the Colosseum, as a quarry for years—eventually reverting to what the Italians call a *campo vaccino* (cow pasture). But excavations in the 19th century began to bring to light one of the world's most historic spots.

By day, the columns of the now-vanished temples, the stones from which long-forgotten orators spoke, are mere shells. Bits of grass and weed grow where a triumphant Caesar was once lionized. But at night, when the Forum is silent in the moonlight, it isn't difficult to imagine that the Vestal Virgins are still guarding the sacred fire in the temple. (Historical footnote: The function of the maidens was to keep the sacred fire burning—but their own flame under control. Failure to do the latter sent them to an early grave . . . alive!)

You can spend at least a morning wandering through the ruins of the Forum alone. If you're content with just looking at the ruins, you can do so at your leisure. But if you want to give meaning to the stone, you'll have to purchase a detailed plan, as the temples are hard to locate otherwise.

Some of the ruins are more important than others, of course. The best of the lot is the handsomely adorned Temple of Castor and Pollux, erected in the 5th century B.C. in honor of a battle triumph. The Temple of Faustina, with its lovely columns and frieze (griffins and candelabra), was converted into the San Lorenzo in Miranda Church.

The senators used to meet in the Curia, walking on marble floors. Diocletian reconstructed the Senate, and it was later transformed into a medieval church. Across from the Curia is the "Lapis Niger," a black marble slab said to be the tomb of Romulus, legendary founder of the city (you can go downstairs).

The Temple of the Vestal Virgins is a popular attraction. Some of the statuary, mostly headless, remains. The Temple of Saturn was rebuilt in the days of the Republic in the 1st century B.C.

The Temple of Julius Caesar was ordered constructed by Octavian, in honor of the place where Caesar's body was cremated following his assassination. Rather oddly placed is the Church of Santa Maria Antiqua, with Christian frescoes that go back to the 7th century A.D.

Finally, the two arches are memorable: the Arch of Septimius Severus, erected in A.D. 203 with bas-reliefs, and the Arch of Titus, with much better carving, commemorating a victory in Jerusalem.

The Roman Forum, on via dei Fori Imperiali, can be reached by taking bus 27, 30, 85, 87, or 88, or the subway to the Colosseo station. It is open from 9 a.m. to 3 p.m. daily except Tuesday, when it is closed. You must leave no later than an hour before sunset. On holidays you may visit from 9 a.m. to 1 p.m., exiting no later than 2 p.m. Admission costs 5,000 lire ($3.80) for adults, free for children under 12 if accompanied by adults. On the first and third Saturday and the second and fourth Sunday of the month, admission is free to all. The same hours are in effect and the same ticket will admit you to the next major attraction. Telephone 679-0333 for information.

(4) PALATINE HILL

A long walk up from the Roman Forum leads to one of the seven hills of Rome. The Palatine, tradition tells us, was the spot on which the first settlers built their huts, under the direction of Romulus. In years to come the hill was turned into an elegant patrician residential district—attracting such citizens as Cicero. In time, however, it was gobbled up by imperial palaces—drawing such a famous and infamous roster of tenants as Caligula (he was murdered here), Nero, Tiberius, and Domitian.

Only the ruins of its former grandeur remain today, and you really need to be an archeologist to make sense of them, as they are more difficult to understand than those in the Forum. But even if you're not interested in the past, it's worth the climb for the magnificent sweep of both the Roman and Imperial forums, as well as the Capitoline Hill and the Colosseum.

Of all the ruins to inspect, none is finer than the so-called **House of Livia** (the "abominable grandmother" of Robert Graves's *I, Claudius*). Actually, recent archeological research indicates that the house was in fact the "casa" of her husband, Augustus. Livia used to slip him maidens noted for their discretion. A guard who controls the gate will show you the mythological frescoes reminiscent of those discovered at Herculaneum and Pompeii.

The Imperial Palace—the **Domus Augustana**—is an easy walk away, lying in the virtual heart of the Palatine. Domitian called the palace home. In the middle of the once-lavish estate—now stripped to the brick—is a large peristyle, with a fountain. The same emperor also ordered the building of the Palatine Stadium or "Hippodrome" below. In addition, Domitian was responsible for a once-remarkable structure, the Palace of Flavii, with its triclinium or great hall. When not overseeing real-estate construction, Domitian was seeing to it that his name would become immortal in the history of vice.

When the glory that was Rome has completely overwhelmed you, you can enjoy a respite in the cooling **Farnese Gardens,** laid out in the 16th century, incorporating some of the designs of Michelangelo.

(5) THE COLOSSEUM

In spite of the fact that it's a mere shell of itself, the **Colosseum** remains the greatest architectural inheritance from Ancient Rome. Called the Amphitheatrum Flavium, the elliptically shaped bowl was ordered built by Vespasian in A.D. 72 and was launched by Titus in A.D. 80 with a many-weeks-long bloody combat between gladiators and wild beasts.

At its peak, under the cruel Domitian, the Colosseum could seat 50,000 spectators. The Vestal Virgins from the temple screamed for blood, as more and more exotic animals were shipped in from the far corners of the empire to satisfy jaded tastes (lion vs. bear, two humans vs. hippopotamus). Not-so-mock naval battles were staged (the canopied Colosseum could be flooded), in which the defeated combatants might have their lives spared if they put up a good fight. One of the most enduring legends linked to the Colosseum—that is, that Christians were fed to the lions here—is considered to be without foundation by some historians.

Long after it ceased to be an arena to amuse sadistic Romans, the Colosseum was struck by an earthquake. Centuries later it was used as a quarry, its rich marble facing stripped away to build palaces and churches.

On one side, part of the original four tiers remain—the first three levels being constructed in Doric, Ionic, and Corinthian to lend it variety. The Colosseum (tel. 735-227) is at the piazzale del Colosseo (subway to "Colosseo"). The Colosseum is open daily from 9 a.m. to 7 p.m. If you wish to visit the upper levels, admission is 3,000 lire ($2.30). It closes at 4 p.m. in winter, and is open only from 9 a.m. to 1 p.m. on Wednesday.

Also at the piazzale del Colosseo is the **Arch of Constantine,** one of Rome's most enduring landmarks, having been built in A.D. 315 to celebrate a military victory of Constantine—and it's still in relatively good shape. Under this arch marched the victor and the vanquished.

After visiting the Colosseum, it is also convenient to explore the **Domus Aurea,** or the Golden House of Nero on via Labicana, facing the Colosseum. Adjacent to the Forum, Nero built one of the most sumptuous palaces of all time. Floors were made of mother-of-pearl, furniture of gold. The area that is the Colosseum today was an ornamental lake, reflecting the grandeur and glitter of the Golden House. Nero constructed the estate after that disastrous fire that swept over Rome in A.D. 64. The hollow ruins—long stripped of their lavish decorations—lie near the entrance of the Oppius Park, extending on one of the two Esquiline heights.

During the Renaissance, painters such as Raphael chopped holes in the long-buried ceilings of the Domus Aurea to gain admittance. Once there, they were inspired by the frescoes and the small "grotesques" of cornucopia and cherubs. The word "grotto" came from this palace, as it was believed to have been built underground. Remnants of these original almost-2,000-year-old frescoes remain, along with fragments of mosaics. The Domus Aurea is usually open daily from 9 a.m. until two hours before sunset. However, it is likely to be closed during the lifetime of this edition.

(6) A WALKING TOUR OF IMPERIAL ROME

The Imperial Forums

Even in the days of the Republic, the population explosion was a problem. Julius Caesar saw the overcrowding and began to expand, starting what were known as the **Imperial Forums** in the days of the empire. After the collapse of Rome and during the Dark Ages, the Forums were lost to history until Mussolini set out to restore the grandeur of Rome. He knew that one way to do that was to remind his compatriots of their glorious past. He cut through the years of debris and junky buildings to carve out the **via dei Fori Imperiali,** linking the piazza Venezia to the Colosseum. Excavations began at once, and much was revealed. Today the boulevard makes for one of the most fascinating walks in Rome. All the Imperial Forums can be seen from street level.

Starting at the Colosseum, with your back to it, begin walking up via dei Fori Imperiali, keeping to the right side of the street. Those ruins across the street are what's left of the colonnade that once surrounded the **Temple of Venus and Roma.** Next to it, you'll recognize the back wall of the Basilica of Constantine. Shortly, you'll come to a large outdoor restaurant, where via Cavour joins the boulevard you're on. Just beyond the small park across via Cavour are the remains of the **Forum of Nerva,** built by the emperor whose two-year reign (A.D. 96–98) followed that of the paranoid Domitian.

The Forum of Nerva is best observed from the railing that skirts it on via dei Fori Imperiali. You'll be struck by just how much the ground level has risen in 19 centuries. The only really recognizable remnant is a wall of the Temple of Minerva with two fine Corinthian columns. This forum was once flanked by that of Vespasian, which is, however, completely gone. It's possible to enter the Forum of Nerva from the other side, but you can see it just as well from the railing.

The next forum we come to was the **Forum of Augustus,** built before the birth of Christ to commemorate the emperor's victory over the assassins Cassius and Brutus in the Battle of Philippi (42 B.C.). Fittingly, the temple that once dominated this forum—and whose remains can still be seen—was that of Mars Ultor, or Mars the Avenger. In the temple once stood a mammoth statue of Augustus, which has unfortunately completely vanished. Like the Forum of Nerva, you can enter the Forum of Augustus from the other side (cut across the wee footbridge).

Continuing along the railing, you'll see next the vast semicircle of **Trajan's Market,** 95 via Quattro Novembre, whose teeming arcades stocked with merchandise from the far corners of the Roman world long ago collapsed, leaving only a few ubiquitous cats to watch after things. The shops once covered a multitude of levels, and you can still wander around many of them. In front of the perfectly proportioned semicircular façade—designed by Apollodorus of Damascus at the beginning of the 2nd century—are the remains of a great library, and fragments of delicately colored marble floors still shine in the sunlight between stretches of rubble and tall grass. While the view from the railing is of interest, Trajan's Market is worth the descent below street level. To get there, follow the service road you're on until you come as far as the monumental Trajan's Column on your left, but turn right here and go up the steep flight of stairs that leads to via Nazionale. At the top of the stairs, about a half block farther on the right, you'll see the entrance to the market, which is open daily except Monday from 9 a.m. to 1 p.m. Admission is 1,500 lire ($1.15). Telephone 671-03-613 for information.

Before you head down through the labyrinthine passageways, you might like to climb the **Tower of the Milizie,** a 12th-century structure that was part of the medieval headquarters of the Knights of Rhodes. The view from the top (if it's open) is well worth the climb. From the tower, you can wander where you will through the ruins of the market, admiring the sophistication of the layout and the sad beauty of the bits of decoration that still remain. When you've examined the brick and travertine corridors, head out in front of the semicircle to the site of the former library; from here, scan the retaining wall that supports the modern road and look for the entrance to the tunnel that leads to the **Forum of Trajan.**

Once through the tunnel, you'll emerge in the latest and most beautiful of the Imperial Forums, designed by the same man who laid out the adjoining market. There are many statue fragments, and pedestals bearing still-legible inscriptions, but more interesting is the great **Basilica Ulpia,** whose gray marble columns rise roofless into the sky. Beyond the basilica is **Trajan's Column,** in magnificent condition, with intricate bas-relief sculpture depicting Trajan's victorious campaign, although from

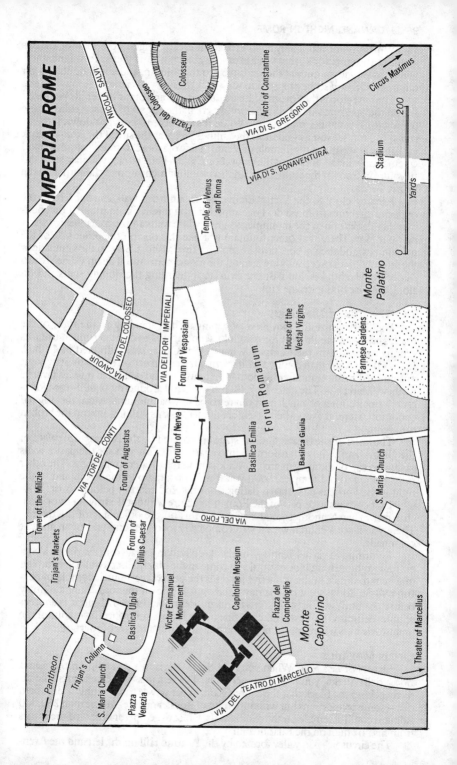

IMPERIAL ROME

Colosseum

Piazza del Colosseo

VIA NICOLA SALVI

Arch of Constantine

VIA DI S. GREGORIO

VIA DI S. BONAVENTURA

Circus Maximus

Temple of Venus and Roma

Stadium

Yards

0   200

VIA DEL COLOSSEO

VIA CAVOUR

VIA DEI FORI IMPERIALI

Forum of Vespasian

Forum Romanum

House of the Vestal Virgins

Monte Palatino

Farnese Gardens

Forum of Nerva

Basilica Emilia

Basilica Giulia

VIA TOR DE' CONTI

Forum of Augustus

VIA DEL FORO

S. Maria Church

Tower of the Milizie

Trajan's Markets

Forum of Julius Caesar

Capitoline Museum

Pantheon

Basilica Ulpia

Trajan's Column

Victor Emmanuel Monument

Piazza del Compidoglio

Monte Capitolino

S. Maria Church

Piazza Venezia

VIA DEL TEATRO DI MARCELLO

Theater of Marcellus

your vantage point you'll only be able to see the earliest stages. At the base of Trajan's Column the emperor's ashes were kept in a golden urn. If you're fortunate, there will be someone on duty at the stairs next to the column, and you'll be able to get out there. Otherwise, be prepared to walk back the way you came.

The next stop is the **Forum of Julius Caesar,** the first of the Imperial Forums. It lies on the opposite side of via dei Fori Imperiali, the last set of sunken ruins before the Victor Emmanuel monument. While it's possible to go right down into the ruins, you can see just as well from the railing. This was the site of the Roman stock exchange, as well as of the Temple of Venus, a few of whose restored columns stand cinematically in the middle of the excavations. From here, retrace your last steps until you're in front of the white Brescian marble monument around the corner on the piazza Venezia.

Keeping close to the Victor Emmanuel monument, walk to your left, in the opposite direction from via dei Fori Imperiali. You might like to pause at the fountain that flanks one of the monument's great white walls and splash some icy water on your face. There is another fountain just like this one on the other side of the monument, and they're both favorite spots for tired visitors. Stay on the same side of the street, and just keep walking around the monument. You'll be on via del Teatro Marcello, which takes you past the twin lions guarding the sloping stairs and on along the base of Capitoline Hill.

The Theater of Marcellus

You'll recognize the two rows of gaping arches, standing to the right of the road, said to be the models for the Colosseum. It was in a theater much like this (Pompey's theater in the Campus Martius) that Caesar was murdered in 44 B.C. Julius Caesar is the man credited with starting the construction of this theater, but it was finished many years after his death by Augustus, who dedicated it to his favorite nephew, Marcellus. The date: 11 B.C. You can stroll around the 2,000-year-old arcade, a small corner of which has been restored to what presumably was the original condition. Here, as everywhere, there are numerous cats stalking around the broken marble.

The bowl of the theater and the stage are covered by the Renaissance palace of the Orsini family, now transformed into apartments. You can see the palace walls sitting on top of the ancient arches. Walk around the theater to the right. The other ruins belong to old temples. Soon you'll walk up a ramp to the street, and to the right is the Porticus of Octavia, dating from the 2nd century before Christ. Note how later cultures used part of the Roman structure without destroying its original character. There's another good example of this on the other side of the theater. There you'll see a church with a wall completely incorporating part of an ancient colonnade.

Returning to via del Teatro Marcello, keep walking away from the piazza Venezia for two more long blocks, until you come to the **piazza Bocca della Verità.** The first item to notice in this attractive piazza is the perfect rectangular **Temple of Fortuna Virile.** You'll see it on the right, standing a little off the road. Built a century before the birth of Christ, it's still in magnificent condition. Behind it is another temple, dedicated to Vesta. Like the one in the forum, it is round, symbolic of the prehistoric huts where continuity of the hearthfire was a matter of survival.

Circus Maximus

Shades of *Ben Hur.* When you're at Santa Maria in Cosmedin on the piazza Bocca della Verità, you're just a block away. The remains of the great arena lie directly behind the block that the church is on. What we see today is only a large field of awesome proportions but without a trace of Roman marble. At one time 250,000 Romans could assemble on the marble seats, while the emperor observed the games from his box high on the Palatine Hill.

The circus lies in a valley formed by the Palatine Hill on the left and the Aventine Hill on the right. Next to the Colosseum, it was the most impressive structure in Ancient Rome and was certainly in one of the most exclusive neighborhoods. Emperors lived on the Palatine, while the great palaces of patricians sprawled across the Aventine, which is still a rather nice neighborhood. For centuries the pomp and ceremony of imperial chariot races filled this valley with the cheers of thousands.

When the dark days of the 5th and 6th centuries fell on the city, the Circus Maximus seemed a symbol of the complete ruination of Rome. The last games were held in 549 on the orders of Totilla the Goth, who had seized Rome in 546 and established himself as emperor. He lived in the still-glittering ruins on the Palatine and apparently thought that the chariot races in the Circus Maximus would lend credence to his charade of empire. It must have been a pretty miserable show, since the decimated population numbered something on the order of 500 souls when Totilla had recaptured the city. The Romans of these times were caught between Belisarius, the imperial general from Constantinople, and Totilla the Goth, both of whom fought bloodily for control of Rome. After the travesty of 549, the Circus Maximus was never used again, and the demand for building materials reduced this, like so much of Rome, to a great dusty field.

To return to other parts of town, head for the bus stop adjacent to the Santa Maria in Cosmedin Church, or walk the length of the Circus Maximus to its far end and pick up the subway to Terminal Station.

(7) CAPITOLINE HILL (CAMPIDOGLIO)

Of the Seven Hills of Rome, Campidoglio is considered the most sacred—its origins stretching way back into antiquity (an Etruscan temple to Jupiter stood on this spot). The most dramatic approach to the Capitoline Hill is to walk up to via di Teatro Marcello from the piazza Venezia, the center of Rome.

On your left, you can climb the steps designed by Michelangelo. At the top of the approach is the perfectly proportioned square of the piazza di Campidoglio, also laid out by the Florentine genius.

Michelangelo positioned the bronze equestrian statue of Marcus Aurelius in the center. A most remarkable treasure, the statue was made in the 2nd century A.D. All other imperial bronze equestrian statues have been lost to history, but this one was discovered in the mud of the Tiber. The bronze emperor on his horse, it is believed, once rode atop a column—hence, the seeming distortion of the present work when viewed up close. Since 1981, the statue has been removed for restoration. It may not be returned to the piazza because of bad pollution in the area and might end up in a museum. Its status was not known at press time.

One side of the piazza is open; the others are bounded by the Senatorium (Town Council), the statuary-filled Palazza dei Conservatori, and the Capitoline Museums (see "Museums and Galleries"). The Campidoglio is dramatic at night (walk around to the back for a regal view of the floodlit Roman Forum). On your return, head down the small steps on your right. You'll pass two caged wolves, a commemorative gesture to the "Capitoline Wolf," who is said to have suckled Romulus and Remus, legendary founders of Rome. If you care to climb the other steps adjoining Michelangelo's approach, they'll take you to Santa Maria d'Aracoeli (see "Churches of Rome").

(8) CASTEL SANT' ANGELO

From its vantage landmark position on the Tiber (at largo Castello), this overpowering structure was originally built in the 2nd century A.D. as a tomb for the Emperor Hadrian, and it continued as an imperial mausoleum until the time of Caracalla. Cylindrically shaped, it is an imposing and grim castle with thick walls. If it looks like a fortress, it should, as that was its function in the Middle Ages (built over the Roman walls and linked by an underground passageway to the Vatican, much used by the fleeing papacy trying to escape unwanted visitors, such as the sacker of the city in 1527, Charles V).

In the 14th century it became a papal residence, enjoying various connections with Boniface IX, Nicholas V, even Julius II, patron of Michelangelo and Raphael. But its legend rests largely on its link with Pope Alexander VI, whose mistress bore him two children—Cesare and Lucrezia Borgia.

Of all the ladies of the Renaissance in Italy, Lucrezia is the only one who could command universal recognition in the Western world, her name a virtual synonym for black deeds, such as poisoning. Again, popular legend is highly unreliable: many of the charges against her that her biographers have suggested (such as incestuous involvements with her brother and father) may have been successful attempts to blacken her name. In addition to being a link with an infamous family, she was a patroness of the arts and a devoted charity worker, especially after she moved to Ferrara. Of course, her brother, Cesare, is without defense—a Machiavellian hero who is remembered accurately as a symbol of villainy and cruel spite.

Today the highlight of the castle is a trip through the Renaissance apartments, with their coffered ceilings and lush decoration. Their walls have witnessed some of the arch treachery of the High Renaissance—plots and intrigues. Later, you can go through the dank cells that once rang with the screams of Cesare's victims of torture, such as Astorre Manfredi of Faenza, who was finally relieved of his pain by murder.

Perhaps the most famous figure imprisoned here was Benvenuto Cellini, the eminent sculptor and goldsmith, remembered chiefly for his classic, candid autobiography. Cellini kept getting into trouble—murdering people, etc.—but was jailed here on a charge of "peculation" (embezzlement of public funds). He escaped, was hauled back to jail, but was finally freed.

Now an art museum (tel. 687-5036), the castle shelters halls displaying the history of the Roman mausoleum, along with a wide-ranging selection of ancient arms and armor. Don't fail to climb to the top terrace for another one of those dazzling views of the Eternal City. The museum, which can be visited on your way to St. Peter's, is open from 2 to 6:30 p.m. on Monday, 9 a.m. to 1 p.m. Tuesday through Saturday, and 9 a.m. to noon on Sunday. Admission is 3,000 lire ($2.30).

(9) APPIAN WAY AND THE CATACOMBS

Of all the roads that led to Rome, the Appia Antica—built in 312 B.C.—was the queen. It eventually stretched all the way from Rome to the seaport of Brindisi, through which trade with the colonies in Greece and the East was funneled. According to the Christian tradition, it was on the Appian Way that an escaping Peter encountered the vision of Christ, which caused him to go back into the city to face subsequent martyrdom.

Along the Appian Way the patrician Romans built great monuments above the ground, while the Christians met in the catacombs beneath the earth. The remains of both can be visited today. In some dank, dark grottoes (never stray too far from either your party or one of the exposed lightbulbs), you can still discover the remains of early Christian art.

Only someone wanting to write a sequel to *Quo Vadis* would want to visit all the catacombs. Of those open to the public, the Catacombs of St. Calixtus and those of St. Sebastian are the most important. Both can be reached by taking bus 118, which leaves from near the Colosseum close to the Metro station.

The Tomb of St. Sebastian, called the Catacombs di San Sebastiano, lies at via Appia Antica 136 (tel. 788-7035). The tomb of the martyr is in the basilica (church). His original tomb was in the catacomb that is under the basilica. From the time of Emperor Valerian until the reign of Emperor Constantine, the bodies of Saint Peter and Saint Paul were hidden in the catacomb. The big church was built here in the 4th century, and this is the only Christian catacomb in Rome that is always open. None of the catacombs, incidentally, is a grotto; all are dug from tufo, a soft volcanic rock.

The tunnels here, if stretched out, would reach a length of seven miles. In the tunnels and mausoleums are mosaics and graffiti, along with many other pagan and Christian objects, even from centuries before Constantine. Visiting hours are 9 a.m.

to noon and 2:30 to 5 p.m. Friday through Wednesday (summer schedules are a bit longer). The catacombs are closed on Thursday, and otherwise charge an admission of 3,000 lire ($2.30).

The **Catacombs of St. Calixtus** (Catacombe di San Callisto), via Appia Antica 110 (tel. 513-6725), to quote the words of Pope John XXIII, "is one of the oldest and the most ancient of the Christian sanctuaries." It was also probably the best of all the cemeteries of the Christian communities, and, after the Vatican, was the place in which all the popes of the 3rd century were buried. Actually, in the late 2nd century there were distinct units that later became united. The name comes from the deacon, Calixtus, who was put in charge of the wealth of the church in the 3rd century, although he himself is buried in the Cemetery of Calepodius on via Aurelia.

The Catacombs of St. Calixtus comprise a complex of underground crypts and galleries rediscovered in 1852, extending for more than 15 miles. Visitors are conducted by a guide to the Crypts of the Popes (9 of the 16 popes of the 3rd century who were interred in the area are buried here) and to the Cubiculum of St. Cecilia (patron saint of music), an early Christian martyr. She received three ax strokes on her neck, the maximum number allowed by Roman law, which failed to kill her outright. She reportedly died after three days of agonizing pain and bleeding. Farther along, visitors will notice the Crypts of the Sacraments, so called because the original frescoes (2nd century A.D.) allude to the Holy Eucharist, Baptism, Penance, and a variety of early Christian symbols, most notable being the fish. The catacombs were for the dead a resting place and for the living a place of worship and meeting, not homes or hiding places, as some believe. Visiting hours are 8:30 a.m. to noon and 2:30 to 5:30 p.m. Thursday through Tuesday in summer, closing at 5 p.m. in winter. Admission is 3,000 lire ($2.30). These particular catacombs are kept open all year except on Wednesday, January 1, Easter, and Christmas. To reach them, you board bus 118 at St. John in Lateran, the Colosseum, or Circus Maximus, or else bus 218 from St. John in Lateran to Fosse Ardeatine. Ask the driver to drop you at the Catacombs of St. Calixtus.

Of the Roman monuments, the most impressive is the **Tomb of Cecilia Metella,** on via Appia Antica, within walking distance of the catacombs. Cylindrically shaped, the tomb honors the wife of one of the military commanders of Caesar. Why such an elaborate tomb for such an unimportant person in history? Cecilia Metella happened to be singled out for enduring fame because her tomb remained and the others decayed.

(10) THE PANTHEON

Of all the great buildings of Ancient Rome, only one remains intact: the Pantheon ("all the gods"). Built in 27 B.C. by Marcus Agrippa, it was later reconstructed by Emperor Hadrian in the first part of the 2nd century A.D. This remarkable building is listed among the architectural wonders of the world because of its concept of space and its dome. Byron described the temple as "simple, erect, austere, severe, sublime."

Once it was ringed with white marble statues of pagan gods, such as Jupiter and Minerva, in its niches. Animals were sacrificed and burned in the center, the smoke escaping through the only means of light, an opening at the top 27 feet in diameter. The Pantheon is 142 feet wide, 142 feet high. Michelangelo came here to study the dome before designing the cupola of St. Peter's (the dome of the Pantheon is two feet larger than that of St. Peter's).

Other statistics are equally impressive. The walls are 25 feet thick, and the bronze doors leading into the building weigh 20 tons each. The temple was converted into a church in the early 7th century.

About 125 years ago, the tomb of Raphael was discovered in the Pantheon (fans still bring him flowers). Victor Emmanuel II, king of Italy, was interred here.

The admission-free Pantheon lies at the piazza della Rotonda (take bus 87 or 94). It's open daily except Monday from 9 a.m. to 1 p.m. and 2 to 5 p.m. (from 9 a.m. to 1 p.m. on Sunday); from October to April it can be visited only in the afternoon.

(11) THE PIAZZA DI SPAGNA (SPANISH STEPS)

The Spanish Steps were the last view of the outside world that Keats saw before he died in a house at the foot of the stairs (see "Poets' Corner"). The steps—filled, in season, with flower vendors, young jewelry dealers, and photographers snapping pictures of tourists—and the square take their names from the Spanish Embassy, which used to have its headquarters here.

At the foot of the steps is a nautically shaped fountain that was designed by Pietro Bernini (Papa is not to be confused with his son, Giovanni Lorenzo Bernini, who proved to be a far greater sculptor of fountains). About two centuries ago, when the foreign art colony was in its ascendancy, the 136 steps were flanked with young men and women wanting to hire out to pose for the painters—the men with their shirts unbuttoned to show off what they hoped was a Davidesque physique, the women consistently draped like Madonnas.

At the top of the steps is not only a good view, but the 16th-century church of Trinità dei Monti, built by the French, with twin towers.

(12) THE FOUNTAINS OF ROME

Rome is a city of fountains—a number of such exceptional beauty that they're worth a special pilgrimage. Some of the more famous ones are the Four Seasons and Bernini's Triton Fountain at the piazza Barberini, but the two that hold the most enduring interest are the Fountains of Trevi and the waterworks at the piazza Navona.

The **piazza Navona,** surely one of the most beautifully baroque sites in all of Rome, is like an ochre-colored gem, unspoiled by new buildings or even by traffic. The shape results from the Stadium of Domitian, the ruins of which lie underneath the present constructions. Great chariot races were once held here, some of them rather unusual. There was one, for instance, where the head of the winning horse was lopped off as he crossed the finish line and carried by runners to be offered as a sacrifice by Vestal Virgins on top of the Capitoline Hill. Historians also note that the piazza Navona was, in medieval times, flooded by the popes and used to stage mock naval encounters. Today the most strenuous activities are performed by occasional fire-eaters who go through their evening paces before an interested crowd of Romans and visitors.

Beside the twin-towered façade of the **Church of Saint Agnes** (17th century), the piazza boasts several other baroque masterpieces. In the center is Bernini's **Fountain of the Four Rivers,** whose four stone personifications symbolize the world's greatest rivers—the Ganges, Danube, della Plata, and Nile. It's fun to try to figure out which is which (hint: the figure with the shroud on its head is the Nile, so represented because the river's source was unknown at the time the fountain was constructed). The fountain at the south end, the **Fountain of the Moor,** is also by Bernini and dates from the same period as the church and the Fountain of the Four Rivers. The **Fountain of Neptune,** which balances that of the Moor, is a 19th-century addition. During the summer there are outdoor art shows in the evening, but a visit during the day is in order. It's the best time to inspect the fragments of the original stadium remaining under a building on the north side of the piazza. If you're interested, walk out at the northern exit and turn left for a block. It's astonishing how much the level of the ground has risen since ancient times.

As you elbow your way through the summertime crowds around the **Trevi Fountain** (Fontana di Trevi) at the piazza di Trevi, you'll find it hard to believe that this little piazza was nearly always deserted before *Three Coins in the Fountain* brought the tour buses. Today it's a must on everybody's itinerary. The fountain is an 18th-century extravaganza of baroque stonework presided over by a large statue of Neptune. While some of the statuary is the work of other artists, the man who gets credit for the entire project is Nicolo Salvi. The tradition of throwing coins into the fountain is an evolution of earlier customs. At one time visitors drank water from the fountain. Later they combined that with an offering to the spirits of the place. Nowadays, no one dares to drink the water, but many still make the offering. To do it properly, hold your lire coin in the right hand, turn your back to the fountain, and toss the coin over your shoulder, being careful not to bean anyone behind you. Once done, the spirit of the fountain will see to it that you will one day return to Rome. Or at least that's the tradition. On one corner of the piazza you'll see an ancient church with a strange claim to fame. In it are contained the hearts and viscera of several centuries of popes. This was the parish church of the popes when they resided at the Quirinal Palace on the hill above, and for many years each pontiff willed those parts of his body to this church.

The **piazza Barberini** lies at the foot of several Roman streets: via Barberini, via Sistina, and via Veneto among them. It would be a far more pleasant spot were it not for the considerable amount of traffic swarming around its principal feature, Bernini's **Fountain of the Triton.** Day and night for more than three centuries, the strange figure sitting in a vast open clam has been blowing water from his triton. Off to one side of the piazza is the clean aristocratic side façade of the Palazzo Barberini. Rome has always been a city of powerful families. The Renaissance Barberini reached their peak when a son was elected pope—Urban VIII. It was this Barberini pope who encouraged Bernini and gave him so much patronage.

As you go up the via Veneto, look for the small fountain on the right-hand corner of the piazza Barberini. There stands another of Bernini's works, the small **Fountain of the Bees.** At first they look more like flies, but they are the bees of the Barberini, the crest of that powerful family complete with the crossed keys of St. Peter above them. The keys were always added to a family crest when a son was elected pope.

---

2. The Secondary Sights

MUSEUMS AND GALLERIES

For those not tossing their lire into the Trevi Fountain—and who can stick around for a more extended stay—I'll now discuss some other important sights, museums, and galleries:

National Roman Museum (Museo Nazionale Romano)

At via delle Terme di Diocleziano (tel. 460-856), near the piazza dei Cinquecento, which fronts the railway station, this museum (also called the Museum of the Thermae) occupies part of the 3rd-century (A.D.) Baths of Diocletian and a section of a convent that may have been designed by Michelangelo. Today it houses one of the finest collections of Greek and Roman sculpture and early Christian sarcophagi in Europe.

The Ludovisi Collection is the apex of the museum, particularly the statuary of the Gaul slaying himself after he's done in his wife (a brilliant copy of a Greek original from the 3rd century B.C.).

Another prize is a one-armed Greek Apollo. A galaxy of other sculptured treasures include: *The Discus Thrower of Castel Porziano* (an exquisite copy); *Aphrodite of Cirene* (a Greek original); and the so-called *Hellenistic Ruler,* a Greek original of an athlete with a lance. A masterpiece of Greek sculpture, *The Birth of Venus* is in the Ludovisi throne. The *Sleeping Hermaphrodite* (Ermafrodito Dormiente) is an original Hellenistic statue. Don't fail to stroll through the cloisters, filled with statuary and fragments of antiquity, including a fantastic mosaic. At press time restoration was in progress.

The museum is open daily except Monday from 9 a.m. to 2 p.m. (holidays and Sunday, 9 a.m. to 1 p.m.); 4,000 lire ($3.05) for admission.

National Museum of Villa Giulia (Etruscan)

A 16th-century papal palace in the Villa Borghese gardens shelters a priceless collection of art and artifacts of the mysterious Etruscans, who predated the Romans. Known for their sophisticated art and design, the Etruscans left as their legacy sarcophagi, bronze sculptures, terracotta vases, and jewelry, among other items.

If you have time only for the masterpieces, head for Sala 7, with its remarkable Apollo from Veio from the end of the 6th century B.C.—clothed, for a change. The other two widely acclaimed pieces of statuary in this gallery include *Dea con Bambino* (a goddess with a baby) and a greatly mutilated, but still powerful, Hercules with a stag. In the adjoining room, Sala 8, you'll see the lions' sarcophagus from the mid-6th century B.C., excavated at Cerveteri, north of Rome.

Finally, one of the world's most important Etruscan art treasures is the bride and bridegroom coffin from the 6th century B.C., also dug out of the tombs of Cerveteri (in Sala 9). Near the end of your tour, another masterpiece of Etruscan art awaits you in Sala 33: the *Cista Ficoroni,* a bronze urn with paw feet, mounted by three figures, dating from the 4th century B.C.

The address of the museum is piazza di Villa Giulia 4 (tel. 360-1951); take tram 30 or 19. It is open daily except Monday from 9 a.m. to 7 p.m. (on Sunday from 9 a.m. to noon) and charges 4,000 lire ($3.05) for admission.

The Borghese Gallery and Museum

Housed in a handsome villa in the Villa Borghese gardens on via Pinciano (tel. 858-577), the gallery contains some of the finest paintings in Rome, with a representative collection of Renaissance and baroque masters, along with important Bernini sculpture. Among these is the so-called *Conquering Venus* by Antonio Canova, Italy's greatest neoclassic sculptor. Actually, the early-19th-century work created a sensation in its day, for its model was Pauline Bonaparte Borghese, sister of Napoleon (if the French dictator didn't like to see his sister naked, he was even more horrified at the Canova version of himself totally nude). In the rooms that follow are three of Bernini's most widely acclaimed works: *David, Apollo and Daphne* (his finest piece), and finally, *The Rape of Persephone.*

The paintings form a display of canvases almost too rich for one visit. If pressed for time, concentrate on three works by Raphael (especially the young woman holding a unicorn in her lap and the *Deposition from the Cross*).

Caravaggio (1569–1609), the master of chiaroscuro and leader of the realists is on view. His paintings include such works as the *Madonna of the Palafrenieri.* Rubens's favorite theme, the elders lusting after Susanna, is displayed. Titian's *Sacred and Profane Love* is exhibited, along with three other works by the same master.

The gallery is open Tuesday through Saturday from 9 a.m. to 1:30 p.m., on Sunday from 9 a.m. to 1 p.m.; entrance is free. Currently, only the sculptures are on view, but that may have changed by the time of your visit.

After visiting the gallery, you may want to joint the Italians in their strolls through the Villa Borghese, replete with zoological gardens and small bodies of water. Horse shows are staged at the piazza di Siena.

Capitoline Museum and Palace of the Conservatory

At the piazza del Campidoglio are two museums housing some of the greatest pieces of classical sculpture in the world. The **Capitoline Museum,** or Musei Capitolini (tel. 678-2862), was built in the 17th century, based on an architectural sketch by Michelangelo. The exhibit was originally a papal collection, founded by Sixtus IV in the 15th century.

In the first room is a statue that brings instant recognition the world over, *The Dying Gaul,* a work of majestic skill, a copy of a Greek original that dates from sometime in the 3rd century B.C. But in a special gallery all her own is *The Capitoline Venus,* demurely covering herself—the symbol of feminine beauty and charm down through the centuries (a Roman copy of the Greek original from the 3rd century B.C.). Finally, *Amore* (Cupid) and *Psyche* are up to their old tricks.

The **Palace of the Conservatori** across the way was also based on an architectural plan by Michelangelo. It is rich not only in classical sculpture but paintings as well. One of the most notable bronzes—a work of incomparable beauty—is the *Spinario* (the little boy picking a thorn from his foot). The Greek classic bronze dates from the 1st century B.C. In addition, you'll find *Lupa Capitolina* (the Capitoline Wolf), a rare Etruscan bronze that may possibly go back to the 6th century B.C. (Romulus and Remus, the legendary twins that the wolf suckled, were added at a later date). The palace also contains a "Pinacoteca"—mostly paintings from the 16th and 17th centuries. Notable canvases include Caravaggio's fortune-teller and his curious John the Baptist; the Holy Family by Dosso Dossi; Romulus and Remus by Rubens; and Titian's *Baptism of Christ.*

Both museums are open from 9 a.m. to 1:30 p.m. daily except Monday (to 1 p.m. on Sunday, and also from 5 to 8 p.m. Tuesday and Thursday; from 8:30 to 11 p.m. on Saturday from April to the end of September). Off-season hours are 9 a.m. to 1:30 p.m. daily except Monday (to 1 p.m. on Sunday, and also from 5 to 8 p.m. on Saturday). Admission is 4,500 lire ($3.40). The same ticket admits you to both museums.

National Gallery of Modern Art

At viale delle Belle Arti 131, the museum is in the Villa Borghese gardens, a short walk from the Etruscan Museum. With its neoclassic and romantic paintings and sculpture, it's a dramatic change from the glories of the Renaissance and the Romans. Its 75 rooms house the largest collection in Italy of 19th- and 20th-century artists, including a comprehensive collection of modern Italian paintings.

Also included are important works of Balla, Boccioni, DeChirico, Morandi, Manzù, Marini, Burri, Capogrossi, and Fontana, and a large collection of Italian optical and pop art.

Look for Modigliani's *La Signora dal Collaretto* and the large *Nudo.* Several important sculptures, including one by Canova, are on display in the museum's gardens. The gallery also houses a large collection of foreign artists, including French impressionists Degas, Cézanne, and Monet, and the post-impressionist van Gogh. Surrealism and expressionism are well represented in works by Klee, Ernst, Braque, Miró, Kandinsky, Mondrian, and Pollock. In addition to the paintings, you'll find sculpture by Rodin. The collection of graphics, the storage rooms, and the department of restoration can be visited by appointment Tuesday through Friday. Gallery hours are daily except Monday from 9 a.m. to 2 p.m. (on Sunday to 1 p.m.) On Wednesday, Thursday, and Friday, it is also open from 3 to 7:30 p.m. Admission is 4,000 lire ($3.05). Trams 19 and 30 service the museum, or if you're taking the subway, go on Line A. For more information about the museum and its exhibitions, telephone 802-751.

Palazzo Doria Pamphilj

Off via del Corso, the museum offers visitors a look at what it's really like to live in an 18th-century palace. The mansion, like many Roman palaces of the period, is partly leased to tenants (on the upper levels), and there are even shops on the street level, but all this is easily overlooked after you enter the grand apartments of the historical princely Doria Pamphilj family, which traces its line back to before the great 15th-century Genoese admiral Andrea Doria. The regal apartments surround the central court and gallery of the palace. The 18th-century decor pervades the magnificent ballroom, drawing rooms, dining rooms, and even the family chapel. Gilded furniture, crystal chandeliers, Renaissance tapestries, and portraits of family members are everywhere. The Green Room is especially rich in treasures, with a

15th-century Tournay tapestry, paintings by Memling and Filippo Lippi, and a semi-nude portrait of Andrea Doria by Sebastiano del Piombo. The Andrea Doria Room is dedicated to the admiral and to the ship of the same name. It contains a glass case with mementos of the great maritime disaster.

Skirting the central court is a picture gallery with a memorable collection of frescoes, paintings, and sculpture. Most important among a number of great works are the portrait of *Innocent X* by Velázquez, called one of the three or four best portraits ever painted; *Salome* by Titian; and works by Rubens and Caravaggio. Notable also are *Bay of Naples* by Pieter Brueghel the Elder and Raphael's portrait of Principessa Giovanna d'Aragona de Colonna, the subject looking remarkably like Leonardo's *Mona Lisa*. Most of the sculpture came from the Doria country estates. It includes marble busts of Roman emperors, bucolic nymphs, and satyrs. Even without the paintings and sculpture, the gallery would be worth a visit—just for its fresco-covered walls and ceilings. Both the apartments and gallery are open to the public on Tuesday, Friday, Saturday, and Sunday from 10 a.m. to 1 p.m. Admission is 3,000 lire ($2.30) for the gallery and another 3,000 lire for the private apartments. The entrance is at piazza dei Collegio Romano 1A (tel. 679-4365).

The Museum of Palazzo Venezia

At the piazza Venezia, in the geographic heart of Rome, is the building that served until the end of World War I as the seat of the Embassy of Austria. During the Fascist regime (1928–1943), this was the seat of the Italian government. The balcony from which Mussolini used to speak to the Italian people is from the 16th century, built during the reign of Paulus III Farnese. Standing on the part of the Capitoline Hill overlooking the piazza is the 19th-century monument to Victor Emmanuel II, king of Italy, a lush work that has often been compared to a birthday cake. Here you'll find the Tomb of the Unknown Soldier created in World War I. Less known is the museum (tel. 679-8865) founded in 1916 in the former papal residence that dates back to the 15th century. You can now visit the rooms and halls containing oil paintings, antiques, porcelain, tapestries, ivories, ceramics, and arms. No one particular exhibit stands out. It is the sum total that adds up to a major attraction.

The museum is open daily from 9 a.m. to 2 p.m. (on Sunday until 1 p.m.), costing 4,000 lire ($3.05) for admission.

Galleria Nazionale d'Arte Antica

The Palazzo Barberini is one of the most magnificent baroque palaces in Rome. Entered at via Quattro Fontane 13, right off the piazza Barberini, it was begun by Carlo Maderno in 1627 and completed in 1633 by Bernini, whose lavishly decorated rococo apartments, called the Gallery of Decorative Art, are on view. The palace houses the Galleria Nazionale (tel. 475-0184), which is open Tuesday through Saturday from 9 a.m. to 2 p.m.; to 1 p.m. on Sunday; closed Monday. It charges 3,000 lire ($2.30) for admission.

The bedroom of Princess Cornelia Costanza Barberini and Prince Giulio Cesare Colonna di Sciarra still stands just as it was on their wedding night, and throughout a series of rooms, many household objects are displayed in the decorative art gallery. In the chambers, with their frescoes and hand-painted silk linings, you can see porcelain from Japan and Bavaria, canopied beds, and a baby carriage made of wood.

On the first floor of the palace, a splendid array of paintings includes works that date back to the 13th and 14th centuries, most notably the *Mother and Child* by Simone Martini. Also praiseworthy are paintings by Florentine artists from the 15th century, including art by Beato Angelico and Filippo Lippi. In some salons are displayed 15th- and 16th-century paintings by such artists as Andrea Solario and Francesco Francia. Il Soloma has some brilliant pictures on display at the gallery, including *The Rape of the Sabines* and *The Marriage of St. Catherine*. One of the best-known paintings is Raphael's beloved *La Fornarina,* the baker's daughter who was his mistress, posing for his Madonna portraits. Titian is represented by a stern portrait of Philip II. Other artists exhibited include Tintoretto, El Greco, and Holbein the Younger. Many visitors come here just to see two magnificent Caravaggios: *St. John the Baptist* and *Narcissus.*

The Museo di Arte Ebraico della Comunitá Israelitica di Roma

At lungotevere Cenci (Tempio), the museum of Hebraic art is the permanent exhibition of the Jewish community of Rome. It contains Jewish ritual objects and scrolls from the 17th to the 19th centuries as well as copies of tombstones, paintings, prints, and documents illustrating 2,000 years of Jewish history in Rome. The collection of silver ceremonial objects is important, as is a selection of ancient ceremonial textiles. Documents of Nazi domination are of exceptional interest. It is open from 9:30 a.m. to 2 p.m. and 3 to 5 p.m. Monday through Thursday, from 9:30 a.m. to 1:30 p.m. on Friday, and from 9:30 a.m. to 12:30 p.m. on Sunday; closed Saturday. Admission is 2,000 lire ($1.50). For more information, phone 685-5051.

THE ALTAR OF PEACE

On the banks of the Tiber, across via di Ripetta, the **Ara Pacis Augustae** is one of the treasures of antiquity, although it is housed in a glass-and-concrete structure. It was built in 13 B.C. to honor Augustus and the peace he brought to the Roman world, and it was reassembled in 1938 from the original fragments which up to then had been housed in the National Museum. Portraits in marble include those of such imperial family members as Augustus, his wife, Livia, and Tiberius. Even the daughter of Augustus, Julia, is depicted, a woman known for her sexual excesses. Bas-reliefs illustrate the deeds of the emperor. The Altar of Peace (tel. 671-02-071) may be viewed from 9 a.m. to 1:30 p.m. Tuesday through Saturday, to 1 p.m. on Sunday; closed Monday. Admission is 1,500 lire ($1.15).

Across from the pavilion housing the Ara Pacis stands the **Mausoleum of Augustus,** a pile of bricks that has stood in a wide piazza for some 2,000 years. It was ordered constructed by Augustus as his tomb and the burial place of the imperial family. Once it was adorned with marble and statues and was bounded by porticoes. It was crowned by a conical mound of earth that had been heavily planted with graceful cypress trees. A statue of the emperor dominated the top. In medieval times it was converted to a fortress, and it had several other roles as it gradually withered, stripped of its richness and adornment. Invading barbarians long ago smashed the imperial remains, stealing the golden urns. Now all you can do is stand at the gates looking in upon this scene of former glory. Instead of golden urns you'll see a lot of hungry cats looking for food.

MODERN ROME

At the height of Mussolini's power, he launched a complex of modern buildings—many of them in cold marble—to dazzle Europe with a scheduled world's fair. But Il Duce got strung up, and E.U.R.—the area in question—got hamstrung. The new Italian government that followed inherited the uncompleted project, and decided to turn it into a center of government and administration. It has also developed into a residential section of fairly deluxe apartment houses. Most of the cold granite edifices fail to escape the curse of "Il Duce moderno," but the small "city of tomorrow" is softened considerably by a man-made lagoon, which you can row across in rented boats.

Italy's great modern architect, Milan-born Pier Luigi Nervi, designed the **Palazzo della Sport** on the hill. One of the country's most impressive modern buildings, it was the chief site of the 1960 Olympics. Another important structure is the **Palazzo dei Congressi** in the center, an exhibition hall with changing displays of industrial shows. It's well worth a stroll. You'll also spot versions of architecture reminiscent of Frank Lloyd Wright, "Aztec modern," and a building that evokes the design of the United Nations in New York.

If you want to turn your jaunt into a major outing, you can visit the museum of Roman civilization, or **Museo della Civiltà Romana** (tel. 592-6135), on the piazza Giovanni Agnelli, housing Fiat-sponsored reproductions that recapture life in Ancient Rome. Its major exhibition is a plastic representation in miniature of what Rome looked like at the apex of its power. You'll see the impressive Circus Maximus, the Colosseum as it looked when intact, the Baths of Diocletian—and lots more. The museum is open Tuesday through Saturday from 9 a.m. to 1:30 p.m. On Sunday, it is open from 9 a.m. to 1 p.m. and on Thursday evening, it is open from 4 to 7 p.m.; closed Monday. It charges 4,000 lire ($3.05) for admission. To reach E.U.R., take the Metro to E.U.R. Fermi (underground Line B). (E.U.R. can be visited en route to Ostia Antica and the Lido of Rome.)

For still another look at Mussolini's architectural achievements, head across the river from E.U.R. to the **Foro Italico**. Shades of 1932! This complex of sports stadiums blatantly honors Il Duce. At the entrance to the forum, an obelisk bears the name MVSSOLINI so firmly engraved that to destroy the lettering would be to do away with the monument. It stands defiantly. Visitors on a sunny day walk across the mosaic courtyard with DVCE in the pavement more times than La Rosa has noodles. The big attraction of this freakish site is the "Stadium of Marbles," encircled with 50 marble nude athletes—draped discreetly so as not to offend the eyes of the Golden Madonna on the hill beyond. Take bus 32 or 48 to the piazzo Lauro de Bosis when you tire of looking at the forums of ancient dictators and want to see that of a more contemporary one.

THE CHURCHES OF ROME

St. Peter's is not the only church you should see in Rome. The city's hundreds of churches—some built with marble stripped from ancient monuments—form a major sightseeing treasure. I've highlighted the best of the lot, including four patriarchal churches of Rome that are extraterritorial, belonging to the Vatican. Others are equally worth viewing, especially one designed by Michelangelo. My selections follow:

Basilica of San Giovanni in Laterano

At the piazza di San Giovanni in Laterano is the seat of the archbishop of Rome. St. John's—not St. Peter's—is the cathedral of Rome. Originally built in the 4th century by Constantine, the cathedral has suffered the vicissitudes of Rome, being badly sacked and forced to rebuild many times. Only fragmented parts of the baptistery remain from the original structure.

The present building is characterized by its 18th-century façade by Alessandro Galilei (statues of Christ and the Apostles ring the top). Borromini gets the credit (some say blame) for the interior, built for Innocent X. It is said that in the misguided attempt to redecorate, frescoes by Giotto were destroyed (remains believed to have been painted by Giotto were discovered in 1952 and are displayed). In addition, look for the unusual ceiling, the sumptuous transept, and explore the 13th-century cloisters.

The popes used to live next door at the Lateran Palace before the move to Avignon in the 14th century. But the most unusual sight is across the street at the "Palace of the Holy Steps," called the **Scala Sancta**. It is alleged that these were the actual wooden steps that Christ climbed when he was brought before Pilate. These steps are supposed to be climbed only on your knees, as you're likely to see the faithful doing throughout the day.

Basilica of St. Mary Major (Santa Maria Maggiore)

At the piazza di Santa Maria Maggiore, the third great church of Rome was founded in the 5th century, then later rebuilt. Its campanile, erected in the 14th century, is the loftiest one in the city. Much doctored in the 18th century, the church's façade is not an accurate reflection of the treasures inside. The basilica is especially noted for the 5th-century Roman mosaics in its nave, as well as for its coffered ceiling, said to have been gilded with gold brought from the New World. In the 16th century Domenico Fontana built a now-restored "Sistine Chapel." In the following century Flaminio Ponzo designed the Pauline (Borghese) Chapel in the baroque style. The church contains the tomb of Bernini, Italy's most important architect during the flowering of the baroque in the 17th century. Ironically, the man who changed the face of Rome with his elaborate fountains was buried in a tomb so simple it takes a sleuth to track it down (to the right near the altar).

The Basilica of St. Paul

On via Ostiense lies the fourth great patriarchal church of Rome. Tracing its origins back to Constantine, it burned in the 19th century and was subsequently rebuilt. This basilica is believed to have been erected over the tomb of St. Paul, much as St. Peter's was built over the tomb of that saint. Inside, its windows appear at first to be stained glass, but they are alabaster—the effect of glass created by the brilliant light shining through. With its forest of single-file columns and its mosaic medallions (portraits of the various popes), it is one of the most streamlined and elegantly decorated churches in Rome. Its single most important treasure is a 12th-century candelabrum, designed by Vassalletto, who is also responsible for the remarkable cloisters—in themselves worth the trip "outside the walls." The Benedictine monks and students sell a fine collection of souvenirs, rosaries, and bottles of Benedictine. The visit to the basilica and cloisters is free. The gift shop is open every day except Sunday and religious holidays.

St. Peter in Vincoli

From the Colosseum, head up a "spoke" street, via degli Annibaldi, to a church founded in the 5th century A.D. to house the chains that bound St. Peter in Palestine. The chains are preserved under glass. But the drawing card is the tomb of Julius II, with one of the world's most famous pieces of sculpture, *Moses* by Michelangelo. As readers of Irving Stone's *The Agony and the Ecstasy* know, Michelangelo was to have carved 44 magnificent figures for Julius's tomb. That didn't come about, of course, but the pope was given one of the greatest consolation prizes—a figure intended to be "minor" that is now numbered among Michelangelo's masterpieces. Of the stern, father symbol of Michelangelo's *Moses,* Vasari, in his *Lives of the Artists,* wrote: "No modern work will ever equal it in beauty, no, nor ancient either."

Church of Santa Maria Degli Angeli

At piazza della Repubblica 12 (tel. 460-812), adjoining the National Roman Museum near the railway station, stood the "tepidarium" of the 3rd-century Baths of Diocletian. But in the 16th century, Michelangelo—nearing the end of his life—converted the grand hall into one of the most splendid churches in Rome. Surely the artist wasn't responsible for "gilding the lily"—that is, putting trompe-l'oeil columns in the midst of the genuine pillars. The church is filled with tombs and paintings, but its crowning treasure is the statue of St. Bruno by the great French sculptor Jean-Antoine Houdon. His sculpture is larger than life and about as real. No admission is charged, and you can visit throughout the day.

Church of St. Clement

From the Colosseum, head up via di San Giovanni in Laterano, which leads to the Basilica of Saint Clement at via Labicana 95 (tel. 731-5723). This isn't just another Roman church. Far from it. In this church-upon-a-church, centuries of history peel away like stalks of fennel which the Romans eat for dessert. In the 4th century a church was built over a secular house of the 1st century A.D. beside which stood a pagan temple dedicated to Mithras (god of the sun). Down in the eerie grottoes (which you can explore on your own—unlike the catacombs on the Appian Way), you'll discover well-preserved frescoes from the 1st through the 3rd centuries A.D. You can visit the grottoes from 9 a.m. to noon and 3:30 to 6 p.m. daily (from 10 a.m. on Sunday), for a well-spent 1,000 lire (75¢). After the Normans destroyed the lower church, a new one was built in the 12th century. Its chief attraction is its bronze-orange mosaic (from that period) which adorns the apse, as well as a chapel honoring St. Catherine of Alexandria (murals by Masolino de Panicale who decorated the Brancacci Chapel in the Church of Carmine in Florence in the 15th century).

Church of Santa Maria in Cosmedin

At the piazza della Verità is a charming little church that was founded in the 6th century, but subsequently rebuilt—and a campanile was added in the 12th century in the Romanesque style. The church is ever popular with pilgrims to Rome drawn here not by its great art treasures but by its "Mouth of Truth," a large disk under the portico. According to tradition, it is supposed to chomp down on the hand of any liar who inserts his or her paw (although Audrey Hepburn escaped with her mitt untouched in *Roman Holiday*). On my last visit to the church, a little woman, draped in black, sat begging a few feet from the medallion. A scene typical enough —except this woman's right hand was covered with bandages.

The Church of Santa Maria D'Aracoeli

Sharing a spot on Capitoline Hill (but unfortunately reached by a long flight of steps different from those leading to the piazza di Campidoglio), this landmark church was built for the Franciscans in the 13th century. According to legend, Augustus once ordered a temple erected on this spot, where a sibyl, with her gift of prophecy, forecast the coming of Christ. On the interior of the present building, you'll find a nave and 2 aisles, 2 rows with 11 pillars each, a Renaissance ceiling, and a mosaic of the Virgin over the altar in the Byzantine style. If you're sleuth enough, you'll also find a tombstone carved by the great Renaissance sculptor Donatello.

THE POETS' CORNER OF ROME

At the foot of the Spanish Steps, the **Keats-Shelley Memorial,** at piazza di Spagna 26 (tel. 678-4235), is the 18th-century house where Keats died of consumption on February 23, 1821—carefully tended by his close friend, Joseph Severn. "It is like living in a violin," wrote the Italian author Alberto Savinio. The apartment where Keats spent his last months shelters a museum, with a strange death mask of Keats as well as the "deadly sweat" drawing by Severn and many other mementos of Keats, Shelley, and Byron. For those interested in the full story of the involvement of Keats and Shelley in Italy, a good little book compiled by Neville Rogers is sold on the premises. The memorial house is open from 9 a.m. to 1 p.m. and 3 to 6 p.m. in summer, from 9 a.m. to 1 p.m. and 2:30 to 5:30 p.m. in winter, weekdays; closed Saturday and Sunday. Admission is 3,500 lire ($2.65).

Near St. Paul's Station, in the midst of a setting of cypress trees, lies the old **Protestant Cemetery** where John Keats was buried. In a grave nearby, Joseph Severn, his "death-bed" companion, was interred beside him six decades later. Dejected and feeling his reputation as a poet diminished by the rising vehemence of his critics, Keats asked that the following epitaph be written on his tombstone: "Here lies one whose name was writ in water." A great romantic poet Keats certainly was, but a prophet, thankfully not.

Shelley, author of *Prometheus Unbound,* was drowned off the Italian Riviera in 1822—before his 30th birthday. His ashes rest alongside those of Edward John Trelawny, fellow romantic and man of the sea. Trelawny maintained that Shelley may have been murdered, his boat being overrun by petty pirates bent on robbery. Although it's not part of "English Rome," it's good to tie in a visit to the Protestant Cemetery with the neighboring **Pyramid of Caius Cestius,** which adjoins it on the piazzale Ostiense (bus 30). Dating from the 1st century B.C., it is about 90 feet high, and looks as if it belongs to the Egyptian landscape. The pyramid can't be entered, but it's fun to circle and photograph. Who was Caius Cestius? A judge of sorts, a man less impressive than his tomb.

ROME'S MOST MACABRE SIGHT

It's the **Cemetery of the Capuchin Fathers,** in the Church of the Immaculate Conception, via Vittorio Veneto 27, a short walk from the piazza Barberini. You enter the cemetery from the first staircase on the right of the church, at the entrance to the friary. Guidebooks of old used to rank this sight along with the Forum and the Colosseum as the top attractions in the city. Qualifying as one of the most horrifying sights in all Christendom, it is a cemetery of skulls and crossbones woven into "works of art." To make this allegorical dance of death, the bones of more than 4,000 Capuchin brothers were used. Some of the skeletons are intact, draped with Franciscan habits. The creator of this chamber of horrors? The tradition of the friars is that it was the work of a French Capuchin. Their literature suggests that the cemetery should be visited keeping in mind the historical moment of its origins, when Christians had a rich and creative cult for their dead, when great spiritual masters meditated and preached with a skull in hand. Those who have lived through the days of crematoriums and other such massacres may view the graveyard differently, but to many who pause to think, this macabre sight of death has a message. It's not for the squeamish. Charging no admission, the cemetery is open in summer daily from 9 a.m. to noon and 3 to 7 p.m. (winter hours, 9:30 a.m. to noon and 3 to 6 p.m.).

VILLA DORIA PAMPHILJ

This park was opened to the public in 1971 and acquired from Princess Orietta Doria Pamphilj. (The princess is descended from the world-famous naval commander Andrea Doria.) Behind the Vatican, the park is about half as large as Central Park in New York, but is more than double the dimensions of the previously described Villa Borghese. Villa Pamphilj fills a sad lack in the Roman capital, providing some much-needed green space. At one time the park belonged to Pope Innocent X, who planted it with exotic shrubbery, trees, and flowers.

THE QUIRINAL

In a wide pink piazza in the heart of Rome stands the palace of the president of Italy. It was the home of the king of Italy until the end of World War II, and before that, it was the residence of the pope. In antiquity, this was the site of Augustus's Temple of the Sun. The steep marble steps that lead to Santa Maria in Aracoeli on the Capitoline Hill once led to that temple. The great baths of Constantine also stood nearby, and that's the origin of some of the fountain statuary.

JANICULUM HILL (GIANICOLO)

From many vantage points in the Eternal City, the views are magnificent. Scenic gulpers, however, have traditionally preferred the outlook from Janiculum Hill (across the Tiber), not one of the "Seven Hills" but certainly one of the most visited (a stopover on many coach tours). The view is seen at its best at sundown, or at dawn when the skies are often fringed with mauve. Janiculum was the site of a battle between Giuseppe Garibaldi and the forces of Pope Pius IX in 1870—an event commemorated today with statuary. To reach "Gianicolo" without a private car, take bus 41 from Ponte Sant' Angelo.

BATHS OF CARACALLA

Named for the Emperor Caracalla, the baths were completed in the early part of the 3rd century. The richness of decoration has been carted off, and its lushness can only be judged from the shell of brick ruins that remain. Regrettably, you can no longer visit these baths to attend operas such as Verdi's *Aïda*. Authorities had to close the baths to the opera production, because pollution was damaging the monument. However, these imperial baths on via della Terme di Caracalla can be visited daily from 9 a.m. to 3 p.m. for an admission of 3,000 lire ($2.30).

PAPAL AUDIENCES

Private audiences with the pope are very difficult to obtain. Public audiences with the pope are held regularly, usually on Wednesday morning. The actual hour of this gathering is likely to vary. Sometimes it's 11 a.m., but it could also be at 10 a.m. if it's an especially hot day. In summer, audiences take place in St. Peter's Square. However, in the off-season, they are held regularly at 11 a.m. in the large Paul IV Hall, close to the south side of St. Peter's. Anyone is welcome.

To attend a general audience, you can obtain a free ticket from the office of the Prefecture of the Pontifical Household, which lies at the far reach of the northern colonnade of St. Peter's Square. Hours are 9 a.m. to 1 p.m. on Tuesday and from 9 a.m. until right before the papal appearance on Wednesday.

Prospective visitors should write to **Prefetto della Casa Pontificia,** 00120 Vatican City (tel. 06-6982), indicating the language they speak, the day they would like to come, and the hotel where they will be staying.

In summer the pope appears on Sunday at his summer residence at Castel Gandolfo. He says a few words at noon, prays, and bestows his blessing upon the throng gathered there.

ORGANIZED TOURS

Because of the sheer volume of the artistic riches of Rome, some visitors prefer to begin their stay with an organized tour. While few things can really be covered in any depth on one of these "overview tours," they are sometimes useful for getting the feel and geography of a complicated city. One of the leading tour operators (among the zillions of possibilities) is **American Express,** whose offices are at piazza di Spagna 38 (tel. 67-641).

Tours are usually by chartered bus and sometimes require a minimum number of participants. Those who book the tours request that participants planning to visit churches not wear shorts or sleeveless shirts. Some of the inner-city tours last 3 hours, although a few of the more ambitious ones can last a bone-breaking 17 hours or more!

Tour options include an orientation tour of Rome and the Vatican, a tour of a scattering of Rome's ancient monuments, a run through the Sistine Chapel and the Vatican Museums, a tour of the Appian Way with stopovers at the catacombs, and afternoon or evening tours to Tivoli. Tours of Rome in English, lasting 3 hours, cost 25,000 lire ($19) plus museum fees. A four-hour tour to Tivoli goes for 40,000 lire ($30.50).

Be realistic about what any tour offers. For example, a one-day tour of Pompeii and Capri is not recommended because the itinerary is too ambitious, particularly in summer when brochures warn that "service to the Blue Grotto may at times be taxed beyond capacity." *Caveat emptor.*

---

3. Shopping in Rome

I won't pretend that Rome is Italy's finest shopping center (Milan and Venice are), nor that its shops are unusually inexpensive—many of them aren't. But even on the most elegant of Rome's thoroughfares there are values mixed in with the costly boutiques, and I've therefore arranged this chapter to discuss the city's top shopping streets. The method, obviously, is to stroll these streets, ferreting out the best values they offer, comparison-shopping on those stretches that hold no particular appeal to the budget-minded tourist.

I don't know who numbered Rome's streets—doubtless it was done centuries ago—but many times you'll find that the numbers start on one side of the street, run all the way down that side in sequence to the far end of the street, then change sides and run all the way back. Therefore, 500 is sometimes across the street from 1. So, duly warned, you're ready to stroll what I consider the city's major shopping thoroughfares.

VIA FRATTINA

Via Frattina runs off piazza di Spagna and is probably the busiest shopping street in town. You'll frequently find it closed to traffic, converted into a pedestrian mall thronged with shoppers moving from boutique to boutique.

Starting at piazza di Spagna, as you walk down the street, in between antique shops and beauty parlors, you'll see one boutique after another.

Anticoli Gloves Factory, piazza Mignanelli 22 (tel. 679-6873), is the oldest factory in Rome, with the largest selection in gloves. Near the American Express office and the piazza di Spagna, this factory outlet offers bargain prices on its merchandise. Not only gloves are for sale, but belts, wallets, handbags, scarves, ties, and souvenirs.

Anatriello Bottega del Regalo, via Frattina 123 (tel. 678-9601), is chock-full of high-quality gifts such as silver candelabra, elegant table lighters, and tea sets.

Vanilla, via Frattina 37 (tel. 679-0638), a boutique for women, offers an unusual collection of offbeat items, including handmade, elaborately decorated sweaters and imaginative accessories.

At **Brighenti,** via Frattina 7-8 (tel. 679-1484), you might run across Gina Lollobrigida or Sophia Loren shopping for some "seductive fantasy." It is strictly *lingerie di lusso,* or perhaps better phrased, *haute corseterie.*

Castelli, via Frattina 54 (tel. 678-0066), is a perfume-cosmetic-jewelry boutique, with another branch at via Condotti 61. The no. 54 branch comes complete with a full-service beauty salon and fashion section. Here you can luxuriate in every kind of beauty treatment, including sauna baths and body massage. However, no appointments can be made over the phone.

Fornari, via Frattina 71-72 (tel. 679-2524), has been providing fine silver to an international clientele for more than half a century. The via Frattina showroom consists of two floors, on which are displayed the precision-crafted items that have earned this establishment the reputation of being the finest silversmith in Rome. Elegant silver trays and boxes, complete tea services, small gift items, handsome silver table settings, and many fine antique pieces as well as modern gift items are on display and can be shipped anywhere in the world. It's great fun to browse around inside, inspecting the objects in elegantly curved brass-and-glass cases. In addition, the store has a whole section of dishes, glassware, and everything related to wedding listings for brides.

VIA FRANCESCO CRISPI

This is a short street that crosses via Sistina a block from the top of the Spanish Steps. Within a block of the intersection in either direction are several excellent shops for small, not overly expensive gifts.

Giovanni B. Panatta Fine Art Shop, via Francesco Crispi 117 (tel. 679-5948), in business since 1890, is up the hill toward the Borghese Gardens. Here you'll find excellent prints in color and black-and-white, covering a variety of subjects from 18th-century Roman street scenes to astrological charts. Also, there is a good selection of antique reproductions of medieval and Renaissance art—extremely attractive and reasonably priced as well.

Pappagallo, via Francesco Crispi 115 (tel. 678-3011), is a suede and leather factory. The staff at this "parrot" make their own goods here, including bags, wallets, suede coats—all manner of leather items. The quality is fine too, and the prices are reasonable.

At the corner of via Sistina is **A.Grispigni,** via Francesco Crispi 59 (tel. 679-0290), with a large assortment of leather-covered boxes, women's purses, compacts, desk sets, and cigarette cases. Many items are inlaid with gold, including Venetian wallets and Florentine boxes.

More leather is down the street at **A. Antinori,** via Francesco Crispi 47 (tel. 679-0713). This well-established shop is a place for distinctive, high-quality gifts, including billfolds, all kinds of attractive Venetian and Florentine boxes, desk sets, cigarette cases, bags, frames, albums, purses, and luggage items.

VIA SISTINA

This street, after via Frattina, is good for browsing, and women visitors will occasionally find exciting items on sale. The boutiques begin at piazza Trinità dei Monti, at the top of the Spanish Steps. Moving down via Sistina toward the piazza Barberini, you'll discover one small shop after another. Among them:

Leather boots and bags are sold at **Elena,** via Sistina 81-82 (tel. 678-1500).

Tomassini di Luisa Romagnoli, via Sistina 119 (tel. 461-909), offers delicately beautiful lingerie and negligees, all original designs by Luisa Romagnoli. Her creations of frothy nylon, shimmery Italian silk, and fluffy cotton come ready to wear or can be custom made.

Pancani, via Sistina 117 (tel. 461-434), has a wispy boutique look in muted pastels. Inventory at this small shop (whose ceiling contains a fanciful fresco by the well-known Roman artist Novella Parigini) includes well-cut clothes, sometimes in cashmere, for younger women.

VIA CONDOTTI

This is the poshest shopping street in Rome, but many of the larger stores have a few small and moderately priced items. Wise shoppers are advised to take a look at the goods displayed on the Spanish Steps before touring via Condotti. Here, artisans good and bad lay out their wares on old velvet clothes, usually paintings, beads, silver and turquoise jewelry, some of it quite good—and bargain for the best offer. If nothing here interests you, then head down via Condotti. New Yorkers will regard many of the stores on Condotti as direct transplants from Fifth Avenue (although it was usually the other way around).

Krizia, piazza di Spagna 77 (tel. 679-3419), near the corner of the famous street but still on the piazza, is the only outlet in Rome for some of Italy's most lighthearted and best-received women's designers.

Then, starting from the top of the street, near the Spanish Steps, you'll find an array of shops which, as many visitors to Rome sometimes ruefully admit, sends them into an absolute orgy of spending. Some highlights include—

Gucci, via Condotti 8 (tel. 679-0405), is a legend, of course, an established firm since 1900. Its merchandise consists of high-class leather goods, such as suitcases, handbags, wallets, shoes, and desk accessories. It also has departments complete with elegant men's and women's wear. Sold there are beautiful shirts, blouses, and dresses, as well as ties and scarves in numerous designs, and many accessories, including Gucci's own perfume.

Bulgari, via Condotti 10 (tel. 679-3876), has the jewels to wear with anything. The shop, considered the most extravagant in Rome, was founded by a Greek immigrant, Sotirio Bulgari, who used to hawk his handmade silver on the Spanish Steps in the 19th century.

Federico Buccellati, via Condotti 31 (tel. 679-0329), is one of the best-known gold- and silversmiths in Italy, selling neo-Renaissance creations that will change your thinking about the way gold and silver are designed. Here you will discover the Italian tradition and beauty of handmade jewelry created by Buccellati.

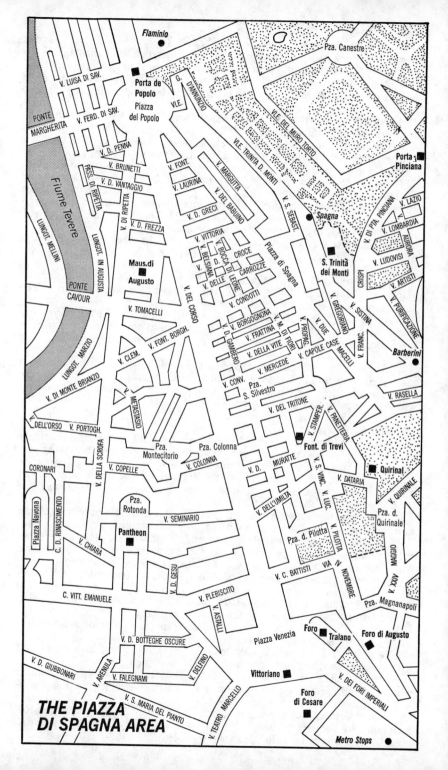

THE PIAZZA
DI SPAGNA AREA

Salvatore Ferragamo, via Condotti 73-74 (tel. 679-1565), sells elegant women's clothing, shoes, and accessories in an atmosphere full of Italian style. A few stores away, at via Condotti 66 (tel. 678-1130), the same designer sells ready-to-wear, shoes, and accessories for men. The name became famous in America when such silent-screen stars as Pola Negri and Greta Garbo began appearing in Ferragamo shoes.

Across the street, **Fornari,** via Condotti 80 (tel. 679-4285), specializes in sumptuous small jewelry and gift items for both sexes. The collection includes gold and silver jewelry, striking rings in traditional and modern designs, unusual bracelets, watches, silver key rings, chains, and necklaces, plus an array of charms.

Other good spots for (at least) window-shopping include: **Cucci,** via Condotti 67 (tel. 679-1882)—not to be confused with Gucci. This has been a leading name in custom tailoring and shirt-making since 1912. Here you'll find beautifully made knitwear, sport shirts, and cashmere sweaters for both women and men. Many original designs are always available. Cucci's also features handsome ties and scarves, along with an exclusive line of handmade moccasins.

Fragiacomo, via Condotti 35 (tel. 679-8780), sells shoes for both men and women in a champagne-colored showroom with gilt-touched chairs and big display cases.

Max Mara, via Condotti 46, at largo Goldoni (tel. 678-7946), is one of several branches, considered one of the best outlets in Rome for women's clothing. The fabrics are appealing, and the alterations are free.

Sergio Valente Beauty Center, via Condotti 11 (tel. 679-1268), offers every cosmetic indulgence—fashion hair styling, coloring, scalp treatments, facials, manicures, massages, and sauna—in bright, luxurious surroundings. English is spoken.

Note: Via Condotti is actually at the heart of a stylish shopping area that extends into the side streets in both directions. You might enjoy browsing on some of these other streets, particularly amid the aforementioned boutiques (for men and women) on via Frattina, and along via della Vite.

VIA BORGOGNONA

Sandwiched between the already-recommended vias Condotti and Frattina is yet another of Rome's exclusive shopping streets, via Borgognona, beginning near the piazza di Spagna. This street has some of the most elegant clothing in Rome—but at high prices. In fact, observers of the Rome fashion scene are beginning to think that stores on this fashionable street are quickly approaching the desirability of the addresses on the adjacent via Condotti.

Carlo Palazzi, via Borgognona 7E (tel. 678-9143), in a 16th-century palazzo near the Spanish Steps, provides modern man with the possibility of creating or refurbishing his wardrobe with beautiful suits and shirts, either off the rack or custom made. Amid the antique/modern decor and sculptures, you can also choose from a wide selection of knitwear, ties, belts, and whatever else a discerning man wears.

Givenchy, via Borgognona 21 (tel. 678-4058), is a Rome outlet for this Paris fashion house, one of the great couturiers.

Gucci Boutique, via Borgognona 25 (tel. 679-0405), holds the Italian colors in this exclusive boutique devoted to the finest in leather handbags (soft, superb finish), as well as a stunning collection of belts and other Gucci fashion items such as scarves, ties, luggage, women's shoes, and wallets.

Fendi, via Borgognona 36A-39 (tel. 679-7641), is for fun furs, amusing and witty, as well as stylish purses and leather goods for women.

Scotch House, via Borgognona 36 (tel. 678-2660), is an attractively cramped women's boutique with helpful saleswomen and a floor-to-ceiling collection of fashions by leading European designers.

Gianni Versace Uomo, via Borgogona 29 (tel. 679-5292), is the biggest Roman outlet for the famous designer's men's wear line. The daring clothes are displayed in a long format of stone floors and white-lacquered walls.

Missoni, via Borgognona 38B (tel. 679-7971), is the main outlet in Rome for this imaginative designer who is known for spectacular knitwear in kaleidoscopic patterns and colors.

Gianfranco Ferre, via Borgognona 6 (tel. 679-7445), is the outlet for his men's line. His women's line is sold at no. 42B on this same street (tel. 678-0256). The clothing for women has been called "adventurous."

VIA VENETO AND VIA BARBERINI

There's quite a bit of shopping here, especially along the via Veneto (at high tabs).

Ribot, via Veneto 98A (tel. 483-485), offers exclusive ties; Peter Scott and Ribot exclusive cashmeres; all Burberry lines including suits, jackets, and sports-wear; plus Italian shoes made by Sutor exclusively for Ribot. It also stocks Boss men's wear. It is in front of the Excelsior Hotel.

The elegant store of **Raphael Salato,** via Veneto 104 (tel. 484-677), near the Excelsior Hotel, is where the style-conscious woman goes for the latest in shoe fash-ions. The selection of unusual and well-crafted shoes is wide. In addition, Raphael Salato stocks an exclusive line of children's shoes, plus bags and leather fashions. Other stores in Rome include via Veneto 149 (tel. 493-507) and piazza di Spagna 30 (tel. 679-5646).

Bruno Magli, via Veneto 70A (tel. 464-355) and via Barberini 94 (tel. 486-850), offers dressy footwear for both sexes. Magli also has shops at via del Gambero 1 (tel. 679-3802) and via Cola di Rienzo 237 (tel. 351-972).

Also in the area are several other stores of note:

Angelo, via Bissolati 34 (tel. 464-092), is a custom tailor for discerning men. Angelo has been featured in such publications as *Esquire* and *Gentleman's Quarterly.* He employs the best craftspeople and cutters, and his taste in style and design is impeccable. Custom shirts, suits, dinner jackets, even casual wear can be made on short notice. A suit, for instance, takes about three days. If you haven't time to wait, Angelo will ship anywhere in the world.

Limentani Franco, via Barberini 78 (tel. 475-1122), is a specialty leather shop with a good assortment of handbags, T-shirts, silk ties, leather wallets, and gloves. It has quality items at moderate prices.

La Barbera, via Barberini 74 (tel. 483-628), has been in business since 1837, building a substantial reputation in the field of optical equipment. The store also carries a full spectrum of related wares: cameras, films, binoculars, opera glasses, and microscopes. You can have prescription glasses reproduced in 48 hours. For those fashionable hangouts on the via Veneto and the piazza del Popolo, take a look at Barbera's collection of sunglass frames—more than 5,000 varieties.

VIA DEL CORSO

Now that traffic has been curtailed on this main thoroughfare of Rome, a vari-ety of unusual shops has sprung up.

Elsy, via del Corso 106 (tel. 679-2275), features women's clothing on two lev-els of ultramodern, warmly accented floor space.

Dominici, via del Corso 14 (tel. 361-0591). An understated façade, a few steps from the piazza del Popolo, shelters an amusing and lighthearted collection of men's and women's shoes in a variety of vivid colors. The style is aggressively young-at-heart, and the children's shoes are adorable.

VIA NATIONALE

One of the city's busiest shopping thoroughfares, via Nazionale runs from pi-azza della Repubblica (with its great Fountain of the Naiads in front of the Baths of Diocletian) down almost to piazza Venezia. There is an abundance of leather stores that are more reasonable than those in many other parts of Rome, as well as a wel-come new element—some stylish and moderately priced boutiques.

Our first stop is near the beginning of via Nazionale. **Cesare Diomedi Leather Goods,** via Vittorio Emanuele Orlando 96-97 (tel. 464-822), offers one of the most outstanding collections of leather goods in Rome. And leather isn't all you'll find in this small, two-story shop with its attractive winding staircase. There are many other distinctive gift items—small gold cigarette cases, jeweled umbrellas—that make this a good stopping-off point for that last important item. Upstairs is a wide assortment of elegant leather luggage and accessories.

Down via Nazionale, at the corner of via Torino, is **Arte dell' Arredamento,** via Nazionale 6 (tel. 461-1034), offering an outstanding collection of fabrics and Oriental rugs. Another shop is via Torino 24 (tel. 475-1377).

At **Marte's,** via Nazionale 14-16 (tel. 461-048), you'll find boots and casual shoes for both sexes.

Marisa, via Nazionale 234A (tel. 461-669), has boutique items and fashions for the style-conscious career woman.

Winton, via Nazionale 209-210 (tel. 475-5918), features restrained but chic fine leather and suede clothing for men and women. It also offers a good assortment of men's shirts, trousers, and ties, plus sweaters for both sexes.

Louis, via Nazionale 198 (tel. 464-614), is a moderately priced shoe emporium for both men and women.

Alexia, via Nazionale 76 (tel. 475-1438), offers good buys in purses and shoes for women, as well as a stylish selection of leather coats and accessories and furs.

Opposite the travertine marble palace of the Banca d'Italia is **Socrate,** via Nazionale 89B (tel. 484-530), dispensing low-key, excellently cut, high-quality men's clothing, much of it wool and suede.

Borsalino, via IV Novembre 157B (tel. 679-4192), is chock-full of rakish hats reminiscent of the 1930s. The most famous hatmaker in all of Italy—the world, even—offers all sorts of other styles too, for both women and men. The store sells well-made trousers and suits as well.

VIA DEI CORONARI

Like via Condotti, this street should be seen whether or not you buy. Buried in a colorful section of the Campus Martius (Renaissance Rome), via dei Coronari is an antiquer's dream, literally lined with magnificent vases, urns, chandeliers, breakfronts, chaises, refectory tables, candelabra—you name it. You'll find the entrance to the street just north of the piazza Navona. Turn left outside the piazza, past the excavated ruins of Domitian's Stadium, and the street will be just ahead of you. There are more than 40 antique stores within the next four blocks, and on my last trip I saw in the windows brocade dining chairs, inlaid secretaries, marble pedestals, claw and ball tables, gilded consoles, and enamel clocks, among countless other treasures. Keep in mind that stores are frequently closed between 1 and 4 in the afternoon.

BOOKSTORES

There are at least two good ones in Rome selling English-language publications. The **Lion Bookshop,** via del Babuino 181 (tel. 360-5837), has only U.S. and British books, including a section for children, the whole range of Penguin books, photographic books on Rome and Italy, and the most recent paperback fiction. Try also the **Economy Book Center,** via Torino 136 (tel. 474-6877), open from 9:30 a.m. to 7:30 p.m. daily except Sunday, selling American and English paperback books, both new and used. This store is one block from the Repubblica Metro station and numerous bus lines.

MISCELLANEA

For a treasure trove of liquors (including liqueurs and wines), honey, and herbal teas made in monasteries and convents all over Italy, seek out **AiMonasteri,** corso Rinascimento 72 (tel. 654-2783). The owners also concoct creams and balms from fruits and flowers. You can buy excellent chocolates and other sweetmeats here as well. The shop will ship some items home for you. You can make your selections in a quiet atmosphere reminiscent of a monastery, even though the shop is only two blocks from Bernini's Four Rivers Fountain in the piazza Navona.

At **E. Fiore,** via Ludovisi 31 (tel. 481-9296), near the via Veneto, you can choose a jewel and have it set according to your specifications. Or make your selection from a rich assortment of charms, bracelets, necklaces, rings, brooches, corals, pearls, and cameos. Also featured are elegant watches, silverware, and goldware. Fiore's also does expert repair work on your own jewelry and watches.

Basile, via Mario dei Fiori 29 (tel. 678-9244), is the only store in the city that sells women's clothes from the Milanese factories of this famous Italian clothier. This store positively reeks of Italian taste and style, and the service is gracious. Apparel, of course, is always well made and can be worn in the most sophisticated of circles.

Murano Veneto, via Marche 13, behind the Hotel Excelsior (tel. 474-1995), offers a magnificent collection of Venetian blown glass, including chandeliers, art objects, fine mirrors, sculptures, and giftware, in a variety of colors and styles. Shipments are guaranteed.

Galleria d'Arte Schneider, rampa Mignanelli 10 (tel. 678-4019), an art gallery run by an American professor of art, Robert E. Schneider, is worth a visit. It's near the Spanish Steps.

Lembo, via XX Settembre 25A (tel. 463-759), is an excellent place to find gifts —crystal and china pieces, glassware, sterling, and the like.

THE FLEA MARKET

This sprawling open-air market is held in Rome every Sunday morning—at which time every peddler from Trastevere and the surrounding "Castelli Romani" sets up his temporary shop. The vendors are likely to sell merchandise ranging from secondhand paintings of madonnas (the Italian market's glutted with these), to termite-eaten Il Duce wooden medallions (many of the homes of the lower-income groups still display likenesses of the murdered dictator), to pseudo-Etruscan hairpins, to bushels of rosaries, to 1947 television sets, to books printed in 1635. Serious shoppers can often ferret out a good buy. Go to the flea market in Trastevere, near the end of viale Trastevere (bus 75 to Porta di Portese, then a short walk away to via Portuense) to catch the workday Roman in an unguarded moment. If you've ever been impressed with the bargaining power of the Spaniard, you haven't seen anything till you've viewed an Italian.

The market is open Sunday from around 7 a.m. to 1 p.m. By 10:30 a.m. the market is full of people. Some of the vendors get there as early as midnight to get their choice space.

---

4. Rome After Dark

When the sun goes down, lights across the city bathe palaces, ruins, fountains, and monuments in a theatrical white light. There are actually few evening occupations quite as pleasurable as a stroll past the solemn pillars of old temples or the cascading of torrents of Renaissance fountains glowing under the blue-black sky. Of the fountains, the **Naiads** (piazza della Repubblica), the **Tortoises** (piazza Mattei), and of course, the **Trevi** are particularly beautiful at night. The **Capitoline Hill** is magnificently lit after dark, its measured Renaissance façades glowing like jewel boxes surrounding the statue of Marcus Aurelius. Behind the Senatorial Palace is a fine view of the **Roman Forum.** If you're staying across the Tiber, the **piazza San Pietro** (in front of St. Peter's Basilica) is particularly impressive at night without tour buses and crowds. And a combination of illuminated architecture, Renaissance fountains, and, frequently, sidewalk shows and art expositions is at the **piazza Navona.** If you're ambitious and have a good sense of direction, try exploring the streets to the west of piazza Navona, which look like a stage set when they're lit at night.

There are no inexpensive nightclubs in Rome, so be duly warned. Another important warning: During the peak of the summer visiting days, usually in August, all nightclub proprietors seem to lock their doors and head for the seashore. Many of them seem to operate alternate clubs at coastal resorts. Some of them close at different times each year, so it's hard to keep up-to-date with them. Always have your hotel check to see if a club is operating before you make a trek to it. Many of the legitimate nightclubs, besides being expensive, are highlighted by hookers plying their trade. Younger people fare better than some more sedate folk, as the discos open and close with free-wheeling abandon.

To a Roman, a night on the town means dining late at a trattoria. The local denizens like to drink wine and talk after their meal, even when the waiters are putting chairs on top of empty tables.

CAFES, BARS, AND COFFEEHOUSES

Unless you're dead set on making the Roman nightclub circuit, you may experience a far livelier scene simply by sitting late at night on the via Veneto or the piazza del Popolo (see below)—all for the cost of an espresso.

On the Via Veneto

Back in the 1950s—a decade that *Time* magazine gave to Rome, in the way it conceded the '60s to London—via Vittorio Veneto rose in fame and influence as the choicest street in Rome, crowded with movie stars, aspirant and actual, their directors, and a fast-rising group who were card-carrying members of the so-called jet set. Fashions, of course, are one of the most fickle elements in social culture. Today the *belle gente* (the beautiful people), movie stars, and directors wouldn't be caught dead on the via Veneto—even with night-owl sunglasses. In the course of time, the via Veneto has moved into the mainstream of world tourism and lays its own claim to having interest (no first-timer should miss it). It's about as in and undiscovered today as pretzels. But you may want to spend some time there.

Gran Caffè Doney, via Veneto 139-143 (tel. 493-405), is one of Rome's most enduring cafés. It was born in Florence in 1822, coming to Rome in 1884 to a location not now known. The via Veneto café opened in 1946. Legend has it that only foreigners go there, but they must like it, as they return year after year. In fact, Doney is now considered more fashionable than the Caffè de Paris (see below). While you're eating lunch at a sidewalk table, pedestrians walk right through the maze, inspecting your chicken salad sandwich. Cocktails cost from 10,000 lire ($7.60) and sandwiches begin at 12,000 lire ($9.10). Service is from 8 a.m. to 1:30 a.m. in the cafeteria, the pastry and chocolate shop, and the bar. From 10 a.m. to 12:30 a.m., you can also order light lunch or dinner, as well as items listed above. From 8 p.m. to midnight September to June, piano music is played. If you've got it, flaunt it at the Doney every night except Monday.

A rival café across the street, the **Caffè de Paris,** via Veneto 90 (tel. 465-284), rises and falls in popularity, depending on the decade. In the '50s a haven for the fashionable, it is now a popular restaurant in summer where you can occupy a counter seat along a bar or else select a table inside. However, if the weather's right, the tables spill right out onto the sidewalk, and the passing crowd walks through the maze. A coffee costs 4,000 lire ($3.05) if you sit outside. Hours are 8:30 a.m. to 1:30 a.m. daily.

A perennial favorite is **Harry's Bar,** via Veneto 148 (tel. 474-5832). Every major Italian city (Florence and Venice, for example) seems to have a Harry's Bar, and Rome is no exception, although the one here has no connections with those of the other Italian cities or the one in Paris. This haunt of the IBF—International Bar Flies—at the top of via Veneto is elegant, chic, and sophisticated. In summer, sidewalk tables are placed outside, but off-season the ambience is more intimate, with walls of tapestry, ornate wood paneling, carved pilastering, and Florentine sconces. In back is a small dining room, serving good but outrageously expensive food. A whisky costs from 8,000 lire ($6.10). The bar is open from 11:30 a.m. to 1 a.m. Closed Sunday.

Piazza del Popolo

The piazza is haunted with memories. According to legend, the ashes of Nero were enshrined there, until 11th-century residents began complaining to the pope about his imperial ghost. The Egyptian obelisk seen there today dates from the 13th century B.C., removed from Heliopolis to Rome during the reign of Augustus. Originally it stood at the Circus Maximus. The present piazza was designed by Valadier, the architect of Napoleon, in the early 19th century. The twin baroque churches also stand on the square, overseeing the never-ending traffic.

Café Rosati, piazza del Popolo (tel. 361-1418), attracts Fellini and Zeffirelli types, plus an assortment of guys and dolls of all kinds and persuasions who drive up in Maseratis and Porsches. The Rosati, which has been around since 1923, is really a sidewalk café/ice-cream parlor/candy store/confectionery that has been swept up in the fickle world of fashions. The later you go, the more interesting is the action. Whisky at a table begins at 8,500 lire ($6.45). It's open daily from 7:30 a.m. to 1 a.m. (closed Tuesday in winter).

Canova Café, piazza del Popolo (tel. 361-2231). Although management has filled the interior with boutiques selling expensive gift items, which include luggage and cigarette lighters, many Romans still consider this *the* place to be on the piazza del Popolo. The Canova has a sidewalk terrace for pedestrian-watching, plus a snackbar, a restaurant, and a wine shop inside. In summer you'll have access to a courtyard whose walls are covered with ivy and where flowers grow in terracotta planters. Expect to spend 3,900 lire ($2.95) for a cappuccino at a table. A complete set meal is offered for 35,000 lire ($26.50) and up. Food is served from 12:30 to 3 p.m. and 8 to 11 p.m., but the café is open from 7:30 a.m. to midnight. Closed Monday.

Near the Pantheon

Many visitors to the Eternal City now view the piazza della Rotonda, across from the Pantheon, reconstructed by the Emperor Hadrian in the first part of the 2nd century A.D., as the "living room" of Rome. This is especially true on a summer night. The most desirable café here is **Di Rienzo,** piazza della Rotonda 8-9 (tel. 656-9097), which is open daily from 7 a.m. to 2 a.m. In fair weather you can sit at one of the sidewalk tables (if you can find one free), contemplating life on the square and the Pantheon. In cooler weather you can retreat inside the elegant café, whose walls are inlaid with the type of marble found on the floor of the Pantheon. You can visit and order only a coffee at 2,500 lire ($1.90), or you can order a complete meal, costing from 25,000 lire ($19). Many types of pasta appear on the menu, as does risotto alla pescatora (fishermen's rice) or several meat courses such as roast veal. You can also order pizzas.

A Café in Trastevere

Just as the piazza del Popolo lured the chic and sophisticated from the via Veneto, several cafés in the district of Trastevere, across the Tiber, threaten to do the same for Popolo. Fans who saw Fellini's *Roma* know what the **piazza Santa Maria,** deep in the heart of Trastevere, looks like. The square—filled with milling throngs in summer—is graced with an octagonal fountain and a church dating from the 12th century. On the piazza, despite a certain amount of traffic, children run and play, and occasional spontaneous guitar fests are heard when the weather's good.

Café-Bar di Marzio, piazza di Santa Maria in Trastevere 14B (tel. 580-9095), is a warmly inviting place, strictly a café (not a restaurant), with both indoor and outdoor tables at the edge of the square with the best view of its famous fountain. Whisky costs from 6,000 lire ($4.55). Hours are 7 a.m. to 1 a.m. daily except Monday.

A Grand Café on the Corso

The monumental **Café Alemagna,** via del Corso 181 (tel. 678-9135), is usually filled with busy shoppers. On the premises is just about every kind of dining facility a hurried resident of Rome could want, including a stand-up sandwich bar with dozens of selections from behind a glass case, a cafeteria, and sit-down area with waiter service. The decor includes high coffered ceilings, baroque wall stencils, globe lights, crystal chandeliers, and black stone floors. Pastries cost from 2,300 lire ($1.75) at a table. It is open daily except Sunday from 7:30 a.m. to 11:50 p.m.

The Most Fashionable Coffeehouse

Off and on since 1760, **Antico Caffè Greco,** via Condotti 86 (tel. 679-1700), has been the poshest and most fashionable coffee bar in Rome, and it holds the title today. Attired in the trappings of the turn of the century, it has for years enjoyed a reputation as the gathering place of the literati. Previous sippers included Stendhal, Goethe, even D'Annunzio. Keats would also sit here and write. Today, however, you're more likely to see dowagers on a shopping binge and American tourists. In the front is a wooden bar, but beyond this is a series of small salons, decorated in the 19th-century style with oil paintings in gilded frames. You sit at marble-topped tables of Napoleonic design, against a backdrop of gold or red damask, romantic paintings, and antique mirrors. Waiters are attired in black tailcoats. A cup of cappuccino costs 4,000 lire ($3.05). The house specialty is a paradiso, made with lemon and orange, costing 4,200 lire ($3.20). Light sandwiches go for 3,000 lire ($2.30). There's plenty of atmosphere here. The café is open daily except Sunday from 8 a.m. to 9 p.m., closing for one week in August and on Saturday afternoon in July and August.

Wine Drinking

One of the best selections is found at **Enoteca Fratelli Roffi Isabelli,** via della Croce 76 (tel. 679-0896). A stand-up drink within its darkly antique confines might be the perfect ending to a visit to the nearby Spanish Steps. Set behind an unflashy façade, this place is the best repository for Italian wines, brandies, and grappa in this chic shopping district. You can opt for a postage-stamp table in back, if you desire, or else stay at the bar with its impressive display of wines which lie stacked upon shelves in every available corner. The place is open daily except Sunday and Thursday afternoon from 10 a.m. to 1:30 p.m. and 5 to 8:30 p.m. Whiskey or a grappa costs from 5,000 lire ($3.80); a glass of wine begins at 3,000 lire ($2.30).

For the Best Espresso

A popular spot is **Caffè Sant'Eustachio,** piazza Sant'Eustachio 82 (tel. 686-1309). Strongly brewed coffee might be considered one of the elixirs of Italy, and many Romans will walk many blocks for what they consider a superior brew. One of the most celebrated espresso shops is on a small square near the Pantheon, where the city water supply comes from a source outside Rome that the Emperor Augustus funneled into the city with an aqueduct in 19 B.C. Rome's most experienced judges of espresso claim that the water plays an important part in the coffee's flavor, although steam forced through ground Brazilian coffee roasted on the premises has an important effect as well. Stand-up coffee at this well-known place costs 900 lire

(70¢). If you sit, you'll pay 2,000 lire ($1.50). Purchase a ticket from the cashier for as many cups as you want, and leave a small tip (about 100 lire, 10¢) for the counterman when you give him your receipt. It's open from 8 a.m. to 1 a.m. every day except Monday, although on Saturday it stays open until 1:30 a.m.

SOOTHING THE SWEET TOOTH

For devotees of *gelato* (addictively tasty ice cream), **Giolitti,** via Uffici del Vicario 40 (tel. 678-0410), is one of the most popular gathering spots in nighttime Rome. In the evening, this colorful section of Rome throngs with strollers with a sweet tooth. Satisfying that craving admirably is a whipped-cream-topped Giolitti cup of gelato, costing 5,000 lire ($3.80) at a table. Some of the sundaes look like Vesuvius about to erupt. During the day, good-tasting snacks are served also. Many take gelato out to eat on the streets; others enjoy it in the post-Empire splendor of the salon inside. You can have your "coppa" from 7 a.m. to 2 a.m. every day except Monday. There are many excellent, smaller *gelateria* throughout Rome, wherever you see the cool concoction advertised as *"produzione propia"* (homemade).

NIGHTCLUBS

Drink prices in Roman nightclubs often begin at 10,000 lire ($7.60), but can range as high as 25,000 lire ($19) or more (for a first drink) if some special entertainment is offered.

Gil's, via Romagnosi 11A (tel. 361-1348), is a chic rendezvous. The designer wanted to give the impression that you are entering a mammoth tent of some sheik in the Sahara. Sand-filled aquariums line the walls. This is definitely an '80s kind of club, unlike some Roman nightspots where the nostalgic aura of the '50s lingers. Gil, incidentally, one of the leading makeup artists in Rome, is said to be one of the owners. Doors open at 10:30 p.m. nightly, but no one shows up until much later. Evening clothes are the appropriate garb. It closes at 3:30 a.m. and on Monday. Drinks cost from 20,000 lire ($15.20).

La Cabala, in the Hostaria dell'Orso, via dei Soldati 25 (tel. 686-9609). In this 14th-century Renaissance palazzo, the clientele usually wears stunning clothes (but not formal). Two guitarists and a pianist entertain, and it's fun to sip and admire the scenery. It's magnificent Roman splendor, but it may be shut down in summer—so telephone in advance. The building housing the hostaria and bar has a rich history. It was once a simple inn, constructed in 1300. Reportedly, St. Francis of Assisi once stayed here, as did Dante during the Jubilee Year. Later, as a hotel, it was to attract such guests as Rabelais, Montaigne, and Goethe. It is open from 10:30 p.m. "until." A compulsory first drink costs 25,000 lire ($19).

L'Arciliuto, piazza Monte Vecchio 5 (tel. 687-9419), is one of the most romantic candlelit spots in Rome. It was the former studio of Raphael. From 10 p.m. when it opens to 11 p.m., there is a show with music. The first drink costs 25,000 lire ($19); the second, 10,000 lire ($7.60). The setting and atmosphere are intimate. Highly recommended, it is hard to find, but is within walking distance of piazza Navona. Closed Sunday.

Gilda, via Mario dei Fiori 97 (tel. 678-4838), is noted both for its adventurous combinations of nightclub, disco, and restaurant and for the glamorous acts it books. In the past they have included Diana Ross and splashy, Paris-type revues, often with young women from England and the United States. The artistic direction assures first-class shows, a well-run restaurant, an attractive bar, and recently released disco music played between the live musical acts. The restaurant opens at 9:30 p.m. and occasionally presents shows. An international cuisine is featured, with meals costing 60,000 lire ($45.50) to 110,000 lire ($83.50). The nightclub, opening at 11 p.m., presents music of the '60s as well as modern recordings. A first drink costs 25,000 lire ($19) to 30,000 lire ($22.75).

Jackie O', via Boncompagni 11 (tel. 461-401), is still around. Nowadays the doorman is far less strict about whom he will let into these glittering precincts.

There is a restaurant serving very expensive food inside, as well as a piano bar. You go to the Jackie O' section for dancing and to another area for dining. This was—and still is to some extent—a haven for what used to be called "the beautiful people." Open daily from 11 p.m. to 3 a.m., it charges 25,000 lire ($19) for your first drink.

Easy Going, via della Purificazione 9 (tel. 474-5578). Rome has never been able to match the variety of gay nightclubs of New York or San Francisco, but this amusingly decorated two-level club near the piazza Barberini is by far the best-known gay disco in the Italian capital. Set behind speakeasy-style, white-lacquered doors with a peephole, the club charges an entrance fee of 10,000 lire ($7.60) to 15,000 lire ($11.50) per person, which gives the guest the right to one drink. This can be consumed at the upstairs bar, whose walls and cubbyholes are decorated with pseudo-baroque frescoes of cherubs, or at the downstairs level, which is the more popular and where the illustrations are far more risqué. There is a slickly contemporary bar area, and a very small dance floor where would-be models from *Gentleman's Quarterly* stand in poses of studied indifference. It is open Monday through Saturday from 10 p.m. to 4 a.m.

Mississippi Jazz Club, borgo Angelico 16 (tel. 654-0348), is the best place in Rome to hear jazz. A jazz concert with Dixieland is presented on Saturday from 11:30 p.m. to 1:30 a.m. In air-conditioned comfort, you can enjoy this laid-back atmosphere of American music with Italian style. You get good drinks at the bar, and if you're hungry, the waiter will serve you a pizza. An entrance fee of 20,000 lire ($15.25) includes your first drink.

EVENINGS IN TRASTEVERE

Roman rusticity is combined with theatrical flair at **Teatro Tiberino,** via di Santa Dorotea 6 (tel. 589-2986), the "people's theater" where the famous actor Petrolini made his debut.

Dressed in regional garb of Italian provinces, the waiters serve with drama. The cuisine isn't subtle—still, it's good and bountiful. Such dishes as the classic saltimbocca (ham with veal) are prepared, preceded by tasty pasta (including one with a sauce made with red peppers)—everything aided by the wines from the "Castelli Romani." Accompanying the main dishes is a big basket of warm, country-coarse herb bread (you'll tear off hunks). Expect to pay 70,000 lire ($53.25) to 80,000 lire ($60.75) for a full meal. Some two dozen folk singers and musicians in regional costumes perform, making it a friendly, festive affair. The theater opens at 8:30 p.m., and the folklore show, featuring both Roman and Neapolitan favorites, is presented from 9:30 to 10:30 p.m. It's closed Sunday.

Da Meo Patacca, piazza dei Mercanti 30 (tel. 581-6198), would certainly have pleased Barnum and Bailey. On a gaslit plaza from the Middle Ages in Trastevere, it serves bountiful self-styled "Roman country" meals to flocks of tourists. The atmosphere is one of extravaganza—primitive, colorful, theatrical in a carnival sense —but good fun if you're in the mood. From the huge open spit and the charcoal grill, many tempting platters are served. Downstairs is a vast cellar, studded with waves of strolling musicians and singers—a smash hit. Utilizing a taverna theme, the restaurant is decked out with wagon wheels, along with garlands of pepper and garlic. And the offerings are as adventurous as the decor: wild boar, wild hare, quail, corn on the cob, even pork and beans. You can also get thick-cut sirloins and chicken on a spit. The antipasti—many succulent tidbits—are a good opener. Expect to spend from 40,000 lire ($30.50) up for a meal here. In summer, you can dine at outdoor tables. Open from 8 to 11 p.m. daily.

Featured at **Da Ciceruacchio** are charcoal-broiled steaks and chops, along with lots of local wine. Located on the same piazza at via del Porto 1 (tel. 580-6046), it was once a sunken jail—the ancient vine-covered walls dating from the days of the Roman Empire. Bean soup is a specialty. The grilled mushrooms are another good opening, as is the spaghetti with clams. For a main course, I'd recommend scampi with curry or charcoal-broiled meats. You can dine here daily except Monday from 8 p.m. to midnight for 40,000 lire ($30.50) and up.

Also on the same square is **Ar Fieramosca,** piazza dei Mercanti 3A (tel. 589-0289), which is named after a medieval knight hero. The place is super-rustic, with large 15th-century fireplaces, waiters dressed as fishermen, and strolling musicians. Charcoal-grilled meats and seafood and a huge buffet are featured, and there are beer and wines on tap. The restaurant is also known for its pizzas. Expect to pay at least 40,000 lire ($30.50) for a complete meal. It is open from 7 p.m. to midnight daily except Sunday.

FILMS

In Trastevere, not too far from the piazza Santa Maria, the little **Pasquino** draws a faithful coterie of English-speaking fans, not only Italians, but expatriates. To find out what is playing, call 580-36-22. The location is at vicolo del Piede, a small street deep in the district, across the Tiber. The average films—and usually they are of recent vintage—cost 6,000 lire ($4.55).

CULTURE

You may want to attend the Rome opera house, **Teatro dell'Opera,** piazza Beniamino Gigli 1 (tel. 461-755), off the via Nazionale, should you be in the Italian capital for its season, usually from the end of December till June. Tickets for this historic theater cost 10,000 lire ($7.60) to 80,000 lire ($60.75). The sale of tickets begins two days before a performance is scheduled. The first five nights are always more expensive.

Concerts, given by the orchestra of the Academy of St. Cecilia, take place on the piazza del Campidoglio in summer. In winter, they are held in the concert hall on via della Conciliazione. Tickets for symphonic music range from 15,000 lire ($11.50) to 35,000 lire ($26.50); for chamber music, from 12,000 lire ($9.10) to 23,000 lire ($17.50). From the end of June, concerts at the piazza del Campidoglio cost 8,000 lire ($6.10) to 20,000 lire ($15.25). Details, such as prices and schedules, are available by phoning the academy at 654-1044.

5. Ring Around Rome

Most capitals of Europe are ringed with a number of scenic attractions. For sheer variety, Rome tops all of them. Just short miles away, you can walk in silence across the cemetery of U.S. servicemen killed on the beaches of Anzio in World War II, or go back to the dawn of Italian history and explore the dank tombs the Etruscans left as their legacy.

You can wander around the ruins of the "queen of villas of the ancient world" (Hadrian's), or be lulled by the music of baroque fountains in the Villa d'Este. You can drink the golden wine of the Alban hill towns ("Castelli Romani"), or turn yourself bronze on the beaches of Ostia di Lido—or even explore the ruins of Ostia Antica, the ancient seaport of Rome.

Unless you're rushed beyond reason, allow at least three days for taking a look at the attractions in the environs. I'll highlight the best of the lot, beginning with:

TIVOLI

Known as Tibur to the ancient Romans, Tivoli was the playground of emperors. Today its reputation continues unabated: it is the most popular half-day jaunt visitors take from Rome. The ruins of Hadrian's Villa as well as the Villa d'Este, with their fabulous fountains and gardens, remain the two chief attractions of Tivoli—and both should be seen, even by those who must curtail their sightseeing in Rome. The town of Tivoli lies 20 miles from the capital, out the via Tiburtina. Even if you don't have a car, you won't have to take a guided tour, as a motorcoach leaves from via Volturno, around the corner from via Gaeta in Rome (piazza dei Cinquecento) nearly every 20 minutes.

Right inside the town, we can look at two villas before heading to the environs of Tivoli and the ruins of Hadrian's Villa.

The Villa d'Este

Like Hadrian centuries before, Cardinal Ippolito d'Este of Ferrari believed in heaven on earth. In the mid-16th century he ordered a villa built on a hillside (entered from the piazza Trento). The dank Renaissance structure, with its second-rate paintings, is hardly worth the trek from Rome, but the gardens below—designed by Pirro Ligorio—dim the luster of Versailles.

Visitors descend the cypress-studded slope to the bottom, and on their way are rewarded with everything from lilies to gargoyles spouting water, torrential streams, and waterfalls. The loveliest fountain—on this there is some agreement—is the **Fontana dell'Ovato,** designed by Ligorio. But nearby is the most spectacular achievement—the hydraulic organ fountain, dazzling visitors with its water jets in front of a baroque chapel, with four maidens who look tipsy. The work represents the French genius of Claude Véanard.

Don't miss the moss-covered, slime-green **Fountain of Dragons,** also by Ligorio, and the so-called **Fountain of Glass** by Bernini. The best walk is along the promenade with 100 spraying fountains. The garden, filled with rhododendron, is worth hours of exploration, but you'll need frequent rest periods after those steep climbs. Admission is 5,000 lire ($3.80). The villa can be visited from 9 a.m. to 6:45 p.m. daily, to 4 p.m. off-season.

While at Tivoli, you may want to visit another attraction—

The Villa Gregoriana

Whereas the Villa d'Este dazzles with man-made glamour, the Villa Gregoriana relies more on nature. At one point on the circuitous walk carved along a slope, visitors stand and look out onto the most spectacular waterfall (Aniene) at Tivoli. The trek to the bottom on the banks of the Anio is studded with grottoes, plus balconies opening onto the chasm. The only problem is, if you do make the full journey, you may need to have a helicopter lowered to pull you up again (the climb back is fierce). From one of the belvederes is an exciting view of the Temple of Vesta on the hill. The gardens were built by Pope Gregory XVI in the 19th century. The villa is open from 9 a.m. to one hour before sunset daily, except Monday, and costs 1,500 lire ($1.15) to enter.

Hadrian's Villa on the Outskirts of Tivoli

Of all the Roman emperors dedicated to *la dolce vita,* the globe-trotting Hadrian spent the last three years of his life in the grandest style. Less than four miles from Tivoli he built one of the greatest estates ever erected in the world, filling acre after acre with some of the architectural wonders he'd seen on his many trips.

Perhaps as a preview of what he envisioned in store for himself, the emperor even created a representation of hell centuries before Dante got around to recording its horrors in a poem. A patron of the arts, a lover of beauty, and himself something of an architect, Hadrian directed the staggering construction task that created not a villa, but a self-contained world for a vast royal entourage and the hundreds of servants and guards they required to protect them, feed them, bathe them, and satisfy their libidos.

On the estate were erected theaters, baths, temples, fountains, gardens, and canals bordered with statuary. The palaces and temples Hadrian filled with sculpture, some of which now rests in the museums of Rome. In the centuries to follow, barbarians, popes, and cardinals, as well as anyone who needed a slab of marble, carted off much that made the villa so spectacular. But enough of the fragmented ruins remain for us to piece together the story.

For a glimpse of what the villa used to be, see the plastic reconstruction at the entrance. Then, following the arrows around, look in particular for the Marine Theater (the ruins of a round structure with Ionic pillars); the Great Baths, with some of the mosaics intact; and the Canopus, with its group of caryatids, their images reflected in the pond, as well as a statue of Mars. For a closer look at some of the items excavated, you can visit the museum on the premises and a new museum and visitors center near the villa parking area. Hadrian's Villa (Villa Adriana, to Italians) is open daily from 9 a.m. to sunset (about 7:30 p.m. in summer, 5 p.m. in winter), and charges 4,000 lire ($3.05) for admission. From Tivoli, take bus 2 to the gateway of the villa.

Dining in Tivoli

Restaurant Sibilla, via della Sibilla 50 (tel. 0774/20281), is a landmark restaurant with a 2nd-century B.C. temple in its private garden. In fair weather, you can choose one of a collection of tables running right up to the foundation of what the owners claim is the oldest remaining temple in Italy. Called the Temple of Vesta (also known as Sibilla), it is occasionally visited by art historians who travel many miles just to see it. You, however, can combine your cultural visit with well-prepared regional cooking, scents from the overhead wisteria, and the views across the precipice to a crashing waterfall. An elegant interior room has terracotta walls, old lace in gilt frames, and a mosaic tile floor. Specialties are cannelloni, trout freshly caught in the Anio, and a mouthwatering soufflé. If you decide to dine here, you'll be interested to know that you have been preceded by French author and statesman Vicomte Chateaubriand in 1803 and by Princess Margaret of Britain. The price of a complete meal, depending on what you order, will range from 40,000 lire ($30.50) up. It's open daily from noon to 10:30 p.m.

Albergo Ristorante Adriano, Villa Adriana (tel. 0774/529-174), might be the perfect stopover point either before or after you visit Hadrian's Villa. At the bottom of the villa's hill, in an ochre-colored building a few steps from the ticket office, it offers terrace dining under plane trees in summer or indoor dining in a high-ceilinged room with terracotta walls, neoclassical moldings, and Corinthian pilasters painted white. Menus include roast lamb, saltimbocca, a variety of veal dishes, deviled chicken, a selection of salads and cheeses, and simple desserts. Expect to spend about 28,000 lire ($21.25) to 38,000 lire ($29). Hours are noon to 3 p.m. and 8 to 10 p.m.; closed Monday and in August.

OSTIA

If you want to see all of Rome—both ancient and modern—take the Metropolitana (subway) at Terminal Station. With your bikini in hand, ride it until you reach the stop at Ostia Antica, about 16 miles from Rome. However, remember to change trains at the stop called "Piramide." There you can catch another train which stops right at Ostia Antica. You can then walk to the ruins (see below). Later, you can board the underground again for the Lido di Ostia, the beach.

Ostia Antica

At the mouth of the Tiber, Ostia was the port of Ancient Rome. Through it were funneled the riches from the far corners of the empire. It was founded in the 4th century B.C., but the engineering work of dredging it into a major port and naval base was carried out primarily under two later emperors: Claudius and Trajan.

A thriving prosperous city developed, full of temples, baths, theaters, and patrician homes. Ostia Antica flourished for about eight centuries from the date of its founding, eventually withering, as the wholesale business of carting off its art treasures began. Gradually it became little more than a malaria bed, a buried ghost city that faded into history.

But in the 19th century a papal-sponsored commission launched a series of diggings, although the major work of unearthing was carried out under Mussolini's orders from 1938 to 1942, having to stop because of the war. The city is only partially dug out today, but it is believed that all the chief monuments have been uncovered.

Ostia Antica is one of the major attractions in the environs of Rome, particularly interesting to those who can't make it to Pompeii. All the principal monuments are clearly labeled. The most important spot in all the ruins is the piazzale delle Corporazioni, an early version of Wall Street. Near the theater, this square contained nearly 75 corporations, the nature of their business identified by the pattern of mosaics preserved.

Greek dramas were performed at the ancient theater, built sometime in the early days of the Empire. The classics are still aired here in summer (check with the tourist office for specific listings), but the theater as it looks today is the result of much rebuilding. Every town the size of Ostia had a forum. Uncovered during the excavations were a number of pillars of the ancient Ostia Forum. At one end is a 2nd-century B.C. temple honoring a trio of gods, Minerva, Jupiter, and Juno (little more than the basic foundation remains). In addition, there is a well-lit museum within the enclave, displaying Roman statuary along with some Pompeii-like frescoes. Exploring the ruins, which takes at least a couple of hours, costs 5,000 lire ($3.80) admission. Summer hours are 9 a.m. to 6 p.m. (closes at 5 p.m. in winter). Closed Monday.

To reach Ostia Antica, take bus 57 from via Nazionale to Piramide, then a train to Ostia Antica. Many readers prefer this way of going there to the subway method.

Lido di Ostia

Italy may be a strongly Catholic country, but the Romans don't allow religious conservatism to affect their bathing attire. Shapely Italian girls know how to wear a wild bikini. This is the beach where the denizens of the capital frolic on the seashore, at times creating a merry carnival atmosphere, with dance halls, cinemas, and pizzerias. The Lido is set off best at Castelfusano, against a backdrop of pinewoods. This stretch of shoreline is often referred to as the Roman Riviera.

CASTELLI ROMANI

For both the Roman emperor and the wealthy cardinal in the heyday of the Renaissance, the Castelli Romani (Roman Castles) exerted a powerful lure. They still do. Of course, the Castelli are not castles, but hill towns—many of them with a history that is ancient. The wines from the Alban Hills will add a little *feu de joie* to your life. The ideal way to explore the hill towns is by car. But you can get a limited preview by taking one of the motorcoaches that leaves every 20 minutes from Rome on the viale Carlo Felice. My selection of a string of the most interesting towns follows, beginning with—

Marino

About 14 miles from Rome, out the via Appia, this hillside town is the most easily reached of Rome's satellites. It was the birthplace of the poetess Victoria Colonna, whose platonic relationship with Michelangelo greatly influenced his life. In spite of its charming fountains and interesting churches, it has been encroached upon by "moderno," which drains much of its charm.

Other towns in the Castelli Romani are more intriguing—except at grape-harvesting time in October. Marino is the liveliest spot in all of Italy. The fountains start spouting wine (you can drink all you want—free), as Baccharalian revelry reigns supreme. The only trick is to avoid the snake-like line of homeward-bound

Romans afterward. When stone sober, the Romans drive as if the Madonna were their own special protector. When filled with the golden wine of the Alban Hills, they descend like the Normans in their sack of the city.

Castelgandolfo

Since the early 17th century this resort on Lake Albano, 16 miles from Rome, has been the summer retreat of the popes. As such, it attracts thousands of pilgrims yearly, although the papal residence, Villa Barberini, and its surrounding gardens, are private—open only on special occasions. As a sardonic side note, the pope's summer place incorporates part of Domitian's imperial palace (but the pastimes have changed).

On days that the pope grants a mass audience, thousands of visitors—many of whom arrive by foot—stream into the audience hall about 100 yards long. Built by Pius XII, the air-conditioned structure protects the faithful from the elements. The late pope once expressed alarm at the thousands of people waiting out in the rain to see him. On a summer Sunday, the pope usually appears on a small balcony in the palace courtyard, reciting with the crowd the noon Angelus prayers.

The seat of the papacy opens onto a little square in the center of the town, where holiday-makers sip their wine—nothing pontifical here. A chair lift transports visitors from the hillside town to the lake, where some of the aquatic competitions were held in the 1960 Olympics. The Church of St. Thomas of Villanova, on the principal square, as well as the fountain, reveal Bernini's hand. If you need more selling, remember that Castelgandolfo was praised by such an eminent guidebook writer as Goethe.

Rocca di Papa

Easily approached from Frascati is the star sapphire in the Castelli Romani crown. Towering over all, the medieval village lies near what was supposedly the camping grounds of Hannibal's legions. The most colorful time to visit is on market day, but any time can be good for the athletic. The narrow lanes are filled with kinks, swirls, ups and downs—more suitable for the donkeys of Rocca di Papa than those who grew up in the elevator era. The snug little houses hug the slopes like cliff dwellings. A greater peak still—3,130 feet high—is Monte Cavo, to be driven, not walked, from Rocca di Papa. It's the most scenic spot in the hill towns.

Nemi

The Romans flock here in droves, particularly from April through June, for the succulent strawberry of the district—acclaimed by some gourmets as the finest in Europe. (In May, there's a strawberry festival.) Nemi was also known to the ancients. To the huntress Diana, a temple was erected on Lake Nemi—said to be her "looking glass."

In A.D. 37, Caligula built luxurious barges to float on the lake. Mussolini had Nemi drained in another era. The Caligula barges, as predicted, were discovered. Regrettably, it was a dangerous time to excavate them from the lake's bottom, as they were senselessly destroyed by the Nazis during their infamous retreat.

The 15th-century Palazzo Ruspoli, a baronial estate, is the focal point of Nemi, but the hill town itself invites exploration—particularly the alleyways the local denizens call streets and the houses with balconies jutting out over the slopes. While darting like Diana through the Castelli Romani, try to time your schedule for lunch in Nemi.

WHERE TO DINE. Offering a large array of the dishes of the region, as well as a "rustico" atmosphere, **La Taverna,** via Nemorense 13 (tel. 06/936-8135), is worth the trouble of reaching it. In April the fragole (wild strawberries) signs go out. Spring is also the time to order pappardella al sugo de lepre (large noodles with wild game sauce), worthy of the goddess of the hunt. For a main dish, I suggest the chef's specialty, arrosto di abbacchio e maiale (it consists of both a pork chop and grilled lamb). If you want to have a Roman feast, accompany it with large roasted mushrooms, priced according to size, and a small fennel salad. To top off the galaxy of goodies, it's traditional to order sambucca, a clear white drink like anisette, "with a fly in it." The "fly," of course, is a coffee bean, which you suck on for added flavor. Meals cost 40,000 lire ($30.50). It's open from 12:30 to 2 p.m. and 8 to 10 p.m. daily except Wednesday.

Frascati

About 13 miles from Rome out via Tuscolana, Frascati is one of the most beautiful of the hill towns—known for the wine to which it lends its name and its villas. Romans drive up on a Sunday just to drink vino. Although bottles of Frascati are exported—and served in many of the restaurants and trattorie of Rome—tradition holds that the wine is best near the golden vineyards from which it came. Some 1,073 feet above sea level, the town bounced back from the severe destruction caused by bombers in World War II.

If you stand in the heart of Frascati, the piazza Marconi, you'll see the most important of the estates: **Villa Aldobrandini.** The finishing touches to this 16th-century villa were applied by Maderno, who designed the façade of St. Peter's. Only its gardens (free) may be visited. With its grottoes, yew hedges, statuary, and splashing fountains, it makes for an exciting outing. To visit the gardens, which are open only in the morning, go to Azienda di Soggiorno e Turismo, piazza Marconi 1 (tel. 942-0331). Open from 9 a.m. to 1 p.m. Tuesday through Saturday, they are closed on Sunday.

If you have a car, you can continue past the Villa Aldobrandini to **Tuscolo,** about three miles beyond the villa. An ancient spot with the ruins of an amphitheater dating from the 1st century B.C., Tuscolo offers what may be one of Italy's greatest views—with the campagna laid out before you.

You may also want to go to the bombed-out **Villa Torlonia.** Its grounds have been converted into a public park, whose chief treasure is the "Theater of the Fountains," also designed by Maderno.

WHERE TO DINE. In Frascati, **Cacciani Restaurant,** via Armando Diaz 4 (tel. 06/942-0378), is the choicest restaurant in a town where the competition's always been tough (Frascati foodstuffs once attracted Lucullus, the epicurean). A large, modern restaurant, with a terrace commanding a view of the valley, Cacciani in the past drew such celebs as Clark Gable. The kitchen is exposed to the public, and it's fun just to watch the women clean the sand off the spinach. To get you started, I recommend the pasta specialties—such as fettuccine (thin noodles) or rigatoni alla vaccinara (tail of the ox in tomato sauce). For a main course, the baby lamb with a special sauce of white wine and vinegar is always reliable. There is a large choice of wines, which are kept in a cave under the restaurant. Meals cost from 36,000 lire ($27.25). Hours are noon to 3 p.m. and 7 to 10 p.m.; closed Tuesday.

Cantina Comandini, via E. Filiberto (no phone), at the steps of the station, right off the central piazza Roma, is a wine cellar that's reason enough for going over the hill to Frascati. On a hot summer day, to sneak away to this cool wine cellar and sample the golden dry vino is reason enough to live. It's cheap: only 3,500 lire ($2.65) per liter. The owners, the Comandini family, sell wine in this rustico tavern from their own vineyards. They'll also show visitors the grottoes where the choicest wine is stored. In the evening there is singing. The cantina is open from noon to 2 p.m. and 7 to 10 p.m.; closed Sunday. To sum up, here you'll find good revelry, Bacchus style.

PALESTRINA

If you go out via Prenestina for about 24 miles, you'll eventually come to Palestrina, a medieval hillside town overlooking a wide valley. When U.S. airmen flew over in World War II, bombing part of the town, they scarcely realized they were launching Palestrina as an important tourist attraction. The debris cleared, a pagan temple—once one of the greatest in the world—emerged: the **Fortuna Primigenia**, rebuilt in the days of the empire but dating from centuries before.

Palestrina antedates the founding of Rome by several hundred years. It resisted being conquered by the early Romans, and later took the wrong side in the civil war between Marius and Sulla. When the eventual victor (Sulla) won, he razed every stone in the city except the Temple of Fortune, and then built a military barracks on the site. Later it became a favorite vacation spot for the emperors and their entourages, sheltering some of the most luxurious villas of the Roman Empire.

In medieval feuds between the Colonna and the Vatican, the city was repeatedly destroyed. Its most famous child was Pier Luigi da Palestrina, recognized as the father of polyphonic harmony.

The **Barberini Palace,** high on a hill overlooking the valley, today houses Roman statuary found in the ruins, plus Etruscan artifacts, such as urns the equal of those in the Villa Giulia Museum in Rome. But the most famous work—worth the trip itself—is the "Nile Mosaic," an ancient Roman work, well preserved, the most remarkable one ever uncovered. The mosaic details the flooding of the Nile, depicting a shepherd's hut, mummies, ibises, Roman warriors—and lots more. From November to February daily hours are 9 a.m. to 4 p.m.; in March and October, to 5 p.m.; in September, to 5:30 p.m.; in May, to 6:30 p.m.; and June through August, to 7:30 p.m. Admission is 4,000 lire ($3.05).

You'll also find a cathedral here, dating from 1100, with a bell tower that remains mostly intact from the date of its construction. It rests on the foundation of a much earlier pagan temple. To reach Palestrina, you can take a bus leaving from the viale del Castro Pretorio, near the Central Station.

Food and Lodging

Albergo Ristorante Stella (Restaurant Coccia), piazza della Liberazione 3, Palestrina, 00036 Roma (tel. 06/955-8172), is a buff-colored hotel set in the commercial center of town on a cobblestone square filled with parked cars, trees, and a small fountain. The simple lobby is filled with warm colors, curved leather couches, and autographed photos of local sports heroes. The 25 bedrooms rent for 26,000 lire ($19.75) daily in a single and 45,000 lire ($34.25) in a double. The restaurant is sunny, filled with a cluttered kind of modernity. There is a small bar where you might have an apéritif before lunch. Meals cost from 25,000 lire ($19).

ANZIO AND NETTUNO

These two towns are peaceful seaside resorts today, but to many Americans and English they conjure up bitter memories. On January 22, 1944, an Allied amphibious task force landed the U.S. VI Corps at Anzio and Nettuno, as a prelude to the liberation of Rome. Fighting against terrific odds, the Allies lost many lives.

In Nettuno the Italian government presented 77 acres to the United States for a cemetery. The graves are visited today by wives, brothers, sisters, and other relatives who lost men in the campaign. The cemetery contains graves not only of those who died on the beaches of Anzio and Nettuno (where holiday-makers now revel), but also of those who were killed in the Sicilian campaign.

The fields of Nettuno contain 7,862 U.S. dead—39% of those originally buried (the others have been returned home by their relatives). In Nettuno, a Graves Registry office helps visitors locate the markers of particular servicemen. The neatly manicured fields are peppered with crosses and stars of David, plus the saddest sight of all: 488 headstones that mark the graves of the unknowns. The cemetery is open from 8 a.m. till 6 p.m. daily.

In Anzio, you can visit the British cemetery filled with war dead. One memorial to B. J. Pownell, a gunner in the Royal Artillery, seems to symbolize the plight of all the young men who died on either side. "He Gave the Greatest Gift of All: His Unfinished Life." Gunner Pownell was struck down on January 29, 1944. He was 20 years old.

Anzio was the birthplace of both Nero and Caligula. Many wealthy Romans once erected villas there at the port said to have been founded by Antias, the son of Circe and Odysseus. In the ruins of Nero's fabulous villa, the world-famous statue of *Apollo Belvedere* was discovered.

Motorists can visit Ostia Antica in the morning, Anzio and Nettuno in the afternoon. Tourists dependent on public transportation can either take a train from Terminal Station in Rome, or a bus from via Carlo Felice in the capital.

FREGENE

The fame of this coast city north of the Tiber dates back to the 1600s when the land belonged to the Rospigliosi, a powerful Roman family. Pope Clement IX, a member of the wealthy family, planted a forest of pine extending along the shoreline for 2½ miles and half a mile deep to protect the land from the strong winds of the Mediterranean. Today the wall of pines makes a dramatic backdrop for the golden sands and luxurious villas of the resort town.

For food or accommodations, there is the following recommendation:

La Conchiglia, piazzale a Mare 4, Fregene, 00050 Roma (tel. 06/646-0229), means "the shellfish" in Italian—an appropriate name for this hotel and restaurant right on the beach, offering views of the water and of the pine trees. Its circular lounge is painted white, with curving wall banquettes built in and facing a cylindrical fireplace with a raised hearth. It seems a setting for one of those modern Italian films, with its cubical upholstered chairs. However, the resort aura is created by the large green plants. Facing the terrace, the bar in the cocktail lounge is also circular. The rooms are comfortable and well furnished, costing 100,000 lire ($76) per person daily for full board in high season. It's also possible to stop by for a meal. The food is good. Try, for example, spaghetti with lobster and grilled fish. Many excellent meat dishes are offered. Meals cost from 36,000 lire ($27.25). The restaurant's in the garden, shaded by bamboo. Oleander flutters in the sea breezes.

THE ETRUSCAN ZONE

As you walk through the Etruscan Museum in Rome (Villa Giulia), you'll often see the word *Caere* written under a figure vase or a sarcophagus. This is a reference to the nearby town known today as Cerveteri. Caere was one of the great Etruscan cities of Italy, its origins dipping back into antiquity—maybe to the 9th century B.C. Of course, the Etruscan town has long faded, but not the **Necropolis of Cerveteri.** The effect is eerie, and it is often called a "city of the dead."

When you go beneath some of the mounds, you'll discover the most striking feature of the necropolis—the tombs are like rooms in Etruscan homes. The main burial ground is called the Necropolis of Banditaccia. Of the graves thus far uncovered, none is finer than the Tomba Bella (sometimes called the Reliefs' Tomb), the burial ground of an Etruscan family by the name of Matuna. Articles such as utensils, even house pets, were painted in stucco relief. Presumably these paintings were representations of items the dead family would need in the world beyond.

The necropolis, 1¼ miles north of Cerveteri, is open May 1 to September 30 from 9 a.m. to 7 p.m. (other months, 10 a.m. to 4 p.m.); closed Monday. Admission is 3,000 lire ($2.30). Cerveteri can be reached by motorcoach from Rome, leaving from via Lepanto. If you're driving, head out **via Aurelia**, northwest of Rome, for a distance of 28 miles.

If you wish to see even more striking and more recently excavated tombs, go to **Tarquinia,** about 13 miles above the port of Civitavecchia.

The medieval turrets and fortifications atop the rocky cliffs overlooking the sea seem to contradict the Etruscan name of Tarquinia. Actually, Tarquinia is the adopted name of the old medieval community of Corneto, in honor of the major Etruscan city that once stood nearby. The main attraction within the town is the

Tarquinia National Museum, piazza Cavour (tel. 0766/856-036), which is devoted to Etruscan exhibits and sarcophagi excavated from the necropolis a few miles away. The museum is housed in the Palazzo Vitelleschi, a Gothic palace dating from the mid-15th century. Among the exhibits are gold jewelry, black vases with carved and painted bucolic scenes, and sarcophagi decorated with carvings of animals and relief figures of priests and military leaders. But the biggest attraction of all is in itself worth a drive all the way from Rome. This is the almost life-size pair of winged horses taken from the pediment of a Tarquinian temple. The finish is worn here and there, and the terracotta color shows through, but the relief stands as one of the greatest Etruscan masterpieces ever discovered. The museum is open daily except Monday from 9 a.m. to 2 p.m. (to 1 p.m. on Sunday), and charges 4,000 lire ($3.05) admission.

Just 4 miles southeast of the town is the **Etruscan necropolis** (tel. 0766/856-308), covering more than 2½ miles of rough terrain near where the ancient Etruscan city once stood. Thousands of tombs have been discovered here, some of which have not been explored even today. Others, of course, were discovered by looters, but many treasures remain even after countless pieces were removed to museums and private collections. The paintings on the walls of the tombs have helped historians reconstruct the life of the Etruscans—a heretofore impossible feat without a written history. The paintings depict feasting couples in vivid colors mixed from iron oxide, lapis lazuli dust, and charcoal. One of the oldest tombs (from the 6th century B.C.) depicts young men fishing while dolphins play and colorful birds fly high above. Many of the paintings convey an earthy, vigorous, sex-oriented life among the wealthy Etruscans. The tombs are generally open daily except Monday. Using the same ticket, you can visit both the museum and the necropolis. Hours for the latter are 9 a.m. to 6 p.m. daily except Monday (to 2 p.m. in winter).

VITERBO

The 2,000 years that have gone into the creation of the city of Viterbo make it one of the most interesting day trips from Rome. Just a two-hour drive on the autostrada north (to the Orte exit), Viterbo traces its history back to the Etruscans. The bulk of its historical architecture, however, dates from the Middle Ages and the Renaissance, when the city was a residence—and hideout—for the popes. The old section of the city is still surrounded by thick stone walls that once protected the inhabitants from papal (or antipapal, depending on the situation at the time) attacks.

The only way to see Viterbo properly is on a walking tour of the medieval town, wandering through the narrow cobbled streets and pausing in front of its remarkable structures. Beginning at the piazza del Plebiscito, which is dominated by the 15th-century town hall, one is impressed by the fine state of preservation of Viterbo's old buildings. The courtyard and attractive fountain in front of the town hall and the 13th-century governor's palace are a favorite meeting place for townfolk and visitors alike.

Just down via San Lorenzo is the **Palazzo San Lorenzo,** the site of Viterbo's cathedral, which sits atop the former Etruscan acropolis. The Duomo, dating from 1192, is a composite of architectures, from its pagan foundations to its Renaissance façade to its Gothic bell tower. Next door is the 13th-century Palazzo Papale, built as a residence for the pope, but also serving as a hideout when the pope was in exile. It was also the site of three papal elections. The outside staircase and the colonnaded loggia all go to make up one of the finest examples of civil Roman architecture from the Gothic period.

The finest example of medieval architecture in Viterbo is the **San Pellegrino Quarter,** reached from the piazza San Lorenzo by a short walk past the piazza della Morte. This quarter, inhabited by working-class Viterboans, is a maze of narrow streets, arched walkways, towers, steep stairways, and ornamental fountains.

Worth a special visit is the **Convent of Santa Maria della Verità,** dating from 1100. The church is interesting enough, with 15th-century frescoes by Lorenzo da

Viterbo, student of Piero della Francesca. But the real reason for visiting the convent is to see the Etruscan collection in the **Municipal Museum (Museo Civica),** housed in the cloisters. Among the contents of the museum are several Etruscan sarcophagi, including a red-haired lady and a red-faced fat man with a broken nose. The collection also includes sculpture (an excellent Etruscan lion) and pottery. Adjoining the museum is a picture gallery containing a painting of the dead Christ, the finest work by Sebastiano del Piombo, a student of Michelangelo's. It is open Monday through Saturday from 8:30 a.m. to 1:30 p.m. and 3:30 to 6 p.m. January to April and October to December, from 8:30 a.m. to 1:30 p.m. and 3:30 to 7:30 p.m. May to September. On Sunday and holidays year round, it is open from 8:30 a.m. to 1:30 p.m. Admission is 2,000 lire ($1.50).

Villa Lante, at Bagnaia, a suburb of Viterbo, which Sacheverell Sitwell called, "the most beautiful garden in Italy," is a worthy contender with Villa d'Este at Tivoli for that title. Water from Mount Cimino flows down to the handsome fountains of the villa, running from terrace to terrrace until it reaches the central pool of the magnificent garden, with statues, stone banisters, and shrubbery. Two symmetrical Renaissance palaces make up the villa.

About eight miles east of Bagnaia at Bomarzo lies the **Parco dei Mostri** (park of Monsters), which Prince Vicino Orsini had built in a deep valley, overlooked by the Orsini Palace and the houses of the village. On the other side of the valley are stone cliffs. Prince Orsini's park, Bosco Sacro (Sacred Wood), is filled with grotesque figures carved from natural rock. The figures probably date from about 1560, since Annibale Caro, a Renaissance poet, refers to them in a letter he wrote in 1564. They rise mysteriously from the wild Tuscan landscape, covered with strangling weeds and moss. Nature and art have created a surrealistic fantasy: the Mouth of Hell (an ogre's face big enough for people to walk into the gaping orifice), a crude Hercules slaying an Amazon, nymphs with butterfly wings, a huge tortoise with a statue on its shell, a harpy, a mermaid, snarling dogs, lions, and much, much more. If you need to refresh yourself after this excursion to the edge of madness, you'll find a snack shop near the entrance. The park is open daily from 9 a.m. to dusk. Admission is 5,000 lire ($3.80).

Dining Near Viterbo

Instead of dining at Viterbo, I suggest a detour to La Quercia, less than two miles from the medieval center. There you'll find **Aquilanti** (tel. 0761/341-701). La Quercia is the seat of the Basilica of the Madonna of Quercia, with its cloister by Bernini, its bell tower of Sangallo, and its ceramic portal by della Robbia. Commanding a view of an Etruscan burial ground, the dining room does not disappoint those seeking good-quality Italian fare. Specialties include fettuccine allo stennarello, ravioli de ricotta e spinaci all'etrusca, plus vitella (veal) alla montanara, as well as a fabulous array of fruit and vegetables. The wine is from Orvieto. Expect to pay 30,000 lire ($22.75) to 40,000 lire ($30.50), plus service. Hours are daily except Tuesday from noon to 3 p.m. and 7:30 to 10 p.m.

MANZÙ

In the village of **Ardea,** the **Raccolta Manzù** (tel. 06/916-1022) is housed in a simple but effective museum. A short drive through the pine- and eucalyptus-studded countryside outside Rome, it is a unique tribute to Giacomo Manzù, a remarkable sculptor, strongly influenced by the 15th-century works of Donatello and Rosso. His combination of classicism and individuality is especially apparent in his ecclesiastical figures. His portraits of his friend Pope John XXIII (they both came from Bergamo), and especially the huge bronze sculpture of *Il Grande Cardinale,* demonstrate this. Look for the oversize pram with the likenesses of the children atop it. Also on display are articles of jewelry created by Manzù.

The collection assembles more than 400 pieces (sculpture, drawings, etchings and lithographs, and gold and silver jewelry) from among the most significant works by Manzù over his half-century-long artistic career. Archives and documents are also collected in this museum. It is open every day except Monday; Tuesday through Friday, hours are 9 a.m. to 7 p.m.; Saturday, Sunday, and holidays, it is open only from 9 a.m. to 1:30 p.m. Admission to the museum is free. The collection is now a special wing of the National Gallery of Modern Art in Rome.

FIUGGI FONTE

Beautiful landscapes and healthy mountain air have combined with "the waters" to make this resort renowned for its curative powers since the 13th century. Michelangelo, his neck strained from painting the Sistine Chapel, went here for the cure, a fact commemorated by a hotel named after him. The resort lies 38 miles south of Rome and can easily be tied in with a sightseeing visit to the previously described Palestrina. The spa is so little known by North Americans that visitors can add it to their list of offbeat European sights.

Food and Lodging

Grand Hotel Vallombrosa & Majestic, via Vecchia Fiuggi 120, 03014 Fiuggi Fonte (tel. 0775/55-531), is unknown to many seasoned Italian travelers. It's a hotel spa that is spacious, airy, and contemporary. Life here moves at a slow pace, the tranquil quality enhanced by trees and gardens. The establishment is just 300 feet from the spa baths. Within the hotel are generous lounges, a guest tavern, plus a cozy bar and restaurant. In the garden, the heated swimming pool is a further draw. All the well-furnished and comfortable bedrooms contain private bath and air conditioning. For full board, you pay 150,000 lire ($114) per person daily in high season, service and taxes included. The hotel is open from mid-May to September.

FLORENCE (FIRENZE)

When the last Renaissance artist capitulated to the baroque and pundits began to evaluate the era, the question was asked, "Why was Florence the city chosen for the 'rebirth'?" Some long-forgotten individual emerged with the opinion that the Renaissance didn't choose Florence, but Florence chose the Renaissance as its own bambino.

The Florentines are a unique lot. A Genoese sailor could persuade Isabella to finance his expedition to the Americas, but it took a Florentine by the name of Amerigo Vespucci to get the country named after himself. The Florentines are the champions of the vigorous life. To adapt another saying, they believe in taking the dilemma by the horns. Thus the Florentine Dante wrote the *Divine Comedy* in the vernacular—and not only persuaded his readers to accept such a "vulgar" work but helped make the Tuscan dialect and language *the* tongue of Italy.

To appreciate Florence, to understand its treasures, we need to know something, however meager, of the boldness and tenacity of its people. So we'll check into our hotel first, look over the city's restaurants, and then, in the following chapter, set out on our task.

GETTING THERE

A major stopover in Europe for holders of the Eurailpass, Florence lies in the heart of Italy. If you're coming north from Rome, count on a two- to three-hour trip depending on your connection. Bologna is just an hour away by train, and if you decide to see Venice first, it's only four hours' traveling distance by train from Florence. Jet-setters cannot fly directly from North America to Florence. If you're flying from New York, the best air connection is to Milan where you can board a domestic flight to the Galileo Galilei Airport at Pisa, 58 miles to the west of Florence. Express trains run between the two cities in an hour. If you're driving, you'll find that Florence, because of its central location, enjoys good autostrada connections with the rest of Italy, especially Rome and Bologna.

1. Orientation

Florence is a city seemingly designed for walking. It's amazing how nearly all the major sights can be discovered on foot. The only problem is, the sidewalks in summer are so crowded that I can only hope you don't suffer from claustrophia.

The city is split by the Arno River, which usually looks serene and peaceful, but can turn ferocious with flood waters on rare occasions. The major part of Florence, certainly its monumental and historical core, lies on the north or "right" side of the river. But the "left" side is not devoid of attractions. Many long-time visitors frequent the left bank for its tantalizing trattoria meals, and also maintain that the shopping here is less expensive. Even the most cursory visitor will want to cross over to the left bank to see the Pitti Palace with its many art treasures and walk through the Giardini di Boboli, a series of formal gardens, the most impressive in Florence. In addition, you'll also want to cross over to the left bank heading for the belvedere piazzale Michelangelo for one of the most panoramic vistas of this city of the Renaissance. To reach it, follow viale Michelangelo up the flank of the hill (one easy way to go is to take bus 13 from the train station).

The Arno is spanned by eight bridges, of which the Ponte Vecchio is the most celebrated and most central, flanked as it is with jewelry stores. Many of these bridges were ancient structures until the Nazis, in a hopeless and last-ditch effort, senselessly destroyed them in their "defense" of Florence in 1944. With tenacity, Florence rebuilt its bridges, often using, whenever possible, pieces from the destroyed structures. The Ponte S. Trinità is the second most important bridge spanning the Arno. After crossing it, you can continue along via de Tornabuoni, which is the most important right-bank shopping street (don't look for bargains, however). At the Ponte Vecchio you can walk, again on the right bank, along via Por Santa Maria which will become Calimala. This will lead you into the heartbeat piazza della Repubblica, a commercial district known for its cafés such as the Caffè Gilli.

From there, you can take via Roma, leading directly into the piazza di San Giovanni, with the baptistery, and its neighboring sister, the larger piazza Duomo, with its world-famous cathedral and bell tower by Giotto. From the far western edge of the piazza Duomo, you can take via del Proconsolo south to the piazza della Signoria, with its landmark Palazzo Vecchio and its sculpture-filled Loggia della Signoria. Most visitors will arrive at the piazza della Stazione, the rail station, which adjoins the piazza di Santa Maria Novella, containing one of the great churches of Florence. From here, most of the major hotels are within easy reach.

High in the hills, overlooking Florence, is the ancient town of Fiesole, with its Roman ruins and splendid cathedral.

TRANSPORTATION

The major sights in the small city of Florence are within walking distance of most hotels, but you might prefer to use the public transportation provided by **buses.** If you do, you must purchase your bus ticket before boarding one of the public vehicles. For 700 lire (55¢), you can ride on any bus (public, that is) in the city for a total of 70 minutes. Bus tickets can be purchased from tobacconists and news vendors.

Taxis can be found at stands at nearly all the major squares in Florence. If you need a radio taxi, call 4390.

For **railway** information, phone 2767.

Bicycles are a practical means of transportation in Florence. You can rent a bicycle from **Ciao & basta,** whose headquarters are at Costa dei Magnoli 24 (tel. 234-2726), although no bicycles are available there. Rental facilities are near the railway station, piazza Stazione, corner of via L'Alamanni, open daily 24 hours a day January to December (tel. 213-307); and piazza Pitti near the Pitti Palace, open daily from 9:30 a.m. to 7 p.m. June to October.

PRACTICAL FACTS

To ease your adjustment into the capital of Tuscany, I have compiled some useful addresses and information that you may need during your visit. The **telephone area code** for Florence and Fiesole is 055.

American Express: The Florentine branch of **American Express** is at via Guicciardini 49A (tel. 278-751). It is open Monday through Friday from 9 a.m. to 12:30 p.m. and 3 to 7 p.m., and on Saturday from 9 a.m. to noon; closed Sunday.

Consulate: American visitors may wish to go to the U.S. Consulate, lungarno Amerigo Vespucci 38 (tel. 055/298-276).

Drugstore: Pharmacy service is available 24 hours a day at Molteni, via Calzaiuoli 7R (tel. 263-490).

Emergencies: Emergency telephone numbers are: for **fire,** 222-222; for an **ambulance,** 212-222; for **police,** 113; and for **road service,** 116.

Library: An American studies library of the University of Florence, the **American Library** (Biblioteca di Storia e Letteratura Nordamericana), is at via S. Gallo 10 (tel. 296-114), open from 9 a.m. to 1 p.m. Monday through Friday.

Medical care: Night service of a **doctor** is available by calling 477-891. To reach a hospital, call the **General Hospital of Santa Maria Nuova,** piazza Santa Maria Nuova 1 (tel. 27-741).

Post Office: Open all the time, the **Central Post Office** is on via Pelliceria. **Telegrams** can be sent from here on a 24-hour basis. You can also send telegrams by phoning 186.

Religious Services: There is a **Baptist** church at via Borgognissanti 6 (tel. 210-537), and a Hebrew **synagogue** at via Farini 4 (tel. 210-763). Florence also has a **Lutheran** church at lungarno Torrigiani 11 (tel. 295-252). If you're **Catholic,** you can walk into virtually any church in the city. The American Episcopalian church is **St. James,** at via Rucellai 9 (tel. 294-417).

Tourist Information: This is available at the **Azienda Autonoma di Turismo,** located at via Tornobuoni 15 (tel. 216-544). The number for the information office is 217-459. The offices are open from 9 a.m. to 1 p.m. daily except Sunday.

THE HOTEL SITUATION

Florence was always a leader in architecture. Consequently, with the decline and fall of the great aristocratic families of Tuscany, many of the city's grand old villas and palaces have been converted into hotels. For sheer charm and luxury, the hotels of Florence are among the finest in Europe. There are not too many tourist cities where you can find a 15th- or 16th-century palace—tastefully decorated and most comfortable—rated as a second-class pensione (boarding house). Florence is well equipped with hotels in virtually all price ranges and of widely varying standards, comfort, service, and efficiency. However, during the summer season there simply aren't enough rooms to meet the demand, and if you arrive without a reservation you may not find a place for the night and will have to drive to the nearby resort of Montecatini where you'll always stand a good chance of securing accommodations. My recommendations in every major government classification follow, beginning with—

2. Deluxe and First-Class Hotels

LUXURY LEADERS OF FLORENCE

Even with your eyes wide open, you will be justified in daydreaming you're a Medici or other elegant patron of Leonardo da Vinci or Michelangelo when you check into one of these deluxe hotels.

Hotel Excelsior, piazza Ognissanti 3, 50123 Firenze (tel. 055/264-201), set on a Renaissance square, is the ultimate in well-ordered luxury during a stopover in Florence. Demand for the elegant bedrooms is so great that during peak season most of the accommodations are reserved many weeks in advance. Once part of the hotel was owned by Carolina Bonaparte, sister of Napoleon. The present hotel was formed in 1927 by the fusion of two other hotels, the De la Ville and the Italie. Several of the bedrooms have terraces, and many open onto views of the Arno. The rooms offer lots of comfortable chairs, well-appointed space, and opulent baths with heated racks, thick towels, and high-ceilinged comfort. Singles range from 210,000 lire ($160) to 290,000 lire ($220) daily, and doubles cost 320,000 lire ($243) to 420,000 lire ($319)—but be duly warned that taxes and I.V.A. are extra.

Il Castello is the hotel's deluxe restaurant, attracting an upper-crust clientele who, in summer, come either to drink beside the piano or on the flowered terrace of this hotel's roof garden, or else to dine under a canopy by candlelight. On the sixth floor, the garden is open only from May to October (in winter, it moves back downstairs again). But in summer the hotel closes its downstairs dining room in favor of the breezes and the panoramic views of the Arno that visitors enjoy from this terrace. Meals are served from noon to 3 p.m. and 7 to 11 p.m. daily. A dinner costs 90,000 lire ($68.50) to 100,000 lire ($76). The cuisine is Mediterranean with Tuscan specialties and a few items that are always "fresh from today's market." Reservations are always imperative. For details on the hotel's popular bar, the Donatello, turn to Section 5 of Chapter VI.

Plaza Hotel Lucchesi, lungarno della Zecca Vecchia 38, 50122 Firenze (tel. 055/264-141), is one of the most charming and best-managed hotels in Florence, offering many of the facilities and services of the city's famous five-star hotels, but at about half the price. Originally built in 1860, and gracefully renovated many times since then, it lies along the banks of the Arno, a ten-minute walk from the Duomo and a few paces from the imposing Church of Santa Maria della Croce. Its interior decor includes lots of glossy mahogany, acres of marble, and masses of fresh flowers which its sophisticated owner/manager, Vernero Ciofi, considers a necessity. There's a sun-flooded lobby-level restaurant, the site of copious morning breakfast buffets and elegant dinners. Diners often enjoy the melodies of a resident pianist/singer. The comfortably appointed bar reigns supreme as the hotel's social center. Each of the 97 handsomely furnished and beautifully kept bedrooms contains all the modern equipment and comfort you'd expect from such a stellar property. Each has a meticulously tiled bath, color TV, radio, phone, air conditioning, and frigo-bar. About 20 accommodations open onto private terraces or balconies, some with enviable views over the heart of historic Florence. With breakfast included, singles rent for 200,000 lire ($152) daily and doubles go for 275,000 lire ($209).

Villa Medici, via il Prato 42, 50123 Firenze (tel. 055/261-331), centrally located between the railway station and the Arno, creates its own world once you walk through its glass doorways. This 1960 luxury hotel has all the trappings and extra services (air conditioning, radios, phones in all the rooms, a barbershop, hairdressing salon, cleaning and pressing facilities) needed to attract the famous and glamorous, even kings and princesses. The super-size, handsomely maintained bedrooms —all with private bath or shower—combine both traditional and modern features in decor. Rates depend on whether you request a private bath or shower. Single rooms range from 202,000 lire ($154) to 268,000 lire ($204) daily, and doubles run 303,000 lire ($230) to 453,000 lire ($344). The big draw at the Medici is its private garden, with its open-air, onion-shaped swimming pool for the use of guests at no additional charge—it's complete with poolside tables and changing rooms. On the rooftop terrace you can enjoy a view of Brunelleschi's dome and Giotto's bell tower. Dining is in the Lorenzo de' Medici Restaurant, offering both an international and Florentine cuisine. In summer meals are also served by the pool.

Savoy Hotel, piazza della Repubblica 7, 50123 Firenze (tel. 055/283-313), is a dignified hotel sheltered behind a buff-colored façade with neoclassical trim carved from gray stone. It sits in what might be called the commercial center of Florence (but also the historic district), in an area filled with fine stores, a few blocks from the duomo. The predictably upper-class interior includes potted plants, patterned carpeting, and coffered ceilings. An accommodating bar area has frescoed walls reminiscent of a trompe-l'oeil view from an 18th-century balcony, with jardinières and parrots. Each of the well-furnished rooms has a private bath, with singles renting for 220,000 lire ($167) to 330,000 lire ($251) daily and doubles going for 340,000 lire ($258) to 520,000 lire ($395). Rooms are at their highest in May, September, and October, which are considered the most desirable months to visit Florence.

Villa La Massa, via La Massa 8, 50010 Candeli (tel. 055/630-051), lies on the outskirts of Florence at Candeli, about a ten-minute drive from the city, a distance of four miles from the railway station. In its special classification, the villa—the 15th-century home of the Count Giraldi family—is favored by numerous celebrities in summer. One of the loveliest spots in all the hill country, the villa is on a projection of parkland with tennis courts that has the Arno snaking around on three sides. All the spacious drawing rooms, private library, and dining salons open onto a central covered courtyard-lounge, with a surrounding arched passageway. The bedrooms on the floor above open onto this courtyard or the river and gardens. A single with bath rents for 179,000 lire ($136) to 219,000 lire ($166) daily, and a double with bath goes for 280,000 lire ($213) to 384,000 lire ($292). Half board costs 210,000 lire ($213) to 289,000 lire ($220) per person daily. Some rooms have hydromassage.

The 44 bedroom, all with private bath and air conditioning, are lavishly furnished with antiques or fine reproductions. The public areas are equally adorned. The glittery bar was once an altar, and the Corinthian-columned dining room is formal, with a vaulted ceiling and a stone fireplace—ideal for baronial meals. In addition, you'll find a sun terrace and a small swimming pool, along with flowers and shade trees. There's another building, near the riverside, where dining is accompanied by dance music. A cellar (Club La Cave) offers an American-style bar and occasional entertainment. A hotel bus transports visitors into the city.

Grand Hotel Villa Cora, viale Machiavelli 18-20, 50125 Firenze (tel. 055/229-8451), is a grandiose Renaissance neoclassic palace on the hill near Michelangelo Square above the city. Built by Baron Oppenheim and once lived in by the Italian ambassador to the U.S., the luxury hotel stands in its own formal gardens, with a special recreation area, including an open-air swimming pool. The villa was chosen as a residence for the ex-Empress Eugénie, widow of Napoléon III, to whom Florence gave a warm and deferential welcome. The public rooms have architectural splendor, with the drawing rooms opening off the domed circular rotunda. Marble, ornate bronze, white-and-gilt doors, frescoed ceilings, parquet floors, and silk damask walls characterize the decor. Some of the bedrooms—the more expensive ones —are one-of-a-kind, although the others are well furnished with tasteful reproductions of the 19th-century pieces. All are air-conditioned, with frigo-bar. Singles with shower rent for 188,000 lire ($143) to 273,000 lire ($208) daily; doubles with bath or shower from 264,000 lire ($330). In the restaurant, Taverna Machiavelli, you can enjoy fine food. In warm weather meals are also served in the open air near the swimming pool. From the rooftop solarium, a panoramic view of the rooftops of Florence unfolds.

Hotel Regency, piazza Massimo d'Azeglio 3, 50121 Firenze (tel. 055/245-247), lies a bit apart from the shopping and sightseeing center of Florence, but happily is only a 15-minute stroll to the cathedral. Although its location is away from the center (a blessing for tranquility seekers), it is conveniently and quickly reached by taxi. This well-built, old-style villa, a member of *Relais & Châteaux,* has its own garden across from a park in a residential area of the city. This luxurious hideaway, filled with stained glass, paneled walls, and reproduction antiques, offers 38 exquisitely furnished rooms. In a single, expect to pay from 320,000 lire ($243) daily, 415,000 lire ($315) to 460,000 lire ($350) in a double. There are some special rooms on the top floor with walk-out terraces. The attractive paneled dining room serves excellent food, or you can take your meals in the well-lit winter garden. The owner, who also has the prestigious Lord Byron in Rome, has a capable staff at the Regency.

Grand Hotel, piazza Ognissanti 1, 50123 Firenze (tel. 055/278-781), is a bastion of luxury, fronting a little Renaissance piazza across from the Excelsior. A hotel of history and tradition, the Grand is known for its halls and salons. Its legend grew under its name, Continental Royal de la Paix. In both the 19th and 20th centuries it has attracted many famous personages. Its rooms and suites have a refined elegance, and the most desirable overlooks the Arno. Each of its bedrooms contains all the silks, brocades, and real or reproduction antiques you'd expect from such a highly regarded establishment. The prices also achieve grandeur: 210,000 lire ($160) to 290,000 lire ($220) daily in a single, 320,000 lire ($243) to 420,000 lire ($319) in a double or twin. Breakfast and taxes are not included. Highlight of the hotel is the Winter Garden, an enclosed court lined with arches, which has been restored.

FIRST-CLASS HOTELS

Florence has many first-class accommodations, my selection of which is listed below by geographical position.

Near the Railway Station

Hotel Croce di Malta, via della Scala 7, 50123 Firenze (tel. 055/282-600), is housed within a stately palace whose soaring interior was modernized in the early 1970s. It's one of the few hotels in Florence with its own swimming pool, whose curved edges are partially shaded by the rear garden's 100-year-old magnolia. The stylish lobby has massive stone columns between which the architects placed rounded doorways like you'd expect on "Star Trek." In sharp contrast, the bedrooms are classically elegant, filled with Florentine furniture and frescoed headboards showing landscapes that might have been interpreted by an artist of the early Renaissance. Some of the more expensive accommodations are duplexes with their own sleeping loft set midway between the floor and high ceilings. Each of the 98 accommodations contains a private bath, frigo-bar, radio, and phone. With breakfast included, singles cost 155,000 lire ($118) to 189,000 lire ($144) daily, and doubles go for 210,000 lire ($160) to 261,000 lire ($198). Apartments rent for 300,000 lire ($228) to 326,000 lire ($248) for two people daily. Rates depend on the season. On the premises is a whimsically decorated restaurant, Il Coccodrillo, serving well-prepared food from 35,000 lire ($26.50) a meal.

Hotel Kraft, via Solferino 2, 50123 Firenze (tel. 055/284-273), was created by the son of one of Italy's greatest hoteliers (the father, Herman Kraft, of Berne, Switzerland, sparked the Excelsior in the 19th century). The present-day Kraft is far removed from the baroque—rather, it meets the requirements of today quite beautifully. It's at the side of a square, close by the railroad station and almost next to the Arno and the American Consulate. Fine antiques or reproductions are used in the comfortable bedrooms. Many have little terraces, perfect for morning coffee, and all have baths. A single with bath costs an inclusive 195,000 lire ($148) daily; two people pay 270,000 lire ($205). Taxes, air conditioning, and service are included. The Kraft is crowned on top with a dining room opening onto a covered terrace. Several terraces higher is an open-air swimming pool. Imagine swimming with a view of the Duomo, the piazzale Michelangelo, and Fiesole. Being so near the opera house, the Kraft is popular with maestros and singing stars.

Grand Hotel Baglioni, piazza Unità Italiana 6, 50123 Firenze (tel. 055/218-441), for years was a landmark hotel near the railway station. Completely renovated, the first-class hotel offers a total of 220 accommodations, all with private bath and air conditioning, plus mini-fridge, radio, and color TV. In high season, a single rents for 196,000 lire ($149) daily, and a double goes for 271,000 lire ($205). However, in the off-season the tariff drops to 164,500 lire ($125) in a single, 230,000 lire ($175) in a double. Candlelight meals, and good ones at that, are served on the panoramic roof garden of the hotel. A set luncheon or dinner costs 48,000 lire ($36.50). The period furnishings and the excellent standard of service make this hotel one of the leaders in Florence. The Melarancio Restaurant is ideal for quick breakfasts, business lunches, and also late-night snacks.

Grand Hotel Minerva, piazza S. Maria Novella 16, 50123 Firenze (tel. 055/284-555), is one of the most streamlined choices near the railway station. Its 108 rooms all have private bath or shower, mini-fridge, radio, color TV, and air conditioning. The bedrooms are pleasantly furnished with modern pieces. A single room with bath or shower costs from 173,000 lire ($139) daily; a double begins at 228,000 lire ($173). Half board is 49,000 lire ($37.25) per person in addition to the room rate. The most popular feature of the Minerva is its rooftop swimming pool, a choice spot considering the view of the city. The hotel is well protected against noise, billing itself as "the really quietest hotel of the town."

Hotel Pullman Astoria, via del Giglio 9, 50123 Firenze (tel. 055/298-095), at one time housed the offices of a now-defunct newspaper. In the 17th century John Milton wrote parts of *Paradise Lost* in one of the bedrooms. Pullman renovated the 14th-century building into one of the most original hotels in Florence. The stylish lobby is illuminated with a skylight that shines into a copy of a mural by Botticelli and a heroic collection of metallic horses more or less on permanent display. From the bedrooms on the upper floors, you'll have a view over the terracotta rooftops of Florence. If you choose to stay in one of the stylishly comfortable bedrooms of this hotel, be sure to inspect the conference rooms of what used to be the adjoining Palazzo Gaddi, whose frescoes are filled with chubby cherubs. On the premises is a garden-style restaurant with wall murals, beamed ceilings, and Empire lyre-backed chairs. Singles rent for 180,000 lire ($137) daily, and doubles go for 275,000 lire ($209).

Hotel Londra, via Jacopo da Diacceto 16-20, 50123 Firenze (tel. 055/262-791), is a modern, first-class hotel close to the museums and monuments of Florence, the shopping areas, and the railroad station. The marble tile floor of the lobby is beautified by a large Oriental carpet, and the lounges are furnished with big, comfortable chairs, of brown leather in one area and olive-green velvet in another. There is a small American bar with an adjacent piano bar, where music is produced nightly after dinner. The dining room, with a polished hardwood floor, opens in summer onto the walled terrace garden where meals are served amid greenery. The wood-paneled bedrooms are comfortably furnished and well lighted, each with private bath complete with bidet and hairdryer. All units have direct-dial phone, refrigerator, color TV, radio, and air conditioning. Singles rent for 173,000 lire ($132) daily and doubles begin at 228,000 lire ($173). The lighted room numbers beside each door are helpful. You can descend to the reception area by elevator or carpeted stairs. The hotel has a large private garage for customers.

Atlantic Palace Hotel, via Nazionale 12, 50123 Firenze (tel. 055/284-959). Late in 1985 a group of entrepreneurs transformed what had been a run-down hotel into a four-star model of imaginative design, using the shell of a 17th-century monastery as a foundation. Today this is one of the most alluring hotels in the vicinity of the railway station. Each of its oversize bedrooms has some kind of memorable ceiling, often with heavy beams crisscrossed with old tiles or with rows of hand-painted panels set into geometric patterns. Accommodations contain reproductions of antiques, frigo-bar, air conditioning, color TV, radio, and modern tile bath. Depending on the season, singles range from 130,000 lire ($98.75) to 180,000 lire ($137) daily, and doubles run 180,000 lire ($137) to 260,000 lire ($198). Some triples are also rented, costing 300,000 lire ($228) to 350,000 lire ($266). All tariffs include a buffet breakfast.

Near Cascine Park

Anglo-American Regina Hotel, via Garibaldi 9, 50123 Firenze (tel. 055/282-114), occupies an old Florentine palace. Its streetside buildings enclose a covered garden room, lounge, and loggia—spring-like all year. The older parts of the hostelry have exquisite architectural features, as does the dining room, with its ornate plaster designs on the wall—cameo-like in pink, red, and white. Crystal chandeliers and towering gilt mirrors grace the public salons. The lobby has tent-like draperies covering the sloping skylights, with an elegant dining room with Victorian chairs. There's also an English club–style bar. Other facilities include a barbershop, a beauty parlor, a sauna, and an inside garden and loggia. The bedrooms, 118 in all, each have bath or shower, direct-dial phone, radio, and air conditioning. In a twin-bedded accommodation, the cost for a room and a continental breakfast peaks at 250,000 lire ($190) daily, dropping to 180,000 lire ($137) in a single. A table d'hôte dinner at the hotel costs from 45,000 lire ($34.25). The hotel is well placed near the Arno, close to the opera house and the U.S. Consulate. A garage for your car is available nearby.

Off Via Tornabuoni

Hotel de la Ville, piazza Antinori 1, 50123 Firenze (tel. 055/261-805), stands on the most elegant and exclusive street of the historic center close to the Arno. It has a conservatively contemporary appearance, with a decor that includes flowering plants, mirror-bright marble floors, and many distinct sitting areas. All the soundproof bedrooms have air conditioning, frigo-bar, color TV, and direct-dial phone. Single rooms rent for 196,000 lire ($149) daily, and doubles go for 272,000 lire ($207) to 340,000 lire ($258), the price depending on the size of the accommodation. An extra bed can be set up in any unit for an additional 93,000 lire ($71). A continental breakfast is included in the prices. The hotel has an American piano bar, a grill room, a restaurant, and a laundry, as well as a garage and parking area for patrons.

On the Arno

Hotel Principe, lungarno Vespucci 34, 50123 Firenze (tel. 055/284-848), is a real "find." Its façade is dignified, like an old embassy town house, and its 22 bedrooms have been well adapted. Each bedroom is treated differently, reflecting the high taste level of the owner, who blends antique and modern. Every room has a private bath—the original mammoth marble ones are retained on the lower two floors. Ask for one of the terrace rooms, where tables and chairs are set out for breakfast fronting the Arno. Double glass doors protect the bedrooms from street noises. There is central air conditioning. Singles with bath rent for 135,000 lire ($103) daily, and doubles run 220,000 lire ($167), including taxes and service. Finally, one of the nicest features of the hotel is its little walled garden in back where drinks are served.

Lungarno, borgo San Jacopo 14, 50125 Firenze (tel. 055/264-211). As you stand on the banks of the Arno, looking at the façade of the ten floors of the hotel, you find it difficult to believe it was built entirely in the 1960s. It's proof that a modern, comfortable hotel can be created in the old style without sacrificing conveniences of the 20th century. Imagine sitting in a stone tower suite, enjoying a room-long view through a picture window of the rooftops of Florence, including the duomo and campanile. Throughout the hotel is a collection of contemporary watercolors and oils. Around the fireplace is a "clutter wall" of framed art. On sunny days guests congregate on the upper terrace, enjoying drinks and a view of the bridges spanning the Arno. The bedrooms are consistently well designed and attractive, each having its own color theme. For the average accommodations, including service, taxes, and air conditioning, the rate in a single with shower is 150,000 lire ($114) daily, 220,000 lire ($167) in a double with bath.

Augustus e dei Congressi, piazzetta dell'Oro, 50123 Firenze (tel. 055/283-054), is for those who require modern comforts in a setting of historical and monumental Florence. The Ponte Vecchio is just a short stroll away, as is the Uffizi Gallery. The exterior is rather pillbox modern but the interior seems light, bright, and comfortable. The expansive lounge and drinking area is like an illuminated cave, with a curving ceiling and built-in conversational areas interlocked on several levels. Some of the bedrooms open onto little private balconies with garden furniture. Single rooms with shower rent for 100,000 lire ($76) to 150,000 lire ($114) daily, and doubles with private bath go for 140,000 lire ($106) to 200,000 lire ($152), with an extra sitting room going for 100,000 lire ($76). Air conditioning, satellite TV, service, and taxes are included.

Near the Duomo

In a well-preserved structure, **Hotel Monna Lisa** (yes, that's the right spelling), borgo Pinti 27, 50121 Firenze (tel. 055/247-9751), is a privately owned Renaissance palazzo. On a narrow street where carts once were driven, the palace façade is forbiddingly severe, in keeping with the style of its day. But when one enters the reception rooms, the atmosphere is inviting. Most of the great old rooms overlook either an inner patio or the garden in the rear. Each of the salons is handsomely furnished in a restrained way, utilizing many fine antiques and oil paintings. The gracious owner is Countess N. D. Oslavia Ciardi-Dupré. The bedrooms, which vary greatly, have private bath and air conditioning. Everywhere is a stamp of individuality and good taste. Breakfast is included in the price of 230,000 lire ($175) daily for a double, 160,000 lire ($122) for a single. No other meals are offered.

At Galluzzo

Relais Certosa, via Colle Ramole 2, 50124 Firenze (tel. 055/204-7171), a four-star hotel of exceptional merit, is set on five acres of land with tennis courts. The relais was originally a guesthouse for the monastery near here, but that gave way during the Renaissance to the villa that stands today. In the 19th century it was a farm. After centuries of use in private hands, it became a hotel in the 1970s, its original purpose fulfilled. The hotel could easily become your home in Florence. Convenient for motorists who want to avoid the hysterical center of Florence, the location is only ten minutes from the monumental district of the city and five minutes from the Rome-Milan expressway (A1 exit, marked "Firenze/Certosa"). Open all year, its rooms are well furnished with individual climate control, private bath, color TV, and mini-bar. Somehow the owners, the Bettoja family, have managed to blend Renaissance charm and style with today's comforts. The atmosphere is a special Florentine one. Singles rent for 188,000 lire ($143) daily, and doubles run 255,000 lire ($194), including a continental breakfast, service, and tax. All rooms face a park with views of the Tuscan hills and the Certosa monastery. For some of the best Tuscan dining in the area, you can patronize the Greenhouse Restaurant even if you're not a guest of the hotel. It offers regional specialties as well as continental dishes. Guests also enjoy a garden and terrace for drinks and snacks, a bar and piano bar, a heated swimming pool, a sauna, and a solarium. There's also space for 200 cars.

At Colli

Hotel Villa Carlotta, via Michele di Lando 3, 50125 Firenze (tel. 055/220-530). The lavish renovations that the owner poured into her distinguished establishment transformed it into one of the most charming smaller hotels in Florence. It was built during the Edwardian age as a private villa and acquired in the 1950s by Carlotta Buchholz, who named it after herself. When her daughter, Evelina Pagni, took the administrative reins, she enlarged the ground floor with a glassed-in extension, filled it with Persian carpets and family heirlooms, and restored the elaborate plaster detailing of the formal interior. The aura here is still very much that of a private villa. It's set in a residential section of the city, behind a neoclassical façade whose entrance columns are capped with stone lions and flanked with venerable cypresses. In 1985 all 27 bedrooms were upgraded with the addition of a sheathing of pink or blue silk wallpaper, reproduction antiques, silk bedspreads, private safety-deposit boxes, and crystal chandeliers. Each of the units also benefits from air conditioning, mini-bar, color TV, and views of the surrounding garden. High-season rates, with breakfast included, are 270,000 lire ($205) daily in a double, 195,000 lire ($148) in a single. The dining room serves meals ranging from the presentation of fresh salads to full culinary regalias, always accompanied by top-notch service and personal touches. The hotel lies only ten pedestrian minutes from the Ponte Vecchio, which by taxi cuts the time in half.

Torre di Bellosguardo, via Roti Michelozzi 2, 50125 Firenze (tel. 055/229-8145), is a treasure, not too well known. A four-star hotel, it consists of a 14th-century tower surrounded by a majestic villa. The location is on top of a hill about a mile and a half from the city walls with a spectacular view over Florence. The hotel is framed by an avenue of cypresses in the Tuscan style. The tower was from a manor house constructed here by a Florentine nobleman and friend of Dante. Two magnolia trees lead into a sunny veranda. Guests enter a frescoed ballroom. There are fewer than 20 bedrooms, no two alike. Your room might have a gilded four-poster or a 16th-century rosette-studded ceiling. Singles, doubles, and family accommodations are available, each with private bath and direct-dial phone. Singles rent for 200,000 lire ($152) daily; doubles cost 220,000 lire ($167) to 260,000 lire ($198). The garden around the hotel is almost like a park, with a series of terraces stretching toward Florence. In the garden is a swimming pool. This hotel merits a high recommendation.

---

3. Medium-Priced Hotels

OFF THE PIAZZA DELLA SIGNORIA

Opposite the Bargello Museum, **Grand Hotel Cavour,** via del Proconsolo 3, 50122 Firenze (tel. 055/295-290), is an elaborate palace built in the 13th century between via del Proconsolo and via Ricciarda (now via Dante Alighieri), on an important corner of the city, near the Badia Church, between the houses of the Cerchi and Pazzi families. The hotel belonged to the Cerchis, and in the lounge you can see where the old courtyard was laid out. In the basement, a historic well is called Beatrice's Well. The Portinaris, family of Dante's beloved Beatrice, lived nearby, and it is possible that the young woman actually drew water from the well. Certainly, such a chore was done by Beatrice's nurse, Monna Tessa. The Hotel Cavour came into being when Florence was the capital of Italy (1860–1865), and it was nicknamed "The Senators' Hotel" because it was frequented by the members of the highest assembly of the new state. The Cavour maintains its architectural splendor. The coved main lounge, with its frescoed ceiling and crystal chandelier, is of special interest, as is the old chapel, now used as a dining room. The altar and confessional are still there. The ornate ceiling and stained-glass windows reflect superb crafting. The Cavour attained a curious supremacy in Florence: in 1905, the first water elevator in town was installed to grant comfortable access to the upper floors. The hotel is now also centrally heated. All 92 bedrooms have private bath and phone. Singles rent for 80,000 lire ($60.75) daily. Twin-bedded rooms go for 110,000 lire ($83.50).

ON THE ARNO

Right at the entrance of the Arno-spanning Ponte Vecchio, **Hotel Continental,** lungarno Acciaiuoli 2, 50123 Firenze (tel. 055/282-392), occupies some choice real estate. Through the lounge windows and from some of the bedrooms, you can see the little jewelry and leather shops flanking the much-painted bridge. Despite its perch in the center of historic Florence, the hotel cut its teeth in the '60s, so its style of accommodation is utilitarian, with functional furniture, softened by the placement of decorative accessories. You reach your bedroom either by the elevator, or by climbing a wooden staircase (note that parts of the old stone structure have been retained). The air-conditioned bedrooms are furnished with Italian provincial pieces, color coordinated. The management likes to put up North Americans, knowing they'll be attracted to the roof terrace, a vantage point for viewing the piazzale Michelangelo, the Pitti Palace, the duomo, the campanile, and Fiesole. Artists fight to get the tiny simple rooms up in the tower ("Torre Guelfa dei Consorti"). All 62 bedrooms have private bath or shower. Singles cost 84,000 lire ($63.75) to 134,000 lire ($102) daily, and doubles go for 138,000 lire ($105) to 198,000 lire ($151). A continental breakfast is included.

Hotel Balestri, piazza Mentana 7, 50122 Firenze (tel. 055/214-743). The buff-colored front of this hotel faces a quiet square, while its side looks out over the Arno and the traffic running along its quay. Built as a private home in 1888 (the date is set into the floor of the entryway in contrasting shades of marble), the hotel has a lobby with vaulted ceilings, red-and-white stone floors, Oriental rugs, and modern paintings. The reception is friendly, and the hotel has been run by the same family for generations. Breakfast is included in the room price of 95,000 lire ($72.25) daily for a single, 136,000 lire ($103) for a double. All units contain private baths.

Hotel Columbus, lungarno Cristoforo Colombo 22A, 50136 Firenze (tel. 055/677-251), is a modern hotel, built and furnished with good taste, offering 99 rooms with bath or shower and private balcony. Although it's set quite a distance from the city's major attractions, it is still only a 20-minute walk from the Ponte Vecchio. The air-conditioned public rooms, with light-inviting windows, have pleasant, informal furnishings. The dining room has round tables, with ladder-back chairs, potted greenery, and a sense of space. Each of the bedrooms is compact, in the motel fashion, with everything built in: bedside table, lights, and all. There's no fussy decor—severe but restful. Singles are charged 1,000 lire ($61.50) daily in rooms with private bath; doubles, 122,000 lire ($92.75) with private bath. Breakfast, taxes, and service are included.

NEAR PIAZZA SS. ANNUNZIATA

On one of the most quietly elegant squares in Florence, you find **Loggiato dei Serviti,** piazza SS. Annunziata 3, 50121 Firenze (tel. 055/219-165). Built in the early 1500s as a monastery, it has served, in one capacity or another, as a hotel since the turn of this century. Its entrance lies beneath the soaring arcades facing the Renaissance Hospital of the Innocents and an imposing equestrian statue. More than any other hotel in the neighborhood, its bedrooms evoke the aura of an austerely elegant monastery, with vaulted or beamed ceilings, some of which are painted with Renaissance-inspired designs. Each contains a TV, phone, and a private bath. With breakfast included, singles cost 86,500 lire ($65.75) daily, and doubles rent for 136,500 ($104). A duplex suite, accommodating up to four people, goes for

200,000 lire ($152) to 300,000 lire ($228). All the rates include breakfast, taxes, and service.

NEAR THE OPERA

In the heart of Florence, **Queen Palace Hotel,** via Solferino 5, 50123 Firenze (tel. 055/296-818), is in a quiet, fashionable area near the opera house, the U.S. Consulate, and several big hotels. The rooms, hidden behind an 18th-century palazzo façade, have comfortable proportions and have been fully modernized, all with air conditioning, frigo-bar, and color TV. The general manager, Mrs. Francesca Scaglione Grazzini, charges 126,000 lire ($95.75) daily in a single, 178,000 lire ($135) in a double, 250,000 lire ($190) in a triple, and 275,000 lire ($209) for two persons in a suite with a bedroom and a living room. Breakfast and taxes are included in the tariffs.

AT COLLI

On the edge of Florence, **Villa Belvedere,** via Benedetto Castelli 3, 50124 Firenze (tel. 055/222-501), stands in grounds that once belonged to the Medici, although the present building is a reconstruction. It's suitable for those wanting a tranquil setting, gardens for sunbathing, a swimming pool for quick dips, and a tennis court for exercise. The 27 rooms, with private bath and air conditioning, are efficient and well planned. The villa is closed in December, January, and February. Singles pay 140,000 lire ($106) daily for a room and a continental breakfast. Doubles are charged from 190,000 lire ($144) for a room and breakfast.

Note: Some doubles, renting for 210,000 lire ($160), have a veranda with a panoramic view of Florence. The use of the swimming pool, tennis court, and garage parking is free, and tax is included in the tariffs. The villa lies on the Siena-Roma road (take bus 11 or 37; the stop is Poggio Imperiale).

---

4. Budget Lodgings

OFF THE PIAZZA DELLA SIGNORIA

Within a few minutes' walk of the Ponte Vecchio and the Signoria, **Porta Rossa,** via Porta Rossa 19, 50123 Firenze (tel. 055/287-551), has a history dating from the 13th century, although the present structure is from the 19th. Its original construction was ordered by a silk merchant who offered to house dozens of his competitors here during their visits to Florence. To eliminate their presence at the markets the following day, he drugged their wine, causing them to sleep late into the following afternoon. To this day the symbol of the house is the poppy, whose likeness is carved above the windows and doors.

The lobby, the breakfast room, and the beautiful bar area are outfitted in a 19th-century style the manager calls "decadent romantic." This includes vaulted lunette ceilings, stained-glass inserts, and lavishly carved paneling. Clients who sleep here today are following in a tradition set long ago by such distinguished overnighters as Stendhal and Balzac. True to the origins of the hotel, the clients still include visiting merchants who exhibit their merchandise to wholesalers in the sprawling bedrooms. The labyrinthine interior reveals slightly faded antiques, old jardinières, dingy plaster, and carved stone at virtually every corner.

Your room will probably (that's probably) be high-ceilinged and sparsely furnished. Accommodations rent for 79,500 lire ($60.50) daily in a single with bath. Doubles with bath cost 119,500 lire ($90.75).

NEAR THE RAILWAY STATION

A handsome structure, **Villa Azalee,** viale Fratelli Rosselli 44, 50123 Firenze (tel. 055/214-242), is a remake of a gracious 19th-century corner villa, with a big garden. The owners have provided a personal touch in both atmosphere and decor. The decorating is tasteful: tall, white-paneled doors with ornate brass fittings, parquet floors, crystal chandeliers, and antiques intermixed with credible reproductions. The lounge is as in a private home, and the bedrooms have distinction (one, in particular, boasts a flouncy canopy bed). Rooms with bath cost 88,000 lire ($67) daily for a single, 140,000 lire ($106) for a double, including breakfast, taxes, service, and air conditioning.

Nuova Italia, via Faenza 26, 50123 Firenze (tel. 055/287-508), is a renovated hotel in a 17th-century building in the center of Florence. The hotel consists of 24 rooms, all with private baths. All the bedrooms have pieces by Salvarani, a well-known Italian furniture maker. Rooms are pleasantly furnished, and a phone comes with each unit. The rate in a single ranges from 52,000 lire ($39.50) daily to 58,000 lire ($44); in a double, from 80,000 lire ($60.75) to 92,000 lire ($70). A continental breakfast is included. Some large rooms are particularly suitable for families, to whom the management—the Viti family—grants special reductions. The location is only one block from the railway station, near the San Lorenzo market (the flea market) and the Medici Chapels. A garage is also nearby.

Hotel Mario's, via Faenza 89, 50123 Firenze (tel. 055/212-039), has been completely restored and refurnished in 16th-century Florentine style. Mario Noce is a gracious host, and he and his staff speak English. His three-star hotel is spotless, and all 16 rooms have private baths. Singles rent for 30,000 lire ($45.50) to 75,000 lire ($57) daily; doubles and twins go for 95,000 lire ($72.25) to 110,000 lire ($83.50), and triples run 125,000 lire ($95) to 150,000 lire ($114). Rates include a generous breakfast, taxes, and service. Although you'll find cheaper inns in Florence, the service, hospitality, and good level of innkeeping make Mario's worth your while.

OFF THE PIAZZA DELL'INDIPENDENZA

An "E" for effort is due **Rapallo,** via Santa Caterina d'Alessandria 7, 50129 Firenze (tel. 055/472-412), as all its rooms have indications of attempts to make them liveable and comfortable, including air conditioning in summer. Without succeeding in being typical of Florence, it is, nevertheless, newish (completely revamped), fresh, and inviting. The lounge, ingeniously using small space, is brightened by planters, Oriental rugs, and barrel stools set in the corners for drinking and conversation. The bedrooms—30 in all, some with private bath—are furnished mostly with blond-wood suites, quite pleasant, and all have private safe, direct-dial phone, and frigo-bar. The twin-bedded rooms have end-to-end beds, à la Scandinavia. A single with shower costs 77,000 lire ($52.50) daily. Doubles go for 120,000 lire ($91.25) with complete plumbing facilities. Breakfast, service, and taxes are included in the rates.

Hotel Splendor, via S. Gallo 30, 50129 Firenze (tel. 055/483-427). Although it lies within a ten-minute walk of the duomo, the residential neighborhood it occupies is a world away from the milling hordes of the tourist district. The hotel takes over three high-ceilinged floors of a 19th-century apartment building. Its elegantly faded public rooms evoke the kind of family-run pensione which, early in the century, attracted genteel visitors from northern Europe for prolonged art-related visits. This is the domain of the Masoero family, whose 31 rooms contain an eclectic array of semi-antique furniture and much of the ambience of bedrooms in a private house. About 20 of the accommodations contain a private bath, and each has a phone. With a buffet breakfast included, bathless rooms cost 51,000 lire ($38.75) daily in a single, 75,000 lire ($57) in a double. Units with bath rent for 55,000 lire ($41.75) single, 89,000 lire ($67.75) double.

5. The Pick of the Pensiones

ALONG VIA TORNABUONI

Near the Arno and the piazza S. Trinità, **Tornabuoni Beacci,** via Tornabuoni 3, 50123 Firenze (tel. 055/212-645), is on the principal shopping street of Florence. The pensione occupies the three top floors of a 14th-century palazzo. All its living rooms have been furnished in a tatty provincial style, with bowls of flowers, parquet floors, a formal fireplace, old paintings, murals, and rugs. The hotel was completely renovated recently, but it still bears an air of gentility. The roof terrace, surrounded by potted plants and flowers, is for late-afternoon drinks or breakfast. The view of the nearby churches, towers, and rooftops is worth experiencing. The names in the guest book are numerous, including in days of yore many personalities such as John Steinbeck, the Gish sisters, and Fredric March. The bedrooms are moderately well furnished. Every room of the first-class pensione has private bath. The half-board rate ranges from 120,000 lire ($91.25) to 236,000 lire ($179) daily for two persons, with taxes and service included. It offers good value, and there's an elevator, a bar, and air conditioning.

La Residenza, via Tornabuoni 8, 50123 Firenze (tel. 055/284-197), lies right in the hub of Florence, on an elegant shopping street of fashion houses, boutiques, and palaces. It occupies the top floors of a 16th-century Renaissance building, just a few blocks from American Express and the Arno, right next door to the Palazzo Strozzi. The palace housing the pensione belongs to the descendants of the Tornabuoni, the family of Lorenzo de' Medici's mother. The pensione offers freshness, comfort, and style. The elevator is a mahogany-and-glass jewel rising up the interior of the stone stairwell, whose entrance is graced by a statue of a bashful Venus. The dining room is elegant with high ceilings, and antiques are extensively used. The rooms have been redecorated with reproductions and color-coordinated pieces, and some have private balconies. You can have morning coffee in the roof garden, enjoying the wisteria, pots of flowering plants, and especially the view. With breakfast included, bathless singles cost 63,500 lire ($48.25) daily, while singles with bath go for 79,000 lire ($60). Doubles with bath and breakfast are tabbed at 122,500 lire ($93). These prices are all inclusive. The bathrooms here have been recently renovated, and all rooms have direct-dial phones.

NEAR THE PONTE VECCHIO

Directly on the Arno, **Quissana e Ponte Vecchio,** lungarno Archibusieri 4, 50122 Firenze (tel. 055/216-692), stands near the Ponte Vecchio and within an easy walk of the Uffizi Gallery. A late-19th-century Florentine pensione, it is serviced by an elevator that takes you to its 40-room apartment upstairs which has been furnished in a home-like fashion. Singles rent for 80,000 lire ($60.75) daily with private bath. A double goes for 129,000 lire ($98) with private bath. A continental breakfast is included. The pensione's nicest feature is a loggia overlooking the Arno. Some scenes of E. M. Forster's *A Room with a View* were filmed here.

ON THE LEFT BANK

In existence since the 15th century, **Pensione Annalena,** via Romana 34, 50125 Firenze (tel. 055/222-403), has gone through many owners, including the Medici. Once a convent, it has, in the past three-quarters of a century, been a haven for artists, poets, sculptors, and writers (Mary McCarthy once wrote of its importance as a cultural center). During a great deal of that period it was the domain of the late sculptor Olinto Calastri. Now it is owned by Claudio Salvestrini, who attracts paying guests who are sympathetic to the special qualities of the Annalena. For rooms with a continental breakfast, singles with bath cost 89,500 lire ($68) daily; doubles are 188,500 lire ($143) with private bath. Service and taxes are included.

During the war, the Annalena was the center of much underground work, as many Jews and rebel Italians found safety hidden away in an underground room behind a secret door. The pensione lies about a five-minute walk from the Pitti Palace, ten from the Ponte Vecchio.

Pensione Pitti Palace, via Barbadori 2, 50125 Firenze (tel. 055/282-257), a few steps from the Ponte Vecchio, near the Pitti Palace, is a well-run pensione, the personal statement of Amedeo Pinto and his American-born wife, Mary Ann. Both are helpful, offering advice about how to cope with the tourist life in Florence (they'll even give you a map to send you on your way). They serve breakfast in their high-ceilinged dining room. One of the sitting rooms is especially cozy, decorated with warm colors and what look like family portraits. The 40 rooms rent for 118,000 lire ($89.75) daily in a double with private bath, from 77,000 lire ($58.50) in a single with bath. Bathless doubles are priced at 96,000 lire ($73), while bathless singles go for 61,000 lire ($46.25).

NEAR SANTA CROCE

A rare find in Florence, **Rigatti,** lungarno Diaz 2, 50122 Firenze (tel. 055/213-022), is an establishment doing what it can to preserve the aura of an elegant private palace still studded with many of the original frescoes and antiques. The loyal clientele includes teachers, art historians, and an international collection of friends of the cultivated family running it, the Rigatti. The owners are Gabriella di Benedictus and her brother, Luigi, both of whom are descendants of the Rigatti family who set up the pensione in 1907 in a 14th-century palazzo. Set on the banks of a noisy Arno quay, the hotel's entrance takes clients up a narrow sidewalk, through massive wooden doors, and up a small elevator to the second floor. There, a series of elegantly furnished high-ceilinged rooms with rococo lighting fixtures, musical instruments, and 19th-century chairs create a baronial setting that extends into the simple and comfortable bedrooms. The windows of these open onto carved stone columns that look out, depending on the exposure, over the river, a garden filled with azaleas, or a narrow side street of Renaissance buildings. On the upper floor, a covered loggia with views of the piazza della Signoria offers a place where guests are sometimes able to order coffee or drinks. A generous continental breakfast is included in the price, which with bath ranges from 51,000 lire ($38.75) daily in a single and from 81,000 lire ($61.50) in a double. The Rigatti is closed during most of December, January, and February.

PIAZZA DELLA REPUBBLICA

Founded in 1879, **Pensione Pendini,** via Strozzi 2, 50123 Firenze (tel. 055/211-170), is still family owned and run, offering an old-fashioned environment in a distinguished setting of Florence. Your room may overlook the active piazza or front an inner courtyard (more peaceful). One of the oldest pensiones in Florence, it has 37 rooms, and the location is on the fourth floor of an arcaded building. A single with bath goes for 60,000 lire ($45.50) to 74,000 lire ($56.25) daily; doubles run 85,000 lire ($64.50) to 115,000 lire ($87.50). The all-purpose lounge is furnished family style with a piano and card tables. The breakfast room is pleasantly and modestly provincial, and some of the bedrooms have quite a lot of character, with reproductions of antiques. The Pendini is not for everyone, but it's one of the long-enduring favorites among pensione devotees visiting Florence.

Hotel Pensione Maxim, via dei Medici 4, 50123 Firenze (tel. 055/217-474), in the center of Florence, is a well-run accommodation where your host is English-speaking Paolo Maioli. His rooms are spacious, comfortable, modernized, and clean. Singles and doubles are rented with and without bath, costing 35,000 lire ($26.50) to 40,000 lire ($30.50) daily in a single, rising to 51,000 lire ($38.75) to 61,000 lire ($46.25) in a double. Some of the accommodations are suited for either triples or quads. A continental breakfast is served in an inviting room, and it is included in the tariffs quoted along with service and taxes.

NEAR PIAZZA DELLA SS. ANNUNZIATA

Small and charming, the **Hotel Morandi alla Crocetta,** via Laura 50, 50121 Firenze (tel. 055/234-4747), is administered by one of the most experienced hoteliers in Florence, a sprightly matriarch, Katherine Doyle, who came to Florence from her native England when she was 12. It contains all the elements needed for a Florentine pensione, lying on a little-visited backstreet. The structure that contains it was built in the 1500s as a convent. The bedrooms have been tastefully restored, filled with framed examples of 19th-century needlework, beamed ceilings, and antiques. Each contains a renovated private bath, phone, color TV, radio, and frigobar. In the best Tuscan tradition, the tall windows are sheltered from the summer sunlight with heavy draperies. Singles cost 63,000 lire ($48) daily; doubles, 96,000 lire ($73). You register in a high-ceilinged and gracefully austere salon filled with Persian carpets.

NEAR PIAZZA D'AZEGLIO

A good, inexpensive choice, the **Albergo Losanna,** via Alfieri 9, 50121 Firenze (tel. 055/245-840) is a tiny—only nine rooms—family-run place off viale Antonio Gramsci, between the piazzale Donatello and the piazza d'Azeglio. It offers utter simplicity and cleanliness. Bus 6 stops a block and a half away (get off at Mattonaia). The bedrooms are homey and well kept. A single room without bath costs 38,500 lire ($29.25) daily, the price increasing to 59,000 lire ($44.75) in a bathless double. A double with bath rents for 62,000 lire ($47), and a single with bath is 42,000 lire ($32). The tax is added, but a continental breakfast is included. There's free parking on a quiet street.

NEAR THE OPERA

Just a block from the Arno, **Ariele,** via Magenta 11, 50123 Firenze (tel. 055/211-509), calls itself "Your Home in Florence." It's an old corner villa that has been converted into a roomy pensione. The building is impressive architecturally, with large salons and lofty ceilings. The furnishings, however, combine antique with functional. The bedrooms are a grab bag of comfort. There are 30 units, all with bath or shower. Singles range in price from 68,000 lire ($51.75) daily; doubles, from 92,000 lire ($70); and triples, from 120,000 lire ($91.25). The tariffs include a continental breakfast, taxes, and service.

Pensione Bretagna, lungarno Corsini 6, 50123 Firenze (tel. 055/263-618), run by the helpful Guidi family, offers bed-and-breakfast in one of the earliest Renaissance palaces of Florence. Depending on the plumbing, singles go for 42,000 lire ($32) to 51,000 lire ($38.75) daily; doubles, 67,000 lire ($51) to 81,000 lire ($61.50), the latter with private bath. All rates include breakfast, taxes, and service. Accommodations are furnished in a basic style, but the public rooms with their gilded stuccowork and painted ceilings testify to the splendor of former times. Off the drawing room, a balcony overlooks the Arno.

NEAR THE DUOMO

About two blocks from the duomo, **Soggiorno Brunori,** via del Proconsolo 5, 50122 Firenze (tel. 055/263-648), is an unpretentious little pensione in the center of the historic district. Its comfortably simple bedrooms are outfitted in angular furniture, soft colors, and modern baths. The English-speaking management charges 46,000 lire ($35) daily for doubles with bath, the cost rising to 63,000 lire ($48) for triples with bath. Bathless doubles cost 36,000 lire ($27.25), while bathless triples are priced at 51,000 lire ($38.75).

NEAR THE RAILWAY STATION

The building that houses the **Pensione Serena,** via Fiume 20, 50123 Firenze (tel. 055/213-643), was erected in 1905 as an apartment house. Today it still contains a scattering of stained-glass doors and ornate plaster ceilings, but the furnishings are considerably simpler than was the case in the building's heyday. The owner of this seven-room pensione makes guests feel comfortable and welcome as soon as they walk in. After riding the elevator to the first floor, guests register in the wide hallway and are taken to a spaciously high-ceilinged, but dimly illuminated bedroom. Doubles without shower cost 35,000 lire ($26.50) daily, going up to 44,000 lire ($33.50) with shower. Breakfast is additional.

Pensione Elite, via della Scala 12, 50123 Firenze (tel. 055/215-395), is a little pensione worthy of mention. Modest in scale and appointments, it lies about a two-block walk from the main railway station. It's also convenient for exploring most of the major attractions of monumental Florence. The owner, Maurizio Maccarini, speaks enough English to get by, and he's a helpful, welcoming host. His charges are based on the plumbing, as some of his units contain a private shower, for which you'll pay more, of course. Singles without shower cost 25,000 lire ($19) nightly, with doubles priced from 36,000 lire ($27.25) to 41,000 lire ($31.25). Triples range from 51,000 lire ($38.75) to 56,000 lire ($42.50).

Soggiorno Erina, via Fiume 17, 50123 Firenze (tel. 055/284-343), lies in a position convenient to the railway station, along a street lined with residential buildings. It sits on the third floor of a 19th-century building whose façade is ornamented with sculpted faces peering from above the windows. The wrought-iron elevator requires a 10-lira coin before it will take you to the hotel's third-floor reception area, or else you can take the stairs. Seven double bedrooms stretch off a wide central hallway. The place is basic and simple, but newcomers are made to feel welcome. Doubles rent for 61,000 lire ($43.25) daily. Each unit has a private bath and a few offer balconies.

Albergo Ester, largo Fratelli Alinari 15, 50123 Firenze (tel. 055/212-741), sits opposite via Fiume, in a middle-class apartment building a few minutes' walk from the railway station. Take a creaking elevator to the second floor. The lobby is unpretentious, but several of the rooms are quite spacious, and all of them are clean but basic. Bathless rooms rent for 25,000 lire ($19) daily in a single, 36,000 lire ($27.25) in a double. No breakfast is served, but there are many cafés in the neighborhood.

NEAR PONTE S. TRINITA

A simple pensione, **Soggiorno Castelli,** borgo SS. Apostoli 25, 50123 Firenze (tel. 055/214-213), has seven comfortable rooms on the upper floor of a 200-year-old palazzo. Set about a block from the Arno on a narrow street in the old city, it charges 55,000 lire ($41.75) to 62,000 lire ($47) daily in a double, depending on the plumbing. A bathless single rents for 36,000 lire ($27.25). Breakfast is included.

After checking into your hotel (and assuming you've escaped the board requirement, at least for one meal), you'll begin an even more interesting search—this time for a restaurant that may represent your introduction to Florentine cuisine.

6. The Restaurants of Florence

The Tuscan cuisine should please most North Americans (except for some of the hair-raising specialties), as it's simply flavored, without rich spices, based on the hearty, bountiful produce brought in from the hills. Florentine restaurants are not generally acclaimed by gourmets as much as those of Rome, but many dishes are prepared so well that the Tuscan kitchen is considered among the finest in Italy.

Florentines often assert that the cooking in the other regions of Italy "offends the palate."

The case was stated most critically by Mary McCarthy, who wrote: "The food in the restaurants is bad, for the most part, monotonous, and rather expensive. Many of the Florentine specialties—tripe, paunch, rabbit, and a mixture of the combs, livers, hearts, and testicles of roosters—do not appeal to the foreign palate." The statement is funnier than it is true, although I concede the point about some of the specialties.

But one of the most typical platters is the Florentine beefsteak, savored by foreigners and locals alike. I don't know where Ms. McCarthy dined in Florence, which admittedly has many expensive citadels dispensing viands at "Grand Duke" prices. On the other hand, the city often stuns its many visitors with its sheer preponderance of good moderately priced eating establishments.

The one Italian wine all foreigners recognize, the ruby-red Chianti, usually in a straw bottle, comes from Tuscany. Although shunned by some wine snobs, it is a fit complement to many a local repast.

Armed with a knife and fork, we'll eat our way down through the pick of the restaurants. I hasten to point out that the reference to "down" is in price only. Many of my most memorable and top-level dinners have been in some of the completely unheralded trattorie and "buca" (cellar) restaurants of the city.

THE TOP RESTAURANTS

Considered by many gourmets as the best restaurant in Italy, **Ristorante Enoteca,** via Ghibellina 87, near St. Croce (tel. 242-777), also has one of the finest wine cellars. Housed on the ground floor of the 15th-century Giacometti-Ciofi Palace in the center of historic Florence, this restaurant might be called a moveable feast in more than one sense. Depending on the weather, the service moves from a covered niche at the base of a heroic statue of Apollo to an open-air courtyard with a view of the stars and a series of vine-covered lattices, to one of two formal interior rooms where the furnishings include a porphyry fireplace, Renaissance antiques, and modern paintings. Of course, masses of flowers and silver candelabra are scattered throughout, but the main feature here is the personalities of the Nice- and Modena-born owners, Annie Feolde and Giorgio Pinchiorri. She is the chef, and he is the sommelier. The establishment began as a wine bar (that's roughly what *enoteca* means in Latin). When Annie began cooking in 1979, she quickly raised the level of cuisine to those high-quality heights that no Florentine restaurant could match. Guests have ranged from Danny Kaye to the princess of Holland. The representatives of *Relais & Châteaux* showed up, including the establishment among their prestigious listings. When I first inspected the kitchens here, the phone was almost constantly ringing with calls from the Four Seasons in New York.

The food is an inspired blend of French moderne and Italian cuisine, with a fixed-price menu degustation at around 80,000 lire ($60.75) and a cuisine du marché fixed-price meal at around 90,000 lire ($68.50). For 80,000 lire ($60.75), a menu degustation is offered, consisting of old Tuscan recipes that have been largely forgotten or impossible to find in other restaurants. The specialties change daily, but notable offerings include cannelloni of salmon with a mousseline of fresh clams, caramelized ricotta with a fondue of fresh peppers, and other equally imaginative recipes. Some of these dishes in the hands of a lesser chef might be an abject failure. But in the hands of that statuesque red-haired queen of the Florentine kitchen, Annie Feolde, they are usually nothing less than sublime. The restaurant, open from 12:30 to 1:30 p.m. and 8 to 10 p.m., is closed all day Sunday and for Monday lunch and during the entire month of August.

Da Dante–Al Lume di Candela, via delle Terme 23R (tel. 294-566), is uniquely located in a 13th-century tower that was partially leveled when its patrician family fell from grace (the prestige of Tuscan families was once reflected in how high their family towers soared). With its sophisticated tavern decor, the restaurant offers a typically Florentine cuisine, under the guiding, deft hand of the padrone in the kitchen. In a candlelit atmosphere, it makes for a romantic dining place, having drawn celebrities in the past. This restaurant has been much improved since Dante Poggiali took over. He knows and anticipates the whims of discerning patrons. Among his main-course specialties, I recommend the entrecôte alla Diana or perhaps the veal kidney in a tempting sauce. The most spectacular dessert is the crêpes suzette, served only for two persons. For a full, satisfying lunch, expect to pay 36,000 lire ($27.25), and for a worthy dinner, your tab is likely to run as high as 60,000 lire ($45.50). The bistro, which lies off the major shopping artery, via Por Santa Maria, near the straw market, is open from noon to 2 p.m. and 6:30 to 11 p.m.; closed Sunday, Monday at lunch, and August 10 to August 25.

Harry's Bar, lungarno Vespucci 22R (tel. 296-700), is an enclave of expatriate and well-heeled visiting Yankees. From its prime position on the Arno, it deserves its well-earned reputation. You not only get a welcome from Leo at the bar and the staff in the dining room, but here you'll find the easiest place in Florence to meet your fellow Americans and (at least for a while) escape from some of the glory of the Renaissance. On a recent visit I heard three words of Italian from a frustrated woman from Alabama who was kindly assured by the Tuscan waiter (in English) that she need struggle no more. As if by inner radar, martini drinkers and hungry diners know they'll be able to order from an international menu—small, but select, and beautifully prepared. Several soups are featured daily, including cream of green pea or cream of chicken. The gamberetti (crayfish) cocktail is most tempting. Harry has created his own tortellini (stuffed pasta), but Harry's hamburger and his club sandwich are the most popular items. The chef also prepares about a dozen specialties every day: breast of chicken "our way," grilled giant-size scampi, and a lean broiled sirloin steak. An apple tart with fresh cream nicely finishes off a meal, which will cost from 45,000 lire ($34.25). Harry's is open from noon to 3 p.m. and 5:30 p.m. to midnight daily except Sunday. Closed from early December to early January.

Sabatini, via de' Panzani 9A (tel. 282-802), despite its unchic location near the railway station, has long been extolled by Florentines and visitors alike as the finest of the characteristic restaurants of the city. To celebrate my return visit to this restaurant, I ordered the same main course I had when I was originally researching this guide. It was boiled Valdarno chicken with a savory green sauce. Back then I had complained to the waiter that the chicken was tough. He'd replied, "But, of course!" The Florentine likes chicken with muscle, not the hot-house variety so favored by Americans. Having eaten a lot of Valdarno chicken since those long-ago days back in the '60s, I was more appreciative of Sabatini's dish. But on a subsequent visit I found some of the other main courses more delectable, especially the veal scaloppine with artichokes. Of course, you can always order a good sole meunière and the classic beefsteak Florentine. American-style coffee is also served, following the Florentine cake, called zuccotto. Count on spending 50,000 lire ($38) to 75,000 lire ($57) per person. The restaurant is open from 12:30 to 3:30 p.m. and 7:30 to 11:30 p.m. daily except Monday. Reservations are important.

Ristorante Oliviero, via della Terme 51 (tel. 287-643), has a long tradition and a top-drawer reputation, and is frequented by some of the most fashionable denizens of Florence. Its cuisine is appropriate for the city of Donatello: original and imaginative dishes. Come here only with a large appetite for rich and, at the same time, subtle food. Under the clever eye of the director, guests are welcomed from all over the world to consummate service and courtesy. To begin your dinner, I recommend the crêpes alla fiorentina. Among fish dishes, the filet of sole Oliviero would please Neptune. Delicie di vitello alla moda du chef is another specialty. For dessert, either crêpes suzette or a soufflé for two is recommended. Expect to spend from 55,000 lire ($41.75) up. The restaurant is open from 7:30 p.m. to 1 a.m. nightly except Sunday. After-theater dinner is served. At 8 p.m. there's music in the piano bar. The restaurant is closed for vacation in August.

MODERATE TO BUDGET DINING
For fine meals at reasonable prices, sample the following establishments.

Near the Duomo
Giannino in San Lorenzo, borgo San Lorenzo 37R (tel. 212-206), a short walk from the duomo, prepares some of the finest steaks and roasts in Florence. Serving diners upstairs and down, Giannino crackles with an open-fire grill, usually chock-full of golden brown roast chickens turning on the spit. Thus its reputation as a rosticceria. Many diners come here for one of the juicy, charcoal-grilled Florentine steaks. For starters, tortellini alla panna is a house specialty. To finish, the Florentine cake, zuccotto, will completely destroy your waistline but please your tastebuds. Count on spending from 35,000 lire ($26.50) up if you order à la carte. Giannino is further suited to low budgeteers: it serves a 19,000-lira ($14.50) tourist menu, for which you must specifically ask the waiter. Late at night you may want to drop in for a pizza, as the restaurant's also a pizzeria. The best one I've tried here is the pizza capricciosa, made with ham, mushrooms, and cheese. Giannino shuts down on Thursday but is open other days from 11:30 a.m. to 10:30 p.m.

Trattoria Coco Lezzone, via del Parioncino 26R (tel. 287-178). In Florentine dialect, the establishment's name refers to the sauce-stained apron of the extroverted chef who established this place more than a century ago. Today some of the heartiness of the Tuscan countryside can be purchased for the price of a meal at this duet of tile-covered rooms on a backstreet a short walk from the duomo in the historic district of Florence. Reservations in this crowded, bustling trattoria are never accepted. Florentine "blue bloods" wait with workers crowding in on their lunch hours for a seat at one of the long tables. Go early before the rush begins if you want a seat. The fare includes generous portions of boiled meats with a green sauce, pasta fagiole (beans), ossobuco, tripe, or beefsteak Florentine. Full meals cost 36,000 lire ($27.25) to 45,000 lire ($34.25) per person, and are served from noon to 3 p.m. and 7:30 to 10:30 p.m. daily except Sunday and Tuesday evening in winter. In summer, the place is also closed on Saturday and Sunday.

Near Ponte S. Trinità
Ristorante Natale, lungarno Acciaioli 80R (tel. 213-968), between the Ponte Vecchio and the Ponte S. Trinità, is an excellent choice for good food and leisurely dining along the Arno. A big refrigerator case greets you as you enter from the riverside quay. The decor includes paintings and old photos of the street life of Florence, plus wrought-iron chandeliers with dragons and their slayers hanging from the vaulted ceilings. I've found that this restaurant's kitchen is among the best in Florence—and its prices are below those of more-heralded establishments nearby. You might begin with fried squash blossoms in springtime or fresh asparagus and peas. Daily specials include veal piccata, beefsteak Florentine, fried chicken with zucchini, and scampi flambé. Full meals range upward from 38,000 lire ($29). A second room in the back offers additional seating. The restaurant is open from noon to 3 p.m. and 7:15 to 10:30 p.m. daily except Tuesday; also closed from the third week in July to the third week in August.

Near the Piazza della Signoria
Il Cavallino, via della Farine 6 (tel. 215-818), is the kind of discreetly famous restaurant where Florentines invariably go just to be with one another. It is on a tiny street (which probably won't even be on your map) that leads into the piazza della Signoria at its northern end, not far from the equestrian statue. There's usually a gracious reception at the door, especially if you called ahead for a reservation. The walls are dotted with unusual art, and seating is divided into three rooms, two of which have vaulted ceilings and peach-colored marble floors. The main room looks

out over the piazza right in the heartbeat of Florence. Menu items include typical Tuscan fare, including an assortment of boiled meats in a green herb sauce, grilled filet of steak, breast of chicken Medici style, a mixed fish fry, grilled sole, and the inevitable Florentine spinach. The restaurant, charging from 38,000 lire ($29) for a complete meal, is open from noon to 2:30 p.m. and 7 to 9:30 p.m.; closed on Wednesday and in August.

Paoli, via dei Tavolini 12R, near the piazza della Signoria (tel. 216-215), between the duomo and the piazza della Signoria, is one of the finest restaurants in Florence, turning out a host of specialties. But it could be recommended almost solely for its medieval-tavern atmosphere, with arches and ceramics stuck into the walls like medallions. The walls are adorned with frescoes. Its pastas are homemade. The fettuccine alla Paoli is served piping hot. The chef also does a superb rognoncino (kidney) trifolato and a sole meunière. A recommendable side dish is piselli (garden peas) alla fiorentina. If you select a complete meal from the specialties described, expect to pay around 36,000 lire ($27.25) to 48,000 lire ($36.50). Food is served from noon to 2:30 p.m. and 7 to 10:30 p.m. daily except Thursday.

Trattoria Antico Fattore, via Lambertesca 1 (tel. 261-215), on a backstreet near the Uffizi, is an inviting place where the owners speak English and cook good Tuscan food. As you enter the trattoria, with its dark wood and marble furniture, you're greeted by a tempting array of antipasti, ranging from marinated anchovies to salami to ham to fried zucchini flowers—what have you. Follow your pasta selection with a Florentine steak or other grilled or roast meats. Local fare, which includes chicken and guinea fowl as well as tasty Tuscan desserts, is all fresh cooked. You can have some of the good regional bread with your meal, or perhaps you'd prefer the chunky rolls called *stinchi,* pronounced "stinky." Meals cost from 35,000 lire ($26.50). The trattoria is open from 12:30 to 2:30 p.m. and 7:30 to 10:30 p.m. Tuesday through Saturday; closed Sunday and Monday.

Da Pennello, via Dante Alighieri 4R (tel. 294-848), is a family-style place, operated informally. The waiters speak some English. The food is top-notch, produced with skill by the women in the kitchen. The trattoria offers many Florentine specialties on its à la carte menu. A filling and good-tasting dish is spaghetti alla carbonara. Da Pennello is known for its wide selection of antipasti, and, if you wish, you can fill your plate with it, making a meal out of these delectable hors d'oeuvres. The kitchen here makes its own ravioli. To follow, you can have deviled roast chicken. Typically Italian dishes include a plate of mixed roasts and a Florentine beefsteak. The chef posts daily specials, and sometimes it's best to order one of these, as the food offered was bought fresh that day at the market. A Florentine cake, zuccotto, rounds out the meal. You can count on spending from 35,000 lire ($26.50) if you order à la carte. The restaurant, serving from noon to 2:30 p.m. and 7:30 to 9:30 p.m., is on a narrow street, near Dante's house, about a five-minute walk from the Duomo in the direction of the Uffizi. Closed Sunday night, Monday, in August, and from December 25 to January 3.

Da Ganino, piazza dei Cimatori (tel. 214-125), is a well-established restaurant, staffed with the kind of waiters who take the quality of your meal as their personal responsibility. This little-known restaurant has vaulted ceilings, glazed walls, and an array of paintings by Florentine artists. Someone will recite to you the frequently changing specialties of the day, including well-seasoned versions of Tuscan beans, spinach risotto, grilled veal liver, grilled veal chops, and Florentine beefsteak on the bone. The cost of your gastronomic sins will be figured on a paper tablecloth. The bill will usually average 40,000 lire ($30.50). The place is open daily except Sunday from 1 to 3 p.m. and 8 p.m. to 1 a.m. Small and intimate, it lies on a square in the center of town.

Near the Railway Station

Le Fonticine, via Nazionale 79R (tel. 282-106), used to be part of a convent until the gracious owner, Silvano Bruci, converted both it and its adjoining garden into one of the most hospitable restaurants of Florence. Today the richly decorated interior contains all the abundance of an Italian harvest, as well as the second passion of Signor Bruci's life, his collection of original paintings. The first passion, as a meal here reveals, is the cuisine that he and his elegant wife produce from recipes she collected from her childhood in Bologna.

Proceed to the larger of the establishment's two dining areas, and along the way you can admire dozens of portions of recently made pasta decorating the table of an exposed grill. At the far end of the room, a wrought-iron gate shelters the wine collection that Mr. Bruci has amassed, like his paintings, for many years. The food, served in copious portions, is both traditional and delectable. Begin with a platter of fresh antipasti, then follow with samplings of three of the most excellent pasta dishes of the day. This might be followed by such main dishes as fegatina di pollo (chicken), three different preparations of veal scaloppini, and a full repertoire of the classic Italian cuisine. Full meals cost from 45,000 lire ($34.25) per person and are served daily except Saturday and Sunday from noon to 3 p.m. and 7:30 to 10:30 p.m. Closed late July to late August.

Near the Piazzale Michelangelo

La Loggia, piazzale Michelangelo 1 (tel. 234-2832). You shouldn't have any trouble locating this popular restaurant housed in a 100-year-old former art gallery. It occupies one of the most prominent positions in Florence, a panoramic piazza where all first-time visitors appear to drink in the view of the City of the Renaissance. The food is good too. Service may be a bit chaotic, but when you get to order, you might like to try the giant porcini and ovoli mushrooms among the favorite antipasti. Florentine steaks are usually tender here, grilled over an open fire. Try also the risotto con fagioli (beans). For a perfect finish for your meal, try a herb drink, Amaro Montenegro. Another specialty of the bartender is a heavenly apéritif of champagne and peaches. Expect to spend 35,000 lire ($26.50) to 52,000 lire ($39.50) for a complete meal. Open from noon to 2:30 p.m. and 7 to 10:30 p.m.; it's closed Wednesday and two weeks in mid-August.

Near Piazza G. Salvemini

Da Noi, via Fiesolana 46R (tel. 242-917), lies on a narrow street about a ten-minute walk north from the duomo. Bruno Tramontana and his Swedish wife, Sabina Bush, have established a tiny enclave of moderately priced gourmet food. Reservations are essential, as there are only seven tables. Amid a consciously simple decor, you can enjoy such specialties as ravioli stuffed with shrimp, tagliatelle with wild boar, veal with an artichoke-flavored cream sauce, turbot en papillote, salmon in a Pernod sauce, and grilled prawns in a cognac sauce. For an antipasto selection, try the terrine of duck liver in sherry sauce. Lunch or dinner costs 50,000 lire ($38) to 60,000 lire ($45.50), and is served from 1 to 2 p.m. and 8 to 10:30 p.m. daily except Sunday, Monday, and in August.

At the Piazza Antinori

Buca Lapi, via del Trebbio 1R (tel. 213-768), a cellar restaurant founded in 1880, is big on glamour, good food, and the almost *gemütlich* enthusiasm of fellow diners. Its decor alone—under the Palazzo Antinori—makes it fun: vaulted ceilings covered with travel posters from all over the world. There's a long table of interesting fruits, desserts, and vegetables. The cooks know how to turn out the most classic dishes of the Tuscan kitchen with superb finesse. Specialties include pâté di fegato della casa, a liver pâté; cannelloni; scampi giganti alla griglia, a super-size shrimp; and bistecca alla fiorentina (local beefsteak). In season, the fagioli toscani all'olio—Tuscan beans in the native olive oil—are considered a delicacy by many palates. For dessert, you can order the international favorite, crêpes suzette, or the local choice, zuccotto, a Florentine cake that's "delicato." Meals cost from 45,000 lire ($34.25) per person and are served from 12:30 to 2:30 p.m. and 7:30 to 11 p.m.

Evenings can be quite festive, as the singing becomes contagious. The restaurant is closed Sunday and at lunch on Monday.

Caninetta Antinori, piazza Antinori 3 (tel. 292-234). Hidden behind the severe stone façade of the 15th-century Palazzo Antinori is one of Florence's most popular restaurants and one of the city's few top-notch wine bars. Small wonder that the cellars should be supremely well stocked since the restaurant is one of the city's showplaces for the vintages of the oldest and most distinguished wine company in Tuscany or Umbria. It has become the preferred rendezvous point for wine lovers who appreciate an overview of the assembled wines of the region, readily available and cheerfully served. Vintages can be consumed by the glass at the stand-up bar or by the bottle as an accompaniment for the Italian meals served at wooden tables. The room is not especially large, and the decorative statement is from the floor-to-ceiling racks of aged and artfully undusted wine bottles set on their sides in wooden racks. The overflow from the ground floor goes up to the overhead balcony. It is open from 12:30 to 2:30 p.m. and 7 to 10:30 p.m. weekdays, and is closed Saturday, Sunday, and in August. Full meals, not counting the wine, range from 32,000 lire ($24.25), but you can eat for less if you want to sample only the snacks, such as salads, sandwiches, and other light dishes.

Buca Mario, Piazza Ottaviani 16R (tel. 214-179), is one of the most famous cellar restaurants of Florence, in business for around a century. Its location is right in the monumental historic center. Tables are placed beneath vaulted ceilings, and you'll often find that some of the waiters have worked in the States. They might suggest such dishes as an array of Florentine pastas, beefsteak, Dover sole, and beef carpaccio, followed by a tempting selection of desserts. Lunch or dinner is likely to cost from 38,000 lire ($29) and service is from 12:15 to 2:30 p.m. and 7:15 to 10:30 p.m. Friday through Tuesday; closed Wednesday and Thursday.

Near the Piazza Taddeo Gaddi

Pierot, piazza Taddeo Gaddi 25R (tel. 702-100), is housed in a 19th-century building constructed during the reign of Vittorio Emmanuel. Before World War II these premises were a food store, but for at least 40 years Pierot has been a restaurant fixture of Florence. Owned by Enrico Bolognini, the restaurant is unusual in that it specializes in seafood, and therefore is considered a bit of an oddity in landlocked Florence. The seasonal menu varies with the availability of ingredients, but might include linguine with a creamy crabmeat sauce, pasta with clams, and a succulent version of squid and beets (yes, you heard right). Meals are served daily except Sunday from noon to 3 p.m. and 7 to 11:30 p.m. Annual vacation is in August. Lunches cost from 25,000 lire ($19), with dinners going for 35,000 lire ($26.50) and up. More expensive fish dishes will cost more, of course.

Trattoria Vittoria, via Fonderia 52R (tel. 225-657), is unheralded and untouristy, but it serves some of the finest fish dishes in Florence. A big, bustling trattoria, it offers you a chance to dine in one of three rooms. Service is frenetic. Most of the fresh fish dishes of the day are priced according to weight. Sole is the most expensive, although you can also order equally tempting lower-priced dishes. Two outstanding choices to begin your meal include risotto alla marinara and spaghetti alla vongole (clams). The mixed fish fry gives you a little bit of everything. Desserts are homemade and extremely rich. Depending on your choice of plates, your final bill is likely to range from 45,000 lire ($34.25) to 55,000 lire ($41.75). Open from noon to 2:30 p.m. and 7:30 to 10:30 p.m.; it's closed Wednesday.

Near Piazza S. Croce

Cibrèo, via dei Macci 118R (tel. 234-1100), is a plain little restaurant where Fabio and Benedetta Picchi turn out far-from-plain food. The decor consists of flowers in beer mugs, with posters on the walls. The food is served indoors where patrons can watch the activity in the kitchen around the charcoal oven, or in summer tables are placed on the back sidewalk. Here you can observe the shoppers in the big open food market held in the square during the morning. Fabio's soups are special (he serves no pasta), and you might choose the potato and chickpea or pumpkin potage. Tuscan dishes are well prepared here, and there are also such international specialties as brains baked en papillote, a Turkish offering. No cocktails are served, but you can have wine with your meal. Expect to pay 50,000 lire ($38) to 60,000 lire ($45.50) for a complete dinner. Food is served from 12:30 to 2:20 p.m. and 8 to 10:30 p.m. Tuesday through Saturday; closed Sunday, Monday, and in August.

Ristorante Leo in Santa Croce, via Torta 7R (tel. 210-829), offers good food in a trio of appealingly decorated dining rooms. It has a convenient location a few paces from the piazza that prefaces the Church of Santa Croce. An array of water-colors, some of them satirical portraits of past clients, decorate the walls. Full meals cost from 35,000 lire ($26.50), and might include ravioli with salmon, pappardella with rabbit, fondue bourguignonne, and kidneys flambé. Succulent grills such as steak and chicken are regularly featured as well. Meals are served daily except Monday from noon to 2:30 p.m. and 7:30 to 10:30 p.m.

On the Left Bank

Trattoria Cammillo, borgo S. Iacopo 57 (tel. 212-427), is one of the most popular—and perhaps the finest—of the left bank dining spots, housed on the ground floor of a former Medici palace. It's good enough to lure the snobbish own-ers of the boutiques, who cross the Arno regularly to feast here. They know they'll get such specialties as tortellini alla panna or zuppa alla certosina to begin their feast. The characteristic trattoria also does a scaloppa alla parmigiana and that old standby, beloved by the locals, Florentine tripe. Meals cost 38,000 lire ($29) to 72,000 lire ($54.75). In modest but attractive surroundings, the trattoria is between the Ponte Vecchio and the Ponte S. Trinità. Because of increased business, one is likely to be rushed through a meal. Open from noon to 2:30 p.m. and 7 to 10:15 p.m., it's closed Wednesday, Thursday, the first three weeks in August, and from just before Christmas to mid-January.

Mamma Gina, borgo S. Iacopo 37 (tel. 296-009), is a rustic left bank restau-rant that's a winner for fine foods prepared in the traditional manner. This trattoria is exceptional, well worth the trek across the Ponte Vecchio. The trattoria is a center for hearty Tuscan fare. The chef does an excellent tortellini verde (a green pasta dish). You can follow with any number of fish or meat dishes. Meals cost 37,000 lire ($28) to 47,000 lire ($35.75) and are served from noon to 2:30 p.m. and 7 to 10 p.m. Closed Sunday and the first three weeks in August. Mamma Gina is ideal for lunch after visiting the Pitti Palace.

Near the Ponte Vecchio

Ristorante Walter e Nandina, borgo SS. Apostoli 684 (tel. 213-024), is an ele-gant old favorite with both Florentines and visitors alike. A family-run restaurant, it is just off the Arno, lying about a four-minute walk from the Uffizi (in fact, it's an excellent choice for lunch if you're viewing the galleries). Tables are set out on the square in front, within view of a soaring commemorative column and a baroque church, but back in the kitchen for your background music there is a symphony of the rattling of pots and pans. Fresh flowers are placed on the tables under vaulted ceilings and iron chandeliers. If you arrive early, you can have an apéritif in the inti-mate and plushly upholstered cocktail lounge near the entrance. The cuisine consists of dishes from provinces and cities such as Rome, Tuscany, and Venice, and might include taglierini with flap mushrooms, spinach crêpes, curried breast of capon, veal piccatina, several kinds of beefsteak, and a changing array of daily specials. Full meals cost from around 45,000 lire ($34.25) and are served from noon to 3 p.m. and 7:30 to 10:30 p.m. every day except Sunday.

Buca dell'Orafo, via dei Girolami 28 (tel. 213-619), is a little dive (one of the many cellars or "buca"-type establishments beloved by Florentines). An *orafo* is a goldsmith, and it was in this part of Florence that the goldsmith trade grew up. The buca, owned by Piero Parretti and Lamberto Monni, once part of an old goldsmith's shop, stands near the Ponte Vecchio, reached via a street under a vaulted arcade right off the piazza del Pesce. The trattoria is usually stuffed with its habitués, so if you want a seat, go early for either lunch or dinner. Over the years the chef has made little concession to the foreign palate, turning out instead genuine Florentine specialties, including tripe and mixed boiled meats with a green sauce and stracotto e fagioli, which is beef braised in a sauce of chopped vegetables and red wine, served with beans in a tomato sauce. For a savory beginning, try the fennel-flavored salami or asparagus in the spring. Florentine beefsteak is the most expensive item on the menu. Meals cost from 40,000 lire ($30.50) and are served from 12:30 to 2:30 p.m. and 7:30 to 10:30 p.m. except on Sunday, Monday, and in August. There's a feeling of camaraderie among the diners here.

Near Piazza Goldoni

Trattoria Garga, via del Moro 40R (tel. 298-898). Some of the most creative cuisine in Florence is served in an amicably cramped dining room barely large enough for 30 people. The establishment is run by Giuliano Gargani and his Canadian wife, Sharon, a happy combination of personalities that began when a strawberry blonde met "Signor Right." The building's thick Renaissance walls contain paintings by both Florentine and American artists, the decor complemented by hanging oil lamps and operatic arias which emerge along with the heavenly odors from a postage-stamp-size kitchen. Many of the menu items are so unusual that Sharon's bilingual skills are put to good use. You can enjoy a fine array of salads, including a well-dressed combination of artichokes, hearts of palm, fresh lettuce, and parmigiana cheese. Other dishes include tagliatelle with garlic, tomatoes, anchovies, and smoked salmon, along with octopus with chile peppers and garlic, boar with juniper berries, grilled marinated quail, and "whatever strikes the mood" of Giuliano. Full meals cost from 40,000 lire ($30.50) and are served from 1 to 3 p.m. and 8 to 10:30 p.m. daily except Sunday, and no lunch is served Monday. Call ahead for a table.

Near the Piazza della Santa Maria Novella

La Carabaccia, via Palazzuolo 190R (tel. 214-782). Two hundred years ago a *carabaccia* was a workaday boat, shaped like a hollowed-out half onion and used on the Arno to dredge silt and sand from the river bottom. The favorite onion soup of the Medici was zuppa carabaccia, which this restaurant still features today. It is a creamy white onion soup served with croutons (and not in the French style, the chef rushes to tell you). Carabaccia is still a style of Florentine cuisine that presents a meat, such as boar, with stewed onions on the side. You can, of course, eat more than onions here. The menu changes every day and is based on the use of fresh local ingredients. There is always one soup, followed by four or five pastas, including crespelle (crêpe) of such fresh vegetables as asparagus or artichokes. A daily fish dish is also featured. The restaurant is run by a quartet of Florentine friends. Full meals cost from 30,000 lire ($22.75) and are served from 12:30 to 2:30 p.m. and 7:30 to 10:30 p.m. daily except Monday at lunch and all day Sunday (watch for the annual closing in August). The decor of the restaurant features white walls decorated with objects of ceramic and copper.

Sostanza, via del Porcellana 25R (tel. 212-691), has for years been a tucked-away little trattoria where working people could go to get excellent food inexpensively. But in more recent times the invading sophisticates have been pouring in to share tables with them. You enter through a hole-in-the-wall into a small dining room, with crowded family tables. The rear kitchen is open, its secrets exposed to diners. When you taste what comes out of that kitchen, you'll know that fancy decor would be superfluous. Specialties include breaded chicken breast and a succulent T-bone steak. You might also want to try tripe here the Florentine way—that is, cut into strips, then baked in a casserole with tomatoes, onions, and parmesan cheese. A fine beginning is the tortellini and a fit ending is Florentine cake. A standard dinner will cost from 35,000 lire ($26.50). Open from noon to 2:10 p.m. and 7:30 to 9:30 p.m., it's closed Saturday, Sunday, and in August.

Otello, via Orti Oricellari 36R (tel. 215-819), near the railway station. "Mangi, mangi, mangi!" the waiter urges. That means, "Eat, eat, eat!" And the Otello has plenty of victuals to stir the most lethargic of appetites. To begin with, one of the most tempting arrays of Tuscan antipasti is wheeled to your table. Even tender roast pork is part of the offering, and this opening feast represents merely the hors d'oeuvres. The price of this inaugural plateful is based on what you order. For main courses, the Florentine beefsteak is priced according to weight. But I recommend arrosto misto, also priced according to what you have—a cart is wheeled to your table containing "everything that walks or flies," and you're asked by the waiter to make your selection. Incidentally, because of Italian hunting laws, the small birds so favored by Italians are served only in winter. Two other good main dishes include chicken curry and veal scaloppine Otello. If you can manage pasta as well, I suggest taglierini all'Otello. For desserts, the specialty is zuccotto alla fiorentina, a rich Florentine cake. For a complete meal, expect to spend from 60,000 lire ($45.50) per person. The restaurant is open from noon to 3 p.m. and 7:30 to 11 p.m.; closed Tuesday.

Le Mossacce, via del Proconsolo 55R (tel. 294-361), patronized by a long list of faithful Tuscan devotees of its cuisine, is conveniently located midway between two of the city's most famous monuments, the Bargello and the duomo. This small 35-seat restaurant was originally established as such at the turn of the century. Within its 300-year-old walls, a team of hard-working waiters serve fixed-price meals costing 16,000 lire ($12.25) each. These meals include selections from a wide range of Florentine and Italian specialties, including ribollita (a thick regional soup), cannelloni, heavily seasoned baked pork, and involtini. Full meals are served Monday through Friday from noon to 2:30 p.m. and 7 to 9:30 p.m., on Saturday from 7 to 9:30 p.m.; closed all day Sunday, and its annual closing is for three weeks in August.

For Lira Watchers

Vecchia Firenze, borgo degli Albizi 18 (tel. 234-0361), is a combination of atmosphere and budget meals. It's housed in an old palace, with an elegant entrance, which you enter through high doors. Some of the tables are in the courtyard; others are inside the vaulted dining rooms. Part of the past, the restaurant is lit by a wrought-iron chandelier. It's not elaborately voguish—in fact, it caters to students and the working people of Florence, who eat here regularly. They never seem to tire of its offerings. Usually one gets both a first and a second course (a choice of a dozen different items), as well as fruit, a quarter liter of wine, bread, and service. You might begin with a tagliatelle Vecchia Firenze, then follow with a quarter of a roast chicken or sole in butter. A repast here is likely to cost 25,000 lire ($19) to 35,000 lire ($26.50), served from noon to 3 p.m. and 7 to 10 p.m. daily except Monday.

Giannino in San Lorenzo, borgo S. Lorenzo 31 (tel. 218-219), is a self-service cafeteria with a rustic decor, only a short walk from the Duomo. The food is several notches above what you might expect in cafeteria fare, and the portions are large and filling. Pastas are dished out from huge serving pans fresh from the kitchen. The meat dishes are equally good, especially a breaded veal cutlet in the Milanese style. Count on spending 20,000 lire ($15.25) up for a complete meal. At night, pizzas are a specialty. Food is served from 11:30 a.m. to 10:30 p.m.; closed Friday. The same owners run a more expensive restaurant next door.

For Vegetarians

Almanacco, via della Ruote 30R (tel. 475-030), is considered more of a private vegetarian club than a traditional restaurant. This popular eating house serves only vegetarian food, in a room filled with wooden tables, basket-shaped lamps, and a cafeteria-style setup where an employee ladles out portions onto plates and trays.

First-time diners are required to pay a membership fee of 2,000 lire ($1.50), after which they receive a membership card and access to the brick-floored interior. Within sight lines of a waiting cashier, you select your dinner from a chalkboard, filling in the items you want on a preprinted form. Full meals are served Tuesday through Friday from 12:45 to 2:30 p.m. and 7:45 to 10:30 p.m.; on Saturday and Sunday, only dinner is served. It's closed Monday and during most of August. A full three-course meal without wine costs from 12,000 lire ($9.10). Wine is served from a brimming carafe, although some vegetarians feel more comfortable with a bottle of organic, preservative-free Italian wine. Menu items vary with the seasonality of Italy's produce, but typical items include pasta with vegetarian sauces, rice with pumpkin, eggplant parmigiana, and country-derived pizza with thick crusts, along with an array of freshly composed salads.

THE ATTRACTIONS OF FLORENCE

Florence was the fountainhead of the Renaissance, the city of Dante and Boccaccio. Characteristically, it was the city of Machiavelli; uncharacteristically, of Savonarola. For three centuries it was dominated by the Medici family, patrons of the arts, masters of assassination. But it is chiefly through its artists that we know of the apogee of the Renaissance: Ghiberti, Fra Angelico, Donatello, Brunelleschi, Botticelli, and the incomparable Leonardo da Vinci and Michelangelo.

In Florence we can trace some of the steps by which man freed himself from the shackles of medievalism and entered an age of "rebirth." For example, all modern painters owe a debt to an ugly, awkward, unkempt man who died at 27. His name was Masaccio (Vasari's "Slipshod Tom"). Modern painting began with his frescoes in the Brancacci Chapel in the Church of Santa Maria del Carmine. You can go see them today. Years later Michelangelo was to paint a more celebrated Adam and Eve in the Sistine Chapel, but even so great an artist was never to realize the raw humanity of Masaccio's Adam and Eve fleeing from the Garden of Eden.

Ralph Roeder in a 1930 book, *The Man of the Renaissance,* wrote: "In the broadest sense the Renaissance might be described as one of those recurring crises in the annals of the race when a ferment of a new life, like a rising sap, bursts the accepted codes of morality and men revert to Nature and the free play of instinct and experience in its conduct."

To understand more fully the remarkable achievement of which Roeder wrote, I'll begin with the impressive ecclesiastic architecture.

---

1. The Top Sights

In the heart of Florence, at the piazza del Duomo and the piazza S. Giovanni (named after John the Baptist), is a complex of ecclesiastical buildings that form a triumvirate of top sightseeing attractions.

(1) GIOTTO'S BELL TOWER

Giotto, if we can believe the accounts of his contemporaries, was the ugliest man ever to walk the streets of Florence. In an ironic touch, he left to posterity the most beautiful bell tower or campanile in Europe, rhythmic in line and form. That Giotto was given the position of "capomastro" and grand architect (and pensioned for 100 gold florins for his service) is remarkable in itself, as his fame rests on his genius in freeing painting from the confinements of Byzantium. The campanile was designed by Giotto in the remaining two or three years of his life, and he died before its actual completion.

The final work was admirably carried out by Andrea Pisano, who was one of the greatest Gothic sculptors in Italy (see his bronze doors on the nearby Baptistery). The 274-foot tower, a most "Tuscanized" Gothic, with bands of colored marble, can be scaled for a panorama of the sienna-colored city, a view that surely will rank among your most memorable—encompassing the enveloping hills and Medici villas. If a medieval pageant happens to be passing underneath (a likely possibility in spring), so much the better. After Giotto's death, Pisano, as well as Luca della Robbia, did some fine bas-relief and sculptural work, now in the Duomo Museum, at the base of the tower. Charging 3,000 lire ($2.30) for admission, Giotto's campanile at piazza del Duomo is open Monday through Saturday in summer from 9 a.m. to 7:30 p.m. and in winter from 9 a.m. to 5:30 p.m.

(2) THE BAPTISTERY

Named after the city's patron saint, Giovanni (John the Baptist), the present octagonally shaped building dates from the 11th and 12th centuries. The oldest structure in Florence, the baptistery is a highly original interpretation of the Romanesque style, with its bands of pink, white, and green marble. Visitors from all over the world come to gape at its three sets of bronze doors.

In his work on two sets of doors, Lorenzo Ghiberti reached the pinnacle of his artistry in "quattrocento" Florence. To win his first commission on the north door, the then-23-year-old sculptor had to compete against such formidable opposition as Donatello, Brunelleschi (architect of the dome crowning the cathedral), and Siena-born Jacopo della Quercia. Upon seeing Ghiberti's work, Donatello and Brunelleschi conceded. By the time he completed the work, Ghiberti was around 44 years old. The gilt-covered panels represent scenes from the New Testament, including the *Annunciation,* the *Adoration,* and Christ debating the doctors in the temple—a flowing rhythmic narration in bronze.

After his long labor, the Florentines gratefully gave Ghiberti the task of sculpting the east door (directly opposite the entrance to the duomo). On seeing the doors, Michelangelo is said to have exclaimed, "The Gateway to Paradise!" Given carte blanche, Ghiberti designed his masterpiece, choosing as his subject familiar scenes from the Old Testament, including Adam and Eve at the creation. This time, Ghiberti labored over the rectangular panels from 1425 to 1452 (he died in 1455).

Shuttled off to adorn the south entrance and to make way for Ghiberti's "gate" to paradise were the oldest doors of the baptistery, by Andrea Pisano, mentioned earlier for his work on Giotto's bell tower. For his subject, the Gothic sculptor represented the "Virtues" as well as scenes from the life of John the Baptist, whom the baptistery honors. The door was completed in 1336. On the interior (just walk through Pisano's doors—no charge), the dome is adorned with 13th-century mosaics, dominated by a figure of Christ. It's open from 9 a.m. to 12:30 p.m. and 2:30 to 5:30 p.m. daily.

The third part of the ecclesiastical compound is the dominant sight of the city.

(3) THE CATHEDRAL OF S. MARIA DEL FIORE (THE DUOMO)

Il Duomo, graced by Brunelleschi's dome, is the crowning glory of Florence. But don't rush inside too quickly, as the view of the exterior, with its bands of white, pink, and green marble—geometrically patterned—is the best feature, along with the dome, of course.

One of the world's largest churches, the Duomo of Florence represents the flowering of the "Florentine-Gothic" style. Begun in 1296, it was finally conse-crated in 1436, although finishing touches on the façade were applied as late as the 19th century. Actually, the cathedral was designed by Arnolfo di Cambio in the closing years of the 13th century, the funds being raised in part by a poll tax. As was typical of the history of cathedrals, construction stretched over centuries. In tribute to Arnolfo di Cambio's original foundation, it was miraculous that it supported the double-thick dome of Brunelleschi.

The efforts of Brunelleschi to build the dome (1420–1436) would make the subject of a film, as did Michelangelo's vexations over the Sistine Chapel. Before his plans were eventually accepted, the architect was once tossed out on his derrière and denounced as an idiot. He eventually won the commission by a clever "egg trick," as related in Vasari. His dome—a "monument for posterity"—was erected without supports. When the time came for Michelangelo to construct a dome over St. Pe-ter's, he said in tribute to Brunelleschi's earlier cupola in Florence: "I am going to make its sister larger, yes, but not lovelier."

Inside, the overall effect of the cathedral is bleak, except when you stand under the cupola, frescoed in part by Giorgio Vasari, to whom I owe a debt in this book (as do authors of all other books dealing with Italian Renaissance art) for his *Lives of the Painters,* written in the 16th century. Some of the stained-glass windows in the dome were based on designs by Donatello (Brunelleschi's friend) and Ghiberti (Brunelleschi's rival). If you resisted scaling Giotto's bell tower, you may want to climb Brunelleschi's ribbed dome. And if so, you can, daily except Sunday from 10:30 a.m. to 5 p.m. for 3,000 lire ($2.30) admission. The view is well worth the trek.

Also in the cathedral are some terracottas by Luca della Robbia. In 1432 Ghi-berti, taking time out from his gateway to paradise, designed the tomb of St. Zenobius. Recent excavations in the depths of the cathedral have brought to light the remains of the ancient Cathedral of S. Reparata (tombs, columns, and floors), proba-bly founded in the 5th century, and transformed in the following centuries until it was demolished to make way for the present cathedral. Admission is 1,500 lire ($1.15). The cathedral is open from 10 a.m. to 5 p.m. daily.

Incidentally, during some 1972 excavations the tomb of Brunelleschi was dis-covered. New discoveries indicate the existence of a second tomb near that of the architect of the dome. Giotto's tomb, which has never been found, may be in a right nave of the cathedral, beneath the campanile that bears his name.

After coming out of the entrance to the cathedral, turn to the right, then head down via Ricasoli to our next stop.

(4) THE ACADEMY GALLERY (MICHELANGELO'S *DAVID*)

This museum, at via Ricasoli 60 (tel. 214-375), contains paintings and sculp-ture, but is completely overshadowed by one work, Michelangelo's colossal *David,* unveiled in 1504. One of the most sensitive accounts I've ever read of how Michel-angelo turned the 17-foot "Duccio marble" into David is related in "The Giant" chapter of Irving Stone's *The Agony and the Ecstasy.* Stone describes a Michelangelo "burning with marble fever" who set out to create a *David* who "would be Apollo, but considerably more; Hercules, but considerably more; Adam, but considerably

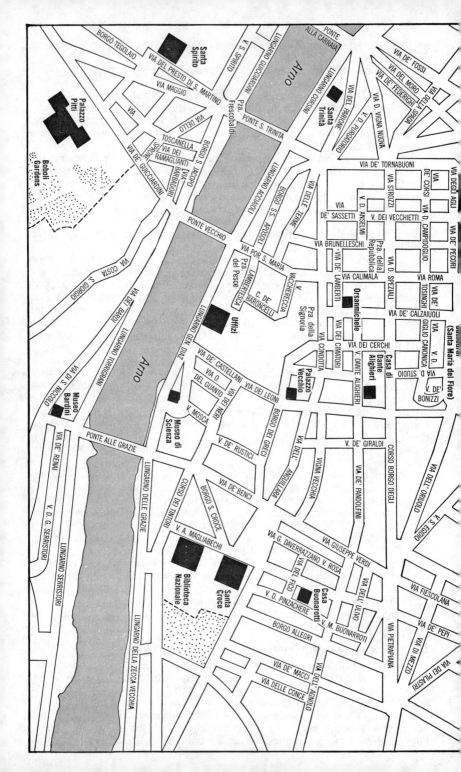

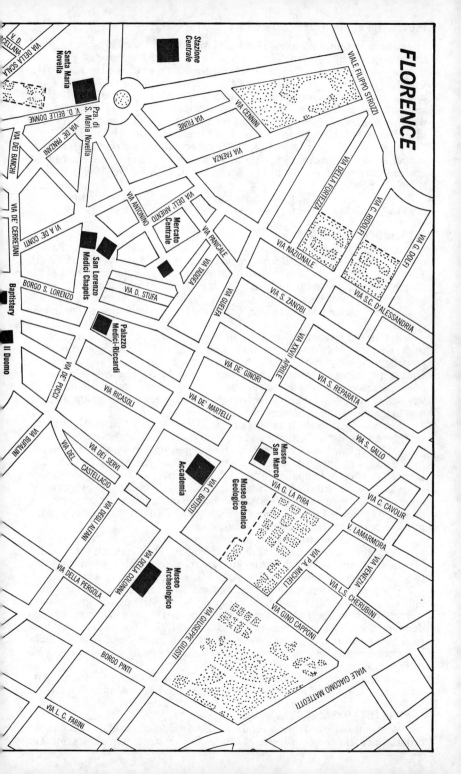

more; the most fully realized man the world had yet seen, functioning in a rational and humane world." How well he succeeded is much in evidence today.

David once stood in the piazza della Signoria but was removed in 1873 to the academy (a copy was substituted). Apart from containing the masterwork, the sculpture gallery also is graced with Michelangelo's unfinished quartet of slaves, carved around 1520 and intended for the ill-fated tomb of Julius II, and his *St. Matthew,* which he worked on (shortly after completing *David*) for the Duomo. His unfinished *Palestrina Pietà* displayed here is a much later work, dating from 1550.

In the connecting picture gallery is a collection of Tuscan masters, such as Botticelli, and Umbrian works by Perugino (teacher of Raphael). You can visit the academy daily except Monday from 9 a.m. to 2 p.m. for 4,000 lire ($3.05). It closes at 1 p.m. on Sunday.

While still suffused with the rich legacy of Michelangelo, it's only fitting that we pay a call on another venue for his work.

(5) THE MEDICI CHAPELS

A mecca for all pilgrims, the Medici tombs are sheltered adjacent to the Basilica of San Lorenzo (see "Churches of Florence") on piazza Madonna (tel. 213-206). The tombs, housing the "blue-blooded" Medici, are actually entered in back of the church by going around to the piazza Madonna degli Aldobrandini. First, you'll pass through the octagonally shaped, baroque "Chapel of the Princes," with its colored marble but cold decoration. In back of the altar is a collection of Italian reliquaries.

But the real reason the chapels are visited en masse is the "New Sacristy," built to the design of Michelangelo. Working from 1521 to 1534, the Florentine artist created the Medici tomb in a style that foreshadowed the coming of the baroque. One of the greatest names in the history of the Medici family—Lorenzo the Magnificent—a ruler who seemed to embody the qualities of the Renaissance itself, was buried near Michelangelo's uncompleted *Madonna and Child* group, a simple monument that evokes a promise unfulfilled.

Sardonically, the finest groups of sculpture—of world renown—were reserved for two Medici "clan" members, who (in the words of Mary McCarthy) "would better have been forgotten." Both are represented in sculptured figures by Michelangelo as armored, regal, idealized princes of the Renaissance. In fact, Lorenzo II, Duke of Urbino, depicted as "the thinker," was a young man (just out of his teens before he died) who was deranged. Clearly, Michelangelo was not working to glorify these two Medici dukes. Rather, he was chiseling for posterity. The other two figures on Lorenzo's tomb are most often called *Dawn* and *Dusk,* with the morning represented as woman; the evening, man.

The two best-known figures—Michelangelo at his most powerful—are *Night* and *Day* at the feet of Giuliano, the duke of Nemours. *Night* is chiseled as a woman in troubled sleep; *Day,* a man of strength awakening to a foreboding world. These two figures were not the sculptural works of Michelangelo's innocence.

Discovered in a sepulchral chamber beneath the Medici Chapel was the world's only group of mural sketches by Michelangelo. Access is through a trap door and a winding staircase. The walls apparently had been used by the great artist as a giant doodling sheet. Drawings include a sketch of the legs of Duke Giuliano, Christ risen, and a depiction of the Laocoön, the Hellenistic figure group. In all, 50 drawings were found, done in charcoal on plaster walls. The public can sometimes view these sketches in the choir.

The chapels are open from 9 a.m. to 2 p.m. Tuesday through Saturday, to 1 p.m. on Sunday, charging 4,350 lire ($3.30) for admission. Closed Monday.

(6) THE UFFIZI GALLERY

When the last grand duchess of the Medici family died, the end of her line, she bequeathed to the people of Tuscany a wealth of Renaissance, even classical, art. The paintings and sculpture had been accumulated by the powerful grand dukes in three centuries of rule that witnessed the height of the Renaissance. Vasari designed the palace in the 16th century for Cosimo I.

The Uffizi contains the finest collection of art in Italy, and ranks along with the Prado and Louvre as one of the greatest art galleries in the world. To describe its offerings would take a very thick volume all its own, and to see and have time to absorb all the Uffizi paintings would take at least two weeks. I'll present only the sketchy highlights to get the first-timer through a citadel of madonnas and bambini, mythological figures, and Christian martyrs. The Uffizi is nicely arranged—that is, grouped into periods or schools to show the development and progress of Italian art, which later branches out to include European masters in general.

The first room begins with classical sculpture, but then you meet up with those rebels from Byzantium, Cimabue and Giotto, his pupil, with their madonnas and bambini. Since the Virgin and Child seem to be the overriding theme of the earlier of the Uffizi artists, it's enlightening just to follow the different styles over the centuries, from the ugly, almost midget-faced babies of the post-Byzantine works to the chubby, red-cheeked cherubs that glorified the baroque.

Look for Simone Martini's *Annunciation,* a collaborative venture. The halo around the head of the Virgin doesn't conceal her pouty mouth. Fra Angelico of Fiesole, a 15th-century painter, lost in a world peopled with saints and angels, is represented making his Uffizi debut with a *Madonna and Bambino,* naturally. A special treasure is a work by Masaccio, who died at an early age, but is credited as the father of modern painting. In his madonnas and banbini we see the beginnings of perspective in painting. Two important portraits are by Piero della Francesca, the 15th-century painter (go to Arezzo to see his frescoes). Fra Angelico's *Coronation of the Virgin* is in this salon.

Another room is outstanding for the work of another friar—this one Filippo Lippi, a rebel among the brethren, who painted a far superior *Coronation* along with a galaxy of charming madonnas.

The Botticelli rooms are popular, especially with visitors who come here to contemplate "Venus on the Half-Shell." The room contains the finest works by Sandro Botticelli. Before being captured by Venus, don't miss *Minerva Subduing the Centaur,* a most important painting which brought about a resurgence of interest on the part of painters in mythological subjects. The canvas was one of many Uffizi treasures shipped to Germany in World War II. Botticelli's *Allegory of Spring* or *Primavera* is a Uffizi gem; it's often called a symphony because you can listen to it. Set in a citrus grove, the painting depicts Venus with Cupid hovering over her head. "The Wind" is trying to capture a nymph; but the three graces, in a lyrical composition, form the painting's chief claim to greatness. Mercury looks out of the canvas to the left. But it is the *Birth of Venus*—Botticelli's supreme conception of life—that packs them in. Flora is trying to cover the nude goddess, while the gods of the wind are puffing up a storm. Before leaving the room, look for Botticelli's *Adoration of the Magi,* in which we find portraits of the Medici (the vain man at the far right is Botticelli). Also here is Botticelli's small allegorical *Calumny.*

Nobody should miss *The Adoration of the Shepherds,* a triptych, superb in detail, commissioned for a once-important Tuscan family and painted by Hugo van der Goes, a 15th-century artist. In another room we come across another of Leonardo da Vinci's unfinished paintings, this one the brilliant *Adoration of the Magi,* and in the same room is Verrocchio's *Baptism of Christ,* not a very important painting, but noted because da Vinci painted one of the angels when he was 14 years old, already a child prodigy. Also in this salon hangs da Vinci's *Annunciation,* a painting of the early years of his genius—with its twilight atmosphere, each leaf painstakingly in place. Proof that Leonardo was an architect? The splendid Renaissance palace he designed is part of the background.

The most beautiful room in the gallery with its dome of pearl shells contains the *Venus of the Medici,* occupying center stage, one of the most reproduced of all Greek sculptural works. Also displayed are *Apollo* and *The Wrestlers,* from Greek originals of the 3rd and 4th centuries B.C.

In the rooms to follow are works by Perugino, Dürer, Mantegna, Giovanni Bellini, Giorgione, and Correggio. Finally, don't miss Michelangelo's contribution to the Uffizi, his *Holy Family,* as well as Raphael's *Madonna of the Goldfinch,* plus his portraits of Julius II and Leo X. There is also what might be dubbed the Titian salon, as that painter of the High Renaissance takes over with two of his interpretations of Venus (one depicted with Cupid). When it came to representing voluptuous females on canvas, Titian had no rival. In other rooms are important Mannerists: Parmigianino, Veronese, Tintoretto (*Leda and the Swan*). In the rooms nearing the end are works by Rubens, Caravaggio (*Bacchus*), and Rembrandt.

The Uffizi, at loggiato degli Uffizi 6 (tel. 218-341), between the piazza della Signoria and the Arno, is open daily except Monday from 9 a.m. to 7 p.m. and charges 5,000 lire ($3.80) for admission. On Sunday and holidays, hours are 9 a.m. to 1 p.m. Last entrance is 45 minutes before closing.

(7) THE PIAZZA DELLA SIGNORIA

This square, although never completed, is one of the most beautiful in Italy— the center of secular life in the days of the Medici. Through it pranced church robbers, connoisseurs of entrails, hired assassins seeking employment, chicken farmers from Valdarno, book burners, and many great men—including Machiavelli on a secret mission to the Palazzo Vecchio, and Leonardo da Vinci, trailed by his inevitable entourage.

On the square is the Fountain of Neptune, the sea god surrounded by creatures from the deep, as well as frisky satyrs and nymphs. It was designed by Ammannati, who later repented for chiseling Neptune in the nude. But Michelangelo, to whom Ammannati owes a great debt, judged the fountain inferior.

Near the fountain is a spot where Savonarola walked his last mile. The zealous monk, of course, was a fire-and-brimstone reformer who rivaled Dante in conjuring up the punishment hell would inflict on sinners. Two of his chief targets were Lorenzo the Magnificent and the Borgia pope, Alexander VI, who excommunicated him. Savonarola whipped the Florentine faithful into an orgy of religious fanaticism, but eventually fell from favor. Along with two other friars, he was hanged in the square. Afterward, as the crowds threw stones, the pyre underneath the men consumed their bodies. It is said that the reformer's heart was found whole, grabbed up by souvenir collectors. His ashes were tossed in the Arno. The year was 1498.

For centuries Michelangelo's *David* stood in the piazza della Signoria, but it was moved to the Academy Gallery in the 19th century. The work you see on the square today is an inferior copy, commonly assumed by many first-time visitors to be Michelangelo's original.

In the 14th-century **Loggia della Signoria** (sometimes called Loggia dei Lanzi) is a gallery of sculpture, depicting fierce, often violent scenes. The most famous and the best piece is a rare work by Benvenuto Cellini, the goldsmith and tell-all autobiographer. Of his exquisite, but ungentlemanly, *Perseus* holding the severed head of Medusa, critics have said it is the most significant Florentine sculpture since Michelangelo's *Night* and *Day.* Two other well-known, although less skilled, pieces are Giambologna's *Rape of the Sabines* and his *Hercules with Nessus the Centaur.*

For those on the mad rush, I suggest saving the interior of the **Palazzo Vecchio** (see "Palaces and More Museums") for another day.

(8) THE PITTI PALACE

The Palatine Gallery, on the left bank (a five-minute walk from the Ponte Vecchio) at the piazza Pitti (tel. 210-323), houses one of Europe's great art collections, with masterpieces hung one on top of the other, as in the days of the Enlightenment. If for no other reason, it should be visited for its Raphaels alone. The Pitti, built in the mid-15th century (Brunelleschi was the original architect), was once the residence of the powerful Medici family.

There are actually several museums in this complex, including the most important, the **Galleria Palatina,** repository of old masters. Other museums include the **Appartamenti Monumentali,** which the Medici family once called home, and the **Museo degli Argenti,** 16 rooms devoted to displays of the "loot" acquired by the Medici dukes. Others are the **Coach and Carriage Museum** and the **Galleria d'Arte Moderna.** Exhibits also include **Museo della Porcellane** (porcelain) and **Galleria del Costume.** After passing through the main door, proceed to the Sala di Venere (the Room of Venus), which appropriately belongs to Titian, the favorite admirer of that goddess. In it are his *La Bella,* of rich and illuminating color (entrance wall), and his portrait of Pietro Aretino, one of his most distinguished works. On the opposite wall are Titian's *Concert of Music,* often attributed to Giorgione, and his portrait of Julius II.

In the Sala di Apollo (on the opposite side of the entrance door) are Titian's *Man with Gray Eyes*—aristocratic, handsome, a romanticist—as well as his Mary Magdalene with her plunging décolletage. On the opposite wall are Van Dyck portraits of Charles I of England and Henrietta of France.

In the Sala di Marte (entrance wall) is an important *Madonna and Child* by Murillo of Spain, as well as the Pitti's best-known work by Rubens, *The Four Philosophers.* On the left wall is one of Ruben's most tragic and moving paintings, depicting the *Consequences of War*—an early *Guernica.*

In the Sala di Giove (entrance wall) are Andrea del Sarto's idealized John the Baptist in his youth, Fra Bartolomeo's *Descent from the Cross,* and one of Rubens's most exciting paintings (even for those who don't like art): a romp of nymphs and satyrs. On the third wall (opposite the entrance wall) is the Pitti's second famous Raphael, the woman under the veil, known as "La Fornarina," his bakery-girl mistress.

In the following gallery, the Sala di Saturno, look to the left on the entrance wall to see Raphael's *Madonna of the Canopy,* plus other works, such as portraits, by that Renaissance master. On the third wall near the doorway is the greatest Pitti prize, Raphael's *Madonna of the Chair,* his best-known interpretation of the Virgin —in fact, probably one of the six most celebrated paintings in all of Europe.

In the Sala dell'Iliade (to your left on the entrance wall) is a work of delicate beauty, Raphael's rendition of a pregnant woman, painted while he was still searching for a personal style. On the left wall is Titian's *Portrait of a Gentleman,* which he was indeed. (Titian is the second big star in the Palatine Gallery.) Finally, as you're leaving, look to the right of the doorway to see one of Velázquez's interpretations of the many faces of Philip IV of Spain.

In the rooms that follow, the drama of the salons remains vivid—enhanced by portraits by Justus Sustermans, who could be almost as devastating as Velázquez.

Major works in the Sala di Prometeo include Filippo Lippi's *Madonna and Child,* as well as two Botticelli portraits. In the Sala dell'Educazione di Giove hangs Caravaggio's *Sleeping Cupid,* and in the Sala della Giustizia you'll find Tintoretto's *Virgin and Child,* a vintage work by that Venetian master.

The Pitti is open daily except Monday from 9 a.m. to 2 p.m. (til 1 p.m. on Sunday), and charges 4,000 lire ($3.05) for admission. The modern-art gallery requires a separate ticket costing 4,000 lire ($3.05).

(9) THE NATIONAL MUSEUM (BARGELLO)

At via del Proconsolo 4 (tel. 210-801) is a fortress palace, dating from the 13th century, that once resounded with the cries of the tortured echoing through its dark underground chambers. Today it's a vast repository of some of the most important sculpture of the Renaissance, housing works by both Michelangelo and Donatello.

Here, you'll see another of Michelangelo's Davids (referred to in the past as *Apollo*), chiseled perhaps 25 to 30 years after the statuesque figure in the Academy

Gallery. The Bargello *David* is totally different—even effete when compared to its stronger brother. The gallery also displays Michelangelo's grape-capped *Bacchus* (one of his earlier works), tempted by a satyr. Among the more significant sculpture is Giambologna's *Winged Mercury.*

The Bargello displays two versions of Donatello's John the Baptist—one emaciated, the other a younger and much kinder edition. Donatello, of course, was one of the outstanding and original talents of the early Renaissance. In this gallery you'll learn why. His *St. George* is a work of heroic magnitude. According to an oft-repeated story, Michelangelo, upon seeing it for the first time, commanded it to "March!" Donatello's bronze *David* in this salon is one of the most remarkable figures of all Renaissance sculpture—the first "free-standing" nude since the Romans stopped chiseling. As depicted, *David* is narcissistic, a stunning contrast to Michelangelo's latter-day virile interpretation. For the last word, however, I'll have to call back our lady of the barbs, Mary McCarthy, who wrote: "His David . . . wearing nothing but a pair of fancy polished boots and a girlish bonnet, is a transvestite's and fetishist's dream of alluring ambiguity."

Look for at least one more notable work, another *David*—this one by Andrea del Verrocchio, one of the finest of the 15th-century sculptors. The Bargello contains a large number of terracottas by the della Robbia clan.

The museum, a short walk from the piazza della Signoria, is open daily except Monday from 9 a.m. to 2 p.m. (on Sunday from 9 a.m. to 1 p.m.), and charges 3,000 lire ($2.30) admission.

(10) SAN MARCO MUSEUM

Museo di San Marco, via G. La Pira 1 (tel. 210-741), is a handsome Renaissance palace, the walls of its cells decorated with frescoes by the mystical Fra Angelico, one of Europe's greatest 15th-century painters. In the days of Cosimo dei Medici, San Marco was built by Michelozzo as a Dominican convent. It originally contained bleak, bare cells, which Angelico and his students then brightened considerably with some of the most important works of this pious artist of Fiesole, who learned to portray recognizable landscapes in strong, vivid colors. One of his better-known paintings found here is *The Last Judgment,* peopled with angels on the left dancing in a circle, with lordly saints towering overhead.

But hell, as depicted on the right, is naïve—Dantesque—infested with demons, reptiles, and sinners, boiling in a stew. If not that, then the denizens of the deep are devouring each other's flesh . . . or worms. Much of hell was created by his students, as Angelico's brush was inspired only by the Crucifixion, madonnas and bambini—or landscapes, of course. Here also are his *Descent from the Cross* and an especially refined interpretation panel of scenes from the life of Mary, including the *Flight into Egypt.*

In a room after the Lavabo are frescoes by another friar—this one Bartolomeo, who lived from 1475 to 1517 and worked with Raphael. Note his *Madonna and Child with Saints.* In the Capitolo is a fading, but powerful *Crucifixion* by Angelico.

Turn right at the next door and you'll enter a refectory devoted to the artistic triumph of Domenico Ghirlandaio, the man who taught Michelangelo how to fresco. In Ghirlandaio's own work in this room, a *Last Supper,* he was rather realistic, giving his saints tragic faces, while silently evoking a feeling of impending doom.

Upstairs on the second floor—at the top of the hallway—is Angelico's masterpiece, *The Annunciation,* a perfect gem of a painting. From here, you can walk down the left corridor, exploring the cells of the Dominicans, enhanced by frescoes by Angelico and his pupils. Most of the poorly lit frescoes depict scenes from the Crucifixion.

After turning to the right, you may want to skip the remaining frescoes, as they appear to be uninspired student exercises. But at the end of the corridor is the cell of Savonarola, the scene of his arrest. The cell contains portraits of the reformer by Bartolomeo, who was plunged into acute melancholy by the jailing and torturing of his beloved teacher. You'll also find pictures of the reformer on the pyre at the piazza della Signoria.

If you retrace your steps to the entrance, then head down still another corridor, you'll see more frescoes, past a library with Ionic columns designed by Michelozzo. Finally, you'll come to the cell of Cosimo dei Medici, with a fresco by Gozzoli, who worked with Angelico.

A state museum, San Marco is open daily except Monday from 9 a.m. to 2 p.m. and charges 3,000 lire ($2.30) for admission. On Sunday it's open till 1 p.m.

A TIP FOR EXPLORING FLORENCE

Readers traveling to Florence on limited time (two or three days) should be there toward the middle or end of the week if possible. Most museums close at 12:30 or 1 p.m. on Sunday and are closed all day Monday, so it's wise to plan your visit accordingly.

2. The Secondary Sights

THE CHURCHES OF FLORENCE

The wealth of architecture, art, and treasures of Florence's churches is hardly secondary, but if you want to see even a sampling of the best, you'll have to schedule an extra day or more in the City of the Renaissance.

Church of Santa Croce

The piazza Santa Croce is the Pantheon of Florence, sheltering the tombs of everyone from Michelangelo to Machiavelli, from Dante (he was actually buried at Ravenna) to an astronomer (Galileo) who—at the hands of the Inquisition— "recanted" his concept that the earth revolves around the sun. Just as the Santa Maria Novella was the church of the Dominicans, Santa Croce was the church of the Franciscans, said to have been designed by Arnolfo di Cambio.

In the right nave (first tomb) is the Vasari-executed monument to Michelangelo, whose body was smuggled back to his native Florence from its original burial place in Rome. Along with a bust of the artist are three allegorical figures representing the arts. In the next memorial a prune-faced Dante looks down, a poet honored belatedly in the city that exiled him. Farther on, still on the right, is the tomb of Machiavelli, whose *The Prince* became a virtual textbook in the art of wielding power. Nearby is a lyrical bas-relief, *The Annunciation* by Donatello.

The "Trecento" frescoes are reason enough for visiting Santa Croce— especially those by Giotto to the right of the main chapel. Once whitewashed, the Bardi and Peruzzi Chapels were "uncovered" in the mid-19th century in such a clumsy fashion that they have had to be drastically restored. Although badly preserved, the frescoes in the Bardi Chapel are most memorable, especially the deathbed scene of St. Francis. The cycles in the Peruzzi Chapel are of John the Baptist and St. John. In the left transept is Donatello's once-controversial wooden *Crucifix*— too gruesome for some Renaissance tastes, including that of Brunelleschi, who is claimed to have said: "You [Donatello] have put a rustic upon the cross." (For Brunelleschi's "answer," go to Santa Maria Novella.) Incidentally, the Pazzi Chapel, entered through the cloisters, was designed by Brunelleschi, with terracottas by Luca della Robbia.

Additionally, inside the monastery of this church the Franciscan fathers established the **Leather School** at the end of World War II. The purpose of the school was to prepare young boys technically to specialize in Florentine leather work. The school has flourished and produced many fine artisans who continue their careers here. Stop in and see the work when you visit the church.

Church of Santa Maria Novella

At the piazza Santa Maria Novella, near the railway station, is one of the most distinguished churches of Florence, begun in 1278 for the Dominicans. Its geometric façade, with bands of white and green marble, was designed in the late 15th century by Leon Battista Alberti, an aristocrat who was the true Renaissance man (that is, philosopher, painter, architect, poet). The church in good harmony borrows from the Romanesque, Gothic, and Renaissance styles.

In the left nave as you enter (third large painting) is the great Masaccio's *Trinity,* a curious work that has the architectural form of a Renaissance stage setting, but whose figures—in perfect perspective—are like actors in a Greek tragedy. If you view the church at dusk, you'll see the stained-glass windows in the fading light casting kaleidoscopic fantasies on the opposite wall.

Head straight up the left nave to the Gondi Chapel for a look at Brunelleschi's wooden *Christ on the Cross,* said to have been carved to compete with Donatello's same subject in Santa Croce (see above). According to Vasari, when Donatello saw Brunelleschi's completed Crucifix, he dropped his apron full of eggs intended for their lunch. "You have symbolized the Christ," Donatello is alleged to have said. "Mine is an ordinary man." (Some art historians reject this story.)

In the late 15th century Ghirlandaio contracted with a Medici banker to adorn the choir with frescoes, illustrating scenes from the lives of Mary and John the Baptist. Michelangelo, only a teenager at the time, is known to have studied under Ghirlandaio (perhaps he even worked on this cycle).

If time remains, you may want to visit the cloisters, coming first to the "Green Cloisters," then the splendid Spanish Chapel frescoed by Andrea di Bonaiuto in the 14th century (one panel depicts the Dominicans in triumph over heretical wolves). The cloisters may be inspected from 9 a.m. to 2 p.m. (to 1 p.m. on Sunday) for 3,000 lire ($2.30); closed Friday.

Church of San Lorenzo

At the piazza San Lorenzo is Brunelleschi's 15th-century Renaissance church, where the Medici used to attend services from their nearby palace on via Larga, now via Camillo Cavour. Most visitors flock to see Michelangelo's "New Sacristy" with that artist's *Night* and *Day* (see the Medici chapels under "The Top Sights"), but Brunelleschi's handiwork deserves some time too.

Built in the style of a Latin cross, the church is distinguished by harmonious grays and rows of Corinthian columns. The Old Sacristy (walk up the nave, then turn left) was designed by Brunelleschi and decorated, in part, by Donatello (see his terracotta bust of St. Lawrence).

After exploring the Old Sacristy, go through the first door (unmarked) on your right, then turn right again and climb the steps.

The **Laurenziana Library** (entered separately from piazza San Lorenzo 9) was designed by Michelangelo to shelter the expanding library of the Medici. Beautiful in design and concept, approached by exquisite stairs, the library is filled with some of Italy's greatest manuscripts—many of them handsomely illustrated. The library is open from 9 a.m. to 1 p.m. Monday through Saturday (free); closed Sunday. The study room is open from 8 a.m. to 2 p.m. After a visit here, you may want to wander through the cloisters of San Lorenzo, with their Ionic columns.

Santa Maria del Carmine

At the piazza Santa Maria del Carmine, a long walk from the Pitti Palace on the left bank, is a baroque church, a result of rebuilding after a fire in the 18th century. Miraculously, the renowned Brancacci Chapel was spared—miraculous in that it contains frescoes by Masaccio, who ushered in the great century of "Quattrocento" Renaissance painting. Forsaking the ideal, Masaccio depicted man and woman in their weakness and their glory.

His technique is seen at its most powerful in the expulsion of Adam and Eve from the Garden of Eden. The artist peopled his chapel, a masterpiece of early perspective, with scenes from the life of St. Peter, the work originally begun by his master, Masolino. Note especially the fresco "tribute money," and the baptism scene with the nude youth freezing in the cold waters.

No less an authority than Leonardo da Vinci commented on the decline by imitation in painting following Giotto's breakthrough. But upon seeing Masaccio's work, he wrote: "Masaccio showed by his perfect works how those who take for their ideal anything but nature—mistress of all masters—tire themselves in vain." Masaccio did the upper frescoes, but because of his early death, the lower ones were completed by Filippino Lippi (not to be confused with his father, Filippo Lippi, a greater artist).

It is open in summer from 7 a.m. to noon and 4 to 6 p.m. daily. In winter it keeps the same hours, except that it closes at 5 p.m.

The Synagogue of Florence

This synagogue, at via Farini 4 (tel. 245-252), is in the Moorish style, inspired by Constantine's Byzantine church of Hagia Sophia. Completed in 1882, it was badly damaged by the Nazis in 1944 but has been restored to its original splendor. A museum is upstairs. You can visit the synagogue daily except Saturday and Jewish holidays. Admission is free. For the exact timetable of visits and prayers, please phone the secretary.

PALACES AND MORE MUSEUMS

The most famous and most imposing palace in Florence is, without doubt, the—

Palazzo Vecchio

At the piazza della Signoria is the secular "Old Palace" (tel. 27-681), dating from the closing years of the 13th century. Its remarkable architectural feature is its 308-foot tower, an engineering feat that required supreme skill on the part of the builder. Once home to the Medici, the Palazzo Vecchio (also called Palazzo della Signoria) is occupied today by city employees, but much of it is open to the public.

You can visit the 15th-century "Hall of the 500" ("Dei Cinquecento"), the most outstanding part of the palace, filled with Vasari & Co. frescoes as well as sculpture. As you enter the hall, look for Michelangelo's *Victory*. It depicts an insipid-looking young man treading on a bearded older man (it's been suggested that Michelangelo put his own face on that of the trampled man).

Later you can stroll through the rest of the palace, through its apartments and main halls. You can also visit the private apartments of Eleanor of Toledo, wife of Cosimo I, and a chapel, begun in 1540 and frescoed by Bronzino. In the Cancelleria is the original of Verrocchio's bronze putto (dating from 1476) from the courtyard fountain. This work is called both *Winged Cherub Clutching a Fish* and *Boy with a Dolphin*. The palace also shelters a 16th-century *Portrait of Machiavelli* which is attributed to Santi di Tito. Once Donatello's famous bronze group, *Judith Slaying Holofernes,* stood on the piazza dei Signoria, but it was brought inside.

The salons, such as a fleur-de-lis apartment, have their own richness and beauty. Following his arrest, Savonarola was taken to the Palazzo Vecchio for more than a dozen torture sessions, including "twists" on the rack. The torturer pronounced him his "best" customer. Charging 6,000 lire ($4.55) for admission, the palace is open Monday through Friday from 9 a.m. to 7 p.m. and on Sunday from 8 a.m. to 1 p.m.; closed Saturday.

Palazzo Medici-Riccardi

At via Camillo Cavour 1 (tel. 27-601), a short walk from the duomo, was the home of Cosimo dei Medici before he took his household to the Palazzo della

Signoria. Built by palace architect Michelozzo in the mid-15th-century, the brownstone was also the scene, at times, of the court of Lorenzo the Magnificent. Art lovers visit today chiefly to see the mid-15th-century frescoes by Benozzo Gozzoli in the Medici Chapel.

Gozzoli's frescoes, depicting the *Journey of the Magi*, form his masterpiece—in fact they are considered a hallmark in Renaissance painting in that they abandoned ecclesiastical themes to celebrate emerging man (he peopled his work with the Medici, the artist's master Fra Angelico, even himself). Gozzoli's ability as a landscape artist and a distinguished portraitist (each man in the procession is a distinctly identifiable individual—often elaborately coiffed and clothed) is seen at its finest here. The chapel is open from 9 a.m. to 12:30 p.m. and 3 to 5 p.m. daily except Wednesday (on Sunday till noon). The entrance is free.

The gallery of Luca Giordano, which has to be entered by another stairway, was frescoed by that artist in the 18th century, but his work seems merely decorative. The apartments, where the prefect lodges, are not open to the public. The gallery, incidentally, may also be viewed free.

Archeological Museum

At via della Colonna 38 (tel. 247-8641), a short walk from the piazza della SS Annunziata, this museum houses one of the most outstanding Egyptian and Etruscan collections in Europe. Its Egyptian mummies and sarcophagi are on the first floor, along with some of the better-known Etruscan works. Pause to look at the lid to the coffin of a fat Etruscan (unlike the blank faces staring back from many of these tombs, this overeater's countenance is quite expressive).

One room is graced with three bronze Etruscan masterpieces, among the rarest objets d'art of these relatively unknown people. They include the *Chimera*, a lion with a goat sticking out of its back. The lion's tail—in the form of a venomous reptile—lunges at the trapped beast. The others are a statue of *Minerva* and one of an *Orator*. These pieces of sculpture range from the 5th to the 1st centuries B.C. Another rare find is an original Greek bronze of a young man, the so-called *Idolino from Pesaro*. The François vase on the ground floor, from the year 570 B.C., is celebrated. The museum is open from 9 a.m. to 2 p.m. daily except Monday, charging 3,000 lire ($2.30) for admission. It closes at 1 p.m. on Sunday.

Duomo Museum

At piazza del Duomo 9 (tel. 213-229), across the street but facing the apse of Santa Maria del Fiore, is a museum beloved by connoisseurs of Renaissance sculptural works. It shelters the sculpture removed from the campanile and the duomo—not only to protect the pieces from the weather, but from visitors who wanted samples. A major attraction of this museum is the unfinished *Pietà* by Michelangelo, which is in the middle of the stairs. It was carved between 1548 and 1555 when the artist was in his 70s. In this vintage work, a figure representing Nicodemus (but said to have Michelangelo's face) is holding Christ. The great Florentine intended it for his own tomb, but he is believed to have grown disenchanted with it and to have attempted to destroy it. The museum has a Brunelleschi bust, as well as della Robbia terracottas.

You'll see bits and pieces from what was the old Gothic-Romanesque fronting of the cathedral, with ornamental statues, as conceived by the original architect, Arnolfo di Cambio. One of Donatello's early works, *St. John the Evangelist*, is here—not his finest hour certainly, but anything by Donatello is worth looking at. That is especially true of one of his most celebrated works of art, his *Magdalene*, placed in the room with the cantorie. This wooden statue by Donatello once stood in the Baptistery, and had to be restored after the flood of 1966. Dating from 1454-1455, it is stark and penitent.

A good reason for visiting the museum is to see the marble choirs—"cantorie"—of Donatello and Luca della Robbia (the works face each other, and are housed in the first room you enter after climbing the stairs). The Luca della Robbia choir is more restrained, but still "Praises the Lord" in marble—with "clashing cymbals, sounding brass" . . . a reaffirmation of life. In contrast, all restraint breaks loose in the "cantoria" of dancing cherubs in Donatello's choir. It's a romp of chubby bambini. Of all of Donatello's works, perhaps this one is the most lighthearted. But, in total contrast, don't miss Donatello's *Zuccone,* which some consider to be one of his greatest masterpieces; it was done for Giotto's bell tower. The museum is open Monday through Saturday March 1 to September 30 from 9 a.m. to 8 p.m. and October 1 to February 28 from 9 a.m. to 6 p.m. Admission is 3,000 lire ($2.30). On Sunday all year, it is open only from 10 a.m. to 1 p.m., and admission is free.

EVEN MORE SIGHTS

As you're swiftly learning, the sights of Florence are virtually endless.

Boboli Gardens

Behind the Pitti Palace are the gardens through which the Medici romped. They were originally laid out by that great landscape artist Tribolo in the 16th century. The Renaissance gardens are the scene of the annual open-air "Maggio Musicale." The Boboli is ever popular for a promenade or an idyllic interlude in a pleasant setting. It's filled with fountains and statuary, such as a *Venus* by Giambologna in the "Grotto" of Buontalenti. You can climb to the top of the Fortezza di Belvedere for a dazzling view of the city. The admission-free gardens are open daily in summer from 9 a.m. to 6:30 p.m. They close in winter at 4:30.

Piazzale Michelangelo

For a view of the wonders of Florence below and Fiesole above, hop aboard bus 13 from the central station and head for the piazzale Michelangelo, a 19th-century belvedere overlooking a view seen in many a Renaissance painting. It's best at dusk, when the purple-fringed Tuscan hills form a frame for Giotto's bell tower, Brunelleschi's dome, and the towering hunk of stones sticking up from the Palazzo Vecchio. Dominating the square is another copy of Michelangelo's *David.*

Warning: At certain times during the day the square is so overcrowded with tour buses and trinket peddlers with claptrap souvenirs that the balcony is drained of its chief drama. If you go at midday in summer, you'll find that the view of Florence is still intact—only you may be run down by a Vespa if you try to enjoy it.

Ponte Vecchio

Spared by the Nazis in their bitter retreat from the Allied advance in 1944, "The Old Bridge" is the last remaining medieval *ponte* spanning the Arno (the Germans blew up the rest). The existence of the Ponte Vecchio was again threatened in the flood of 1966—in fact, the waters of the Arno swept over it, washing away a fortune in jewelry from the goldsmiths' shops that flank the bridge.

Today the restored Ponte Vecchio is closed to traffic except the *pedoni* type. The little shops continue to sell everything from the most expensive of Florentine gold to something simple—say, a Lucrezia Borgia poison ring. Once the hog butchers of Florence peddled their wares on this bridge.

Foundling Hospital

At piazza SS. Annunziata 12 is the **Hospital of the Innocents,** or Galleria dello Spedale degli Innocenti (tel. 243-670), the oldest of its kind in Europe. The building, and especially the loggia, with its Corinthian columns, was conceived by Brunelleschi, marking the first architectural bloom of the Renaissance in Florence. In the cortile are terracotta medallions, in blues and opaque whites, of babes in swaddling clothes, the work of Andrea della Robbia.

Still used as a hospital, the building also contains an art gallery. Notable among its treasures is a terracotta *Madonna and Child* by Luca della Robbia, plus works by

Andrea del Sarto and Filippo Lippi. One of the gallery's most important paintings is an *Adoration of the Magi,* by Domenico Ghirlandaio (the chubby Bambino looks a bit pompously at the Wise Man kissing his foot). The gallery is open daily except Wednesday from 9 a.m. to 2 p.m. (to 1 p.m. on Sunday). No admission is charged.

Bardini Museum

At piazza de' Mozzi (tel. 234-2437), the Bardini Museum grew out of the collections of one Stefano Bardini who died in 1922. In his heyday in the 19th century he was known as a major art dealer, and grew wealthy buying and selling art. He saved a lot for himself, as this collection clearly reveals. The only regret I have is that he short-sightedly demolished a 13th-century church to build a palace to house his collection; however, he at least used some of the architectural remnants in his new palace. Visiting hours are 9 a.m. to 2 p.m. Monday through Saturday and 8 a.m. to 1 p.m. on Sunday; closed Wednesday. Admission is 3,000 lire ($2.30).

This museum seems little visited and even less known, except among art connoisseurs, those who make a point to visit *every* museum in Florence. Bardini seems to have followed no particular guidelines in his collection, and thus one is likely to get a little bit of everything, from Greek and Roman sculpture, even Etruscan. Antique musical instruments are exhibited along with church altars. Naturally, he was able to acquire some stunning Renaissance furniture, along with paintings by such old masters as Lucas Cranach and Tintoretto. He also collected terracotta reliefs, the favorite mother and child theme from the della Robbias.

Horne Museum

Herbert Horne, an art historian, immortalized himself upon his death in 1916, having collected the nucleus for this exhibition, appropriately called the Horne Museum and found at via dei Benci 6 (tel. 244-661). It can be visited Monday through Saturday from 9 a.m. to 1 p.m.; closed Sunday. Admission is 3,000 lire ($2.30). A bachelor, and also a prominent figure in the pre–World War I expatriate colony that flourished in Florence, English-born Horne was a great collector. This is even more remarkable when one considers that he was not wealthy.

But he knew art, and he shopped for "bargains," especially in the art of the Renaissance. He was mainly interested in painting. His greatest acquisition was the Giotto portrait of Saint Stephen, dating from the early 14th century. Other minor masterpieces were also acquired, including works by Filippo Lippi, Simone Martini, Dosso Dossi, and Masaccio.

HOUSES OF ARTISTS AND WRITERS

What better place to start than at the house once owned by Michelangelo.

Casa Buonarroti

At via Ghibellina 70 (tel. 241-752), a short walk from Santa Croce, stands the house that Michelangelo managed to buy for his nephew. Turned into a museum by his descendants, the house was restored in 1964. It contains some fledgling work by the great artist, as well as some models by him. Here you can see his *Madonna of the Stairs,* which he did when he was about 17 years old, as well as a bas-relief he did later, depicting *The Battle of the Centaurs.* The casa is enriched by many of the drawings of Michelangelo shown to the public in periodic exhibitions. The house is open daily except Tuesday from 9:30 a.m. to 1:30 p.m., charging 4,000 lire ($3.05) for admission.

Casa Guidi

At piazza S. Felice 8 (tel. 284-393), just across from the Pitti Palace, not far from the Arno, is the former residence of Elizabeth Barrett and Robert Browning. They chose this location less than a year after their clandestine marriage in London, and it became their home for the remaining 14 years of their life together. Casa

Guidi is where their son was born and where they wrote some of their best-known works. Elizabeth died here in 1861. Her tomb can be visited at the English cemetery in Florence. After her death, a heart-broken Browning left Florence, never to return (he died in Venice in 1889 and is buried in Westminster Abbey in London). The poets' son, Pen, acquired the residence in 1893, intending to make a memorial to his parents; however, he died before completing his plans. The rooms were first opened to the public in 1971 when the Browning Institute, an international charitable organization, acquired the apartment. "White doves in the ceiling" and frescoes of "angels looking down from a cloud," both of which Elizabeth wrote about, will interest Browning aficionados.

Today the rooms are open from 3 to 6 p.m. Monday through Friday, as well as by appointment on Saturday, Sunday, and holidays. From December 15 to February 1 they are open only by appointment. Admission is free, but contributions to the Browning Institute through the Friends of Casa Guidi are welcome. In a more cynical age, there is the possibility of rejecting the Brownings' life in Florence as "sentimental." Regardless, it's admirable what the institute has done to pay homage to the two 19th-century poets who were the center of the Anglo-Florentine community, much as Keats and Shelley were the stars in "English Rome." Elizabeth Barrett Browning wrote regarding Casa Guidi that "the charm of a home is a home to come back to." As such, the institute is maintaining the house for future generations.

Dante's House

For those of us who were spoon-fed hell but spared purgatory, a pilgrimage to this rebuilt medieval house may be of passing interest, although it contains few specific exhibits of note. Dante was exiled from his native Florence in 1302 for his political involvements. He never returned, and thus wrote his *Divine Comedy* in exile, conjuring up fit punishment in the *Inferno* for his Florentine enemies. Dante certainly had the last word. The house is reached by walking down via Dante Alighieri, but the entrance to the museum is at via Santa Margherita 1 (tel. 283-343). The admission-free casa is open daily except Wednesday from 9:30 a.m. to 12:30 p.m. and 3:30 to 6:30 p.m. from 9:30 a.m. to 12:30 p.m. on Sunday. Between July 1 and August 31, the house is closed for approximately three weeks.

Museo Stibbert

The eclectic collection of arms and armor, paintings by major and minor artists, tapestries, furniture, porcelain, and costumes for men and women, particularly the apparel of warriors of many civilizations, which was the life interest of Frederick Stibbert can be seen at Museo Stibbert, via F. Stibbert 26 (tel. 475-520). Florentine-born Stibbert, son of an upper-class English father and a Florentine mother, made his 62-room villa, set in an elegant park, into his own personal museum, which he left on his death in 1906 to the city of Florence. It is on the Montughi hill just outside the city. From the entrance into the Malachite Room with red-brocade-covered walls, you go through Louis XV, Louis XVI, and Empire salons, Italian rooms, Turkish corridors, and samurai arsenals. The museum is unusual in that it houses the most extensive collection known of Near Eastern armor, plus that of Oriental warriors, as well as complete sets of the finery of European knights worn during at least two centuries. Of special interest are three rooms whose walls and doors are completely covered with embossed and painted leather. The park in which the villa stands is a mixture of English horticulture and exotic flora, with a pond and a little Egyptian pavilion. Monday through Saturday (closed Thursday) visits are by guided tour only, beginning on the hour from 9 a.m. to 1 p.m. On Sunday, only part of the museum can be visited, from 9 a.m. to 12:30 p.m. Admission is 2,000 lire ($1.50).

Leonardo's Hometown

At Vinci, 27 miles from Florence, you can visit the **Leonardo da Vinci Museum** (tel. 055/56055) in the 11th-century castle there. Leonardo was born in the town in 1452. The museum contains photographic documentation of drawings and paintings by Leonardo, together with a magnificent collection of models built after Leonardo's original sketches, constituting a testimonial to the vastness and versatility of his genius. A library containing some 13,000 volumes about Leonardo's works is in the museum. Charging adults 3,000 lire ($2.30) for admission, it is open daily from 9 a.m. to noon and 2 to 6:30 p.m. The house where the great painter, mathematician, physicist, and engineer was born lies one mile to the north of Vinci on the Anchiano road.

AMERICAN MILITARY CEMETERY

On a 70-acre site, the **Florence American Cemetery and Memorial** (tel. 055/202-0020) lies about 7½ miles south of the city on the west side of via Cassia, the main highway connecting Florence with Siena and Rome. One of 14 permanent American World War II military cemetery memorials built on foreign soil by the American Battle Monuments Commission, the Florence memorial is on a site liberated August 3, 1944, which later became part of the zone of the U.S. Fifth Army. It is astride the Greve River and framed by wooded hills. Most of the 4,402 servicemen and women interred here died in the fighting that occurred after the capture of Rome in June 1944. The cemetery is open daily: from 8 a.m. to 6 p.m. May 15 to September 15 and from 8 a.m. to 5 p.m. September 16 to May 14. The SITA city bus stops at the cemetery entrance every two hours except on holidays, when there is usually no bus service. The bus follows via Cassia.

---

3. A Walking Tour of Florence

This tour begins at the piazza de' Pitti, where you may or may not elect to visit the art treasures of the Pitti Palace or walk through the Boboli Gardens in back of the palace. Head up via di Guicciardini toward the Ponte Vecchio until you reach this ancient, shop-flanked bridge spanning the river. Pause at the top of the bridge where a vista from the double-sided belvedere offers views of the Arno on both sides. The calm waters you see today belie the unpredictable torrents that, as they did in 1966, are capable of sweeping over sections of the bridge.

After crossing the bridge, turn right, walking alongside the Arno, passing beneath a riverside arcade pierced both longitudinally and latitudinally by a series of arches which open from four directions like a Renaissance study in perspectives. Traffic whizzes beside you, funneling into the tiny piazza del Pesche. The riverside promenade that supports you now changes its name to the lungarno degli Archibusieri, which, a few steps later, gives way to lungarno Anna Maria Luisa de' Medici, just at the end of your sheltering arcade. Note the almost medieval view of the Ponte Vecchio from this spot.

In about 40 paces you'll come to a soaring canopy of one of the most impressive arcades in Florence. This closes off the Arno side of the three-sided colonnades of the Uffizi Gallery. Walk between the rhythmically spaced arches of the arcades onto flagstones, which in sunny weather support dozens of hawkers and vendors. The Tower of the Signoria opens to your sight as you approach it.

At the piazza della Signoria, stop to admire the sculpture-filled Loggia della Signoria and the Palazzo Vecchio. Pass the fountain of Neptune and turn right just before the equestrian statue. Head onto the far corner of the square, taking a small street flanking the side of the Palazzo Vecchio. This street, via de' Gondi, in one block takes you to the piazza di San Firenze. Cross this street and climb seven stone steps of the baroque palace in front of you and turn to contemplate your first view of the very top of Brunelleschi's dome on the duomo.

Proceed down a narrow alley where a yellow-and-black sign points the way to the Basilica of Santa Croce. The name of the street is the borgo de' Greci. You emerge onto the piazza di Santa Croce, for a view of the pink, green, and white bands that ornament the façade of the Basilica of Santa Croce. After visiting the church, take a small street in front of it, called via Torta. Continue along to the first intersection, going along via della Burella, a narrow, flagstone-covered neighborhood street. At the end, you'll come to via dell'Acqua.

Turn right and walk a short distance until the foreboding brownstone bulk of the Palazzo Bargello now soars above you. Turn left on the street via della Vigna Vecchia, which parallels the side of the Bargello. At the end of this narrow street, your sightlines will expand into the piazza di San Firenze. Go right onto via del Proconsolo. You won't be able to see it yet, but you'll be headed to the duomo.

The sidewalk is very narrow, often crowded, and somewhat a threat because of traffic. But, suddenly, there explodes the intricately patterned façade of what might be Italy's most obvious symbol of the Renaissance, the red-tile dome of the duomo. Head across the crosswalk and continue more or less in a straight line along the periphery of shops and buildings ringing the edges of the rear side of the duomo. Stop at no. 9 on the piazza del Duomo, if you have time, and visit the Museo del Duomo. As you leave the museum, continue to ring the periphery of the piazza until you reach a pedestrian crosswalk, which leads you to a point between the cathedral's entrance and the doors of the baptistery. The baptistery actually sits on its own satellite square, the piazza di San Giovanni.

After visiting the duomo and the baptistery, cross the same street you approached them from. Turn left as soon as you reach via Martelli and walk 1½ blocks until you turn right at borgo San Lorenzo. Walk a short distance until you reach the piazza di San Lorenzo. Pass to the right of the roughly textured façade of the Basilica of San Lorenzo and go along the side of this building. Continue in a crescent-shaped arc, always following the periphery of this huge church. You'll reach the wooden doors leading to the Medici chapels. At this point, you'll be on the piazza di Madonna degli Aldobrandini.

Take via del Giglio, walking straight across the busy traffic of via Panzani. Continue straight along via del Giglio until its end, via de Banchi, where you turn right. This will take you to the piazza Santa Maria Novella. After visiting the church, take via delle Belle Donne and follow it past a granite column. Cross via del Moro, taking via del Trebbio. Follow this narrow street, past the Buca Lapi restaurant, until you come to the piazza degli Antinori. Turn right onto the most famous shopping street of Florence, via dei Turnabuoni. Walk along this street, checking out its many elegant shops, until you pass the soaring column of the piazza Trinità, up to the banks of the Arno again. At a point between a pair of statues, flanking the entrance to the Ponte Trinità, consider that your tour has ended and plan which route of attack you'll follow while visiting the other treasures of Florence.

---

4. Shopping in Florence

Skilled craftsmanship and traditional design unchanged since the days of the Medici have made Florence a goal for the serious shopper. Florence is noted for its hand-tooled leather goods and its various straw merchandise, as well as superbly crafted silver jewelry. Its reputation for fashionable custom-made clothes is no longer what it was, having lost its position of supremacy to Milan.

The whole city of Florence strikes many visitors as a gigantic department store. Entire neighborhoods on both sides of the Arno offer good shops, although those along the medieval Ponte Vecchio (with some exceptions) strike most people as too touristy.

Of course, Florence's Fifth Avenue is via dei Tornabuoni, with its flag-ship Gucci stores for leather and Ferragamo for stylish but costly shoes.

The better shops are for the most part along Tornabuoni, but there are many on via Vigna Nuova, via Porta Rossa, and via degli Strozzi. You might also stroll on the lungarno along the Arno.

BOOKS

A vast array of books is carried by **Libreria BM Book Shop,** via Borgognissanti 4R (tel. 294-575). In fact, it is one of the finest such stores in Europe. Browsers are encouraged, aided, and informed. Many customers come here just to look over the collection of art books. The bookshop is near the Excelsior Hotel.

Paperback Exchange, via Fiesolana 31R (tel. 247-8154), has thousands and thousands of books, both fiction and nonfiction, on its shelves. Books are recycled. That is, you can trade in your old paperbacks, and if they're acceptable, you're granted discounts on the advertised price on the cover of any more volumes you purchase. It's very democratic and very cheap if you want to catch up on your reading while in Florence. In addition to the used books, a new stock of paperbacks has been added, including current bestsellers, classics, and the like, as well as modern and contemporary literature with emphasis on Italy, plus travel guides.

CLOTHING (MEN AND WOMEN)

In the commercial center of town near the duomo, **Romano,** piazza della Repubblica (tel. 296-890), is a glamorous clothing store for women. The owners commissioned a curving stairwell to be constructed under the high ornate ceiling. But even more exciting are their well-stocked leather and suede goods, along with an assortment of dresses, shoes, and handbags, many at very high prices if you're willing to buy for quality.

Bellucci Italian Classics, borgo San Lorenzo 14R, offers good-quality men's clothing. The service here is excellent, and the prices better than at many other shops. The ready-to-wear selection is from top Italian manufacturers, specializing in classic jackets, suits, trousers, and seasonal outerwear. There is special-order tailoring service, allowing selection of style, fabric, and detailing, with arrangements for having the finished product sent to you at home.

EMBROIDERY

Superior work is found at **Rifredi School of Artistic Embroidery,** via Carlo Bini 29 (tel. 422-0575). However, it's a 15-minute ride from the center of town (take bus 14, 28, or 20). Awaiting your inspection is an array of delicate embroidery of artistic design, including tea and breakfast sets, tablecloths, bed linen, handkerchiefs, and women's lingerie.

FABRICS

In business for more than a half century, **Casa dei Tessuti,** via de' Pecori 20 (tel. 215-961), is a shop for connoisseurs, those seeking one of the largest and highest-quality selections of materials in linen, silk, and wool (along with cottons). The Romoli family, longtime proprietors, are proud of their assortment of fabrics, and rightly so, and are known for their selections of designs and colors.

FLORENTINE PAPER

The leading stationery store in Florence is **Giulio Giannini Figlio,** piazza Pitti 36-37R (tel. 212-621). Much of its merchandise is so exquisite that it qualifies as a gift store. The English-speaking staff is most helpful. This has been a family business for nearly 140 years.

GALLERIES

One of Tuscany's oldest foundries, **Peter Bazzanti & Son,** lungarno Corsini 44-48 (tel. 215-649), offers shoppers the chance to buy bronze or marble copies of the sculptures they've admired in many of Italy's finest museums. This company's retail outlet sits beside the Arno in a sprawling series of high-ceilinged rooms crammed with more than 3,000 copies of sculpture originally created by the Etruscans, the ancient Romans, or Renaissance artists. You can purchase what might become a family heirloom. Small gift items in onyx, marble, or bronze are also sold. Anything you purchase can be crated and shipped, regardless of size.

Galleria Masini, piazza Goldoni 6R (tel. 294-000), a few minutes' walk from the Grand Hotel Excelsior and other leading hotels, has been established for more than 100 years and is still owned by the Masini family. Their selection of modern and contemporary paintings by top artists is extensive. Even if you're not a collector, this is a good place to select a picture which will be a lasting reminder of your visit to Italy—and you can take it home duty free.

GIFTS

At the piazza del Pesce–Ponte Vecchio, **Menegatti** (tel. 215-202) has a wide collection of items. Pottery from Florence, Faenza, and Deruta is offered, along with della Robbia reproductions made in red clay like the originals. Items can be sent home if you arrange it at the time of purchase.

Balatresi Gift Shop, lungarno Acciaiuoli 22R (tel. 287-851), is presided over by Umberto and Giovanna Balatresi, who have stocked their shop full of treasures, among which are Florentine mosaics created for them by Maestro Marco Tacconi, arguably the greatest mosaicist alive today, as well as original ceramic figurines by the sculptor Giannitrapani, exclusive Fabergé reproductions, and a fine selection of hand-carved alabaster. Many Americans come into this store in August to do their Christmas shopping.

HANDCRAFTS

The society for the exportation of Italian artistic products, **S.E.L.A.N.,** via Porta Rossa 107R (tel. 212-995), right off the piazza S. Trinità, is a star choice for traditional designs in Italian ceramics. A wide assortment of merchandise is offered.

JEWELRY

Buying jewelry is almost an art in itself, so proceed with caution. Florence, of course, is known for its jewelry. You'll find some stunning antique pieces, and if you know how to buy, some fine bargains.

Faraone-Settipassi, via Tornobuoni 25R (tel. 215-506), is one of the most distinguished jewelers of the Renaissance city, drawing a well-heeled patronage.

Mario Buccellati, via Tornabuoni 69-71 (tel. 296-579), specializes in exquisite handcrafted jewelry and silver. A large selection of intriguing pieces at high prices is offered. Bucellati is closed in August.

G & G Gold, lungarno Acciaioli 52R (tel. 210-040). There are dozens of jewelry stores in Florence, but one that has an interesting selection and an easy-to-reach location sits on the quays of the Arno a few steps from the Ponte Vecchio.

LEATHER

Universally acclaimed, Florentine leather is still the fine product it always was —smooth, well shaped, and vivid in such colors as green and red.

S. Luti & Son, via Parione 28-32R (tel. 287-047), offers hundreds of fine-quality articles and has been in the leathergoods business since 1922. It has a large selection of high-fashion women's handbags, as well as many fine gift items and travel articles. Businesspeople can select from a wide range of contemporary attaché cases and well-styled traditional briefcases. The construction is of top-notch quality. Via Parione is one of the oldest streets in Florence, in the historical center running perpendicular to via Tornabuoni and parallel to the Arno. In summer, the shop closes on Saturday afternoon.

John F., lungarno Corsini 2, near S. Trinità Bridge (tel. 298-985), is a high-fashion house of leather in a Florentine palace. The leather clothing is of exclusive design, and the salon shows models from the crème de la crème of its collection.

Although Italian male patronage is high, the shop also dresses some of the chicest Florentine women. Accessories made here, including handbags and leather articles, are well crafted and beautifully styled. John F. has just opened a new jewelry store, **Aurum,** lungarno Corsini 16 (tel. 284-259), situated between the John F. store and the boutique for women, **Mariposa,** at no. 18-20 (tel. 284-259). All three stores are operated by the same family, forming a shopping complex of high quality where you can find the work of some of the most famous Italian designers.

Bojola, via Rondinelli 25R (tel. 211-155), is another leading name in leather. Sergio Bojola has distinguished himself in Florence by his selections for many types and tastes, both in synthetic materials and beautiful leathers. Hundreds of customers are always enthusiastic about the variety of items found here, reflecting first-class quality and craftsmanship. Since 1861, when Felice Bojola, Sergio's grandfather, became known as a craftsman, making little umbrellas and walking sticks, the Bojolas have excelled in handcrafted items of refined and discreet style. Today Sergio and his sons design many collectors' items in leather, silver, and other materials, as well as offering for purchase such valuables as crystal and silver boxes, antique "necessaries," and little sun umbrellas.

Leonardo Leather Works, borgo de' Greci 16A (tel. 292-202), actually concentrates on two of the oldest major crafts of Florence: leather and jewelry. Leather goods include wallets, bags, shoes, boots, briefcases, clothing, travel bags, belts, and gift items, with products by famous designers. No imitations are permitted here. The jewelry department has a large assortment of gold chains, bracelets, rings, earrings, and charms. The gold, all 18 karat, is sold by weight.

LINGERIE AND LINENS

A leader in this field is **Loretta Caponi,** via Borgognissanti 12R (tel. 213-668), who not only offers beautiful nightgowns and other items of clothing (many of them hand-embroidered), but also features linens such as pillowcases. All the merchandise is lovely, and you'll at least want to drop in for a visit. However, understandably, for such quality you must pay a lot.

THE MARKETS

After checking into a hotel, the most intrepid shoppers head for the **piazza del Mercato Nuovo (straw market)** called *Il Porcellino* by the Italians because of the bronze reclining pig resting there. The market stands in the monumental heart of Florence, an easy stroll from the Palazzo Vecchio. Open daily from 9 a.m. to 7 p.m., it sells not only straw items but leathergoods as well, along with an array of typically Florentine merchandise, such as frames, trays, hand-embroidery, table linens, and hand-sprayed and painted boxes in traditional designs.

However, even better bargains await those who make their way through pushcarts to the stalls of the open-air **Mercato Centrale,** in and around borgo San Lorenzo, in the vicinity of the railway station. If you don't mind bargaining, which is imperative here, you'll find an array of merchandise that includes raffia bags, Florentine leather purses, salt-and-pepper shakers, straw handbags, and art reproductions.

Warning: In some of these markets you may think you've found Puccis, Guccis, and Louis Vuittons selling for peanuts. You can be sure that such low-priced merchandise is imitation. Most often, it is easily recognized as fake.

MOSAICS

In the old quarter of Santa Croce lies the **Arte Musiva,** largo Bargellini 2-4 (tel. 241-647). Florentine mosaics are universally recognized for their distinction. Bruno Lastrucci, the director of Arte Musiva, is one of the most renowned living exponents of this art form. You can visit the shop Monday through Saturday from 9 a.m. to 7 p.m. and on Sunday from 9 a.m. to 1 p.m. and 3 to 6 p.m. In the workshop you can see artisans plying their craft; some of the major mosaicists of Italy are here. In addition to traditional Florentine, modern mosaic has been developed. A selection of the most significant works is permanently displayed in the gallery. These include decorative panels, linings, and tiles, as well as "figures," "landscapes," and "still lifes" of the great masters of the past.

PHARMACY

Perhaps the most fascinating pharmacy in Italy is **Officina Profumo–Farmaceutica di Santa Maria Novella,** via della Scala 16N (tel. 216-276). To the northwest of the Church of Santa Maria Novella, it opened its doors to the public in 1612, offering a selection of herbal remedies that were created by friars of the Dominican order. Those closely guarded secrets have been retained, and many of the same elixirs are still sold today. You've heard of papaya as an aid to digestion, but what about elixir of rhubarb? A wide selection of perfumes, scented soaps, shampoos, and of course, potpourris, along with creams and lotions, are handsomely presented in these old-fashioned precincts, which almost qualify as a sightseeing attraction.

PUCCI

The name needs little introduction. Marquis Emilio Pucci's palazzo is at via Pucci 6 (tel. 283-061), near the duomo. You'll find a sampling of high-quality fashion in his boutique on the second floor. It is on this same floor that his latest fashions are presented to the world in his much-photographed showroom.

SHOES

Both men and women can buy shoes at **Lily of Florence,** via Guicciardini 2R (tel. 294-748), in American sizes. For women, Lily distributes both her own Lily of Florence designs and Petra brand shoes, also sold in top U.S. department stores. The men's shoes here are by Bally of Switzerland. Color comes in a wide range, and leather texture is of good quality. The styling is refined, the prices reasonable.

Salvatore Ferragamo, via Tornabuoni 16 (tel. 292-123), has long been one of the most world-famous names in shoes. Although he started in Hollywood before the outbreak of World War I, the headquarters of this famed shoemaker was installed here in the Palazzo Feroni, on the most fashionable shopping street of Florence, before the outbreak of World War II. Ferragamo sells shoes known for their durability and style for both men and women, along with some of the most elegant boutique items in the city, including ready-to-wear, scarves, handbags, and other merchandise.

SILVER

There are many charming little antique stores clustered around the Ponte Vecchio that sell silverware. I regard **Peruzzi Brothers,** at Ponte Vecchio 60, corner of borgo San Jacopo 2-4 (tel. 292-027), as among the finest silversmiths in the city, specializing in the best chased Florentine silverware as well as handmade jewelry. The firm has been doing business since 1880.

STRAW

A display house for manufacturers of straw and raffia goods, **Emilio Paoli,** via della Vigna Nuova 24-28R (tel. 214-596), offers women's handbags, hats, skirts, raffia shoes, table mats, baskets, and cane furniture. The exhibits in the showroom are tasteful, and designs show considerable flair.

---

5. Florence After Dark

Not an exciting prospect, unless you like simply to walk through the narrow streets or head up toward Fiesole for a view of the city at night (truly spectacular). The typical Florentine begins his evening early, perhaps at one of the cafés listed below.

Café Rivoire, piazza della Signoria 5R (tel. 214-412), offers a classy, amusing, and interesting old-world ambience looking directly onto the statues of one of my favorite squares in the world. You can sit at one of the metal tables set up on the flagstones outside, or at one of the tables in a choice of inner rooms filled with marble detailing and unusual oil renderings of the piazza outside. If you don't want to sit at all, try the mahogany and green-marble bar, where many of the more colorful characters making the Grand Tour of Europe talk, flirt, or gossip. A member of the staff will serve you an espresso for 850 lire (65¢) or a whisky for 4,000 lire ($3.05). There is also a selection of small sandwiches, omelets, and ice creams. The café is noted for its hot chocolate as well. It is open daily except Monday from 8 a.m. to midnight.

Giacosa, via Tornabuoni 83 (tel. 296-226), is a deceptively simple-looking café whose stand-up bar occupies more space than its limited number of sitdown tables. Set behind three Tuscan arches on a fashionable shopping street in the center of the old city, it has a warmly paneled interior, a lavish display of pastries and sandwiches, and a reputation as the birthplace of the Negroni. That drink, as you probably know, is a combination of gin, Campari, and red vermouth. Other drinks served here include Singapore slings, Italian and American coffee, and a range of apéritifs. Sandwiches and omelets range upward from 8,000 lire ($6.10), and ice creams, for which the café is famous, begin at 6,000 lire ($4.55). Light lunches are served. The café, open from 7 a.m. to 11 p.m., shuts down all day on Sunday.

Monna Lisa, via Faenza 4 (tel. 210-298), is a restaurant with an orchestra, popular with the over-30 set. You can go not only for dinner, but can dance to live music. It is open daily except Monday from 8 p.m. to 2 a.m. The dinner costs from 50,000 lire ($38).

Gilli, piazza della Repubblica 39R (tel. 213-896), said to be the oldest and most beautiful café in Florence, occupies a desirable position in the center of the city, a few minutes' walk from the duomo. It was founded in 1733, when the piazza della Repubblica had a different name. You can sit at a small, brightly lit table near the bar, or else retreat to an intricately paneled pair of rooms to the side, enjoying the flattering light from the Venetian glass chandeliers. A cappuccino costs 4,000 lire ($3.05), and daily specials, sandwiches, toasts, and hard drinks are sold, along with an array of "tropical" libations. Open from 8 a.m. to midnight daily.

Giubbe Rosse, piazza della Repubblica 13-14R (tel. 212-280). The waiters of this place still wear the red coats they did when the establishment was founded in 1888. Originally a beerhall, it is today an elegantly paneled café, bar, and restaurant filled with turn-of-the-century chandeliers and polished granite floors. You can enjoy a drink or cup of coffee at one of the small tables near the zinc-topped bar. An inner dining room has a soaring vaulted ceiling of reddish brick and an Italian menu where meals cost from 35,000 lire ($26.50). Light lunches are a specialty, as well as full American breakfasts. Hours are 8 a.m. to 10 p.m. daily except Thursday.

Perhaps nothing could be more unexpected in this city of Donatello and Michelangelo than a club called the **Red Garter,** via de'Benci 33 (tel. 234-4904), right off the piazza Santa Croce. The American Prohibition era not only lives on, it's been exported. Visitors to the Red Garter can hear a variety of music, ranging from rock to banjo. The club is open from 8 p.m. to 1 a.m. Sunday through Thursday, to 1:30 a.m. on Friday and Saturday, attracting young people from all over the world. A mug of Heineken lager on tap goes for 5,000 lire ($3.80), and most tall drinks, made from "hi-jacked hootch," as it's known here, cost from 7,000 lire ($5.30).

Space Electronic Discoteque, via Palazzuolo 37 (tel. 29-30-82), is a multi-media light-and-sound spectacular on two large floors. On the ground floor—containing a unique aquarium/bar, giant carnival heads, and wall-to-wall mirrors—you can have a quiet drink while seated in one of the comfortable, secluded flower-shaped booths. The floor above offers up-to-date disco music transmitted via a high-quality sound system. The stainless-steel dance floor is large and the light show is sophisticated, with lasers, a multimedia starship, and closed-circuit television. The management and employees create a relaxing atmosphere. The disco is open seven days a week from 9:30 p.m. to 1:30 a.m. and accommodates a crowd of all ages. The first drink costs 15,000 lire ($11.50). A second drink goes for 7,000 lire ($5.30).

Yab-Yum Club, via dei Sassetti 5R (tel. 282-018). In Indian dialect, the name of this place means "rendezvous point," and that is precisely what hordes of Florentine disco lovers use it for. The entrance takes you down an illuminated staircase flanked with Plexiglass columns containing bubbling water and a sort of blend between the electronic age and neoclassicism. Often entertainers are presented, occasionally including acrobats and costumed dancers. Banquettes are arranged theater style around the dance floor, where tunes include American and British music. Near the piazza della Repubblica, the club is open from 10 p.m. to 3:30 a.m. daily except Monday. The first drink costs 20,000 lire ($15.25); the second drink, 10,000 lire ($7.60).

River Club, lungarno Corsini 8 (tel. 282-465), was once the baroque Orsini palace, but it has been converted into one of the poshest and most sophisticated nightclubs in Italy, featuring a disco, a semi-nude floor show, and a piano bar. You can sit at the bar, with its double-barreled baroque fountain and monumental figures of Adam and Eve. The bar stools opposite the fountain are often adorned with "hostesses." To see the floor show at 12:30 a.m., you must go into the adjoining ornate room. A six-piece orchestra plays until dawn on most nights. At the tables, regular whisky costs 16,000 lire ($12.75) for your first drink. The club is open daily except Sunday from 10 p.m. to 2:30 a.m.

Donatello Bar, in the Hotel Excelsior, piazza Ognissanti 3 (tel. 264-201), lies just off the lobby of this grand hotel. Many of the bar's guests, both residents and nonresidents of the hotel, prefer to visit in the late afternoon or early evening, when the stained-glass windows and baroque sculpture are shown in what might be their best light. The bar is open from 11 a.m. to 1:30 a.m. every day. This place is the choicest watering spot in Florence. You are likely to see everyone from Milanese industrialists to French movie stars. In any event, the piano music encourages conviviality that makes the 12,000-lire ($9.10) and up price per drink worth it. In your nightlife prowl of Florence, you might also want to have a drink in the hotel's roof garden, should your visit be during the summer months.

Finally, to cap your evening, you may want to do what the Florentines do. Head for **Gelateria Vivoli,** via Isola delle Stinche 7R (tel. 292-334). This little establishment, run by Piero and Sergio Vivoli, serves the finest ice cream I've tasted in Italy. Buy your ticket first and select your flavor, including such delights as blueberry, fig, melon, and other fruits in season, as well as chocolate mousse, even coffee ice cream flavored with espresso. A special ice cream is made from rice. The gelati range in price from 2,000 lire ($1.50) to 5,000 lire ($3.80). The establishment offers a number of semifreddi concoctions—an Italian ice cream using cream as a base instead of milk. Semifreddi are hardly obtainable outside Italy, and the most popular flavors are almond, marengo (a type of meringue), and zabaglione (eggnog). Other flavors include limoncini alla crema (candied lemon peels with vanilla-flavored ice cream) and aranciotti al cioccolate (candied orange peels with chocolate ice cream). In a backstreet near the church and cloisters of Santa Croce, the Vivolis have renovated the establishment with a white marble and chrome interior, spotlights, and palm trees. The gelateria is open daily except Monday from 9 a.m. to 1 a.m.; closed Sunday during the lunch hour, on holidays, and for three weeks in August.

6. Fiesole

For more extensive day trips, refer to the following chapter. But Fiesole is a virtual suburb of Florence.

When the sun shines too hot on the piazza della Signoria, and tourists try to prance bare-backed into the Uffizi, Florentines are likely to head for the hills—usually to Fiesole. But they will probably encounter more tourists, as this town—once an Etruscan settlement—is the most popular outing from the city. Bus 7, leaving from the piazza San Marco, a breathtaking 25-minute ride, will take you there and give you a fine view along the way. You'll pass fountains, statuary, and gardens strung out over the hills like a scrambled jigsaw puzzle.

THE SIGHTS

When you finally arrive at Fiesole, by all means don't sit with the throngs all afternoon in the central square sipping Campari (although that isn't a bad pastime). Explore some of Fiesole's attractions. You won't find anything as dazzling as the Renaissance treasures of Florence, however, as the charms of Fiesole are subtle. Fortunately, all major sights branch out within walking distance of the main piazza, beginning with—

The Duomo

At first this cathedral may seem austere, with its cement-gray Corinthian columns and Romanesque arches. But it has its own beauty. Dating from A.D. 1000, it was much altered during the Renaissance. In the Salutati Chapel are important sculptural works by Mino da Fiesole. Around to the side of the cathedral is the—

Bandini Museum

This ecclesiastical museum (tel. 59-701) belongs to the Fiesole Cathedral Chapter, established in 1913. On the ground floor are della Robbia terracotta works, as well as art by Michelangelo and Nino Pisano. On the top floors are paintings by the best Giotto students, reflecting such ecclesiastical and worldly themes as the Four Triumphs (Love, Chastity, Time, God) of Florence (1442–1493), most of them the work of Tuscan artists of the 14th century. The museum is open daily from 9:30 a.m. to noon and 3 to 6 p.m. in summer; from 10 a.m. to noon and 3:30 to 5:30 p.m. in winter. Admission is 3,000 lire ($2.30).

The Roman Theater and Archeological Museum

On this site is the major surviving evidence that Fiesole was an Etruscan city six centuries before Christ, and later a Roman town. In the 1st century B.C. a theater was built, the restored remains of which you can see today. Near the theater are the skeleton-like ruins of the baths, which may have been built at the same time. Try to visit the Etruscan-Roman museum, with its many interesting finds dating from the days when Fiesole—not Florence—was supreme (a guide is on hand to show you through). The museum and theater are open from 9 a.m. to 7 p.m. daily in summer. From October to March, hours are 10 a.m. to 4 p.m. daily except Monday. Admission is 2,500 lire ($1.90).

The hardest task you'll have in Fiesole is to take the steep goat-climb up to the—

Convent of San Francesco

You can visit the Franciscan church, in the Gothic style, but it's of routine interest, with mediocre frescoes (some in contemporary dress). In the basement, however, is a museum devoted to objets d'art from China (collected by a father who was sent there as a missionary), along with Etruscan and Roman artifacts, even an Egyptian sarcophagus. The real reason to make the climb is for the unforgettable view. The museum is open from 10 a.m. to noon and 3 to 6 p.m. Monday through Saturday, closing at 5 p.m. in winter. Sunday hours are 10 to 11 a.m. and 3 to 5 p.m. No admission is charged, but you should make a donation.

WHERE TO STAY

An ancient monastery of unsurpassed beauty is **Villa San Michele,** via Doccia 4, Fiesole, 50014 Firenze (tel. 055/59-451). The setting is memorable, even breathtaking. On a hill just below Fiesole, the monastery, complete with gardens, was built in the 15th century on a wide ledge. After being damaged in World War II, the villa was carefully restored. It is said that the façade and the loggia were designed by Michelangelo. A curving driveway, lined with blossoming trees and flowers, leads to the entrance. A ten-arch covered loggia continues around the view side of the building to the Italian gardens at the rear. On the loggia, chairs are set out for drinks and moonlight dinners. Most of the bedrooms open onto the panoramic view, or the inner courtyard. Each room is unique, some with iron or wooden canopy beds, antique chests, Savonarola chairs, formal draperies, old ecclesiastical paintings, candelabra, and statues—in other words, a stunning tour de force of rich but restrained design. Poets and artists have stayed at San Michele, singing its praise. Half board costs 400,000 lire ($304) to 560,000 lire ($426) daily in a single, 330,000 lire ($251) to 425,000 lire ($323) per person in a double. The hotel is open from March to November.

Hotel Aurora, piazza Mino da Fiesole 39, Fiesole, 50014 Firenze (tel. 055/59-100), on the main square of town in a modernized 1890s building, is concealed behind an ochre façade set with green shutters. The terrace of the restaurant in back (closed from November to January) offers typical Italian meals and views of hanging vines and city lights. You can also eat inside. The hotel has a high, beamed reception area and functional furniture. Units with private bath cost 130,000 lire ($98.75) daily in a single, from 210,000 lire ($160) in a double. A la carte meals are served in the dining room, averaging around 35,000 lire ($26.50).

Pensione Bencista, via B. da Maiano 4, Fiesole, 50014 Firenze (tel. 055/59-163), has been the family villa of the Simoni family for years. It was built around 1300, with an addition made to the existing building about every 100 years after that. In 1925 Paolo Simoni opened the villa to paying guests. Its position, high up on the road to Fiesole, is commanding, with an unmarred view of the city and the hillside villas. A ten-minute ride from the heart of Florence, it is reached by bus 7 from the station, the piazza Duomo, and the piazza San Marco. The driveway to the formal entrance, with its circular fountain, winds through olive trees. The widely spread-out villa has many lofty old rooms—unspoiled and furnished with family antiques. Bedrooms vary in size and interest, some having private bath, but most with hot and cold running water only. Half board is from 70,000 lire ($53.25) per person daily in a room without bath, 88,000 lire ($67) per person with bath. In chilly weather, guests meet each other in the evening in front of a huge fireplace. The Bencista is suitable for families who might want to leave their children in the country while taking jaunts into the city.

WHERE TO DINE

For good food in a pleasant ambience, go to **Le Lance** at San Domenico (tel. 599-090). The airy and sunny construction of this hillside restaurant could almost be something you'd find in southern California, except for the lights of Florence that stretch below you. The low-lying building has maximum amounts of glass windows and exposed stone, as well as plantings. This restaurant is popular with city residents on summer nights. Dining is either indoors on rush-bottomed chairs, or on a terrace illuminated with carriage lights and surrounded by shrubbery. Menu specialties include mixed Tuscan hors d'oeuvres from a well-stocked table in the center of the room, fresh mozzarella with fresh tomatoes, fresh spinach parmigiana, beefsteak Florentine (priced by the kilogram), cutlets of lamb with artichokes, risotto with champagne, and sole meunière. Meals begin at 45,000 lire ($34.25). The restaurant, open from 12:30 to 2 p.m. and 7:30 to 10:30 p.m., is closed on Monday and Tuesday at lunch.

Trattoria Le Cave di Maiano, via delle Cave 16 (tel. 591-33), at Maiano, is a mere 15-minute drive from the heart of Florence. It's an old family-run establishment, which for many years has been an esoteric address to discerning Florentines. It's imperative, incidentally, that you reserve a table before heading here. The trattoria is a garden restaurant, with stone tables and large sheltering trees, which create a setting for the excellent cooking. Inside, the restaurant is in the tavern style, with a beamed ceiling. Le Cave is open for lunch and dinner from 12:30 to 2 p.m. and 7:30 to 10:30 p.m. every day except Thursday, Sunday night, and in August. I recommend highly the antipasto and the homemade green tortellini. For a main course, there is a golden grilled chicken or perhaps a savory herb-flavored roast lamb. For side dishes, I suggest fried polenta, Tuscan beans, and fried potatoes. As a final treat, the waiter will bring you homemade ice cream with fresh raspberries. Enjoying a complete meal of the described specialties will cost you 35,000 lire ($26.50) to 50,000 lire ($38).

SIENA, PISA, AND THE HILL TOWNS

The hill towns of Tuscany and Umbria are prized not only for their essential beauty (for example, the unspoiled medieval severity in the heart of Siena and San Gimignano)—but for their spectacular art treasures, created by such "hometown boys" as Leonardo da Vinci. From Florence, you can explore numerous nearby cities, including Pisa, Lucca, and Siena, as well as San Gimignano with its medieval towers.

And if you're traveling between Rome and Florence, why not veer off the autostrada and visit a string of yet other hill towns that are, in essence, sanctuaries of the past?

1. Siena

After Florence, it's altogether fitting, certainly bipartisan, to call on what has been labeled in the past her natural enemy. In Rome we saw classicism and the baroque; in Florence, the Renaissance; but in the walled city of Siena we stand solidly planted back in the Middle Ages. On three sienna-colored hills in the center of Tuscany, "Sena Vetus" lies in Chianti country. Perhaps preserving its original character more markedly than any other city in Italy, it is a showplace of the Italian Gothic (of a different character from Gothic in the French or Flemish sense).

William Dean Howells, the American novelist (*The Rise of Silas Lapham*), called Siena "not a monument but a flight." About 31 miles south of Florence and regrettably too often visited on a quick day's excursion, it is a city of contemplation and profound exploration. It is characterized by Gothic palaces, almond-eyed madonnas, mansions of long-faced aristocrats, letter-writing St. Catherine (patron saint of Italy), narrow streets, and medieval gates, walls, and towers.

Although such a point of view may be heretical, one can almost be grateful that Siena lost its battle with Florence. Had it continued to expand and change after reaching the zenith of its power in the 14th century, chances are it would be markedly different now, influenced by the rising tides of the Rennaissance and the baroque (represented today only in a small degree). But Siena retained its uniqueness (I've read that certain Sienese painters were still showing the influence of Byzantium in the late 15th century).

A visit to Siena at any time can be of enduring interest, although the best time if you're seeking a spectacle is usually on July 2 or August 16, the occasion of the **"Palio delle Contrade."** This is a historical pageant and tournament known throughout Europe, drawing thousands annually. In the horse race, each bareback-riding jockey represents a *contrade* (the wards into which the city is divided). The race requiring tremendous skill, takes place on the shell-shaped piazza del Campo, the historic heart of Siena. Before the race, much pageantry evoking the 15th century parades by, with colorfully costumed men and banners. The flag-throwing ceremony, depicted in so many travelogue films, takes place at this time. And just as enticing is the victory celebration.

Reader Pam King writes: "Don't buy expensive tickets for the day of the Palio. It's free to stand in the middle—and a lot more fun. Just get there real early, bring a book and a Thermos. For a great dinner and loads of fun, join one of the 17 *contraces* attending a *cena* (supper) that is held outdoors the night before the race."

The Siena telephone area code is 0577.

THE SIGHTS

There's much to see here. Let's start with the **Palazzo Comunale (Pubblico).** Standing in the heart of Siena, the "town hall" opens onto the shell-shaped **piazza del Campo,** described by Montaigne as "the finest of any city in the world." Pause before entering the palazzo to enjoy the "Fonte Gaia," the fountain of joy, with embellishments by Jacopo della Quercia (the present sculptured works are reproductions; the badly beaten original ones are found in the town hall).

The skyline of Siena is characterized by its lithe **Torre (tower) del Mangia,** dating from the 14th century and soaring to a height of 335 feet. The tower is open in summer Monday through Saturday from 9 a.m. to 6:30 p.m. and on Sunday from 9:30 a.m. to 1 p.m. Off-season hours are Monday through Saturday from 9:30 a.m. to 1:30 p.m. and on Sunday from 9:30 a.m. to 1 p.m. Admission is 2,500 lire ($1.90).

Keeping the same hours and visited on the same ticket is the brick **Palazzo Pubblico,** dating from 1288 to 1309 (tel. 292-111), filled with important artworks by some of the leaders in the Sienese school of painting and sculpture. This collection is the Museo Civico. Upstairs in the museum is the "Sala della Pace," frescoed from 1337 to 1339 by Ambrogio Lorenzetti, and showing allegorically the idealized effects of good government and bad government. In this depiction, the most notable figure of the Virtues surrounding the king is "La Pace" (Peace). To the right of the king and the Virtues is a representation of Siena in peaceful times.

On the left, Lorenzetti showed his opinion of "ward heelers," but some of the sting has been taken out of the frescoes, as the evil-government scene is badly damaged. Actually, these were propaganda frescoes in their day, commissioned by the party in power, but they are now viewed as among the most important of all secular frescoes to come down from the Middle Ages.

In the "Sala del Mappamondo" is Simone Martini's *Majesty*, the Madonna enthroned with her Child, surrounded by angels and saints. It is his earliest-known documented work (c. 1315). The other remarkable Martini fresco (on the opposite wall) is the equestrian portrait of Guidoriccio da Fogliano, general of the Sienese Republic, in ceremonial dress. The palazzo is open April to October, Monday through Saturday, from 9 a.m. to 6:30 p.m. to 1 p.m. on Sunday. Off-season hours are 9 a.m. to 1:30 p.m. Admission is 5,000 lire ($3.80).

Il Duomo

At the piazza del Duomo stands an architectural fantasy. With its colored bands of marble, the Sienese cathedral is an original and exciting building, erected in the Romanesque and Italian Gothic styles and dating from the 12th century. The dramatic façade—designed in part by Giovanni Pisano—dates from the 13th century, as does the Romanesque bell tower.

The zebra-like interior, with its black-and-white stripes, is equally stunning. The floor consists of various embedded works of art, many of which are roped off to preserve the richness in design, which depict both biblical and mythological subjects. Numerous artists worked on the floor, notably Domenico Beccafumi. For most of the year, a large part of the cathedral floor is covered to protect it.

The octagonally shaped, 13th-century pulpit is by Niccolò Pisano (Giovanni's father), who was one of the most significant Italian sculptors before the dawn of the Renaissance (see his pulpit in the baptistery at Pisa). The Siena pulpit is considered his masterpiece, revealing in relief such scenes as the slaughter of the innocents and the Crucifixion. The elder Pisano finished the pulpit in 1268, aided by his son and other artists. Its pillars are supported by four marble lions, again reminiscent of the Pisano pulpit at Pisa.

In the chapel of the left transept (near the library) is a glass-enclosed box with an arm that tradition maintains is that of John the Baptist, used to baptize Christ, and Donatello's bronze of John the Baptist. To see another Donatello work in bronze—a bishop's gravemarker—look at the floor in the chapel to the left of the pulpit's stairway. And don't miss the inlaid wooden stalls in the apse, some based on designs by Riccio. A representational blue starry sky twinkles overhead. Il Duomo can be visited daily from 9 a.m. to 7 p.m. in summer, from 8 a.m. to 5 p.m. off-season.

Piccolomini Library

Founded by Cardinal Francesco Piccolomini (later Pius III) to honor his uncle (Pius II), the library is renowned for its cycle of frescoes by the Umbrian master Pinturicchio. His panels are well preserved, although they were frescoed in the early 16th century. In Vasari's words, the panels illustrate "the history of Pope Pius II from birth to the minute of his death." Raphael's connection with the frescoes, if any, is undocumented. In the center is an exquisite *Three Graces*, a Roman copy of a 3rd-century B.C. Greek work from the school of Praxiteles. The library is open daily from 9 a.m. to 7:30 p.m. in summer, from 10 a.m. to 1 p.m. and 2:30 to 5 p.m. off-season. Admission is 1,500 lire ($1.15).

To the right of (facing) the cathedral is the—

Opera Metropolitana

Housing paintings and sculptures originally created for the cathedral, this museum at the piazza del Duomo deserves some attention. On the ground floor you'll find much interesting sculpture, including works by Giovanni Pisano and his assistants. But the real reason the museum is visited hangs on the next floor in the "Sala di Duccio": his fragmented *La Maestà*, a Madonna enthroned, painted from 1308 to 1311. The panel was originally an altarpiece by Duccio di Buoninsegna for the cathedral, filled with dramatic moments illustrating the story of Christ and the Madonna. A student of Cimabue's, Duccio was the first great name in the school of Sienese painting.

In the rooms upstairs are the collections of the treasury, and on the very top floor is a display of paintings from the early Sienese school. The museum, charging 4,000 lire ($3.05) for admission, is open April to September Monday through Saturday from 9 a.m. to 7:30 p.m., on Sunday to 1 p.m. In winter the hours are 9 a.m. to 1:30 p.m.

From the museum, a walk down some nearby steps in back of the cathedral takes us to—

The Baptistery

On the piazza San Giovanni, the façade of the baptistery dates from the 14th century, but remained uncompleted over the passing centuries. In the center of the interior is the baptismal font by Jacopo della Quercia, containing some bas-reliefs by Donatello and Ghiberti. Open daily from 9 a.m. to 1 p.m. and 3 to 7 p.m.

Pinacoteca Nazionale (Picture Gallery)

Housed in the 14th-century Palazzo Buonsignori at via San Pietro 29 (tel. 281-161) is the national gallery's collection of the Sienese school of painting, which once rivaled that of Florence. Displayed here are some of the giants of the pre-Renaissance. Most of the paintings cover the period from the late 12th century to the mid-16th century.

The principal treasures are found on the second floor, where you'll contemplate the artistry of Duccio in the early salons. The gallery is rich in the art of the two Lorenzetti brothers, Ambrogio and Pietro, who painted in the 14th century. Ambrogio is represented by an *Annunciation* and a *Crucifix,* but one of his most celebrated works, carried out with consummate skill, is an almond-eyed Madonna and her Bambino surrounded by saints and angels. Pietro's most important entry here is an altarpiece—*The Madonna of the Carmine*—made for a church in Siena in 1329. Simone Martini's *Madonna and Child* is damaged but one of the best-known paintings here.

In the salons to follow are works by Giovanni di Paolo (*Presentation at the Temple*) and Sano di Pietro with his eternal fixation on the Madonna and Child. In one room is a masterpiece of Giovanni Antonio Bazzi (called "Il Sodoma," allegedly because of his sexual interests). It is a picture of Christ at a column, a work of such plastic quality it almost qualifies for publication in a body-beautiful magazine.

From May to September the gallery is open daily except Monday from 8:30 a.m. to 7 p.m. (on Sunday to 12:45 p.m.). The admission is 3,000 lire ($2.30).

St. Catherine's Sanctuary

Of all the personalities associated with Siena, the most enduring legend surrounds that of St. Catherine, acknowledged by Pius XII in 1939 as the patron saint of Italy. The mystic, the daughter of a dyer, was born in 1347 in Siena. She was instrumental in persuading the papacy to return to Rome from Avignon. The house where she lived has now been turned into a sanctuary—really a church and oratory, with many works of art, on the spot where her father had his dyeworks. The sanctuary, called Santuario e Casa di Santa Caterina, is on costa di S. Antonio (tel. 280-330). It is open Monday through Saturday and holidays from 9 a.m. to 12:30 p.m.

and 3:30 to 6 p.m. Admission is free, but an offering is expected. Nearby at the 13th-century Basilica of Domenico is a chapel dedicated to St. Catherine. Frescoed by Il Sodoma, it includes his celebrated "swoon."

HOTELS IN SIENA

You'll *definitely* need hotel reservations for the Palio. Make them far in advance, and secure your room with a deposit.

The First-Class Choices

Park Hotel Siena, via di Marciano 16, 53100 Siena (tel. 0577/44-803), is a luxurious hotel whose physical plant was originally commissioned in 1530 by one of Siena's most famous Renaissance architects. A difficult access road leads around a series of hairpin turns (watch the signs carefully) to a buff-colored villa set with a view over green trees and suburbanite houses about a 12-minute drive southwest of the city center. The landscaping, swimming pool, double-glazed windows, uphol-stered walls, and plush carpeting have set new standards around here. The hotel is well tended, with stylish modern decoration, a comfortably furnished series of pub-lic salons, and up-to-date bathrooms. Singles rent for 238,000 lire ($181) daily, and doubles peak at 344,000 lire ($261). Tariffs include a continental breakfast and taxes. Meals in the restaurant might include wild-mushroom salad with black truf-fles, tortellini with spinach and ricotta, and a regularly featured series of regional dishes from Tuscany, Umbria, or Emilia-Romagna.

Certosa di Maggiano, via Certosa 82, 53100 Siena (tel. 0577/288-180), had been lying in dusty disrepair until 1975, when Anna Grossi Recordati renovated it and began attracting some of the world's social luminaries into its 700-year-old inte-rior. It was built as a monastery by Certosinian monks early in the 13th century, and they maintained their vegetable gardens in an area just beyond the stone walls. These have been transformed into elegant gardens dotted with old masonry, flowering shrubs, arcaded terraces, a tennis court, and a swimming pool. The public rooms fill the spaces between what used to be the ambulatory of the central courtyard, and include a stylish and plush collection of intimately proportioned gathering places (including a re-creation of a Renaissance library), filled with antiques and old ma-sonry. A medieval church with a separate entrance adjoins the hotel and still holds mass on Sunday. The entire hotel contains only 14 rooms, one of which has a private walled garden. It's filled with lighthearted summer furniture, and has attracted such guests as the late Richard Burton, the prime minister of Austria, and the president of Italy.

On warm days, breakfast is served in the courtyard, within sight of the ancient well, which adds a decorative note to the otherwise severe stonework. Doubles rent for 290,000 lire ($220) daily, while singles go for 250,000 lire ($190), with a conti-nental breakfast included. The vaulted dining room contains seven tables, a marble fireplace, and entire walls full of modern ceramics. It's open to nonresidents who reserve. It serves guests a set lunch for 80,000 lire ($60.75), and a table d'hôte din-ner for 95,000 lire ($72.25). The hotel is not easy to find, set away from the center of town on a narrow road barely wide enough for two cars. You might phone for direc-tions before you set out to find it, although the city has made efforts to post signs for general directions.

Villa Scacciapensieri, via di Scacciapensieri 10, 53100 Siena (tel. 0577/41-441), is one of the lovely old villas of Tuscany, where you can stay in a personal and tasteful atmosphere. The hostess, Mrs. Emma Nardi, opened her hotel in the sum-mer of 1934, and each year has continued to make important improvements, as-sisted in the work and supervision by her nephews, Riccardo and Emanuele Nardi. Standing on the crest of a hill, with a panoramic view of Tuscany's Chianti hills and Siena about two miles away, the villa is approached by a private driveway under shade trees. The bedrooms are individually designed and exquisitely appointed. Open from March until the end of December, the first-class hotel charges 135,000 lire ($103) daily in a single, 195,000 lire ($148) in a double. A look at one season's guest book tells the story: European princesses, Renata Tebaldi, and André Kostelanetz. Evenings in the informal drawing room are worth the trip; guests chat as they gather around the log fire burning on a raised hearth in winter. The gardens open onto many vistas. There is bus service into Siena (an eight-minute ride) every 15 minutes. Additions include a handsomely landscaped swimming pool and tennis court, plus a completely equipped "villino," with charming sleeping and sitting areas. The restaurant of the hotel is becoming better known, offering not only panoramic views, but quality Tuscan food and wine. You can dine here daily except Wednesday for about 50,000 lire ($38), but it is advisable to call and make a reservation.

Jolly Hotel Excelsior, piazza La Lizza, 53100 Siena (tel. 0577/288-448), set in the commercial center of the newer section of town, is a distinguished member of this nationwide chain. It is sheltered behind an imposing red-brick façade set with neoclassical stone trim. The renovated lobby is stylishly Italian, with terracotta trim and white columns, plus an illuminated bar set up at the far end. The 126 bedrooms offer convenient modern comfort for 175,000 lire ($133) daily in a single and 280,000 lire ($213) in a double, with a continental breakfast included. A restaurant is on the premises.

The Medium-Priced

Grand Hotel Villa Patrizia, via Fiorentina 58, 53100 Siena (tel. 0577/50-431), is a white-walled villa set into a well-planned park dotted with old trees and sculpture. Outside the city, the hotel is simply and attractively furnished, offering both an outdoor pool and a tennis court. Singles range from 70,000 lire ($53.25) to 140,000 lire ($106) daily, and doubles go for 105,000 lire ($79.75) to 210,000 lire ($160).

Garden Hotel, via Custoza 2, 53100 Siena (tel. 0577/47-056), is a well-styled country house, built by a Sienese aristocrat in the 16th century. On the edge of the city, high up on the ledge of a hill, it commands a view of Siena and the surrounding countryside, the subject of many a painting. The hotel stands formal and serene, with an entrance on the garden side and a long avenue of clipped hedges. There's a luxurious sense of space and an aura of freshness. Some of the 67 rooms are in the old villa, the others in an adjoining building. All have bath or shower. The rate for a single is 52,000 lire ($39.50) daily; for a double 85,000 lire ($64.50). These rates include taxes and service. An enjoyable spot for morning coffee is the breakfast room, with its flagstone floor, decorated ceiling, and view of the hills. You can take you other meals in an open-air restaurant on the premises. There is a swimming pool also. In addition, the hotel has opened a four-star annex offering the latest comforts in rooms all with private baths or showers.

Castagneto Hotel, via dei Cappuccini 55, 53100 Siena (tel. 0577/45-103), is a modestly proportioned brick villa set behind a graveled parking lot, near a garden with birds and trees on the western outskirts of Siena. It was renovated into a hotel in 1973 with a total of 11 unpretentious rooms in clean and functional working order. The price is right at 80,000 lire ($60.75) daily in a double. Open from mid-March to November.

Albergo Chiusarelli, via Curtatone 11, 53100 Siena (tel. 0577/280-562), is housed in an ochre-colored building with Ionic columns and Roman caryatids supporting a second-floor loggia. It looks much older, but the building was constructed around 1900. The interior has been almost completely renovated into a functional format that includes a modern bath and electric hairdryer in each room. The hotel is just at the edge of the old city, and is convenient to the parking areas at the sports stadium a five-minute walk away. The 50 accommodations rent for 61,000 lire ($49.25) daily in a double and 40,000 lire ($30.50) in a single, breakfast not included. A bar and restaurant are on the basement level, serving full meals for around 28,000 lire ($21.25).

Best for the Budget

Palazzo Ravizza, Pian dei Mantellini 34, 53100 Siena (tel. 0577/280-462), has lots of old-fashioned charm. A first-class pensione in Siena, it's really an old palace, within walking distance of the major attractions. In the front is a formal façade, in the rear a terraced garden with shade trees and benches for viewing the sweeping countryside. For years the home of great Tuscan families, it is owned and managed by sensitive people who have not allowed drastic modernization, except for the installation of water basins and a few private baths. There are 30 well-furnished bedrooms (21 bathrooms), each with a distinct personality, utilizing fine old furniture. Singles rent for 56,000 lire ($42.50) daily with bath; doubles cost an inclusive 93,000 lire ($70.75). From March to December the pension accepts guests on the half-board plan, charging from 84,000 lire ($63.75) in a single, from 74,500 lire ($56.50) per person in a double. The living room and drawing rooms of the second floor possess antiques, including a grand piano. All the rooms are interesting architecturally, with many coved ceilings.

Albergo Centrale, via Calzoleria 24, 53100 Siena (tel. 0577/280-379), a minute's walk from the piazza del Campo, is rated fourth class by the government, and it's inexpensive and clean. Many students have stayed here who come to Siena to attend the School of Language and Culture, mainly to learn Italian (the Sienese "tongue" is said to be pure—that is, free of dialect). The Centrale is housed in an old building, typical of its surrounding structures, and is reached by a stairway (no elevator, of course). They have no singles, but doubles cost 57,000 lire ($43.25) daily with bath. The 20 rooms are basic.

Villa Terraia, via dell'Ascarello 13, 53100 Siena (tel. 0577/221-108), is a country villa, on the rise of a hill about two miles from Siena. It's not only moderate in price, but a restful place at which to stay should you happen to be touring Tuscany by car. Open from the first of April until the end of October, this little two-star hotel has long been a haven for artists and musicians. The bedrooms are different in shape, decor, and size, and much of the villa has the aura of a country home. Depending on the plumbing, singles cost 37,000 lire ($28) to 51,000 lire ($38.75) daily, doubles run 64,000 lire ($48.75) to 80,000 lire ($60.75), with breakfast included. To reach the villa, head out Simone Martini, cross viale Lippo Memmi, turning right on viale Sardegna, until you come to via dell'Ascarello, about a ten-minute drive through undulating hills.

In the Environs

Villa Belvedere, Belvedere, 53034 Colle di Val d'Elsa (Siena) (tel. 0577/920-966), about 7½ miles from Siena, halfway between that city and San Gimignano, is in a villa built in 1795. It was the residence of Ferdinand III, archduke of Austria and grand duke of Tuscany, in 1820 and of Grand Duke Leopold II in 1845. Surrounded by a large park, the hotel has bar service, a garden with a panorama, and elegant dining rooms. The bedrooms—13 doubles and 2 singles—all have private bath, phone, and central heating. They are furnished with antiques and overlook the park. Bed-and-breakfast costs 60,000 lire ($45.50) daily in a single, 98,000 lire ($74.50) in a double. You can arrange for half board, costing 90,000 lire ($68.50) in a single, 79,000 lire ($60) per person in a double. Typical Tuscan and classic Italian dishes are served.

DINING IN SIENA

Even half-day trippers sometimes find themselves in Siena for lunch, and that's a happy prospect, as the Sienese are good cooks, in the best of the Tuscan tradition.

Al Marsili (Ristorante Enoteca Gallo Nero), via del Castoro 3 (tel. 472-154). This beautiful restaurant, the best in Siena, stands near the duomo in a neighborhood packed with medieval and Renaissance buildings. You dine beneath criss-crossed ceiling vaults whose russet-colored brickwork was designed centuries ago. Specialties of the chef include a rigatoni with zucchini, selections of antipasti from an abundantly stocked table, gnocchi with duck sauce, and a scallop of veal with chive sauce, followed by well-prepared desserts. Full meals, costing 35,000 lire ($26.50) to 42,000 lire ($32), are served from 12:30 to 2:30 p.m. and 7:30 to 10 p.m. daily except Monday, and reservations are important.

Al Mangia, piazza del Campo 43 (tel. 281-121), is one of the finest restaurants in the heart of the city, with outside tables overlooking the Town Hall. The food is not only well cooked, but appetizingly presented. To begin with, the house specialty is cannoli alla Mangia. If then you crave some savory Tuscan main dish, try a bollito di manzo con salsa verde (boiled beef with green sauce). Another excellent course is the ossobuco with artichokes, and in season wild boar is featured. For dessert, there's one specialty that transcends identification with its hometown and is known all over Europe: panforte, made of spicy delights, including almonds and candied fruits. Expect to spend 35,000 lire ($26.50) to 50,000 lire ($38) per person to dine here. It is open from 12:30 to 2:30 p.m. and 7:30 to 10 p.m.; closed Monday and in February.

Nello La Taverna, via del Porrione 28 (tel. 289-043), offers an ambience that is about as typical of the Sienese region as anything you'll find. On a narrow stone-covered street about half a block from the piazza del Campo, the establishment, as its name implies, offers a tavern decor that includes brick walls, hanging lanterns, racks of wine bottles, and sheaves of corn hanging from the ceiling. Best of all, you can view the forge-like kitchen with its crew of uniformed cooks busily preparing your dinner from behind a row of hanging copper utensils. Specialties include a salad of fresh radicchio, green lasagne ragoût style, and lamb cacciatore with beans. The best wines, according to the owner, come from the region. Your waiter will gladly suggest a local vintage for you. A la carte dinners begin at 35,000 lire ($26.50). The restaurant, open from 12:30 to 2:30 and 7:30 to 10 p.m., is closed on Sunday night and Monday.

Guido, vicolo Pier Pettinaio 7 (tel. 280-042), is a medieval Tuscan restaurant, about 100 feet off the promenade street near the piazza del Campo. It's decked out with crusty old beams, time-aged brick walls, arched ceilings, and iron chandeliers. My approval is backed up by the public testimony of more than 300 famous people, who have left autographed photographs to adorn the walls of three dining rooms—film stars, diplomats, opera singers, and car-racing champions. There's an open grill for steaks, chickens, and roasts. You may want to order some of the specialties on the à la carte list. Thus, you can have assorted antipasti, which are most rewarding. For a main dish, you may want to stick to the roasts, especially the piccione (pigeon) with potatoes. Desserts are good too. A complete meal is likely to run 40,000 lire ($30.50) to 60,000 lire ($45.50). Food is served daily from 12:30 to 2:30 p.m. and 7:30 to 10 p.m.

Grotta Santa Caterina-da Bagoga, via della Galluzza 26 (tel. 282-208), in a brick building midway up a narrow, steeply inclined cobblestone street, is an unpretentious gathering place popular with local residents. Inside are brick arches, lots of rustic detailing, plants, and wooden chairs. You are served such specialties as eight kinds of scaloppine, beef with truffles, or chicken cooked in beer. Rabbit in champagne is a favorite, and the kitchen will also prepare a wide variety of mixed roast meats, including veal, pork, and lamb. Set meals are offered for 25,000 lire ($19), and you are likely to spend around 35,000 lire ($26.50) and up by ordering à la carte. The restaurant is open from 12:30 to 3 p.m. and 7:30 to 10 p.m. It's closed Sunday night, all day Monday, and for three weeks in the middle of July.

WINE TASTING

Owned and operated by the Italian government, **Enoteca Italica Permanente,** Fortezza Medicea (tel. 288-497), serving as a showcase for the finest wines of Italy, would whet the palate of even the most sophisticated wine devotee. An unusual architectural setting is designed to show bottles to their best advantage. The establishment lies just outside the entrance to an old fortress, at the bottom of an inclined ramp, behind a massive arched doorway. Marble bas-reliefs and wrought-iron sconces, along with regional ceramics, are set into the high brick walls of the labyrinthine corridors, the vaults of which were built by Cosimo de Medici in 1560. On the premises are several sunny terraces for outdoor wine-tasting, an indoor stand-up bar, and voluminous lists of available vintages, which are for sale either by the glass or by the bottle. Count yourself lucky if the bartender will agree to open an iron gate for access to the subterranean wine exposition. There, in the lowest part of the fortress, carpenters have built illuminated display racks containing bottles of recent vintages. Open from 3 p.m. to midnight every day of the week, the enoteca sells wine by the glass, ranging from 1,500 lire ($1.15).

2. San Gimignano

A golden lily of the Middle Ages! Called the Manhattan of Tuscany, the town preserves 13 of its noble brick towers, which give it a skyscraper skyline. The approach to the walled town is dramatic, but once it must have been fantastic, as San Gimignano in the heyday of the Guelph and Ghibelline conflict had as many as 75 towers. Today its fortress-like severity is softened by the subtlety of its quiet, harmonious squares, and many of its palaces and churches are enhanced by Renaissance frescoes, as San Gimignano, like Florence and Siena, could afford to patronize major painters.

San Gimignano's telephone area code is 0577.

THE SIGHTS

In the center of town is the palazzo-flanked **piazza della Cisterna** (see my hotel recommendations)—so named because of the 13th-century cistern in its heart. Connecting with the irregularly shaped square is its satellite, the **piazza del Duomo.** The square's medieval architecture—towers and palaces—is almost unchanged, the most beautiful spot in town.

The present **duomo** dates essentially from the 13th century. Inside, the cathedral is richly frescoed. In the right aisle, panels trace scenes from the life of Christ—the kiss of Judas, the Last Supper, the flagellation, and the Crucifixion—painted by an artist most often known as Barna da Siena. In the left aisle are frescoes by Bartolo di Fredi, a mid-14th-century cycle representing scenes from the Old Testament, including the massacre of Job's servants.

The chief attraction is the **Chapel of Santa Fina,** designed by Giuliano da Maiano. It was frescoed in about 1475 by Domenico Ghirlandaio, who depicted scenes from the life of Saint Fina, as in the memorable deathbed panel. Ghirlandaio, you may recall, was Michelangelo's fresco teacher. The chapel is open the same hours as the civic museum (see below), and you can use your ticket from the museum to enter.

Around to the left of the cathedral on a little square (the piazza Luigi Pecori) is the **Museum of Sacred Art,** an unheralded museum of at least passing interest for its medieval tombstones and wooden sculpture. It also has an illustrated-manuscript section and an Etruscan section. Admission is with your ticket from the civic museum.

Palazzo del Popolo, a palace designed by Arnolfo di Cambio in the 13th century, with a tower built a few years later that is believed to have been the tallest "skyscraper" (about 178 feet high), a symbol of the *podestà* or mayor. You can scale the tower and be rewarded with a bird's-eye view of this most remarkable town and visit the palace as well.

Installed upstairs is the **Museo Civico,** notably the Sala di Dante, where the Guelph-supporting poet spoke out for his cause in 1300. Look for one of the masterpieces of San Gimignano—the *Maestà,* or Madonna enthroned, by Lippo Memmi (later "touched up" by Gozzoli).

The first large room you enter upstairs contains the other masterpieces of the museum—a *Madonna in Glory,* with Saints Gregory and Benedict, painted by Pinturicchio when perspective was flowering. Flanking it are two different portraits of the *Annunciation* by Filippino Lippi. On the opposite wall, note the magnificent primitive *Crucifix* by Coppo di Marcovaldo.

The museum is open April 1 to September 30 Tuesday through Sunday from 9:30 a.m. to 12:30 p.m. and 3:30 to 6:30 p.m. Off-season, it is open from 9:30 a.m. to 12:30 p.m. and 2:30 to 5:30 p.m. Closed Monday. Admission is 4,000 lire ($3.05), which also allows you to climb the Torre Grossa.

The **Church of Sant' Agostino.** At the piazza Sant' Agostino, this handsome Gothic church was built in the 13th century. It is visited today chiefly by those wanting to see the mid-15th-century cycle of 17 frescoes on the choir by Benozzo Gozzoli. The panels, depicting scenes from the life of St. Augustine, are noted for their backgrounds and for the attention the artist paid to architectural detail and costumes. You can also explore the cloisters, with their simple, but beautiful, architectural lines. It's a pleasant stroll from the town center. The church can be visited daily from 8 a.m. to noon and 3 to 7 p.m. in summer, only from 2 to 5 p.m. in winter.

THE HOTELS

A second-class hotel, **La Cisterna,** piazza della Cisterna, 53037 San Gimignano (tel. 0577/940-328), is modernized but still retains its medieval lines, having been built at the base of some 14th-century patrician towers. In its heyday La Cisterna was the palazzo of a Tuscan family of nobility. Many tourists visit it just for the day, patronizing Le Terrazze restaurant (see my dining recommendation). The bedrooms are generally large, with some of the more superior lodgings opening onto terraces with views of the Val d'Elsa (the hotel surmounts a hilltop). The Cisterna has 46 bedrooms, equipped with private bath or shower. Singles with bath rent for 52,500 lire ($40) daily; doubles with bath, 87,000 lire ($66) to 95,000 lire ($72.25). The half-board rate ranges from 72,000 lire ($54.75) to 81,000 lire ($61.50) per person daily. Within two minutes after leaving the front door, you'll be at all the major sightseeing attractions. The hotel is open from early March to early November.

Bel Soggiorno, via San Giovanni 41, 53037 San Gimignano (tel. 0577/940-375), lies on a narrow street running through the town, its rear bedrooms and dining room opening on the lower pastureland and the bottom of the village, a splendid view of the Val d'Elsa. The front is in the unspoiled Tuscan style, with an entryway and arched windows. Although rated only third class by the government, the lodgings offered are far superior to what you might expect. The rooms are small and pleasantly revamped, and they offer excellent views (some have antiques and terraces). All of them were designed in the high Tuscan style by an architect from Milan. In all, the Bel Soggiorno contains 26 rooms. Doubles cost 80,000 lire ($60.75) daily, singles 55,000 lire ($41.75), with breakfast included. In high season you'll be asked to have your meals here—which is no great hardship, as the cuisine is excellent. The half-board rate is 65,000 lire ($49.50) per person. Part of the dining room juts out into space, with three sides of glass. Done in the medieval style, it contains murals depicting the hunting of wild boar. There's a country fireplace with crude chairs. Outsiders can drop in for meals, except on Monday when it's closed.

If no rooms are available at the Bel Soggiorno, you can book into the **Pescille,** Verso, Castel San Gimignano, 53037 San Gimignano (tel. 0577/940-186), which many guests consider superior. Here, a single room costs from 50,000 lire ($38) daily and a double begins at 80,000 lire ($60.75). Meals are served daily, costing

35,000 lire ($26.50) to 55,000 lire ($41.75) per person. The restaurant is closed Wednesday. The Pescille, lying almost three miles from the center of the town and therefore best for motorists, is closed in January and February.

WHERE TO DINE

In La Cisterna Hotel, **Ristorante Le Terrazze,** on the piazza della Cisterna (tel. 940-328), offers a panoramic view through glassed-in windows opening onto the Val d'Elsa. The setting is one of a country inn. The food is an assortment of produce from the surrounding Tuscan farm country. Many soups and pastas make for fine beginnings, and the risotto alla Cisterna is a specialty of the house. In meats, the house specialties are vitello alla Cisterna with beans in butter, breaded lamb cutlet with fried artichokes, a worthy repast, and faraona arrosto (roast guinea fowl) with fried potatoes. Depending on your choice of specialties, your final tab is likely to be anywhere from 32,000 lire ($24.25) to 50,000 lire ($38). The restaurant is open from 12:30 to 2:30 p.m. and 7:30 to 10 p.m. Closed Tuesday, Wednesday at lunch, and November to mid-March.

3. Montecatini Terme

The best known of all Italian spas, Montecatini Terme has long been frequented for its cures and scenic location. It is a peaceful Tuscan town set among green hills of the valley called Valdinievole. The location is 19 miles northeast from Florence and 26 miles from the Pisa International Airport.

The spa's fame began in the latter part of the 18th century when the grand duke of Tuscany, one Pietro Leopoldo, opened a thermal spa here. But centuries before that it had been discovered by the Romans. The fame of Montecatini spread rapidly, and by 1890 at least it was a regular stopover for some of the titled aristocrats of Europe. In the 20th century it drew such luminaries as Gary Cooper, Rose Kennedy, and Gabriel D'Annunzio.

Many visitors are just regular tourists who enjoy a restful stopover in a spa town; others come to lose weight, to take the mud baths, and to visit the sauna-cum-grotto.

The mineral waters are said to be the finest in Europe, and the most serious visitors go to the 19th-century Tettuccio spa, with its beautiful gardens, to fill their cups from the curative waters.

The spa is filled with dozens of hotels and pensiones, and many would-be visitors to Florence—unable to find a room in that overcrowded city—journey to Montecatini instead. The spa has a season lasting from April to October.

When you tire of all that rest, you can take a cableway up to Montecatini Alto, enjoying its panoramic view. The funicular leaves from viale Diaz. Montecatini Alto was important in the Middle Ages, containing about two dozen towers that were demolished in 1554 on orders of Cosimo Medici I. You can walk along narrow streets to the ruins of a fortress here, paying a short visit to St. Peter's Church. You'll invariably come across the main square, named for the poet Guiseppe Giusti. From the hillside town, you can see Florence on a clear day.

The telephone area code for Montecatini is 0572.

WHERE TO STAY

Established in 1870, the **Grand Hotel e la Pace,** via della Toretta 1, 51016 Montecatini Terme (tel. 0572/75-801), is a veritable residential palace with flowered sun terraces, lying within walking distance of the Montecatini Thermal Establishment. The hotel epitomizes to many of its famous guests the kind of discreet palace hotel unique to Europe. The lounges are luxuriously stunning, combining high ceilings, frescoes, paneling, soaring columns, lots of gilt, and all the ornate detailing that characterized 19th-century architecture. Everything is impeccably maintained. Singles range from 220,000 lire ($167) daily, while doubles cost 400,000 lire ($304). Suites, of course, are more expensive. Full board goes for 200,000 lire ($152) to 265,000 lire ($201) per person daily. Many of the guests prefer a lunch beside the pool, followed by dinner inside a dining room that might be intimidatingly grandiose except for the service offered by the thoughtful staff.

In addition to being a grand hotel, the hotel is a natural health spa as well. Guests can choose one- or two-week programs, but can, of course, stay for shorter periods too. Guests have at their disposal specialized doctors, dieticians, sports directors, and physiotherapists. For those who just want a taste of the spa life—all the rage these days—there are saunas, Swiss showers, underwater massages, a masseur and masseuse, a solarium, a swimming pool, and a fine gymnasium. You can join the celebrity register, which has included such notables as Truman Capote, Sophia Loren, Lady Churchill, and Princess Grace. The hotel is open from April 1 until the end of October.

Grand Hotel Croce di Malta, viale IV Novembre 18, 51016 Montecatini Terme (tel. 0572/75871). In a residential section a short walk from the center of the resort, the imposing white façade of this pleasant hotel rises from behind a screen of shrubbery and an outdoor terrace. The interior is tastefully and attractively filled with conservatively modern furniture and lots of exposed marble set into rooms that have been discreetly renovated into a refreshing style. One of my favorite middle-bracket hotels, this establishment charges from 120,000 lire ($91.25) daily in a single and from 200,000 lire ($152) in a double. Unlike many hotels at the spa, this one is open all year.

Grand Hotel Vittoria, viale della Libertà 2A, 51016 Montecatini (tel. 0572/79271), is a pleasantly old-fashioned hotel set away from the center of town amid a dignified collection of private homes. Considered one of the best of the middle-bracket hotels, it has neoclassical detailing and an ornate double stairwell built of travertine and flanked with masses of flowers. Verdi stayed here shortly after the hotel opened in 1905, just before it went through various transformations including a short time as a monastery. It served as the headquarters for the Germans and later the Americans in World War II. Many of the hotel's regular clients are repeat visitors who stay for extended periods. Meals in the sunny dining room are also gastronomic events. The spacious and high-ceilinged rooms can be reached either by elevator or via a sloping ornate stairwell, whose balustrade is turn-of-the-century wrought iron. Near the gardens are a small swimming pool, a tennis court, and a covered terrace whose flagstones are sheltered from the direct sunlight by an arbor of edera vines. With half board included, per-person rates range from 72,000 lire ($54.75) to 110,000 lire ($83.50) daily, depending on the season.

Grand Hotel du Park et Regina, viale Diaz 8, 51016 Montecatini Terme (tel. 0572/60098). Inside a turn-of-the-century pink-and-white neoclassical building whose entrance is across from the city gardens, this hotel offers what are said to be the oldest spa facilities in the town. On the front terrace during sunny weather, strains of classical music can sometimes be heard from the bandshell across the street. From the carved stone balconies (which envelop every other window of the façade), guests can see the garden's many flowering trees, which have been set into big terracotta pots. On the premises are a sauna, an outdoor swimming pool, an accommodating staff, and an elegant high-ceilinged dining room with windows on three sides. Rates are slightly higher in August and September, when half board costs 88,000 lire ($67) per person daily. The rest of the year, singles with breakfast cost 80,000 lire ($60.75) daily, and doubles with breakfast go for 110,000 lire ($83.50).

Biondi Hotel, viale IV Novembre 83, 51016 Montecatini Terme (tel. 0572/71341), stands in a residential section of town on a quiet tree-lined street. Its design stresses its strong vertical lines and shuttered windows, which illuminate the comfortable bedrooms. Many families seem to like the informality of the place. Meals in the spacious dining room are often accompanied by piano music. Full board ranges from 60,000 lire ($45.60) to 80,000 lire ($60.75) per person daily. The hotel has an indoor swimming pool and a guarded car park.

WHERE TO DINE

Most visitors to Montecatini book into one of the hotels on the full- or half-board plan. However, if you can sneak away for one meal, try the following:

Gourmet, via Amendola 6 (tel. 771-012). On my first visit here, I overcame my suspicion of any restaurant that styles itself or its cuisine as "gourmet." Too often that isn't the case. However, this Gourmet lives up to its billing. My most recent risotto with fresh spring asparagus was a worthy treat, followed by tournedos in a sauce made with green peppercorns. A dining companion opted for the Florentine beefsteak, which was properly seasoned and politely presented. The food is the best at the spa. The chef offers essentially an international cuisine, as befits the many nationalities of the guests attracted to Montecatini. The elegant restaurant is made even more so with its art nouveau touches and stained glass. Service is impeccable. Meals cost 35,000 lire ($26.50) to 65,000 lire ($49.40) and are served from 12:30 to 2:30 p.m. and 7:30 to 10 p.m. It is closed on Tuesday and the first three weeks in August.

---

4. Pisa

One of the best short stories Katherine Anne Porter ever wrote was called "The Leaning Tower." A memorable scene in that story dealt with a German landlady's sentimental attachment to a five-inch plaster replica of the Leaning Tower of Pisa, a souvenir whose ribs caved in at the touch of the fingers of one of her prospective clients. "'It cannot be replaced,' said the landlady, with a severe, stricken dignity. 'It was a souvenir of the Italian journey.'" Ironically, the year (1944) Miss Porter published her "Leaning Tower," a bomb fell near the real campanile, but fortunately, it wasn't damaged.

Few buildings in the world have captured imaginations as much as the Leaning Tower of Pisa. It is probably the single most instantly recognizable building in all the Western world. Perhaps people are drawn to it as a symbol of man's fragility, or at least the fragility of his works.

The Leaning Tower may be a landmark powerful enough to entice visitors to come to call, but once there, they usually find other sights to explore. I'll survey the top attractions first, as most visitors pass through just for the day.

The telephone area code for Pisa is 050.

THE SIGHTS

In the Middle Ages, Pisa reached the apex of its power as a maritime republic, before it eventually fell to its rivals, Florence and Genoa. As is true of most cities at the zenith, Pisa turned to the arts, making contributions in sculpture and architecture. Its greatest legacy remains in the piazza del Duomo, which D'Annunzio labeled the "Piazza dei Miracoli" (miracles). Here you'll find an ensemble of the top three attractions—original "Pisan-Romanesque" buildings, including the duomo, the baptistery, and the Leaning Tower itself. Nikolaus Pevsner, in his classic *An Outline of European Architecture,* wrote: "Pisa strikes one altogether as of rather an alien character—Oriental more than Tuscan." I'll begin with—

Il Duomo

Dating back to the 1060s, the cathedral was designed by Buscetto, although Rainaldo in the 13th century erected the unusual façade, with its four layers of open-air arches, which diminish in size as they ascend. Reminiscent of the baptistery in Florence, the Pisa cathedral is marked by three bronze doors—rhythmic in line—

which were damaged in a disastrous fire in 1596, but have been restored. The south door is considered the most notable, and was designed by Bonanno in 1180.

In the restored interior, the chief art treasure is the pulpit by Giovanni Pisano. Actually the pulpit, damaged in the cathedral fire, was finally rebuilt only in 1926, employing bits and pieces of the original, which was finished by Pisano in 1310. The pulpit is polygonally shaped, held up by porphyry pillars and column statues symbolizing the Virtues (two posts are supported on the backs of lions). The relief panels depict scenes from the Bible. The pulpit is similar to an earlier one by Giovanni's father, Niccolò Pisano, in the baptistery across the way.

There are other treasures too—Galileo's lamp (according to unreliable tradition, the Pisa-born astronomer used the chandelier to formulate his laws of the pendulum), mosaics in the apse said to have been designed by Cimabue, the tomb of Henry VII of Luxembourg, a *St. Agnes* by Andrea del Sarto, a *Descent from the Cross* by Il Sodoma, and a *Crucifix* by Giambologna. It's open daily from 7:40 a.m. to 1 p.m. and 3 to 7 p.m.

The Baptistery

Begun in 1153, the baptistery is like a Romanesque crown capped by Gothic. Although it is at its most beautiful on its exterior, with its arches and columns, it should be visited inside to see the hexagonally shaped pulpit made by Niccolò Pisano in 1260. Supported by pillars resting on the backs of a trio of marble lions, the pulpit contains bas-reliefs of the Crucifixion, the Adoration of the Magi, the presentation of the Christ child at the temple, and the Last Judgment (many angels have lost their heads over the years). Column statues represent the Virtues. At the baptismal font is a contemporary John the Baptist by a local sculptor. The echo inside the baptistery shell has enthralled visitors for years. Hours are daily from 9 a.m. to 12:50 p.m. and 3 to 6:50 p.m. (to 5 p.m. in winter).

The Leaning Tower

Construction began on the eight-story campanile in 1174 by Bonanno, and there has been a persistent legend that the architect deliberately intended that the bell tower lean (but that claim is undocumented). If it stood up straight, the tower would measure about 180 feet.

Another legend is that Galileo let objects of different weights fall from the tower, then timed their descent to prove his theories on bodies in motion. From 8 a.m. to 7 p.m. in summer, to 5 p.m. off-season, you can scale the tower for 4,000 lire ($3.05) admission. The sensation of climbing the tilting steps, 294 in all, and going out on the loggia may upset your sense of balance, at least. From the top of the tower a magnificent view is spread before you. How long you'll be able to climb the tower is a matter of conjecture. The tower is no longer ailing, but is in serious danger of collapse. The government has announced an international competition to solicit plans to save the monument. The tower is said to be floating on a sandy base of water-soaked clay, leaning at least 14 feet from the perpendicular.

Museo dell'Opera

On the piazza Arcivescovado, the Museum of the Opera (tel. 502-720), opened in 1986, exhibits works of art removed from the monumental buildings on the piazza. The heart of the collection, on the ground floor, consists of sculptures spanning the 11th to the 13th century. The most famous exhibit is an ivory *Madonna* and the *Crucifix* by Giovanni Pisano. Also exhibited is the work of French goldsmiths, which was presented by Maria de' Medici to the Archbishop Bonciani in 1616. Upstairs are many paintings from the 16th to the 18th century. Some of the textiles and embroideries date from the 15th century. Another section of the museum is devoted to Egyptian, Etruscan, and Roman works of art. In summer, visiting hours are 8 a.m. to 7:30 p.m. daily, and 9 a.m. to 4:30 p.m. daily in winter. Admission is 4,000 lire ($3.05).

Camposanto

This cemetery was originally designed by Giovanni di Simone in 1278, but a bomb hit it in 1944. In more recent times, it has been partially restored. It is said that earth from Calvary was shipped here by the Crusaders on Pisan ships (the city was a great port before its water receded). The cemetery is of interest because of its sarcophagi, statuary, and frescoes. Notable frescoes, badly damaged, were by Benozzo Gozzoli, who illustrated scenes from the Old Testament, paying special attention to the architectural details of his cycle. One room contains three of the most famous frescoes from the 14th century: the *Triumph of Death*, the *Last Judgment,* and the *Inferno,* with the usual assortment of monsters, reptiles, and boiling caldrons. The *Triumph of Death* is the most interesting, with its flying angels and devils—superb in composition. In addition, you'll find lots of white-marble bas-reliefs—including Roman funerary sculpture. The cemetery may be visited daily from 9 a.m. to 12:45 p.m. and 3 to 6:50 p.m. (it closes at 5 p.m. in winter) for 2,000 lire ($1.50) admission.

The National Museum of St. Matthew

This handsome, well-planned museum on lungarno Mediceo contains a good assortment of paintings and sculpture, many of which date from the 13th and 14th centuries. In the museum are statues by Giovanni Pisano; Simone Martini's *Madonna and Child with Saints,* a polyptych, as well as Nino Pisano's *Madonna del Latte* (milk), a marble sculpture; Masaccio's *St. Paul,* painted in 1426; Domenico Ghirlandaio's two *Madonna and Saints* depictions; works by Strozzi and Alessandro Magnasco; and very old copies of works by Jan and Peter Brueghel. The national museum is open Tuesday through Saturday (closed Monday) from 9 a.m. to 1 p.m. and 3 to 6 p.m., and from 9 a.m. to 2 p.m. on Sunday, in summer; daily from 9 a.m. to 2 p.m. in winter. Admission is 3,000 lire ($2.30). You enter from the piazza San Matteo. In Italian, the museum is called Museo Nazionale e Civico di San Matteo (tel. 23-750)

HOTELS IN PISA

Pisa has good accommodations in all price ranges, as you'll see by the following recommendations:

Hotel Cavalieri, piazza della Stazione 2, 56100 Pisa (tel. 050/43290), is the best hotel in Pisa, lying with a view over the monumental train station and the piazza in front of it, just two miles from Pisa International Airport. It was built in 1948, in a design that emphasizes strong angles and postwar modernity. Since then it was practically rebuilt from the inside out. Today the rooms are filled with plush furniture, paneling, and large expanses of glass. Each room is air-conditioned, containing a frigo-bar, TV, radio, up-to-date bathroom, and the kind of comfort that made ex-British Prime Minister Edward Heath, opera star Eduardo de Filippo, and actor Vittorio Gassman feel at home here. The hotel also hosts dozens of business travelers, who appreciate the serenity of the bar and restaurant for their meetings. Singles cost 175,000 lire ($133) daily, and doubles rent for 250,000 lire ($190). Parking is often possible in the square in front of the station or, for better security, in the near-by garage.

Grand Hotel Duomo, via Santa Maria 94, 56100 Pisa (tel. 050/561-894), is a blending of the talents of an architect and decorator who set out to create a stream-lined modern hotel in the heart of Pisa, a short walk from the Leaning Tower. The air-conditioned hotel offers 90 bedrooms, all with handsome private bath. Contemporary it is, in a buff-colored stucco, with a covered roof garden for those uninterrupted views. Inside, there's a liberal use of marble, crystal chandeliers, even tall murals in the dining room, one of which is an artist's rendering of a verdant, blooming Pisa. A garage is on the premises. With a continental breakfast included, singles cost 135,000 lire ($103) daily; doubles 195,000 lire ($148). The bedrooms are well furnished, with parquet floors, big windows, built-in headrests, individual lights, phone, and air conditioning.

Hotel D'Azeglio, piazza Vittorio Emanuele II no. 18, 56100 Pisa (tel. 050/500-310), is a first-class hotel in the vicinity of the railway station and the air terminal, in the historic and commercial center of Pisa. On the premises is an American bar and roof garden with a view of the city. A garage is adjacent to the hotel, and each of the rooms is air-conditioned, with color TV and frigo-bar. Well-furnished singles cost 130,000 lire ($98.75) daily, and doubles go for 170,000 lire ($129).

California Park Hotel, via Aurelia at km. 338, 56100 Pisa (tel. 050/890-726), only lacks palm trees to make it true to its name. Just outside the city, the hotel is a tidy, modern group of bungalows, gathered around an open-air swimming pool, with fir trees. It's a good stopover for motorists, especially in summer. The rooms are equipped with modern amenities, wall-to-wall draperies, built-in headboards, and comfortable beds. The pool has plenty of space for long-distance swimmers. All rooms have private bath. Singles cost from 75,000 lire ($57) daily, and doubles begin at 100,000 lire ($76), tax included.

Royal Victoria, lungarno Pacinotti 12, 56126 Pisa (tel. 050/502-130), is conveniently located on the Arno, within walking distance of most of the jewels in Pisa's crown. Its tastefully decorated lounge sets the hospitable scene. Most rooms are devoted to the past only through painted ceilings, spaciousness, and the warmth of antiques suitable to contemporary comfort. Bathless singles rent for 30,000 lire ($22.75) daily, and singles with bath go for 54,000 lire ($41). Doubles rent for 40,000 lire ($30.50) without bath, 75,000 lire ($57) with bath.

Hotel Arno, piazza della Repubblica 6, 56100 Pisa (tel. 050/501-820), is one of the best of the second-class hotels, conveniently situated in a quiet position in front of the Tribunal. This modern hotel has 34 rooms, all with private shower. It is furnished throughout with pieces of a functional design. Singles rent for 54,000 lire ($41) daily, and doubles go for 75,000 lire ($57), including service and taxes. For full board, add 46,000 lire ($35) per person to the room rate. A lunch or dinner costs from 25,000 lire ($19).

DINING IN PISA

Pisan fare has greatly improved in recent years, particularly since the opening of the restaurant immediately following.

Ristorante Sergio, lungarno Pacinotti 1 (tel. 48-245). Residents of Pisa flock here. It sits on the banks of the Arno, in a building whose walls are 1,000 years old. In days of yore, when it was an inn, it sheltered such illustrious guests as Montaigne, Shelley, and Garibaldi. A long bar area is near the entrance, flanked by a massive stone wall that is dotted with medieval wrought-iron keys, woodcarvings, and rare wines. Dining is on two levels, on comfortably rustic chairs pulled up to beautifully set tables. The service is impeccable, with help offered at each of the proper moments by Sergio Lorenzi's gracious wife and daughter. The bouquets, as well as many of the herbs and vegetables, come from the family garden.

All of the finest ingredients combine with Sergio's talents to form a unique *cucina Toscana* that has been presented by him on cooking lectures throughout Europe and North America. A *gran menu del giorno* is offered for 75,000 lire ($57), although a luncheon menu is also popular at 50,000 lire ($38). My favorite is the 80,000 lire ($60.75) menu dégustation, offered only in the evening. It features a portion of many different courses, all of them superb. These might include a rich salad with truffles, a re-creation of an ancient Tuscan recipe for vegetable and meat soup, and a range of delicacies that make this the best-rated restaurant in Pisa. The collection of wines is superb, and the waiter will be pleased to help you in selecting one. The restaurant is open from 12:30 to 3 p.m. and 7:30 to 10 p.m.; closed all day Sunday, for Monday at lunch, for one week in July, and in January and February.

Al Ristoro dei Vecchi Macelli, via Volturno 49 (tel. 20-424), is one of the best restaurants in Pisa, a comfortably rustic building near the piazzetta di Vecchi

Macelli. Residents of Pisa claim that the cuisine is prepared with something akin to love, and prove their devotion by returning frequently. After selecting from a choice of two dozen varieties of seafood antipasti, you can enjoy a homemade pasta with scallops and zucchini or fish-stuffed ravioli in a shrimp sauce. Other dishes include gnocchi with pesto and shrimp and roast veal with a truffle-flavored cream sauce. Full meals, costing 42,000 lire ($32) to 70,000 lire ($53.25) are served from 12:30 to 2:30 p.m. and 7:30 to 10 p.m. daily except Wednesday, Sunday lunch, and for two weeks in August. Reservations are necessary.

Buzzino, via Cammeo 42 (tel. 562-141), is conveniently reached from the piazza dei Miracoli (the square of miracles with the Leaning Tower). It slightly resembles a Santa Barbara hacienda, with a clerestory window that filters light down upon the interior brick wall and ladderback dining chairs. The waiter will point out specialties on the à la carte menu, among them fresh fish. Although the restaurant resembles "the businessperson's choice," the food is really good. The chef does a nice scaloppine. If you order at random, you're likely to spend around 45,000 lire ($34.25) for a fine repast, with wine. Open from noon to 3 p.m. and 7 to 11 p.m.; closed Tuesday.

Emilio, via Roma 26-28 (tel. 26-028), stands midway between the Arno and the tower. It's convenient for lunch, although dinner is equally appetizing. The antipasti buffet is tempting, especially the seafood dishes. The menu features the usual Italian fare, and the food is well prepared and particularly good. For a full meal, expect to pay anywhere from 28,000 lire ($21.25) to 38,000 lire ($29). With your repast, I'd suggest a local red wine, Bellavista. The dining room is decorated with a painting collection, and overhead is a pair of glittering globular chandeliers. Fresh flowers are placed on every table. Closed Monday, but open other days from 12:30 to 2:30 p.m. and 7:30 to 10 p.m.

---

5. Lucca

At the time of the collapse of the Roman Empire, Lucca was virtually the capital of Tuscany. Periodically in its valiant, ever-bloody history, it functioned as an independent principality, similar to Genoa. This autonomy attests to the fame and prestige that Lucca enjoyed. Now, however, it is largely bypassed by time and travelers, rewarding the discriminating few.

Linda Arking summarized its special appeal this way: "Thriving, cosmopolitan, and perfectly preserved, Lucca is a sort of Switzerland of the south. Banks have latticed Gothic windows; shops look like well-stocked linen cupboards. Plump children play in landscaped gardens, and geraniums bloom from the roofs of medieval tower houses."

Its city walls, built largely in the days of the Renaissance, enclose the old town, the zone of the most interest to visitors, of course. For orientation, you may want to walk (even drive your car) along the tree-shaded ramparts, a distance of 2½ miles.

Afterward, I suggest that you head to the piazza San Martino to visit the **duomo,** dating back to 1060, although the present structure was mainly rebuilt. The façade is exceptional, evoking the "Pisan-Romanesque" style, but with enough originality to distinguish it from the duomo at Pisa. Designed mostly by Guidetto da Como in the early years of the 13th century, the west front contains three wide ground-level arches, surmounted by a trio of scalloped galleries with taffy-like twisting columns (each one a different design), tapering in size. Towering to the side is a quadrangular campanile or bell tower.

The relic of St. Martin (the name of the cathedral) is the *Volto Santo,* a crucifix carved by Nicodemus (so tradition has it) from the Cedar of Lebanon. The face of Christ was supposedly chiseled onto the statuary. The main art treasure in the duomo is Jacopo della Quercia's tomb of Ilaria del Carretto, who died in 1405 (while still young), the wife of Paolo Guinigi. The marble effigy of the young lady, in regal robes, rests atop the sarcophagus—the cathedral's diffused mauve light in the afternoon casting a ghostly glow on her countenance. The tomb in the transept is fringed with chubby bambini.

At the piazza San Michele, a short walk away, the **Church of San Michele** often surprises first-timers to Lucca, who mistake it for the duomo. A 12th-century church, it is the most memorable example of the style and flair the denizens of Lucca brought to the Pisan-Romanesque school of architecture. Its west front, again employing the scalloped effect, is spanned by seven arches on the ground level, then surmounted by four tiers of galleries, utilizing imaginatively designed columns. Dragon-slaying St. Michael, wings outstretched, rests on the frieze-like peak of the final tier. Inside, seek out a Filippo Lippi painting of four saints.

Within the city walls, the **Church of San Frediano** is one of the most important and famous in Lucca. Romanesque in style, it was erected when Lucca enjoyed its greatest glory, in the 12th and 13th centuries. Its white façade is severe, relieved by a 13th-century mosaic of Christ ascending. Its campanile or bell tower rises majestically. The interior is dark, and visitors often speak in whispers. But the bas-reliefs on the Romanesque font add a note of comic relief. Supposedly depicting the story of Moses, among other themes, it shows Egyptians in medieval armor chasing after the Israelites. Some are riding two on a horse. Two tombs in the basilica were the work of Jacopo della Quercia, the celebrated Sienese sculptor. They are in the fourth chapel on the left.

Lucca's telephone area code is 0583.

HOTELS IN LUCCA

If you're planning to spend the night, you'll find Lucca adequately supplied with good lodgings. None will be finer than the stunning choice immediately following.

Hotel Villa La Principessa, 55050 Massa Pisana (Lucca) (tel. 0583/370-037), is set on the highway (not to be confused with the autostrada) between Lucca and Pisa, on a drive that calls for an abrupt negotiation with a jutting stone wall. Three miles from the center, the hotel is sheltered by hedges, flowering trees, and the best kinds of detailing of another era. It was built in 1320 as the private home of one of the dukes of Lucca (his name was Castruccio Castracani, and he was later depicted by Machiavelli as "the ideal prince"). Later, when the hills around Lucca were dotted with the homes of members of the Napoleonic court, the house was rebuilt into the severe Tuscan style. In 1805 Princess Elisa Baciocchi Bonaparte made the villa her home. Today it's owned by the Mugnani family, who maintain this *Relais & Châteaux* property for a distinguished clientele.

After parking, you'll pass below a high and severely designed façade crowned with a three-arched loggia on the upper floor. The decor includes red plaid rugs, scarlet walls, Tuscan antiques, and lots of space to walk in. The inner salons have 25-foot ceilings, flowered brocaded upholstery covering the walls, masses of flowers, and aristocratic oil portraits. The other public rooms include an English-style club bar, a breakfast room with framed copies of Tuscan coats-of-arms (about 100 of them) on the corn-colored walls, and a dining room in vivid colors, with 19th-century tables, copies of Chinese Chippendale chairs, and a superb cuisine. Visitors enjoy interludes in the elaborate gardens, where roses and wisteria grow over brick columns and where many of the trees are centuries old. On the premises are an outdoor swimming pool and a series of terraces. Singles cost from 200,000 lire ($152) daily, and twin-bedded rooms rent for 270,000 lire ($205) to 320,000 lire ($243). Half board is an additional 95,000 lire ($72.25) per person per day.

Napoleon, viale Europa 1, 55100 Lucca (tel. 0583/53-141), is a second-class hotel of 63 rooms. Lying outside the city walls, near the autostrada, the Napoleon stands alone off the highway, like a miniature citadel of comfort. There's a circular glass-enclosed stairway attached to the front. Effort has been expended in coordinating colors, the furnishings, and designs—much of which was successful, creating an island of plushness. Throughout the lounges is exhibited a permanent art collection, and there are areas with modern tables and chairs for relaxing. All the air-conditioned bedrooms have private bath or shower and phone. The rooms are handsome, in the contemporary style, but softened with decorator touches. Singles with bath go for 85,000 lire ($64.50) daily, and doubles with bath run 135,000 lire ($103). There's plenty of parking space.

Hotel Ilaria, via del Fosso 20, 55100 Lucca (tel. 0583/47-558), is a little (17 rooms) hotel on a tiny but swiftly flowing canal just outside one of the massive city walls. The Ilaria mixes rustico with moderno in its interior—and keeps both clean and well groomed. Many of the pleasingly furnished but simple rooms overlook a view of irregular roofs and balconies with flowers and vines. No meals are offered, other than a continental breakfast. You pay 62,000 lire ($47) daily in a double with bath, 38,000 lire ($29) in a single with bath. Bathless singles cost 31,000 lire ($23.50). A raised sun terrace on the back of the house is for the use of hotel guests.

DINING IN LUCCA

Once a country post office, **Buca di Sant' Antonio,** via della Cervia 1 (tel. 55-881), is one of the finest regional restaurants in Tuscany, specializing in game dishes. Right off the piazza San Michele, it is tucked away on a hard-to-find mews, but the quality of its produce keeps the visitors and habitués returning. The interior is intimate in the rustic idiom, with a fireplace and such "quaint bits" as copper pots. To begin your meal (if you're there in the right season, autumn), you can order pappardelle alla lepre, a noodle concoction with rabbit and a spiced sauce. To be regional, you can partake of codfish with polenta, although you may prefer one of the game dishes. Featured in season are faraona (guinea fowl) and capretto (kid). The restaurant charges from 28,000 lire ($21.35) to 40,000 lire ($30.50) for a complete meal. It is open from 12:30 to 2:30 p.m. and 7:30 to 10 p.m.; closed on Sunday night, all day Monday, and for most of July. Call for a reservation before going there.

Da Giulio-in Pelleria, via San Tommaso 29 (tel. 55-948), is like a return to another day in cuisine. The owner is Paolo Sari, who is noted for his earthy, savory cuisine laden with herbs. Strong seasonings, lots of olive oil, and liberal garlic characterize his food. You might try Tuscan funghi with a sauce of mushrooms and sausage, or local tripe, or a squid-and-eel concoction. You can begin with a hearty vegetable soup or one of his pasta dishes. Meals cost from 20,000 lire ($15.25), and hours are noon to 3 p.m. and 7:30 to 10:30 p.m. It is closed Sunday, Monday, and in August.

Ristorante Sergio, piazza Bernardini 7 (tel. 49-944), offers well-prepared Italian cookery in a setting capped by undulating ceilings. At the top of a flight of stairs from the square below, the restaurant has a modern setting, including fresh flowers on the tables. Menu items offer a series of pastas, including penne with cream sauce or maccheroni Lucca style. The cuts of meat are usually first class, including a range of scaloppine dishes and roast meats, which might be accompanied by risotto Sergio style. Your dessert could be a rich zuppa inglese, a layer cake with fresh and candied fruits smothered in whipped cream. Try one of the wines of the province, especially a ruby-colored Chianti Classico, finishing with an espresso. The menu changes daily. They offer three fixed-price meals, costing 50,000 lire ($38), 60,000 lire ($45.50), and 80,000 lire ($60.75). The restaurant is open from noon to 2:30 p.m. and 7 to 9:30 p.m.; closed on Monday night and all day Tuesday.

6. Arezzo

The most landlocked of all towns or cities of Tuscany, Arezzo lies about 50 miles southeast of Florence, a one-hour train ride from that city. Originally an

Etruscan settlement, later a Roman center, Arezzo flourished in the Middle Ages before its capitulation to Florence.

The walled town grew up on a hill, but large parts of the ancient city, including native son Petrarch's house, were bombed during World War II before the area fell to the Allied advance in the summer of 1944. Apart from Petrarch, famous sons of Arezzo have included Vasari, the painter-architect remembered chiefly for his history of the Renaissance artists, and Guido of Arezzo (sometimes known as Guido Monaco), who gave the world the modern musical scale before his death in the mid-11th century.

The Arezzo telephone area code is 0575.

THE SIGHTS

The biggest event on the Arezzo calendar is the **"Giostra (joust) del Saraceno,"** staged the first Sunday of September at the piazza Grande. Horsemen in medieval costumes reenact the lance-charging ritual—with balled whips cracking in the air—as they have since the 13th century. But at any time of the year, the **piazza Grande** should be visited for the medieval and Renaissance palaces and towers that flank it, including the 16th-century Loggia Palace by Vasari.

If you have only an hour for Arezzo, run—don't walk—to the **Church of St. Francis,** piazza di San Francesco, a Gothic church finished in the 14th century for the Franciscans. In the church is a fresco cycle—*Legend* (or *Story*) *of the True Cross*—that Piero della Francesca painted, his masterpiece. Working in the 1450s, the artist of the "Quattrocento" Renaissance was largely ignored by the world for centuries (except by art historians), but now enjoys his position in the foreground of popular taste.

His frescoes are remarkable for their grace, clearness, dramatic light effects, well-chosen colors, and ascetic severity. If the cycle appears composed with consummate precision, it may be recalled that Vasari credited della Francesca as a master of the laws of geometry and perspective. The frescoes depict the burial of Adam, Solomon receiving the queen of Sheba at the court (the most memorable scene in the cycle), the dream of Constantine with the descent of an angel, as well as the triumph of the Holy Cross with Heraclius, among other subjects. The church can be visited daily from 7 a.m. to noon and 2:30 to 7 p.m.

Church of Santa Maria della Pieve, corso Italia (in the rear it opens onto the piazza Grande), is a Romanesque structure, with a front of three open-air loggias (each pillar designed differently). On the front side is a 14th-century bell tower, known as "the hundred holes," as it's riddled with windows. Inside, the church is bleak and austere, but there's a notable polyptych of the *Virgin with Saints* by one of the Sienese Lorenzetti brothers (Pietro), painted in 1320. It is open daily from 8 a.m. to 12:30 p.m. and 3 to 7 p.m. in summer, from 8 a.m. to 6 p.m. in winter.

A short walk away is **Petrarch's House,** via dell'Orto 28A (tel. 24-700), rebuilt after war damage. Born at Arezzo in 1304, Petrarch was, of course, the great Italian lyrical poet and humanist, who immortalized his love, Laura, in his sonnets. His house may be visited daily from 10 a.m. to noon and 3 to 4 p.m.

Il Duomo: Built in the so-called pure Gothic style—rare for Tuscany—the cathedral was begun in the 13th century, but the final touches (the façade) weren't applied until the outbreak of World War I. Its art treasures include a *Mary Magdalen* by della Francesca, stained-glass windows by Marcillat, and a main altar in the Gothic style. Hours are 7 a.m. to noon and 3:30 to 7:30 p.m. daily.

WHERE TO STAY

Most visitors seem to whiz through Arezzo just for the day. But if you're seeking lodgings, you'll find the following:

Continentale, piazza Guido Monaco 7, 52100 Arezzo (tel. 0575/20-251), is a honeycomb-modern invasion on an old tree-filled piazza. Every room has its own small balcony. The Continentale is at its best on its roof terrace with its potted trees, tables for drinks, and panoramic view of the city. Inside, the lounges and private rooms are spic-and-span modern, most streamlined. The bedroom furnishings are also utilitarian, with color added to make them breezy and cheerful. The all-year hotel has 74 rooms, most with bathroom. Singles go for 50,000 lire ($38) daily. Couples pay 85,000 lire ($64.50) for rooms with bath.

DINING IN AREZZO

The best restaurant in Arezzo is **Buca di San Francesco,** via San Francesco 1 (tel. 23-271). In fact, it holds its own admirably in all of Tuscany. Not only is the food sumptuous—prepared and served with style—but the atmosphere is appropriate: the buca is decorated in the 14th-century fashion, with a frieze of Tuscan colors, blues and sienna. One dish worth veering off the autostrada for is the anise-flavored pollo del Valdarno arrosto (roast chicken of the province). When the diners pick the bones, the pleased waiter throws up his hands with a "thank you, thank you." For 28,000 lire ($21.25) to 40,000 lire ($30.50) per person, you can have a meal that includes not only a minestrone *and* a pasta, but the roast chicken as well, along with a fresh garden salad, Chianti, and dessert. For an appetizer, try the superb green noodles with a rich meat sauce, oozing with creamy cheese and topped off with a big hunk of fresh butter. The cellar lies just across the way from della Francesca's eternal frescoes. Closed Monday night, Tuesday, and in July.

From Arezzo, a 50-mile drive takes us to—

---

7. Perugia

For one of their greatest cities, the Etruscans chose a setting of remarkable beauty—much like Rome, with a group of hills overlooking the Tiber River Valley. In Perugia we can peel away the epochs. For example, one of the town gates is called the **Arco di Augusto,** or Arch of Augustus. The loggia spanning the arch dates from the Renaissance, but the central part is Roman. Builders from both periods used the reliable Etruscan foundation, the work of architects who laid stones to last. Perugia was one of a dozen major cities in the galaxy of the mysterious Etruscans.

Today the city is the uncrowned capital of Umbria, retaining much of its Gothic and Renaissance charm, although it's been plagued with wars and swept up in disastrous events. To capture the essence of the Umbrian city, you must head for the **piazza IV Novembre** in the heart of Perugia. During the day the square is overrun. Try, then, to go to the piazza late at night when the old town is sleeping. That's when the ghosts come out to play.

Perugia's telephone area code is 075.

THE SIGHTS

As the villages of England compete for the title of most picturesque, so the cities of Italy vie for the honor of having the most beautiful square. As you stand on the **piazza IV Novembre,** you'll know that Perugia is among the top contenders for that honor.

In the heart of the piazza is the **Fontana Maggiore** (Grand Fountain), built sometime in the late 1270s by a local architect, a monk named Bevignate. But its artistic triumph stems from the sculptural work by Niccolò Pisano and his son, Giovanni. Along the lower basin of the fountain—the last major work of the elder Pisano—is statuary symbolizing the arts and sciences, Aesop's fables, the months of the year and signs of the zodiac and scenes from the Old Testament and Roman history. On the upper basin (mostly the work of Giovanni) is allegorical sculpture, such as one figure representing Perugia, as well as saints, biblical characters, even local officials of the city in the 13th century.

After viewing the marvels of the fountain, you'll find that most of the other major attractions either open onto the piazza IV Novembre or lie only a short distance away.

The exterior of the **Cathedral of San Lorenzo** is rather raw looking, as if the builders were suddenly called away to pour boiling oil on the heads of invaders, and never returned. The basilica is built in the Gothic style, dating from the 14th and 15th centuries. Inside, you'll find the *Deposition* of Frederico Barocci. In the museum housing the cathedral works is displayed Luca Signorelli's *Virgin Enthroned*, with saints. Signorelli was a pupil of della Francesca.

On the opposite side of the Piazza IV Novembre is the **Palazzo dei Priori** (Palace of the Priors), corso Vannucci, the town hall, considered one of the finest secular buildings in Italy, dating from the 13th century. Its façade is characterized by a striking row of mullioned windows. Over the main door is a Guelph (member of the papal party) lion and a griffin of Perugia, holding chains once looted from a defeated Siena. You can walk up the stairway—the Vaccara—to the pulpit. By all means explore the interior, especially the vaulted Hall of the Notaries, frescoed with stories of the Old Testament and from Aesop.

Upstairs in the Palace of the Priors is the **National Gallery of Umbria** (tel. 20-316), housing the most comprehensive collection of Umbrian art from the 13th up to the 18th century. Among the earliest paintings of interest is a *Virgin and Child* by Duccio de Buoninsegna, the first important master of the Sienese school. You'll see statuary by the Pisano family, who designed the Grand Fountain out front, and by Arnolfo di Cambio, the architect of the Palazzo Vecchio in Florence.

Tuscan artists are well represented—the pious Fra Angelico's *Virgin and Child* with saints and angels, as well as the same subject treated differently by Piero della Francesca and Benozzo Gozzoli.

You'll also see works of native-son Perugino, among them his *Adoration of the Magi*. Perugino, of course, was the master of Raphael. Often accused of sentimentality, Perugino does not enjoy the popularity today that he did at the peak of his career, but he remains a key painter of the Renaissance, noted especially for his landscapes.

The gallery also displays art by Pinturicchio, whose most notable work was the library of the Duomo of Siena. Pinturicchio studied under Perugino. Vasari had few kind words for Pinturicchio: "It seems that fortune's favorites are those who must depend on her alone, unaided by any ability, and of this we have an instance in Pinturicchio of Perugia, whose reputation was far greater than he deserves." In this salon, you can decide for yourself.

The gallery, charging 4,000 lire ($3.05) for admission, is open Monday through Saturday from 9 a.m. to 1:30 p.m. and 3 to 7 p.m. Sunday. It is open only in the afternoon on Sunday.

Collegio del Cambio (tel. 61-379). Right off the piazza IV Novembre, at corso Vannucci 25, the medieval exchange building opens onto the main street of Perugia, corso Vannucci (Vannucci was the real name of Perugino). The collegio is visited chiefly by those seeking to view the Hall of the Audience, frescoed by Perugino and his assistants, including a teenage Raphael. On the ceiling Perugino represented the planets allegorically. The Renaissance master peopled his frescoes with the Virtues, sybils, and such biblical figures as Solomon. But his masterpiece is his own countenance. It seems rather ironic that—at least for once—Perugino could be realistic. Another room of interest is the Chapel of S. J. Battista, containing many frescoes painted by a pupil of Perugino, G. Nicola di Paolo. The exchange is open Tuesday through Saturday from 9 a.m. to 12:30 p.m. and 2:30 to 5:30 p.m. from March to the end of October and just before Christmas to early January. Otherwise, hours are from 8 a.m. to 2 p.m. On Sunday and holidays it is open from 9 a.m. to 12:30 p.m.; closed Monday. Admission is 1,500 lire ($1.15).

An escalator has been installed to take passengers from the older part of Perugia at the top of the hill and the upper slopes to the lower city. During construction of this means of transportation, the old fortress, Rocca Paolina, that had been covered over to make the park and viewing area at the end of corso Vannucci in the last century, was rediscovered, along with buried streets. The old streets and street names have been cleaned up, and the area is well lighted, with an old wall exposed and modern sculpture added. The escalator, with stops at several levels, is a marvel in itself.

HOTELS IN PERUGIA

Suitable accommodations in most price ranges can be found in Perugia. But since the town has so few recommendable hotels, you are always advised to arrive with a reservation.

Hotel Brufani, piazza Italia 12, 06100 Perugia (tel. 075/62-541), at the top of the city, was built by Giacomo Brufani in 1884 on the ruins of the ancient Rocca Paolina. It is placed on a cliff edge of town, only a few yards from the main street of Perugia, corso Vannucci. A view of the Umbrian landscape so beloved by painters is offered in most of the 24 rooms and three suites of this five-star hostelry, which was completely renovated in 1984 and is now owned by SINA Hotels of Italy. It is fully air-conditioned, and all rooms are equipped with radio, color TV (with CBS news from the U.S.), and mini-bar. Doubles cost 190,000 lire ($144) to 257,000 lire ($195) daily. There are no single rooms, but 140,000 lire ($106) to 190,000 lire ($144) is charged for single occupancy of a double unit. The higher prices are for high season. The hotel has a good café-restaurant, Mr. Collins (see below), named for the great-grandfather of Mr. Bottelli who succeeded the original owner, Mr. Brufani, nearly a century ago.

Hotel Posta, corso Vannucci 97, 06100 Perugia (tel. 075/61-345). Goethe slept here. So did Hans Christian Andersen. The hotel sits on the main street of the oldest part of Perugia, behind an impressively ornate façade, which was originally sculpted in the 1700s. Each of the 65 bedrooms contains a private bath, and units are, for the most part, functional and modernized. A handful of the more elegant Venetian rooms are found on the first floor. With breakfast included, singles rent for 50,000 lire ($38) daily; doubles, 80,000 lire ($60.75).

Hotel La Rosetta, piazza Italia 19, 06100 Perugia (tel. 075/20-841). Since 1922, when this Perugian landmark was established, it has expanded from a seven-room pensione to a sprawling and labyrinthine complex with 96 rooms. With its frescoed ceiling, room 55 has been declared a national treasure. (The bullet holes that papal mercenaries shot into the ceiling in 1848 have been artfully preserved.) The other, less grandiose accommodations include decors ranging from slickly contemporary to Victorian to the 1950s era. Each unit is peaceful, clean, and comfortable, regardless of decor. Singles cost 55,000 lire ($41.75) to 60,000 lire ($45.50) daily; doubles, 110,000 lire ($83.50) to 190,000 lire ($144). The in-house restaurant is recommended separately.

DINING IN PERUGIA

A choice of dining experiences and ambience is offered at **Mario Ragni/Il Pappagallo,** via dei Priori 78-82 (tel. 21-889). The vaulted cellars containing these unusual restaurants were originally assembled in the 1600s. Today they work as a backdrop for the creative cuisine of Mario Ragni, who almost singlehandedly produces the most sophisticated dishes in Perugia. First, there is Il Pappagallo, where amid a lighthearted decor of red plastic tables and chairs you can serve yourself from an array of Italian delicacies changed daily. A bottle of Spumanti comes with the fixed-price meal of 75,000 lire ($57) per person. The true gastronomes of the town, however, head for the lowest level of the cellar, where a surprise meal is prepared every day according to the whims and fancies of the maestro himself. My most recent meal included such dishes as fresh salmon with armagnac-flavored mascarpone and pistachios, peeled and marinated grapes with asparagus-coiffed shrimp, tricolor gnocchi with a gorgonzola sauce, an original and delectable form of Oriental veal, and many other courses, each served with a suitable wine. The price is 90,000 lire

($68.50) per person. Reservations are necessary. The cellars serve food from 12:30 to 2:30 p.m. and 7:30 to 10 p.m.; closed Sunday and in August.

Mr. Collins, in the Hotel Brufani, piazza Italia 12 (tel. 62-541), is a café-restaurant operating on the ground floor of the hotel, with a private entrance from piazza Italia. Guests can enjoy an open-air café in front of a small park from May to October. Light snacks are available, and before you go inside, you can study the à la carte menu outside the entrance. You can select anything from a dish of spaghetti to a complete meal of traditional Italian cuisine, served daily from 12:30 to 2:30 p.m. and 7:30 to 9:30 p.m. At the Collins, you're likely to spend from 42,000 lire ($32) for a meal, although you can get by for less.

La Rosetta, piazza Italia 19 (tel. 20-841), has gained more fame than the hotel in which it's lodged. Food-smart Italian travelers manage to arrive here at mealtime: it's that good and reasonable. You'll find three areas in which to dine: an intimate wood-paneled salon, a main dining area divided by Roman arches and lit by brass chandeliers, and a courtyard enclosed by the walls of the villa-style hotel. Under shady palm trees you can have a leisurely meal. The menu choice is vast, but a few specialties stand out over the rest. To begin, the finest dishes are either spaghetti alla Norcina (with a truffle sauce) or vol-au-vent di tortellini Rosetta. Among the main dishes, the outstanding entry is scaloppine alla perugina. The vegetable choices are fresh and tasty, and several desserts, such as fresh fruit and ice cream, are the pick of the after-dinner choices. Expect to spend 25,000 lire ($19) to 40,000 lire ($30.50) for a complete meal. The restaurant, open from 12:30 to 2:30 p.m. and 7:30 to 10 p.m., is closed Monday.

La Taverna, via delle Streghe 8 (tel. 61-028). The entrance to this provincial tavern is at the bottom of one of the narrowest alleyways in town. Prominent illustrated signs indicate its position off via Vannucci at the bottom of a flight of steps. You enter a high-ceilinged room filled with overflowing displays of antipasti. Four dining rooms radiate outward from there, each filled with exposed brick and oil paintings. The menu includes arrays of pasta, polentas, soups, and a typical list of fish, meats, and liver. Full dinners are reasonably priced at 30,000 lire ($22.75) to 46,000 lire ($35). Food is served from 12:30 to 2:30 p.m. and 7:30 to 10 p.m. daily except Monday and the last two weeks in July.

Trattoria Ricciotto, piazza Dante 19 (tel. 21-956), is a rustically elegant restaurant. It's owned and operated by members of the Betti family, who cook, serve the food, uncork the wine, and welcome visitors to Perugia. The restaurant offers a variety of well-prepared specialties. These include, for example, fettuccine with artichokes, a spicy combination of lentils with sausage, suckling pig, baby veal dishes, and a full array of grilled meats and well-prepared vegetables. Open from 12:30 to 2:30 p.m. and 7:30 to 10 p.m., it is closed every Sunday and in July, and reservations are suggested. Expect to pay from 40,000 lire ($30.50) per person, not counting one of the wide assortment of regional wines.

Falchetto, via Bartolo 20 (tel. 61-875). Owner and chef Alessandro Alunni has never been afraid to try new recipes on his loyal clientele of habitués. Many of the dishes take traditional themes and add a certain zest that has won critical approval for the medieval-style restaurant he works so hard to maintain. A few of the menu items include tagliatelle with truffles, grilled trout, prosciutto several different ways, pasta with chickpeas, and grilled filet of goat. A short walk from the piazza Piccinino (where you'll be able to park), the restaurant is open from 12:30 to 2:30 p.m. and 7:30 to 10 p.m. daily except Monday. Expect to pay about 22,000 lire ($16.75) to 35,000 lire ($26.50) per person.

THE CAFE LIFE

On the main shopping street of town, **Sandri Pasticceria,** corso Vannucci 32 (tel. 61-012), offers drinks, cakes, pastries, sandwiches, and rolls to clients who cluster around the shiny marble-topped bar area. If you order Milanese cutlet, Parmesan eggplant, chicken salad, or one of the many other hot or cold dishes, you can perch on a red stool or sit at a small table. Main courses cost from 9,000 lire ($6.85); pasta and rice, from 4,000 lire ($3.05); and vegetables, 2,000 lire ($1.50). Only the finest ingredients are used. You can also buy the city's famous candies and specialties gleaned from many other places displayed on the antique carved wooden shelves. The bar is lit by crystal chandeliers and candles in silver holders. Hours are 8:15 a.m. to 11 p.m. daily except Monday.

Caffè del Cambio, corso Vannucci 29 (tel. 61-065). My favorite café in Perugia is favored by the town's many university students. The first room is the most impressive. Capped with a vaulted ceiling, it contains racks of pastries, cases of ice cream, a long stand-up bar, and a handful of tiny tables. The low-ceilinged room in back is smokier, more crowded, and, to some, much livelier. If you stand, a whisky costs 3,200 lire ($2.45) to 4,400 lire ($3.35). If you sit, the prices are 50% more. Hours are 8 a.m. to midnight daily.

ON THE OUTSKIRTS

Ten miles from Perugia stands **Le Tre Vaselle,** via Garibaldi 48, 06089 Torgiano (tel. 075/982-447), which many discriminating guests prefer to make their base for exploring the Umbrian countryside. A very old house has been transformed into a luxurious *Relais & Châteaux*. Its stucco façade, regularly pierced by arched doorways and shuttered windows, is framed by the greenery of a baroque garden. Inside, the soaring ceilings are capped with hand-hewn timbers or vaulted stonework whose amber-colored reflections highlight the combinations of new and old furniture. Some of the public rooms contain grandly proportioned fireplaces, near which secluded seating areas give guests the chance to relax with a drink. In addition to its up-to-date conference facilities, the establishment contains a modern dining room where regional specialties are carefully prepared. A la carte meals cost from 60,000 lire ($45.50). The cozy bedrooms are comfortable and contemporary, an occasional antique softening their angular line. The 48 bedrooms rent for 180,000 lire ($137) daily in a single, 260,000 lire ($198) in a double. A widely acclaimed wine museum designed to appeal to scholars, wine enthusiasts, and other visitors is on the premises.

---

8. Gubbio

Gubbio, 25 miles from Perugia, is one of the best-preserved medieval towns in Italy, its origins going back to dim times. It has modern apartments and stores on its outskirts, but once you press through that, you are firmly back in the Middle Ages as you walk the best-known streets of its medieval core, especially via XX Settembre, via dei Consoli, via Galeotti, and via Baldassini. All these streets are found in the old town or **Città Vecchia,** set against the steep slopes of **Monte Ingino.** If the weather is right, you can take a cable car up to the mountain at a height of 2,690 feet. Service is daily from 8 a.m. to 1 p.m. and 2 to 8 p.m., a round-trip ticket costing 3,000 lire ($2.30).

Back in Gubbio, after having surveyed a panoramic view, you can set about exploring a town that knew its golden age in the 1300s. That exploration might begin at the piazza della Signoria, the most important square. On this square you can visit the **Palazzo dei Consoli** or consuls' palace, a Gothic edifice housing the famed bronze *tavole eugubine,* a series of tablets as old as Christianity, which were discovered in the 15th century. The tablets contain writing in the mysterious Umbrian language. The museum has a display of antiques from the Middle Ages and a collection of paintings. It is open May to September daily from 9 a.m. to 12:30 p.m. and 3:30 to 6 p.m., charging an admission of 2,000 lire ($1.50). Off-season, its hours are 9 a.m. to 1 p.m. and 3 to 5 p.m. daily.

The other major sight is the **Palazzo Ducale,** or ducal palace, which is open daily except Monday from 9 a.m. to 2 p.m. (to 1 p.m. on Sunday), charging an admission of 2,000 lire ($1.50). This palace is associated with the memories (not always good ones) of the ruling dukes of Urbino. It was built by Federico of Montefeltro. After visiting the palace, you can go inside the **duomo,** or cathedral, across the way. It is a relatively unadorned pink Gothic building with some stained-glass windows from the 12th century. It has a single nave.

Gubbio has other attractions, including the **Church of St. Francis,** built in the Gothic style, and a **Roman theater,** dating from the era of Augustus. But you may want to save the rest of your time to explore many of the shops in town that make ceramics, some of which are known for their unique iridescent red luster. Gubbio is also known for many famous processions and festivals, including the Procession of the Dead Christ on Good Friday and the Corsa dei Ceri on May 15, when hourglass-shaped wooden towers are hauled through the streets.

The telephone area code for Gubbio is 075.

WHERE TO STAY

The most scenically located hotel in town, the **Albergo Bosone,** via XX Settembre 22, 06024 Gubbio (tel. 075/927-2008), is at the meeting point of an almost endless flight of stone steps and a narrow street in the upper regions of town. A Tuscan-style Romanesque arch caps the doorway of this three-story medieval palace whose façade is embellished with neoclassical trim. The cozy bedrooms rent for 45,000 lire ($34.25) daily in a single, 65,000 lire ($49.50) in a double. The hotel closes in February.

Hotel San Marco, via Perugina 5, 06024 Gubbio (tel. 075/927-2349). Its unpromising location on the busiest streetcorner in town is its only real drawback. In summer, guests tend to gravitate to the chairs on the arbor-covered terrace in back where uniformed waiters serve food and drink. The hotel has a notable restaurant, Lo Struzzichino, whose simple napery-covered tables are sheltered with russet-colored brick vaulting. The 66 airily modern bedrooms cost 40,000 lire ($30.50) daily in a single, 60,000 lire ($46.50) in a double. Each unit contains a private bath and phone. The town's parking lot is across the street. The hotel is closed in January.

Hotel Gattapone, via Beni 11, 06024 Gubbio (tel. 075/927-2489), is a pleasant hotel at the bottom of a narrow alleyway whose flagstone pavement is spanned with soaring medieval buttresses. Guests enter a modernized lobby, heading for a sun-flooded breakfast room where large windows offer glimpses of a tiny garden. The establishment contains only 15 bedrooms. The furnishings are modern, but a few have handcrafted details such as timbered ceilings and inset arches of chiseled stone. Each comes with a private bath and phone. Singles cost a modest 32,000 lire ($24.25) daily, doubles 50,000 lire ($38), with breakfast included. The hotel closes in January.

WHERE TO DINE

The most elegant restaurant in town is **Alla Fornace di Mastro Giorgio,** via Mastro Giorgio 2 (tel. 927-5740). Set above the town's commercial center, to the side of an endless set of gently sloping steps, this building was constructed of stones that look as old as the Umbrian hills that surround it. Because restaurant owner Ignazio Mongelli is a transplant from the extreme south of Italy, his cuisine sometimes reflects a bit of Puglia's Mediterranean flair. Such specialties are served as fresh salmon in a herb sauce, a crêpe of white Umbrian truffles, a torte of mussels with rice, and several varieties of seasonal game dishes, along with such marine fare as seafood brochettes with basil. The pappardelle with rabbit and truffles is heavenly. Full meals, served from 12:30 to 2:30 p.m. and 7:30 to 10 p.m. daily except Monday and in February, cost 28,000 lire ($21.25) to 45,000 lire ($34.25).

Ristorante Federico da Montefeltro, via della Repubblica 35 (tel. 927-3949), stands beside steeply inclined flagstones in the oldest part of the city within a tavern-style duet of rooms ringed with exposed stone and pine planking. Many of the specialties are based on ancient regional recipes. You might be tempted by a display of antipasti before ordering such dishes as chicken cooked with oil, garlic, rosemary, and wine, or else roast suckling pig, several varieties of polenta, tagliatelle (ribbon pasta), and such traditional fare as veal, beef, and truffle platters. You'll be served a local version of unleavened bread fried in oil as part of the meal, costing from 30,000 lire ($22.75). The restaurant is open from 12:30 to 2 p.m. and 7 to 10 p.m. daily except Thursday between October and March. It is closed in February. It was named for the feudal lord who built the ducal palace of Gubbio.

Taverna del Lupo, via B. Ansidei 21a (tel. 927-1269). Several of the ceilings of this warmly decorated establishment are supported by barrel vaults and ribbing of old stone. From the glow of iron chandeliers, you can select your favorite antipasti from the prominent display. Other dishes include a flavorful risotto with artichokes, a house lasagne, charcoal-grilled meats, and several kinds of pasta, along with Florentine beefsteaks and fresh vegetables. Full meals, costing 35,000 lire ($26.50) to 45,000 lire ($34.25), are served from 12:30 to 2:30 p.m. and 7:30 to 10 p.m. daily except Monday and in January.

---

9. Assisi

Ideally placed on the rise to Mount Subasio, watched over by the medieval Rocco Maggiore, this purple-fringed Umbrian hill town, about 15 miles from Perugia, retains a mystical air. The site of many a pilgrimage, Assisi is forever linked in legend with its native son, St. Francis. The gentle saint founded the Franciscan order and shares honors with St. Catherine of Siena as the patron saint of Italy. But he is remembered by many, even non-Christians, as a lover of nature (his preaching to an audience of birds is one of the legends of his life).

The telephone area code of Assisi is 075.

THE TOP SIGHT

An important church, the **Basilica of St. Francis,** consisting of both an upper and lower church, at the piazza di San Francesco, houses some of the most important cycles of frescoes in Italy, works by such pre-Renaissance giants as Cimabue and Giotto. Both churches were built in the first part of the 13th century. The basilica and its paintings form the most significant monument to St. Francis.

Upon entering the upper church through the principal doorway, look to your immediate left to see one of Giotto's most celebrated frescoes, that of St. Francis preaching to the birds. In the nave of the upper church you'll find the rest of the cycle of 27 additional frescoes, some of which are by Giotto, although the authorship of the entire cycle is a subject of controversy. Many of the frescoes are almost surrealistic—in architectural frameworks—like a stage setting that strips away the walls and allows us to see the actors inside. In the cycle we see pictorial evidence of the rise of humanism that was to lead not only to Giotto's but Italy's split from the rigidity of Byzantium.

Proceed up the nave to the transept, turning left. Here is a masterpiece of Cimabue's, the *Crucifixion.* Time has robbed the fresco of its former radiance, but has not diminished its power and ghost-like drama. The cycle of badly damaged frescoes in the transept and apse are other works by Cimabue and his paint-smeared helpers.

From the transept we proceed down the stairs through the two-tiered cloisters to the lower church, which will put us in the south transept. Look for Cimabue's faded but masterly *Virgin and Child* with four angels and St. Francis looking on from the far right. The fresco is badly lit, but is often reproduced in detail as one of Cimabue's greatest works. On the other side of the transept is the *Deposition* (descent) *from the Cross,* a masterpiece by that Sienese artist Pietro Lorenzetti, plus a

Madonna and Child with St. John and St. Francis (stigmata showing). In a chapel honoring St. Martin of Tours, Simone Martini of Siena painted a cycle of frescoes, done with great skill and imagination, depicting the life and times of that saint. Finally, under the lower church is the crypt of St. Francis.

Visiting hours in summer are 8 a.m. to 7 p.m. daily (in winter, from 8 a.m. to noon and 2 to 6 p.m.).

OTHER SIGHTS

The **Church of San Rufino.** Built in the mid-12th century at the piazza San Rufino, the Duomo of Assisi is graced with a Romanesque façade, greatly enhanced by rose windows, all making it one of the finest churches in the hill towns, as important as the one at Spoleto. Adjoining the cathedral is a bell tower or campanile. Inside, the church has been baroqued, an unfortunate decision and a loss of the purity that the front suggests. St. Francis and St. Clare were both baptized here.

The **Basilica of Santa Chiara** (Clare), on the piazza Santa Chiara, is dedicated to "the little plant of Blessed Francis," as St. Clare liked to describe herself. Born in 1193 into one of the richest and noblest families of Assisi, Clare was to give all her wealth to the poor and to found, together with St. Francis, the Order of the Poor Clares. She was canonized by Pope Alexander IV in 1255. Pope Pius XII declared her Patroness of Television in 1958, based on a vision she said she had on Christmas Eve of 1252 in which she saw the manger and heard the friars sing in the Basilica of St. Francis while she was bedridden in the Monastery of San Damiano. The frescoes that once decorated the walls of this basilica were almost completely destroyed by whitewash applied over them in the 18th century. Indeed, only a shortage of funds saved those in the Basilica of St. Francis from a similar fate. In the Chapel of the Crucifix, to the right of the nave, is displayed what is possibly the world's most famous cross, the crucifix that is alleged to have spoken to St. Francis in the Church of San Damiano, indicating to him his vocation with the words: "Go, Francis, and repair my church which, as you see, is falling into ruin." On the end wall of the same chapel, behind a double grille, you may see some of the most important relics extant of St. Clare and St. Francis. A Poor Clare nun of the neighboring Protomonastery of St. Clare offers visitors a brief explanation of them. Downstairs in the crypt, the mortal remains of St. Clare repose on a wooden table inside a simple urn. The church, in Italian Gothic style, built in the 13th century, is characterized by its façade of alternating rose-and-white decorative stripes.

The **Temple of Minerva** opens onto the **piazza del Commune,** the heart of Assisi. The square is a dream for a lover of architecture from the 12th through the 14th centuries. A pagan structure, with six Corinthian columns, the Temple of Minerva dates from the 1st century B.C. With Minerva-like wisdom, the people of Assisi let it stand, turning it into a baroque church inside so as not to offend the devout. Adjoining the temple is the 13th-century Tower of the People, built by Ghibelline supporters.

The **Rocca Maggiore** (Great Fortress) strides a hill overlooking Assisi. It should be visited if for no other reason than the view of the Umbrian countryside possible from its ramparts. The present building—now in ruins—dates from the 14th century, and the origins of the structure go back beyond that. There's no admission charged to enter the fort, but the nonsalaried guard expects a tip. The fortress is open daily in summer from 9 a.m. to noon and 2 to 6 p.m.

The **Eremo delle Carceri** (Prisons' Hermitage) (tel. 812-301). In a setting 2½ miles east of Assisi (out via Eremo delle Carceri), the hermitage is from the 14th and 15th centuries. The "prison" is not a penal institution—rather a spiritual retreat. It is believed that St. Francis retired to this spot for meditation and prayer. Visitors can go down into the grotto to see the stone bed on which (tradition says) St. Francis slept. Out back is a gnarled, moss-covered ilex (or live oak) tree, more than 1,000 years old, where St. Francis is believed to have blessed the birds, after which blessing they are said to have flown in the four major directions of the compass to symbolize that Franciscans, in coming centuries, would spread out from Assisi all over the world. The monastery contains some faded frescoes. One of the handful of friars who still inhabit the retreat will show you through. The retreat is open daily from 8 a.m. to sunset, charging no admission, but donations are gratefully accepted to defray the cost of maintenance. In keeping with the Franciscan tradition, the friars at Le Carceri are completely dependent on alms for their support.

HOTELS IN ASSISI

Space in Assisi tends to be tight—so reservations are important. Still, for such a small town, Assisi has a goodly number of accommodations. I will begin with the most expensive. Those on a strict budget should read from the bottom of the list.

Hotel Subasio, via Frate Ella 2, 60081 Assisi (tel. 075/812-206), is a first-class hotel with a decidedly old-fashioned aura. The Subasio has been the unquestioned choice of many a famous visitor—the king and queen of Belgium, the queen of the Netherlands, Charlie Chaplin, Merle Oberon, Marlene Dietrich, and James Stewart. The hotel is linked to the Church of St. Francis by a covered stone arched colonnade, and its dining terrace (extremely good food) is perhaps the most dramatic in Assisi. Your table will be shaded by a sprawling vine. Dining is also an event on the vaulted medieval loggia. The bedrooms at the front open onto balconies with a good view. The rooms are furnished with Italian flair. All contain baths, showers, TVs, frigobars, and air conditioning. Singles rent for 85,000 lire ($64.50) daily, and doubles go for 130,000 lire ($98.75).

Hotel Giotto, via Fontebella 41, 06082 Assisi (tel. 075/812-209), is a most up-to-date and well-run hotel, built at the edge of town on several levels. Near the Basilica of St. Francis, and opening onto panoramic views, the Giotto offers little formal gardens and terraces for meals or sunbathing. It has spacious modern public rooms and an elevator. All of its well-furnished bedrooms—70 in all—have private baths. Bright colors predominate, and there's a Parmeggiani mural (modern artist from Bologna) over the drinking bar. Singles cost 70,000 lire ($53.25) daily, and doubles or twins go for 120,000 lire ($91.25), with breakfast included. Full board is offered for 155,000 lire ($118) per person daily. The hotel is open from mid-March to mid-November.

Umbra, via degli Archi 6, 06081 Assisi (tel. 075/812-240), is the most centrally located accommodation in Assisi, in a position right off the main square with its Temple of Minerva. The outdoor terraced dining room forms an important part of the hotel's entryway. You enter through old stone walls covered with vines, and walk under a leafy pergola. The lobby is compact and functional. The bedrooms are efficient, with comfortable beds; some have a tiny balcony overlooking the crusty old rooftops and the Umbrian countryside. Many of the 25 rooms have private bath or shower. Singles rent for 45,000 lire ($34.25) daily; doubles run 65,000 lire ($49.50).

St. Anthony's Guest House, via Galeazzo Alessi 10, 06081 Assisi (tel. 075/812-542), is special. It's for those desiring an economical and comfortable accommodation in a medieval villa turned guesthouse. On the upper ledges of Assisi, St. Anthony's Guest House contains its own terraced gardens and views. Run by members of the Franciscan Sisters of the Atonement (an order originating in Graymoor, New York), the guesthouse offers good rooms and complete tranquility. Visitors who pass through the large entrance door are greeted with a smile. In all, 40 people are accommodated here and are charged 35,000 lire ($26.50) per person daily, based on double occupancy, with private bath. This tariff includes breakfast and lunch. No evening meal is served. The sisters are dedicated to social work and to St. Francis, and finding this former villa was the answer to a prayer. They joyfully go about their work and serve good breakfasts and midday meals in a restored 12th-century dining room.

DINING IN ASSISI

The best place to dine is **Il Medioevo,** via dell'Arco dei Priori 4 (tel. 813-068), one of the gastronomic staples and architectural oddities of Assisi. The foundations on which the restaurant rests are at least 1,000 years old. During the Middle Ages and again in Renaissance times it was successively enlarged and modified, until today it is considered an authentic medieval gem of heavy stonework. Fresh ingredients and skill go into the food preparation. You might order, for example, roast duck with vinegar sauce, a fritto misto containing baby squid among other ingredients, several preparations of lamb, and succulent pastas laced with fish and/or vegetables. Meals cost from 30,000 lire ($22.75), and are served daily except Wednesday from noon to 2:30 p.m. and 7:30 to 9:45 p.m.

Down a walk of old steps, at **La Taverna dell'Arco da Bino,** vicolo San Gregorio 8 (tel. 812-383), you'll find some of the best cuisine to be found outside the second-class hotels. The tavern captures the atmosphere of the 14th century, with original vaulted ceilings and stone walls. In the days of St. Francis, this was the abode of monks. Nowadays it's run by owners known for their good food and such wine as the locally produced Bianco dell' Umbria. Your first plate might be melon and figs. Main dishes include piccione (pigeon), served in a sauce of fresh sage, lemon, capers, olive oil, and black olives, or veal scaloppine in marsala wine. Much of the meat and vegetables come from a farm the family has in the Umbrian countryside. Desserts are homemade and luscious. Among a wide choice of set meals, a three-course repast will run 15,000 lire ($11.50) to 25,000 lire ($19). Open from 12:30 to 2:30 p.m. and 7:30 to 9:30 p.m., the restaurant is closed on Tuesday and in January and February.

Ristorante Buca di San Francesco, via Brizi 1 (tel. 812-204), set below street level in the basement of an ancient palace, is outfitted with stone walls. The menu changes frequently, according to the availability of ingredients. One of the specialties is spaghetti alla buca, as well as onion soup. Grilled meats are always featured, and sometimes they are served with truffles, so popular in the Umbrian countryside. Expect to spend from 35,000 lire ($26.50) for a full meal. The restaurant is open from 12:30 to 2:30 p.m. and 7:30 to 9:30 p.m.; closed Monday.

Umbra, via degli Archi 6 (tel. 812-240). The shaded garden of this pleasant restaurant is calm and quiet enough to have pleased St. Francis (well, almost). On a warm day you'll probably hear birds chirping. In the heart of the old city, not far from the cathedral, the establishment is the personal statement of the owner and his staff of capable helpers. Menu items include dishes that range from the fanciful to the classically popular. In any event, ample use is made of truffles. The best cuts of meat are generally used, along with very fresh vegetables. Meals, served from noon to 2 p.m. and 7:30 to 9 p.m., cost 35,000 lire ($26.50) to 48,000 lire ($36.50). The restaurant is closed on Tuesday and from mid-November to mid-December.

---

10. Spoleto

Hannibal couldn't conquer it, but Gian-Carlo Menotti did—and how! Before Maestro Menotti put Spoleto on the tourist map, it was known mostly to art lovers, teachers, and students. Today the chic and fashionable, the artistic and arty flood the Umbrian hill town to attend performances of the world-famed **"Festival dei Due Mondi"** (Festival of Two Worlds), most often held in June and July. Menotti searched and traveled through many hill towns of Tuscany and Umbria before making a final choice. When he saw Spoleto, he fell in love with it. And quite understandably.

Long before Tennessee Williams arrived to première a new play, Thomas Schippers to conduct an opera, *Macbeth,* Shelley Winters to do three one-act plays by Saul Bellow, Spoleto was known to St. Francis and to Lucrezia Borgia, the latter having occupied the 14th-century castle that towers over the town, the Rocca dell'Albornoz. The town is filled with palaces of Spoletan aristocracy, medieval streets, and towers for protection from a time when visitors weren't as friendly as those of today. There are churches, churches, and more churches—some of which, such as **San Gregorio Maggiore,** were built in the Romanesque style in the 11th century.

But the tourist center is the **piazza del Duomo,** with its cathedral and **Teatro Caio Melisso** (Chamber Theater). Although few visitors may know it, Mr. Menotti has a small house with a terrace opening onto the square. The cathedral is a hodge-podge of Romanesque and medieval architecture, with a 12th-century campanile. Its façade is of exceptional beauty, renowned especially for its mosaic by Salsterno. The interior should be visited if for no other reason than to see the cycle of frescoes in the chancel by Filippo Lippi. His son, Filippino, also an artist, designed the tomb for his father. The keeper of the apse will be only too happy to unlock it for you. These frescoes, believed to have been carried out largely by students, were the elder Lippi's last work; he died in Spoleto in 1469. Vasari writes, "Some said he was poisoned by certain persons related to the object of his love." As friars went in those days, Lippi was a bit of a swinger, having run off with a nun, Lucrezia Buti, who later posed as the Madonna in several of his paintings.

Spoleto should be visited even when the festival isn't taking place, as it's a most interesting town. It has a number of sights worth seeking out, including the remains of a **Roman theater** lying off the piazza della Libertà. Motorists wanting a view can continue up the hill from Spoleto around a winding road (about five miles) to **Monteluco,** 2,500 feet above sea level. An ancient spot, Monteluco is peppered with summer villas.

A note on the festival: Dates, programs, and ticket prices change yearly. In Spoleto, the general offices of the festival are at via Giustolo 10.

Spoleto's telephone area code is 0743

HOTELS IN SPOLETO

Spoleto offers an attractive range of hotels, but when the "two worlds" crowd in at festival time, the going's rough (last season a group of students bedded down on the piazza del Duomo). In an emergency, the tourist office at piazza della Libertà 7 (tel. 0743/28-111) can probably arrange for you to stay in a private home—at a low price. The office is open only during regular business hours, but it's imperative to telephone in advance for a reservation. Many of the private rooms are often rented well in advance to artists appearing at the festival. Innkeepers are likely to raise all the prices listed below to whatever the market will bear.

Gattapone, via del Ponte, 06049 Spoleto (tel. 0743/36-147), is more a spectacle than a hotel. Probably the only 16-room hotel in Italy to be rated first class, it's among the clouds, high on a twisting road leading to the ancient castle and the 13th-century Ponte delle Torri, a bridge 250 feet high. The hotel and restaurant occupy two separate stone cottages, side by side—one devoted to guest rooms, the other to serving meals. The buildings cling closely to the road, and each descends the precipice overlooking the gorge. The hotel has had its view side equipped with a two-story picture window and an open spiral stairway leading from the intimate lounge to the bedrooms. Each of the rooms—doubles only, all with private bath—is individually furnished, with comfortable beds, antiques, and plenty of space. A superior double room costs from 145,000 lire ($110) daily; a twin goes for 96,000 lire ($73). The restaurant is open March to October only.

Dei Duchi, on the piazza della Libertà, viale Matteotti 4, 06049 Spoleto (tel. 0743/44-541), is a well-designed, modern hotel, within walking distance of the major sights—yet it perches on a hillside with views and terraces. Near the Roman theater, Dei Duchi is graced with walls of natural brick, open-to-the-view glass, tropical plants, and lounges with modern furnishings and original paintings. Every bedroom has its own balcony, bedside lights, and telephone, plus brightly colored bed coverings, wood-grained furniture, built-in-cupboards—quite a good layout. Depending on the season, singles with private bath or shower cost 55,000 lire ($41.75) to 80,000 lire ($60.75) daily, and doubles with bath or shower rent for 78,000 lire ($59.25) to 115,000 lire ($87.50). In high season, half board is required, costing from 130,000 lire ($98.75) per person daily. You have a choice of two dining rooms, each airy, light, and roomy.

Clarici, piazza della Vittoria 32, 06049 Spoleto (tel. 0743/46-706), is rated only third class, but it's airy and modern—all its rooms featuring a private bath or shower. Each accommodation has a private balcony, opening onto a view. The hotel doesn't emphasize style, but the creature comforts: soft low beds, built-in wardrobes, phones, steam heat, an elevator. There's a large hanging terrace for sunbathing or sipping drinks. Open all year, the hotel charges 45,000 lire ($34.25) daily for a single with shower, 65,000 lire ($49.50) for a double with shower, inclusive.

Hotel Charleston, piazza Collicola 10, 06049 Spoleto (tel. 0743/38-135). The tile-roofed, sienna-fronted building that contains it was originally built in the 17th century. Today it serves as a pleasantly accessorized hotel, conveniently located in the historic center. Each of the 18 bedrooms has a ceiling accented with beams of honey-colored planking, comfortable mattresses, a color TV, frigo-bar, and a phone. Singles cost 49,000 lire ($37.25) daily; doubles 67,000 lire ($51). On the premises is a sauna, as well as a bar and a library and sitting room with sofas and a writing table.

DINING IN SPOLETO

Outside the heart of town, at **Il Tartufo,** piazza Garibaldi 24 (tel. 40-236), near the amphitheater, you may be introduced to the Umbrian tartufo (truffle). This immaculately kept, excellent taverna serves at least nine regional specialties using the black tartufo of Spoleto. An ever-popular dish—and a good introduction for neophyte palates who may never have tried truffles—is fettuccine al tartufo. Alternatively, you may want to start your meal with an omelet—for instance, frittata al tartufo. Main dishes of veal and beef are also excellently prepared. For such a small restaurant, the menu is large. Count on spending from 45,000 lire ($34.25) up. The restaurant, open from 12:30 to 3 p.m. and 7:30 to 10 p.m., is closed on Wednesday and from mid-July to early August.

Tric-Trac da Giustino, on the piazza del Duomo, at via dell'Arringo 10 (tel. 44-592), is frequented by an international clientele at the Festival of Two Worlds. The setting on this landmark square is in an atmosphere evoking the 16th century. The restaurant as well as Giustino's American bar is beneath Signor Menotti's house. The food is well prepared, the service excellent. For a full-course meal, expect to pay 15,000 lire ($11.50) to 50,000 lire ($38). The restaurant and bar are open daily from 9 a.m. to 2 a.m.

---

11. Orvieto

Built on a pedestal of volcanic rock above vineyards in a green valley, Orvieto is the closest hill town to Rome and, as such, is often visited by those who lack the time to explore other targets in Umbria.

Lying on the Paglia, a tributary of the Tiber, Orvieto is 75 miles north of Rome. This hill town sits on an isolated rock some 1,035 feet above sea level. Crowning the town is its world-famed cathedral. A road runs from below up to the piazza del Duomo.

Considered the most spectacularly sited hill town in Umbria (but not the most spectacular town), Orvieto was founded by the Etruscans, who were apparently drawn to it because of its good defensive possibilities. Likewise, long after its days as a Roman colony, Orvieto was to become a papal stronghold. It was a natural fortress, as its cliffs rise starkly from the valley below, even though Orvieto, when you finally reach it, is relatively flat. Although the tall, sheer cliffs on which the town stands saved it from the incursion of railroads and superhighways, which are down in the valley, time and traffic vibrations have caused disintegration in the soft volcanic rock so that work is imminently necessary to shore up the town.

It is known for its white wine which, everybody agrees, is best enjoyed at a wine bar on the piazza del Duomo, as you contemplate the façade of the cathedral. If you visit on a Saturday morning, you can see the pottery market that takes place on the piazza del Popolo.

The telephone area code for Orvieto is 0763.

THE SIGHTS

Erected on the site of two older churches, the **Cathedral of Orvieto,** dedicated to the Virgin, was begun in 1288 (maybe even earlier). The purpose was to commemorate the "Miracle of Bolsena." This alleged miracle came out of the doubts of a priest who questioned the Transsubstantiation (that is, the incarnation of Jesus Christ in the Host). However, so the story goes, at the moment of Consecration, the Host started to drip blood. The priest doubted no more, and the Feast of Corpus Christi was launched.

The cathedral is known for its elaborately adorned façade, rich statuary, marble bas-reliefs, and mosaics. Pope John XXIII once proclaimed that on Judgment Day God would send his angels down to earth to pick up the façade of this cathedral and transport it back to heaven.

There is a rose window over the main door. But the most controversial part of the cathedral is the modern bronze portals that many art historians journey from around the world to see. The doors were the work of Emilio Greco, an eminent sculptor. He took as his theme the Misericordia, the seven acts of corporal charity. One panel depicts Pope John XXIII's famous visit to the prisoners of Rome's Queen of Heaven jail in 1960. Some critics have called the doors "outrageous"; others have praised them as "one of the most original works of modern sculpture." You decide for yourself.

On the west façade, the richly sculptured marble was based on designs of Lorenzo Maitani of Siena. It is divided into three gables. Four wall surfaces around the trio of doors were adorned with sculpture in relief, also based on designs of Maitani. He worked on the cathedral façade until his death in 1330. The bas-reliefs depict scenes from the Bible, including the Last Judgment. After the death of Maitani, Andrea Pisano took over, but the actual work carried on until the dawn of the 17th century. For decades every guidebook writer has suggested that the cathedral façade is best viewed at sunset. However, there is nothing wrong with dawn's early light.

Inside, the nave and aisles were constructed in alternating panels of black and white stone. You will want to seek out the Cappella del Corporale with its mammoth silver shrine based on the design of the façade of the cathedral. Considered a masterpiece, the 1338 work, richly embellished with precious stones, was the work of Ugolino Vieri of Siena, and it was designed to shelter the Holy Corporal from Bolsena (the cloth in which the bleeding Host was wrapped). The most celebrated chapel inside is the Chapel of San Brizio, containing frescoes of the Apocalypse, the work of two great artists, Luca Signorelli and Fra Angelico, who completed the cycle between 1499 and 1504. Michelangelo was said to have been inspired by the frescoes at the time he was contemplating the Sistine Chapel. Pietro del Minella created the richly carved choir stalls.

The famous **Il Pozzo di San Patrizio** (St. Patrick's Well) is an architectural curiosity. In its day it was considered an engineering feat. The pope, Clement VII, ordered the well built, fearing that Orvieto might come under siege and its water supply be cut off. Next to the piazzale Cahen, the well was entrusted to the design of Antonio da San Gallo the Younger in 1527. It is some 200 feet deep, cut into volcanic rock (about 42 feet in diameter). Two spiral staircases, with about 250 steps, lead into the wells. These spiral ramps never meet. The well can be visited daily, May to October from 9 a.m. to 7 p.m. and November to April from 9:30 a.m. to 1 p.m. and 3 to 5 p.m. Admission is 3,000 lire ($2.30).

Next to the cathedral, the **Palazzo dei Papi** (Palace of the Popes) houses the Museo dell' Opera del Duomo. Opening onto the piazza del Duomo, the large palace was built of volcanic rock. Over the centuries it provided a refuge for 32 popes. The building dates from 1264. Many works of art from the Middle Ages are displayed in the museum, along with church vestments, sculpture, woodwork, and some utensils excavated from an Etruscan burial ground. It also has a *Madonna* by Simone Martini as well as sculptures by Maitani and Arnolfo di Cambio. Hours in summer are 9 a.m. to 12:30 p.m. and 3 to 6 p.m. daily except Monday, from 9 a.m. to 12:30 p.m. and 2:30 to 5 p.m. in winter. Admission is 3,000 lire ($2.30).

Across from the cathedral is the **Museo Archeologico Claudio Faino,** housed in a 17th-century palace. Originally a private collection, the museum contains many Etruscan artifacts found in and around Orvieto. In addition to the stone sarcophagi, terracotta portraits, and vials of colored glass left by the Etruscans, the museum also contains many fine Greek vases. Hours are 9 a.m. to 1 p.m. and 3 to 7 p.m. daily. Admission is free.

If you still have time after walking through the old quarter of Orvieto, lying to the west of the piazza della Repubblica, you may want to visit other palaces and churches in the town. Of special interest is the **Church of San Domenico,** containing a tomb of Cardinal de Braye who died in the 13th century. The tomb was by Arnolfo di Cambio.

WHERE TO STAY

Most visitors pass through Orvieto just for the day, returning to Florence, Rome, or exploring other hill towns, such as Assisi. The fortunate few who remain may want to consider one of the following accommodations.

Hotel La Badia, at La Badia, 05019 Orvieto (tel. 0763/90-359), three miles from Orvieto, has been called one of the most memorable of the Italian country-style inns. It combines history with all the modern comforts. Built on a hill that faces the rocky foundations of the old Etruscan fortress of Orvieto, the location served as a Benedictine abbey (Badia in Italian) in the 8th century A.D. It was upgraded to a monastery in the 12th century when a church was erected nearby with a tower donated by a local noblewoman. In the 19th century the buildings were renovated by an aristocratic family called Fiumi, who did what they could to preserve the irreplaceable stonework. Today a hotel, the finest in and around Orvieto, La Badia is graced with tennis courts, a swimming pool, a well-chosen collection of antiques, and a plush series of comfortable bedrooms, many with views over the surrounding countryside. The 22 units rent for 108,000 lire ($82) to 121,000 lire ($92) daily in a standard single; doubles cost 155,000 lire ($118) to 181,000 lire ($138). Even more expensive suites are also available. Most guests stay here on half-board terms, costing 185,000 lire ($141) to 198,000 lire ($151) daily in a single, 154,500 lire ($117) to 167,500 lire ($127) per person in a double. The hotel is closed in January and February.

If you don't have a car, or if you prefer to stay in Orvieto proper, the **Hotel Maitani,** via Maitani 5, 05018 Orvieto (tel. 0763/42-011), is the best choice. It's also ideal for sightseeing, as it lies right around the cathedral. Rooms, 40 in all, are quiet at night and tastefully and comfortably furnished. I've found the staff helpful and accommodating. A single rents for 80,000 lire ($60.75) daily, and a double goes for 125,000 lire ($95).

If all the above accommodations charge prices too high for your wallet, try the little **Hotel Corso,** corso Cavour 343, 05018 Orvieto (tel. 0763/42-020). A short walk from the cathedral, it is utterly simple, containing only eight rather basically furnished accommodations. However, for such a functional no-frills stopover, the price is right. A single pays from 33,000 lire ($25) daily; a double, 50,000 lire ($38).

WHERE TO DINE

A much-frequented trattoria in the town is **Cucina Monaldo,** via Angelo da Orvieto 7 (tel. 41-634). Cooking is reliable and substantial, but hardly innovative. The chef sticks unashamedly to the cuisine of Orvieto, using only time-tested recipes. That means roast loin of veal, a homemade prosciutto, pasta e fagioli (beans), or cannelloni with truffles (in season) or fresh mushrooms. You might finish with one of the local cheese selections. Full meals, costing from 30,000 lire ($22.75), are served from noon to 2:30 p.m. and 4:30 to 10 p.m. The restaurant is closed Monday and from July 15 to 30.

Dell'Ancora, via di Piazza del Popolo 7-11 (tel. 42-766). Both locals and visitors are attracted to this restaurant from whose kitchen emerge well-prepared meats and fresh vegetables. The meats are grilled, roasted, or sautéed at the customer's request and are accompanied by vegetables fresh from the Umbrian countryside. Specialties include fried lamb and tripe Roman style, veal with tuna sauce, and elegantly prepared chicken. The zuppa inglese for dessert is a good, if fattening, choice. Expect to spend around 32,000 lire ($24.25) for a full meal. The restaurant is open from 12:30 to 2:30 p.m. and 7:30 to 10 p.m. Closed on Thursday in January.

BOLOGNA AND EMILIA-ROMAGNA

Lying in the northern reaches of central Italy, the district of Emilia-Romagna is known for gastronomy and for its art cities, such as Modena and Parma. Once-great families, including the Renaissance dukes of Ferrara, rose in power and influence, creating courts that attracted painters and poets, notably Tasso and Ariosto. (For other centers in this region, refer to the Byzantine city of Ravenna and the Adriatic resort of Rimini in the following chapter.)

Bologna, the capital of Emilia, stands at the crossroads between Venice and Florence, and is linked by express highways to both Milan and Tuscany. By centering in the ancient university city of Bologna, you can branch out in all directions: north for 32 miles to Ferrara; southeast for 31 miles to the ceramics-making town of Faenza; northwest for 25 miles to Modena with its Romanesque cathedral; or 34 miles farther northwest to Parma, the legendary capital of the duchy of the Farnese family in the 16th century. Busseto, home territory of Verdi, lies in the Po Valley, 80 miles northeast of Bologna.

With the exception of Ferrara, which makes a good stopover for motorists heading south from Venice and Busseto, all our sightseeing destinations lie on the ancient Roman road, via Emilia, that began in Rimini and stretched all the way to the Roman colony of Piacenza, a temptress that often attracted invading barbarians.

This ancient land (known to the Romans as "Aemilia," and to the Etruscans before them) is rich in man-made attractions—the cathedral and baptistery of Parma, for instance—and in scenic beauty (the green plains and the slopes of the Apennines). Emilia is one of the most bountiful farming districts in Italy, and sets a table highly praised in Europe—both for its wines and for its imaginatively prepared pasta dishes.

First, we'll drop anchor in—

1. Bologna

The manager of a hotel in Bologna laments: "You Americans! You spend a week in Florence, a week in Venice. Why not six days in Florence, six days in Venice . . . and two days in Bologna?" A good question. Bologna is one of the most sadly over-looked (by tourists) cities of Italy, enough so that I've found cavernous accommodation space here in July and August, when the hotels in Venice and Florence were packed as tightly as a can of Progresso clam sauce.

"But what is there to see in Bologna?" is a question also asked. True, it boasts no Uffizi or Doges' Palace. What it does offer is a beautiful city considered by some to be the most architecturally unified in Europe—a panorama of marbled sidewalks and porticos that, if spread out, would surely stretch all the way to the border.

A city of sienna-colored buildings, perhaps a suitable shade for its left-wing politics, Bologna is the leading city of Emilia. Its rise as a commercial power was almost assured by its strategic location as the geographic center between Florence and Venice. Its university, the oldest in Europe, has for years generated a lively interest in art and culture.

Bologna is also considered to be the gastronomic capital of Italy. Gourmets flock here just to sample the food—the pasta dishes (tortellini, tagliatelle, lasagne verde), the meat and poultry specialties (zampone, veal cutlet bolognese, tender breasts of turkey in sauce suprême), and, finally, mortadella, the incomparable sausage of Bologna, as distant a cousin to baloney as porterhouse is to the hot dog.

The city seems to take a vacation in August, becoming virtually dead. Everywhere you see the sign proclaiming *Chiuso* ("closed").

The telephone area code for Bologna is 051.

GETTING THERE

Bologna, because of its strategic location, lies at the center of vast road and rail connections in Italy. Coming over the Apennines, the Autostrada del Sole A1 runs northwest to Milan just before reaching the outskirts of Bologna. The A13 super-highway cuts northeast to Ferrara and Venice and the A14 dashes east to Rimini, Ravenna, and the towns along the Adriatic. Rail connections are fast and frequent to such cities as Milan, Florence, and Venice, which you may also be visiting. For even quicker visits, Bologna also has a domestic airport, the Borgo Panigale, lying four miles north of the center and serviced by such domestic carriers as Aermediterranea and ATI.

GETTING AROUND

Walking, of course, is the only way you'll really see Bologna. Because the city is so compact and so many of its attractions are clustered near each other, strolling from sight to sight is quite possible. City buses leave for most points from either piazza Nettuno or piazza Maggiore. Free maps are available at the storefront office of the A.T.C. in the Palazzo del Podesta, right between the piazza Nettuno and the piazza Maggiore in the heart of town. Tickets can be purchased at one of many booths throughout Bologna. Once on board, however, you must have your ticket validated. Taxis are on radio call (dial either 534-141 or 376-2727).

HOTELS IN BOLOGNA

Before we sample the culinary and sightseeing wares, I'll survey the hotels, beginning with the most expensive, then descending in price.

The Deluxe Choice

Grand Hotel Baglioni, via dell'Indipendenza 8, 40121 Bologna (tel. 051/225-445), was originally built in the 19th century as the headquarters of a local bishop, the famous and very rich Cardinal Lambertini. It was transformed into a hotel in the early 1900s and thoroughly renovated in the 1980s. Reopened after a decade, it boasts a desirable location in the center of Bologna, close to the main square and Neptune's fountain. Its façade is crafted of the same reddish brick that distinguishes many of the older buildings of the city. The interior is noted for its wealth of wall and ceiling frescoes, many of which were painted by two of Bologna's most famous 19th-century artists, the Carracci brothers. Each of its 122 accommodations contains reproductions of antique furniture, air conditioning, color TV, mini-bar, and radio. The suites have hydromassage in the bathtubs. Classified as a five-star property, it charges 230,000 lire ($175) to 260,000 lire ($198) daily in a single, with doubles going for 330,000 lire ($251) to 390,000 lire ($296). Breakfast, tax, and service are included.

First-Class Hotels

Royal Hotel Carlton, via Montebello 8, 40121 Bologna (tel. 051/249-361), is L-shaped, rises six stories high, and has a triangular garden. It is in the modern style, with a balcony and picture window for each bedroom. It is only a few minutes' walk from the railway station and many of the national monuments. Inside, the decorator infused the establishment with warmth. One of the most dramatic staircases in Bologna sweeps from the second floor in an elegant crescent to a point near the comfortable American bar. The large stone-floored lobby contains leather sofas and sculpture, whose futuristic forms increase the impression that this is a stylish hotel well suited for the dozens of businesspeople who stop here on work-related visits to Bologna. The carpeted bedrooms offer such amenities as color TV, radio, frigo-bar, and air conditioning. Singles cost 230,000 lire ($175) daily, and doubles go for 310,000 lire ($236), with a continental breakfast included. The grill restaurant serves good food in an ambience of style and comfort. Motorists appreciate the easy parking in the hotel's underground garage.

Grand Hotel Elite, via Aurelio Saffi 36, 40301 Bologna (tel. 051/437-417), on the outskirts of Bologna, close to Autostrada A1, is highly recommendable. It makes a bold architectural and decorative statement, with tastefully applied primary colors contrasting with bone white. Wood paneling creates a warm ambience. The bedrooms are well designed and decorated. They contain radio, direct-dial phone, and individually controlled air conditioning and heating, and many offer bar and refrigerator areas. Singles rent for 140,000 lire ($106) daily, and doubles go for 200,000 lire ($152). Even if you're not staying at the hotel, you may want to patronize the dining room, Cordon Bleu, featuring an array of international specialties, plus classic dishes from Emilia. Also popular is an *enoteca* American bar, with comfortable tufted banquettes. Closed from late July to late August.

Internazionale, via dell'Indipendenza 60, 40121 Bologna (tel. 051/245-544), is in a typical classic palace-style building, over an arched sidewalk colonnade, with a contemporary extension. However, its interior has been given the lush Italian moderne look. Lounges are dominated by overscale plastic armchairs, autumnal colors, and contemporary paintings. The 140 bedrooms have style, each containing a tile bath. All have been given that decorator touch. Rates are 150,000 lire ($114) daily in a single, 225,000 lire ($171) in a double. A continental breakfast is included.

Jolly, piazza XX Settembre 2, 40121 Bologna (tel. 051/248-921), is one of the golden nuggets in this ubiquitous hotel chain. Nicely placed right off the piazza Medaglie d'Oro, it avoids much of the deafening noise of the heavy traffic. The first-class, fully air-conditioned, 176-room hotel offers private baths and phones in all its rooms. The bedrooms escape the usual Jolly simplicity; many have mahogany period furniture and Oriental rugs, combined with soft draperies and pastel colors. A double room rents for 250,000 lire ($190) daily, and a single goes for 165,000 lire ($125). These rates include service and taxes. The drinking lounge, in wood paneling, is a good spot for an apéritif or an after-dinner coffee.

Hotel Milano Excelsior, viale Pietramellara 51, 40121 Bologna (tel. 051/246-178), is a first-class hotel near the piazza Medaglie d'Oro. It has all the trappings and fringe benefits associated with hostelries in its classification: air conditioning, private bath with every soundproof room, an American bar, and a restaurant decorated with crystal chandeliers. Frequented largely by a commercial clientele, the Milano Excelsior has a completely modern decor, except that a number of its bedrooms have been filled with the romantic designs of the past. A couple is charged from 250,000 lire ($190) daily; singles pay from 175,000 lire ($133). The hotel offers excellent service and an unusually attentive staff. The hotel dining room, the Ristorante Felsineo, serves tasty Emilian cookery. There is a garage connected to the hotel.

A Second-Class Hotel

Alexander, viale Pietramellara 47, 40121 Bologna (tel. 051/247-118), is perhaps the best of the hotel buys near the main hub of automotive and rail traffic, the piazza Medaglie d'Oro, for the wayfarer who wants maximum comfort at moderate price. Perched near the more expensive Hotel Milano Excelsior, the Alexander tempts with its quite good bedrooms, which contain brightly painted foyers, compact furnishings, and neat, tidy baths. The thickness of the double glass in the windows helps to blot out street noises. The main lounge is crisply and warmly paneled in wood, with lounge chairs placed on Turkish rugs. All 108 bedrooms have private bath and phone, and they are air-conditioned as well as heated properly in winter. A double costs 250,000 lire ($190) daily; a single, 165,000 lire ($125). Closed in August.

Best for the Budget

Tre Vecchi, via dell'Indipendenza 47, 40121 Bologna (tel. 051/231-991), is clean and bright, with most of its sections recently renovated. It has no restaurant and serves only breakfast. In spite of the location on a much-traveled street, most of the accommodations are noiseless because of the hotel's isolation. A double costs from 95,000 lire ($72.25) daily; a single, 75,000 lire ($57). Children up to 6 years old are sheltered in their parents' room at a 20% discount. Each room has a TV, frigo-bar, and air conditioning. On the floors are several lounges where you can relax and watch television.

Regina Hotel, via dell'Indipendenza 51, 40121 Bologna (tel. 051/248-878), has been much improved. It offers attractive rooms, 61 in all, and a modern lounge dotted with black leather sofas. The personnel who run the place are helpful, and the maids keep everything clean. The hotel has no restaurant, but there is a pleasant bar. Rooms are small and comfortably furnished, and except for a handful of singles, each is equipped with a private bath or shower. Singles rent for 70,000 lire ($53.25) daily; doubles, 95,000 lire ($72.25). The location is right off the piazza dell'Agosto.

DINING IN BOLOGNA

Even though Bologna is the reigning queen of Italian cuisine, she does not charge regal prices in her restaurants. One of the city's finest gourmet citadels, Al Pappagallo, is not at all super-priced by North American standards. And, happily, Bologna—being a university town—has a number of good dining spots catering to a student clientele. I'll begin with the top restaurants, then descend in price.

Ristorante Al Pappagallo, piazza della Mercanzia 3C (tel. 232-807), draws a faithful coterie of gastronomes, some of whom consider it one of the finest restaurants in Italy. Diners have included Einstein, Hitchcock, and Toscanini. "The Parrot" is housed on the ground floor of a Gothic mansion, across the street from the landmark 14th-century Merchants' Loggia (a short walk from the leaning towers). Under a beamed ceiling and crystal chandeliers, diners from many lands are introduced to the Bolognese cuisine. For the best possible introduction, begin your meal with lasagne verde al forno (baked lasagne which gets its green color from minced spinach). And then, for the main course, the specialty of the house: filetti di tacchino, superb turkey breasts baked with white wine, parmigiano cheese, and truffles. With your meal, the restaurant serves the amber-colored Albana wine and the sparkling red Lambrusco, two of the best-known wines from the vineyards of Emilia. Meals cost daily 50,000 lire ($38) to 70,000 lire ($53.25). It is open from 12:30 to 2:30 p.m. and 8 to 10:20 p.m. except Sunday night and Monday; closed the first three weeks in August and a week in mid-January.

Ristorante Notai, via dei Pignattari 1 (tel. 228-694). Hidden behind a lattice- and ivy-covered façade next to the cathedral, within view of one of the most beautiful squares in Italy, this popular restaurant draws from a loyal clientele of local residents. Music lovers and relaxing businesspeople appreciate the upstairs piano bar, where low-slung couches and a high-tech bar alternate with posters of Italian and American show-biz types. The decor of the establishment combines belle-époque with Italian flair and includes artwork, hanging Victorian lamps, and clutches of beautifully arranged flowers on each table, all in a subdued color scheme of creams and beiges. The Notai, owned by a well-known restaurateur and wine expert, Nino Castorina, has been praised by a variety of Italian food critics for having what is said to be the best food in a town distinguished for its fine restaurants. Specialties include a salad delizia (with scampi, carpaccio, fruit, salad greens, olive oil, lemon, and seasonings), as well as tagliatelle Notai, homemade foie gras, calves' liver Grand Marnier, Florentine beefsteak, and chateaubriand with béarnaise sauce. A la carte meals range from 55,000 lire ($41.75) to 75,000 lire ($57). Open from noon to 3 p.m. and 8 p.m. to midnight; it is closed on Sunday.

Antica Osteria Romagnola, via Rialto 13 (tel. 263-699), in spite of its location in Bologna, serves many dishes inspired by recipes from the south. Unusual and well-flavored risottos might launch many a repast. Or you can make a selection of antipasti, as the kitchen puts much effort into a savory selection of dishes. The array of pastas is also impressive, including ravioli with essence of truffles, fusilli with zucchini, or pasta whipped with asparagus tips. You might also select a terrine of ricotta and arugula, the latter considered an aphrodisiac by the ancient Romans. For your main course you might try a springtime specialty of roast goat with artichokes and potatoes or filet mignon prepared with basil. Meals cost 38,000 lire ($29) to 52,000 lire ($39.50), and service is daily from 1 to 2:30 p.m. and 8 to 10:30 p.m. The restaurant closes in August.

Rostaria Antico Brunetti, via Caduti di Cefalonia 5 (tel. 234-441), is sheltered in a 12th-century tower just off the piazza Maggiore in the heart of Bologna. The restaurant reportedly is the oldest in town, dating back to 1873. Antico Brunetti has distinguished itself for its gramigna verde alla moda dello chef, green spaghetti with a sauce made with sausage. Other dishes worth trying are the lasagne, a kind of *pasta asciutta*, made with sheets of green pasta with tomato sauce and cheese inside; and mama's tortellini, those little stuffed squares of dough in a ragoût. With the tortellini, I suggest ordering a bottle of Lambrusco di Sorbara, one of the most straightforward and best-known wines of Italy. It is a brilliant ruby-red and has a natural sparkle. For a main course, I prefer the traditional cotoletta al prosciutto, veal cutlet with a slice of ham and cheese, topped with white truffles or Italian mixed fry, also with veal. The dessert specialty is chocolate cake. Expect to spend from 40,000 lire ($30.50) for a complete meal, available from noon to 2:30 p.m. and 7 to 10:30 p.m. Closed Sunday night and Monday.

Rosteria da Luciano, via Nazario Sauro 19 (tel. 231-249), is seriously challenging the competition for supremacy. It serves some of the best food in Bologna. On a side street, within walking distance of the center, it has an art deco style and contains three large rooms with a real Bolognese atmosphere. The front room, opening onto the kitchen, is preferred. As a novelty, there's a see-through window on the street, looking directly into the kitchen. The chefs not only can't keep any secrets from you, but you get an appetizing preview of what awaits you before you step inside. To begin your gargantuan repast, request the tortellini Petroniani. Two well-recommended main dishes include the fritto misto all'Italiana and the scaloppe al cartoccio. A dramatic dessert is the crêpes flambés. Meals cost 45,000 lire ($34.25) to 60,000 lire ($45.50). Hours are 12:30 to 2:30 p.m. and 7:30 to 10:30 p.m. Closed Tuesday night, Wednesday, and in August.

Al Cantunzien, piazza Verdi 4 (tel. 238-356), occupies a "small corner" on an arcaded piazza with ochre-tinted Renaissance buildings. It faces the Teatro Communale. Behind brass-fitted doors are small and intimate tables set against stucco walls and lots of wood trim. It is air-conditioned in summer. The former-Communist mayor with his family often comes here for a long-drawn-out feast (but French champagne?). The restaurant has a long tradition. Once it was a stop-over for chauffeurs. The chef is especially noted for his many varieties of pasta, including several made with spinach. My favorites are green noodles al Cantunzien (stuffed with sausages). For a main course, I recommend the cotoletta Eva farcita ("stuffed Eve's rib"), the suprema di pollo (chicken suprême flamed with cognac), followed by a dining oddity, fritto di frutta (a mixed fruit fry). A complete meal will run 35,000 lire ($26.50) to 45,000 lire ($34.25). For your wine, I suggest Sangiovese, a dark ruby-red "brut" wine whose name translates as "the blood of Jove." Closed Wednesday and in August, it's open other days from 12:30 to 2:30 p.m. and 7:30 to 10:30 p.m.

Montegrappa da Nello, via Montegrappa 2 (tel. 236-331), has a faithful list of habitués who swear by its pasta dishes. Franco Bolini is your host. He insists that all produce be fresh. His restaurant, just a short walk from the piazza Maggiore, offers tortellina Montegrappa, a pasta favorite served in a cream-and-meat sauce. The restaurant is also known for its fresh white truffles and mushrooms. You can try these in an unusual salad, including porcini, the large wild mushrooms. Another salad I prefer is made with truffles, mushrooms, parmesan cheese, and artichokes (again, fresh). For a main course, I suggest misto del cuoco—a mixed platter from the chef, featuring a selection of his specialties, including zampone, cotoletta bolognese, and scaloppina with fresh mushrooms. Expect to pay from 45,000 lire ($34.25) for a complete meal, offered from noon to 3 p.m. and 8 p.m. to midnight. Walk on through the ground-floor dining area, heading for the large kitchen and dining room below. The restaurant is closed Monday and in August.

Grassilli, via del Luzzo 3 (tel. 222-961), is a good bet for conservatively regional cooking with few deviations from time-tested formulas that have made the Bolognese cuisine famous. In an ochre building across from an antique store, on a narrow cobblestone alleyway a short block from the two leaning towers, the restaurant has a summertime streetside canopy for outdoor dining. At night it can be festive, and your good time will probably be enhanced if you order such specialties as tortellini in a mushroom cream sauce, the chef's special tournedos, maccheroni with fresh peas and prosciutto, a range of grilled and roasted meats, and many tasty desserts. Expect to pay 46,000 lire ($35) to 70,000 lire ($53.25) per person. The restaurant, open from 12:30 to 2:30 p.m. and 7:30 to 10 p.m., is closed on Wednesday and from mid-July to mid-August.

Ristorante Le Tre Frecce, strada Maggiore 19 (tel. 231-200), an attractive restaurant near the two leaning towers, is directed by the Salsini family, and it lies under an arcade of a medieval mansion whose stonework shows the slow weathering of many centuries. The remodeled interior retains its high Gothic ceilings, old portraits, and much of the stonework of the original house. A balcony has been constructed over one of the two rooms for additional seating, while a bar is set on a raised dais with a view over the crowd of contented diners. Service here is excellent, and the menu includes such time-honored favorites as tagliatelle bolognese, green gnocchi with gorgonzola, filetta di manzo, salmon with chive sauce, and veal scallopine with fresh asparagus. Full meals, served from 12:30 to 2:30 p.m. and 7:30 to 10:30 p.m., cost from 42,000 lire ($32) per person. It is closed on Sunday night, Monday, and in August.

Trattoria La Braseria, via Testoni 2 (tel. 264-584), is a pleasant, modernized little restaurant, with wood paneling and many original paintings. Only a short walk from the basilica, it is often frequented by athletes—footballers, mountain climbers, and swimmers. Typical main dishes include tortellacci al vino rosso (big green ravioli stuffed with meat and served in a red wine sauce), gnocchetti alla monsignore (potato pasta with vegetables and mushrooms), and tagliata di manzu (grilled thin-cut beef with red chicory, artichokes, and truffles, or other ingredients depending on the season). A complete meal costs from around 35,000 lire ($26.50). Food is served from 12:30 to 2:30 p.m. and 7:30 to 10:30 p.m. The trattoria is closed Sunday, from just after Christmas to January 10, and for ten days in mid-August.

Trattoria Da Pietro, via De Falegnami 18A (tel. 230-644), may win you over with its local color, a fit foil for the typical regional dishes served here, including foods from Umbria, Lazio, and Tuscany as well as Bolognese dishes. The trattoria has just a few tables on the lower level. An elaborate display of foods—fresh strawberries, oranges, sausages, apples, strings of garlic, peppers, green tomatoes, fresh asparagus, cherries—is a Lorelei lure. The upper level has several family-style tables, at which you're likely to see a gathering of artists. The English-speaking owner is also likely to say: "Forget about the menu. We'll tell you what we have." Anywhere from 35,000 lire ($26.50) should be sufficient for a substantial meal here. It is open from noon to 2:30 p.m. and 7:15 to 10:30 p.m.; closed Sunday evening and all day Monday.

A Gastronomic Retreat on the Outskirts

To an increasing degree, gastronomes from all over Europe and America are traveling to the unlikely village of Imola, lying 21 miles southeast of Bologna, to savor the cuisine of what some food critics consider the best restaurant in Italy. The restaurant can also be easily reached from Ravenna and Rimini.

San Domenico, via Gaspare Sacchi 1 (tel. 0542/29000). The cuisine here is sometimes compared to cuisine moderne creations in France. However, owner Gianluigi Morini claims that his delectable offerings are nothing more than adaptations of festive regional dishes rendered lighter and subtler, then served in more manageable portions. He was born in this rambling stone building whose simple façade faces the courtyard of a neighboring church. For 25 years Signor Morini worked at a local bank, returning home every night to administer his restaurant. Now his establishment is among the primary attractions of Emilia-Romagna.

A tuxedo-clad member of his talented young staff will escort you to a table near the tufted leather banquettes whose dark colors offset the candles, baroque silver, and hanging lamps whose fabric matches that of the tented ceilings. Meals include heavenly concoctions made with the freshest ingredients. You might select goose liver pâté studded with white truffles, fresh shrimp in a creamy sweet bell-pepper sauce, roast rack of lamb with fresh rosemary, stuffed suprême of chicken wrapped in lettuce leaves, or fresh handmade spaghetti with shellfish. Signor Morini has collected some of the best vintages in Europe for the past 30 years. Full meals cost from 100,000 lire ($76) per person and are served from 12:30 to 2:30 p.m. and 8 to 10:30 p.m. Reservations are essential. Closed Monday, for the first two weeks in January, and late July to mid-August.

THE SIGHTS

Of all the cities of Italy, Bologna is perhaps the easiest to cover on foot, as most of the major sights are in and around the **piazza Maggiore,** the heart of the city. And such a handsome center it is, dominated by—

The Church of Saint Petronius

Sadly, the façade of this enormous Gothic basilica was never completed. The church honors the patron saint of Bologna. The builders went to work in 1390, but after three centuries the church was still not completed, although Charles V was crowned emperor here in 1530. However, Jacopo della Quercia of Siena did grace the central door with Renaissance sculpture, considered a masterpiece. Inside, the church could accommodate the traffic of Grand Central Station. The central nave is separated from the aisles by pilasters, shooting upward to the flying arches of the ceiling. Of the 22 art-filled chapels, the most interesting is the Bolognini Chapel, the fourth chapel on the left as you enter. It is embellished with frescoes representing heaven and hell (the cannibalistic scenes from hell, the sadism and torture, attract the most attention). The purity and simplicity of line represent some of the best of the Gothic in Italy. Open daily from 7:30 a.m. to 7 p.m.

As you come out of the basilica, head left to the second attractive square of Bologna, the **piazza del Nettuno,** adjoining the piazza Maggiore. In the center of this satellite square is—

The Fountain of Neptune

Characteristic of the pride and independence of Bologna, this fountain has gradually become the symbol of the city, but it was in fact designed by a Frenchman named Giambologna by the Italians (his fame rests largely on the work he did in Florence). Considered irreverent by some, vulgar to other tastes, magnificent by more liberal appraisers, the 16th-century fountain depicts Neptune with rippling muscles, with a trident in one arm and a heavy foot on the head of a dolphin. Around his feet are four cherubs, also with dolphins. At the base of the fountain nestle four sirens, each spouting five different streams of water from her breasts.

After checking out the sirens, head across the street for—

The Palazzo Comunale

Built in the 14th century, the **town hall** has seen major restorations, but happily retains its splendor. Enter through the courtyard, then proceed up the steps on the right to the **Communal Collection of Fine Arts** (free; open Monday and Wednesday through Saturday from 9 a.m. to 2 p.m., on Sunday from 9 a.m. to 12:30 p.m.; closed Tuesday and midweek holidays). The collection includes many paintings from the 18th- and 19th-century Emilian school.

The Basilica of St. Domenico

At piazza St. Domenico 13, the basilica (tel. 239-310) dates from the 13th century, but has seen many alterations and restorations. The church houses the tomb of St. Domenico, in front of the Cappella della Madonna. The sculptured tomb—known as an arca—is a masterpiece of the Renaissance, a joint enterprise of Niccolò Pisano, Guglielmo (friar), Niccolò dell'Arca, Alfonso Lombardi, and the young Michelangelo. The choir stalls, the second major artistic work in the basilica, were carved by Damiano da Bergamo, another friar, in the 16th century.

The Leaning Towers

At the piazza di Porta Ravegnanna (one of the most interesting of the old squares of Bologna), the towers keep defying gravity year after year. The Due Torri were built by patricians in the 12th century. In the Middle Ages, Bologna had dozens of these skyscraper towers, anticipating Manhattan. They were status symbols: the more powerful the family, the taller the tower. The smaller one, the Garisenda, is only 162 feet high, leaning approximately 10½ feet from true perpendicular. The taller one, the Asinelli (334 feet high, a walk up nearly 500 steps), inclines almost 7½ feet. Those who scale the Asinelli (2,000 lire, or $1.50, admission) should be awarded a medal, but instead they're presented with a panoramic view of the tile roofs of Bologna and the hills beyond. Hours are 9 a.m. to 6 p.m. daily.

Afterward, take a walk up what must be the most elegant (from the architectural point of view) street in Bologna, the **strada Maggiore,** with its colonnades and mansions.

The Church of St. Stephen

From the leaning towers, head up via Santo Stefano to see a virtual community of churches, linked together like Siamese twins. The first church you enter is the Church of the Crucifix, relatively simple with only one nave plus a crypt. It was built in the 11th century. To the left is the entrance to the Church of Santo Sepolcro, its present structure dating principally from the 12th century. Under the altar is the tomb of patron saint Petronius. Continuing left, we enter another rebuilt church, this one honoring saints Vitale and Agricola. The present building, graced with three apses, also dates from the 11th century. Reentering Sepolcro, we take the back entrance this time into the Courtyard of Pilate, onto which several more chapels open. Through the courtyard entrance to the right, proceed into the Romanesque cloisters, dating from the 11th and 12th centuries. The names on the wall of the lapidary honor Bolognese war dead. The ecclesiastical complex is open daily from 9 a.m. to noon and 3 to 6 p.m. (admission is free).

The Church of San Giacomo Maggiore

At via Zamboni 15, on the piazza Possini, the Church of St. James (tel. 225-970) originally was a Gothic structure in the 13th century; but like so many others, it has been altered and restored at the expense of its original design. Still, it is one of Bologna's most interesting churches, filled with art treasures. The Bentivoglio Chapel is the most sacred haunt, even though time has dimmed the luster of its frescoes. Near the altar, seek out a Madonna and Child enthroned, one of the most outstanding works of the artist Francesco Francia. The holy pair are surrounded by angels and saints, as well as a half-naked Sebastian to the right. Nearby is a sepulchre of Antonio Bentivoglio, designed by the Sienese Jacopo della Quercia, who labored so long over the doors to the Basilica of San Petronio. In the Chapel of Santa Cecilia, you'll discover important frescoes by Francia and Lorenzo Costa.

The Civic Archeological Museum

At Dell'Archiginnasio 2 (on the street that runs to the left when facing the Basilica of San Petronio), housed in this museum (tel. 233-849) is one of the major Egyptian collections in Italy, as well as important Etruscan discoveries found in Emilia. As you enter, look to the right in the atrium to see a decapitated marble torso, said to be that of Nero. Upstairs are cases of the relics, tools, and artifacts of prehistoric man. But interest is greater in the Egyptian collection—notably an array of mummies and sarcophagi. The chief attraction among this collection is the cycle of bas-reliefs from Horemheb's tomb. The museum's greatest single treasure is Phidias's head of *Athena Lemnia,* a copy of a Greek work, dating from the 5th century B.C. As you go from room to room, search out the miniature Byzantine casket, carved from ivory. The relics of the Etruscans comprise the best part of the museum. Look for a highly stylized *Askos Benacci,* depicting a man on a horse that is perched on yet another animal. Also displayed are an intriguing terracotta urn and a vase depicting fighting Greeks and Amazons. A bronze Certosa jar dates from the 6th century B.C. The museum is open Tuesday through Saturday from 9 a.m. to 2 p.m. and on Sunday from 9 a.m. to 12:30 p.m.; closed Monday. Admission is 2,500 lire ($1.90).

The National Picture Gallery (Pinacoteca Nazionale)

At via Belle Arti 56 (tel. 243-222), the most significant works of the school of painting that flourished in Bologna from the 14th century to the heyday of the baroque have been assembled under one roof in this second-floor *pinacoteca.* In addition, the gallery houses works by other major Italian artists, such as Raphael's *St. Cecilia in Estasi.* Guido Reni (1575–1642) of Bologna steals the scene with his *St.*

Sebastian and his *Pietá*, along with his equally penetrating *St. Andrea Corsini, The Slaying of the Innocents,* his idealized *Samson the Victorious, The Flagellation of Christ,* the *Crucifixion,* and his masterpiece—*Ritratto della Madre*—a revealing portrait of his mother that must surely have inspired Whistler. Then, don't miss Vitale de Bologna's (1330–1361) rendition of St. George slaying the dragon—a theme in European art that parallels Moby Dick in America. Also displayed are works by Francesco Francia, and especially noteworthy is a polyptych attributed to Giotto. The gallery is open Tuesday through Saturday from 9 a.m. to 2 p.m. and on Sunday from 9 a.m. to 1 p.m.; closed Monday and holidays. Admission is 3,000 lire ($2.30).

Municipal Medieval Museum

Stop in at the 15th-century Palazzo Ghisilardi Fava to see a collection of Gothic sculptures, medieval ivories, glass, and weapons of the Middle Ages, as well as many other artifacts from that era. The museum, called **Museo Civico Medievale,** at via Manzoni 4 (tel. 228-912), is open Monday through Saturday from 9 a.m. to 2 p.m. and on Sunday from 9 a.m. to 12:30 p.m.; closed Tuesday and on mid-week holidays. Admission is 2,500 lire ($1.90).

---

2. Ferrara

When Papa Borgia, otherwise known as Pope Alexander VI, was shopping around for a third husband for the apple of his eye, darling Lucrezia, his gaze fell on the influential house of Este. From the 13th century this great Italian family had dominated Ferrara, building up a powerful duchy and a reputation as builders of palaces and patrons of the arts. Alfonso d'Este, son of the shrewd but villainous Ercole I, who was the ruling duke of Ferrara, was an attractive, virile candidate for Lucrezia's much-used hand (her second husband had already been murdered, perhaps by her brother, Cesare, who was the apple of nobody's eye—with the possible exception of Machiavelli).

Although the Este family may have had private reservations (after all, it was common gossip that the pope "knew" his daughter in the biblical sense), they finally consented to the marriage. As the duchess of Ferrara, a position she held until her death, Lucrezia was to have seven children (all by Alfonso, I trust). But one of her grandchildren, Alfonso II, wasn't as prolific as his forebear, although he had a reputation as a roué. He left the family without a male heir. The greedy eye of Pope Clement VIII took quick action on this, gobbling up the city as his fief in the waning months of the 16th century. The great house of Este went down in history, and Ferrara sadly declined under the papacy.

Incidentally, Alfonso II was a dubious patron of Torquato Tasso (1544–1595), author of the epic *Jerusalem Delivered,* a work that was to make him the most celebrated poet of the late Renaissance. The legend of Tasso—who is thought to have been either insane, paranoid, or at least tormented—has steadily grown over the centuries. Not that it needed any more boosting, but Goethe fanned that legend through the Teutonic lands with his late-18th-century drama *Torquato Tasso.* It is said that Alfonso II at one time made Tasso his prisoner.

About 30 miles from Bologna, Ferrara today is still relatively undiscovered, especially by the globe-trotting North American. The city is richly blessed with much of its legacy intact, including a great cathedral and the Este Castle, along with enough ducal palaces to make for a hysterically frantic day of sightseeing. Its palaces, for the most part, have long been robbed of their lavish furnishings, but the faded frescoes, the paintings not carted off, the palatial rooms, are ghostly reminders of the vicissitudes of power.

The telephone area code for Ferrara is 0532.

THE SIGHTS

We'll begin our tour in the center of the city at the landmark—

Este Castle

A moated, four-towered castle (lit at night), this proud fortress began as a brick-layer's dream near the end of the 14th century, although its face has been lifted and wrenched around for centuries. It was home to the powerful Este family. Here the dukes went about their daily chores: murdering their wives' lovers, beheading or im-prisoning potential enemies. Today used for the provincial administration offices and prefecture, many of its once-lavish rooms may be inspected—notably the Salon of Games, the Room of Games, and the Room of Dawn, as well as a chapel that once belonged to Renata di Francia, daughter of Louis XII. The castle is open from 9 a.m. to 12:30 p.m. and 2:30 to 5 p.m. daily except Monday. No admission is charged.

The Duomo

A short stroll from the castle, the duomo weds a delicate Gothic with a more virile Romanesque. The offspring: an exciting marble façade. Behind the cathedral is a typically Renaissance campanile (bell tower). Inside, the massive structure is hea-vily baroqued, as the artisans of still another era festooned it with trompe l'oeil. The entrance to the **Duomo Museum** (tel. 32-969) lies to the left of the atrium as you enter. It's worth a visit just to see works by Ferrara's most outstanding painter, Cosmè Tura, of the 15th century. Aesthetically controversial, the big attraction here is Tura's St. George slaying the dragon to save a red-stockinged damsel in distress. Opposite is a work by Jacopo della Quercia depicting a sweet, regal Madonna with a pomegranate in one hand and the Child in the other. This is one of della Quercia's first masterpieces. Also from the Renaissance heyday of Ferrara are some bas-reliefs, notably a "Giano bifronte," a mythological figure looking at the past and the future, along with some 16th-century *arazzi*, or tapestries, woven by hand. The museum is open June to September daily from 10 a.m. to noon and 4 to 6 p.m. From October to March, it is open daily from 10 a.m. to noon and 3 to 5 p.m. There is no admis-sion charge, but a contribution is appreciated.

The Schifanoia Palace

Housing the **Museo Civico d'Arte Antica** at via Scandiana 23 (tel. 62-038), the first part of Schifanoia Palace was built in 1385 for Alberto V d'Este, but the most significant portion was the one ordered by Borso d'Este (1450–1471). The work began in 1465, and the wall section was completed in 1467. The main body of the building, constructed in 1391, was later raised by one floor and was finished off with painted merlons. In 1470 work started on the big marbled portal.

The museum was founded in 1758 at the Paradiso Palace, the head office of the Ariostea Public Library and of the Civil University, which contributed to the meth-ods and activities of the museum. The first part of the collection then exhibited, which consisted of coins and medals, was enhanced by donations of archeological finds, antique bronzes, small Renaissance plates, and painted objects. In 1897 the museum was transferred to its present site. Art lovers are lured to its Salon of the Months to see the cycle made up of subject matter chosen by Cosmè Tura, the offi-cial court painter for the Estes. Tura was founder of the Ferrarese School, one of whose followers, Francesco del Cossa, was the outstanding artist of the Schifanoia cycle, painting the March, April, and May scenes. The cycle depicts life of the time in the city, but the frescoes form a complex presentation, leading to varying interpretations as to the meaning. The museum is open from 9 a.m. to 7 p.m. daily except on major public and religious holidays. Admission is 2,500 lire ($1.90).

The Este Tomb

At the Monastery of Corpus Domini, via Pergolato 4 (tel. 34-820), run by veiled sisters, Lucrezia Borgia, the most famous woman of the Renaissance, lies buried, her secrets with her. The much-married duchess gave up her wicked ways in Rome when she became the wife of Alfonso I (except for, perhaps, a discreet love affair with the handsome, romantic Venetian poet Bembo). The woman whose very name (perhaps erroneously) has become synonymous with evil lies under a flat slab, a simple tomb. Frankly, it's not much of a sight, but it would be heretical to come all this way and not pay your respects to the seductive enchantress who in crimson velvet died on a warm Emilian morning on June 24, 1519, having only days before given birth to a daughter. Visiting hours are 9:30 a.m. to noon and 4 to 5:30 p.m. daily. There is no charge for admission, but the visitor should always offer some money because of the service the order the Poor Clares offers.

The Palace of Ludovic the Moor

This ducal Renaissance palace, at via XX Settembre 124 (tel. 66-299), makes a handsome background for the priceless collection of Etruscan works discovered in the necropolis at Spina (in the environs of Comechio). The **National Archeological Museum** (Museo Archeologico Nazionale di Spina), in the building, houses the booty unearthed from the Etruscan tomb. Downstairs is a salon with admirable frescoes by Garofalo. In another room are two hand-hewn trees (pirogues) that date from late Roman years. Afterward, you may want to stroll through the gardens behind the palace. The museum is open from 9 a.m. to 2 p.m. daily except Monday. Admission is free.

The Diamond Palace

Another sparkler to d'Este splendor, the Palazzo dei Diamanti, corso Ercole d'Este 21 (tel. 21-831), is so named because of the diamond-shaped stones on its façade. Of the handful of museums sheltered here, the **National Picture Gallery** (Pinacoteca Nazionale) is the most important, holding the works of the Ferraresi artists—notably the trio of old masters, Tura, del Cossa, and Roberti. The collection covers the chief period of artistic expression in Ferrara from the 14th to the 18th century. The gallery charges 3,000 lire ($2.30) for admission and is open from 9 a.m. to 2 p.m. daily except Monday (on Sunday from 9 a.m. to 1 p.m.).

The Romei House

At via Savonarola 30, this 15th-century palace, **Casa Romei** (tel. 37-437), was the property of a rich man, John Romei, a friend and confidant of the fleshy Duke Borso d'Este, who made the Este empire a duchy. John (or Giovanni) was later to marry one of the Este princesses, although we don't know if it was for love or for power or both. In later years, Lucrezia and her gossipy coterie—the ducal carriage drawn by handsome white horses—used to descend upon the Romei house, perhaps to receive Borgia messengers from Rome. The house is near the Este tomb. Its once-elegant furnishings have been carted off, but the chambers—many with terracotta fireplaces—remain, and the "casa" has been filled with frescoes and sculpture. Noted especially for its graceful courtyards, the Romei House may be visited from 8:30 a.m. to 1:30 p.m. daily. Admission is 2,500 lire ($1.90).

La Palazzina Marfisa d'Este

This palace, at corso Giovecca 170 (tel. 36-923), was part of a larger complex of buildings erected for Francesco of Este, and given to his natural daughter, Marfisa, married in 1578 to Alfonsino of Este and in 1580 to the Marquis Alerano Cybo of Carrara. Legends surrounding this woman, reputedly of exceptional beauty (according to Tasso), have attributed to her a sentimental restlessness, with her house being a place with traps and secrets, inhabited by ghosts. In fact, this was a luxurious residence, somewhat isolated today because of the destruction of the Este complex. The pictorial decorations and floral motifs, together with the hunting scenes in two adjoining rooms, are attributed to Ferrarese painters of the late 16th century. Also in the house are exquisite furniture, a bust of Ercole I by Sperandio of Mantua, a female bust by Antonio Lombardo (1458–1516), and other paintings. Charging 2,000 lire ($1.50) admission, the "small palace" is open daily from 9 a.m. to 12:30 p.m. In summer, afternoon hours are 3 to 6 p.m., 2 to 5 p.m. in winter.

WHERE TO STAY

Near the main post office, **Astra Hotel,** viale Cavour 55, 44100 Ferrara (tel. 0532/26-234), is one of the most prominent and best-recommended hotels in town. Behind a dignified travertine-and-brick façade, the hotel has a sunny lobby and a conservatively modern interior dotted with comfortable furniture. Singles with complete bath cost 100,000 lire ($76) daily; doubles, also with bath, 160,000 lire ($122). All the well-furnished rooms are air-conditioned and soundproof, and contain mini-bar and phone.

Ripagrande Hotel, via Ripagrande 23, 44100 Ferrara (tel. 0532/34-733), is one of the most unusual hotels in town, occupying one of the city's Renaissance palaces. Rich coffered ceilings, walls in Ferrarese brickwork, 16th-century columns, and a wide stairway with a floral cast-iron handrail characterize the broad entrance hall. On the inside are two Renaissance courtyards decorated with columns and capitals. The hotel has 40 rooms, about half of which are junior suites equipped with a cooking corner and living and sleeping areas connected to an internal stairway. The furnishings are modern and in good taste, with phones, TVs, and mini-bars. A double room costs 190,000 lire ($144) daily, and a suite for two rents for 210,000 lire ($160) to 250,000 lire ($190). Tariffs include a buffet breakfast. The hotel has an elevator, garage, and parking.

Hotel Europa, corso della Giovecca 49, 44100 Ferrera (tel. 0532/21-438), is housed in a 17th-century palace that is said to have been visited by Napoleon, Casanova (hopefully, he was not alone), and Verdi. It is furnished in part with antiques in the Venetian style and has some old murals. Rooms are comfortably furnished, and most contain a private bath or shower, costing from 50,000 lire ($38) daily in a single, from 80,000 lire ($60.75) in a double. The hotel, which has a solarium, shuts down the first three weeks in August.

Hotel Carlton, via Garibaldi 93, 44100 Ferrara (tel. 0532/33-141), is housed in a six-story building set directly on the piazza Sacrati. Its stone- and wood-trimmed lobby has a winding stairwell and a terracotta bas-relief of St. George killing that dragon. The 73 comfortably modern bedrooms with baths rent for 38,000 lire ($29) daily in singles, 70,000 lire ($53.25) in doubles.

WHERE TO DINE

Behind a classic brick façade on a busy square, **Grotta Azzurra,** piazza Sacrati 43 (tel. 37-320), sounds like a restaurant you might encounter on the sunny isle of Capri, not in Ferrara. However, the cuisine is firmly entrenched in the northern Italian kitchen. It is best to visit in the autumn when favorite dishes include wild boar and pheasant. Usually these dishes are served with the characteristic polenta. Many sausages, served as antipasti, are made with game as well. The chef also prepares esoteric dishes such as a boiled calves' head and tongue. A favorite is stuffed pork leg, which is also boiled. He's also an expert at grilled meats, especially pork, veal, and beef. If you're rushed, a number of dishes are indicated that can be prepared in just 15 minutes. You might begin with a tasty helping of creamy lasagne. The restaurant, charging 25,000 lire ($19) to 38,000 lire ($29) for a complete meal, is open from 12:30 to 2:30 p.m. and 7:30 to 9:30 p.m. It is closed Wednesday and the first two weeks in July.

Its major rival, **Buca San Domenico,** piazza Sacrati 22 (tel. 37-006), lies right across the same square. This is the restaurant that should have the Neapolitan name since it specializes in pizza, at least 25 different kinds. You can also select a full meal here for around 32,000 lire ($26.50), enjoying it against a backdrop of a tavern decor. The soups are good, especially the mushroom and asparagus (with fresh ingredients). There is also a wide selection of pasta dishes to begin with, followed by such classic dishes as sole meunière. If you're fond of kidneys, the chef knows how to prepare them in interesting variations. He also serves two types of carpaccio. The buca, open from 12:30 to 2:30 p.m. and 7:30 to 10 p.m., is closed Monday and in July.

La Provvidenza, corso Ercole 1° d'Este 92 (tel. 21-937), stands on the same street as the Palazzo dei Diamanti, a sightseeing attraction already mentioned. It has a farm-style interior, with a little garden where its habitués request tables in fair weather. The antipasti table spread before you is the finest I have seen—or sampled—in Ferrara. It includes everything from fresh anchovies, mozzarella with sweet yellow peppers, fresh asparagus in spring, and several kinds of shellfish. Really hearty eaters order a pasta, such as fettuccine with smoked salmon, before tackling the main course, perhaps perfectly grilled and seasoned veal chops. The dessert choice is wide and luscious. Take a large appetite to this local favorite and count on spending around 30,000 lire ($22.75) and up for a meal here, available from noon to 2:30 p.m. and 8 to 10 p.m. It is closed Monday and for part of August. Always call for a reservation.

Riparestaurant, via Ripagrande 21 (tel. 34-942), is a room of the previously recommended Ripagrande Hotel, set aside as a restaurant seating 150 people, double that when good weather makes it possible to dine in the Renaissance courtyard. In pleasant surroundings diners can taste the Ferrarese cuisine as well as regional and national dishes. Tradition reigns here with the classic Ferrarese bread, the salama da sugo, cappellacci di zucca, and pasiccio di maccheroni. For dessert, I recommend pampepato. Each dish is accompanied by excellent wines. A complete meal costs from 35,000 lire ($26.50) up. The restaurant is open from 12:30 to 2:30 p.m. and 7:30 to 10 p.m. daily except Monday; also closed from July 25 to August 25.

Ristorante Italia "da Giovanni," largo Castello 32 (tel. 35-775), faces the castle moat—a view to enjoy. It isn't the scenic site nor the 1900s decor, however, that makes the Italia a good eating spot in the city, but its *tipico* Ferrarese cuisine. Inside, the air-conditioned restaurant is equipped to prepare and serve fine food. A black-jacketed maître d' seats you, and the service is superb. For the best of the specialties, try macaroni alla Giovanni and grilled fish. Assorted boiled meats will be brought to your table and carved in front of you. Many dishes are served with truffles. For dessert, try a large helping of Italia's homemade ice cream. Depending on the specialties you select, the final tab is likely to range from 40,000 lire ($30.50) to 60,000 lire ($45.50). Hours are 12:30 to 2:30 p.m. and 7:30 to 10 p.m. daily except Tuesday and in August.

3. Faenza

Positioned halfway between Bologna and Rimini on the Adriatic, Faenza lent its name to a form of ceramics (majolica) known as "faïence." The town flourished in ceramics, an art form that reached its height in Faenza in the 16th century, thereafter declining. That legacy is preserved in the museum described below.

The telephone area code for Faenza is 0546.

INTERNATIONAL MUSEUM OF CERAMICS

On viale Baccarini, this museum is probably the world's greatest china shop. Originally founded in 1908, it rose again following a 1944 bombing. The "international" in its title is deserving and accurate. Housed here are works that range the world over, including pre-Columbian pottery from Peru. Of exceptional interest are the Etruscan and Egyptian ceramics, as well as a wide-ranging collection from the Orient, and even from the days of the Roman Empire.

But deserving most attention is the modern ceramic art. So impressed were they by Faenza's reputation that many of the greatest contemporary artists have contributed their statement in ceramics. You'll find Picasso vases and a platter with his dove of peace, a platter in rich colors by Chagall, a surprise from Matisse, and a framed ceramic plaque of the crucifixion by Georges Rouault. Another excellent work, the inspiration of a lesser-known artist, is a ceramic woman by Dante Morozzi. The museum is open from 9:30 a.m. to 1 p.m. and 3:30 to 6:30 p.m. (afternoon hours are 2:30 to 5:30 off-season). On Sunday, it closes at 1 p.m., and it shuts down all day Monday. Admission is 4,000 lire ($3.05).

WHERE TO DINE

To create the restaurant **Amici Miei,** corso Mazzini 54 (Galleria Gessi) (tel. 661-600), the owner rented the basement of the Gessi Palace and transformed it into the kind of place where everybody from artists to politicians feels free to congregate within view of the old-fashioned costumes and antiquities you'd expect to find in a museum. If you want to try a glass of each of the local vintages, there is a wine bar on the premises. Guests who remain to dine find an imaginative menu whose offerings change with the season. Specialties include warm prosciutto in a fruit sauce, a fondue of truffled cheese, green tortelloni with fresh asparagus, pickled filet of beef with basil and an essence of mace, and roast of veal with rhubarb and radicchio. That might be followed by such delightful desserts as pears with a cheese mousse. Full meals cost from 45,000 lire ($34.25) per person, and are served daily except Monday and in August from 12:30 to 2:30 p.m. and 7:30 to 9:30 p.m. Reservations are suggested.

---

4. Modena

After Ferrara fell to Pope Clement VIII, the duchy of the Este family was established at Modena (25 miles northwest of Bologna) in the closing years of the 16th century. Lying in the Po Valley, the provincial and commercial city possesses a great many art treasures that evoke that more glorious past. And, too, the chefs of Modena enjoy an outstanding reputation in hard-to-please gastronomic circles. Traversed by the ancient Roman road via Emilia, Modena (pronounced *Mo*-dena) is often visited by European art connoisseurs, less frequently by overseas travelers.

Many visitors who care little about antiquities come to Modena just to visit the plants that make the sports cars of Ferrari and Maserati. Those who can veer from northern Italy's mainline attractions for two or three hours will be richly rewarded.

Modena's telephone area code is 059.

THE SIGHTS

The action begins at the **piazza del Duomo,** with its—

The Duomo

One of the glories of the Romanesque in northern Italy, the Duomo of Modena was built in a style familiar to those who've been to Lombardy. It was founded in the summer of the closing year of the 11th century, and designed by an architect named Lanfranco, although Viligelmo was the decorator (given to sometimes bizarre tastes).

The work was carried out by Campionesi masons from Lake Lugano. The cathedral, consecrated in 1184, was dedicated to St. Geminiano, the patron saint of Modena, a 4th-century Christian and defender of the faith. Towering from the rear is the "Ghirlandina" (so named because of a bronze garland), a 12th- to 14th-century campanile, 285 feet high. Leaning slightly, the bell tower guards the replica of the *Secchia repita* (stolen bucket), garnered as booty from a defeated Bolognese.

The façade of the duomo features a 13th-century rose window by Anselmo da Campione, Viligelmo's main entryway, its pillars supported by lions, as well as Viligelmo bas-reliefs depicting scenes from Genesis. But don't confine your look to the front. The south door, the so-called Princes' Door, was designed by Viligelmo in the 12th century, and is framed by bas-reliefs that illustrate scenes in the saga of the patron saint. You'll find an outside pulpit from the 15th century, with emblems of Matthew, Mark, Luke, and John.

Inside, the overall effect is gravely impressive, with a vaulted ceiling—all wisely and prudently restored by the Modenese during the first part of the 20th century, so that its present look resembles the original design. The gallery above the crypt is an outstanding piece of sculpture, supported by four lions. The pulpit, also intriguing, is held up by two hunchbacks. The crypt, where the body of the patron saint was finally taken, is a forest of columns. In it, you'll find Guido Mazzoni's *Holy Family* group in terracotta, which was completed in 1480.

After visiting the crypt, head up the stairs on the left, where the custodian (tip expected) will lead you to the **Museum of the Cathedral**. In many ways the most intriguing of the duomo's art, the "metopes" displayed here used to adorn the architecture. Like gargoyles, these profane bas-reliefs are a marvelous change of pace from solemn ecclesiastical art. One, for example, is part bird, part man—with one hoof. But that's not all: he's eating a fish whole. The cathedral is open daily from 10 a.m. to noon and 3:30 to 6 p.m. Admission is free.

Estense Gallery and Library

These two attractions are sheltered in the 18th-century **Palazzo del Musei** at largo Sant' Agostino 48.

The Estense Gallery (tel. 235-004) is noted for its paintings from the Emilian or Bolognese schools from the 14th to the 18th century. The nucleus of it was created by the Este family, in Ferrara's and afterward Modena's heyday as duchies. Some of the finest work is by Spanish artists, including a miniature triptych by El Greco of Toledo and a portrait of Francesco I d'Este by Velázquez. Other works of art include Bernini's bust of Francesco I, plus paintings by Cosmè Tura, Correggio, Veronese, Tintoretto, Carracci, Reni, and Guercino. The gallery is open from 9 a.m. to 2 p.m. on Tuesday, Wednesday and Friday; from 9 a.m. to 7 p.m. on Thursday and Saturday; and from 9 a.m. to 1 p.m. on Sunday. Closed Monday. Admission is 2,000 lire ($1.50).

Considered one of the greatest libraries in southern Europe, the Estense Library contains around 500,000 printed works and 13,000 manuscripts. An assortment of the more interesting volumes are kept under glass for tourists to inspect (ask the attendant to unlock the door). Of these, the most celebrated is the 1,200-page Bible of Borso d'Este, bordered with stunning miniatures.

WHERE TO STAY

In the old part of town, the **Canalgrande Hotel,** corso Canalgrande 6, 41100 Modena (tel. 059/217-160), is housed in a pink stucco palace. It has elaborate mosaic floors, voluptuous Victorian-era furniture, intricately carved and frescoed ceilings, and gilded chandeliers. There's a beautiful garden behind the hotel whose central flowering tree seems filled with every kind of bird in Modena. Some visitors might find the monumental oil paintings of the salons too much like a museum. A tavern lies below the hotel, under the basement's vaulted ceiling. Singles rent for 118,000 lire ($89.75) daily; doubles, 169,000 lire ($128).

Hotel Roma, via Farini 44, 41100 Modena (tel. 059/222-218), is a buff-and-white neoclassical building about two blocks from the cathedral. It's one of my favorite hotels in its category in Modena, and is preferred above many others by opera stars who gravitate to Pavarotti's hometown for concerts and auditions. The windows and doors are soundproof, presumably so anyone can imitate his or her favorite diva while practicing an aria.

The bedrooms are all freshly papered, with high ceilings, tasteful colors, and comfortable and attractive bedrooms. The building dates from the 17th century, when it belonged to the duke of Este. The lobby is a long skylit room with an arched ceiling and a bar and a snackbar at the far end. Singles cost 56,000 lire ($42.50) daily; doubles, 79,000 lire ($60).

DINING IN MODENA

As a city noted for gastronomy, Modena offers a number of good restaurants at varying price levels. But for a memorable experience, head for—

Fini, rua Frati Minori 54 (tel. 223-314). This restaurant alone is well worth making the trip to Modena. Proudly maintaining the high reputation of the city's kitchen, Fini (owned by the Hotel Real-Fini, but in a different part of the city) is one of the best restaurants you're likely to encounter in Emilia-Romagna. In spite of its modern decor, the restaurant was founded in 1912. This is a favorite restaurant of Pavarotti when he visits Modena.

For an appetizer, try the green lasagne or the tortellini (prepared in six different ways here—for example, with truffles). For a main dish, the gran bollito misto reigns supreme. A king's feast of boiled meats, accompanied by a selection of four different sauces, is wheeled to your table. Included on this board of meats is zampone, the specialty of Modena. As prepared at Fini's it is stuffed pigs' trotters boiled with beef, a calves' head, ox tongue, chicken, and ham. After all this rich fare, you may settle for the fruit salad. From a wide range of specialties, you should be able to select a three-course meal with wine at a price ranging from 45,000 lire ($34.25) to 65,000 lire ($49.50). The restaurant is open from 12:30 to 2:30 p.m. and 7:30 to 10 p.m. Wednesday through Sunday; closed Monday, Tuesday, and late July to late August. For wines, Lambrusco is the local choice, and it's superb. The Fini is splashed with Picasso-esque murals and equipped with banquettes.

Ristorante Da Enzo, via Coltellini 17 (tel. 225-177), off the piazza Giuseppe Mazzini (car parking), is kinder to wallets while still alluring to the palate. Four specialties are noteworthy—lasagne verde, tortellini, boiled meats, and zampone. If you order à la carte, expect to spend 25,000 lire ($19) to 35,000 lire ($26.50). The menu is in English. The restaurant upstairs is closed Saturday, but hours otherwise are 12:30 to 2:30 p.m. and 7:30 to 10 p.m.

---

5. Parma

Straddling via Emilia, Parma was the home of Correggio, Il Parmigianino, Bodoni (of type fame), Toscanini, and parmesan cheese. It rose in influence and power in the 16th century as the seat of the Farnese duchy, then in the 18th century under Bourbon rule. For years Parma has been a favorite of art lovers.

It is also a mecca for opera lovers, as Verdi, the great Italian composer, whose works included *Il Trovatore* and *Aïda,* was born in the small village of Roncole, to the north of Parma, in 1813. In time his operas would echo through the opera house, the Teatro Regio, that was ordered constructed by Marie Louise. Because of Verdi, Parma became a center of music, and even today the opera house is jam-packed in season. It is said that the Teatro Regio is the most "critical Verdi house" in Italy.

The telephone area code for Parma is 0521.

THE SIGHTS

Let's begin our tour of Parma at the piazza del Duomo in—

The Duomo

Built in the Romanesque style in the 11th century, with Lombard lions from the 13th century guarding its main porch, the dusty-pink duomo stands side by side with a campanile (bell tower)—in the Gothic-Romanesque style—completed in 1294. The façade of the cathedral is highlighted by three open-air loggias. Inside, two darkly elegant aisles flank the central nave. The octagonally shaped cupola was frescoed by the "divine" Correggio. Master of light and color, Correggio (1494–1534) was one of Italy's greatest painters of the High Renaissance. His fresco here, *Assumption of the Virgin,* foreshadows the baroque. The frescoes were painted from 1522 to 1534. In the transept to the right of the main altar is a Romanesque bas-relief, the *Deposition from the Cross,* by Benedetto Antelami—somber, each face bathed in tragedy. Made in 1178, the bas-relief is the best-known work of the 12th-century artist, who is considered the most important sculptor of the Romanesque in northern Italy. The cathedral is open all year, daily from 7:30 a.m. to noon and 3 to 7 p.m. For Antelami's real achievement, however, head across the square to the—

Baptistery

Listed among the greatest Romanesque buildings in northern Italy, the baptistery was the work of Antelami, begun in 1196, although the date of its actual completion is in doubt. Made of salmon-colored marble, it is spanned by four open tiers (the fifth one closed off). Inside, the baptistery is richly frescoed with biblical scenes: a *Madonna Enthroned* and a *Crucifixion.* But it is the sculpture by Antelami that forms the most worthy treasure and provides the basis for that artist's claim to enduring fame, especially his portrayal of the "months of the year." The baptistery is open from 9 a.m. to noon and 3 to 6 p.m. daily April to June; from 9 a.m. to 12:30 p.m. and 3:30 to 7 p.m. daily in July and August. Off-season hours are 9 a.m. to noon and 3 to 5 p.m.; closed Monday. Admission is 3,000 lire ($2.30).

Abbey of St. John (San Giovanni Evangelista)

In back of the duomo at the piazzale San Giovanni is a church (tel. 39-067) of unusual interest. After admiring the baroque front, pass into the interior to see yet another cupola by Correggio. Working from 1520 to 1524, the High Renaissance master depicted the *Vision of San Giovanni.* Vasair liked it so much he became completely carried away in his praise, suggesting the "impossibility" of an artist's conjuring up such a divine work and marveling that it could actually have been painted "with human hands." Correggio also painted a St. John with pen in hand in the transept (over the doorway to the left of the main altar). Il Parmigianino, the second Parmesan master, also did some frescoes in the chapel at the left of the entrance. You can visit the abbey from 9 a.m. to 7 p.m.; closed Monday. Admission is 2,000 lire ($1.50).

Other Sights

After viewing this complex of ecclesiastical buildings, you'll find the second batch of attractions conveniently sheltered under one roof at the **Palazzo della Pilotta.** At via della Pilotta 5, this palazzo once housed the Farnese family in Parma's heyday as a duchy in the 16th century. Badly damaged by bombs in World War II, it has been restored and turned into a palace of museums, the most important of which is the **National Gallery** (tel. 33-309). Filled with the works of Parmesan artists from the late 15th century to the 19th century—notably paintings by Correggio and Parmigianino—the National Gallery offers a limited, but well-chosen, selection of art. In one room is an unfinished head of a young woman attributed to da Vinci. Correggio's *Madonna della Scala* (of the stairs), the remains of a fresco, is also displayed. But his masterpiece—one of the celebrated paintings of northern Italy—is *St. Jerome with the Madonna and Child*. Imbued with a delicate quality, it represents age, youth, love—a gentle ode to tenderness. In the next room is Correggio's *Madonna della Scodella* (with a bowl), with its agonized faces. You'll also see Correggio's *Coronation*, a golden fresco, a work of great beauty, and his less successful *Annunciation*. One of Parmigianino's best-known paintings is here, *St. Catherine's Marriage*, with its rippling movement and subdued colors.

The gallery may be visited from 9 a.m. to 2 p.m. for an admission fee of 5,000 lire ($3.80). On Sunday it's open from 9 a.m. to 1 p.m. Closed Monday.

With the same ticket, you're entitled to view **St. Paul's Chamber,** which Correggio frescoed with mythological scenes, including one of Diana. The chamber lies on via Macedonio Melloni.

On the same floor as the National Gallery is the **Farnese Theater,** evocative of Palladio's theater at Vicenza. Originally built in 1618, the structure was bombed in 1944 and has been restored. Still in the same palazzo, you can explore the **National Archeological Museum** (Museo Archeologico Nazionale di Parma) (tel. 33-718). This most interesting museum houses Egyptian sarcophagi, Etruscan vases, Roman and Greek-inspired torsos, a bronze portrait of a boy from the 1st century A.D., Bronze Age relics, and a most celebrated exhibition called "Tabula Alimentaria," a bronze-engraved tablet dating from the reign of Trajan and excavated at Velleia in the province of Piacenza. The museum is open Tuesday through Saturday from 9 a.m. to 2 p.m., on Sunday from 9 a.m. to 1 p.m.; closed Monday.

In the same palazzo is the **Bodoni Museum,** a collection of graphic arts and rare manuscripts, including a rare edition of Homer's *Iliad*. Hours are 9 a.m. to noon daily except Sunday. Admission is free. Also, the Palatine Library exhibits works from the fallen house of Bourbon.

Arturo Toscanini's Birthplace, via Rodolfo Tanzi 13, is the house where the musician and conductor was born in 1867. This Italian orchestral conductor was unquestionably the greatest of the first half of the 20th century, and one of the most astonishing musical interpreters of all time. He spent his childhood and youth in this house, which has been turned into a museum with interesting relics and a record library, containing all the recorded works that he conducted. It is open from 10 a.m. to 1 p.m. Monday through Saturday; closed Sunday. There is no admission charge.

Finally, to round out your day, go to one of the shops and buy a bottle of "Parma Violet" perfume.

HOTELS IN PARMA

The choice is limited but adequate. However, during the fairs held in May and September it will be virtually impossible to get a room unless you reserve well in advance.

Palace Hotel Maria Luigia, viale Mentana 140, 43100 Parma (tel. 0521/281-032), is welcome on the Parma hotel scene. Bold colors and molded plastic built-ins set the up-to-date mood, and bedrooms are made particularly comfortable by soundproof walls, air conditioning, and TV. There's a very Italian-looking American bar on the premises, and garage space. All rooms come with bath and go for 130,000 lire ($98.75) daily for a single, 190,000 lire ($144) for a double. The hotel has one of the best restaurants in Parma, Maxim's, which serves excellent Italian and international specialties daily except Sunday and in August. Dinners range from 45,000 lire ($34.25) up. The hotel is near the station.

Park Hotel Stendhal, piazzetta Bodoni 3, 43100 Parma (tel. 0521/208-057), sits on a quiet square close to the opera house, a few minutes' walk from many of the city's important sights. It offers 60 rooms, all with private bath or shower. Singles go for an inclusive 115,000 lire ($87.50) daily, and doubles run 170,000 lire ($129). The bedrooms of the hotel are well maintained, furnished with contemporary pieces, and each has color TV, a frigo-bar, and air conditioning. There's a traditional

American bar and lounge, with comfortable armchairs for before- and after-dinner drinks. The hotel has a closed garage.

International via Reggio 51A, 43100 Parma (tel. 0521/994-247), is one of the best of the second-class choices. In a quiet area but convenient for the town center, airport, and fairs, it opened in 1988. The 76 bedrooms have such modern conveniences as private bath or shower, air conditioning, TV, radio, mini-bar, and phone. Singles rent for 70,000 lire ($53.25) daily, and doubles go for 100,000 lire ($76), with breakfast included. Parma specialties are served in the hotel restaurant, and there is ample parking.

Milano, viale Bottego 9, 43100 Parma (tel. 0521/773-031), is near the railway station and a busy thoroughfare. It is an old hotel without pretenses, but its bedrooms are fairly large, adequately furnished, and clean. The front rooms face a noisy boulevard. The hotel has 47 rental units, most of them with private bath or shower. Bathless singles cost 32,000 lire ($24.25) daily; bathless doubles, 55,000 lire ($41.75). With bath, singles go for 47,000 lire ($35.75); doubles, 72,000 lire ($54.75). The hotel's restaurant serves good Parma specialties.

The **Hotel Button,** strada Vitale 7, 43100 Parma (tel. 0521/208-039), is another local favorite and one of the best bargains in town. This is a family-owned and -run hotel, and you're made to feel welcome. It stands just off the heartbeat piazza Garibaldi. Far cheaper than the Palace Hotel Maria Luigia and the Park Hotel Stendhal, it rents 41 pleasantly and comfortably furnished rooms, a single costing from 50,000 lire ($38) daily, a double peaking at 74,000 lire ($56.25). The hotel doesn't have a restaurant—in Parma this is no problem at all—but will serve you a continental breakfast for an extra charge. The hotel takes a holiday in July.

Prìncipe, via Emilia Est 46, 43100 Parma (tel. 0521/493-847), about a ten-minute walk from the center of town, is considered the best bargain hotel in Parma. The 33 comfortably furnished rooms cost from 54,000 lire ($41) daily in a single and from 74,500 lire ($56.50) in a double. The place is clean and pleasant, although the front rooms are somewhat noisy. There are frequent buses from here to the center of Parma and to points of interest. The Prìncipe has a restaurant, which is closed on Sunday from December through March, and the hotel is closed the first two weeks in August.

DINING IN PARMA

The chefs of Parma are far more skillful than the innkeepers. Of course, parmesan cheese has added just the right touch to thousands of Italian dinners, and the word "parmigiana" is familiar to diners in American-Italian restaurants.

Parizzi, strada della Repubblica 71 (tel. 285-952). Under a skylit patio, the people of Parma, known for their exacting tastes and demanding palates, enjoy the rich cuisine for which their town is celebrated. There are those who say that this restaurant serves the best food in town, although Angiol d'Or (see below) also has its devotees. After you're shown to a table in one of the good-size dining rooms, a trolley cart filled with antipasti is wheeled before you, containing shellfish and salmon among its many delectable offerings. The stuffed vegetables are especially good (try the zucchini). The owner's name is Ugo Parizzi, the son of a deli owner, who knows his cuts of meat. You might begin with the chef's specialty, crêpes alla parmigiana— that is, crêpes stuffed with fontina, Parma ham, and ricotta or with truffles in September. In May you'll want to try the asparagus fresh from the fields. A good main course is the veal scaloppine with fontina and ham. Desserts include zabaglione laced with marsala. The restaurant is open from 12:30 to 2:30 p.m. and 7:30 to 10:20 p.m.; closed Sunday night and Monday and for most of August. It charges 35,000 lire ($26.25) to 45,000 lire ($34.25), which is a reasonable price considering what you get. Reservations are important.

Angiol d'Or, vicolo Scutellari 1 (tel. 282-632), lies at the corner of the piazzo del Duomo, attracting a devoted clientele of local residents and frequent visitors, many of whom claim that this restaurant serves the finest food in Parma. It is certainly the most elegant, enjoying more luxurious touches than the equally highly rated Parizzi just previewed. The chef at Angiol d'Or specializes in both international dishes and local fare. If you order anything "alla parmigiana," including risotto, you'll fare well indeed. Try also the cannoli alla parmigiana. The chef is a hearty exponent of the cuisine of northern Italy, and many of the recipes are inspired not only by the traditions of Parma but of Bologna and Modena as well. In the intimate, well-appointed restaurant, you can expect to be served a full meal ranging in price from 38,000 lire ($29) to 65,000 lire ($49.50). The local wines to order are Lambrusco and Malvasia. The restaurant is open from 12:30 to 2:30 p.m. and 7:30 to 10:30 p.m.; closed Sunday night and Monday.

La Greppia, strada Garibaldi 39 (tel. 33-686), has an unpretentious decor and a location near the opera house, yet it is near the top of every gourmet's list of the finest dining rooms of Parma. Through a plate-glass window at one end of the dining room, you can see the chef at work.

My most recent pasta dish came baked with radicchio, my favorite lettuce. Try, if featured in autumn, tortelli stuffed with a spicy pumpkin purée. However, chances are your tortelli will be stuffed with chopped spinach and ricotta, over which a rich butter, a light cream sauce, and, naturally, grated parmesan cheese have been spread. For a main dish, I recently enjoyed the grilled sole, which was excellent, my dining companion preferring thinly sliced raw beef like steak tartare, which the Italians call carpaccio. The tarts made with fresh fruit are succulent desserts. Even better, the chef is known for his compelling chocolate cake, which one reviewer claimed was much better than the famed Sachertorte served at the Hotel Sacher in Vienna. La Greppia is closed on Thursday and Friday, unusual for a restaurant. It serves meals for 40,000 lire ($30.50) to 65,000 lire ($49.50) from 12:30 to 2:30 p.m. and 7:30 to 10 p.m., and reservations are necessary.

Al Canòn d'Or, via Nazario Sauro 3 (tel. 285-234), is considerably down the price scale, but known for its quality meals at a moderate price. The owner pays a lot of attention to the food, turning out a worthy cuisine in a city where diners are often hard to please. The place is closed on Sunday and in August, otherwise offering meals for 28,000 lire ($21.25) to 38,000 lire ($29) from 12:30 to 2:30 p.m. and 7:30 to 10 p.m.

EXCURSIONS FROM PARMA

Admittedly, the French novelist Stendhal (who died in 1842, his real name being Marie Henri Beyle) isn't read as much as he once was. But he is still widely appreciated. In addition to *The Red and the Black,* his other famous novel was *The Charterhouse of Parma,* which was acclaimed in its day for its vivid depiction of contemporary manners.

The charterhouse, or **Certosa di Parma** (tel. 0521/492-247), about 2½ miles from Parma, can still be visited today. Dating from 1282, it was reconstructed over the years and serves as a school. You can wander its halls, some of which are frescoed, weekdays from 9 a.m. to noon and 3 to 6 p.m. (2 to 4 p.m. in winter). Its weekend hours are 9 a.m. to noon, and admission is free, with the school's permission.

If you'd like to pick up the trail of Stendhal, you can drive to **Colorno,** a small town some nine miles from Parma. There you'll be directed north for 2½ miles to Sacca, where you'll easily spot the **Stendhal–da Bruno** (tel. 0521/815-493). The inn that Stendhal actually patronized here is long gone, but the present building was constructed on the site. It was here, reportedly, that Stendhal got the inspiration to write *La Chartreuse de Parme.*

If the weather is behaving, ask for a table on a terrace adorned with a trellis of heavy vines. On the banks of the Po, this restaurant is a family affair. From the ovens in the back emerge delectable roast duck, pork, and lamb. Fish, including sea bass, is the main dish specialty. If you don't want fish, ask for an arrosti misti, a plate of mixed roasts. However, the seafood antipasti are excellent, and surely you'll be tempted. The restaurant also has many fine wines from the Emilia-Romagna district.

Count on spending 35,000 lire ($26.50) to 50,000 lire ($38), the latter price if you order the fresh fish. The restaurant is open from 12:30 to 2:30 p.m. and 7:30 to 9:30 p.m.; closed on Tuesday, from late July to early August, and the first two weeks in January.

6. Busseto

"The town of Verdi" is a phrase neatly summing up Busseto. The noted composer lived here and nearby most of his life, and aficionados come to follow the Verdi trail, visiting his birthplace, the church where he was baptized, the villa where he lived after he gained fame, and the various paths he trod in Busseto.

The provinces of Piacenza, Parma, and Cremona meet at this Po Valley town, and its history is long, from centuries before Verdi brought it lasting fame. As late as 1820 Busseto was still protected by massive city walls, dominated by a fortress from at least the 11th century.

The telephone area code of Busseto is 0524.

SIGHTS

The **castle** (*rocca*) of Busseto was reconstructed in the 13th century by a prince, Obert the Great, who became the subject of Verdi's first opera, *Oberto*. The moated fortress stands on one side of the piazza Giuseppe Verdi, the town's main square. At the top of the square is a large seated statue of the composer. The main street of Busseto, via Roma, is colonnaded on either side, its arches opening onto the Verdi Square around which are ecclesiastical highlights of the town.

A trip through the Verdi shrines can be taken separately or by means of a three-part ticket purchased at the castle for 5,000 lire ($3.80). The first stop is at the **Verdi Opera House** built by Busseto and dedicated to the composer in 1845. The small theater is a miniature of La Scala, and Verdi, a frequent guest, conducted here at least once. All 27 of his operas have been performed here.

The **municipal museum** in the Palazzo Pallavicino is the second part of the ticket. The baroque palace outside the city walls, built by the same family that constructed the fortress, contains musical instruments, manuscripts, and portraits connected with Verdi.

To see the master's **birthplace,** your trek (and the third portion of your ticket) takes you to the town of Roncole Verdi, which was called Le Roncole when the musician was born there. The village is about 2½ miles southeast of Busseto toward Piacenza. The stone cottage where the Verdi family lived, and from which Papa Verdi operated a tavern and grocery store, is not furnished today, but visitors can walk through the low-ceilinged rooms. The Roncole church where Giuseppe was baptized and where he later was the organist can also be visited. The organ and the little room it occupies are just as they were in Verdi's day.

The three-part tour can be taken daily except Monday from 9:30 a.m. to 5:30 p.m., but the Verdi birthplace is closed from 12:30 to 2:30 p.m.

Sant'Agata, two miles northwest of Busseto on the road to Cremona, is the estate and the villa that Verdi built up from a farmhouse after he gained fame. It is privately owned and occupied, but the grounds and part of the house can be visited. It was here that the composer finally got around to marrying the diva, his beloved Giuseppina, in 1859. It is said that much of the financing for the restoration of the villa was paid for by the royalties from *Rigoletto*. A guided tour takes visitors through the bedchambers of Guiseppina and of Verdi, where many of his personal effects are preserved. You can also see a replica of the room in a Milan hotel where Verdi died in 1901. The room has been faithfully reproduced, and there's even a glass case containing the music master's death mask. Sant'Agata is open from 9 a.m. to noon and 2 to 4 p.m. April 1 to October 1; closed Monday. Admission is 4,000 lire ($3.05).

WHERE TO STAY AND DINE

The best hotel in Busseto is **I Due Foscari,** piazza Carlo Rossi 15, 43011 Busseto (tel. 0524/92-337). It's run by a Verdian tenor, Marco Bergonzi. He's not always there, however, as he is often on tour. He rents out only 20 rooms, each one comfortably furnished, costing from 40,000 lire ($30.50) daily in a single and from 65,000 lire ($49.50) in a double. No food is served on Monday, but otherwise you can enjoy an excellent meal costing from 32,000 lire ($24.25) to 50,000 lire ($38). The hotel is named for an early Verdi work, one of his more obscure operas.

If you make the pilgrimage to Roncole Verdi, you'll be well advised to dine at the **Guareschi Ristorante** (tel. 92-495), which serves some of the finest food I've discovered in this region, although unfortunately it's open only for lunch from 12:30 to 3 p.m. The cannelloni Rigoletto is named of course for the Verdi opera. However, the restaurant takes its name from the author of the *Don Camillo* series. The cannelloni, incidentally, is every bit as good as the opera. You might, as a prelude to your meal, want some of the mortadella (it's not baloney) of Busseto. The kitchen also turns out excellent green fettuccine as well as rigatoni and tortellini. Many of its meat dishes are served alla parmigiana, and often fried polenta accompanies a main course. Desserts are rich and good tasting, and everything is backed up by some fine regional wines. Count on spending 40,000 lire ($30.50) to 60,000 lire ($45.50) for a complete meal. The restaurant is closed on Friday and in July, December, January, and February. It's best to call for a reservation and to make sure they're open.

ALONG THE ADRIATIC

The brisk air of the Adriatic Sea sweeps across the marshy land, dunes, and pine woods. The aromas of the Romagna kitchen waft across the lobby of a boarding house. Clusters of bodies line the sandy beaches for miles. Ravenna evokes the melancholy memories of the Byzantium in the West. But Rimini makes you forget them again, as you're swept up in a carnival-like atmosphere with northern Europeans in pursuit of fun by the seashore. And at sunset you can hike up Mount Titano to the little Republic of San Marino for a view—high, wide, and handsome.

1. Ravenna

Ravenna, where Dante Alighieri came to die, is one of Italy's greatest art cities —but different from all the rest. The sea long receded, Ravenna is another landlocked city in the way that Pisa is. The waters left behind one of the greatest collections of mosaics in the Western world—many created to decorate 5th- and 6th-century basilicas, during the flowering of Ravenna's artistic expression within the confines of Byzantine and early-Christian art.

Ravenna's telephone area code is 0544.

THE SIGHTS

If Ravenna existed in some remote corner of Italy, the chances are it would be overrun by visitors and sprinkled with first-class hotels. But all too often it's relegated to a quick day's jaunt from either Venice or Rimini. Steeped in industry and ravaged by World War II bombings, Ravenna still evokes its illustrious past. But you must follow an inviolable rule: never decide whether to enter a church just by looking at its exterior. Like the Alhambra at Granada, many of Ravenna's basilica façades appear unprepossessing, but contain a wealth of Byzantine mosaics inside. Incidentally, the mosaic business—now reactivated—is going strong once more in Ravenna.

To Ravenna went the dubious privilege of being the capital of the Roman Empire in the West. Flavius Honorius, emperor of the West, moved his court to Milan after the sack of Rome. But, again threatened by barbarian hordes, he set up his capital in Ravenna, near his Adriatic fleet for those quick getaways should the need arise. The court was graced with the presence of the legendary Galla Placidia, sister of Honorius, who ruled for a time in place of her son, Valentinian III. With the fall of the Roman emperors, Odoacer came to call, then Theodoric. The Ostrogothic king Theodoric converted to Christianity and left many great monuments and reminders of his peaceful reign in Ravenna. He governed for more than 30 years at the end of the 5th century and the beginning of the 6th century. Eventually, Justinian recaptured the city (539), returning it to the folds of the Roman Empire in the East. Ravenna became the outpost of Byzantium in the West. For the glory left behind during all these periods, let's explore—

The Neone Baptistery

At the piazza del Duomo, near the cathedral, the octagonally shaped baptistery (tel. 39-196) was built in the 5th century. In the center of the cupola is a tablet showing John the Baptist baptizing Christ. The circle around the tablet depicts in mosaics the 12 crown-carrying Apostles, dramatic in deep violet-blues and sparkling golds. From April to September the baptistery is open from 9 a.m. to 12:30 p.m. and 2:30 to 6 p.m., till 5 p.m. in winter. It is closed Sunday afternoon. The entrance fee is 1,000 lire (75¢). The baptistery originally serviced a cathedral that no longer stands. The present-day Duomo of Ravenna was built around the mid-18th century and is of little interest except for some unusual pews. Beside it is a campanile from the 11th century, perhaps earlier. For a sight far more appealing, walk around in back of the duomo to the—

Archepiscopal Museum and Church of St. Andrea

Opening onto the piazza Arcivesçovado, this twofold attraction is housed in the Archbishop's Palace, dating mainly from the 6th century. In the museum, the major exhibit is a throne carved out of ivory for Archbishop Maximian (some of the panels missing), dating from around the mid-6th century. In the chapel or oratory dedicated to St. Andrea are brilliant mosaics. Pause a while in the antechamber and look over the entrance for a most intriguing mosaic. Here is an unusual representation of Christ as a warrior, stepping on the head of a lion and a snake. Although haloed, he wears partial armor, evoking "Onward, Christian Soldiers." The chapel —built in the shape of a cross—contains other mosaics that are "angelic," both figuratively and literally. Busts of saints and apostles stare down at you with the ox-eyed look of Byzantine art. The museum is open from 9 a.m. to 12:30 p.m. and 2:30 to 6 p.m. (till 5 p.m. in winter) Tuesday through Saturday, from 9 a.m. to 1 p.m. on Sunday; closed Monday.

The next cluster of sights is centered a short walk from the piazza Baracca, beginning with the—

Church of St. Vitale

On via San Vitale sits an octagonally shaped dome-surmounted church that dates from the mid-6th century. Inside, its mosaics—in brilliant greens and golds, lit by poetic light from translucent panels—are among the most celebrated not only in Ravenna, but the Western world. Covering the apse is a mosaic rendition of a clean-shaven Christ, striding the world, flanked by saints and angels. To the right is the mosaic of Empress Theodora and her court, and to the left the man who married the courtesan-actress, Emperor Justinian, and his entourage. If you can tear yourself away from the mosaics long enough, you might admire the church with its marble decoration. Seven large arches span the temple, but the frescoes of the cupola are unimaginative. St. Vitale is open (free) daily from 8:30 a.m. to 7:30 p.m. In winter the hours are 8:30 a.m. to 5 p.m.

The Mausoleum of Galla Placidia

Standing beside the Church of St. Vitale, and built in the 5th century, this is a chapel so unpretentious that you'll think you're at the wrong place. But inside it contains mosaics of exceptional merit—dripping with antiquity, but not looking it. Popular tradition has it that the cross-shaped structure houses the tomb of Galla Placidia, sister of Honorius. But there is evidence that this claim may be false. Translucent panels bring the mosaics alive in all their grace and harmony—rich and vivid with peacock-blue, moss-green, Roman gold, eggplant, and Navajo orange. The mosaics in the cupola literally glitter with stars. It keeps the same hours as St. Vitale.

In the courtyard of St. Vitale is the entrance to the—

National Museum (Museo Nazionale)

This museum contains archeological objects from the early Christian and Byzantine periods—icons, fragments of tapestries, medieval armaments and armory, sarcophagi, ivories, ceramics, and bits of broken pieces from the stained-glass windows of St. Vitale. Charging 3,000 lire ($2.30) for admission, it is open from 8:30 a.m. to 7 p.m. On Sunday and holidays, it is open from 8:30 a.m. to 1:30 p.m. It is closed all day Monday.

The Adrian Baptistery

Lying right off the piazza Ariani, the Baptistery deserves a visit. Dating from the 5th century, the octagonally shaped structure is also noted for its mosaics. In the center of the cupola is a portrait of John the Baptist baptizing Christ, and the figure of an old man who represents the Jordan River. Like spokes in a wheel, the 12 Apostles—all haloed—branch out. The admission-free oratory is open daily from 8:30 a.m. to 12:30 p.m. and 2:30 p.m. to sunset.

Basilica of St. Apollinare Nuovo

On via di Roma (at the intersection of via Alberoni), this church, dating from the 6th century, was founded by Theodoric. In the nave are some of Ravenna's finest mosaics, illustrating the procession of virgins and martyrs, with their typically rounded faces, in brilliant greens, golds, and whites. On the left are 22 haloed virgins, plus the Madonna and her Bambino, as well as three Wise Men and four angels. On the right wall, Christ is depicted seated on his throne with four angels and 26 martyrs carrying crowns. Repetitious in part, the processionals create a stunning effect. At one end of the panel depicting the martyrs is a representation of the Palace of Theodoric. Supporting the walls are two dozen Corinthian columns. The admission-free basilica is open daily from 9 a.m. to 12:30 p.m. and 2:30 to 6 p.m. In winter, it closes at 5 p.m. Adjoining the church is an impressive circular campanile of the 10th century.

Dante's Tomb

On via Dante, right off the piazza Garibaldi, the final monument to Dante Alighieri, "the divine poet," isn't much to look at—graced as it is with a bas-relief in marble. But it's a far better resting place than he assigned to some of his fellow Florentines. The author of the *Divine Comedy,* in exile from his hometown of Florence, died in Ravenna on September 14, 1321. To the right of the small temple is a mound of earth in which Dante's urn went "underground" from March 1944 to December

1945. It was feared in Ravenna that his tomb might suffer in the bombings. Near the tomb is the Church of San Francesco, dating from the 5th century, in which the poet's funeral was held.

Theodoric Mausoleum

Less than a mile from the above-mentioned attractions (out on via della Industrie), the mausoleum honors Theodoric, king of the Ostrogoths (A.D. 474–526). Although stripped of its art, the two-story tomb, made of Istrian stone, is starkly awesome. In the upper chamber is a porphyry sarcophagus, but the remains of Theodoric have long disappeared, of course. The museum is open from 8:30 a.m. to 2:30 p.m. daily except Monday. Admission is 3,000 lire ($2.30).

The Basilica of St. Apollinaire in Classe (also Classis)

About 3½ miles south of the city (it can be visited on the way to Ravenna if you're heading north from Rimini), the church dates from the 6th century, having been consecrated by Archbishop Maximian. Before the waters receded, Classe was a seaport of Rome's Adriatic fleet. Dedicated to St. Apollinaire, the bishop of Ravenna, the early basilica stands side-by-side with a campanile—both symbols of faded glory now resting in a lonely low-lying area. Inside is a central nave, flanked by two aisles, the latter containing tombs of ecclesiastical figures in the Ravenna hierarchy. The floor—once carpeted with mosaics—has been rebuilt (look at the fenced-off section to the right of the entrance for a sense of what it once looked like). Along the central nave are frescoed tablets. Two dozen marble columns line the approach to the apse, where you find the major reason for visiting the basilica. The mosaics are exceptional, rich in gold and turquoise, set against a background of top-heavy birds nesting in shrubbery. St. Apollinaire stands in the center, with a row of lambs on either side lined up as in a processional (the 12 lambs symbolizing the Apostles, of course). The basilica may be visited from daily 9 a.m. to noon and 2 to 6 p.m. (till 5 p.m. in winter). No admission is charged.

HOTELS IN RAVENNA

Generally they are an uninspired lot—but adequate and perfectly suitable for overnighting.

Park Hotel Ravenna, viale delle Nazioni 181, 48023 Marina di Ravenna (tel. 0544/531-743), eight miles from the heart of Ravenna. Some visitors prefer a beachside resort after visiting the narrow and crowded streets of Ravenna. The best one in the area is the Park Hotel, an oasis with a large swimming pool and many resort activities. Its arching windows are separated from a popular beach by a copse of evergreens. Two tennis courts stretch almost to the foundation of the establishment's white walls whose interiors contain public areas ranging from airy tile-floored lounges to warm re-creations of country taverns. Between April and October, the 146 modern and sunny rooms rent for 95,000 lire ($72.25) to 120,000 lire ($91.25) daily in a single, 150,000 lire ($114) to 180,000 lire ($137) in a double.

Jolly Hotel, piazza Mameli 1, 48100 Ravenna (tel. 0544/35-762). This four-story hotel, built in 1950, contains two elevators and a conservative decor that includes a bunker-like façade, stone floors, and lots of paneling. Considered the best hotel within Ravenna, and usually preferred by traveling businesspeople, it has 75 rooms, each of which has air conditioning, radio, TV, mini-bar, and modern bath. With a continental breakfast included, singles rent for around 115,000 lire ($89.50) daily; doubles, 175,000 lire ($133).

Bisanzio, via Salara 30, 48100 Ravenna (tel. 0544/27-111), stands in the heart of town, just a few minutes' walk from many of Ravenna's treasures, such as the Basilica of St. Vitale and the Mausoleum of Galla Placidia. A pleasantly coordinated modern hotel, it's a dignified place at which to stay, with bedrooms that have attractive Italian styling. To brighten the wood paneling are wall-to-wall draperies and Oriental carpets. It's ideal for those who want the comfort of a well-organized hotel, with good bedrooms, offering simplicity, compactness, and tile bath and shower in all rooms. Other amenities are air conditioning, phone, and color TV in the rooms, plus an American bar and an uncluttered breakfast room with softly draped windows. Singles go for 82,000 lire ($62.30) daily; doubles, 155,000 lire ($118). Guests have use of a garden, and parking is available.

Hotel Centrale Byron, via IV Novembre 14, 48100 Ravenna (tel. 0544/22-225), is an art deco–inspired hotel a few steps from the piazza del Popolo. The lobby is an elegantly simple combination of white marble and brass detailing. The public rooms stretch "railroad style" in a long narrow format past a reception desk, an alcove sitting room, a long hallway, and a combination TV room, bar, and snacking and breakfast room area. The 57 rooms, each with bath or shower, color TV, and direct-dial phone, rent for 53,000 lire ($40.25) daily in a single, 80,000 lire ($60.75) in a double. Some rooms have air conditioning available for an extra fee.

DINING IN RAVENNA

The best choice in town, **Ristorante Tre Spade,** via G. Rasponi 37 (tel. 32-382), is an appealing restaurant set behind a rounded set of canopies about a block from the piazza del Popolo. You enter a beautifully appointed room with wood detailing, half-paneled walls, lace curtains, a corner bar, and a big antipasti table, along with dozens of culinary accessories and lots of 19th-century military-inspired engravings. Specialties include an asparagus parfait accompanied by a zesty sauce of bits of green peppers and black olives, and an appetizing assortment of carpaccio (thinly sliced raw meat covered with sliced sheets of parmesan cheese with raw artichoke hearts in olive oil). This might be followed by taglioni with smoked salmon sauce, veal cooked with sage, spaghetti with fruits of the sea (which includes clams in their shells), green gnocchi in gorgonzola sauce, or roast game in season, plus a good collection of wines. The menu changes frequently, and daily specials are offered according to the market. The restaurant suggests reservations, and usually charges from 45,000 lire ($34.25) for a complete meal. It is open from 12:30 to 2:30 p.m. and 7:30 to 10:30 p.m.; closed Monday and from late July to late August.

Bella Venezia, via IV Novembre 16 (tel. 22-746), a few steps from the piazza del Popolo, is the kind of well-known restaurant that many of the city's hotel managers recommend to their clients. Next to the Hotel Centrale Byron, the restaurant offers well-prepared, typically Italian food, including a wide range of pasta, vegetable, and meat dishes. Full meals range from 35,000 lire ($26.50) to 45,000 lire ($34.25) and are served from 12:30 to 2:30 p.m. and 7:30 to 10 p.m. every day of the week except Sunday. The restaurant is also closed in January.

Ristorante La Gardèla, via Ponte Marino 3 (tel. 27-147), a few steps from one of Ravenna's most startling leaning towers, is spread out over two levels of paneled walls lined with racks of wine bottles. The waiters bring out an array of typical but savory dishes. These include fried squid, pork liver, veal chops, baked green lasagne, Parma ham, and beefsteak. Meals range upward from 25,000 lire ($19). The restaurant is open from noon to 2 p.m. and 7:30 to 9:30 p.m.; closed Thursday and during most of August.

A WINE BAR

In the 16th-century Palazzo Rasponi, **Ca de Ven,** via Corrado Ricci 24 (tel. 30-163), honors the Robin Hood of the region, Passatore. This folk hero of the 19th century was a bearded ferryboat operator whose robbing of the rich to give to the poor was somewhat suspect. Some people said he gave mainly to the poor (but pretty) girls he liked. At any rate, his likeness appears on the neck of the bottles at this wine bar. Food of the region served here includes pizza and the almond cake, marzipane. They don't offer normal meals, but you can order a big crêpe, called a piadine, which is often stuffed with ham like a sandwich, costing 2,800 lire ($2.15). The establishment is open from 10 a.m. to 2 p.m. and 5:30 to 10:20 p.m. daily except Monday.

Thirty-three miles south of Ravenna, you'll find—

2. Rimini

The leading resort along the Adriatic, Rimini basks in the *gemütlich* sun from May to October, then settles down for a long winter's nap. First discovered by the Germans, Rimini was splashed with *Zimmer frei* signs, as the Emilians moved in from the hinterlands to open one pensione after another, based on the soundness of the West German mark. Then the cheap charter flights from Copenhagen and Stockholm brought more hordes—this time the Vikings, not in horn helmets but in the briefest of bikinis.

The English—who know a good bargain—began to fly in, drawn by the low prices of the Adriatic resort, which are considerably cheaper than similar accommodations on the French and Italian Rivieras. New signs—"English tea like mother makes"—started to compete with the beer and wurst billboards. Now North Americans are discovering that Rimini is a great place at which to wind down between vaporetto rides in Venice and too much cold marble in Florence.

Rimini can be a curvaceous mermaid to some, a battle-scarred sea dragon to others. Go there if you adore invasions of holiday-makers—some of whom have had more than the traditional quarter liter of wine for lunch. The beaches are wide and long. The sand is a healthy beige—that is, if you can see the beach under the layers of snow-white bodies cooking a lobster-red under the hot July sun.

To arrive in peak season without a reservation guarantees that you'll get a quickly assembled *From Here to Eternity* cot in the maid's pantry. In contrast, those efficient itinerary mappers who always know where they'll be at any given hour—four months in advance—are luxuriating in the beachfront rooms with the picture windows.

Rimini has more beds than San Marino has postage stamps. Most of the hostelries line the beach. Some of the dreary third-class boarding houses away from the beach are hot and bonebare of facilities. Rimini also has a water shortage in summer, so don't be surprised if you're greeted with a dying gurgle when you turn on the tap.

If approached in the right spirit, Rimini can spell fun in the sun. But if you're haunted by fears of the population explosion, get thee to a nunnery.

The telephone area code for Rimini is 0541.

THE SIGHTS

With so much interest centered on the beaches and the modern hotels, it's easy to forget that Rimini is also an ancient seaport. In the center of the city stands the **Arch of Augustus** (27 B.C.), commemorating the joining of the two great Roman roads, the Emilia and the Flaminia. But the real interest in Rimini centers on the Malatesta family, who were to the Adriatic city what the Medici were to Florence. The Malatesta grip on Rimini was tightened to a stranglehold in the 14th century.

The most memorable story of that reign starred Paolo and Francesca, the ill-fated Romeo and Juliet of Rimini. According to legend, Francesca though she was going to marry Paolo, nicknamed the handsome, but was tricked into wedding his deformed brother, Gianciotto. The cripple later killed both his wife and his brother, who were lovers. Dante immortalized them in the lines: ". . . these two who go together and seem to be so light in the wind." The divine poet wasn't carried away with any school-girl romance, however. Unable to condone adultery, he sentenced them both to his Inferno.

The drama of Paolo and Francesca took place, it is said (but some historians discount it), at the 13th-century **Gradara Castle,** which is best visited on an A.T.R. tour departing daily in summer at 3 p.m. (it's less than an hour's ride, a distance of only 18 miles, to Gradara) from the piazza Tripoli. Of course, you can visit Gradara on your own. It's most interesting, encircled by fortress-like medieval walls. The Castle La Rocca was built by the Grifi family, belonging later to the Malatesta and the Sforza. From mid-May to mid-September the castle is open daily except Monday from 3 to 7 p.m. At other times of the year, visiting hours are 9 a.m. to 1 p.m. (9 a.m. to noon on Sunday and holidays). It is closed on Monday, and charges 3,000 lire ($2.30) for admission.

Sigismondo was another member of the Malatesta clan, the subject of numerous legends because of his penchant for getting rid of his wives. The true love of the Rimini lord was his beautiful mistress, Isotta. To show his devotion, and being Italian, he erected a church to her (the **Malatesta Temple** on via Leon Battista Alberti). The military leader and art patron hired Leon Battista Alberti to design it. Throughout the Renaissance temple—today a sort of Malatesta pantheon—are representations of elephants and roses, the Malatesta symbol, and the initials of Isotta and Sigimondo knotted together into a dollar sign (with only one line). The present-day temple, heavily damaged in the war, has been restored. A church, it remains marvelously secular somehow. It can be visited from 7 a.m. to noon and 3 to 7 p.m. daily April to September, closing at 5 p.m. off-season.

HOTELS IN RIMINI

My hotel recommendations, in several price ranges, follow.

A Deluxe Choice

Grand Hotel, piazzale Indipendenza, 47037 Rimini (tel. 0541/56-000), treasures the splendor of the past. The only luxury hotel in Rimini, it takes forgivable pride in its palace architecture, its park setting beside a private beach, its 18th-century French and Venetian antiques and crystal chandeliers. Note some of the attractions—a free-form swimming pool, private cabañas with shower on the hotel beach as well as a bar-grill where you can lunch in your bikini, the Lady Godiva video disco, a piano bar, air conditioning, and schools for waterskiing, sailing, and windsurfing. The handsomely outfitted rooms—119 in all—come equipped with bath, phone, radio, color TV, and frigo-bar. The Grand charges 145,000 lire ($110) daily in a single, 280,000 lire ($213) in a double. You can stay here on full-board terms for 190,000 lire ($144) to 250,000 lire ($190) per person daily. In the evening, guests can dance to orchestra music on the terrace, cooled by the sea breezes of the Adriatic. The hotel has an international restaurant in the veranda-salon and a typical bar-restaurant, L'Ombrellone, on the private beach.

First-Class Choices

Hotel Imperiale, viale Vespucci 16, 47037 Rimini (tel. 0541/52-255), is positioned directly on the beach. Air-conditioned, it offers well-furnished rooms that contain TV, radio, frigo-bar, direct-dial phone, digital clock with automatic alarm, and balcony with views directly on the sea. In the high season of July and August, a single rents for 160,000 lire ($122) daily, a double goes for 240,000 lire ($182). The hotel has two restaurants, one offering a panoramic view from its sixth-floor location, a stretch of 19 miles of Adriatic coastline. The other dining spot, the Melograno, is open every evening. Other facilities include a gymnasium, a sauna, a massage room, a heated swimming pool, a garden, a solarium, and a car park which is guarded by closed-circuit TV. The hotel staff will also arrange for tennis, waterskiing, sailing, fishing, and horseback riding.

Ambasciatori, via Amerigo Vespucci 22, 47037 Rimini (tel. 0541/55-561), is one of the finest first-class hotels in Rimini. Its breezy moderno is uplifting, with walls of glass opening around a courtyard that faces the sea. Even the elevator's positioned for a view: in a glass shaft outside the building. The bedrooms are restrained, with slickly coordinated color schemes. There's a glassed-in sitting area that opens onto a private balcony. In case the Adriatic breezes wane, there is air conditioning.

Each room has its own private bath. With half board included, rates range from 120,000 lire ($91.25) to 165,000 lire ($125) per person daily, based on double occupancy. The dining room opens toward the sea, as does the breakfast room. The lounges, with rattan furnishings and comfortable armchairs, are well styled, with shafts of violet-and-blue marble floors. The hotel has its own cabañas on a private beach. These are free, but you pay extra for umbrella and chair. You can arrange to lunch at the beach. The hotel has rakishly angled balconies and a sun terrace and café in front, near its unusually shaped outdoor pool.

Hotel Bellevue, piazzale Kennedy 12, 47037 Rimini (tel. 0541/54-116), is a pleasingly contemporary white-walled palace rising above a flowered park about a block from the sea, close to the center of town. Its comfortably furnished public rooms are filled with deep leather chairs, while the bedrooms are streamlined and often have a private balcony. A full range of sporting facilities is close at hand, and at night the piano bar on the premises is lively. Each unit has a color TV, modern bath, and direct-dial phone. Singles range from 110,000 lire ($83.50) daily; doubles, 180,000 lire ($137).

A Second-Class Selection

Aristeo, viale R. Elena 106, 47037 Rimini (tel. 0541/381-150), is a modern structure with private swimming pool, open all year. Its spacious bedrooms, each with a small private balcony overlooking the Adriatic, plus color TV and direct-dial phones, are equipped with private bath and utilitarian but comfortable furnishings. Even during the peak season (July and August), the rates are quite reasonable, at 52,000 lire ($39.50) to 70,000 lire ($53.25) daily for a single room, 62,000 lire ($47) to 88,000 lire ($66.75) for a double. During the rest of the year rates drop to 42,000 lire ($32) to 50,000 lire ($38) for a single and 42,000 lire ($32) to 68,000 lire ($51.75) for a double. Full board ranges from 42,000 lire ($32) to 64,000 lire ($48.75) per person daily, depending on the season and the room.

The Budget Class

Astra, viale Regina Elena 80, 47037 Rimini, (tel. 0541/21-264), was created for sun worshippers and lovers of the sea. Decked out with private balconies and a rooftop solarium, it enjoys an anchor spot right on the beachfront. Every room here is set for vacation action—simple, Italian modern, quite basic in fact, but with the required conveniences. All of the rooms have their own private shower. Full board costs from 35,000 lire ($26.50) per person daily. The hotel is open from May 20 to September 20.

Spiaggia Marconi, viale Regina Elena 100, 47037 Rimini (tel. 0541/380-368), is a good oceanfront choice—a fairly large (44-room) family-run elevator hotel. Facing the main boulevard, it has shady trees and a graveled terrace on one side, with its own bathing cabins on the seafront. Most of the bedrooms—furnished with utilitarian pieces—have a private shower. The peak-season (July and August) rate is 40,000 lire ($30.40) daily for singles, 80,000 lire ($60.75) for doubles, inclusive. Of course, if you check in off-season, or get one of the bathless rooms, the rates will be 20% cheaper. The family of Antonio Marconi may win your heart. Signora Marconi speaks English. She serves memorable meals, with abundant portions, including, on occasion, tender slices of sautéed veal with garden-fresh asparagus and a bowl of crisp salad greens, with two desserts to finish. The open-air modern living and dining room is enhanced with plenty of glass letting in the view of the sea. There's free parking. The hotel is open May to October.

RESTAURANTS IN RIMINI

If you ever escape from your hotel's board requirements, you'll find some good fish dishes from the Adriatic served at the city's limited number of fine restaurants. For the best of the lot, try one of the following recommendations.

Belvedere, Al Molo di Levante (tel. 50-178). Known throughout the resort for its fish, this airy restaurant is often completely filled with appreciative diners. Many of its tables look out over the water through big windows that flood the interior with light. The seafood antipasti is the preferred beginning, to be followed by spaghetti with seafood or a pungent risotto. Diners order as a main course a grilled fish based on the catch of the day. Full meals, costing from 45,000 lire ($34.25), are served between March and October, usually seven days a week from 12:30 to 3 p.m. and 7:30 to 10:30 p.m. (closes on Monday in their less busy seasons).

Taverna degli Artisti, viale Vespucci 1 (tel. 28-519), lies at the Parco dell' Indipendenza, and is a good center for dining if you are in the beach area. In summer it offers its dishes at sidewalk tables. Fish is king around here, and the chef always seems willing to fry you a batch of Adriatic delicacies. But pasta is also important. The kitchen has the widest selection of any restaurant in town, and, in season, you can order a plate of it from noon to 4 a.m. All the pasta dishes are cooked to order (not precooked, as they are in so many other places). The so-called new line of pasta dishes has proven to be most popular. They include spaghetti crudaiola (that is, spaghetti with a sauce of uncooked tomatoes, basil, parsley, black olives, tuna fish, pecorino cheese, anchovies, little red peppers, and olive oil), and garganelli (a homemade macaroni with a sauce of peperonata and ricotta cheese on top). In all, about 30 different types of pasta are served in addition to the regular menu. The restaurant charges 35,000 lire ($26.50) to 52,000 lire ($39.50) for a complete meal. It is closed on Wednesday in low season and regularly from mid-December until the first of the year.

3. Urbino

Go here for a look at the medieval. This ancient town, where Raphael was born and spent his boyhood, stands on a hill about 1,500 feet above sea level. Dominated by a ducal palace, the town is filled with streets both narrow and crooked. Urbino is similar to San Gimignano in that much hasn't changed since the 15th century. For the North American, it is somewhat off the beaten tourist path, although it lies just 44 miles from Rimini, a car ride that usually takes about 1½ hours.

In the main piazza of Urbino, a monument was erected in 1897 to honor its son, Raphael. This mellow old artistic city, bathed in a golden-yellow light, was once surrounded by walls, the outline of which can still be traced. Many old palaces which stood in the days when Urbino was plagued with Gothic wars are standing now.

The flowering of Urbino occurred during the era of Federico (1444–1482). As a patron of arts and letters the duke presided over a noble court, and under his patronage Urbino reached the zenith of its power and influence. His son, Guidobaldo, continued in his father's footsteps.

The Urbino telephone area code is 0722.

THE SIGHTS

A tour of the beautiful old town will take about two hours. The most important attraction is the **Palazzo Ducale,** housing the **Galleria Nazionale delle Marche,** at the piazza Duca Federico (tel. 27-60). It is generally open from 9 a.m. to 2 p.m. Monday through Saturday and 9 a.m. to 1 p.m. on Sunday. Admission is 4,000 lire ($3.05).

Erected by a Dalmatian architect, Luciano Laurana, in 1465–1482, the ducal palace is of harmonious design, a symphony of elegance. After admiring the palace, you take a grand staircase to the left (facing the building) which leads to the National Art Gallery in the apartments above. In addition to looking at pictures of the Renaissance, you can observe the palace's original decorations, including Montefeltro coats-of-arms, sculptured doorways, and friezes. After a large-scale restoration project, many of the paintings have been returned to their original luster (well, almost).

Less preferred are the works of the Counter-Reformation on the second floor. However, the ducal apartments contain some art of the Renaissance, notably a *Madonna* by Verrocchio. Uccello painted the *Profanation of the Host* beginning in 1465, a work that often appears in books on art history. The great artist Piero della Francesca, who wrote his celebrated book on the science of perspective in Urbino, left behind a *Madonna of Senigallia*. Seek out, in addition, his *Flagellation Scene*, as well as a *Gathering of the Apostles* by Just van Gand.

The most important painting in the collection is Raphael's *The Mute One*. It is the portrait of a "gentlewoman," her face, like *Mona Lisa*'s smile, usually called enigmatic by art historians. Painted in 1507, the picture now rests in a Plexiglas cage, having been stolen in 1975, one of the country's most sensational art thefts. However, it was found in good condition two years later and returned to Urbino.

The best for last: The ducal study is decorated with stunning inlays often attributed to Botticelli. They are mounted on panels depicting well-known men. Just van Gand painted some of the portraits.

While in Urbino, you can visit **Casa Natale di Raffaello,** Raphael's birthplace, at via Raffaello Sanzio 57. Its hours are 9 a.m. to 2 p.m. daily except Monday (to 1 p.m. on Sunday). Admission is 3,000 lire ($2.30). The building contains a small medieval shop and a 15th-century courtyard. On the second floor of the house is a museum with coins, books, and portraits.

If time remains, try to see, in addition, the **Oratorio di San Giovanni,** which is open daily from 10 a.m. to noon and 2:30 to 5 p.m. all year, charging an admission of 1,000 lire (75¢). In 1414 the brothers Lorenzo and Giacombo Salimbeni da San Severino frescoed the walls of the oratory with scenes from the life of John the Baptist. To reach the chapel from the piazza della Repubblica, head up via Barocci. The oratory will be on your left.

WHERE TO STAY

Sleekly and somewhat impersonally modern, the **Albergo Montefeltro,** via Pian Severo 2, 61029 Urbino (tel. 0722/328-324), nevertheless enjoys a panoramic perch, lying a short distance from the monumental heart of Urbino against a backdrop of dark-green hills. The place is well cared for, and the staff is cooperative. Rooms are comfortable and pleasantly maintained, a single renting for 42,000 lire ($32) daily; a double, 65,000 lire ($49.50). Units are equipped with private shower and toilet. In all, 65 rooms are offered, each with balcony and phone. The public lounges are ample, and the dining room serves both national and regional specialties. In addition to a popular bar, the Montefeltro also offers ample parking facilities.

Hotel Due Querce, via della Stazione 35-37, 61029 Urbino (tel. 0722/25-09), is a simple little place constructed against a backdrop of the hills of Montefeltro. Rooms are airy and spacious, containing private bath or shower for the most part. Singles range in price from 33,000 lire ($25) daily; doubles, 42,000 lire ($32). On nippy nights, a fireplace is kept burning in the lounge. Facilities include a bar as well as a terrace with a fine view.

WHERE TO DINE

Most visitors are in Urbino at lunchtime. If that is the case with you, the best place for dining is **Il Nuovo Coppiere,** via Porta Maja 20 (tel. 320-092), which offers tasty specialties of the Marche district. The management takes trouble to see that its food looks and tastes inviting and appetizing. The menu isn't expensive, but the kitchen uses good materials and cooks with no pretensions. For a complete meal, served from 12:30 to 2:30 p.m. and 7:30 to 10:30 p.m., expect to pay from 35,000 lire ($26.50). The restaurant shuts down on Wednesday and in February.

Ristorante Self-Service Franco, via di Poggio 1 (tel. 24-92), a block from the main entrance to the palace/museum, is a place where you can get good, wholesome meals for around 12,000 lire ($9). A lot of local people (Urbinati) eat here. The price includes a first course of soup or pasta, a second course of meat (beef, veal, or chicken) with vegetables, or excellent fish on Friday, as well as bread and wine. Hours are noon to 3 p.m. and 7 to 10 p.m. daily except Sunday.

4. San Marino

The world's oldest and smallest republic, San Marino is 14 miles from Rimini, reached either by autostrada in your own private car or by bus, which leaves frequently in front of the railway station in Rimini. Southern Europe's other peapod nations, Vatican City and Monaco, have less land space, but they aren't republics. San Marino may not have enough land for a decent crow's flight (24 square miles), but it isn't exactly bursting at the seams with population either.

San Marino, also the name of the capital, strides the top slopes of Mount Titano. The origins of San Marino go back to the 4th century A.D. Local tradition holds that Marino, a Dalmatian slave later made a saint, founded the republic. Except for Cesare Borgia's invasion in 1503, and periodic attempts to seize it, the state has enjoyed relative freedom. Napoleon passed this way, finding the nation "amusing," even benevolently offering it more territory. But the people wisely turned him down. Officially neutral in both world wars, San Marino suffered Allied bombs in World War II (for which Great Britain later paid an indemnity).

Of course, the adjective "sovereign" applied to San Marino shouldn't be interpreted too literally. Whenever a republic is small and completely surrounded by a larger nation, it can only exist at that nation's good grace. Unlike Monaco, San Marino does not have access to the sea (Rimini is its port). In the postwar years, when San Marino, in the grand tradition of Monaco, opened a gambling casino to attract much-needed revenue, the Italian government brought such pressure that the tiny republic was forced to abandon the operation and the badly needed lucre.

San Marino, instead, has been forced to rely almost entirely on visitors and postage stamps. Prized by collectors the world over, the postage stamps are sold in nearly every shop in San Marino.

On December 15, 1972, San Marino issued its first series of coins in 35 years. On orders from Mussolini, it had stopped minting coins in 1938, relying entirely on the use of Italian lire. Minted in Rome and even designed by an Italian sculptor, the new coins depict such scenes as Garibaldi and his wife, Anita, taking refuge in the little country after the collapse of the Roman republic in 1849.

The telephone area code for San Marino is 0541.

SIGHTS

The country is blessed with one superstar attraction: a view seen from one of its trio of medieval towers, Guaita, Cesta, and Montale. Among these specific sights to visit are—

Palazzo del Governo

In the center of town is this Gothic-Florentine-style building, erected toward the end of the 19th century. It's well worth a visit. In spring and autumn it's usually open daily from 8:30 a.m. to 12:45 p.m. and 2:45 to 7 p.m. From June 15 to September the government palace remains open from 8 a.m. to 8 p.m.; in August, to 11 p.m. Admission is 3,000 lire ($2.30), and this also entitles you to visit the fortress, the Arms Museum, the Museum of History, the picture gallery, and the Church of San Francesco.

Dominating San Marino is a **fortress** or castle that looms like a great ship in the sky. From one of its towers, you can see Rimini, the Adriatic, even the Dalmatian Coast (Yugoslavia).

The Arms Museum

At the top of another hill, also offering a splendid view, is this fairly routine museum filled with such medieval armaments as hatchets, used back in the days when people killed each other one at a time instead of en masse. Hours are the same as those of the Palazzo del Governo.

San Marino Basilica

This basilica looks like a first national bank, but it is graced by a splendid campanile to its side. When the bells sound, it's a wonder that San Marino doesn't wake up and flee. The interior is less austere, with a central nave and two aisles, adorned with Corinthian columns.

DINING IN SAN MARINO

Chances are you'll be more in need of a good restaurant than a good hotel, as most visitors hike through San Marino in a day, then strike out for another frontier by evening.

Righi-Ristorante La Taverna, piazza della Libertà (tel. 991-196), combines two attractive restaurants in different price ranges, both anchored to a site that looks over the valleys of the Apennine landscape. The upper room is a rustic and spacious inn, with provincial exposed brick, a deep fireplace, and dozens of tastefully arranged agrarian touches. The antipasti are especially appetizing, loaded onto a big central table. The establishment's policy of making all of its pasta "at home" has given several American apprentice chefs an extensive education in its subtleties. Specialties include scaloppini à la Righi (cooked in beer with celery and carrots), and many other typically Italian meat and vegetable dishes. Expect to pay around 35,000 lire ($26.50) for a full meal, wine not included.

With your dinner, why not order a bottle of Moscato, a characteristic wine of San Marino? Downstairs is a wine boutique, where you can sample a glass of many of the vintages before you buy. A few steps away, a ground-floor taverna is dotted with hunting trophies set proudly under coffered ceilings. A tourist menu is served here that offers good value for 25,000 lire ($19), including pasta, a main course, fruit, bread, and service. Tables from the taverna fill an area of the outdoor stone terrace in the summer, providing both indoor and outdoor dining. The establishment with all its extensions is closed on Wednesday in winter and the month of February. But it's open every day in summer. Hours are 12:30 to 2:30 p.m. and 7:30 to 9:30 p.m.

Buca di San Francesco, piazzetta Placito Feretrano 3 (tel. 991-462), is a basement restaurant at which guests arrive via a flight of weathered stone steps. On a hillside, just off a small square in the center of the old city, the restaurant's entrance is marked with a canopy and a view into the two stone-walled rooms flanked with a big zinc-capped bar. In summer, management sets outdoor tables onto the pavement outside, although many guests usually prefer the interior with its massive stonework. A specialty is a mixed roast plate of the house, which could be accompanied by a wide assortment of pasta and antipasti. These include lasagne, tortellini, and tagliatelle, a choice of six daily soups, grilled pork, veal dishes (scaloppine alla sammarinese with cheese and mushrooms and cutlet milanese or bolognese), and a selection of other typically Italian dishes. Meals range from 25,000 lire ($19) and are served daily from 12:30 to 2:30 p.m. and 7:30 to 9:30 p.m. The buca is open from March to October.

Ristorante Diamond, via XXV Marzo 72 (tel. 991-003), is a grotto dug out of rock and sheltered by a roughly hewn stone façade. The restaurant is divided into a stand-up bar, accented with a large porcelain bas-relief of a winged horse fighting a dragon, and a simple eating area set on a slightly lower level. In summer, wooden tables, picnic style, are placed outside, two steps from the throngs of milling tourists and the maze of souvenir shops packed into the narrow street. Food items include a large pasta menu, including tortellini, roast veal or chicken, veal cutlet milanese, and what is advertised as an English tea. Full meals are usually well prepared, ranging from 22,000 lire ($16.75) to 30,000 lire ($22.75). Service is daily from 12:30 to 2:30 p.m. and 7:30 to 9:30 p.m. Doubles in the adjacent five-room hotel rent for 50,000 lire ($38).

WHERE TO STAY

The clean and contemporary **Grand Hotel Marino,** viale Antonio Onofri 31, 47031 Repubblica di San Marino (tel. 0541/992-400), is on the serpentine hillside road leading up to the old city. Parking is on the premises, so it's a convenient way for a motorist to settle into San Marino before walking on to the nearby medieval section. The decor of the hotel includes polished marble floors and lots of light-grained paneling. Many of the comfortable rooms have panoramic views over the fertile valley below. Singles cost 60,000 lire ($45.50) daily; doubles, 75,000 lire ($57).

Hotel Titano, contrada del Collegio, 21, 47031 Repubblica di San Marino (tel. 0541/991-007), is a first-class hotel in the center of the old town. Views from its tile outdoor terrace encompass much of the surrounding countryside, as well as a few of the more monumental buildings of the city's core. The marble and parquet-floored interior is filled with soft colors and a combination of reproduction rococo and modern furniture. Motorists should park in city parking lot no. 5. The 50 comfortably furnished rooms rent for 56,500 lire ($43) daily in a single and 74,500 lire ($56.50) in a double. Full board is 93,000 lire ($70.75) in a single and 81,500 lire ($62) per person in a double. The hotel is open from March 15 to November 15.

VENICE

One rainy morning as I was leaving my hotel—a converted palazzo—a decorative stone fell from the lunette, narrowly missing me. For a second, it looked as if I was a candidate for the gondola funeral cortège to the island of marble tombs, San Michele. In dismay I looked back at the owner, a woman straight from a Modigliani portrait. From the doorway, she leaned like the Tower of Pisa, mocking the buildings of her city. Throwing up her hands, she sighed: "Venezia, Venezia," then turned and went inside.

Stoically, she had long ago surrendered to the inevitable decay that embraces Venice like moss at the base of the pilings. Venice is preposterous, a monument to both the folly and the obstinacy of man. It shouldn't exist . . . but it does, much to the delight of thousands upon thousands of tourists, gondoliers, lacemakers, hoteliers, restaurateurs, and glassblowers.

Fleeing the barbarians, Venetians centuries ago left drydock and drifted out to a flotilla of "uninhabitable" islands in the lagoon. Survival was difficult enough, but no Venetian has ever settled for mere survival. The remote ancestors of the present inhabitants created the world's most beautiful city.

However, to your children or their children, Venice may be a mirage of the past. It is sinking at a rate of about 2½ inches every decade. It is estimated that one-third of the city's art will have deteriorated hopelessly within the next decade or so if action is not taken to save it. Clearly Venice is in peril. One headline recently read, "The Enemy's at the Gates."

Working on a campaign to save Venice, John R. McDermott put the case this way: "Venice is under assault by uncontrolled tides, pollution, and old age. Atmospheric acid is eating away its art treasures—stone, bronze, and pigment—and the walls of its buildings are being eroded by floods; industrial waste is polluting its water. Unless these conditions are alleviated and repairs made, some of the loveliest art in the world will be lost forever and eventually the city itself could cease to exist as we know it now."

GETTING THERE

You can now fly from North America to Venice via Rome on Alitalia. Many more visitors arrive by train, which pulls into the Stazione di Santa Lucia. Travel time by train from Milan is 3½ hours; from Florence, 4 hours; and from Bologna, 2 hours. Venice also has autostrada links with the rest of Italy, with direct hookups with such cities as Trieste, Milan, and Bologna.

1. Orientation

Venice, lying 2½ miles from the Italian mainland and 1¼ miles from the open seas of the Adriatic, is an archipelago of some 117 islands. Most visitors, however, concern themselves only with the piazza San Marco and its vicinity. In fact, the entire city has only one "piazza," which is San Marco. Venice is divided into six quarters which local residents call "sestieri," including the most frequented, San Marco, but also Santa Croce, San Paolo, Castello, Cannaregio, and Dorsoduro, the last of which has been compared to New York's Greenwich Village.

Many of the so-called streets of Venice are actually canals, 150 in all. A canal is called a "rio," and a total of 400 bridges span these canals. If Venice has a main street, it is the Grand Canal, which is spanned by three bridges: the Rialto, the Academy Bridge, and the stone Railway Bridge, the last dating from the 20th century. The canal splits Venice into two unequal parts.

Get used to a lot of unfamiliar street designations. A street running alongside a canal is called a *fondamenta,* and major thoroughfares are known as *salizzada, ruga,* or a *calle larga.* But what is a *sottoportego?* That's a passageway beneath buildings. You'll often encounter the word "campo" when you come to an open-air area. That is a reference to the fact that such a place was once grassy, and cattle in days of yore grazed there.

Since you can't hail a taxi, at least not on land, what you do in Venice is walk. Walk and walk. People from North America who get in their cars to drive two blocks back home often find themselves walking for miles and miles in Venice. Of course, such walks can be broken up by vaporetti or boat rides.

Those arriving by plane will land at Mestre, with its Marco Polo Aeroporto. Boats depart directly from the airport, taking visitors to a terminal near the piazza San Marco. It's less expensive to take a bus from the airport, a trip of less than five miles. You cross the Ponte della Libertà to the Stazione Santa Lucia, the railway station of Venice where even more visitors arrive. You will be at the piazzale Roma, where you can make transportation connections (see below) to most parts of Venice, including the Lido. It is at this point that first-time visitors encounter the Canal Grande or Grand Canal, a channel leading to the Canale di San Marco, which itself heads directly to the Adriatic.

South of a section of Venice called Dorsoduro, which is south of the Grand Canal, is another major channel, Canale della Giudecca. That separates Dorsoduro from the large island of La Giudecca. At the point where Canale della Giudecca flows into the Canale di San Marco, you'll spot the little Isola di San Giorgio Maggiore, with its church by Palladio. The most visited islands in the lagoon, aside from the Lido, are Murano of glass-making fame, Burano, and Torcello, each of which we'll visit in due course.

Once you land and explore the piazza San Marco and its satellite, the piazzetta San Marco, you can head down Riva degli Schiavoni, with its deluxe and first-class hotels, or else follow the signs along the Mercerie, the major shopping artery of Venice, leading to the Rialto, site of the market area.

But with all the directions in the world, with all the signposts and maps, know that the best thing for an explorer in Venice is to get lost.

ARRIVAL IN VENICE

All roads lead not necessarily to Rome but in this case to the docks on the mainland of Venice. The arrival scene at the unattractive piazzale Roma is filled with nervous expectation, and even the most veteran traveler can become confused. Whether you arrive by train, bus, auto, or airport limousine, there is one common denominator—everyone walks to the nearby docks to select a method of transport to his or her hotel. The cheapest way is by vaporetto, the more expensive by gondola or motor launch.

Car Parks

If you arrive in Venice by auto, there is a multitiered car park near the vaporetti, gondola, and motor-launch docks. You'll find it at the end of the road on your transportation to your hotel. You'll be charged 20,000 lire ($15.25) to 31,000 lire ($23.50) per day, depending on the size of your car. However, I must warn you that from spring to fall this municipal car park is nearly always filled, and often people have to park great distances away at Mestre. However, there is one method that always seems to work, even when the dispatchers assure you that there is "not one spot left." Offer a bribe! It usually helps get you parked.

Porters

Another tricky problem. If you need help with your luggage to reach a remote accommodation tucked into the inner regions of Venice, the chances are that you'll be dependent on the Venetian porter. The porter can carry your luggage aboard the vaporetto or water taxi (you pay his boat fare), then lead you through the winding narrow streets until he reaches your hotel. In this capacity, he'll double as a guide, eliminating the need to pore over tiny lettering on a map.

Between two points in the city, give the porter 7,700 lire ($5.85) for one or two pieces of luggage and 2,150 lire ($1.65) for each additional piece. If your hotel lies near one of the public vaporetto stops, you can sometimes struggle with your own luggage until you reach the hostelry's reception area. In any event, the one time-tested rule for Venice-bound travelers is that excess baggage is bad news, unless you are willing to pay dearly to have it carried for you.

The rates started here are the official fees for porters, but they are valid only at the time of this writing and will surely go up in the lifetime of this edition. If, however, a porter thinks you're unaware of the city's official guidelines, he may try to charge you more—sometimes *much* more. Protests mean little to these battle-toughened veterans who have stood off the most robust of visitors in sirocco winds under the blazing August sun.

Vaporetti

Much to the chagrin of the once-ubiquitous gondolier, the motorboats of Venice provide inexpensive, frequent, if not always fast transportation in the canal-riddled city. The average fare on the *accelerato* (which makes every stop) is 1,700 lire ($1.30), which will take you from St. Mark's to the Lido. The average fare on the *diretto* (only express stops) is 2,500 lire ($1.90)—say, from the railway station to the Rialto Bridge. Visitors to Venice may avail themselves of an 8,000-lira ($6.10) ticket which allows them to travel all day long on any of the many routes of the city's boat services. This all-inclusive ticket is a bargain. In summer, these vaporetti are often fiercely crowded.

Water Taxi—Motor Launch

It costs more than the public vaporetto, but you won't be hasseled as much when you arrive with your luggage if you hire one of the city's many private motor launches. You may or may not have the cabin of one of these sleek vessels to yourself, since the captains fill their boats with as many passengers as the law allows before taking off. Your porter will have an uncanny radar for showing you to one of the inconspicuous piers where a water taxi waits.

You always have to negotiate the fare before getting in. The sailors seem to follow in the footsteps of the most cunning of doges. To their credit, the captains of Venice's motor launches are usually adroit about depositing you with your luggage at the canalside entrance to your hotel or on one of the city's smaller waterways, which lies within a short walking distance of your destination.

Gondolas and Gondoliers

In *Death in Venice,* Thomas Mann wrote: "Is there anyone but must repress a secret thrill, on arriving in Venice for the first time—or returning thither after long absence—and stepping into a Venetian gondola? That singular conveyance, come down unchanged from ballad times, black as nothing else on earth except a coffin— what pictures it calls up of lawless, silent adventures in the plashing night; or even more, what visions of death itself, the bier and solemn rites and last soundless voyage!"

Mann reflected the point of view of German romanticism, but he didn't tell all the story. The voyage on a gondola isn't likely to be so "soundless"—at least not when time comes to pay the bill. When riding in a gondola, two major agreements have to be reached: (1) the price of the ride; (2) the length of the trip. If you vaguely suggest in any way one of Barnum's suckers, you're likely to be taken on both counts. It's a common sight in Venice to see a gondolier huffing and puffing to take his passengers on a "quickie," often reducing the hour to 15 minutes. The gondolier, with his eye on his watch, is anxious to dump his load and pick up the next batch of passengers. Consequently, his watch almost invariably runs fast.

There is an accepted official rate schedule for gondoliers, but I've never known anyone to honor it. The actual fare depends on how effective you are in standing up to the gondolier's attempt to get more money out of you. Many visitors hire a gondolier for anywhere from 65,000 lire ($49.50) up—emphasis on the *up*—per 50 minutes. In fairness to the gondoliers, it must be said that they have an awful job, romanticized out of perspective by the world. For they must row boatloads of tourists across hot, smelly canals with such endearments screamed at them as "No sing! No pay!" And these fellows must make plenty of lire while the sun shines, as their work ends when the first cold winds blow in from the Adriatic.

A Last Comment

It may seem that excessive attention is devoted here to porters, water taxis, vaporetti, and gondoliers, but I've seen too many visits to Venice marred by a hassle that dampens the tourist's enthusiasm for the city at the outset. Providing you can overcome the problem of getting yourself and your luggage transported safely— and without fisticuffs—to your hotel, you'll probably be set to embark on one of the grandest experiences of a lifetime: the exploration of Venice.

OTHER TRANSPORTATION INFORMATION

If you need to find out about flight arrivals or departures at **Marco Polo Airport,** call 661-111.

Buses leave for points on the mainland of Italy from the piazzale Roma.

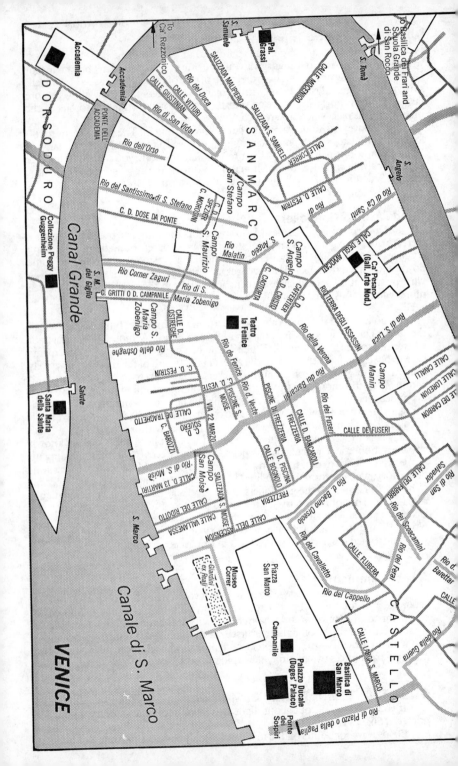

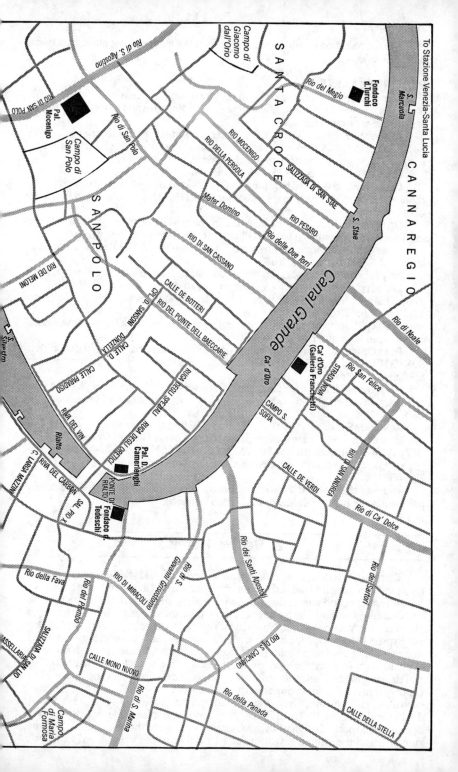

The **train station** is called Santa Lucia. For information about rail connections, dial 715-555.

PRACTICAL FACTS

Some questions that may come to mind will have been answered in the ABCs section in Chapter II. However, for some specific Venetian addresses, read on. The **telephone area code** for Venice is 041.

American Express: The office of American Express in Venice is at San Mosè 1471 (tel. 520-0844), in the San Marco area. City tours and mail handling (provided you are a customer) can be obtained here.

Consulate: There is no U.S. Consul in Venice.

Currency Exchange: There are many banks in Venice where you can exchange money. For example, try the **Banca d'America e d'Italia,** San Marco 2216 (tel. 520-0766).

Drugstore: If you need a drugstore in the middle of the night, call 192 for information about one that is open. Pharmacies take turns staying open late.

Emergencies: Phone numbers are: 113 for **police;** 523-0000 for an **ambulance;** 522-2222 to report a **fire.**

Helpful Phone Numbers: To check on the time, call 161; for the weather, 191.

Laundry: For laundering clothes, try **Lavaget,** Cannaregio 1269 (tel. 715-976), at Ponte della Guglie. It is open Monday through Friday from 8:30 a.m. to 12:30 p.m. and 3 to 7 p.m.

Medical Care: For a hospital, get in touch with the **Civili Riunti di Venezia,** campo Santi Giovanni e Paolo (tel. 520-5622).

Post Office: In Venice, the major post office is at Fondaco dei Tedeschi (tel. 528-9317), in the vicinity of the Rialto Bridge. It is open daily except Sunday from 8:30 a.m. to 7 p.m.

The post office also maintains a **telegram** service 24 hours a day. You can also call Italcable at 170, if you wish to send an international telegram. Otherwise, call 186.

Religious Services: If you're Catholic, you'll find churches all over Venice (you can hardly miss one). There is a Jewish **synagogue** in the Ghetto Vecchio (tel. 715-012). A **Methodist** church is at Santa Maria Gormosa 5170 (tel. 522-7549); an **Anglican (Episcopal)** church, St. George's, in Dorsoduro at campo San Vio 870 (tel. 520-0571).

Tourist Information: Visitors can receive information at the **Ente Provinciale per il Turismo,** piazza San Marco 71C (tel. 522-6356).

---

2. Deluxe Hotels

Cipriani, isola della Giudecca, 30133 Venezia (tel. 041/520-7744), is a select resort villa on a small island across from the piazza San Marco. It was conceived as a private residence and guesthouse emphasizing personal comfort, the creation of the late Giuseppe Cipriani, the founder of Harry's Bar and the one real-life character in Hemingway's Venetian novel. Nowadays it's owned and run by Venice Simplon Orient Express Hotels. Opened in 1958, it's the only hotel in Venice with an Olympic-size swimming pool, and there are also tennis and sauna. There's even an exclusive Sea Gull Club, reserved for hotel guests. In the evening, an orchestra plays for informal dancing in the Gabbiano grill-bar, or on terraces overlooking the lagoon. The Cipriani prides itself on serving an authentic Venetian cuisine. Rooms have different exposures, facilities, and sizes. A single ranges from 505,000 lire ($384) daily. A double begins at 750,000 lire ($570). The rooms have splendid views, either of the lagoon to the south, the Palladian San Giorgio Maggiore to the east and north, or the vineyards and the domed Redentore and Le Zitelle to the west. A private launch service ferries guests, at any hour, to and from the hotel's own pier and the piazza San Marco. The hotel accepts guests, who have ranged from Margaret Thatcher to Barbra Streisand, from mid-March to November.

Gritti Palace, campo Santa Maria del Giglio 2467, 30124 Venezia (tel. 041/ 794-611), is a stately setting on the Grand Canal, a renovated palazzo of the 15th-century doge Andrea Gritti. "Our home in Venice" to Ernest Hemingway, it has for years drawn a select clientele of some of the world's greatest theatrical, literary, political, and royal figures, including Queen Elizabeth and Prince Philip, Greta Garbo, Herbert von Karajan, and Winston Churchill. The Gritti has 100 rooms, all air-conditioned and containing private baths. The range and variety seem almost limitless, from elaborate suites to relatively small single rooms. But in every cast, the stamp of glamour is evident. Antiques are often used in both the bedrooms and public rooms. For splurge living, ask for Hemingway's old suite or the Doge Suite once occupied by W. Somerset Maugham. The management is used to catering to the whims of the famous, but it doesn't overlook the needs and desires of first-timers. The Gritti charges a peak-season 450,000 lire ($342) daily for a single, 655,000 lire ($498) for a double.

The cuisine served here is among the best in Venice. At Ristorante Club del Doge, an intimate room whose size is more than doubled in summer when tables are placed on a platform standing over the canal, meals are served daily from 12:30 to 2:30 p.m. and 7:30 to 11:30 p.m. The cuisine is mainly Mediterranean. Expect to spend from 100,000 lire ($76) per person for a meal.

Danieli Royal Excelsior, riva degli Schiavoni 4196, 30122 Venezia (tel. 041/ 522-6480), was built as a grand showcase by the Doge Dandolo in the 14th century. In 1822 it was transformed into a deluxe "hotel for kings." Placed in a most spectacular position, right on the Grand Canal, it has sheltered not only kings, but princes, cardinals, ambassadors, and such literary figures as George Sand and her 24-year-old lover, Alfred de Musset. In time the palace was to play host to such men as Charles Dickens, D'Annunzio, and Wagner. The palace fronts the canal with the New Danieli Excelsior, a modern wing. Two neighboring palaces as well have been incorporated into this *serenissima* ensemble.

You enter into a four-story-high stairwell, with Venetian arches and balustrades. Throughout you wander in an atmosphere of silk-flocked walls, gilt mirrors, ornate furnishings, marble walls, decorated ceilings, and Oriental carpeting. Even the balconies opening off the main lounge have been illuminated by stained-glass skylights. More intimate is the beamed-ceiling drinking lounge, with leather armchairs. The hotel possesses a rooftop dining room, giving you an undisturbed view of the canals and "crowns" of Venice. The bedrooms, 231 in all, range widely in price, dimension, decor, and vistas, with the ones opening onto the lagoon going for more, of course. Doubles cost 515,300 lire ($392) to 571,200 lire ($434) daily, the latter price for those facing the canal. Singles rent for 358,800 lire ($273) to 394,500 lire ($300). The service charge is included in the price, as is a continental breakfast.

Hotel Bauer Grünwald & Grand Hotel, campo San Mosè 1459, 30124 Venezia (tel. 041/523-1520), combines an ornate 13th-century palazzo facing the Grand Canal with a massive concrete wing that was the talk of Venice when it was built back in the '60s. The entrance is a huge rectangular room with an elegant decor of warm colors and gilt trim. Bedrooms range from the opulently antique—fit for a Medici—to more conservatively decorated units in the newer section. A canalside terrace is dotted with striped gondola tie-ups and a baroque statue of a torch-bearing Amazon jutting out from the corner. In summer the Settimo Cielo roof garden is ideal for dancing to music under a Venetian moon. Rooms, rather spacious for the most part, rent for 200,000 lire ($152) to 250,000 lire ($190) daily in a single and 270,000 lire ($205) to 390,000 lire ($296) for a double, with a continental breakfast included. Prices vary widely with the seasons.

Hotel Monaco & Grand Canal, calle Vallaresso 1325, 30124 Venezia (tel.

041/520-0211), is intimate and refined, capturing the essence of Venice with its breathtaking view of the Grand Canal. Harry's Bar is right across from the hotel, which used to be the Palazzo Erizzo-Vallaresso, dating back to the 18th century. It has been a hotel for more than 100 years. In high season, a twin-bedded room with bath rents for 360,000 lire ($274) daily; a single goes for 230,000 lire ($175). The hotel harbors one of the city's leading restaurants, named for the Grand Canal, where you can partake of Venetian specialties of highest quality, coupled with impeccable service and a panorama. In season, meals are also served on the terrace along the canal. This five-star hostelry is a favorite with discriminating Italians, particularly in the fall and winter seasons. It was the choice place in Venice of Simone de Beauvoir and Jean-Paul Sartre. More recently, Prince Rainier has stayed here as well.

Londra Palace, riva degli Schiavoni 4171, 30122 Venezia (tel. 041/520-0533), is an elegant hotel with 100 windows on the Venetian lagoon, formed by two palaces that were joined together about 80 years ago, a few yards from St. Mark's Square. The hotel's arguably most famous patron was Tchaikovsky, who wrote his Fourth Symphony in room 108 in December 1877. He also composed several other works here. The cozy reading room off the main lobby is decorated like a section of an English club, with leaded windows and blowups of some of Tchaikovsky's sheet music set into frames along the paneled walls. Other public rooms contain modern paintings, some showing an apocalyptic end by drowning of Venice. The hotel also has a popular piano bar and an excellent restaurant, Les Deux Lions, recommended below. The 70 bedrooms rent for 206,000 lire ($157) to 418,000 lire ($318) daily for a twin or double, 132,000 lire ($100) to 254,000 lire ($193) in a single. A continental breakfast is included in all tariffs. Vaporetto stop: San Zaccaria.

---

3. Other Top Hotels

NEAR THE PIAZZA SAN MARCO

A longtime favorite on the Grand Canal is **Hotel Europa & Regina,** via XXII Marzo 2159, 30124 Venezia (tel. 041/520-0477), reached by motorboat at its canal side or through a courtyard on via XXII Marzo. The hotel was formed by combining two Venetian palaces, both facing the Grand Canal and the Church of La Salute, with a restaurant terrace and a café terrace between them. This five-star deluxe hotel contains 189 accommodations, the majority of which offer canal views. They are beautifully furnished, with varying decor. Singles cost 150,000 lire ($114) to 210,000 lire ($160) daily; doubles, 250,000 lire ($190) to 330,000 lire ($251). The terrace restaurant serves meals averaging 70,000 lire ($53.25).

Gabrielli-Sandwirth, riva degli Schiavoni 4110, 30122 Venezia (tel. 041/523-1580), was originally built in 1238 as a Venetian-Gothic palace, but today its peach-colored stone and stucco façade stands a few paces from some of the most expensive and glamorous hotels in Venice. Later in its history, a duet of medieval houses were joined together to its high-ceilinged core to form a labyrinth of interior courtyards, rambling hallways, and a total of 115 tastefully conservative bedrooms. Each of these rooms has a private bath and phone, renting for 250,000 lire ($190) to 350,000 lire ($266) daily in a double or twin, 160,000 lire ($122) to 215,000 lire ($163) in a single, with breakfast included. This is the only hotel on the riva degli Schiavoni with its own garden, an idyllic enclave banked on one side by a canal, with espaliered roses, palm trees, and lattice-supported vines. From the panoramic rooftop sun terrace, a handful of chairs and dozens of flowering pots accent views of the Grand Canal and the Venetian lagoon such as Guardi might have painted. The dining room, outfitted in a turn-of-the-century art nouveau style, contains three of the most beautiful Murano chandeliers in Venice. Public rooms in the hotel have beamed ceilings and a marble-covered charm.

Saturnia-Internazionale, via XXII Marzo 2399, 30124 Venezia (tel. 041/520-8377), is a 14th-century Venetian palazzo near piazza San Marco, part and parcel of old Venice. Wherever you wander throughout this palace, you'll find richly embellished beauty—the grand hallway with its wooden staircase, heavy iron chandeliers, fine paintings, beamed ceiling; the dining salon with its more rustic decor, including regal chairs and pillars of bricks; or the more intimate dining gallery in a nautical theme. The air-conditioned bedrooms are spacious, furnished with chandeliers and Venetian antiques and enriched with tapestry rugs, gilt mirrors, and ornately carved ceilings. Many of these bedrooms overlook the quiet and dignified garden in the back. The cost of staying here varies according to the season. All of the hotel's 95 bedrooms have private bath. Singles in high season (mid-March to the end of October) cost 220,000 lire ($167) daily; doubles, 330,000 lire ($251). Rates are inclusive of a buffet breakfast, taxes, and service. The cuisine is excellent.

Hotel Luna, calle dell' Ascensione 1243, 30124 Venezia (tel. 041/528-9840), is the oldest hotel in Venice. Founded in 1474 as a monastery by the Congrega di Fratti della Luna, it took in traveling pilgrims on their way through Venice. The tradition of hospitality remains for the thousands of visitors who have found a room at this comfortable hotel near the piazza San Marco. Some of the rooms look over the Grand Canal, and most of them have high ceilings, renovated interiors, marble floors, air conditioning, and parquet floors. Flowers are in the hallways of the upper floors, which can be reached by elevator or by a wide marble staircase. Singles range from 230,000 lire ($175) daily and doubles begin at 370,000 lire ($281). Vaporetto stop: San Marco.

AT RIVA DEGLI SCHIAVONI

At the widest part of the Grand Canal is the **Hotel Metropole,** riva degli Schiavoni 4149, 30122 Venezia (tel. 041/520-5044), once a house with a small musical chapel where Antonio Vivaldi taught and composed music from 1703 to 1740 and the study where he composed *The Four Seasons* concerto suite, now the hotel lounge. An easy walk from the piazza San Marco, this hotel is in a four-story building with green shutters, white trim, and a buff-colored stone façade. As you cross over the red-and-white checkerboard of the lobby's marble floor, you'll pass beneath a red-and-gold depiction of the lion of St. Mark attached to the ceiling.

This is a good hotel, dotted with unusual detailing and craftsmanship and filled with lots of antiques and personal touches. A bar and snackbar with a zodiac theme lies just off the lobby. The hotel has an attractive sitting room and even a boat landing has a side canal for water taxi and gondola embarkations. Built at the beginning of the 17th century, the premises were used as a private residence, then as a military hospital, and finally, in 1909, as a hotel. Totally renovated in 1985, the 64 bedrooms are filled with elegantly conservative furniture, Venetian glass chandeliers, painted headboards, and marble baths. Many of the accommodations overlook either the lagoon, one of the lesser canals leading into it, or a Venetian garden. Singles rent for 135,000 lire ($103) to 225,000 lire ($171) daily, while doubles range from 175,000 lire ($133) to 325,000 lire ($247). Prices vary with the accommodation and the season, although breakfast is included in the price. Vaporetto stop: San Zaccaria.

4. Medium-Priced Hotels

NEAR PIAZZA SAN MARCO

Filled with the accumulated charm of its 800-year history, the elegant **Hotel Cavaletto e Doge Orseolo,** calle del Cavaletto 1107, 30124 Venezia (tel. 041/520-0955), occupies a prime position a few paces from St. Mark's Square. It lies on a narrow cobblestone street between the arched footbridge and an unused baroque church in one of the most historic sections of Venice. The hotel was created by ancestors of its sophisticated owner, Eduardo Mario Masprone, when a trio of buildings was unified into one rambling and well-managed unit in the early 1900s. In the 1100s the oldest of the three was the private home of one of the most famous of the early Venetian patriarchs, Doge Orseolo, who, according to plaques on the front, "was esteemed by Caesars of the East and West." The family trees and names of other doges connected with the site are proudly displayed in some of the bedrooms. In the 1300s, part of what is now the hotel served as one of the city's first taverns.

Today the Cavaletto is best viewed from its sinuously curved rear, where a flotilla of moored gondolas use a stone-sided harbor, one of only two such basins in Venice. A quartet of well-trained concierges seem to have the client's interests at heart. From a position in the airily comfortable lounge, a metal plaque indicates the position, about three feet off the floor, of the high-water flood mark in the 1960s. The hotel also has a big-windowed restaurant, with reflected sunlight from the lagoon dappling the high ceiling. Excellent meals of a high international standard are served here for 65,000 lire ($49.50). There's also a kind of *dolce vita* bar where a relaxing cocktail might be the perfect end to a day. Each of the hotel's 81 bedrooms is comfortably outfitted with glass chandeliers from nearby Murano, hardwood floors, and elegantly Italian-inspired furniture. Rooms contain a private bath, air conditioning, phone, TV, and radio. Many have views of canals and ancient stones. Singles cost 175,000 lire ($133) daily, and doubles peak at 295,000 lire ($224), with a continental breakfast included.

Hotel La Fenice et des Artistes, campiello de la Fenice 1936, 30124 Venezia (tel. 041/523-2333), offers widely varying accommodations in two buildings. One building is rather romantic in decor, with an architecturally rich staircase leading to beautifully decorated bedrooms (one accommodation was once described as "straight out of the last act of *La Traviata,* enhanced by small gardens and terraces"). Your satin-lined room may have an inlaid desk and a wardrobe painted in the Venetian manner to match a baroque bed frame. Capping the decor are velvet bedcovers, gilt mirrors, and crystal chandeliers. Other chambers are far less glamorous. Both buildings that comprise the hotel are at least 100 years old, and are connected at lobby level. The older of the two has no elevator, and while the newer has an elevator, its modern bedrooms have conservative, rather sterile furniture. These more contemporary rooms meet with little favor from readers, so your reaction to this hotel will depend entirely on your room assignment. Singles range from 97,000 lire ($73.75) to 112,000 lire ($85) daily, and doubles range from 140,000 lire ($106) to 150,000 lire ($114). Some more expensive suites are available. This hotel, one of the most famous in Venice, occupies a desirable location behind the opera house. The vaporetto stop is no. 15 (San Marco).

Hotel Flora, via XXII Marzo 2283A, 30124 Venezia (tel. 041/520-5044), has a jewel setting, right in the full swing of Venetian life, yet set back on a narrow lane in a peaceful garden overlooking the so-called Palazzo of Othello. The little hotel (44 rooms) has its own central patio garden with a graveled terrace and pots of rambling blossoming vines and plants. Some rooms overlook either of these gardens. The hotel is run by an old Venetian family, the Romanellis. Some of the rooms have Oriental rugs on terrazzo floors, furniture subtly colored in the Venetian fashion, desks, armchairs, and private bath or shower. Singles with bath go for 113,000 lire ($86) daily. Bathless doubles cost 132,000 lire ($100); doubles with bath, 171,000 lire ($130). No board terms are offered, although arrangements can be made for you to take your meals at two nearby restaurants. Some of the rooms are quite small and cramped, and whether or not you like this hotel depends on the room you're assigned.

Bonvecchiati, calle Goldoni 4488, 30100 Venezia (tel. 041/528-5017), halfway between the Rialto Bridge and the piazza San Marco, stands proudly on its little square, looking much like the private villa of a titled Venetian family. The owner,

Giovanni Deana, is a noted collector of modern art. Paintings acquired by him are in most of the lounge halls, corridors, living rooms, even gracing some of the bedrooms. Most of the units are furnished with antiques or good reproductions, and all have bath or shower. A single rents for 109,000 lire ($82.75) daily, and a double goes for 165,000 lire ($125). The full-board rate ranges from 127,000 lire ($96.50) to 180,000 lire ($137) per person daily, depending on the season. The interior dining room—all in white and ivory, with fluted columns and a central crystal chandelier—has a balcony for overflow dining. But the favored spot for meals is the outside canopied terrace, bordering the canal and decorated with potted plants, lanterns, and garden furniture. The drinking bar is warmed by a collection of copper pots hanging from the beamed ceiling. The lounges are more like personalized living rooms, with paintings and Turkish carpets.

Hotel Panada, calle dei Specchieri 646, 30124 Venezia (tel. 041/520-9088), lies along a narrow street a few steps from St. Mark's Square. Its 1981 renovation transformed a run-down 19th-century hotel into a clean and bright air-conditioned enclave with red-and-white marble floors, a charming bar, and 46 cozy bedrooms. Each of these offers a tile bath, a phone, gilt-framed mirrors, and Venetian furniture painted with pastel-colored landscapes of flower arrangements. Singles cost from 115,000 lire ($87.50) daily, and doubles begin at 180,000 lire ($137), with breakfast included.

Boston Hotel, Ponte dei Dai 848, 30124 Venezia (tel. 041/528-7665), is a 50-room hotel, built in 1962, just a whisper away from St. Mark's. Open from mid-March through October, it's run by an attractive couple, Mario and Adriana Bernardi, who have instilled their good taste here. The hotel was named after an uncle who left to seek his fortune in Boston . . . and never returned. The little living rooms combine the old and the new, containing many antiques and Venetian ceilings. For the skinny guest, there's a tiny, self-operating elevator and a postage-stamp-sized street entrance. Most of the bedrooms with parquet floors have built-in features, snugly designed beds, chests, and wardrobes. Fortunately, several have tiny balconies opening onto canals. For the rooms with a private bath or shower, the single rate is 100,000 lire ($76) daily; the double rate, 160,000 lire ($122). A continental breakfast is included in the tariffs quoted.

Hotel Concordia, calle Larga San Marco 367, 30124 Venezia (tel. 041/520-6866), is the only hotel in Venice that contains rooms looking out over St. Mark's Square. Completely renovated, the century-old hotel, now a winning four-star choice, is housed in a centrally air-conditioned, five-story russet-colored building with stone-trimmed windows. The name of the hotel is spelled out in mosaics just below your feet as you enter. A series of gold-plated marble steps takes you to the lobby. There, you'll find a comfortable bar area, friendly service, and elevators to whisk you to the labyrinthine corridors upstairs. All 55 bedrooms are in Venetian antique style and have phones, radios, color TVs, electronic safes, and mini-bars, plus private baths/showers and hairdryers. Depending on the season and the quality of the room, singles rent for 100,000 lire ($76) to 160,000 lire ($122) daily, and doubles or twins go for 140,000 lire ($106) to 280,000 lire ($213). Tariffs include a continental breakfast.

Savoia & Jolanda, riva degli Schiavoni 4187, 30122 Venezia (tel. 041/524-4130), is in a prize position on Venice's main street, with a lagoon as its front yard. Most of the bedrooms—56 in all—have a view of the boats and the Lido. While its exterior has much of old Venice to win you, the interior is somewhat spiritless. But the staff makes life here comfortable and relaxed. The bedrooms are neutral modern, with plenty of space for daytime living (desk and armchairs). Most of them have a private bath, for which singles pay 110,000 lire ($83.50) daily; doubles, 165,000 lire ($125). Rates quoted are charged in peak season.

Giorgione, SS. Apostoli 4587, 30001 Venezia (tel. 041/522-5810), is a glamorized little hotel near the Ca' d'Oro vaporetto stop. In spite of its modernization, its decor is traditionally Venetian. The lounges and dining rooms are equipped with fine furnishings and decorative accessories. Likewise, the bedrooms are designed to coddle guests, being very comfortable as well as stylish. Singles with bath peak at 115,000 lire ($87.50) daily, and doubles go for 175,000 lire ($133), all tariffs including breakfast, taxes, and service. The owner hawkeyes the running of the dining room, seeing that the cuisine is first-rate. The hotel also has a typical Venetian garden. It's rated second class by the government, but the Giorgione has a higher standard than many of the first-class establishments.

Hotel Carpaccio, San Tomà 2765, 30125 Venezia (tel. 041/523-5946). Don't be put off by the narrow, winding alleyways leading up to the wrought-iron entrance of this second-class hotel. The building was meant to be approached by gondola. Once you're inside, you'll realize that your location in the heart of the oldest part of the city justifies your confusing arrival. This building used to be the Palazzo Barbarigo della Terrazza, and part of it is still reserved for private apartments. Owner Guido Tassotto, who studied in London, maintains 20 tasteful and spacious rooms filled with serviceable furniture. The salon is decorated with gracious pieces, marble floors, and a big arched window whose exterior is crowned with a bearded head of stone looking, along with you, over the Grand Canal. The hotel is closed in winter, but at other times singles rent for 71,000 lire ($54) to 110,000 lire ($83.50) daily, depending on whether or not the unit has a bath. Doubles cost 127,000 lire ($96.50) to 171,000 lire ($130), the latter price for a room with bath. Bathless triples rent for 167,000 lire ($127), and triples with bath go for 222,000 lire ($169). Breakfast, the only meal served, is included in the rates. Vaporetto stop: San Tomà.

Hotel Montecarlo, calle dei Specchieri 463, 30124 Venezia (tel. 041/520-7144), only a two-minute walk from St. Mark's Square, was established some years ago in a 17th-century building. It was recently renovated to include modern baths. Your walk to your bedroom leads through upper hallways lined with paintings by Venetian artists. The double rooms are comfortably proportioned and decorated with functional furniture; however, the handful of singles are very, very small. Venetian glass chandeliers in the rooms add a festive note, and each unit has a private bath, phone, TV, and for an extra charge, air conditioning. Singles cost from 116,000 lire ($88.25) daily, doubles start at 171,000 lire ($130), with breakfast included.

Hotel Kette, piscina San Mosè 2053, 30124 Venezia (tel. 041/520-7766), lies a five-minute walk from St. Mark's Square. You'll be welcomed inside by a pleasant receptionist, and will find a decor of copies of Victorian armchairs, Oriental carpets, and a pair of cast-iron columns flanking the stairwell. Each of the compact bedrooms contains air conditioning, a private bath, color TV, direct-dial phone, electronic safe, and a hairdryer. The 54 units rent in high season for 115,000 lire ($87.50) daily in a single, 180,000 lire ($137) in a double, with low-season rates quoted at 70,000 lire ($53.25) for a single and 100,000 lire ($76) for a double. Prices include a continental breakfast.

Hotel Bel Sito, campo Santa Maria del Giglio 2517, 30124 Venezia (tel. 041/522-3365), near the Gritti Palace Hotel, is considered one of the finest small hotels of Venice. It sits behind a baroque façade with green shutters and a view of the elaborately decorated church of Santa Maria del Giglio. There's no elevator, so guests walk to the upper floors (four in all) for access to the 33 bedrooms, all of which have private baths or showers and are air-conditioned. No meals are served other than breakfast, which is included in the price of a room. Singles cost from 106,800 lire ($81.25) daily; doubles, from 158,500 lire ($120); and a three-bedded room, from 205,000 lire ($156). Vaporetto stop: Santa Maria del Giglio.

Hotel San Cassiano Ca' Favretto, calle della Rosa 2232, 30145 Venezia (tel. 041/524-1768), used to be the studio of the 19th-century painter Giacomo Favretto. The views from the hotel's gondola pier and from the four-arched porch of the dining room encompass the lacy façade of the Ca' d'Oro, which is sometimes considered the most beautiful building in Venice. The hotel was constructed in the 14th century as a palace. Giancarlo Manao, who purchased the property in 1978, worked closely with Venetian authorities to preserve the original details, which include a 20-foot beamed ceiling in the entrance area. Today the architectural plans from the many renovations hang in gilt frames above the antiques in the lobby. Patrons have included George McGovern and guests of the American Embassy. Fifteen of the 35 conservatively decorated rooms overlook one of two canals, and many of them are filled with antiques or high-quality reproductions. Singles begin at 115,000 lire ($87.50) daily, and doubles, at 175,000 lire ($133), with a continental breakfast included. Each unit contains a radio, mini-bar, TV, and air conditioning. Vaporetto stop: San Stae.

Hotel Casanova, Frezzeria 1285, 30124 Venezia (tel. 041/520-6855), a few steps from the piazza San Marco, was a former private home. Today transformed into a hotel, it contains 45 bedrooms and an elegant collection of church art and benches from old monasteries. These sit on flagstone floors near oil portraits. The reception manager will give you your key to a modernized bedroom with comfortably contemporary furnishings and TV. Singles cost 90,000 lire ($68.50) to 132,000 lire ($100) daily, depending on the season. Doubles rent for 130,000 lire ($98.75) to 180,000 lire ($137), and triples are priced at 160,000 lire ($122) to 217,000 lire ($165). Vaporetto stop: San Marco.

AT CAMPO SANTA MARIA DEL GIGLIO

Built as a palace in the 1550s, the **Hotel Ala,** campo Santa Maria del Giglio 2494, 30124 Venezia (tel. 041/520-8333), has an entrance flanked by a pair of stone lions that look out over the same square that opens onto the Hotel Gritti Palace. The establishment was converted into a hotel in the 1960s. It's under the same management as the Raffaele restaurant, reviewed in the restaurant section. It has simple lounges, a modest interior decor, and 80 clean bedrooms that cost from 125,000 lire ($95) daily in a single and 187,000 lire ($142) in a double, with a continental breakfast and air conditioning included.

NEAR THE ACCADEMIA

Set on a small waterway, the **American Hotel,** campo San Vio 628, 30123 Venezia (tel. 041/520-4733), lies across the Grand Canal from the most heavily touristed areas in an ochre building. The lobby is filled with murals, warm colors, and antiques, and the location is the kind preferred by anyone wanting to avoid the crowds that descend on Venice in summer. This peaceful and pleasantly furnished hotel contains 29 rooms, each of which has a bath or shower, color TV, direct-dial phone, and mini-bar, as well as air conditioning. Depending on the season, singles cost 75,000 lire ($57) to 120,000 lire ($91.25) daily; doubles, 120,000 lire ($91.25) to 180,000 lire ($137); and triples, 150,000 lire ($114) to 230,000 lire ($175). All tariffs include breakfast, taxes, and service. Vaporetto stop: Accademia.

---

5. Budget Lodgings

NEAR THE RIALTO BRIDGE

Spanning the main waterway at its center, the **Hotel Rialto,** riva del Ferro 5147, 30124 Venezia (tel. 041/520-9166), opens right onto the Grand Canal at the foot of the Ponte di Rialto, the famous bridge flanked with shops. Its bedrooms are quite satisfactory. They combine modern or Venetian furniture with the complexities of ornate Venetian ceilings and wall decorations. The beds are comfortable. The hotel has been considerably upgraded to second class, and more private baths or showers have been installed. The most expensive double chamber, overlooking the Grand Canal, costs 176,000 lire ($134) daily in high season, and singles run 115,000 lire ($87.50), including a continental breakfast. Vaporetto stop: no. 7.

Hotel Marconi & Milano, riva del Vin 729, 30100 Venezia (tel. 041/522-2068), was built in the year 1500, when Venice was at the height of its supremacy on the seas, but now it incorporates a later addition. The older portion, once a wine shop, has been absorbed into the hotel and is bound to titillate lovers of the ornate. Drawing-room furnishings, for instance, are appropriate for visiting bishops. The hotel lies less than 50 feet from the much-painted Rialto Bridge (vaporetto stop no. 7). The Savoldi Scherer family operates everything, combining an Italian flair with German efficiency (the German owner married the daughter of the founder). Only four of the lovely old rooms open directly onto the Grand Canal; the others face side and rear streets. The bedrooms are less inspired, with semi-modern furnishings. Bathless singles rent for 42,000 lire ($32) daily; bathless doubles run 76,000 lire ($57.75), and doubles with bath go for 97,500 lire ($74). Breakfast, service, and taxes are included. It's fun to have meals in the L-shaped room, sitting rather formally in Gothic chairs. But in summer, you'll want to dine at a sidewalk table on the Grand Canal, or in the Venetian-style tea room. The hotel is closed in winter.

Hotel da Bruno, salizzada san Lio 5726A, 30122 Venezia (tel. 041/523-0452), combines good rooms and excellent meals. You can't go wrong if you enjoy Italian locanda life. The innkeeper has 30 rooms to rent. Half these rooms have private shower. The bedrooms are quite satisfactory—nicely furnished, compact, tidy. Ignore the tiny lobby and the lack of a lounge, and concentrate on a good night's sleep. Bathless singles go for 43,000 lire ($32.75) daily; with shower, for 57,000 lire ($43.25). Doubles rent for 78,500 lire ($59.75) without bath, 99,500 lire ($75.50) with private shower. Da Bruno is halfway between the Rialto Bridge and the piazza San Marco (vaporetto stop no. 7 is closer). It is open from mid-March to the end of October.

Hotel Mignon, SS. Apostoli 4535, 30131 Venezia (tel. 041/523-7388), is a small third-class hotel not far from the Rialto Bridge and the Ca' d'Oro vaporetto stop. After a facelift, it now offers some accommodations with private bath. Fortunately for lone travelers there are many single rooms, a rarity in Venice. Most of the chambers overlook a private garden where breakfast is served, even afternoon tea. Bathless singles cost 39,500 lire ($30) daily; bathless doubles, 69,500 lire ($52.75). In the double with private bath, the charge is 69,500 lire ($68). Breakfast, service, and taxes are included. In winter, a 15% discount is granted.

NEAR THE PIAZZA SAN MARCO

Off the beaten track for most visitors, **San Mosè,** piscina San Mosè, 2058, 30124 Venezia (tel. 041/520-3755), provides much-needed peace and privacy, only a short walk from St. Mark's and near the theater, La Fenice. It's on a cul-de-sac, a little canal (Canale dei Barcaroli) overlooking the private garden of a neighboring palace. The owner suggests that you arrive by gondola if you can afford it; otherwise, it's a few minutes' walk from vaporetto stop no. 15. The hotel's 16 bedrooms have been renovated, decorated in part in a typical draped Venetian style. All rooms have private shower and toilet, color TV, radio, air conditioning, direct-dial phone, and mini-bar. Singles cost 118,000 lire ($89.75) daily; doubles, 181,000 lire ($137.50). A continental breakfast, the only meal served at the hotel, is included in the rates. Special discounts are quoted off-season.

Hotel Do Pozzi, corte do Pozzi 2373, calle XXII Marzo, 30124 Venezia (tel. 041/520-7855), is small, modern, and centrally located, just a short stroll from the Grand Canal. More of a little country tavern than a hotel, it opens onto a paved front courtyard, with potted greenery. To complete the picture, you can arrive via taxi, boat, gondola, or vaporetto. The sitting and dining rooms are furnished with antiques (and near antiques)—all intermixed with utilitarian modern. Baths have been added, and a major refurbishing has given everything a fresh touch. The price for a single room with shower, including a continental breakfast, is 115,000 lire ($87.50) daily. A twin-bedded room with bath or shower is 185,000 lire ($141). Air conditioning is included in the rates.

Hotel Lisbona, calle Barozzi 2153, 30124 Venezia (tel. 041/528-6774), is a simple and unpretentious hotel, which benefits from its location near St. Mark's Square. It's next door to the far more expensive Hotel Europa & Regina and across a narrow canal from the costly Hotel Bauer Grünwald. Each of the Lisbona's 15 rooms is clean and simply furnished in the style of the year of the hotel's opening (1975). Most units contain a modern bath, mini-bar, radio, and phone. The Zibetto family are the owners. With bath, doubles cost 100,000 lire ($76) daily, singles, 60,000 lire ($45.50). A limited number of bathless singles are available for 50,000 lire ($38).

Hotel Bisanzio, calle della Pietà, 3651, 30122 Venezia (tel. 041/520-3100), is a peaceful three-story hotel with green shutters and a plaque honoring it as the former home of the sculptor Alessandro Vittoria. Near St. Mark's Square and set back from the riva degli Schiavoni, the hotel is quieter and cheaper than many of its famous neighbors along the quay. The interior has gray marble floors, a uniformed staff, a bar, and a conservatively modern decor that includes stone floors and lots of exposed wood. The bedrooms, whose keys are attached to brass replicas of sea horses, rent for 100,000 lire ($76) daily in a single, 140,000 lire ($106) in a double. Vaporetto stop: San Zaccaria.

Hotel Città di Milano, campiello San Zulian 590, 30124 Venezia (tel. 041/522-7002). You go through a winding series of narrow streets of Venice to reach this small hotel 300 feet from St. Mark's Square. However, usually reliable signs point the way. It is mainly known for its restaurant (see separate recommendation). Its 26 accommodations are simple, but they are clean and centrally located. The reception area is usually filled with pedestrian traffic from the adjoining restaurant. Bathless rooms rent for 41,000 lire ($31.25) daily for a single, 74,500 lire ($56.50) in a double. Units with private bath cost 55,000 lire ($41.75) in a single, 95,500 lire ($72.50) in a double, with a continental breakfast included.

AT CAMPO SANTA MARIA FORMOSA

On a narrow street, the **Hotel Scandinavia,** campo Santa Maria Formosa 5240, 30122 Venezia (tel. 041/522-3507), has its entrance set behind a dark-pink façade just off one of the most colorful squares in Venice. You'll have to climb a steep marble staircase decorated with red-and-white cut-velvet wallpaper to the reception desk, whose nearby window offers a panoramic view of the piazza. The public rooms are filled with copies of 18th-century Italian chairs, Venetian glass chandeliers, autumnal colors, and a re-created rococo decor. The 30 rooms rent for 110,000 lire ($83.50) daily in a single, 165,000 lire ($125) in a double. Vaporetto stop: San Zaccaria (but a good walk).

NEAR THE ARSENALE

One of the most unusual hotel finds in Venice, **La Residenza,** Castello 3608, campo Bandiera e Moro, 30122 Venezia (tel. 041/528-5315), is operated by Franco Tagliapietra from its location in a pleasingly proportioned 14th-century building that looks a lot like a miniature version of the Doge's Palace. It's on a residential square where children play soccer and old persons feed the pigeons. After gaining access (just press the button outside the entrance), you'll pass through a stone vestibule lined with ancient Roman capitals before ringing another bell at the bottom of a flight of stairs. First an iron gate and then a door will open into an enormous salon with elegant antiques, 300-year-old paintings, and some of the most marvelously preserved walls in Venice. Applied in 1750, they swirl to the top of the 20-foot ceilings in flamboyant curves of pink and green, with the color contained within, not applied over, the stucco.

The 14 bedrooms are far less opulent than the public salons, and are furnished with contemporary pieces and functional accessories. The more choice ones are usually booked far in advance, especially for carnival season. With a continental breakfast included, doubles rent for 100,000 lire ($76) daily, while the lone single costs 55,000 lire ($41.75). The hotel is closed every year from around mid-November to mid-December and from mid-January to mid-February. Vaporetto stop: Arsenale.

NEAR CAMPO SAN ROCCO

The tastefully decorated, small **Hotel Falier,** salizzada San Pantalon 130, 30125 Venezia (tel. 041/522-8882), has an elegant reception area with stone Doric columns, red-and-white marble floors, and lots of paneling. In 1984 the owners combined their back-alley hotel with a streetside shop, and renovated each of the 19 bedrooms into what eventually became almost a completely new hotel. It's in an area of Venice, a commercial and working-class district, not visited by your average tourist. Neighboring streets are lined with shops and local restaurants. Two peaceful and sunny terraces, at different levels of the establishment, are dotted with flowers and outdoor furniture. Bathless rooms rent for 35,000 lire ($26.50) daily in a single and 70,000 lire ($53.25) in a double. Rooms with private bath cost 43,000 lire ($32.75) in a single, 88,000 lire ($67) in a double.

---

6. The Pick of the Pensiones

NEAR THE SALUTE

Opening onto the bright Guidecca Canal, **La Calcina,** zattere al Gesuati 780, 30123 Venezia (tel. 041/520-6466), lies in what used to be the English enclave of Venice before the area developed a broader base of tourism. In a less-trampled, secluded, and dignified district of Venice, it's reached by taking the vaporetto to the Accademia station. John Ruskin, who wrote *The Stones of Venice,* stayed here in 1877, and he charted the ground for his latter-day compatriots. The pensione is absolutely clean, and the furnishings are almost deliberately simple and unpretentious. The rooms are comfortable, and most of them come equipped with bath or shower. A bathless double costs 76,000 lire ($57.75) daily, rising to 92,000 lire ($70) with a bath or shower. A bathless single is tabbed at 47,000 lire ($35.75). Triples cost 98,000 lire ($74.50) to 115,000 lire ($87.50), depending on the plumbing. A continental breakfast is included.

Pensione Seguso, zattere al Gesuati 779, 30123 Venezia (tel. 041/522-2340), is a terracotta-colored house whose foundation dates from the 15th century. Set at the junction of two canals, this 36-room hotel is off the beaten track, on a less-traveled side of Venice, across the Grand Canal from the piazza San Marco. Its relative isolation made it attractive to such tenants as Ezra Pound and John Julius Norwich and his famous mother, Lady Diana Cooper. The interior is furnished with the family antiques of the Seguso family, who have maintained the hotel for the past 70 years. Small tables are set up near the hotel entrance, upon which breakfast is served on sunny days. Half board is obligatory in the elegantly upper-crust dining room, where reproduction antiques, real heirlooms, and family cats vie for the attention of the many satisfied guests. Open from March 1 until the end of November, the hotel charges half-board rates of 74,500 lire ($56.50) daily for a single without bath, 86,000 lire ($65.25) for a single with bath or shower or else a view. Half board in twin-bedded rooms costs 70,250 lire ($53.50) to 79,500 lire ($60.50) per person, the price depending on the plumbing or the view, with taxes included. Vaporetto stop: Accademia.

Pensione alla Salute "Da Cici," fondamenta Ca' Balà 222, in Dorsoduro, 30123 Venezia (tel. 041/522-2271), is a centuries-old palazzo in a secluded and charming part of Venice (vaporetto stop no. 14). It avoids the usual mass-tourism features, linking itself with the inner image of the city. Poetically oriented, it's been an offbeat haven for numerous writers and artists, including Ezra Pound at one time. Right on a small waterway that empties into the Grand Canal, "Da Cici" is furnished in a standard way, but most serviceably. The level of cleanliness is good. A bathless single rents for 37,000 lire ($28) daily, increasing to 48,000 lire ($36.50) in a single with bath or shower. A bathless double rents for 63,000 lire ($48), going up to 83,000 lire ($63) with bath or shower.

NEAR THE RIALTO

On its own canal, **Caneva,** ramo della Fava 5515, 30122 Venezia (tel. 041/522-8118), is midway between the Rialto Bridge and the piazza San Marco. Most of its functional bedrooms overlook either the canal or courtyard, with its potted trees and balconies. The owner, Mr. Gino, keeps his rooms tidy and employs a helpful staff. Most of his rooms are bathless, for which he charges singles 35,000 lire ($26.50) daily; couples pay 58,000 lire ($44). A few rooms have private bath or shower, for which you pay 46,500 lire ($35.25) in a single, from 76,500 lire ($58.25) in a double, including a continental breakfast.

NEAR THE ACCADEMIA

The well-recommended **Locanda Montin,** fondamenta di Borgo 1147, 31000 Venezia (tel. 041/522-7151), is an old-fashioned Venetian inn whose adjoining restaurant is one of the most loved and frequented in the area. In the Dorsoduro section, an area marked with residences across the Grand Canal from the most popular tourist zones, the establishment is officially listed as a fourth-class hotel. But its accommodations are considerably larger and better than that rating would suggest. Containing only seven rooms, none of which has a private bath, the locanda or inn charges around 45,000 lire ($34.25) a night for a double, which is such a bargain that many of the units are filled even in off-season. Reservations are virtually mandatory, owing to the fame of this locanda. Because it has virtually all the business it can handle, the inn is difficult to locate, marked only by a small carriage lamp etched with the name of the establishment extending over the pavement. Vaporetto stop: Accademia.

Pensione Accademia, fondamenta Bollani 1058, in Dorsoduro, 30123 Venezia (tel. 041/521-0188), the most patrician of the pensioni, is in a villa whose garden extends into the angle created by the junction of two canals. Iron fences, twisting vines, and neoclassical sculpture are a part of the setting, as well as Gothic-style paneling. Venetian chandeliers, and Victorian-era furniture. The building served as the Russian Embassy before World War II, and as a private house before that. There's an upstairs sitting room flanked with two large windows and a formal rose garden, which is visible from the breakfast room. The bedrooms are spacious, with original furniture from the 19th century. Depending on the facilities and the season, singles rent for 40,000 lire ($30.50) to 83,000 lire ($63) daily, and doubles go for 74,000 lire ($56.25) to 145,000 lire ($110), including a continental breakfast. The Pensione Accademia was the fictional residence of Katharine Hepburn when she was in Venice shooting *Summertime.* (Incidentally, it was at this time that she fell into a Venetian canal and got a permanent eye infection!) Vaporetto stop: Accademia.

ON THE RIVA DEGLI SCHIAVONI

Right on the lagoon, **Casa Paganelli,** riva degli Schiavoni 4687, 30122 Venezia (tel. 041/522-4324), occupies some of the most gold-plated real estate in the city, yet is a relatively simple pensione. Its owner, Francesco Paganelli, is charming and hospitable, and his lobby still contains a collection of modern art that was left by former artist guests, including Ben Nicolson. The hotel is in two Venetian houses, each of which is at least two or three centuries old (both once belonged to a convent). The hotel was opened by Francesco's grandfather in 1874 and has been thriving ever since. Signor Paganelli represents the third generation of innkeepers in the Paganelli family. Frankly, the bedrooms continue to draw a mixed report from readers. The place has its devotees who appreciate its unique atmosphere. Other potential guests seeking greater comfort might find better amenities elsewhere. The hotel contains 23 very simple bedrooms, most of which offer a private bath. Rooms with bath rent for 57,000 lire ($43.25) daily in a single, 100,000 lire ($76) in a double. Bathless rooms cost 43,000 lire ($32.75) in a single and 79,000 lire ($60) in a double. Prices are reduced by about 10% in winter. One of the two buildings contains a restaurant popular with both visitors and locals. Half-board terms range from 70,000 lire ($53.25) to 85,000 lire ($64.50) per person daily, with taxes and service included.

NEAR THE PIAZZA SAN MARCO

Off the lagoon, the **Doni Pensione,** calle de Vin 4656, 30122 Venezia (tel. 041/522-4267), sits in a private position, off the lagoon, about a three-minute walk from St. Mark's. Most of its 13 bathless rooms either overlook a little canal, where four or five gondolas are usually tied up, or a garden with a tall fig tree. Simplicity prevails, especially in the pristine and down-to-earth bedrooms, but the level of cleanliness is high. The rates are compensatingly low: 56,000 lire ($43) daily for two people with breakfast, including taxes and service. The pensione is at vaporetto and motorboat stop no. 16.

LA GIUDECCA

On the island of La Giudecca, **Casa Frollo,** Giudecca 50, 30123 Venezia (tel. 041/522-2723), is a 26-room gem of a pensione about a four-minute boat ride from San Marco. This is the sort of place where you can visualize young travelers of other days and their strict chaperones sitting in the big garden studying guidebooks to plan their exploration of Venice. Just down the quay from the posh Cipriani, Casa Frollo rents singles without bath for 42,000 lire ($32) daily, and singles with bath for 56,000 lire ($42.50). Bathless doubles cost 76,500 lire ($58.25); doubles with bath go for 97,500 lire ($74). Breakfast is included in the rates. It is open from April to the end of November. From the car terminal or train station, take a boat on Line 5 to Zitelle.

---

7. Hotels On the Lido

A DELUXE HOTEL

When the mammoth **Excelsior Palace,** lungomare Marconi 41, 30126 Venezia Lido (tel. 041/526-0201), was built, it was the biggest resort hotel of its kind in the world. It did much to make the Lido fashionable. At first glance it appears to be a castle—no, a government building; no, a hotel of sweeping magnitude with rooms that range in style and amenities from cozy singles to suites. The Excelsior is a monument to *La Dolce Vita.* It's also the preferred hotel of the dozens of film industry spokespeople who book practically every one of the rooms leading off the interminable corridors of the upper floors at festival time. Most of the social life here takes place around the angular swimming pool, traversed like lines on a Mondrian painting with two bridges, or on the flowered terraces leading up to the cabañas on the sandy beach. Clients can rent boats from a pier extending far into the Adriatic, the entrance to which passes between two guardian sphinxes. One of these, like the original in Cairo, is missing its nose, although the overall effect is undeniably high-style Italian.

All the rooms—some of them big enough for tennis games—have been modernized, often with vivid colors that look like reminders of summer, regardless of the season. On the premises is one of the most elegant dining rooms on the Adriatic, the Tropicana, with a soaring ceiling, thousands of embellishments, and meals costing around 140,000 lire ($106). The Blue Bar on the ground floor has piano music and views of the beach. On the premises are six tennis courts, and the hotel maintains a private launch for hourly runs to the other CIGA hotels on the Grand Canal. Singles range from 415,000 lire ($315) daily; doubles run 550,000 lire ($418) and up. The hotel is closed from mid-October until mid-April.

A FIRST-CLASS HOTEL

An enormous establishment, the **Hotel des Bains,** lungomare Marconi 17, 30126 Venezia Lido (tel. 041/765-921), was built in the grand era of European resort hotels, with its own wooded park and private beach with individual cabañas along with a kind of confectionary façade from the turn of the century. Thomas Mann stayed here several times before making it the setting for his novella, *Death in Venice,* and later it was used as a stage for the film of the same name. The renovated interior exudes the flavor of the leisurely life of the aristocratic belle-époque era most strongly in its high-ceilinged main salon, whose paneling is a dignified combination of Gothic with art deco.

Overlooking the sea, the April-to-October hotel has 191 well-furnished, fairly large rooms, all with private bath and shower. Room-and-breakfast rates range from 227,800 lire ($173) to 260,000 lire ($198) daily in a single, 357,000 lire ($271) to 412,000 lire ($313) in a double. An additional 61,000 lire ($46.25) per person is charged for half board. Guests dine in a large veranda dining room cooled by Adriatic sea breezes. The food is top-rate, the service superior. Special features include many resort-type amenities at Golf Club Alberoni, such as tennis courts, a large swimming pool, a private pier, and a park with shade trees and flowering shrubbery. A motorboat shuttles you back and forth between Venice and the Lido.

THE MIDDLE BRACKET

In its price bracket, the **Quattro Fontane,** via Quattro Fontane 16, 30126 Venezia Lido (tel. 041/526-0227), is one of the most charming hotels on the Lido. The trouble is, a lot of people know that, so it's likely to be booked (and it's open April to October only). Like a chalet from the Dolomites, this former summer home of a Venetian family, built in the late 19th century, is most popular with the discriminating British, who like a home-like atmosphere, a garden, a helpful staff, rooms with superior amenities, and good food served at tables set under shade trees. The hotel has been enlarged and now offers 72 rooms, more than two-thirds with private shower bath, and all with air conditioning. Singles cost 135,000 lire ($103) to 190,000 lire ($144) daily, and doubles go for 210,000 lire ($160) to 290,000 lire ($220), depending on the plumbing. Full-board terms range from 190,000 lire ($144) to 235,000 lire ($179) per person daily. Many of the rooms are furnished in part with antiques.

Hotel Helvetia, Gran Viale 4-6, 30126 Venezia Lido (tel. 041/526-0105), near the commercial center of the Lido, is a four-story, russet-colored, 19th-century building with stone detailing. On a side street near the lagoon side of the island, the hotel is owned by two brothers who acquired it from an earlier Swiss owner who'd named it for his homeland. The quieter rooms face away from the street. The older wing has belle-époque high ceilings and attractively comfortable furniture. The newer wing is more streamlined, dating from around 1950, and has been renovated into a style appropriate to the conservative management who maintain this establishment. Breakfast is served, weather permitting, in a flagstone-covered wall garden behind the hotel. Open from April 1 until October 31, the hotel charges 100,000 lire ($76) to 135,000 lire ($103) daily in a single and 160,000 lire ($122) to 190,000 lire ($144) in a double, depending on the plumbing. A continental breakfast is included in the price. The hotel's location is an easy walk from the vaporetto stop from Venice.

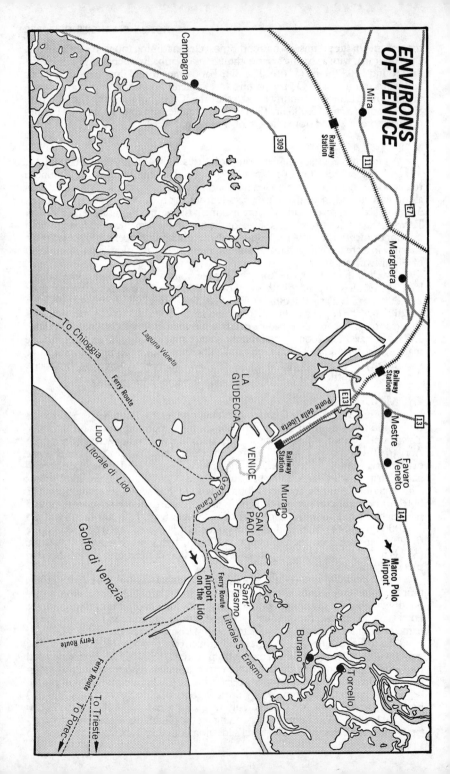

ENVIRONS
OF VENICE

Mira

Railway
Station

309

11

E7

Marghera

To Chioggia

Laguna Véneta

Ferry Route

LA
GIUDECCA

Ponte della Libertà

Railway
Station

E13

Mestre

13

Favaro
Veneto

VENICE

Grand Canal

Murano

SAN
PAOLO

14

Marco Polo
Airport

Lido

Litorale di Lido

Golfo di Venezia

Ferry Route
Airport
on the Lido

Sant'
Erasmo

Litorale S. Erasmo

Burano

Torcello

Ferry Route

To Trieste

To Poreč

Campagna

THE BUDGET RANGE

Built in 1857, the **Hotel Belvedere,** piazzale Santa Maria Elisabetta 4, 30126 Venezia Lido (tel. 041/526-0115), is still run by the same family. Restored and modernized, it also offers a popular restaurant (recommended later). The location is across from where the vaporetto from Venice stops. Unusual for the Lido, the hotel is open all year. It offers 25 simply furnished double rooms, each with shower, direct-dial phone, and radio. Furnishings are functional and rooms are small, but for the Lido at least prices are reasonable. Singles rent for 85,000 lire ($64.50) daily, doubles go for 125,000 lire ($95), and triples run 165,000 lire ($125). The hotel has parking in its garden.

---

8. Villas in the Environs of Venice

Villa Cornèr della Regina, via Corriva 10, 31050 Cavasagra (tel. 0423/481-481), is one of the grandest country hotels in the environs of Venice. A magnificent Palladian-style villa, once occupied by Italian armies in World War I, it was in this century a palatial private residence, receiving such visitors as J. Paul Getty and Maria Callas. In 1980 the property was acquired by Count Nicolò Dona dalle Rose, who comes from an important Venetian family that has included three doges. He had the villa and its adjacent farm buildings turned into a hotel, the farm buildings converted into both hotel rooms and time-share apartments. The Countess Giuliana Dona dalle Rose tastefully furnished the elegant hall, drawing rooms, suites, and bedrooms, using period furniture. In all, it evokes the era of the Venetian Republic. There are only 2,000 Palladian-inspired buildings in the world (the most famous New World version is Thomas Jefferson's Monticello), but this is one of the very few that has been transformed into a hotel.

The villa is set in a park with 22 acres of vineyards and gardens filled with 32 statues. Lying only a 30-minute drive from Venice, Villa Cornèr, on property once owned by the queen of Cyprus, offers air-conditioned suites or bedrooms. Depending on your room assignment, standard singles cost 130,000 lire ($98.75) daily, and doubles go for 180,000 lire ($137), including a continental breakfast, service, and VAT. The hotel offers a first-class restaurant, serving Italian and international specialties, and an array of sports facilities, including a heated swimming pool, a sauna, and hard tennis courts. Call for directions.

Villa Condulmer, in Zerman, outside Mogliano, 31020 Mogliano Veneto (tel. 041/457-100), is a 17th-century villa ten miles from Venice. Surrounded by its own huge grounds, it accepts discerning visitors from mid-March to mid-November. Built on the ruins of a monastery, the villa still maintains its classic architectural richness, with ornately paneled walls, parquet floors, frescoed ceilings, antiques, and Venetian crystal chandeliers. Food from the hotel's own gardens is served in the intimate gold-and-white dining room. The drinking lounge is also cozy, containing a baronial fireplace. The bedrooms are graciously large, furnished in a classic deluxe style. The highest tariffs are charged from May to September. Singles rent for 70,000 lire ($53.25) daily, and doubles go for 200,000 lire ($152). A restaurant serves meals for 50,000 lire ($38). The hotel is really a resort, complete with an 18-hole golf course, two tennis courts, and a large, free-form swimming pool.

Hotel Villa Cipriani, via Canova 298, 31011 Asolo (tel. 0423/55-444), is a 16th-century villa situated amid Italy's loveliest hills: a perfect retreat for the romanticist who'd enjoy staying in the house where the legendary actress Eleonora Duse and the poet Robert Browning once lived. The town is known for the fortress of Queen Cornaro, the open-air antique market, and the view of a hundred horizons. And, of course, for its tranquility and mild climate. It's about an hour's drive from Venice, a total of 40 miles, reached by the national road linking Venice to Treviso and Asolo, through the valley of the Venetian villas. The hotel, once owned by Signor Cipriani of Harry's Bar, now belongs to CIGA hotels. Still maintaining its original architectural beauty, it has been converted to receive guests. The decor is understated and comfortable, and includes a small, well-manicured garden, a terrace where you can take meals, and a dining room with views over the hills. A meal in the restaurant (with wine) costs from 85,000 lire ($64.50) per person. The best fresh fish in the market is used, plus fresh vegetables grown in the hotel's garden. The 31 bedrooms all have private bath, color TV, and air conditioning. One person pays 180,000 lire ($137) to 250,000 lire ($190) daily; two people, 210,000 lire ($160) to 270,000 lire ($205). The rooms are attractively furnished.

9. The Restaurants of Venice

Although Venice doesn't grow much foodstuff, and is hardly a victory garden, it is bounded by a rich agricultural district and plentiful vineyards in the hinterlands. It is from the Adriatic that the city gets the choicest items on its menu, although the fish dishes, such as scampi, tend to be expensive. The many rich and varied specialties prepared in the Venetian kitchen will be surveyed in the restaurant recommendations to follow. For Italy, the eating establishments of the city are high-priced. However, there are many trattorie catering to moderate budgets. I'll first take up my fork at the most expensive, then descend in price level.

THE TOP RESTAURANTS

Facing the Teatro della Fenice, **Antico Martini,** San Marco 1983, campo San Fantin (tel. 522-4121), is elegantly situated. The leading restaurant of Venice, it elevates the Venetian cuisine to its highest level, even—or especially—if you stick to the local fare. Because it serves such good food, it has enjoyed a long list of distinguished patrons, including Lord Olivier, Sir John Gielgud, Leonard Bernstein, Igor Stravinsky, and Balanchine. An excellent beginning is the risotto di frutti di mare, creamy Venetian style with plenty of fresh seafood, which may vary according to the season. For a main dish try the fegato alla veneziana (best when covered with a liberal sprinkling of freshly ground pepper), which is tender liver fried with onions and served with a helping of polenta, a yellow cornmeal mush praised by Goldoni. Also good is the roast baby lamb. A complete meal will probably cost 70,000 lire ($53.25) to 100,000 lire ($76). An interesting local wine, especially with fish dishes, is the yellow Tocai. Decor? Inside, the walls are paneled; elaborate chandeliers glitter overhead; gilt-framed oil paintings adorn the walls. Outside, the courtyard is favored in summer. The restaurant's in the tradition of a Venetian palazzo.

Actually, it was founded in 1720 as a coffeehouse, serving the popular Turkish brew in the heyday of trade with the Ottoman Empire. A wine grower from Tuscany acquired the coffeehouse as a bad debt in 1921. That long-ago proprietor was the father of the present owner, Emilio Baldi, who runs the present Antico Martini with just the right amount of dash and flair. Hours are noon to 2:30 p.m. and 7:30 to 11:30 p.m., but the restaurant does not serve lunch on Wednesday and is closed all day Tuesday.

Harry's Bar, calle Vallaresso 1323 (tel. 523-6797), serves some of the best food in Venice. Its fame was spread by Ernest Hemingway. A. E. Hotchner, in his *Papa Hemingway,* quoted the writer as saying, "We can't eat straight hamburger in a Renaissance palazzo on the Grand Canal." So he ordered a five-pound "tin of beluga caviar" to, as he said, "take the curse off it." Harry, by the way, is an Italian named Arrigo, son of the late Commendatore Cipriani. Like his father, Arrigo is an entrepreneur extraordinaire known for the standard of his cuisine. His bar is a watering spot for martini-thirsty Americans—a wide mixture that includes both Madison Avenue types and the sunflower girls of Kansas. The vodka martini is dry and well chilled. Hemingway and Hotchner always ordered Bloody Marys. Some superb libations are made with the juice of fresh peaches grown in the lagoon (one, called a Bellini, consists of champagne and fresh peach juice—truly delectable). The food is good, and you can have your choice of dining in the bar downstairs, or the room with a view upstairs. I recommend the Venetian fish soup, followed by the scampi thermidor with rice pilaf, and topped off by a chocolate mousse. Meals cost 75,000 lire ($57) to 120,000 lire ($91.25). The restaurant and bar are open from 10:30 a.m. to 11 p.m.; closed on Monday and in January. From October to March, it also closes on Sunday evening.

Taverna La Fenice, campiello de la Fenice 1938, (tel. 522-3856), is one of the most romantic dining spots in Venice. The interior is elegant, but in summer guests dine outside under a canopy, beside the Teatro La Fenice where Stravinsky introduced *The Rake's Progress*. The service is smooth and efficient, and English is spoken. The most appetizing beginning is a selection of seafood antipasti. The fish in this selection is fresh caught from the Adriatic. You might enjoy the cannoli alla Fenice, rigatoni Fenice, or tagliatelle alle noci di mare (seafood pasta). Main-dish specialties include cartoccio Fenice (fish cooked in a paper bag) and steak Elisabeth cooked at your table. Complete meals begin at 60,000 lire ($45.50) to 90,000 lire ($68.50). The place is open from noon to 3 p.m. and 7 p.m. to midnight (till 1 a.m. if there is a performance at the theater); closed Sunday from the first week of January to the first week of February.

La Caravella, calle Larga XXII Marzo 2398 (tel. 520-8901). Next door to the Hotel Saturnia-Internazionale, it attracts, with its gracious ambience, an elegant pub atmosphere with time-mellowed paneling. Many of the specialties are featured nowhere else in town. For a different beginning, try a smooth gazpacho—the cold "liquid salad" of Andalusia. Standard dishes include chateaubriand for two persons and the spring chicken cooked in a paper bag. However, the best item to order is one of the poached fish dishes, such as bass—all priced according to weight and served with a tempting sauce. The bouillabaisse in the style of Marseilles is also excellent. After all that, the ice cream in champagne is welcome. Expect to pay 70,000 lire ($53.25) to 100,000 lire ($76). It is open from noon to 3 p.m. and 7 p.m. to midnight. From November to March, it is closed all day Wednesday and Thursday for lunch. In summer, however, it remains open daily.

Do Forni, calle dei Specchieri 468 (tel. 523-7729). Centuries ago this was the site where bread was baked for some local monasteries, but today it's the most frenetically busy restaurant in Venice, even when the rest of the city slumbers under a wintertime Adriatic fog. That means you must always arrive with a reservation. A few blocks from St. Mark's Square, it is divided into two sections, separated by a narrow alleyway. The Venetian cognoscenti prefer the front part, decorated in *Orient Express* style. The larger section at the back is like a country tavern, with ceiling beams and original paintings. The English menu is entitled "food for the gods," listing such specialties as spider crab in its own shell, champagne-flavored risotto, calves' kidney in a bitter mustard, and sea bass in papillotte, to name only a few items. Full meals cost from 65,000 lire ($49.50), but could go higher if you order lobster. Hours are noon to 3 p.m. and 7 to 11 p.m. Except in summer, Do Forni is closed Thursday, and its annual vacation is in late November and early December.

Other Top Restaurants

Trattoria Alla Colomba, San Marco-Piscina-Frezzeria 1665 (tel. 522-1175), close to the piazza San Marco, is the queen of the trattorie of Venice. The restaurant is decorated with a small gallery of modern paintings, including works by well-known Italian and internationally known artists. The popularity of the trattoria is mainly due to the excellence of its cuisine, which includes such specialties as minestre di fagioli (bean soup), risotto di frutti di mare alla pescatora (risotto with seafood), risotto di funghi del Montello (risotto with mushrooms of the local hills of Montello), baccalà alla vicentina (milk-simmered dried cod, seasoned with onions, anchovies, and cinnamon, and served with polenta), and granzeola (shellfish of the Adriatic). Fruits and vegetables are produced locally on the islands near Venice. The cost of an excellent meal is likely to run 50,000 lire ($38) to 75,000 lire ($57). Open from noon to 3 p.m. and 7 to 11 p.m. daily from May to September. The rest of the year it is likely to be closed on Wednesday.

Les Deux Lions, in the Londra Palace Hotel, riva degli Schiavoni 4171 (tel. 522-5032), offers a big-windowed view of a magnificent 19th-century equestrian statue ringed with heroic women taming lions. On the ground floor of this well-known hotel on the banks of the Grand Canal, the restaurant is filled with colors of scarlet and gold, a motif of lions patterned into the carpeting, and English pub-style furniture. An adjoining piano bar is a popular nightspot. Menu items include typical French and international specialties. You might begin with foie gras de canard (duck liver), then follow with entrecôte béarnaise or salmon with champagne. The chef also prepares an excellent sole with "fruits of the sea." Summer dining is on an outdoor terrace with a view of the pedestrian traffic from the nearby piazza San Marco. Meals, served from noon to 3 p.m. and 7 to 10:30 p.m., range upward from 75,000 lire ($57). The restaurant is closed on Tuesday. Vaporetto stop: San Zaccaria.

Ristorante Noemi, calle dei Fabbri 909 (tel. 522-5238), is a simple but tasteful room whose main decorative feature is a multicolored marble floor pieced into abstract patterns. It stands on a narrow street behind a russet stucco façade with swag curtains covering big glass windows, a short walk from the piazza San Marco. Specialties include many items bordering on *nuova cucina*, such as thin black spaghetti with cuttlefish "in their own sauce," fresh salmon crêpes with cheese, shrimp soup in pink spumante, spider crab dressed in its shell, baked eel (with white wine, garlic, and bay leaf), medallion of turkey in fresh orange sauce, roast shoulder of veal (with chile peppers, olives, bacon, and capers), followed by the special lemon sorbet of the house, made with sparkling wine and fresh mint. A la carte meals range from 40,000 lire ($30.50) to 68,000 lire ($51.75). The restaurant, serving from noon to 2:45 p.m. and 7 to 10:30 p.m., is closed Sunday night, all day Monday, and from mid-January to mid-February.

Ristorante a la Vecia Cavana, rio Terra SS. Apostoli 4624 (tel. 528-7106), is off the tourist circuit and well worth the trek through the winding streets to find it. "Cavana" is a place where gondolas are parked, a sort of liquid garage. The site of this restaurant used to be such a place. When you enter, you'll be greeted with brick arches, stone columns, terracotta floors, framed modern paintings, and a photograph of 19th-century fishermen relaxing after a day's catch. It's an appropriate introduction to a menu that specializes in seafood. These include a mixed grill from the Adriatic, fried scampi, fresh sole, squid, three different types of risotto (each prepared with seafood), and a spicy zuppa di pesce (fish soup). Another specialty of the house is antipasti di pesce Cavana, which includes an assortment of just about every sea creature. A la carte meals range from 35,000 lire ($26.50) to 50,000 lire ($38). The restaurant is open from noon to 3 p.m. and 7:30 to 10 p.m.; closed Tuesday. You might see an occasional movie star here.

"Al graspo de ua," calle des Bombaseri 5093 (tel. 520-0150), is one bunch of grapes you'll want to pluck. For that special meal, it's a winner. Decorated in the old taverna style, it offers several dining rooms. One has a beamed ceiling, hung with garlic and copper bric-a-brac. Considered among the best fish restaurants in Venice, "al graspo de ua" has been patronized by such celebs as Elizabeth Taylor, Jeanne Moreau, Rossano Brazzi, even Giorgio de Chirico. You can help yourself to all the hors d'oeuvres you want—known on the menu as "self-service mammoth." You can order the gran fritto dell'Adriatico, a mixed treat of deep-fried fish from the Adriatic. Desserts are good, especially the peach Melba. Your meal, served from noon to 3 p.m. and 7 to 11 p.m., will cost 55,000 lire ($41.75) to 75,000 lire ($57). The air-conditioned restaurant is near the Rialto Bridge (vaporetto stop no. 7). Closed Monday, Tuesday, and from just before Christmas to early January.

Ristorante Corte Sconta, calle del Pestrin 3884 (tel. 522-7024), is contained behind a narrow storefront that you'd probably ignore if you didn't know about this place. On a narrow alley whose name is shared by at least three other streets in Venice (this particular one is near campo Bandiere Moro and San Giovanni in Bragora), the restaurant has a multicolored marble floor, plain wooden tables, hanging metallic lights, and no serious attempt at decoration. The place has become well known, however, as the kind of sophisticated gathering place that is quietly talked about throughout Venice. As the depiction of the satyr chasing the mermaid above the entrance implies, this is a fish restaurant, serving a variety of gilled creatures (much of the "catch" is largely unknown in North America). If you don't like fish, a tender filet of beef is available. The restaurant's specialties include a mixed fish fry from the Adriatic (which includes scampi), a wide selection of grilled fish, Venetian antipasti, a few well-chosen pasta dishes, and both a zuppa di pesce and a risotto di pesce. A good selection of wines adds to the enjoyment of your meal. There's a big stand-up bar in an adjoining room that seems almost a private fraternity of the locals. Meals range upward from 55,000 lire ($41.75). The restaurant is open from 12:30 to 2:30 and 7:30 to 9:30 p.m.; closed Sunday, Monday, and from mid-June to mid-July. Vaporetto stop: Arsenale.

Il Cortile, via XXII Marzo 2402 (tel. 520-8938), is connected to the more expensive Caravella Restaurant, part of the Hotel Saturnia-International, and uses the same kitchen, but this attractive place charges less money and offers just as much atmosphere. In summer folding chairs are set beneath the abbreviated canopy of the central courtyard, permitting candlelit meals in a garden setting. In colder weather, guests select one of a pair of rustically elegant rooms covered with a painted and paneled ceiling, reflecting the music of a live pianist. Bouquets of flowers and wrought-iron chandeliers add to the enjoyment of full meals, costing from 60,000 lire ($45.50) per person. Specialties include ossobuco with a saffron-flavored risotto, grilled quail with polenta, a mixed grill of fish, Venetian eel, grilled turbot, and several preparations of lobster, along with sea bass, truffled calves' kidney, and veal piccata. There is a changing array of daily specials derived from local recipes. Hours are 7 to 10:30 p.m.; closed Monday and Tuesday.

MEDIUM- AND BUDGET-PRICED RESTAURANTS

The best of these in Venice can be found in the following areas—

Near La Fenice and Piazza San Marco

Al Teatro, campo San Fantin 1917 (tel. 523-7214), is a ristorante-pizzeria on a piazzetta adjoining the opera house. You can let your mood dictate your dining spot for the evening, as there are several rooms from which to choose. In fair weather tables are placed out on the charming little square. Downstairs, one can order pizza and several regional dishes, including zuppa d'orzo e fagioli (a soup made with barley in fresh cream of beans). A noodle dish worthy of an award is tortelloni Lucia (made with butter, eggs, cheese, and bits of pork). This is one of the many specialties the maître d' prepares right at your table. For dessert, try a mixed fresh fruit salad (macedonia) with ice cream or tiramesù, a typical Venetian cake. Meals begin at 40,000 lire ($30.50) and are served from noon to 2:30 p.m. and 7 to 11:30 p.m. The upper-floor dining rooms are decorated in the rustic manner. Closed Monday.

Ristorante da Raffaele, San Marco 2347 (fondamenta delle Ostreghe) (tel. 523-2317), a five-minute walk from the piazza San Marco and a minute from the Grand Canal, has long been one of my favorite canalside restaurants in Venice. The outdoor tables offer the kind of charm and special atmosphere unique to the city. However, the inner rooms have become more popular with both Venetians and visitors alike. The huge inner sanctum has a high-beamed ceiling, 17th- to 19th-century pistols and sabers, exposed brick, wrought-iron chandeliers, a massive fireplace, and copper pots (hundreds of them), all contributing to the rustic ambience. If you go to the rest room, you pass through part of one of the kitchens, itself worth a visit. The food is excellent, beginning with a choice of tasty antipasti or well-prepared pastas.

Seafood specialties include scampi, squid, or a platter of deep-fried fish from the Adriatic. The grilled meats are also succulent, followed by rich, tempting desserts. An average meal will cost around 45,000 lire ($34.25). The crowded conviviality is part of the experience. The restaurant is open from noon to 3 p.m. and 7 to 10:30 p.m.; closed on Thursday and December 10 to January 25.

Vini Da Arturo, calle degli Assassini 3656 (tel. 528-6974), attracts many devoted habitués, including artists and writers. Here you get some of the most delectable of the local cooking—and not just the standard cliché Venetian dishes. One local restaurant owner, who likes to dine here occasionally instead of at his own place, explained, "The subtle difference between good and bad food is often nothing more than the amount of butter and cream used." Instead of plain pasta, a tantalizingly sophisticated dish to order is spaghetti alla gorgonzola. The beef is also good, especially when prepared with a cream sauce flavored with mustard and freshly ground pepper. Salads are made with crisp, fresh ingredients, often in unusual combinations. For a complete meal, served from noon to 2:30 p.m. and 7 to 10:30 p.m. daily, expect to spend from 70,000 lire ($53.25). The place is small, only seven tables, so reservations are important. The location is between the Fenice Opera House and St. Mark's Square.

Da Ivo, ramo di Fuseri 1809 (tel. 528-5004), has such a faithful clientele you'll think at first you're in a semiprivate club. The rustic atmosphere is both cozy and relaxing, and your well-set table flickers to the glow of candlelight. A big plate-glass window frames a vista of an offshoot canal where gondolas and their passengers glide by. Homesick Florentines go here for some fine Tuscan cookery from that land of "milk and honey." In season, game, prepared according to ancient traditions, is cooked over the open fire. Of course, it is Tuscan beef that is best, and it's preferred charcoal grilled with a minimum of condiment and sauce, simply seasoned with pepper, salt, and oil. A popular appetizer in Florence is anything prepared on "crostini"—that is, toasted bread. On my latest rounds, my hearty bread was browned to perfection and spread with a pâté-like paste made of chopped chicken livers and anchovies (it's recommended even to people who don't like anchovies). On a cold day one December my heart and plate were warmed when I ordered a homemade tagliatelli. Over it were spread slivers of tartufi bianchi, the pungent white truffle from the Piedmont district that is unforgettable to the palate. A complete meal will cost 65,000 lire ($49.50) to 75,000 lire ($57) per person. Da Ivo is open from noon to 2:40 p.m. and 7 p.m. to midnight daily except Sunday.

Ai Barbacani, calle del Paradiso 5746 (tel. 521-0234). Within a brick-lined series of dining rooms, by the light of flickering candles in the evening, you can enjoy some of the freshest fish in Venice. Unusual for a Venetian restaurant, the fish is grilled over a charcoal fire. When you enter, the catch of the day is laid out on ice for your perusal. In addition to fish, a limited meat selection is available, along with an array of antipasti and pastas. Try gnocchi à la seppie. Full meals, costing from 70,000 lire ($53.25) with fish, 40,000 lire ($30.50) without fish, are served daily except Monday from noon to 3 p.m. and 7 to 11 p.m.

Ristorante Città di Milano, campiello San Zulian 599 (tel. 528-5437), is on a hidden square built around a Renaissance well a short distance from the piazza San Marco, within view of the peeling walls of an old church. Dining can be outdoors on the flagstones at a group of tables sheltered by a canopy and separated from the square by a ring of shrub-covered lattices. In winter or in bad weather, diners usually gravitate indoors to a series of rooms dotted with modern lithographs. The restaurant serves such specialties as crêpes with salmon, spaghetti with cuttlefish, risotto with scampi, mixed grilled fish, mixed grilled meat, and the excellent dessert, tiramesù, a Venetian cake. Daily blackboard specials are posted. Expect to pay around 44,000 lire ($33.50) for a meal. The restaurant, open from noon to 3 p.m. and 7 to 10 p.m., is closed on Monday. The hotel attached to this restaurant is endorsed earlier in this chapter.

All'Angelo, calle Larga San Marco 408 (tel. 522-2000), is the restaurant portion of a small hotel that draws a large clientele of artists. Paintings cover the bare brick walls. Here you can have some of the more popular Venetian specialties. From the à la carte listings, four are especially recommended: the mixed fish fry from the Adriatic, tender calves' liver fried with onions, scaloppine marsala, and sweetbreads, also cooked in marsala. Seafaring tastes may be attracted to the Venetian bouillabaisse or the grilled sturgeon. An average repast will cost from 60,000 lire ($45.50). A set menu, however, goes for 30,000 lire ($22.75). For those who flunked Italian, the menu's in English. The service is efficient without appearing to be so. There's no pretentious drama, but superb victuals are prepared. If the weather's right, aim for a sidewalk table. Hours are 11 a.m. to midnight; closed Tuesday.

Al Gambero, calle dei Fabbri 4685 (tel. 522-4384), is a canalside restaurant with a sidewalk terrace, one of the best of the appealingly priced dining spots of Venice. The food is good and well prepared, with all sorts of taste treats. The least expensive way to dine here is to order a 17,000-lire ($13) fixed-price meal, which might include spaghetti or pastina in brodo, followed by Hungarian goulash or calves' liver fried with onions in the Venetian style. Other main dishes are likely to include a veal cutlet milanese or perhaps baked chicken accompanied by roast potatoes and a mixed salad. Afterward, you're faced with the fruit of the season or a selection of Italian cheese. Many typical Venetian dishes are offered on a menu costing 26,000 lire ($19.75). They include spaghetti with onion and anchovy sauce, gnocchi al castrà (potato dumplings with stewed lamb sauce), castrà in tecia (stewed lamb with polenta), stewed cuttlefish, and fresh sardines, marinated with onions and vinegar. Expect to pay a cover charge of 1,500 lire ($1.15) per person if you order à la carte. The restaurant is open from noon to 2 p.m. and 6 to 11:30 p.m. daily except Thursday.

In the Dorsoduro

Locanda Montin, fondamenta di Borgo 1147 (tel. 522-7151), is the kind of rapidly disappearing Venetian inn that virtually every literary and artistic figure in Venice has visited since it opened just after World War II. Famous clients have included Ezra Pound, Jackson Pollock, Mark Rothko, and many of the assorted artist friends of the late Peggy Guggenheim, whose museum is just around the corner. Other luminaries have included Jimmy Carter, who, after a long day at a summit conference, requested dinner at a traditional Venetian restaurant. The inn is owned and run by the Carretins, who have covered the walls with paintings donated by or purchased from their many friends and clients. The building was constructed in the 17th century and used for many years as a storage place for the masses of firewood needed to chase away the chill of a Venetian winter.

Today its arbor-covered garden courtyard is filled with regular clients, many of whom allow their favorite waiter to select most of the items for their meal. The frequently changing menu is printed daily on the back of reproductions of one of the restaurant's paintings. Specialties of the chef include antipasti Montin, which includes a cold assortment of fruits of the sea. There is always an array of fresh pasta, plus a variety of salads, grilled meats, and fish caught in the Adriatic. Dessert might be a semifreddo di fragoline, a tempting chilled liqueur-soaked cake, capped with whipped cream and wild strawberries. Expect to pay from 40,000 lire ($30.50) for a full meal, served from 12:30 to 3:30 p.m. and 7:30 to 10:30 p.m. The locanda lies in one of the least-trampled sections of Venice, the Dorsoduro, across the Grand Canal from the piazza San Marco. The restaurant is closed on Tuesday evening and all day Wednesday.

La Furatola, calle Lunga San Barnaba 2870A (tel. 520-8594), is very much a neighborhood hangout, but it has captured the imagination of Venetian restaurant aficionados. It's in the Dorsoduro section, along a narrow flagstone-paved street which you'll need a good map and a lot of patience to find. Perhaps you'll have lunch here after a visit to the Church of San Rocco, only a short distance away. Push past double glass doors and enter a simple dining room. The specialty is fish brought to your table in a wicker basket so that you can judge its size and freshness. A display of seafood antipasti is set out near the entrance. Full meals cost from 40,000 lire ($30.50) and are served from 12:30 to 2:30 p.m. and 7:30 to 9:30 p.m. daily except Wednesday evening, all day Thursday, and in July and August.

East of the Piazza San Marco

Arcimboldo, Castello Calle dei Furlani 3219 (tel. 528-6569). The small street containing this exciting restaurant might not be on your map, although most Venetians locate it by walking to the end of the calle dei Furlani, in the heart of the oldest part of the inner city. Opened in 1982, the restaurant is perfect for devotees of the freshest kinds of vegetables. The chefs present an imaginative array of dishes inspired by the fruits of the Italian harvest. The sunny decor includes fresh colors of pastel greens and blues, plus an absorbing collection of original paintings by friends of the owners, and huge baskets of carefully arranged vegetables-as-art that vie for attention with the fresh flowers of the day. The name of the restaurant evokes the Renaissance painter who arranged vegetables into portraits of his contemporaries (a radish for a chin, a carrot for a nose). A copy of one of Guiseppe Arcimboldo's most famous works, *Summer,* hangs prominently as a suggestion of the kinds of specialties served here. You might enjoy fresh asparagus, a variety of eggplant dishes, zucchini in white wine with endive and artichokes, veal liver in butter and sage, veal kidneys with parsley and garlic, beef with pink peppercorns, and tagliolini with smoked salmon. Expect to spend around 60,000 lire ($45.50) per person. The restaurant, open from 8 p.m. to 2 a.m., is closed Tuesday. Vaporetto stop: San Zaccaria.

Hostaria da Franz, fondamenta San Isepo 754 (tel. 522-0861). Much of the experience of this place derives from the promenade its visit requires through a residential neighborhood rarely visited by tourists. It lies a long walk from St. Mark's Square beside a narrow canal whose waters are bordered by children, pets, flapping laundry, and grandiose monuments to 19th-century military heroes. Long ago the troops of the Austro-Hungarian armies used this building as a barracks, but today you'll find a bar, a pleasant dining room spanned with weathered beams, and an ebullient reception. The place is small and popular, so call ahead for a table. In summer, elegant candlelit tables are placed along the river. Your meal might include a pasticcio of fresh fish, fish-flavored gnocchi, and a satisfying choice of fresh seafood. These even include lobster flown in from the waters off North America. The maître d' recommends one of the local vintages to accompany your meal, which will cost from 45,000 lire ($34.25), served from 12:30 to 3 p.m. and 7 p.m. to midnight. Readers Tim and Joyce Foresman, of Green Valley, Nevada, warn that most maps spell this establishment's street name as "Rio di S. Giuseppe," although local street signs refer to it as "Rio di S. Isepo." No meals are served on Tuesday off-season and in January. Vaporetto stop: no. 18, Giardini.

Near the Rialto

Restaurant da Bruno, Castello Calle del Paradiso 5731 (tel. 522-1480), is like a country taverna in the center of Venice, about halfway between the Rialto Bridge and the piazza San Marco. On a narrow street, the restaurant attracts its crowds by grilling meats on an open-hearth fire. Get your antipasti at the counter and watch your prosciutto order being prepared—paper-thin slices of spicy flavored ham wrapped around breadsticks (grissini). In the right season, da Bruno does some of the finest game specialty dishes in Venice. If featured, try in particular its capriolo (roebuck) and its fagiano (pheasant). A typical Venetian specialty—prepared well here—is the zuppa di pesce (fish soup). After that rich fare, you may settle for a macedonia of mixed fruit for dessert. Expect to pay 30,000 lire ($22.75) to 40,000 lire ($30.50) for a complete meal from noon to 3 p.m. and 6:45 to 10 p.m. Closed Tuesday and from mid-July to the first of August.

Trattoria Madonna, calle de la Madonna 594 (tel. 522-3824), near the Rialto Bridge, is one of the most characteristic trattorie of Venice. Unfortunately, it's usually so crowded you can't get in. On a narrow street, it lures with its fish specialties. To get you started, I suggest the antipasto frutti di mare (fruits of the sea). At the fish counter, on ice, you can inspect the sea creatures you'd like to devour. The mixed fish fry is a preferred dish. Depending on your selection of fish, a complete meal will cost from 35,000 lire ($26.50). The restaurant, open from noon to 3 p.m. and 7:15 to 10:15 p.m., is closed on Wednesday and in January and August 4 to August 18. Take the vaporetto to the Rialto stop.

Fiachetteria Toscana, San Giovanni Crisostomo 5719 (tel. 528-5281). A street-level dining room spanned by old ceiling beams contains amusing modern art and an impressive display of the day's catch. A country-style wooden staircase leads past marble columns to an upper room and additional tables. Menu specialties mainly consist of different varieties of fish, including an octopus-and-celery salad, spider crab in its own shell, grilled razor clams, seafood risotto with champagne, and baked eel. A red chicory salad from Treviso is the perfect accompaniment. Meals cost from 50,000 lire ($38) and are served from 12:30 to 2:30 p.m. and 7:30 to 10:30 p.m. daily except Tuesday and July 1 to July 15. Vaporetto stop: Rialto.

At San Polo

Osteria da Fiore, calle del Scalater 2202 (tel. 721-308). The breath of the Adriatic seems to blow through this place, although how the wind finds this little restaurant tucked away in a labyrinth I don't know. One never knows what's likely to be on the menu. An imaginative and changing fare is offered, depending on the availability of fresh fish and produce. If you have a love of foods maritime, you'll find them here —everything from scampi (a sweet Adriatic prawn, cooked in as many different ways as there are chefs) to granzeola, a type of spider crab. In days gone by I've recalled everything from fried calamari (cuttlefish) to bottarga (dried mullet roe to be eaten with olive oil and lemon). For your wine, I suggest Prosecco, which has a distinctive golden yellow color and a bouquet that is refreshing and fruity. It's been around for centuries, and is in fact one of the best-known wines of Venetia, made with grapes from the Conegliano. The proprietors extend a hearty welcome to match their fare. A complete meal, inclusive, should run about 45,000 lire ($34.25) to 65,000 lire ($49.50) per person. Hours are 12:30 to 2:30 p.m. and 8 to 9:30 p.m. The trattoria is closed on Sunday and Monday. The restaurant is also closed for the entire month of August and from Christmas to New Year's. Vaporetto stop: Silvestro.

Trattoria Antica Besseta, calle Savio 1395 (tel. 721-687). If you manage to find this place (go armed with a good map), you'll be rewarded with a true Venetian cuisine at its most unpretentious. Head for the campo San Giacomo dell'Orio, then negotiate your way across infrequently visited piazzas and winding alleys. Push through saloon doors into a bar area filled with African masks and modern art. The dining room in back is ringed with paintings and illuminated with wagon-wheel chandeliers. Nereo Volpe, his wife, Maurizia, and one of their sons are the guiding force, the chefs, the buyers, and even the "talking menus." The food depends on what looked good in the market that morning. Full meals, costing from 45,000 lire ($34.25), include roast chicken, fried scampi, fritto misto, spaghetti in a sardine sauce, various roasts, and a selection from the day's catch. The Volpe family produces two kinds of their own wine, a pinot blanc, and a cabernet. Meals are served from 12:30 to 2:30 p.m. and 7:30 to 9:30 p.m. daily except Tuesday and Wednesday. Closed in July and August.

La Giudecca

Harry's Dolci, fondamenta San Biago (tel. 522-4844), on the Isola della Giudecca. The people at the famed Harry's Bar have established their latest enclave far from the maddening crowds of St. Mark's Square on this little-visited island. From the quayside windows of this chic place, you can watch sea-going vessels, everything from yachts to lagoon-based barges. White napery and uniformed waiters grace a modern room, where no one minds if you order only coffee and ice cream, perhaps a selection from the large pastry menu (the zabaglione cake is divine). A full meal, served from 1:30 to 3:30 p.m. and 7:30 to 10 p.m., costs from 35,000 lire ($26.50) and includes carpaccio Cipriani, chicken salad, club sandwiches, gnocchi, and house-style cannelloni. Dishes are deliberately kept simple, but each is well prepared. The place is closed Monday and from November 10 to March 10. Take the vaporetto to stop 5 to Santa Eufemia where you'll see the restaurant's awnings on a building beside the wharf.

On the Lido

If you're visiting the Lido just for the day, you may want to dine there. Outside of the big hotels, the best food is served at the **Ristorante Belvedere,** piazzale Santa Maria Elisabetta 4 (tel. 526-0115). Don't be put off by its location, across from where the vaporetto from Venice stops. In such a place, you'd expect a touristy establishment. Actually, the Belvedere attracts some of the finest people of Venice, who come here as an excursion knowing they can get some of the best fish dishes along the Adriatic. Sidewalk tables are placed outside, and there is, as well, a glass-enclosed portion for windy days. The main dining room is attractive, with cane-backed bentwood chairs and big windows. In back, reached through a separate entrance, is a busy café. Main dishes include the chef's special sea bass, along with grilled dorade (or sole), fried scampi, and other selections. You might begin with the special fish antipasti or spaghetti en papillote. Regular meals cost from 40,000 lire ($30.50). The restaurant is open from noon to 2:30 p.m. and 7 to 9:30 p.m.; closed Monday.

XI

THE ATTRACTIONS OF VENICE

1. ST. MARK'S SQUARE
2. THE GRAND CANAL
3. MUSEUMS AND GALLERIES
4. SCUOLE AND CHURCHES
5. A WALKING TOUR OF VENICE
6. SHOPPING IN VENICE
7. THE LIDO AND LAGOON
8. VENICE AFTER DARK

Venice is the courtesan of Europe, appearing at times to have been created specifically to entertain her legions of callers. Ever since the body of St. Mark was smuggled out of Alexandria and entombed in the basilica, Venice has been hostess to a never-ending stream of visitors—famous, infamous, and otherwise—from all over the world.

In the pages ahead, we'll explore her great art and architecture. But unlike Florence, Venice would reward her guests with treasures even if they never ducked inside a museum or church. In the city on the islands, the frame eternally competes with the picture inside.

"For all its vanity and villainy," wrote Lewis Mumford, "life touched some of its highest moments in Venice."

To begin our search for its special and unique beauty, we'll head for—

1. St. Mark's Square

The **piazza San Marco** was the heartbeat of the Serenissima in the heyday of Venice's glory as a seafaring republic, the crystallization of her dreams and aspirations. If you have only one day for Venice, you need not leave the square, as the city's major attractions, such as the Basilica of St. Mark and the Doges' Palace, are centered there or nearby.

The traffic-free square, inhabited by tourists and pigeons, and sometimes by Venetians, is a constant source of bewilderment and interest—its moods changing as quickly as the characters in a Goldoni play. If you rise at dawn, you can almost have the piazza to yourself, watching the sun come up—the sheen of gold mosaics glisten into a mystic effect of incomparable beauty. At midmorning (9 a.m.) the overstuffed pigeons are fed by the city (if you're caught under the whir, you'll think you're witnessing a remake of Hitchcock's *The Birds*). At midafternoon the tourists reign supreme, and it's not surprising in July to witness fisticuffing over a camera angle. At sunset, when the two "Moors" in the Clock Tower strike the end of another day, lonely sailors begin a usually frustrated search for those hot spots that characterized Venice of yore but not of today. Deep in the evening, the strollers parade by or stop for espresso at the fashionable Florian Caffè—and sip while listening to a band concert.

Thanks to the effort of the conqueror of Venice, Napoleon, the square was unified architecturally, the emperor adding the Fabbrica Nuova, bridging the Old and New Procuratie. Flanked with medieval-looking palaces, Sansovino's Library, elegant shops and colonnades, the square is now finished—unlike the piazza della Signoria at Florence. On the piazza San Marco promenaded the wealthy of the old-world Europe of the 18th and 19th centuries. Among specific sights to inspect individually, we'll first explore the:

BASILICA OF ST. MARK

The so-called Church of Gold (tel. 522-5697) dominates the square. One of the world's greatest and most richly embellished churches, it looks as if it had been moved intact from Istanbul. A conglomeration of styles, it owes a heavy debt to Byzantium, but incorporates other designs, such as Romanesque and Gothic, with free-wheeling abandon. Like Venice, it is adorned with booty from every corner of the city's once far-flung mercantile empire—capitals from Sicily, columns from Alexandria, porphyry from Syria, sculpture from old Constantinople.

The basilica is capped by a dome that—like a spider plant—sends off shoots, in this case a quartet of smaller-scale cupolas. Spanning the façade is a loggia, surmounted by replicas of the four famous St. Mark's horses—the "triumphal quadriga."

On the façade are rich marble slabs and mosaics that depict scenes from the lives of Christ and St. Mark. One of the mosaics re-creates the entry of the evangelist's body into Venice, transported on a boat. St. Mark's body, hidden in a pork barrel, was smuggled out of Alexandria in 828 and shipped to Venice. The evangelist dethroned Theodore, the Greek saint who up to then had been the patron of the city that had "outgrown" him.

In the atrium are six cupolas filled with mosaics illustrating scenes from the Old Testament, including the legend of the Tower of Babel. Once the private chapel and pantheon of the doges, the basilica stuns with its interior, a wonderland of marbles, alabaster, porphyry, and pillars. Visitors walk in awe across the undulating multicolored ocean floor, patterned with mosaics.

To the right is the admission-free baptistery, dominated by the Sansovino-inspired baptismal font, on which a bronzed John the Baptist is ready to pour water. Look back at the aperture over the entryway to see a mosaic, the dance of Salome in front of Herod and his court. Wearing a star-studded russet-red dress and three white fox tails, Salome dances under a platter holding John's head. Her glassy face is that of a Madonna, not an enchantress.

After touring the baptistery, proceed up the right nave to the doorway to the treasury (tesoro), open from 9:30 a.m. to 5:30 p.m. Monday through Saturday and 1:30 to 5 p.m. on Sunday, and charging 500 lire (40¢) for admission. The oft-looted treasury contains the inevitable skulls and bones under glass, plus goblets, chalices, and Gothic candelabra.

The entrance to the presbytery is nearby (use the same ticket). In it, on the high altar, is the alleged sarcophagus of St. Mark, resting under a green marble blanket, held up by four sculptured, Corinthian-style alabaster columns. The Byzantine-style

Pala d'Oro, from Constantinople, is the rarest treasure at St. Mark's—made of gold and studded with precious stones.

On leaving the basilica, head up the stairs in the atrium for the **Marciano Museum** and the Loggia dei Cavalli. The star attraction of the museum is the world-famed Quadriga, four horses looted from Constantinople by Venetian crusaders in the sack of that city in 1204. These horses once surmounted the basilica but were removed because of damage by pollution. They were subsequently restored. This is the only quadriga (which means a quartet of horses yoked together) to have survived from the classical era. They are believed to have been cast in the 4th century. Napoleon once carted these much-traveled horses off to Paris for the Arc du Carousel, but they were returned to Venice in 1815. Hours are 10 a.m. to 5:30 p.m. Monday through Saturday, and from 2 to 4:30 p.m. on Sunday. It closes at 4:45 p.m. Monday through Saturday off-season. Admission is 500 lire (40¢). The museum, with its mosaics and tapestries, is especially interesting, but walk out onto the loggia for a view of the piazza San Marco.

THE PALACE OF THE DOGES

Off St. Mark's Square, entered through the magnificent 15th-century Porta della Carta at the piazzetta, the Doges' Palace (tel. 522-4951) is part of the legend and lore of Venice. Like a frosty birthday cake in pinkish-red marble and white Istrian stone, the Venetian-Gothic palazzo—with all the architectural intricacies of a paper doily—gleams in the tremulous Venetian light. Considered by many to be the grandest civic structure in Italy, it dates back to 1309, although a fire in 1577 destroyed much of the building.

If you enter from the piazzetta, past the four porphyry Moors, you'll stand in the middle of the splendid Renaissance courtyard, one of the latest styles in a palace that has experienced the work of many architects of widely varying tastes. You can take the "giants' stairway" to the upper loggia—so called because of the two Sansovino mythological statues.

The fire made ashes of many of the palace's greatest masterpieces, and almost spelled doom for the building itself, as a new architectural fervor of the post-Renaissance was in the air. But sanity prevailed. Many of the greatest Venetian painters of the 16th century adorned the restored palace, replacing the canvases or frescoes of the old masters.

After climbing the Sansovino "stairway of gold," you'll enter some get-acquainted rooms. Proceed to the Anti-Collegio salon housing the palace's greatest artworks—notably Veronese's *Rape of Europa,* far left on the right-hand wall. One critic called the work "delicious." Tintoretto prevails with his *Three Graces* and his *Bacchus and Adriadne.* Some critics consider the latter his supreme achievement. In the adjoining Sala del Collegio, you'll find allegorical paintings on the ceiling by Veronese. Proceeding to the right, you enter the Sala del Senato o Pregadi, with its allegorical painting by Tintoretto in the center of the ceiling.

In the Sala del Consiglio dei Dieci, with its gloomy paintings, the dreaded Council of Ten (often called "The Terrible Ten" for good reason) used to assemble to decide who was in need of decapitation. In the antechamber, bills of accusation were dropped in the lion's mouth.

Now trek downstairs through the once-private apartments of the doges to the grand "Maggior Consiglio," with its allegorical *Triumph of Venice* on the ceiling, painted by Veronese. What makes the room outstanding is Tintoretto's *Paradise,* over the Grand Council chamber—said to be "the largest oil painting in the world." Paradise seems to have an overpopulation problem, perhaps a too-optimistic point of view on Tintoretto's part. Tintoretto was in his 70s when he began this monumental work. He died only six years later. The second grandiose hall, entered from the grand chamber, is the Sala dello Scrutinio, with paintings telling of past glories of Venice.

Reentering the "Maggior Consiglio," follow the arrows on their trail across the Bridge of Sighs, linking the Doges' Palace with the Palazzo delle Prigioni, where the cellblocks are found, the ones that lodged the prisoners who felt the quick justice of the "Terrible Ten." The "sighs" in the bridge's name stemmed from the sad laments of the numerous victims led across it to certain torture and possible death. The cells are just dank remnants of the horror of medieval justice.

The palace is open daily in summer from 8:30 a.m. to 7 p.m. (from 9 a.m. to 3 p.m. in winter), and it charges 5,000 lire ($3.80) per person.

PIAZZETTA SAN MARCO

If St. Mark's Square is the drawing room of Europe, then the satellite piazzetta is the antechamber. Hedged in by the Doges' Palace, Sansovino's Library, and a side of St. Mark's, the tiny square faces the Grand Canal. Two tall granite columns are mounted by a winged lion, representing St. Mark, and a statue, supposedly that of the dethroned patron St. Theodore, taming a dragon. Both columns came from the East in the 12th century.

During the heyday of the Serene Republic, dozens of victims either lost their heads or were strung up here, many of them first being subjected to torture that would have made the Marquis de Sade flinch. One, for example, had his teeth hammered in, his eyes gouged out, and his hands cut off before being strung up. Venetian justice became notorious throughout Europe.

If you stand with your back to the canal, looking toward the south façade of St. Mark's Basilica, you'll see the so-called *Virgin and Child* of the poor baker, a mosaic which honors Pietro Fasiol (also Faziol), a young man unjustly sentenced to death on a charge of murder.

To the left of the entrance to the Doges' Palace are four porphyry figures, which, for want of a better description, the Venetians called "Moors." These puce-colored fellows are huddled close together, as if afraid. Considering the decapitations and torture that have occurred on the piazzetta, I shouldn't wonder.

THE CAMPANILE

One summer night back in 1902, the bell tower of the Basilica of St. Mark—suffering from years of rheumatism in the damp Venetian climate—gave out a warning sound that sent the elegant and fashionable coffee drinkers scurrying from the Florian Caffe in a dash for their lives. But the campanile gracefully waited till the next morning—July 14—before it tumbled into the piazza. The Venetians rebuilt their belfry, and it's now safe to ascend. In campanile-crazed Italy, where visitors must often ascend circuitous stairs, it's good to report that the Venetian version has a modern elevator. For 3,000 lire ($2.30), you can ride it for a pigeon's view of the city—any time in summer from 9:30 a.m. to 10:30 p.m. (from 10 a.m. to 4 p.m. in winter). It's a particularly good vantage point for viewing the cupolas of St. Mark's Basilica. For information, phone 522-4064.

THE CLOCK TOWER

At St. Mark's Square is one of the most typical and characteristic of Venetian scenes—that of the two Moors striking the bell atop the Clock Tower (Torre dell'Orologio; tel. 523-1879). The *torre* soars over the Old Procuratie. The clock under the winged lion not only tells the time, but is a boon to the astrologer: it matches the signs of the zodiac with the position of the sun. If the movement of the Moors striking the hour seems slow in today's fast, mechanized world, remember how many centuries the poor wretches have been at their task without time off. (The "Moors" originally represented two shepherds of the white race, but reproduced in bronze, they have grown darker with the passing of time, so they came to be called Moors by the Venetians). The tower usually may be scaled from 9 a.m. to noon and 3 to 5 p.m. It is closed Monday. Currently, it is closed for restoration. Check its status at the time of your visit.

2. The Grand Canal

Peoria may have its Main Street, Paris its Champs-Elysées—but Venice, for uniqueness, tops all of them with its Grand Canal. Lined with palazzi—many in the elegant Venetian-Gothic style—this great road of water is today filled with vaporetti, motorboats, and gondolas. Along the canal the boat moorings are like peppermint sticks. It begins at the piazzetta San Marco on one side and Longhena's Salute Church on the opposite bank. At midpoint it is spanned by the Rialto Bridge, lined with budget shops. Eventually, the canal winds its serpentine course to the railway station. I can guarantee that there's not a dull sight en route.

Of course, the gloriously coiffured ladies Longhi painted have faded with high tide. Many of the lavish furnishings and tapestries that adorned the interiors of the palaces were hauled off to museums or ended up in the homes of the heirs of the rising mercantile class of two centuries ago. In the sad decline of the city, Venetian nobility didn't get less noble; they only went broke.

Some of the major and most impressive buildings along the Grand Canal may be visited, as they have been converted into galleries and museums (see below). Others have been turned into cooperative apartments. Venetian housewives aren't the incurable romantics that the foreign visitors are. A practical lot, these women can be seen stringing up their laundry in front of thousands upon thousands of tourists.

Along this canal one foggy day came Madame Amandine Lucile, Aurore Dudevant, née Dupin (otherwise known as George Sand), with her effete, poetic young lover (Alfred de Musset), rescued from his mother's skirttails. John Ruskin came this way to debunk and expose in his *The Stones of Venice*. Robert Browning, burnt out from the loss of his beloved Elizabeth and his later rejection at the hands of Lady Ashburton, came here to settle down in a palazzo, where he eventually died. Of more recent vintage, Eleonora Duse came this way with the young poet to whom she had given her heart, Gabriele d'Annunzio. Even Shakespeare came here in his fantasies (and intrepid guides will point out the "Palazzo de Desdemona").

3. Museums and Galleries

Venice is a city of art. Decorating her palazzi and adorning her canvases were artists such as Giovanni Bellini, Carpaccio, Giorgione, Titian, Lotto, Tintoretto, Veronese, Tiepolo, Guardi, Canaletto, and Longhi, to name the more important ones. In the museums and galleries to follow, important works by all these artists are exhibited, as well as a number of modern surprises, such as the Guggenheim Collection.

Open hours are often subject to major variations, so keep this in mind as you go sightseeing. Many visitors who have budgeted only two or three days for Venice often express disappointment when for some unknown reason a major attraction will close abruptly. If you have time for only one gallery, make it—

GALLERY OF THE ACADEMY

At the campo della Carità (vaporetto stop no. 12), in the **Gallerie dell' Accademia** (tel. 522-2247), the pomp and circumstance, the glory that was Venice, lives on in a remarkable collection of paintings spanning the 14th to the 18th century. The hallmark of the Venetian school? Color and more color. From Giorgione to Veronese, from Titian to Tintoretto, with a Carpaccio cycle thrown in, the Accademia has samples—often their best—of its most famous sons. I'll highlight only some of the most-renowned masterpieces for the first-timer in a rush.

You'll first see works by such 14th-century artists as Paolo and Lorenzo Veneziano, who crossed the Byzantine bridge into a Gothic garden (see the latter's

Annunciation). Next, you'll view Giovanni Bellini's *Madonna and Saint* (poor Sebastian, not another arrow), and Carpaccio's fascinating, although gruesome, work of mass crucifixion. Moving on, head for the painting on the easel by the window, attributed to the great Venetian artist Giorgione. On this canvas, he depicted the *Madonna and Child*, along with the mystic St. Catherine of Siena and John the Baptist (a neat trick for Catherine, who seems to have perfected transmigration to join the cast of characters).

Two of the most important works with secular themes are Mantegna's armored *St. George*, with the dragon slain at his feet, and Hans Memling's 15th-century portrait of a young man. A most unusual *Madonna and Child* is by Cosmè Tura, the master of Ferrara who could always be counted on to give a new twist to an old subject. The Tuscan master Piero della Francesca is represented with *St. Jerome.*

The madonnas and bambini of Giovanni Bellini, expert in his harmonious blending of colors, are the subject of another room. None but the major artists could stand the test of a salon filled with the same subjects, but under Bellini's brush each Virgin achieves her individual spirituality. Giorgione's *Tempest,* displayed here, is the single most famous painting at the Accademia. It depicts a baby suckling from the breast of its mother, while a man with a staff looks on. What might have emerged as a simple pastoral scene on the easel of a lesser artist comes forth under Giorgione as a picture of a rare and exceptional beauty. Summer lightning pierces the sky, but the tempest seems in the background—far away from the figures in the foreground, who are menaced without knowing it.

The masterpiece of Lorenzo Lotto, a melancholy portrait of a young man, can be seen before you come to a room dominated by Paolo Veronese's *The Banquet in the House of Levi*—in reality, a "Last Supper" that was considered a sacrilege in its day, forcing Veronese to change its name to indicate a secular work. Impish Veronese caught the hot fire of the Inquisition by including in the mammoth canvas dogs, a cat, midgets, blackamoors, Huns, and drunken revelers. Four large paintings by Tintoretto—noted for their swirling action and powerful drama—depict scenes from the life of St. Mark. Finally, painted in his declining years (some have suggested in his 99th year before he died from the plague), is Titian's majestic *Pietà.*

Many other works by Veronese (an epic *Crucifixion,* an *Annunciation,* and the *Battle of Lepanto,* in which the Venetians triumphed over the Turks) and by Tintoretto (a golden *Cain and Abel* and an *Adam and Eve*) can be viewed. Tiepolo, the great decorative painter, has figures writhing across one wall, plus two curious 3-D works in the corners.

After a long and unimpressive walk, search out Canaletto's *Porticato.* Yet another room is heightened by Gentile Bellini's stunning portrait of St. Mark's Square, back in the days (1496) when the horses glistened with gold in the sunlight. All the works in this salon are intriguing, especially the re-creation of the *Ponte de Rialto,* then a covered wood bridge, by Carpaccio.

The cycle of narrative paintings that Vittore Carpaccio did of St. Ursula for the Scuola (School) of Santa Orsola is displayed. No. 578 is the most famous, showing Ursula asleep on her elongated bed, a dog nestled on the floor, as the angels come for a visitation. But all the works are excellent, a virtuoso performance by an artist. Finally, on the way out, look for Titian's *Presentation of the Virgin,* a fit farewell to this galaxy of great Venetian art.

The Gallerie dell' Accademia is open from 9 a.m. to 2 p.m. daily (holidays to 1 p.m.), charging 4,000 lire ($3.05) for admission.

CORRER MUSEUM

At the opposite end of St. Mark's Basilica, housed in the Procuratie Nuove, this museum (tel. 522-5625) traces the development of Venetian painting from the 14th to the 16th century. But on the second floor are the red-and-maroon robes once worn by the doges, plus some fabulous street lanterns, as well as an illustrated copy of *Marco Polo in Tartaria.* You can see Cosmè Tura's *La Pietà* a miniature of renown from the genius in the Ferrara School. This is one of his more gruesome works, a bony, gnarled Christ sprawled on the lap of the Madonna. Farther on, search out a Schiavone *Madonna and Child* (no. 545), my candidate for the ugliest bambino ever depicted on canvas (no wonder the mother looks askance).

One of the most important rooms at the Correr is filled with three masterpieces: *La Pietà* by Antonello da Messina; a *Crucifixion* by Hugo van der Goes, the Flemish painter; and a *Madonna and Child* by Dieric Bouts, who depicted a baby suckling from his mother in a sensual manner. The star attraction of the Correr is the Bellini salon, including works by founding padre Jacopo and his son, Gentile. But the real master of the household was the other son, Giovanni, the major painter of the 15th-century Venetian school (see his *Crucifixion* and compare it with his father's treatment of the same subject).

A small, but celebrated, portrait of St. Anthony of Padua by Alvise Vivarini is here, plus works by Bartolomeo Montagna. The most important work in the gallery, however, is Vittore Carpaccio's *Two Venetian Ladies,* popularly known as the "Courtesans." A lesser work, *St. Peter,* with the daggers in him, hangs in the same room—perhaps a hara-kiri victim for his having to share quarters with "women like that!" The Correr, charging 3,000 lire ($2.30) for admission, is open from 10 a.m. to 4 p.m. (from 9 a.m. to 12:30 p.m. on Sunday); closed Tuesday.

CA' D'ORO

This is one of the grandest and most handsomely embellished palaces along the Grand Canal (vaporetto stop no. 6). Although it contains the important **Franchetti Gallery** (tel. 523-8790), the House of Gold (so named because its façade was once gilded) competes with its own paintings. Built in the first part of the 15th century in the ogival style, it has a lacy Gothic look. Baron Franchetti, who restored and filled it with his own collection of paintings, sculpture, and furniture, presented it to Italy in World War I.

You enter into a stunning courtyard with a multicolored patterned marble floor, filled with statuary (a lovely garden out back). Then proceed upstairs to the lavishly appointed palazzo. One of the gallery's major paintings is Titian's voluptuous *Venus.* She coyly covers one breast, but what about the other?

In a special niche reserved for the masterpiece of the Franchetti collection is Andrea Mantegna's icy-cold *St. Sebastian,* riddled with what must be a record number of arrows. You'll also find works by Carpaccio.

Don't fail to walk out onto the loggia for a view of the Grand Canal. Open daily from 9 a.m. to 2 p.m. (from 9 a.m. to 1 p.m. on holidays). Admission is 2,000 lire ($1.50).

CA' REZZONICO

This 17th- and 18th-century palace (tel. 522-4543) along the Grand Canal (vaporetto stop no. 11) is where Robert Browning set up his bachelor headquarters. Pope Clement XIII also stayed here. It's a virtual treasure house, known for both its baroque paintings and furniture. First, you enter the Grand Ballroom, with its allegorical ceiling, then proceed through lavishly embellished rooms with Venetian chandeliers, brocaded walls, portraits of patricians, tapestries, gilded furnishings, and touches of chinoiserie. At the end of the first walk is the Throne Room, with its allegorical ceilings by Giovanni Battista Tiepolo.

On the first floor you can walk out onto a balcony for a view of the Grand Canal as the aristocratic tenants of the 18th century saw it. After this another group of rooms follow, including the library. In these salons look for a bizarre collection of paintings. One, for example, depicts half-clothed women beating up a defenseless naked man (one amazon is about to stick a pitchfork into his neck, another to crown him with a violin). In the adjoining room another woman seems ready to chop off a man's head, and in still another painting a woman is hammering a spike through a man's skull. Enough torture by the ladies to please Leopold von Sacher-Masoch.

Upstairs you'll find a survey of 18th-century Venetian art. As you enter the main room from downstairs, head for the first salon on your right (facing the canal), which contains the best works of all, paintings from the brush of Pietro Longhi. His most famous work, *The Lady and the Hairdresser,* is the first canvas to the right on the entrance wall. Others depict the life of the idle Venetian rich. On the rest of the floor are bedchambers, a chapel, and salons—some with badly damaged frescoes, including a romp of satyrs.

The palace is open from 10 a.m. to 3:30 p.m. Monday through Thursday, 10 a.m. to 3:30 p.m. on Saturday, and 9 a.m. to 12:30 p.m. on Sunday; closed Fridays. Admission is 3,000 lire ($2.30).

GUGGENHEIM COLLECTION

At Ca'Venier dei Leoni, an unfinished palazzo (vaporetto stop no. 14 or on foot from the Accademia), is one of the most comprehensive and brilliant modern art collections in the Western world, revealing both the foresight and critical judgment of its founder. The collection is housed in the former Venetian home of Peggy Guggenheim, who died in 1979. The house, at Dorsoduro 701 (tel. 520-6288), may be visited from early April to the end of October daily except Tuesday from 11 a.m. to 6 p.m. Admission is 5,000 lire ($3.80) for adults and 3,000 lire ($2.30) for students. Peggy Guggenheim, in the tradition of her family, was a lifelong patron of contemporary painters and sculptors. Founder of the Art of This Century Gallery in New York in the '40s, she created one of the most avant-garde galleries for the works of contemporary artists. Critics were impressed not only by the high quality of the artists sponsored, but by her methods of displaying them.

As her private collection increased, she decided to find a larger showcase and selected Venice, steeped in long tradition as a haven for artists. While the Solomon Guggenheim Museum was going up in New York to Frank Lloyd Wright's specifications, she was creating her own gallery in Venice. Guests wander through, enjoying art in an informal and relaxed way. Max Ernst was one of Peggy Guggenheim's early favorites, as was Jackson Pollock (she provided a farmhouse where he could develop his painting technique). Displayed here are works not only by Pollock and Ernst, but also by Picasso (see his cubist *The Poet* of 1911), Duchamp, Chagall, Mondrian, Brancusi, Delvaux, Magritte, and Miró, and a garden of modern sculpture including works by Giacometti and Moore. Temporary modern art shows are presented during the winter months when the permanent collection is closed. Since Peggy Guggenheim's death, the collection has been administered by the Solomon R. Guggenheim Foundation, which also operates the Solomon R. Guggenheim Museum in New York.

THE NAVAL MUSEUM AND ARSENAL

The **Naval Museum of Campo San Biasio** (Museo Storico Navale) on the riva degli Schiavoni (tel. 520-0276) is filled with cannons, ships' models, and fragments of old vessels dating back to the days when Venice was master of the Adriatic. The prize exhibit is a gilded model of the *Bucintoro,* the great ship of the doge that surely would have made Cleopatra's barge look like an oil tanker in comparison. In addition, you'll find models of historic and modern fighting ships, of local fishing and rowing craft, and a collection of 24 Chinese junks, as well as a number of maritime *ex voto* from churches of Naples.

If you walk along the canal branching off from the museum, you come first (about 270 yards from the museum and before the wooden bridge) to the **Ships' Pavilion** where historic vessels are displayed. Proceeding on along the canal, you soon reach the **Arsenal** at the campo de l'Arsenal, guarded by stone lions, Neptune with a trident, and other assorted ferocities. You'll spot it readily enough because of its two towers, flanking each side of the canal. The Arsenal in its day turned out galley after galley at speeds usually associated with wartime production.

The museum and pavilion are open from 9 a.m. to 1 p.m. (to noon on Saturday). Closed on holidays. The same ticket, costing 1,000 lire (75¢), admits you to both.

FORTUNY MUSEUM

The 15th-century Palazzo Pesaro degli Orfei, at campo San Benedetto 3780 (tel. 520-0995), is now Museo Fortuny, where you can see the home and work surroundings of Mariano Fortuny, who lived here for almost 50 years. The Spanish-born Fortuny was known for his fabric and dress designs, especially his pleated silk Grecian gowns popular around the turn of the century. However, he was also engaged in theater set design, in painting, and in photography. In his fabric designs, he used motifs of Islam, France, Greece, Africa, and Italy, as well as pre-Columbian civilizations. In the museum and the artist's former living quarters, you can see murals, fabrics (including a fine Oriental rug simulated on velvet), portraits, his own copies of old masters, and other interesting decorative pieces. The museum is open daily except Monday from 9 a.m. to 7 p.m. Admission is 5,000 lire ($3.80). From the campo San Benedetto, you enter through a courtyard, going upstairs to a loggia.

---

4. Scuole and Churches

SCUOLA DI SAN ROCCO

Of the scuole of Venice, none is as richly embellished as this one, filled with epic canvases by Tintoretto. By a clever trick, he won the competition to decorate the darkly illuminated early-16th-century building. He began painting in 1564, and the work stretched on till his powers as an artist waned. The paintings sweep across the upper and lower halls, mesmerizing the viewer with a kind of passion play. In the grand hallway, they depict New Testament scenes, devoted largely to episodes in the life of Mary (the *Flight into Egypt* is among the best). In the top gallery are works illustrating scenes from both the Old and New Testaments, the most renowned being those devoted to the life of Christ. In a separate room is what is considered Tintoretto's masterpiece—his mammoth *Crucifixion*, one of the world's most celebrated paintings. In it he showed his dramatic scope and sense of grandeur as an artist, creating a deeply felt scene that virtually comes alive—filling the viewer with the horror of systematic execution, thus transcending its original subject matter.

The school, charging 5,000 lire ($3.80) for admission, is open April 1 to October 31 from 9 a.m. to 1 p.m. and 3:30 to 6:30 p.m. daily. From November 1 to March 31, hours are 10 a.m. to 1 p.m. Monday through Friday and 10 a.m. to 1 p.m. and 3 to 6 p.m. on Saturday and Sunday. Last tickets are sold at 12:30 and 6 p.m. For more information, phone 523-4864. Vaporetto stop: no. 10.

SANTA MARIA DEI FRARI

Known simply as the Frari, the Venetian-Gothic church is at campo dei Frari (tel. 522-2637), only a short walk from the Scuola di San Rocco (vaporetto stop no. 10, San Tomà). The church is filled with some great art. First, the best—Titian's *Assumption* over the main altar, a masterpiece of soaring beauty, depicting the ascension of the Madonna on a cloud "puffed up" by floating cherubs. In her robe, but especially in the robe of one of the gaping saints below, "Titian red" dazzles as never before.

On the first altar to the left as you enter is Titian's second major work here—a *Madonna Enthroned,* painted for the Pesaro family in 1526. Although lacking the power and drama of the *Assumption,* it nevertheless is a brilliant painting in the use of both color and light effects. But Titian surely would turn redder than his madonna's robes if he could see the latter-day neoclassical tomb built for him on the opposite wall. The kindest word for it: large.

Facing it is a memorial to Canova, the Italian sculptor who led the revival of classicism. To return to more enduring art, head to the sacristy for a Giovanni Bellini triptych on wood, painted in 1488. The Madonna is cool and serene, one of Bellini's finest virgins. Also see an almost primitive-looking woodcarving by Donatello of *St. John the Baptist*. The basilica is open daily from 9 a.m. to noon and 2:30 to 5 p.m., and charges 800 lire (60¢) for admission.

SCUOLA DI SAN GIORGIO DEGLI SCHIAVONI

At St. Antonino Bridge (fondamenta dei Furlani) off the riva degli Schiavoni is the second important school (tel. 522-8828) to visit in Venice. Between 1502 and 1509, Vittore Carpaccio painted a pictorial cycle here of exceptional merit and interest. Of enduring fame are his works of St. George and the dragon, my favorite art in all of Venice—certainly the most delightful. For example, in one frame St. George charges the dragon on a field littered with half-eaten bodies and skulls. Gruesome? Not at all. Any moment you expect the director to call "Cut!" The pictures relating to St. Jerome are appealing but don't compete with St. George and his ferocious dragon.

April to October, hours are Tuesday through Saturday from 9:30 a.m. to 12:30 p.m. and 3:30 to 6:30 p.m. (on Sunday from 9:30 a.m. to 12:30 p.m.). From November through March, hours are 10 a.m. to 12:30 p.m. and 3:30 to 6 p.m. (on Sunday from 10 a.m. to 12:30 p.m.). The school is closed Monday, and charges an admission of 3,000 lire ($2.30).

CHIESA MADONNA DELL'ORTO

At campo dell'Orto, this church provides a good reason to walk to this fairly remote northern district of Venice (vaporetto stop no. 6). At the church on the lagoon, you'll be paying your final respects to Tintoretto. The brick structure with a Gothic front is famed not only because of its paintings by that artist, but because the great master is buried in the chapel to the right of the main altar. At the high altar are Tintoretto's *Last Judgment* (on the right) and his *Sacrifice of the Golden Calf* (left)—two monumental paintings that curve at the top like a Gothic arch. Over the doorway to the right of the altar is Tintoretto's superb portrayal of the presentation of Mary as a little girl at the temple. The composition is unusual in that Mary is not the focal point—rather, a pointing woman bystander dominates the scene. The first chapel to the left of (facing) the main altar contains a masterly work by Cima de Conegliano, showing the presentation of a sacrificial lamb to the saints (the plasticity of John's body evokes Michelangelo). Finally, the first chapel on the left (as you enter) is graced with an exquisite Giovanni Bellini *Madonna and Child* (note the eyes and mouth of both mother and child, a work of consummate skill). There are two other pictures on the apse representing *The Presentation of the Cross to St. Peter* and *The Beheading of St. Christopher* (1551–1555). Besides the five paintings of the apse are works by Tintoretto and his school. Two paintings are by Palma the Younger: *The Annunciation* and *The Crucifixion* (where the influence of his master, Tintoretto, is seen).

In summer, daily hours are 9:30 a.m. to noon and 4 to 7 p.m., from 9:30 a.m. to noon and 3 to 4:30 p.m. in winter. For information, phone 719-933.

CHURCH OF SAN SEBASTIANO

This is at campo San Bastian, and can be reached by waterbus line 5, stopping at San Basilio. It's also possible to tie in a visit here with one to Ca' Rezzonico. If so, take line 1, getting off at stop no. 11. Continue down calle Larga San Barnaba to San Sebastiano. In a city as rich in art as Venice, this small Renaissance church might easily have been overlooked. However, it's well worth a visit, as it contains the only frescoes of Paolo Veronese in Venice (also his first), plus canvases of exceptional beauty, the cycle illustrating the story of San Sebastian and of Esther. The master, who died in 1588, is buried near the side altar on the left. The church also contains paintings by Titian, Tintoretto, and an architectural monument by Sansovino.

The Church of San Sebastiano is not a museum. It is a functioning Catholic church, which can be visited by phoning the rector for an appointment (tel. 528-2487).

CHURCH OF SAN ZACCARIA

Behind St. Mark's Basilica on the square named after San Zaccaria is a Gothic church (tel. 522-1257) with a Renaissance façade. The church is filled with works of art, notably Giovanni Bellini's *Madonna Enthroned*, painted with saints (second altar to the left). Many have found this one of Bellini's finest madonnas, and it does have beautifully subdued coloring, although it appears rather static. Apply to the sacristan to see the Sisters' Choir, with works by Tintoretto, Titian, Il Vecchio, Anthony van Dyck, and Bassano. The paintings aren't labeled, but the sacristan will point out the names of the artists. In the Sisters' Choir are five armchairs in which the Venetian doges of yore sat. And—the best for last—see the faded frescoes of Andrea del Castagno in the shrine honoring San Tarasio.

The church is open daily from 10 a.m. till noon and 4 to 6 p.m.

CHURCH OF SAN GIORGIO

It sits on the little island of San Giorgio Maggiore, across the water from the piazzetta San Marco. To visit it, take the Giudecca-bound vaporetto (no. 8) or motorboat (no. 5) on the riva degli Schiavoni, getting off at the first stop, right in the courtyard of the church (tel. 528-9900). The building was designed by Palladio, the great Renaissance architect of the 16th century—perhaps as a consolation prize for his not being chosen to rebuild the Doges' burnt-out Palace. The logical rhythm of the Vicenza architect is played here on a grand scale. But inside it's almost too stark (Palladio was not much on gilded adornment). The chief art hangs in the main altar —two epic paintings by Tintoretto—one to the left, the *Fall of Manna,* and then the far more successful *Last Supper* to the right. It's interesting to compare Tintoretto's *Cena* with that of Veronese at the Academy. Afterward, you may want to take the elevator for 2,000 lire ($1.50) to the top of the belfry for a view of the greenery of the island itself (look for the Greek-style Teatro Verde), the lagoon, and the Doges' Palace across the way. In a word, it's unforgettable.

The church is open daily from 10 a.m. to 12:30 p.m. and 2:30 p.m. to closing which ranges from 4 to 6:30 p.m., depending on the season.

SANTA MARIA DELLA SALUTE

Like the proud landmark that it is, this church—the pinnacle of the baroque movement in Venice—stands at the mouth of the Grand Canal, overlooking the piazzetta San Marco (vaporetto stop no. 14). One of the most historic churches in Venice, it was built by Longhena in the 17th century as an offering to the Virgin for delivering the city from the grip of the plague. It was erected on enough pilings to support the Empire State Building (well, almost). Surmounted by a great cupola, the octagonal basilica makes for an interesting visit, as it houses a small art gallery in its sacristy (tip the custodian)—a marriage feast of Cana by Tintoretto, allegorical paintings on the ceiling by Titian, and a mounted St. Mark and poor St. Sebastian with his inevitable arrow. The latter works, however, did not earn for Titian the title of "Il Divino."

The admission-free basilica is open daily from 7 a.m. to noon and 3 to 7 p.m.

CHURCH OF SS. GIOVANNI E PAOLO

On the campo of the same name, this church, also known as "Zanipolo," is often called the pantheon of Venice, as it houses the tombs of many doges. One of the great Gothic churches of Venice, the building was erected between the 13th and 14th centuries. Inside, it contains artwork by many of the most noted Venetian painters. As you enter, you'll find a retable (right aisle) by Giovanni Bellini (including a St. Sebastian filled with arrows). In the Rosary Chapel are ceilings by Veronese, depicting New Testament scenes, including *The Assumption of the Madonna*. To the right of the church is one of the world's best-known equestrian statues—that of Bartolomeo Colleoni (paid for by the condottiere), sculptured in the 15th century by Andrea del Verrochio. The bronze has long been acclaimed as his masterpiece, although it was completed by another artist. The horse is far more beautiful than the armored military hero, who looks as if he had just stumbled upon a three-headed crocodile. Open daily from 9 a.m. to noon and 3 to 6 p.m. (closes at 5 p.m. in winter). To the left of the pantheon is the **Scuola di San Marco,** with its stunning Renaissance façade (it's now run as a civic hospital).

THE GHETTO

The Ghetto of Venice, instituted in 1516 by the Venetian Republic, stands in the northwestern corner of Venice. Once Venetian Jews were confined to a walled area and obliged to wear distinctive red or yellow marks (cloth circles or hats). The walls were torn down long ago, but much remains of the past. One of the most beautiful synagogues, the **Scola Tedesca,** has been restored, the program financed by funds from West Germany. This is the German "Scola," one of five synagogues: the others are the Spanish one that is the oldest continuously functioning synagogue in Europe, the Italian, the Levantine-Oriental, and Scola Canton. Tours usually include three synagogues (sometimes two), with the museum and tourist service run by a partnership providing tourists with multilingual guides.

The museum is open daily from 10:30 a.m. to 1 p.m. and 2:30 to 5 p.m. from mid-March to the end of June, from 9:30 a.m. to 5 p.m. from July to the end of October. Admission to the museum is 2,000 lire ($1.50); the guided tour of the synagogues is included for 6,000 lire ($4.55). For more information, get in touch with the **Jewish Community Museum,** Cannaregio 2902 in the campo di Ghetto Nuovo (tel. 715-359).

While in the area, you can explore on your own, seeing houses huddled close together, narrow streets, and a little museum documenting hundreds of years of Venetian Jewish life. In all, it represents a complex that is unique in the world.

5. A Walking Tour of Venice

There are potentially hundreds of byways, alleyways, and canals stretching across the faded splendor of Venice. This two-hour walking tour will give you at least an exterior view plus a general orientation to the layout of parts of the city, often showing lesser-known sights, which can best be seen from the outside, on foot. Later, you can pick and choose at your leisure the sights you most want to revisit, especially those requiring interior inspections.

Our tour begins, appropriately enough, at the heartbeat **piazza San Marco,** or St. Mark's Square, perhaps the most famous in Italy. Here and on its satelite square, the **piazzetta San Marco,** you can explore the major attractions of the city, including the **Basilica of St. Mark,** the **Palace of the Doges,** the **Campanile,** and the **Clock Tower.**

The Renaissance mariners who supplied the lifelines leading to their Adriatic capital realized that the most impressive view of the city was, and perhaps still is, visible only from the water. To better see this unforgettable view, I suggest that you take a brief vaporetto ride across the Grand Canal to the rhapsodically baroque white walls of **Santa Maria della Salute.** Buy your ticket at either of two vaporetti stops:

no. 16 (San Zaccaria), just east of St. Mark's Square, or no. 15 (San Marco Giardinetti), which lies just west of the square along the Grand Canal. Enjoy the short water ride and the view before getting off on the opposite canal at stop no. 15 at the pier marked "Salute." There you can look back across the Grand Canal at the rows of palazzi, many of which have been turned into glamorous hotels.

Walk to the right-hand side of the church along the campo della Salute, past a pair of wooden bridges, and continue until you reach the third bridge, the only one of the three made of stone. Cross this bridge, heading onto rio Terràdei Catecumeni. After one block, turn left onto calle Constantina. Now walk toward the water, along a wide flagstone-covered walkway divided by a single row of trees struggling to survive in the salt air of Venice. The waterway you'll soon reach separates this section of Venice from the rarely visited island of **Giudecca.** Turn right, admiring the faraway baroque churches and houses, as well as the industrial cranes of Venice's industrialized mainland sister, Mestre, to the north.

This is much more of a neighborhood than the area around the piazza San Marco. It has often been compared to New York's Greenwich Village because of the artists and writers traditionally attracted to it; many, of course, came to avoid the stratospheric prices charged on the opposite side of the Grand Canal. With water to your left, and a changing panorama of brick and stone buildings to your right, you'll cross over the high arches of several bridges, always continuing along the canalside walkway which, in characteristically Venetian fashion, will change its name at least three times.

At the third and last bridge, the Ponte della Calcina, at the campiello della Calcina, notice two of the most famous pensiones of Venice, La Calcina, where John Ruskin stayed, and the Pensione Seguso, both previously recommended. The name of the pavement that supports you here is the zattere ai Gesuati. You'll notice a pair of wooden platforms, managed by local cafés and separated from one another by dry-docked steel-hulled ships. After perhaps a coffee, you reach the acanthus pilasters of the baroque **Chiesa dei Gesuati.** After visiting the church, take the street to its right-hand side, rio Terrà Antonio Foscarini.

Admire the campo Santa Agnese, the square set to the side of the church where bells call the neighborhood to mass. Now, continue north along rio Foscarini until you reach the Grand Canal and the **Gallerie dell'Accademia.** You can either visit this great gallery of art or else save it for another day. Cross the bridge, noticing the West German consulate beside the elegant garden to the left. When you step off the bridge, you'll be on the campo San Vidal. At this point, the city of Venice has graciously mapped out one of the most logical walking tours in the city, posting prominently displayed yellow signs with black lettering on dozens of appropriate street corners.

Your walk, if you follow the signs, will take you back to St. Mark's Square through dozens of claustrophobic alleys, crumbling from exposure to the Adriatic winds, and into gloriously proportioned squares whose boundaries are often ornamented with exquisite detailing. From this point on, follow the signs that say "per S. Marco." You can afford to ignore your map and lose yourself in the Renaissance splendor in this most unusual city. At the campo San Vidal, the pavement will funnel you in only one possible direction. After several twists and turns, you'll be in the huge expanse of the **campo San Stefano.** Keep walking across the square, past a wood-and-iron flagpole capped with the Lion of St. Mark. Midway along the right-hand side of the square, follow the "per S. Marco" sign down a tiny alleyway called the calle del Spezier. The alley funnels across a bridge and then changes its name to calle del Piovan. This will open to the wide expanses of the **campo San Maurizio.** Walk directly across the square, looking for yet another "per S. Marco" sign, taking you over another set of bridges.

This square funnels into the narrow calle Zaguri. Cross another canal's arched bridge and enter the campiello de la Feltrina. Keep following the signs to San Marco. Soon you'll come to one of the most famous squares of Venice, shaped roughly like a crucifix. One end opens onto the Grand Canal, near the most famous hotel in Venice, the Gritti Palace. The full name of the square is the campo Santa Maria Zobenigo O del Giglio, a name usually shortened to **campo del Giglio.** The square is dominated by a larger-than-life-size statue, guarding the baroque façade of the **Chiesa di Santa Maria del Giglio.** Founded in the 9th century, but reconstructed in the 17th century, it contains canvases by Tintoretto and Rubens.

As you exit from the church, follow once again the signs to San Marco, going down an alleyway, calle de le Ostreghe. Cross the high arch of a canal-spanning bridge, then stop in for a stand-up espresso or cappuccino, and perhaps one of the tasty sandwiches served at the Bar Ducale on the far side. When you exit, follow the street through several twists and turns onto the **calle Larga XXII Marzo.** Its many shops make this one of the most-frequented streets of Venice.

Notice the faraway **Church of San Mosè,** whose ornate façade fills the space at the end of the street. At this point, midway down the calle Larga XXII Marzo, I recommend a short detour off to the left. Notice the gold, white, and red sign pointing to "al teatro la Fenice." The street this points to is calle del Sartor da Veste. Turn neither to the left or right, but follow it over two bridges, into what is often considered one of the most intimate summertime "living rooms" of Venice, the **campo San Fantin.** In fair weather, the enclosed square is dotted with tables set out by the best restaurant in Venice, Antico Martini, and its lesser rivals. Here you'll find the **Teatro La Fenice** and the **Church of St. Fantin.** After visiting the church, retrace your steps along the street you took previously. From the end of the square, its name appears as calle del Cafetier. This walk will take you back over the pair of bridges leading once again to calle Larga XXII Marzo.

Turn left, heading in the direction of San Mosè Church. By now the "per S. Marco" signs will lead you through the **campo San Mosè,** with the modern bulk of the Hotel Bauer Grünwald and Grand Canal on your right. Take the street to the left of the church, noticing the sign, "per S. Marco," as you pass by the American Express office heading straight along the street which, by now, has changed its name once again, this time to calle Seconda de l'Ascension. Continue straight under an arched tunnel to the sweeping expanses of St. Mark's Square, where you'll surely be ready for a coffee at the Caffè Florian.

Later, walk through the square, passing to the left of the Basilica of St. Mark, stopping perhaps to admire a pair of lions carved from red porphyry. As you gaze with the lions back across the wide expanse of the square, notice the arched tunnel piercing the base of the Clock Tower. Pass beneath the Moorish bellringers and the zodiacal representations of the clock face. Here you will be on the major shopping street of Venice, the **Mercerie.** Of course, this is the popular name of the street. It actually has many longer names, preceded by the word "merceria." From now on, your guiding light will be the signs saying "per Rialto." They will be either formally positioned at strategic corners in yellow or black or scrawled sometimes graffiti-style on the sides of buildings.

Once at the **Rialto,** I suggest you board a vaporetto back to the piazza San Marco. This ride along the palazzi-flanked banks of the **Grand Canal** is not only one of the grandest experiences in all of Italy, but in the entire world.

---

6. Shopping in Venice

Venetian glass and lace are known throughout the world. But selecting quality products in either craft requires a shrewd eye. There is much that is tawdry and shoddily crafted in Venetian shops. Some of the glassware hawked isn't worth the cost of shipping it home. Yet other pieces represent some of the world's finest artistic and ornamental glass. Murano is the island where glass is made, and the women on Burano put in painstaking hours turning out lace. If you're interested in some little glass souvenir of your stay, perhaps an animal or a bird, you'll find such items sold in shops all over Venice. Most shops are open daily except Sunday from 9 a.m. to 12:30 p.m. and 3 to 7:30 p.m. If you want to make a serious purchase, read on.

VENETIAN GLASS

Perhaps the finest and most reliable dealer in Venetian glass in the city is **Salviati s.r.l.,** San Gregorio 195 (tel. 522-2532). On St. Mark's Square, it keeps two small shops. If you apply there, you'll be escorted to its main showrooms and museum of antique glass on the Grand Canal. From April to the end of September, hours are 9 a.m. to 7 p.m. Monday through Saturday and 9 a.m. to 12:30 p.m. Sunday. After September, hours are 9 a.m. to 12:30 p.m. and 3 to 6 p.m. Monday through Saturday. Salviati has displays in great museums of the world, including the Vatican and the Museum of Modern Art in New York.

Another premier house of Venetian glass is **Pauly & Co.,** San Marco Ponte Consorzi (tel. 520-9899). This award-winning house exports all over the world. You can wander through its 30 salons, enjoying an exhibition of artistic glassware, later seeing a furnace in full action. There is no catalog offered; Pauly's production, which is mainly to order, consists of continually renewed patterns, subject to change and alteration based on customer desire.

VENETIAN LACE

For serious purchases, **Jesurum,** Ponte Canonica 4310, behind St. Mark's Basilica (tel. 520-6177), is the best place. This elegant shop, a center of famous lacemakers and fashion creators, has been located in a 12th-century church since 1870. They offer Venetian handmade or machine lace and embroidery on table, bed, and bath linens. Quality and originality are guaranteed, and special orders are accepted. The exclusive linens created here are expensive, but the inventory is large enough to accommodate most budgets.

JEWELRY

The most highly refined selection of exquisite Venetian jewelry is found at **Nardi Sergio,** piazza San Marco 68-71 (tel. 522-5733). For old pieces, fine silver, antique jewelry, and new and original designs, it is stunning.

LEATHER

With three shops near each other at San Marco Ascensione 1291, 1301, and 1305, **Vogini** (tel. 522-2573) offers every kind of leatherwork, especially women's handbags, which are exclusive models by such makers as Roberta di Camerino, Moshino, Soprani, and Celine. There's also a large assortment of handbags in petit-point, and the collection of artistic Venetian leather is of the highest quality, as well as fine men's and women's wear and shoes. The travel-equipment department contains a large assortment of trunks and wardrobe suitcases as well as dressing cases—many of the latest models in luggage.

BRASS OBJECTS

Founded in 1913, **Valese Fonditore,** San Marco 793 (tel. 522-7282), a short walk from the piazza San Marco, is a showcase outlet for one of the most famous of several foundries making Venice their headquarters. Many of its brass copies of 18th-century chandeliers that grace fine homes in the United States are produced by this company. Many visitors to Venice invest in these brass castings which eventually become family heirlooms. If you're looking for a brass replica of the sea horses decorating the sides of gondolas, this shop stocks them in five or six different styles and sizes.

PAPER

You can browse or buy at **Legatoria Piazzesi,** Santa Maria del Giglio 2511 (tel. 522-1202), among displays of patterned, hand-printed paper, perhaps selecting paper-covered objects in bright colors as souvenirs of Venice. *Legatoria* means bookbindery, and some of this work is still done on special order, but the shop mainly offers such objects as scrapbooks, address books, diaries, Venetian carnival masks, and paperweights. Of course, you can also find writing paper, monogrammed, and decorative pieces. The shop does not ship purchases.

GRAPHICS

For the right—and light—souvenir of Venice, **Osvaldo Böhm,** San Mosè 1349-1350 (tel. 522-2255), has a rich collection of photographic archives specializing in Venetian art, original engravings and maps, lithographs, watercolors, and Venetian masks. Also you can see modern graphic works and some fine handcrafted bronzes.

CHILDREN'S WEAR

In Venice, **Maricla,** via XXII Marzo 2401 (tel. 523-2202), is called the boutique *per bambini e giovinette,* which means for babies and young girls. It also has a fine collection of lingerie for women, as well as exquisite embroideries.

BARGAINS

If you're seeking some bargain-basement buys, head not for any basement but to one of the little shops that line the **Rialto Bridge.** The shops there branch out to encompass fruit and vegetable markets as well. The Rialto isn't the Ponte Vecchio in Florence, but what it offers isn't bad, particularly if your lire are running short. You'll find a wide assortment of merchandise here, ranging from angora sweaters to leather gloves. Quality is likely to vary widely, so plunge in with utmost discrimination.

---

7. The Lido and Lagoon

Along the white sands of the Lido strolled a hand-holding Eleonora Duse and Gabriele d'Annunzio (*Flame of Life*); Goethe in Faustian gloom; a clubfooted Byron trying to decide with whom he was in love that day; de Musset pondering the fickle ways of George Sand; Thomas Mann's Gustave von Aschenbach with his eye on Tadzio in *Death in Venice.* But gone is the relative isolation of yore. The de Mussets of today aren't mooning over lost loves: they're out chasing bikini-clad new ones.

Near the turn of the century the Lido began to blossom into a fashionable beachfront resort, complete with deluxe hotels and its Municipal Casino (see "Venice After Dark"). Lido prices are usually stratospheric. It is not a haven for budget-minded tourists.

Even if you aren't lodging at the Lido, you may still want to come over for a swim in the Adriatic. And if you don't want to cross the thresholds of the rarefied citadels of hotel beachfront property—with huts lining the beach like those of some tropical paradise—you can try the Lungomare G. d'Annunzio Public Bathing Beach at the end of the Gran Viale (piazzale Ettore Sorger), a long stroll from the vaporetto stop. You can book cabins—called *camerini*—and enjoy the sand. Rates change seasonally.

To reach the Lido, take vaporetto 6 (the ride takes about 15 minutes). The boat departs from a landing stage near the Doges' Palace.

But don't confine your look at the Venetian lagoon just to the Lido. Venice is surrounded by islands, at least three of which make for a memorable day's outing by vaporetto transportation.

MURANO

In the lagoon is the island where glassblowers have for centuries performed oral gymnastics turning out those fantastic chandeliers (some with porpoise arms) that Victorian ladies used to prize so highly, along with heavily ornamented glasses so ruby-red or so indigo-blue you can't tell if you're drinking blackberry juice or pure wood-grain. Happily, the glassblowers are still plying their trade, although increasing competition—notably from Sweden—has forced sophistication into some of the designs. Still, the tasteful ware must be sought out in a glass menagerie where some of the animals (reptilian chalices) should never have been released, much less allowed inside your home.

Murano remains the chief expedition from Venice, but it doesn't take even second place in the beauty contests (Burano and Torcello are far shapelier). How to visit: You can combine a tour of Murano with a trip around the lagoon. To reach it, take vaporetto 5 at riva degli Schiavoni, a short walk from the piazzetta San Marco. The boat docks at the landing platform at Murano where—lo and behold—the first furnace awaits conveniently.

As you stroll through Murano, you'll find that the factory owners are only too glad to let you come in and see their age-old crafts (try to arrive in midmorning when the furnaces are going full blast). These managements aren't altogether altruistic, of course. While browsing through the showrooms, you need stiff resistance to keep the salesmen at bay. And it's possible to bargain down the initial quoted offer by salespeople. Don't—repeat, don't—pay the marked price on any item. That's merely the figure at which to open negotiations.

An exception to that is made-on-the-spot souvenirs, which are turned out at Murano. For example, you might want to purchase a horse streaked with blue. The artisan takes a piece of incandescent glass, huffs, puffs, rolls it, shapes it, snips it, and behold—he has shaped a horse. The showrooms of Murano also contain a fine assortment of Venetian crystal beads, in every hue of the rainbow. You may find some of the best work to be the experiments of apprentices. On one recent occasion a clerk was trying to steer me toward a tawdry vase when I spied some delicately hued glass based on Etruscan designs. The clerk was apologetic—"just the work of students." But I purchased an exquisite Etruscan-style vase and a she-wolf whose distant ancestor suckled Romulus and Remus.

While on the island, you can visit a Renaissance palazzo housing the **Museo Vetrario di Murano** (tel. 739-586). It is open in summer daily except Wednesday from 10 a.m. to 4 p.m. (on Sunday from 9:30 a.m. to 12:30 p.m.). In winter, opening time is the same, with closing at 3 p.m. Admission is 3,000 lire ($2.30). Inside is a spectacular collection of Venetian glass.

The **Church of San Pietro Martire** dates from the 1300s but was rebuilt in 1511. Richly decorated, it offers a respite from the glass factories, with its paintings by Tintoretto and Veronese. Its proud possession is a *Madonna and Child Enthroned* by Giovanni Bellini, plus two superb altarpieces by the same master.

Even more notable is **Santi Maria e Donato,** campo San Donato, which is open daily from 8 a.m. to noon and 4 to 7 p.m. A stellar example of the Venetian Byzantine style, in spite of its 19th-century restoration, it dates from the 7th century from Greece. The interior is known for its mosaic floor—a parade of peacocks and eagles, as well as other creatures—and a 15th-century ship's-keel ceiling. Over the apse is an outstanding mosaic of the Virgin against a gold background, dating from the early 1200s.

You can take the same ferry back, but why not get off at fondamente Nuove, then slowly stroll through an unheralded section of the city that will bring you closer to the quiet charm and serene beauty of Venice?

Where to Dine

Trattoria Busa alla Torre, campo San Stefano 3 (tel. 739-662), offers well-prepared fish dishes and an unusual location at the top of a flight of stairs in a 13th-century building. The decor conjures up memories of other family restaurants along the Venetian coast. Here, specialties include recipes unique to Murano, including scampi alla Busa, a variety of bluefish, good sardines, and a wide array of fish anti-pasti, along with a mixed Adriatic fish fry and the ubiquitous fish-flavored risotto and fish soup. The restaurant is open from 9 a.m. to 8 p.m. every day but Sunday. Expect to spend around 50,000 lire ($38) for a meal with fish.

Al Corallo, fondamenta dei Vetrai 73 (tel. 739-636), is usually filled with a wide variety of clients from all walks of life. Specialties here are typically Venetian, and the service is polite. Local clients choose this restaurant for a well-deserved meal after a morning of hard physical work, blending with the tourists. A substantial dinner will likely cost from 35,000 lire ($26.50). The restaurant, open from noon to 3:30 p.m. and 7 to 8:30 p.m., is closed on Tuesday and from mid-December to mid-January.

Ai Vetrai Già ai Piavoleti, fondamenta Manin 29 (tel. 739-293), one of the leading restaurants of Murano, entertains and nourishes its guests in a large, fashionably decorated room not far from the Canale dei Vetrai. If you're looking for fish prepared in the local style, with what might be called the widest selection in Murano, this is it. Most varieties of crustaceans and gilled creatures are available on the spot. However, if you phone ahead and order food for a large party, as the Venetians sometimes do, the owners will prepare what they call "a noble fish" on special command. Expect to spend from 40,000 lire ($30.50) for a full meal. The restaurant is open daily from noon to 5 p.m. only; closed on Wednesday off-season.

BURANO

An island riddled with canals, Burano became world famous as a center of lacemaking, a craft that reached its pinnacle in the 18th century (recall Venetian point?). The visitor who can spare a morning to visit this island will be rewarded with a charming little fishing village far removed in spirit from the grandeur of Venice, but lying only half an hour away by ferry. Boats leave from fondamente Nuova, which overlooks the Venetian graveyard, well worth the trip all on its own.

Once at Burano, you'll discover that the houses of the islanders come in varied colors—sienna, robin's-egg or cobalt blue, barn-red, butterscotch, grass green. If you need a focal point for your excursion, it should be the **Scuola Merietti** in the center of the fishing village at piazza Baldassare Galuppi. The Burano School of Lace was founded in 1872 as part of a resurgence movement aimed at restoring the age-old craft that had earlier declined, giving way to such other lacemaking centers as Chantilly and Bruges. By going up to the second floor you can see the lacemakers, mostly young girls, at painstaking work, and can purchase hand-embroidered or handmade-lace items.

After visiting the lace school, you can walk across the square to the **Duomo** and its leaning campanile (inside, look for the *Crucifixion* by Tiepolo). However, do so at once, because the bell tower is leaning so precariously it looks as if it will topple at any moment.

Where to Dine

If you're on the island at mealtime, you may want to join a long line of people who have patronized the rather simple-looking *caratteristico* **Trattoria de Romano,** via Baldassare Galuppi 223 (tel. 730-030), around the corner from the lace school. For about 50,000 lire ($38), you can enjoy a superb dinner there, which consists of risotto di pesce (the Italian version of the Valencian paella); followed by fritto misto di pesce, a mixed fish fry from the Adriatic, with savory bits of mullet, squid, and shrimp. The tab also includes refreshing wine, fresh fruit, and service. Hours are noon to 2:30 p.m. and 7 to 8:30 p.m.; closed Tuesday and for certain parts of winter.

Ostaria ai Pescatori (a.k.a. Trattoria dei Pescatori), piazza Baldassare Galuppi 371 (tel. 730-650). The family that pools its efforts to run this well-known restaurant maintains strong friendships with the local fishermen, who often reserve the best parts of their daily catch for preparation in the kitchen here. The cooking is performed by the matriarch of an extended family. The place has gained a reputation as the preserver of a type of simple and unpretentious restaurant unique to Burano. Locals in dialect call it a *buranello*. Clients often take the vaporetto from other sections of Venice (the restaurant lies close to the boat landing) to eat at the plain wooden tables set up either indoors or on the small square in front. Specialties feature all the staples of the Venetian seaside diet, including fish soup, risotto di pesce, pasta seafarer's style, and a wide range of crustaceans, plus grilled, fried, or baked fish. Expect to spend 50,000 lire ($38) to 60,000 lire ($45.50) per person, which might include a bottle of fruity wine from the region. The restaurant is open daily except Monday from noon to 3 p.m. and 7 to 9 p.m. It takes a vacation in January.

A short boat ride takes you from Burano to—

TORCELLO

Of all the islands of the lagoon, Torcello—the so-called Mother of Venice—offers the most charm. If Burano is behind the times, Torcello is positively antediluvian. In the footsteps of Hemingway, you can stroll across a grassy meadow, traverse an ancient stone bridge, and step back into that time when the Venetians first fled from invading barbarians to create a city of Neptune in the lagoon. Torcello has two major attractions: a church with Byzantine mosaics good enough to make the Empress Theodora at Ravenna turn as purple with envy as her robe, and a *locanda* (inn) that converts trippers into inebriated angels of praise. But, first, the spiritual nourishment before the alcoholic sustenance—

The **Cattedrale di Torcello,** also called Church of Santa Maria Assunta (tel. 730-084), was founded in A.D. 639 and subsequently rebuilt. Whipped by the winds of the Adriatic, it stands in a lonely grassy meadow beside a campanile dating from the 11th century. It is visited chiefly because of its Byzantine mosaics. Clutching her child, the weeping Madonna in the apse is a magnificent sight. On the opposite wall is a powerful *Last Judgment.* Byzantine artisans, it seems, were at their best in portraying hell and damnation. At Santa Maria Assunta they do not disappoint. In their Inferno they have re-created a virtual human stew, the fires stirred by wicked demons. Reptiles slide in and out of the skulls of cannibalized sinners. Open daily from 10 a.m. to 12:30 p.m. and 2 to 6:30 p.m. Admission is 1,000 lire (75¢).

Where to Dine

After a whiff of this Dantesque nightmare, you'll need one of "Harry's" martinis.

Locanda Cipriani (tel. 730-150), just across from the church, is an inn extraordinaire. The term *locanda* usually denotes an unusually inexpensive lodging, rated under the lowliest pensione. But not so at this place. The country inn is well appointed with an open-air dining loggia. The chef features a number of high-priced dishes, with suggested dinners on the menu ranging from 65,000 lire ($49.50) to 100,000 lire ($76) for a big spread. Specialties: cannelloni, fish soup (most savory), and a rice pilaf, a big, saffron-colored portion. For an appetizer, try the gnocchi, a Roman-inspired dish, made with a semolina base. It's open from noon to 3 p.m. and 7 to 10 p.m. mid-March until November 10. Closed Tuesday.

Final warning: If you go on your own, don't listen to the savvy gondoliers who hover at the ferry quay. They'll tell you that both the cathedral and the locanda are "miles away." Actually, they're both reached after a leisurely 12- to 15-minute stroll along the canal.

8. Venice After Dark

In the olden days, wealthy Venetians were rowed down the Grand Canal, serenaded by gondoliers. To date, no one has improved on that age-old custom. But it can be very expensive.

CAFES

Strolling through St. Mark's Square, having a cup of espresso at one of its cafés, and listening to a band concert may be even better.

The most famous café is the **Florian,** piazza San Marco 56 (tel. 528-5338), open daily except Wednesday from 9 a.m. to midnight. Dating from 1720, it is romantically and elegantly decorated—pure Venetian salons with red plush banquettes, intricate and elaborate murals under glass, and art-nouveau lighting and lamps. Considered the most fashionable and aristocratic rendezvous in Venice, the Florian roster of customers has included such figures as Casanova, Lord Byron, Goethe, Canova, de Musset, and Madame de Stäel.

Special cocktails include a Bellini or a mimosa, each costing from 11,000 lire ($8.35), with most long drinks priced at 14,000 lire ($10.75). Most visitors, however, order an espresso at 4,000 lire ($3.05). During concerts, if you sit down at a sidewalk table a surcharge of 3,500 lire ($2.65) will be imposed.

Quadri, piazza San Marco 120 (tel. 522-2105), stands on the opposite side of the square, the sunny side. It, too, is elegantly decorated in an antique style. It should be, as it was founded in 1638. Wagner used to drop in for a drink when he was working on *Tristan and Isolde.* Its prices are virtually the same as at the Florian, and it, too, imposes that surcharge on drinks ordered during concert periods. A coffee costs 3,000 lire ($2.30), but if there's music, the price goes up to 3,800 lire ($2.90). Hours are daily except Monday from 9:30 a.m. to 11 p.m. During the peak weeks of summer it remains open on Monday, however.

Café Lavena, piazza San Marco 134 (tel. 522-4070), is a popular but intimate café under the arcades of the piazza San Marco. The establishment was frequented by Richard Wagner during his stay in Venice. He composed some of his greatest operas here. It has one of the most beautifully ornate glass chandeliers in town—the kind you'll love even if you have Venetian glass—hanging from the ceiling between the iron rails of an upper-level balcony. The dozens of maroon glass "Aunt Jemima" heads perched on each of the chandeliers is a good example of Italian wit. You'll spend 900 lire (70¢) for a small coffee. Hours are 9:30 a.m. to midnight daily. The most interesting tables are near the plate-glass window in front, although there's plenty of room at the stand-up bar as well.

Want more in the way of nightlife? All right, but be warned: the Venetian nightclub owners may sock it to you when they present the bill. The Lido is the star bet in your search for twinkling colored lights, the featured attraction being the—

MUNICIPAL CASINO

If you want to risk your luck and your lire, you can take a boat ride on the Casino Express, leaving from the stops of the railway station, piazzale Roma and piazzetta San Marco, and delivering you to the landing dock of the Casino Municipale, lungomare G. Marconi 4 (tel. 526-0626), which stands near the Hotel Excelsior Lido. Open daily from 3 p.m. to 2:30 a.m. from April to September only, the casino is considered one of the most spectacular in Europe, certainly one of the most famous. The Italian government wisely forbids its nationals to cross the threshold unless they're working on the staff. But foreign visitors who remembered to bring their passports are admitted for a fee of 15,000 lire ($11.50). Once inside, guests can enjoy food and entertainment at one of the floor shows, or else just gamble, playing such games as roulette, craps, chemin de fer, and blackjack.

In winter, the casino action moves to the **Palazzo Vendramin Calergi,** Cannaregio 2040, strada Nuova (tel. 720-444), the palace on the Grand Canal where Wagner died in 1883. Hours are 3 p.m. to 2:30 a.m. daily.

THE BARS

The Londra Palace Hotel's **Do Leoni,** riva degli Schiavoni 4171 (tel. 520-0533), leads the ranks of piano bars. The interior is a rich blend of scarlet-and-gold carpeting with a motif of lions, English pub-style furniture, and Louis XVI–style chairs, along with plenty of exposed mahogany. An outdoor terrace is more nautical in feeling, with drinks served at canvas director's chairs surrounded with lots of shrubbery. The view is of a 19th-century bronze statue of a collection of Amazonian lion tamers, the lagoon, and the foot traffic along the Grand Canal. The hotel's deluxe restaurant has already been previewed. However, from 8 p.m. (till 1 a.m.), entertainment takes over, the piano adding musical warmth. A whisky costs from 9,000 lire ($6.85).

Martini Scala, campo San Fantin 1980 (tel. 522-4121), is a piano bar with live music and singers, with full dinners or just snacks served until early morning. The music in this completely redecorated place consists mostly of songs from the '50s and '60s. It's possible to dance here although it is not a dance hall. Particularly popular are the after-theater dinners, drawing crowds who have attended presentations at La Fenice, whose entrance is just on the right of the nightclub. In this deluxe atmosphere, specialties served include petto d'oca affumicato con pompelmo e rucola (smoked goose breast with grapefruit and arugula), gnocchi burro e salvia (dumplings with butter and sage), and salmone al burro nero (fresh salmon with black butter and olives). Expect to pay 45,000 lire ($34.25) to 50,000 lire ($38) for a three-course repast, including a good house wine. Drinks cost from 10,000 lire ($7.60). Hours are 8 p.m. to 3:30 a.m. daily except Tuesday in winter, 10 p.m. to 3:30 a.m. in summer.

In July and August, **Settimo Cielo** (roof garden of the deluxe hotel, Bauer Grünwald), San Mosè 1440 (tel. 523-1520), is ideal for tripping the light fantastic under a Venetian moon—that is if you don't mind shelling out 14,000 lire ($10.75) per drink. There's no floor show, but the piano bar is good. It opens nightly at 9 p.m. (no set closing hour).

Bar Ducale, San Marco 2354 (calle delle Ostreghe) (tel. 521-0002), occupies a tiny corner of a building near a bridge over a narrow canal. Customers stand at the zinc bar facing the carved 19th-century Gothic-reproduction shelves. A specialty is a mimosa cocktail, but the sandwiches are one of the bar's attractions. The ebullient owner learned his craft at Harry's Bar before going into business for himself. Today his small establishment is usually mobbed every day of the week, except on Tuesday when it's closed. Other days it's open from 8:30 a.m. to 9 p.m., ideal for an early-evening apéritif as you stroll about. A whisky costs from 2,500 lire ($1.90).

Bar ai Speci, in the Hotel Panada, calle dei Specchieri 646 (tel. 520-9088), is a charming corner bar a short walk from St. Mark's Basilica. Its richly grained paneling is offset by dozens of antique mirrors, each different, whose glittering surfaces reflect the rows of champagne and scotch bottles and the clustered groups of Biedermeier chairs. The bar is open daily for guests of the hotel, but closed on Monday to outsiders. Hours are 5 p.m. to midnight; whisky costs 5,000 lire ($3.80) to 7,000 lire ($5.30).

FOLK MUSIC

At the **Alla Grotta,** calle dell'Angelo 407 (tel. 520-9299), performers alternate between operatic arias and old Venetian love ballads, the audience occasionally joining in. And you can drown your own blues in purple wine. In a cellar, the Grotta is incredibly touristy, but that's a characteristic it shares with nearly every other establishment in Venice. The action starts after dinner at 10 p.m. and continues till 1 a.m. Entrance costs 18,000 lire ($13.75). Closed in winter.

WINE DRINKING

A wine bar with a selection of more than 250 Italian and imported wines, **Vino Vino,** calle del Cafetier 2007-A (tel. 522-4121), attracts a heterogeneous clientele: a Venetian countess may be sipping prosecco near a gondolier eating polpette. Loved by snobs, young people, and tourists with little money left, the place offers wines by the bottle or glass, including Italian grappas. Dishes of Venetian popular cuisine are served, including sarde in saor, nervetti, folpetti, pastas, fagioli, spezzatino, baccalà (codfish), and polenta. The two rooms are always jammed like a vaporetto in rush hour, and there is take-away service if you can't find a place. Hours are 10 a.m. to 1 a.m. daily. Expect to spend 15,000 lire ($11.50) to 20,000 lire ($15.25) for a meal, from 800 lire (60¢) to 8,500 lire ($6.45) for a glass of wine.

Enoteca Volto, calle Cavalli di San Marco 4081 (tel. 522-8945), lies off fondamenta del Carbon. Considering the rarity of some of the vintages served at this wine bar, the tiny room that shelters it is unpretentious. Yet it is a Venetian institution. Found on a narrow street, it offers more than 2,000 labels, as well as dozens of varieties of beer. There are few places to sit, but that doesn't bother some of the more dedicated drinkers, a few of whom have patronized the place since it was established in 1936. Wine costs 1,000 lire (75¢) to 4,000 lire ($3.05) per glass. Salty snacks and small pizzas are also sold, and the enoteca, open from 8:45 a.m. to 1:20 p.m. and 4:15 to 9 p.m., closes every Sunday and for all of August.

ICE CREAM

For many, strolling to **Gelateria Paolin,** campo San Stefano 2962A (tel. 522-5576), a large colorful square, and ordering some of the tastiest ice cream (*gelato*) in Venice, is nightlife enough. That's the way many a Venetian spends the evening in summer. This ice-cream parlor (*gelateria*) stands on the corner of the busy square. You can order your ice cream to go or eat it at one of the sidewalk tables. Many interesting flavors are offered, including pistachio. But you may want to be adventurous and try something known as "Málaga" The gelateria is open from 7:30 a.m. to midnight in summer (till 9 p.m. in winter), but is closed on Friday.

THE FILM FESTIVAL

Since 1952 Venice has played host to an annual festival of the cinema, usually beginning in the last days of August and running into the first two weeks of September. Steadily mushrooming in popularity, the festival attracts top stars and directors, all accompanied by a glittering assortment of the international set. Motion pictures are most often presented in their original languages, with Italian subtitles. Films are shown at the **Palazzo de Cinema,** on the Lido near the Municipal Casino.

The very fortunate time their visit to Venice to coincide not only with the film festival, but with the spectacular regatta, usually held on the first Sunday in September. The Grand Canal fills with richly ornamented craft, and spectators from the balconies of the palazzi watch the race of the gondolas. The regatta is an ancient Venetian custom—worth the trip to Venice just to see the period costumes.

THEATER-GOING

One of the most famous theaters in Europe, **La Fenice,** San Marco 2549 (campo San Fantin) (tel. 522-3954), has existed since the 19th century (an earlier structure was gutted by fire). In the 18th-century heyday of La Fenice, Carlo Goldoni, a Venetian playwright and master of comedy, presented his buffoons night after night —and play after play—to the delight of high society. Italy has yet to produce another master of comedy to topple Goldoni from his pedestal near the Rialto Bridge. To cap the perfect visit, try to attend either a concert or an opera at this theater. Check locally to see if anything is being presented at the time of your visit.

XII

VERONA, PADUA (PADOVA), AND VICENZA

1. VERONA
2. PADUA (PADOVA)
3. VICENZA

Tearing yourself away from the piazza San Marco is a task for those of iron will. But Venice doesn't possess a regional monopoly on art or treasures. Of the cities of interest easily reached from Venice, three tower above the rest. They are Verona, the home of the eternal lovers, Romeo and Juliet; Padua, the city of Mantegna, with its frescoes by Giotto; and Vicenza, city of Palladio, with its streets of Renaissance palazzi and its villa-studded hills. The miracle of all of these cities is that Venice did not siphon off their creative drive completely, although the Serene Republic dominated them for centuries.

The first and most important sightseeing center is the longest distance from Venice—

1. Verona

The home of a pair of star-cross'd lovers, Verona was the setting for the most famous love story in the English language, Shakespeare's *Romeo and Juliet*. A long-forgotten editor of an old volume of the bard's plays once wrote: "Verona, so rich in the associations of real history, has even a greater charm for those who would live in the poetry of the past." It's not known if a Romeo or a Juliet ever existed, but the remains of Verona's recorded past are much in evidence today. Its Roman antiquities, as only one example, are unequaled north of Rome.

In the city's medieval age of flowering under the despotic, cruel Scaligeri princes, Verona reached the pinnacle of its influence and prestige, developing into a town that even today is considered among the great cities of Italy. The best-known member of the ruling Della Scala family, Cangrande I, was a patron of Dante. His sway over Verona has often been compared to that of Lorenzo the Magnificent over Florence.

Verona's telephone area code is 045.

THE SIGHTS

Verona is found alongside the snaking Adige River, about 71 miles from Venice. It's most often visited on a quickie half-day excursion from that city (easily reached on the autostrada), but Verona deserves more time. It's meant for wandering and for contemplation. If you're rushed, head first to the old city to begin your exploring at the—

Piazza dei Signori

Opening onto this square, the handsomest in Verona, is the Palazzo del Governo, where Cangrande extended the shelter of his hearth and home to that fleeing Ghibelline, Dante Alighieri. The marble statue in the center of the square, the expression as cold as a Dolomite icicle, is of the "divine poet." But unintimidated pigeons perch on his pious head. Facing Dante's back is the late-15th-century Loggia del Consiglio, surmounted by five statues. The most attractive building on the square, the loggia is frescoed. Five different arches lead into the piazza dei Signori, the innermost chamber of the heart of Verona. From the piazza, the arch to the right of the building will take you to the—

Arche Scaligere

These outdoor tombs, surrounded by highly decorative wrought iron, form a kind of open-air pantheon of the Scaligeri princes. One tomb, that of Cangrande della Scala, rests directly over the door of the Santa Maria Antica Church, dating from the 12th century, with many Romanesque features. It is crowned by a copy of an equestrian statue (the original is now at the Castelvecchio). The tomb nearest the door is that of Mastino II; the one behind it—and the most lavish of all—that of Cansignorio. Adjoining the piazza dei Signori is the—

Piazza delle Erbe

The old Roman forum, this lively, palace-flanked square is today the setting of the fruit and vegetable market . . . and milling Veronese, both shoppers and vendors. In the center of the square is a fountain dating from the 14th century and a Roman statue dubbed *The Virgin of Verona*. The pillar at one end of the square, crowned by a chimera, symbolizes the many years that Verona was dominated by the Serenissima. Important buildings and towers include the House of Merchants, dating from the early years of the 14th century; the Gardello Tower, built by one of the Della Scala princes; the restored former city hall and the Lamberti Tower, soaring about 260 feet; the Maffei Palace in the baroque style; and finally, the Casa de Mazzanti.

From the vegetable market, you can walk down **via Mazzini,** the most fashionable street in Verona, to the **piazza Brà,** with its neoclassical town hall and the Renaissance palazzo, the Gran Guardia. But the reason for a visit is to view—

The Arena

Evoking the Colosseum in Rome, the elliptically shaped amphitheater on the piazza Brà dates from the 1st century A.D. Standing today are four arches of the "outer circle" and a complete "inner ring." For nearly half a century it's been the setting of a summer opera house, usually from mid-July to mid-August. More than 20,000 people are treated to Verdi or Mascagni, for example. The Arena is open from 9 a.m. to 6 p.m. in summer and charges 3,000 lire ($2.30) for admission. Closed Monday.

Reservations can be made and tickets purchased at the box office of the arena daily from 9 a.m. to 12:20 p.m. and 3 to 5:30 p.m. Reservations can also be made by letter, enclosing a bank draft or money order for the necessary amount of payment and indicating the date of performance, the section, and the number of tickets desired. Customers are taken care of on the basis of the availability of seats on receipt of the order. Write to Ente Lirico Arena di Verona, piazza Brà 28, 37100 Verona (tel. 045/590-109). Phone orders are not accepted.

Castelvecchio

Ordered built by Cangrande II in the 14th century, the Old Castle (tel. 594-734) is alongside the Adige River (and reached by heading out via Roma). It stands near the Ponte Scaligero, the bridge bombed by the Nazis in World War II and subsequently reconstructed. The former seat of the Della Scala family, the restored castle has been turned into an **art museum,** with important paintings from the Veronese school and works by other masters of northern Italy. On the ground floor are displays of 14th- and 15th-century sculpture, and on the upper floor you will see masterpieces of painting from the 15th to the 18th century.

In the Sala Monga is Jacopo Bellini's *St. Jerome,* in the desert with his lion and crucifix. Two sister-like portraits of Saint Catherina and Veneranda by Vittore Carpaccio grace the Sala Rizzardi Allegri. The Bellini family is also represented here by a lyrical *Madonna con Bambino* painted by Giovanni, the master of that subject.

Between the buildings is the most charming equestrian statue I've ever seen, that of Cangrande I, grinning like a buffoon, with a dragon sticking out of his back like a projectile. In the Sala Murari dalla Corte Brà is one of the most beguiling portraits in the castle—Giovanni Francesco Caroto's grinning red-haired boy with a caricature. In the Sala di Canossa are paintings by Tintoretto, a *Madonna Nursing the Child* and a *Nativity,* and by Veronese, a *Deposition from the Cross* and the *Pala Bevilacqua Lazise.*

In the Sala Bolognese Trevenzuoli is a rare self-portrait of Bernardo Strozzi, and in the Sala Avena, among paintings by the most famous Venetian masters such as Gianbattista and Giandomenico Tiepolo and Guardi, hangs an almost satirical portrait of an 18th-century patrician family by Longhi.

The castle is open from 8:30 a.m. to 7 p.m. daily except Monday. Admission is 3,000 lire ($2.30).

Church of San Zeno Maggiore

This near-perfect Romanesque church and campanile, at the piazza San Zeno, a long walk along the river from the Castelvecchio, is graced with a stunning entrance —two pillars supported by puce-colored marble lions and surmounted with a rose window. On either side of the portal are bas-reliefs depicting scenes from the Old and New Testaments, as well as a mythological story portraying Theodoric as a huntsman lured to hell (the king of the Goths defeated Odoacer in Verona). The panels, nearly 50 in all, on the bronze doors are a remarkable achievement of primitive art, sculpted perhaps in the 12th century. They reflect, of course, a naïve handling of their subject matter—see John the Baptist's head resting on a platter. The artists express themselves with such candor that they achieve the power of a child's storybook. Inside, the church is divided into a central nave and two aisles. Somber, severe, it contains a major Renaissance work at the main altar, a triptych by Andrea Mantegna, showing the Madonna and Child enthroned with saints. Although not remarkable in its characterization, it reveals the artist's genius for perspective.

The church can be visited from 7 a.m. to noon and 3 to 7 p.m. daily.

Church of Sant'Anastasia

In piazza Sant'Anastasia, the same square as the deluxe Hotel Due Torri, the church dates from the 13th century. Its façade isn't complete, yet nevertheless it is considered the finest representation of the Gothic design in Verona. Many artists in the 15th and 16th centuries decorated the interior, and few of the works seem worthy of being singled out for special mention. The exception, however, is the Pellegrini Chapel, with the reliefs in terracotta by the Tuscan artist Michele. The interior consists of one nave, flanked by two aisles, and the overall effect is impressive, especially the patterned floor. As you enter, look for two hunchbacks. Open daily from 9 a.m. to noon and 2:30 to 5:30 p.m. (to 6 p.m. in summer).

Il Duomo

At the piazza del Duomo, the cathedral of Verona is outdistanced in interest by San Zeno, but it still merits a visit. A blend of the Romanesque and Gothic styles, its façade contains (lower level) sculptured reliefs by Nicolaus, made in the 12th century, depicting scenes of Roland and Oliver, who were two of the legendary dozen knightly paladins attending Charlemagne. In the left aisle (first chapel) is an *Assumption* by Titian. The other major work of art is the rood screen in front of the presbytery, with Ionic pillars, designed by Samicheli. Open daily from 9 a.m. to 12:30 p.m. and 2:30 to 5:30 p.m. (to 6 p.m. in summer).

Basilica of San Fermo

At the piazzo San Fermo, a Romanesque church dating from the 11th century forms the foundation of the 14th-century Gothic basilica that surmounts it. Through time it's been used by both the Benedictines and the Franciscans. The interior is unusual, with a single nave and a splendid roof constructed of wood and exquisitely paneled. The most important work in the basilica is Pisanello's frescoed *Annunciation*, to the left of the main entrance (at the Brenzoni tomb). Delicate and graceful, the work reveals the artist's keen eye for architectural detail and his bizarre animals.

Roman Theater (Teatro Romano)

Originally built in the 1st century A.D., the Teatro Romano, now in ruins, climbs the foot of St. Peter's Hill. For nearly a quarter of a century a Shakespearean festival has been staged here on certain dates in July and August, and, of course, it makes for a unique theater-going experience to see *Romeo and Juliet* or *Two Gentlemen of Verona* in this setting. The theater (tel. 800-0360) is across from the Adige River (take the Ponte di Pietra). It is open Tuesday through Sunday from 8 a.m. to 6 p.m. (closes at 2 p.m. in winter); closed Monday. Admission is 3,000 lire ($2.30).

After seeing the remains of the theater, you can take an elevator to the 10th-century Santa Libera Church towering over it. In the cloister of St. Jerome is the **Roman Archeological Museum,** with its interesting mosaics and Etruscan bronzes.

Giardino Giusti

One of the oldest and most famous gardens in Italy, the Giardino Giusti was created at the end of the 14th century. These well-manicured Italian gardens, studded with cypress trees, form one of the most relaxing and coolest spots in all of Verona for strolls. You can climb all the way to the "monster balcony" for an incomparable view of the city. The romantic Arcadians of the 18th century met here in a setting appropriate to their idealized beliefs.

What we see today is the layout given the gardens by Alessandro Vittoria, who worked with Palladio. All its 16th-century characteristics—the grottoes, the statues, the fountains, the mascarons, the box-enclosed flower garden, and the maze—have remained intact. In addition to the flower displays, you can admire the statues by Lorenzo Muttoni and Alessandro Vittoria, interesting Roman remains, and the great cypress mentioned by Goethe.

The gardens have been visited by the illustrious over the centuries, including Addison, De Brosses, Mozart, Goethe, and Emperor Joseph II. The gardens, with their adjacent 16th-century palazzo, form one of Italy's most interesting urban complexes. The maze, constructed with myrtle hedges, faithfully reproduces the 1786 plan of the architect Trezza. Its complicated pattern and small size make it one of the most unusual in Europe.

The gardens lie near the Roman Theater, only a few minutes' walk from the heart of the city. They are open daily from 8 a.m. to sunset, charging an admission of 4,000 lire ($3.05). For information about the gardens, call 877-492.

Juliet's Tomb

Outside the city, the so-called **Tomba di Giulietta** (tel. 25-361) is sheltered in a Franciscan monastery entered on via Luigi da Porto, off via del Pontiere. "A grave? O, no, a lantern . . . For here lies Juliet, and her beauty makes this vault a feasting presence full of light." Don't you believe it! Still, the cloisters, in the vicinity of the Adige River, are graceful. Adjoining the tomb is a **museum of frescoes,** dedicated to G. B. Cavalcaselle. Both these places are open to the public daily from 8:30 a.m. to 7 p.m. (close an hour earlier in winter), charging an admission of 3,000 lire ($2.30).

Juliet's House

La Casa di Giulietta, via Cappello 23 (tel. 38-303), is a small house with a balcony and a courtyard. With a little bit of imagination it's not difficult to hear Romeo saying: "But, soft! what light through yonder window breaks? It is the east, and Juliet is the sun!" The house is open from 8:30 a.m. to 7 p.m.; closed Monday. Entrance is 3,000 lire ($2.30).

Sightseeing Tip

At the **Ente Provinciale per il Turismo,** via Valverde 34 (tel. 30-086), you'll be able to pick up a map before setting out on a tour of Verona.

A Shopping Note

Verona attracts devotees of antiques who satisfy their whims by wandering around corso Santa Anastasia, via Massalongo, via Sottoriva, and adjacent streets. Here you'll find any number of shops selling porcelain, furniture, ornaments, tapestries, paintings, and prints. In addition, the historic center of Verona, particularly via Cappello and via Mazzini, is full of shops of nearly every description, ranging from fashionable boutiques to handcraft shops and department stores. The already-previewed piazza delle Erbe, of course, sells every conceivable kind of goods—well, almost.

HOTELS IN VERONA

Verona boasts a deluxe hotel, the Due Torri. After that, the level of accommodations drops considerably, making most of the lodgings more suitable for overnighting than lingering. Hotel rooms tend to be scarce during the Country Fair in March and the opera and theater season in July and August.

A Deluxe Choice

Hotel Due Torri, piazza Sant'Anastasia 4, 37121 Verona (tel. 045/595-044), is almost a sightseeing attraction in addition to a hotel. Rebuilt in 1958 in the original style, it hides secret glamour behind a streamlined façade. Originally the Due Torri belonged to the Scaligeri ruling princes and has in its time sheltered such notables as Mozart, Goethe, and Emperor Alexander I of Russia (in the city in 1822 for the Congress of Verona). Enrico Wallner did a brilliant job of creating one of the most unusual luxury hotels in Italy. To attain the perfection he sought, he launched a massive antique hunt for fine pieces of the 18th and 19th centuries. When you check in, the concierge shows you color photographs of what the rooms are like, and you can choose your own theme. The range is splendid—Directoire, Empire, Louis XVIII, even the Germanic Biedermeier. Few hotels in Europe have such tasteful and well-thought-out rooms. There are 96 such impressive bedchambers, all with private bath, central heating, and air conditioning (most are soundproof as well). Single rooms rent for 170,000 lire ($129) to 210,000 lire ($160) daily, and twins and doubles go for 260,000 lire ($198) to 313,000 lire ($238). The old oil paintings inserted in ceiling panels make for a floating art gallery. The little salons available on each floor are equally distinguished. If you order dinner, expect to pay from 55,000 lire ($41.75) for a gourmet-level meal, served in the restaurant, All'Aquila. Menus are based on typical local and light cuisine. This is one of the most distinguished restaurants of Verona, and even if you're not a guest of the hotel you can visit for a meal. Food is served daily from 12:30 to 2:30 p.m. and 7:15 to 10 p.m.

First-Class Hotels

Columba d'Oro, via C. Cattaneo 10, 37121 Verona (tel. 045/595-300), is an old villa in the center of town, with moss-green shutters and balconies. Inside, it is efficiently organized to accommodate voyagers in an atmosphere that hovers between semi-traditional and contemporary. The 49 bedrooms, all with private bath or shower, are nicely furnished, with matching fabrics and comfortable pieces. The single rate is 102,000 lire ($77.50) daily. The high-season charge for doubles is 140,000 lire ($106). The hotel's service is good.

Hotel Accademia, via Scala 12, 37121 Verona (tel. 045/596-222), is an elegant centrally located hotel whose marble-floored lobby is covered with Oriental rugs, a medieval tapestry, and two marble columns flanking the polished stone stairwell leading to the bedrooms. There's a warmly paneled, modern bar at the far end of the lobby, just past the elevator and a monochromatic mural of old Verona. Rooms are comfortable and well kept, each with private bath or shower, mini-bar, direct-dial phone, color TV, and air conditioning. A single costs 115,000 lire ($87.50) daily, and a double goes for 170,000 lire ($129) to 215,000 lire ($163), with a continental breakfast included. The hotel has a covered garage.

The Medium-Priced Range

Milano Hotel, vicolo Tre Marchetti 11, 37127 Verona (tel. 045/596-011), is a 49-room hotel, one minute from the Roman Arena. Its public rooms are furnished in a functional style. The bedrooms are neatly laid out with utilitarian simplicity but remain restful, although too small in many cases. All the accommodations contain private bath or shower, a single costing from 70,000 lire ($53.25) daily, a double going for 88,000 lire ($67). Other facilities include a garage and an elevator.

Giulietta e Romeo, vicolo Tre Marchetti 3, 37121 Verona (tel. 045/800-3554), has two balconies on the street façade, most appropriate for the Romeo and Juliet of today. By leaning out either balcony, you can see the Roman Arena. The hotel has a slight formality to it, with a fumed oak lobby. The recently remodeled hotel has 29 rooms, all with private bath or shower. The rate in a single room is 56,000 lire ($42.50) daily. Doubles go for 80,000 lire ($60.75).

The Budget Range

Aurora, piazza delle Erbe, 37121 Verona (tel. 045/594-717), is a tower-size building—three rooms on each landing—stacking up six flights and serviced by an elevator. This little hotel opens off the piazza delle Erbe, the center of the city. It's modest, immaculate, and comfortable. Many of the rooms overlook the market square. Each floor has its own toilet and bath, and each room is equipped with an individual water basin. Bathless rooms cost 33,000 lire ($25) daily in a single, 58,000 lire ($44) in a double. Doubles with bath rent for 75,000 lire ($57); singles with bath go for 38,000 lire ($23). Breakfast, service, and taxes are included.

Hotel de' Capuleti, via del Pontiere 26, 37122 Verona (tel. 045/800-0154), is an attractively simple little hotel, which lies in a convenient position a few steps from Juliet's (supposed) Tomb and the chapel where she was said to be married. The reception area has stone floors and leather-covered couches, along with a tastefully renovated decor that's reflected upstairs in the comfortable bedrooms, each with toilet, shower, and individually controlled air conditioning. The hotel charges from 74,000 lire ($56.25) daily for a single and from 95,000 lire ($72.25) for a double.

Hotel San Luca, via Volto San Luca 8, 37122 Verona (tel. 045/591-333), is a contemporary hotel whose entrance is below a covered passage leading into a major boulevard, the corso Porta Nuova, just beyond the city walls. The well-maintained lobby has two-tone marble floors and lots of sunlight. The simple and attractive bedrooms rent for 90,000 lire ($68.50) daily in a single and 125,000 lire ($95) in a double, with a continental breakfast included.

WHERE TO DINE

The oldest eating place in Verona, **Ristorante 12 Apostoli,** vicolo Corticella San Marco 3 (near the piazza delle Erbe, up via Pelliciai; tel. 596-999), has been in business for two centuries. It's a festive place at which to dine, steeped in tradition, with frescoed walls and two dining rooms separated by brick arches. It's operated by the two Gioco brothers. Giorgio is the artist of the kitchen, changing his menu daily in the best tradition of great chefs, while Franco directs the dining room. Just consider some of these delicacies: salmon baked in a pastry shell (the fish is marinated the day before, seasoned with garlic, stuffed with scallops); or chicken stuffed with shredded vegetables and cooked in four layers of paper. To begin with, I recommend the tempting antipasti alla Scaligera. Another specialty is cotoletta 12 Apostoli. Even the spaghetti alla salmi d'olive is superb. For your dessert, you can order the homemade cake, a big piece. Count on spending at least 55,000 lire ($41.80) to 75,000 lire ($57) for a really top-notch repast with wine. The restaurant, serving from 1:30 to 2:30 p.m. and 7:30 to 10 p.m., is closed Sunday night, all day Monday, and for three weeks beginning sometime in mid-June.

Ristorante il Desco, via Dietro San Sebastiano 7 (tel. 595-358), is a handsome restaurant, one of the best in Verona. In the historic center, in a tastefully renovated palazzo that's one of the civic prides of the city, the restaurant is ably directed by Elia Rizzo. The menu steers closer to the philosophy of nouvelle cuisine à l'italienne than almost anything else in town. Specialties make use of the freshest of ingredients, including a purée of shrimp, taglierini with crabmeat, calamari salad with shallots, tortellini with sea bass, risotto with radicchio and truffles, and tagliolini with fresh mint, lemon, and oranges. The wine cellar is superb, and your sommelier will help you with a choice if you're unfamiliar with regional vintages. The cheese selection includes a wide range, featuring choices from France. Expect to spend from 75,000 lire ($57) for a full meal, served from 12:30 to 2 p.m. and 7 to 9:30 p.m. The restaurant is closed on Sunday and in June. Reservations are strongly advised.

Nuova Marconi, via Fogge 4 (tel. 595-295), is one of the most glamorous restaurants in Verona. It's in an ochre villa with canopies on a narrow street just around the corner from the piazza Signori. The exterior doors are covered with an art-nouveau wrought-iron grill, while the interior has stone columns, silk-shaded lamps, lots of framed paintings, and some of the best food in Verona (many claim *the* best). The restaurant is the winner of many culinary prizes, serving such specialties as beef filet Maria Callas, filet of fresh salmon in sauce, salmon gnocchi, seafood in a basil sauce, and luscious desserts. Dining is on two levels, and the service is agreeable. The restaurant is open from noon to 2:30 p.m. and 7:30 to 10 p.m.; closed Sunday. Expect to spend 55,000 lire ($41.75) to 70,000 lire ($53.25).

Ristorante Re Teodorico, piazzale di Castel San Pietro (tel. 49-990), is perched in a choice scenic position, high on a hill at the edge of town, with a panoramic view of Verona and the Adige River. From its entrance, you descend a cypress-lined road to a ledge-hanging restaurant, suggestive of a lavish villa. Tables are set out on a wide flagstone terrace edged with a row of classical columns and an arbor of red and yellow rose vines. Specialties on the à la carte menu include fondue bourguignonne, filet of sole cooked in white wine, and rognone di vitello (calves' kidneys). The desserts are as heavenly as the view, for example, zabaglione in marsala wine or a banana flambé with Cointreau. For a complete meal, expect to pay from 55,000 lire ($41.75) per person. Hours are 12:30 to 2:30 p.m. and 7:30 to 9:30 p.m. The restaurant is closed Wednesday and in November.

VeronAntica, via Sottoriva 10 (tel. 800-4124), is a distinguished local restaurant housed on the ground floor of a five-story townhouse. It lies a short block from the river, across from a cobblestone arcade similar to the ones used in the film *Romeo and Juliet.* This is an establishment that attracts the Veronese themselves—not just tourists. Reservations are absolutely necessary, particularly at night when the address is made even more romantic by a hanging lantern dimly illuminating the street. The chef knows how to prepare all the classic Italian dishes as well as some innovative ones too. The restaurant, open from 12:30 to 2:30 p.m. and 7:30 to 10:30 p.m., charges 40,000 lire ($30.50) to 60,000 lire ($45.50) for an elegant repast. It is closed all day Sunday and for Monday lunch, and also from mid-July through the first three weeks of August.

Torcoloti, via Zambelli 24 (tel. 800-6777), offers an elegant and refined atmosphere and one of the best reputations in the city for turning out skillfully prepared specialties. Menu items include gnocchi verde with gorgonzola, Italian antipasti (which includes smoked salmon), tortellini with ricotta and fresh spinach, grilled filet of pork, tournedos, pasta with mushrooms, and filet of veal castellana (stuffed with fresh mushrooms and prosciutto). Full meals, served from 12:30 to 2:30 p.m. and 7:30 to 9:30 p.m., range from 40,000 lire ($30.50) to 50,000 lire ($38). The restaurant is closed all day Sunday and on Monday night, and also takes a holiday from early June till early July.

Al Bragozzo, via del Pontiere 13 (tel. 30-035), lies at the edge of the historic district, a short walk from the river and Juliet's so-called tomb. It is also across the street from one of Verona's more popular budget hotels, De' Capuleti, already previewed. This restaurant lies behind a crumbling stucco façade whose windows are topped with canopies. It is arguably the best fish restaurant in the city, serving a fresh array of crustaceans and Adriatic fish, which can be baked, grilled, or fried, according to your preference. The calamari are very good, as are the scampi, usually priced by the gram. Expect to spend 30,000 lire ($22.75) to 50,000 lire ($38) for a meal. Hours are 12:30 to 2:30 p.m. and 7:30 to 10 p.m. The restaurant is closed Monday and from the last week of June to mid-July.

2. Padua (Padova)

Padua no longer looks as it did when Burton tamed shrew Taylor in the Zeffirelli adaptation of Shakespeare's *The Taming of the Shrew,* which was set in old Padua. But it remains a major art center of Venetia, some 25 miles west of Venice. Shakespeare called Padua a "nursery of arts." A university that grew to fame throughout Europe was founded here as early as 1222 (in time, Galileo and the poet Tasso were to attend). Petrarch also lectured here, and Padua University has remained one of the great centers for learning in Italy. The historic main building of the university is called Il Bo, which was the name of an inn with an ox as its sign. The chief entrance to Il Bo, is on via Otto Febbraio. Incidentally, Il Bo was the major font of learning in the heyday of the Venetian Republic. Of particular interest is an anatomy theater, dating from 1594, the first of its kind in Europe. Guided tours of the university are conducted from 9 a.m. to noon and from 3 to 5 p.m. except on Saturday afternoon and Sunday.

Padua is sometimes known as "La Città del Santo" (the city of the saint), the reference being to St. Anthony of Padua, who is buried at a basilica the city dedicated to him. "Il Santo" was an itinerant Franciscan monk (who is not to be confused with St. Anthony of Egypt, the monastic hermit who could resist all temptations of the Devil). Padua lies about a 45-minute train ride from Venice, easily reached on a one-day round trip. If you're driving, a fast ride along the A4 from Venice should put you in Padua in about 25 minutes.

The telephone area code for Padua is 049.

THE SIGHTS

If you're on a tight schedule when you visit Padua, then I recommend that you confine your sightseeing to (1) the Cappella degli Scrovegni (Giotto frescoes) and (2) the Basilica di San Antonio.

Cappella degli Scrovegni (also Arena Chapel)

In the public gardens off the corso Garibaldi, the modest (on the outside) chapel (tel. 650-845) is the best reason for visiting Padua. Sometime around 1305 and 1306 Giotto did a cycle of more than 35 (remarkably well-preserved) frescoes inside, which (along with those at Assisi) form the basis of his claim to fame. Like an illustrated storybook, the frescoes unfold biblical scenes. The third bottom panel (lower level on the right) depicts Judas kissing a most skeptical Christ, perhaps the most reproduced and widely known panel in the cycle. On the entrance wall is Giotto's *Last Judgment,* with hell winning out in sheer fascination. The master's representation of the *Vices and Virtues* is bizarre, revealing the depth of his imagination in personifying the nebulous evil or the elusive good. One of the most dramatic of the panels is the raising of Lazarus from the dead, a masterly balanced scene, rhythmically ingenious for its day. The swathed and cadaverous Lazarus, however, looks indecisive as to whether he'll join the living again.

The chapel is open April 1 to September 30 from 9 a.m. to 5:30 p.m., October 1 to March 30 from 9 a.m. to 5 p.m. Sunday hours are 9:30 a.m. to 12:30 p.m. Admission is 5,000 lire ($3.80). An easy walk from the chapel leads to the:

Chiesa degli Eremitani

One of the tragedies of Padua was that this church at piazza Eremitani 9 (tel. 31-410) was bombed in World War II. Before that time it housed one of the greatest art treasures in Italy, the Ovetari Chapel frescoed by Andrea Mantegna. The cycle of frescoes was the first significant work by Mantegna (1431–1506). The church was rebuilt, but you don't resurrect 15th-century frescoes, of course. Inside, in the chapel to the right of the main altar, are fragments left after the bombing, a glimpse at what we lost in Mantegna's work. The most interesting fresco saved is a panel depicting the dragging of St. Christopher's body through the streets. Note also the *Assumption of the Virgin.* Mantegna is recommended even to those who don't like "religious painting." Like da Vinci, the artist had a keen eye for architectural detail. A mass is held daily at 9 a.m. The church is open daily, with visitors admitted from 8:15 a.m. to noon and 3:30 to 6:30 p.m. in summer, to 5:30 p.m. in winter. On Sunday and religious holidays visits begin at 9 a.m. No admission is charged, but donations for the maintenance of the parish are appreciated.

Museo Civico agli Eremitani, piazza Eremitani 8, adjacent to the church, is operated by the city of Padua. Primarily an archeological museum, it also has a few Renaissance and modern pieces. Hours are 9 a.m. to 5:30 p.m. Tuesday through Saturday and 9:30 a.m. to 5:30 p.m. on Sunday; closed Monday. Admission is 5,000 lire ($3.80). The entrance is near the church.

Basilica di San Antonio

Dating from the 13th century and dedicated to St. Anthony of Padua, interred within, the basilica, on the piazza del Santo (tel. 663-944), is a synthesis of styles, with mainly Romanesque and Gothic features. It has eight cupolas. Campanili and minarets combine to give it an Eastern appearance. Inside, it is richly frescoed and decorated, and usually filled with pilgrims devoutly touching the saint's marble tomb. One of the more unusual relics is in the treasury—the seven-centuries-old, still-uncorrupt tongue of St. Anthony.

The greatest art treasures are the Donatello bronzes at the main altar, with a realistic *Crucifix* (fluid, lyrical line) towering over the rest. Seek out, too, the Donatello relief depicting the removal of Christ from the cross, a unified composition expressing in simple lines the tragedy of Christ, the sadness of the mourners—an unromantic approach. The basilica is open daily from 6:30 a.m. to 7:45 p.m. (closes at 7 p.m. in winter).

In front of the basilica is one of Italy's best-known statues—this one by Donatello. Donatello broke with the regimentation and rigidity of medievalism in the 15th century by sculpting an undraped *David*. Likewise, in the work in front of the basilica, he restored the lost art of the equestrian statue. Though the man it honors—called "Gattamelata"—is of little interest to art lovers, the statue is of prime importance. The large horse is realistic, as Donatello was a master of detail. He cleverly directs the eye to the forceful, commanding face of the Venetian military hero. Gattamelata was a dead ringer for Lord Laurence Olivier.

Museo Civico

At piazza Eremitani, this picture gallery is important, filled with minor works by major Venetian artists, dating from the 14th century. Look for a wooden *Crucifix* by Giotto and two miniatures by Giorgione (Leda and her amorous swan, and a mother and child in a bucolic setting). Other works include Giovanni Bellini's *Portrait of a Young Man* and Jacopo Bellini's miniature *Descent into Limbo*, with its childlike devils. The 15th-century Arras tapestry is also on display. Other works are Veronese's *Martyrdom of St. Primo and St. Feliciano*, plus Tintoretto's *Supper in Simone's House* and his *Crucifixion* (the latter probably the finest single painting in the gallery). The museum is open Monday through Saturday from 9 a.m. to 1:30 p.m., charging an admission of 2,000 lire ($1.50). On Sunday and holidays, its hours are 9:30 a.m. to 1 p.m.

Palazzo della Ragione

At the piazza delle Erbe, and dating from the early 13th century, this "Palace of Law" (tel. 661-377) is listed among the remarkable buildings of northern Italy. Ringed with loggias and with a roof shaped like the hull of a sailing vessel, it sits in the marketplace of Padua. Climb the steps and enter the grandiose Salone, an assembly hall that's about 270 feet long. In the hall is a gigantic wooden horse dating from the 15th century. The walls are richly frescoed, the symbolic paintings replacing frescoes by Giotto and his assistants that were destroyed in a fire in 1420. The hall is open daily except Monday from 9:30 a.m. to 12:30 p.m. and 2:30 to 5:30 p.m. Admission is 2,000 lire ($1.50).

HOTELS OF PADUA

On a busy boulevard, the **Hotel Plaza,** corso Milano 40, 35139 Padova (tel. 049/656-822), is a commercially oriented hotel faced with brown ceramic tiles and cement-trimmed square windows in pairs. The entrance is under a modern concrete arcade, which leads into a contemporary lobby. Its angular lines are softened with an unusual Oriental needlework tapestry, brown leather couches, and a pair of gilded baroque cherubs. The rooms are comfortable and well decorated. The bar, which you can reach through a stairwell and upper balcony dotted with modern paintings, is a relaxing stopover place for a drink. There is also a restaurant on the premises, plus a parking garage. Well-furnished singles rent for 100,000 lire ($76) daily; doubles 150,000 lire ($114).

Europa-Zaramella, largo Europa 3, 35137 Padova (tel. 049/661-200), built in the '60s, is considered first runner-up among hotels. Near the Padua post office, it contains 57 handsome bedrooms, all with private bath and air conditioning. The single rate ranges from 65,000 lire ($49.50) daily, and doubles begin at 90,000 lire ($68.50), tax inclusive. The bedrooms are tasteful, with bare pastel walls and built-in furnishings, compact and serviceable. The rooms open onto small balconies. The public rooms are enhanced by cubist murals, free-form ceramic plaques, and furniture placed in conversational groupings. The American bar is popular, as is the dining room. The Zaramella Restaurant features a good Paduan cuisine, with an emphasis on seafood dishes from the Adriatic. Meals cost from 40,000 lire ($30.50).

Majestic Hotel Toscanelli, piazzetta dell'Arco 2, 35122 Padova (tel. 049/663-244), is in a pastel-pink building on a cobblestone square in the heart of town. Wrought-iron balconies protect the French windows, whose edges are trimmed with stone. There's even a Renaissance well and dozens of potted shrubs in front. Inside, you'll find an octagonal bar whose walls are shingled with nostalgic mementos. The lobby has white marble floors, Oriental rugs, and a format that includes an upper balcony and a comfortable mishmash of old and new. There's also a restaurant in the basement called the Toscanelli (see my restaurant recommendation). Singles range from 71,500 lire ($54.25) to 76,000 lire ($57.75) daily; doubles cost about 111,000 lire ($84.25) to 119,000 lire ($90.50). All units contain private bath, TV, air conditioning, and phone. Parking is on the premises.

Hotel Donatello, piazza del Santo, 35123 Padova (tel. 049/875-0634), is a renovated hotel with an ideal location near the Basilica of St. Anthony. Its buff-colored façade is pierced by an arched arcade, and the oversize chandeliers of its lobby combine with the checkerboard marble floor for a pleasing and hospitable ambience. To prepare you for the eventual sight of Padua's famed wooden horse, the management has placed a big illuminated photo of it in the lobby. On the premises is one of my preferred restaurants, the Sant' Antonio (see my restaurant recommendation). Well-furnished double rooms rent for 120,000 lire ($91.25) daily; singles 90,000 lire ($68.50). All units contain private baths.

Hotel Leon Bianco, piazzetta Pedrocchi 7, 35122 Padova (tel. 049/875-0814), is a small, tasteful hotel recently modernized and restructured. Across from the historic Caffè Pedrocchi, it sits at the center of a pedestrian zone. In good weather, breakfast—the only meal served here—may be taken in the roof garden. All rooms come with color TV, mini-bar, direct-dial phone, and air conditioning. Singles rent for 78,000 lire ($59.25) daily, doubles go for 115,000 lire ($87.50), and triples run 160,000 lire ($122), all tariffs including breakfast.

DINING IN PADUA

The most elegant and best-rated dining place in Padua, **Ristorante El Toulà,** via Belle Parti 11 (tel. 875-1822), was established in 1982 in a building that had housed an earlier restaurant for 200 years, under ceiling beams that are at least 400 years old. The age of the physical plant, however, did not stop a team of designers from creating a sensual decor of Italian style at its best. The ground-floor level includes a slick black bar, near an equally black piano, which provides music for diners savoring an apéritif on the leather couches or for the late-night crowd who drop in for an evening drink at closing time. The main dining area offers the kind of excellent service that this most sophisticated of nationwide restaurant chains is eager to provide. The palate-pleasing menu items change monthly, but might on any given day include blinis with caviar, crostino (a flaky appetizer) with mozzarella, sweet peppers, and anchovy sauce, or asparagus milanese, five kinds of homemade pasta, five kinds of risotto (one with caviar and fresh salmon), Westphalian salmon with capers, along with a wide assortment of veal, beef, and chicken, topped off by freshly baked pastries and dessert crêpes. A full meal here—a regalia by anyone's standards—costs from 55,000 lire ($41.75). The restaurant is open from 12:30 to 2:30 p.m. and 8 to 10:30 p.m.; closed Sunday, for lunch on Monday, and in August.

Ristorante Dotto, via Squarcione 23 (tel. 875-1490), takes its name from the *dottori* (doctors) of the university for which Padua is famous. The discreet, elegant restaurant is in the heart of the city, suitable not only for an academic or business meal but also for an intimate tête-à-tête dinner. Try their pasta fagiole, grilled sole, risotto made with fresh asparagus, or the chef's pâté. You could top all this off with a feathery dessert soufflé, the most elaborate of which must be ordered at the beginning of a meal. Dinners range from 45,000 lire ($34.25). The restaurant, open from 12:30 to 2:30 p.m. and 7:30 to 9:30 p.m., is closed on Sunday, Monday night, and in August.

Toscanelli, piazzetta dell'Arco 2 (tel. 663-244), is connected to the Majestic Hotel Toscanelli, already previewed, but reachable through a separate entrance from under an arcade. The decor includes warm colors and ceiling beams, lots of exposed brick, and a kitchen that is visible from behind a plate-glass window. There's even an open grill for the proper preparation of fish, scampi, and meats. Many of the specialties are Tuscan, although dishes also include international recipes such as fondue bourguignonne and sauerkraut Alsatian style. The zuppa di pesce (fish soup) is especially recommendable. Meals, served from 12:30 to 2:30 p.m. and 7 p.m. to midnight, cost 30,000 lire ($22.75) to 50,000 lire ($38). The restaurant is closed Sunday and from mid-July to mid-August.

Ristorante Sant' Antonio, in the Hotel Donatello, piazza del Santo (tel. 875-0634), offers what might turn out to be the most rewarding view of Saint Anthony's Basilica. A series of outdoor tables are set up in summer, although the L-shaped interior is pleasant as well, outfitted with tones of white, beige marble floors, and bentwood chairs. All the standard Italian dishes are served here, many of them so familiar to foreign visitors that they may not need to ask for the English menu. However, it's available if you want it. Closed Wednesday, the restaurant serves full meals beginning at 35,000 lire ($26.50) from 12:30 to 2:30 p.m. and 7:30 to 9:30 p.m.

Trattoria da Placido, via Santa Lucia 59 (tel. 875-2252), is one of the most reliable choices for good food at moderate prices in Padua. It doesn't spend its money on decor, although the ambience is warm and inviting. You dine here on traditional Italian fare, including bollito misto (a mixed selection of boiled meats with a green herbal sauce), fettuccine alla boscaiola, baccalà (dried codfish) alla vicentina, and cuttlefish alla veneziana. However, the chef will surprise you and serve a salad, for example, of radicchio that is commonplace in Italy, but a gourmet treat in North America. Meals range from 26,000 lire ($19.75) to 35,000 lire ($26.50) and are served from 12:30 to 2:30 p.m. and 7:30 to 9:30 p.m. The restaurant is closed Saturday night, all day Sunday, and in August.

A Famous Coffeehouse

Caffè Pedrocchi, piazzetta Pedrocchi 6 (tel. 875-2020), off the piazza Cavour, is a neoclassical landmark. It was opened by Antonio Pedrocchi in 1831 and was hailed at the time as the most elegant coffeehouse in Europe. Its green, white, and red rooms reflect the national colors of Italy. On sunny days you might want to sit under one of the two stone porches, architectural oddities in themselves, although in winter you'll have plenty to distract you inside. There, the sprawling bathtub-shaped travertine bar has a brass top and brass lion's feet. The velvet banquettes have maroon upholstery, red-veined marble tables, and Egyptian-revival chairs. And if you tire of all this 19th-century outrageousness, you can retreat to a more conservatively decorated English-style pub on the premises, whose entrance is under a covered arcade a few steps away. Cappuccino costs 2,500 lire ($1.90) at the stand-up bar, around 3,800 lire ($2.90) at a table. Although drinks cost more than they would in a lesser café, you haven't heard the heartbeat of Padua until you've been at the Pedrocchi. Open daily from 7:30 a.m. to 2 a.m.

---

3. Vicenza

In the 16th century Vicenza was transformed into a virtual laboratory for the architectural experiments of Andrea Palladio, a Paduan who arrived there in 1523.

One of the greatest architects of the Renaissance, Palladio peppered the city with palazzi and basilicas, and the surrounding hills with villas for patrician families.

The architect was particularly important to England and America. In the 18th century Robert Adam was especially inspired by him, as reflected by many country homes in England today. Then, through the influence of Adam and others even earlier, the spirit of Palladio was imported across the waves to America (take, for example, Jefferson's Monticello or plantation homes in the antebellum South). Palladio even lent his name to this style of architecture—"Palladianism"—identified by regularity of form, massive, often imposing size, and an adherence to lines established in ancient Greece and Rome.

Vicenza's telephone area code is 0444.

THE SIGHTS

To introduce yourself to the "world of Palladio," head for the heart of Vicenza—

Piazza dei Signori

In this classical square stands the **Basilica Palladiana,** partially designed by Palladio. The loggias consist of two levels, the lower tier with Doric pillars, the upper with Ionic. In its heyday this building was much frequented by the aristocrats among the Vicentinos, who were lavishly spending their gold for villas in the neighboring hills. They met here in a kind of social fraternity, probably to talk about the excessive sums being spent on Palladio-designed or -inspired projects. Originally, the basilica was in the Gothic style, and served as the Palazzo della Ragione (justice). The roof collapsed following a 1945 bombing, but has been subsequently rebuilt. To the side is the Tower of the Piazza, dating from the 13th century and soaring approximately 270 feet high. Across from the basilica is the **Loggia del Capitanio** (guard), designed by Palladio in his waning years. On the square are two pillars, one supporting a chimera, another a saint.

Olympic Theater (Teatro Olimpico)

The masterpiece and last work of Palladio—ideal for performances of classical plays—is one of the world's greatest theaters (and still in use). It was completed in 1585, five years after Palladio's death, by Vincenzo Scamozzi, and the curtain went up on the Vicenza première of Sophocles' *Oedipus Rex.* The arena seating area, in the shape of a half-moon, is encircled by Corinthian columns and balustrades. The simple proscenium is abutted by the arena. What ordinarily is the curtain in a conventional theater is a permanent façade, U-shaped, with a large central arch and a pair of smaller ones flanking it. These three openings have forced perspective on the raked stage. The reproductions represent the ancient streets of Thebes, combining architectural detail with trompe l'oeil. Above the arches (to the left and right) are rows of additional classic statuary on pedestals or in niches. Over the area is a dome, with trompe-l'oeil clouds and sky, giving the illusion of an outdoor Roman amphitheater.

At the piazza Matteotti, the attraction may be visited daily mid-March to mid-October from 9:30 a.m. to 12:20 p.m. and 3 to 5:20 p.m. (on Sunday from 9:30 a.m. to 12:15 p.m.). In winter it closes at 4 p.m. Admission to the theater and the Museo Civico (see below) is 3,000 lire ($2.30). For more information, phone 234-381.

City Museum (Museo Civico)

Across the street from the entrance to the Olympic Theater, the museum is housed in the Palazzo Chiericati, one of the most outstanding buildings by Palladio. Begun in the mid-16th century, it was not finished until the latter 17th century, during the baroque period. Today the palazzo is visited chiefly for its excellent collection of Venetian paintings on the second floor. Works by lesser-known artists—

Paolo Veneziano, Bartolomeo Montagna, and Jacopo Bassano—are displayed alongside paintings by such giants as Tintoretto, Veronese, Tiepolo. Notable items include Tintoretto's *Miracle of St. Augustine,* as well as Veronese's *The Cherub of the Balustrade* and his *Madonna and Child.* Also intriguing are Tiepolo's *Time and Truth* and Giovanni Battista Piazzetta's *Ecstasy of San Francesco.*

The museum (tel. 321-348), at the piazza Matteotti, is open Tuesday through Saturday from 9:30 a.m. to noon and 2:30 to 5 p.m. and on Sunday from 10 a.m. to noon. It is closed on Monday. Admission is 3,000 lire ($2.30) to the museum and the theater previewed above.

Santa Corona Church

Off the corso Palladio, a short walk from the Olympic Theater, the church was founded in the mid-13th century, and designed in the Gothic style. Much altered over the centuries, it should be visited if for no other reason than to see Giovanni Bellini's *Baptism of Christ* (fifth altar on the left). In the left transept, a short distance away, is another of Vicenza's well-known works of art—this one by Veronese depicting the three Wise Men paying tribute to the Christ child. The high altar with its intricate marble work is also of interest. A visit to Santa Corona is more rewarding than a trek to the duomo (cathedral), only of passing interest.

It is open daily from 9:30 a.m. to 12:15 p.m. and 3:30 to 6 p.m. (closed Monday morning).

Basilica of Monte Berico

High on a hill overlooking the town and the surrounding villas, the basilica, 87 Viale 10 Giugno (tel. 320-999), is the Sacré-Coeur of Vicenza. Lit at night, the church is reached by car or a hiker's walk up a colonnaded street. But the real reason for climbing the hill is to walk out onto the belvedere near the church. You'll see the town spread beneath your feet—a sight of splendor day or night.

The basilica is open daily from 7 a.m. to noon and 2:30 to 7 p.m. (to 6 p.m. in winter).

La Rotonda

On the southeast border of the town, past the Arco delle Scalette (the landmark "arch of the tiny steps" from the late 16th century), is another of the most famous creations of that maestro, Palladio. Like the Olympic Theater, the Rotonda (tel. 321-793) was started by Palladio but left for completion by his pupil, Scamozzi. Many great estates in Europe and America found their inspiration in this elegant domed villa. The Rotonda is a private residence and therefore can't be visited except from 10 a.m. to noon and 3 to 6 p.m. on Wednesday from March 15 to November 15. Admission is 5,000 lire ($3.80). However, the grounds are open daily except Monday from 10 a.m. to noon and 3 to 6 p.m. Admission is 3,000 lire ($2.30).

Villa Valmarana

In the same area, a mile southeast of the center of Vicenza, is the Villa Valmarana, called "Dwarf's Villa" (tel. 321-1803). It comprises two buildings, the villa and the guesthouse, not creations of Palladio but built as a private estate at the end of the 17th century. It is visited today for its beautiful frescoes by Giambattista Tiepolo in the villa and by Giandomenico Tiepolo in the guesthouse, painted in the last half of the 18th century. The attraction is open from 3 to 6 p.m. daily from the end of March to the first of November, and also from 10 a.m. to noon on Thursday, Saturday, and Sunday. It is closed in the afternoon on Sunday and holidays. Admission is 4,000 lire ($3.05).

HOTELS IN VICENZA

A good stopover is the **Hotel Europa,** viale San Lazzaro 11, 36100 Vicenza (tel. 0444/564-111). The interior of this roadside hotel is nicer than its boxy façade would imply. It's the most modern hotel in Vicenza (built in 1980), lying 1¼ miles southwest of the center on the road to Verona. It's a favorite of business travelers who use it during the winter, tourists who come in summer, and high-ranking officers of the nearby American military base who appreciate the leather-accented bar during off-hours. The lobby is outfitted with black cowhide chairs, splashes of spring colors, and a big photographic blowup of the Palladian buildings of Vicenza. Each of the 72 comfortable bedrooms has a TV, radio, air conditioning, mini-bar, and of course, a modern bath. Singles rent for 85,000 lire ($64.50) daily, and doubles go for 120,000 lire ($91.25), with a buffet breakfast included. City bus no. 1 makes frequent runs between the hotel and the center of town.

Hotel Campo Marzio, viale Roma 21, 36100 Vicenza (tel. 0444/545-700). This contemporary hotel is ideally situated in a peaceful part of the historic center of Vicenza, adjacent to a park. The hotel has undergone complete renovation. The sunny lobby has a conservatively comfortable decor that extends into the 35 bedrooms, all fully air-conditioned and with color TV, direct-dial phone, radio, and mini-bar. With a buffet breakfast and taxes included, the rate for singles is 104,900 lire ($79.75) daily; for doubles, 159,800 lire ($121). A cozy restaurant offers gourmet dining Monday through Friday.

Hotel Cristina, corso San Felice 32, 36100 Vicenza (tel. 0444/234-280), is a cozy hotel with an inside courtyard where visitors can park. It has a well-maintained contemporary format and a desirable location near the city center. The decor consists of large amounts of marble and parquet flooring and lots of exposed paneling, coupled with comfortable furniture in both the public rooms and the high-ceilinged bedrooms, although some of the accommodations are small. Singles with bath cost 60,000 lire ($45.50) daily; doubles with bath go for 85,000 lire ($64.50).

The **Continental,** viale Trissino 89, 36100 Vicenza (tel. 0444/505-476), is among the best choices for an overnight stopover in a town not known for its hotels. Renovated in a modern style, the Continental offers a total of 55 comfortably appointed bedrooms, all with air conditioning, color TV, mini-bar, and bath/shower. Singles cost from 57,000 lire ($43.25) daily and doubles begin at 81,000 lire ($61.50). The hotel has a good restaurant where meals cost 25,000 lire ($19) to 38,000 lire ($29); however, there is no meal service on Saturday, Sunday, or in August. There is a solarium on the premises.

WHERE TO DINE

A Venetian-style palace, **Scudo di Francia,** Contrà Piancoli 4 (tel. 320-898), houses the best restaurant in Vicenza. Within a short walk of the piazza Signori, the restaurant has a sunny decor accented with gilt wall sconces, high ceilings, and a garden visible through its rear windows. Its service and food presentation are the finest in the area. Menu choices change frequently, but are likely to include filet of beef with green peppercorns, Venetian-style liver, ossobuco with polenta, fettuccine with fresh spring peas, and risotto with fresh asparagus, plus a range of fresh antipasti such as artichoke salad with parmesan cheese along with such delicacies as smoked salmon. A la carte meals range upward from 40,000 lire ($30.50), and the restaurant, open from 12:30 to 2:30 p.m. and 8 to 10 p.m., is closed Sunday night, all day Monday, and in August.

Ristorante Pedavena, viale Verona 93 (tel. 563-064), is one of the better dining spots in town, although its inconvenient position on a four-lane highway on the road leading to Verona makes it difficult for nonmotorists. It's housed in a chalet stucco building with stone-trimmed wrought-iron accents. There's a parking lot in front, plus a summer beer garden sheltered from the busy street with a wall and a row of leafy trees. There's a wide assortment of pasta, along with such selections as arrosti misti (mixed roast meats), scaloppine with asparagus, entrecôte, and an array of fresh salads. Full meals cost 35,000 lire ($26.50) to 45,000 lire ($34.25). The restaurant serves from 12:30 to 2:30 p.m. and 7:30 to 10 p.m.; closed Monday year round and on Sunday night in winter.

Ristorante Grandcaffè Garibaldi, piazza dei Signori 5 (tel. 544-147). The most impressive café in town has a design worthy of the city of Palladio. In the heartbeat center, it has a wide terrace in front and a high-ceilinged interior with an ornate ceiling, marble tables, and a long glass case of sandwiches which you can select before you sit down (the waitress will bring them to your table). Prices are slightly cheaper if you stand up at the bar. On the premises is an upstairs restaurant, with trays of antipasti and arrangements of fresh fruit set up on a central table. The menu's array of familiar Italian specialties are among the best in town, a full meal costing from 35,000 lire ($26.50). Open from 12:30 to 2:30 p.m. and 7:30 to 10 p.m., the restaurant and café are closed Tuesday night and all day Wednesday.

Antica Trattoria Tre Visi, Contrà Porti 6 (tel. 238-677), deserves to be better known. A short walk from the basilica, the restaurant is on the ground floor of a Venetian-style palazzo dating from 1489. The decor is in the rustic style, with a fireplace, ceramic wall decorations, baskets of fresh fruit, and tavern chairs. You can see the kitchen from the main dining area. An array of Italian specialties is suggested, and you can select from a choice of set meals or order à la carte, with meals costing from 45,000 lire ($34.25). Together with the rich choice of international and local specialties, you can enjoy a good selection of wines of the Vicenza region. The owner, Luigi Barbiero, will be pleased to suggest and help you with your choice. Hours are 12:30 to 2:30 p.m. and 7:30 to 10:30 p.m. It is closed Sunday night, all day Monday, and from July 15 to August 8.

TRIESTE, THE DOLOMITES, AND SOUTH TYROL

The limestone Dolomites are a peculiar mountain formation of the northeastern Italian Alps. Some of their peaks soar to a height of 10,500 feet. One of Europe's greatest natural attractions, the Dolomites are a year-round pleasure destination, with two high seasons: in midsummer, and then in winter when the skiers slide in.

At times the Dolomites form fantastic shapes, combining to create a landscape that looks primordial, with chains of mountains peaking like giant dragon's teeth in contrast to lofty masses of detritus. Clefts descend precipitously along jagged rocky walls, while at other points a vast flat tableland—spared by nature's fury—emerges.

The provinces of Trent and Bolzano (Bozen in German) form the Trentino–Alto Adige region. The area is rich in health resorts, attracting many German-speaking visitors to its alpine lakes and mountains. Many of its waters—some of which are radioactive—are said to have curative powers.

South Tyrol is surrounded by the Dolomite Alps. Until 1919 South Tyrol was part of Austria, and even though it today belongs to Italy, it is still very much Tyrolean in character, both in its language (German) and in its dress.

Today the Trentino–Alto Adige region functions with a great deal of autonomy.

Before I proceed to details, readers with an extra day or so to spare may first want to postpone their Dolomite or Tyrolean adventure for a detour to—

1. Trieste

On the half-moon Gulf of Trieste, opening into the Adriatic, Trieste is 72 miles northeast of Venice. A shimmering, bright city, with many neoclassical buildings, it perches at a remote point in Italy.

As an Adriatic seaport, Trieste has had a long history, with many changes of ownership. The Habsburg emperor, Charles VI, declared it a free port in 1719. But by the time the 20th century rolled around it was an ocean outlet for the Austro-Hungarian Empire. Came the war and a secret deal among the Allies, and Trieste was ceded to Italy in 1918, marking its decline. In the late summer of 1943 Trieste again fell to foreign troops—this time the Nazis. The arrival of Tito's army from Yugoslavia in the spring of 1945 changed its destiny once more. A postwar attempt to turn it into a free territory failed. In 1954, after many a hassle, the American and British troops withdrew as the Italians marched in, with the stipulation that the much-disputed Trieste would be maintained as a free port.

Trieste has known many glamorous literary associations, particularly in the pre–World War II years. As a stopover on the *Orient Express,* it became a famed destination. Dame Agatha Christie came this way, as did Graham Greene. As part of his elopement with Nora Barnacle, James Joyce arrived in Trieste in 1904. Out of both work and money, Joyce got a job teaching at the Berlitz School. He was to live here for nearly ten years. It is believed that he began his masterpiece, *Ulysses,* while living in Trieste. He wrote *A Portrait of the Artist as a Young Man* here.

Author Richard Burton, known for his *Arabian Nights* translations, lived in Trieste from 1871 until he died, about 20 years later.

The Teatro Verdi, the opera house, enjoys a deserved reputation throughout Italy, and many compare it favorably with La Scala.

The telephone area code for Trieste is 040.

THE SIGHTS

The heart of Trieste is the neoclassic **piazza dell'Unità d'Italia,** said to be the largest in Italy fronting on the sea. Opening onto the square is the town hall with a clock tower, the Palace of the Government, and the main office of the Lloyd Triestino ship line. Flanking the square are numerous cafés and restaurants, popular at night with the denizens of Trieste who sip an apéritif, then later promenade along the seafront esplanade.

After visiting the main square, you may want to view Trieste from an even better vantage point. If so, head up the hill for another cluster of attractions. You can take an antiquated tram, leaving from the piazza Oberdan, getting off at Obelisco. There, at the belvedere, the city of the Adriatic will be spread out before you.

Cathedral of San Giusto

Dedicated to the patron saint (Just) of Trieste, who was martyred in A.D. 303, the basilica was consecrated in 1330, incorporating a pair of churches that had been separate until then. The front is in the Romanesque style, enhanced by a rose window. Inside, the nave is flanked by two pairs of aisles. To the left of the main altar are found the best of the Byzantine mosaics in Trieste (note especially the blue-robed Madonna and her Child). The main altar and the chapel to the right contain less interesting mosaics. To the left of the basilica entrance is a small campanile from the 14th century, which you can scale on foot for a view of Trieste and its bay. At its base are preserved the remains of a Roman temple from the 1st century A.D. I prefer to take a taxi to the top (or else bus 24), then walk back down, allowing a leisurely 15 minutes. From the basilica you can walk to the nearby—

Castle of San Giusto

Constructed in the 15th century by the Venetians on the site of a Roman fort, this fortress maintained a sharp eye on the bay, watching for unfriendly visitors arriving by sea. From its bastions, panoramic views of Trieste unfold. Inside is a museum (tel. 766-956) with a collection of arms and armor. It is open from 9 a.m. to 1 p.m. daily except Monday. Admission is 1,000 lire (75¢).

In July and August, open-air performances—Hungarian dancers, for instance—are staged in the **Cortile delle Milizie**. An elegant taverna, Bottega del Vino, caps your exploration within the city proper.

Miramare

Overlooking the Bay of Grignano, the castle (tel. 224-143) was erected by Archduke Maximilian, the brother of Franz Joseph, the Habsburg emperor of Austria. Maximilian, who married Princess Charlotte of Belgium, was the commander of the Austrian navy in 1854. In an ill-conceived move, he and "Carlotta" sailed to Mexico in 1864, where he became the emperor in an unfortunate reign. He was shot in 1867 in Querétaro, Mexico. His wife lived until 1927 in a château outside Brussels, having been driven insane by the Mexican episode. You may remember the movie, probably on late at night, about Maximilian and Carlotta. It was called *Juarez*, starring Bette Davis, Paul Muni, and Brian Aherne.

On the ground floor of the castle, you can visit the bedroom of Maximilian (built like a ship's cabin) and that of Charlotte, as well as an impressive receiving room and more parlors, including a chinoiserie salon. Miramare may be visited Monday through Saturday from 9 a.m. to 1:30 p.m. for 3,000 lire ($2.30) admission. On holidays and Sunday, the hours are 9 a.m. to 12:30 p.m. Enveloping the castle are magnificently designed park grounds (Parco di Miramare), ideal for pleasant strolls (no admission fee, open till sunset). In summer, a son et lumière presentation in the park of the castle depicts Maximilian's tragedy in Mexico. Tickets to the presentation, staged from June to September, cost from 4,500 lire ($3.40). To reach Miramare, take bus 6 from the center of town until the end of the line. There transfer to line 36, which will transport you to the castle.

The Giant Cave (Grotta Gigante)

About nine miles from Trieste, in the heart of the limestone plateau called "Carso" that surrounds the city, you can visit the **Giant Cave,** an enormous cavern and one of the most interesting phenomena of speleology. First explored in 1840 via the top ceiling entrance, this huge room, some 446 feet deep, was opened to the public in 1908. It is the biggest single-cave room ever opened and one of the world's largest underground rooms. A visit, costing 6,000 lire ($4.55) for adults and 4,000 lire ($3.05) for children 6 to 12, can be made only with a guide and takes nearly an hour. Near the entrance is the **Man and Caves Museum,** opened in 1963 and unique in Italy. Tours are given daily from 9 a.m. to noon and 2 to 5 p.m. every 45 minutes, in March and October; from 10 a.m. to noon and 2:30 to 4:30 p.m. every 30 minutes, November to February; and 9 a.m. to noon and 2 to 7 p.m. every 30 minutes, April to September. For information, phone 327-312 or 60-317 from 3 to 7 p.m. Monday through Friday. Bus 45 will take you to the cave from the center of the city, or you can reach it through Villa Opicina or by taking the strada del Friuli road beyond the marble white Victory Lighthouse as far as Prosecco. On the freeway, you can take the exit at Prosecco.

WHERE TO STAY

The now-glamorous **Hotel Duchi d'Aosta,** piazza dell'Unità d'Italia 2, 34121 Trieste (tel. 040/62-081), began about 200 years ago with the establishment of a restaurant for the dock workers who toiled at the nearby wharves. In 1873 one of the most beautiful façades in Trieste was erected to cover the existing building in a white neoclassical shell with delicate carving, arched windows, and a stone crown of heroic sculptures. The design is a lot like that of an 18th-century palace, with an effect that is enhanced with views over the fountains and lamps of the major square of Trieste and the sea beyond it. The hotel was practically rebuilt from the inside in the 1970s. Today the 52 bedrooms are a favorite of business travelers who come to Trieste, appreciating the food in the ground-floor restaurant (see my restaurant recommendation for Harry's Grill), and the 19th-century ambience of the Victorian-style public rooms. Each of the accommodations has a well-stocked mini-bar concealed behind panels, antiqued walls, built-in radio, TV, modern bath, and tasteful combinations of furniture. Singles cost from 155,000 lire ($118) daily, and doubles begin at 210,000 lire ($160). Parking is in one of the limited number of spaces on the street outside.

Another leading choice is the **Savoia Excelsior Palace,** riva del Mandracchio 4, 34124 Trieste (tel. 040/7690), which stands proudly next to the headquarters of the Lloyd Triestino shipping palazzo, right off the piazza dell'Unità. Fronting the water, the hotel has witnessed much of the pageantry of Trieste. A first-class hotel, it offers 154 rooms, many furnished in bold modern designs and all having air conditioning, phone, radio, and color TV. Singles peak at 175,000 lire ($133) daily; doubles, 250,000 lire ($190). In respect to the past, there's a tea room, but an American bar adds a contemporary touch.

Jolly Hotel, Corso Cavour 7, 34132 Trieste (tel. 040/7694), rises from a convenient spot in the center of town behind a two-tone concrete façade. The public rooms are decorated in a conservatively plush decor that includes velvet armchairs, appealing colors, and an array of conference rooms frequently used for local gatherings and social celebrations. The modern bedrooms include air conditioning, TV, radio, mini-bar, and direct-dial phone, as well as comfortable bedding and up-to-date bath. Prices range from 150,000 lire ($114) daily in a single to 210,000 lire ($160) in a double.

Hotel Al Teatro, capo di piazza G. Bartoli 1, 34100 Trieste (tel. 040/64-123). The theatrical mask carved into the stone arch above the entrance is an appropriate symbol of a hotel that is favored by many of Trieste's visiting opera stars. Behind a beige-colored neoclassical façade a few steps from the seaside panorama of the piazza del' Unità d'Italia, the hotel has 47 comfortable rooms connected to one another by wide upstairs hallways and a stone stairwell. The simply furnished and slightly old-fashioned rooms have parquet floors, lots of space, and comfortable but minimal furniture. The hotel was built in 1830 as a private house and later served as the headquarters of the British army in the aftermath of World War II. Bathless rooms cost from 32,000 lire ($24.25) daily in a single and from 52,000 lire ($39.50) in a double. Accommodations with private bath rent for 45,000 lire ($34.25) in a single and 73,000 lire ($55.50) in a double.

Hotel Città di Parenzo, via Artisti 8, 34100 Trieste (tel. 040/630-119), is the economy special of Trieste. On a narrow street in the 19th-century business district, it is relatively secluded from the major traffic artery, although overnight guests may still hear the inevitable sounds of a Vespa. The marble wall-covering of the lobby extends into the hall. The 43 simple bedrooms are furnished YMCA-style. The English-speaking reception charges 32,500 lire ($24.75) daily for a single with bath, 53,000 lire ($40.25) for doubles with bath. No meals are served, but breakfast is available at a little café across the street. The hotel is named after an old seaport about 30 miles from Trieste, a favorite destination of the former owners.

WHERE TO DINE

For good food, go to **Ristorante Harry's Grill,** in the Hotel Duchi d'Aosta, piazza dell'Unità d'Italia 2 (tel. 62-081). The adjoining bar is one of the most popular rendezvous spots in town, particularly for the business community. The establishment has no relation to any of the many other Harry's restaurants or bars scattered throughout Italy. The big lace-covered curtains illuminate the paneling, the polished brass, and the chandeliers of blue glass from Murano. In summer, tables are set up in the traffic-free piazza dell'Unità d'Italia, the heartbeat of the center. Illuminated with light from the carriage lamps set into the stonework of the hotel, the outdoor terrace, with a separate area for bar clients, is sheltered by a canopy to protect clients from the Adriatic winds that sometimes sweep in from the sea. The Mediterranean-inspired cuisine includes such specialties as fresh shrimp with oil and lemon, pasta and risotto dishes, boiled salmon in sauce, veal in madeira sauce, butter-fried calves' liver with onions, and an array of beef and fish dishes. Full meals, served daily from 12:30 to 3 p.m. and 7:30 to 10 p.m., cost 50,000 lire ($38) to 95,000 lire ($72.25). Reservations are suggested.

Antica Trattoria Suban, via Comici 2 at San Giovanni (tel. 54-368). In 1865 the founder established a country tavern with a spacious terrace opening onto a view of the hills near Trieste. Today the surrounding landscape contains glimpses of the industrial age, but the brick and stone walls, the terrace, and the country feeling are still intact. The cuisine is both hearty and delicate at the same time. The chefs concoct specialties from fresh ingredients from surrounding farmlands. Specialties include a flavorful risotto with herbs, basil-flavored crêpes, beef with garlic sauce, a perfectly prepared chicken Kiev, and veal croquettes with parmesan and egg yolks. The chef's handling of grilled meats, some recipes for which are derived from neighboring Yugoslavia, is adept, and the rich pastries are worth the extra calories. Full meals, priced from 38,000 lire ($29) to 60,000 lire ($45.50), are served from 12:30 to 2:30 p.m. and 7:30 to 10 p.m. daily except Monday lunch, all day Tuesday, and in August. This place is best reached by taxi.

Elefante Bianco, riva Tre Novembre 3 (tel. 60-889). To get a table at this talked-about "white elephant," you have to reserve early before the crowds form. Its reputation has caught on with the fashion-oriented people of Trieste. The restaurant, on a busy street fronting the harbor, is behind lattices and a semicircular wooden platform. The centerpiece of the garden-style interior is an abundantly stocked table of fruit and antipasti above a white porcelain elephant festooned with trailing ivy. The young and cooperative waiters serve a light and healthy cuisine, including such tempting specialties as pasta with truffles or salmon, tagliolini with shrimp, grilled beef with fresh rosemary, grilled shrimp marinated with oranges and champagne, and well-prepared beefsteak flavored with herbs. Full meals, costing from 45,000 lire ($34.25), are served from 1 to 3 p.m. and 8 to 11:30 p.m. daily except Sunday.

Al Granzo, piazza Venezia 7 (tel. 306-788), is one of the leading seafood restaurants of Trieste. Try to get a seat on its waterfront terrace facing the fish market. Here you might order a brodetto, a traditional bouillabaisse spiced with saffron and other herbs, or vermicelli with black mussels, or perhaps a risotto with fruits of the sea. For your main-course selection, I recommend the fish of the day. You can make your own choice from a wagon where the fish rest on a bed of ground ice. Good with fish is a local Tocai Friulano, which is aromatic, harmonious, and somewhat tart in flavor, its color a lemon-yellow tending to pale-green. Expect to pay 30,000 lire ($22.75) to 45,000 lire ($34.25) for a complete meal. The restaurant, open from 12:30 to 3 p.m. and 7:30 to 10 p.m., is closed on Wednesday.

LaBottega del Vino di San Giusto, Castello di San Giusto (tel. 733-235), is the rustic and medieval-style wine cellar inside the castle whose view encompasses most of Trieste. Within the castle precincts, you reach a massive arched door set into an ivy-covered wall leading off the central courtyard. An upper floor is often used for private parties, while the heavily timbered lower level is dotted with wooden tables for the tasting of a large selection of Italian wines. Amid a setting of massive stone columns, 1,000-year-old walls, and iron wall sconces, guests can also enjoy full meals ranging from 40,000 lire ($30.50). These include all the classic Italian dishes such as veal piccata, risotto with scampi and curry or with champagne, a few pasta dishes, and a limited selection of fish. The most elaborate offering is chateaubriand with béarnaise sauce, which could be accompanied by one (or two) of the establishment's large selection of red and white Italian wines. These include Asti Spumanti and even champagne if you're feeling extravagant. Evening music is provided. The place is open from 6:30 p.m. to 2 a.m.; closed Tuesday.

Buffet Benedetto, via XXX Ottobre 19 (tel. 61-655), is a good example of the kind of establishment that's popular in Trieste. Near the front door, there's a high-ceilinged room crowded with jars of local produce, wine, and regional foodstuffs, as well as a collection of stand-up diners who order a plate of food from behind a glass display case. Many of them are crowded elbow to elbow. Many diners prefer to pass through the deli-buffet section into one of two inner rooms (there might be a wait at lunchtime). There, a uniformed waiter will recite menu items to you in rapid Italian, of which you will probably understand some of the more commonly known specialties. The antipasti, when I was last there, consisted of a cold salad of fresh shrimp mixed with squid and served with a lemon and mild creamy sauce. Other menu items include thinly sliced prosciutto, a huge bowl of rigatoni with tomato sauce, baked lasagne, Florentine steaks, saltimbocca, eggplant parmigiana, and several kinds of beef. Full meals at the tables range from 30,000 lire ($22.75). Stand-up meals at the buffet cost substantially less, and no one will mind if you have only a dish of pasta as a main course. Both sections are open from noon to 3 p.m. and 7 to 10 p.m.; closed Monday and all of August.

Al Bragozzo, riva Nazario Sauro 22 (tel. 303-001), is one of the best-known fish restaurants at the port. The outdoor tables, sheltered by a canopy, are popular in summertime, although the paneled dining room is the better place to dine during inclement weather. Primarily a fish restaurant serving meals for 35,000 lire ($26.50) and up, it offers such food items as calamari, a well-prepared Adriatic fish fry, risotto with seafood, zuppa di pesce, a few meat dishes, and a variety of dessert crêpes. Hours are 12:30 to 2 p.m. and 7:30 to 10 p.m. daily except Monday; closed from mid-June to early July.

Bagutta Triestino, via Carducci 30 (tel. 761-839), is a restaurant on a busy commercial street surrounded by 19th-century buildings. The interior contains a zinc bar near the entrance, warm colors, and a high ceiling covered with planks. The large Italian menu contains seven kinds of spaghetti, filet of beef cooked in ten different ways, Swiss fondue bourguignonne (served only to two or more people), radicchio grown in the environs of Trieste, and a large and tempting selection of antipasti. A dessert specialty is gubana, a cake soaked in grappa. Meals range upward from 35,000 lire ($26.50). The manager, who is also a sommelier, has a varied selection of high-quality wines. Open from 12:30 to 3 p.m. and 7:30 to 10 p.m., the restaurant is closed Sunday and Monday.

If you are intrigued with the idea of a buffet, you might try **Da Pepi,** via Cassa di Risparmio 3 (tel. 68-073), with a groaning counter display of "the works." Try, in particular, a long, thinnish sausage known as luganiga. This tasty sausage is sometimes broiled with tomato sauce. The boiled beef called *Rindfleisch* in Vienna is simmered to perfection, and the sauerkraut is distinctive in flavor. For your drink, select either a liter of the robust local wine or a beer, perhaps an import from Czechoslovakia or Austria. A hearty meal here, served from noon to 2 p.m. and 7 to 9 p.m. daily except Sunday, is likely to cost 25,000 lire ($19).

For one of the best bargains in Trieste, I suggest **Ai Due Triestini,** via Cadorna 10 (tel. 303-759), which is a tavern behind the piazza dell'Unità. Run by a husband-and-wife team, the little trattoria covers its tablecloths with plastic and doesn't even bother to print a menu. Some of the cookery leans heavily on the influence of neighboring Austria. Try, for example, spezzatino, chunks of beef in a goulash ragoût, with fresh peas and potatoes. The Hungarian goulash is quite good, as is a rich strudel in the tradition of Budapest. Many diners order beer with their meals, and others come in just to ask for a glass of wine, served from one of the casks which line a wall. My latest tab came to only 28,000 lire ($21.25). Hours are 12:30 to 2:30 p.m. and 7:30 to 10 p.m. daily.

A CAFE OF TRIESTE

The inner chamber of the heart of Trieste is **Caffè degli Specchi,** piazza dell'Unità de'Italia (tel. 60-533). You can sit at a sidewalk table in an area surrounded by shrubs, with a view of a sunset over the open sea on one side and the rhythmically neoclassical buildings of the most important piazza in Trieste on the other. In summer, the sidewalk tables face one of the liveliest congregations of people in town. However, when the cold Adriatic wind blows, everybody retreats behind the giant plate-glass windows. With its contemporary icicle-like chandeliers and its wide selection of clients, the café has very much an Eastern European aura. You can have a whisky here for 5,000 lire ($3.80). The café is closed on Tuesday.

---

2. Udine

The little hill town of Udine, lying some 44 miles northwest of Trieste and 85 miles north of Venice just off the autostrada leading to the Dolomites, is memorable mostly for the paintings by Giambattista Tiepolo, in the duomo (cathedral) and the Archbishop's Palace. Much of the town was damaged by a 1976 earthquake, but fortunately the buildings housing the best of Tiepolo's art were spared. The little town is easily reached by road or by a two-hour train ride from Venice. It is in the Friuli–Venezia Giulia region.

The telephone area code for Udine is 0432.

SIGHTS

The piazza della Libertà, at the foot of the castle-crowned hill around which the town developed, contains the **Communal Palace,** a pink-and-white-striped smaller version of the Doges' Palace in Venice, as well as a triumphal arch by Palladio. The 16th-century **Loggia di San Giovanni** has a clock tower whose Moorish figures striking the hours are similar to those at Venice.

The partially restored castle on the hill was the seat of the area's authorities from the Most Serene Republic of Venice during its heyday after the early 15th century. Before that, it was the seat of the patriarchs of Aquilea, under whose rule the cathedral took shape. The campanile of the **duomo** is from that era, with an Annunciation and the Archangel Gabriel on one of its sides. The works of Tiepolo grace the chapels of the cathedral. See especially the trompe-l'oeil frescoes in the Chapel of the Holy Sacrament. The **Oratory of Purity** (Oratorio della Purità), to the right of the cathedral, is notable for the painting of the Assumption of the Virgin on the ceiling. The duomo can be visited daily except from 12:30 to 2 p.m. To see the oratorio, ask one of the cathedral sacristans to open it. There is no admission charge to either the duomo or the oratorio.

The **Archbishop's Palace** (Palazzo Arcivescovile) contains a wealth of Tiepolo frescoes which can be seen by asking the guard at the entrance. The breathtaking work of the artist is everywhere, with the gallery upstairs being chief among the rooms to see. The palace is open from 9 a.m. to noon Monday through Friday. Admission is free.

FOOD AND LODGING

Once a visitor settles into the well-known **Astoria Hotel Italia,** piazza XX Settembre 24, 33100 Udine (tel. 0432/505-091), many of the historic sites of Udine will be within a short walking distance. It sits on one of the centrally located hubs of town, a few blocks from the cathedral. Its 80 bedrooms are comfortably outfitted with up-to-date accessories, with a well-managed restaurant on the premises. Singles rent for 114,000 lire ($86.75) daily; doubles, 149,000 lire ($113). In an elegant and high-ceilinged dining room, visitors are pampered by a polite staff, and served such specialties as mussel soup, pungently aromatic varieties of grilled beef, and roast veal along with seasonal mushrooms and vegetables. Full meals, served every day of the year, cost from 40,000 lire ($30.50).

Alla Vedova, via Tavagnacco 8 (tel. 470-291), is a venerable Udine establishment, where many of its patrons have celebrated their wedding parties or taught their children how first to behave in a public restaurant. A handful of warmly decorated rooms is clustered around an open courtyard, where a crew of grillmasters produce racks of basted chickens, whose aroma permeates the other rooms. A specialty is risotto with wild duck meat, often preceded by portions of country ham or slices of garlic-flavored sausages. Unfortunately for many summer visitors, the establishment is closed during August. Otherwise, it serves from 12:30 to 3 p.m. and 7:30 to 10 p.m. daily except Sunday night and all day Monday. Full meals cost 35,000 lire ($26.50) to 45,000 lire ($34.25).

Alla Buona Vite, via Treppo 10 (tel. 21-053), is one of the most sophisticated dining spots in town. Its Venetian-born owners serve a tempting menu based mainly on fresh seafood, each dish served with a little flair. If your weakness is pasta garnished with shellfish, this place offers several varieties, each of which tastes better with a bottle from the wine cellar. Additionally, an array of turbot, sole, and John Dory is strictly fresh and well prepared. Full meals, served from 12:30 to 2:30 p.m. and 7 to 10 p.m., cost 32,000 lire ($24.25) to 50,000 lire ($38). The establishment is closed Sunday night, all day Monday, and in August.

---

3. Cortina d'Ampezzo

This fashionable resort some 100 miles north of Venice is your best center for exploring the snow-powdered Dolomites. Its reputation as a tourist mecca dates back to before World War I, but its growth in recent years has been phenomenal. Cortina d'Ampezzo draws throngs of nature lovers in summer, and both Olympic-caliber and neophyte skiers in winter. The Dolomite haven is a hotel owner's Shangri-la, charging maximum prices in July and August as well as in the three months of winter.

The town "signora" of propaganda once insisted: "Just say Cortina has *everything*." Statements of propaganda chiefs, even when they come from charming Italian ladies, are suspect—but in this case she's nearly right. "Everything," in the Cortina context, means—first and foremost—people of every shape and hue: New York socialites in their old Balenciaga gowns rub elbows in late-night spots with frumpy Bremen hausfraus. Young Austrian men, clad in Loden jackets and stout leather shorts, walk down the streets with feathers in their caps and gleams in their eyes. French girls in red pants sample Campari at café tables, while the tweedy English sit at rival establishments drinking "tea like mother made."

Then, too, "everything" means location. Cortina is in the middle of a valley ringed by enough Dolomite peaks to cause Hannibal's elephants to throw up their trunks and flee in horror. Regardless of which road you choose for a motor trip, you'll find the scenery rewarding. Third, "everything" means good food. Cortina sets an excellent table, inspired by the cuisine of both Venice and Tyrol. Fourth, "everything" means sporting facilities in both summer and winter—chiefly golf, horseback riding, curling, tennis, fishing, mountain climbing, skiing, skating, and swimming. The resort not only has an Olympic ice stadium, but an Olympic bobsled track and ski jump (the 1956 Olympics were held at Cortina, publicizing the resort all over the world). In addition, it has a skiing school, an Olympic-size ice-skating rink, a large indoor swimming pool, an Olympic downhill track, and a cross-country track.

Fifth, "everything" means top-notch hotels, pensiones, private homes, even mountain huts for the rugged. The locations, facilities, types of service, price structures, and decor in these establishments vary considerably, but I've never inspected an accommodation here that wasn't clean. Most of the architecture of Cortina, incidentally, seems more appropriate to Zell am See, Austria, than an Italian town.

In brief, Cortina is for the leisurely life—no fuss and bother about those dutiful visits to museums, basilicas, and historical monuments. The emphasis is on fun: fun from the early morning when the heartiest visitors make an early trip to the peaks, fun till the last patron—his head reeling with Italian wine—exits from the lowliest taverna.

The Faloria-Cristallo area in the surroundings of Cortina is known for its 18½ miles of ski slopes and 10 miles of fresh-snow runs.

One of the main attractions in Cortina is to take a cable car "halfway to the stars," as the expression goes. On one of them, at least, you'll be just a yodel away from the pearly gates. It's the **Freccia Nel Cielo** (or "arrow of the sky"). For information about departures, phone 0436/5052. Beginning at 9 a.m., departures leave every 20 minutes, ending at 5 p.m. in winter, 5:30 p.m. in summer. The cable car operates daily from mid-December to mid-April and from July through September. Each stage of the three-stage trajectory costs 8,000 lire ($6.10) to 16,000 lire ($12.25) round trip. The first station is Col Druscie at 5,752 feet. The second station, Ra Valles, stands at 8,027 feet, and the top station, Tofana di Mezzo, is at 10,543 feet. At Tofana on a clear day, you can see as far as Venice.

The telephone area code for Cortina d'Ampezzo is 0436.

HOTELS IN CORTINA D'AMPEZZO

The pickings are ample—and in all price ranges.

The Upper Bracket

Miramonti Majestic Grand Hotel, 32043 Cortina d'Ampezzo (tel. 0436/42-01) is one of the grandest hotels in the Dolomites. It consists of two ochre-colored buildings with alpine hipped roofs set a short distance from the center of town. There's a gazebo built in the same style as the hotel on the right as you ascend the curved driveway leading up to the dignified façade, and a backdrop of jagged mountains behind the thick stucco walls and the dozens of gingerbread balconies. The rustic interior is filled with warmly appealing colors, lots of exposed timbers, and about the most elegant clientele in Cortina. The well-furnished bedrooms look more like the accommodations in a private home than those in a hotel, complete with matching wallpaper and bedspreads, built-in closets, and all the modern amenities. A sporting facility is on the premises, with an indoor swimming pool, exercise and massage equipment, a sauna, hydrotherapy, and physical therapy. Other sports facilities for winter and summer exercises are close nearby. In season, half board costs 160,000 lire ($122) to 240,000 lire ($182) daily per person, based on double occupancy, with a minimum stay of one week. Singles pay a supplement of 20,000 lire ($15.25) daily. The hotel is open in July and August and from just before Christmas to early April.

Cristallo Palace, via Menardi 42, 32043 Cortina d'Ampezzo (tel. 0436/42-81), is a large (81 rooms) establishment in the grand tradition of European resort hotels. It offers excellent bedrooms, lots of facilities, and top-notch service (many of the staff are virtually "retainers" of the Cristallo). The managing director keeps the standards high. The meals produced here are raison d'etre for booking an accommodation. The bedrooms are good-size, all with private baths, color TVs, direct-dial phones, and mini-bars, featuring attractive furnishings and picture-window views of the Dolomites. The hotel is open only from July to September and December 20 through March. Half board, which is obligatory in season, peaks at 280,000 lire ($213) daily in a single, 262,000 lire ($199) per person in a double or twin. Facilities include hard tennis courts, an open-air swimming pool, and terraces for sunning and drinks.

The Medium-Priced Range

De la Poste, piazza Roma 14, 32043 Cortina d'Ampezzo (tel. 0436/42-71), built like a Tyrolean mountain chalet, enjoys a central and sunny position in a pedestrian zone. It has long been a celebrity favorite, attracting such guests as King Hussein and Queen Noor. Its amenities are top-rate, with 80 rooms and an equal number of private baths. Open wooden balconies and terraces encircle the building, giving bedrooms sun porches. All the bedrooms have double windows and French doors, chintz draperies and bedspreads, and built-in wardrobes, many home-like touches. The hotel is closed from mid-October to mid-December, but otherwise receives guests, charging them 180,000 lire ($137) daily in a single room, 280,000 lire ($213) in a double. Full-board terms are 160,000 lire ($122) to 280,000 lire ($213) per person. The get-acquainted, woodsy bar, evoking a country tavern, is one of the liveliest spots in town. The hotel, once a postal inn, is the most popular place in Cortina for après-ski drinks.

Parc Hotel Victoria, corso Italia 1, 32043 Cortina d'Ampezzo (tel. 0436/32-46), is one of the best hotels in the center of town, a modern structure created in the Tyrolean style, with many good-size balconies opening onto views of the mountaintops. It's a successful place, combining the old chalet decor with contemporary, roomy areas, lots of amenities. All rooms contain private bath, TV, mini-bar, and plenty of steam heat in the winter months. The various living rooms and dining rooms are furnished with reproductions of old country furniture (bare-pine tables, peg-legged chairs). The regional fireplace with a raised hearth is the focal point for after-dinner gatherings. The hotel is open from mid-July to the end of September and December 20 to the end of March. In ski season, a single rents for 130,000 lire ($98.75) daily, and a double goes for 220,000 lire ($167). It's possible to book in here at full-board terms, ranging from 155,000 lire ($118) to 260,000 lire ($198) per person, with taxes and service included, the price depending on the season.

Hotel Corona, via Cesare Battisti 5, 32040 Cortina d'Ampezzo (tel. 0436/32-51), is one of the first hotels built at the resort, dating from 1935. It enjoys a loyal collection of clients who would stay nowhere else during a stopover in Cortina. For anyone interested in modern Italian art, a stopover here is an event. The interior walls are painted a neutral white as a foil for the hundreds of carefully inventoried artworks displayed, acquisitions of Luciano Rimaldi, the athletic manager, over the past 25 years. (He is also a ski instructor and coached Princess Grace in her downhill technique shortly before her death.) He later served as head of the Italian ice hockey team during the 1988 Winter Olympics at Calgary. It has been said that many of the most important artists of Italy (and a few from France) from 1948 to 1963 are represented here with artwork, not only painting, but sculpture and ceramic bas-reliefs. The hotel doesn't overlook sports either. It was chosen for the World Cup competition by a U.S. ski team just before they headed for the Sarajevo Olympics. The hotel prefers clients to take full board in high season (the kitchen will prepare a lunch bucket for skiers). With full board included, the per-person rates range from 110,000 lire ($83.50) to 190,000 lire ($144) daily in high season, from 80,000 lire ($60.75) to 130,000 lire ($78.75) in low. The hotel is open from December 20 to the end of March and July to mid-September.

Ancora, corso Italia 62, 32040 Cortina d'Ampezzo (tel. 0436/32-61), a "Romantik Hotel," is the domain of that hearty empress of the Dolomites, Flavia Bertozzi, who, in addition to attracting sporting guests from all over the world, also plays host to modern art exhibitions and classical concerts. This "hostess with the mostest" believes in her guests' having a good time. The antique sculptures and objets d'art filling the hotel were gathered from Signora Flavia's trips to every province of Italy. Hers is a revamped hotel enclosed on two sides by terraces with outdoor tables and umbrellas—the town center for sipping and gossiping. Garlanded wooden balconies encircle the five floors, with most bedrooms opening directly onto these sunny porches. Almost all the well-furnished and comfortable bedrooms have private bath. Based on the plumbing, the full-board rate is 170,000 lire ($129) to 250,000 lire ($190) per person daily in season. The bedrooms are especially pleasant—many with sitting areas—and you sleep under brightly colored woolen blankets. All is kept shiny clean, the service is polite and efficient, and the food is good. The hotel receives guests from June 20 to mid-September and December 20 to mid-April.

The Budget Range

Motel Agip, via Roma 118, 32040 Cortina d'Ampezzo (tel. 0436/861-400), offers many amenities as a member of this popular Italian hotel chain. It's a good bet if you arrive in Cortina in the off-season, when virtually everything else is closed. Its convenient location on the main road just outside the center of town—coupled with its clean, comfortable, contemporary, and no-nonsense format—have gained increasing favor with its many visitors. The bedrooms are predictably furnished and fairly quiet, the management helpful. The restaurant serves good food, featuring regional specialties. The 42 rooms cost 92,000 lire ($70) daily in a single, 150,000 lire ($114) in a double, with a continental breakfast included.

Menardi, via Majon 112, 32043 Cortina d'Ampezzo (tel. 0436/24-00), is an eye-catcher in the upper part of Cortina, looking like a great country inn, with its wooden balconies and shutters. Its rear windows open onto a meadow of flowers and a view of the rough Dolomite crags. The inn is 100 years old. It is run by the Menardi family, who still know how to speak the old Dolomite tongue, Ladino. Decorated in the Tyrolean fashion, each bedroom has its distinct personality. The 41 bedrooms each have private bath. The full-board rate ranges from 75,000 lire ($57) to 128,000 lire ($97.25) per person daily, inclusive, depending on the season. Considering what you get—the quality of the facilities, the reception, and the food —I'd rate this one as the best for the money in Cortina. The living rooms and dining rooms have home-like furnishings—lots of knick-knacks, pewter, antlers, spinning wheels. The Menardi is open from mid-June to mid-September and December 21 to April 1. Should this hotel be full, the family will book you into their second accommodation, containing only eight rooms, each with private bath and a balcony opening onto the Dolomites.

Hotel du Nord, via la Verra 1, 32042 Cortina d'Ampezzo (tel. 0436/47-07). Set in the upper reaches of the resort's northern periphery, alongside the road leading to the Brenner Pass, this is one of the most genuinely charming cost-conscious hotels in Cortina. Built like a chalet, and ringed with balconies on three sides, it evokes the mountain buildings of nearby Austria, but with Italian flair. It dates from 1956, with a new wing completed in 1970. Each of its 34 bedrooms contains furniture crafted from local pinewood, a phone, and a private bath. With full board included, per-person rates range from 75,000 lire ($57) to 100,000 lire ($76) daily, based on double occupancy.

Rooms in Private Homes

The **tourist office,** piazzetta San Francesco 8 (tel. 0436/32-31), has a list of all the private homes in and around Cortina that take in paying guests, lodging them family-style for a moderate cost. It's a good opportunity to live with a Dolomite family in comfort and informality. For information, you can get in touch with the tourist office. Even though there are nearly 3,500 rooms available, it's best to reserve in advance, especially from August 1 to 20 and December 20 to January 7, when bookings reach their peak. The tourist office, however, will not personally book you into a private home. Those arrangements you must make independently.

THE TOP RESTAURANTS

My favorite restaurant in Cortina, and one of the finest in the area, is **Ristorante Tivoli,** località Lacedel (tel. 866-400), set within a low-slung alpine chalet whose rear seems almost buried in the slope of the hillside. Standing high above the resort, about a mile from the center, it is beside the road leading to the hamlet of Pocol. Vastly popular with a chic and stylishly athletic European clientele, it derives its excellence from the hard-working efforts of the Calderoni family. Their gracious members seem to perform all the services necessary to make this place one of the most fun and interesting at the resort. Full meals cost from 40,000 lire ($30.50) per person, and are served from 12:30 to 3 p.m. and 8 to 10 p.m. daily (closed Monday in low season). Reservations are recommended for meals which might include stuffed rabbit in an onion sauce, duck filet with bacon and greens, veal filet with basil and pine nuts, or salmon flavored with saffron. The pastas are made in the kitchen the day they are consumed. Examples include ravioli stuffed with spinach, cream, mushrooms, and truffles, or tagliatelle with goose liver. For dessert, you might sample an aspic of exotic fruit. The bustling kitchens are visible from the vestibule as you enter, adding to the warmth and pleasure of the restaurant. It is closed from Easter to mid-July and early October to the end of November.

The most elegant dining spot, **El Toulà**, via Ronco 123 (tel. 33-39), is a wood-framed structure with picture-window views and an outside terrace. It is perched about a five-minute drive from the center of Cortina, in the direction of Pocol. The restaurant commands a panoramic view. It is the current Dolomite favorite of the fancy folk and the international set, and is one of several El Toulà branch establishments throughout Italy. You get excellently prepared dishes here, including squab grilled to perfection and served with an expertly seasoned sauce and veal braised with a white truffle sauce. The filet of beef is also recommended. A complete meal averages anywhere from 55,000 lire ($41.75) to 75,000 lire ($57). It is open from 12:30 to 2:30 p.m.; closed on Monday except in high season when it's open daily. El Toulà is in business from mid-July to early September and December 20 to Easter.

Ristorante Bellavista–Il Meloncino, località Gillardon 17 (tel. 861-043). The sweeping view of Cortina and the mountains beyond it is only one of the attractions of this small and rustic restaurant set at the top of one of the village's easiest ski runs. If you're driving, you'll need to follow the signs to Falzarego from the center of town, stopping in the satellite suburb of Gillardon. The building looks like little more than a log hut, although members of the Franco Melon family have added wind-sheltered terraces and a nearby barbecue grill on wheels that looks like an adaptation of a Conestoga wagon. You're likely to meet the more experienced members of the Cortina social scene here, all of whom enjoy the unusual specialties prepared in the establishment's tiny kitchen. These include risotto with fruit (offered from June to September only), homemade liver pâté, scaloppine dishes, roast mountain goat, grilled beef in several variations, ample use of fresh mushrooms, and homemade ice cream. Full dinners cost 35,000 lire ($26.50) to 50,000 lire ($38). The restaurant, open from 12:30 to 2:30 p.m. and 8 to 11 p.m., is closed Tuesday and for all of June and November.

Da Beppe Sello, via Ronco 67 (tel. 32-36), is in reality a third-class hotel, but habitués of Cortina know it as a village-edge chalet providing regional meals that are generous and tasty. In summer, the al fresco dining on the terrace is preferred; all other times, guests retreat inside the snug Tyrolean dining room. The restaurant is closed from early April to mid-May and mid-September to the end of October. Look for some of these specialties: gnocchi di patate (potato dumplings) or roast chicken with savory bay leaves—delightful. The fried trout is also superb. The average meal will cost 35,000 lire ($26.50) unless you order some of the more elaborate specialties. If you do, you could spend as much as 45,000 lire ($34.25). Hours are 12:30 to 2 p.m. and 7:30 to 9:30 p.m., but there is no service on Tuesday.

A SHOPPING NOTE

Good purchases are available at the **Art House,** corso Italia 96 (tel. 38-98), which offers about the best collection in the area of copper, brass, and pewter fashioned into about a thousand different variations ranging from the most practical to

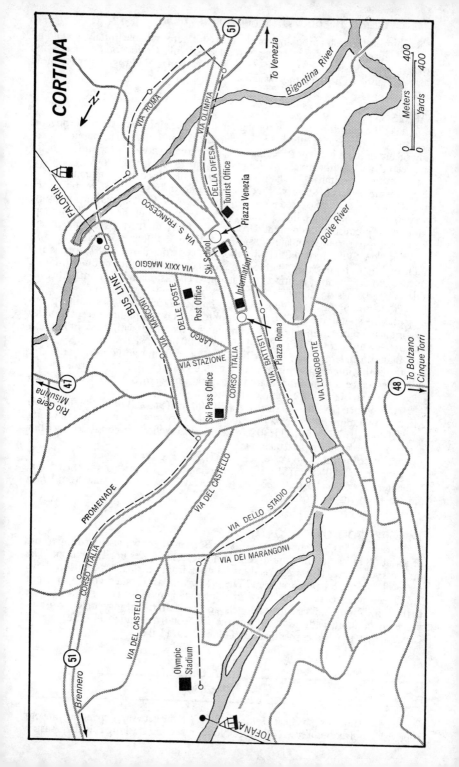

the whimsical. If you're looking for the best cookware available in Italy, you'll find copper saucepans and casseroles that would satisfy Julia Child. You might also find that massive brass door knocker you've been seeking, along with pewter mead glasses. Gabriele Caspari is the owner.

APRES SKI

Like the nightlife scattered through many of the alpine resorts in Europe, the bar and disco scene virtually closes down in the warm months. The popularity rating of any of them is about as fleeting as the mountain snow in June, although, for the record, a few of the more enduring establishments are listed below.

Limbo, corso Italia 97 (tel. 860-026), is a popular disco and restaurant, attracting pleasure seekers of all ages. It is closed in summer, but sees winter action when the skiers flock here. The disco is open nightly from 10:30 p.m. to 3 a.m., charging an entrance fee of 10,000 lire ($7.60). A whisky costs about the same. The restaurant on the premises is open nightly from 8 p.m. to 3 a.m. (perhaps the only restaurant in Cortina serving that late). A meal costs from 35,000 lire ($26.50).

Monkey Club, in the Hotel Cristallo, via Menardi 42 (tel. 42-81), opens at 9 p.m. nightly in high season, with piano music continuing until midnight. Plush, secure, and fashionable, it attracts sophisticated clients, many of whom gather beside a carved limestone fireplace. A beer costs from 5,500 lire ($4.20).

Piano Bar, in the Hotel Venezia, corso Italia 209 (tel. 32-91), is another popular gathering spot in the traffic-free center of town. It opens nightly except Monday in winter at 9 p.m. closing the music at midnight. It reopens with music in July and August. A whisky costs 6,000 lire ($4.55) to 8,000 lire ($6.10).

Bilbo Club, largo Poste (tel. 861-168), is open from midnight to 3 or 4 a.m. nightly, both winter and summer, charging 20,000 lire ($15.25) for a drink and the price of entrance. The interior is dark and rustically modern, the crowd, young disco clients from all over Europe and North America.

Aria, Ronco (tel. 867-393), charges 20,000 lire ($15.25) or 25,000 lire ($19) entrance, including the price of your first drink. Very modern, it caters to a young set, and does so nightly from 11:30 p.m. to 4 a.m. You enter a bar on street level, but descend to the basement to dance.

Hippopotamus, largo Poste (tel. 23-33), caters to the young disco market. It charges patrons 20,000 lire ($15.25) to enter, including the price of your first drink. You enter a street-level bar, descending to the "cave" to dance any time from 10:30 p.m. to 4 a.m. nightly.

THE GREAT DOLOMITE ROAD

From Cortina d'Ampezzo in the east to Bolzano in the west is a circuitous route of about 68 miles. It ranks among the grandest scenic drives in all of Europe. The first pass you'll cross (Falzarego) is about 11 miles from Cortina. At 6,900 feet above sea level, it offers a panoramic view. The next great pass is called Pordoi, at about 7,350 feet above sea level, loftiest point along the highway (you can take a cable car to the top). You'll find restaurants, hotels, and cafés. In the spring, edelweiss grows in the surrounding fields. After crossing the pass, you'll descend to the little resort of Canazei, then much later pass by the sea-blue Carezza Lake.

---

4. Bolzano

The terminus of the Great Dolomite Road (or the gateway, depending on your approach), Bolzano is a town of mixed blood, reflecting the long rule that Austria enjoyed until 1919. Many names, including that of the town (Bozen), appear in German. As the recipient of considerable Brenner Pass traffic (55 miles north), the city is a melting pot of Italians and both visitors and residents from the Germanic lands. The capital of a province of the same name, Bolzano lies in the center of the Alto Adige region. It is traversed by two rivers, the Isarco and Talvera, one of which splits the town into two sections.

Bolzano makes a good headquarters for exploring the Dolomites and the scenic surroundings, such as Renon (Ritten in German) on the alpine plateau, with its cog train; the village of San Genesio, reached by cable north of Bolzano; and Salten, 4,355 feet up, an alpine tableland. Bolzano is a modern industrial town, yet a worth-while sightseeing attraction in its own right. It has many esplanades for promenad-ing along the river. The most interesting street is the colonnaded via dei Portici. You can begin your stroll down this street of old buildings at either the piazza Municipio or piazza delle Erbe, the latter a fruit market for the orchards of the province.

Bolzano's telephone area code is 0471.

HOTELS IN BOLZANO

A choice place to stay, **Park Hotel Laurin,** via Laurino 4, 39100 Bolzano (tel. 0471/980-500), recaptures the glamour of the past, the nostalgia of yesteryear. The 106 well-furnished and ample-size bedrooms each have private bathroom. The only hotel in Bolzano in its first-class classification, the Park Laurin charges 125,000 lire ($95) daily in a single. The rate in a double is 175,000 lire ($133), inclusive. Its private garden is dominated by old shade trees and a flagstone-enclosed swimming pool. Guests are drawn to the high-beamed and spacious lounge, with its brass chan-deliers and its groupings of antiques and reproductions, as well as its baronial fire-place and deeply set windows. The garden terrace is a sunpocket, ideal for lunches or breakfast. The evening meals are served in the interior dining room to the accompa-niment of a softly playing orchestra or in the restaurant in the garden with its com-fortable open-air American bar. A lunch or dinner costs from 45,000 lire ($34.25) per person.

Grifone-Greif, piazza Walther 6, 39100 Bolzano (tel. 0471/977-056). Strate-gically on the piazza Walther with its Salzburg spirit of ornate buildings and open-air cafés, the year-round Grifone-Greif has a traditional look out front, where there's a sidewalk café under a canopy. In the rear, however, is a garden swimming pool and a revamped modern façade with upper-floor balconies. The 131 rooms vary in size and amenities, although all are comfortable and well maintained. The rate is 120,000 lire ($91.25) daily in a single with bath, 160,000 lire ($122) for a double with bath, inclusive. In fair weather, you can dine in the open-air restaurant, shel-tered by a canopy. Excellent South Tyrolean and Italian meals are served in a garden atmosphere.

Hotel Alpi, via Alto Adige 35, 39100 Bolzano (tel. 0471/970-535), is a taste-fully contemporary hotel whose exterior is dotted with recessed balconies, large aluminum-framed windows, and the flags of many nations. The spacious public rooms are richly covered with paneling, exposed stone, and ceramic wall sculptures, which, with the comfortable upholstered seating areas, make for a pleasant hotel. In the commercial center of town, the hotel has a bar, a restaurant, a well-trained staff, and 110 cozy rooms, priced from 85,000 lire ($64.50) daily in a single, 125,000 lire ($95) in a double. Each unit has a modern bathroom. Meals begin at 35,000 lire ($26.50) in the hotel's restaurant.

Luna Mondschein, via Piave 15, 39100 Bolzano (tel. 0471/975-642), offers comfortable accommodations in an establishment that combines old-fashioned service with modern amenities. The interior has high ceilings, many of them cof-fered or adorned with plaster detailing, lots of exposed wood, and a combination of up-to-date furniture with copies of the 19th-century accessories. The restaurant, which spills over into a garden section in summer, is one of the best in town. Singles cost from 70,000 lire ($53.25) daily; doubles begin at 110,000 lire ($83.50). Full meals in the restaurant, which is closed every Sunday between November and March, cost from 35,000 lire ($26.50) per head.

Scala Hotel Stiegl, via Brennero 11 (Brennerstrasse 11), 39100 Bolzano (tel. 0471/976-222), is one of the best of the middle-bracket hotels of Bolzano. Its trilingual staff speaks fluent English, among other languages, and keeps the interior spotless. The neobaroque yellow-and-white façade is well maintained, with plenty of ornamentation scattered symmetrically over its five-story expanse. On the premises is an outdoor pool, plus a summer garden restaurant specializing in Tyrolean dishes. The hotel affords easy access to the train station and the historic center of town. Its well-furnished rooms, 60 in all, rent for 60,000 lire ($45.50) daily in a single, 95,000 lire ($72.25) and up in a double. Meals begin at 25,000 lire ($19). The hotel has parking spaces for 50 cars.

Herzog, piazza del Grano 2, 39100 Bolzano (tel. 0471/976-267), is a small, Old-World inn, in the heart of Bolzano. It attracts everybody who likes a nostalgic atmosphere. Each room is decorated with hand-painted furniture from Austria. Many units have a shower and some have a private bath. There are 4 singles and 21 doubles. Depending on the plumbing, singles cost 30,000 lire ($22.75) to 35,000 lire ($26.50) daily; doubles, 55,000 lire ($41.75) to 75,000 lire ($57). Breakfast is included in all the tariffs. The little breakfast room overlooks the old piazza.

DINING IN BOLZANO

The most elegant restaurant in Bolzano, **Da Abramo,** piazza Gries 16 (Grieserplatz 16) (tel. 280-141), took great pains to introduce a chicly modern airiness to its physical decor. In a sienna-colored villa across the river from the historic center of town, the restaurant offers a summer garden covered with vine arbors, plus a labyrinthine arrangement of rooms. The accessories include brass lamps. Full meals range upward from 40,000 lire ($30.50) and might include, depending on the mood of the chef, veal in a sauce of tuna and capers, roast quail with polenta, fish soup, spaghetti carbonara, vegetarian antipasti, codfish Venice style, a vast array of shellfish and seafood, tagliatelle with prosciutto, and beefsteak flambé with cognac. Reservations are suggested, and the restaurant is open from 12:30 to 2:30 p.m. and 7:30 to 9:30 p.m.; closed Sunday.

Chez Frédéric, via Armando Diaz 12 (tel. 271-011), is altogether exceptional for the area, serving some of the finest food outside the major hotel dining rooms. Located across the river, it is decorated in an inviting style. In summer, tables are set outside in the courtyard. Everything is cooked to order and served in an efficient manner. To begin your meal, I recommend an order of speck, a Tyrolean dish of meat sliced razor-thin, the color of dried beef. As a main dish, the pepper steak is also recommended, or you may prefer the chateaubriand for two persons. The chef's recommendation, and I concur, is fegato col uvetta (liver with grapes). Desserts are rich, fattening, and smooth-tasting. Depending on your beef selection, the average meal here will range in price from 25,000 lire ($19) to 42,000 lire ($32). The restaurant, open from 12:30 to 2:30 p.m. and 7:30 to 9:30 p.m., is closed Tuesday.

Zur Kaisertron', via della Mostra 1 (Mustergasse 1) (tel. 970-770). The food is excellent, the decor appealing, and the management preserves the bicultural ambience for which Bolzano is known. The restaurant is housed in an Austrian yellow-and-white baroque building a block from the cathedral. For warm-weather dining, there's a canopy-covered wooden platform in front surrounded with greenery. From 12:30 to 2:30 p.m. and 7:30 to 9:30 p.m., you'll be welcomed by a member of the staff and ushered to a table under vaulted ceilings. Light comes from open windows or wrought-iron chandeliers. Favorite dishes include an assortment of alpine dried beef, beef goulash with polenta, trout with salmon, spaghetti with clams, creamy soups, and a range of other frequently changing items. Expect to spend 35,000 lire ($26.50) and up for a full meal. The restaurant is closed Saturday night and all day Sunday.

Maretsch Restaurant, at Castle Maretsch (tel. 979-439), is part of a modern conference complex set in a medieval castle. The castle lies about a five-minute walk from most of the major hotels in the old-town sector of Bolzano. The location is near the Talfer Promenade in a tranquil setting of vineyards. The restaurant serves lunch and dinner daily except Sunday for 40,000 lire ($30.50) and up. Hours are 9 a.m. to 3 p.m. and 5:30 to 11 p.m. daily. The food is both traditional Italian and Central European. You might prefer the chef's goulash or a bollito misto, a selection of boiled meats (including tongue), covered with a herb-flavored sauce. Guests dine under vaulted ceilings in cooler weather, enjoying the outside tables in the castle courtyard in summer.

---

5. Merano

Once the capital of Tyrol (before Innsbruck), Merano (Meran) was ceded to Italy at the end of World War I, but it retains much of its Austrian heritage. In days gone by it was one of the most famous resorts in Europe, drawing kings and queens and a vast entourage from many countries, who were attracted to the alpine retreat by the grape cure. (The eating of luscious Merano grapes is supposed to have medicinal value.) After a slump, Merano now enjoys popularity, especially in autumn when the grapes are harvested. Before the last war Merano also became known for its radioactive waters, in which ailing bathers supposedly secured relief for everything from gout to rheumatism.

The Passirio River cuts through the town (and along it are many promenades, evoking the heyday of the resorts of the 19th century). In the Valley of the Adige at the foot of Küchelberg, Merano makes a good base for excursions in several directions, particularly to Avelengo. A bus from Sandplatz will deliver you to a funicular connection, in which you can ascend 3,500 feet above sea level to Avelengo, with its splendid vista and mountain hotels and pensions.

Merano is richly endowed with vacation-type facilities and attractions, such as open-air swimming pools at its Lido, tennis courts, and a race track (Grand Prix in September).

The telephone area code for Merano is 0473.

AMERANO SIGHT

On the Tappeinerweg promenade, the **Museo Agricolo Brunnenburg** is housed in a castle owned by the daughter and grandson of Ezra Pound, who lived in Merano from 1958 to 1964. The museum has displays of Tyrolean country life, including a blacksmith's shop and a grain mill. There are also ethnology exhibits, plus a room dedicated to Pound. Open daily except Tuesday from 9:30 to 11:30 a.m. and 2 to 5 p.m. Admission is 1,500 lire ($1.15). You can reach the castle by taking the bus to Dorf Tirol, every hour on the hour from Merano, or by climbing the Tappeinerweg.

HOTELS IN MERANO

The resort is also well stocked with hotel beds, and offers many superior accommodations at moderate prices.

A Deluxe Choice

Kurhotel Palace, via Cavour 2 (Cavourstrasse 2), 39012 Merano (tel. 0473/34-734), is a turn-of-the-century re-creation of a baroque palace that has been set into the most beautiful formal gardens in town. The ceilings of the gilt-and-cream-colored public rooms are supported by a series of Corinthian columns similar to the ones adorning the yellow-and-white façade. The furniture, in part, seems to be good-quality copies of 18th-century designs, and the crystal chandeliers are massive. From the rear terrace there's a view of the large marble slabs that have been arranged into a chessboard on the lawn. From there you'll be able to see the groupings of small inquisitive cherubs set onto the hotel's ornate roofline that appear to be squinting down into the gardens. These contain a free-form pool whose waters flow below a modern tile annex for an indoor extension of the swimming area.

Many of the bedrooms have their own stone or wrought-iron balconies, which look over roses, palms, and palmettos. Although it has been in business for more than 80 years, the hotel has up-to-date comforts. A wide variety of accommodation is offered. Depending on the size, season, and view, halfboard ranges from 130,000 lire ($98.75) to 180,000 lire ($137) daily in a single, 120,000 lire ($91.25) to 150,000 lire ($114) per person in twin-bedded rooms, with taxes and service included. Special packages for health and diet are offered. A fully equipped department with complete spa, beauty, health, and fitness programs under medical supervision is offered in the indoor pool area, as well as sauna, solarium, hot whirlpool, and thermal treatments.

First-Class Choices

The **Bristol** (Grand Hotel), via Ottone Huber 14, 39012 Merano (tel. 0473/49-500), has 138 large, well-furnished rooms, each with its own private bath or shower. Some are equipped with ornate pieces, and private balconies envelop the building. Open from March to October, the Bristol charges from 85,000 lire ($64.50) daily in a single with a continental breakfast, to 145,000 lire ($110) in a double on the same arrangement. To stay here on full-board terms for three or more days, a guest pays 114,000 lire ($86.75) daily in a single, from 102,000 lire ($77.50) per person daily based on double occupancy. The food (open-air restaurant) has been highly praised. The tax is included. While the rooms are comfortable and the baths handsomely tiled (with bidets), it is the roof garden with the heated swimming pool and view that holds the attraction. A garden with centenary trees surrounds the building. Among its facilities, the hotel offers health cures, spa and cosmetics treatments, and special dietary preparation.

Villa Mozart, via San Marco 26, 39012 Merano (tel. 0473/30-630), and its Ristorante Andrea, via Galilei 44 (tel. 37-400), are the statement of Andreas Hellrigl, a cook by profession and writer of books on South Tyrolean cuisine. Hellrigl's small hotel (20 beds) is decorated and furnished in the Jugend style of the Vienna Secessionists, a contemporary and similar motif of art nouveau. His use of glass, mirrors, geometrical design, and stark black and white throughout the handsome structure is striking and effective. All bedrooms have bath, direct-dial phone, color TV, radio, and drink cabinet. They rent for 178,000 lire ($135) per person daily for half board, with service, taxes, and use of the indoor pool included. The hotel also has a sauna, solarium, garden terrace, and covered parking.

The most outstanding feature of this sophisticated hostelry is the restaurant in which Hellrigl's expertise shows in the haute cuisine, based on the dishes of the South Tyrol. His specialties, adapted to modern palates, include fresh asparagus covered with a chervil-flavored cream sauce, beef bordelaise with a purée of fresh parsley, and a ragoût of snails flavored with basil and served with plenta. Expect to spend 50,000 lire ($38) to 80,000 lire ($60.75) for a meal. The restaurant enjoys a following among locals and visitors alike, and reservations are strongly advised. The Andreas, open daily except Monday from 12:30 to 2:30 p.m. and 7:30 to 9:30 p.m., closes for most of January and February. Cooking courses are offered for those wishing to learn how an expert does it.

Hotel Meranerhof, via Manzoni 1 (Manzonistrasse 1), 39012 Merano (tel. 0473/30-230), is a centrally located, rather fashionable hotel. On the banks of the river, near one of the popular pedestrian promenades of Merano, the hotel contains an elegant bar that curves around one of the well-furnished sitting rooms. The ceiling of the lobby is supported by stone columns into which elaborately curlicued bas-reliefs have been carved. There's lots of gilding on the ornate Austrian furniture, and modern crystal chandeliers cast a prismatic glow over everything. A swimming pool set into the lawn in back of the hotel beckons, and a series of massage facilities are available upon request. With full board included, the conservatively elegant bedrooms rent for 95,000 lire ($72.25) to 100,000 lire ($76) per person daily.

Riz Stephanie, via Cavour 12 (Cavourstrasse), 39012 Merano (tel. 0473/37-745), is housed in a mustard-colored building with ornate wrought-iron balconies that look over well-maintained flowering gardens. It began life during World War I as a private hospital, and it was turned into a hotel in 1969. Today soft, salmon-colored velvet covers many of the walls, alternating with gilt trim, white accents, and tastefully conservative furniture. The lobby bar has a secluded terrace for drinks amid the flowers, and the hotel's rear wing stretches toward a small swimming pool set amid exotic trees. Many of the accommodations contain private balconies and all the modern conveniences. With full board, prices range from 95,000 lire ($72.25) to 110,000 lire ($83.50) per person daily. Open March to October.

The Middle and Budget Range

Hotel Aurora, Kurpromenade 38, 39012 Merano (tel. 0473/33-028), is an appealing hotel set behind a salmon-colored façade on the most popular pedestrian promenade in town. Many of the rooms have an angled balcony better to enjoy the views of the river, although some of the German-speaking guests seem to congregate in a sunny café terrace, or when it's full, in the light-grained sitting room. The hotel is open from mid-March to mid-November, when it seems to be the most popular place in town. With full board included, rates range from 66,000 lire ($50.25) daily in a single, 110,000 lire ($83.50) in a double.

Hotel Garni Seisenegg, via Giardini 1 (Gartenstrasse 1), 39012 Merano (tel. 0473/37-212). The usual way of reaching this family-run hotel is via a narrow walled alley from the center of town. The path will lead you into the private walled garden of a modern ochre-colored hotel set amid towering trees. From the sun terrace, you can see the steeple of a 15th-century church in the commercial part of town, a short distance away, and hear a rushing stream and the chattering of birds. The hotel was built in 1961 on the site of a 17th-century house, whose walls were completely incorporated into the new structure. The owner keeps this pleasant hotel open from mid-March until early November every year. With a continental breakfast included, rates range from 100,000 lire ($76) daily in a double, 56,000 lire ($42.50) in a single.

DINING IN MERANO

The board requirement is an old and established tradition at Merano. But if you're lodging at a hotel that doesn't require meals, or are just passing through for the day, then consider the following:

Andrea, via Galileo Galilei 44 (tel. 37-400), is known to gastronomes on both sides of the Alps, one of the most respected dining spots in the region. Laden with atmosphere, the cozy dining room is directed by Oberrauch Walter and Nothdurfter Pepi. Full meals, costing from 78,000 lire ($59.25), are served from noon to 2 p.m. and 7:30 to 10 p.m. daily except Monday; closed from the beginning of January to March 15. Specialties include a marinaded salmon, Angus beef with parsley purée and red wine sauce, and cheese gnocchi with fruit sauces. Reservations are vital.

Flora, via Portici 75 (tel. 31-484), serves a sophisticated Tyrolean and Italian cuisine of consistently good quality in its conservatively elegant confines. Full meals, costing from 50,000 lire ($38), include ravioli stuffed with chicken and exotic mushrooms, pasta blackened with squid ink, rack of lamb cooked in a shell of salt, and marinated trout with fine herbes. Open from 12:30 to 2:30 p.m. and 7:30 to 9:30 p.m., the place is closed Sunday and from mid-January to the end of February.

6. Bressanone

At the confluence of the Isarco and the Rienza Rivers, Bressanone is more often referred to by its German name of Brixen. It is very much an old Tyrolean town, with buildings characterized by oriel windows. It is also one of the most attractive towns in the Trentino–Alto Adige area.

Its **cathedral** dates from the 13th century, although it was extensively remodeled in the 18th century. Adjoining the duomo are some cloisters originally constructed in the 12th century. These cloisters are frescoed, some of the paintings going back to the 14th century.

Also of interest, San Giovanni Battista or **St. John the Baptist's Chapel** was originally from the 11th century. It has some frescoes (many from the 13th century). Naturally, among other subjects, they depict the beheading of John.

About two miles north of the town, you can take a guided tour through the **Convento di Novacella** (tel. 22-189) at 10 or 11 a.m., and 2, 3, or 4 p.m. However, it is closed on Sunday and holidays. Admission is 3,000 lire ($2.30). The monastery dates from 1142, but it was extensively remodeled centuries later, including the 18th. The monastery contains a library, valuable manuscripts, and some 15th-century cloisters. See, in particular, the Chapel of St. Michael.

Bressanone's telephone area code is 0472.

WHERE TO STAY AND DINE

As intriguing as Bressanone is, many people come here mainly for its famous **Elephant Hotel,** via Rio Bianco 4, 39042 Bressanone (tel. 0472/32-750), a Renaissance inn that took its name from a royal elephant which slept there for two weeks in the winter of 1550 and 1551. It was being sent to Vienna as a gift to the Emperor Ferdinand of Austria from King John III of Portugal. The poor beast had already survived a rough trip from Goa by ship to Genoa. A fresco was commissioned of the elephant (which, understandably, was drawing big crowds back in those days), and it is still there today.

Karl-Heinz Falk runs the inn today, attracting visitors who often cross the border from Austria to spend the weekend here. Many of his 43 rooms are furnished with antiques (in a few cases from the 17th century). Oil paintings, mainly 19th-century works, decorate some of the walls. Herr Falk runs one of the finest inns in the province, growing his own fruit and vegetables in the nearby walled garden and luring guests with a swimming pool. A single room rents for 70,000 lire ($53.25) daily, while a double costs from 140,000 lire ($106). Many guests who visit (and aren't registered at the hotel) come just for the food. A complete meal costs 32,000 lire ($24.25) to 46,000 lire ($35). Both traditional Italian dishes and Tyrolean fare are served in the dining room. Tafelspitz, a boiled-beef dish beloved by the Emperor Franz Joseph of Austria, is regularly featured, but you can also enjoy pasta as well, especially the spinach- and ricotta-stuffed ravioli. Those with gargantuan appetites may want to order the Elefantenplatte, a medley of various grilled, fried, and boiled meats. However, there must be at least four in your party, although the platte could feed far more. Meals are served from 12:30 to 2:30 p.m. and 7:30 to 9:30 p.m. daily except Monday.

An excellent *Relais & Chateaux* selection is the **Hotel Dominik,** via Terzo di Sotto 13, 39042 Bressanone (tel. 0472/30-144), where Monika and Dominik Demetz welcome you to their ochre-colored hostelry housing 29 spacious bedrooms, a bar, and a restaurant. Built in the late 1970s, the hotel has comfortable and relaxing public rooms furnished with antiques, an indoor swimming pool, a fitness room, a sauna, and a solarium. Terraces and gardens are inviting places for guests to relax, and there is a large garage for your car. Cornell University–trained Dominik manages his establishment graciously, and his restaurant offers excellent cuisine and good wines. All the bedrooms face the south, and doubles have sitting areas and loggias or terraces so that guests can look out over the Tyrolean surroundings. All the units have a bath and other modern conveniences. The charges for half board are 95,000 lire ($72.25) to 125,000 lire ($95) per person daily. Closed from early January to mid-March and in November.

7. Trent (Trento)

Another northern Italian city that basks in its former glory, this medieval town on the left bank of the Adige is known throughout the world as the host of the Council of Trent (1545–1563). Beset with difficulties, such as the rising tide of "heretics," the Ecumenical Council convened at Trent, a step that led to the Counter-Reformation.

On the main rail line from the Brenner Pass, Trent is visited mainly as a stopover en route to other points. The city has much old charm, offset somewhat by unbridled industrialization. For a quick glimpse of the old town, head for the **piazza del Duomo,** dominated by the **Cathedral of Trent.** Built in the Romanesque style and much restored over the centuries, it dates from the 12th century. In the center of the square is a mid-18th-century Fountain of Neptune, armed with a triton.

The ruling prince-bishops of Trent, who held sway till they were toppled by the French in the early 19th century, resided at the medieval **Castello del Buonconsiglio,** reached from the via B. Clesio. Now the old castle has been turned into a provincial museum, with collection of paintings and fine art, some quite ancient, including early medieval mosaic. The **Museo del Risorgimento,** also at the castle, is a museum containing mementos related to the period of national unification between 1796 and 1948. The museums are open from 9 a.m. to noon and 2 to 5:30 p.m. (close at 5 p.m. in winter); closed Monday. Admission is 2,000 lire ($1.60).

Lean on attractions, Trent still makes a good base for exploring the sports resort of **Monte Bondone,** with its panoramic view (chair lifts), about 8½ miles from the city center; **Paganella,** slightly more than 6 miles from Trent (the summit, nearly 7,000 feet high, is reached by cable); and the **Brenta Dolomites.** The latter excursion, which will require at least a day for a good look, will reward you with some of the finest mountain scenery in Italy. From Trent, you'll first pass by **Lake Toblino,** then travel a winding, circuitous road for much of the way, past jagged boulders. A ten-minute detour from the main road is suggested at the turnoff to the Genova valley, with its untamed scenery—at least to the thunderous **Nardis waterfall.** A good stopover point is the fast-rising little resort of **Madonna di Campiglio.**

The telephone area code for Trent is 0461.

HOTELS IN TRENT

Direly in need of a counter-reformation, the hotels of Trent are better for overnighters than fortnighters. My recommendations follow, beginning with the more expensive—

Grand Hotel Trento, via Alfieri 3, 38100 Trento (tel. 0461/981-010), was designed in the 1950s-style format of an L-shaped floor plan with one curved extension stretching toward the city park just across the street. The interior has everything you'd expect in a commercially oriented hotel, including a decor of gray and red marble floors, contemporary furniture, a prominent and comfortable bar, and a restaurant called Al Caminetto, with an adjoining terrace café. Each of the 94 rooms contains a mini-bar, TV, radio, and phone. Doubles rent for 170,000 lire ($129) daily; singles, 120,000 lire ($91).

Hotel Buonconsiglio, Romagnosistrasse 16-18, 38100 Trento (tel. 0461/980-089), is conveniently located on a busy street in the center of town near the railway station. The bigger-than-life-size sculptures (one of which is the hotel's namesake), the abstract modern paintings, and the warmly inviting color scheme contribute to the coziness of the lobby area. The staff speak some English. One of the bigger public rooms contains a bar. Each of the comfortable and well-decorated accommodations contains private bath, frigo-bar, air conditioning, and television. Singles rent for 110,000 lire ($83.50) daily; doubles, 150,000 lire ($114).

Hotel America, via Torre Verde 50, 38100 Trento (tel. 0461/983-010), is a simple and attractive hotel with iron balconies and a vine-wreathed arbor sheltering the main entrance. The owner worked in America for a while before naming the hotel after one of his favorite places. Singles in this centrally located establishment rent for 60,000 lire ($45.50) daily, and doubles go for 90,000 lire ($68.50). All units contain a modern bath.

Hotel Monaco, via Torre d'Augusto 25, 38100 Trento (tel. 0461/983-060). If you look up at the towering cliffs that surround this modern hotel in the center of town, you'll get the idea that you're in the bottom of a rock quarry. That doesn't detract from the comfortable accommodations in this three-story hotel with its prominent balconies and its strong horizontal lines. There is ample parking outside, as well as a bar, restaurant, and sidewalk terrace. Singles cost 75,000 lire ($57) daily; doubles, 125,000 lire ($95).

Albergo Accademia, vicolo Colico 6, 38100 Trento (tel. 0461/981-011), is a 40-room alpine inn in the center of town. It is made up of three buildings that have been joined to make a comfortable, attractive hostelry. One of the buildings is believed to be of 11th- or 12th-century origin, based on a brick wall similar to the city walls, found during renovation work. According to legend, the older part of the Accademia was used to house church leaders who attended the Council of Trent in the 16th century. The inn stands behind the Renaissance Church of Santa Maria Maggiore. The rooms are done in light natural wood, with singles renting for 75,000 lire ($57) daily; doubles, 115,000 lire ($87.50). The suite at the top of the house has a terrace from which you can see the town and the mountain. The alpine influence is carried out in the bar and the restaurant. You can get a good meal for two, with a bottle of wine, for 40,000 lire ($30.50).

DINING IN TRENT

A visit to **Restaurant Chiesa,** Parco San Marco (tel. 985-577), involves tasting the largest array of dishes I've ever seen made with apples. Owners Sergio and Isabella Chiesa recognized that Eve's favorite fruit, which grows more abundantly around Trent that practically anywhere else, was the base of dozens of traditional recipes. After augmenting them with a few creations of their own, they established a popular restaurant in 1974 in what had been the 17th-century home of the Count Wolkenstein. The restaurant stands at the back of a large walled garden (you'll have to ring the bell set into the iron gate before gaining access). Once inside, you can choose one of the three large, rustically appointed rooms, with ceiling beams, stone columns, racks of regional pottery, a central serving area, and baskets and barrels filled with the owners' favorite fruit. Specialties include risotto with apple, apple strudel, liver pâté with apple, apple cocktail Eva (made with beef and spices), filet of perch with apple, and a range of other well-prepared specialties (a few of which, believe it or not, do not contain apples). However, several meat dishes are cooked in cider. A rich dessert might be followed by apple cider. Full meals range upward from 45,000 lire ($34.25), and reservations are suggested. The restaurant is open from 12:30 to 2:30 p.m. and 7:30 to 9:30 p.m. daily except Sunday.

Hostaria del Buonconsiglio, via Suffraggio 23 (tel. 986-619), is a rustic restaurant in an old building whose interior is warmly decorated. Its menu is determined by whatever is at the market and in season on any particular day. Meals cost 38,000 lire ($29) and up. The establishment is open daily except Sunday from noon to 2 p.m. and 7 to 10 p.m. daily.

Birreria Forst, via Oss-Mazzurana 38 (tel. 35-590), is a good budget-category dining choice set in a redesigned palazzo in the center of Trent. The ground-floor level focuses around a horseshoe-shaped chrome-covered bar behind which beer on tap and varieties of the local wine are served. Below a high ceiling fashioned from half-rounded beams and rough planks, diners enjoy pizzas or meals from 20,000 lire ($15.25). If you don't want to eat in the bar section, there is a separate dining area at the top of a curved staircase at the back of the room. Menu specialties include mixed grill of the house, tripe parmigiana, goulash with potatoes, speck with mushrooms, and typical Italian specialties. The restaurant, open from 9:30 a.m. to midnight, is closed on Monday.

THE LAKE DISTRICT

1. **LAKE GARDA**
2. **LAKE COMO**
3. **LAKE MAGGIORE**

Flower-bedecked promenades . . . lemon trees and villas . . . parks and gardens . . . tunnel-like roads . . . crystal-clear blue waters . . . great natural beauty. A lake district holiday may sound a bit dated, like a penny-farthing bicycle or an aspidistra in the bay window. But the lakes—notably Garda, Como, and Maggiore—combine to form one of the most enchanting splashes of scenery in northern Italy.

Like the lake district in northwestern England, the Italian lakes have attracted poets and writers, everybody from Goethe to Gabriele d'Annunzio. But after World War II the Italian lakes seemed to be largely the domain of English and German women, the matronly types who prefer to do a lot of walking in groups. In my more recent swings through the district, I've noticed an increasing joie de vivre and a rising influx of the under-25 set, particularly at such resorts as Limone on Lake Garda.

Even if your time is limited, you'll want to have at least a look at—

1. Lake Garda

The most easterly of the northern Italian lakes, Garda is also the largest, stretching 32 miles in length (and 11½ miles in width at its fattest point). Sheltered by mountains, its scenery, especially the part on the western shore that reaches from Limone to Salo, has often been compared to that of the Mediterranean: olive, orange, and lemon trees, even palms. The almost transparent lake is ringed with four art cities: Trent to the northeast, Brescia to the west, Mantua (Mantova) to the south, and Verona to the east.

The eastern side of the lake is more rugged, less trampled, but the western resort-studded strip is far more glamorous to the first-timer. On the western side, a circuitous road skirts the lake through one mole-like tunnel after another. You can park your car at several secluded belvederes for a panoramic lakeside view. In spring the scenery is splashed with color, everything from wild poppy beds to oleander. Garda is well served by buses, or you can traverse the lake on steamers or motorboats, leaving from a number of harbors.

From our last stopover in Trent, it's only a 27-mile drive southwest to—

RIVA DEL GARDA

Astride the narrowing northern point of Garda, in the province of Trento, 195 feet above sea level, Riva is the oldest and most traditional resort along the lake. It consists of both an expanding new district and an old town, the latter centered at the piazza III Novembre. On the harbor are the **Tower of Apponale,** dating from the 13th century, and the **Rocca,** built in 1124 and once owned by the ruling Scligeri princes of Verona. The latter has been turned into a museum.

On the northern banks of the lake, between the Benacense plains and towering mountains, Riva offers the advantages of the Riviera and Dolomites. Its climate is classically Mediterranean, mild in winter and moderate in summer. Vast areas of rich vegetation combine with the deep blue of the lake. Many come for health cures; others for business conferences, meetings, and fairs. Riva is popular with tour groups from the Germanic lands and from England. It is linked to the Brenner-Modena motorway (Rovereto Sud/Garda Nord exit), the railway (Rovereto station), and is near Verona Airport Villafranca.

Information is available from **Azienda Autonoma di Siggiorno,** Palazzo dei Congressi, 38066 Riva del Garda (tel. 0464/554-444).

The telephone area code for Riva del Garda is 0464.

Where to Stay in Riva del Garda

Hotel du Lac et du Parc, viale Rovereto 44, 38066 Riva del Garda (tel. 0464/520-202), is the best hotel in town, in the deluxe category. Its design might be California or Spanish in style. Set back from the busy road behind a shrub-filled parking lot dotted with stone cherubs, the hotel has several outbuildings closer to the street, containing restaurants and additional rooms. The interior of the main building is freshly decorated, with arched windows, lots of spacious comfort, and an enclosed and manicured lawn visible from the lobby. There's a huge dining room, two additional restaurants, an attractive bar, unusual accessories, and a comfortably sprawling format, each corner of which gives the impression of being part of a large private home. Established as a hotel 100 years ago, the current structure is from 1953. It was renovated by the Zontini family. The well-trained staff speaks a variety of languages, and seems genuinely concerned with the well-being of their guests. A garden stretches behind the hotel, containing a swimming pool, lakeside beach, and two tennis courts. With half board included, the charge is 130,000 lire ($98.75) per person daily in a double; singles pay a supplement of 5,000 lire ($3.80). The hotel is open from April to October.

A first-class choice, the **Lido Palace Hotel,** viale Carducci 10, 38066 Riva del Garda (tel. 0464/552-664), is a grand lakeside retreat, surrounded by gardens and only a five-minute walk to the town center. The formal tree-lined drive reinforces the feeling of entering a private estate. The hotel was completely renovated and reopened in 1983. It has 63 twin-bedded rooms with modern furnishings, private bath or shower, toilet, and phone. A single unit costs from 105,000 lire ($79.75) daily; a double begins at 180,000 lire ($137). Full-board rates range from 125,000 lire ($95) per person per day. High season is from July to mid-September, but the hotel is open from late March to October.

In the medium-priced bracket, the **Hotel Sole,** piazza III Novembre 35, 38066 Riva del Garda (tel. 0464/552-686), apparently had far-sighted founders, snaring the best position on the waterfront. Although rated second class by the government, and charging second-class prices, the hotel has all the amenities worthy of a first-class rating. It's an overgrown villa and has a large stack of rooms with arched windows and surrounding colonnades. Its interior has time-clinging traditional rooms. The beamed-ceiling lounge centers around a cone-sloped hooded fireplace, with clusters of antique chairs set on islands of Oriental carpets. The character and quality of the bedrooms vary considerably according to their position (most of them have views of the lake). Some are almost suites, with living room areas; the smaller ones are less fortunate. Nevertheless, all the rooms are comfortable and are maintained spotlessly. All units have private bath or shower. In a single, the rate ranges from 42,000 lire ($32) to 62,000 lire ($47) daily; in doubles, from 70,000 lire ($53.25) to 100,000 lire ($76). Depending on your room assignment, the half-board charge is 54,000 lire ($41) to 78,000 lire ($59.25) per person daily. You can dine in the formal interior room or on the flagstone lakeside terrace.

Hotel Venezia, viale Rovereto 62, 38066 Riva del Garda (tel. 0464/522-216), one of the most attractive budget-category hotels in town, is housed in an angular modern building whose main section is raised on stilts above a private parking lot. The complex is surrounded by trees on a quiet street bordered with flowers and private homes. The reception area is at the top of a flight of red-marble steps. There's an attractively landscaped private pool surrounded by palmettos, while Victorian reproduction chairs fill the spaces below the tables in the clean and sunny dining room. There's only a total of 24 rooms here, each pleasantly furnished. With full board, rates range from 69,000 lire ($52.50) to 75,000 lire ($57) per person daily, depending on the season.

Hotel Luise, viale Rovereto 9, 38066 Riva del Garda (tel. 0464/552-796), is a contemporary hotel set a few hundred yards away from the shore of the lake. It has its own free-form swimming pool as well as a nearby tennis court. The paneled interior contains big windows and comfortable furniture. With full board included, rates, based on double occupancy, range from 70,000 lire ($53.25) to 80,000 lire ($60.75) per person daily. All units contain private bath and are tastefully restrained, with built-in necessities.

Where to Dine

Most guests in Riva del Garda dine either on half- or full-board terms at their hotel. However, there are a few good independent eateries, none better than the recommendation below.

Ristorante San Marco, viale Roma 20 (tel. 554-477), lies on one of the main shopping streets of the resort, set back from the lake. If you arrive early for your reserved table, you can enjoy an apéritif at the bar up front. The food is classically Italian, and the cookery and service are excellent. You might begin with one of the pasta selections, such as spaghetti with clams or tortellini with prosciutto. Many good fish dishes are presented daily, including sole (prepared several ways) and grilled scampi. Among the meat selections, try the tournedos opera or the veal cutlet bolognese. The restaurant charges 38,000 lire ($29) to 50,000 lire ($38) for a complete dinner. Food is served from 12:30 to 2:30 p.m. and 7:30 to 9:30 p.m. It is closed Monday and in February. The owners speak English.

WARNING TO MOTORISTS

The twisting roads that follow the shores of Lake Garda would be enough to rattle even the most experienced driver. Couple the frightening turns, dimly lit tunnels, and emotional local drivers (who know every bend in the road and you don't), with convoys of tour buses and trucks that rarely stay in their lane, and you have what might be one of the more frightening drives in Italy.

Be especially careful, and don't be afraid to use your horn around blind curves. Also, be warned that Sunday is an especially risky time to drive, since everyone on the lake and from the nearby cities seems to take to the roads after a long lunch with lots of heady wine.

Leaving Riva, the first resort you'll approach while heading south on the western shore (about six miles away) is—

LIMONE SUL GARDA

Characteristic of Garda's western shore is the *limonaie*, hillside terraces of lemon and orange groves. Taking its name from the fruit of the lemon trees, Limone is one of the liveliest resorts along the lake.

Snuggling close to the lake, Limone is reached by descending a narrow, precipitous road. The village nestles on a narrow hunk of land space. Shopkeepers, faced with no building room, dug right into the rock (in one such resulting grotto, you can get a cavewoman coiffure).

For those seeking recreation, there are 2½ miles of beach from which you can bathe, sail, or surf. Playing fields, tennis courts, mini-golf, soccer, and other sports activities, as well as discos and local musical entertainment, are available to the visitor who wants to make Limone a holiday base.

If you're bypassing Limone, you may still want to make a detour south of the village to the turnoff to Tignale in the hills. You can climb a modern highway to the town for a sweeping vista of Garda, one of the most scenic spots on the entire lake.

The Limone sul Garda telephone area code is 0365.

Hotels in Limone sul Garda

Hotel Capo Reamol, strada Statale, 25010 Limone sul Garda (tel. 0365/954-040). You won't get even a glimpse of this hotel from the main highway between Riva del Garda and Limone, because it nestles on the side of the lake well below road level. Be alert to traffic as you pull into a roadside area indicated by a sign 1¼ miles north of Limone, and then follow the driveway down a steep and narrow hill into a lower-level parking lot. Since the hotel is built on a series of terraces stretching down to the edge of the lake, you'll have to go down, not up, to your freshly decorated bedroom after registering at the reception desk. The bar, restaurant, and sports facilities are on the lowest level, sheltered from the lakeside breezes by windbreaks. Many of the public rooms are painted in pastel shades. Clients can swim in the lake or in the pool, and rent windsurfers on the graveled beach. There's a disco in a tavern which profits, like everything else in the hotel, from views of the water. The hotel charges 110,000 lire ($83.50) to 120,000 lire ($91.25) per person daily for a room and full board. Open April to October.

Hotel Le Palme, via Porto 36, 25010 Limone sul Garda (tel. 0365/954-681), completely renovated, is a well-known antique Venetian-style villa, with period furniture, standing in the shade of two centuries-old palm trees, in the historic center of Limone, opening directly onto the shores of Lake Garda. The hotel is rated second class, but there is nothing second-rate about its facilities and amenities. Although extensively remodeled for the installation of more private baths, it retains many of its original architectural features. The hotel offers 28 well-furnished bedrooms, each individually decorated, containing a private bath, phone, and radio. On the second floor is a comfortable reading room with a TV set, while on the floor above there is a wide terrace in the open air. On the ground floor is a large dining room with decorative sculpture, opening onto a wide terrace where one can also order meals and drinks in fair weather. The cuisine, backed up by a good wine list, is excellent. In high season a single room rents for 44,000 lire ($33.50) daily, and a double goes for 70,000 lire ($53.25). For full board, the charge is 72,000 lire ($54.75) to 80,000 lire ($60.75) per person daily. Because of the popularity of the hotel, it is best to make reservations. Open from April to October.

GARDONE RIVIERA

In the province of Brescia, the western shore of Gardone Riviera is well equipped with a number of good hotels and sporting facilities. Its lakeside promenade attracts a wide range of predominantly European tourists for most of the year. When it used to be chic for patrician Italian families to spend their holidays by the lake, many of the more prosperous built elaborate villas not only in Gardone Riviera, but in neighboring Fasano (some of these have been converted to receive guests). The town also has the biggest man-made sight along the lake, which you may want to visit even if you're not lodging for the night.

Gardone Riviera's telephone area code is 0365.

The Main Sight

Vittoriale (tel. 20-130) was once the private home of Gabriele d'Annunzio (1863–1938), the poet and military adventurer, another Italian who believed in *La Dolce Vita*, even when he couldn't afford it. Most of the celebrated events in D'Annunzio's life—such as his love affair with Eleonora Duse, his bravura takeover as a self-styled commander of a territory being ceded to Yugoslavia—occurred before 1925. In the remaining years of his life and up until he died in the winter before World War II, the national hero lived the grand life at his private estate on Garda.

North of the town, Vittoriale is open daily except Monday from 8:30 a.m. to 12:30 and 2 to 6 p.m. (closes at 5 p.m. off-season). Admission to both the house and museum is 3,000 lire ($2.30). The furnishings and decor passed for avant garde in their day, but evoke the Radio City Music Hall of the '30s when viewed now. D'Annunzio's death mask is of morbid interest, and his bed with a "Big Brother" eye adds a curious touch of Orwell's *1984* (over the poet's bed is a faun casting a nasty sneer). The marble bust of Duse seems sadly out of place, but the manuscripts and old uniforms perpetuate the legend. In July and August, D'Annunzio plays are presented at the amphitheater on the premises. To sum up, it's a bizarre museum to a dated hero of yesteryear.

Hotels in Gardone Riviera

Grand Hotel, via Zanardelli 72, 25083 Gardone Riviera (tel. 0365/20-261). When it was built in 1881, this was the most fashionable hotel on the lake and one of the biggest resort hotels of its kind in Europe. In World War II its elegantly proportioned bedrooms served as hospital accommodations, first for the Germans and later for the Americans. Later the hotel's reputation as a glamorous and desirable resting place convinced Churchill to stay for an extended period in 1948, where he fished, wrote letters, and recovered from his end-of-the-war defeat in the British elections. Today the establishment still boasts a distinguished clientele, including Fiat owner Agnelli, plus a collection of habitués who return year after year. The hotel is one of northern Italy's great reminders of turn-of-the-century grandeur. It isn't difficult to get lost in the almost endless high-ceilinged corridors, although the focus of your visit will usually bring you back to the main salon, whose sculpted ceilings, parquet floors, and elegantly comfortable leather chairs make it an ideal spot for reading or watching the lake. The dining room offers the kind of good food and oldtime splendor that could easily be imagined on a movie set. In fact, an Italian historical film, called *Mussolini and I*, was shot here. The hotel, whose massive tower is visible for miles around, contains 180 rooms, 90% of which face the lake, avoiding the roadside noise. A series of garden terraces, a private beach, and a swimming pool are scattered throughout the extensive gardens. Half board costs 97,000 lire ($73.50) to 125,000 lire ($95) per person daily. Prices, of course, vary with the season. The hotel is open from mid-April until the beginning of October.

Monte Baldo Hotel, 25083 Gardone Riviera (tel. 0365/20-951), is composed of both an old and a new building separated from one another by a lakeside garden dotted with trees and an oval-shaped swimming pool. The older building is adorned with baroque detailing, such as stone demigoddesses looking benignly out over the water and elaborately crafted balustrades. The newer building, clean and attractive in its own right, has recessed balconies and shutters fastened to the white stucco walls. Double rooms in either building rent for 80,000 lire ($60.75) per person daily, with full board included. Accommodations that face the busy street are slightly less expensive. The hotel is open from mid-April until the end of September.

Parkhotel Villa Ella, viale dei Colli 32, 25080 Gardone Riviera (tel. 0365/21-030), is an isolated hotel set amid trees, copies of Roman statues, and lots of flowers. On a hillside above the lake, at the end of a winding series of country roads that take you past ruins of older buildings, the hotel has a combination of new and old architecture whose earliest sections date from 1910. Singles begin at a low of 70,000 lire

($53.25) daily, and doubles at 120,000 lire ($91.25). It's also possible to stay here on full-board terms, costing from 60,000 lire ($45.50) per person off-season to a high of 75,000 lire ($57) per person in peak season. A swimming pool is on the premises, and slightly cheaper units are available in the nearby annex. The hotel is open from April to September.

In the budget range, **Bellevue Hotel,** 25083 Gardone Riviera (tel. 0365/20-235), a villa perched up from the main road, has many terraces surrounded by trees and flowers—and an unforgettable view. You can stay here, enjoying the advantages of lakeside villa life. Franco Pizzi, who owns and manages the hotel, opens his large rooms to guests from April to October. The furnishings in the bedrooms are modern, and everything is kept shipshape. Each room has a private bath or shower. The lounges have comfort, and the dining room affords a view through the arched windows. The quality of the meals is excellent (no skimpy helpings here). The full-board rate is 52,000 lire ($39.50) to 60,000 lire ($45.60) per person daily, depending on the season.

Where to Dine at Gardone Riviera

Most visitors to this resort take their meals at their hotels; however, there is at least one good independent dining selection.

Ristorante La Stalla, strade per il Vittoriale (tel. 21-038), is a charming restaurant frequented by local families, who sometimes drive for miles just to dine here. In a handcrafted stone building with a brick-columned porch, outdoor tables, and an indoor ambience loaded with rustic artifacts and crowded tables, the restaurant is set in a garden ringed with cypresses on a hill above the lake. To get there, follow the signs up il Vittoriale, as if you were going to D'Annunzio's former home, to a quiet street with singing birds and residential houses. Sunday afternoon is the most crowded time to visit, and reservations are always a good idea.

Specialties will be recited by one of the uniformed waiters. Depending on the shopping that day, they might include farfale with walnuts, cream and speck, tagliatelle with gorgonzola, macaroni with four cheeses, spaghetti siciliana (with pesto and anchovies), fusili with garlic, oil, and basil, a well-prepared array of grilled meats such as veal or beef, fish (especially trout), a tasty assortment of antipasti, and a wide range of desserts. Expect to spend 30,000 lire ($22.75) to 50,000 lire ($38) for a full meal, served from 12:30 to 2:30 p.m. and 7:30 to 9:30 p.m. Closed Tuesday except from July to September.

Hotels in Fasano del Garda

Fasano is a satellite resort of Gardone Riviera, lying 1¼ miles to the north. Many prefer it to Gardone. If you're so inclined, you might want to consider the following recommendation.

Hotel Villa del Sogno (Villa of Dreams), 25080 Gardone Riviera (tel. 0365/20-228). This 1920s re-creation of a Renaissance villa offers sweeping views of the lake and a series of spaciously comfortable old-fashioned bedrooms that might be a good choice for your stay in the lake area. Set a few hundred yards above the water, with easy access to its private beach, the hotel also has a pool and is ringed with terraces filled with café tables and pots of petunias and geraniums, which combine with bougainvillea and jasmine to brighten and scent the surroundings. The baronial stairway of the interior, as well as many of the ceilings and architectural details, were crafted from wood. Open from April to mid-October, the hotel charges 115,000 lire ($87.50) to 135,000 lire ($103) per person daily for full board.

At the southern side of Lake Garda stands our final stopover.

SIRMIONE

Perched at the tip of a narrowing strip of land, Sirmione juts out for 2½ miles into Lake Garda. Noted for its thermal baths (used in the treatment of deafness), the town is a major resort that blooms in spring and wilts in late autumn. It's reached by heading north after veering from the autostrada connecting Milan and Verona.

The resort was a favorite of Giosuè Carducci, the Italian poet who won the Nobel Prize for literature in 1906. In Roman days it was frequented by still another poet, Catullus. Today the **Grotte di Catullo** is the chief sight, an unbeatable combination of Roman ruins and a panoramic view of the lake. You can wander at leisure through the remains of this once-great villa. At the far end of town, the archeological site is open from 9 a.m. to an hour before sunset; closed Monday. The admission is 3,000 lire ($2.30). For more information, phone 916-157.

At the entrance to the town stands the moated 13th-century **castle** that once belonged to the powerful Scaligeri princes of Verona. Architecturally, the medieval castle is distinguished by its crenellated battlements. You can climb to the top and walk the ramparts. It is open (admission free) from 9 a.m. to 1 p.m. and 2:30 to 6:30 p.m. (9 a.m. to 2 p.m. off-season); closed Monday.

The telephone area code for Sirmione is 030.

Hotels in Sirmione

During peak season, motorists have to have a hotel reservation to take their vehicle into the crowded confines of the town. However, there is a large car park at the entrance to the town. In hotels, Sirmione is adequately endowed. The following are my recommendations:

A first-class choice is the **Villa Cortine Palace,** via Grotte 12, 25019 Sirmione (tel. 030/916-021), luxuriously set apart from the town center, surrounded by imposing and sumptuous gardens. The century-old grounds have a formal entrance through the fluted columns of a colonnade. There are winding lanes lined with cypress trees, wide-spreading magnolias, and flower-bordered marble fountains with classic sculpture. Through the trees merges a partial view of the lake and the nearby private waterside beach area. A newer structure with well-furnished rooms and private baths adjoins the mellow and pillared main building. In comfort and convenience, the bedrooms are unequaled in Sirmione. Open from March 25 to October 25, the hotel charges a peak-season rate of 260,000 lire ($198) to 285,000 lire ($217) per person daily for full board, which is obligatory. The interior has one formal drawing room, with much gilt and marble, very palace-like.

Hotel Eden, piazza Carducci 18, 25019 Sirmione (tel. 030/916-481), opened in 1984 in a totally renovated format that required four years of labor. The exterior, whose foundations date from the 12th century, is covered with pink stucco with stone trim around each of the big windows. The awning-covered entrance opens into a beautifully polished hall, where the gray and pink marble covering the floors came from India. Breakfast or drinks can be enjoyed on a flagstone-covered terrace surrounded with flowers. A winding stone staircase leads to the tastefully contemporary bedrooms, each of which is outfitted with pastel shades. Each of the units has its own marble-trimmed bath, air conditioning, TV, radio, and phone, and are among the most up-to-date bedrooms in Sirmione. In the center of the old city, the hotel charges 120,000 lire ($91.25) daily for a double, with a buffet breakfast and tax included. A limited number of singles are available for 80,000 lire ($60.75). The hotel stays open from March until October.

Hotel Sirmione, piazza Castello, 25019 Sirmione (tel. 030/916-331), is set near the castle at the water's edge, behind an ochre façade with awnings and shutters. A swimming pool juts out on a narrow strip of land just above the lake, within sight of a small marina loaded with sailing craft. The functionally furnished bedrooms often have private balconies. With full board included, rooms rent for 115,000 lire ($87.50) to 125,000 lire ($95) per person daily. Prices vary with the season and room assignment, and the hotel is open from April to October.

Grand Hotel Terme, viale Marconi 1, 25019 Sirmione (tel. 030/916-261), is a rambling, three-story hotel at the entrance of the old town, on the lake next to the Scaligeri Castle. The wide marble halls and stairs lead to balconied bedrooms. Half board costs 212,000 lire ($161) daily in a single, 182,000 lire ($138) per person in a double. Constructed in 1948, the hotel has contemporary furnishings, plus a number of spa and physical-therapy facilities, along with an entrenched position as the grand dowager hotel of the town. A swimming pool and a pleasant lawn are on the premises. The food served in the indoor-outdoor dining room is excellent, with such offerings as prosciutto and melon, risotto with snails, fettuccine with fresh porcini, and a wide choice of salads and fruits. The hotel is open from Easter to October.

In the medium-priced range is the **Olivi,** via San Pietro 5, 25019 Sirmione (tel. 030/916-110), a creation of its sun-loving owner, Cerini Franco. At his hotel, each room is light and view oriented. Furthermore, its location is excellent, on the rise of a hill in a grove of olive trees, at the edge of town. The all-glass walls of the major rooms never let you forget you're in a garden spot of Italy. Even the compact and streamlined bedrooms—60 in all—have walls of glass leading out onto open balconies. All the rooms are air-conditioned and contain private baths. The cost of a double is 105,000 lire ($79.75) to 110,000 lire ($83.50) daily, dropping to 70,000 lire ($53.25) in a single, including breakfast. In high season, it's best to take the full-board arrangement: 90,000 lire ($68.50) to 111,000 ($84.25) per person daily. Closed in January.

Hotel Continental, Punta Staffalo 7-9, 25019 Sirmione (tel. 030/916-031), lies in a lakeside building with spacious recessed balconies. Its gardens are well maintained and include evergreens and a large rectangular swimming pool. The interior contains polished stone floors and low-slung chairs. Designed with easy access to spa facilities, the hotel has 60 rooms, all of which have private bath, mini-bar, phone, balcony, and air conditioning. With full board included, prices range from 125,000 lire ($95) per person daily.

Hotel Broglia, via Piana 36, 25019 Sirmione (tel. 030/916-305), is contained within a modern building near the spa facilities. Its contemporary interior has big windows and light-grained paneling, while the gardens outside have a flagstone-covered terrace and a swimming pool set into the hillside. Full-board rates range from 115,000 lire ($87.50) to 125,000 lire ($95) per person daily. Each of the accommodations has a private bath, balcony, and phone. Open from April to October.

Flaminia Hotel, piazza Flaminia 8, 25019 Sirmione (tel. 030/916-078), is one of the best second-class hotels in Sirmione, with a number of facilities and ammenities. One of the more modern accommodations, it lies near the town center right on the lakefront, with a terrace extending out into the water. The bedrooms, all with private bath, phone, and TV, come off fairly well, dominated as they are by French doors opening onto private balconies. Couples are charged a peak-season rate of 115,000 lire ($87.50) daily. A few singles are rented at 75,000 lire ($57). Breakfast is included. The rooftop terrace provides an excellent view of Garda. The lounges are furnished with functional modern. Open from March to October.

Dining in Sirmione

In the heart of town, **La Rucola,** vicolo Strentelle 5 (tel. 916-326), lies on a small alley a few steps from the main gate leading into Sirmione. This establishment looks like a vine-laden, sienna-colored country house. Full meals, served in a modernized interior, range from 35,000 lire ($26.50) to 50,000 lire ($38) and could include grilled scampi, langoustines, mixed grilled fish, and a more limited meat selection. Meats are most often grilled or flambéed, including Florentine beefsteak and Venetian calves' liver Rasputin. Good pasta dishes include spaghetti with clams and several local varieties. Many of the desserts are made for two persons, including crêpes suzette and banana flambé. The restaurant, open from 12:30 to 2:30 p.m. and 7:30 to 9:30 p.m., is closed on Thursday and in January.

Antica Taverna del Marinaio, via Romagnoli (tel. 916-056), offers a lakeside terrace ringed with shrubbery whose inner-town location across from the Hotel Eden makes it a favorite. The view is of the water and a nearby landing wharf for sailboats. The restaurant specializes in fresh fish and charcoal-broiled meats. These include ravioli soup, mussels with lemon sauce, broiled turbot for two persons, grilled eel, rock lobsters, and risotto with seafood. Desserts are often flambéed, and, in season, are made with fresh peaches and strawberries. Full meals range from 40,000 lire ($30.50) and are served from 12:30 to 2:30 p.m. and 7:30 to 9:30 p.m. In the cooler weeks, clients can retreat to an attractively modern interior. The restaurant is closed Monday, and stays open only from March to November 10.

Ristorante Grifone da Luciano, via delle Bisse 5 (tel. 916-097), one of the most attractive restaurants in town, is separated from the castle by a row of shrubbery, a low stone wall, and a moat. From your seat on the flagstone terrace, you'll have a view of the crashing waves and the plants that ring the dining area. The headquarters of this establishment is technically an old stone house surrounded with olive trees. Many of the diners gravitate toward the low-lying glass-and-metal extension stretching toward the lake. The tables inside are covered with candles and flowers. Food items include many varieties of fish and many of the standard dishes of the classic Italian kitchen. Meals range from 30,000 lire ($22.75) to 40,000 lire ($30.50). The restaurant is open from 12:30 to 2:30 p.m. and 7:30 to 9:30 p.m. mid-March to October every day of the week but Wednesday.

Ristorante al Pozzo da Silvio, via Statale 15 (tel. 919-138), is outside Sirmione at Colombare, some two miles away but it's worth the trip. It offers family-style dining and a country Italian decor. You can enjoy savory culinary specialties of the owner and chef, Olga Bicchi, who is in partnership with her husband, Silvio Tonoli, from whom the restaurant gets its name. You can try samplings from their antipasti table, to be followed by dried codfish Lake Garda style (with polenta), ossobuco, perhaps rabbit stew cacciatore. Full meals, costing from 30,000 lire ($22.75), are served from 12:30 to 2:30 p.m. and 7:30 to 9:30 p.m.; closed all day Wednesday, and Thursday at lunch. The annual closing is in November.

2. Lake Como

Everything noble, everything evoking love—that was how Stendhal characterized fork-tongued Lake Como. Others have called it "the looking glass of Venus." More than 30 miles north of Milan, it is, next to Garda, the most heavily visited of Italian lakes. A shimmering deep blue, the lake spans 2½ miles at its widest point. With its flower-studded gardens, its villas built for the wealthy of the 17th and 18th centuries, its mild climate, Larius (as it was known to the Romans) is among the most scenic spots in all of Italy.

For a short, but still fairly comprehensive, one-day motor tour, I suggest going first to Como at the southern tip of the lake. From there, you can travel up the eastern shore of the west branch to Bellàgio, the best-known resort. From Bellàio, you can either stop over or else traverse the lake by car-ferry to Villa Carlotta and Tremezzo on the western shore, then head south down the strip to Milan again. I've found this to be a more scenic routing than along the eastern branch of Como, called the Laga di Lecco.

COMO

This is both the name of the lake and its principal city. At the southern tip of the lake, Como is known for its silk industry. Most visitors will pass through here to take a boat tour of the lake. If you do so, you'll cross the piazza Cavour, the lakeside square and the center of local life.

Because Como is also an industrial city, I have generally shunned it for overnighting, preferring to anchor into one of the more attractive resorts along the lake, including Bellàgio. However, train passengers who don't plan to rent a car may prefer Como (the city, that is) for convenience.

For centuries the destiny of the town has been linked to that of Milan. This means that Como prospered along with Milan, but also shared many of its bigger sister's misfortunes. Como lies 25 miles to the north of Milan.

Como is called the world capital of silk, the silkmakers of the city joining communal hands with the fashion designers of Milan. Como has been making silk since Marco Polo first returned with silkworms from China. However, Como today isn't engaged in mulberry and worm cultivation, and hasn't been since the end of World War II. Those arduous labors, including the spinning of raw silk, are done in China. Como imports its thread from China.

Designers such as Giorgio Armani and Bill Blass pass through Como, discussing with silk manufacturers the patterns they want.

Before rushing off on a boat for a tour of the lake, you may want to look at the **Cathedral of Como,** which dates from the 14th century when the master builders of the city began its construction in the Lombard-Gothic style. Before it was finished the Renaissance was in flower, and it wasn't until the 1700s that the duomo was officially "crowned." The exterior of the cathedral, frankly, is more interesting than the interior. Dating from 1487, it is lavishly decorated, with statues, including those of Pliny the Elder and the Younger, whom one writer once called "the beautiful people of ancient Rome." Inside, look for the 17th-century tapestries depicting scenes from the Bible.

Como's telephone area code is 031.

Hotels in Como

Hotel Barchetta Excelsior, piazza Cavour 1, 22100 Como (tel. 031/266-531), is a first-class hotel set at the edge of the main square in the commercial section of town. Major additions have been made to the hotel, including the alteration of its restaurant and an upgrading of the bedrooms, which are comfortably furnished, often with a balcony overlooking this heartbeat square and the lake. All accommodations have private baths, refrigerators, color TVs, radios, direct-dial phones, and air conditioning, and most have lake views. Singles rent for 126,000 lire ($95.75) to 149,000 lire ($113) daily in a single, for 164,000 lire ($125) to 192,000 lire ($146) in a double, with an American breakfast included. There's a parking lot behind the hotel, plus a covered garage just over 50 yards away.

Metropole & Suisse, piazza Cavour 19, 22100 Como (tel. 031/269-444), offers good value in accommodations, which are clean and convenient. Near the cathedral on this major lake-fronting square, the hotel is composed of three lower floors dating from around 1700, plus upper floors that were added about 60 years ago. The hotel began life as a waterfront store at the edge of what was then part of the lake (the square you see today is a landfill dating from 1850). The creator of the hotel was Swiss, and he was photographed with the staff in 1892, a picture that hangs behind the reception desk. Each of the bedrooms is different, rich with character for the most part. Many repeat clients have staked out their favorite rooms. A parking garage and the city marina are nearby. A popular restaurant, Imbarcadero, under separate management, fills most of the ground floor of the hotel. Each of the 71 bedrooms has its own private bath. Singles cost 100,000 lire ($76) daily, and doubles go for 130,000 lire ($98.75). The hotel is closed from mid-December to mid-January.

Where to Dine in Como

Ristorante Imbarcadero, piazza Cavour 20 (tel. 277-341), established more than a decade ago in a 300-year-old building near the edge of the lake, is filled with a pleasing blend of carved Victorian chairs, panoramic windows with a view of the marina and potted palms. You'll be greeted at the door with the sight of a long, streamlined bar area and a member of the uniformed staff. The outdoor terrace set up on the square in summer is ringed with shrubbery and illuminated with evening candlelight. The chef makes his own tagliatelle, or you may want to order spaghetti with garlic, oil, and red pepper. Main courses include steak tartare, veal cutlet milan-ese, trout with almonds, and whitefish. Desserts are often lavish productions, in-cluding banana flambé and crêpes suzette. Meals range in price from 35,000 lire ($26.50) to 55,000 lire ($41.75). The restaurant serves from 12:30 to 2:30 p.m. and 7:30 to 9:30 p.m. daily except Monday; closed the first week in January.

CERNOBBIO

Less than three miles northwest of Como, Cernobbio is a small, fashionable resort frequented by the wealthy of Europe because of its deluxe hotel, the 16th-century Villa d'Este. But its idyllic anchor on the lake has also attracted a less affluent tourist, who'll find a number of third-and even fourth-class accommodations as well.

The telephone area code for Cernobbio is 031.

The Deluxe Hotel Choice

Grand Hotel Villa d'Este, 22010 Cernobbio (tel. 031/511-471), is a kingdom unto itself. This historic and splendid palace, surrounded by what must be the finest hotel gardens in Italy, has roots deep in the past. Built in 1557 by Cardinal Tolomeo Gallio, it has in turn been the Italian refuge for a number of celebrated figures, in-cluding Maria Feodorovna, empress of Russia (wife of Czar Nicholas I) and Caro-line Amalia of Brunswick, princess of Wales and later the wife of England's George IV (her parties were the scandal of Europe). The ancestors of the villagers grew ac-customed to the arrival of golden coaches. Today's residents settle for a parade of Rolls-Royces. A hotel since 1873, the villa is a romantic, unusual establishment for a select group of international guests. The interior lives up to its reputation: each room is unique. The Salon Napoléone with its frescoed ceiling has silken wall drap-eries made especially for the little Corsican's visit. Queen Caroline's boudoir is a miniature stuccoed salon, now an intimate reading room. The Canova Room con-tains a statue of Venus attributed to Canova. The Grand Ballroom is mostly for ban-quets; the entrance lobby is graced with a vaulted ceiling and marble columns; the Canova Bar, all white and gold, offering piano music, opens onto the terrace; and, finally, the dining room is a kind of garden salon.

To all this splendor one adds the beauty of the bedrooms and suites—each has its own distinction, and each is furnished with antiques or reproductions. In other days the favorite room of the duke of Windsor and his duchess used to adjoin the personal choice of Prince Rainier and Princess Grace. Open from April to October, the hotel charges from 360,000 lire ($274) daily in a single, from 560,000 lire ($426) in a double. Of course, even more expensive corner rooms or bed-sitting rooms are offered. The cuisine is a culinary celebration. The head chef, presiding over a staff of nearly 50 persons, is an artist, known for tantalizing the palate of the gourmet. If you're stopping by just for dinner, expect to pay from 65,000 lire ($49.50) up for a complete meal. The recreation facilities are "fit for a king"—a "floating" filtered swimming pool on Lake Como; one of the finest 18-hole golf courses (at Montofano) in Italy; sailing, motorboating, fishing, eight top-grade red-clay tennis courts. In the evening there is dancing on an octagonal floor, with lake-side garden tables for drinks, plus a private disco club. Most splendid of all are the old gardens, with their wide-sweeping avenues of pointed trees, opening onto long vistas, highlighted by bits of architectural ruins and sculpture. The hotel is open April to October.

A Medium-Priced Accommodation

Hotel Asnigo, via Noseda 2, 22012 Cernobbia (tel. 031/510-062), calls itself *un piccolo Grand Hotel.* Commanding a view of Como from its hillside perch at piazza Santo Stefano, this is a good little (30 bedrooms) first-class hotel set in its own garden. Its special and subtle charms have long been known to a lake-loving set of British visitors as it dates from 1914. An Englishwoman writes: "Last summer I did something not recommendable to your readers: I went on a trip to Italy with my nephew and his wife from America, who quite frankly patronize a higher type of establishment than I do. Naturally, they were lured to the Villa d'Este on Como. I, fortunately, was able to find a splendid little hotel in the hills, the Asnigo. The proprietor was most helpful; the meals flawless and beautifully served; the room spotlessly clean and comfortable. After being a dinner guest one night at the Villa d'Este, I returned the hospitality the following evening by inviting my relatives for a most enjoyable meal at my hotel. At least they learned that good food and comfort are not the sole domain of a deluxe hotel." I echo her sentiments. The hotel charges from 115,000 lire ($87.50) daily in a single with bath. A twin with bath rents for 175,000 lire ($133).

A 45-minute drive north from Como will take you to—

BELLAGIO

Sitting on a promontory at the point where Lake Como forks, Bellàgio is with much justification given the label of "The Pearl of Larius." A sleepy veil hangs over the town's arcaded streets and its little shops. Bellàgio is rich in memories, having attracted fashionable, even royal visitors, such as King Leopold I of Belgium, who used to own the 18th-century Villa Giulia. To reach many of the spots in town, you must climb streets that are really stairways. Its lakeside promenade blossoms with flowering shrubbery. From the town, visitors can take tours of Lake Como and enjoy several sports such as rowing and tennis, or else they can lounge at Bellàgio Lido.

If time allows, try to explore the gardens of the **Villa Serbelloni,** the Bellàgio Study and Conference Center of the Rockefeller Foundation (not to be confused with the Grand Hotel Villa Serbelloni by the waterside in the village). The villa is not open to the public, but the park can be visited on guided tours starting at 10 a.m. to 4 p.m., and lasting for 1½ hours. Tours are conducted daily except Monday from mid-April to mid-October at a cost of 3,000 lire ($2.30) per person, the proceeds going to local charities.

The most important tourist attraction of Bellàgio are the gardens of the **Villa Melzi** museum and chapel. The villa was built in 1808 for Duke Francesco Melzi d'Eril, vice-president of the Italian republic founded by Napoleon. Franz Liszt and Stendhal are among the illustrious guests who have stayed here. The park has many well-known sculptures, and if you're here in the spring, you can enjoy the azaleas. Today it is the property of Duke Gallarati Scotti, who opens it daily from 9 a.m. to 6 p.m. April to the end of October. Admission is 3,000 lire ($2.30).

The Bellàgio telephone area code is 031.

Hotels in Bellàgio

Good choices are available in a number of categories, in hotels that have appealed to everyone from Napoleon to Mark Twain.

In the deluxe category, the **Grand Hotel Villa Serbelloni,** 22021 Bellàgio (tel. 031/950-216), is for those born to the grand style of life, a lavish old hotel that was frequented by a number of prewar crowned heads of Europe. Prominently placed, it stands proud and serene, at the edge of town against a backdrop of hills. Surrounded by its own gardens of flowers and semitropical plants, it is perched on the lakefront, and guests sunbathe on the waterside terrace or doze under a willow tree. Inside, the public rooms rekindle the spirit of the baroque: the grand drawing room with a painted ceiling, marble columns, a glittering chandelier, and ornate gilt furnishings; a painted vaulted ceiling, baronial fireplace, fluted classic columns; or the mirrored neoclassical dining room. The bedrooms are wide ranging, from elaborate suites with a recessed tile bath, baroque furnishings and lake-view balconies to more chaste quarters. Rooms are priced according to view, the most expensive opening onto the lake. Doubles cost from 315,000 lire ($239) daily; singles, from 220,000 lire ($167). Most guests stay here on the full-board plan, paying 215,000 lire ($163) to 290,000 lire ($220) per person daily. On the shore of the lake, the hotel is surrounded by a beautiful garden and park that are often visited by the general public. The Villa Serbelloni is open from mid-April to October 20.

Hotel du Lac, piazza Mazzini, 22021 Bellàgio (tel. 031/950-320), was built 150 years ago, at a time when the waters of the lake came directly up to the front door of the ochre façade. Today there's a generous terraced expanse of flagstones in front, on which are café tables and an arched arcade. Arturo and June Leoni (he is pure Italian, and she is half English, half Brazilian) are the down-to-earth owners who, with the help of their son, Luca, have maintained and renovated this property bit by bit over the past 30 years. The hotel is imbued with conservative comfort, with an adjoining bar, a large glassed-in restaurant with a terrace, and a rooftop garden where guests can bask in the sun or relax in the shade while enjoying a view over the lake. The bedrooms, 50 in all, contain bath or shower and hairdryer. For bed and a buffet breakfast, the cost is 60,000 lire ($45.50) to 70,000 lire ($53.25) daily in a single and 96,000 lire ($73) to 106,000 lire ($80.50) in a double in peak season. Half board goes for 64,000 lire ($48.75) to 74,000 lire ($56.25) per person. The hospitable proprietors keep their hotel open between mid-April and mid-October. It is in the center of town.

Hotel Florence, piazza Mazzini, 22021 Bellàgio (tel. 031/950-342), is a green-shuttered 19th-century villa whose entrance is under a vaulted arcade near the ferryboat landing stage. Wisteria climbs over the iron balustrades of the lake-view terraces. The Florence is one of the most charming middle-bracket choices in the resort. The reception desk is at one end of an entrance hall whose ceilings are supported by massive timbers, old vaulting, and Doric columns made of granite. There's even a Tuscan fireplace, with finely chiseled carving and a globe-like wrought-iron chandelier. The main section of this hotel was built around 1720, although most of what you see today was added around 1880. For 150 years the hotel has been run by a member of the Ketzlar family, who originally acquired it as a private villa, turning it into one of the artistic centers of the lake area. Today you'll probably be welcomed by the beautiful and charming Roberta Ketzlar (who studied foreign languages and worked for a short time as a Milanese radio announcer), her brother, Ronald, and their mother, Friedl. Their 45 bedrooms are scattered amid spacious upstairs sitting and dining areas, and often have high ceilings, antiques, and lake views. Depending on the exposure, doubles with bath cost 87,000 lire ($66) to 97,000 lire ($73.75) daily. Open mid-April to mid-October.

Excelsior Splendide, 22021 Bellàgio (tel. 031/950-225), in a Liberty-style building (Italian art nouveau), has comfortable rooms facing the lake, as well as a swimming pool in the garden and a lakeside terrace for dining and drinking. The hotel is attractive, the service efficient. For a room with bath or shower and a buffet breakfast, the rate is 42,000 lire ($32) to 47,000 lire ($35.75) per person daily, with taxes and service included. There are ample lounge facilities.

From Como, car-ferries ply back and forth across the lake to **Cadenabbia** on the western shore. Cadenabbia is another lakeside resort, with hotels and villas, the most important of which you'll surely want to visit—

THE VILLA CARLOTTA

Directly south of Cadenabbia on the run to Tremezzo, the Villa Carlotta (tel. 40-405) is the most-visited attraction on Lake Como—and with good reason. In a serene setting, the villa is graced with gardens of exotic flowers and blossoming shrubbery, especially rhododendrons and azaleas. Its beauty is tame, cultivated, much like a fairytale that recaptures the halcyon life available only to the very rich of the 19th century. Dating from 1847, the estate was named after a Prussian princess,

Carlotta, who married the duke of Sachsen-Meiningen. Inside the villa are a number of art treasures including Canova's *Cupid and Psyche,* and a number of neoclassical statues by Bertel Thorvaldsen, the Danish sculptor who died in 1844. Also displayed are neoclassical paintings, furniture, and a stone-and-bronze table ornament that belonged to Viceroy Eugene Beauharnais. From March 15 to March 31 and in October, it is open daily from 9 a.m. to noon and 2 to 4:30 p.m. From the first of April until the end of September, it is open from 9 a.m. to 6 p.m. Admission is 5,000 lire ($3.80).

From the villa, it's only a minute's drive to—

TREMEZZO

Another popular west-shore resort, Tremezzo opens onto a panoramic view of Lake Como. Around the town is a district known as Tremezzina, with luxuriant vegetation that includes citrus trees, palms, cypresses, and magnolias. Tremezzo is the starting point for many excursions. Its accommodations are much more limited than those in Bellàgio.

The telephone are code for Tremezzo is 0344.

Where to Stay in Tremezzo

Grand Hotel Tremezzo Palace, 22019 Tremezzo (tel. 0344/40-446), was built at the beginning of this century, but has seen much modernization since then. This grand old hotel rests on a lakeside ledge, surrounded by spacious terraced gardens and keeping good company with the neighboring Villa Carlotta. Its situation is ideal, especially under palm trees by the open-air swimming pool or on the lakeside lido. The 98 bedrooms for the most part are spacious, with private bath or shower and direct-dial phones. All rooms that face the lake contain private balconies. You're given a choice of a lakeside or a park view. In a twin or double, the price peaks at 170,000 lire ($129) a night, dropping to 105,000 lire ($79.75) in a single. The hotel also has three restaurants with excellent service and an international regional cuisine, with meals costing from 45,000 lire ($34.25). You can enjoy meals on an open-air terrace overlooking the lake. In the hotel's large park are two swimming pools, a tennis court, a putting green, and a jogging track. The private Club l'Escale with a disco and piano bar, a billiard room, landing stage, heliport, and meeting center complete the facilities.

Hotel Bazzoni and Du Lac, via Regina 26, 22019 Tremezzo (tel. 0344/40-403). There was an older hotel on this spot during Napoleon's era, although it was bombed by the British five days after the official end of World War II. Today the reconstructed hotel is a collection of glass and concrete walls, with prominent balconies at the edge of the lake. It is one of the best hotels in a resort town filled with hotels with grander formats but much less desirable accommodations. Each of the 125 bedrooms has a private bath. The main restaurant, on the ground floor, has a baronial but unused fireplace, contemporary wall frescoes of the boats on the lake, and scattered carvings. The pleasantly furnished sitting rooms include antique architectural elements from older buildings. A summer restaurant near the hotel's entrance is constructed like a small island of glass walls. The establishment is closed from the end of November until mid-March. The rest of the year, it charges 85,000 lire ($64.50) daily in a single, 78,000 lire ($59.25) per person in a double, including full board.

Where to Dine in Tremezzo

Al Veluu, Rogaro di Tremezzo (tel. 40-510), one mile north of the resort in the hills, is the ideal stopover point for visitors looking for a regional restaurant with plenty of charm and lots of personalized attention. Owner Carlo Antonini, who set up his terraced restaurant after a career as a steward with Alitalia, is an important element in the relaxed and sophisticated format of this excellent restaurant. "Al Veluu" (which means "the sail" in the local dialect) was a reminder to him of the time he spends with his friends sailing his boat on Lake Como, which is visible in a panoramic sweep from one of the terrace's well-prepared tables. The rustic dining room with its fireplace and big windows is a welcome refuge in inclement weather. But in summer, the terrace lures all.

Most of the vegetables and produce come freshly picked from the garden, which lies just across the curving road leading up from the lake. Even the butter is homemade, and the best cheeses come from a local farmer whose home is visible among the rocks and trees of a nearby mountain. Menu items include gamberoni (giant shrimp) and fresh fish prepared in several different ways, plus pasta with salmon or in a pesto sauce, carpaccio, grilled beef, veal cutlet milanese or piccata style, and a series of luscious desserts that might include banana flambé, zabaglione, or crêpes suzette. On weekends the menu is augumented with lakefish and meats in many varieties from the outdoor grill. The restaurant is open from 12:30 to 2:30 p.m. and 7:30 to 10 p.m. daily except Tuesday and from November to March. Reservations are suggested, and meals range usually from 40,000 lire ($30.50) to 50,000 lire ($38).

MENAGGIO

This is a little satellite resort of Tremezzo, lying directly north along the lake.

Grand Hotel Victoria, via Castelli 11, 22017 Menaggio (tel. 0344/32-003), is one of the best hotels on the lake, and one that is moderate in price considering its grand format. The hotel was built in 1806 along a quiet lakeside road bordered with chestnut trees. It was renovated in 1983 into a format almost as luxurious as the original, with attention paid to the preservation of ornate plasterwork whose tendrils and curlicues entwine the ceiling vaults. Architectural details include lavish use of marble, big windows, and carving on the white façade that resembles the heads of what looks like water sprites.

Some sections of the establishment have been purchased for private use by vacationing individuals, but the majority of the rooms rent for 184,000 lire ($140) daily in a double, 117,000 lire ($89) in a single. The modern furniture in the bedrooms includes a mini-bar, phone, radio, and TV, plus plushly appointed private bath with wall tiles designed by Valentino. There's a swimming pool in the back garden, and (as many members of the staff will tell you) the beach in front of the hotel is the best spot on Lake Como for windsurfing, especially between 3 and 7 p.m.

Guests enjoy drinks on the outdoor terrace near the stone columns of the tree-shaded portico, or in the antique-filled public rooms. The restaurant has well-prepared food, art-nouveau chandeliers, and an embellished ceiling showing all the fruits of an Italian harvest scattered amid representations of lyres and mythical beasts. Menu specialties include saltimbocca, steak tartare, turtle soup, homemade ravioli, veal cutlet milanese, filet of sole, and crêpes suzette. Expect to spend from 45,000 lire ($34.25) for a full meal. Half board is offered for 150,000 lire ($114) daily in a single, 260,000 lire ($198) in a double.

3. Lake Maggiore

The shores of this lake wash up on the banks of Piedmont and Lombardy in Italy, but its more austere northern basin (Locarno, for example) lies in the mountainous region of Switzerland. At its longest point, it stretches a distance of more than 40 miles (and is 6½ miles at its widest stretch).

A wealth of natural beauty awaits the visitor: mellowed lakeside villas, dozens of gardens with lush vegetation, sparkling waters, panoramic views. A veil of mist seems to hover at times, especially in the early spring and late autumn.

Maggiore is a most rewarding lake to visit from Milan, especially because of the Borromean Islands in its center (most easily reached from Stresa). The fortunate visitor will be able to motor around the entire basin. But those on a more limited schedule may find the western, resort-studded shore the most scenic. From Milan, a drive northwest for about 51 miles will take you to Stresa, the major resort on Lake Maggiore.

The launching of a 320- by 18-foot floating fountain, with 110-foot, multicolored waterjets, on Lake Maggiore was part of an attempt to update the region's belle-époque image and to increase its popularity.

STRESA

On the western shore, Stresa has skyrocketed from a simple village of fisherfolk to a first-class international resort. Its vantage on the lake is almost unparalleled, and its level of hotel accommodations is superior to that of the other Maggiore resorts of Italy. Scene of sporting activities and an international Festival of Musical Weeks (beginning in late August), it swings into action in April, then dwindles in popularity at the end of October. Depending on traffic, Stresa is reached in one hour from Milan on the Simplon Railway.

Stresa's telephone area code is 0323.

Hotels in Stresa

I'll survey the best of accommodations in Stresa—in price categories ranging from deluxe to fourth class:

Hôtel des Iles Borromées, lungolago Umberto I no. 67, 28049 Stresa (tel. 0323/30-431), set on the edge of the lake in a flowering garden, has an ornate façade looking over the water. The Borromean Islands are visible from many of the bedrooms. All the accommodations have been furnished in an Italian/French Empire style, including rich ormolu, burnished hardwoods, plush carpets, and pastel color schemes. The baths look as if every quarry in Italy had been scoured for matched marble. The hotel opened its doors for the first time in 1863, attracting titled notables. Alexandra, the grand duchess of Russia, carved her name into one of the hotel's window panes with a diamond ring in 1870. But it wasn't until the opening of the Sempione Tunnel in 1906 that the hotel (and Stresa) could profit from the beginning of mass tourism. Famous guests of yesterday have included J. P. Morgan and Eleanora Duse. Hemingway ordained that the hero of *A Farewell to Arms* should stay here to escape from World War I.

The public rooms, elegantly capped with two-tone ornate plasterwork and crystal chandeliers, were even the scene of a top-level meeting among the heads of state of Italy, Great Britian, and France in an attempt to stave off World War II. Today all this splendor can be part of your vacation, but it won't come cheaply. Singles rent for 200,000 lire ($152) daily, and doubles go for 300,000 lire ($228). The restaurant is as dignified as you'd expect. Full meals cost upward from 90,000 lire ($68.50) per person. The hotel, open all year, also has a medically supervised health and exercise program. In the Centro Benessere, you could not be in better hands. A specialized medical team will help you relax, give you a thorough checkup, and get you back into fine shape with personalized exercise schedules and carefully planned diets.

Regina Palace, lungolago Umberto I no. 27, 28049 Stresa (tel. 0323/30-171), was built in 1908 in a boomerang-shaped design whose central curve faces the lakefront. The hotel looks almost like the spinnaker of a sailboat running downwind. Foremost among its architectural features are art deco illuminated glass columns (lit from within) that are capped with gilded Corinthian capitals. A wide marble stairwell is flanked with carved oak lions, while the elaborately patterned ceiling of the main lobby is illuminated with natural light. There's a swimming pool in the rear, and a guest roster that has included George Bernard Shaw, Ernest Hemingway, Umberto I of Italy, Princess Margaret, and Gina Lollabrigida. Lately, about 90% of the guests are American, many of them with tour groups who stream through Stresa. The hotel contains 172 rooms, priced from 120,000 lire ($91.25) to 190,000 lire ($144) per person daily, including full board. Tennis courts are on the premises, and there is ample parking. Bedrooms are equipped with all the modern comforts, and many have views of the Borromean Islands, so famous in Italian romantic novels. Closed in January.

Hotel La Palma, lungolago Umberto I, 28049 Stresa (tel. 0323/32-401). The designs crafted into the wrought-iron balconies of this tasteful hotel reflect the palms for which the hotel is named. Set into gardens across a road from the lake, the hotel boasts an azalea-covered terrace in front, a private swimming pool, and 118 comfortably furnished bedrooms. About 90% of them face the lake and have a private balcony. All of the units contain private bath, hairdryer, and color TV. The hotel, built in 1964, charges 180,000 lire ($137) to 210,000 lire ($160) daily for two people in the same room for half board. Singles, also with half board, pay 120,000 lire ($91.25) to 130,000 lire ($98.75). The hotel is open from the first of March until mid-November.

The medium-priced range offers the **Hotel Astoria,** lungolago Umberto I no. 31, 28049 Stresa (tel. 0323/32-566), expressly for sun-seekers who want a modern hotel with its own heated swimming pool, Turkish bath, small gym, roof garden, and Jacuzzi. Standing right on the lake, it features triangular balconies—one to each bedroom—jutting out for the view. Most of its streamlined, spacious bedrooms have private baths as well. Open from March 20 to October, the hotel in high season charges 120,000 lire ($91.25) daily for a single with shower, 160,000 lire ($122) for a double with bath. Service, town tax, I.V.A., and a continental breakfast are included in the rates. The full-board cost reaches a peak of 135,000 lire ($103) per person. The public lounges have walls of glass opening toward the lake view and the garden. The portion of the dining room favored by most guests is the wide-paved, open-air, front terrace, where under shelter you dine on a good cuisine while enjoying Maggiore as the chef d'oeuvre.

Hotel Moderno, via Cavour 33, 28049 Stresa (tel. 0323/30-468), true to its name, is a contemporary 53-bedroom hotel a block from the lake and boat-landing stage. The hotel has been completely modernized, with good beds and rhapsody phones for direct dialing and automatic wakeup calls. The rooms, all with bath or shower and toilet, are personalized. Single rates range from 55,000 lire ($49.50); doubles cost 80,000 lire ($60.75). Open March to October, the hotel also charges 55,000 lire ($41.75) to 60,000 lire ($45.50) per person for half board. In addition to its regular dining room, the Moderno also offers two open-air restaurants, the candlelit veranda, Gazebo, in one of the most characteristic streets of Stresa, and La Damigiana in the rear patio shaded by a wisteria. In all, the Moderno is one of the best hotels for value in Stresa.

Meuble Primavera, via Cavour 39, 28049 Stresa (tel. 0323/31-286), is open all year. The owner, Signor Maurizio Ferraris, has the happy and relaxed temperament you expect from a host. His family-run hotel is kept immaculately clean. Fully tiled floors and wood furniture are used throughout. Some of the front bedrooms have windows over via Cavour, facing an old church. They also have balconies of red geraniums. A double without bath costs 40,000 lire ($30.50) to 50,000 lire ($38) daily. With bath, two people pay 50,000 lire ($38) to 70,000 lire ($53.25). Singles with bath rent for 40,000 lire ($30.50) to 50,000 lire ($38). All tariffs include a continental breakfast served in the first-floor lounge, where you may chat with Signor Maurizio at night over a glass of grappa.

Albergo Ariston, corso Italia 60, 28049 Stresa (tel. 0323/31-195), is a good bargain. The hotel is listed as third class, but its amenities are superior. Rooms are well kept and attractively furnished. A single with toilet (no bath) costs from 38,000 lire ($29) daily; a single with toilet and private bath or shower goes for 45,000 lire ($34.25). A double with private bath costs from 60,000 lire ($45.50), and the half-board rate is 55,000 lire ($41.75) per person daily. It's possible for nonresidents to stop for a meal, ordering a lunch or dinner with wine from 28,000 lire ($21.25). The food is served on the terrace, which has a beautiful view of the lake and gardens. Your hosts are the Balconi family.

Hotel Italie et Suisse, piazza Marconi 1, 28049 Stresa (tel. 0323/30-540), is considered one of the best bargains at the resort. For a spacious double overlooking Lake Maggiore, with bath and toilet and a small balcony, the charge is 66,000 lire ($50.25) daily, while singles pay 48,000 lire ($36.50). There are 37 comfortably furnished rooms, some with queen-size bed. The Albergo also serves food, with meals costing from 22,000 lire ($16.75). It receives guests from mid-March to mid-November.

Dining in Stresa

Ristorante Emiliano, corso Italia 48 (tel. 31-396). As its name suggests, both the owners and the cuisine come directly from the Emilia-Romagna region of Italy. Directed by Romano Felisi, the restaurant is filled with a kind of decor that makes it the most elegant nonhotel restaurant in Stresa. It also serves the best food at the resort. The entrance is sheltered from cloudbursts by a wrought-iron and glass canopy, which even extends partially over the tops of the outdoor tables with their view of the lake. Inside, the half-paneled walls are accented with candlelight. Menu specialties feature a frequently changing array of delicacies, which on any given day might include pasta with smoked salmon, rack of spring lamb with rosemary, risotto with scampi, or fried squash blossoms and truffles. Ever had macaroni with fresh asparagus and liver? Surely you've never tasted their adaptation of an ancient Emilian peasant dish of tortelloni stuffed with a combination of potatoes and mushrooms. The restaurant is open from 12:30 to 2:30 p.m. and 7:30 to 10 p.m. daily except Tuesday, and is completely shut down from November to December 20. Meals cost 70,000 lire ($53.25) to 130,000 lire ($98.75).

Petit Pam Pam, piazza San Michele 4 (tel. 31-177), is a cozily rustic restaurant at the top of a short flight of stairs a few blocks from the lake. The decor includes autumnal colors, wrought-iron accents, an array of original paintings, and so many bottles stacked in every available nook that a meal here is a lot like dining in a wine cellar. You'll hear an international medley of languages, and you'll be able to sample a mainly Italian menu that includes pizzas priced at 5,000 lire ($3.80) and up. There is also a large fish menu, including antipasti di mare, large grilled shrimp, sole in butter, and various fruits of the sea. You might also prefer various types of prosciutto, grilled beefsteak, spaghetti carbonara, or fondue bourguignonne (the latter served only for two persons). A la carte meals cost 40,000 lire ($30.50) to 45,000 lire ($34.25). The restaurant is open from noon to 2 p.m. and 6 p.m. to midnight; closed Thursday.

Taverna del Pappagallo, Principessa Margherita 4B (tel. 30-411), is an informal little garden restaurant and tavern operated by the Ghiringhelli brothers, who turn out some of the least-expensive meals in Stresa. Specialties of the house include gnocchi (semolina dumplings), many types of scaloppine, scalamino allo spiedoe fagioli (grilled sausage with beans), and saltimbocca alla romana (a veal and ham dish). At night pizza is king (try the piazza Regina). A complete meal will range in price from 30,000 lire ($22.75). The taverna service has a personal family touch. The restaurant is open from noon to 2:30 p.m. and 7 p.m. to midnight. It is closed Tuesday and Wednesday.

THE BORROMEAN ISLANDS

The heart of Lake Maggiore is occupied by this chain of tiny islands, which were turned into sites of lavish villas and gardens by the Borromeo clan. From the harbor at Stresa, you can buy an excursion ticket on a boat that will take you to the three major islands. Boats leave about every 30 minutes in peak season, and the trip takes three hours.

The major stopover is on the **Isola Bella** (Beautiful Island), which should be visited if you have time for only one sight. Dominating the island is the 17th-century Borromeo Palazzo (tel. 30-556). When approached from the front, the figurines in the garden evoke the appearance of a wedding cake. On conducted tours, you are shown through the light and airy palace, from which the views are remarkable. Napoleon slept here. A special feature is the six grotto rooms, built piece by piece like a mosaic. In addition, there is a collection of quite good tapestries, with gory cannibalistic animal scenes. Outside, the white peacocks in the garden enchant year after year. The palace and its grounds are open March to October from 9 a.m. to 5 p.m. daily. To visit the palace and its gardens costs 5,000 lire ($3.80).

The **Isola Madre** (Mother Island) is the largest of the chain, visited chiefly because of its botanical gardens. You wander through a setting ripe with pomegranates, camellias, wisteria, rhododendrons, bougainvillea, hibiscus, hydrangea, magnolias, even a cypress tree from the Himalayas. The 17th-century palace on the grounds may also be visited. It contains a rich collection of 17th- and 18th-century furnishings. Of particular interest is a collection of 19th-century French and German dolls belonging to the Countess Borromeo. Livery of various kinds belonging to the house of Borromeo is also exhibited. The unique 18th-century marionette theater of the house of Borromeo, complete with scripts, stage scenery, and devices for sound, light, and other special effects, is on display. Peacocks, pheasants, and other birds live and roam freely on the grounds. Visiting hours are 9 a.m. to 5:30 p.m. daily. The price of admission to both the palace and grounds is 6,000 lire ($4.55).

The **Isola dei Pescatori** (Fishermen's Island) is without major sights or lavish villas, but in many ways it is the most colorful. Less a stage setting than its two sisters, it is inhabited by fisherfolk who live in cottages. Good walks are possible in many directions.

The telephone area code for the islands is 0323.

THE VILLA TARANTO

Back on the mainland near the resort of Pallanza, north of Stresa, the botanical gardens spread over more than 50 acres of the Castagnola Promontory, which juts out into Lake Maggiore. In this dramatic setting between the mountains and the lake, more than 20,000 species of plants from all over the world thrive in a well-tended and cultivated institution, begun in 1931 by a Scotsman, Capt. Neil McEacharn. Plants range from rhododendrons and azaleas to specimens from such faraway places as Louisiana and Canada. Seasonal exhibits include fields of Dutch tulips (80,000 of them), Japanese magnolias, giant water lilies, cotton plants, and rare varieties of hydrangeas. The formal gardens of the villas are carefully laid out with ornamental fountains, statues, and reflection pools. Among the more ambitious creations of the gardens are the elaborate irrigation system which pumps water from the lake to all parts of the gardens, and the Terrace Gardens, complete with waterfalls and swimming pool.

The villa gardens are open every day from 8:30 a.m. till sunset, April 1 through October 31. Professional guides will take you on tours, which last more than an hour. You may also take a round-trip boat ride from Stresa, which docks at the Villa Taranto pier adjoining the entrance to the gardens. You pay an admission of 6,000 lire ($4.55) for adults, 5,000 lire ($3.80) for children 6 to 14. For information, phone 506-667.

MILAN AND FIVE LOMBARD CENTERS

The vicissitudes of the history of Italy are reflected in Lombardy as perhaps in no other region. All conquerors from barbarians to Napoleon have marched across its plain. Even Mussolini came to his end here. He and his mistress—both already dead—were strung up in a square in Milan as war-weary residents vented their rage upon the two bodies.

Among the most progressive of all the Italians, the Lombards have charted an industrial empire unequaled in Italy. Often the dream of the underfed and jobless worker in the south is to go to "Milano" for the high wages and the good life.

But Lombardy isn't all manufacturing. Milan, as we'll soon see, is filled to the brim with important attractions, and nearby are four old art cities—Bergamo, Brescia, Cremona, and Mantua (Mantova), as well as the Carthusian Monastery of Pavia.

1. Milan

Up to now we've been paying homage to the past. In the capital of Lombardy we meet the Italy of today and of tomorrow. The progressive Milanese are creating a powerful manufacturing and commercial metropolis, advanced in design and fashion. The past lingers on in its many art treasures spared from the heavy World War II bombing, including the Gothic cathedral and Leonardo da Vinci's memorable *Last Supper.* Nevertheless, the banking center of Italy is firmly entrenched in the 20th century.

As a railway terminus in the Po Valley, it is without peer in Italy: the Simplon,

Bernina, and Gotthard lines link northern Italy with the heartland of Europe. The city tends to be fiercely hot in summer (rooms with air conditioning are advised for those who can afford them) and fiercely cold in winter.

A word of warning: Milan really closes up in August, except for hotels, of course. Reader Pam King, of New Haven, Connecticut, writes: "It didn't really bother us, but some people might care, as it's a little eerie. We found only one out of every seven or eight stores open."

GETTING THERE

Milan ranks with Rome as one of the easiest cities in Italy to reach by public transportation. It is serviced by two airports, the **Aeroporto di Linate,** 4½ miles to the east from the inner city, and the **Aeroporto della Malpensa,** 31 miles to the northwest. In general, Malpensa airport is used for most transatlantic flights, whereas Linate is for flights within Italy and Europe. Buses for Linate leave from the Porta Garibaldi station every 20 minutes between 5:40 a.m. and 8:40 p.m. (stops are made at the Stazione Centrale). Buses for Malpensa leave from the Stazione Centrale every 2½ hours before international and intercontinental flight departures. This, I assure you, is a much cheaper method than taking a taxi. Milan is also serviced by the finest rail connections in Italy. The main rail station for arrivals is the already mentioned **Stazione Centrale.** Milan is also reached by bus from various connections within Italy, and has autostrada links for motorists.

RAILWAY INFORMATION

The National Railways information office is at the Stazione Centrale (tel. 67-500), and it's open from 7 a.m. to 10:30 p.m. daily.

AN ORIENTATION

The **piazza del Duomo** lies in the heart of historical Milan. This square, containing the Milan cathedral, is also the geographical heart of the ever-growing city. Milan is encircled by three "rings," including a road, the **Cerchia dei Navigli** following, more or less, the outline of its former medieval walls. The road runs along what was formerly a series of canals—hence the name "navigli." The second ring is known both as **Bastioni** or **Viali,** and it follows the outline of the Spanish Walls from the 16th century. It is now a tram route (take no. 29 or 30). A much more recent ring is the Circonvallazione Esterna, which connects you with the main roads coming into Milan.

If you're traveling within the Cerchia dei Navigli, which is relatively small, you can do so on foot. It is not recommended that you attempt to drive within this circle unless you're heading for a garage. All the major attractions, including Leonardo's *Last Supper,* the Scala, and the duomo lie within this ring.

One of Milan's most important streets, **via Manzoni,** begins near the Teatro alla Scala, and will take you to the piazza Cavour, a key point for the traffic arteries of Milan. The **Arch of Porta Nuova** marks the entrance to via Manzoni. This "archi," as they call it in Italian, is a remnant of the medieval walls. To the northwest of the piazza Cavour lie the Giardini Pubblici, and to the northwest of these important gardens is the **piazza della Repubblica.** From this square the Vittor Pisani leads into the **piazza Duca d'Aosta,** site of the cavernous Stazione Centrale.

Back at the piazza Cavour, you can head west along via Fatebenefratelli into the **Brera** district, whose major attraction is the Accademia di Brera at via Brera 28. This district in recent years has become a major center in Milan for offbeat shopping and after-dark diversions.

GETTING AROUND

A special 3,200 lira ($2.45) one-day travel pass, good for unlimited use on the city's tram, bus, and subway network, is available in Milan at the tourist office, **Ente Provinciale per il Turismo,** at via Marconi 1 (tel. 02/809-662).

The city **bus system** covers most destinations within Milan, at a cost of 800 lire (60¢), as does the **subway** at the same fare. Some subway tickets are good for continuing trips on city buses at no extra charge, but they must be used within 75 minutes of purchase. These fares are presented only for your general guidance, and may go up in the lifetime of this edition.

To phone a **taxi**, dial 67-67. Fares start at 4,000 lire ($3.05).

PRACTICAL FACTS

For Milan, the **telephone area code** is 02. If you need to make long-distance calls, try, if possible, to avoid going through your hotel switchboard, which imposes staggering surcharges. The best place is the Central Post Office (see below), where telephone booths and operators maintain a 24-hour service.

American Express: There is an American Express bank at via Brera 3 (tel. 85-571). However, for mail, tour bookings, and other services, go to via Vittor Pisani 19 (tel. 67-09).

Babysitters: To find a babysitter, get in touch with Al Centro Baby-Sitters, via Ciro Menotti 18 (tel. 271-1903). You might also try Baby's Club, via Cusani 5 (tel. 805-6039).

Consulate: You will find the **U.S. Consulate,** at largo Donegani 1 (tel. 02/652-841), open from 9 a.m. to noon and 2 to 4 p.m. Monday through Friday.

Drugstore: If you need a drugstore, you can find an all-night pharmacy by phoning 192 for information.

Emergencies: Important phone numbers are: **police,** 62-261; to report a **fire,** 34-999; and to seek **first aid,** 3883, or **ambulance,** 7733.

Newspapers: Foreign newspapers, including the *International Herald-Tribune,* can be found at all major newsstands, among them those at the Stazione Centrale and the piazza del Duomo. If you read Italian (even just a little bit), you can pick up information about present attractions and coming events, such as cinema and theater schedules, by buying the daily *La Repubblica,* a useful newspaper. If you're seeking secondhand bargains, you can learn about sales in *Secondamano,* which comes out only on Monday and Thursday.

Post Offices: Most branches are open from 8:30 a.m. to 1:30 p.m. Monday through Saturday. The Central Post Office is at via Cordusio 4 (tel. 869-0735), and it is open Monday through Friday from 8:15 a.m. to 8 p.m. and on Saturday from 8:15 a.m. to 2 p.m. To reach it, take the subway to the Cordusio stop.

Religious services: Catholic services in English are conducted at Santa Maria Annunciata, piazza del Duomo 18 (tel. 804-441).

Tourist Information: One of the first things you may need in Milan is some information. If so, you'll find the **Azienda di Promozione Turistica del Milanese** on the piazza del Duomo at via Marconi 1 (tel. 809-662), particularly helpful, dispensing free maps and whatever advice they can. There is a branch in the Galleria Vittorio Emanuele (tel. 870-565) and another at the Stazione Centrale (tel. 669-0532) for arriving train passengers.

HOTELS IN MILAN

In the city are some deluxe as well as a super-abundance of first- and second-class hotels, most of which are big on comfort but short on romance. In the third- and fourth-class bracket and on the pensione (boarding house) level there are dozens of choices—many of which rank at the bottom of the totem pole of comparably classed establishments in all of Italy's major cities, with the exception of Naples. Many of these hotels are filled with often unemployed workers who have come north hoping for a new job and opportunity as long as their meager funds hold out. Some places are outright dangerous, and others so rock-bottom and unappealing as to hold little interest for the average visitor. In several places, men sit around in the lobby in their bathrobes watching soccer games on the one TV set.

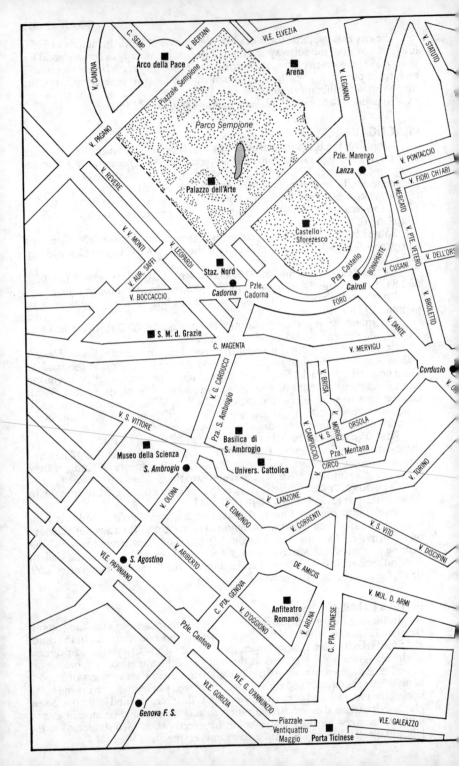

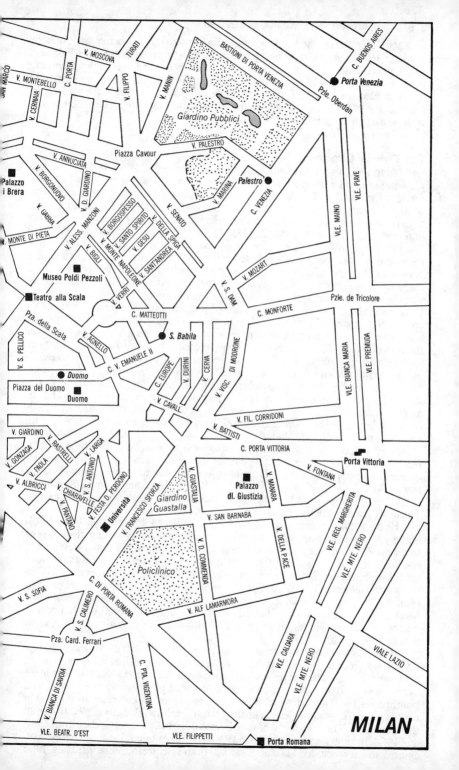

My recommendation is—if you can afford it—to stay in a better grade of hotel in Milan, leaving your serious budgeting to such tourist meccas as Rome, Florence, and Venice, which have clean, comfortable, and often architecturally interesting third- and fourth-class hotels and pensiones. However, for the serious economizer I have included some budget recommendations for Milan, which, I am told, represent the best of the lot. They are presented as safe and (hopefully) clean shelters, but with no particular enthusiasm on my part.

The Deluxe Choices

Milano Hilton, via Galvani 12, 20124 Milano (tel. 02/69-83), is a modern glass-and-steel cube rising a few blocks from the main railway station. Its 339 comfortably furnished bedrooms contain everything you'd expect in terms of high-quality accommodations, as well as many extras. These include TV, air conditioning, private bath and phone, a well-stocked mini-bar, and radio. Singles cost 265,000 lire ($201) to 410,000 lire ($312) daily; doubles, 360,000 lire ($274) to 500,000 lire ($380). There is no additional charge for children occupying the same room as their parents. This all-purpose hotel could suit either a tourist or a business person, and the mix of clients in the London Bar, with its richly upholstered chairs, contains a comfortable collection of both. The marble-trimmed lobby has four elevator banks. The hotel spent millions of lire renovating the upstairs restaurant, Da Giuseppe, whose warmly chosen shades of gilt and brown, along with its belle-epoque accessories, recall the era of Verdi, whose portrait hangs behind a frequently used grand piano. A portrait of Verdi's mistress, Giuseppina Strepponi, hangs on the opposite wall. Their juxtaposition helps to create the kind of intimacy that goes well with the Italian and international dishes that are the specialties of the house.

Excelsior Gallia, piazza Duca d'Aosta 9, 20124 Milano (tel. 02/62-77), originally completed in 1933 by members of the Gallia family, was enlarged in the 1960s. Its decor is more art nouveau than its year of construction suggests. The hotel lies near the main railway station and is one of the most expensive in Milan. Bedrooms fall into two categories: those modern and comfortable in the newer wing and those more graciously old-fashioned in the original core. Each accommodation comes with color TV with satellite reception, refrigerator, and many other amenities. Some units have a Jacuzzi in their bathroom, and others open onto private balconies fronting a busy square. Depending on the accommodation, singles range from 200,000 lire ($152) to 280,000 lire ($213), and doubles cost 260,000 lire ($198) to 380,000 lire ($289). Service is included, but breakfast and tax are extra. The hotel also has a noted restaurant.

Hotel Palace, piazza della Repubblica 20, 20124 Milano (tel. 02/63-36), blithely ignores the pell-mell commercial world around it, standing aloof on the slight rise of a hill, with a formal car entrance and a facade of 11 floors with tiers of balconies. It is near the railway station. Primarily a business hotel catering to some of the most prominent figures in Europe, the Palace also welcomes tourists and occasional entertainers (Gina Lollobrigida has been a guest here). The bedrooms are furnished with pastel upholstery, carpeting, and reproductions of Italian antiques. Modern conveniences include heated towel racks and mini-bars concealed behind mahogany chests. Singles range from 350,000 lire ($266) daily; doubles, from 500,000 lire ($380).

Hotel Principe e Savoia, piazza della Repubblica 17, 20124 Milano (tel. 02/62-30), was built in 1927 to fill the need for a luxurious hotel in the vicinity of the Stazione Centrale. Substantial and luxurious, it offers good solid comfort in an overscale atmosphere that includes crystal, detailed plasterwork, fine carpets, and polished marble. The bedrooms are spacious and modernized. Many are paneled in hardwoods, all containing leather chairs, stylish furniture, and modern bath with all the accessories. The Prìncipe, whose elaborately ornamented wings date from 1947 and 1954, has housed what might be a Who's Who of modern Western society. Notable guests have included Luciano Pavarotti, Ingrid Bergman, Alexander Haig, Julio

Iglesias, Henry Ford, a wide assortment of the Rockefellers, Evita Peron, Maria Callas, Jerry Lewis, and the duke of Windsor. The spacious bar area leading off the main lobby is the social focal point of the hotel. Rates are 220,000 lire ($167) to 300,000 lire ($228) daily in a single, 320,000 lire ($243) to 440,000 lire ($334) in a double.

The First-Class Range

Grand Hotel Duomo, via San Raffaele 1, 20121 Milano (tel. 02/88-33), a former palace, is on a traffic-free side street leading directly up to the stone lacework of the side of the cathedral. The lobby is modern, with tall ceilings and a gilded mural showing flute players cavorting in a zoological garden. The low velvet chairs and the chrome and glass accents add an unusual perspective on the many older buildings that abound in this section of town. Business people from many countries seem to prefer this hotel, patronizing its restaurant. The side of the hotel that faces the piazza del Duomo is built in a style similar to the arches and arcades of the 19th-century Galeria a few steps away. It is also within walking distance of La Scala. The bedrooms have been renovated into a warmly tinted modern format with all the conveniences. Accommodations, with a continental breakfast included, cost 220,000 lire ($167) daily in a single, 320,000 lire ($243) in a double.

Plaza Grand Hotel (Grande Albergo Plaza), piazza Diaz 3, 20123 Milano (tel. 02/805-8452), is a dramatically angular hotel set on a square centered around a modern metallic sculpture a few blocks from the duomo. The hotel's severe stone façade opens into a gray-and-white marble-covered lobby divided with mirrors and curved walls into a series of sunlit seating areas, one of which contains a bar. An aquarium bubbles in one corner of the lobby, softening the almost hi-tech ambience of the stylish decor. Each bedroom contains a private bath, phone, radio, TV, air conditioning, soundproofing, and a mini-bar. Singles rent for 230,000 lire ($175) daily; doubles, 290,000 lire ($220).

Grand Hotel et de Milan, via Manzoni 29, 20121 Milano (tel. 02/801-231). This was the grandest hotel in Milan when it opened in 1870. Today, visitors who appreciate the hotel's proximity to many of the best shops of Europe can immerse themselves in the 19th-century luxury that appealed to Verdi when he lived in one of the spacious apartments. The hotel sits behind an elegantly proportioned stone facade whose window frames are carved into fanciful garlands of leaves and flowers. The high-ceilinged lobby contains statues of Moors holding lamps, 19th-century watercolors displayed on wooden easels, elaborate plaster detailing, and an aura of what might have been a wealthy bohemian home of a century ago. The skylit bar area is the perfect place to read one of the newspapers, which hang, library-style, on wooden dowels near a carved marble mantelpiece adorned with bronze statues. The bill of the hotel's first overnight guest is nostalgically displayed in a frame near the cashier's desk. Including drinks, dinner, and a lot of extras, a single room rented for 51 lire. Today, however, singles are considerably more expensive, costing 235,000 lire ($171) daily. Doubles rent for 320,000 lire ($243). A small restaurant stands next to the bar.

Jolly President, largo Augusto 10, 20122 Milano (tel. 02/77-46), adds contemporary glamour to this popular chain. In the heart of the city, the Milan Jolly is slick and attractive. Its lounges, dining rooms, and cocktail bar successfully blend the modern with the traditional. Its restaurant, Il Verziere, offers a first-class cuisine. The decor throughout is in good taste, although not daring or unconventional. Each of the 220 well-furnished bedrooms, renovated in 1987, contains a private bath or shower, picture windows, and built-in furnishings. Bedside tables have gadgets to operate music and lights. All rooms have an adjoining lounge area with desks. The inclusive rate in a single is 280,000 lire ($213) daily; in a double, 330,000 lire ($251).

Il Leonardo da Vinci, via Senigallia 6, 20161 Milano (tel. 02/64-031), is a world unto itself—a hotel, an apartment residence, a congress center, and a sports center—located about a 30-minute run from the center of Milan, three miles from the main railway station beside the motorway ring. Motorists can use an underground garage and a large parking area. This complex offers 290 roomy accommodations, each furnished in bright colors, with private bath, taped music, color TV, frigo-bar, direct-dial phone, and individually controlled air conditioning. A single room rents for 200,000 lire ($152) daily, and a double goes for 284,000 lire ($216), including a buffet breakfast. In the main lobby of the hotel are a piano bar, a shopping center, a hairdresser for both men and women, and boutiques. You can even obtain medical service. From there, you can enter the Monna Lisa restaurant, which offers regional dishes of Lombardy as well as selections from the standard international repertoire. There is also Il Moro coffeeshop for meal if you're rushed. The Leonardo da Vinci also offers a sauna, a massage room, a disco, and an indoor swimming pool.

Hotel Executive, viale don Luigi Sturzo 45, 20154 Milano (tel. 02/62-94), inaugurated in 1973, is one of the largest hotels in Italy, with 420 double-bedded rooms. All rooms have private bath, air conditioning, radio, TV, and direct-dial phone. The modern furnishings and the service are efficient. Its Gibigiana Restaurant, with some of the best meat dishes in Milan, is well known. You can have an excellent meal for 60,000 lire ($45.50) and up. For a single room the rate is 250,000 lire ($190) daily, 300,000 lire ($228) for a double. Public facilities include a bar and a garage for 500 cars.

Carlton Hotel Senato, via Senato 5, 20121 Milano (tel. 02/798-583). The façade of this hotel appears like a collection of private ochre-fronted villas joined into a single unit behind an iron fence. The modernized interior is set up to receive the dozens of traveling businesspeople who check in weekdays from other sections of Europe and from America. Each of the 71 well-furnished bedrooms contains wall-to-wall carpeting and a high-ceilinged format, along with a private bath, frigo-bar, color TV, and phone. Singles cost 165,000 lire ($125) daily; doubles, 210,000 lire ($160). The hotel has a restaurant and bar on the premises, and also has a parking garage.

Hotel Cavour, via Fatebenefratelli 21, 20121 Milano (tel. 02/650-983), is a leading first-class hotel, containing 113 rooms with private tub or shower bath. The cost is 195,000 lire ($148) daily in a double, 170,000 lire ($129) in a single—tax and service included. The modern decor is far better than average—in fact, rather elegant. The hotel is spotlessly clean, offering good service and an excellent location, a short walk from the duomo and La Scala.

Windsor, via Galileo Galilei 2, 20124 Milano (tel. 02/63-46), which was erected and furnished in 1968, is an accomplishment. In spite of its "moderno," it maintains a warm ambience. A generous use of vibrant colors, plus a wise selection of traditional furnishings, with an accent on comfort, have made the Windsor a satisfactory hotel in its price range. A corner building of sienna-colored marble, it was built midway between the railway station and the duomo on a tree-lined boulevard. Each of its 114 bedrooms comes equipped with a bath and a shower, plus a direct-dial phone, a radio, TV, and your own drink-stocked refrigerator. You get free air conditioning as well, and there is also a garage. Singles rent for 160,000 lire ($122) daily, and doubles go for 195,000 lire ($148). The accommodations contain wall-to-wall draperies, with built-in headboards and chests. Public facilities include a cozy bar, as well as a breakfast room, with tall panels of wood and walls of curtained glass.

Hotel Gran Duca di York, via Moneta 1A, 20123 Milano (tel. 02/874-863). When it was built by the Catholic church in the 1890s, this Liberty-style palace was used as a residence for dozens of priests who staffed the nearby duomo. Among them was the cardinal of Milan, who was later to become Pope Pius XI. Today visitors can rent one of the 36 pleasantly furnished and well-kept bedrooms, each with a private bath sheathed with patterned tiles and containing a phone, radio, and TV. Singles cost 110,000 lire ($83.50) daily; doubles, 130,000 lire ($98.75); and triples, 180,000 lire ($137). Behind the ochre-and-stone façade, visitors will find a bar in an alcove of the severely elegant lobby, where a suit of armor and leather-covered armchairs contribute to the restrained tone.

Hotel Manzoni, via Santo Spirito 20, 20121 Milano (tel. 02/705-700), charges reasonable prices considering its location near the most fashionable shopping streets of Milan. It lies behind a façade of stone slabs on a fairly quiet one-way street. Each of its 52 bedrooms is outfitted with comfortable functional furniture, carpeting, and a compact bath, with color coordination. A brass-trimmed winding staircase leads from the lobby into a bar and TV lounge. Singles rent for 95,000 lire ($70) daily; doubles, 135,000 lire ($103). The cooperative English-speaking staff will point the way to the hotel's garage.

The Medium-Priced Range

Antica Locanda Solferino, via Castelfidardo 2, 20121 Milano (tel. 02/659-9886). When Curzio Castelli established his country-style hotel in 1976, the surrounding neighborhood was considered a depressed backwater of downtown Milan. Since then, however, the location has improved into an avant-garde community of actors, writers, and poets, and this inn takes some of the credit for the transformation. Castelli, a former road construction engineer in the jungles of Central and South America, believed the time was right for a personalized approach to innkeeping, and got off to a fortuitous beginning when members of the editorial staff of *Gentleman's Quarterly* stayed here soon after the hotel opened for one of their fashion investigations in Milan. Since then, Lindsay Kemp and Marcello Mastroianni have been among the fashionable clients who either stay in one of the old-fashioned bedrooms or else dine at the ground-floor restaurant (see my restaurant recommendation).

Each bedroom is different, reflecting the floor plan of the 19th-century building that houses it. The furnishings include Daumier engravings, art nouveau or late-19th-century bourgeois pieces, and various armoires purchased from a nearby hotel that went out of business. Staying between the white walls whose doors are surrounded with handcrafted moldings is like lodging in a room 50 years ago. But the baths are modern, and all units contain a phone. If you didn't know you were in the heart of the most industrialized city of Italy, you'd think you were in a small village. Double rooms cost 91,600 lire ($69.50) daily. Since the hotel is small and often fully booked, it's wise to make reservations as far in advance as possible.

Hotel Augustus, via Napo Torriani 29, 20124 Milano (tel. 02/657-5741), is just far enough away from the railway station to miss the commotion, yet close enough for convenience. It's a medium-size hotel with 56 bedrooms, most compact and modern. Throughout is a blending of marble, wood paneling, and contemporary furnishings. The rooms are small and well furnished, containing air conditioning. Nearly all the bedrooms have either private bath or shower with freshly scrubbed appliances, including bidet. The elevator hotel charges 111,000 lire ($83.50) daily in a single with bath, 169,000 lire ($128) for a double with bath. Every room has a frigo-bar. Breakfast and taxes are included in the rates.

Lord Hotel Internazionale, via Spadari 11, 20123 Milano (tel. 02/862-420), benefits from a convenient location a few blocks from the duomo. Renovated in 1989, the hotel contains 46 rooms, about half of which face a courtyard that is considerably quieter than the busy shopping street outside. The stone-floored lobby contains upholstered chairs and a bar. Each of the comfortable rooms has a bath, radio, phone, air conditioning, and TV. If you can motor your way through the labyrinthine streets, the hotel will arrange for garage service. Singles cost 95,000 lire ($72.25) daily, and doubles run 140,000 lire ($106) with breakfast.

Casa Svizzera, via San Raffaele 3, 20121 Milano (tel. 02/807-738), right off the piazza Duomo, is one of the most modern hotels in the city center, now that it has been rebuilt. Two elevators service five floors of rooms. Soundproofing keeps out the noise. Air conditioning can be independently regulated in each accommodation. Each of the 45 bedrooms contains a private bath, renting from 107,000 lire

($81.25) daily in a single, 150,000 lire ($114) in a double- or twin-bedded room. These tariffs include a Swiss breakfast. The bedrooms are furnished in a home-like fashion. Features include paneled double windows, frigo-bar, and TV.

The Budget Range

Albergo Bolzano, via Boscovich 21, 20124 Milano (tel. 02/669-1451), has been considerably renewed and upgraded. Each room contains a private bath or shower, and soft music is played in the background. Other amenities added include air conditioning. Some version of English is spoken, and the hotel has a helpful management, making this a welcome oasis. The tariff for bed-and-breakfast in a single is 88,300 lire ($67) a night, rising to 136,600 lire ($104) in a double or twin. Ideal for families, some triple and quadruple units are also rented. The hotel has a patio and a comfortable lounge as well. It is only about 500 feet from the main railway station.

Hotel Star, via dei Bossi 5, 20121 Milano (tel. 02/871-703). The major drawback to this family-run hotel is its location on a narrow street that the Milanese seem to consider their private racetrack. Despite that, its position a few blocks from La Scala and the duomo make it an acceptable low-cost hotel. The dimly lit lobby contains comfortable armchairs, a TV, a bar, and marble floors. The Ceretti family rents out 28 simple rooms, each with phone, shower, sink, toilet, and air conditioning. Accomodations are kept clean, and cost 82,000 lire ($62.25) daily in a single, 120,000 lire ($91.25) in a double or twin.

London Hotel, via Rovello 3, 20121 Milano (tel. 02/872-988), is a pleasant little hotel near the center of town, convenient for sightseeing and shopping. It is just off via Dante between Miravegli and Foro Buonaparte, a brief walk to the piazza del Duomo. Francesco Gambino, who heads this family-operated establishment, speaks English. Bedrooms are air conditioned in summer. A single with private bath, shower, and breakfast costs 66,000 lire ($50.25) daily; a double with the same amenities goes for 106,400 lire ($80.75).

Hotel Kennedy, viale Tunisia 6, 20124 Milano (tel. 02/29400934), on the sixth floor of an office building (reached by elevator), is an immaculate accommodation, whose young owners offer 12 pleasant rooms with shower. The units are small but comfortable, and the owners watch out for the well-being of their guests. Singles cost 35,000 lire ($26.50) daily, doubles with shower go for 70,000 lire ($53.25), and triples with shower rent for 28,000 lire ($21.25) per person. After midnight the door is locked, but they will give you a key.

The Pick of the Pensiones

Pensione Londra, piazza Argentina 4, 20124 Milano (tel. 02/228-400). If you're under 30, attractive, and looking for work as a model in Milan, the chances are that you'll gravitate to this pensione on the seventh floor of a 19th-century building on the north side of Milan. The establishment is directed by Franco Volante, who in his spare time heads the Milanese branch of the Turin soccer club. Of course, he welcomes more than models, having a devoted list of regular habitués from many walks of life. There are only 17 rooms, which are comfortable and adequate for the budgeteer. Studio shots of the dozens of American and Canadian models who have stayed here during exploratory searches of the local fashion houses are displayed above the espresso machine in the TV/breakfast room. About half the rooms face the noisy piazza, while the quieter ones look onto a more tranquil courtyard. Only a few of the rooms contain a private bath. Depending on the plumbing, singles range from 30,000 lire ($22.75) to 41,000 lire ($31.25) daily, and doubles cost 43,500 lire ($33) to 60,500 lire ($46).

If you prefer an establishment with an older and more conservative clientele, you might be happier at the **Pensione Parva Domus,** piazza Argentina 4, 20124 Milano (tel. 02/204-1138), in the same building. The name of this establishment comes from a Latin proverb which means a "small and quiet house." That is exactly what owner Rodolfo Begni, a former merchant seaman, has created on the sixth floor of a commercial building on a noisy square in a neighborhood filled with wide streets and tall buildings. You'll be greeted at the door by the sight of a bubbling aquarium, a cozily furnished TV room, and a collection of homey knickknacks. It is comfortable, clean, and you get not only a budget room, but advice from the well-mannered host. The quieter rooms face an inner courtyard. Since there are only ten rooms in the establishment, it might be a good idea to reserve well in advance. Bathless singles cost from 30,000 lire ($22.75) daily; bathless doubles from 46,000 lire ($35). Doubles with bath are rented at 66,000 lire ($50.25).

Pensione Arno, via Lazzaretto 17, 20124 Milano (tel. 02/652-782), is a hospitable place to stay, a short walk from the Stazione Centrale. The rooms are attractive, and the owner is responsive to requests from guests. A double with a shower costs from 65,000 lire ($49.50) daily, dropping to 45,000 lire ($34.25) in a bathless double. Singles without bath rent for 32,000 lire ($24.25).

DINING IN MILAN

The cooking of Lombardy is distinctive, relying heavily on the country butter, and reaching its finest levels of accomplishment in Milan. Even the minestrone tastes different. The specialty is risotto, rice cooked in consommé and flavored with saffron. The vines of Lombardy yield tender grapes, and the grapes are transformed into such aromatic wines as Barbagallo, Buttaffucco, and something called "Inferno." The wide economic levels of the population—from textile manufacturer to working person—are reflected in the prices of the restaurants, ranging from the haute-cuisine type to the pizza parlor. First, the most expensive—

The Top Choices

Gualtiero Marchesi, via Bonvesin de la Riva 9 (tel. 741-246). The namesake of this restaurant has been cited for years as the patron saint of the "cucina nuova" in Italy. The most creative chef in Italy, Signor Marchesi has invented more original dishes than any competitor in Milan. In fact, *Time* magazine has rated him among the top ten chefs in the world. Many consider his establishment the finest restaurant in the entire country. A piece of futuristic sculpture sits on each of the limited number of tables in this coolly dignified restaurant where, it is said, the bland decor lights up as soon as the owner, a consummate showman, enters the dining room. The menu may have changed radically by the time you arrive, depending on Signor Marchesi's inspiration. However, you are likely to find rice with herbs and scampi, twice-cooked filet of red mullet (first sautéed, then braised), ragoût of kidneys, cold spaghetti with chives and caviar, and lobster with a purée of sweet peppers. You might also try the crayfish, cooked very al dente, with cucumbers and olive oil, or sample an unusual form of half-opened ravioli. The kitchen uses only super-fresh ingredients. Reservations are vital. Meals run 90,000 lire ($68.50) to 130,000 lire ($98.75), but could cost twice as much. Hours are 12:30 to 2 p.m. and 7:30 to 11:30 p.m. The restaurant is closed all day Sunday, Monday at lunch, and in July.

Savini, Galleria Vittorio Emanuele 11 (tel. 805-8343), provides a heavenly introduction to the aromatic cookery of Lombardy and has attracted everybody from Puccini to Pavarotti. Perched in the heart of the great glass-enclosed arcade opposite the duomo, this "classico" restaurant, dating from 1867, draws the elite, both the out-of-towner and the discriminating local who wants some of the most savory viands in the city. Guests sit on the terrace outside, or else dine in the Old-World main room, with its crystal chandeliers and glittering silverware. Waiters in black jackets hover over you to see that you enjoy every mouthful. The smallest tab you are likely to receive is 70,000 lire ($53.25), although you can easily spend 100,000 lire ($76). Many of the most memorable dishes are unassuming, for example the specialty of Lombardy—costoletta alla milanese, the most tender veal coated with an egg batter and breadcrumbs, then fried a rich brown. The pièce de résistance of Milan, most often ordered before the main course, is risotto alla milanese—that is, rice simmered in a broth and dressed with whatever the artiste in the kitchen selects that night. Savini is excellently stocked with a wide-ranging choice of wines (the staff will gladly assist you). Closed Sunday and about ten days in mid-August, but open otherwise from noon to 3 p.m. and 7:30 to 11 p.m.

Giannino, via Amatore Sciesa 8 (tel. 545-2948), continues to enchant its loyal patrons and to win new adherents every year who sing its praises. Rightly, it's considered one of the top restaurants in all of Lombardy and has been since its founding in 1899. It has a chef who approaches every day as if he must make his reputation anew. Diners have a choice of several attractively styled rooms, but eyes rivet on the tempting under-glass offerings of the *specialità gastronomiche milanesi* from the behind-the-glass kitchen. The choice is excellent, including such characteristic Lombard dishes as the tender, breaded veal cutlet and the risotto simmered in broth and coated with parmesan cheese. It's difficult to recommend any specific dish, as everything I've ordered, or even seen going by, piqued my taste. However, I have special affection for one dish—tagliolini con scampi al verde, fresh homemade noodles with prawn tails in green herb sauce. Also superb are the cold fish and seafood salad and the beautifully seasoned orata al cartoccio (a European fish). This fish is baked in a brown paper bag with shrimp and butter along with fresh herbs. Expect to pay anywhere from 65,000 lire ($49.50) to 100,000 lire ($76) for a complete meal. Giannino, open from noon to 2:30 p.m. and 8 to 10:30 p.m., is closed on Sunday and in August.

El Toulà, piazza Paolo Ferrari 6 (tel. 870-302), lies right behind La Scala in the business district, drawing the VIP crowd at lunch, the opera-goers—the cream of Milanese society—in the evening. It is smart, fashionable, elegant, and also expensively priced. But the service and food are impeccable, as this is the same "Hayloft" whose owners run El Toulà in Rome, one of that city's greatest restaurants. Popular before and after the theater, El Toulà offers service that is faultless and a superb wine cellar. Some of its specialties, particularly veal and beef dishes, are those served in its Roman counterpart, although there are variations unique to Lombardy. Expect to pay 80,000 lire ($60.75) to 100,000 lire ($76) for a complete meal. The restaurant is open from noon to 2:30 p.m. and 8 to 10:30 p.m.; closed Sunday and the first three weeks of August.

Gallia's Restaurant, in the Hotel Excelsior Gallia, piazza Duca d'Aosta 9 (tel. 62-77), is one of the best—perhaps *the* best—of the hotel restaurants of this highly competitive city. It is decorated with the sumptuous flourish. This stylish dining room lies within this previously recommended hotel. It is open daily from 12:30 to 2:30 p.m. and 7:30 to 10:30 p.m., charging from 70,000 lire ($53.25) for a very elegant meal. Your repast might include smoked swordfish, spaghetti with zucchini flowers and shrimp, succulent slices of braised foie gras, and risotto with porcini mushrooms. For the most part, the cooking is very Italian cuisine moderne, influenced by the kitchens of both Milan and Naples. Reservations are always necessary.

La Scaletta, piazza Stazione Porta Genova 3 (tel. 835-0290), emerges near the top in the highly competitive world of Milanese restaurants. Here, Italian cuisine moderne, is practiced by the chefs with a certain flair. In an elegant setting, which some diners have likened to a small and exclusive London club, the restaurant serves in two rooms. It is closed Sunday and Monday, but open other days from noon to 1:15 p.m. and 8 to 9:30 p.m.—relatively short serving hours for Milan. Because this place is so popular with the business community of the city, reservations are essential, as far in advance as possible. The quality of the ingredients is superb. The chefs demand that every item be fresh, whether it be fish or vegetables. The veal dishes are heavenly. You might begin with a tripe terrine in gelatin or a scampi salad, before giving serious attention to your main course. Meals cost 65,000 lire ($49.50) and up, with an emphasis on *up*. The restaurant takes a vacation in August.

First-Class Restaurants

Taverna del Gran Sasso, piazza Principessa Clotilde 10 (tel. 659-7578), not only provides regional meals, but it is a joyride as well. It is an old taverna, filled with lots of sentimental baubles. Its walls are crowded ceiling to floor with copper molds, ears of corn, strings of pepper and garlic, and cart wheels. A tall open hearth burns with a charcoal fire, and a Sicilian cart is laden with baskets of bread, dried figs, nuts, and kegs of wine. As you enter, you'll find a mellowed wooden keg of wine with a brass faucet (you're to help yourself, using glass mugs). The policy is country festive —that is, you can eat all you want for 43,000 lire ($32.75), including wine. An abbreviated luncheon menu is offered for 22,000 lire ($16.75). The cuisine features a number of specialties from the Abruzzi district in the south of Italy—regional dishes such as maccheroni alla chitarra, a distinctively shaped macaroni with a savory meat sauce. The first course offers at least ten choices; the second, two; the third, four; the fourth, five; and there are six or seven desserts to choose from for the final selection. The waiters and waitresses wear folk apparel, and they join in the spirit of the place—often singing folk songs. Hours are noon to 1:45 p.m. and 7:45 to 10:30 p.m. The restaurant is closed on Friday at lunchtime, all day Sunday, and in August.

Antico Boeucc, piazza Belgioioso 2 (tel. 790-224). This restaurant, established in 1682, is a trio of rooms in a severely elegant old palace, within walking distance of the Duomo and the major shopping streets of Milan. Throughout you'll find soaring stone columns and modern art. In summer, guests gravitate to a terrace for open-air dining. The hearty specialties, the standard of the kitchen, come from the different regions of Italy. You might enjoy a spaghetti in clam sauce, a salad of shrimp with arugula and artichokes, or grilled liver, veal, or beef with aromatic herbs. In season, sautéed zucchini flowers accompany some dishes. Full meals cost from 50,000 lire ($38) and are served from 12:30 to 2:30 p.m. and 7:30 to 10:30 p.m. daily except Saturday and for lunch Sunday. Closed in August.

Peck's Bottega del Vino, via Victor Hugo 4 (tel. 876-774), is owned by the famous delicatessen of Milan, which many gastronomes consider the Milanese equivalent of Fauchon's in Paris. In an environment filled with shimmering marble and modern Italian paintings, an alert staff will serve an elegant fixed-price menu degustation for 65,000 lire ($49.50) per person. The fresh specialties include a classic version of risotto milanese, rack of lamb with fresh rosemary, rollatini of salmon with a "rape" sauce, ravioli alla fonduta, and lombo di vitello with artichokes, followed by chocolate meringue for dessert. Reservations are necessary for meals served from noon to 2:30 p.m. and 7 to 10:30 p.m., and the restaurant is closed on Sunday and in July.

St. Andrews, via Sant'Andrea 23 (tel. 793-132). This restaurant has given much pleasure to many people for many years. It offers one of the finest kitchens in Lombardy, preparing both international and regional food. Try, for example, marinated salmon, green apple salad, sea bass pie with a potato crust, or the apple tart. At lunch it has somewhat the atmosphere of a private club, and is apt to be filled with businesspeople talking about the affairs of Italy. The armchairs are covered in black leather, the paneling is dark wood, and the lighting discreet from hooded lamps. Formally attired waiters give superb service. The cuisine is superior, a complete meal costing in the neighborhood of 80,000 lire ($60.75) to 120,000 lire ($91.25). The restaurant is open from noon to 4 p.m. and 7 to 2 a.m.; closed Sunday and in August.

The Middle Bracket

Alfio-Cavour, via Senato 31 (tel. 780-731). There's a luminous quality to the lavish displays of antipasti served with relish at this family-run restaurant. It stems partly from the Tahitian-style decor, where trees grow through the glass panels of a greenhouse-like roof and vines entwine themselves among bamboo lattices. You'll be seated in the clear light of what used to be a private garden. The restaurant is best known for its serve-yourself display of antipasti, where the polite but sharp-eyed staff bills you for what you select. A pasta specialty is the flavorful spaghetti pescatore, with bits of seafood. You might follow with large grilled shrimp or a "gran misto" fish fry, or else one of the many excellent beef or veal dishes. Full meals, served from 12:30 to 3 p.m. and 7:30 to 11 p.m., cost 60,000 lire ($45.50) to 70,000 lire ($53.25), and the restaurant is closed all day Saturday, Sunday at lunch, and in August.

Ristorante Solferino, via Castelfidardo 2 (tel. 659-9886), is a country-style inn with all the accoutrements you'd expect to find in an agrarian community on the outskirts of town rather than in the center of a busy city. Below a beamed ceiling, next to racks of wine bottles and among the fashion stars, you can dine on such specialties as risotto Grande Milano, Milanese veal with vegetables, gnocchi with salmon, carpaccio, and tagliata Solferino, following with a dessert known as "Milanese custard." An average meal will cost from 40,000 lire ($30.50). The establishment maintains a limited number of bedrooms upstairs (see my hotel recommendation), as well as a less formal and much less expensive buffet-style restaurant just around the corner. Hours are 12:45 to 2:30 p.m. and 7:30 to 11:30 p.m. Reservations are appreciated. The restaurant is closed on Saturday for lunch, all day Sunday, and for part of August.

Piero, via Ajaccio 7 (tel. 715-373), with a little garden outside, is one of the most favored dining spots in Milan. The owners welcome you and invite you to try some of their many specialties. From May to October they offer veal fricassée with mushrooms (known as funghi porcini). Another seasonal offering is a guinea fowl known as "faraona." Other special dishes are penne, a type of pasta, with eggplant, along with spaghetti savonese. However, the unusual menu is likely to change every day, so you don't really know what's offered until you get there. It's cheerful and well run, but is likely to become an uproar when it gets overrun with hungry diners, everybody speaking at top decibel level. A good wine to order is Sasella, which is a bright ruby-red and considered one of the finest of the Valtellina wines. Expect to pay from 50,000 lire ($38). The restaurant, serving food from 12:30 to 2:30 p.m. and 7:30 to 10:30 p.m., is closed Saturday at lunch, all day Sunday, and for ten days in August.

Osteria del Vecchio Canneto, via Solferino 56 (tel. 659-8498), is the sister of Gran Sasso, previously recommended. What Gran Sasso does with regional cookery, Canneto achieves with the denizens of the deep. For the set price of 50,000 lire ($38), you're given a staggering seafood dinner, 16 courses if you want it. You can order pasta, but nearly everything else is from the sea. A more limited lunchtime menu is offered for 30,000 lire ($22.75). The cellar location where you're greeted by a foghorn is as crowded as its seafood platter. Go here only if you have a gargantuan appetite and are in the mood for noisy, good fun. The restaurant is open from 12:15 to 2 p.m. and 7 to 10:30 p.m.; closed all day Sunday, Monday at lunch, and in August.

Al Porto, piazzale Generale Cantore (tel. 832-1481), is another seafood restaurant, except this one is located in a customs house from the 18th century. It offers one of the best seafood menus in town, and all dishes are well prepared and beautifully served. A complete meal costs from 60,000 lire ($45.50). Specialties include risotto di frutti di mare, scampi alla livornese, and orata (dorado) al cartoccio. For dessert, I'd suggest the gelato with whisky. The restaurant is open from 12:30 to 2:30 p.m. and 7:30 to 11:30 p.m. It is closed all day Sunday, Monday at lunch, and in August.

Trattoria Bagutta, via Bagutta 14 (tel. 702-767), patronized heavily by artists, is the most celebrated of the trattorie in Milan, dating from 1927. A venerable-looking establishment, it is slightly hard to find in its side-street location. The Bagutta is known for the caricatures—framed and frescoed—that cover its walls. Of the many large and bustling dining rooms, the rear one with its picture windows is most enticing. The food is lushly tempting, drawing on the kitchens of Lombardy, Tuscany, and Bologna for inspiration. Assorted antipasti are offered. Main-dish specialties include fried squid and scampi, lingua e pure (tongue with mashed potatoes), and scaloppine alla Bagutta. A complete meal here, served from 12:30 to

2:30 p.m. and 7:30 to 10:30 p.m., will cost from 50,000 lire ($38). The Bagutta enjoys a vogue among out-of-towners who consider it chic to patronize the sophisticated little trattoria, as opposed to the more deluxe restaurants. Closed Sunday and for part of August.

A Santa Lucia, via San Pietro all'Orto 3 (tel. 793-155), pulls out hook, line, and sinker to lure you with some of the best fish dinners in Milan. A festive place at which to dine, the restaurant is decked out with photographs of pleased celebs, who attest to the skill of its kitchen. You can order such specialties as a savory fish soup, a meal in itself; fried baby squid; or good-tasting sole. Spaghetti alle vongole evokes the tang of the sea with its succulent clam sauce. Pizza also reigns supreme. Try either the calzone of Naples or the pizza Napoletana, the classic dish of the city on the bay. Both are made with mozzarella. Diners spend from 50,000 lire ($38) for a meal here. The restaurant is open only for dinner, from 8 p.m. to 2 a.m., and is closed Monday and in August.

Peck, via Victor Hugo 4 (tel. 876-774), offers one of the best mealtime values in Milan, served in a glamorous cafeteria associated with the most famous delicatessen in Italy (a high-priced restaurant is in the basement). Only a short walk from the duomo, Peck has a stand-up bar in front, and, in the rear, a well-stocked series of display cases containing specialties fresh from the establishment's treasure trove of produce. Armed with a plastic tray, you can sample such tempters as artichoke-and-parmesan salad, seafood salads, marinated carpaccio, slabs of tender veal in an herb sauce, risotto marinara, and selections from a carving table laden with a juicy display of roast meats. Full meals, served from noon to 2:30 p.m. and 7 to 10:30 p.m., are priced at 50,000 lire ($38). Closed Sunday.

The Budget Range

Biffi, Galleria Vittorio Emanuele (tel. 805-7961), is located in the most popular shopping arcade of Milan. The decor tries to re-create the nostalgic era of the gallery's construction, with its belle époque globe lights, bentwood chairs, and polished brass. Despite the glass canopy high above the heads of the sidewalk diners, there's a striped awning over the pavement in front, with uniformed waiters hovering in the background. The interior contains a self-service buffet one floor above ground level, while the small tables of the ground floor offer such Italian specialties as roast veal and risotto parmigiana, and set menus (including wine, service, and tax) for 31,000 lire ($23.50). A la carte meals, which can be as simple or as elaborate as you want, usually begin at around 45,000 lire ($34.25). Open from 12:30 to 3 p.m. and 7:30 to 10:30 p.m., it is closed on Sunday.

Magolfa, via Magolfa 15 (tel. 832-1696), is one of the dining bargains of the city, offering a gargantuan meal for 45,000 lire ($34.25). The building is a country farmhouse with checkered cloths. It's likely to be crowded, as is every other restaurant in Milan that offers such value. If you don't mind its location away from the center of town, you'll be treated to some very good regional cookery emerging fresh from battered pots and pans. A general air of conviviality reigns. There is music of local origin nightly. This old Milan restaurant is open from 8 p.m. to midnight but closed on Sunday and in August.

Al Chico, via Sirtori 24 (tel. 294-6883), is a good neighborhood restaurant, specializing in such fare as onion soup and fondue bourguignonne. Tuscan specialties such as Florentine beef steak are also featured. A complete meal here will cost from 42,000 lire ($32), and portions are tasty and satisfying. The place is usually crowded, but it's worth the wait for a table. The service is good, and the basic materials that go into the dishes are fresh and well selected at the market. Of course, you'll want to order Chianti, that most typical of all Italian wines, to go with your meal. Good house wines from Tuscany are stocked. Hours are noon to 3 p.m. and 7 to 10:30 p.m.; closed Saturday at lunch, all day Sunday, and in August.

Burghy, piazza del Duomo (tel. 871-129), is a Milanese copy of McDonald's set at the far end of the square facing the cathedral. The colorful Formica and wood-grained decor will remind you of every other fast-food place you've ever been in, except for the ancient granite columns supporting the ceiling near the cashiers. There's ample seating, the hamburgers are well prepared and thicker than you'd expect, and perhaps best of all, the staff refuses tips. A large cheeseburger costs around 3,500 lire ($2.65). The coffee, unlike other American-inspired items on the menu, comes Italian style, served as espresso in a polystyrene cup. Open from 10:30 a.m. to midnight daily except Wednesday.

Trattoria Officina, viale le Monza 140 (tel. 257-1127), offers one of the best restaurant values in Milan to the hordes of regulars who line up every evening at 8 for the first "shift" of diners. The fixed-price menu of 18,000 lire ($13.75) offers a limited choice of variation for each of the abundant courses. No à la carte is offered, but that doesn't seem to bother anyone. It's open daily except Monday, serving until 10:30 p.m.

Al Tempio d'Oro, via delle Leghe 23 (tel. 285-0709), near the central railway station, offers inexpensive and well-prepared meals in an ambience similar to what you might have found if an ancient Greek temple had decided to serve beer on tap along with international food specialties. The crowd scattered among the ceiling columns is relaxed, and they contribute to an atmosphere that is somewhat like that of a beer hall. A full meal goes for 27,000 lire ($20.50), although no one will mind if you just stop by for a drink. It is open daily except Sunday from 8 p.m. to 3 a.m.

Pizzeria Positano, via Piero della Francesca 52 (tel. 331-9946), is an excellent pizza restaurant, serving the kind of pies you would otherwise have to go to Naples to find. A richly aromatic fish antipasti could precede a pasta and a meat dish, which would be served to you for around 40,000 lire ($30.50), with wine included. Pizzas alone cost from 7,000 lire ($5.30). The Positano is open from noon to 2:30 p.m. and 7 p.m. to midnight daily except Wednesday.

BARS AND CAFES

Every city in Italy seems to have a café reeking of 19th-century detailing and memories of Verdi or some such famous person. They usually offer a wide variety of pastries and a particular kind of clientele who gossip, sip espresso, munch in-between-meals snacks, and compare notes on comparative shopping values in the area.

In Milan, that action takes place at the **Café Cova,** via Montenapoleone 8 (tel. 793-187). Amid a chic assemblage of garment district personnel, along with the shoppers who support them, the café follows a routine it established back in 1817. This involves concocting gallons of the heady espresso to keep everyone's nerves jumping. They also dispense staggering amounts of pralines, chocolates, brioches, and sandwiches from behind a glass display case. The more elegant sandwiches contain smoked salmon and truffles. Clients drink their espresso from fragile gold-rimmed cups at one of the small tables in an elegant inner room or standing up at the prominent bar. Most of the action takes place at the bar, so you really don't need a table unless you're exhausted from too much shopping. Coffee at the bar costs from 1,000 lire (75¢). Hours are 8 a.m. to 8 p.m., but when the surrounding stores close on Sunday, the café remains dark.

Taveggia, via Visconti di Modrone 2 (tel. 791-257), offers the kind of Old-World ambience that is a rarity now in the hustle-bustle atmosphere of modern Milan. Behind ornate glass doors set into the 19th-century façade, Tabeggia is reputed to make the best cappuccino and espresso in town. To match this quality, a variety of brioches, pastries, candies, and tortes is offered. Freshly made on the premises, they can be enjoyed while standing at the bar of walnut burl and shining marble counters or seated in the Victorian tea room. All service at the tables is slightly more expensive, as is the rule in Europe. A cappucino costs 1,300 lire ($1). Taveggio is open from 8 a.m. to 8 p.m.; closed Monday.

THE TOP ATTRACTIONS

Despite its modern architecture and industry, Milan is a city of great art. The serious sightseer will give the metropolis at least two days for exploration. If your schedule is frantic, see (1) the duomo; (2) Da Vinci's *Last Supper* at the Santa Maria della Grazie; and (3) the important Brera Picture Gallery.

The Duomo

In the very center of Milan, opening onto the heart of the city's life, the piazza del Duomo, the impressive lacy Gothic cathedral (tel. 870-907) ranks with St. Peter's in Rome and the cathedral at Seville, Spain, as the largest in the world. It is 479 feet long and 284 feet wide at the transepts. Dating from 1386, the church has seen numerous architects and builders. The conqueror of Milan, Napoleon, even added his own decorating ideas to the facade in the early years of the 19th century. The imposing structure of marble is the grandest and most flamboyant example of the Gothic style in Italy.

Built in the shape of a Latin cross, the cathedral is divided by soaring pillars into five naves. The overall effect is like a marble-floored Grand Central Station—that is, in space—with far greater dramatic intensity. In the crypt rests the tomb of San Carlo Borromeo, the cardinal of Milan. To experience the duomo at its most majestic, you must ascend to the roof, either by elevator for 3,500 lire ($2.65) or by steps for 1,500 lire ($1.15), from which you can walk through a "forest" of pinnacles, turrets, and marble statuary—like a promenade in an early Cocteau film. The gilded Madonna towers over the tallest spire.

Across the square, the **Museo del Duomo,** piazza del Duomo (tel. 860-358), is housed in the Palazzo Reale or royal palace. It is like a picture storybook of the cathedral's six centuries of history. It is open daily except Monday from 9:30 a.m. to 12:30 p.m. and 3 to 6 p.m., charging an admission of 4,000 lire ($3.05).

The museum has exhibits of statues and decorative sculptures, some dating from the 14th century. Also shown are antique art objects, stained-glass windows (some from the 15th century), and ecclesiastical vestments, many as old as the 16th century.

Santa Maria delle Grazie (*The Last Supper*)

Off the corso Magenta, on the piazza Santa Maria delle Grazie, this Gothic church was erected by the Dominicans in the mid-15th century. A number of its more outstanding features, such as the cupola, were designed by the great Bramante. But "trippers" from all over the world flock here to gaze upon a mural in the convent next door. In what was once a refectory, the incomparable Leonardo da Vinci adorned one wall with his *The Last Supper*. Commissioned by Ludovico the Moor, the painting was finished about 1497. The gradual erosion of the painting makes for one of the most intriguing stories in art. Narrowly escaping bombing in 1943, it is being restored. What remains today, however, is Leonardo's "outline"—and even it is suffering badly. As one Italian newspaper writer put it: "If you want to see 'Il Cenacolo,' don't walk—run!" A painting of grandeur, the composition portrays Christ at the moment he announces to his shocked apostles that one of them will betray him. Vasari called the portrait of Judas "a study in perfidy and wickedness." The *Cenacolo Vinciano* (tel. 490-7588) is open Tuesday through Saturday from 9 a.m. to 1:30 p.m. and 2 to 6 p.m., on Sunday and Monday from 9 a.m. to 1:15 p.m. Admission is 4,000 lire ($3.05).

Pinacoteca di Brera

At via Brera 28 (tel. 808-387), one of Italy's finest art galleries contains an exceptionally good collection of both Lombard and Venetian masters. Like a Roman emperor, Canova's nude Napoleon—a toga draped over his shoulder—stands in the courtyard (fittingly, a similar statue ended up in the duke of Wellington's house in London). The gallery is open daily except Monday from 9 a.m. to 2 p.m. (closes at 1 p.m. on Sunday), charging 4,000 lire ($3.05) for admission.

Among the notable artworks, a *Pietà* by Lorenzo Lotto is a work of great beauty, as is Gentile Bellini's *St. Mark Preaching in Alexandria* (it was finished by his brother, Giovanni). Seek out Andrea Mantegna's *Virgin and the Cherubs,* a great work from the Venetian school. Two of the most important prizes at the Brera are Mantegna's *Dead Christ* and Giovanni Bellini's *La Pietà,* as well as Carpaccio's *St. Stephen's Debating.*

Other paintings include Titian's *St. Jerome,* as well as such Lombard art as Bernardino Luini's *Virgin of the Rose Bush* and Andrea Solarion's *Portrait of a Gentleman.* One of the greatest panels is Piero della Francesca's *Virgin and Child Enthroned with Saints and Angels and the Kneeling Duke of Urbino in Armor.* Seek out, in addition, the *Christ* by Bramante. One wing is devoted to modern art, offering works by such artists as Boccioni, Carrà, and Morandi. One of my favorite paintings in the gallery is Raphael's *Wedding of the Madonna,* with a dance-like quality. *The Last Supper at Emmaus* is another moving work, this one by Caravaggio.

OTHER SIGHTS

Truly fabulous, the **Poldi Pezzoli Museum,** via Manzoni 12 (tel. 794-889), is done in great taste and rich with antique furnishings, tapestries, frescoes, and Lombard woodcarvings. It also displays a remarkable collection of paintings by many of the old masters of northern and central Italy, including Andrea Mantegna's *Madonna and Child,* Giovanni Bellini's *Cristo Morto,* and Filippo Lippi's *Madonna, Angels, and Saints* (superb composition). One room is devoted entirely to Flemish artists, and there is a collection of ceramics and also one of clocks and watches. The museum grew out of a private collection donated to the city in 1871. It is open daily except Monday from 9:30 a.m. to 12:30 p.m. and from 2:30 p.m. to 6 p.m., staying open till 7:30 p.m. on Sunday. From April 1 to September 30 it is closed Sunday afternoon. Admission is 4,000 lire ($3.05).

At the piazza Castello sits **Castle Sforzesco,** the Castle of Milan. The ancient fortress was rebuilt by Francesco Sforza, who launched another governing dynasty. It is believed that both Bramante and Leonardo da Vinci may have contributed architectural ideas to the fortress. Following extensive World War II bombings, it was painstakingly restored and continued its activity as a Museum of Ancient Art called the **Museo d' Arte Antica** (tel. 62-36). Displayed on the ground floor are sculpture from the 4th century A.D., medieval art mostly from Lombardy, and armor. The most outstanding exhibit, however, is Michelangelo's *Rondanini Pietà,* on which he was working the week he died. In the rooms upstairs, besides a good collection of ceramics, antiques, and bronzes there is the important section of the picture gallery, rich in paintings from the 14th to the 18th century, including works by Lorenzo Veneziano, Mantegna, Lippi, Bellini, Crivelli, Foppa, Bergognone, Cesare da Sesto, Lotto, Tintoretto, Cerano, Procaccini, Morazzone, Guardi, and Tiepolo. The castle is open from 9:30 a.m. to noon and 2:30 to 5:30 p.m., and charges no admission. Closed Monday and January 1, Easter, May 1, August 15, and Christmas.

At piazza Pio XI 2, near the duomo, the **Ambrosiana Picture Gallery** and library (tel. 800-146) were founded in the early 17th century by Cardinal Federico Borromeo. On the second floor, the *pinacoteca* contains a remarkable collection of art, mostly from the 15th through the 17th century. Among the notable works are a *Madonna and Angels* by Botticelli; works by Brueghel (impressive detail, among the best art in the gallery); paintings by Lombard artists, including Bramantino's *Presepe,* in earthy, primitive colors, plus a curious miniature *St. Jerome with Crucifix* by Andrea Solario, along with works by Bernardino Luini. The museum owns a large sketch by Raphael on which he labored before painting *The School of Athens* for the Vatican. The most celebrated treasures are the productions of Leonardo da Vinci's *Codice Atlantico.* (In Milan, the master had as a patron the powerful

Ludovico Sforza, known as "The Moor.") After seeing the sketches (in facsimile), you can only agree with Leonardo's evaluation of himself as a genius without peer. Attributed to him is a portrait of a musician, believed to have been that of Franchino Gaffurio. The library contains many medieval manuscripts, shown for scientific examination only. The visiting hours are 9:30 a.m. to 5 p.m. (closed Saturday), and the charge is 3,000 lire ($2.30) for admission.

If you're a devotee of Leonardo da Vinci, as I am, you may want to visit the **Museo Nazionale della Scienza e della Tecnica Leonardo da Vinci,** via San Vittore 21 (tel. 462-709), which is open daily except Monday from 9 a.m. to 5 p.m., charging an admission of 4,000 lire ($3.05). This is a vast museum complex where you could practically spend a week devouring the exhibits. However, for the average visitor, the most interesting section is the Leonardo da Vinci Gallery, which displays copies and models from this Renaissance genius.

Other exhibits trace the rail industry in Italy, with 20 real locomotives. There is a reconstruction pharmacy from a convent, along with a monastic cell, even a sewing machine collection. You'll also see antique carriages plus exhibits relating to astronomy, telecommunications, watchmaking, goldsmithery, motion pictures, and the subjects of classic physics.

The **Civica Galleria d'Arte Moderna** (Civic Modern Art Gallery), via Palestro 16 (tel. 760-028-19), used to be known as the royal villa before its name was changed to the Villa Comunale. Constructed between 1790 and 1793, it was designed by the architect Leopold Pollack. For a short time it was the residence of Napoleon and Eugène de Beauharnais. The gallery has a large collection of works from the Milanese neoclassical period, along with many paintings showing the development of Italian Romanticism. It is predictably rich in Lombard artists. Important collections donated to the modern art gallery are those of Carlo Grassi and the Vismara art accumulation. Also important is the Marino Marini Museum, which was opened in 1973. Marini, a famous Italian sculptor, has some 200 works displayed, including not only sculpture, but paintings and graphics, all a gift of the artist himself. You'll recognize the names of many celebrated artists on parade: Picasso, Matisse, Rouault, Renoir, Modigliani, Corot, Millet, Manet, Cézanne, Bonnard, and Gauguin. Hours are 9:30 a.m. to noon and 2:30 to 5:30 p.m., except on Tuesday when it is closed. No admission is charged.

At piazza San Eustorgio 1, the 9th-century **Basilica of San Eustorgio** (tel. 835-1583), has a bell tower dating from the 13th century, built in the Romantic style by patrician Milanese families. It has the first tower clock in the world, made in 1305. Originally, this was the tomb of the Three Kings (4th century A.D.). Inside, its greatest treasure is the "Capella Portinari" designed by the Florentine Michelozzo in the style of the Renaissance (the sacristan will let you inside for 500 lire, or 40¢). The chapel is frescoed and contains a bas-relief of angels at the base of the cupola. In the center is an intricately carved tomb, supported by marble statuary of the 13th century by Balduccio of Pisa. Inside are the remains of St. Peter Martyr. The basement has a Roman crypt.

At piazza Sant Ambrogio 15 the **Church of San Ambrogio** (tel. 872-059) was originally erected by St. Ambrose in the later years of the 4th century A.D. The present structure was built in the 12th century in the Romanesque style. The remains of St. Ambrose rest in the crypt. The church, entered after passing through a quadrangle, is rather stark and severe, in the style of its day. The atrium is its most distinguishing architectural feature. In the apse are interesting mosaics from the 12th century. The Lombard tower at the side dates from 1128, and the façade with its two tiers of arches is impressive.

The **Cimitèro Monumentale** (Monumental Cemetery), piazzale Cimitèro Monumentale 1 (tel. 659-9938), has catered for more than 100 years to the whims of the elite of Milan's society. Actually, the only requirements for burial in the cemetery are first, that you are dead, and second, that you can buy your way into a plot. Some families have paid up to 200 million lire just for the privilege of burying their dead here. The graves are marked, not only with brass plates or granite markers, but also with Greek temples, elaborate obelisks, or such original works as an abbreviated version of Trajan's column.

This outdoor museum has become such an attraction that a superintendent has compiled an illustrated guidebook—a sort of "Who *was* who." Among the cemetery's outstanding sights are a sculpted *The Last Supper*. Several fine examples of art nouveau sculpture dot the hillside, and there's a tasteful example of Liberty-style architecture (Italy's version of art nouveau) in a tiny chapel designed to hold the remains of Arturo Toscanini's son, who died in 1906. Among the notables buried here are Toscanini himself and novelist Alessandro Manzoni. In the Memorial Chapel is the tomb of Salvatore Quasimodo, the 1959 Nobel Prize winner for literature. Here also rest the ashes of Ermann Einstein, father of the scientist. In the Palanti Chapel is a monument commemorating the 800 Milanese citizens slain in Nazi concentration camps. A model of this monument is displayed in the Museum of Modern Art in New York. From April 1 to September 30, hours are 8:30 a.m. to 6 p.m. From October 1 to March 31, visiting times are 8:30 a.m. to 5 p.m. Closed Monday.

SHOPPING IN MILAN

London has Harrods, Paris has all the big-name boutiques you can think of, and Rome and Florence instill an acquisitial fever in the eyes of anyone who even window-gazes. Milan, however, is blessed with one of the most unusual concentrations of shopping possibilities in Europe. Most of the boutiques are infused with the style, humor, and sophistication that has made Milan the dynamo of the Italian fashion industry, a place where the sidewalks fairly sizzle with the hard-driving entrepreneurial spirit that has been part of the northern Italian textile industry for centuries.

One well-heeled shopper from Florida recently spent the better part of her vacation in Italy shopping for what she called "the most unbelievable variety of shoes, clothes, and accessories in the world." A visitor's walk on the fashion subculture's focal point, via Montenapoleone, one of Italy's three great shopping streets, a mile-long strip that has become a showcase for famous (and high-priced) makers of clothes and shoes, with excursions into the side streets, will quickly confirm that impression.

Note carefully that the beauty does not come cheaply in the garment industry, and the attention you receive will often be based directly on the salesperson's impression of how much money you plan to spend. But as a handful of American models, along with design imitators from around the world, know, there are indeed riches to be discovered.

Early-morning risers will be welcomed only by silent streets and closed gates. Most shops are closed all day Sunday and Monday (although some open on Monday afternoon). Some stores open at 9 a.m. unless they're very chic, and then they are not likely to open until 10:30 a.m. They remain open, for the most part, until 1 p.m., reopening again between 3:30 and 7:30 p.m.

Via Montenapoleone

This street of fashion gives the impression of being almost a self-contained community, filled with all the politics and drama of any pressurized collection of fashion retailers. Behind the 19th-century façades that line its wide and straight-as-an-arrow path, you'll find dozens of shops, a cross section of which include the following:

Beltrami, via Montenapoleone 16 (tel. 702-975), offers an enormous two-story collection of fine leathergoods for men and women, along with a well-lit decor in great style.

Missoni, via Montenapoleone 1 (tel. 700-906). The decor looks more like that of a chic art gallery than a store. It's the only Missoni outlet in Milan, contained at the top of a flight of black stairs decorated with fashionable accessories. Inventory includes knitwear for both men and women, along with a collection of avant-garde garments in silk, cotton, and wool.

Gucci, via Montenapoleone 2 and 5 (tel. 545-6621), is the Milanese headquarters for the most famous leathergoods distributor in Italy. Spread out between two neighboring stores, these chic addresses offer unfailing quality and conservative excellence.

Old America, via Bagutta 9, with a side entrance on via Montenapoleone (tel. 706-019), is one of several high-quality antique stores scattered among the clothiers. When the store was founded 30 years ago, it sold only American furniture, although stocks of that have become so rare that this shop now sells mainly Scottish and English styles. A bigger annex of the same store is on two comfortably cluttered floors at another outlet (via Bagutta 6), a few blocks away.

Mario Buccellati, via Montenapoleone 4 (tel. 702-153), offers the best-known —and perhaps the most expensive—silver and jewels in Italy. The designs are nothing short of rhapsodic, and the quality is the highest. You'll be ushered into the tastefully appointed showroom within what turns out to be a formidable security system.

Tanino Crisci, via Montenapoleone 3 (tel. 791-264), sells shoes for both men and women, and elegant ones at that, in an English club–style decor of leather-covered carved chairs.

Mila Schön, via Montenapoleone 6 (tel. 701-333), sells the men's line from the well-known designer. An adjacent store, at via Montenapoleone 4 (tel. 701-803), offers women's clothes by the same designer.

Galleria Geri Antichità, via Montenapoleone 8 (tel. 760-007-85), with an even bigger annex a few steps away at via Bagutta 13, sells antiques from Italy that would be hard to find in North America.

Rossetti, via Montenapoleone 1 (tel. 791-650), displays shoes for both men and women, along with a limited but elegant selection of clothing.

Salvatore Ferragamo, via Montenapoleone 3 (tel. 700-054). The label is instantly recognizable, the quality high at this store for women's ready-to-wear, shoes, and accessories. On the other side of the street at via Montenapoleone 24 (tel. 706-660), Salvatore Ferragamo sells men's wear.

Donini, via Montenapoleone 7 (tel. 702-568), sells the kind of women's lingerie that might fulfill a Joan Collins fantasy. Some of the embroidery is made by hand. An array of infants' clothes is offered too.

Galtrucco, via Montenapoleone 27 (tel. 702-978), is a two-floor collection of elegant men's suits, shirts, and knitwear. The clothes are well made and attractively conservative. Another outlet of the same store is at piazza del Duomo 2 (tel. 876-256), where thousands of miles of yard goods are sold on the ground floor. It's ideal if you plan to take up sewing. There is also a department with men's and women's garments.

Don't ignore the side streets, as mentioned, which contain abundant opportunities for conspicuous consumption.

Via della Spiga

Krizia Boutique, via della Spiga 23 (tel. 708-429). If you like Krizia, you love Krizia. The clothes are witty, well designed, and avant garde. This outlet has two floors, including women's knitwear, evening dresses, and even a collection of baby clothes.

Kashiyama, via della Spiga 19 (tel. 781-469), could outfit practically any male with a *Gentleman's Quarterly* look. Clothes are elegantly casual, including designs by Basile, Montana, and several other famous designers. The ideal client of this store would be in his 20s and very thin.

Spiga 31 di R. Bilancioni, via della Spiga 31 (tel. 793-502), sells informal and youth-oriented clothes for women.

Gianfranco Ferre, via della Spiga 32 (tel. 798-170) is the women's outlet, the only one in Milan, for this famous designer.

Smart Lady, via della Spiga 42 (tel. 760-001-001), is the kind of women's boutique where each item is brought out for a client's approval and displayed on well-polished granite tables. Inventory includes womens underwear, panties, lace-trimmed slips, and a carefully selected collection of sweaters, nightgowns, and dresses in cotton, linen, and silk.

In the same neighborhood, you will approach—

Via San Andrea

Giorgio Armani, via San Andrea 9 (tel. 792-757), is housed with the style we've come to expect from Armani in a large aircraft hangar type of showroom. The format combines both men's and women's clothes with panache.

Lange, via San Andrea 11 (tel. 794-133), is a specialist in unusual blouses and risqué evening dresses, usually in silk voiles. Women's suits are in eye-catching styles that are sometimes perfect for daytime.

Domenico Piva, via San Andrea 1 (tel. 760-006-78), next door to the Museo di Milano, sells an important collection of 17th- and 18th-century Venetian and Milanese furniture, paintings, ceramics, and objets d'art.

Fendi, via San Andrea 16 (tel. 791-617), contains a small collection of furs, a chic clientele, and a spacious format of women's purses, shoes, and a small rack of expensive, well-tailored dresses.

Comme des Garçons, via San Andrea 10A (tel. 760-009-05), is one of the most unusual stores in the district, designed in a monochromatic combination of Japanese simplicity and avant-garde clothes, many of which are made from linen. Rei Kawakubo is the female designer who produces many of these garments that appeal to the ultra chic.

Miscellany

Other shops in Milan, a random sampling, include the following:

Fratelli Prada, Galleria Vittorio Emanuele (tel. 876-979), in the gallery near the duomo, offers luggage, wallets, umbrellas for men and women, and attractively styled shoes for women.

Bernasconi, in the Galleria Vittorio Emanuele (tel. 872-334), founded in 1872, is one of the oldest and most prestigious silver vendors in Milan.

Rizzoli, Galleria Vittorio Emanuele 79 (tel. 807-348). One of the biggest publishers in Italy operates its own well-stocked bookstore in the famous covered gallery near the duomo. An excellent selection is offered, including titles in English.

Renco, corso Venezia 29 (tel. 76-000-235). Many of the taller, broader, bigger, and better-developed men and women of North America used to hunt in vain for Italian clothing that would fit properly. Today the sartorial skills of Italy can be appreciated even by full-figure sizes, thanks to this well-stocked store where even designer clothes come in sizes considered "larger than normal" in Italy.

La Rinascente, piazza del Duomo (tel. 88-52), bills itself with accuracy as Italy's largest fashion department store. Here you'll find a vast array of clothing for men, women, and children. The basement carries a wide variety of giftware for the home, including handiwork from all regions of Italy. The information desk on the ground floor will answer your questions. Enjoy a refreshing break in your shopping with a drink at the bar or an excellent meal in the seventh-floor restaurant.

Incidentally, the name of the store was suggested by the poet Gabriele d'Annunzio, for which he received a compensation of 5,000 lire. The store was officially opened right before Christmas in the closing year of World War I, but it burned down on Christmas Eve. Rebuilt, it later met total destruction in an Allied bombing in 1943. But it has always rallied back from disaster and now is better than ever, particularly in its choice of merchandise.

Finally, visitors should know about a shopping area specializing in low-cost, youth-oriented clothes including jeans, punk-rock sneakers, and informal printed shirts and blouses. The clothes on **via Torino** are a long way from being couture, but if you need another garment during your stopover in Milan, you can take a walk up this street near the duomo.

MILAN NIGHTLIFE

As in Rome, many of the top nightclubs in Milan shut down for the summer, when the cabaret talent and the bar girls pack their bags and head for the hills or the seashore. Some clubs that remain open are more suited for Milano factory owners spending a night on the town with salesmen from Central Europe. Tabs tend to be stratospheric, entertainment second rate, and the atmosphere in many of them depressing.

Opera

If you have only a night for Milan and are here mid-December to May, try to attend a performance at the world-famous **Teatro alla Scala,** piazza della Scala (tel. 88-791). Built to the designs of Piermarini, the neoclassic opera house was restored after World War II bomb damage. The greatest opera stars appear here, and the Milanese first-night audience is considered among the hardest to please in the world. Tickets are also extremely hard to come by.

Opera lovers will also want to visit the **Museo Teatrale alle Scala** (tel. 805-3418), in the same building. Charging 4,000 lire ($3.05) for admission, it is open from 9:30 a.m. to noon and 2 to 6 p.m.; closed Sunday. Launched in 1913, it contains a rich collection of historical mementos and records of the heady world of opera. Among them are busts and portraits of such artists as Beethoven, Chopin, Donizetti, Verdi, and Puccini. Two halls are devoted to Verdi alone, including scores written in his own hand and the spinet on which he learned to play. Rossini's eyeglasses and his pianoforte tuning key are in a vitrine, and there are many other such treasures, including a death-cast of Chopin's left hand. A small gallery honors Toscanini, with his batons, medals, and pince-nez on display. One of the greatest thrills for opera lovers who may not be in Milan at the time of a performance at La Scala—or may not be able to get tickets—will be the view from the third floor. From here, you can look down on the theater's ornate auditorium with its velvet draperies.

Favorite Bars

Piano bars are all the rage in town. Many of these cozy bars are in the Brera district, among them **Club 2,** via Formentini 2 (tel. 873-533), where in addition to show tunes you also hear good jazz. Drinks cost around 9,000 lire ($6.85) at the piano bar, 18,000 lire ($13.75) in the jazz club. The establishment is open from 8:30 p.m. to 2:30 a.m. daily.

Moscatelli, corso Garibaldi 93 (tel. 655-4602), in the Brera district, has been out of fashion for so long that it's almost fashionable again. This bar has a pillar in its center, which is decorated by a mirror mosaic. Its video jukebox has brought entertainment to thousands. Try a glass of their sparkling wine and soak up the oldtime ambience any day except Monday from 10:30 a.m. to 7:30 p.m. and 9:30 p.m. to 2 a.m. A bottle of wine averages 18,000 lire ($13.75).

A Video Bar

Facsimile, via Tallone 11 (tel. 738-0635), is a popular rendezvous point where rock-conscious Milanese can commune with their favorite video stars in living color. The avant-garde decor is almost entirely gray and red, and the rock video might be the same kinds of images a New Yorker might view on a lonely Friday night. There are outdoor tables for star-gazing. Drinks range from 1,000 lire (75¢) to 3,500 lire ($2.65). The bar is open from 7 p.m. to 2 a.m. daily except Thursday.

Jazz

Il Capolinea, via Ludovico il Moro 119 (tel. 470-524). In the early '60s when Giorgio Vanni, the jazz drummer, founded this place, it was the first of its kind in the city. It's on the border of the Navigli district, reached by tram 19, which heads for the "end of the line." Some of the greatest names in jazz have appeared here. Drinks cost from 8,000 lire ($6.10), and the club is open every day but Monday from 8 p.m. to 2 a.m.

Floor Shows

Club Astoria, piazza Santa Maria Beltrade 2 (tel. 808-787), is a popular night-club, one of the most frequented in town, especially by the expense-account junket crowd. When there's a performance, a drink might cost around 30,000 lire ($22.75), which seems to take the place of a cover charge. Hours are 10 p.m. to 4 a.m. daily.

Discos

Prego Club, via Besenzanica 3 (tel. 407-5653), is one of the best-known discos in Milan, in an electronics-filled labyrinth that contains a big dance floor, a wide range of colored lights, and the kinds of uninhibited aura that has made it one of the "historic" discos of Milan. Light shows and films are shown on the walls, except when there's a live concert, of course. The recorded music is kept up-to-date. Every night there is a different show, and they are priced according to what is being presented, ranging in price from 10,000 lire ($7.60) to 20,000 lire ($15.25), including a first drink. The club is open nightly except Monday from 10 p.m. to either 3 a.m. or 4 a.m.

Rolling Stone, corso XXII Marzo 32 (tel. 733-172), features heavy-metal rock and a difficult-to-define ocean of aggressively energetic exhibitionists in their teens and 20s. Members of the crowd often include visiting rock stars from many nations who have business of one kind or another in Milan. Entrance ranges from 12,000 lire ($9.10) and up, and the club is open from 11 p.m. to 2:30 a.m. They don't have a fixed closing day.

A Gay Club

No Ties, foro Bonaparte 68 (tel. 872-780), is a stylish hangout for stylish gay men in Milan, although it draws straights as well. The inspiration for the layout probably came from the United States, as well as a few of the participants, although you get a representative cross section of Europe. The establishment, open from 11 p.m. to 3 a.m., is closed on Monday, Tuesday, and Wednesday. You should count on spending 12,000 lire ($9.10) to 15,000 lire ($11.50) for a first drink and door charge. If you show up in a tie, it will be clipped off.

Films

English-language films are shown in their original version at **Angelicum,** piazza San Angelo 2 (tel. 655-1712). Tickets usually cost 7,000 lire ($5.30). Doors open at 5 p.m.

Using Milan as a base, you can drive 31 miles on the motorway northeast of the city to—

2. Bergamo

A two-in-one city, Bergamo is crowned by the hilltop Città Alta, the old walled town fortified by the Venetians during their long centuries of dominance. With the

Bergamesque Alps in the background, it makes for a Lombard setting of dramatic intensity, earning the praise of Stendhal. At its base is the more modern lower town, with its wide streets and shops.

The telephone area code for Bergamo is 035.

SIGHTSEEING IN BERGAMO

For the sightseer, the higher the climb the more rewarding the view. By funicular, you can go from the upper town to the hill of San Vigilo crowning it at its loftiest point. The Città Alta is replete with narrow circuitous streets, old squares, splendid monuments, and imposing and austere medieval architecture that prompted D'Annunzio to call it a city of muteness.

The heart of the upper town is the **piazza Vecchia,** which has witnessed most of the town's upheavals and a parade of conquerors ranging from Attila to the Nazis. On the square is the Palazzo della Ragione, the town hall; an 18th-century fountain designed by Contarini; and the Palazzo Nuova of Scamozzi, the library of Bergamo.

A vaulted arcade connects the piazza Vecchia with the piazza del Duomo. Opening onto the latter is the cathedral of Bergamo, with little bite in its baroque teeth. The church on this square that is interesting is **Santa Maria Maggiore.** D'Annunzio, in rough translation, said it seemed "to blossom in a rose-filtered light." Built in the Romanesque style, the church was founded in the 12th century. At a much later date it was baroqued on its interior, with its disturbingly busy ceiling. The Flemish and Tuscan tapestries displayed are exquisite, incorporating such themes as the *Annunciation* and the *Crucifixion.* The choir dates from the 16th century, having been designed by Lotto. Fronting the main altar is a series of inlaid panels by Capodiferro di Lovere, depicting such themes as Noah's Ark and David and Goliath.

Also opening onto the cathedral square is the **Colleoni Chapel,** honoring the already inflated ego of the Venetian military hero. The Renaissance chapel, its inlaid marble façade reminiscent of Florence, was designed by Giovanni Antonio Amadeo, who is chiefly known for his creation of the Certosa in Pavia, south of Milan. For the *condottiere,* Amadeo built an elaborate tomb, surmounted by a gilded equestrian statue (Colleoni, of course, was the subject of one of the most famous equestrian statues in the world, now standing on a square in Venice). The tomb sculpted for the soldier's daughter, Medea, is much less elaborate. Giovanni Battista Tiepolo painted most of the frescoes on the ceiling.

Facing the cathedral is the baptistery, dating from the mid-14th century and rebuilt at the end of the 19th century. The original architect of the octagonal building was Giovanni da Campione.

In the lower town is Bergamo's chief attraction, the—

Carrara Academy

Filled with a wide-ranging collection of the works of home-grown artists, as well as Venetian and Tuscan masters, the academy draws art lovers from all over the world. The gallery charges 2,000 lire ($1.50). Throughout the year, the gallery is open from 9:30 a.m. to 12:30 p.m. and 2:30 to 5:30 p.m. It is closed on Tuesday, however. The location is at piazza Giacomo Carrara 82A (tel. 339-425). On the top floor are the most important works—so head there first if your time is limited.

The Botticelli portrait of *Giuliano di Medici* is well known, and another room contains three different versions of Giovanni Bellini's favorite subject, the *Madonna and Child.* It's interesting to compare his work with that of his brother-in-law, Andrea Mantegna, whose *Madonna and Child* is also displayed, as is Vittore Carpaccio's *Nativity of Maria,* seemingly inspired by Flemish painters.

Farther along you encounter a most original treatment of the old theme of the "Madonna and Child"—this one the work of Cosmè Tura of Ferrara. Also displayed are three tables of a predella by Lotto; a portrait of the *Holy Family with St.*

Catherine (wonderful composition) by Lotto, and Raphael's *St. Sebastian.* The entire wall space of another room is taken up with paintings by Moroni (1523–1578), a local artist who seemingly did portraits of everybody who could afford it. In the salons to follow, foreign masters, such as Rubens, Van der Meer, and Jan Brueghel, are represented, along with Guardi's architectural renderings of Venice and Longhi's continuing parade of Venetian high society.

WHERE TO STAY

The best hostelry in town is the **Hotel Excelsior San Marco,** piazza della Repubblica 6, 24100 Bergamo (tel. 035/232-132), a modern establishment at the edge of a city park dotted with flowers. It's actually about midway between the old and new towns, both of which might be visible from the balcony of your room. The lobby area contains a small bar, reddish stone accents, and low-slung leather chairs. The most prominent theme of the ceiling frescoes is that of the lion of St. Mark. The in-house restaurant, Tino Fontana, is reviewed separately (see below). Rooms are attractively furnished and most comfortable, with singles renting for 115,000 lire ($87.50) daily, while doubles cost 175,000 lire ($133). Half board, with meals taken in the excellent restaurant, is available at 160,800 lire ($122) daily in a single and 134,400 lire ($102) per person, based on double occupancy.

Hotel Capello d'Oro, viale Papa Giovanni XXIII 12, 24100 Bergamo (tel. 035/232-503), is a renovated corner building on a busy street in the center of the newer section of town. The 19th-century façade has been covered with stucco, and the public rooms and bedrooms are functional, high ceilinged, and clean, and might be suitable for an overnight stopover. Rooms are adequately furnished. The cost of a single is 70,000 lire ($53.25) daily, and a double goes for 79,500 lire ($60.50), with breakfast included.

Agnello d'Oro, via Gombito 22, 24100 Bergamo (tel. 035/249-883), is a little spellbinder, an intimate, old-style country inn right in the heart of the Città Alta, facing a handkerchief square with a splashing fountain. It's a beguiling background for good food or a good bed. When you enter the cozy reception lounge, you should ring an old bell to bring the owner away from the kitchen. You dine at wooden tables, sitting on carved ladderback chairs. Among the à la carte offerings are three worthy regional specialties. Try casoncelli alla bergamasca, a succulent ravioli dish or quaglie farcite (quail stuffed and accompanied by slices of polenta). If someone chooses the risotto al profumo di bosco (with mushrooms and truffle cream), he or she is presented with a dish painted by the manager. A complete meal costs 30,000 lire ($22.75) to 55,000 lire ($41.75). The room becomes the tavern lounge between meals. Wine is served in unusual pitchers. The restaurant is closed Monday and in January.

The bedrooms are quite good (some beds set in recesses) and nicely furnished. Ask for one of the front rooms, with French doors, heavy shutters, and miniature balconies with potted vines. Every accommodation has a private bath. The rate in a single is 32,200 lire ($24.50) daily, 53,400 lire ($40.50) for a double.

WHERE TO DINE

In the heart of the Città Alta, the **Taverna dei Colleoni,** piazza Vecchia 7 (tel. 232-596), is known to many a gourmet who journeys here to try regional dishes of exceptional merit. Architecturally it continues the design concept of the square. The sidewalk tables are popular in summer, and the view is part of the reward for dining there. Inside, the decor suggests medievalism, but with a fresh approach. The ceiling is vaulted, the chairs are leather, and there's a low-floor dining room with a wood-burning fireplace. Specialties include gioielli alla Colleoni, tagliatelle alla Colleoni, and filetto di bue (beef filet) alla Colleoni. A complete meal costs 45,000 lire ($32.50) to 80,000 lire ($60.75). The restaurant is open from 12:30 to 2:30 p.m. and 7:30 to 9:30 p.m. daily except Monday; closed the first three weeks in August.

Ristorante Tino Fontana, in the Hotel Excelsior San Marco, piazza della

Repubblica 6 (tel. 215-321), accessible from the lobby of the best hotel in town, was renovated in 1984 into a format that qualifies it as the best-appointed restaurant in town. The modern curved stairwell leading up to it is covered with birch paneling. The spacious design is laid out like a garden terrace, with balconies visible. Menu items could include asparagus milanese, lamb cutlets in a thyme-flavored cream sauce, risotto with artichoke hearts, fettuccine with pesto, herbed salmon with chive sauce, veal Cordon Bleu with asparagus tips, and a house version of tagliatelle alla romana, with prosciutto, walnuts, eggs, and a robustly flavored meat sauce. Expect to pay 60,000 lire ($45.50) to 70,000 lire ($53.25) for a full dinner. The restaurant is closed on Sunday but open other days from noon to 2:30 p.m. and 7:30 to 10:30 p.m.

Antico Ristorante dell'Angelo, borgo Santa Caterina 55 (tel. 237-103). Don't be misled by the "antico" in the restaurant's title. That may suggest that it's old-fashioned; however, the cuisine here leans strongly toward the kinds of nouvelle creation that can turn traditional Italian recipes into unusual treats with undeniable flair. Pierangelo Cornaro is the owner, and his staff turns out such specialties as tortelloni stuffed with sea bass and served with a fresh basil sauce, filet of sea bass with olive oil and an essence of tomatoes, savarin of rice and sole, baby partridge cooked in grappa, and what the chef has named a "violin" of calves' brains with grapes. Each of the dessert pastries is made in-house and might be the perfect way to end a big meal here. Expect to spend from 60,000 lire ($45.50) for a complete meal. The restaurant, open from noon to 3 p.m. and 7:45 to 10:30 p.m., is closed every Monday and for the last three weeks of August.

Ristorante da Vittorio, viale Papa Giovanni XXIII 21 (tel. 218-060), is a well-known and popular restaurant on the main boulevard of the newer section of town. Set on a corner, the establishment lights its entrance with lanterns. You enter a long and narrow hallway, richly paneled with dark wood and, in summer, lined with tables laden with all the fruits of the Italian harvest. The menu is amazingly complete, offering more than a dozen kinds of risotto, more than 20 kinds of pasta, and around 30 meat dishes, as well as just about every kind of fish that swims, somewhere, in the waters around Italy. The service is efficient, all of it directed by members of the Cerea family who by now are among the best-known citizens of Bergamo. Expect to spend 70,000 lire ($53.25) to 90,000 lire ($68.50) in this attractive place. Open from 12:30 to 2:30 p.m. and 7:30 to 9:30 p.m.; it is closed on Wednesday and in August.

---

3. Brescia

Near lakes Garda and Iseo, Brescia is an ancient town, the capital of a province of the same name. It is on the main route between Verona and Milan and makes for a good stopover. In the medieval period it was a duchy, but it has known many rulers, including the Romans, the Scaligeri of Verona, the Visconti of Milan, and the Venetians. One of the most disastrous moments in its history was the looting and burning of the town by French troops under Gaston de Foix in 1512. The ferocity of its fight for independence from the Austrians in 1849 earned for it the title of Lioness of Italy. Its last battle was in the spring of 1945, when Allied forces seized the town. Brescia's telephone area code is 030.

THE SIGHTS

The historic heart of town is the **piazza della Loggia,** on which the Brescian Renaissance reached its fullest bloom architecturally. The Palazzo della Loggia dates from 1492, but was actually built in stages. The architecture on the square certainly owes a debt to other cities. The top part of the loggia evokes a Palladio design in Vicenza, and the clock tower (*orologio*), with its two "moors," is reminiscent of a similar tower on the piazza San Marco in Venice. Also opening onto the square is the Monte Vecchio di Pietà, dating from 1484.

A short walk away will take you to the **piazza del Duomo,** where you'll find both an old and a "new" cathedral, as well as the Broletto, the latter built in medieval times as the first town hall. It is joined by a tower, called the Torre del Popolo. The Duomo Vecchio, from the 11th century, is often referred to as the Rotunda because of its shape. It was erected over a church dating from the 6th century A.D., and modernization has destroyed much of what must have been its original drama (be sure to explore the crypt). Adjoining is the rather juiceless "new cathedral" designed by Giovanni Battista Lantana in the 17th century.

Actually, the most interesting attraction in Brescia is the—

Tosio-Martinengo Civic Picture Gallery, via Martinengo da Barco 1 (tel. 59-120), off the piazza Moretto in the Martinengo da Barco Palace, is a *pinacoteca,* filled with the most important works of the artists of the Brescian school, as well as with a scattered sampling from the old masters of northern Italy. Among the more notable works are Raphael's *The Redeemer* and Lotto's *The Adoration of the Shepherds.* One salon is devoted to the leading painter of Brescia, Moretto (see his *Annunciation* and his *Christ and an Angel* from the 16th century), and to Romanino. Works by other leading Lombard artists, such as Moroni, Foppa (the chief force in the early Renaissance in Brescia), and Savoldo, are also displayed. The gallery is open from 10 a.m. to 12:45 p.m. and 2 to 6 p.m. daily except Monday from June to the end of September. From October to May, hours are 9 a.m. to 12:45 p.m. and 2 to 5 p.m. daily except Monday. Admission is 2,000 lire ($1.50).

Try also to visit the Capitolium, housing the **Civic Museum of the Roman Period,** at the piazza del Foro. This Corinthian temple, built by Vespasian in A.D. 73, contains a prize exhibit: the *Statue of Victory,* a Roman bronze (discovered in 1826) that was inspired by Praxiteles and his pupils. Additional exhibits include such bronzes as the *Bacchic Ass,* as well as a collection of bas-reliefs, ceramics, and mosaics. From June to September, it is open daily except Monday from 10 a.m. to 12:45 p.m. and 2 to 6 p.m. From October to May, hours are 9 a.m. to 12:45 p.m. and 2 to 5 p.m. daily except Monday. Admission is 2,000 lire ($1.50).

WHERE TO STAY

The top choice is the **Hotel Vittoria,** via della Giornate 10, 25121 Brescia (tel. 030/280-061). Originally built in 1933, and thoroughly renovated in 1986, this hotel is considered one of the pure examples of art deco architecture in Brescia. In the center of the city, midway between three of the most historic squares, it boasts a marble-sheathed façade of orange and brown which extends into the interior of the lobby. On the premises are a French provincial-style bar, a restaurant, and 65 comfortably modern bedrooms. Each of these has a decor of warm earth tones and a private bath. The only accommodations without private facilities are two interconnected rooms (actually a suite) sharing a common private bath. Year-round rates are 166,500 lire ($127) daily in a single, rising to 213,000 lire ($162) in a double. Breakfast is included, but state tax is an extra 19%. A privately owned parking garage lies immediately behind the hotel.

Another leading choice is the **Master,** via Apollonia 72, 25128 Brescia (tel. 030/399-037), offering high-grade comfort in its 76 well-furnished rooms. These rent for 100,000 lire ($76) daily in a single, 160,000 lire ($122) in a double. The service is polite, and, all in all, the Master makes for a comfortable overnight stopover. Drinks and occasional buffets are presented in the garden. There is also a solarium. The hotel lies slightly north of the center of town in the "Castello zona."

Ambasciatori, via Santa Maria Crocifissa di Rosa 90, 25124 Brescia (tel. 030/308-461), is another suitable choice, which lies even farther afield than the Master. You reach it by heading north of the castle district along via Lombroso. It's a modern building in a good position, renting a total of 66 comfortably furnished rooms. These cost from 58,000 lire ($44) daily in a single, 90,000 lire ($68.50) in a double. The hotel also has a good restaurant, serving meals from 25,000 lire ($19) up. There is no service on Sunday and in August.

Igea, viale Stazione 15, 25124 Brescia (tel. 030/44-221), is an economical choice in the station area. It offers a total of 71 moderately comfortable bedrooms at a good price: 65,000 lire ($49.50) daily in a single, 110,000 lire ($83.50) in a double. The place is reliable if your needs are not too demanding. It has a suitable restaurant, serving inexpensively priced meals, costing from 25,000 lire ($19). The restaurant is closed Sunday.

WHERE TO DINE

One of the main reasons to go to Brescia is **La Sosta,** via San Martino della Battaglia 20, off Vittorio Emanuele II (tel. 295-603). The cuisine is excellent and the setting beguiling, making "The Stop" a well-named establishment. It's a preserved 17th-century stable, converted into a glamorous dining hall. At first glance it seems more like a vaulted chapel of a royal palace, indicating that its former equine occupants were given the regal treatment. Tables are set along the aisles, the naves, and around tall marble pillars. Around the walls are equestrian paintings and prints. Look carefully at the pillars and you'll see large rings where horses were once tied up. In the centeraisle is a 20-foot food display table that guests preview before taking their seats. Delectable dishes include a cheese-and-shrimp soufflé get you started, perhaps spaghetti carbonara or an array of outstanding antipasti. Other selections include fresh marinated salmon with green peppercorns, sole and salmon with celery and champagne, and marinated deviled quail. Meals cost 40,000 lire ($30.50) to 60,000 lire ($45.50). If you use the side entrance, be sure to catch the vast open hearth where meats and fish are grilled. A few tables are set around the fire for more informal dining, a choice spot on nippy evenings. Hours are 12:30 to 2:30 p.m. and 7:30 to 9:30 p.m. Closed Monday and the last three weeks in August.

4. Cremona

This city of the violin is found on the Po River plain, 53 miles east of Milan. Music lovers from all over the world flock here, as it was the birthplace of Monteverdi (the father of modern opera), and of Stradivari (latinized to Stradivarius), who made violin-making an art. Born in Cremona in 1644, Antonio Stradivari became the most famous name in the world of violin-making, far exceeding the skill of his teacher, Andrea Amati. The third great family name associated with the craft, Guarneri, was also of Cremona.

At the **Antonio Stradivari Museum,** via Palestro 17 (tel. 23-349), you can see a collection of models, designs, and shapes and tools of Stradivari. It is open from Tuesday through Saturday from 10 a.m. to 12:15 p.m. and 3:15 p.m. to 5:45 p.m. On Sunday, it is open from 9:30 a.m. to 12:15 p.m., and it's closed on Monday all year. Admission is 1,000 lire (75¢).

Most of the attractions of the city are centered on the harmonious **piazza del Comune.** The Romanesque cathedral dates from 1107, although its actual consecration was in 1190. Over the centuries, Gothic, Renaissance, even baroque elements were incorporated. In the typical Lombard style, the pillars of the main portal rest on lions, an architectural detail matched in the nearby octagonal baptistery from the 13th century. Surmounting the portal are some marble statues in the vestibule, with a Madonna and Bambino in the center. The rose window over it, from the 13th century, is inserted in the façade like a medallion.

Inside, the cathedral consists of one nave flanked by two aisles. The pillars are draped with Flemish tapestries. Five arches on each side of the nave are admirably frescoed by such artists as Boccaccio Boccaccino (see his *Annunciation* and other scenes from the life of the Madonna, painted in the early 16th century). Other artists who worked on the frescoes were Gian Francesco Bembo (*Adoration of the Wise Men* and *Presentation at the Temple*), Gerolamo Romanino (scenes from the life of Christ), and Altobello Melone (a *Last Supper*).

Beside the cathedral is the **Torrazzo,** dating from the latter 13th century and enjoying a reputation as the tallest campanile (bell tower) in Italy. From the same period, and also opening onto the piazza, are the Loggia dei Militi and the Palazzo Communale in the Gothic style as uniquely practiced in Lombardy.

The Cremona telephone area code is 0372.

WHERE TO STAY

Roads from many parts of northern Italy converge on the busy square on which the comfortably contemporary **Hotel Continental,** piazza della Libertà 26, 26100 Cremona (tel. 0372/434-141), stands. There isn't that much of a difference between this hotel and scores of other pleasantly up-to-date hotels in Italy, except for the obvious pride in the musical history of Cremona that is displayed by the staff. They will be eager to point out the illuminated glass cases built into the lobby walls. These contain a copy of a violin made by Stradivarius and an original by Amati. There are also instruments made by master luthiers of Cremona, some of whom seem to be on a first-name basis with the management. A bronze bust of Verdi looks out over the lobby. A restaurant capable of seating 500 people is on the premises. Each of the hotel's rooms has a private bath, as well as a phone, TV, and sound-insulated windows. Doubles cost 115,000 lire ($87.50) daily; singles, 75,000 lire ($57).

Motel Agip, località San Felice, 26100 Cremona (tel. 0372/434-101), is at the San Felice exit of the superhighway between Piacenza and Brescia. Many a late-night traveler in this part of Italy has been rescued by the availability of a room in this member of a nationwide chain. Checking in has a certain ease. The motel is a modern establishment with 77 comfortable bedrooms, outfitted with bath, hairdryer, color TV, phone, and refrigerator. Rates go from 74,000 lire ($56.25) daily in a single to 126,000 lire ($95.75) in a double. All rooms are soundproofed against the noise of the nearby highway. A good restaurant on the premises serves copious amounts of food. Parking is also easy here.

WHERE TO DINE

Near the duomo, **Ceresole,** via Ceresole 4 (tel. 23-322), is an elegant and well-known culinary institution of the city. Behind a masonry façade on a narrow street, the establishment has windows covered with elaborate wrought-iron grills. The cuisine is prepared by Lucia Giura and Anna Freghieri, whose husbands, Rino and Saverio Botte, work in the dining room. Reservations are important. Specialties include rice with rhubarb, a wide array of delicately seasoned fish (some of them served with fresh seasonal mushrooms and truffles), whiting with a green peppercorn–flavored cream sauce, and grilled baby piglet. Some of the dishes are based on long-standing and time-honored recipes of the region, including spaghetti alla marinara and ravioli with radicchio. Full meals cost from 50,000 lire ($38) and are served from 12:30 to 2:30 p.m. and 7:30 to 9:30 p.m. The restaurant is closed Sunday evening, all day Monday, and for most of August.

Antica Trattoria del Cigno, via del Cigno 7 (tel. 21-361), is a popular restaurant attracting a crowd of local residents, who appreciate the historic atmosphere and well-prepared Italian meals. You'll spend around 30,000 lire ($22.75) for a full meal. The restaurant is open from 12:30 to 2:30 p.m. and 7:30 to 10:30 p.m.; closed all day Sunday and at lunch Monday.

5. Mantua (Mantova)

Once a duchy, Mantua knew a flowering of art and architecture under the ruling Gonzaga dynasty that held sway over the town for nearly four centuries. Originally an Etruscan settlement, later a Roman colony, it has known many conquerors, including the French and Austrians in the 19th century. Virgil, the great Latin poet, has remained its most famous son (he was born outside the city in a place called Andes).

Mantua is an imposing city, at times even austere, despite its situation near three lakes, Superior, di Mezzo, and Inferiore. It is easily reached from a number of cities in northern Italy, lying about 25 miles from Verona, 95 miles from Milan, and 42 miles from Parma. It is very much a city of the past.

The telephone area code for Mantua is 0376.

THE SIGHTS

If you're just passing through, at least try to save time for its chief attraction—

The Gonzaga Palace

At the piazza Sordello, the ducal apartments of the Gonzagas may be visited. With more than 500 rooms and 15 courtyards, the group of palaces is considered by many to be the most remarkable in Italy—certainly when judged from the standpoint of size. Like Rome, the compound wasn't built in a day, or even in a century. The earlier buildings, erected to the specifications of the Bonacolsi family, date from the 13th century. The latter 14th century and early 15th saw the rise of the Castle of St. George, designed by Bartolino da Novara. The Gonzagas also added the Palatine Basilica of St. Barbara by Bertani.

Over the years the historic monument of Renaissance splendor has suffered the loss of many of the art treasures collected by Isabella d'Este during the 15th and 16th centuries, in her efforts to turn Mantua into "La Città dell' Arte." Her descendants, the Gonzagas, sold the most precious objects to King Charles I of England in 1628, and two years later, most of the rich collection remaining was looted during the sack of Mantua. Even Napoleon did his bit by carting off some of the objects still there.

The painting collection is rich, including works by Tintoretto and Sustermans, and a "cut-up" Rubens. The display of classical statuary is impressive, gathered mostly from the various Gonzaga villas at the time of Maria Teresa of Austria. Among the more inspired sights are the Zodiac Room, the Hall of Mirrors with vaulted ceiling constructed at the beginning of the 17th century, the River Chamber, the Apartment of Paradise, the Apartment of Troia with frescoes by Giulio Romano, and a scale reproduction of the Holy Staircase in Rome. The most-interesting and best-known room is the Camera degli Sposi (bridal chamber), frescoed by Andrea Mantegna in the castle. Winged cherubs appear over a balcony at the top of the ceiling. Look for a curious dwarf and a mauve-hatted portrait of King Christian I of Denmark. There are many paintings by Domenico Fetti, along with a splendid series of nine pieces of tapestry woven in Brussels and based on cartoons by Raphael. A cycle of frescoes on the age of chivalry by Pisanello has been recently discovered.

A guide takes visitors on a tour pointing out the many highlights. The Ducal Palace of Mantua is open daily from 9 a.m. to 2 p.m. all year. It is also open except on

Sunday and Monday from 2:30 to 6:30 p.m. in summer, to 5 p.m. in March and October, and to 4:30 p.m. from November to February. Admission is 4,000 lire ($3.05). For more information, telephone 320-283.

Two other sightseeing attractions include—

The Basilica of Sant'Andrea

Built to the specifications of Leon Battista Alberti, this church opens into the piazza Mantegna, just off the piazza delle Erbe, with its fruit vendors. The actual work on the basilica, started in the 15th century, was carried out by a pupil of Alberti's, Luca Fancelli. However, before Alberti died in 1472, it is said that he knew he had "buried the Middle Ages." The church was finally completed in 1782 when Juvara crowned it with a dome. As you enter, the first chapel to your left contains the tomb of the great Mantegna (the paintings are by the artist's son, except for the *Holy Family* by the old master himself). The sacristan will light it for you. In the crypt you'll encounter one of the more fanciful legends in the history of church relics: St. Andrew's claim to possess the blood of Christ, "the gift" of St. Longinus, the Roman soldier who is said to have pierced his side. Beside the basilica is a campanile (bell tower), dating from 1414.

Palazzo Te

This Renaissance palace (tel. 323-266), built in the 16th century, is known for its frescoes by Giulio Romano and his pupils. At the edge of the city, it is reached on viale Te Federigo II. Federigo II, one of the Gonzagas, ordered the villa built as a place where he could slip away to see his mistress. The name is said to have been derived from the word *Tejeto,* which in the local dialect means "a cut to let the waters flow out." This was once marshland drained by the Gonzagas for their horse farm. The frescoes in the various rooms, dedicated to everything from horses to Psyche, rely on mythology for subject matter. The Room of the Giants, the best known, has a scene depicting heaven venting its rage on the giants who have moved threateningly against it.

To visit the palace, you must go on a guided tour. Hours are 9:30 a.m. to 12:30 p.m. and 2:30 to 5 p.m. Tuesday through Saturday. Sunday hours are 9 a.m. to 12:30 p.m. from June to mid-August. Admission is 2,500 lire ($1.90). Closed Monday.

HOTELS IN MANTUA

Near the center of the old city, stands the **Rechigi Hotel,** via P. F. Calvi 30, 46100 Mantua (tel. 0376/320-781), a comfortable modern hotel, one of the best in Mantua. Its lobby is warmly furnished, with an alcove bar. The owners maintain the property well, and they have decorated the attractively furnished rooms in good taste. Singles rent for 85,000 lire ($64.50) daily and doubles go for 120,000 lire ($91.25). All accommodations contain modern bath, phone, and air conditioning. There's a parking garage and a restaurant on the premises.

Mantegna Hotel, via Fabio Filzi 10, 46100 Mantua (tel. 0376/350-315), is in a commercial section of town, a few blocks from one of the entrances to the old city. This six-story hotel has bandbox lines and a façade of light-gray tiles. The lobby is accented with gray-and-red marble slabs, along with enlargements of details of paintings by (as you probably guessed) Mantegna. About half the units look out over a sunny rear courtyard, although the rooms facing the street are fairly quiet as well. The hotel represents good value for the rates charged: 55,000 lire ($41.75) daily in a single with bath, 85,000 lire ($64.50) in a double with bath. If you're on a serious budget, ask for a bathless double at 55,000 lire ($41.75).

Hotel Dante, via Corrado 54, 46100 Mantua (tel. 0376/326-425). Built in 1968, this boxily modern hotel was constructed with a car park under the recessed entrance area and a pleasant marble-accented interior, parts of which look out over a flagstone-covered courtyard. The hotel's location on a narrow and quiet street assures peaceful lodging. The 40 rooms, all with private bath and phone, rent for 55,000 lire ($41.75) daily in a single, 85,000 lire ($64.50) in a double.

DINING IN MANTUA

One of the best restaurants in town, **Ristorante II Cigno** (The Swan), piazza Carlo d'Arco 1 (tel. 327-101), is the kind of establishment that gastronomes would drive miles out of their way to enjoy. Its entrance lies under a terracotta plaque of the restaurant's namesake, a swan, which looks over a cobblestone square in the old part of Mantua. The exterior of the building is a faded ochre, with wrought-iron cross-hatched window bars within sight of easy parking on the piazza outside. After passing through a large entrance hall studded with trompe-l'oeil frescoes, gray and white cherubs cavorting in the ceiling coves, and Renaissance antiques, you'll come into the elegant dining room whose clear light and dozens of framed artworks make a meal here a rare celebration. Appetizers are likely to include a liver pâté, and you might follow that with the tortelli di zucca, and egg pasta with a filling of puréed pumpkin. Other dishes from which to choose are filet of eel in basil, a homemade terrine of duck and white truffles, sautéed liver with grapes, duck in duck-liver sauce lightly flavored with orange, a savory concoction of risotto with about six seasonal vegetables, and a juicy capon. Lamb is available in autumn and winter only. Expect to spend from 60,000 lire ($45.50) for a full meal. The restaurant, open from 12:30 to 2:30 p.m. and 7:30 to 9:30 p.m., is closed Monday and Tuesday. Reservations are recommended.

Competing with II Cigno for best-restaurant honors is **l'Aquila Nigra** (the Black Eagle), vicolo Bonacolsi 4 (tel. 350-651), in a Renaissance mansion on a narrow passageway by the Bonacolsi Palace. Among the excellent food served in the elegant rooms, which may come as a surprise after going through the more mundane entrance hall, you can choose from such dishes as pike from the Mincio River, called luccio, served with salsa verdi and polenta, as well as other specialties of the region. You might order a pasta or the gnocchi alle ortiche (potato dumplings tinged with puréed nettles) as part of your meal, served from noon to 2:30 and 7:30 to 9:30 p.m. Expect to spend 35,000 lire ($26.50) to 45,000 lire ($34.25) for a complete dinner. The eagle folds its wings and rests on Sunday night and Monday. Reservations are advised.

Ristorante Romani, piazza delle Erbe 13 (tel. 323-627), has the advantage of being located under an ancient arcade on what might be the most beautiful square in Mantua. It's a cozy, intimate family-run establishment whose decor consists of hundreds of antique copper pots hanging randomly from the single barrel vault of the plaster ceiling. A well-stocked antipasti table is placed near the door, and it's loaded with delicacies. In summer, tables spill out into the square, offering guests a chance to drink in the surrounding architecture as well as the aromas from the kitchen. Specialties include agnolotti (a form of Mantovan tortellini) with meat, cheese, sage, and butter, as well as risotto alla mantovana (with pesto). Other palatable dishes include noodles with mushrooms or salmon, roast filet of veal (deboned and rolled), and a well-made blend of fagioli (white beans) with onions. A full meal with wine costs from 30,000 lire ($22.75). The restaurant is open from 12:30 to 2:30 p.m. and 7:30 to 9:30 p.m.; closed Wednesday night, all day Thursday, and in July.

---

6. Pavia

About 19 miles south of Milan, the **Certosa** (Charter House) of Pavia marks the pinnacle of the Renaissance statement in Lombardy. The Carthusian monastery is five miles north of the town of Pavia. Gian Galeazzo Visconti founded the Certosa in 1396, but it was not completed until years after. The result: one of the most harmonious structures in Italy.

The façade, studded with medallions and adorned with colored marble and sculptural work, was designed in part by Amadeo, who worked on the building in the latter 15th century. Inside, much of its rich decoration is achieved by frescoes reminiscent of an illustrated storybook. You'll find works by Perugino (*The Everlasting Father*) and Bernardino Luini (*Madonna and Child*). Gian Galeazzo Visconti, the founder of the Certosa, is buried in the north transept.

Through an elegantly decorated portal you enter the small cloisters, noted for their exceptional terracotta decorations. In the second and larger cloisters is a continuous chain of elaborate "cells," attached villas with their own private gardens and loggia. Admission free, the charterhouse keeps its longest hours from May to August when it's open daily from 9 to 11:30 a.m. and 2:30 to 6 p.m. In March and April and again in September and October, it's open from 9 to 11:30 a.m. and 2:30 to 5 p.m. From November through February, its hours are 9 to 11:30 a.m. and 2:30 to 4:30 p.m. Closed on Monday.

The telephone area code for Pavia is 0382.

DINING IN PAVIA

Chances are, you'll be in Pavia only for a meal, as most North American visitors return to Milan or press on to other destinations instead of spending the night. If it's good food you want, try one of the following recommendations:

Trattoria Ferrari-da Tino, via dei Mille 111 (tel. 31-033), is a typical trattoria-style restaurant with rustic accessories, known for its robust specialties. These include country-style ravioli, breast of duck, veal stew with onions, a heady mixture of fresh vegetables in puff pastry, tagliatelle with fresh asparagus tips, and other savory dishes. A full meal with wine costs around 35,000 lire ($26.50). Food is served from 12:30 to 2:30 p.m. and 7:30 to 9:30 p.m., but not on Sunday night, all day Monday, and from mid-July to the end of August.

Osteria della Madonna, via dei Liguri 28 (tel. 302-833). You'll be able to promenade through the center of the old city before climbing the steps of the historic building that houses this attractive restaurant. Your fellow diners come from any walk of Pavian life, and all of them are drawn by the efforts of the owner, Giuseppe Ferrari. At lunch, served from noon to 2:30 p.m., the menu is simple but wholesome, both tasty and filling, costing 20,000 lire ($15.25). In the evening, from 7:30 to 10 p.m., reservations are suggested when the concoctions get more elaborate. For example, you might be served medallions of veal in a mustard sauce, filet of turbot, or a selection of beef dishes. Count on paying about 35,000 lire ($26.50) for a full meal then. The restaurant closes every Sunday and in August.

PIEDMONT AND THE VALLE D'AOSTA

Towering, snow-capped alpine peaks; oleanders, poplars, and birch trees; sky-blue lakes; river valleys and flower-studded meadows; the chamois and the wild boar; medieval castles; Roman ruins and folklore; the taste of vermouth on home ground; Fiats and fashion—northwest Italy is a fascinating area to explore.

Piedmont is largely agricultural, although its capital, Turin, is one of Italy's front-ranking industrial cities (with more mechanics per square foot than in any other location in Europe). The influence of France is strongly felt, in both the dialect and the kitchen.

Valle d'Aosta (really a series of valleys) has traditionally been associated with Piedmont, but in 1948 it was given wide-ranging autonomy. Most of its residents (in this least-populated district in Italy) speak French. Closing in the Valle d'Aosta to the north on the French and Swiss frontiers are the tallest mountains in Europe, including Mont Blanc (15,780 feet), the Matterhorn (14,690 feet), and Monte Rosa (15,200 feet). The road tunnels of Great St. Bernard and Mont Blanc (opened in 1965) connect France and Italy.

---

1. Turin (Torino)

The capital of Piedmont, Turin gave birth to the Italian Risorgimento (unification). During the years when the United States was fighting its Civil War, Turin became the first capital of a unified Italy, a position it later lost to Florence. Much of the history of the city was associated with the house of Savoy, a dynasty that reigned for nine centuries, even presiding over the kingdom of Italy. Victor Emmanuel II, the king of Sardinia (incidentally, Turin was the capital of Sardinia), was proclaimed king of Italy in 1861. The family ruled, at times in name only, until the monarchy was abolished in 1946.

Following extensive World War II bombings, Turin found renewed prosperity, largely because of the Fiat manufacturers based there. The city has been called the

Detroit of Italy. Many buildings were destroyed, but much of its 17th- and 18th-century look remains. Turin is well laid out, with wide streets, historic squares, churches, and parks. For years it has had a reputation as the least visited and least known of Italy's major cities. Easily reached, Turin (Torino in Italian) is on the Po River, 140 miles west of Milan, 108 miles northeast of Genoa.

GETTING THERE AND ORIENTATION

Both Alitalia and ATI fly into the **Caselle Airport,** lying about nine miles north of Turin. Actually, this is quite an important airport, receiving international flights as well. Of course, Turin is a major rail terminus, with arrivals at **Stazione di Porta Nuova.** For example, it takes only 1½ hours to reach Milan by train from Turin, but anywhere from 9 to 11 hours to come from Rome, depending on the connection. Turin also has autostrada links. If you're coming from France via **Mont Blanc Tunnel,** you can pick up the autostrada at Aosta. You can also reach Turin by autostrada from both the French and Italian Rivieras, and there is an easy link from Milan.

The Stazione di Porta Nuova is in the very center of town. The **Po River,** which runs through Turin, lies to the east of the station. One of the main arteries running through Turin is **corso Vittorio Emanuele II,** directly north of the station. Turin is also a city of fashion, with excellent merchandise in its shops, and you'll want to walk along the major shopping street, **via Roma,** which begins north of the station, leading eventually to two squares that join each other, the piazza Castello and the piazza Reale. In the middle of via Roma, however, is the **piazza San Carlo,** which many consider the heartbeat of Turin.

Railway Station: The central station, or Stazione Centrale, Corso Vittorio Emanuele II (tel. 544-471), is where you are likely to arrive in Turin. It is in the heart of the city.

Airport: Most visitors will probably arrive in Turin by car or by train. However, Turin's Caselle Airport (tel. 57-781) has flights to such cities as London, Paris, and Frankfurt.

Taxi: To summon a taxi, phone 57-30.

PRACTICAL FACTS

For Turin, the **telephone area code** is 011. Public telephones are at via Roma 18, bis via Arsenale 13, and the Stazione di Porta Nuova.

American Express: The representative of American Express in Turin, Malan Viaggi, is at via Accademia delle Scienze 1 (tel. 513-841). It's closed Saturday afternoon and all day Sunday. Some services are not available on Saturday.

Consulate: You'll find the **U.S. Consulate** at via Pomba 23 (tel. 011/517-437).

Drugstore: If you need an all-night **drugstore,** try the Alleanza Cooperative Torinese, via Nizza 65 (tel. 659-259).

Emergency Phone Numbers: In a **life-threatening emergency,** dial 113. To seek **first aid** or to call an **ambulance,** phone 57-47. A major **police** station is at via Avogradro 41 (tel. 533-853).

Medical Care: For a **hospital,** there is the Ente Ospedliero Opere Pie Ospitaliere, via Venezia 18 (tel. 60-61).

Post Office: The main post office is at via Alfieri 10. It is closed on Sunday.

Religious Services: English-language services are conducted at the Chiesa Evangelica di Lingua Inglese, via San Pio V 15 (tel. 682-838).

Tourist Information: If you're seeking specific information about Turin, go to the office of **A.P.T.,** via Roma 226 (tel. 535-181), open from 8 a.m. to 7 p.m. Monday through Friday and 8 a.m. to 12:30 p.m. Saturday. There is another office at the train station, Porta Nuova (tel. 531-327), open from 8 a.m. to 7 p.m. Monday through Friday and 8 a.m. to 12:30 p.m. on Saturday.

HOTELS IN TURIN

Generally the hotels lack distinction, except in the expensive range. Like Milan, Turin is an industrial city first, a tourist center second. Most of its hotels were built after the war with an eye toward modern comfort but not necessarily style. My recommendations follow, beginning with—

The Deluxe Choices

Turin Palace Hotel, via Sacchi 8, 10128 Torino (tel. 011/515-511), is a graceful hotel in the tradition of plush surroundings and attentive service. Its entrance is under three arches of an arcade across from the Porta Nuova train station, behind glass doors set into a white marble façade. Its convenience to the center of town and its fashionable address prompted the Empress Elizabeth of Austria to stay here in 1893, when she was accompanied by a baron, a countess, three friends, and eight servants. Today the clientele is likely to include top-level management from the General Motors headquarters in Detroit during their business trips to Turin, an event for which the hotel usually brings out masses of arranged flowers. The public rooms contain a scattering of full-size oil portraits as well as opulent chairs and console tables of massively carved and gilded woods. These have been supplemented with an assortment of tastefully contemporary furniture as well. The upper hallways have wide expanses of carved oak detailing, often in a shell motif that repeats itself, along with recessed and illuminated glass cases containing gilded Oriental statues. The 125 bedrooms and baths are soundproof, containing such conveniences as air conditioning, phone, radio, TV, and frigo-bar. A hotel garage is on the premises, a service much appreciated in a town where everyone seems to own a car. Singles rent for 245,000 lire ($186) daily, while doubles cost 310,000 lire ($236).

Jolly Hotel Principi di Piemonte, via Gobetti 15, 10123 Torino (tel. 011/519-693), reflects an increasing appreciation for luxury living in Turin. A favorite choice of Fiat czars, the hotel is found in the center of the city, near the railway station. Owned by the country's Jolly chain, it employed some of Italy's finest architects and designers in its wholesale revamping. Each of the 107 bedrooms—all with private bath—reflects an individualized style, but yet contains such practical equipment as radio, TV, and frigo-bar. In general, a variety of styles has been used, employing both antiques and reproductions, as well as modern items. Each room is air-conditioned and contains a phone. The rate in a single is 220,000 lire ($167) daily, rising to 270,000 lire ($205) in a double. The public rooms are grand in style and furnishings, using bas-relief ceilings, gold wall panels, silk draperies, Louis XVI–style chairs, and baroque marble sideboards. There are several dining rooms, both formal and informal, as well as a fashionable drinking lounge.

The First-Class Range

Villa Sassi, via Traforo del Pino 47, 10132 Torino (tel. 011/890-556), is a classic 17th-century-style estate at the edge of the city, surrounded by its own park grounds and approached by a winding driveway. Long ago converted into a top-grade hotel and restaurant (see "Dining in Turin," below), it offers a dozen rooms to wayfarers. The original, impressive architectural details are still intact, including the wooden staircase in the entrance hall. The drawing room invites with its overscale mural and life-size sculpted baroque figures holding bronze torchiers. The intimate drinking salon continues the same theme, with its draped red-velvet walls, bronze chandelier, black dado, and low seat cushions. Each bedroom has been decorated in individual style (the fabrics and colors are harmonious, and the furniture is a combination of antiques and reproductions). The manager sees that all is run in a personal way, with "custom-made" service. The rooms have either private bath or shower, for which the single rate is 200,000 lire ($152) daily; the double, 280,000 lire ($213). You may want to take full board for 280,000 lire ($213) per person, tax inclusive, but a minimum stay of three days is required. The villa is closed in August.

Hotel Concord, via Lagrange 47, 10122 Torino (tel. 011/557-6756), is across from the hysterical traffic of a street running alongside the Porta Nuova train station. It sits behind a grandly proportioned façade dotted with cast-iron balconies and large stones chiseled into blocks of high-relief contrasts. The entire hotel was modernized in 1982. What you'll see today is two tones of marble covering much of the lobby, a bank of elevators leading to a stylish bar and restaurant one floor above street level, and a busy series of commercially oriented guests. The simply furnished and comfortable bedrooms rent for 175,000 lire ($133) daily in a single and from 228,000 lire ($167) in a double, including a continental breakfast. All units contain modern bath, individually controlled air conditioning, double-glazed and soundproof windows, radio, private phone, TV, and frigo-bar.

The Medium-Priced and Budget Range

Hotel Stazione e Genoa, via Sacchi 14, 10128 Torino (tel. 011/545-323), is under the same 19th-century arcade as the far more expensive Hotel Turin Palace, near the Porta Nuova train station. This attractive hotel was renovated in 1984. The warmly futuristic lobby area is covered with carpeting and rare wood. The design throughout the labyrinthine hallways is redolent of the best kinds of Italian style, while the comfortable bedrooms contain modern tile bath, TV, and private phone. This hotel is, in my opinion, the best medium-priced hotel in Turin, with a location that's difficult to match and an English-speaking staff. Singles cost 85,000 lire ($64.50) daily, and doubles rent for 120,000 lire ($91.25).

Hotel Victoria, via Nino Costa 4, 10123 Torino (tel. 011/533-710), is a small but substantial hotel whose accommodations are better than its second-class classification would imply. Although simply designed, the bedrooms have a personal touch to them that stems partly from the use of one color to a room. Graceful furniture, and large expanses of stained-glass windows contribute to a feeling of luxury in the public rooms. Each of the comfortable bedrooms contains its own private bath or shower. Rates in a single are 85,000 lire ($64.50) daily; in a double, 120,000 lire ($91.25).

Hotel Luxor, corso Stati Uniti 7, 10128 Torino (tel. 011/531-529), was built in 1961 and completely renovated in 1981. The stylish lobby is accented with oak trim, fresh flowers, and well-placed mirrors, all of which welcome passengers disembarking from the nearby Porta Nuova train station. There's a bar in the lobby. The bedrooms are less stylish than the public rooms, but they have comfort. It's better to ask for a room facing the back, which on summer nights would be quieter than those opening onto the street. Each of the 63 rooms has a private bath, frigo-bar, phone, and radio. Singles cost 88,000 lire ($67) daily, and doubles rent for 126,000 lire ($95.75).

Hotel Genio, corso Vittorio Emanuele 47, 10125 Torino (tel. 011/650-8264), is a simple, centrally located hotel with a conservatively modern decor that includes a high-ceilinged reception area and upper-grade furniture. The bedrooms contain a comfortable blend of contemporary with late-19th-century pieces, and have double windows for soundproofing. Singles rent for 90,000 lire ($68.50) daily; doubles, 130,000 lire ($98.75).

Hotel Bramante, via Genova 2, 10126 Torino (tel. 011/697-997), is a bit distantly located, near the Museo dell'Automobile, but it's one of the best of the reasonably priced hotels of Turin. At 90,000 lire ($68.50) daily in a single, 105,000 lire ($79.75) in a double, that's a good price for Turin. The rooms, 42 in all, are comfortably and pleasantly equipped. The hotel has no restaurant, serving breakfast only, but it does offer a bar-lounge.

Hotel Goya, bis via Prìncipe Amedeo 41, 10123 Torino (tel. 011/874-951), sports a modern façade of beige brick on a quiet street in the center of the city. The lobby contains a small bar area just behind the reception desk. There's no garage on the premises, so parking on the street might be a problem. The hotel belongs to a chain in Turin, many members of which bear the names of famous artists. Doubles cost 130,000 lire ($98.75) daily; singles, 75,000 lire ($57).

Hotel Piemontese, via Berthollet 21, 10125 Torino (tel. 011/669-8101), is contained in a 19th-century building about two short blocks from a weekend outdoor vegetable market. The façade is ornamented with iron balconies and ornate stone trim. The restructured interior is clean and well maintained, the bedrooms and public places having undergone a complete restoration in 1987. Rooms are simple but comfortable, costing 60,000 lire ($45.50) daily in a single, rising to 75,000 lire ($57) in a double. Breakfast, the only meal served, is taken in an airy, sunny room. There is also a private garage reserved for clients of the hotel.

DINING IN TURIN

Turin gave the world vermouth, for which martini drinkers have been in the eternal debt of the Carpano family. The Piedmont kitchen is a fragrant delight, differing in many respects from the Milanese, especially in its liberal use of garlic. What it lacks in subtlety is often made up in large portions of hearty fare.

The Top Restaurants

El Toulà–Villa Sassi, via Traforo del Pino 47 (tel. 890-556), is a spacious, 17th-century villa on the rise of a hill at the edge of the city, four miles from the center on the road to Chieri. Against the background of a stylish antique-decorated villa, a modern dining room has been built, with walls of glass extending toward the gardens (most of the tables have an excellent view). Some of the basic foodstuff is brought in from the villa's own farm—not only the vegetables, fruit, and butter, but the beef as well. At the villa, it's recommended that you order à la carte unless you're a guest of the hotel. For an appetizer, try either the frogs' legs cooked with broth-simmered rice, or fonduta, a Piedmont fondue, made with fontina cheese, richly flavored with eggs, milk, and butter, to which the white truffles of the region are added. Another local dish to Piedmont is agnolotti, a form of meat-stuffed pasta like ravioli. If featured, you may want to try the prized specialty of the house: camoscio in salmi—that is, chamois (a goat-like antelope) prepared in a sauce of olive oil, anchovies, and garlic, laced with wine and served with polenta. Count on spending at least 75,000 lire ($57), maybe 100,000 lire ($76), for a complete dinner. Hours are noon to 2 p.m. and 8 to 10:30 p.m.; closed Sunday and in August.

Del Cambio, piazza Carignano 2 (tel. 546-690), is a classic and traditional restaurant of old Turin. Here, you can dine in comparative grandeur, in a setting of white-and-gilt walls, crystal chandeliers, and gilt mirrors. It's utterly Old World. The restaurant was founded in 1757, and it is not only the oldest restaurant in Turin, but maybe in all of Italy. Camillo Cavour, his much-frequented corner immortalized with a bronze medallion, was one of its loyal patrons. The 19th-century tradition of the waiters' wearing long white aprons continues. The white truffle of Piedmont is used with finesse in many of the chef's specialties. The chef has received many culinary honors, and unfortunately I have room to mention only a few of his specialties. To begin with, the assorted antipasti are excellent. The best pasta dish is the regional agnolotti piemontesi. Among the main dishes singled out for special praise are fondue with truffles from Alba and beef braised in Barolo wine. Fresh vegetables are always available. Rounding out the repast is a homemade tart. Expect to spend 75,000 lire ($57) and up for a complete meal. The restaurant is open from 12:30 to 3 p.m. and 7:30 to 10:30 p.m. daily except Sunday and in August.

Ristorante Vecchia Lanterna, corso Re Umberto 21 (tel. 537-047), is located appropriately on a street named after a king whose power was greatest during the era when many of the restaurant's furnishings were completed. This is one of Turin's most popular upper-bracket restaurants, one that requests reservations, and usually proves to be a rewarding gastronomic experience. The bar area near the entrance has belle époque lighting fixtures, heavy gilt mirrors, ornate 19th-century furniture, and Oriental rugs over carpeting. The dining room reminds guests of those of old Venice. The antipasti selection is a treat. It includes a choice of king crab Venetian style, asparagus flan, pâté de foie gras, grilled snails on a skewer, and marinated trout. This could be followed by gnocchi stuffed with fondue cheese, ravioli stuffed with duck and served with a truffle sauce, your choice of risotto, or snail soup. Main courses change frequently depending on the season, but often include goose liver piccata on a bed of fresh mushrooms, sea bass Venetian style, garnished frogs' legs, and many other tempting taste sensations. A menu dégustation is available for 88,000 lire ($67). Expect to spend 70,000 lire ($53.25) for a full meal ordered from the à la carte menu. The restaurant, open from noon to 3 p.m. and 8 p.m. to midnight, is closed Saturday at lunch, all day Sunday, and in August.

The Middle and Budget Range

Ristorante C'era una Volta, corso Vittorio Emanuele 41 (tel. 655-498). You'll enter through carved oak doors from the busy street, riding an elevator to one floor above ground level. Many of the clients of this restaurant are faithful devotees. The decor is in the typical Piedmontese style with hanging copper pots and thick walls of stippled plaster. Menus cost from 50,000 lire ($38) and feature an apéritif, a choice of seven or eight antipasti, and a selection of two each of both a first and a main course, with vegetables, dessert, and coffee. Virtually everything served is inspired by Piedmontese tradition. Go only for dinner, from 8:30 to 9:30 p.m., and never on Sunday or in August. The translation of the restaurant's name is "Once upon a time."

Trattoria Ostu Bacu, corso Vercelli 226 (tel. 264-579), is a small restaurant, the kind discriminating Fiat executives try to keep a secret. The owners are the Barla family, and they prepare the regional specialties that have made the place so popular. These include agnolotti (ravioli stuffed with spinach, beef, and tomatoes), a mixed fish fry (which many guests travel across the city to enjoy), a bagna cauda of roast meats, veal rolled into tender and savory main dishes, honey torte, and a full array of homemade pastries. The ambience attracts some of the better-heeled diners of Turin who might show up when they want to avoid the formality of deluxe citadels such as Villa Sassi. The wines are excellent vintages from Piedmont. The restaurant is open from noon to 3 p.m. and 7 to 11 p.m.; closed Sunday and in July. Expect to spend from 38,000 lire ($29) per person.

Ristorante Tre Galline, via Bellezia 37 (tel. 546-833). The historic lodgings inside an early-17th-century palazzo is not the only reason for this restaurant's success. The proprietor and chef concocts the kind of regional specialties that even the most diehard Piedmontese loyalist can't seem to resist. No one puts on airs here. Portions are more than generous, and when the bill comes, you won't faint. Some of the best risottos in the city are served here, along with bagna cauda, fonduta with truffles, braised beef, and an especially savory agnolotti. The wine cellar is well stocked with Piedmontese vintages. The restaurant, serving from 12:30 to 2:30 p.m. and 7:30 to 10 p.m., is closed Sunday, Monday, and in August. Expect to spend 38,000 lire ($29) and up per person.

Da Giuseppe, via San Massimo 34 (tel. 812-2090), is a place where you can feast to your stomach's content. There is no menu, and you can partake of dish after dish, brought to you hot or cold, as the contents and temperature of the day dictate. Eggplant, spinach flan, steak tartare alla Alba, lamb piemontese, and luscious profiteroles all tempt you, together with other dishes of merit. You pay a fixed price of 40,000 lire ($30.50) for your meal, available daily from 12:30 to 2:30 p.m. and 7:30 to 10 p.m. Reservations are required.

Da Mauro, via Maria Vittoria 21 (tel. 839-7811), is the best of the low-cost trattorie. Generally packed (everybody loves a bargain), it is within walking distance of the piazza San Carlo. The food is conventional, but manages to have character, as the chef borrows freely from most of the gastronomic centers of Italy. An excellent pasta specialty is tortellini di nagro alla cardinale. Most main dishes consist of well-prepared fish, veal, and poultry. Desserts such as Italian cheesecake and ice cream are consistently enjoyable. A tourist menu is offered for 20,000 lire ($15.25), and an à la carte meal will cost from 33,000 lire ($25). Hours are 12:30 to 2:30 p.m. and 7:30 to 10 p.m.; closed Monday and in July.

A Famous Coffeehouse

Caffè Torino, piazza San Carlo 204 (tel. 545-118), is the best re-creation in Turin of the days of Vittorio Emanuele. There's a brass inlay of a bull set into the flagstone under the sheltering arcade in front. Inside, there are about as many seating areas as there are colors of marble set into the floor and walls. A deli-style counter area surrounded with cabriole-legged stools offers snacks, which you can choose from a case. You have to eat on one of the stools, however, since some arbitrary rule prohibits eating at one of the sit-down tables in the adjacent café area. If you want a full meal, a uniformed waiter will serve it to you in an elegantly decorated side room. If you want only a quick caffeine fix or a gulp of midafternoon wine, there's a stand-up bar near the entrance. Despite the complexity of the seating areas, the decor is beautiful, including frescoed ceilings embellished with depictions of wines and flowers, along with crystal chandeliers. Throughout the establishment, there's a 19th-century kind of formality worthy of the elegant square on which the café is located. A sit-down beer costs 6,500 lire ($4.95); a sit-down coffee, 3,500 lire ($2.65). Full meals begin at 40,000 lire ($30.50). The café is open daily except Tuesday from 8 a.m. to 1 a.m.

SIGHTSEEING IN TURIN

To begin your exploration, head first for the **piazza San Carlo,** the loveliest and most unified square in the city, covering about 3½ acres. Heavily bombed in the last war, it dates from the 17th century, and was built to the design of Carlo di Castellamonte. In the heart of the piazza is an equestrian statue of Emanuele Filiberto. The two churches are those of Santa Cristina and San Carlo. Some of the most prestigious names in Italy have sat on this square, sipping coffee and plotting the unification of Italy.

You'll find the most interesting museums housed in the Guarini-designed, 17th-century **Science Academy Building,** via Accademia della Scienze 6 (tel. 544-091). The collection of the **Egyptian Museum** is so vast that it's rated second only to the one at Cairo. Of the statuary, that of Rameses II is the best known, but there is one of Amenhotep II as well. A room nearby contains a rock temple consecrated by Thutmosis III in Nubia. In the crowded wings upstairs, the world of the pharaohs lives on (one of the prize exhibits is the "Royal Papyrus," with its valuable chronicling of the Egyptian monarchs from the 1st through the 17th dynasties). The funerary art is exceptionally rare and valuable, especially the chapel built for Meie and his young wife, and an entirely reassembled tomb (that of Kha and Mirit, 18th dynasty), discovered in a well-preserved condition at the turn of the century. The museum is open Tuesday through Sunday from 9 a.m. to 2 p.m. and charges 3,000 lire ($2.30) for admission. Closed Monday.

In the same building, you can visit the **Sabauda (Savoy) Gallery** (tel. 547-440), one of the richest in Italy, whose collection was acquired over a period of centuries by the house of Savoy. It is open from 9 a.m. to 2 p.m. on Tuesday, Thursday, Saturday, and Sunday, and from 2:30 to 7:30 p.m. on Wednesday and Friday; closed Monday. The charge for admission is 3,000 lire ($2.30). The gallery has the largest exhibition of the Piedmontese masters, but is well endowed in Flemish art as well. Of the latter, the best-known painting is Sir Anthony Van Dyck's *Three Children of Charles I.* Other important works include Botticelli's *Venus,* Memling's *Passion of Christ,* Rembrandt's *Sleeping Old Man,* Duccio's *Virgin and Child,* Mantegna's *Holy Conversation,* Jan van Eyck's *The Stigmata of Francis of Assisi,* Veronese's *Dinner in* *the House of the Pharisee*, intriguing paintings by Brueghel, Ballotto's *Views of Turin*, and a renewed section of the royal collections between 1730 and 1832.

The Renaissance **Cathedral of John the Baptist** is of major interest to visitors as it contains Guarini's Chapel of the **Holy Shroud.** Acquired by Emanuele Filiberto (whose equestrian statue you saw in the piazza San Carlo), the shroud is purported to be the one that Joseph of Arimathea wrapped around the body of Christ when he was removed from the cross. Detailed charts in front of the holy relic claim to show evidence of a hemorrhage produced by the crown of thorns. The chapel, crowned by a baroque dome, is at the piazza IV Marzo, a short walk from the entrance to the Royal Palace. Recent scientific testing has shown the fabric to be only six or seven centuries old; therefore, it could not have dated from the time of Jesus. The shroud, however, has always been the subject of controversy. When it was first exhibited in 1354, a French bishop denounced it as a fraud. The mystery is far from ended. The life-size image of a crucified body looks like a photographic negative. Photography had not been invented. Therefore, how the image was imprinted remains a miracle. You can rest assured that the final word has not been sounded in this matter. The shroud rests in a silver box behind bulletproof glass. The chapel is open from 7:30 a.m. to noon and 3 to 5:30 p.m. (on Sunday from 9:45 a.m. to noon); closed Monday.

The Royal Palace (Palazzo Reale): At the piazza Castello, the palace that the Savoys called home was begun in 1645. Its halls, columned ballroom by Palagi, tea salon, and "Queen's Chapel" are richly baroqued. The original architect was Amedeo de Castellamonte, but numerous builders were to supply ideas and skill before the palazzo was finally complete. As in nearly all ducal residences of that period, the most bizarre room is the one bedecked with flowering chinoiserie. The throne room is of interest, as is the tapestry-draped banqueting hall. Le Nôtre, a Frenchman, mapped out the gardens, which may be visited. In the building you can also visit the Royal Armory or Ameria Reale, with its large collection of arms and armor, with many military mementos. The palace (tel. 546-731) is open from 9 a.m. to 2 p.m. daily except Monday and there is a charge of 3,000 lire ($2.30) for admission.

In the **Carlo Biscaretti di Ruffia Automobile Museum,** corso Unità d'Italia 40 (tel. 677-666), outside the heart of the city in a colossus of a modern exhibition hall, historic "buggies" are handsomely displayed. The exhibitions span the years—ranging from a model of Valturio's "wind machine" (made 20 years before Columbus sailed for America), to the first Fiat car (turn of the century), to a pre–World War II Mercedes-Benz. The museum is open daily except Monday from 9 a.m. to 12:30 p.m. and 3 to 7 p.m., and charges 4,000 lire ($3.05) admission.

---

2. St. Vincent

Easily reached by air, road, and rail, St. Vincent is an ideal center for exploring the Aosta Valley. Towering over the region are great mountain peaks—Mont Blanc, the Matterhorn, Monte Rosa, and Gran Paradiso. In Billia mountain-safari Landrovers you can discover the most out-of-the-way corners of the valley, or can head for a day of skiing at two of the most famous ski resorts in Italy, Courmayeur or Breuil-Cervinia.

In 1770 Abbé Jean-Baptiste Perret, a chemist, discovered St. Vincent's mineral-water spring, and since then the water's therapeutic qualities have been known to aid in various ailments of the liver and stomach, among other disorders. But most visitors come to St. Vincent to enjoy the high life as the resort is hailed as "the alpine Riviera," and the casino here is one of only four in Italy.

Grand Hotel Billia, viale Piemonte 18, 11027 St. Vincent (tel. 0166/3446), is the queen of the Italian Alps. One of the most unusual hotels in Italy, and certainly one of the best equipped, it was originally built in a neo-Flemish design in the late 19th century. But over the years it has been modernized and expanded until now it has 250 handsomely equipped and well-maintained bedrooms, with many amenities. Each unit is stylish and comfortable, with a phone, color TV, in-house movies, and a mini-bar—in all, a great deal of classy allure, as reflected by the porphyry and marble used in the public rooms. Singles begin at 220,000 lire ($167) daily; doubles, at 310,000 lire ($236). On the grounds are well-tended gardens, as well as a mineral spring and spa, a sauna, a well-stocked shopping arcade, an excellent restaurant serving both Italian and international specialties, a bar with a pianist, and a clientele eager to rejuvenate themselves in the mountain air of the Valle d'Aosta. The hotel sits atop a forested knoll, with an outdoor pool and the gray rocks of the mountains forming a backdrop.

The Aostan government approved the establishment of a casino here, within a modern annex, and today, on any given weekend, this elegant oasis attracts gamblers from all corners of Europe. The casino is connected to the hotel via the most flamboyant pop-art tunnel in Italy. Entrance to the casino, open daily from 4 p.m. to 6 a.m., requires the presentation of a passport and a 10,000-lira ($7.60) fee. The complex also houses Nightclub 33, opening for dinner at 9 p.m. Dining is optional: you can also attend just for the Las Vegas–style revue, with each drink costing 15,000 lire ($11.50). The club boasts the most glittering and lavish cabaret in the Italian Alps, featuring feather-clad artistes from Paris to Manila. An array of musical stars, including on one occasion Ella Fitzgerald, also appears.

3. Aosta

In the capital of the Valle d'Aosta stands the **Arch of Augustus,** built in 24 B.C., the date of the Roman founding of the town. Aosta was important in Roman times, and the further remains of a theater, the Praetorian Gate, and the Forum provide other evidence of its occupation and growth under domination from the south. The town is also enriched by its medieval relics. The Gothic **Church of Sant'Orso,** founded in the 12th century, is characterized by its landmark steeple designed in the Romanesque style. You can explore the crypt, but the cloisters, with capitals of some three dozen pillars depicting biblical scenes, are more interesting.

Lying on a major artery, Aosta makes for an important stopover point, either for overnighting or as a base for exploring the Valle d'Aosta or taking the cable car to the Conca di Pila, the mountain that towers over the town. My hotel recommendations follow.

Aosta's telephone area code is 0165.

HOTELS IN AOSTA

The leading choice is the **Hotel Valle d'Aosta,** corso Ivrea 146, 11100 Aosta (tel. 0165/41-845), in good modern design. Open all year, the hotel lies behind a zigzag concrete façade on a busy road leading from the old town to the entrance of the autostrada. It serves as a prominent stopover for motorists using the Great Saint Bernard and Mont Blanc tunnels into Italy. The sunny lobby has beige stone floors, lots of paneling, and deep leather chairs. A restaurant is on the premises, under a different management, and the lobby contains an oversize bar area. Of the 104 bedrooms, about half contain TV, while all of them have a frigo-bar, double windows, suitable comfort, and views angled toward the mountains. Doubles rent for 145,000 lire ($110) daily, while singles cost from 100,000 lire ($76). Breakfast and garage costs are extra.

Le Pageot, via G. Carrel 31, 11100 Aosta (tel. 0165/32-433). Built in 1985, this is one of the best value hotels in town. Sheathed within a modern and angular façade of brown brick and big windows, it contains only 18 functional but clean and comfortable bedrooms. Each of these has a phone, radio, and private bath, renting for 50,000 lire ($38) daily in a single, 85,000 lire ($64.50) in a double. The well-lit public areas contain a breakfast room, floors crafted from carefully polished slabs of mountain granite, and a TV room. The hotel's name translates from an antiquated local dialect into the word for bed.

Hotel Roma, via Torino 7, 11100 Aosta (tel. 0165/40-821), is on a peaceful alleyway behind a cubist-oriented white stucco building surrounded by the balconies and windows of what look like private apartment buildings. The entrance is at the top of an exterior concrete stairwell. The public rooms include a warmly paneled bar area, big windows, and a home-like, decor filled with bright colors and rustic accessories. Silvio Lepri and Graziella Nicoli, the owners, charge 45,000 lire ($34.25) to 50,000 lire ($38) daily in a single and 62,000 lire ($47) to 79,000 lire ($60) for a double. Prices depend on the season. Each of the comfortable rooms has a private bath. Half board can be arranged at a nearby restaurant. There's a garage on the premises, plus public parking a short distance away.

WHERE TO DINE

The most outstanding restaurant in the Valle d'Aosta is **Ristorante Cavallo Bianco,** via Aubert 15 (tel. 362-214). There's no à la carte menu offered at this Aostan restaurant, which is filled with antiques. Each of the satisfied clients chooses one of two fixed-price menus, one at 65,000 lire ($49.50), another at 90,000 lire ($68.50). The menus offer a choice of a main course, and are usually prepared with infinite care by the family in charge. At lunch, a 50,000-lira ($38) menu is offered. Individual food items change daily, depending on the availability of very fresh produce at the markets. The restaurant is housed on the second floor of a building set at the far end of a courtyard whose entrance is under a vaulted tunnel leading from the street. Because of the weathered wooden stairwell and balustrades, the gracefully massive fireplace, the beamed ceilings, and the cabriole-legged chairs, the establishment might look very much like a 17th-century French country inn, except for the Aostan flagstones covering the roof. Hours are 12:30 to 2 p.m. and 8 to 9:30 p.m. The place is closed Sunday night and Monday except in July and August.

Ristorante Le Foyer, corso Ivrea 146 (tel. 32-136), is set beside a busy traffic artery on the outskirts of town. Other than during two weeks in July and January, full meals are served daily except Tuesday from 12:15 to 2:15 p.m. and 7:15 to 9:30 p.m. A flavorful and cost-conscious fixed-price menu is offered for 35,000 lire ($26.50), with à la carte going for 40,000 lire ($30.50). Specialties are served with panache in a wood-sheathed dining room illuminated from a wall of oversize windows. These include carpaccio of salmon with three peppers, a salad of smoked trout with orange, fondue valdostana (whose main ingredient is the local Fontina cheese), and such grilled fresh fish as salmon.

Vecchia Aosta, piazza Porte Pretoriane 4 (tel. 361-186), is probably the most unusual restaurant in Aosta, lying in the narrow niche between the inner and outer Roman walls of the Porta Pretoriane. The old building containing it was modernized to include proof of the superb building techniques of the Romans, whose chiseled stones are sometimes visible between patches of modern wood and plaster. Full meals are served on at least two different levels in a labyrinth of nooks and isolated crannies, daily except Wednesday from noon to 3 p.m. and 7:30 to 10 p.m. Meals cost 35,000 lire ($26.50) and might include homemade ravioli, stuffed turkey, pepperoni flan, eggs with cheese fondue and truffles, and a cheese-laden version of Valdostan fondue.

Ristorante Piemonte, via Porte Pretoriane 13 (tel. 40-111), is on a relatively traffic-free street lined with shops. This is one of the best of the low-cost trattorie within the walls of the old town. Amid a family-run ambience of vaulted ceilings and tile floors, you can savor such specialties as bagna cauda, cannelloni of the chef, risotto with roast pork, good roast beef, and an array of refreshing desserts, which could include fresh strawberries with lemon. Fixed-price meals cost around 20,000 lire

($15.25), with à la carte dinners beginning at 35,000 lire ($26.50). The restaurant is open from noon to 3 p.m. and 7 to 10 p.m.; closed on Sunday and during most of January.

Ristorante Agip, corso Ivrea 138 (tel. 44-565). Normally you think of Agip as a place to get gas or perhaps to secure motel lodgings for the night. However, in Aosta they operate only a restaurant (no rooms), next to a garage on the main highway attracting motorists going to and from the Mont Blanc Tunnel. The location is on a major artery, and you might want to stop here if you're rushed and don't have time to go into the old town of Aosta. Some tables are placed outside in summer, and there is generally adequate parking. In addition to classic Italian recipes, you get specialties here from the Valdostan kitchen. Full meals—and generous helpings—cost from 30,000 lire ($22.75). Hours are noon to 2:30 p.m. and 7:30 to 9:30 p.m. The restaurant is closed Monday, except in July and August when it is open every day.

A 22-mile drive from Aosta takes you to—

---

4. Courmayeur and Entrèves

Courmayeur is Italy's best all-around ski resort, with a "high season" attracting the alpine excursionist in summer, the ski enthusiast in winter. Its popularity was given a considerable boost with the opening of the Mont Blanc road tunnel, feeding traffic from France into Italy (estimated run of the trip, 20 minutes). The cost for an average car is 22,000 lire ($16.75) one way, 28,000 lire ($21.25) round trip.

With Europe's highest mountain in the background, Courmayeur sits snuggly in a valley. To the north of the resort is the alpine village of Entrèves, sprinkled with a number of chalets (some of which receive paying guests).

In the vicinity, you can take a cable-car lift—one of the most unusual in Europe —across Mont Blanc all the way to Chamonix, France. It's a ride across glaciers that is altogether frightening, altogether thrilling, but for steel-nerved adventure seekers only. This is a spectacular achievement in engineering. Departures on the **Funivie Monte Bianco** are from La Pallud, near Entrèves. The three-stage cable car heads for the intermediate stations, Pavillon and Rifugio Torino, before reaching its peak at Punta Helbronner at 11,254 feet. At the latter, you'll be on the doorstep of the glacier and the celebrated 11¼-mile Vallée Blanche ski run to Chamonix (France), which is most often open at the beginning of February every year. The round-trip price of the cable ride is 26,000 lire ($19.75) per person. Departures are every 20 minutes in summer and winter, and service is daily from 8 a.m. to 4:20 p.m. At the top is a terrace for sunbathing, a bar, and a snackbar. Panoramic views unfold of 40 alpine peaks.

The telephone area code for Courmayeur and Entrèves is 0165.

HOTELS IN COURMAYEUR

Courmayeur has a number of good and attractive hotels, many of which are open seasonally. Always reserve in high season, either summer or winter. I'll begin my survey with—

The Deluxe Choices

Hotel Pavillon, strada Regionale 60, 11013 Courmayeur (tel. 0165/842-420), a selection of the prestigious *Relais & Châteaux,* is easily the swankiest and most important hotel at the resort, even though it is quite small, with only 40 bedrooms. Many of the clients warming themselves around the stone fireplace are from England, Germany, and France, adding a continental allure. Built in 1965, and designed like a chalet, the hotel stands on the outskirts. In its basement is a full array of hydrotherapy facilities, as well as a covered swimming pool visible from the entrance vestibule. One of my favorite restaurants in town will be previewed later, but it's an Argentine steakhouse found on these premises. The bedrooms lie behind leather-covered doors, with built-in furniture, a color TV, and comfortably conservative de-cor. All but two accommodations contain private balconies, and each, of course, has a private bath. Depending on the season, and with full board included, the per-person rates are 115,000 lire ($87.50) to 200,000 lire ($152) daily, based on double occupancy. Singles pay daily supplements of 15,000 lire ($11.50) to 30,000 lire ($22.75), depending on the season. The hotel, only a short walk to the funicular that goes to Plan Checrouit, is open from December to April and June to September.

Grand Hotel Royal e Golf, via Roma 87, 11013 Courmayeur (tel. 0165/843-621), is the queen of the mountain. Built in 1950, it juts dramatically above the heart of the resort between the most fashionable pedestrian walkway and a thermally heated outdoor swimming pool. Much of its angular façade is covered with meticu-lously fitted rocks, which fit neatly into the surrounding mountainous landscape. The hotel's social center is a large and warmly comfortable lounge, flanked on one side with a bar and on another with a dias on which a piano provides nightly enter-tainment in season. One of the resort's pockets of posh, Il Grill dell'Hotel Cipriani, is on the lobby level and will be previewed later. Open from July through September and December through April, the hotel charges 260,000 lire ($198) to 280,000 lire ($213) per person daily, double occupancy, in high season with full board included. Off-season, those tariffs drop to 165,000 lire ($125) to 190,000 lire ($144) per per-son daily, double occupancy, also with full board.

The Upper Bracket

Palace Bron, località Plan Gorret, 11013 Courmayeur (tel. 0165/842-545), about 1¼ miles from the heart of the resort, is considered one of the most tranquil oases for a vacation in Courmayeur. It's a white-walled chalet whose windows bene-fit from a commanding view over all of Courmayeur and the mountains beyond. It's the most noteworthy building on the pine-studded hill that supports it. This is con-sidered one of the plushest addresses in town. Guests are often made to feel like members of a baronial private household rather than patrons of a hotel. Summer residents benefit from an outdoor pool dug into the side of the steeply sloping mountain, while winter visitors appreciate the proximity of the many ski lifts in the area. Walking from the center of town to the chalet is a good way to exercise after the filling cuisine of the well-managed kitchen. There's a nearby parking lot for motor-ists who prefer to drive the long, steep distance. The hotel is open from December 20 to April and from July to September. Its 20 bedrooms are handsomely furnished and well maintained. Guests can book in here on the full-board plan, paying 150,000 lire ($114) to 200,000 lire ($152) per person daily, depending on the sea-son.

The Medium and Budget Range

Hotel Courmayeur, via Roma 158, 11013 Courmayeur (tel. 0165/842-323), right in the center of the resort, was constructed so that most of its rooms would have unobstructed views of the nearby mountains. A number of the bedrooms, fur-nished in the mountain chalet style, also have wooden balconies and private bath or shower. The hotel is closed in October and November. A single with private bath or shower rents for 50,000 lire ($38) daily; a double, for 80,000 lire ($60.75). To stay here on a full-board arrangement will cost 70,000 lire ($53.75) to 110,000 lire ($83.50) per person in peak season.

Hotel del Viale, viale Monte Bianco 74, 11013 Courmayeur (tel. 0165/842-227), resounds with the alpine theme. An old-style mountain chalet, it perches at the edge of town. Clients enjoy the indoor-outdoor life: the front terrace with tables set out under trees in fair weather, the cozy and pleasant rooms inside in the chillier months. In the winter guests gather in the taproom to enjoy après-ski life, drinking

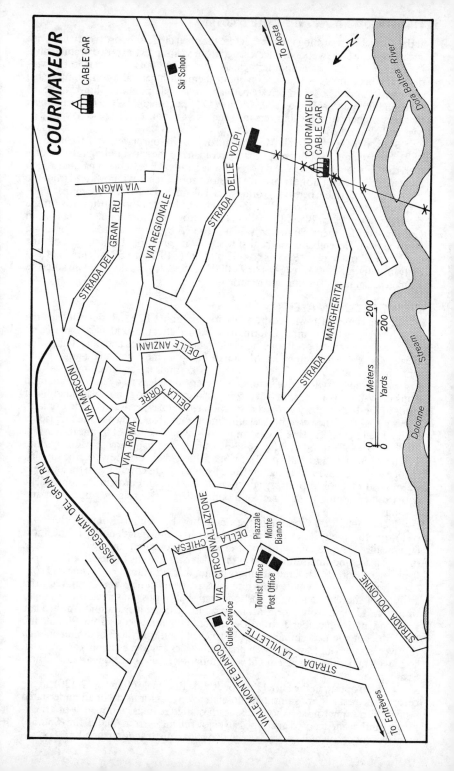

at the pine tables, warming their feet before the open fire. The house is enriched with such pieces as a large wooden pillar rescued from a wine press, exposed beams, hanging copper kettles, a grandmother's clock, pewter, and pots of flowers in the window. The bedrooms have a rustic air about them, with natural wood, comfortable and clean. All units contain private bath and toilet, phone, and radio. Half board costs 55,000 lire ($41.75) to 100,000 lire ($76) per person daily. The friendliness that prevails here turns wallflowers into edelweiss bouquets. The place is closed in May and November.

Bouton d'Or, off piazzale Monte Bianco, 11013 Courmayeur (tel. 0165/842-380). Named after the buttercups that cover many of the surrounding hills in summer, this 25-room hotel is owned by the Casale family. The exterior is painted a deep mustard yellow, with stone trim and a flagstone roof. French windows lead from the clean and comfortable bedrooms onto small balconies. Each of the rooms has a private bath or shower, a phone, TV, and radio. The hotel is about 100 yards (in the direction of the Mont Blanc Tunnel to France) from the most popular restaurant in Courmayeur, Le Vieux Pommier, which is owned by the same family. Guests are received from December until the first week of May and from the last week of June until the end of October. Rooms cost 53,000 lire ($40.25) to 59,000 lire ($44.75) daily in a single, 87,000 lire ($66) to 97,000 lire ($73.75) in a double. The hotel has a garage, a sauna, a solarium, and a garden.

DINING IN COURMAYEUR

In the center of town, **Cadran Solaire,** via Eoma 122 (tel. 844-609), is the most interesting restaurant in Courmayeur. Named after the sundial (*cadran solaire*) that embellishes the upper floor of its chalet façade, it is owned and operated by Leo Garin, whose also-recommended Maison de Filippo is the most sought-after restaurant in the Val d'Aosta. The restaurant is as unusual architecturally as it is gastronomically. Try to arrive before your reserved table is ready for a before-meal drink in a vaulted bar whose massive stones were crafted into almost alarmingly long spans in the 16th century using construction techniques perfected by the Romans. A few steps away, the rustically elegant dining room has its own stone fireplace, a beamed ceiling, wide plank floors, and a fun-loving clientele. Full meals, costing 50,000 lire ($38) to 60,000 lire ($45.50), are served daily except Monday from 12:30 to 2:30 p.m. and 7:30 to 10 p.m. Specialties, like the shadows on the sundial, change with the season, but might include fresh asparagus covered with tuna sauce, a warm salad of smoked trout, spaghetti with zucchini and prosciutto, pappardelle with exotic mushrooms, and rack of mountain lamb. Desserts are sumptuous and luscious.

Il Grill dell'Hotel Cipriani, in the Grand Royal e Golf, via Roma 87 (tel. 843-621), on the lobby level of this previously recommended hotel, is the most fashionable—and certainly the most expensive—restaurant in town. It contains only 30 places for diners interested in the cuisine inspired by the legacy of "Harry" Cipriani, of Harry's Bar fame. Its allure comes from its cultivated cuisine and consciously spartan decor whose main interest is a carved Gothic screen, removed from an English church, standing against one wall. Full meals are served only at night from 7 to 11 p.m. daily except Monday; annual closing is from mid-April to late June and mid-September to mid-December. Full meals cost from 90,000 lire ($68.50), but guests, seemingly, happily pay that for the privilege of dining on such relatively simple but fresh and well-prepared dishes as pasta e fagioli, carpaccio, risotto with radicchio, and rosettes of veal Cipriani style. Reservations are always necessary in season.

Le Bistroquet, in the Hotel Pavillon, strada Regionale 60 (tel. 842-420), in the cellar of the best and most intimate hotel in town, has for its decor an understated replica of an Argentine steakhouse. Beneath vaulted ceilings, within view of a theatrically flamboyant exposed grill, you can enjoy full meals from 40,000 lire ($30.50) each. Dozens of cowhides draped over wooden banquettes add to the allure. Specialties include bagna cauda piemontese, several kinds of air-dried beef, risotto flavored with red radishes and Asti Spumante, two kinds of fondue, filet of trout perfumed with thyme, and many different steaks and grills. Meals are served daily except Monday from 12:30 to 2:30 p.m. and 7:30 to 9:30 p.m. Annual closing lasts from late April to late June and from late September to late November.

Le Vieux Pommier, piazzale Monte Bianco 25 (tel. 842-281). Before the construction of this restaurant could begin, there was an apple tree that had to be cut down. Grieving for its loss, the owners decided to erect its gnarled skeleton as the focal point of this warmly decorated establishment on the main square of town. One of its recent guests was filmmaker Ingmar Bergman, who, like everyone else, appreciated the exposed stone, the copper-covered bar, the heavy ceiling beams, and thick pine tables arranged in an octagon around the heavily ornamented tree.

Today Alessandro Casale directs the kitchen. He is the son of the warm-hearted woman who established the restaurant, Madame Berthod. He is assisted by his wife, Lydia, and they have traveled on tours of Europe, teaching the technique of their regionally inspired cuisine. Your meal might consist of three kinds of dried alpine beef, followed by noodles in a ham-studded cream sauce, an arrangement of three kinds of pasta or four types of fondue, including a regional variety with Fontina, milk, and egg yolks. Then it's on to chicken suprême en papillote or four or five unusual meat dishes that require cooking mountain style, right at your table. Six kinds of grilled meats are also offered, all of them tasty and flavored with aromatic herbs. Desserts are refreshingly sweet, especially the chocolate cream parfait. Your meal is usually finished off by coffee served in the style of the Valle d'Aosta. A full dinner will cost 25,000 lire ($19) to 40,000 lire ($30.50) per person. The restaurant, open from 12:30 to 2:30 p.m. and 7 to 10:30 p.m., is closed Monday and in October.

Leone Rosso, via Roma 73 (tel. 842-324), lies within a stone- and timber-fronted house on its own slightly isolated courtyard, a few paces from the busy pedestrian traffic of via Roma. It serves well-prepared, competently seasoned Aostan specialities, including fondues, a thick and steaming version of regional minestrone, tagliatelle with mushrooms en papilotte, and an array of rich, creamy desserts. Full meals cost from 25,000 lire ($19) on the fixed price, 45,000 lire ($34.25) for à la carte specialties, and are served daily except Thursday from noon to 2:30 p.m. and 7:30 to 10 p.m. This place is not to be confused with the Red Lion pub recommended separately.

AFTER DARK

The life expectancy of the average disco in an alpine resort such as Courmayeur is about as long as that of a snow crystal in July. They can be fun, however, and might offer a chance to meet someone. As of this writing, the après-ski crowd is attracted to the electronic rhythms at the following establishments:

The American Bar, via Roma 43 (tel. 842-126). Not to be confused with a less desirable bar with the same name at the end of the same street, this is one of the most popular bars on the après-ski circuit. It's rowdy and sometime outrageous, but most often a lot of fun. You might want to peruse the message board for notes from long-departed friends, but most guests end up in one of the duet of rooms, beside either an open fireplace or a long, crowded bar. The place is open in winter from 10 a.m. to 1:30 a.m. daily. It is sometimes closed on Tuesday, but never in peak season. A large beer costs 3,500 lire ($2.65); a glass of white wine goes for 2,500 lire ($1.90) and up.

Café Posta, via Roma 51 (tel. 842-272), is as sedate as its neighbor, the American Bar, is undisciplined. Many guests prefer to remain in the warmly decorated bar area, never knowing about the large and comfortable salon awaiting them with a glowing fireplace in an adjacent room. A piano provides live entertainment nightly in season from 10 p.m. to 1:30 a.m. The place changes its stripes throughout the day, opening as a morning café at 8 a.m. A whisky and soda costs 5,000 lire ($3.80).

The Red Lion, via Roma 54 (tel. 843-704). Within a warmly paneled ambience reminiscent of Britain, you'll encounter an array of skiers, foaming mugs of beer, and bar snacks. Open daily from 10 a.m. to 1:30 a.m., it charges 5,000 lire ($3.80) for a beer, 3,000 lire ($2.30) to 7,000 lire ($5.30) for whisky.

Abat Jour, via Regionale (tel. 842-990). Popular with a younger, sometimes teenage clientele, it boasts a rustic decor, loud new wave music, and a 10,000-lira ($7.60) entrance fee. The admission price includes a drink. After that, other drinks cost 5,000 lire ($3.80) to 7,000 lire ($5.30). The club rocks from 9:30 p.m. to 1:30 a.m. daily in season.

Le Clochard, Frazione Dolonne (tel. 843-053), is probably the most sophisticated and mature disco in town, catering to an over-25 crowd and charging an entrance fee of 15,000 lire ($11.50), going up to 20,000 lire ($15.25) on Saturday. Inside are plenty of supple couches on which to roost, along with a blazing fireplace and lots of exposed stone. Drinks cost from 4,000 lire ($3.05) each. Hours are 9:30 p.m. to 1:30 p.m. daily.

Tiger Club, in the Hôtel des Alpes in Entrèves (tel. 89-273), has a very modern decor, a clientele of indeterminate age, and some of the best dance music around. Residents of the Hôtel des Alpes pay an entrance fee of 6,000 lire ($4.55); nonresidents, 10,000 lire ($7.60). A whisky and soda costs from 6,000 lire ($4.55), and the place is open nightly in season from 9 p.m. to 2 a.m.

FOOD AND LODGING AT ENTRÈVES

The convenient and modern **Hôtel des Alpes,** 11013 Courmayeur Entrèves (tel. 0165/89-981), has concrete walls and timbered balconies standing out against the rocks and cliffs behind it. Midway between Courmayeur and Entrèves, the building consists of a central six-story core with a low extension stretching out to one side. The interior contains frequently burning fireplaces angled into pleasing designs, panoramic windows flanked with plants, and contrasting textures of exposed stucco, wood, stone, and thick carpets. The bedrooms are comfortable and well maintained. In high season, singles cost 120,000 lire ($91.25) daily, and doubles run 160,000 lire ($122), including breakfast. Low-season tariffs are reduced to 95,000 lire ($72.25) daily in a single and 120,000 lire ($91.25) in a double. Again, depending on the season, full board costs 85,000 lire ($64.50) to 130,000 lire ($98.75) per person daily. The hotel opens the first week of December and stays open until around April 20; in summer, it does business only from June 20 until September 20.

La Grange Meublé, 11013 Courmayeur-Entrèves (tel. 0165/89-274). This will be one of the first buildings you'll see as you enter this rustic alpine village, a short distance from Courmayeur in the direction of the Mont Blanc Tunnel. A few stones of the foundation probably date from as early as the 1300s, when the building was used as a barn for the cows that grazed on the neighboring slopes. What you'll see today is a stone building whose balconies and gables are outlined against the steep hillside into which it is built. The Berthod family transformed what had been a dilapidated property into a rustic and comfortable hotel in 1979, surrounding the establishment with summer flowerbeds. Today it's managed by Bruna Berthod Perri and her nephew, Stefano Pellin. Their youth and enthusiasm are evident. The unusual physical decor is accented with a grandfather clock in the lobby, along with a collection of antique tools and a rhythmic series of thick timbers, stucco, and exposed stone walls. The bar is open only to residents of the hotel, and music is offered. There are also an exercise room and a sauna. Comfortable double rooms with bath, phone, TV, and frigo-bar cost 81,000 lire ($61.50) in high season, 71,000 lire ($54) in low. No singles are available. A rich breakfast is the only meal served, but there is the possibility of choosing your menu in different restaurants cooperating with La Grange. The hotel is closed in May, June, October, and November.

La Brenva, 11013 Courmayeur-Entrèves, (tel. 0165/89-285). Many skiers from Courmayeur make a special trek to Entrèves just to have a drink at the old-fashioned bar area of this hotel and restaurant, where a copper espresso machine is surmounted by a brass eagle, and where many of the decorative accessories are at least a century old. The core of the building was constructed in 1884 as a rustic hunting lodge for Victor Emmanuel. In 1897 it became the closest hotel to the base of Mont Blanc, and in 1980 the Vaglio family enlarged its stone foundations with the addition of extra bedrooms and a larger eating area.

The restaurant consists of three rooms, each lined with exposed stone walls, wide flooring planks, hunting trophies, copper pots, and straw-bottomed chairs. Fires burn almost all the time in winter, and many diners prefer an apéritif in the unusual salon, within view of the well-chosen paintings. On any given day the menu could include prosciutto, fonduta for two, carbonada with polenta, scaloppine with fresh mushrooms, Valle d'Aostan beefsteak, and zabaglione for dessert. Full meals cost 35,000 lire ($26.50) to 50,000 lire ($38), served from 12:30 to 1:30 p.m. and 7:30 to 10:30 p.m.

The 14 simple and comfortable bedrooms each have a private bath, TV, phone, and lots of peace and quiet. Many of them have covered loggias. With half board included, they rent for 95,000 lire ($72.25) per person daily, depending on the season. La Brenva is a Provençal word for the thousands of larches that cover the surrounding mountainside.

La Maison de Filippo (tel. 89-968) since 1965 has offered the complete gastromic experience of the Valdostan kitchen in a *tipico* atmosphere. A colorful tavern, it is the creation of Leo Garin, who was once featured in both *Playboy* magazine and *Town & Country*. His establishment is for those who enjoy a rustic atmosphere, bountiful regional food, and a festive mood. The fare is served either in the mellowed rooms inside, or in the beer garden in summer, with a full view of Mont Blanc. Mr. Garin features local specialties on an all you-can-eat basis. Some call his mansion the "Chalet of Gluttony."

A typical meal? The first course might begin with a selection of antipasti, followed by a two-foot-long platter of about 60 varieties of sausage, with a cutting board and knife. Then there will be a parade of pasta dishes. For a main course, you can pick everything from fondue to camoscio (chamois meat) to trout with an almond-and-butter sauce, to roast duck with an orange glaze. You may even prefer the Valdostan boiled dinner, with pungent hamhock, cabbage, and potatoes. Accompanying are huge hunks of coarse country bread from a wicker basket (the size of a laundry bin). For dessert, crêpes suzette are an ever-popular favorite, along with a selection of the regional cheese. At the end of the banquet, an aptly titled grail of friendship makes for an exciting event. Meals are served from 12:30 to 2:30 p.m. and 8 to 10:30 p.m., and the tavern is closed from June to July 15 and in November, as well as on Tuesday.

Many French people ride through Mont Blanc Tunnel just to dine here. Inside, the three-story open hallway seems like a rustic barn, with an open worn wooden staircase leading to the various dining nooks. You pass casks of nuts, baskets of fresh fruits, window ledges with bowls of salad, fruit tarts, wooden boxes spilling over with spices, onions, gourds, and loaves of freshly baked bread. It's one of the most charming inns in all the valley. Expect to pay 38,000 lire ($29) for a so-called normal meal or up to 50,000 lire ($38) if you prefer five huge courses.

A 31-mile drive northeast of Aosta takes us to—

5. Breuil-Cervinia

A major ski resort, Breuil-Cervinia has enough alpine terrain to satisfy all but the most insatiable of scene-gulpers. With the Matterhorn (Monte Cervino) towering majestically in the background, the resort occupies a superb setting, including a man-made one that has burst into full bloom in recent years. Many of its hotels and chalets have that new look to them, much like a Klondike town. The air is crystal fresh, and there are walks in all directions. For the most exciting look at mountain scenery, take the run to the Plateau Rosa at 11,415 feet above sea level.

The most adventurous of skiers, armed with an international lift ticket and a passport, can follow a series of cable cars and specially marked trails all the way to the Swiss resort of Zermatt.

The telephone area code for Breuil-Cervinia is 0166.

HOTELS IN BREUIL-CERVINIA

In hotels, Breuil-Cervinia is amply stocked, with new ones sprouting up along the hillside. My recommendations follow:

The Upper Bracket

Grand Hotel Cristallo, 11021 Breuil-Cervinia (tel. 0166/948-121). Massive and convex, its severe façade was built in the 1950s, those *la dolce vita* days of Gina Lollobrigida and Aristotle Onassis. With its stout timbers, gray stone, and white stucco, it's still going strong, renting not only regular rooms but apartments and suites as well. One of the highest hotels at the resort, it stands in lonely grandeur amid snowbacks, about a quarter of a mile above the center. It's said to have one of the biggest indoor pools of any high-altitude hotel in Europe, as well as an array of streamlined but comfortable public rooms. These include a bar/pizzeria, a unisex hairdresser, a cabaret (in season only), a piano bar, a mini-club for children, two saunas, and a Turkish bath. The Cristallo also shelters the premier restaurant at the resort. It is open from late June through August and from just before Christmas to April. Each of its bedrooms has a private bath, solid built-in furniture whose angles are softened with coordinated fabrics, and mini-bar. Depending on the season, and with half board included, per-person rates in a double range from 120,000 lire ($91.25) to 220,000 lire ($167) daily. The hotel is richly decorated with original art.

Hotel Hermitage, 11021 Breuil-Cervinia (tel. 0166/948-918), my favorite nest at the resort, was built in the 1970s and set a short but steep walk above the center. This hotel is considered the finest and most stylish in Breuil-Cervinia. It's owned and managed by members of the Neyroz family, who, for my money, are the most gracious hosts in the valley, equally adept at entertaining a fur-coat-clad Ferrari group from Milan or a couple on their honeymoon from Michigan. Its chalet-inspired design includes a warm but streamlined interior decor with lots of exposed pine and granite, high ceilings, and a spacious, airy feeling. In the heart of the reception area is a roaring fireplace where, as snow whirls around the great snaggletooth pyramid of Matterhorn, you are likely to see couples drinking grappa, a heady elixir. The Hermitage contains one of the most alluring swimming pools at the resort. Sinuously curved, it is illuminated with huge windows against which snowdrifts pile softly as if to stress the difference between the cozy interior and the savage cold outside. Facilities also include a steambath and a sauna. The hotel is small, only 32 well-furnished bedrooms, so each guest gets personal treatment, often from a family member. Rooms on the north open onto majestic views of the towering Matterhorn, whereas those with southern exposure are sun traps. Accommodations are either double or twin bedded, and each has a private bath. With half board included, the per-person rate is 130,000 lire ($98.75) daily.

The Medium-Priced Range

Hotel Europa, 11021 Breuil-Cervinia (tel. 0166/948-660), at the foot of the Matterhorn, lying at the head of the main artery of the resort, is competent and comfortable. A family-run hotel, it is operated by the Odissio-Zavattaro clan. Designed with clean angles, it is a no-nonsense hotel often avidly appreciated by its ski clientele, who check in from December 10 to May. Those interested in viewing the Mat-

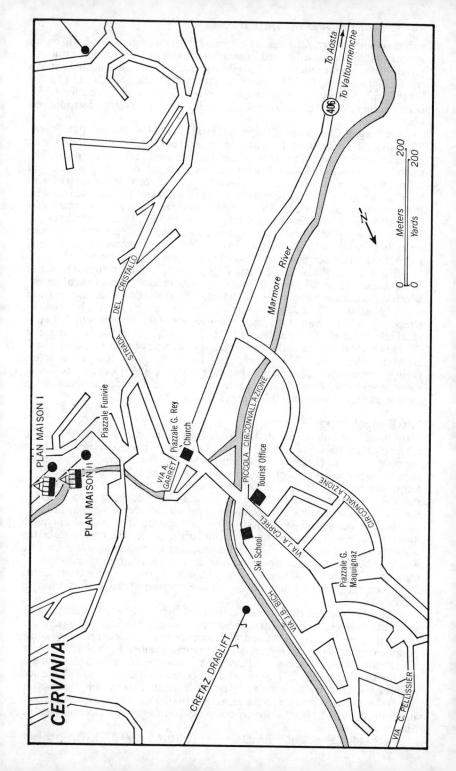

terhorn in summer can also book in here from July to mid-September. Its 40 rooms are cozy and modern, well heated in winter, each with its own triangular balcony, private bath, and earth-tone fabrics. Singles cost 50,000 lire ($38) daily and doubles run 81,000 lire ($61.50). Full board ranges from 90,000 lire ($68.50) to 110,000 lire ($83.50) per person. On the premises is a large dining room serving food from both Piedmont and Valle d'Aosta. Other facilities include a terrace solarium and a bar.

Les Neiges d'Antan, località Perrères, 11021 Breuil-Cervinia (tel. 0166/948-775), about 2½ miles from the center, offers small but well-furnished rooms in an alpine chalet. It is one of the most peaceful and tranquil hotels at the resort. The location's name is technically called Perrères, and motorists will see signs indicating it from the center of Breuil-Cervinia. Many of the interior walls are covered with wood, accented with mountain artifacts, and filled with a usually contented clientele that seems to appreciate the isolation. The 30 rooms rent for anywhere from 65,000 lire ($49.50) to 90,000 lire ($68.50) per person daily for full board in high season. Even if you're not staying there, the restaurant might make a popular excursion from town. In summer, they organize tours in the mountains with mules. Both the hotel and restaurant are open from early December to May and July to September.

Breuil, 11021 Breuil-Cervinia (tel. 0166/949-537), is the preferred choice of many skiers, who book its 45 comfortably furnished rooms solidly in high season, which lasts from December to April. The resort hotel also does a summer business when it reopens in July and August. Right in the heart of the town, the hotel is contemporary and well maintained. Each of its well-heated (in winter) rooms has a private bath or shower. The rate ranges from 55,000 lire ($41.75) daily in a single to 90,000 lire ($68.50) in a double. However, it's customary to stay here on the half-board rate of 95,000 lire ($72.25) per person daily. Skiers gather here for their après-ski in winter, enjoying the American bar and the wood-paneled lounge. The dining room serves some of the best food in the area, with many Valdostan specialties, a complete meal costing from 40,000 lire ($30.50).

The Budget Range

Chalet Valdôtain, strada Statale, 11021 Breuil-Cervinia (tel. 0166/949-428), is a family affair, offering a home-like touch. The Morello family operates this chalet opposite Lago Bleu (Lake Blue), two miles or so from the center. An alpine structure, it makes good use of wood and picture windows, and the bedrooms are tastefully restrained (a typical one has pine floors, with walls partly in white and partly in pine). A single rents for 70,000 lire ($53.25) daily, and a double goes for 120,000 lire ($91.25). On the full-board plan, guests pay 90,000 lire ($68.50) to 110,000 lire ($83.50) per person daily. Meals in the large restaurant, decorated in typical mountain style with great fir beams and a large grill in the center seem to taste better when the logs are lit in the fieldstone fireplace. The get-together point is the bar, which is like a living room, decorated with fir wood, making for an ambience of comfort and warmth. In addition, you can also spend an evening in the tavern disco. In summer the place is open from June 15 to September 30, reopening in winter from December to April.

Hotel Breithorn, 11021 Breuil-Cervinia (tel. 0166/949-9024). Built in 1929 as a private Valdostan home, this establishment became a hotel in 1935, one of the first in the area. Its intricately fitted stone exterior rises six abrupt stories above a position on the southern periphery of the commercial center. Each of its 24 rooms has a phone, a tile-covered bath, and alpine furniture crafted from local pine. Singles rent for 45,000 lire ($34.25) daily, and doubles cost 80,000 lire ($60.75), including breakfast. On the premises is an alpine-inspired dining room with windows on three sides, potted geraniums, and a menu of such rib-sticking fare as pasta e fagioli and grilled steaks. The hotel is closed from mid-September to early December and in May and June.

Leonardo Carrel, 11021 Breuil-Cervinia (tel. 0166/949-077), is an excellent refuge for skiers and mountain climbers, standing as it does at the foot of the Alps, with a stream at its edge, along with woods and pastures. Owned by Ada and Leonardo Carrel (a professional guide and ski instructor), it offers a chance to enjoy alpine chalet life. The stone-and-wood house, with its overhanging roof (three tiers of sun balconies), is just outside the village. In it, the Carrels have provided a private bath or shower for every one of the ten bedrooms, unusual for a hotel rated fourth class. The interior walls in most rooms are in knotty pine; accommodations are simply furnished. In the peak season, they prefer to accept guests—usually serious skiers—for a seven-day minimum. The daily rate for half board is 50,000 lire ($38) per person, rising to 59,000 lire ($44.75) for full board. The dining room, in knotty pine, with freshly starched white curtains and tablecloths, is an appropriate place for the meals prepared by Mrs. Carrel, who knows the specialties of the Valle d'Aosta. The hotel is open all year.

WHERE TO DINE

The reputation of many restaurants in the area is well deserved for its fine food and regional fare. Most guests dine at their hotel on some board arrangement; however, there are some independent eateries. Or you can visit another hotel dining room for a change of pace, as there are several good ones.

Hotel Hermitage Restaurant (tel. 948-998), already previewed as a desirable hotel, is also considered a leader in cuisine. The Neyroz family insist on the freshest of ingredients in their kitchen, and they hire a competent staff to run both the kitchen and the attractive dining room, with its huge windows. Nonresidents who call for a table are welcome. At a huge fireplace chickens are grilled to perfection, even on occasion a chamois. Chamois is also served as an air-dried meat, part of the antipasti selection. You can also order international specialties, such as snails in garlic butter. Two types of fondues are offered, along with mouthwatering pasta dishes. For a change of fare, try risotto al radicchio as an opening course, followed by, say, filet Hermitage in a mushroom sauce. Regional dishes are highly regarded by the staff, including the traditional soup of the valley, valpeileunentse (made with cheese and cauliflower). Everything is prepared to order, so prepare to wait. A fixed-price menu costs 40,000 lire ($30.50). Hours are 1 to 2:30 p.m. and 8 to 9:30 p.m. daily.

Les Neiges d'Antan, località Perrères (tel. 948-775), previewed as a hotel, is, in the opinion of many, the finest dining room in Breuil-Cervinia. A ten-minute ride from the center, it stands in a quiet and isolated valley. The cuisine mixes, in the words of one food critic, "the professionalism and fantasies" of the owner, Maurizio Bich. His major interests are said to be fine wine, the guitar, and opera. Certainly food, at least mountain-style fare, might be added to that list. The decor of the restaurant is rustic, with a fireplace grill, and old-fashioned recipes, handed down from generation to generation, are kept alive here. A small coach takes clients to and from the town. For antipasti, try a platter of air-dried alpine beef, followed by, say, polenta with baby quail. For a main course, the charcoal-grilled meats are superb. You might also sample trout pan-fried in butter. The kitchen serves some of the best cheese in the region as well, along with tempting desserts. The check will come to around 38,000 lire ($29), and service is daily except Monday from 12:30 to 2:30 p.m. and 7:30 to 9:30 p.m. Closed in July, October, and November.

Ristorante Matterhorn (tel. 948-518), in the center of the resort, has a rustic decor with lots of wood like a chalet. Ezio and Mirco Dominici, two brothers from Rimini on the Adriatic, rule over this hearty domain. Proof of the pudding is that they are nearly always full in season, so reservations are important. From their oven come pizzas along with an array of grilled meats. However, they are known mainly for their fish, which is shipped in from their native Rimini. They are adept at preparing any of the famous dishes of the Romagna kitchen, including such tempting pastas as tortellini and ravioli. Try their gnocchi in a flavorful sauce as well. The restaurant is open daily from noon to 3 p.m. and 7 p.m. to midnight; a meal costs from 30,000 lire ($22.75).

AFTER DARK

A café, nightclub, and cinema, the **Hostellerie des Guides,** 11021 Breuil-Cervinia (tel. 0166/949-473), reigns supreme in the region as the most sought-after gathering place for the athletically chic. It boasts loyalists from as far away as the Himalayas. All this was created by one of the world's most celebrated mountaineers, Mirko Minuzzo, who climbed Mount Everest on a 1973 Italian expedition. The establishment rises abruptly from the center of town, a bit like a modernized fortress. Inside, the inn offers 14 "constantly booked" accommodations, costing 110,000 lire ($83.50) daily in a double with breakfast—that is, if you can get in.

However, everybody is invited to the street-level café, where scores of photographs record the world's most daring wilderness feats in locales ranging from Greenland to Nepal. There are also cases filled with artifacts from India, pairs of elephant tusks flanking a long couch, and, most important, huge windows. An Irish coffee, ideal on a cold night, costs 12,000 lire ($9.10). The café is open daily from 7 a.m. to midnight.

In the basement, the Scotch Club disco is outfitted with a round brass-topped dance floor, a bar carved from mahogany, and a separate annex whose labyrinth of couches is designed only for conversation. Open nightly in season from 10 p.m. to 4 a.m., it charges a 15,000-lira ($11.50) entrance in low season, going up to 20,000 lire ($15.25) in high season. Also in the basement is a small, intimate movie theater.

GENOA, THE TWO RIVIERAS, AND ELBA

For years the retreat of the wintering wealthy, the twin Italian Rivieras now enjoy the broadest base of tourism. Even in winter (the average temperature in January hovers around the 50° Fahrenheit mark) the Rivieras are popular, but not for swimming. Some of the hotels in San Remo, for example, charge high-season prices then, unique for European beach resorts. The balmy weather is made possible by the protection provided by the Ligurian Apennines that loom in the background.

The winding coastline of the Rivieras, particularly the one that stretches from the French frontier to San Remo, is especially familiar to movie-goers, as it's been used as a background for countless flicks about sports-car racing, jewel thieves, spy thrillers, even off-the-record romances. Over the years the northwestern coast of Italy has known the famous and the infamous, especially literary figures: Shelley (who drowned off the shore), D'Annunzio, Byron, Katherine Mansfield, George Sand, D. H. Lawrence.

The Mediterranean vegetation is characterized by pines, olives, citrus trees, and cypresses. The Western Riviera—the Riviera di Ponente—from the border to Genoa is sometimes known as the Riviera of Flowers because of its perfumey profusion of blossoms. Starting at the French border, Ventimiglia becomes the gateway city to Italy. Along the way you'll encounter the first big resort, Bardighera, followed by San Remo, the reigning queen, although her crown has been tarnished since her more lustrous days at the turn of the century.

Genoa, dividing the two Rivieras, is the capital of the Ligurian region—a big, bustling port city that has charm for those willing to spend time seeking out its treasures.

On the Riviera di Levante (eastern), a triumvirate of small, dramatically situated resorts—Rapallo, Santa Margherita, and Portofino (the yachtsman's favorite) —take the edge. Proceeding down the coast, you'll come to Viareggio, a mammoth summer watering spa. La Spezia, a naval port perched on a gulf, is included not so much for its own attractions, but as a base for exploring the Cinque Terre. Finally, south of Pisa you can take a ferry at Piombino for the most isolated beach strips of them all, on the Isle of Elba in the Tuscan archipelago.

Starting at the French frontier, we'll base first in—

---

1. San Remo

Ever since Emperor Frederick wintered in a villa, the reputation of San Remo has grown, attracting first the turn-of-the-century wealthy, including many French people, the English, and later the Americans. Positioned about 10 miles from the French frontier, 85 from Genoa, the flower-filled resort seems dated by today's standards, although attempts have been made to upgrade it. But its casino, race track, 18-hole golf course, its deluxe Royal Hotel, still attract the fashionable. Its climate is considered the mildest on the entire western Riviera coast.

Even if you're just passing through, you might want to stop off and visit La Città Vecchia (also known as La Pigna), the old city on the top of the hill. Far removed in spirit from the burgeoning sterility near the water, old San Remo blithely ignores the present, capturing and holding the past behind the façades of its tiny houses on narrow, steep lanes. In the new town, the palm-flanked passeggiata dell'Imperatrice attracts the promenader. For a scenic view, you can take the funicular to Monte Bignone at 4,265 feet.

San Remo's telephone area code is 0184.

HOTELS IN SAN REMO

There are plenty of accommodations in San Remo, in all price categories.

A Deluxe Choice

Royal, corso Imperatrice 80, 18038 San Remo (tel. 0184/79-991), seems like a mirror reflection of the Beverly Hills Hotel, complete with terraces and gardens, a heated free-form saltwater swimming pool, a forest of palm trees, bright flowers, and hideaway nooks for shade. The activity centers around the garden terrace, as there is little emphasis put on the public lounges (decked out in the grand old dowager style). Your lunch, for example, will be served in fair weather on the veranda under an arbor of orange roses. The bedrooms vary considerably—some are tennis-court size with private balconies, many have sea views, and others face the hills. All the rooms have phone, radio, color TV and bar-freezer, and the furnishings range from traditional to semi-modern—in other words, a lottery chance. The hotel is closed from October to mid-December, otherwise charging 185,000 lire ($141) daily in a single room, 320,000 lire ($243) in a double. The maximum half-board rate is 235,000 lire ($179) per person. An orchestra gives a concert in the afternoon and plays for dancing in the evening (festive occasions call for formal dress). On the premises are an American bar, facilities for children, hairdressers, a sauna, a solarium, mini-golf, a gym, a tennis court, covered and open-air car parks, and a garage with a mechanic.

The Upper Bracket

Grand Hotel Londra, corso Matuzia 2, 18038 San Remo (tel. 0184/79-961), was built around 1900 as a two-story hotel and later expanded into the imposing structure you see today. It's within a ten-minute walk of the commercial district, although it lies in a park with a view of the sea. The well-furnished interior is filled with framed engravings, porcelain in illuminated cases, warm colors, gilt mirrors, brass detailing, and a bar. Many of the bedrooms have wrought-iron balconies whose curves are repeated in the art-nouveau iron-and-glass canopy extending over the entryway. With full board included, rooms rent for 155,000 lire ($118) to 180,000 lire ($137) per person daily. The hotel is closed from October 10 to December 20. On the premises is a saltwater swimming pool.

Hotel Astoria West End, corso Matuzia 8, 18038 San Remo (tel. 0184/70-791). Its immaculate white façade is grand enough to be a wedding-cake version of Buckingham Palace. Set imperially above well-maintained gardens, across from the main artery running alongside the sea, the hotel lies next door to the Londra. Its interior has retained many of the original building's elaborate plaster ceilings. The colors are stylish and refreshing, especially in the airy bar section where brass-and-teakwood stools pull up to a red-marble countertop. Everywhere there are lots of provincial panels, and an outdoor terrace is set under a glass-and-wrought-iron canopy. Fanciful iron chairs are scattered throughout the semitropical garden and near the pool. Built in 1860, this is one of the two or three oldest hotels in San Remo. It was completely renovated in 1982, although the architects kept the soaring cast-iron columns of the stairwell, the carved-oak elevators, and the 120-year-old chandeliers. Liza Minnelli stayed here once in the only room on the premises with a working fireplace. The beautifully up-to-date rooms rent for 95,000 lire ($72.25) to 155,000 lire ($117.75) daily in a single and 110,000 lire ($83.50) to 145,000 lire ($110) per person in a double, the higher tariffs charged in high season. Half board is included.

Hotel Méditerranée, corso Cavallotti 76, 18038 San Remo (tel. 0184/571-000). The traffic in front of this steel-and-glass structure might appear hysterical, especially in peak season, but once you're inside, or in the rear garden with its Olympic-size pool, you'll scarcely be aware of it. The stylish public rooms contain pleasing color combinations that go well with the many plants and the generously sized modern sculpture filling part of the polished floor space. There's a drinking area with a metallic ceiling and bar stools with chrome bases. The Aloha restaurant offers a Polynesian theme under a rustic inclined shelter. The comfortable rooms cost from 160,000 lire ($122) per person daily, with full board included. Air conditioning and car-park services are extra. Children under 6 receive a 30% reduction.

The Medium-Priced Range

Hotel Paradiso, via Roccasterone 10, 18038 San Remo (tel. 0184/85-112), is lodged on a hillside in a former residential sector now turned into a resort district. Those who visit appreciate the family ownership, the quiet position, and the comfortable amenities. You enter onto a paved parking area. The rooms overlook the lower terrace, banked with semitropical vines and flowers. The dining room, where Italian specialties are served, has its own airy look, with three walls of glass. The old-fashioned drawing room, on the other hand, is decorated with gilt mirrors and crystal chandeliers. The bedrooms are well furnished, containing private bath or shower, mini-bar, direct-dial phone, and TV on request. The seafront rooms all have large balconies with potted geraniums in various colors, the handiwork of the owner Signora Gaiani. Single rooms cost from 59,000 lire ($44.75) daily, and doubles go for 92,000 lire ($70). Full board is offered for 94,000 lire ($71.50) to 99,000 lire ($75.25) per person, depending on the accommodation and the season.

Hotel Miramare, corso Matuzia 9, 18038 San Remo (tel. 0184/882-381), is a well-maintained building whose white exterior looks vaguely Moorish, especially since it's set at the back of semitropical gardens bordering the busy thoroughfare on which it's located. A curved driveway leads past palmettos to the front entrance, whose lobby is filled with marble floors, gilt-frame mirrors, French portrait busts, 19th-century bronzes, and an art nouveau painting above the reception desk. After passing through the public rooms, you discover a seaside garden with sculptures and plenty of verdant hideaways. The bedrooms are clean and comfortable. An additional eight rooms are contained in a neighboring annex whose white walls look out over the garden. Closed from September 22 to December 21, the hotel charges from 90,000 lire ($68.50) daily in a single, from 150,000 lire ($114) in a double. Accommodations in the annex are slightly less expensive. A covered swimming pool is in one of the outbuildings.

The Budget Range

Hotel Bel Soggiorno Juana, corso Matuzia 41, 18038 San Remo (tel. 0184/83-703), is centrally located, near the main sea promenade Imperatrice and the beaches. Attractively furnished and inviting, it provides each room with a phone, bath (or shower), and toilet. A double room with bath or shower rents for 70,000 lire ($53.25) daily; a single with bath or shower goes for 45,000 lire ($34.25). Because the food is good, many prefer to stay here on the half-board plan, at terms ranging from 70,000 lire ($53.25) per person daily. There's a large reception area, plus plenty of living rooms for lounging. The management of Luciana Maurizi de Benedetti has also provided a nice garden to sit out and enjoy the sun and plants. There's also a garage.

Hotel Mare Luce, corso Matuzia 3, 18038 San Remo (tel. 0184/85-505). As you're walking along the flowered promenade away from the commercial center of town, you'll notice a flowering garden enclosed on one side by a gilded coat-of-arms emblazoned on the neighboring walls of a Polish Catholic church. At the back of the garden is the building that until 1945 housed a refugee center that Poles throughout Europe used as a base for finding friends and relatives. Today it's one of the most pleasant, reasonably priced hotels in the resort. The furniture in the public rooms is bathed in sunlight from the big windows. From the flowering garden, visitors can see the grounds and façades of surrounding hotels, which are far more expensive. The 23 bedrooms rent for 42,000 lire ($32) daily in a single going up to 60,000 lire ($45.50) in a double. The hotel is closed from November 1 until December 20.

Hotel Eletto, via Matteotti 44, 18038 San Remo (tel. 0184/85-614), is on the main artery of town, near more expensive hotels. It has a 19th-century façade with cast-iron balconies and ornate detailing. The rear of the 35-room hotel is set in a small garden with about the biggest tree in San Remo casting a welcome shade over the flowerbeds. This pleasant stopover point contains public rooms filled with carved panels, old mirrors, and antique furniture, along with windows on two sides. The dining room is sunny and well maintained. Singles cost from 40,000 lire ($30.50) daily; doubles, 70,000 lire ($53.25).

DINING IN SAN REMO

In San Remo you'll be introduced to the Ligurian cuisine, a table characterized by the Genovese style of cooking, with a reliance on seafood dishes. If featured on the menu, try the buridda, which is the Ligurian version of Mediterranean bouillabaisse. The white wines from the five villages (the Cinque Terre) are highly valued.

Da Giannino, lungomare Trento e Trieste 23 (tel. 504-014). The chef, Anna Tiburzio, is the guiding light behind this excellent restaurant, the finest in San Remo. In a conservatively comfortable decor of elegance, you can enjoy such specialties as a changing array of warm seafood antipasti, a flavorful risotto laced with cheese and a pungently aromatic green sauce, and a selection of main courses that change with the availability of ingredients. Some of the more exotic selections are likely to include a marinated cuttlefish gratiné. The wine list includes many of the better vintages of both France and Italy. Meal prices range from 65,000 lire ($49.75) to 85,000 lire ($64.50), and service is from 12:30 to 2:30 p.m. and 7:30 to 10 p.m. The restaurant is closed all day Sunday and for lunch on Monday. Reservations are strongly advised.

Pesce d'Oro, corso Cavalloti 300 (tel. 576-332), serves some of the finest food on the Italian Riviera. The location is so unprepossessing—right in the midst of a mechanics' alley—you'll think you're at the wrong address. However, once inside you should place yourself in the hands of Signor Visconti, who is both the chef and the owner. Perhaps he'll suggest a pasta to begin with, the lasagne al pesto (a sauce made with olive oil, garlic, pine seeds, cheese, and fresh basil), or the highly recommendable farfalline al'pizzico—a blending of potatoes, spinach-flavored pasta butterflies, and fresh string beans. Among the seafood dishes, the zuppa di frutti di mare is outstanding, as is the spiedino di scampi. Fresh fish is featured daily, except on Monday, when the "Golden Fish" is closed. Expect to pay anywhere from 50,000 lire ($38) to 75,000 lire ($57) for a complete meal, served from noon to 2:30 p.m. and 7:30 to 10 p.m. Closed from February 15 to March 15.

La Lanterna, via Molo di Ponente al Porto 8 (tel. 86-055), is a harborside restaurant where the smart set goes for top-notch fish dinners and a big whiff of local atmosphere. You'll find a good table under parasols, so you can keep an eye trained on the yachting set ("No, darling, we're definitely not going to Hydra this year!"). Most dishes are beautifully cooked and served by a willing staff. Meals include an excellent fish soup, called brodetto di pesce con crostini, followed by a mixed Ligurian fish fry or a meat course, such as scaloppine in a marsala wine sauce. Your tab will be 28,000 lire ($21.25) to 42,000 lire ($32). Hours are 12:30 to 2:30 p.m. and 7:30 to 10 p.m. daily except Thursday; closed from mid-December to mid-February.

Il Bagatto, via Matteotti 145 (tel. 85-500), provides good meals in a tavern setting, with dark beams, provincial chairs, even overscale pepper grinders brought to the tables. The location is in the shopping district of the town, about two blocks from the sea. My most recent dinner began with a choice of creamy lasagne or savory hors d'oeuvres. The scaloppine with marsala sauce was especially pleasing, as was (on another occasion) tender calves' liver with bacon. All orders were accompanied by potatoes and a choice of vegetables, then followed by crème caramel for dessert. And the pièce de résistance is the Valencian paella—a whopping order with bite-size pieces of fish floating in a sea of rice. Expect to spend from 50,000 lire ($38). The restaurant, open from 12:30 to 2:30 p.m. and 7:30 to 10 p.m., shuts down every Sunday and for all of June.

SAN REMO AFTER DARK

The high life holds forth at the **San Remo Casino** (tel. 79-901), which is built in a turn-of-the-century style known as "Liberty," an ornate mixture of classical with art nouveau. For decades fashionable visitors have frequented this temple, dining in the highest style in the elegant restaurant, reserving tables at the roof garden's cabaret, or testing their luck with Lady Fortune at the gaming tables. Like a white-walled palace built at the top of a steep flight of stone steps above the main artery of town, the casino perhaps lacks the lushness of its nearby sister at Monte Carlo, yet still stands pristine and restrained, catering to a conservative audience that doesn't necessarily include the titled aristocrats of yesteryear.

The entrance fee to the casino is 10,000 lire ($7.60) for the French gaming room, which is open every day from 2:30 p.m. to 3 a.m. A jacket and tie are required for men, and the first 10,000 lire ($7.60) worth of chips is free. Entrance to what the management calls the American games section (where there is no dress code) is free. Action there begins at 2:30 p.m. Presentation of a passport is required for entrance, and security is strict.

Not everyone shows up to gamble. The restaurant usually has an orchestra playing everything from waltzes to modified rock and roll, and no one will mind if you get up to dance. It is open daily from 8:30 to 11 p.m. (till 1 a.m. on Saturday and Sunday). A full meal goes for 60,000 lire ($45.60) and up. A roof-garden cabaret is open only during the three months of summer. Drinks there cost from 20,000 lire

($15.25), more when there's a show, which is not without its share of striptease. The bartender can make at least 25 concoctions (he's used to odd requests).

---

2. Genoa (Genova)

It was altogether fitting that "Genoa the Proud" (Superba) gave birth to Christopher Columbus. Its link with the sea and maritime greatness dates back to ancient times. However, Columbus did his hometown a disservice. By blazing the trail to the New World, he caused a devastating blow to Mediterranean ports in general, as the balance of trade shifted to newly developing centers on the Atlantic.

Even so, Genoa today is Italy's premier port, ranking with Marseille in importance. In its heyday (the 13th century), its empire rivaled that of Venice, extending from colonies on the Barbary Coast to citadels on the Euphrates. Apart from Columbus, its most famous son was Andrea Doria (the ill-fated ocean liner was named after him), who wrested his city from the yoke of French domination in the early 16th century.

Like a half-moon, the port encircles the Gulf of Genoa. Its hills slope right down to the water, so walking is likely to be an up- and downhill affair. Because of the terrain, it was quite late in Genoa's development that it saw the opening of the Christopher Columbus Airport.

The center of the city's maritime life, the **Harbor of Genoa** makes for an interesting stroll, particularly in the part of the old town bordering the water. Sailors from many lands search for adventure and girls to entertain them in the little bars and cabarets occupying the back alleyways. Often the streets are merely medieval lanes, with foreboding buildings closing in.

A word of warning: The harbor, particularly after dark, is not for the squeamish. It can be dangerous. If you go wandering, try not to be alone and leave as many valuables in safekeeping as possible. Genoa is rougher than Barcelona, more comparable to Marseille. Not only in the harbor area, but on any side street that runs downhill, a woman is a likely candidate to lose her purse.

The present harbor was the result of extensive rebuilding, following massive World War II bombardments that crippled its seaside installations. The best way to view the overall skyline is from a boat which you take from the Maritime Station at the Ponte dei Mille. The trip lasts one hour. Along the way, you pass naval yards, shipbuilders, steelworkers, and warehouses (yachtsmen anchor at Duca degli Abruzzi)—not a pretty picture entirely, but a fascinating landscape of industrial might.

GETTING THERE AND ORIENTATION

In the middle of the Italian Riviera, Genoa is often reached by train, as it has good rail connections with the rest of Italy. For example, it lies only 1½ hours from the French border. If you're already in Italy, you'll find Milan is a train journey of only 1½ hours; Florence, 3 hours. Alitalia and other carriers also fly into Genoa, winging it in at **Aeroporto Cristoforo Colombo,** four miles west of the center. Motorists will find Genoa lying right along the main autostrada that begins its run at the French border, running along the Ligurian coastline.

Genoa opens onto the Porto di Genova, and most of the section of interest to tourists lies between two main rail stations, **Stazione Prìncipe,** on the western fringe of the town, near the port, and **Stazione Brignole,** to the northeast, opening onto piazza Verdi. A major artery is **via XX Settembre,** which lies between the piazza Ferrari in the west and the piazza della Vittoria in the east. **Via Balbi** is another major artery, beginning its run east of the Stazione Prìncipe, off piazza Acquaverde. At the end of via Balbi you'll come to the piazza Nunziata. From

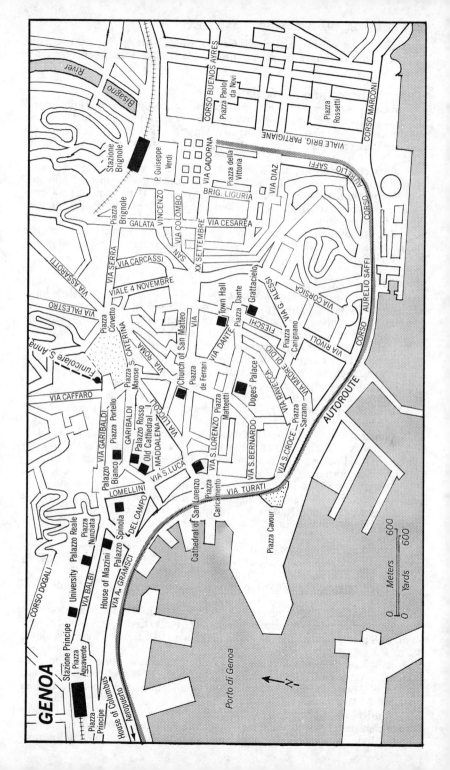

there, it is just a short walk along via Cairola, which leads to the most important touristic street of Genoa, the palazzo-flanked **via Garibaldi** (but more about that later).

Other Transportation Information

Railway Stations: Genoa has two major rail stations, the Stazione Prìncipe and the Stazione Brignole. Chances are that you'll arrive at the Prìncipe, which is nearest to the harbor and the old part of the city. However, both trains and municipally operated buses run between the two stations. For information about trains, call 284-081.

Airport: Genoa has an airport with limited service. It's the Aeroporto Internazionale di Genova C. Colombo. For information about flights, call 600-861.

Ferry Information: It is highly likely that you are in Genoa waiting for a ferryboat to take you to such offshore destinations as Sardinia or Sicily. If so, the number to call for information is the Stazione Marittima (tel. 267-128).

Gas Station: If you don't mind self-service, there is an Agip gas station open at night. It's along the viale Brigate Partigiane. You must possess the right change.

Taxi: To call a radio taxi, dial 2696.

PRACTICAL FACTS

For Genoa, the **telephone area code** is 010. If you need to make a long-distance call, it's cheaper to go to the office at via XX Settembre 139, which is open 24 hours a day. Otherwise, your hotel is likely to impose heavy surcharges. You can also place calls at both the Brignole and Prìncipe railroad stations until 9:30 p.m.

American Express: The representative of American Express in Genoa is Aviomar S.N.C., via Vernazza 48R (tel. 595-551). But you should be a client—that is, carry an American Express card or use the company's traveler's checks—before you have your mail sent to them.

Babysitters: If you need a babysitter, get in touch with **Casa della Giovane,** via Galata 38B (tel. 561-621), which receives calls only Monday through Friday from 3 to 5:45 p.m.

Consulate: In Genoa, the **U.S. Consulate** is at piazza Portello 6 (tel. 282-741).

Currency Exchange: To exchange money, you'll find service at **Delfino,** via Balbi 161R. However, both the Brignole and Prìncipe railway stations have exchange offices open daily from 7 a.m. to 10 p.m.

Drugstores: Genoa has several all-night pharmacies, including **Europa,** corso Europa 676R (tel. 380-239), and **Ghersi,** corso Buenos Aires 74R (tel. 541-661).

Emergency Phone Numbers: Dial 113 for assistance in a **general emergency.** If it's **automobile trouble,** call A.C.I., Soccorso Stradale (tel. 116). For an **ambulance,** call 595-951.

Laundry: Looking for a laundry? You'll find them at strategic points throughout the city. Two recommendable ones are **Galata,** via Galata 76R, and **De Paoli,** via Palestro 11R. They operate during regular business hours.

Lost Property: The lost and found office is the **Comune,** via Garibaldi 9 (tel. 20-981).

Medical Care: If you're in need of a doctor, call **A.I.A.D.** (tel. 566-158).

Post Office: The post office, at via Dante 161, also has a telex. Hours are 8:15 a.m. to 8 p.m. Monday through Friday and 8 a.m. to 1 p.m. on Saturday; closed Sunday.

Religious Services: If you're Catholic, you can go into almost any church in Genoa. If you're Protestant there's the Chiesa Evangelica Metodista, via Da Persico 40 (tel. 672-664), and if you're Jewish there's the Tempio Israelitico, on via Bertora (tel. 891-513).

Tourist Information: Visitors can get information at the major office of **Ente Provinciale peril Turismo,** via Roma 11 (tel. 581-407), and it's open from 8 a.m. to 2 p.m. Monday through Friday, until 1 p.m. on Saturday; closed Sunday. Information booths dispensing tourist literature can also be found at the rail stations and at the airport.

THE SIGHTS

Back in the heart of the city, you can stroll down **via Garibaldi,** the street of the patricians, on which noble Genovese families erected splendid palazzi in late Renaissance times. The guiding hand behind the general appearance and most of the architecture was Alessi, who grew to fame in the 16th century (he once studied under Michelangelo). Among the structures you'll want to visit, as they contain important galleries and museums, is the—

Palazzo Rosso

At via Garibaldi 18 is this 17th-century palace (tel. 282-641), once the home of the Brignoles. Restored after bombings in World War II, it contains a good collection of paintings, with such exceptional works as an *Ecce Homo* by Caravaggio and a *St. Catherine* by Tintoretto. Perhaps its best-known exhibit is Sir Anthony Van Dyck's portraits of Pauline and Anton Giulio Brignole-Sale from the original collection and the magnificient frescoes by Gregorio De Ferrari (*Spring* and *Summer*) and Domenico Piola (*Autumn* and *Winter*). There are also collections of old coins, ceramics, and sculpture, and a display of gilded baroque statuary. The gallery is open daily except Monday from 9 a.m. to 7 p.m. On Sunday, guided tours are offered at 10:30 a.m. and 3:15 p.m. Admission is 2,000 lire ($1.50).

Across from the red palace is the white palace, at no. 11 on the same street.

Palazzo Bianco Gallery

Donated to the city by the duchess of Galliera, along with her collection of art, the palace was built in the 17th century, although its appearance today reflects the work of later architects. Also gravely damaged during the war, the palace was rebuilt afterward, its designers using the opportunity to reflect the most recent advances in museum planning. The most significant paintings—from the Dutch and Flemish schools—include Gerard David's *Virgin of the Pappa* and Van der Goes's *Jesus Blessing the Faithful,* as well as works by Sir Anthony Van Dyck and Peter Paul Rubens. A wide-ranging survey of European and local artists is presented—with paintings by Zurbaran, and works by Bernardo Strozzi (a whole room) and Alessandro Magnasco (excellent painting of a scene in a Genovese garden). This gallery, at via Garibaldi 11 (tel. 291-803), is open daily except Monday from 9 a.m. to 7 p.m., with guided tours on Sunday at 10:30 a.m. and 3:15 p.m. Admission is 2,000 lire ($1.50).

From via Garibaldi, you can head down via della Maddalena to the next attraction, the—

National Gallery (Galleria Nazionale)

Housed in the Palazzo Spinola, piazza della Pellicceria 1 (tel. 294-661), is another painting collection. (This palace was originally designed for the Grimaldi family in the 16th century as a private residence, although the Spinolas took it over eventually.) Its notable works include Sir Anthony Van Dyck's *Child and His Dog,* Joos Van Cleve's *Madonna in Prayer,* Antonello da Messina's *Ecce Homo,* and Giovanni Pisano's *Giustizia.* The gallery, charging 2,000 lire ($1.50) admission, is open daily except Monday from 9 a.m. to 5 p.m. (to 1 p.m. on Sunday).

Via Garibaldi eventually becomes via Balbi, another palazzi-flanked street. The chief attraction here is the—

Royal Palace (Palazzo Reale)

The Royal Palace, via Balbi 10, was started about 1650, and work continued until the early years of the 18th century. It was built for the Balbi family, then sold to the Durazzo. It later became one of the royal palaces of the Savoia in 1824. King Charles Albert modified many of the rooms around 1840. Like all Genovese palazzi, some of these subsequent alterations marred original designs. Its Galleria d'Arte (tel. 206-851) is filled with paintings and sculpture, works of art by Van Dyck, Tintoretto, G. F. Romanelli, and L. Giordano. Frescoes and antiques from the 17th to the 19th century are displayed. Seek out, in particular, the Hall of Mirrors and the Throne Room. It is open daily except Sunday from 9 a.m. to 1:30 p.m., charging an admission of 2,000 lire ($1.50).

Although Genoa is noted for its medieval churches, towering over all of them is the—

Cathedral of San Lorenzo

At the piazza San Lorenzo (Lawrence), the cathedral is distinguished by its bands of black and white marble adorning the façade in the Pisan style. In its present form it dates from the 13th century, although it was erected upon the foundation of a much earlier structure. Alessi, referred to earlier, designed the dome, and the campanile (bell tower) dates from the 16th century. The Chapel of John the Baptist, with interesting Renaissance sculpture, is said to contain the remains of the saint for whom it is named. The treasury is worth a visit, especially for its Sacred Bowl, thought to be the Holy Grail when Crusaders brought it back from Caesarea in the early 12th century (Eastern traders probably made goodly sums off naïve Christians pursuing relics of Christ for the church back home). Hours of the treasury are 9 to 11:30 a.m. and 3 to 5:30 p.m. Tuesday through Saturday and from 10 a.m. to noon on Sunday.

Cimitèro di Staglieno

This has to be the most spectacular cemetery in the world. It is a collection of architectural wonders on a reduced scale—everything from a Gothic cathedral to an Egyptian pyramid to a Romanesque basilica to a Moorish mosque. The schmaltzy Victorian statuary is larger than life. The tombs of the great families of Genoa are found here. Giuseppe Mazzini, the Italian patriot, was buried here in 1782. The cemetery lies about three miles from the center of Genoa. Take road 45.

House of Columbus

A last sight that tour buses are fond of pointing out is the so-called house of Columbus, a dilapidated, vine-covered building at the piazza Dante, off the vico Dritto Ponticello (not to be visited inside). What it is, is an 18th-century reconstruction at the site of what may have been the house of the explorer.

HOTELS IN GENOA

Generally hotels are second rate but some good finds await those who search diligently. *Warning:* Some of the cheap hotels and pensiones in and around the waterfront are to be avoided. My recommendations, however, are suitable for married couples or women traveling alone.

A Deluxe Choice

Hotel Columbia, via Balbi 40, 16126 Genova (tel. 010/261-841), is the most luxurious hotel in Genoa. When it was built in 1926, it was the ultimate statement in expansive perspectives and grandly ornate design, outfitted in a 19th-century style that might make you think it's from an earlier era. The hotel served as headquarters of both the Germans and the Americans (in that order) during and after World War II. Today the pink-and-gilt dining room is likely to include businesspeople. Some of the closets of the oversize bedrooms are as big as small rooms in other hotels, and the bedrooms have Venetian glass chandeliers, large-scale furniture, high ceilings, French windows, air conditioning, and baths. They rent for 150,000 lire ($114) to 200,000 lire ($152) daily in a single, 210,000 lire ($160) to 260,000 lire ($198) in a double. Even more luxurious rooms and suites are available. To reach the hotel, take the exit from the autostrada at the Genova West side and proceed in the direction of the Stazione Prìncipe, just across the street from the Columbia.

The Upper Bracket

Hotel Savoia Majestic, via Arsenale di Terra 5, 16126 Genova (tel. 010/261-641), is the second-grandest hotel in Genoa, ranking just after the Columbia, right across the street. Built across from the train station in 1887, it was renovated in 1919 and again in 1950, which gave the public rooms many of the postwar accessories that are still there. It's said that this was one of the first hotels in Europe to have both its public rooms and private bedrooms air-conditioned. The clients tend to be overnighters from the business community of Europe. If you select this hotel, you should know that the decor of the high-ceilinged bedrooms ranges from modern to conservatively old-fashioned. Each accommodation has a frigo-bar, TV, phone, and air conditioning. Singles cost 150,000 lire ($114) daily, and doubles go for 210,000 lire ($160), including a continental breakfast. The lobby and reception area of this hotel is shared with another establishment, the Londra & Continentale.

Bristol-Palace, via XX Settembre 35, 16121 Genova (tel. 010/592-541), has a number of features that make one's stay in Genoa special. Its obscure entrance behind colonnades on a commercial street is misleading. The salons and drawing rooms are furnished nicely with traditional pieces—many antiques are utilized, some of which appear to be of museum caliber. The dining room, in the Louis XVI style, is the most inspired, an ornately carved ceiling highlighting a mural of cloud-riding cherubs in the center. The larger of the bedrooms have an old-fashioned elegance, are spacious and comfortable, and tastefully furnished. Most of the rooms have private bath, and all have the proper amenities, such as bedside lamps and phone. A single room rents for 160,000 lire ($122) daily, a double goes for 230,000 lire ($175), including a continental breakfast, service, and tax. The hotel's stairway is one of the most stunning in Genoa. The English bar is a favorite rendezvous point.

Plaza, via Martin Piaggio 11, 16122 Genova (tel. 010/893-642), is newer than its modified classic façade suggests. It was actually built in 1950 to replace an older hotel destroyed by an air raid in World War II. Its location is one of its finest assets, just off the piazza Corvetto with its equestrian statue, flower-bordered walks, and trees. The interior of the well-run hotel has been completely renewed, providing comfort and convenience. The bedrooms—97 in all, with either private bath or shower—are above average. Many have tiny sitting areas and modern, functional furnishings, plus refrigerator bar and color TV. The inclusive rate in a single is 130,000 lire ($98.75), 200,000 lire ($152) daily in a double. Air conditioning is included. On the premises are an American bar and a grill room.

The Medium-Priced Range

City Hotel, via San Sebastiano 6, 16123 Genova (tel. 010/592-595), is one of the best hotels in its category, located in a starkly angular stucco and travertine postwar building in the middle of a crumbling series of town houses that cluster along the narrow streets leading up to it. The location is one of the hotel's best features, near Corvetto Square and via Garibaldi. The staff will welcome you upon your arrival in the warm and comfortable wood-and-granite lobby and usher you to one of the modern rooms. In these, the parquet floors, specially designed furniture, and up-to-date amenities will isolate you from city life. A cocktail bar with snacks and a full breakfast are included in the attractions. Singles cost 95,000 lire ($72.25) to 135,000 lire ($103) daily; doubles, 140,000 lire ($106) to 180,000 lire ($137).

Albergo Viale Sauli, viale Sauli 5, 16121 Genova (tel. 010/561-397), is on the second floor of a modern concrete office building just off a busy shopping street in the center of town. The hotel is scattered over three floors, each of them reachable by elevator from the building's lobby. The public rooms are a high-ceilinged paneled trio of bar, breakfast room, and reception area, all with big windows and lots of comfort. Enore Sceresini is the opera-loving owner, and his clients usually include businesspeople who appreciate the cleanliness and comfort. Each of the units has marble floors and a spacious bath. Singles cost 75,000 lire ($57) daily; doubles, 104,000 lire ($79).

Hotel Nuova Astoria, piazza Brignole 4, 16122 Genova (tel. 010/873-316), was established in 1978 on the site of an older hotel, whose legacy included lots of polished paneling, wrought-iron accents, beige marble floors, and a baronial carved fireplace in one of the public rooms. The hotel sits on an uninspiring square that contains a filling station and whose view encompasses a traffic hub and many square blocks of apartment buildings. Each of the 75 bedrooms contains a private bath. There's a bar on the premises, but no restaurant. Singles rent for 90,000 lire ($68.50) daily; doubles, 120,000 lire ($91.25).

Hotel Londra & Continentale, Stazione Prìncipe, 16126 Genova (tel. 010/261-641). The lobby and reception personnel of this establishment are shared by another hotel, the Savoia Majestic, which is better rated. The Londra & Continentale, however, maintains its own identity in a modern format where each of the recently renovated rooms has a private bath, frigo-bar, and air conditioning. It's only a few steps from the main railway station, and there is parking on the premises. Rooms are neatly and attractively laid out. Singles cost 140,000 lire ($106) daily; doubles, 200,000 lire ($152).

Hotel Vittoria Orlandi, via Balbi 33-45, 16126 Genova (tel. 010/261-923). Since this hotel is constructed on one of the hillsides for which Genoa is famous, its entrance lies under a tunnel whose mouth opens at a point about a block from the Stazione Prìncipe. An elevator will take you up to the reception area, where you'll be greeted by one of the five Gerolla brothers who, along with their wives, maintain and direct this comfortable and medium-priced hotel. The establishment welcomes a wide variety of guests, some of them staying for only one night, in the simple but clean rooms. Many of the units have balconies. About half the units are air-conditioned, and all of them have a tile private bath. Best of all, the hotel is quiet because of the way it's sheltered from the busy boulevards by other buildings. Singles cost 50,000 lire ($38) daily; doubles, 75,000 lire ($57).

The Budget Range

Hotel Assarotti, via Assarotti 42, 16122 Genova (tel. 010/885-822), a substantial, well-run, 24-room establishment—no fuss, no frills—has been renovated. Off a busy boulevard, it occupies a floor of a large building with 19th-century ornamentation. The undersize lounges are furnished in a lackluster fashion, with deep leather armchairs. The bedrooms, all with modern private bath or shower, are nondescript in style but functional from the point of view of comfort (the larger, more handsome doubles are parceled out first). The single rate is 35,000 lire ($26.50) daily; doubles 60,000 lire ($45.50).

Hotel Brignole, vico de Corallo 13R, 16122 Genova (tel. 010/561-651), is a pleasant hotel on a hard-to-find street near the piazza Brignole, from which it takes its name. It's sandwiched between commercial and residential buildings, with laundry flapping in the wind from the nearby buildings and a storefront on its lower level. After climbing an interior stairwell, you'll find yourself in an unpretentious lobby leading into clean and simple rooms, each with a tile bath. The hotel is scattered over three floors of the building, without an elevator. Service is helpful. Singles rent for 60,000 lire ($45.50) daily; doubles, 90,000 lire ($68.50).

Hotel Agnello d'Oro, via Monachette 6, 16126 Genova (tel. 010/262-084). When the Doria family owned this structure and everything around it in the 1600s, they carved their family crest on the walls of the building near the top of the alley to announce to all of Genoa the point at which their property began. The symbol is a golden lamb, and you are still able to see one at the point where the narrow street joins the busy boulevard leading to the Stazione Prìncipe. The hotel, which was named after the animal on the crest, is a 17th-century building which includes vaulted ceilings and paneling in the lobby. About half the units are in a newer wing, but if you want the oldest accommodations, ask for nos. 6, 7, or 8. Today the hotel is maintained by a family, who have installed a small bar off the lobby. With bath, singles rent for 55,000 lire ($41.75) daily; doubles, 75,000 lire ($57).

DINING IN GENOA

You'll find lots of restaurants and trattorie, many of which are strung along the harbor. The Genovese cuisine has been praised for its kitchen. The following recommendations will give you several chances to judge it for yourself. By ordering anything with *pesto* at the end, you'll be sampling the best-known regional concoction, a sauce made with olive oil, garlic, pine seeds, cheese, and fresh basil.

Ristorante Vittorio al Mare, Belvedere Firpo 1, (tel. 312-872) at Boccadasse, right on the waterfront, lies at the edge of the city. It's a modern establishment, with unmarred views of the sea, but its decor is so unprepossessing that you'd hardly know it serves the finest dishes in Genoa. The cuisine is not subtle, in the typical fashion of the seaport, but even such routine dishes as scalloppine al marsala or veal cutlet milanese, roast veal or grilled entrecôtes, seem distinguished here. The fish courses are highly recommended, especially the mixed fish fry and the burrida (the local bouillabaisse with savory spices). The average meal ranges in price from 58,000 lire ($44) to 85,000 lire ($64.50). Only the finest ingredients are used, and the service generally pleases. The restaurant, open from 9 a.m. to 2 a.m., is closed on Monday.

Gran Gotto, via Fiume 11R (tel. 564-344), facing a park, is a top-notch trattoria with a good atmosphere and a fine kitchen. The concentration is on seafood, but the meat and pasta dishes aren't neglected either. In fact, the most typical offering, trenette al pesto, is quite famous, a pasta of paper-thin noodles (depending on the artistry of the chef) that is served with the characteristic pesto. The delicately simmered risotto is also tempting. The main dishes are most reasonably priced and of high standard, including the mixed fish fry or the French baby squid. The zuppa di pesce, like a Mediterranean bouillabaisse, has made many a luncheon for many a gourmet. The rognone al cognac is another superb choice—tender calves' kidneys that have been cooked and delicately flavored in cognac. From the à la carte menu, you can compose a meal for anywhere from 46,000 lire ($35) to 70,000 lire ($53.25). A favorite spot with the Genovese, the restaurant, open from 12:30 to 2:30 p.m. and 7:30 to 10 p.m., is closed on Sunday and the last three weeks in August.

Ristorante Il Primo Piano, via XX Settembre 36 (tel. 540-284). Dining at one of the tables of this elegant establishment one floor above street level is like getting a discreet view of an Italian family hard at work at their shared goal of running an excellent restaurant. Menu items include a rich assortment of fresh fish, fricassée of lamb, stuffed veal Genovese style, and desserts such as frozen zabaglione. Reservations are suggested. Full meals cost around 45,000 lire ($34.25) and are served from 12:30 to 2:30 p.m. and 7:30 to 10 p.m. The restaurant closes on Sunday and in August.

Ristorante Saint Cyr, piazza Marsala 4 (tel. 886-897). My favorite time to come to this restaurant is at night, when some of the most discriminating palates in Genoa might be seen munching on culinary dishes prepared with generous adaptations of regional recipes. The food items change every day, although a recent menu featured rice with truffles and cheese, a timbale of fresh spinach, a charlotte of fish, and a variety of braised meats, each delicately seasoned and perfectly prepared. The restaurant is open for lunch, when the clientele is likely to be conservatively dressed businesspeople discussing shipping contracts. Ferruccio and Lina Corti are the owners (he works in the dining room, she supervises the kitchen). There's a good selection of wines to accompany your meal. A full dinner will cost from 45,000 lire ($34.25). Open from 12:30 to 2:30 p.m. and 7:30 to 10 p.m., the restaurant is closed on Saturday, Sunday, and in August.

Ristorante Aladino, via Ettore Vernazza 8 (tel. 566-788), is a warmly accommodating restaurant, an elegant place in the center of Genoa. The cuisine at times can reach high points in classic Italian cookery. The chefs know how to glorify otherwise mundane dishes by the use of fresh ingredients, and they also use plenty of cream, truffles, and fresh mushrooms. You might enjoy taglierini with fresh basil or a mascarpone of fresh brie with truffles and polenta, along with whitefish soup, spaghetti in puff pastry with fresh seafood, and a filet of beef layered with carpaccio. A full meal will cost from 65,000 lire ($49.50). The restaurant is open from noon to 3 p.m. and 7:30 to 10 p.m. every day except Sunday for lunch and dinner.

Ristorante Zeffirino, via XX Settembre 20 (tel. 591-990), on a cul-de-sac just off one of the busiest boulevards of Genoa, has hosted celebrities ranging from Frank Sinatra to Pope John Paul II who arrived with a 40-member entourage. At least 14 members of the Zeffirino family prepare what is said to be the best pasta in the city from recipes collected all over Italy. These include lesser-known varieties such as quadrucci, pettinati, and cappelletti, as well as the more familiar tagliatelle and lasagne. Following one of these platters, you can select from a vast array of meat and fish, along with 1,000 kinds of wine. Ligurian specialties, including risotto alla pescatore and beef stew with artichokes, are featured. Reservations are a good idea, and full meals, offered from noon to 3 p.m. and 7 p.m. to midnight daily except Wednesday, cost 60,000 lire ($45.50) to 70,000 lire ($53.25).

Ristorante Cardinali, via Assarotti 60, near piazzo Corvetto (tel. 870-380), is a popular restaurant. Menu specialties include a delectable pâté en croûte, an array of well-flavored grilled meats, and about the best fondue bourguignonne in town. Full dinners cost from 60,000 lire ($45.50), and are accompanied by a selection of excellent wines. The restaurant, open from noon to 2:30 and 8 to 10:15 p.m., is closed Sunday and during parts of August.

Ristorante Ippogrifo, via Raffaele Gestro 9 (tel. 592-764), is in the Foce district near the International Fair of Genoa. It's a modern restaurant with air conditioning. The setting is intimate, and the cuisine is one of a high level. Some of the finest dishes—both an international repertoire and regional specialties from the Ligurian kitchen—are presented with flair. The average meal ranges in price from 40,000 lire ($30.50). The restaurant is open from noon to 3:30 p.m. and 7 p.m. to midnight; closed Thursday.

Il Cucciolo, viale Sauli 33 (tel. 546-470). When you're in Genoa, you perhaps want to dine as the Genovese do. However, if you're going to be around for a while, you may want to vary the diet by dining in one of the best Tuscan restaurants in the city. That is, if you can find it. Go armed with a good map, as it lies on one of those "hidden" squares of the city, with near-impossible parking. Should you go at night, lanterns are placed festively outside, adorning this ground-floor restaurant in a 19th-century building. You not only get good Tuscan food, especially beefsteak Florentine, but excellent wines as well. The restaurant is closed Monday and in August, but otherwise serves well-prepared meals from noon to 3 p.m. and 7:30 to 10:30 p.m. costing 45,000 lire ($34.25) to 55,000 lire ($41.75). The service is efficient, and the reception is gracious.

Trattoria del Mario, via Conservatori del Mare 35R, piazza Banchi (tel. 297-788), is one of the best dining spots in the old town, offering a minimum of atmosphere but a maximum of taste. Its location may be somewhat hard to find, but the Genovese have been marking a trail to its door. It features such specialties as trenette al pesto, which is made with the local, almost perfumed basil. The trenette is a pasta-like fettuccine that has been tossed with slices of potato and thin strips of green beans. You might begin your meal with the cold seafood salad known as insalata di pesce. The array of antipasti includes roast sweet yellow peppers, stuffed tomatoes, and mushrooms. An unusual and exciting dish is lettuce leaves that have been stuffed with a nutmeg-scented ground veal. As an accompanying dish you can order thin slabs of zucchini that have been deep-fried a golden brown. Expect to pay from 35,000 lire ($26.50) to 50,000 lire ($38) for a fine repast. Hours are 12:30 to 2:30 p.m. and 7:30 to 10 p.m. Closed Saturday.

A Grand Café

Caffè Mangina, via Roma 91R (tel. 564-013), is one of the most elegant cafés in town, filled with embellishments from the 19th century and often with genteel residents of the surrounding neighborhood. Even the zinc-top bar is supported by what antique connoisseurs would consider a fine piece of furniture. Cappuccino costs 2,300 lire ($1.75) at a table. You can admire the equestrian statue of Victor Emmanuel II in the piazza Corvetto while you sip your beverage. Hours are 7:30 a.m. to 8 p.m.; closed Monday.

---

3. Rapallo

A front-ranking seaside resort—known for years to a chic and wealthy crowd who live in villas studding the hillside—Rapallo occupies a remarkable site overlooking the Gulf of Tiguillio. In summer, the heart of Rapallo takes on a crowded, somewhat carnival air, as hordes of bathers occupy the rocky sands along the beach. In the area is an 18-hole golf course plus an indoor swimming pool, a riding club, and a modern tourist harbor. You can also take a cable car to the Sanctuary di Montallegro, then walk to Monte Rosa for what is considered one of the finest views on the Ligurian coast. There are many summer boat trips possible, not only to Portofino but to the Cinque Terre.

Rapallo has had a long history, often liked to the vicissitudes of Genoa, 21 miles away. It became part of the Repubblica Superba in 1229, but Rapallo had existed long before that. Its cathedral dates from the 6th century when it was founded by the bishops of Milan. Once walls enclosed the medieval town, but now only the Saline Gate remains. Rapallo has also been the scene of many an international meeting, the most notable of which was the 1917 conference of wartime allies.

The telephone area code for Rapallo is 0185.

HOTELS IN RAPALLO

I'll survey a full price range before moving on to Santa Margherita Ligure.

The Deluxe Choice

Grand Hotel Bristol, via Aurelia Orientale 369, 16035 Rapallo (tel. 0185/273-313), is a sparkling renovation of one of the Riviera's grand old buildings. It is easily one of the most glamorous hotels along the coast. Originally built in 1908, it was reopened in 1984 as the personal brainchild of a multimillionaire who died shortly after its transformation. The turn-of-the-century pink-and-white façade, with surrounding shrubbery and iron gates, was spruced up but basically unchanged during the five-year rebuilding program. The interior, however, which was mostly gutted, now contains five elegant restaurants in several degrees of formality, a series of conference rooms, and a free-form swimming pool, one of the biggest in the region, whose inviting waters are visible from many of the bedrooms.

The kitchens are about the most modern anywhere, and the polite staff is dressed in formal morning suits. The lush modern decor includes tasteful colors and stylish accessories. Perhaps best of all, the architects knew what to do with the unused space under the twin Victoria towers on the top floor. There, enclosed within the sloping walls, you'll find an unusual piano bar, complete with live music, plush upholstery, comfortable chairs, and views that stretch up and down the coast. Some of the bedrooms have private terraces, and all of them contain a frigo-bar, TV, springtime colors, modern bath, electronic window blinds, lots of mirrors, and tree-of-life motifs wallpapered onto the spaces above the oversize beds. Singles cost 140,000 lire ($106) to 200,000 lire ($152) daily; doubles, 240,000 lire ($182) to 320,000 lire ($243). The most formal of all the hotel's restaurants is outfitted in shades of dusty rose, with massive silver cutlery, an army of waiters, and fixed-price lunches and dinners costing around 60,000 lire ($45.50). A full range of sporting facilities is available at the hotel, which is closed November to just before Christmas.

The Upper Bracket

Eurotel, via Aurelia Ponente 22, 16035 Rapallo (tel. 0185/60-981), is a vivid sienna-colored structure indented with a series of arched and recessed loggias, plus a curved extension jutting over the front entrance. It's one of the highest hotels in town, set above the port at the top of a winding road where you'll have to negotiate the oncoming traffic with care. The hotel has one of the only two swimming pools in town, plus a collection of condominiums on the premises that are usually occupied during part of the year by their owners. The lobby has marble floors and a helpful staff. All units overlook the water, containing built-in cabinets and beds that fold, Murphy style, into the walls. In addition, all accommodations contain air conditioning, color TV, frigo-bar, balcony, and private bath. A bar and restaurant are on the premises. Full board ranges from 140,000 lire ($106) to 165,000 lire ($125) per person daily.

The Middle Bracket

Hotel Riviera, piazza 4 Novembre, 16035 Rapallo (tel. 0185/50-248), is a modernized Victorian-era villa set on a waterside street corner at the edge of a row of villas, all containing hotels. There's a big glassed-in terrace serving drinks in a decor of exposed wood, marble floors, and Italian modern furniture. The comfortable bedrooms either face the water or a rear garden, the latter much quieter. With half board included, rates range from 80,000 lire ($60.75) to 85,000 lire ($64.50) per person daily. The establishment is closed in November and during most of December.

Hotel Astoria, via Gramsci 4, 16035 Rapallo (tel. 0185/273-533), is a symmetrical cream-and-white villa with a baroque trim. On a waterside street near the beach cabañas, it was one of five turn-of-the-century villas all in a row, which have since been turned into hotels. There's a well-maintained rose garden in front. The well-furnished bedrooms are equipped with frigo-bar, color TV, radio, and air-conditioning. About half the rooms have a sea view, although the rear rooms are much quieter. Doubles rent for 150,000 lire ($114) daily; singles, 90,000 lire ($68.50). Breakfast, which costs extra, can be served in your room, in the breakfast room, or in the garden.

Hotel Moderne & Royal, viale Gramsci 6, 16035 Rapallo (tel. 0185/50-601), is a gracious, old 50-room villa, on the sea, with tables and umbrellas set out on its front terrace. The villa has art nouveau wrought-iron balconies and a carved winged cherub's head capping its uppermost gable. When it was originally built, what is now the hotel was five units of summer villas. They were united and transformed into a hotel after World War II. Most of its public rooms have high-arched windows to drink in the view of the promenade, with its row of palm trees. Directly across the promenade is Rapallo's swimming beach, with its rows of cabañas and bikini-clad inhabitants. All the accommodations contain private bath except for a few singles. Singles with bath rent for 97,000 lire ($73.75) daily, and doubles with bath go for 108,000 lire ($82), with full board included. Local and international cuisine is served in the dining room.

The Budget Range

Hotel Giulio Cesare, corso Colombo 62, 16035 Rapallo (tel. 0185/50-685), is a bargain for the Italian Riviera. A modernized four-story villa, it stands on the "right" side of Rapallo. The genial owner, Antonio Camisa, has been skillful in renovating the establishment, keeping expenses down to keep room rates lower. Lying on the coast road, about 90 feet from the sea, his hotel offers 33 bedrooms, all with private bath. The bedrooms, featuring a good view of the Gulf of Tiguillo, are furnished with tasteful reproductions, resulting in a home-like ambience (most of

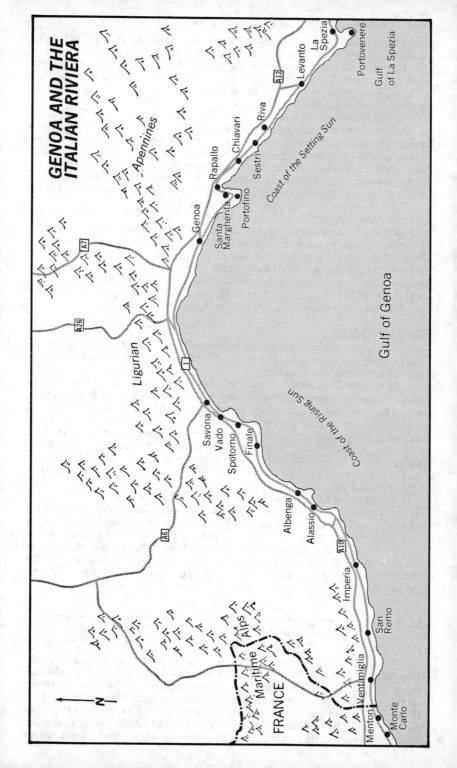

them have sun balconies). Bed and breakfast cost 35,000 lire ($26.50) per person daily. The charge for half board is 55,000 lire ($41.75) per person, while those staying here on a full-board arrangement pay 65,000 lire ($49.50) per person per day. Ask for the rooms on the top floor if you want a better view and a quieter situation. The meals are prepared with flair, and fine ingredients are used (the fish dishes are superb). The hotel is closed in November.

Hotel Miramare, via Vittorio Veneto 27, 16035 Rapallo (tel. 0185/50-293), is on the water near a stone gazebo. This is a jazz age (1929) re-creation of a Renaissance villa whose exterior frescoes have faded in the salt air. The gardens in front have been replaced by a glass extension that contains a clean and contemporary restaurant where an aquarium bubbles near the entrance. The accommodations inside are rather unimaginative, but comfortable and high-ceilinged. Many of them have iron balconies stretching toward the harbor. Single rooms with bath rent for 40,000 lire ($30.50) daily; doubles with bath, 70,000 lire ($53.25).

Hotel Bel Soggiorno, via Gramsci 10, 16025 Rapallo (tel. 0185/54-527), is a 22-bedroom Victorian building with ornate gables, green shutters, and a desirable location near a city park at the edge of the water. The lobby contains photographs from 1904 showing what the street looked like then. The modernized interior has big windows, leather armchairs, and a helpful staff. This is a good budget choice for a stopover, especially because of the garden terrace in front, complete with palmettos and shrubbery. Full board costs from 75,000 lire ($57) per person daily. All accommodations contain a private bath. Closed in November.

WHERE TO DINE

Most guests stay in Rapallo on the half- or full-board plan. However, those visiting for the day or wanting an extra meal outside their domicile will want to know of the following recommendations.

Ristorante De Monique, lungomare Vittorio Veneto 6 (tel. 50-541), offers a nautical decor in a big-windowed setting overlooking the boats of a marina. This is one of the most popular seafood restaurants along the harbor, especially in summer, when the tavern chairs are almost completely filled. As you'd expect, fish is the specialty, including seafood salad, fish soup, risotto with shrimp, spaghetti with clams or mussels, grilled fish, and both tagliatelle and scampi "Monique." A la carte dining can run the tab up to 45,000 lire ($34.25) per person. Open from 12:30 to 2:30 p.m. and 7:30 to 10 p.m., the restaurant is closed every Tuesday and from January 20 to February 20.

Ristorante Elite, via Milite Ignoto 19 (tel. 50-551), is set back from the water on a busy commercial street in the center of town. Mainly fish is served, the menu for which depends on the catch of the day. Your dinner might consist of mussels marinara, minestrone Genovese style, risotto marinara, trenette al pesto, scampi, zuppa di pesci, sole meunière, turbot, or a mixed fish fry from the Ligurian coast. A limited selection of the standard meat dishes is available too. Meals average 30,000 lire ($22.75) per person, and are served from 12:30 to 2:30 p.m. and 7:30 to 10 p.m. daily except Thursday and in November.

4. Santa Margherita Ligure

A resort rival to Rapallo, Santa Margherita Ligure also occupies a beautiful position on the Gulf of Tiguillio. With a most attractive harbor, usually thronged with fun-seeking life, the spa offers the widest range of accommodations in all price levels on the eastern Riviera. Its promenade, palm trees swaying in the wind, and beds of flowers give it a festive appearance. But typical of the Riviera, its beach combines rock and sand. The location is 19 miles from Genoa and 3 miles from Portofino, to which Santa Margherita Ligure is linked by a narrow road. It's on the Rome-Genoa rail link. The climate of Santa Margherita Ligure is mild, even in the winter months, when many elderly clients visit the resort.

The town dates back to A.D. 262. The official name of Santa Margherita Ligure was given to the town by Victor Emmanuel II in 1863. Before that, it had known many other names, including Porto Napoleone, an 1812 designation from Napoleon.

You can visit the richly embellished Basilica of Santa Margherita d'Antiochia, with its Italian and Flemish paintings, along with relics of the saint from whom the town takes its name.

The telephone area code for Santa Margherita Ligure is 0185.

HOTELS
I'll survey the pick of the lot, beginning with the most expensive.

Deluxe Choices
Imperial Palace, via Pagana 19, 16038 Santa Margherita Ligure (tel. 0185/288-991), is like an ornate gilded palace required for one's "season on the Riviera." It commands a position at the edge of the resort, built against a hillside and surrounded by semitropical gardens. All along its water edge, a festive recreation center has been created, with an oval flagstone swimming pool on a terrace, an extended stone wharf for sunbathing, and a two-decker open-air restaurant and cabañas. Bikini-clad women and men of the international set feel at home here. The public rooms of the Imperial Palace live up to the hotel's name—old courtly splendor dominates, with vaulted gilt and painted ceilings, satin-covered antiques, ornate mirrors, and inlaid marble floors. The dining room is also formal, with white colonnades and arches and mahogany chairs, an appropriate background for the superb meals. The waiters have flair. The music room, with its grand piano and satin chairs, is still enjoyed at teatime. The bedrooms vary widely—from royal suites to simple singles away from the sea. Many of the rooms have elaborate ceilings, balconies, brass beds, chandeliers, and white antiqued furniture. Every chamber has a private bath or shower as well as TV, piped-in music, frigo-bar, and direct-dial phone. The hotel is closed from November to April, otherwise charging from 215,000 lire ($163) daily in a single, from 395,000 lire ($300) in a twin or double. For full board, the price is 255,000 lire ($194) to 280,000 lire ($213) per person.

Grand Hotel Miramare, via Milite Ignoto 30, 16038 Santa Margherita Ligure (tel. 0185/287-013). It was on the terrace of this hotel in 1933 that Marconi succeeded in transmitting for the first time by means of microwaves telegraphic and telephonic signals to a distance of more than 90 miles. Today the building has a festive confectionary look that is enhanced by the blue shutters and dazzling white façade. It lies a three-minute walk from the center of town, standing across a busy boulevard from a stony beach. The hotel is surrounded by gardens whose meticulously maintained rear side is visible through huge plate-glass windows. To one side is a curved outdoor swimming pool with heated sea water. This adjoins a raised sun terrace dotted with parasols and iron tables. The restaurant has many Victorian touches, including fragile chairs and blue-and-white porcelain set into the plaster walls. Full board costs 170,000 lire ($129) to 228,000 lire ($173) daily for a single, 145,000 lire ($110) to 203,000 lire ($154) per person in a double. Children sharing their parents' room are granted reductions according to their age.

The Middle and Upper Bracket
Hotel Continental, via Pagano 8, 16038 Santa Margherita Ligure (tel. 0185/286-512). The façade you'll see from the winding road leading into town is grandiose, adorned with a Doric portico, balustrades, and fancy carving. After you enter the high-ceilinged and airy public rooms, however, you'll see the terraced gardens that stretch down to a rocky spit where guests can swim if they don't feel like using the pool. The bedrooms are filled with conservative furnishings, and often have tall

French windows leading onto balconies ringed with wrought iron. A nearby annex contains additional lodging, and there's a garage facility (which you'll be grateful for) on the premises. The view from the restaurant encompasses the curved harbor of the center of town, a few miles away. With full board included, rates range from 142,000 lire ($108) to 180,000 lire ($137) per person daily depending on the season.

Park Hotel Suisse, via Favale 31, 16038 Santa Margherita Ligure (tel. 0185/289-571), is set in its own garden nest above the town center, with a panoramic view of the sea and harbor. It has seven floors, all of modern design, with deep private balconies that are al fresco living rooms for some of the bedrooms. On the lower terrace is a large, free-form, saltwater swimming pool surrounded by an edge of semitropical vegetation. A modernistic water chute, diving boards, a café with parasol tables for refreshments—all give one the experience of seaside life without the disadvantages. The bedrooms opening onto the rear gardens, sans sea view, cost slightly less; the rooms are decked out with contemporary furnishings in bold colors. Open all year, the hotel in high season charges 105,000 lire ($79.75) daily for a single with bath, 200,000 lire ($152) for a double with bath. The half-board rate is around 115,000 lire ($87.50) to 150,000 lire ($114) per person daily.

Lido Palace Hotel, via Andrea Doria 3, 16038 Santa Margherita Ligure (tel. 0185/285-821). Set on the harbor in the middle of town, the ornate bulk of this mustard- and cream-colored building rises imposingly above the palms and the many bathers of the public beach. It was built sometime between 1910 and 1920 and has been kept attractive through restoration ever since. The hotel's accommodations are mainly junior suites for two to four people. All the units have views of the Golfo del Tigullio and are insulated from traffic noise. They are all equipped with bath, air conditioning and central heating, direct-dial phone, mini-bar, color TV, and kitchenette. Rates depend on the season and room assignment. With service and taxes included, singles cost 75,000 lire ($57) to 145,000 lire ($110) daily, and a twin-bedded room with bath and sitting room rents for 160,000 lire ($122) to 190,000 lire ($144).

Hotel Regina Elena, lungomare Milite Ignoto 44, 16038 Santa Margherita Ligure (tel. 0185/287-003), is housed in a modern boxy building painted in pastel shades, separated from a stony beach by the busy thoroughfare leading to Portofino. A nearby annex contains additional rooms. Although the hotel was built in 1908, few of the turn-of-the-century details remain after a renovation. The dining room is the most interesting part of the hotel, contained within a 12-sided structure whose walls are almost entirely made of glass. A conference center is below the ground level of the parking lot, so many of the guests of the hotel might be involved with some business function. Rates, with full board included, range from 130,000 lire ($98.75) to 170,000 lire ($129) per person daily.

Hotel Minerva, via Maragliano 34, 16038 Santa Margherita Ligure (tel. 0185/286-073). The premises were built in 1952 as a private villa, but were later expanded into this comfortable sienna-colored hotel. It's above the resort, at the end of a residential street lined with trees and flowers. You climb a flight of flagstone steps through a private garden to reach the black marble floors, Corinthian columns, and sofas of the sunny public rooms. The Metaldi family are the owners, charging 58,000 lire ($44) daily for a single, 96,000 lire ($73) for a double, with breakfast included. Full board costs 61,000 lire ($46.25) to 85,000 lire ($64.50) per person daily, depending on the season. Each of the accommodations has a private bath and phone. There's a pleasant bar off the lobby.

The Budget Range

Albergo Conte Verde, via Zara 1, 16038 Santa Margherita Ligure (tel. 0185/287-139), offers one of the freshest and warmest welcomes in town for the low-budget traveler. Only two blocks from the sea, the third-class hotel has been revamped, its rooms simple but adequate (a few private baths are available in the doubles). The hotel is closed from November to Christmas. Other months it charges 52,000 lire ($39.50) daily for a single with bath, 72,000 lire ($54.75) for a bathless double, and 90,000 lire ($68.50) for a double with bath, all these prices including breakfast. Full board costs 55,000 lire ($41.75) to 85,000 lire ($64.50) per person daily, inclusive. The terrace in front of the hotel has swing gliders, and the lounge has period furnishings, including rockers. All is consistent with the villa exterior of shuttered windows, flower boxes, and a small front garden and lawn where tables are set out for refreshments.

Hotel Jolanda, via Luisito Costa 6, 16038 Santa Margherita Ligure (tel. 0185/287-513), is in reality two buildings joined together by a patio that serves as an open-air dining room. It is about two blocks from the sea and the piazza Caprera. One of the Siamese halves is an old-style villa, in the semi-baroque style; the other is in straightforward modern, with rows of balconies. There is no sea view, but the pensione is on a peaceful little street, away from the noise of heavy traffic. Open all year, the Jolanda in high season charges 26,000 lire ($19.75) daily in a bathless single, 42,000 lire ($32) in a bathless double. The most expensive room, a double with bath, is 55,000 lire ($41.75). The full-board rate ranges from 50,000 lire ($38) to 60,000 lire ($45.50) per person. The decor is rather jazzy but the welcome's nice.

DINING

Hotels and boarding houses have the upper hand. However, a few select establishments offer quality meals.

Trattoria Cesarina, via Mameli 2C (tel. 286-059), lies beneath the arcade of a short but monumental street running into the piazza Fratelli Bandiere. In a decor of bentwood chairs and sophisticated lighting, you can enjoy the best food in town. Specialties include arrays of meat, vegetable, and seafood antipasti, along with classical Italian dishes such as taglierini with seafood and pappardella in a fragrant sauce of sausages, plus seasonal fish, best served grilled, which has been caught off the nearby coast. Full meals cost around 70,000 lire ($53.25) and are served from 12:30 to 2:30 p.m. and 7:30 to 10 p.m. daily except Wednesday. Reservations are important, especially in midsummer.

Ristorante La Ghiaia, in the Lido Palace Hotel, via Andrea Doria 5 (tel. 283-708). The translated name of this establishment means "sea rocks," and that is precisely what you'll see from the panoramic windows overlooking the water. Set on the ground floor of one of the town's most centrally located hotels, the modern decor includes clear colors and paintings throughout the sunny dining rooms. Outdoor tables are shielded from the pedestrian traffic by rows of shrubbery. A la carte dinners cost 45,000 lire ($34.25) to 70,000 lire ($53.25). Your meal might begin with antipasti di mare, taglioni di salmon, zuppa di pesce, risotto di mare (rice with seafood), or spaghetti con aragosta (spaghetti with lobster). Fresh fish is priced by the gram, including turbot, scampi, gamberini, and sea bass. The restaurant, open from 12:30 to 2 p.m. and 8 to 10 p.m., is closed every Wednesday and in November.

Ristorante Bassa Prora, via Garibaldi 7 (tel. 286-586). The perfect decor for the yachting set can be found on the street just across from the marina. The bar is fashioned into a mosaic of sea pebbles, while the hanging nautical brass lamps illuminate the vaulted ceilings that taper into hardwood paneling dotted with paintings. Menu specialties include scampi verde, gamberini on a spit, spaghetti with clams, grilled beefsteak, veal piccata with tomatoes, lasagne al pesto, and zuppa di pesce. Meals range from 35,000 lire ($26.50) to 55,000 lire ($41.75) and are served from 12:30 to 2:30 p.m. and 7:30 to 10 p.m. The restaurant is closed Monday night, all day Tuesday, and from mid-September to mid-October.

Trattoria all'Ancora, via Maragliano 7 (tel. 280-559), lies behind a stone façade about a block from the water. This family-run restaurant is decorated with a rustically nautical decor, ample rows of wine bottles, and tavern chairs. Waitresses serve a local clientele that could include a crew of fishermen and electricians taking their midday rest, an extended family with unruly children, or a well-dressed couple celebrating an anniversary. Spaghetti with marinara sauce is proudly presented as one of the specialties of the house. The menu usually features a plate of the day, which most often consists of some kind of fish. Examples include insalata di mare, risotto marinara, minestrone genovese, grilled or fried shrimp, fritto misto, and lasagne and tagliatelle di Portofino served with various sauces, including pesto genovese. Meals cost from 40,000 lire ($30.50). The restaurant is closed every Monday and from December 20 till March 1. It would be wise to reserve a table, especially in the evening and on a weekend. Meals are served from 12:30 to 2:30 p.m. and 7:30 to 10 p.m.

About a four-mile drive from Santa Margherita Ligure along one of the most beautiful coastal roads in all of Italy and you're at—

---

5. Portofino

Elizabeth Taylor used to make her way from boutique to boutique, a "page boy" supplying fresh iced drinks and village mothers thrusting bambini in her face (they'd read in the tabs that she liked to adopt children). Later, a speedboat whisked Taylor Inc. to a palatial yacht moored off the peninsula.

You're likely to see anybody and anything in Portofino—and usually do.

Favored by the yachting set, the resort occupies an idyllic position on a harbor that mirrors the pastel-washed little houses fronting it. In the '30s it enjoyed a reputation with artists; later, a chic crowd moved in—and they're still there, occupying villas in the hills and refusing to surrender completely to popsicle-eating "trippers" who pour in during the day. Then the expatriate, well-heeled habitués flee, only to reemerge at the martini hour when the last tour bus has pulled out.

The thing to do in Portofino: during the day—but preferably before sunset—start on a walk that leads toward the tip of the peninsula. You'll pass the entrance to an old castle (where a German baron once lived), old private villas, towering trees, and much vegetation, until you reach the lighthouse. Allow an hour at least. When you return to the main piazza, proceed to one of the two little drinking bars on the left side of the harbor that rise and fall in popularity.

Once Portofino was a sleepy fishing village. Its history goes back to Roman times. Pliny called it "Portus Delphini." It was the private domain of Benedictines before it was incorporated into the Republic of Genoa in 1414, becoming, in 1815, a part of the Kingdom of the Two Sicilies.

Before beginning that walk to the lighthouse, as mentioned, you can climb steps from the port leading to the little parish Church of St. George. A panoramic view of the port and bay is possible from the terrace here. In summer, you can also take boat rides around the coast to such points as San Fruttuoso.

Portofino's telephone area code is 0185.

HOTELS IN PORTOFINO

In hotels, Portofino is severely limited, and in high season you may be forced to book a room in nearby Santa Margherita Ligure or Rapallo.

A Deluxe Choice

Albergo Splendido, 16034 Portofino (tel. 0185/269-551), a *Relais & Châteaux* selection, provides a luxury base for those who moor their yacht in the harbor below, or have closed down their Palm Beach residence for the summer. For decades the name Splendido has cropped up at every mention of Portofino. Reached from the village by a steep and winding road—flanked with twisting, silvery olive trees and banks of flowers growing against stone walls—the hotel might well have been a monastery. Here, on one of the pergola verandas, you can enjoy a panorama of the sea and rugged Riviera coastline. There are many tile terraces with arbors of wisteria and roses, and many flagstone paths lined with pink geraniums, rhododendrons, and palms.

Inside, a refreshing country-house flavor prevails, characterized by informality. The 73-room villa is rambling, with several levels of public rooms, terraces, and "oh, that view" bedrooms. Each private room is furnished in a personal way—no two alike. Traditional old pieces include antique desks and comfortable sofas and armchairs in small sitting areas. Prices are expensive, varying according to the season and the room assigned. Guests are booked in here on the half-board plan, ranging from 314,000 lire ($239) to 386,500 lire ($294) per person daily. Tariffs include the service charge. On two levels, the dining room is divided by a row of arches and furnished with Biedermeier chairs, flower bouquets, and a fine old tapestry. The restaurant terrace not only enjoys a view but also serves traditional dishes of typical Ligurian cooking. Parking is free. The hotel is open from the end of March to the end of October.

The Medium-Priced Range

Albergo Nazionale, 16034 Portofino (tel. 0185/269-575), is at stage center, right on the harbor. An old villa with many roof levels, it is modest, yet well laid out. Its interior rooms are tastefully decorated, and its little lounge has a brick fireplace, coved ceiling, antique furnishings, and good reproductions. Most of the bedrooms, furnished in a mixture of styles (hand-painted Venetian in some of the rooms), have a view of the harbor. The room price is 180,000 lire ($137) to 257,300 lire ($196) daily for a double unit with sitting room. There are no singles. All accommodations contain private bath, and taxes and service are included.

The Budget Range

Hotel Eden, 16034 Portofino (tel. 0185/269-091), just 150 feet away from the harbor in the heart of the village, is a little 14-room albergo, a budget holdout in an otherwise high-fashion resort. Set in its own garden (hence, its name), it is a good place at which to stay. While there is no view of the harbor, there is a winning vista from the front veranda, where breakfast is served. The hotel is run by Mr. Ferruccio, and life here is decidedly casual. Open all year, the albergo charges 70,000 lire ($53.25) daily in a single, this rate increasing to 160,000 lire ($76) to 130,000 lire ($99.25) in a double with bath. Breakfast is included. The Ristorante da Ferruccio is well known in the area, and many nonresidents visit to sample the Ligurian specialties. Open from April to November.

Hotel San Giorgio, 16034 Portofino (tel. 0185/269-261), is a good hotel set on a hill above the port. The bedrooms are clean, not very elaborate, and comfortable, all with TV, radio, phone, and mini-bar, and most with private bath. Singles with bath cost 70,000 lire ($53.25) daily; doubles with bath, 110,000 lire ($83.50). The family-owned hotel is closed in January and February.

RESTAURANTS IN PORTOFINO

Reached by climbing steps, **Il Pitosforo,** Molo Umberto I no. 9 (tel. 269-020), draws a raft of raves and, most likely, cries of protest when the tab is presented. While not blessed with an especially distinguished decor, its position right on the harbor gives it all the native chic it needs, and has ever since Bogey and Baby or Taylor and Burton came this way. The food is worthy. Zuppa di pesce is a delectable Ligurian fish soup, or you may prefer the bouillabaisse, which is always reliable here. The pastas are especially recommendable, including lasagne al pesto, wide noodles prepared in the typical Genovese sauce. Fish dishes include mussels alla marinara and paella valenciana for two, saffron-flavored rice studded with sea fruit and chicken. Expect to pay at least 100,000 lire ($76) per person for a meal. The restaurant, open from noon to 3 p.m. and 7 to 11 p.m., is closed Tuesday, Wednesday at lunch, and January and February.

Delfino, piazza Martiri dell'Olivetta 40 (tel. 269-081), right on the harbor-fronting village square, is the other most fashionable dining spot in Portofino. It's in a harborside, sienna-colored building with forest-green shutters. It is both nautically rustic and informally chic. Less expensive than Il Pitosforo, it offers virtually the same type of food, such as lasagne al pesto. Again, the fish dishes provide the best reason for lifting your fork: zuppa di pesce (a soup made of freshly caught fish with a secret spice blend), risotto with shrimp, and a mixed fish fry. The latter is exceptional, a whole platter loaded with shrimp, sole, squid, and other sea creatures. If you can't stand fish but are trapped into dining with those who do, then know that the chef at Delfino prides himself on his sage-seasoned vitello all'uccelletto, a roast veal with a gamey taste. Depending on your choice of fish dishes, expect a final tab ranging from 75,000 lire ($57) up. Try to get a table near the front so as to enjoy the parade of visitors and villagers. Hours are noon to 3 p.m. and 7 to 11 p.m.; closed Thursday and from November 1 to December 26.

Ristorante Puny (tel. 269-037) is becoming better known as it competes with the two established leaders of Portofino's portside restaurants. The Puny is set up on the stone square whose edge opens onto the harbor. Because of its location, it's practically in the living room of Portofino, within sight of the evening activities that make the town famous as a hangout for the rich. Green-painted tables are set under trees at night on a slate-covered outdoor terrace. Inside, the nautical decor is ringed with walls of stippled stucco, with a zodiac theme inlaid in brass above the bar area. The menu includes peppardelle Portofino, antipasto of the house, spaghetti with clams, grilled sole, carne pizzaiola, and an array of freshly caught fish. Meals range from 45,000 lire ($34.25) to 65,000 lire ($49.50). Open from noon to 3 p.m. and 7 to 11 p.m., the restaurant is closed Thursday and in January and February.

Da U'Batti, vico Nuovo 17 (tel.269-379). Informal, chic, and colorful, this place sits on a narrow cobblestone-covered piazza a few steps above the port. A pair of barnacle-encrusted anchors, hanging above the arched entrance, hint at the seafaring specialties that have become this establishment's trademark. Co-owner and chef Felice Bianchi, and his partner, Giancarlo Foppiano, serve delectable shrimp, crayfish, and lobster, as well as the catch of the day. Taglierini with pesto sauce is another specialty. Set menus cost 70,000 lire ($53.25). Two sittings at lunch are at 12:30 and 1:30 p.m.; dinner, at 8 and 9:30 p.m. The place is closed on Monday and November 20 to mid-February.

THE BAR SCENE

Portofino's **La Gritta American Bar,** on the calata Marconi (tel. 269-126), vies for business with its rival a few storefronts away. Between the two of them, they have attracted the biggest names in show business or whatever: from Onassis to Frank Sinatra to John Wayne. These celebrities have intermingled with dozens of tourists and a collection of U.S. Navy personnel in this small, well-appointed restaurant. As James Jones, author of *From Here to Eternity,* noted: "This is the nicest waterfront bar this side of Hong Kong." That is true, but it's always wise to check your bar tab carefully before you stagger out looking for a new adventure. La Gritta means "The Crab" in Genovese dialect. Long drinks cost from 12,000 lire ($9.10) apiece. Closed Thursday.

Scafandro American Bar, calata Marconi 10 (tel. 269-105), is one of the village's chic rendezvous points, a place that has attracted a sophisticated array of guests. The seating arrangements inside contribute to the general feeling of well-being, since they're three-quarter-round banquettes, pulled up to teakwood tables with brass detailing. The members of your party will be illuminated by hanging dome lights, while in a corner sits a brass and copper headset removed from a 19th-century diver's costume. If one of the world's celebrities doesn't happen to come in while you're there, you can always study one of the series of unusual nautical engravings adorning the walls. A cappuccino costs from 5,000 lire ($3.80); a whisky, from 9,000 lire ($6.85). Open from 8:30 a.m. to 3 a.m. daily except Tuesday.

DINING IN THE ENVIRONS

In the small town of Recco, ten miles from Portofino, **Manuelina,** via Roma 278 (tel. 0185/75-364), lies less than a mile from the center of town. It is a large restaurant, offering terrace dining in fair weather and good service. It's also a secret address known to owners of villas in Portofino who take their special guests here for a festive meal which costs from 50,000 lire ($38) to 65,000 lire ($49.50). The pasta dishes are so good you may want to order two of them (or share, in the fashion of a Chinese restaurant). I suggest pansotti alla salsa di noci, a type of ravioli filled with Swiss chard and eggs, and served with a rich-tasting sauce of ricotta, garlic, olive oil, and ground walnuts. The chef also does a sublime focaccia al formaggio, a cheese-stuffed dumpling that is served deep-fried until it is a golden brown. If featured, I suggest a soup made with a rare and much-prized sea delicacy (eagerly sought by gastronomes) called datteri di mare, and it's made with tiny razor clams. For a main course, a selection of mixed grilled seafood will be served. The restaurant is open from 12:30 to 2:30 p.m. and 7:30 to 10 p.m.; closed Wednesday, the last ten days in July, and from mid-January to mid-February. Always call before striking out.

---

6. La Spezia

An important naval port in Italy, La Spezia lies at the center of the "gulf of the writers," its waterfront promenade lined with palm trees. Heavily bombed in World War II because of its strategic military value, it is a modern town today, about 70 miles south of Genoa.

La Spezia makes a good base for exploring sights, often remote, along the coast. For example, south of town, opening onto the gulf, is the little village of **Santa Terenzo,** which converts into a popular resort in summer, attracting a lot of young people. Totally lacking the élan of the more highly polished beach meccas, it was discovered by Shelley in 1822, the year he drowned off the coast. His Magni house is at via P. Mantegazza 15, on the waterfront ("I still inhabit this divine bay, reading dramas, sailing, and listening to the most enchanting music").

The telephone area code for La Spezia is 0187.

WHERE TO STAY

Across from a palm-dotted park, **Jolly Hotel del Golfo,** via XX Settembre 2, 19100 La Spezia (tel. 0187/27-200), has an angular façade of masonry-rimmed windows opening toward views of the water. The lobby contains an elegant bar, checkerboard marble floors, Oriental rugs, and conservatively comfortable furniture. There's a TV, plus radio and air conditioning in each room, also a private bath. The restaurant is attractive, and you get the same fine service that seems to be a hallmark of this nationwide chain. With a continental breakfast included, singles rent for 120,000 lire ($91.25) daily, and doubles are priced at 185,000 lire ($141).

Residence Hotel, via del Tino 62, 19100 La Spezia (tel. 0187/504-141), was built on a busy highway about two miles from the center of town. Its balconied façade looks more like that of an apartment building than a hotel, a fact appreciated by the many Italian visitors who wouldn't stay anywhere else in La Spezia. The lobby has low-slung leather-upholstered chairs, rugs, carved and gilded mirrors, and modern accessories. Many of the bedrooms contain 19th-century chests of drawers whose solid craftsmanship softens the angularity of the contemporary architecture. Each of the accommodations is equipped with a private bath, color TV, phone, radio, mini-bar, and air conditioning, plus a balcony. There's a safe on the premises for valuables. Singles cost 85,000 lire ($64.50) daily and doubles begin at 125,000 lire ($95). A continental breakfast is included in the tariffs.

WHERE TO DINE

The high-quality **Ristorante La Posta,** via Don Minzoni 24 (tel. 34-419), is the best. The items available from the kitchen are not limited to what's actually printed on the menu. Specialties include peppardelle Brittany style, fettuccine with crabmeat, sea date soup (made of mussels called dattero), chateaubriand of the house, sole with tarragon, and filet of wild boar. Full meals range from 35,000 lire ($26.50) to 45,000 lire ($34.25) and are served from noon to 3 p.m. and 7:30 to 10:30 p.m. The restaurant is closed Saturday, Sunday, and in August.

Da Dino, via Da Passano 19 (tel. 21-360), ranks among my favorites in the area, a short walk from the water lying behind the major boulevard, viale Italia. This is in many ways a typical trattoria, but it invariably ends up on every visiting Italian's list as the place to go, ranking next to the just-previewed La Posta. The food and service are good, and reasonable in price, with meals costing 25,000 lire ($19) and up. The kitchen turns its major attention to fruits of the sea. Try the mixed grill from the bay, containing scampi and shrimp, among other creatures of the deep. The pasta dishes are also good. It is likely to be the busiest at lunch. Hours are noon to 3 p.m. and 7:30 to 10 p.m.; closed Sunday night, all day Monday, and from June 25 to July 10.

ON THE OUTSKIRTS AT AMEGLIA

A combined restaurant and hotel, **Paracucchi Locanda dell'Angelo,** viale XXV Aprile, 19031 Ameglia (tel. 0187/64-391), lies midway between Sarzana and Marinella, about two miles southeast of Ameglia, which is itself some 12 miles from La Spezia. The premises are the personal brainchild of Angelo Paracucchi, who managed to include both his first and last name in the establishment's title with an amusing twist. Most visitors are impressed with its slickly opulent contemporary "Italian style." The locanda is considered the best restaurant—as well as the best hotel—in the area. The cuisine, like the architecture, might be called "moderno." It includes imaginative recipes based loosely on the best of rich Italian tradition. Examples might include risotto with fresh crabmeat, mousseline of caviar, or braised beefsteak with chives. You will find, as well, many French adaptations of the Italian cuisine. The specific menu depends on the shopping of the day. Angelo had a distinguished restaurant career in Paris before returning to Italy to impress gastronomes with the finesse of his cookery. Dinners range from 65,000 lire ($49.50) to 80,000 lire ($60.75). Food is served from 12:30 to 2:30 p.m. and 7:30 to 10:30 p.m. The locanda also rents 37 attractive rooms, charging 85,000 lire ($64.50) daily in a single, 130,000 lire ($98.75) in a double.

7. Cinque Terre

North of La Spezia is Cinque Terre, or Five Lands—five little cliffside-hugging towns which originated as fishing villages in the Middle Ages, built at the locations of natural harbors along what is known as the Riviera di Levante, between Genoa and La Spezia where the Apuane Alps send high ridges right to the sea. The alpine ridges and rugged country inland from the harbors caused the five towns to be inaccessible by land for centuries after their origin. The towns are **Riomaggiore, Manarola, Corniglia, Vernazza,** and **Monterosso al Mare,** this last a town popular among sandy-beach devotees.

Today, the Cinque Terre towns can be reached by train or (except for Corniglia and Vernazza) by car. To drive here, take the autostrada A12, going from Genoa to Livorno, then exit at Brugnato, some 20 miles from Monterosso al Mare, going via

Pignone. At Monterosso is a large parking area for use of beach crowds. A local highway leads from La Spezia to Riomaggiore and Manarola, but cars are not allowed to enter the villages and must park outside. Trains stop hourly at all five towns, taking four minutes to go from one to the other. Purchase your ticket at the local station.

Many visitors to the Cinque Terre prefer to walk from town to town along a 12-mile, well-marked trail, whose strong guardrail offers protection where the trail goes around coastal ledges and cliff overhangs. A leaflet about the paths in the area is available at the tourist offices in Monterosso.

Among sights along the way are a 1622 Capuchin convent, a crenellated fortress, ancient buildings, and the fishing boats in the harbor at Monterosso. Vernazza has a plaza on the harbor. Labyrinthine steps lead through the ancient town, and you can see an elegant Renaissance campanile with an octagonal balustrade. Corniglia is not at the water's edge, as are the other four towns. Instead, it is on a promontory that juts out, with a long stairway leading down to the quay where fishing boats tie up. In the town stands a Renaissance chapel built in layers of black basalt and white travertine, giving it a striped effect seen mainly in Tuscany. Corniglia was built in a ravine and has houses climbing both sides of the declivity, with fishing boats lining the one street of the town.

Manarola welcomes visitors to its sidewalk cafés, where you can rest from the walk if you're making your way along the trail. The path leading from it to Riomaggiore, called via dell'Amore, is mostly paved and has guardrails to protect walkers from falling over the cliffs. Riomaggiore rests in the natural valleys, with both an old and a new town. Instead of cars, fishing boats are parked on the street, and a weekly market is held every Thursday. All the five towns are known for their wines.

The telephone area code for the Cinque Terre is 0187.

FOOD AND LODGING

Monterosso al Mare is the only Cinque Terre town I recommend for an overnight stay. **Hotel Porto Roca,** 19016 Monterosso al Mare (tel. 0187/817-502), stands on a high point of land, allowing views of the sea from the balconies that grace most of the bedrooms. The hotel is richly furnished, in part with antiques, giving it a home-like quality. Rates are from 170,000 lire ($129) daily in a single, from 140,000 lire ($106) per person in a double, with half board included. The service and cuisine here are excellent. If you're just visiting for the day, you can enjoy a meal for 50,000 lire ($38) to 70,000 lire ($53.25). The hotel, accessible only by taxi or on foot, is open from March to the first week of November.

---

8. Viareggio

Tuscany on the sea, Viareggio is one of the most fashionable sea resorts in Italy, a mecca of the sun-and-beach lover along the Tyrrhenian coast. It is 18 miles from Pisa, 54 miles from Florence. Guests flock here mainly in summer to enjoy 18 miles of coast, with many long sandy beaches.

It's also a good base for exploring parts of Tuscany, when you tire of the sands. For example, visitors drive to the Carrara marble excavations where Michelangelo worked and sculpted, and they also visit such inland art cities as Lucca.

Viareggio is also known for its carnival, when the whole month of February is turned over to merry-making. Every Sunday the people of the town—hoping to scare up some winter business—have a parade of flamboyantly colored floats along the promenade.

Viareggio is the capital of Riviera della Versilia, which also includes the satellite resort of **Forte dei Marmi,** 8½ miles along the coast. For hotel recommendations there, see my selections, coming up.

Music-lovers will want to visit the **Torre del Lago Puccini,** about three miles southeast of Viareggio. Puccini, born in 1858, composed such classics as *La Bohème* and *Madame Butterfly* there. During the summer season, some of his operas are performed in an open-air theater that takes full advantage of its location on Lake Massaciuccoli, where the composer's tomb and memento-filled villa are open to inspection.

Viareggio's telephone area code is 0584.

WHERE TO STAY

The glossy, modern **Hotel Astor,** viale Carducci 54, 55049 Viareggio (tel. 0584/50-301), is considered the finest at the resort, with a contemporary design that includes a multilevel lobby, comfortable armchairs, a roof garden with a bar and restaurant, lots of marble trim, and a health center. Many of the clients checking in here come for weight loss, massage therapy, and hydrotherapy sessions, although no one will object if clients use their rooms as a base for a vacation on the beach. Many of the well-furnished rooms offer views of the water. Singles rent for 180,000 lire ($137) daily; doubles, 280,000 lire ($213).

Royal Grand Hotel, lungomare Carducci 44, 55049 Viareggio (tel. 0584/45-151), is the grand dowager of Viareggio's hotels. Constructed in the 19th century, it was once the residence of Pauline Bonaparte, the sister of Napoleon, until it was enlarged into what looks like a Florentine palace in 1921. The interior contains a stairwell of carved balustrades stretching the vertical length of the hotel. There's also the biggest hotel garden in town, behind the ornate cream-colored structure, much of it encircled by an ornate wrought-iron fence. Don't come here expecting the same physical decor that greeted the kings and diplomats who arrived during the hotel's heyday. There have been many alterations, some caused by the occupancy of the American army here after World War II, along with modern accessories. There are, nonetheless, many amenities, such as the biggest private pool in town (25 yards), plus an outdoor restaurant with a vine-covered trellis suspended above the marble floor, which might be a delightful place for lunch on a summer day. The hotel charges from 130,000 lire ($98.75) daily in a single, 160,000 lire ($122) for a double, including a continental breakfast. The hotel is closed from October 15 to May 1.

Grand Hotel Excelsior, viale Carducci 88, 55049 Viareggio (tel. 0584/50-726), one of my preferred hotels in Viareggio, housed in a grandiose stone building with a Victorian dome, ornate loggias with balconies and shutters, sits across from a park on the main boulevard running beside the sea. The sunny lobby has a collection of carved 19th-century furniture and a frieze of sculptured seashells running under the ceiling coves. The charges are 130,000 lire ($98.75) daily in a single, 180,000 lire ($137) in a double. Full board, with meals taken in the high-ceilinged dining room, is offered for 100,000 lire ($76) to 140,000 lire ($106) per person daily.

Hotel San Francisco, viale Carducci 68, 55049 Viareggio (tel. 0584/52-666), is a real find, designed almost like something you'd find along the beachfront in California. It's better than some of the more expensive hotels a few blocks away. No one from the staff had ever been to San Francisco when the hotel was first established, although the name seemed appropriate, especially since "all the other possible names were already taken." Today you'll be greeted with a large aerial photograph of the Bay Area's skyline as you enter the pleasantly furnished lobby. There's a small bar, a breakfast room, 31 bedrooms, stone floors, lots of polished paneling, and plenty of plants and sunlight. Singles cost from 55,000 lire ($41.75) daily, doubles from 80,000 lire ($60.75). All units contain private bath, air conditioning, and phone. The hotel is open from February to October.

WHERE TO DINE

The most sophisticated and best eating place in town is **Ristorante Il Patriarca,** viale Carducci 79 (tel. 53-126). It's become a favorite dining spot for the many celebrities who have passed through here. Entire walls of the establishment are covered with their autographed photos, including Anthony Quinn, Frank Sinatra, Ella Fitzgerald, John Wayne, Pavarotti, Nureyev, Chuck Berry, and Giorgio Armani. Enzo Brocchino, the owner, had a career in London, Milan, Rome, and Florence, before launching this excellent restaurant in Viareggio. There's often piano music at night.

Out-of-season foods are flown in frequently from both California and Israel, for a collection of menu specialties that virtually knows no season. Many of the dishes are cooked within view of the dining room on the olivewood grill, sending savory aromas among the ceiling beams, the antiques, the ornate brass lamps, and what might be the funniest movie posters in Italy. There's a glassed-in terrace with rounded banquettes for more intimate dining, masses of fresh flowers, and an antipasti table laden with delicacies that took the chefs hours to prepare. Your meal might consist of fresh eel (a specialty), plus a wide range of meats, fish, salads, the freshest of vegetables, and a delectable array of desserts. Full meals begin at 70,000 lire ($53.25), although it's possible to spend far more, particularly if you order one of the more difficult-to-obtain fish dishes. The restaurant is open from noon to 2:30 p.m. and 7:30 to 11:30 p.m. every day of the week except Wednesday off-season and in October when the staff goes on vacation. Mr. Brocchini also runs the popular Enoclub Harry's Bar.

Ristorante Montecatini, viale Manin 8 (tel. 962-129), stands next to the Plaza Hotel on the city's main boulevard. It's generally acknowledged in Viareggio that to pass up something from the antipasti table would be a mistake, since practically everything on it is the result of hours spent with all the fruits of the sea. Food items are predominantly concocted from different types of fish. These would include whatever is available that day from the local fishermen, as well as zuppa di pesce, sole in champagne, spaghetti in a marinara sauce, penne with shrimp sauce, Ligurian sole, scampi with white beans, fish mousse, and grilled dorade. Among the meat dishes, the chateaubriand of the house with béarnaise sauce is excellent. You'll recognize the establishment by its position in a garden setting at the end of a long flagstone-covered passageway leading into the street. The restaurant charges 45,000 lire ($34.25) to 60,000 lire ($45.50) for a complete meal. Its doors are closed Monday (except in summer) and it's open from 12:30 to 3 p.m. and 7:30 to 10 p.m.

Gran Café Margherita, lungomare Margherita 30 (tel. 962-553). Puccini is said to have composed sections of *La Bohème* at one of the small marble tables, and other regular clients in the past included Toscanini. The glamorous clientele seems appropriate to the extravagant architecture, which makes this one of the most distinctive buildings in town. The restaurant is designed like a quasi-Moorish pavilion, with double towers covered with pastel-colored tiles. The interior is emblazoned with painted panels on its high ceilings, potted palms, formally dressed waiters, carved Victorian-era antiques *à l'Italiennes,* and a big-windowed view of a semitropical garden in back. It's probably the most authentic re-creation of the 19th century in Viareggio. The establishment today considers itself more a restaurant than a café, serving full meals from 45,000 lire ($34.25). These include a mixed grill of various meats, medallions of veal with lemon, chateaubriand with béarnaise sauce, veal liver, sole with fresh tomatoes and basil, risotto with scampi, spaghetti with seafood, a wide selection of antipasti, and a standard collection of desserts. The Gran Café is open from 12:30 to 3 p.m. and 7:30 to 10 p.m.; closed every Wednesday.

FORTE DEI MARMI

One of the leading resorts along the Riviera della Versilia is Forte dei Marmi, which in the last few years has taken much business away from Viareggio, only 8½ miles away. Many frankly prefer the resort to Viareggio, but that is a matter of personal taste. Forte is surrounded by sea, pine woods, beach, and mountains. It is also convenient for exploring such famous cities as Siena, Pisa, Florence, Lucca, and San Gimignano, as well as the marble quarries once frequented by Michelangelo.

The telephone area code for Forte dei Marmi is 0584.

Where to Stay
Augustus Hotel, viale Morin 169, 55042 Forte dei Marmi (tel. 0584/80-202), the best hotel at the resort, is a vacation compound in a spacious park, part of which contains an outdoor swimming pool. The main building is a flat-roofed, balconied structure with stone accents and a thick covering of ivy. The public rooms are finished with lots of exposed marble—sometimes in vivid colors of red and pink—along with light-grained wood. A wing, La Nave, with horizontal lines, cantilevered balconies, and concrete construction, looks like something Le Corbusier could have designed for a Chinese client. A 19th-century, sienna-colored villa, set close to the beach and connected to the rest of the hotel complex via an underground tunnel, offers additional accommodations. Finally, for clients wanting even more privacy, the establishment maintains a handful of villas set either directly on the beach or in the midst of a pine forest. Rates depend on the accommodation. With full board included, each person is charged 230,000 lire ($175) to 265,000 lire ($201) daily. The hotel is open only from May until September.

Hermitage Hotel, via Cesare Battisti, 55042 Forte dei Marmi (tel. 0584/80-022), under the same direction as the nearby Augustus, offers a rustically inviting series of public rooms inside a white stucco building with recessed balconies and textured stone accents. The high-ceilinged public rooms are comfortably outfitted. On the premises are an outdoor pool, a restaurant, an American-style bar, a private beach, and a covered parking garage. With full board included, rates range from 170,000 lire ($129) to 190,000 lire ($144) per person daily, depending on the accommodation. The hotel is open from late May to late September.

9. Isle of Elba

Lying slightly more than six miles from the mainland of Italy, Elba is the largest island in an archipelago linked to Tuscany (Florence).

The string of Tuscan islands, incidentally, includes the legendary Montecristo, 38 miles south of Elba, made famous by the older Dumas in his *The Count of Monte Cristo*—and now containing the remains of a Camaldulensian convent last occupied in the mid-16th century. The tiny isle, lying between the Italian mainland and Corsica, has become a natural preserve and bird sanctuary, administered by the forestry service. Most of the Isle of Montecristo is rocky and bare of vegetation. It is mountainous, occupying about six square miles and having a nine-mile perimeter. Boat trips are made daily from Elba.

Napoleon knew Elba well, but today it's fast being discovered by ever-increasing numbers of foreign visitors, who value its moderate prices and good accommodations. Italy has far more glamorous islands (Capri and Ischia), but Elba makes for an excellent, less trampled base for a holiday by the sea, with a minimum of sights. In many places—*still*—a rustic life holds forth, the people suspicious of strangers, standoffish. But the growing number of visitors coming over are necessarily changing the landscape—and even the Elbani, many of whom have known extremely hard times, are now learning the wily ways of competing for tourist lire.

With 91 miles of coastline—and with lots of hidden coves and occasional beaches away from the maddening crowd—Elba presents the typical Mediterranean landscape of silvery olive trees and hill-climbing vineyards. Its climate is mild, with a tendency toward dryness.

GETTING THERE
A number of means are offered, principally from the port of Piombino on the Italian mainland. The hydrofoil, taking less than 30 minutes, is the quickest method. But motorists will want to board one of the ferryboats that run between

Piombino and Portoferraio (capital of Elba) several times daily (there's more limited service in winter). There is also a ferry service between Piombino and Porto Azzurro on the southern coast of Elba. Space is likely to be tight in summer, so reserve at Toremar; piazzale Premuda at Piombino (tel. 31-100)

THE MAIN SIGHT

Once on the island, you'll want to visit the chief man-made attraction, which is, of course, **Napoleon's Villa** at San Martino, about three miles outside Portoferraio. With everything—quite symbolically—in trompe l'oeil, the villa was the summer home of Napoleon, who ruled over the small principality of Elba following his abdication on April 11, 1814. Only 45, the Corsican was impatient, launching many projects to keep his mind occupied. But it wasn't enough. In late February 1815 he left Elba to begin the famous "Hundred Days" that culminated in Waterloo. He was never to return to Elba, of course; he was exiled the next time to Saint Helena.

The villa is unimpressive, but rich in the memories of its former tenant. The apartments were occupied by Napoleon and Marshal Bertrand. On the grounds today is a 19th-century neoclassic museum (see the statue of *Galatea* by Canova). The residence is open from 9 a.m. to 1:30 p.m. (on Sunday from 9 a.m. to 12:30 p.m.), and charges 3,000 lire ($2.30) admission. Closed Monday and holidays.

The telephone area code for the Isle of Elba is 0565.

We'll dock first at—

PORTOFERRAIO

Elba's capital is a busy harbor, filled with traffic caused by the coming and going of visitors. However, it's not the loveliest spot at which to base for a holiday by the sea, as the resorts in the hinterlands offer far more idyllic settings. (In off-season it provides a more suitable center, as many outlying hotels shut down then.) In the old town is the **Mulini Palazzina,** a Medici fortress containing Napoleonic memorabilia. It charges the same admission and is open the same hours as Napoleon's Villa at San Martino, described above. It is closed Monday.

Where to Stay

Hotel Touring, 57037 Portoferraio (tel. 0565/915-851), offers 31 plain but clean rooms, of which about 80% contain private bath or shower. The rate in a single is 48,000 lire ($36.50) daily, rising to 72,000 lire ($54.75) in a double. Only breakfast is served.

Hotel Nuova Padulella, 57037 Portoferraio (tel. 0565/92-742), lies outside the center and contains slightly more accommodations than the Touring. Its amenities and comforts are comparable, however. Done in a modern style, it stands in a well-situated position overlooking the gulf. The hotel is closed from December to mid-January, and prefers guests on the half-board plan, costing 50,000 lire ($38) to 65,000 lire ($49.50) per person daily. However, the restaurant is closed from November to March.

Where to Dine

La Ferrigna Ristorante (tel. 92-129) has many faithful habitués on the island, and is certainly the finest place to eat in the capital. On my latest rounds, several of the guests were raving about the Gucci "copies" in leather goods they had purchased at the Friday market. In fair weather you can select a table under a canopy. Here you can enjoy Elban cookery at its finest and most regional. Naturally, the chef uses the fish available on the island to his best advantage. You might be daring and order squid served with risotto that has been flavored with the calamaretti ink. If not that, then perhaps some stuffed zucchini will tempt your palate. In spring you are treated to fresh strawberries and asparagus, always a delight, and if you're lucky you'll get some of those large Mediterranean prawns. The staff will suggest what's good on any particular day. The restaurant charges 30,000 lire ($22.75) to 50,000 lire ($38) for a complete meal, served from 12:30 to 2:30 p.m. and 7:30 to 10 p.m. daily. Closed from mid-November to mid-March.

Food and Lodging at Picchiaie

Far better accommodations are found on the immediate outskirts of Portoferraio. To illustrate, try the following accommodation at Picchiaie, about four miles south of Portoferraio.

Picchiaie Résidence, Picchiaie, 57037 Portoferraio (tel. 0565/966-072), is one of the better hotels in the area, receiving guests from mid-May to late September. The hotel doesn't lie on the seacoast, like so many other Elban hostelries, but is set in a beautiful forest. The architect knew how to create a dramatic building, and management added an alluring outdoor swimming pool in lieu of a beach. The service is efficient. If you're visiting only for a meal, expect to spend from 45,000 lire ($34.25). However, should you plan to make the hotel your choice for an Elban holiday, the price is 90,000 lire ($68.50) daily in a single, 140,000 lire ($106) in a double. In peak season, most guests stay here on the full-board plan at rates ranging from 110,000 lire ($83.50) to 135,000 lire ($103) per person daily, with off-season reductions granted.

Food and Lodging at Biodola

Hotel Hermitage, La Biodola, 57037 Portoferraio (tel. 0585/969-932), is one of the oldest and also the finest hotels on the island. It offers bedroom cottages, beautifully furnished, its rooms overlooking the bay on what has been called Elba's "gold coast." You're only a few steps from the sea, and the hotel has its own private beach, along with a garden, swimming pool, and tennis courts. In a pine forest, the hotel receives guests in its 90 rooms from the first week of May until September. Depending on the season, half board ranges from 85,000 lire ($64.50) to 218,000 lire ($166) per person daily, the latter the high-season tariff for a superior room. Single supplements go from 8,000 lire ($6.10) to 17,000 lire ($13) daily. If you're stopping only for a meal, expect to spend from 40,000 lire ($30.50). In summer you can enjoy lunch at the beach restaurant or at the barbecue bar. Tranquility seekers like the seclusion of the place.

Hotel La Biodola, La Biodola, 57037 Portoferraio (tel. 0585/969-966), may have a lower rate than its bigger and grander sister, the Hermitage, but many of its faithful guests frankly prefer it. The location of the Biodola is supreme, right on the best beach of Elba. The accommodations, a total of 68 rooms, are handsomely decorated, often in pastels. In summer large pots of geraniums grow from the balconies, as in Austria. There's a seawater pool in the landscaped grounds, and it is here that most of the guests gather on a summer day. Only boarding guests are accepted in season, and the hotel receives visitors only from mid-April to October 20. Half board in high season costs 125,000 lire ($95) to 169,000 lire ($128) per person daily, double occupancy. In low season, half board begins at a low of 74,000 lire ($56.25) per person daily, rising to 156,000 lire ($119) in doubles. Singles are charged a daily supplement going from 6,000 lire ($4.55) to 16,000 lire ($12.25) daily, depending on the season. Even if you're not a guest, you might want to visit for lunch if you're touring in the area, but you should call first and make a reservation. Meals cost from 50,000 lire ($38). The hotel fills up quickly, and it's also necessary to reserve if you want accommodations in high season.

A drive along the north shore for about seven miles will take you to—

PROCCHIO

An attractive beach on a crystal-blue bay, Procchio is one of the best-equipped resorts on Elba, particularly in hotels in the top bracket.

Hotels in Procchio

Hotel del Golfo, 57030 Procchio (tel. 0585/907-565), about four miles southeast of Marciana Marina, is a self-sustaining private world, overlooking the Gulf of Procchio. A modern, three-story hotel, it stands on its own grounds at the inner bend of the bay, with a sandy beach. The park-like surroundings have many recreational facilities, including a free-form swimming pool with a flagstone terrace, cabañas, an open-air restaurant, and tennis courts. The hotel is built of stone and partially covered with bougainvillea. Most of the bedrooms have private balconies, where it's the custom to have your breakfast. The bedrooms are large, comfortable, and immaculate, some with air conditioning. High-season prices are charged from July 11 to August 20, and the hotel remains open from mid-May to September. All the rooms have private bath or shower, and there are no single rooms. In summer, half board costs 150,000 lire ($114) per person daily. Public rooms are spacious. The dining room has a panoramic view of the sea, and the American bar is cozy.

Hotel Désirée, 57030 Procchio (tel. 0585/907-502), at Spartaia di Procchio, about 3½ miles southeast of Marciana Marina, sits in a top-notch position, off the coast road, with its own gardens and beach. Spacious and up-to-date, it offers sunpocket terraces. The furnishings in the public rooms may suggest air-terminal modern, but the architecture is for those who like a sense of openness, light colors, and tile terraces with garden furniture set out for refreshments. There is a long dining room with two all-glass walls and another of native stone. The bedrooms are contemporary, with streamlined furnishings—immaculately maintained. Désirée receives guests from April 20 to October 1. All rooms contain either private bath or shower. The highest tarriffs are charged in July and August. Depending on the time of year, full board costs from 93,000 lire ($70.75) to 175,000 lire ($133) per person daily.

Continuing along the northern shore for another 4½ miles, we arrive at the resort of—

MARCIANA MARINA

A fishing village some 12½ miles from Portoferraio, Marciana Marina occupies a lovely setting. You can see the fishermen sitting around weaving lobster baskets.

Where to Stay

Albergo Marinella, 57033 Marciana Marina (tel. 0585/99-018), is a renovated seafront hotel-and-restaurant combination, right on the promenade. It's not only economical, but the food is especially good, and you're in the center of the promenade where the cafés provide the town's social activity. Behind the albergo's façade is a spacious lobby, with comfortable lounging chairs and an open fireplace. Away from the sea is a small informal garden, and there are two tennis courts and a swimming pool. The bedrooms are stark white, each with one wall of wood paneling, plus minimum furnishings, and most of them have a view of the sea. All rooms are doubles, and each has a private bath as well. For full board, the rate is 75,000 lire ($57) to 85,000 lire ($64.50) per person daily. High season is in July and August, when reservations are required. The owner is proud of his chef, who carefully selects fresh fish every morning for his dinners and serves his platters with the white Elban house wine from his own cellar. On the open but covered dining terrace, every table seems to be ringside.

Where to Dine

Rendez-Vous da Marcello, piazza della Vittoria (tel. 99-251), is one of the finest restaurants in Elba, one that remains open for most of the year. It serves a rotating series of specialties that adjust themselves to the season on its terrace overlooking the sea. The specialty is fish, and you'll find it concocted in soups, grilled with herbs, or fashioned into several varieties of antipasti. Bouillabaisse is a specialty, and it's said to be the best on the island. In this and many other dishes the chef doesn't skimp on the lobster or crab. You might enjoy the tuna with rosemary, or the spaghetti with crab, perhaps the house fettuccine or the peppardelle with hare sauce. The Florentine beefsteak with olive oil is grilled to perfection. Full meals range from 35,000 lire ($26.50) to 50,000 lire ($38). The restaurant is closed every Wednesday except in summer and from around mid-January to March, serving otherwise from 12:30 to 2:30 p.m. and 7:30 to 10 p.m.

The largest and most important resort on the southern shore is—

MARINA DI CAMPO

A base for trips to Montecristo, Marina di Campo, studded with pine trees, is my favorite among the Elban resorts, offering some of the most superior accommodations. The sandy beach separating it from the sea—slightly more than a mile long—is most inviting, the quintessence of an Elban holiday. The pace is slow; the living's easy.

Where to Stay

Montecristo, 57034 Marina di Campo (tel. 0585/976-861), is the best place to stay in town (the competition is slight). It attracts sun-seekers, often from the Teutonic lands, anytime between April and October. It doesn't have a restaurant, but it offers 43 attractively furnished and comfortable rooms with a continental breakfast, ranging in price from 150,000 lire ($114) daily in a single, from 240,000 lire ($182) in a double. The hotel has a swimming pool and a helpful staff. I've found it fairly easy to get a room in May, but if you're planning a visit in either July or August, it's important to nail down a reservation.

Hotel Dei Coralli, 57034 Marina di Campo (tel. 0585/97-336), is a good-sized nest some 220 yards from the beach, a season-only hotel that accepts guests from June through September. They are placed in a total of 60 pleasantly furnished by plain bedrooms, where singles cost 74,000 lire ($56.25) daily, and doubles go for 122,000 lire ($92.75), including a continental breakfast. No other meals are served.

Santa Caterina, 57034 Marina di Campo (tel. 0585/97-452), is another clean and comfortable hotel that opens its doors in mid-April, shutting them again at the end of September. Summer visitors, especially Europeans, book its 41 bedrooms, which are simply furnished and well maintained. Guests often stay at this one on a full-board arrangement, which begins at 58,000 lire ($44) per person daily in low season, going up to 90,000 lire ($68.50) per person in high.

Where to Dine

In Marina de Campo you can try **La Triglia** (tel. 97-059), which takes its name from the red mullet found in Elban waters. Naturally, that fish is the specialty of the kitchen. You might also try the whiting, which is steamed and offered with melted butter. The delicate fish soup served here is flavorful, and the noble sardine is not neglected either. The food is well prepared, the service polite. The clients are likely to be both local patrons and tourists. The restaurant is closed on Thursday and open only from mid-March to October, when you are likely to pay 30,000 lire ($22.75) to 40,000 lire ($30.50) for a complete meal served from 12:30 to 2:30 p.m. and 7:30 to 10 p.m.

At La Pila, 1½ miles from Marina di Campo, near the airport (an unlikely place for a good restaurant), you'll find **Da Gianni** (tel. 976-965). This small restaurant offers excellent food, served only from March to the end of October from 12:30 to 2:30 p.m. and 7:30 to 10 p.m., with meals costing 30,000 lire ($22.75) to 38,000 lire ($29), which is really a bargain considering the quality of food served here. The restaurant is closed on Friday.

Otherwise, every night you can try one of Bari-born Gianni's offerings, with about a dozen different choices, including beef ragoût and the inevitable Florentine beefsteak. He preserves dried tomatoes in olive oil and basil (among other herbs) as they do in his native southland, and uses them most delectably in pasta dishes. His specialty is risotto with fruits of the sea, and his pièce de résistance is his stufatino, a fish stew. He serves these dishes piping hot in the crocks in which the ingredients were simmered to perfection. His stufatino is his answer to the bouillabaisse served along the French and Italian Rivieras at highly inflated prices. It is rich in shellfish, especially mussels. Squid holds no terror for him, and it shouldn't for you when you see what enterprising dishes he can make with it.

In the southeast sector of the island is—

CAPOLIVERI

One of the choicest spots on the island, particularly noted for views of the sea, the village of Capoliveri occupies one of the more recently emerging resort areas of Elba. It's in the vicinity of Porto Azzurro.

Where to Stay

Antares, 57031 Capoliveri (tel. 0585/940-131), is the best place to stay in the area, but it's not in the center of Capoliveri, rather a distance of five miles away at the Capoliveri Lido. Naturally, it's a summer hotel, receiving guests from April to October. It rents 31 simply furnished but well-kept rooms. Full-board guests are preferred, at a rate that begins at 88,000 lire ($67) per person daily in low season, climbing to 110,000 lire ($53.50) in high. The food is good and filling.

Where to Dine

Il Chiasso, via Nazario Sauro (tel. 968-709). Restaurants such as this depend for their success as much on the personalities of the owner as on the quality of the cuisine. In this case, both are alluring enough to make Il Chiasso one of the best-known restaurants of Elba. Owner Luciano prepares well-seasoned versions of such classic recipes as fish soup. He also makes a "grande zuppa" of four different kinds of shellfish, as well as fish hors d'oeuvres, grilled, flambéed, or roasted fish, or savory grilled shrimp on a skewer. All fish is the catch of the day. There is a selection of meats, vegetables, and homemade desserts. As well as local wine, other important Italian vintages are offered. Full meals, costing from 50,000 lire ($38), are served from 12:30 to 2:30 p.m. and 7 to 10 p.m. daily from Easter to the end of October. It is closed Tuesday off-season.

PORTO AZZURRO

The southern terminus of the ferry, Porto Azzurro is a colorful harbor, suitable for photographing, dining, and overnighting.

Food and Lodging

Belmare, 57036 Porto Azzurro (tel. 0585/95-012), is considered a pioneer of Elban tourism, and it's still going strong, receiving guests in its 27 simply furnished bedrooms. It's more economical to stay here on full-board terms, costing from 65,000 lire ($49.50) per person daily. If you're just passing through, you can dine in the restaurant, enjoying a seafood dinner beginning at 35,000 lire ($26.50). The restaurant closes on Friday. The management is considerate.

NAPLES, ISCHIA, AND POMPEII

In one of the most memorable novels to come out of World War II, *The Gallery* by John Horne Burns, there is this passage: "But I remember best of all the children of Naples. The scugnizz'. Naples is the greatest baby plant in the world. Once they come off the assembly line, they lose no time getting onto the streets. They learn to walk and talk in the gutters. Many of them seem to live there."

The milling Mediterranean city known to the American G.I. of 1944 has changed drastically since its early postwar days. Yet its character seems unalterable. To the foreigner unfamiliar with the complexities of the multifarious "Italys" and their regional types, the Neapolitan is the quintessence of the country—easy to caricature ("O Sole Mio," "Mamma Mia," bel canto). If a native who moved to Rome (Sophia Loren) evokes the Italian woman to you, you'll find more of her look-alikes here than in any other city.

1. Naples

Naples is a city to be savored in bits and pieces, like the zuppa di pesce (fish soup). It is almost too much to take at once. But that is how the city comes upon you, like a runaway car, with tour-ticket sellers, shoeshine boys, hotel hawkers, and pickpockets.

July and August can be extremely unpleasant in Naples, despite the air-conditioning units in many of the hotels (some of which seem to blow out lukewarm air). The average working male on the street solves the problem by pulling off his shirt. And no Neapolitan housewife gets overheated running up and down the steps to convey a message to someone on the street—she handles the situation by screaming out the window. Surely, the Neapolitans are the most spontaneous people on earth, wearing their emotions on the surface of their skin.

The history of Naples (Palaeopolis of old) is ancient, the city having been founded by the Greeks (so it is believed) in the 6th century B.C. Early in the story, the Romans conquered the city, and it was later visited by such fun-and-sun-seeking emperors as Nero, as well as by poets (Virgil wrote the *Georgics* here). Over the years it has known many conquerors—everyone from Roger II of Sicily to Charles of Anjou in the 13th century to the Americans in the 20th. The city was made the capital of the Kingdom of the Two Sicilies by Charles III of Spain in 1734. It is the second-largest port in Italy, topped only by Genoa, and is also experiencing rapid industrial growth.

Warning: More and more readers are expressing disappointment after visiting Naples, complaining that the city on the bay is "rife with thieves." In addition to that, I have found that local transportation is disorganized, and it's hard to come by maps or schedules. Likewise, booking tours is difficult from Naples (easy from lovely Sorrento). The less said about driving a car in Naples, the better. And if, like many visitors, you plan to visit either Naples or the major sight in the environs, Pompeii, on a day trip from Rome, *don't show up on a Monday* when all the most important attractions will be closed.

ORIENTATION

What Naples is, is a fantastic adventure. The best approach, from its bay, is idyllic—a port set against the backdrop of a crystal-blue sky and volcanic mountains. "See Naples and Die" is apt. The rich attractions inside the city and in the environs (Pompeii, Ischia, Capri, Vesuvius, the Phlaegrean Fields, Herculaneum) make Naples one of the five top tourist meccas of Italy. The inexperienced may have difficulty coping with it. The seasoned explorer will find it worthy ground, even venturing down side streets, some of which teem with prostitutes and a major source of their upkeep: the ubiquitous sailor.

Many visitors to Naples confine their visit to the bay-fronting Santa Lucia area, perhaps venturing into another section to see an important museum. Most of the major hotels lie along **via Partenope,** which looks out not only to the Gulf of Naples but the Castel dell'Ovo. To the west lies the Margellina district, site of many restaurants and dozens of apartment houses. The far western section of the city is known as Posillipo.

One of the most important squares of Naples is the **piazza del Plebiscito,** north of Santa Lucia. The Palazzo Reale opens onto this square. On a satellite square, you can visit the **piazza Trento e Trieste,** with its Teatro San Carlo and entrance to the famed Galleria Umberto I. Lying to the east, the third most important square is the **piazza Municipio.** From the piazza Trento e Trieste, you encounter the main shopping street of Naples, **via Toledo/via Roma,** which you can walk as far as the piazza Dante. From that square, take via Enrico Pessina to the most important museum of Naples, opening into the **piazza Museo Nazionale.**

If you arrive by train at the Stazione Centrale, fronting the piazza Garibaldi, to escape from that horror, you can take one of the major arteries of Naples, **corso Umberto,** heading toward the Santa Lucia district. Along the water, many boats, such as those heading for Capri and Ischia, leave from Porto Beverello.

GETTING THERE

In the old days, the custom was to sail into the Bay of Naples, but today's traveler is more likely to drive there, heading down the autostrada from Rome, 136 miles north. Others arrive at the **Stazione Centrale,** on the piazza Garibaldi, having taken a train from Rome. The quickest way to get to Naples from Rome and other major cities of Italy, including Milan, is to fly there on a domestic flight, which will put you into **Capodichino Airport,** four miles from the city.

Railroad Information: The city has two main rail terminals, Stazione Centrale at piazza Garibaldi and Stazione Margelliana at piazza Amadeo. If you want rail information, call 264-644.

NAPLES TRANSPORTATION

Getting around Naples can be a nightmare! Motorists should pay particular attention, as Neapolitans are fond of driving the wrong way on one-way streets and speeding hysterically along lanes reserved for public transportation, perhaps cutting into your lane without warning. Red lights seem to hold no terror for a Neapolitan driver. In fact, you may want to park your car and walk. There are two dangers in that. One is that your car can be stolen, as mine once was, even though apparently "guarded" by an attendant in front of a deluxe hotel. The other danger is that you are likely to get mugged (nearly a third of the city is unemployed, and people have to live somehow).

That leaves public transportation. Chances are, you'll use the suburban rail line, the **Circumvesuviana,** to reach the major towns in the environs, including Pompeii (the chief target of sightseers), Sorrento, and Herculaneum.

Four **funiculars** take passengers up and down the steep hills of Naples. The Funicolare Centrale, for example, connects the lower part of the city to Vomero. Departures are from the piazzetta Duca d'Aosta, just off via Roma. Cable cars run daily from 9 a.m. to 7 p.m. Watch that you don't get stranded by missing the last car back.

It's dangerous to ride **buses** at certain hours. Never have I seen such pushing, shoving, and jockeying for position. On one recent research trip, I saw a middle-aged woman fall from a too-crowded bus, injuring her leg. I was later told that this was a routine occurrence. If you're a linebacker, take your chances; but if you're frail and dainty, leave the buses to the battle-hardened Neapolitans and take other means of transport.

Perhaps a **taxi.** If you survive reckless driving (someone once wrote that all Neapolitans drive like the anarchists they are), you'll only have to do battle over the bill. You will inevitably be overcharged. Many cab drivers claim their meter is broken, and they then proceed to assess the cost of the ride, always to your disadvantage. Some legitimate surcharges are imposed, including night drives and extra luggage. However, many taxi drivers deliberately take you "the long way there" to run up your costs. In repeated visits to Naples, I have never yet been quoted an honest fare. In self-defense, I no longer bother with the meter. Instead I estimate what the fare would be worth, negotiate with the driver, and take off into the night. If you want to take a chance, you can call a radio taxi at 364-444.

Another means of transport, more expensive but far more romantic than the taxi, is a **horse and buggy.** They are still in service; most often taking visitors along the waterfront in Santa Lucia.

You can take a **tram** (no. 4 is the one), which will transport you from the Stazione Centrale to the Margelliana station. It will also let you off at the quayside points where the boats depart for Ischia and Capri.

In addition, the **Metropolitana** line will deliver you from the Stazione Centrale to the west, all the way to the Stazione Margelliana. Get off at the piazza Amadeo if you wish to take the funicular to Vomero.

Fares are reasonable on public transportation, probably costing 600 lire (45¢) per trip at the time of your visit.

TOURS

To visit points of interest, **Tourcar,** piazza Matteotti 1 (tel. 552-3310), has several tours of Naples and its environs. Prices of the trips include your transportation from your hotel to the Tourcar offices or to the quay where you take the hydrofoil to Capri, the services of a knowledgeable guide who speaks English, and entrance fees to the attractions you'll see, returning you to your hotel at the end of the trip.

A half-day tour, from 2 to 6 p.m. takes you to the major points of interest in Naples and to the Solfatara, the ancient volcano 7½ miles west of the city. The charge is 25,000 lire ($19) per person. An excursion to Capri and Anacapri, exclud-

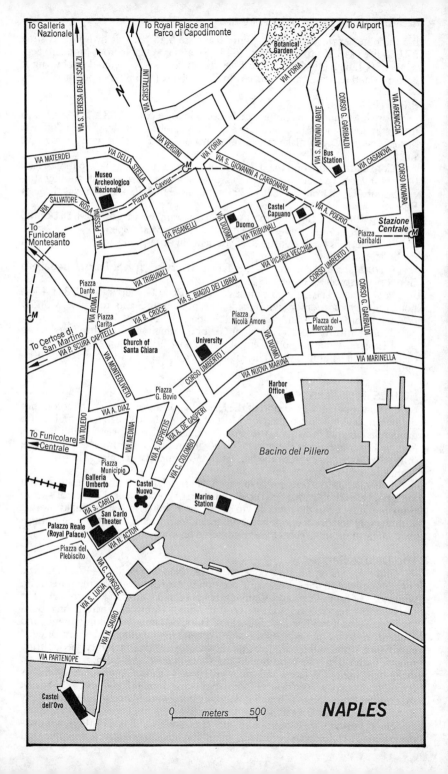

NAPLES

To Galleria Nazionale

To Royal Palace and Parco di Capodimonte

To Airport

Botanical Garden

VIA FORIA

VIA S. TERESA DEGLI SCALZI

VIA CRISTALLINI

VIA S. ANTONIO ABATE

CORSO G. GARIBALDI

VIA ARENACCIA

VIA MATERDEI

VIA DELLA STELLA

VIA VERGINI

VIA FORIA

VIA S. GIOVANNI A CARBONARA

Bus Station

VIA CASANOVA

CORSO NOVARA

Museo Archeologico Nazionale

VIA SALVATORE ROSA

Piazza Cavour

M

VIA E. PESSINA

VIA PISANELLI

VIA DUOMO

Duomo

Castel Capuano

VIA A. POERIO

Piazza Garibaldi

Stazione Centrale M

To Funicolare Montesanto

VIA TRIBUNALI

VIA S. BIAGIO DEI LIBRAI

VIA TRIBUNALI

VIA VICARIA VECCHIA

CORSO UMBERTO I

CORSO G. GARIBALDI

Piazza Dante

VIA ROMA

Piazza Carità

VIA B. CROCE

Piazza Nicolà Amore

Piazza del Mercato

To Certose di San Martino

VIA P. SCURA

CAPITELLI

Church of Santa Chiara

University

VIA DUOMO

VIA MARINELLA

VIA MONTEOLIVETO

Piazza G. Bovio

CORSO UMBERTO I

VIA NUOVA MARINA

Harbor Office

Bacino del Piliero

VIA A. DIAZ

VIA MEDINA

VIA A. DEFRETIS

VIA A. DE GASPERI

VIA C. COLOMBO

VIA TOLEDO

To Funicolare Centrale

Piazza Municipio

Galleria Umberto

Castel Nuovo

Marine Station

VIA S. CARLO

San Carlo Theater

VIA N. ACTON

Palazzo Reale (Royal Palace)

Piazza del Plebiscito

VIA C. CONSOLE

VIA S. LUCIA

VIA N. SAURO

VIA PARTENOPE

Castel dell'Ovo

0 meters 500

ing the Blue Grotto, takes from about 10 a.m. to 6:45 p.m. via hydrofoil, costing 57,000 lire ($43.25) to 57,500 lire ($43.75), and is available from June 1 to September 30. Lunch is included. A half-day trip to Pompeii is offered daily, leaving at 8:15 a.m. and returning at 1 p.m., costing 33,500 lire ($25.50) per person.

PRACTICAL FACTS

For Naples and its environs, the **telephone area code** is 081. If you need to make a long-distance call, you can do so at the Stazione Centrale, where an office is open 24 hours. If you make calls from your hotel, you'll be hit with an excessive surcharge.

Consulate: You'll find the **U.S. Consulate** on the piazza della Repubblica (tel. 081/660-966). The staff has long ago grown weary of hearing about another stolen passport. Open from 8 a.m. to 12:30 p.m. and 3 to 5:30 p.m. Monday through Friday.

Drugstore: If it's an all-night drugstore you want, get in touch with **Di Donna,** piazza Cavour 119 (tel. 299-4940), or call 192 to see what's open.

Emergency phone numbers: If you have an **emergency,** dial 113. To reach the **police,** call 325-025.

Medical Care: If you are in need of medical services, try the **Ente Ospedaliero General,** Castrucci 5 (tel. 440-772).

Post Office: The main post office is on the piazza G. Matteotti (tel. 311-456). Look for the *posta telegrafo* sign outside. It is open from 8 a.m. to 8 p.m. Monday through Saturday and 8 a.m. to noon on Sunday.

Tourist Information: Visitors can ask for information at the **Ente Provinciale per il Turismo** at the Stazione Centrale (tel. 268-779), but don't expect anybody there to be too helpful to you. There is another office at via Partenope 10 (tel. 406-289).

HOTELS IN NAPLES

With the possible exception of the Hotel Excelsior (see below), the accommodations in Naples are often a sad lot. Most of the large hotels lie in the popular (also dangerous) district of Santa Lucia. Many of the so-called first-class establishments line via Partenope along the water. In and around the central railway station are other clusters, many built in the late '50s (and some that seemingly haven't been changed since that faraway time).

Regardless of the price range in which you travel, there's a bed waiting for you in Naples. Regrettably, that bed often isn't clean or comfortable. I'll present a selection of what are generally conceded to be the "best" hotels in Naples, but know that with an exception or two, none of the other candidates leaves me with much enthusiasm. Many of the innkeepers I've encountered seem an indifferent lot.

The Deluxe Range

Hotel Excelsior, via Partenope 48, 80121 Napoli (tel. 081/417-111), has a strong foothold on a most dramatic position in Naples—right on the waterfront, with views of Santa Lucia and Vesuvius. It has been restored and refurbished. The management made efforts to create a country-home ambience. There are many elegant details, such as Venetian chandeliers, Doric columns, wall-filling murals, and bronze torchiers. This same sophistication prevails in the bedrooms, where Oriental rugs blend with traditional elements. Most of them are, in reality, bed/sitting rooms. Each room is air-conditioned and contains a well-maintained private bath, direct-dial phone, TV, radio, and frigo-bar. There is a garage, upon request, which is open 24 hours a day. For a double room, the price is from 385,000 lire ($293) daily; singles cost from 255,000 lire ($194). For dining at the Excelsior, expect to pay from 75,000 lire ($57) for a meal.

Hotel Vesuvio, via Partenope 45, 80121 Napoli (tel. 081/417-044), was originally built in 1880, but was restored about 50 years later to feature a marble- and stucco-sheathed façade strongly evocative of art deco. When it was constructed, it was the first and foremost hotel along the fabled bay, and many aristocratic members of English society flocked here. Curved balconies extend toward Castel dell'Ovo (the Castle of the Egg). Now being overhauled, the hotel remains one of the best in Naples. Today, each of its 175 rooms contains often-lofty ceilings, rich cove moldings, and parquet floors. You'll also find a scattering of antiques set throughout the echoing hallways. Each accommodation contains a renovated bathroom, complete with tiles and lots of space, a color TV, large closets, and a refrigerator and mini-bar. Singles rent for 180,000 lire ($137) daily, and doubles cost 240,000 lire ($182). The hotel also has a first-class restaurant and a comfortable bar that evokes the most stylish decor of the 1950s. The Vesuvio is a member of the prestigious German-based Steigenberger reservation system. To reserve, call toll free 800/223-5652 in the United States, (800/882-4777 in New York State, or 212/593-2988 in New York City).

The First-Class Range

Hotel Majestic, largo Vasto a Chiaia 68, 80121 Napoli (tel. 081/416-500), is one of the finest four-star hotels of Naples, well run and accommodating, with 130 impressive bedrooms, each with bath or shower, color TV, frigo-bar, direct-dial phone, air conditioning, and central heating. Built in 1959 on ten floors, it has been renewed until it is one of the most modern and up-to-date hostelries in a city too often filled with decaying mansions. A favorite with the conference crowd, it lies in the antique district of Naples. At your doorstep will be dozens of fashionable boutiques. Singles rent for 95,000 lire ($72.25) nightly, with doubles costing 160,000 lire ($122). There's a cozy American bar and a restaurant, Magic Grill, serving both Neapolitan dishes and international specialties. Reservations are important, as this hotel is often fully booked.

Jolly Hotel Ambassador's, via Medina 70, 80133 Napoli (tel. 081/416-000), is a skyscraper, Italian style. Neapolitans call it *Il Grattacielo*. Billing itself as the tallest hotel in Italy, it stands as a landmark, a few blocks up from the central harbor. The bedrooms occupy the upper part of the building and afford a magnificent view of the city and of the sea. Of medium size, each has bath or shower, air conditioning, refrigerated bar, automatic wake-up system, direct-dial phone, radio, and color TV. The refurbished rooms have built-in furniture with ample desk surfaces. The top-floor restaurant, with all-glass walls from which you can admire most of the sights of Naples while enjoying regional and international specialties, is remarkable. The Jolly Hotel Ambassador charges 150,000 lire ($114) daily in a single with bath, 198,000 lire ($151) in a double with bath, with a buffet breakfast included, served in the 30th-floor restaurant.

Hotel Royal, via Partenope 38, 80121 Napoli (tel. 081/400-244), occupies a desirable position on this busy street running beside the bay in Santa Lucia. You park in an underground garage, then enter a greenery-filled vestibule where a pair of stone lions flank stairs leading to the modern lobby. Each of the 300 bedrooms contains a balcony, phone, color TV, radio, and contemporary furniture. Some but not all offer a water view. Singles cost 175,000 lire ($133) daily, and doubles go for 260,000 lire ($198), with breakfast included. A saltwater pool with an adjacent flower-dotted sun terrace is on the hotel's roof.

The Medium-Priced Range

Hotel Britannique, corso Vittorio Emanuele 133, 80121 Napoli (tel. 081/660-933), has a Swiss family ownership and a hillside view of the Bay of Naples. It is a remake of a former aristocratic villa. The Britannique is on the curve of a wide hillside boulevard, away from the harbor, providing a panoramic view of it from a distance. Each room contains private bath or shower, air conditioning, direct-dial phone, color TV, and some antique furnishings. Rates are 130,000 lire ($98.75) daily in a single, 180,000 lire ($137) in a twin or double, service and taxes included.

The hotel's restaurant specializes in a continental cuisine. There's also a cocktail lounge and bar. Tropical flowers and plants are found in the hotel's garden.

Hotel Paradiso, via Catullo 11, 80122 Napoli (tel. 081/660-233), might be paradise, but only after you reach it. If you arrive at the central station and head for this address in the Posillipo section, the distance is some 3½ miles. One irate driver claimed that it took about the same amount of time—3½ hours, that is—to reach this address. Once there, however, your nerves are soothed by the view, one of the most spectacular of any hotel in Italy. Before you, the Bay of Naples unfolds, and in the distance Mount Vesuvius looms menacingly. On a clear day you can even see the promontory of Sorrento. The hotel is one of the best in Naples, with 71 well-furnished and comfortably equipped bedrooms, with private bath. Singles cost from 125,000 lire ($95) daily, while doubles go for 185,000 ($141). When you take your breakfast, you may want to linger here before facing the traffic of Naples again. Should you not elect to go out at night, you can patronize the fine restaurant at the Paradiso, enjoying both Neapolitan and Italian specialties, with meals costing from 35,000 lire ($26.50).

Albergo San Germano, via Beccadelli 41, 80125 Napoli (tel. 081/760-5422). Designed like an Italian version of a Chinese pagoda, this brick-and-concrete hotel is ideal for late-arriving motorists who are reluctant to negotiate the traffic of Naples. There is a lobby bar, along with a modern restaurant. A terraced swimming pool and garden are welcome respites after a day in Naples. The hotel's 101 bedrooms are clean, each with a tile bath, phone, and central heating. With breakfast included, singles cost 100,000 lire ($57) daily; doubles, 160,000 lire ($122). To get here from the autostrada, follow its signs to the Tangenziale Napoli (direction Napoli) and exit eight miles later at Agnano Terme. After paying the toll, drive less than a mile toward Naples where you'll see the hotel on your right. You can park your car here and take bus 152 (Sepsa) into the center of Naples, a distance of about four miles.

Hotel Serius, viale Augusto 74, 80125 Napoli (tel. 081/614-844), sits on a palm-lined street of a relatively calm neighborhood known as Fuorigrotto. The hotel was built in 1974 to provide well-organized comfort. The split-level lobby is paneled and contains an intimate bar and several metal sculptures of horses and birds. Parking is free in the hotel's garage. The dining room is pleasant and contemporary. The 69 bedrooms are simply furnished with boldly patterned fabrics and painted furniture. With breakfast included, singles cost 82,000 lire ($62.25) daily; doubles, 120,000 lire ($91.25).

Hotel Miramare, via Nazario Saura 24, 80132 Napoli (tel. 081/427-388), has a superb position, seemingly thrust out toward the harbor on a dockside boulevard. It is central and sunny. Its lobby evokes a little Caribbean hotel, with a semi-tropical look. The bedrooms have been renewed, and now are pleasantly furnished and well maintained by the management. The lower rooms are much too noisy (the curse of most Neapolitan hotels), so request a quieter one upstairs. Open all year, the Miramare charges from 230,000 lire ($175) daily for a double room, 155 lire ($118) for a single. All units contain air conditioning, mini-bars, and private baths or showers, and prices include breakfast. On the premises are an American bar, a restaurant-taverna, a roof garden, and a disco.

The Budget Range

Hotel Rex, via Palepoli 12, 80132 Napoli (tel. 081/416-388), is the most famous budget hotel in Santa Lucia. It has played host to lire-watchers around the world. Some like it and others do not (the mail tends to be mixed). Nevertheless, proof of its popularity is that its 40 bedrooms are often fully booked when other hotels have many vacancies. A lot has to do with the price: 60,000 lire ($45.50) daily in a single and 86,000 lire ($65.25) in a double. Most of the bedrooms contain a private bath. The building itself is lavishly ornate architecturally, but the bedrooms are simple. Breakfast is the only meal served.

Le Fontane al Mare, via Tommaseo 14, 80132 Napoli (tel. 081/416-354), is the best of the boarding houses in the Santa Lucia area. You enter an old-fashioned building with a lot of character, put a small coin in the elevator, and climb to the sixth floor. There you'll find a clean and well-kept pensione, run by a family with a scattering of old furniture. In all, there are 25 bedrooms scattered over the fourth, fifth, and sixth floors. Seven of these have a private bath, and two bedrooms offer a view of the sea. Depending on the plumbing, singles range from 45,000 lire ($34.25) to 55,000 lire ($41.75) daily; doubles cost 60,000 lire ($45.50) to 78,000 lire ($59.25). The pensione has a beautiful terrace overlooking the bay.

Motelagip, at Secondigliano, 80144 Napoli (tel. 081/754-0560), lying 4½ miles to the north of Naples, will appeal to motorists who don't want to chance driving into the city and coping with impossible parking problems. At an Agip you know what you get: standardized rooms and good value, with singles renting for 55,000 lire ($41.75) daily; doubles, 92,000 lire ($70). There are 57 rooms, each with private bath. In all parts of Italy the Agip kitchen emphasizes regional cookery. In its restaurant here, Neapolitan dishes are featured, a complete meal costing from 30,000 lire ($22.75). There is no restaurant service for Saturday lunch or on Sunday.

THE NEAPOLITAN CUISINE

A mixed reaction. Naples is the home of pizza and spaghetti. If you're mad for either of those items, then you'll delight in sampling the authentic versions. However, if you like subtle cooking and have an aversion to olive oil or garlic, you'll not "fare" as well. One of the major problems is overcharging. It is not uncommon for four foreign visitors to have a dinner in a Naples restaurant, particularly those once-famous ones in Santa Lucia, and be billed for five dinners. Service in many restaurants tends to be poor, and when the food arrives it often isn't worth having waited for. Again, as in the hotels, I will attempt to pick out the best of the lot.

La Sacrestia, via Orazio 116 (tel. 664-186). The trompe-l'oeil frescoes in its two-story interior and its name vaguely suggest something ecclesiastical. But that's not the case. Reputed to be the best restaurant in Naples, La Sacrestia is a bustling place, sometimes called "the greatest show in town." It's perched near the top of one of the belvederes of Naples, reached by going along a seemingly endless labyrinth of winding streets from the port. In summer, an outdoor terrace with its flowering arbor provides panoramic seating with a view over the lights of the harbor. Meals emphasize well-prepared dishes with often strong doses of Neapolitan drama. You might, for example, try what is said to be the most luxurious macaroni dish in Italy ("Prince of Naples"), concocted with truffles and mild cheeses. The fettuccine alla Gran Caruso is made from fresh peas, mushrooms, prosciutto, and tongue. Less ornate selections include a full array of pastas and dishes composed of octopus, squid, and shellfish. Meat courses include carpaccio and veal. Expect to spend 65,000 lire ($49.50) to 75,000 lire ($57) for a meal, served from 12:30 p.m. "until the last diner finishes." The place is best reached by taxi. It's closed on Wednesday in winter, Sunday in July, and for all of August, and reservations are suggested.

Rosolino, via Nazario Sauro 5-7 (tel. 415-873), is not defined as a nightclub by its owners, but rather a restaurant with dancing. The stylish and expensive place, set on the waterfront, is divided into two distinct areas. There's a piano bar near the entrance; there you might have a drink before passing into a much larger dining room. There, ringed with stained glass set into striking patterns, you can dine within sight of a bandstand reminiscent of the Big Band era. The food is good, but much of what you'll pay for an evening here will be the music, the decor, and the fun. That could mean a final tab of 100,000 lire ($76) per person with wine. Dishes include rigatoni with zucchini and meat sauce, an impressive array of fresh shellfish, and such beef dishes as tournedos and veal scallopine. There are three different wine lists, including one for French wines and champagne. It is open every evening except Sunday from 8 p.m. to midnight.

La Cantinella, via Cuma 42 (tel. 405-375). You get the impression of Chicago in the '20s as you approach this place, and speakeasy-style doors open after you ring. The restaurant sits beside a busy street skirting the bay in Santa Lucia. Inside, in a room sheathed with Tahiti bamboo, you'll find a well-stocked antipasti table and, get this, a phone on each table. The menu includes four different preparations of risotto (including one with champagne), many kinds of pasta (including penne with vodka and linguine with scampi and seafood), and most of the classic beef and veal dishes of Italy. Best known for its fish, Cantinella serves seafood at its finest when it's grilled. Full meals cost from 45,000 lire ($34.25) and are served from noon to 3 p.m. and 7 p.m. to midnight daily except Sunday and in August.

Ristorante La Fazenda, calata Marechiaro 58A (tel. 769-7420). It would be hard to find a more typically Neapolitan restaurant than this one. The location is in a green area offering a panoramic view that, on a clear day, can include the island of Capri. The decor is rustic, loaded with agrarian touches and filled with an assortment of Neapolitan families, lovers, and visitors who have made it one of their preferred dining locales. In summer the overflow from the dining room spills onto the terrace. Menu specialties include linguine with scampi, an array of fresh grilled fish, sautéed clams, a mixed Italian grill, several savory stews, and many chicken dishes, along with lobster with fresh grilled tomatoes. Full meals range from 50,000 lire ($38). The restaurant, open from 1 to 4 p.m. and 7:30 p.m. to 12:30 a.m., is closed on Sunday and for most of August.

Il Gallo Nero, via Tasso 466 (tel. 643-012). A dinner here is almost like a throwback to the mid-19th century. GianPaolo Quagliata is the owner who, with a capable staff, maintains the villa with its period furniture and accessories. In summer, the elegant outdoor terrace serves as a showplace for the good food served to an enthusiastic clientele. Many of the dishes are based on 100-year-old recipes from the classical Neapolitan repertoire, although a few of them are more recent inventions of the chef himself. You might enjoy the Neapolitan linguine with pesto, rigatoni with fresh vegetables, tagliatelle primavera, or macaroni with peas and artichokes. Fish dishes are usually well prepared, be they grilled, broiled, or sautéed. Meat dishes include slightly more exotic creations such as prosciutto with orange slices, veal cutlets with artichokes, and a savory array of beef dishes. Expect a full meal to cost from 60,000 lire ($45.50). This is primarily an evening restaurant, serving dinner from 6 to 11:30 p.m. Lunch is served only on Sunday, from 12:30 to 3 p.m., but no dinner is served that day. Closed Monday and in August. Reservations are important.

Giuseppone a Mare, via Ferdinando Russo 13 (tel. 769-6002), stands by the sea, offering you a chance to dine in Neapolitan sunshine on an open-air terrace with a view of the bay. The restaurant at Capo Posillipo is known for serving the best and the freshest seafood in the campagna. Diners make their selections from a trolley placed in the heart of the dining room. These denizens of the deep are likely to include everything from crabs to eels. You might precede your fish dinner with some antipasti, such as fritters (a batter whipped up with seaweed and fresh squash blossoms). Naturally, there is linguine with clams, a dish familiar enough in restaurants in North America, except the chef here adds squid and mussels. Much of the day's catch is deep-fried a golden brown. The pièce de résistance is an octopus casserole (try it if you dare!). If the oven's going, you can also order a pizza. Some fine southern Italian wines are served too, especially those from Ischia and Vesuvio. A complete meal, served from 12:30 to 3:30 p.m. and 7:30 to 11:30 p.m., runs 45,000 lire ($34.25) to 60,000 lire ($45.50). The restaurant is closed on Sunday.

Don Salvatore, via Mergellina 5 (tel. 681-817), is no simple lowly pizzeria, but the creative statement of a serious restaurateur, who directs his waterfront establishment with a kind of passion and dedication. Tonino Aversano takes his wine as seriously as the food. The latter is likely to include linguine with shrimp or with squid, or else a linguine facetiously named "Cosa Nostra." There's also an array of fried fish served daily along with a marvelous assortment of fresh Neapolitan vegetables grown in the surrounding countryside. Rice comes flavored in a delicate fish broth, and the wine cellar is said to be the finest in campagna. With a reasonably priced bottle of that wine, full meals cost from 45,000 lire ($34.25). It is open daily except Wednesday from 1 to 4 p.m. and 8 p.m. to 1 a.m. The location is on the seafront near the departure point of hydrofoils for Capri.

Umberto, via Alabardieri 30 (tel. 418-555), might be one of the most atmospheric places to dine in all of Naples. The tasteful dining room has been directed for many a year by the same interconnected family. There's likely to be an evening dance band playing as an accompaniment to the excellent Italian specialties, including pizzas, that make up the establishment's menu. Food items include gnocchi with potatoes, grilled meats and fishes, along with savory stews and a host of pasta dishes. Full meals range from 35,000 lire ($26.50) to 42,000 lire ($32) per person and are served from 12:30 to 3:30 p.m. and 7:30 to 10:30 p.m. The restaurant is closed Wednesday and in August.

La Bersagliera, borgo Marinaro 10 (tel. 415-692), is between the bay and via Partenope. In rustic waterfront surroundings, to the sound of accordion and guitars during dinner, you can select from a menu offering a wide range of fish and other seafoods, veal cutlets milanese or bolognese, tournedos Bersagliera, chicken diavolo and roast chicken, and a complete medley of pasta in all sizes and forms. Expect to pay 38,000 lire ($29) to 50,000 lire ($38) for a complete dinner, service and taxes included. The place is open daily except Tuesday from 12:30 to 3:30 p.m. and 7:30 to 11 p.m.

Dante e Beatrice, piazza Dante 44 (tel. 349-905), is a modest restaurant where the prices are almost as unpretentious as the clientele. Foods are simple, flavorful, and served without fuss to the many workaday clients who seek it out. Menu choices are limited but well prepared, and might include pasta fagiole Naples style, a range of pastas, meat, and fish dishes. Full dinners with wine cost from 35,000 lire ($26.50). The restaurant, open from 12:30 to 3:30 p.m. and 7:30 to 11 p.m., is closed Wednesday and during part of August.

Vini e Cucina, corso Vittorio Emanuele 762. The best ragù sauce in all of Naples is said to be made at this trattoria, which has only ten tables and is known for its home-cookery. I must warn you—it's almost impossible to get in. The owners seem reluctant to give out a phone number, so dedicated diners might do as I do: arrive and wait for a table. The cooking is the best home-style version of the Neapolitan cuisine I have been able to find in this tricky city. The spaghetti, along with that fabulous sauce, is served al dente. Expect to pay from 35,000 lire ($26.50) for a really satisfying meal—that is, if you can get it. The location is in front of the Mergellina station. Open from 11:45 a.m. to 4:30 p.m. and 7 p.m. to midnight. The restaurant is closed Sunday and in August.

Ciro a Santa Brigida, via Santa Brigida 71-73 (tel. 552-4072). Every Neapolitan has his or her favorite pizzeria. Many are on narrow, crooked streets, called *vicoli* in Italian, and are the domain of pickpockets, stray cats, hordes of children, and black-market cigarette vendors. Should you wisely not seek out that secret address some Neapolitan has given you, you'll find some of the best pizzas in town at the address given above. It has been turning out not only pizzas but excellent trattoria food for hordes of faithful customers since 1932, with a few interruptions caused by such catastrophes as world wars when certain ingredients became almost impossible to secure. Those ingredients, at least in Naples, mean good olive oil, fresh tomatoes, and mozzarella. This place has not been caught up in the worldwide craze of putting everything but the kitchen sink on top of a pizza. Near the San Carlo Opera House, this pizzeria and trattoria is almost always crowded with hungry diners. Many guests settle just for the basic pizza Margherita, others preferring more elaborate concoctions such as pizza with fruits of the sea and mushrooms. Pizzas are baked over a wood fire, but, mercifully, the dining rooms are air-conditioned. Fresh fish and good-tasting pastas also appear in the menu. The restaurant is open from 12:30 to 2:30 p.m. and 7:30 to 11 p.m. Closed Sunday and in August. Expect to spend from 35,000 lire ($26.50) for a complete meal.

Drago d'Oro, via Lucilio 11 (tel. 407-810), is one of the leading Chinese restaurants of Naples, decorated in a typical "golden dragon" style with hanging lanterns. The location is in Santa Lucia, behind the deluxe range hotels, Excelsior and Vesuvio. A large menu offers such dishes as chicken with lemon, duck with pineapple, stewed beef in oyster sauce, and steamed or baked dumplings. Meals cost from 25,000 lire ($19), and service is from noon to 3 p.m. and 6 p.m. to midnight; closed Monday. Reservations are rarely needed.

Pizzeria Bellini, via Santa Maria di Costantinopoli 80 (tel. 459-774), with its cramped interior, may look like a pizzeria, but actually it's a full-fledged restaurant. Of course, an array of pizzas is offered, but many clients equally prefer one of the savory pasta selections, including lasagne, bucatini, or vermicelli with clams. You can also order the fresh fish of the day, even roast goat cooked in the style of the campagna. Any of these dishes can be accompanied with a selection of fresh Neapolitan vegetables. Full meals, costing from 40,000 lire ($30.50), are served daily except Sunday from 9 a.m. to 2 a.m. Of course, you can get by for much less if you come here for just a pizza or perhaps a pasta and a salad.

California, via Santa Lucia 101 (tel. 421-752), thinks of itself as "the original American luncheonette in Naples." It provides an oasis for those homesick and hankering for banana splits, ice-cream sundaes, ham and eggs, and pancakes. It's both a counter and a table affair, with a glassed-in sidewalk area. Offered are such typical items as chocolate cake, a hamburger steak, or a hot roast beef sandwich. For the Texan, there's chili con carne. The breakfast specials draw a lively clientele who order a plate of bacon and eggs, as well as "authentic" Kellogg's corn flakes. Meals cost 20,000 lire ($15.25) to 30,000 lire ($22.75). The California is open from 10 a.m. to midnight. Closed Sunday.

The Grand Cafés

The decor of the **Gran Caffè Gambrinus,** via Chiaia 1 (tel. 417-582), the oldest café in Naples (about 150 years old), would fit easily into a grand Bourbon palace. Along the vaulted ceiling of an inner room, Empire-style caryatids spread their togas in high relief above frescoes of mythological playmates. The café is known for its espresso and cappuccino, as well as pastries and cakes whose variety dazzles the eye. These pastries are probably the most famous in Naples. You can also order potato and rice croquettes and fried pizzas for a light lunch. Tea costs 4,000 lire ($3.05); cappuccino goes for 2,500 lire ($1.90) at a table. The café is open from 6 a.m. to 1 a.m. daily except Tuesday. It is near the Galeria Umberto.

Caflish, via Toledo 253 (tel. 412-466), near the Galeria Umberto, welcomes shoppers who come in for a quick glass of orange-flavored brandy, grappa, sambucca, amaretto, or whatever. You can stand at the crowded bar near the entrance for a cup of espresso or select a table in the back room. There, self-service fast food is available. Sandwiches cost from 1,500 lire ($1.15). The place is also known for its rich desserts and ice creams. Open from 8 a.m. to 10 p.m., it closes on Wednesday.

THE SIGHTS OF NAPLES

Before striking out for Pompeii or Capri, you should try to see some of the sights inside Naples. If you're hard pressed for time, then settle for the first three museums of renown.

The Best of the Museums

The **National Archeological Museum,** at the piazza Museo, with its Roman and Greek sculpture, contains one of the most valuable archeological collections in Europe—in particular the select Farnese acquisitions, plus mosaics and sculpture excavated at Pompeii and Herculaneum. The building dates from the 16th century, and it was turned into a museum some two centuries later by Charles and Ferdinand IV Bourbon.

On the ground floor is one of the treasures of the Farnese collections, the nude statues of Armodio and Aristogitone, the most outstanding in the room. A famous bas-relief in a nearby salon depicts Orpheus and his wife, Eurydice, with Mercury, from an original of the 5th century B.C.

The nude statue of the spear-bearing Doryphorus, copied from a work by Polyclitus the Elder and excavated at Pompeii, enlivens another room. See also a gigantic but weary Hercules—a statue of remarkable boldness. A copy of an original by Lysippus, the 4th-century B.C. Greek sculptor for Alexander the Great, it was discovered in the Baths of Caracalla in Rome. On a more delicate pedestal is the decapitated but exquisitely beautiful Venus (Aphrodite). The Psyche of Capua shows why Aphrodite was jealous. The *Group of the Farnese Bull* presents its pageantry of violence from the days of antiquity. A copy of either a 2nd- or 3rd-century B.C. Hellenistic statue—one of the most frequently reproduced of all sculptures— it was also discovered at the Baths of Caracalla. The marble group depicts a scene in the legend of Amphion and Zethus who tied Dirce, wife of Lycus of Thebes, to the horns of a rampaging bull. After this, you will have seen the best of the works on this floor.

The galleries on the mezzanine are devoted to mosaics excavated from Pompeii and Herculaneum. Shown are scenes of cock fights, dragon-tailed satyrs, an aquarium, and the finest item of all, *Alexander Fighting the Persians*.

On the top floor are housed some of the celebrated bronzes dug out of the Pompeii and Herculaneum lava and volcanic mud. Of particular interest is a Hellenistic portrait of Berenice, a comically drunken satyr, a statue of a *Sleeping Satyr*, and *Mercury on a Rock*.

The museum is open from 9 a.m. to 2 p.m. (on Sunday to 1 p.m.), and charges 4,000 lire ($3.05) for admission. Closed Monday. For more information, phone 440-166.

Capodimonte National Gallery and Museum, in the Parco di Capodimonte, off Amadeo di Savoia (tel. 741-3102), is in the 18th-century Palace of Capodimonte (built in the time of Charles III), which stands in a park, haughtily removed from the squalor of Naples. It's got something to be smug about, as it houses one of Italy's finest picture galleries (an elevator takes visitors to the top floor).

Displayed are seven Flemish tapestries, made to the designs of Bernart Van Orley, showing grand-scale scenes from the Battle of Pavia (1525), in which the forces of Francis I of France—more than 25,000 strong—lost to those of Charles V. Van Orley, who lived in a pre-*Guernica* day, obviously didn't consider war a horror, but a romantic ballet.

One of the *pinacoteca*'s greatest possessions is Simone Martini's *Coronation* scene, depicting the brother of Robert of Anjou being crowned king of Naples by the bishop of Toulouse. Linger over the great Masaccio's *Crucifixion*, bold in its expression of grief. The most important room is literally filled with the works of Renaissance masters, notably an *Adoration of the Child* by Luca Signorelli; a *Madonna and Child* by Perugino; a panel by Raphael; a *Madonna and Child with Angels* by Botticelli; and—the most beautiful of all—Filippino Lippi's *Annunciation and Saints*.

Look for Andrea Mantegna's *St. Eufemia* and his portrait of Francesco Gonzaga; brother-in-law Giovanni Bellini's *Transfiguration;* and Lotto's *Portrait of Bernardo de Rossi* and his *Madonna and Child with St. Peter*.

In one room is Raphael's *Holy Family and St. John,* and a copy of his celebrated portrait of Pope Leo X. Two choice sketches include Raphael's *Moses* and Michelangelo's *Three Soldiers*. Displayed farther on are Titians, with Danaë taking the spotlight from Pope Paul III.

Another room is devoted to Flemish art: Pieter Brueghel's *Blind Men* is an outstanding work, and his *Misanthrope* is devilishly powerful. Other foreign works include Joos van Cleve's *Adoration of the Magi*. You can climb the stairs for a panoramic view of Naples and the bay, a finer landscape than any you'll see inside.

The state apartments downstairs deserve inspection. Room after room is devoted to gilded mermaids, Venetian sedan chairs, ivory carvings, a porcelain chinoiserie salon (the best of all), tapestries, the Farnese armory, and a large glass and china collection.

The museum is open in summer from 9 a.m. to 7 p.m. Tuesday through Saturday and 9 a.m. to 1 p.m. Sunday. In the off-season it's open from 9 a.m. to 2 p.m. Tuesday through Saturday and 9 a.m. to 1 p.m. on Sunday. It is always closed Monday. Admission is 4,000 lire ($3.05).

Museo Nazionale di San Martino, in the Vomero residential district (bus 49 or 42), is magnificently situated on the grounds of the Castel Sant'Elmo. It was founded in the 14th century as a Carthusian monastery, but decayed badly until architects reconstructed it in the 17th century in the Neapolitan baroque style. Now a museum for the city of Naples, it displays stately carriages, historical documents, ship replicas, china and porcelain, silver, campagna paintings of the 19th century, military costumes and armor, and the lavishly adorned crib by Cuciniello. A balcony opens onto a fabulous view of Naples and the bay, as well as Vesuvius and Capri. Many come here just to stand on this belevedere in space and drink in the view. The colonnaded cloisters have curious skull sculpture on the inner balustrade. The "Certosa" (Charter House) may be visited from 9 a.m. to 2 p.m. (to 1 p.m. on Sunday) for 3,000 lire ($2.30) admission. Closed Monday. For information, call 377-005.

Other Attractions

The **Royal Palace** (Palazzo Reale), at the piazza Plebiscito, was designed by Domenico Fontana in the 17th century. The eight statues on the façade are of Neapolitan kings. In the heart of the city, the square is one of the most architecturally interesting in Naples, with a long colonnade and a church, San Francesco di Paolo, that evokes the style of the Pantheon in Rome. Inside the Palazzo Reale you can visit the royal apartments, lavishly and ornately adorned in the baroque style with colored marble floors, paintings, tapestries, frescoes, antiques, and porcelain. Charles de Bourbon, son of Philip IV of Spain, became king of Naples in 1734. A great patron of the arts, he installed a library in the Royal Palace, one of the greatest of the south, with more than 1,250,000 volumes. The palace may be visited from 9 a.m. to 2 p.m. (on Sunday to 1 p.m.) for 3,000 lire ($2.30) admission. Closed Monday.

The **New Castle** (Castelnuovo) at the piazza del Municipo was ordered built in the late 13th century by Charles I, king of Naples, as a royal residence for the house of Anjou. Badly ruined, it was later virtually rebuilt in the mid-15th century by the house of Aragon. The castle is distinguished by a trio of three round imposing battle towers at its front. Between two of the towers—guarding the entrance—an arch of triumph was designed by Francesco Laurana to honor the expulsion of the Angevins by the forces of Alphonso I in 1442. It has been described by art historians as a masterpiece of the Renaissance. The Palatine Chapel in the center dates from the 14th century, and the City Commission of Naples meets in the Baron's Hall, designed by Segreta of Catalonia. The New Castle houses municipal offices and is not open to visitors.

Castel dell'Ovo (The Castle of the Egg) is a 2,000-year-old fortress overlooking the Gulf of Naples. The site of the castle was important centuries before the birth of Christ and was fortified by early settlers. In time, a major stronghold guarding the bay was erected and was duly celebrated by Virgil. In one epoch of its long history, it served as a state prison. The view from here is magnificent. It is not open to the public except for special exhibits.

The **Prince of Aragona Pignatelli Cortes Museum,** Riviera di Chiaia (tel. 669-675), is a neoclassical villa lying in a public park, the Villa Pignatelli. The mansion is filled with a collection of porcelain and china, much of it from the 18th century. There is also an impressive collection of antiques. A coach museum can also be visited in a pavilion. Visits are possible daily except Monday from 9 a.m. to 2 p.m. (on Sunday to 1 p.m.) for an admission of 2,000 lire ($1.50).

Nearby is the **Aquarium**, lying between via Caracciolo and the Riviera di Chiaia in a municipal park, Villa Comunale. Established by a German naturalist in the 1800s, the Aquarium is the oldest in Europe. It is said to display about 200 species and marine plants and fish, all found in the Bay of Naples (they must be a hardy lot). Hours are daily except Monday from 9 a.m. to 5 p.m. (on Sunday from 10 a.m. to 7 p.m.), costing an admission of 1,000 lire (75¢). For information, phone 406-222.

The **Catacombs of San Gennaro** (St. Januarius) can only be visited on Saturday and Sunday at 9:30, 10:15, 11, and 11:45 a.m. A guide will show visitors through this two-story underground cemetery, which dates back to the 2nd century and has many interesting frescoes and mosaics. You enter the catacombs on via di Capodimonte (head down an alley going alongside the Madre del Buon Consiglio Church). Admission is 3,000 lire ($2.30).

The **Sansevero Chapel**, via Francesco de Sanctis 19, near the Church of San Domenico Maggiore, is visited mainly by those who wish to view its collection of 18th-century sculpture. The most remarkable piece of work is the *Veiled Christ* by Sammartino. There are also two extraordinary human skeletons of the 18th century, with metal venous apparatus. For an admission of 2,000 lire ($1.50), visits are possible from 10 a.m. to 1:30 p.m. (from 10:30 a.m. on Sunday) daily except Wednesday. For information, call 416-201.

The Churches of Naples

The **Church of Santa Chiara** (Clare), on the palazzo-flanked via Benedetto Croce, was ordered built by Robert the Wise, king of Naples, in the early 14th century. It became the church for the house of Anjou. Although World War II bombers heavily blasted it, it has been returned somewhat to its original look, in the Gothic style as practiced by Provençal architects. The altarpiece by Simone Martini is displayed at the Capodimonte Galleries (see above), leaving the Angevin royal sarcophagi as the principal art treasures, especially the tomb of King Robert in back of the main altar. The Cloister of the Order of the Clares was restored by Vaccaro in the 18th century and is marked by ornate adornment, particularly in the tiles.

The **Duomo** of Naples, on via Duomo, may not be as impressive as some in other Italian cities, but it is visited nevertheless. Consecrated in 1315, it was Gothic in style but the centuries have witnessed many changes. The façade, for example, is from the 1800s. A curiosity of the duomo is its access to the Basilica of St. Restituta, which was the earliest Christian basilica erected in Naples, going back to the 4th century. But an even-greater treasure is the chapel dedicated to St. Januarius (San Gennaro), entered from the south aisle. In a rich 17th-century baroque style, it contains ampullae with the saint's blood, the subject of many religious legends. The chapel is open daily from 8 a.m. to noon.

NAPLES AFTER DARK

A sunset walk through **Santa Lucia** and along the waterfront never seems to dim in pleasure, even if you've lived in Naples for 40 years straight. Visitors are also fond of riding around town in one of the *carrozzelle,* horse-drawn wagons.

As the sun is setting, you may want to drop in at **Il Gabbiano,** via Partenope 27 (tel. 411-666), a sophisticated and charming little piano bar with a glass-fronted façade overlooking the bay. It is also a supper club, serving meals daily from 9 p.m. to 1 a.m. except on Monday. Dinners, costing from 60,000 lire ($45.50), are likely to include such dishes as carpaccio, smoked salmon, penne (a pasta dish) Gabbiano, and beef flambé. Drinks cost from 10,000 lire ($7.60). The management promises, in a poem distributed to guests, that you will be left to dream "and perhaps to forget if you have in your heart a pain." Live music usually begins at 9 p.m. The bar is open till 2 a.m.

Or you can stroll by the glass-enclosed **Galeria Umberto,** off via Roma, in the vicinity of the Theater of San Carlo. The 19th-century gallery, which evokes many a memory for a G.I., is still standing today, although a little the worse for wear. It is a kind of social center for Naples. John Horne Burns used it for the title of his novel, *The Gallery,* in which he wrote: "In August 1944, everyone in Naples sooner or later found his way into this place and became like a picture on the wall of the museum." Through it walked Momma, Giulia, even the melancholy Desert Rat. Perhaps you will be a part of the frame as you're viewed sipping your apéritif.

Attending a performance at the **Theater of San Carlo,** via San Carlo (tel. 797-2111), is to be savored like nectar from the gods. Summer productions are likely to include Puccini's *Madama Butterfly* or Verdi's *Aïda.* Ticket prices range from 15,000 lire ($11.50) to 80,000 lire ($60.75). And if you want to see just the theater, you can visit it daily from 9 a.m. to noon. Guided tours cost 1,500 lire ($1.15). It is closed Monday. The theater was originally built in the baroque style for the Bourbon king Charles III, using such trappings as marble from Siena and crystal from Bohemia. It had to be rebuilt following an 1816 fire and was largely restored and renewed again after extensive bombings in World War II.

On its nightclub and cabaret circuit, Naples probably offers more sucker joints than any other port along the Mediterranean (American sailors are the major objects of prey). If you're starved for action, you'll find plenty of it, and you're likely to end up paying for it dearly and regretting it (maybe even worse).

2. The Environs of Naples

THE PHLAEGREAN FIELDS

One of the bizarre attractions of southern Italy, the Campi Flegrei, as they are known, form a backdrop for a day's adventure of exploring west of Naples and along its bay. An explosive land of myth and legend, the fiery fields contain a semi-extinct volcano (Solfatara), the cave of the Cumaean Sibyl, Virgil's gateway to the "Infernal Regions," the ruins of thermal baths and amphitheaters built by the Romans, deserted colonies left by the Greeks—and lots more. Strike out along via Domiziana, stopping first at—

Solfatara

About 7½ miles west from Naples, in the vicinity of Pozzuoli, the ancient crater of Solfatara hasn't erupted since the final year of the 12th century, but it's been threatening to ever since. Like a fire-spouting dragon, it gives off sulfurous gases and releases scalding vapors through cracks in the earth's surface. In fact, the activity—or inactivity—of Solfatara has been observed for such a long time that the crater's name is used by Webster's dictionary to define any "dormant volcano" emitting vapors. The crater may be visited daily from 9 a.m. to sunset for 3,000 lire ($2.30) admission. For information, telephone 867-2341.

A mile and a half away is—

Pozzuoli

A seaport, Pozzuoli opens onto a gulf of the same name, screened from the Bay of Naples by a promontory. Once the port of Rome, it has been treated unkindly by history, often the victim of ransacking conquerors. The ruins of an amphitheater, built in the last of the 1st century A.D., testify to past greatness. Considered one of the finest surviving examples of the arenas of antiquity, it is particularly distinguished by its "wings"—which, considering their age, are in good condition. The remains can be seen where exotic beasts from Africa were caged before being turned loose in the ring to test their jungle skill against a gladiator. The amphitheater (tel. 867-6007), which may be visited daily from 9 a.m. to two hours before sunset, is said to have entertained 40,000 spectators at the height of its glory. An admission fee of 2,000 lire ($1.50) is charged. In another part of town, the Temple of Serapis was really the "Macellum," or market square, with some of its ruined pillars projecting up today. It was erected during the reign of the Flavian emperors.

Lago d'Averno

Ten miles west of Naples, near Baia, is a lake occupying an extinct volcanic crater. Known to the ancients as the Gateway to Hades, it was for centuries shrouded in superstition. Its vapors were said to produce illness and even death, and Averno could well have been the source of the expression "still waters run deep." Fronting the lake are the ruins of what has been known as the Temple of Apollo from the 1st century A.D. and what was once commonly identified as the Cave of the Cumaean Sibyl. According to legend, the Sibyl is said to have ferried Aeneas, son of Aphrodite, across the lake, where he traced a mysterious spring to its source, the River Styx. In the 1st century B.C., Agrippa turned it into a harbor for Roman ships by digging out a canal.

Baia

In the days of Imperial Rome, the emperors, everybody from Julius Caesar to Hadrian, came here to frolic in the sun while enjoying the comforts of their luxurious villas and Roman baths. Nero is said to have murdered his mother, Agrippina, at nearby Bacoli, with its Pool of Mirabilis. (The ancient "Baiae" was named for Baios, helmsman for Ulysses.) Parts of its illustrious past have been dug out. Ruins of scope and dimension were revealed, including both the Temple of Baiae and the Thermal Baths, said to have been among the greatest erected in Italy. You can explore this archeological district from 9 a.m. to two hours before sunset. It is closed Monday. Admission is 2,000 lire ($1.50).

Cuma

Ancient Cumae was one of the first outposts of Greek colonization in what is now Italy. Twelve miles west of Naples, it is of interest chiefly because it is said to have contained the cave of the legendary Cumaean Sibyl. The cave of the oracle, really a gallery, was dug by the Greeks in the 5th century B.C. and was a sacred spot to them. Beloved by Apollo, the Sibyl is said to have written the *Sibylline Oracles,* a group of books of prophecy purchased, according to tradition, by Tarquin the Proud. You may visit not only the caves, but also the ruins of temples dedicated to Jupiter and Apollo (later converted into Christian churches), from 9 a.m. to two hours before sunset, for 2,000 lire ($1.50) admission. It is closed on Monday. On via Domitiana, to the east of Cuma, you'll pass the Arco Felice, an arch about 64 feet high, built by Emperor Domitian in the 1st century A.D.

HERCULANEUM

The builders of Herculaneum (Ercolano in Italian) were still working to repair the damage caused by an A.D. 62 earthquake when Vesuvius erupted on that fateful August day in A.D. 79. Herculaneum, a much smaller town (about one-fourth the size of Pompeii), didn't start to come to light again until 1709 when Prince Elbeuf launched the unfortunate method of tunneling through it for treasures. The prince was more intent on profiting from the sale of objets d'art than in uncovering a dead Roman town.

Subsequent excavations have been slow and sporadic. In fact, Herculaneum is not completely dug out today. One of the obstacles has been that the town was buried under lava, which was much heavier than the ash and pumice stone that piled onto Pompeii. Of course, this formed a greater protection for the buildings buried underneath—many of which were more elaborately constructed than those at Pompeii, as Herculaneum was a seaside resort for patrician families. The complication of having the slum of Resina resting over the yet-to-be-excavated district has further impeded progress and urban renewal.

Although all the streets and buildings of Herculaneum hold interest, some ruins merit more attention than others. The baths (terme) are divided between those at the forum and those on the outskirts (Terme Suburbane, in the vicinity of the more elegant villas). The municipal baths, which segregated the sexes, are larger, but the ones at the edge of town are more lavishly adorned. The Palestra was a kind of sports arena, where games were staged to satisfy the appetites of the spectacle-hungry denizens.

The typical plan for the average town house was to erect it around an uncovered atrium. In some areas, Herculaneum possessed the harbinger of the modern apartment house. Important private homes to seek out include the "House of the Bicentenary," the "House of the Wooden Cabinet," the "House of the Wooden Partition," and the "House of Poseidon (Neptune) and Amphitrite," the last containing what is perhaps the best-known mosaic discovered in the ruins.

The finest example of how the aristocracy lived is provided by a visit to the "Casa dei Cervi," named the House of the Stags because of sculpture found inside. Guides are fond of showing their male clients a statue of a drunken Hercules urinating. The best of the houses are locked and can only be seen by permission of the gatekeepers, who expect tips for their services.

The ruins may be visited daily except Monday from 9 a.m. to one hour before sunset, for 5,000 lire ($3.80) admission. To reach the archeological zone, take the regular train service from Naples on the Circumvesuviana Railway, a 20-minute ride leaving about every half hour from corso Garibaldi 387 (or take bus 255 from the piazza Municipio). Otherwise, it's a 4½-mile drive on the autostrada to Salerno (turn off at Ercolano).

VESUVIUS

A volcano that has struck terror in Campania, Vesuvius looms menacingly over the Bay of Naples. The date—August 24, A.D. 79—is well known, for it was then that Vesuvius burst forth and buried Pompeii, Herculaneum, and Stabiae under its mass of lava and volcanic mud. Many fail to realize that Vesuvius has erupted periodically ever since (thousands were killed in 1631): the last major spouting of lava occurred in this century (it blew off the ring of its crater in 1906).

The approach to Vesuvius is dramatic, with the terrain growing forlorn and foreboding as you near the top. Along the way you'll see villas rising on its slopes and vineyards (the grapes produce an amber-colored wine known as Lacrimae Christi; the citizens of Pompeii enjoyed vino from this mountainside, as excavations revealed). Closer to the summit, the soil becomes the color of puce and an occasional wildflower appears.

Although it may sound like a dubious invitation to some (Vesuvius, after all, is an active volcano), it is possible to visit the rim—or lips, so to speak—of the crater's mouth. As you look down into its smoldering core, you may recall that Spartacus, in a century before the eruption that buried Pompeii, hid in the hollow of the crater, which was then covered with vines.

To reach Vesuvius from Naples, you can take the Circumvesuviana Railway, or (in summer only) a motor coach service from the piazza Vittoria, which hooks up with bus connections at Pugliano. You get off the train at the Herculano station. A bus goes up the mountain several times a day from just outside the station, costing 1,200 lire (90¢). The bus schedule can be obtained at the tourist information office on the right-hand side of the street connecting the railway station with the Herculaneum excavations. Get off the bus at the beginning of the footpath and walk up the mountain to the rim, about 25 minutes of brisk walking. It's best to hire a guide for about 3,000 lire ($2.30) to take you to the top.

CASERTA

Fifteen miles north of Naples, in the town of Caserta, is one of the largest and greatest palaces of Italy, the Palazzo Reale. The rectangular "Reggia," as it is known, was built in the 18th century for the Bourbon king of Naples, Charles III. The architect was Luigi Vanvitelli, who had dreams of Versailles. The other Bourbon king, Ferdinand IV, son of Charles III, lived here when the palace was completed in 1774. In World War II the Allies commandeered it for use as a military headquarters, and the Nazi army in Italy surrendered here in the spring of 1945.

You can visit the baroque state apartments, with their rich furnishings of the 18th and 19th centuries (some of the present residents, in the grand tradition of the old days at the Louvre, still hang out their laundry). The apartments are open from 9 a.m. to 2 p.m. (to 1 p.m. on Sunday), for 3,000 lire ($2.30) admission. Closed Monday. The Parco Reale (royal park) is spectacular, but it would take at least half a month to walk through it. Vanvitelli adorned the park with statuary, fountains, and cascading waterfalls. If you're not driving to Caserta, you can take a motorcoach leaving about every half hour from the piazza Umberto in Naples.

For out next trip, we head across the Bay of Naples to its largest island.

3. Ischia

Dramatically situated in the bay, Ischia is of volcanic origin. Some of its beaches are radioactive, and its thermal spas claim cures for most anything that ails you—be it "gout, retarded sexual development, or chronic rheumatism."

Called the Green Island or Emerald Island, Ischia is bathed in brilliant light and surrounded by sparkling waters that wash up on many sandy beaches (a popular one: Sant'Angelo). The island is studded with pine groves, and its vineyards produce well-known wines, such as Biancolella. Both a red and a white wine are named after Monte Epomeo, a dead (last eruption: 14th century) volcano that towers over the island at 2,590 feet. From its summit, a spectacular view unfolds. Other popular wines include the red and white Ischia, the latter a favorite accompaniment for most fish platters served on the island.

Ischia is fast rising in popularity, as the number of first-class hotels that went up from the '50s to the '80s reveal. Many wealthy Italians prefer it to Capri, which they consider overrun by foreigners. Before the '50s, Ischia was secluded and relatively unknown, except for those who wanted a quiet oasis. Henrik Ibsen, for example, finished *Peer Gynt* at a villa near Casamicciola. The largest development and concentration of hotels is in the Port of Ischia.

From Naples, the island is reached by ferryboat, hydrofoil, or helicopter. The quickest and easiest way to reach Ischia is to book an *aliscafi* (hydrofoil), with a one-way fare of 11,600 lire ($8.80) per person. The hydrofoil leaves several times daily from Molo Beverello in Naples, taking 40 minutes. An ordinary ferryboat costs 5,800 lire ($4.40) per person. The advantage of a ferry is that you can transport a car. However, count on about an hour and 20 minutes' traveling time.

Once on the island, you can book a boat tour which will encircle Ischia for 10,000 lire ($7.60). The trip takes three hours, including a one-hour stop at Sant'-Angelo. A bus tour of the island costs 14,000 lire ($10.75). It's also possible to take a car tour of Ischia with an English-speaking guide, with two or three stops. For help in arranging these tours, contact the **Azienda di Turismo,** on via Iasolino (tel. 991-146) at Porto d'Ischia.

The telephone area code for Ischia is 081.

PORTO D'ISCHIA

This harbor actually emerged from the crater of a long-dead volcano. Most of the population and the largest number of hotels, as mentioned, are centered here. **Castello Aragonese** once guarded the harbor from raids. At the castle lived Vittoria Colonna, the poetess and confidante of Michelangelo, to whom he wrote the celebrated letters.

References to a fortress on this isolated rock date from as early as 474 B.C. when Geronedi of Siracusa described it in his writings. In the 1300s it was rebuilt by sailors from Aragon. Today it's considered the symbol of Ischia, jutting like a Mediterranean version of France's Mont-St-Michel from the sea surrounding it. It's connected to the oldest part of town by the Ponte d'Ischia, a narrow bridge barely wide enough for a car. If you're driving, you should park on the "mainland" side of the bridge and cross on foot. The fortress is privately owned, and you pay 3,000 lire ($2.30) to use the elevator. After arriving at a point above the cliffs, you pay another 3,000 lire to go inside the fortress. The castle is closed between January and March, but open daily in spring and autumn from 9 a.m. to 6 p.m., till 7 p.m. in summer.

Where to Stay

Porto d'Ischia has the widest range of accommodations in all price ranges. It is challenged by Lacco Ameno, coming up. Visitors interested in a more offbeat experience might consider seeking lodgings at either Forio or Sant'Angelo.

DELUXE HOTELS. The **Hotel Terme Excelsior,** via Emanuele Gianturco 19, 80077 Porto d'Ischia (tel. 081/991-020), is an extravaganza. It's plush, lush, even gush, surrounded by high walls and featuring an oval swimming pool. The small grounds are filled with shade trees and flowers. Inside, the decor should be taken with tongue in cheek, like a saucy Rex Reed interview with a movie star. Ornate fancy furnishings abound, as each room strives to outdo the other. For example, the drinking lounge has a raised fireplace in the center, with four huge, white stone shafts reaching up to a white ceiling with black beams fanning out like a wagon wheel. The circular chimney is a cross between a liberty bell and a cast-iron petticoat. There are porthole windows behind the bar with its intricate swirls of carved wood on its façade. Even the bedrooms have their own special drama, although the decorator has cooled it here; the rooms have French doors opening onto breakfast terraces, and all of them contain private bath. Open from the end of March to mid-October, the hotel requires full-board rates, which range from 251,000 lire ($191) daily per person in high season, dropping to 235,000 lire ($178) per person in low season.

Grand Hotel Punta Molino, lungomare Telese già Colombo, 80077 Porto d'Ischia (tel. 081/991-544), has a sumptuously airy decor, everything set against a forest of pine trees scattered among the volcanic rocks of the surrounding park. The white-walled hostelry occupies a desirable location at the edge of the sea. The outdoor pool is surrounded by small tables and umbrellas. You'll find a richly ornate bar area inside, just off the public rooms. The bedrooms, 88 in all, are handsomely furnished and beautifully maintained. Rates for full board, a requirement, are 210,000 lire ($160) to 270,000 lire ($205) per person daily. Guests are received from late April to the end of October.

FIRST-CLASS HOTELS. The **Hotel Continental Terme,** via Michele Mazzella 74, 80077 Porto d'Ischia (tel. 081/991-588). The core of this sprawling compound is a modern Caribbean-inspired clubhouse where Italian style is highly visible. Wide expanses of glass flood the tile interior with sunlight, exposing residents to views of the gardens outside. My favorite swimming pool re-creates the lush vegetation of a lagoon in Tahiti beneath its canopy of glass. Three other outdoor pools scattered throughout the grounds include an Olympic-size rectangle. On the premises are a well-equipped spa facility, a duet each of bars and restaurants, a disco, a covered garage, tennis courts, and a shuttle service to the beach. Accommodations lie within a diverse collection of balconied town-house villas scattered throughout the grounds. Furnishings are usually substantial in rooms, which are sometimes capped with Napoleonic canopies. The 218 bedrooms each cost 140,000 lire ($106) to 180,000 lire ($137) per person daily with full board. The hotel is open between April and October.

Hotel Moresco, via Emanuele Gianturco 16, 80077 Porto d'Ischia (tel. 081/ 981-355). Its spa facilities and health and beauty center are so complete that some guests check in for the entire duration of their vacation. It sits in a sun-dappled park whose pines and palmettos grow close to the arched loggias of its thick concrete walls. From some angles, the Moorish-inspired exterior looks almost like a cubistic fantasy. Inside, the relatively straightforward design re-creates a modern oasis in the southern part of Spain—matador-red tiles coupled with stark-white walls and Iberian furniture. The Andalusian-style bedrooms each have a terrace or balcony, private bath, phone, radio, color TV, frigo-bar, and air conditioning. Rates for half board are 160,000 lire ($122) to 190,000 lire ($144) per person daily, depending on the season. Open from March to October, the hotel offers a well-landscaped cluster of thermal swimming pools, tennis courts, access to a nearby beach, and several bars and dining areas both in- and out-of-doors. Wide solarium terraces face the sea.

Hotel Terme President, via Osservatorio, 80077 Porto d'Ischia (tel. 081/ 993-970), is terraced into a shrub-covered hillside close to the center of town, the arched openings of its balconies and loggias fronting views of the elliptical swimming pool and the sweeping panorama of the gulf. An indoor pool, part of the hotel's wide range of spa facilities, is proportioned with symmetrical columns and scalloped edges. Everywhere is a feeling of cozy intimacy and well-upholstered comfort. The balconied bedrooms, although small, contain appealing accessories, private bath, and phone. With full board, the charge goes from 75,000 lire ($57) to 105,000 lire ($79.75) per person daily in doubles, depending on the season.

BUDGET ACCOMMODATIONS. La Villarosa, via Giacinto Gigante 13, 80077 Porto d'Ischia (tel. 081/991-316), is the finest pensione in Ischia. Set in a garden of gardenias, banana, eucalyptus, and fig trees, it is like a private villa, charmingly furnished with antiques. The dining room is in the informal country style, with terracotta tiles, lots of French windows, and antique chairs. The meals are a delight, served with a variety of offerings, including the local specialties. And what looks like a carriage house in the garden has been converted into an informal taverna, with more antiques—relaxing, attractive, and ingratiating. Open from mid-March to October, the pensione in high season charges 100,000 lire ($76) to 110,000 lire ($83.50) per person daily for full board, which is required. The staff is selected to maintain the personal atmosphere. The bedrooms are well kept, conveying a homelike flavor.

Villa Paradiso, 80077 Porto d'Ischia (tel. 081/991-501), is an old family villa that accepts paying guests from April to October. The white-and-green villa has its own garden, with date palms, orange and lemon trees, plus a front veranda and a flagstone terrace surrounded by flowers. But it is the forthright geniality of the owner that makes a stay here enjoyable, certainly not the decor. His staff prepares abundant meals and serves them in the Moorish dining room, with its three large windows covered with wrought-iron screens. The bedrooms vary in size—some are overly spacious, with comfortable and efficient furnishings. A few have private bath. The full-board rate ranges from 69,000 lire ($52.50) to 80,000 lire ($60.75) per person daily. It's a two-minute walk from the beach, where you can rent your own changing cabin by the day or week.

Il Monastereo, Castello Aragonese, 80077 Porto d'Ischia (tel. 081/992-435), lies within the most visible symbol of Ischia, the brooding castle whose foundations have rebuffed most invaders since the 4th century B.C. To reach it, take an elevator from the end of the Ponte d'Ischia, which connects the rock to Ischia itself. The

Eletto family operate a small corner of this massive fortress, a private, very old house halfway to the pinnacle. It's classified as a third-class hotel, but its romantic surroundings compensate for the lack of any real opulence. With half board, the per-person rate begins at 40,000 lire ($30.50) daily.

Where to Dine

Ristorante Damiano, via Nuova Circumvallazione (tel. 983-032), offers a sunny terrace with a panoramic view over the pine trees for diners hoping for a relaxing meal. The specialty is fish, and your meal might include it in one of many different ways. Try, for example, a sauté of clams and mussels, perhaps spaghetti with clams, or what might be the best choice of all, one of six different seafood salads made with a variety of sea creatures ranging from shrimp to marinated sea polyps. This is primarily a dinner restaurant, serving lunch only on Saturday and Sunday. The restaurant is closed from the end of September until spring. Expect to spend from 60,000 lire ($45.50) per person for a full meal, served from 12:30 to 3 p.m. and 7:30 p.m. to midnight.

Along the northern coast (frequent bus service) a short ride takes you to—

LACCO AMENO

Jutting up from the water, a rock named Il Fungo ("The Mushroom") is the landmark natural sight of Lacco Ameno. The spa is the center of the good life (and contains some of the best and most expensive hotel accommodations on the island). People come from all over the world either to relax on the beach and be served top-level food or to take the cure. The radioactive waters at Lacco Ameno have led to the development of a modern spa with extensive facilities for thermal cures, everything from underwater jet massages to mud baths.

Where to Stay

Regina Isabella e Royal Sporting, Lacco Ameno, 80076 Ischia (tel. 081/994-322), is the most luxurious spa accommodation on the island, receiving guests—that is, those who can afford to pay the freight—from mid-April to mid-October. Those guests are likely to include everybody from Sophia Loren to Elizabeth Taylor. In a setting of beautiful gardens, the hotel has tile-covered floors along with elegantly decorated lounges. Some of the handsomely furnished, air-conditioned bedrooms, 134 in all, open onto the best views on the island. The accommodations, doubles only, rent for 190,000 lire ($144) to 350,000 lire ($266) daily. Full board in high season begins at 390,000 lire ($296) per person, although this is lowered to 250,000 lire ($190) per person in low season. Guests at this sumptuous, hedonistic resort get maximum comfort in every way. Facilities include a private beach, three swimming pools, a sauna, and a solarium, along with tennis courts and also a protected garage. The daily buffet is notable on the island, a lavish *dolce vita* smörgåsbord. At least a dozen desserts, preceded by a delectable array of antipasti, with lots of seafood, are served, including many classic Italian dishes. Meals begin at 100,000 lire ($76).

Hotel Terme di Augusto, viale Campo 128, Lacco Ameno, 80076 Ischia (tel. 081/994-944). Managed by Sheraton, this is one of the plushest and most modern spa hotels in Ischia, open from mid-April to October. The views from many of the wide expanses of glass encompass flowering gardens rife with cacti and shrubbery. Each of the comfortably outfitted bedrooms has air conditioning, a private bath, balcony, radio, frigo-bar, color TV, and phone. On the premises are a duet of bars and restaurants, both indoor and outdoor pools, tennis courts, reserved beach, and lots of parking space. A shuttle bus runs back and forth to the beach. The 119 bedrooms rent for 132,000 lire ($100) to 154,000 lire ($117) per person daily for full board.

La Reginella, Lacco Ameno, 80076 Ischia (tel. 081/994-300), sits opposite its more glamorous sister, the Regina Isabella. It shares the same ownership and some of the facilities, but charges lower rates. A large villa, it has many patios and tropical planting, and is open from early March to October. The bedrooms—52 in all, each with a private bath or shower—are attractive, with coordinated colors and fabrics and French doors opening onto balconies. Rooms are air-conditioned. Singles cost 147,000 lire ($112) daily, and doubles go for 136,000 lire ($103) per person. The dining room for al fresco meals has a coved ceiling and vines growing profusely around pillars. The inner dining area is pleasant and colorful; the reception lounge is brightened with floral chintz chairs. In the evening, guests gather in the bar. La Reginella guests may use two large thermal water swimming pools—one indoor, one open air—next door.

FORIO

A short drive from Lacco Ameno, Forio stands on the west coast of Ischia opening onto the sea near the Bay of Citara. Long a favorite with artists, it is now developing a broader base of tourism. Locals produce some of the finest wines on the island. On the way from Lacco Ameno, stop at the beach of San Francesco, with its sanctuary. At sunset many visitors head for a rocky spur upon which sits the Church of Santa Maria del Soccorso. The lucky ones get to witness the famous "green flash" over the Gulf of Gaeta. It appears on occasion immediately after the sun sets.

Food and Lodging

Hotel Terme Tritone, Baia di San Francesco, Forio, 80075 Ischia (tel. 081/ 987-471), is set on a carefully landscaped garden at the end of a country road a mile from the center of Forio. Its curving balconies repeat the rounded designs that the stonemasons set into cobblestones of the pine-fringed courtyard in front. The lobby opens onto a view of the establishment's swimming pools, its seaside terraces, and its expanse of beachfront. There's an indoor pool for chilly weather, a spa facility with dozens of massage and hydrotherapy options, and 80 warmly decorated bedrooms. Full board is required at 93,000 lire ($70.75) per person daily, and the hotel is open from March to October.

Hotel Green Flash, via Marina, Forio, 80075 Ischia (tel. 081/997-129). The façade of this portside hotel evokes a green-shuttered, 19th-century kind of stateliness. In contrast, the almost aggressively modern interior is filled with space-age leather or velour-covered chairs and patterned tiles. A rectangular pool fills some of the space of the statue-dotted periphery, while a wide sun terrace rises above the sands of the beach. Filled with pleasant wooden furniture, the summer-style bedrooms have seaview balconies, private baths, and phones. Open from April to October, the hotel charges 60,000 lire ($46.50) to 63,500 lire ($48.25) per person daily for half board, based on double occupancy. Singles pay 68,000 lire ($51.75) for halfboard.

Hotel Santa Lucia, via Citara, Forio, 80075 Ischia (tel. 081/997-670), occupies a rocky perch near the surf, a minute's stroll from the historic center. There's a bit of a houseparty ambience about its open terraces and balconies, its half-rounded outdoor pool, and its location near many of the informal wine and beer cabañas of the coastal road. Owned by a German/Italian alliance of Ute and Vicky D'Abundo, it offers well-scrubbed and tastefully decorated bedrooms filled with pretty colors and views of the sea. Each has its own bath. Depending on the season, doubles cost 70,000 lire ($53.25) to 90,000 lire ($68.50) per person daily, with full board included. There's a contemporary bar, as well as a sun-flooded restaurant and an indoor, thermally heated pool.

Ristorante Romantica, via Marina 46 (tel. 997-345), set near the clusters of drydocked fishing vessels of the old port, is the best place in town for dining outside the hotels. It occupies a Neapolitan building whose façade has been enlarged with the addition of a jutting wooden extension. Everybody from Christian Barnard to Josephine Baker has dined here. Your meal might include one of nine kinds of pasta (one of them a succulent linguine with crayfish), well-seasoned salmon "butterfly style," three kinds of risotto, four different preparations of shrimp, and an array of veal dishes. The most dependable order is the fresh fish from the day's catch. Full meals, costing from 40,000 lire ($30.50), are served from 12:30 to 3 p.m. and 7:30 to 10:30 p.m. daily (closed Wednesday in low season).

SANT'ANGELO
The most charming settlement on Ischia, Sant'Angelo juts out on the southern most tip. The village of fishermen is joined to the "mainland" of Ischia by a 300-foot-long lava-and-sand isthmus. Driving into the town is virtually impossible. In summer, you may have to park a long way away and walk. Its beach is among the best on the island.

Food and Lodging
Hotel Miramare, Sant'Angelo, 80070 Ischia (tel. 081/999-219). Its tile sun terrace cantilevers over a rocky cliff scoured clean by the crashing surf in this Andalusian-style hotel, which benefits from one of the most dramatic perches in town. You can reach it by following a labyrinthine path through the old port. Inside, a summer collection of contemporary furniture complements the plants, which seem to spill over into the gardens of the nearby public spa. The hotel, which is open from April to October, charges 130,000 lire ($98.75) to 150,000 lire ($114) per person daily for full board in high season in one of its 42 comfortable bedrooms.
Casa Celestina, Sant'Angelo, 80070 Ischia (tel. 081/999-213), fills the narrow space between the village's only road and a cliff rising steeply behind it. Its smooth white façade, green shutters, and repetitive wooden balustrades sit across the street from the establishment's cabaña restaurant, where diners get a firsthand view of the crashing surf. The 19 simple bedrooms cost 85,000 lire ($64.50) per person daily for full board. The hotel is open only from April to October.

When Vesuvius erupted in A.D. 79, Pliny the Younger, who later recorded the event, thought the end of the world had come. For our next adventure, we head south from Naples to the scene of the long-ago excitement.

---

4. Pompeii

The ruined Roman city of Pompeii (Pompei in Italian), dug out from the inundation of volcanic ash and pumice stone rained on it by Vesuvius in the year A.D. 79, has sparked the imagination of the world. At the excavations, the life of 19 centuries ago is vividly experienced.

Numerous myths have surrounded Pompeii, one of which is that a completely intact city was rediscovered. Actually the Pompeiians—that is, those who escaped—returned to their city when the ashes had cooled and removed some of the most precious treasures from the thriving resort. They were the forerunners of the later archeologists. But they left plenty behind to be uncovered at a later date and carted off to museums throughout Europe and America.

After a long medieval sleep, Pompeii was again brought to life in the late 16th century, quite by accident, by the architect Domenico Fontana. However, it was in the mid-18th century that large-scale excavations were launched. Somebody once remarked that Pompeii's second tragedy was its rediscovery, that is really should have been left to slumber for another century or two, when it might have been taken care of better. The comment was prompted by the sad state of some of the present ruins and the poor maintenance in general.

The telephone area code for Pompeii is 081.

THE SIGHTS

The most elegant of the patrician villas, the **House of Vettii,** has an Etruscan courtyard, statuary (such as a two-faced Janus), paintings, and a black-and-red Pompeian dining room frescoed with cupids. The house was occupied by two brothers, named Vettii, both of whom were wealthy merchants. As you enter the vestibule, you'll see a painting of Priapus resting his gargantuan phallus on a pair of scales. The guard (that is, for a tip) will reveal other erotic fertility drawings and statuary, although most such material has been removed from Pompeii to the Archeological Museum in Naples (see above). This house is considered the best example of a villa and garden which have been restored. The house is also known for its frescoes of delicate miniatures of cupids.

The second important villa, in the vicinity of Porto Ercolano (Herculaneum Gate), lies outside the walls. Reached by going out viale alla Villa dei Misteri, is the **House of Mysteries.** What makes the villa exceptional, aside from its architectural features, are its remarkable frescoes, depicting scenes associated with the sect of Dionysus (Bacchus), one of the cults that was flourishing in Roman times. Note in some of the backgrounds the Pompeian red. The largest house, called the **House of the Faun** (Casa del Fauno) because of a bronze statue of a dancing faun found there, takes up a city block, with four different dining rooms, along with two spacious peristyle gardens. It sheltered the celebrated Battle of Alexander the Great mosaic, which is now in a museum in Naples.

In the center of town is the **Forum**—rather small, the heart of Pompeian life, known to bakers, merchants, and the wealthy aristocrats who lived luxuriously in the villas. Parts of the Forum were severely damaged in an earthquake 16 years before the eruption of Vesuvius and had not been repaired when the final destruction came. Three buildings that surround the Forum are the **basilica** (the largest single structure in the city) and the **temples of Apollo and Jupiter.** The **Stabian Thermae** (baths)—where both men and women lounged and relaxed in between games of knucklebones—are in good condition, among the finest to come down to us from antiquity. Here you'll see some skeletons in plaster casts. The **Lupanare** titillates visitors with its pornographic paintings. These frescoes are the source of the fattest tips to guides.

In the **Antiquarium** is a number of objects used in the day-to-day life of the Pompeians, including kitchen utensils and pottery, as well as mosaics and sculpture. Note the cast of a dog caught in the agony of death.

The excavations may be visited daily except Monday from 9 a.m. till one hour before sunset for an admission fee of 5,000 lire ($3.80). At the entrance you can hire a guide at a prescribed rate.

To reach Pompeii from Naples, take the 13½-mile drive on the autostrada to Salerno. If you need public transportation, you can board the Circumvesuviana Railway in Naples, departing every half hour. At the railway station in Pompeii, bus connections take you to the entrance of the excavations. There is an entrance about 50 yards from the railway station at Villa Misteri.

HOTELS IN POMPEII

Accommodations appear to be for earnest archeologists only. The best of the lot follow, beginning with—

The Medium-Priced Range

Hotel Villa Laura, via della Salle 13, 80045 Pompei (tel. 081/863-1024), is the best of a rather sorry lot. Actually, this is a good little discovery, lying on a tranquil, somewhat hidden street in this bustling, traffic-filled town. Air-conditioned, it offers 26 comfortably furnished bedrooms, with private bath, phone, and balcony (for the most part). Singles rent for 55,000 lire ($41.75) daily, and doubles cost 90,000 lire

($68.50). In the basement of the hotel is a breakfast room and bar. The hotel also enjoys a garden, and garage facilities are available.

The Budget Range

Hotel Del Santuario, piazza Bartolo Longo 2, 80045 Pompei (tel. 081/863-1020), is the runner-up. Its location is in the very center of the town of Pompeii, opening onto its major square. The entrance faces a small park. The hotel rents 51 simply furnished bedrooms, each clean and well kept. Some are equipped with private bath. Singles rent for 42,000 lire ($32) daily; doubles cost 62,000 lire ($47). Across from the major basilica of Pompeii, the hotel also offers a ristorante, pizzeria, gelateria, and tea room. Meals are good and reasonably priced, costing from 18,000 lire ($13.75). You can enjoy such dishes as beefsteak pizzaiola or a mixed fry of shrimp and squid. Limited car parking is available.

Hotel Europa, piazza Santuario, 80045 Pompei (tel. 081/863-2190), is a hotel of modest dimensions and modest prices. One of the newest hotels to grow up in Pompeii, it is open year round, lying within walking distance of the entrance to the ruins. Every comfortably furnished bedroom has a private bath (or shower) and toilet, as well as a phone. Some open onto balconies. Singles rent for 43,500 lire ($33) daily, with doubles costing 63,000 lire ($48). The hotel has a rooftop terrace with a panoramic view.

Motel Villa dei Misteri, via Villa dei Misteri 1, 80045 Pompei (tel. 081/861-3593), is suitable for motorists. About a mile and a half from the center of town, it offers 41 double rooms with private shower and toilet, renting for 50,000 lire ($38) a night. Along with its own little garden, it features both a swimming pool and a place to park your car. The welcome of the owner and staff may compensate for a certain lack of facilities and amenities. The place could stand a facelift, but many readers have expressed their fondness for it.

WHERE TO DINE

The leading restaurant of Pompeii, **Il Principe,** piazza Bartolo Longo 8 (tel. 863-3342), is not only that, but it is acclaimed as one of the best restaurants in the campagna. Elegant in decor, it offers refined service and an impeccable cuisine. Guests can dine inside its beautiful interior or select a sidewalk table at the corner of the most important square in Pompeii, overlooking the basilica. For your first course, you might start with carpaccio or a salad of porcini (mushrooms); then follow with one of the pasta dishes, perhaps spaghetti vongole (with baby clams). Superb fish dishes, such as sea bass and turbot, are served, and you can also order saltimbocca (sage-flavored veal with ham) or steak Diane. The menu is both Italian and international. Count on spending from 40,000 lire ($30.50) for a meal, and you can do so daily except Monday from 12:30 to 3 p.m. and 7:30 p.m. to midnight. The restaurant closes for three weeks in August.

A good choice is **Zi Caterina,** via Roma 16-22 (tel. 863-1263), conveniently located in the center of town near the basilica, with two spacious dining rooms. The antipasti table might tempt with its succulent seafood, although the pasta fagiole with mussels might also be what you'd want to start your meal. The chef's special rigatoni, with tomatoes and prosciutto, is tempting, as is the array of fish or one of the live lobsters fresh from their tank. Expect to spend 22,000 lire ($16.75) to 40,000 lire ($30.50) per person, if you don't order lobster. The restaurant, open from noon to 11 p.m., shuts down on Tuesday.

THE AMALFI COAST AND CAPRI

Untamed beauty . . . hairpin curves on the serpentine road . . . jagged coasts with sandy beaches filled with bikini-clad bodies and peppermint-striped cabañas . . . olive groves and grape vines . . . rocky peaks floating in cerulean mists . . . secluded inlets once haunted by pirates . . . the wafting aroma of fragrant lemon blossoms . . . cliff-hanging villas of rich expatriates . . . grottoes sapphire blue and emerald green . . . brilliant, shimmering light adored by painters . . . sunsets beloved by romantics.

English-speaking people use the appellation "See Naples and Die" for the bay and Vesuvius in the background. The Germans reserve the saying for the Amalfi Drive. A number of motorists do see the Amalfi Coast and die, as the road is dangerous—not designed for its current stream of traffic, such as summer tour buses that almost sideswipe each other to pass. It's hard to concentrate on the road for the sights. That eminent traveler André Gide called the drive "so beautiful that nothing more beautiful can be seen on this earth."

Capri and Sorrento have long been known to an international clientele. But the emergence into popularity of the resort-studded Amalfi Drive has been a more recent phenomenon. Perhaps it was discovered by German officers in World War II, then later by the American and English servicemen (Positano was a British rest camp in the last months of the war). Later, the war over, many returned, often bringing their wives. The little fishing villages in time became front-ranking tourism centers, with hotels and restaurants in all categories, even nightclubs honky-tonking their attractions. Sorrento and Amalfi are in the vanguard, with the widest range of facilities; Positano has more snob appeal and remains popular with artists; Ravello is still the choice of the discriminating few, such as Gore Vidal, desiring relative seclusion. To cap off an Amalfi Coast adventure, leave on a boat from Sorrento heading for

Capri, which needs no advance billing. Three sightseeing attractions in this chapter —in addition to the towns and villages—are worthy of a special pilgrimage: the Green Grotto between Amalfi and Positano, the Blue Grotto of Capri, and the Greek temples of the ancient Sybarite-founded city of Paestum, south of Salerno.

Heading down from Naples for a distance of 31 miles, we'll stop first at—

---

1. Sorrento

Borrowing from Greek mythology, the Romans placed the legendary abode of the Sirens—those wicked mermaids who lured seamen to their deaths by their sweet songs—at Surrentum (Sorrento). Ulysses resisted their call by stuffing the ears of his crew with wax and having himself bound to the mast of his ship. Perched on high cliffs, overlooking the Bays of Naples and Salerno, Sorrento has been sending out its siren call for centuries—luring everybody from Homer to Lord and Lady Astor. It is the birthplace of Torquato Tasso, author of *Jerusalem Delivered*.

The streets in summer tend to be as noisy as a carnival. The hotels on the racing strip, the corso Italia, need to pass out earplug kits when they tuck you in for the night. Perhaps you'll have a hotel on a cliffside in Sorrento with a view of the "sea of the sirens." If you want to swim in that sea, you'll find both paths and private elevators taking guests down.

To enjoy the beauty of the Amalfi Drive, whose perils are noted above, don't drive it yourself. Take a blue bus marked "Sita," running between either Sorrento or Salerno and Amalfi. In Sorrento, bus stations with timetables are outside the railway station and in the central piazza.

The **tourist information office** in Sorrento is in the Foreigners Club, via Luigi de Mario 45 (tel. 081/878-2104), which winds down to the port where ships to Capri and Naples anchor.

Sorrento's telephone area code is 081.

HOTELS IN SORRENTO

In its first- and second-class hostelries, Sorrento is superior to almost any resort in the south, offering accommodations in all price ranges.

Deluxe Choices

Grand Hotel Excelsior Vittoria, piazza Tasso 34, 80067 Sorrento (tel. 081/807-1044), combines 19th-century glamour with modern amenities. Surrounded by spacious semitropical gardens, with lemon and orange trees, it is built on the edge of a cliff. Three elevators take bathers down to the harbor. There is also a large swimming pool. The grounds were designed and planted when grandeur was a prerequisite for a resort hotel. The terrace theme predominates, especially on the waterside where cold drinks are served at sunset while one gazes at Vesuvius across the bay. Inside, the atmosphere is Old Worldish, especially in the mellow dining room, festive and formal, with ornate, hand-painted ceilings that are a tangle of clouds, sprays of flowers, and clusters of cherubs. While seated in ivory and cane provincial chairs, you'll be served a top-notch Sorrento cuisine. But it is the panoramic view through the windows that makes dining here memorable. The hotel has ten luxury suites, including the one named for Enrico Caruso who stayed in it in 1921. The 125 bedrooms, all with private bath, phone, and radio, have their own drama. Some come with balconies opening onto the perilous cliffside drop. The rooms have a wide mixture of furnishings, with many antique pieces. In high season, the hotel quotes prices of 185,000 lire ($141) daily in a single, 255,000 lire ($194) in a twin, tax inclusive.

Hotel Imperial Tramontano, via Vittorio Veneto 1, 80067 Sorrento (tel. 081/878-1940), when approached by boat from Naples, seems like an integral part

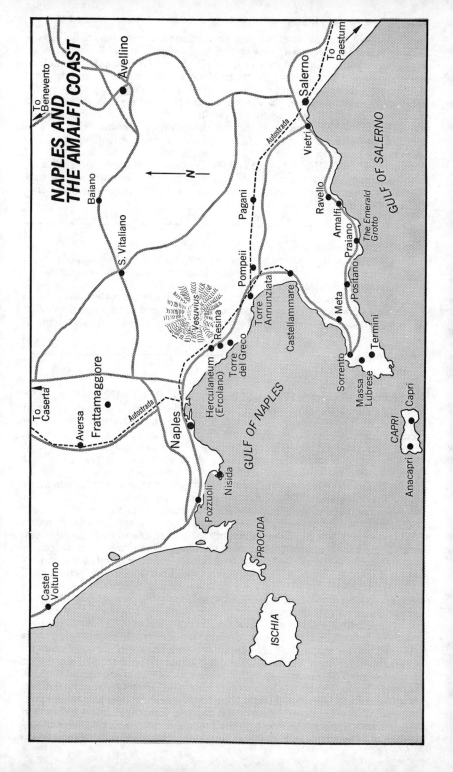

NAPLES AND THE AMALFI COAST

N

To Benevento

Avellino

Baiano

S. Vitaliano

Pagani

Vesuvius

Pompeii

Resina

Torre Annunziata

Torre del Greco

Castellammare

Herculaneum (Ercolano)

To Caserta

Frattamaggiore

Aversa

Naples

Autostrada

Nisida

Pozzuoli

Castel Volturno

GULF OF NAPLES

PROCIDA

ISCHIA

Salerno

To Paestum

Vietri

Autostrada

Ravello

Amalfi

The Emerald Grotto

Praiano

Positano

GULF OF SALERNO

Meta

Sorrento

Termini

Massa Lubrese

CAPRI

Anacapri

Capri

of the high cliff from its imperious position right in the center of town. Built in the villa style, it offers rooms with view balconies, and some of its public lounges open onto garden patios. The drawing room, with English and Italian antiques, modifies its spaciousness by its informal treatment of its furnishings. The bar and drinking lounge are spiked with period pieces—many of them mahogany, Victorian style. The bedrooms, with their tile floors, were designed for long stays. Some have arched French doors and balconies where you can have morning coffee. Furnishings use both antiques and reproductions. All rooms have their own private bath, with a bidet and shower. Rates in high season are 115,000 lire ($87.50) nightly in a single with private bath, 215,000 lire ($163) for a double with bath, inclusive. Full board ranges from 150,000 lire ($114) to 180,000 lire ($137) per person nightly, tax inclusive. In the garden, you can inhale the aroma of sweet-smelling trees and walk down paths of oleanders, hydrangea, acacia, coconut palms, and geraniums. The hotel is open from April to October.

Other Frommer Guides

Frommer's Italy complements 31 other Frommer guides, which highlight the best travel values in all price ranges—from budget to deluxe—with an emphasis on the medium-priced.

Frommer travel guides can be obtained at most bookstores, or by mailing the appropriate amount (turn to the last few pages of this guide for a complete list of titles and prices) to Frommer Books, Prentice Hall Trade Division, 15 Columbus Circle, New York, NY 10023.

First-Class Hotels

Parco dei Prìncipi, via Rota 1, 80067 Sorrento (tel. 081/878-4644), provides some of the best living in Sorrento, combining an integrated contemporary design with the past. The core of this cliffside establishment is the tastefully decorated 18th-century villa of Prince Leopold of Bourbon Sicily. Milan's distinguished architect, Gio Ponti, conceived the present building, and it is a well-coordinated hotel unit. Both houses are placed in the parkland—acres of semitropical trees and flowers, a jungle with towering palms, acacia, olive, scented lemon, magnolias.

A private elevator takes swimmers down the cliff, which affords fantastic views of the Bay of Naples and Vesuvius, to the private beach. There is a mooring pier for yachts and motorboats, and for waterskiing. The public rooms are generous and spacious, utilizing blue-and-white herringbone tile floors and cerulean-blue furniture slickly designed. The bedrooms carry out the sky-blue theme, with striped floors, walls of glass leading to private balconies, built-in desks and headboards with accessories. The rooms are air-conditioned (individually controlled) and each contains a spic-and-span, well-functioning private bath. Open from April to October, the hotel charges 240,000 lire ($182) daily in a double with bath, 180,000 lire ($137) in a single with bath (breakfast included). Note the swimming pool, designed so as not to disturb the century-old trees.

Hotel Bristol, via del Capo 22, 80067 Sorrento (tel. 081/878-4522), is built pueblo style on a hillside at the edge of town. From every room it's possible to have a view of Vesuvius and the Bay of Naples. In a contemporary vein, the hotel lures with its good sense of decor and spaciousness, and with well-appointed public as well as private rooms. The dining room with its terrace and all-glass façade depends on the bay and view for its bait. There's an outer sun-shaded terrace for afternoon drinks from the winter-garden bar. A disco, Chez Nino, is near the large panoramic swimming pool. The bedrooms are warm and inviting, with bright covers and built-in niceties. All of them have private bath or shower, and most have a balcony overlooking the sea. Open all year, the hotel in high season charges 80,000 lire ($60.75) to

150,000 lire ($114) per person daily for full board. A double room with breakfast costs from 175,000 lire ($133); a single goes for 100,000 lire ($76). An added attraction is a Finnish sauna.

Grand Hotel Ambasciatori, via Califano 18, 80067 Sorrento (tel. 081/878-2025). The heavily buttressed foundation that prevents this cliffside hotel from plunging into the sea looks like something from a medieval monastery. Built in a style reminiscent of someone's private villa, it was landscaped to include several rambling gardens whose edges conform to the edge of the precipice. A set of steps and a private elevator lead to the wooden deck of a bathing wharf; there is also a heart-shaped swimming pool. A barbecue is also available in this area. Inside, a substantial collection of Oriental carpets, marble floors, and well-upholstered armchairs provide plush enclaves of comfort. The 103 panoramic air-conditioned bedrooms range from 78,000 lire ($59.25) to 120,000 lire ($91.25) daily in a single, and from 140,000 lire ($106) to 165,000 lire ($125) in a double. Full board costs 160,000 lire ($122) to 190,000 lire ($144) per person daily. Tariffs depend on the season. A garage on the premises provides much-needed parking.

The Medium-Priced Range

Hotel Regina, via Marina Grande 10, 80067 Sorrento (tel. 081/878-2721). Evenly spaced rows of balconies jut out over its well-tended garden. On its uppermost floor, a glassed-in dining room and an outdoor terrace encompass views of the Mediterranean extending as far as Naples and Vesuvius. The 36 clean, functional bedrooms have tile floors, private terrace, and bath, as well as phone. Singles cost 48,000 lire ($36.50) daily; doubles, 86,000 lire ($65.25). The hotel is open between April and October.

Hotel Bellevue Syrena, piazza della Vittoria 5, 80067 Sorrento (tel. 081/878-1024), only a short walk from the central square, is perched at the edge of a cliff at the end of a shaded walkway lined with vines and flowers. Built in the 18th century as a private villa, it has been converted by the entrepreneurial Fluss brothers. A private elevator carries sun worshippers to the beach. Because this was a private home, the size and shape of the bedrooms vary widely. Each, however, is comfortable and clean, with its own bath and phone. Singles range from 70,000 lire ($53.25) to 85,000 lire ($64.50) daily, and doubles run 45,000 lire ($34.25) to 60,000 lire ($45.50) per person. With half board included, tariffs go from 95,500 lire ($72.25) to 110,000 lire ($86.50) daily in a single, from 75,000 lire ($57) to 90,000 lire ($68.50) per person in a double.

The Budget Range

Villa di Sorrento, piazza Tasso 6, 80067 Sorrento (tel. 081/878-1068), is a pleasant villa right in the center of town. Romantic architecturally, it attracts with petite wrought-iron balconies, tall shutters, and vines climbing the façade. The rooms have such small niceties as bedside tables and lamps. All the accommodations have private bath or shower; some have terraces. There is an elevator as well. Open all year, the hotel in high season charges 60,000 lire ($45.50) daily for its singles, 100,000 lire ($76) for its doubles, inclusive.

La Tonnarella, via del Capo 31, 80067 Sorrento (tel. 081/878-1153), is an old-fashioned villa at the outskirts of Sorrento, on a cliff-edge projection of garden terraces opening toward the sea. It's a popular place for dining, but welcomes guests who want sea-view rooms as well. The best feature here—apart from economy and the good meals—is the gardens with oleander, lemon, and eucalyptus trees. There is a bathing beach at the foot of the cliff, with elevator service provided. Sixteen rooms are offered (doubles only), renting in high season at 58,000 lire ($44) per person daily for half board. The units are simple but comfortable, and the view magnificent. All is operated by the Gorgiulo family, who are proud of their kitchen. Meals are served daily and cost from 30,000 lire ($22.75). Space is provided for car parking. The hotel is open from March to November.

Hotel Garni Désirée, bis via Capo 31, 80067 Sorrento (tel. 081/878-1563), lies about half a mile from the center of town at the beginning of the Amalfi Drive. It is a tranquil hotel directed by Mr. and Mrs. Silvio Gargiulo, both of whom speak English. The establishment is ringed with terraces, whose flowered masonry overlooks the Bay of Naples and nearby trees. Some of the bedrooms have views of a waterfall, and all units contain a private bath. This used to be an upper-class private home before it was transformed into the good-value hotel it is today. Many of the attractive personal touches remain as part of the decor. Only breakfast (included in the room price) is served, although there are many good restaurants nearby. You'll recognize the hotel by its green glass lanterns in front and the welcoming awning stretched over the front entrance. Doubles with bath cost from 60,000 lire ($45.50) daily, with breakfast included. A private beach can be reached by elevator. The hotel is open only from April to October.

On the Outskirts at Vico Equense

Capo la Gala Hotel, 80069 Vico Equense (tel. 081/879-8278), at Capo la Gala, about two miles north of Vico Equense, lies only 5½ miles from Sorrento. It is a tasteful, warm, and architecturally unusual establishment built on the rocks a few feet from a stony beach. The location is on a building site that, except for the concrete terraces poured at great expense, could never have sheltered a hotel complex. A series of sundecks is angled to follow the contour of the boulder-studded coastline, and a masonry interior is filled with an airy nautical decor of tile breezeways, rattan and bamboo furniture, and cool tiles. The dining room, ringed with textured stone walls, offers sun-shaded views and well-prepared meals, which you might enjoy after a dip in the seaside swimming pool. The 18 rooms are peaceful and quiet, offering a relaxed getaway. With half board included, the price is 155,000 lire ($118) per person per day. The establishment, which is owned by Tony Savarese, is open from April to October.

DINING IN SORRENTO

A good choice is **O Parrucchiano,** corso Italia 71, (tel. 878-1321), on the busiest street in Sorrento. The building is like an old taverna, the main dining room with an arched ceiling. On the terrace in the rear you can dine in a garden of trees, rubber plants, and statuary. Among the à la carte dishes, the classic items of Italian fare are offered, including the gnocchi (potato dumplings), cannelloni, the mixed fish fry from the Bay of Naples, and a veal cutlet milanese. The chef will also prepare a pizza for you. If you order à la carte, expect to spend 25,000 lire ($19) to 40,000 lire ($30.50) for a complete meal, served from noon to 3:30 p.m. and 7 to 11 p.m. The restaurant is closed Wednesday from November to May.

Ristorante Il Glicine, via San Antonio 2, (tel. 877-2519), sits behind an unimpressive façade between a nursery and a modern apartment building. You'll find it above the main commercial district of town, on a winding road leading to the Sorrento Palace Hotel. A pair of affable partners prepare such specialties from the Abruzzi as green ravioli with an almond sauce, linguine with seafood, penne (a pasta) with a pepperoni sauce, a mixed grill of beef and veal, and unusual preparations of turkey, as well as flavorful homemade pastries. Full meals, served from noon to 3 p.m. and 7 p.m. to midnight daily (closed Wednesday in winter), cost from 35,000 lire ($26.50).

A SHOPPING NOTE

An interesting stop is at **A Gargiulo and Jannuzzi,** piazza Tasso (tel. 878-1041), the best-known maker of marquetry furniture in the region. Demonstrations of the centuries-old technique are presented in the basement, where an employee will juxtapose multihued pieces of wood veneer into patterns of arabesques and flowers. The sprawling showrooms, right in the heart of town, include an array of card tables, clocks, and partners' desks, each inlaid with patterns of elmwood, rosewood, bird's-eye maple, and mahogany. Upstairs is a collection of embroidered napery and table linen. Open daily from 8 a.m. to 10 p.m.

SORRENTO NIGHTLIFE

For fun and games, go to **La Boutique della Birra** (the beer boutique), Villa Pompeiana, via Marina Grande 6 (tel. 877-2428), in an elegant series of rooms first created by Lady Astor, who covered their vaulted periphery with copies of Pompeian frescoes. Today the place is one of the most popular nightspots in town. Within its still noteworthy trio of rooms, you can play pool, drink beer, listen to rock and roll, or whatever. The establishment serves more than 150 kinds of lager, ale, and stout from every part of Europe. You can also order six kinds of hamburgers, 30 different pastas, and more than 40 kinds of sandwiches. In summer, the action moves upstairs onto the panoramic terraces beneath the Ionic columns of the arbors. The menu is less extensive in summer, but you can arrive anytime during the afternoon and evening for snacks "alla Sorrentina" and drinks. Hours are 7:30 p.m. to 1 a.m. daily. Recorded music begins in the garden at 8:30 p.m. A restaurant at the far end of the garden serves relatively formal meals in the evening for 30,000 lire ($22.75) to 70,000 lire ($53.25).

La Mela, corso Italia 263 (tel. 878-1917), is an all-purpose club which begins its evening of festivities with a folkloric show at 8:30 p.m. Lasting for two hours, it includes a Tarantella program of regional songs and dancing. A fee of 20,000 lire ($15.25) gains you entrance to the show as well as a first drink. After 10:30 p.m., the price of admission goes down to 12,000 lire ($9.10) when disco reigns supreme.

DINING AT MASSALUBRENSE

The best table for the "fruits of the campagna" won't be found in Sorrento but at Massalubrense, about 3½ miles away. **Antico Francischiello,** via Partenope 27, 80061 Massalubrense (tel. 081/877-1171), was founded around 1850 by a famous cook whose legend still lives on in gastronomic circles around Sorrento. Today the establishment is directed by a relative of the founder, Signor Gargiulo (a.k.a. Signor Peppino to his clients and friends). With his wife, Pina de Maio, he concocts ingredients, and serves so much of them that his establishment has been called a "gourmand's paradise."

Benefiting from a panoramic view, the restaurant has a format whose size is doubled by an outdoor veranda, which on the hottest days of summer might be too bright even for the most avid sun worshipper. The central altar of this temple to good eating is the antipasti table, crowned with sculpted swans, colored lights, foil decorations, and dozens of antipasti made from virtually every fish and vegetable in the region. The several kinds of bread are homemade, usually from some ancient family recipe. A recent version contained salami, prosciutto, several kinds of cheese, raisins, and red peppers folded into an egg batter. The cannelloni Peppino is a gastronomic masterpiece, prepared with a wholesome and flavorful simplicity. Other specialties include gnocchi Sorrento style, risotto pescatore, grilled or baked fish, mixed meats alla spiedino, and at least two kinds of the house wine, products of the family vineyards. A full meal will range from 25,000 lire ($19) to 50,000 lire ($38) and can be enjoyed from noon to 3 p.m. and 7 to 11 p.m. daily except Wednesday. Signor Peppino also rents out eight rooms, each simply but comfortably furnished, costing 60,000 lire ($45.50) per person daily for half board.

Be alert to the road's numbering system, since it seems to follow a logic all its own.

2. Positano

A hill-scaling, Moorish-style village—traversed by only one road—on the southern strip of the Amalfi Drive, Positano opens onto the Tyrrhenian Sea with its legendary islands of the sirens. The Sirenuse Islands, mentioned in the *Odyssey* by Homer, form the mini-archipelago of Li Galli. Still privately owned, these islands were once purchased by Leonid Massine, the Russian-born choreographer. It is said that the town was "discovered" in the aftermath of World War II when Gen. Mark Clark stationed troops in nearby Salerno. When the U.S. soldiers went on holiday, they learned of the glories of Positano. It has jackrabbited along the classic postwar route of many a European resort: a sleeping fishing village that was visited by painters and writers (Paul Klee, Tennessee Williams), then was taken over by bohemia-sniffing main-drag visitors.

Once Positano was part of the powerful Republic of the Amalfis, a rival of Venice as a sea power in the 10th century. Today smart boutiques adorn the village, and bikinis add vibrant colors to the mud-gray beach where you're likely to get pebbles in your sand castle. Prices have been rising sharply over the past few years. The 500-lire-a-night rooms popular with sunset-painting artists have gone the way of your baby teeth.

The topography of the village, you'll soon discover, is impossible. If you learn to climb the landscape with relative ease, you'll be qualified to hire out as a "scab" during the next donkey sitdown strike. John Steinbeck once wrote: "Positano bites deep. It is a dream place that isn't quite real when you are there and becomes beckoningly real after you have gone."

The telephone area code for Positano is 089.

WHERE TO STAY

Deluxe Hotels

A mile from Positano, **San Pietro,** 84017 Positano (tel. 089/875-455), has only a miniature 15th-century chapel, projected out on a high cliff, for identification. A behind-the-scenes elevator takes you down to the cliff ledges of what is the chicest resort along the Amalfi Coast. By changing elevators at the reception lounge, you can descend even farther to the swimming and boating cove, where you can sunbathe and enjoy the water in seclusion. The suite-like bedrooms are super-glamorous, many containing picture windows beside one's bathtub (there's even a huge sunken Roman bath in one suite). Bougainvillea is rooted on the terraces, reaching into the ceilings of many of the living rooms. The collection of antiques or reproductions is used lavishly in the living room. A dining room is cut into the cliff with room-wide picture windows. San Pietro insists on no advertising, no signs, and zealously guards the privacy of guests. Many are distinguished, including Sir Laurence Olivier, Rudolf Nureyev, and Gregory Peck. Naturally, prices aren't cheap. Tariffs depend on the season. Singles begin at a low of 240,000 lire ($182) daily, climbing to 320,000 lire ($243). Doubles cost 350,000 lire ($266) to 490,000 lire ($327). Half board is available only for a minimum stay of three days, with prices ranging from 235,000 lire ($179) to 380,000 lire ($289) per person daily. The restaurant, charging from 75,000 lire ($57) per meal, is open only to guests of the hotel. The San Pietro is closed from early November to late March.

Le Sirenuse, via Colombo 30, 84017 Positano (tel. 089/875-066), offers an atmosphere in which taste reigns supreme. Everything exists for its sophisticated clientele, which includes numerous artists and writers. The hotel, an old villa perched only a few minutes' walk up from the bay, is owned by the aristocratic Sersale family. The marchesa personally selects all the furnishings, which include fine carved chests, 19th-century paintings and old prints, a spinet piano, upholstered pieces in bold colors, a Victorian settee. A typical touch: the drinking lounge has a polished wooden 16th-century cabinet, derived from an old jewelry shop. The bedrooms, all with private bath and many with Jacuzzi, are varied, with terraces overlooking the village. Your iron bed may be high and ornate, painted red, sharing the space with carved chest and refectory tables. Open all year, the hotel charges high-season prices from June 1 to September 30: 360,000 lire ($294) to 495,000 lire ($376) daily for a double, inclusive, with a continental breakfast. Meals on one of the three terraces are well served, the chef catering to the international palate. You can also take a dip in the hotel's swimming pool.

The Middle Bracket

With only 14 rooms, the **Albergo Miramare,** via Genoino 31, 84017 Positano (tel. 089/875-002), is one of the most charming accommodations in Positano, suitable for those who like the personalized touch that only an individualized little inn can provide. The hotel was converted from a private mansion, which is now well on its way toward a century of life. In the heart of town on a cliff, the hotel is closed from the middle of November to sometime around mid-March when the first of the sun-seeking guests start to check in. The hotel attracts a discriminating clientele drawn to its terraces, both public and private, where one can sip Campari and soda and contemplate the sea. Guests, who reach the hotel after a steep climb, are housed in one of two buildings, each tastefully furnished. In a setting of citrus trees, with lots of flamboyant bougainvillea draped about, you are shown to your room. Your bed will most likely rest under a vaulted ceiling, and the white walls will be thick. Even the bathrooms are romantic. You can stay here at a cost of 116,000 lire ($88.25) to 200,000 lire ($152) per day in a double, depending on the room and the season. Breakfast is included, but half board is an additional 35,000 lire ($26.50) per person per day. The conversation piece of the hotel is a glass bathtub on a flowery terrace. What might seem like questionable taste in Los Angeles—a pink porcelain clamshell serving as a wash basin—becomes charming at the Miramare, even when the water rushes from a sea-green ceramic fish with coral-pink gills.

Palazzo Murat, 84017 Positano (tel. 089/875-177). For atmosphere and baroque nostalgia, this place has no equal in all of Positano. The jasmine and bougainvillea are so profuse within its garden that they spill over their enclosing wall onto the arbors of the narrow street outside. Once this was the sumptuous retreat of Napoléon I's brother-in-law, the king of Naples. Considered the most dashing cavalry leader of his age, he was eventually court-martialed and shot. Today the shell designs capping the windows of the villa look out over a cluster of orange trees and the wrought-iron tendrils of the gate leading into the garden. To enlarge the property, a previous owner erected a comfortable annex in a style compatible with the original villa. Only breakfast is served to occupants of the 28 bedrooms, which are available to visitors from March to October. Doubles cost 155,000 lire, ($118) daily. There are no singles.

Albergo l'Ancora, via Colombo, 84017 Positano (tel. 089/875-318), is a stand-out choice in its classification. A hillside villa turned hotel, it basks in the atmosphere of a private club. It's fresh and sunny here, each room like a bird's nest on a cliff. Designed to accommodate the maximum of sun terraces and sheltered loggias for shade, the hotel is a five-minute climb from the beach (maybe longer if you're past 35). Its main lounge has clusters of club chairs, tile floors, and tear-drop chandeliers. But the bedrooms—catering to couples only—are the stars, with their individualized treatments. Well-chosen antiques, such as fine inlaid desks, are intermixed with more contemporary pieces. The bathrooms in each of the 18 rooms are tiled and contain bidet, and each room opens onto a private terrace. Open from April to October 15, the hotel charges high-season prices from June 1 to September 30: 110,000 lire ($83.50) daily for a double, inclusive. Meals are served on the informal outdoor terrace, under a vine-covered sun shelter. The full-board rate in high season is 110,000 lire ($83.50) per person daily.

Buca di Bacco e Buca Residence, 84017 Positano (tel. 089/875-699), is one of the best of the moderately priced hotels at this resort, and it receives guests from mid-March to mid-October. It also houses one of the best restaurants at Positano (see below). On the main beach of Positano, this hotel and restaurant complex often draws guests who patronize only its bar, one of the best-known rendezvous points along the Amalfi Drive. A large terrace opens onto the beach, and you can enjoy a Campari and soda while still in your bathing suit. The oldest part, the Buca Residence, was an old seaside mansion constructed at the dawn of the 19th century. Rooms are well furnished, with many facilities, including a bath or shower, phone, small refrigerator, and balconies facing the sea. The residence is slightly more expensive than Buca di Bacco. Depending on the season, half-board terms range from 110,000 lire ($83.50) per person daily, climbing to 120,000 lire ($91.25).

Casa Albertina, via Tavolozza 4, 84017 Positano (tel. 089/875-143), is a villa guesthouse, reached by climbing a steep and winding road. Perched on the side of a hill, it offers a view of the coastline. Each bedroom is a gem: color coordinated in either mauve or blue. The rooms are furnished with well-selected pieces, such as gilt mirrors, fruitwood end tables, bronze bed lamps. Each accommodation has its own private bath, as well as wide French doors leading out to one's own balcony. You can have breakfast on the terracotta tile terrace on your own garden furniture. Open all year, the hotel charges its highest rates from June 1 to September 30, when singles cost 100,000 lire ($76) daily and doubles go for 120,000 lire ($91.25). Half board ranges from 85,000 lire ($64.50) to 95,000 lire ($72.25) per person daily in a double, 120,000 lire ($91.25) in a single.

Albergo Ristorante Covo dei Saraceni, 84017 Positano (tel. 089/875-059). You'll find this rambling pink-and-ochre building a few steps above the port. It's a desirable choice for those who want to be in the swim of the summer action. The side closest to the water culminates in a rounded tower of rough-hewn stone, inside of which is an appealing restaurant open to the breezes and a firsthand view of the crashing waves. Open only from April to October, the hotel rents out comfortably furnished, air-conditioned bedrooms, 58 in all, at a cost of 230,000 lire ($175) daily in a double. Half board goes from 154,000 lire ($117) per person.

DINING IN POSITANO

The owner of the sophisticated **Chez Black** (tel. 875-036) is Salvatore Russo, but for his restaurant he uses the suntan-inspired name that his friends gave him in college. Founded after World War II, the restaurant occupies a desirable position close to the sands of the village's shale-colored beach. In summer, it is in the "eye of the hurricane" of action. Its varnished ribbing, glowing sheath of softwood and brass, and yacht-inspired semaphore symbols make it one of the most beautiful restaurants in town. A stone-edged aquarium holds fresh lobsters, while rack upon rack of local wines give diners a choice. Seafood is the specialty, as well as a wide selection of pizzas fresh from a circular oven. Most diners order substantial meals, costing from 40,000 lire ($30.50) and served daily from 12:30 to 3 p.m. and 7:30 to 11 p.m. The best-known dish is the spaghetti with crayfish, but you might also be tempted by linguine with fresh pesto, grilled swordfish, sole, or shrimp, along with an array of veal, liver, chicken, and beef dishes. Reservations are necessary in high season, and the restaurant is closed from January 10 until the end of February.

Buca di Bacco, via Rampa Teglia 8 (tel. 875-699), right on the beach, is one of the top restaurants of Positano. Guests often stop for a before-dinner drink in the bar downstairs, then head for the dining room on a big covered terrace facing the sea for their meals. The tone and theme of the "buca" are set as you enter. On display are various fresh fish, special salads, and fruit, including luscious black figs (in season) and freshly peeled oranges soaked in caramel. An exciting opener is a salad made with fruits of the sea, or you may prefer the zuppa di cozze (mussels), prepared with flair in a tangy sauce. Pasta dishes are homemade, and meats are well prepared with fresh ingredients. A complete meal, served daily from 12:30 to 3:30 p.m. and 8 to 11 p.m., costs 38,000 lire ($29) to 60,000 lire ($45.50).

La Cambusa, Sulla Spiaggia (tel. 875-432). You'll have to navigate multiple series of steps and ramp-like streets to reach the small square where this attractively intimate restaurant sits. There's a veranda for drinks or dining, as well as a pleasant interior if you prefer to be indoors. Your meal might include risotto pescatore, spaghetti with clams, linguine with shrimp, or a specialty of the village, pasta with zucchini. The wide array of meats and fish are well prepared and savory, while desserts are homemade and satisfyingly sweet (chocolate mousse or crème caramel would be good choices). Expect to spend 35,000 lire ($26.50) to 50,000 lire ($38). It is open from 12:30 to 3 p.m. and 7:30 to 11 p.m. every day in summer but closed in November and December.

---

3. Praiano

Known as "the choice" to either Amalfi or Positano, Praiano is a fishing village with a growing number of hotels and restaurants. It's perched on the winding road along the Amalfi Coast, enjoying a beautiful landscape of sea and greenery. Midway between the two towns, a distance of 3½ miles from Positano, Praiano is a good choice for a holiday.

FOOD AND LODGING

A mile from the center of town, the **Hotel Tritone,** 84010 Praiano (tel. 089/874-333), clings to a cliffside below a widened curve of the coast road. After parking beneath one of the arbors beside the pavement, you descend to the lobby's reception area via a combination of stairs and an elevator. There, curved walls of thick concrete open into sweeping windows for a view of neighboring Positano and its rugged coastline. An elevator takes guests down to the beach. The 62 well-furnished bedrooms cost 90,000 lire ($68.50) daily in a single, 170,000 lire ($129) in a double. The hotel's restaurant serves good food, with full-board terms at 125,000 lire ($95) to 150,000 lire ($114) per person. Guests are accepted from the first of April through October.

Tramonto d'Oro, 84010 Praiano (tel. 089/874-008). Its inland side juts abruptly to the edge of the winding road leading through the center of town. On its opposite side, an almost uninterrupted row of windows encompasses most of the jagged coastline. The hotel has a much-needed garage. An elaborately carved oval table sets a gracious note near the reception desk, which leads into a modern bar and dining room. There is an elevator, as well as a swimming pool. Guests are housed in 40 tile-floored and well-furnished bedrooms with their own terraces, private bath, and phone. Doubles with full board cost 70,000 lire ($53.25) to 85,000 lire ($64.50) per person daily.

---

4. Amalfi

From the 9th to the 11th century the seafaring Republic of Amalfi rivaled those great maritime powers, Genoa and Venice. Its maritime code, the *Tavole Amalfitane,* was used in the Mediterranean for centuries. But raids by Saracens and a flood in the 14th century devastated the city. Its power and influence weakened, until it rose again in modern times as the major resort on the Amalfi Drive.

From its position at the slope of the steep Lattari hills, it overlooks the Bay of

Salerno. The approach to Amalfi is most dramatic, whether you come from Positano or from Salerno, 15 miles to the east. Today Amalfi depends on the tourist traffic, and the hotels and pensiones in dead center are right in the milling throng of holiday makers. The finest and most highly rated accommodations lie on the outskirts.

Amalfi's telephone area code is 089.

THE SIGHTS

Evoking its rich past is the **duomo,** the cathedral, in the center of town, named in honor of St. Andrew (Sant'Andrea), whose remains are said to be buried inside in the crypt. Reached by climbing steep steps, the cathedral is characterized by its black-and-white façade and its mosaics. Inside, the one nave and two aisles are all richly baroqued. The cathedral dates back to the 11th century, although the present structure was rebuilt. Its bronze doors were made in Constantinople, and its campanile (bell tower) is from the 13th century, erected partially in the Romanesque style. Adjoining the cathedral are the "Cloisters of Paradise," originally a necropolis for members of the Amalfitan "Establishment."

For your most scenic walk in Amalfi, start at the piazza del Duomo, heading up via Genova. The classic stroll will take you to the **"Valle dei Mulini,"** the Valley of the Mills, so called because of the paper mills along its rocky reaches. (The seafaring republic is said to have acquainted Italy with the use of paper.) You'll pass by fragrant gardens and scented citrus groves.

And for the biggest attraction of all, head west by car or bus to the—

Emerald Grotto (Grotto Smeraldo)

This ancient cavern, known for its light effects, is a millennia-old chamber of stalagmites and stalactites. Three miles west of Amalfi, the grotto is reached from the coastal road via a descent by elevator, which costs 4,000 lire ($3.05). Then you board a boat which traverses the eerie world of the grotto. The stalagmites, unique in that some are under water, rise up in odd formations. Look for the underwater "crib." Visits are possible daily from 9 a.m. to 5 p.m. in March and April, from 8:30 a.m. to 6 p.m. May through September, and from 10 a.m. to 4 p.m. from October through February.

HOTELS IN AMALFI

In accommodations, I recommend the following, beginning with—

The Deluxe Category

Santa Caterina, 84011 Amalfi (tel. 089/871-012), is perched on top of a cliff, with its own elevator taking you down to a private beach and a saltwater pool reserved for hotel guests. This "saint" is one of the most scenic accommodations. You are housed either in the main structure or in one of the small "villas" in the citrus groves along the slopes of the hill. The accommodations are furnished in taste, with an eye toward the comfort of all guests. There are 70 rooms, and most of them contain a private balcony facing the sea that was once filled with the powerful fleet of the Amalfi Republic when it was a formidable sea power. All units have air conditioning and other modern comforts such as frigo-bar, phone, TV, and radio. The furniture respects the tradition of the house, and in every room there is an antique piece. The bathrooms are spacious, with luxurious fittings, and all of them have a hairdryer. It is preferred that in high season guests check in here on the full-board plan, costing 190,000 lire ($144) to 290,000 lire ($220) per person daily.

The food is among the best at the resort, so taking the boarding arrangement is no hardship. Many of the fresh vegetables are grown in the hotel's own garden, and the fish tastes so fresh I suspect the chef has an arrangement with local fishermen who bring in the "catch of the day," which is earmarked for the pampered guests of Santa Caterina. A buffet luncheon is served daily at the open-air restaurant by the swimming pool. Also, once or twice a week, a special evening buffet accompanied by music is held. Nonresidents can order lunch or dinner, costing 50,000 lire ($38) to 80,000 lire ($60.75).

The First-Class Range

Excelsior Grand Hotel, 84011 Amalfi (tel. 089/871-344), three miles from Amalfi at Pogerola, is a modern first-class hotel on the coast. Outdoing the positions of the nearby cliff-hanging monasteries, this extravaganza is perched high up on a mountain. All its rooms, 97 with private baths, are angled toward the view. You get the first glimmer of sunrise, the last rays of golden light. The social center is the 100-foot terrazzo-edged swimming pool filled with filtered mountain spring water. For the lazier, a nearby garden shaded by umbrellas beckons. The hotel structure is unconventional. The core is a high octagonal glass tower rising above the central lobby, with exposed mezzanine lounges and an open staircase leading to the view.

The dining room, with mirrored pillars, ornate blue-and-white tile floors, is a dignified place in which to sample the Italian cuisine with Gallic overtones. The bedrooms are individually designed, with plenty of room. The furnishings, chosen with flair, escape the curse of most hotel rooms. Many good reproductions, some antiques, king-size beds, tile floors, all contrast with the white walls. The private balconies, complete with garden furniture, are the important feature. Open from April to October, the hotel charges 90,000 lire ($68.50) daily in a single, 140,000 lire ($106) in a double. For full board you'll pay 125,000 lire ($95) per person. For those who want a sea experience, the hotel has a private beach, to which it arranges transportation. Several spots were especially created for a festive stay, notably Bar del Night, where an orchestra plays for dancing on weekends.

Hotel Luna e Torre Saracena, 84011 Amalfi (tel. 089/871-002), boasts a 13th-century cloister said to have been founded by St. Francis of Assisi. Now converted into a modern hotel, it is a sun trap. A free-form swimming pool is nestled on the rocks close to the sound of the surf and seagulls. The rather formal dining room has a coved ceiling, high-backed chairs, arched windows opening toward the water, and good food (Italian and international) served in an efficient manner. The long corridors, where monks of old used to tread, are lined with sitting areas and most unmonastic guests. The bedrooms have sea views, private bath, terrace, and modern furnishings. Open all year, the hotel charges its highest prices from April 1 to September 30: from 80,000 lire ($60.75) daily in a single, 130,000 lire ($98.75) to 160,000 lire ($122) in a double, the higher price for a private sitting room. The half-board rate begins at 130,000 lire ($98.75) per person daily. The hotel also has a nightclub projecting toward the sea. In summer, an orchestra plays for dancing.

The Medium-Priced Range

Hotel Belvedere, Conca dei Marini, 84011 Amalfi (tel. 089/831-282), lodged below the coastal road outside Amalfi on the drive to Positano, possesses one of the best swimming pools in the area. Hidden from the view and noise of the heavily traveled road, it is in a prime position, thrust out toward the sea. Terraces of rooms and gardens descend to the water. Well-prepared Italian meals are served either inside (where walls of windows allow for views of the coast) or on the wide front terrace, with its garden furniture. Signor Lucibello, who owns the hotel, sees to it that guests are made content, and provides, among other things, parking space for your car (a bus takes you into Amalfi). All 36 rooms have a freshly kept private bath. The facilities are serviceable and comfortable. Open from April to October, the aptly named Belvedere in high season charges 60,000 lire ($45.50) daily in a single, 110,000 lire ($83.50) for a double, inclusive. Half board costs 100,000 lire ($76) per person daily.

The Budget Range

Hotel dei Cavalieri, 84011 Amalfi (tel. 089/871-333), climbs a rocky hillside above the busy road between Amalfi and Positano. It was built in an angular design of jutting columns and simple detailing in 1976, but it contains so many antiques that the lobby gives the impression of a much older hotel. My favorite is the reception desk, whose massive top is supported by a sextet of growling lions. Upstairs, each of the bedrooms has a tile floor in sparkling patterns and modern bath. About 20% of the 60 guest rooms contain turn-of-the-century bedroom suites, while the furnishings in the other units are neutral but pleasant. Depending on the accommodation and the season, singles cost 41,000 lire ($31.25) to 65,000 lire ($49.50) daily, and doubles are priced from 78,000 lire ($59.25) to 110,000 lire ($83.50), including a buffet breakfast.

Hotel Miramalfi, 84011 Amalfi (tel. 089/871-588), on the western edge of Amalfi, lies below the coastal road and beneath a rocky ledge on its own beach. Family owned, and managed by Francesco Mansi, it offers rooms that wrap around the curving contour of the coastline, giving each an unobstructed view of the sea. The stone swimming pier—used for sunbathing, diving, and the boarding of motor launches for waterskiing—is reached by a winding cliffside path, past terraces of grapevines. A space saver is the rooftop car park. The dining room has glass windows and a few semitropical plants; the food is good and served in abundant portions. Breakfast is provided on one of the main terraces or on your own balcony. Each bedroom—48 in all, with private bath or shower—is well equipped, with built-in headboards, fine beds, cool tile floors, and efficient maintenance. Open all year, the hotel in high season charges from 50,000 lire ($38) daily in its singles, from 80,000 lire ($60.75) for its doubles. The inclusive charge for full board ranges from 85,000 lire ($64.50) per person daily. There are a swimming pool and an elevator to the beach.

Hotel Lidomare, largo Piccolomini 9, 84011 Amalfi (tel. 089/871-332), is a pleasant, small hotel, lying a few steps from the sea. The high-ceilinged bedrooms are airy and clean, containing a scattering of modern furniture mixed with Victorian-era antiques. The Camera family, the owners, charge 36,000 lire ($27.25) daily for a single, 58,000 lire ($44) for a double.

Marina Riviera, 84011 Amalfi (tel. 089/871-104), 50 yards from the beach, offers rooms and terraces overlooking the sea. Directly on the coastal road, it rises on terraces against the foot of the hills, with side verandas and balconies. There is a gracious dining room with high-backed provincial chairs, but meals in the open air are preferred. Two adjoining public lounges are traditionally furnished, and a small bar provides drinks whenever you want them. The refurbished rooms are comfortable, with balcony and such amenities as a hairdryer. Full board costs 65,000 lire ($49.50) to 90,000 lire ($68.50) per person daily.

DINING IN AMALFI

A leading restaurant is **La Caravella,** via Nazionale (tel. 871-029), and, happily, it's inexpensive. A grotto-like, air-conditioned place, it's off the main street next to the road tunnel, only a minute from the beach. The owner is Antonio Dipino. You get well-cooked, authentic Italian specialties, such as spaghetti Caravella with a seafood sauce. Scaloppine alla Caravella is served with a tangy clam sauce, and a healthy portion of zuppa de pesce (fish soup) is also ladled out. You can have a platter of the mixed fish fry, with crisp, tasty bits of shrimp and squid, followed by an order of fresh fruit served at your table in big bowls. For a complete meal, expect to spend 24,000 lire ($18.25) to 35,000 lire ($26.50). Open from 12:30 to 2:30 p.m. and 7:30 to 10:30 p.m.; it's closed on Tuesday and in November.

Da Gemma, via Fra Gerardo Sassa (tel. 871-345), is considered one of the best restaurants in town, one that takes inspired liberties with the regional cuisine and one where diners get a strong sense of the family unity that makes this place popular. The kitchen sends out plateful after plateful of savory spaghetti, sautéed clams, codfish with fresh tomatoes, or sautéed mixed shellfish, fish casserole, and a full range of other "sea creature" dishes. In summer, the intimate dining room more than doubles with the addition of an outdoor terrace. Expect to pay 35,000 lire ($26.50) to 42,000 lire ($32) for a full meal. The restaurant is open from 1 to 3 p.m. and 8 p.m.

to midnight daily except in January and February. It's open only for dinner in August and closes on Wednesday off-season.

Il Tari', via Capuano (tel. 871-832), is a very small, family-run establishment where diners can see the busy goings-on in the tiny kitchen. On the main street of town, the restaurant is unpretentious. The menu items are prepared simply and with flavor. They might include spaghetti with clams, mixed seafood grill, seafood salad, and an array of fish. Full meals range from 25,000 lire ($19) and are served from 12:30 to 3 p.m. and 7:30 to 10:30 p.m. Closed Tuesday and November 5 to December 5.

---

5. Ravello

Known to personages ranging from Richard Wagner to Greta Garbo, Ravello is the choice spot along the Amalfi Drive. Its reigning celebrity at the moment is Gore Vidal, who purchased a villa in town as a writing retreat. The village seems to hang 1,100 feet between the Tyrrhenian Sea and some celestial orbit. From Amalfi, the sleepy (except for summer tour buses) village is approached by a wickedly curvaceous road cutting through the villa- and vine-draped hills that hem in the Valley of the Dragone. Celebrated in poetry, song, and literature are Ravello's major attractions, two villas.

The telephone area code for Ravello is 089.

THE SIGHTS

A long walk past grape arbors and private villas takes you to **Villa Cimbrone**. After ringing the bell for admission and paying a fee of 2,000 lire ($1.50), you'll be shown into the vaulted cloisters (on the left as you enter). Note the grotesque bas-relief. Later, you can stroll (everybody "strolls" in Ravello) through the gardens, past a bronze copy of Donatello's *David*. Along the rose-arbored walkway is a tiny, but roofless, chapel. At the far end of the garden is a cliffside view of the Bay of Salerno, unfolding onto a panorama that the devout might claim was the spot where Satan took Christ to tempt him with the world. It is open daily from 8:30 a.m. to sunset.

Villa Rufolo, near the duomo, was named for its founding patrician family in the 11th century. Once the residence of kings and popes, such as Hadrian IV, it is now remembered chiefly for its connection with Wagner. He composed an act of *Parsifal* here in a setting he dubbed the "Garden of Klingsor." Boccaccio was so moved by the spot that he included it as background in one of his tales. Showing a Moorish influence, the architecture evokes the Alhambra at Granada. The large tower was built in what is known as the "Norman-Sicilian" influence. You can walk through the flower gardens leading to lookout points over the memorable coastline. Throughout the year the villa is open daily in the morning from 9:30 a.m. until 1 p.m. Afternoon hours vary. During the major tourist season (from June 1 to August 31) afternoon hours are 3 to 7 p.m. Other months, the villa usually reopens at 2 p.m., shutting down around 5 p.m. Admission is 1,000 lire (75¢).

HOTELS IN RAVELLO

In accommodations, the choices at Ravello are limited in number, but big on charm.

The Upper Bracket

Hotel Palumbo, 84010 Ravello (tel. 089/857-244), is an elite retreat on the Amalfi coast. A 12th-century palace, it has been favored by the famous ever since

Richard Wagner (who did a lot of composing here) persuaded the Swiss owners, the Vuilleumier family, to take in paying guests. To stay here is to understand why Max Reinhardt, Rossano Brazzi, Humphrey Bogart (filming *Beat the Devil*), Henry Wadsworth Longfellow, Edvard Grieg, Ingrid Bergman, Zsa Zsa Gabor, Tennessee Williams, Richard Chamberlain, Gina Lollobrigida, and a young John Kennedy and his Jacqueline found its situation in the village ideal. D. H. Lawrence even wrote part of *Lady Chatterley's Lover* while staying here.

The hotel offers gracious living in its series of drawing rooms, furnished with English and Italian antiques. Most of the snug but elegantly decorated bedrooms have a tile bath and their own terrace. Some of the bedrooms are in an annex across the street. Open all year, the hotel in high season charges 210,000 lire ($160) to 265,000 lire ($201) per person daily in a double for full board. Meals show the influence of the Swiss-Italian ownership. The food is the finest in Ravello. Even if the dishes that preceded it weren't any good (but they are), it would be worth it to come here to enjoy the hotel's lemon and chocolate soufflés. The selection of dishes is likely to vary, but, chances are, you'll be offered crêpes with five cheeses, spaghetti with gorgonzola, locally caught sole, succulent fresh anchovies, and striped bass stuffed with herbs. Meals, costing from 45,000 lire ($34.25), are served in a 17th-century dining room with baroque accents and a dining terrace opening to the panoramic outdoors. "Fill in" bookings are accepted. The Palumbo also offers its own production of Episcopio wine, served on the premises. The wine originated in 1860 and is stored in 50,000-liter casks in a vaulted cellar.

The Medium-Priced Range

Hotel Giordano e Villa Maria, 84010 Ravello (tel. 089/857-170), are two treasures of the Amalfi coast, lying in tranquil groves between Villa Rufolo and Villa Cimbrone. Your gracious host is Vincenzo Palumbo, who speaks excellent English. Villa Maria, in an old and charming building decorated tastefully with high-quality antiques, overlooks the sea and offers a lovely garden in which the restaurant of the hotel is located. The Giordano, more contemporary, offers a swimming pool (heated in winter) just a few feet from your room. Guests use the facilities of both places, including a solarium, music room, and a dance floor. In season pizza parties are popular. The restaurant serves quality meals with regional specialties not likely to be available elsewhere. Its wine cellar is excellent, and the chef prepares delectable meals with fresh vegetables taken from the garden. The ambience is magnificent, and you can enjoy one of the most spectacular views along the coast. Even if you're not a guest, you may want to dine here, paying from 25,000 lire ($19) for a meal. Rates range from 45,000 lire ($34.25) daily in a single to 75,000 lire ($57) in a double. In 15 minutes, guests can reach the beach by walking along old paths or by public bus leaving every hour from the central square. Ample parking is available.

Hotel Caruso Belvedere, 84010 Ravello (tel. 089/857-111), is a spacious, clifftop hotel, built into the 11th-century remains of what was once the d'Afflitto Palace and is now operated as a hotel by the Caruso family. It has semitropical gardens and a belvedere overlooking the Bay of Salerno. From here, you can look down the terraced mountain slopes and see the rows of grapes used to make the celebrated "Grand Caruso" wine on the premises. The atmosphere is gracious, and the indoor dining room has the original coved ceiling, plus tile floors. It opens onto a wide terrace where meals are also served under a canopy. The cuisine is special here. Naturally, the locally produced wines are served: red, white, or rosé. The bedrooms—26 in all, mainly with private bath, but all with hot and cold running water—have character, some with paneled doors, some with antiques, and some with a private terrace. Open all year, the hotel in high season charges 79,000 lire ($60) to 102,000 lire ($77.50) per person daily for half board. You'll never forget the arcaded walks, the Gothic arches, the pots of geraniums, the orange and purple bougainvillea, and the wine press with its large vats.

Hotel Rufolo, 84010 Ravello (tel. 089/857-133), is a little gem, run by the hospitable Schiavo family. The view from its sundecks is superb, and chairs are placed on a wide terrace and around the swimming pool. The bedrooms are cozy and immaculate, all with bath or shower, and the price, at least for Ravello, is moderate: 112,000 lire ($85) daily for a double room, including a continental breakfast, taxes, and service. Recently enlarged and modernized, the hotel lies in the center of the zone of artistic monuments, between cloisters of pine trees of the Villa Rufolo, from which the hotel takes its names, and the road that leads to the Villa Cimbrone. Food served in the restaurant is more than adequate, and the service is efficient. Mr. Schiavo and his family take good care of their guests.

The Budget Range

Hotel Parsifal, via G. D'Anna 5, 84010 Ravello (tel. 089/857-144), is an exquisite little hotel, incorporating portions of the original convent founded in 1288 by Augustinian monks. These monks had an uncanny instinct for picking the best views, the most inspiring situations in which to build their retreats. The cloister, with stone arches and a tile walk, has a multitude of potted flowers and vines, and the garden spots are the favorite of all, especially the one with a circular reflection pool. Chairs are placed for guests to watch the setting sun and fiery lights illuminating the twisting shoreline. Dining is preferred on the trellis-covered terrace where bougainvillea and wisteria scents mix with that of lemon blossoms. The living rooms have bright and comfortable furnishings, set against pure white walls. The bedrooms, while small, are tastefully arranged. A variety of accommodations are offered—with or without private bath—and a few rooms have a terrace. In high season, the ex-convent charges from 35,000 lire ($26.50) daily in a single, from 56,000 lire ($42.50) in a double.

Albergo Toro, viale Wagner 3, 84010 Ravello (tel. 089/857-211), and the **Villa Amore,** via dei Fusco (tel. 089/857-135), are real bargains—two small and charming villas converted to receive paying guests. The Toro—entered through a garden—lies just off the village square and the cathedral. It has semi-monastic architecture, with deeply set arches, long colonnades, and a tranquil character. The rooms may not have the finest decor—but at these prices, who complains? The owner is especially proud of the meals he serves (the dining room is also available to nonresidents). The hotel in high season (April 1 to October 1) charges 29,500 lire ($22.50) daily for a bathless single, 35,000 lire ($26.50) in a single with bath. A double room without bath costs 51,500 lire ($39.25), rising to 63,000 lire ($48) with bath. The full-board rate ranges from 62,000 lire ($47) per person daily. The Villa Amore charges the same prices. From some of its pleasantly furnished bedroom windows, there is a view of the coastline. In winter, the hotel is open only during the Christmas holidays.

WHERE TO DINE

Most guests take meals at their hotels. But try to escape the board requirement at least once to sample the wares at the following establishments.

Ristorante Garden, via Chiunzi, 84010 Ravello (tel. 089/857-226). Perhaps this pleasant restaurant's greatest claim to fame occurred in 1962 when Jacqueline Onassis, then the wife of President Kennedy, descended from a villa where she was staying to dine here with the owner of Fiat. Today some of that old glamour is still visible on the verdant terrace, which was designed to cantilever over the cliff below. Augusto Mansi charges from 25,000 lire ($19) for a well-prepared meal, which might include one of four kinds of spaghetti, cheese crêpes, an array of soups, a well-presented antipasti table, brochettes of grilled shrimp, a mixed fish fry, and sole prepared in several ways. One of the local wines will be recommended. Meals are served from 12:30 to 3 p.m. and 7:30 to 10:30 p.m. daily except Tuesday. On the premises are ten well-scrubbed rooms, each with its own bath and terrace. Doubles cost 60,000 lire ($45.50), including breakfast.

Cumpa' Cosimo (tel. 857-156). The clientele of this restaurant is likely to include everyone from the electrician down the street to a well-known cinematic personality searching for what is said to be the best home-cooking in town. The kitchen turns out food items sometimes based on old recipes. Try the house version of tagliatelle, followed perhaps by a mixed fish grill, giant prawns, or roast lamb well seasoned with herbs. Many other regional dishes are offered as well. For dessert, try one of several flavors of homemade ice cream. Expect to spend 28,000 lire ($21.25) for a full meal, served daily from 12:30 to 3 p.m. and 7:30 to 10 p.m. In summertime, part of the premises is transformed into a pizzeria. They are closed on Monday from November to March.

---

6. Salerno

Thirty miles south of Naples, the seaport of Salerno, capital of its province, appears on the horizon. It became famous throughout the world on September 9, 1943, when Allied armies established a hard-fought-for beachhead and launched the invasion of the mainland of Europe, the beginning of the end of World War II. Most of its waterfront was destroyed in that daring attack by British commandos.

But there remain in the old town narrow streets from the Middle Ages and a Norman castle capping the hill in the background. The cathedral is characterized by its 12th-century campanile (bell tower) in the Romanesque style. The bronze door (11th century) was shipped from Constantinople to grace the duomo, which was begun by Robert Guiscard. Inside is a remarkable medieval pulpit held up by a dozen columns, with one decorative mosaic pillar standing aloof. In the crypt is the tomb of St. Matthew, the Apostle.

Salerno's telephone area code is 089.

HOTELS IN SALERNO

When stacked against the wonders and the variety of accommodations on the Amalfi Drive, Salerno is a poor sister. But it makes a suitable overnight stopover for motorists bound for Sicily.

Lloyd's Baia Hotel, via de Marinis 2, 84100 Salerno (tel. 089/210-145), clings to the side of a cliff outside the industrial center of town. You'll often see the local business community enjoying its Caribbean-style lounges. The hotel in summer becomes like a seaside resort. At huge expense, a concrete elevator shaft was poised against the cliff's vertical drop to the beach where a pair of rectangular pools hugs the edge of the Gulf of Salerno. Inside the main section of the hotel, a baffling labyrinth of elevators and hallways connects the bar and dining room to the balconied bedrooms. Equipped with TV, modern bath, and phone, rooms cost 105,000 lire ($79.75) to 115,000 lire ($87.50) daily in a single and from 155,000 lire ($118) in a double, with breakfast included.

Hotel Jolly delle Palme, lungomare Trieste 1, 84100 Salerno (tel. 089/225-222), is set apart from the confusion of the heart of the city. It's at the northern tip of a waterside park, with a veranda overlooking the sea and the adjoining public bathing beach. This is a modern establishment, totally functional—short on style, big on creature comforts. The bedrooms, however, are pleasantly furnished. Ask for the sea-view bedrooms, as freight trains run right under the windows in back. Open all year, this Jolly chain member charges 110,000 lire ($83.50) daily in a single with bath, 155,000 lire ($118) in a double with bath.

Albergo Fiorenza, via Trento 145, 84100 Salerno (tel. 089/351-160), occupies the lower floors of a seven-story building on the southern edge of the city. The medium-priced albergo is a clean-cut establishment—neat and uncluttered, only a few hundred feet from the sea. It's in the contemporary style, with a glass lobby, well designed. The bedrooms are compact and Nordic designed, with built-in pieces. All the well-maintained rooms have private bath. The hotel charges 58,000 lire ($44) daily for its singles, 95,000 lire ($72.25) for its doubles, inclusive of taxes, service, and a continental breakfast.

WHERE TO DINE

Salerno used to be called a "gastronomic wasteland" by the harshest of critics. In the past few years there has been a considerable upgrading of the cuisine.

Nicola dei Principati, corso Garibaldi 201 (tel. 225-435), is generally conceded to be the finest restaurant in Salerno. It's not the kind of place that has any stars, but several of its dishes can be memorable and others are at least well prepared and served. The restaurant is a rebuilt structure that grew up on the site of an older restaurant that was destroyed by vandals in a tragic fire. Among the chef's specialties are antipasti, along with an outstanding selection of fish which could vary, depending on the catch of the day. For openers, you might try either the risotto with shellfish or the savory fish soup. You can then follow with grilled fish or grilled meat. A full meal will come to a reasonable 32,000 lire ($24.25) and up. Closed Monday but open other days from 12:30 to 3 p.m. and 7:30 to 10 p.m.

Il Torrione, via Carlo Santoro 15 (tel. 329-037), is a sure bet for a well-prepared cuisine. The chef serves the following specialties for an appreciative clientele: tagliatelle house style, lasagne, penne with seafood, linguine with scampi and mozzarella, fish soup, along with fresh fish (prepared almost any way you like it). There is also a reasonable selection of meat dishes, including veal Cordon Bleu. Expect to spend from 45,000 lire ($34.25) per person. The restaurant is open from 12:30 to 3 p.m. and 7:30 to 10 p.m.; closed Monday and in August.

Antica Pizzeria Del Vicolo della Neve, vicolo della Neve 24 (tel. 225-705), on a tiny street in the oldest part of town, does everything it can to preserve the 19th-century nostalgia of its premises. It's said that the best pizza in town comes from its ovens. But if you're in the mood, you can also order pasta (many variations), grilled meats pizzaiola, pork liver filet, or fish (again, prepared in many different ways, depending on the catch of the day). A glass or a carafe of the house wine might accompany your meal, which shouldn't cost more than 30,000 lire ($22.75) per person. The establishment is open only in the evening from 8 p.m. to 1:30 a.m. every day but Wednesday.

7. Paestum

Dating back to 600 B.C., the ancient Sybarite city of Paestum (Poseidonia) is about 25 miles south of Salerno. Abandoned for centuries, it fell to ruins. But the remnants of its past, excavated in the mid-18th century, are glorious—the finest heritage left from the Greek colonies that settled in Italy. The roses of Paestum, praised by the ancients, bloom two times yearly, splashing the landscape of the city with a scarlet red, a fit foil for the salmon-colored temples that still stand in the archeological garden.

The **basilica** is a Doric temple, dating from the 6th century B.C., the oldest temple from the ruins of the Hellenic world in Italy. The basilica is characterized by 9 columns fronting it and 18 flanking its sides. The Doric pillars are approximately five feet in diameter. Walls and ceiling, however, have long given way to decay. Animals were sacrificed to gods on the altar.

The **Temple of Neptune** is the most impressive of the Greek ruins at Paestum. It and the Temple of Haphaistos ("Theseum") in Athens remain the best-preserved Greek temples in the world, both dating from around 450 to 420 B.C. In front are six columns, surmounted by an entablature. Fourteen columns line the sides. The **Temple of Caeres,** from the 6th century B.C., has 34 columns still standing and a large altar for sacrifices to the gods.

The temple zone may be visited daily from 9 a.m. till two hours before sunset for an admission fee of 3,000 lire ($2.30). Using the same ticket, you can visit the **Archeological Museum,** across the road from the Caeres Temple. It displays the metopes removed from the treasury of the Temple of Hera (Juno). It is open from 9 a.m. to 2 p.m. (until 1 p.m. on Sunday). The museum is closed Monday, which is a bad day to head south in general because of the closings around Naples and Pompeii. New discoveries have revealed hundreds of Greek tombs, which have yielded many Greek paintings. Archeologists have called the find astonishing. In addition, other tombs excavated were found to contain clay figures in a strongly impressionistic vein.

The telephone area code for Paestum is 0828.

WHERE TO DINE

While at Paestum, you may want to take time out for lunch. If so, you'll find the **Nettuno Ristorante,** Zona Archeologica (tel. 811-028), a special place at which to dine. Just at the edge of the ruins, it stands in a meadow, like a country inn or villa. The interior dining room has vines growing around in its arched windows, and from the tables there is a good view of the ruins. The ceilings are beamed, the room divided by three Roman stone arches. Outside, there is a terrace for dining, facing the temples—a marvelous stage for a Greek drama. Under pine trees, hedged in by pink oleander, you can order a complete meal for about 25,000 lire ($19), including such a typical selection as beefsteak or roast chicken, a vegetable or salad, plus dessert. The à la carte suggestions include spaghetti with filets in tomato sauce, veal cutlet, and créme caramel. If you order à la carte, count on spending from 35,000 lire ($26.50). The restaurant, open from 12:30 to 3 p.m. and 7:30 to 10 p.m., is closed on Monday.

WHERE TO STAY

If you'd like to combine serious looks at Italy's archeological past with the first-class amenities of a beachside resort, try the **Strand Hotel Schuhmann,** via Laura Mare, 84063 Paestum (tel. 0828/851-151), a delightful choice for a holiday. From a base here, you can make trips to Amalfi, Sorrento, Pompeii, Capri, Herculaneum, and Vesuvius—let the crowds fight it out on the overcrowded Amalfi Coast. Set in a pine grove removed from traffic noises, the hotel has a large terrace with a view of the sea and a subtropical garden overlooking the Gulf of Salerno and the Amalfi Coast to Capri. Its bedrooms are well furnished and maintained, each with shower or bath, phone, and a balcony or terrace. The half-board rate depends on the season, ranging from 60,000 lire ($46) to 85,000 lire ($64.50) per person daily. The tariffs include service, taxes, private parking, and use of the beach facilities and deck chairs. The Italian cookery is first rate, and even if you're visiting Paestum only on a day trip, consider a meal here, costing from 25,000 lire ($19). The hotel is closed in November.

---

8. Capri

The broiling dog-day July and August sun beating down on Capri illuminates a circus of humanity. The parade of visitors would give Ripley's "Believe It or Not" material for months. In the upper town, a vast snake-like chain of gaudily attired tourists promenades through the narrow quarters (many of the lanes evoking the casbahs of North Africa).

Capri is pronounced *Cap*-ry, not Ca-*pree* as in the old song. The Greeks called it "the island of the wild boars." Before the big season rush is on, Capri is an island of lush Mediterranean vegetation (olives, vineyards, flowers) encircled by emerald waters, an oasis in the sun even before the days of that swinger Tiberius, who moved the seat of the empire here. Writers such as D. H. Lawrence have in previous decades found Capri a haven. Some have written of it, including Axel Munthe (*The Story of San Michele*) and Norman Douglas (*Siren Land*). The latter title is a reference to Capri's reputation as the "island of the sirens," a temptation to Ulysses. Other distinguished visitors have included Gide, Mendelssohn, Dumas, and Hans Christian Andersen.

The telephone area code for Capri is 081.

REACHING THE ISLAND

You can go from Naples by hydrofoil in just 45 minutes, with boats departing from Molo Beverello. The hydrofoil (*aliscafo*) leaves several times daily (some stop at Sorrento). A one-way trip costs from 9,600 lire ($7.30). It's cheaper but longer (about 1½ hours) to go by regularly scheduled ferryboats, a one-way ticket costing 5,000 lire ($3.80). There is no need to have a car in tiny Capri, and they are virtually impossible to drive on the hairpin roads anyway. The island is serviced by funiculars, taxis, and buses.

Many of Capri's hotels are remotely located, especially those at Anacapri, and some are inaccessible by car. I strongly recommend that visitors to the island arrive with as little luggage as possible. However, with even minor baggage, you may need the services of a porter. You'll find the headquarters of the island's union of porters in a building connected to the jetty at Marina Grande. There you can cajole, coddle, coerce, or connive your way through the hiring process where the only rule seems to be that there are no rules.

One positive aspect to the business is that your porter will know where to find the hotel among the winding passageways and steep inclines of the island's arteries. Your best defense during your pilgrimage might be a sense of humor.

"On the isle of Capri," your boat will dock at—

MARINA GRANDE

The least attractive of the island's communities, Marina Grande is the port, bustling with the coming and going of hundreds of visitors daily. It has a little sand-cum-pebble beach, on which you're likely to see American sailors—on shore leave from Naples—playing ball, occasionally upsetting a Coca-Cola over mamma and bambino.

If you're just spending the day on Capri, you should leave at once for the island's biggest attraction, the **Blue Grotto,** open daily from 9 a.m. till one hour before sunset. In summer, boats leave frequently from the harbor at Marina Grande, transporting passengers to the entrance of the grotto for 5,400 lire ($4.10) round trip. Once at the grotto, you'll pay 4,750 lire ($3.60) for the small rowboat that traverses the water. Admission is another 2,000 lire ($1.50).

You'll have to change boats to go under the low entrance to the cave. The toughened boatmen of the campagna are usually skilled at getting heavier passengers from the big boat into the skimpy craft with a minimum of volcanic spills.

The Blue Grotto is one of the best-known natural sights of the campagna. Known to the ancients, it was later lost to the world until an artist stumbled on it in 1826. Inside the caverna, light refraction (the sun's rays entering from an opening under the water) achieves the dramatic Mediterranean cerulean color. The effect is stunning, as thousands testify yearly.

If you wish, you can take a trip around the entire island, passing not only the Blue Grotto, but the Baths of Tiberius, the "Palazzo al Mare" built in the days of the empire, the Green Grotto (less known), and the much-photographed rocks called the "Faraglioni." The motorboats circle the island in about 1½ hours at a cost of 12,000 lire ($9.50) per person.

Connecting Marina Grande with Capri (the town) is a frequent-running funicular, charging 2,600 lire ($2) round trip. However, should you arrive off-season, the funicular, really a cog railway, doesn't operate. Instead, you can take a bus from Marina Grande to Capri at a one-way cost of 1,300 lire ($1).

For information, get in touch with the **Tourist Board,** piazza I. Cerio 11 (tel. 081/837-0424), open daily from 8 a.m. to 2 p.m.

CAPRI

The main town is the center of most of the hotels, restaurants, and elegant shops—and the milling throngs. The heart of the resort is the **piazza Umberto I,** like a grand living room.

Sightseeing in Capri

One of the most popular walks from the main square is down via Vittorio Emanuele, past the deluxe Quisisana, to the **Gardens of Augustus.** The park is the choice spot in Capri for views and relaxation. From this perch, you can see the legendary Faraglioni, the rocks, one inhabited by the "blue lizard." At the top of the park is a belvedere overlooking emerald waters and Marina Piccola. Nearby you can visit the **Certosa,** a Carthusian monastery honoring St. James when it was erected in the 14th century. The monastery is open daily from 9 a.m. to 1 p.m. and 3 p.m. to sunset, and charges no admission.

Back at the piazza Umberto I, head up via Longano, then via Tiberio, all the way to Monte Tiberio. Here, **Villa Jovis** is the splendid ruin of the estate from which Tiberius ruled the empire from A.D. 27 to 37. Actually, the Jovis was one of a dozen villas that the depraved emperor erected on the island. Apparently, Tiberius couldn't sleep, so he wandered from bed to bed. From the ruins there is a view of both the Bay of Salerno and the Bay of Naples, as well as of the island. The ruins of the imperial palace may be visited from 9 a.m. to one hour before sunset for 2,000 lire ($1.50) admission. It is closed on Monday.

Hotels in Capri

Finding your own bed for the night can be a real problem if you arrive in season without a reservation. There is a far greater demand for rooms than there is a supply. Capri is also an exclusive enclave of the wealthy, and even the cheaper accommodations are able to charge high prices. Many serious economizers return to the mainland for the night, unable to pay the steep tariffs of Capri.

THE UPPER BRACKET. The deluxe choice is the **Quisisana & Grand Hotel,** via Camerelle 2, 80073 Capri (tel. 081/837-0788), the favorite nesting place for a regular international clientele. Opened as a small hotel around the turn of the century, the Quisisana was enlarged and became the grand dame of the resort hotels here after World War II. More spacious than its central position would indicate, its private garden is shut off from the crisscross tourism outside its front entrance. A large, rather sprawling, but imposing, structure, it offers a total of 135 bedrooms—from cozy singles to ample suites—opening onto wide arcades with a view of the sea coast. The American bar (which seems appropriate to Berkeley Square, London) is the second-most-frequented spot on the premises, bowing to the swimming pool on the lower terrace. In the main lounge the furnishings are in antique gold. Capri's social center, the terrace of the hotel is where everybody who is anybody goes for cocktails before dinner.

There is a formal dining room, with an entire wall of glass opening onto the park, but a preferred luncheon spot is in the courtyard, where meals are served under a suspended canopy. The head chef is preening proud of his fresh-tasting and attractively displayed fish dishes, as well as his lush fruit and vegetables. The bedrooms, as mentioned, vary greatly—furnished with both traditional and conservatively modern pieces. Open from April to the end of October, the hotel charges a peak-season rate of 262,000 lire ($199) daily for bed and breakfast in a single, 344,000 lire ($261) to 464,000 lire ($353) in a double. Of course, you pay more for the suites. The hotel has sauna and massage facilities, plus a beauty shop.

La Scalinatella (Little Steps), via Tragara 8, 80073 Capri (tel. 081/837-0633), is one of the most delightful hotels of Capri. The establishment is constructed above terraces that offer a magnificent view of the water and of a nearby monastery. The ambience is one of unadulterated luxury, including air conditioning in each of the 28 rooms, a phone beside each of the bathtubs, beds set into alcoves, elaborate wrought-iron accents ringing both the inner stairwell and the ornate balconies, and a sweeping view over the establishment's encircling gardens and its swimming pool. Open only from mid-March to mid-October, the hotel charges 220,000 lire ($167) daily in a single, 400,000 lire ($304) in a double.

FIRST-CLASS CHOICES. In the first-class range, the **Hotel Luna,** viale Matteotti 3, 80073 Capri (tel. 081/837-0433), is in many ways the best hotel on the entire island, worthy of a deluxe rating. On a cliff overlooking the sea and the rocks of Faraglioni, it is almost between the Gardens of Augustus and the Carthusian Monastery of St. James. The creature comforts of the 20th century have been combined nicely with the past. The furnishings have been chosen with a deep respect for excellent, tasteful reproductions of fine antiques—no jarring moderno here. Architecturally, the elaborate tile designs for the floor set the pace. The atmosphere of the drinking lounge is club-like, and the dining room lures with its good-tasting cuisine. The air-conditioned bedrooms, a mixture of contemporary Italian pieces and a Victorian decor, are most successful, some incorporating wood and padded headboards and gilt mirrors over the desk, all consistently well styled. Some of the bedrooms have arched recessed private terraces overlooking the garden of flowers and semitropical plants. The hotel is open from April to October, and charges high-season rates from July through September. The tariff for a double ranges from 230,000 lire ($175) daily, from 110,000 lire ($83.50) in a single. Full board in high season ranges from 170,000 lire ($129) to 220,000 lire ($167) per person daily. All rooms have private baths.

A former private villa, the **Hotel Punta Tragara,** via Tragara 57, 80073 Capri (tel. 081/837-0844), stands at the tip of the most desirable panorama in Capri, but that isn't all that this imaginative hotel has in its favor. Its sienna-colored walls and Andalusian-style accents are designed so that each of the apartment accommodations is subtly different from its neighbor. Outfitted with mottled carpeting, big windows, substantial furniture, and all the modern comforts, each unit opens onto a private terrace or a balcony studded with flowers and vines. Depending on the unit and the season, doubles rent for 190,000 lire ($144) to 245,000 lire ($186) daily and junior suites for two people go for 230,000 lire ($175) to 295,000 lire ($224). Units of two and three bedrooms are available as well. Half board can be arranged for another 60,000 lire ($45.50) per person. On the premises are two swimming pools, one of which is heated, plus multibranched cactus plants in oval terracotta pots, quiet retreats near a baronial fireplace, and a grotto disco.

La Palma, via Vittorio Emanuele 39, 80073 Capri (tel. 081/837-0133), is a gem. Right in the center of Capri, this heartbeat hotel caters to guests seeking first-class amenities and comforts—who are willing to pay the piper for the privilege. Restored and renovated in an appealing style that blends modern and traditional, the hotel has a white-walled exterior with a gracious forecourt with palms and potted shrubs. Each of the 80 bedrooms is handsomely furnished and has private bath. The single rate is 200,000 lire ($152) daily, rising to 300,000 lire ($228) in a double. Guests take half-board terms in peak summer visiting times, paying 180,000 lire ($137) to 230,000 lire ($175) per person daily. Its restaurant, Relais la Palma, is one of the finest dinner choices in Capri if you'd like to make a reservation in the evening. Meals cost 40,000 lire ($30.50) to 60,000 lire ($45.50).

MEDIUM-PRICED HOTELS. The pale azure façade of the **Regina Cristina,** via Serena 20, 80073 Capri (tel. 081/837-744), rises four stories above one of the most imaginatively landscaped gardens of Capri. It was built in 1959 in a sun-flooded design of open spaces, sunken lounges, cool tiles, and *La Dolce Vita* armchairs. Each of the accommodations has its own balcony, lots of calm, a mini-bar, and private bath; few have TV. Singles cost from 115,000 lire ($87.50) daily, and doubles go for 200,000 lire ($152), with breakfast included.

La Pineta, via Tragara 6, 80073 Capri (tel. 081/837-0644), is that rare hotel in Capri that remains open all year. Built in 1952, it has been receiving visitors to Capri ever since. A three-star hotel, it lies along one of the most enchanting walks on the island. A terraced hotel, it lures with its contemporary decor and swimming pool by which you can enjoy lunch daily from noon to 5 p.m. The swimming pool is heated during spring and autumn. Most of the well-furnished bedrooms, 54 in all, are air-conditioned. Prices are 125,000 lire ($95) daily in a single and 185,000 lire ($141) in a double.

Hotel Flora, via Federico Serena 26, 80073 Capri (tel. 081/837-0211), over-looks the Monastery of St. James and the sea, and features terraces edged with olean-der, bougainvillea, and geraniums. There are several tile courtyards with garden furniture, pots of tropical flowers, and spots either to sunbathe or be cooled by the sea breezes. The public and private rooms are a wise blend of the old and new. All of the well-furnished double rooms have private bath. Open April to October, the hotel in high season charges a couple 140,000 lire ($106) daily, including a continental breakfast, service, taxes, and air conditioning. Singles with the same amenities rent for 100,000 lire ($76). There is an annex across the street.

Hotel La Pazziella, via P. R. Giuliani 4, 80073 Capri (tel. 081/837-0044), lies a few pedestrian minutes from the center of Capri behind a small garden and white cement walls. Inside, an expanse of patterned tiles supports the scattering of antique and modern furniture, as well as a handful of plants. The 17 bedrooms each possess air conditioning, frigo-bar, phone, private bath, cool white walls, and tile floors. Sin-gles cost from 110,000 lire ($83.50) daily and doubles begin at 220,000 lire ($167).

BEST FOR THE BUDGET. With a clear view of the sea, **La Vega,** via Occhio Marino 10, 80073 Capri (tel. 081/837-0481), is a sun-pocket little hotel nestled against the hillside. Each of the oversize rooms of this four-level building has a private balcony overlooking the water. Below the rooms is a garden of flowering bushes, and on the lower edge is a free-form swimming pool with a grassy border for sunbathing and a little bar for refreshments. Breakfast is served on a terrace surrounded by trees and large potted flowers. Double rooms with bath rent for 150,000 lire ($114) daily, and singles go for 90,000 lire ($68.50), with a continental breakfast included. The hotel is open from mid-March to October. The rooms have decoratively tiled floors and the beds have wrought-iron headboards.

The budget-priced **Villa Krupp,** via Matteotti 12, 80073 Capri (tel. 081/837-0362), is a sun-pocket villa-turned-guesthouse, overlooking the Gardens of Augus-tus. Surrounded by shady trees, it offers a splendid view of the sea from its lofty ter-races. A family-run place, it has the advantage of intimacy. The front parlor is all glass, opening onto the seaside, with semitropical plants set near Hong Kong chairs, all intermixed with painted Venetian-style pieces. Your bedroom may be large, with a fairly good bathroom. Many of the rooms have a terrace. The villa has only 15 bed-rooms, available all year, for 20,600 lire ($157) to 33,000 lire ($25) daily in a single, 50,500 lire ($38.50) to 59,300 lire ($45) for a double. A continental breakfast, in-cluded in the tariffs, is the only meal offered.

Hotel Florida, via Fuorlovado 34, 80073 Capri (tel. 081/837-0497). You'll have to negotiate a labyrinth of pedestrian alleyways before reaching the white-cement façade of this charming hotel. Owners Giovanni Tarantino and his wife, Costanza, have labored over the small gardens surrounding the property, working to train strands of philodendron over the ceilings of their public rooms. In back, arbors shield tea-drinkers from the sun as they watch tennis games on a pair of courts at the end of an expanse of lawn. Built in 1974, the hotel contains 19 sunny and tile-floored bedrooms, each with its own terrace and private bath. Depending on the season, singles go for 37,000 lire ($28) to 45,000 lire ($34.25) daily, doubles run 65,000 lire ($49.50) to 90,000 lire ($68.50), with breakfast included. An apartment for two costs 105,000 lire ($79.75). The hotel is so popular in high season that repeat visitors often reserve space months in advance. Annual closing is between November 5 and December 20, and, for a supplemental fee, residents can use a swimming pool connected to a neighboring building.

Pensione Villa Bianca, via Belvedere Cesina 9, 80073 Capri (tel. 081/837-8016), is one of the best bargains at the resort. It's run by English-speaking Augusto Ferraro who has been most helpful to readers in the past. A double with a view to the sea costs around 72,000 lire ($54.75) daily, and a double without a sea view rents for 69,000 lire ($52.50) to 70,000 lire ($53.25), with breakfast and taxes included. All rooms have private baths, and those without sea view have the use of a roof terrace. A kitchen is available.

Restaurants in Capri

La Capannina, via Le Botteghe 14 (tel. 837-0732), is my favorite restaurant in all of Capri. It's not pretentious, although a host of famous people, ranging from film actresses to dress designers to royalty, patronize it. A trio of inside rooms is decorated in a sophisticated tavern manner, although the main draw in summer is the inner courtyard, with its ferns and hanging vines. At a table covered with a colored cloth, you can select the finest meals on the island. Wine is from vineyards owned by the restaurant. If featured, a fine opener is Sicilian macaroni. Main-dish specialties include pollo (chicken) alla Capannina and scaloppine Capannina. However, the most savory skillet of goodies is the zuppa di pesce, a soup made with fish garnered from the bay. Some of the dishes, however, were obviously inspired by the nouvelle cuisine school. The restaurant charges 35,000 lire ($26.50) to 55,000 lire ($41.75) for a dinner. Open from 12:30 to 3 p.m. and 7:30 to 10:30 p.m., the restaurant is closed Wednesday (except in August) and from early November to mid-March.

La Pigna, via Roma 30 (tel. 837-0280), a short walk from the bus station, serves the finest meals for the money on the entire island, outside of the hotel dining rooms. A meal here is like attending a garden party in Capri, and this has been true since 1875. The owner loves flowers almost as much as good food. The ambience is one of a greenhouse, with purple petunias, red geraniums, bougainvillea, and lemon trees flourishing in abundance. Much of the produce comes from the restaurant's gardens in Anacapri. The food is excellent, regardless of what you select, but try in particular the pasta specialty, penne (noodles) tossed in a sauce made of eggplant, and the chicken suprême with mushrooms, the house specialty. Another dish I can recommend is the rabbit, which was raised on the farm. It's stuffed with herbs. The dessert specialty is an almond and chocolate torte. Another feature of the restaurant is homemade liqueurs, one of which is distilled from local lemons. Expect to spend from 38,000 lire ($28.90) to 50,000 lire ($38) for a complete meal. The waiters are courteous and efficient, the atmosphere nostalgic, as guitarists stroll by singing sentimental Neapolitan ballads. It is open from noon to 3 p.m. and 8 p.m. to 2 a.m., serving from mid-March until the end of October. It is closed on Tuesday except in July and August.

Ristorante da Tonino Al Grottino, 27 Via Longano (tel. 837-0584), is my pick of the hard-to-find trattorie. Favored by personalities—everybody from Vittorio Gassman to Princess Soraya, Ted Kennedy to Ginger Rogers—it draws a constant stream of hungry diners. To reach it, walk down a narrow alleyway branching off from the piazza Umberto I to an establishment not unlike a bistro in North Africa. The chef knows how to rattle his pots and pans. Bowing to the influence of the nearby Neapolitan cuisine, he offers four different dishes of fried mozzarella cheese, any one highly recommended. A big plate of the mixed fish fry from the seas of the campagne is a favored main dish. The zuppa di cozze (clam soup) is a savory opener, as is the ravioli alla caprese. Truly succulent is a plate of crayfish in homemade mayonnaise. An average meal here will cost 22,000 lire ($16.75) to 35,000 lire ($26.50) per person. It is open from noon to 3 p.m. and 7 to 11 p.m.; closed on Tuesday off-season.

I Faraglioni, via Camerelle 75 (tel. 837-0320). Some of the wits of the island say that the food is only a secondary consideration to the social ferment that usually seems to be part of this popular restaurant. In any event, the kitchen turns out a well-prepared collection of European specialties, which usually base their recipes on seafood from the surrounding waters. Examples might include linguine with lobster, seafood crêpes, rice Crèole, spaghetti with clams, grilled or baked, fish of many different varieties, and a wide assortment of meat dishes, including chateaubriand and veal. Desserts might be made of one of the regional pastries mixed with fresh fruit. A complete meal costs from 50,000 lire ($38), served from 12:30 to 3 p.m. and 7:30 to 10 p.m. The restaurant is open from April to mid-October daily except Monday.

Casa Nova, via Le Botteghe 46 (tel. 837-7642), run by the D'Alessio family, is one of the finest dining rooms in Capri, a short walk from the piazza Umberto I. Its cellar offers a big choice of Italian wines, with most of the favorites of the campagne, and its cooks turn out a savory blend of Neapolitan and Italian specialties. You might begin with a cheese-filled ravioli, then go on to veal Sorrento or even red snapper "crazy waters" (with baby tomatoes). The seafood is always fresh and well prepared. A large buffet of tempting antipasti is always at hand to tempt you into a meal. The restaurant is open seven days a week in the peak summer season, but is closed Thursday off-season. Service is from noon to 3 p.m. and 7 p.m. to midnight. Dinner reservations at casa Nova are needed in summer. Meals cost from 30,000 lire ($22.75). The restaurant is open from April to October.

La Sceriffa, via Acquaviva 29 (tel. 837-7953), stands near the main piazzetta of town, ringed with the tables of its outdoor veranda. This pleasant restaurant offers good food. One of the culinary inventions is a form of linguine "Terra Felice," made with fresh basil, capers, tomatoes, and a healthy shot of cognac. Other dishes might include spaghetti with mussels and clams, fettuccine house style (with eggplant and peppers), a regional form of ravioli, several tasty chicken dishes, and homemade desserts, many of them richly laden with cream. No one will mind if you order a carafe of the house wine, which will bring a full meal to 35,000 lire ($26.50) to 45,000 lire ($34.25). Open from noon to 2:30 p.m. and 7:30 to 10 p.m. April to October, the restaurant also takes a holiday every Tuesday.

Al Geranio, Giardini Augusto, viale Matteotti 8 (tel. 837-0616), is one of the most scenically located restaurants in Capri, standing in the Gardens of Augustus en route to Villa Krupp. It can be easily reached from two of the leading hotels of Capri, the Quisisana and the Luna. You can arrive early to enjoy an apéritif in the bar, furnished in a modern style. The earlier you arrive in summer, the better chance you have of getting an outdoor table. The kitchen turns out a good Mediterranean cuisine likely to include such dishes as fish soup, fried shrimp, swordfish, crêpes with cheese, and cannelloni. A savory dish to order is zuppa di cozze (mussel soup). You might also try Capri-style ravioli. Look also for the daily specials. Meals, served from 12:30 to 3 p.m. and 7:30 to 10 p.m., cost 35,000 lire ($26.50) to 50,000 lire ($38). The restaurant is closed on Thursday and open from April to mid-October.

Da Gemma, via Madre Serafina 6 (tel. 837-0461), has long been a favorite with painters and writers. It's reached from the piazza Umberto I by going up an arch-covered walkway, reminiscent of Tangier. Some tables are arranged for the view. Everything's cozy and atmospheric. The cuisine is provincial, with a reliance on fish dishes. The best beginning is the mussel soup, and pizzas are also featured in the evening. The best main dish to order is the boiled fish of the day with creamy butter, priced according to weight. Desserts are mouthwatering. Expect to spend 30,000 lire ($22.75) to 40,000 lire ($30.50) for a complete meal served from 12:30 to 3 p.m. and 7:30 to 10 p.m. The restaurant is closed on Monday and in November, and has an annex across the street which remains open in winter.

La Cisterna, via Madre Serafina 5 (tel. 837-7236), is an excellent, small restaurant run by two brothers, Francesco and Salvatore Trama. The warm welcome extended by the owners sets the right note to enjoy the fine food. There is a typical set menu, but I prefer to ask what the evening specials are, based on whatever fish was freshest at the dock that afternoon, marinated in wine, garlic, and ginger, and broiled, or perhaps mama's green lasagne. The lightly breaded and deep-fried baby squid and octopus, a mouthwatering saltimbocca, spaghetti with clams, and a filling zuppa di pesce are usually on the menu. For a meal of antipasto, a first course, a second course with one or two side dishes, a dessert, and at least two bottles of Capri wine, you'll pay 35,000 lire ($26.50) to 50,000 lire ($38), and I guarantee you'll have had a banquet. Food is served daily from 12:30 to 3 p.m. and 7:30 to 10 p.m. La Cisterna lies only a short walk from the piazza Umberto I and is reached via a labyrinth of covered "tunnels."

The Café Life

One of the major pastimes in Capri is occupying an outdoor table at one of the cafés on the heartbeat piazza Umberto I. Each arriving visitor picks his or her favorite. They're all about the same. Even some permanent residents (and this is a good sign) patronize **Bar Tiberio,** piazza Umberto I (tel. 837-0268), which is open daily from 7 a.m. to 9 p.m. Larger and a little more comfortable than some of its competitors, this café has tables both inside and outside overlooking the busy life of the square where virtually every visitor to Capri shows up at one time or another. A cappuccino costs 3,000 lire ($2.30), but you can order many other types of drinks as well.

ANACAPRI

Capri is the upper town of Marina Grande. To see the upper town of Capri, you have to get lost in the clouds of Anacapri—more remote, secluded, and idyllic than the main resort, and reached by a daring 1,500-lira ($1.15) round-trip bus ride, more thrilling than any roller coaster. One visitor once remarked that all bus drivers to Anacapri "were either good or dead." At one point in its history Anacapri was connected to its biggest sister only by the "Scala Fenicia," the Phoenician Stairs.

Disembarking at the piazza della Victoria, you'll find a Caprian Shangri-la, a village of charming dimensions.

To continue your ascent to the top, you then hop aboard a chair lift to **Monte Solaro,** the loftiest citadel on the entire island at its lookout perch of 1,950 feet. The ride takes about 12 minutes and operates daily from 9:30 a.m. to sunset, charging 5,500 lire ($4.20) for a round-trip ticket. At the top, the spectacular panorama of the Bay of Naples is spread before you.

You can head out to **Villa San Michele** on viale Axel Munthe. This was the home of Axel Munthe, the Swedish author (*The Story of San Michele*), physician, and friend of Gustav V, king of Sweden, who visited him several times on the island. The villa is left as Munthe (who died in 1949) furnished it, harmonious and tasteful. From the rubble and ruins of an imperial villa built underneath by Tiberius, Munthe purchased several marbles, which are displayed inside. You can walk through the gardens for another in a series of endless panoramas of the island. Tiberius used to sleep out there al fresco on hot nights. The villa may be visited from 9 a.m. to 6 p.m. from May 1 to September 30, from 9:30 a.m. to 5 p.m. in April and October, and from 9:30 a.m. to 4:30 p.m. in March. Admission is 3,000 lire ($2.30). Villa San Michele is a five-minute walk from the piazza Monumento in Anacapri.

Hotels in Anacapri

For a villa with a room for yourself, here are my recommendations, beginning with the first-class **Europa Palace,** via Capodimonte 2, 80071 Anacapri (tel. 081/837-0955). On the slopes of Monte Solaro, the Europa sparkles with *moderne,* turning its back on the past to embrace the semi-luxury of today. Its designer, who had bold ideas, obviously loved wide open spaces, heroic proportions, vivid colors. The landscaped gardens with palm trees and plenty of bougainvillea have a large heated swimming pool, which most guests use as their outdoor living room. Each bedroom contains a private bath (some even with double services), direct-dial phone, radio, color TV, frigo-bar, and air conditioning on request. Special features are four junior suites, each with a private swimming pool. The standard bedrooms rent for 150,000 lire ($114) daily in a single and from 250,000 lire ($190) in a double, tariffs including a continental breakfast, service, and taxes. The hotel's restaurant, Alexandre, is known for the fine cuisine with Mediterranean specialties, even with some nouvelle cuisine. Meals cost from 40,000 lire ($30.50). In the swimming pool area is a snackbar where light lunches and barbecue dishes are served. Open April to October.

In the medium-priced range, there is the **Hotel San Michele di Anacapri,** 80071 Anacapri (tel. 081/837-1427), with its own spacious cliffside gardens and unmarred views. And it has enough shady or sunny nooks to please everybody. Guests linger long and peacefully in its private and well-manicured gardens, the green trees softened by splashes of color from hydrangea and geraniums. The position of this contemporary, well-appointed hotel is just right: near Axel Munthe's Villa San Michele. The view for diners includes the Bay of Naples and Vesuvius. The lounges are pleasantly furnished in an older, more traditional vein, much like the appearance of a country house in France. The bedrooms carry out the same theme, with a deep curtsy to the past, but also with sufficient examples of today's amenities, such as a tile bath in most rooms, good beds, and plenty of space. Singles range from 42,700 lire ($32.50) to 56,200 lire ($42.75) daily, and doubles cost 64,500 lire ($49) to 89,200 lire ($67.75), inclusive.

The budget-priced **Hotel Bellavista,** via Orlandi 10, 80071 Anacapri (tel. 081/837-1463), only a two-minute walk from the main piazza, is a modern retreat, offering a panoramic view. It uses electric, primary colors, a holiday place with authority. Lodged into a mountainside, it has large living and dining rooms, as well as terraces opening toward a view of the sea. The breakfast and lunch terrace has garden furniture, a rattan-roofed sun shelter, and the cozy lounge has an elaborate tile floor and a hooded fireplace on a raised hearth, ideal for nippy nights. The bedrooms are pleasingly contemporary (a few have a bed mezzanine, a sitting area on the lower level, and a private terrace). The 15 rooms rent for 65,000 lire ($49.50) daily in a single, the cost rising to 100,000 lire ($76) in a double. Most guests stay here on the full-board plan, which costs 95,000 lire ($72.25) per person daily. Guests are accepted only from April to October. The restaurant is closed on Monday.

Hotel Loreley, via Orlandi 12, 80071 Anacapri (tel. 081/837-1440), has more to offer than economy: it's a cozy, immaculately kept accommodation, with a homey, genial atmosphere. Opened in 1963, it features an open-air veranda with a bamboo canopy, rattan chairs, and of course, a good view. The rooms overlook lemon-bearing trees that have (depending on the season) either scented blossoms or fruit. The bedrooms are quite large, with unified colors and enough furniture to make for a sitting room. Each of the rooms has a private bath and a balcony. Depending on the plumbing, singles range from 17,900 lire ($13.50) to 29,800 lire ($22.75) daily, while doubles run 34,400 lire ($26.25) to 57,800 lire ($44), including breakfast. The hotel is approached through a white iron gate, past a stone wall. It lies off the road, toward the sea, and is surrounded by fig trees and geraniums.

After Anacapri, we descend to—

MARINA PICCOLA

A little fishing village and beach on the south shore, Marina Piccola is reached by walking down via Krupp (later you can take an bus back up the steep hill to Capri). The village opens onto emerald-and-cerulean waters, with the Faraglioni rocks of the sirens jutting out at the far end of the bay.

Where to Dine

La Canzone del Mare (tel. 837-0104) is a memorable place to spend an afternoon in Marina Piccola. You dine here at a terrace restaurant, then later go for a swim in the luxurious free-form seaside pool. Built on several levels, the dining areas are shaded. This little compound of poshness was created by the late Gracie Fields, the English mill girl with the golden voice who became a star. After a full and dynamic career, starring in many films, countless vaudeville shows, and endless radio and television shows, Miss Fields (the wartime sweetheart of the British) fulfilled a goal by finding the loveliest spot she could in the Mediterranean. She opened this exclusive little restaurant and settled back to enjoy the leisurely life before her death. It is still going strong. The manager will welcome you to a meal, served from 11 a.m. to 5 p.m., that is likely to run in the neighborhood of 55,000 lire ($41.75) to 85,000 lire ($64.50). Seafood dishes are specialties. The club is open from Easter to October.

SICILY

Sicily is an ancient land of myth and legend. The coastal waters washing up on its shores have carried with them a long parade of adventurers from the East. Along with southern Italy, the Greeks called Sicily "Magna Graecia." The Mycenaeans plied their sailing craft into the early settlements, and made contact with the people a millennium and a half before the birth of Christ.

Too long neglected by foreign travelers wooed by the art cities of the north, Sicily today is attracting greater and greater traffic. It is a land of images: volcanic islands, skiing on the slopes of active Mount Etna, a sirocco from the Libyan deserts, horses with plumes and bells pulling gaily painted carts, old villas evoking scenes from *The Leopard,* the scent of almonds in the air, vineyards and citrus groves, Greek temples, coastal plains, classical dramas performed in theaters of antiquity, and the aromatic fragrance of a glass of marsala after downing the Sicilian dessert, cassata.

Sicily, the largest of Mediterranean islands, is a land of dramatic intensity, like a play by native son Luigi Pirandello. For centuries its beauty and charm have attracted the greedy eye of foreigners: the Greeks, Romans, Vandals, Arabs, Normans, Swabians, and the houses of Bourbon and Aragon.

Luigi Barzini wrote: "Sicily is the schoolroom model of Italy for beginners, with every Italian quality and defect magnified, exacerbated and brightly colored." It is the people—bound by tradition and local customs—that provide the greatest interest.

The best centers for touring are Palermo, Agrigento, Syracuse, Catania, and Taormina. If you're considering anchoring into Sicily for a holiday, then Taormina occupies the best site, with the finest choice of hotels in all price ranges.

If you stick to the main road that skirts the coast, encircling the island, you'll get to see most of the major sights, veering inland for such gems as the Greek temple at Segesta and the active volcano of Mount Etna. In the Sicilian archipelago, the islands holding most interest for visitors are Lipari, Vulcano, and Stromboli, which can be visited on a day's excursion from Messina, but it would be better to stay there.

HEADING SOUTH BY CAR

When you head south toward Sicily today, you won't have the transportation headache that plagued Goethe. The autostrada del Sole stretches all the way from Milan to Reggio Calabria, sticking out on the "big toe," the gateway to Sicily.

One day a bridge is supposed to connect Sicily with the mainland, a link that hasn't existed since the island broke away in unrecorded times. The project, it is estimated, would take at least eight years and cost at least a billion dollars. A major problem is that the span is to stretch across the Strait of Messina, a prime earthquake zone.

At present, one way to reach Sicily is to take a ferryboat from via San Giovanni in Reggio Calabria to Messina, costing 1,000 lire (75¢) per passenger. Departures are daily on this state railway ferryboat, vessels leaving from 5 a.m. to 10 p.m. It takes less than an hour to cross. You can take your car on the ferryboat. Much quicker, shaving at least 22 minutes off the crossing time, is an *aliscafo* (hydrofoil). You'll pay 3,700 lire ($2.80). However, the *aliscafo* is recommended, because usually the higher price means fewer passengers—hence, less crowding. You cannot take your vehicle on a hydrofoil.

Near Reggio Calabria, incidentally, is a much smaller community, **Scilla,** famous in Homeric legend. Mariners of old, such as Ulysses, crossed the Strait of Messina from here, and faced the double menace of the two monsters Charybdis and Scylla.

FROM NAPLES TO SICILY BY SEA

One way to reach Palermo is by night ferry from Naples. The ferry leaves Naples at 8:30 p.m., arriving in Palermo the next morning at 6:30. On Friday, there is another departure at 10 p.m. The service is run by **Tirrenia S.A.** For information about this service, call the company's office in Naples at 081/660-333. However, if you're already in Palermo and want to take the ferry service back to Naples, dial 091/585-733. Unfortunately, you will not always find someone who speaks English. Sleeping compartments are often booked days in advance, and there may be space available only on deck.

It is also possible to take a hydrofoil service from Naples to Palermo in summer. Most of these trips, operated by **S.N.A.V.,** leave Naples at 3 p.m., the trip taking five hours.

There is also hydrofoil service from Naples to most of the Aeolian Islands, including Stromboli, Liparo, Milazzo, and Volcano, with schedules different in summer (June to September) from the runs made off-season (October through May). Every travel agent in Naples or the concierge at all the major hotels has an up-to-date schedule of these departures and fares.

FLYING TO SICILY

Flights on **Alitalia,** the national carrier, go at least once a day from such cities as Milan, Naples, Venice, Pisa, Genoa, Bologna, Turin, and Rome. In the case of the more influential cities such as Rome, there are around six flights a day. Flights go to Catania at least once a day from Milan, Pisa, Rome, and Turin.

---

1. Palermo

As the ferryboat docks in the Bay of Palermo, and you start spotting blond, blue-eyed bambini all over the place, don't be surprised. If the fair-haired children don't fit your conception of what a Sicilian should look like, remember that the Normans landed here in 1060, six years before William the Conqueror put in at Hastings, and launched a campaign to wrest control of the island from the Arabs. Both elements were to cross cultures, a manifestation still seen today in Palermo's architecture—a unique style, Norman-Arabic.

The city is the largest port of Sicily, its capital, and the meeting place of a regional parliament granted numerous autonomous powers in postwar Italy. Against a backdrop of the citrus-studded Conca d'Oro plain and Monte Pellegrino, it is a city of wide boulevards, old quarters in the legendary Sicilian style (laundry lapping against the wind, smudge-faced kids playing in the street), town houses, architecturally harmonious squares, baroque palaces, and modern buildings (many erected as a result of Allied bombings in 1943). It also has the worst traffic jams in Sicily.

Palermo was founded by the Phoenicians, but it has known many conquerors, some of whom established courts of great splendor (Frederick II), others of whom brought decay (the Angevins).

PRACTICAL FACTS

For Palermo, the **telephone area code** is 091. For long-distance calls, go to the office on via Lincoln, fronting the main railway station. It is open 24 hours a day.

Airport Information: If you fly from Rome or Naples, you'll land at Cinisi-Punta Raisi, some 19 miles west of Palermo. For information about flights, phone 591-690. It's best to catch a local airport bus, which will take you from the airport to the piazza Castelnuovo. These leave about every hour, and cost 3,600 lire ($2.75) a ride. For the same trip a taxi is likely to charge from 45,000 lire ($34.25)—more if the driver thinks he can get away with it.

American Express: The agent for American Express is Palermois Rugieri, via Emerico Amari 40 (tel. 587-144), which is closed on Sunday but open Monday through Friday from 9 a.m. to 1 p.m. and 4 to 6 p.m., and on Saturday from 9 a.m. to 1 p.m.

Buses: Most municipally operated buses in Palermo charge 600 lire (45¢) for a ticket, which is a cheap way of getting about. Most passengers purchase their tickets at tobacco shops (*tabacchi*) throughout the city before getting on. Otherwise, you'll need some 100-lira coins handy.

Consulate: You'll find the **U.S. Consulate** at via Vaccarini 1 (tel. 091/343-532), open from 9 a.m. to 1 p.m. and 3 to 5 p.m. Monday through Friday.

Crime Warning: Be especially alert. Some citizens here are the most skilled pickpockets on the continent. Keep your gems locked away (in other words, don't flaunt any sign of wealth). Women who carry handbags are especially vulnerable to purse-snatchers on Vespas. Don't leave valuables in your car. In fact, I almost want to say don't leave your car alone, even knowing how impossible that is.

Emergencies: In order to call **police**, report a **fire**, or summon an **ambulance**, dial 113.

Post Office: The major post office is on via Roma, and is open Monday through Friday from 8:30 a.m. to 7:30 p.m., on Saturday to noon. It is closed on Sunday.

Tourist Information: There are offices at strategic points, including the Palermo Airport. The principal office, however, is the **Azienda Autonoma Turismo,** piazza Castelnuova 34 (tel. 583-847).

HOTELS IN PALERMO

Generally you'll find a poor lot, aided by a few fine choices that prove the exception to the rule. Hunt and pick carefully, as many hotels of Palermo are not suitable for the average international wayfarer.

A Deluxe Choice

Villa Igiea Grand Hotel, salita Belmonte 1, 90142 Palermo (tel. 091/543-744), was originally built at the turn of the century as one of Sicily's great aristocratic estates. Today it's considered one of the top two luxury hotels on the island. The exterior resembles a medieval Sicilian fortress whose carefully chiseled walls include crenellated battlements and forbidding watchtowers. It was designed of the same buff-colored stone that Greek colonists used during the Punic wars when they erected a circular temple which, although heavily buttressed with modern scaffolding, still stands in the garden. Nearby, nestled amid a grove of pines and palms, is an art nouveau statue of Igeia, goddess of flowers. The hotel's bar is baronial, with a soaring stone vault. You dine in a grand and glittering room against a backdrop of paneled walls, ornate ceilings, and chandeliers. Everywhere are clusters of antiques. Accommodations vary from sumptuous suites with private terraces to rooms of lesser size and glamour. Each, of course, has a private bath and all the luxuries associated with a grand hotel. Singles cost from 220,000 lire ($167) daily; doubles 360,000 lire ($274). Apartments are more expensive. The hotel, reached by passing through an industrial portside of Palermo, sits on a cliff with a view of the open sea and a nearby shipyard.

Jolly Hotel del Foro Italico, Foro Italico 22, 90133 Palermo (tel. 091/616-5090), provides accommodations in stark moderno. Off a busy boulevard (the Foro Italico, facing the Gulf of Palermo), it invites with shafts of pale blue supporting triangular balconies. Try for the bedrooms on the upper floors or at the rear, which are quieter. One of the best of the more recent hotels (and popular for Sicilian wedding receptions), it offers a contemporary atmosphere, including a swimming pool. The public rooms are efficient, with bright colors and serviceable furnishings. In the bedrooms all is well organized, with lots of built-in pieces, private baths, bedside lamps, phones, and comfortable beds. Open all year, the hotel boasts 290 rooms, making it the largest hostelry in the city. For a single, it charges 125,000 lire ($95) daily, 160,000 lire ($122) in a double, a continental breakfast included. On the premises are a restaurant and an American bar. The Jolly also has a garden, plus a wide parking area.

The Medium-Priced Range

President Hotel, via Francesco Crispi 230, 90133 Palermo (tel. 091/580-733). Its eight-story concrete-and-glass façade rises above the harborfront quays where ferryboats dock before sailing to Naples. This is one of the better and more up-to-date of the middle-bracket hotels in town. You'll pass beneath the façade's soaring arcade before entering the informal stone-trimmed lobby. One of the most appealing coffeeshop/bars in town lies at the top of a short flight of stairs next to the reception area. There's a panoramic restaurant on the uppermost floor, plus a guarded parking garage in the basement. The 129 bedrooms are comfortably furnished, each with air conditioning, private bath, phone, radio, and TV. Singles cost 85,000 lire ($64.50) daily; doubles, 115,000 lire ($87.50).

Motel Agip, via della Regione Siciliana 2620, 90145 Palermo (tel. 091/552-

033), does for the second-class range of hotels what the Jolly does for the first: that is, it provides a modern accommodation for those who want up-to-date amenities. Typical of the Agip chain (owned by a gasoline company), this entry on the Palermo hotel scene offers moderate prices for comfort and value. It's on a wide boulevard at the edge of the city, which makes it more suitable for motorists. The rooms with private bath are compact, with well-planned features, furnished in the traditional motel style, and with comfortable beds. The 105-room motel charges 64,700 lire ($49.25) daily in a single, 117,700 lire ($89.50) in a double. There is air conditioning, on low voltage. On the premises is a restaurant, dispensing the standard Italian dishes with Sicilian variations.

Hotel Ponte, via Francesco Crispi 99, 90133 Palermo (tel. 091/583-744), is a modern building on the main dockside boulevard, one of the best of the second-class hotels near the city center. Its lobby invites with marble floors, large mood-setting murals, deep "comfy" lounge chairs, and a sense of style. All the rooms have private bath and contemporary furnishings, and many offer a balcony. You'll find numerous details usually associated with first-class hotels, including a bidet and shower in the bath, bedside lamps, and a little sitting room area. The rate in a single is 55,000 lire ($41.75) daily, rising to 85,000 lire ($64.50) in a double. Air conditioning is provided for those nights when the sirocco from Africa blows in. In the dining room you'll be served good, abundant meals.

Grande Albergo Sole, corso Vittorio Emanuele 291, 90133 Palermo (tel. 091/581-811), is a pleasant second-class hotel near the center of town. All rooms, comfortable and fresh-looking, come with phone, radio, and air conditioning. Singles range from 50,000 lire ($38) daily, twin-bedded rooms, from 80,000 lire ($60.75). Extras include a television room, day and night restaurants, and a roof garden and terrace for sunbathing.

The Budget Range

Hotel Liguria, via Mariano Stabile 128, 90133 Palermo (tel. 091/581-588), is a well-scrubbed family-run hotel which has won several awards for the quality of its accommodations. To get there, you climb a flight of steps from a busy street in downtown Palermo, passing rows of potted plants along the way. At the upstairs reception desk, Signora Lidia Grosso de Grana will register you into one of her 16 tile-floored accommodations, each of which is suitable for one or two people. Born in Genoa, she named the property after the region of her birth. Many of the rooms are awash with sunlight from the big windows, and each has a clothes press, phone, and comfortable bedding. The rooms are scattered over two floors, costing 40,000 lire ($30.50) daily without a bath, 50,000 lire ($38) with a bath, either single or double occupancy.

Hotel Sausele, via Vincenzo Errante 12, 90127 Palermo (tel. 091/616-1308), is a modern little hotel in the neighborhood of the railway station, the best in a run-down area. It's owned and managed by Swiss-born Monsieur Sausele, who has created a clean establishment in the tradition of his native land. Run efficiently, it is a modest but quite pleasant albergo. Bedrooms are furnished in a most adequate way for a good night's rest. The hotel has an elevator, garage, bar, and TV room. The lounges are air-conditioned. Room rates are 33,000 lire ($25) daily for a bathless single, 55,000 lire ($41.75) for a double without bath. With a private bath, a single rents for 42,000 lire ($32) and a double goes for 67,000 lire ($51). All tariffs include a continental breakfast, service, and taxes.

Moderno Albergo, via Roma 276, 90133 Palermo (tel. 091/588-683), is housed on the upper floor of an old-fashioned building right in the center of the city. There's an elevator to take you to the elegant reception lounge. The hotel has a bar and TV room. All the bedrooms have good beds, phone, and a clean bath with cold and hot running water. The rate in a single with bath is from 30,000 lire ($22.75) daily, 50,000 lire ($38) in a double.

Albergo Cavour, via Manzoni 11, 90133 Palermo (tel. 091/616-2759), is on the fifth floor of an old building conveniently near the central station. The rooms are spacious, and the manager of the albergo sees to it that they are well kept and pleasantly furnished, with comfortable mattresses on the beds. The charge for a single is 18,000 lire ($13.75) daily, and for a double, 24,000 lire ($18.25).

RESTAURANTS IN PALERMO

Take your pick, they come in all shapes and sizes, and in all price ranges.

The Top Restaurants

Gourmand's, via della Libertà 37E (tel. 323-431), is the best restaurant in Palermo for introducing you to the rich, aromatic cookery of Sicily. A corner restaurant in the most elegant commercial district of town, it is a light and airy room filled with original paintings and Chinese-red ceiling lattices. You'll want to admire the richly laden antipasti table before you're ushered to your table. For a first course, I'd suggest spaghetti Gourmand's or an involtini of eggplant. Fresh fish is always available, and you might prefer it grilled as a main course. However, the chef does many Italian dishes well, including veal escalope in the Valdostan style and pepper steak or, if available, roast quail. Risotto with salmon is often featured on the menu, as is rigatoni Henry IV. Meals cost from 50,000 lire ($38) and are served from 1 to 3 p.m. and 8 to 11 p.m. daily except Sunday.

Renato L'Approdo, via Messina Marinha 28 (tel. 470-103), is housed in a former aristocratic residence with a collection of antiques. Run by a husband-and-wife team, it is infused with gaiety. Some visitors are invited to explore the wine cellar, whose contents are said to rival the best of all in Italy, certainly in all of Sicily. For your food selection, consider fish marinated in refined olive oil and flavored with herbs, crêpes filled with seafood, a savory fish soup, swordfish in a sauce made of mandarin oranges, or roast goat flavored with Sicilian herbs. Meals cost from 50,000 lire ($38), and are served daily except Wednesday from 12:30 to 3 p.m. and 8 to 11 p.m.

Friend's Bar, via Brunelleschi 138 (tel. 201-401). The name, in English no less, might sound like a place run by Archie Bunker in a small town in New Jersey. In spite of that incongruity, it is one of the finest restaurants in Palermo. A meal here is considered an event by many Sicilians. Friend's Bar has become one of the sought-after places on the island, one where a reservation for one of the garden seats is almost essential to get past the bar. There is indeed a bar on the premises, although most of the emphasis is on the viands served in the dining room or on the terrace. First, you might enjoy a few of the many delicacies from the antipasti table, followed by one of the many regional specialties such as subtly flavored pastas, trailed by an array of steamed or grilled fish dishes or one of the meat dishes that have made this place so well known locally. The house wine (red) is a good accompaniment for most any meal, which will usually cost about 35,000 lire ($26.50) to 45,000 lire ($34.25) per person. The establishment, open from 1 to 3 p.m. and 8 to 10 p.m., is closed every Monday and in August. It is in a suburb of Palermo, Borgo Nuovo.

The Budget Range

Regine, via Trapani 4A (tel. 586-566), sits about a block off via della Libertà, behind a wood and beveled-glass façade. Its menu features a selection of Italian and international dishes, including spaghetti carbonara, a mixed grill, tournedos with madeira sauce, Cuban-style rice pilaf, game in season, and trenette (a type of pasta) with pesto sauce. Full meals cost 25,000 lire ($19) to 35,000 lire ($26.50) and are served daily except Sunday and in August.

There is one regional restaurant in Palermo that, frankly, deserves more acclaim than it traditionally receives. It's **Al Ficodindia,** via Emerico Amari 64 (tel. 324-214). Its decor is typically Sicilian, a rustic tavern setting for the savory viands dispensed here. The table of antipasti, displayed on an old wagon, is about the best I've encountered in Sicily, each item succulent. On my recent rounds, one diner kept going back for more and more until the waiter pleaded, "But, sir, you should order a main dish." The roast kid (caprettu o furnu) is the chef's specialty, as is a tournedos accompanied by a sauce that contains, among other ingredients, prosciutto. About the cheapest you can get by for is 25,000 lire ($19). Food is served from noon to 4 p.m. and 7 p.m. to midnight; closed Friday.

La Scuderia, viale del Fante 9 (tel. 520-323), is an appealing restaurant directed by dedicated professionals. The inside section is augmented in summer with one of the prettiest flowering terraces in town, a place sought after by everyone from erstwhile lovers to extended families to glamour queens in for a holiday. The location, surrounded by trees, is at the foot of Monte Pellegrino. The sound of falling water, followed by the tunes of a piano player, greets you as you enter. The imaginative cuisine includes a mixed grill of fresh vegetables with a healthy dose of a Sicilian cheese called caciocavallo, along with stuffed turkey cutlet, a wide array of beef and veal dishes, involtini of eggplant, risotto with seafood, veal spiedino, and many tempting desserts, one known as pernice all'erotica. Full meals cost from 55,000 lire ($41.75) and are served from 12:30 to 3:30 p.m. and 8:30 p.m. to midnight. The restaurant is closed Sunday night.

THE TOP SIGHTS

"The four corners" of the city, the **Quattro Canti di Città,** is in the heart of the old town, at the junction of the corso Vittorio Emanuele and via Maqueda. The ruling Spanish of the 17th century influenced the design of this grandiose baroque square, replete with fountains and statues. From here you can walk to—

Piazza Bellini

This square is the most attractive of the plazas of the old city. In an atmosphere reminiscent of the setting for an operetta, you're likely to hear strolling singers with guitars entertaining pizza eaters. Opening onto it is the Church of Santa Maria dell'Ammiragli (also known as "La Martorana"), erected in 1143 with a Byzantine cupola by an admiral to Roger II. Its decaying, but magnificent, bell tower was built from 1146 to 1185. Also fronting the square are the Church of San Cataldo, erected in 1160 in the Arab-Byzantine style with a trio of faded pink cupolas, and the Church of Santa Caterina, from the 16th century.

Adjoining the square is the **piazza Pretoria,** dominated by a fountain designed in Florence in 1554 for a villa, but acquired by Palermo about 20 years later.

A short walk will take you to the—

Cathedral of Palermo

On the corso Vittorio Emanuele, the cathedral (tel. 334-373) is a curious spectacle where East meets West. It was built in the 12th century on the foundation of an earlier basilica that had been converted by the Arabs into a mosque. The cathedral—much altered over the centuries—was founded by an English archbishop known as Walter of the Mill. The "porch," built in the 15th century on the southern front in the Gothic style, is an impressive architectural feature. But the cupola, added in the late 18th century, detracts from the overall appearance, and the interior was revamped unsuccessfully at the same time, a glaring incongruity in styles. In the "pantheon" of royal tombs is that of the Emperor Frederick II, in red porphyry under a canopy of marble. The cathedral is open daily from 7 a.m. to noon and 4 to 6 p.m.

The other church worthy of note is—

San Giovanni degli Eremiti

Saint John of the Hermits stands at via dei Benedettini Bianchi 3 (tel. 296-238). Perhaps in an atmosphere appropriate for the recluse it honors, this little church with its twin-columned cloisters is one of the most idyllic spots in all of Palermo. A medieval veil hangs heavy in the gardens, especially on a hot summer day as you wander around in its cloisters with their citrus blossoms and flowers.

Ordered built by Roger II in 1132, the church adheres to its Arabic influence, sur-mounted by pinkish cupolas, while showing the Norman style as well. It is open daily from 9 a.m. to 2 p.m.

In the vicinity is the—

Palace of the Normans

Palace of the Normans, at the piazza del Parlamento, contains one of the great-est art treasures in Sicily, the **Cappella Palatina** (Palatine Chapel; tel. 488-449). Erected at the request of Roger II in the 1130s, it is considered the finest example of the Arabic-Norman style of design and building. The effect of the mosaics inside is awe inspiring. Almond-eyed biblical characters from the Byzantine art world in lush colors create a panorama of epic pageantry, illustrating such Gospel scenes as the Nativity. The overall picture is further enhanced by inlaid marble and mosaics and pillars made of granite shipped from the East. For a look at still further mosaics, this time in a more secular vein depicting scenes of the hunt, you can visit the Hall of Roger II upstairs, the seat of the Sicilian Parliament, where security is likely to be tight. Visitors are taken through on guided tours. The palace is open only on Mon-day, Friday, and Saturday from 9 a.m. to 12:30 p.m. The chapel is open daily except Wednesday afternoon from 9 a.m. to 1 p.m. (on Sunday from 9 to 10 a.m. and 12:15 to 1 p.m.).

The two most important national museums follow—

Regional Gallery of Sicily

The **Palazzo Abbatellis,** via Alloro 4, houses the Regional Gallery, with impor-tant collections of traditional as well as modern art, including works by local paint-ers of the 15th century. On the ground floor is a good collection of medieval sculpture. The gallery's second most famous work is a 15th-century fresco *Triumph of Death,* in all its gory magnificence. A horseback-riding skeleton, representing death, tramples his victims under hoof. Francesco Laurana's slanty-eyed *Eleonora d'Aragona* is worth seeking out, as are seven grotesque *Drôleries* painted on wood. Of the paintings on the second floor, *L'Annunziata* by Antonello da Messina, a por-trait of the Madonna with depth and originality, is one of the most celebrated paint-ings in Italy. The palace, built in the Gothic-Renaissance style, is open Tuesday through Sunday from 9 a.m. to 2 p.m. and from 3 to 6 p.m. on Tuesday and Thurs-day, and charges 2,000 lire ($1.50) for admission. It closes at 1 p.m. on Sunday. For more information, telephone 616-4317.

Museo Regionale Archeologic

On the piazza Olivella in an ex-convent (tel. 587-825) is one of the greatest archeological collections in southern Italy, where the competition's stiff. Many works displayed here were excavated from Selinunte, once one of the major towns in Magna Graecia (Greater Greece). See, in particular, the Sala di Selinunte, displaying the celebrated metopes that adorned the classical temples, as well as slabs of bas-relief. The gallery also owns important sculpture from the Temple of Himera. The collection of bronzes is exceptional, including the athlete and the stag discovered in the ruins of Pompeii (a Roman copy of a Greek original) and a bronze ram that came from Syracuse, dating from the 3rd century B.C. Among the Greek sculpture is *The Pouring Satyr,* excavated at Torre del Greco (a Roman copy of a Greek original by Praxiteles). The museum is open daily from 9 a.m. to 2 p.m., and also from 3 to 6 p.m. on Tuesday and Friday, and charges 2,000 lire ($1.50) for admission. On Sun-day the hours are 9 a.m. to 1 p.m.

The final attraction in the city is the most bizarre of all.

Catacombe Cappuccini

At the piazza Cappuccini, on the outskirts of Palermo, the catacombs evoke the horrors of the Rue Morgue. The fresco *Triumph of Death* dims by comparison to the real thing. The catacombs, it was discovered, contained a preservative that helped to mummify dead people. Sicilians, everyone from nobles to maids, were buried here in the 19th century, and it was the custom on Sunday to go and visit Uncle Luigi to see how he was holding together. If he fell apart, he was wired together again or wrapped in burlap sacking. The last person buried in the catacombs was placed to rest in 1920—a little girl almost lifelike in death. But many Sicilians of the 19th century are in fine shape, considering—with eyes, hair, clothing fairly intact (the convent could easily be turned into a museum of costume). Some of the expressions on the faces of the skeletons take the fun out of Halloween—a grotesque ballet. The catacombs may be visited on guided tours daily from 9 a.m. to noon and 3 to 5 p.m. (on Sunday and holidays from 9 a.m. to noon only). You should donate at least 1,000 lire (75¢).

AFTER DARK

I always like to begin my evening by heading to **Caffè Mazzara,** via Generale Magliocco 15 (tel. 321-366), where you can sample Sicilian ice cream—among the best in the world—and order coffee that is the densest in all the country. Or perhaps you'll prefer to sit quietly, sipping one of the heady Sicilian wines and enjoying the piano bar. At this café you can anchor in the same corner where Tomasi di Lampedusa in the late '50s wrote a great many chapters of *The Leopard,* one of the finest novels to come out of Italy. Besides an espresso bar and pastry shop on the first floor, there's a so-called American grill on the second floor as well as a dining room, where you can order well-prepared food. If you can't find a place to eat in Palermo on a Sunday, when virtually everything is shut, the Mazzara is a good bet. It is open from 8 a.m. to 11 p.m. daily except Monday. Cappuccino costs 1,300 lire ($1) at the bar.

The world-famed **Teatro Massimo,** opened in 1897, is likely to be closed during the lifetime of this edition. In the meantime, operatic performances are given at **Politeama Garibaldi,** piazza Settimo (tel. 584-334), which was constructed in 1874. I recently saw a performance of Donizetti's *Lucia* here. It is best to have the concierge of your hotel call for seats, which (unless a superstar is appearing) generally range from 40,000 lire ($30.50) to 65,000 lire ($49.50) in the orchestra or 15,000 lire ($11.50) to 22,000 lire ($16.75) in the gallery.

One of the most elegant discos in town is **Speak Easy,** viale Strasburgo 34 (tel. 518-486). Technically, it is a members-only establishment, but most non-residents are welcomed. It is open from 10:30 p.m. to 2:30 a.m. nightly except Monday. Drinks cost 10,000 lire ($7.60) Sunday and Tuesday through Thursday, 13,000 lire ($9.90) on Friday, and 15,000 lire ($11.50) on Saturday.

MONREALE

The town of Monreale is five miles from Palermo, crawling up Monte Caputo and opening onto the Conca d'Oro plain. If you don't have a car, you can reach it by taking trolleybus 8 or 9 from the piazza Indipendenza in Palermo. The Normans under William II founded a Benedictine monastery at Monreale some time in the 1170s. Near the ruins of that monastery a great cathedral was erected.

As with the Alhambra in Granada, Spain, the **Church of Monreale** has a relatively drab façade, giving little indication of the riches inside. The interior is virtually covered throughout with shimmering mosaics, illustrating scenes from the Bible, such as the story of Adam and Eve or Noah and the Ark. The artwork provides a distinctly original interpretation to the old, rigid Byzantine form of decoration. The mosaics make for an Eastern look despite the Western-style robed Christ reigning over his kingdom. The ceiling is ornate, even gaudy. On the north and west façade of the church are two bronze doors in relief depicting biblical stories. The cloisters should also be visited. Built in 1166, they consist of twin mosaic columns, every other pair an original design (the lava inlay was hauled from the active volcano, Mount Etna). They are open daily except Monday from 9 a.m. to 7 p.m. April to September, 9 a.m. to 2 p.m. October to March (on Sunday from 9 a.m. to 1 p.m. all year), charging an admission of 2,000 lire ($1.50). It is also possible to visit the treasury and the Terraces, each costing another 2,000. They are open from 7:30 a.m. to 12:30 p.m. and 3 to 6:30 p.m. The Terraces are actually the rooftop of the church, from which you'll be rewarded with a view of the cloisters.

Food and Lodging

Park Hotel Carrubella, corso Umberto I, 90046 Monreale (tel. 091/640-2187), is one of the highest buildings in town, its terraces providing a sweeping view over the famous church, the surrounding valleys, and the azure coastline of faraway Palermo. To reach it, follow a one-lane road originating at the plaza near the church. It takes you along a serpentine series of terraces. The hotel's spacious interior is filled with semi-luxurious touches, including a black-marble bar built into the rocks of a cliff, gilt-framed mirrors, and deep and comfortable armchairs, along with scattered pieces of sculpture. In the public rooms, as well as in the bedrooms, the floors are covered with rows of Sicilian tiles hand-painted into flowery designs. Each accommodation is comfortably furnished and has its own balcony, a modern bath, air conditioning, and phone. The genial partners who own this place charge from 40,000 lire ($30.50) daily in a single, 60,000 lire ($45.50) in a double. Well-prepared meals are served in the establishment's conservatively elegant dining room.

La Botte, Contrada Lenzitti (S.S. 186) 416 (tel. 414-051). Most of the dishes served here are derived from ancient recipes of Palermo whose origins have long been forgotten. Your meal might include salmon dusted with truffles, a temptingly savory fricassée of tomatoes, mozzarella, and eggplant, or spaghetti with tuna, capers, and olives. Perhaps you'll begin with an aromatic antipasti of such local ingredients as artichokes, tuna, and shrimp. Main courses include freshly grilled shrimp and many traditional Sicilian meat dishes, with full meals costing 38,000 lire ($29). The restaurant is open from 8:30 to 10:45 p.m. Monday through Friday, from 12:30 to 3 p.m. and 8:30 to 10:45 p.m. on Saturday and Sunday. It is closed Monday and in July and August.

MONDELLO LIDO

When the summer sun burns hot, and old men on the square seek a place in the shade, and bambini tire of their games, it's beach weather. For the denizen of Palermo, that means Mondello, 7½ miles to the north. Originally, before this beachfront started attracting the wealthy class of Palermo, it was a fishing village (it still is), and you can see rainbow-colored fishing boats bobbing up in the harbor. A sandy beach, a good one, stretches for about a mile and a half, and it's filled to capacity on a July or August day. You might call it a Palermitan seaside experience. Some women travelers alone have found Mondello more inviting and less intimidating to stay in than downtown Palermo, which, for some, has a rough quality.

Food and Lodging

Mondello Palace Hotel, viale Prìncipe di Scalea 2, 90151 Mondello (tel. 091/450-001), a first-class hotel, is set behind a garden of palms and semitropical shrubs in the geographical center of the resort. Only a road separates it from the beach, yet many clients prefer the swimming pool, whose waters reflect the hotel's contemporary design of rounded corners and prominent balconies. This is the biggest hotel at the resort, and its accommodations are also the finest. Each well-furnished room has a private bath. Most guests stay here on the full-board plan, costing from 165,000 lire ($125) per person daily. Otherwise, singles cost 120,000 lire ($91.25) daily, and doubles go for 180,000 lire ($137).

Splendid Hotel La Torre, via Piano di Gallo 11, 90151 Mondello (tel. 091/450-222). From your comfortable bed you can get up and walk out onto your private terrace overlooking the sea from which the Normans came to invade. Like any Mediterranean resort hotel, La Torre is crowded during the peak summer months so reservations are important. It offers 177 well-furnished chambers, some quite spacious. All are well maintained (at least the 14 units I recently inspected with a maid who wanted to show me everything, including the linen closet). Singles cost from 65,000 lire ($49.50) daily, from 110,000 lire ($83.50) in a double with private bath. During the day there are many sports and recreational activities to occupy your time, including swimming pools, a tennis court, a garden, and plenty of games for children. La Torre is very much a family resort instead of a romantic retreat. It attracts some heavy drinkers as well—the bar opens at 9 a.m. in case you get thirsty, staying open till 1 a.m. The place is not a gourmet haven, but I've enjoyed my meals here, especially the pasta and fish dishes. The cookery is quite good, the choice is ample, and the waiters take good care of you. Expect to spend 36,000 lire ($27.25) to 52,000 lire ($39.50).

Charleston le Terrazze, viale Regina Elene (tel. 450-171), serves the best food, but only from June to September. A buff-colored seaside fantasy of art nouveau, the restaurant has spires and gingerbread detailing. It fronts the sands. The kitchen, fortunately, matches the delights of the eye. The Sicilian staff who work here add to the sense of luxury and refinement. However, it's expensive, so you should bring lots of money—at least 50,000 lire ($38) to 70,000 lire ($53.25) per person. The chef specializes in many dishes, including such favorites as melanzana (eggplant) Charleston (in my modest opinion, the Sicilians do the best eggplant dishes in the world). Try also the pesce spada (swordfish) al gratin and scaloppe Conca d'Oro. For dessert, you can have a spectacular finish to a worthy meal by ordering a parfait di caffè. For a wine, I recommend a Corvo, which comes both "blanco" or "rosso." Of course, with a name like le Terrazze it's got to deliver the mandatory terrace with a view. Hours are 1 to 3 p.m. and 8 to 11 p.m. daily.

If you want something cheaper, but also good, try **Gambero Rosso,** via Piano Gallo 30 (tel. 454-685). Some establishments depend for their identities and creative force on their owners, and this terraced restaurant with its panoramic sea view is one of them. Rosolino Gulizzi is the energetic force, personally supervising everything from the flavoring of the sauces to the table arrangements. Your meal might consist of an appetizer of lobster and shrimp, followed by paella, several stews, shrimp flambé, or other well-seasoned meats. A full list of local wines is available. Full meals, which are served to an appreciative audience from noon to 3:30 p.m. and 7:30 to 11:30 p.m. every day except Monday, range from 32,000 lire ($24.25) to 40,000 lire ($30.50).

TOURING IN THE ENVIRONS

Take a side trip east from Palermo to Bagheria, about 20 miles away, to see the **Villa Palagonia,** at the piazza Garibaldi (tel. 934-543). Built by an eccentric, deformed nobleman at the beginning of the 18th century, it has a garden full of grotesque statuary. Atop the garden wall are stone dwarfs and other freaks, some of them playing musical instruments. One of the rooms of the villa has a ceiling with mirrors creating a bizarre illusionistic effect. If you have an interest in the strange and grotesque, the villa will intrigue you. Goethe has an interesting passage about it in his travel diary. It can be visited from 9 a.m. to 6 p.m. daily. Admission is 2,000 lire ($1.50).

Cefalù

For another day's excursion, I recommend a trek east for 43 miles to this tiny fishing village, which is known all over Europe for its Romanesque cathedral, an outstanding achievement of the Arab-Norman architectural style.

Resembling a military fortress, the **duomo** was built by Roger II to fulfill a vow he made when faced with a possible shipwreck. Construction began in 1131, and in time two square towers dotted the landscape of Cefalú, curiously placed between the sea and a rocky promontory. The architectural line of the cathedral has a severe elegance, and inside are some outstanding Byzantine-inspired mosaics. Seek out especially *Christ the Pantocrator* in the dome of the apse. Capitals in the Sicilian-Norman style are supported by columns.

Before leaving town, head for the **Museo Mandralisca,** via Mandralisca (tel. 0921/21-547), with its outstanding collection of art, none more notable than the 1470 *Portrait of a Man* by Antonello de Messina. Some art critics have journeyed all the way down from Rome just to stare at this handsome work. It is open from 9:30 a.m. to noon and 3:30 to 6 p.m. daily except Sunday, charging an admission of 1,500 lire ($1.15). The museum stands opposite the cathedral.

DINING IN CEFALÙ. After the sights, the restaurants in town, frankly, tend to be mediocre, but that doesn't mean you can't eat well. I've found the best food at **Al Gabbiano da Saro,** viale Lungomare (tel. 0921/21-495). Seafood is the item to order here at this trattoria, making your way through a list of unpronounceable sea creatures. You might begin with zuppa di cozze, a savory mussels soup. The vegetables and pastas are good too. The cookery is consistent, as is the service. If you speak a little Italian, it helps. Expect to spend from 22,000 lire ($16.75). Al Gabbiano is open from noon to 3 p.m. and 7 p.m. to midnight daily except Wednesday; closed from mid-January to mid-February.

Da Nino al Lungomare, viale Lungomare 11 (tel. 0912/22-582), is a reasonably good choice for the cuisine of southern Italy and of Sicily. That means that the kitchen is in no way influenced by trends or food fads. Time-tested recipes are served here, including a delectable risotto marinara. Fresh fish is the featured item. Full meals cost from 35,000 lire ($26.50). It is open daily (except Tuesday in low season) from noon to 3 p.m. and 7 to 11 p.m. It also closes for two weeks in January.

2. Segesta

Now deserted, Segesta (41 miles southwest of Palermo) was the ancient city of the Elymi, a people of mysterious origin, although they have been linked by some to the Trojans. As the major city in the west of Sicily, it was brought into a series of conflicts with the rival power nearby, Selinus (Selinunte). From the 6th through the 5th century B.C. there were near-constant hostilities. The Athenians came from the east to aid the Segestans in 415 B.C., but the expedition ended in disaster, forcing the city to turn eventually for help to Hannibal of Carthage.

Twice in the 4th century B.C. it was besieged and conquered, once by Dionysius and again by Agathocles, the latter a particularly brutal victor who tortured, mutilated, or made slaves of most of the citizenry. Recovering eventually, Segesta in time turned on its old (but dubious) ally, Carthage. Like all Greek cities of Sicily, it ultimately fell to the Romans.

Today it is visited by those wishing to see its remarkable Doric temple, dating from the 5th century B.C. Although never completed, it is in an excellent state of preservation (the entablature still remains). The temple was far enough away from the ancient town to have escaped leveling during the "scorched earth" days of the Vandals and Arabs.

From its position on a lonely hill, the Doric temple commands a majestic setting. Although you can scale the hill on foot, you're likely to encounter Sicilian boys trying to hustle you for a donkey ride. In the peak weeks of summer, classical plays are performed at the temple.

In another spot on Mount Barbaro, a theater, built in the Greek style into the rise of the hill, has been excavated. It was erected in the 3rd century B.C.

In the car park leading to the temple is a café for refreshments.

3. Erice

On the northwestern tip of Sicily, some 60 miles west of Palermo, Erice was famous in ancient days, particularly among mariners who sailed the Mediterranean. The greatest shrine to the goddess of love stood here, attracting sailors from all over the vast sea. Erice became a beacon for vessels on the trade route from European ports to the coast of Africa. The walled town rises half a mile above the sea, a virtual citadel, looking out upon the Egadi Islands (a trio of islands off Trapani), all the way to Tunisia on the North African coast.

In recent years Erice has made some strides as a summer resort, but its facilities are very limited. It is a town of stone, and much of it still retains a flavor of the Middle Ages. Its town walls, mainly medieval, were built upon a Cyclopean base.

Unlike the case in most Sicilian towns, you escape the curse of traffic if you visit Erice. In summer you are forced to leave your vehicle outside the walls and walk through the narrow streets of the town. This is as it should be, because Erice was meant for horses and people, not cars. If you're driving, you'll reach Erice by taking one of two almost recklessly steep, curvy roads. The views are spectacular, but drivers shouldn't take their eyes off the road for a moment.

Erice was named Eryx (after Eros) by the ancients. Virgil wrote that Aeneas erected the temple to Aphrodite, but the monument was eventually destroyed by invaders in 260 B.C. and nothing remains of it, except perhaps a few dusty fragments in a museum. On the site now is a Norman castle, which is enveloped by gardens through which lovely walks are possible. The castle crowns Mount Erice.

Instead of the Temple of Venus you get a church, this one called Chiesa Matrica (Mother of God), dating from the 14th century when it was constructed with stones taken from the pagan temple. The church stands beside a tower from the 13th century, erected by the ruler, Ferdinand of Aragon.

There is a small local museum of antiquities, Museo di Erice, whose main exhibition is a head of Aphrodite, dating from the 4th century B.C.

However, it is not a specific sight that causes Erice to become elbow to elbow with tourists every summer. It is the Sicilian-Norman town taken as a whole, along with its incomparable lofty setting high in the sky.

The telephone area code for Erice is 0923.

WHERE TO STAY

Your best bet is the **Albergo Moderno,** via Vittorio Emanuele 63, 91016 Erice (tel. 0923/869-300), right in the heart of Erice. It offers only 40 bedrooms. Amenities are at a minimum, and pine pieces of furniture form the decor. The major feature is a small balcony on some of the rooms looking out over the Mediterranean. The cost is 55,000 lire ($41.75) daily in a single, 90,000 lire ($68.50) in a double. Many guests stay here on the full-board arrangement, especially in summer, paying 100,000 lire ($76) to 110,000 lire ($83.50) per person. The albergo has a good restaurant, serving seafood among other main dishes, but it's reserved for clients of the hotel. Meals cost from 32,000 lire ($24.25).

Hotel Elimo, via Vittorio Emanuele 75, 91016 Erice (tel. 0923/869-377), is a three-star hotel opened in 1987 in the center of the town near the gate to the road to Trapani. Once part of property belonging to a noble family, the hotel was prepared with careful attention to restoration of the limestone masonry, arches, doorways, windows, and sills of the original structures. The old fireplace and ceiling of the main hall, decorated with ceramic tile, can be appreciated in their original beauty. The three-story hotel has a main entrance, reception hall, waiting room, bar, garden restaurant, and kitchen all surrounding the courtyard where a staircase in 15th-century Trapanese style leads up to the roof terrace where there are a gazebo and winter garden. The 21 bedrooms, all with bath, TV, phone, and other modern amenities, can be reached by an elevator or stairs. Singles cost 51,000 lire ($38.75) daily; doubles, 82,000 lire ($62.25).

Hotel Ermione, Pineta Comunale 43, 91016 Erice (tel. 0923/869-138), is modern and well kept, about an 18-minute walk from the center of town. However, the hotel is scenically located. Rooms contain the usual amenities. In summer, I have found that it's hard to get a room here unless one has reserved well in advance. Singles rent for 57,600 lire ($43.75) daily and doubles go for 89,400 lire ($68). Half board is offered for 86,400 lire ($65.75) per person daily in a double or 97,000 lire ($73.75) in a single. The hotel offers an outdoor swimming pool from which one can enjoy a beautiful view of the valley and coast.

Pensione Edelweiss, cortile Padre Vincenzo, 91016 Erice (tel. 0923/869-420), is the budgeteer's favorite. It is a pension within the walls, but it serves only breakfast. Rooms are clean, but amenities are few. The cost is reasonable: 58,000 lire ($44) daily for a double room with private bath. If you want to book in here on the half-board plan, an arrangement is made whereby you take your meals at their restaurant, Nuovo Edelweiss, in the beautiful central square, where you can enjoy typical Sicilian dishes.

WHERE TO DINE

Near the old Norman castle looking out over the sea, **Taverna di Re Aceste,** viale Conte Pepoli (tel. 869-084), is named after a king whose memory has almost faded with the Mediterranean mists. The physical plant is modern and not particularly glamorous, although the atmosphere and the food might make it worth the trip. The emphasis is placed on seafood, which comes in a rich variety, as well as regional couscous (spelled "cuscus" in dialect) made with fish instead of lamb. Other specialties include beef and veal dishes stuffed with cheese, plus some regional desserts. The restaurant, serving from 12:30 to 3 p.m. and 8 to 10:30 p.m., is closed Wednesday and in November. Full meals cost 32,000 lire ($24.25) to 45,000 lire ($34.25).

Al Ciclope, viale Nasi 49 (tel. 869-183), is an informal restaurant directed by an energetic owner. The restaurant originated some four decades ago around the Cyclops' walls mentioned in the *Aeneid*. It specializes in seafoods, shellfish, and grilled fish. Especially good are the squid and red prawns en brochette and the fish couscous. Other dishes are macaroni with tomatoes, garlic, and basil, and veal roulades Sicilian style. The handmade cakes of Erice make a good dessert. The large menu is supplemented by a lengthy wine list. Full meals cost around 30,000 lire ($22.75) and are served daily from 1:30 to 3 p.m. and 8 to 10 p.m. The restaurant is closed from November to February. There is a large, pleasant patio.

---

4. Trapani

The western most of the main towns of Sicily, Trapani is reached by a good road from Palermo, a distance of 64 miles, or by train, a three-hour ride. It was the Carthaginians in 260 B.C. who spotted this sickle-shaped, desirable strip of land jutting out into the sea and founded a settlement there, within sight of the Egadi Isles. But by 241 B.C. Trapani had passed to the Romans. Over the years, the port was to know many conquerers, beginning with the Vandals and going on to the Arabs and the Spanish. Under the Muslims, Trapani flourished and continued to do so under Norman rule.

When you arrive on the outskirts of Trapani, you'll wonder why you bothered to come here. It is dreary and unattractively modern. Continue on, however, to the old town lying on the narrowing promontory. There you'll find a colorful port and such streets as the main one, corso Vittorio Emanuele, with its baroque façades. You can also walk along the water, perhaps traversing viale Regina Elena for a closeup view of port life. Many people are content just to walk and wander in Trapani, but if you want specific guidance in your sightseeing, pick up a map at the piazza Saturno (tel. 29-000), the official tourist office, and have the following monuments located for you.

The telephone area code for Trapani and the islands is 0923.

THE SIGHTS

Trapani is a city of old churches, including its late-baroque **duomo,** with a *Crucifixion* from the Van Dyck school. See also the **Church of the College** (Chiesa del Collegio), the finest monument left from the baroque age, with its lush decoration of stuccoes and marble inlays. Another notable church is the 15th-century **Church of St. Augustine** (Sant Agostino), erected by the Templars in the Gothic style, with a magnificent radial rose window. Restored after suffering war damage, it stands on the piazza Saturno, considered the most beautiful square of Trapani. Seek out the **Church of St. Maria del Gesù** in the Gothic-Renaissance style, with a marble canopy, the work of Antonello Gagini in 1521, sheltering an enameled terracotta, the *Madonna of the Angels,* by Andrea della Robbia. The most important church is the **Church of the Annunciation** (Santuario dell'Annunziata) from 1315. It has a bell tower and a 16th-century Fisherman's Chapel. But its main treasure stands in back of the high altar, the Chapel of the Virgin, with a Renaissance arch, the work of the Gaginis, and a statue of the *Madonna of Trapani* attributed to Nino Pisano in the 14th century.

In the newer part of Trapani stands the city's most important museum, the **Pepoli National Museum,** housed in a splendid 16th-century palazzo. Among its treasures are a *Pietà* by Naples-born Roberto di Oderisio, and a St. Francis of Assisi receiving the stigmata (c. 1530), a work by Titian. The museum also displays artifacts from archeological digs at such cities as nearby Erice and more-distant Selinunte. It is open from 9 a.m. to 1:30 p.m. Friday through Tuesday, from 9 a.m. to 1:30 p.m. and 4 to 6:30 p.m. on Wednesday and Thursday, charging 2,000 lire ($1.50) for admission.

FOOD AND LODGING

Along the shores of the Trapani peninsula, the **Astoria Park Hotel,** lungomare Dante Alighieri, 91100 Trapani (tel. 0923/62-400), is the best and most up-to-date hotel in the region, less than a mile from the commercial center. It looks like a stylized series of concrete bunkers whose rounded corners were clustered edge to edge along the sands of the beach. Inside, slabs of mottled granite combine with white walls, plants, big windows, and hi-tech accessories. The hotels offers a hatchet-shaped swimming pool, a disco, tennis courts, and a children's playground, plus an American bar. Bedrooms are outfitted with decors of sea-green tiles and big windows, each containing a TV, radio, frigo-bar, and private bath. Many lead out onto a private terrace. With breakfast included, singles cost 60,000 lire ($45.50) daily; doubles, 100,000 lire ($76).

Ristorante P & G, via Spalti 1 (tel. 47-701). Within the walls of this well-known restaurant, you'll enjoy local dishes prepared by one of the region's best-known advocates of Sicilian cuisine. Chef and owner Paolo Gallo (P & G) serves well-researched specialties, which appear on the menu in Sicilian dialect. With a bit of help from the waiters, you can order such dishes as fish soup, a savory array of seafood antipasti, pasta with pesto, a regional adaptation of couscous, grilled brochettes of various meats (often served with an orange salad), and a handful of such international dishes as shrimp with cognac. Expect to spend from 30,000 lire ($22.75) per person for full meals served from 12:30 to 3 p.m. and 8 to 10:30 p.m. daily except Sunday; closed in August.

THE EGADI ISLANDS

One reason to visit Trapani is to explore the Egadi Islands and the Island of Pantelleria (see below). Lying off the coast of Trapani, the Egadi Isles can be viewed from mythical Mount Eryx. Attracting skindivers and the adventurous seeking remote places, they can easily be visited from Trapani, especially in summer, when modern ferryboats and hydrofoils (called *aliscafi*) ply back and forth across the waters, the rides taking only a few minutes, allowing visitors to tour all three if that is their wish. For tickets, schedules, and information, go to **Siremar,** via Ammiraglio Staiti 61 (tel. 0923/40-515) in Trapani.

The largest island, the most developed, and the most visited is **Favignana,** with a port of the same name. It is known for its castle ruins and prehistoric caves. During May, it attracts visitors from all over the world, there to watch a horrible slaughter of tuna fish led into a "chamber of death." Called the *mattanza,* the tradition of rounding up the tuna is centuries old and has assumed almost religious overtones. It's a sorrowful but dramatic sight.

The island **Marettimo** is the most distant and, perhaps for that reason, is considered the most desirable and ruggedly beautiful by some. **Lévanzo** is visited chiefly by those wishing to view its Grotta del Genovese, with painted figures of man and beast from the late prehistoric period. All three islands are noted for their wild landscape and the beauty of their waters. Not yet spoiled by massive tourism, the islanders are generally hospitable, but don't expect many residents to speak English.

Food and Lodging at Favignana

Tourism facilities remained relatively underdeveloped on the island. Most visitors come and go just for the day. However, if you're seeking an accommodation, there is a 12-room inn, the **Egadi,** via Colombo 17, Favignana, 91023 Egadi (tel. 0923/921-232). At this pleasant little place, the welcome is provided by Maria and Giovanni Guccione, who will shelter you in one of their simply furnished bedrooms at a cost of 25,000 lire ($19) daily in a single, 36,000 lire ($27.25) in a double. Meals, which naturally feature fresh fish and are served only from May to September, cost 35,000 lire ($26.50). There are other restaurants on the island, but the food is best here.

THE ISLAND OF PANTELLERIA

The ancient Greeks called this remote island, lying between Sicily and Africa, Cossyra. Some nine miles long by five miles wide, it was settled in prehistoric times. From the center of the island rises the 2,600-foot Montagna Grande, a large extinct crater. It is climbed by those wishing to see both Africa and Europe from either side of the Sicilian Channel.

Known for its thermal springs, the island has a number of treatment centers, including the Bagno Asciutto or dry bath. However, most visitors come mainly in July and August to see the rugged beauty of its coastlines, its many prehistoric caves, and its cerulean-blue waters. Many islanders produce a famous local wine, and underwater fishing is common. The severity of the island's rocks and cliffs has earned for it a designation as a "lunar landscape."

Phoenicians, Romans, Arabs, and Turks all took their turn at conquering Pantelleria, but it was the Arabs who left the most lasting momentos—the farmhouses, called *dammusi,* whose white stucco domes can be seen throughout the countryside. They were first built in the 9th century by farmers wanting to be near their vineyards and fields. Some are still used as farm dwellings, but newer ones today have been built as summer residences.

Motor vessels make the connection to Pantelleria from Trapani. The trip by ferry takes 4½ hours, and departures are daily (except Sunday) at 9 a.m. (subject to change). There is a return at 2 p.m. For tickets and schedules, go to **Agenzia Rizzo,** via Borgo 12 (tel. 0923/911-104) in Trapani. There is also daily air service on **Alitalia** from Palermo, with a return flight on the same day. The flight lasts only 30 minutes and is cheaper than the boat.

Food and Lodging

The island has a limited number of accommodations for those desiring to spend the night; however, reservations are imperative. The best hotels, such as those described below, operate only from June to September, as there isn't enough business to keep them open otherwise.

The finest accommodations are offered at **Del Porto,** via Borgo Italia, 91017 Pantelleria (tel. 0923/911-257), which serves only breakfast. It rents 42 simply furnished but clean and comfortable bedrooms, at a rate of 42,000 lire ($32) daily in a single, rising to 66,000 lire ($50.25) in a double.

Le Lampare del Mursia, Hotel di Fresco, 91017 Pantelleria (tel. 0923/911-2217). Few experienced travelers from the mainland of Europe come here without at least one meal at this sun-flooded restaurant. The cuisine might be called natural. Surrounded by a decor of clear colors within one of the town's hotels, you can enjoy ravioli prepared by a local housewife, a gratinée of deep-water shellfish whose aroma usually fills the kitchen, and an array of fresh fish. There's even a local version of couscous, as well as a choice of perfectly grilled and seasoned meats. Meals cost from 30,000 lire ($22.75) and are served from 12:30 to 2 p.m. and 8 to 9:30 p.m. daily except from the end of October to Easter. You can also stay here on full-board terms of 90,000 lire ($68.50) per person daily.

---

5. Marsala

Once Marsala was the major port of Sicily, but nowadays it is known for its fortified wine, which is often compared to sherry. A walled town, Marsala evokes for many visitors a port on the north coast of Africa. Marsala was built on Capo Boeo, 19 rail miles south of Trapani, 77 miles west of Palermo. Its appearance has greatly altered over the years, and in spite of heavy Allied bombardment in 1943, there is still much left in Marsala to interest the visitor willing to overlook the dreary modern parts.

Long before it was called Marsala, the port was known to the Carthaginians as Lilybaeum when it was their major stronghold in Sicily. Eventually it fell to the Romans, who used it as a launching port for their expeditions against Carthage, ending with the Third Punic War in 147 B.C. In time it fell to the Saracens, who called it Marsa Ali or "Port of Ali." The year 1860 was a big event around here, as Garibaldi landed with some 1,000 men to launch his campaign to liberate Sicily from the Bourbons.

Marsala's telephone area code is 0923.

THE SIGHTS

One of the attractions of Marsala is the **Museo Baglio Anselmi,** a large warehouse-like building that displays a reconstructed version of a Phoenician warship, more than 100 feet long, that was sunk in the First Punic War with Carthage. The fast-moving (in its day) vessel was called a liburnian, and this galley was used by marauding pirates before its adoption by Roman and Carthaginian mariners. Visiting hours are 9 a.m. to 1 p.m. and 4 to 6 p.m. daily except Monday.

The **Cathedral of Marsala** (duomo) stands on the piazza della Repubblica, and is dedicated, ironically, to St. Thomas à Becket. Inside, look for the statuary of St. Thomas the Apostle, a work of Antonello Gagini in 1516. The cathedral was never completed.

A collection of eight 16th-century tapestries illustrating the capture of Jerusalem is displayed in the **Museo degli Arazzi,** via G. Garraffa 57 (tel. 959-903). These were presented by Philip II of Spain. The museum is open from 9 a.m. to 1 p.m. and 4 to 6 p.m. Monday through Saturday and 9 a.m. to 1 p.m. Sunday. Admission is free.

To the northwest of the town is a **Roman house** (reached from viale Vittoria Veneto), which has been excavated in an archeological zone that hardly rivals other archeological gardens in antiquity-rich Sicily. But it makes for an interesting visit as the excavations are on the site of ancient Lilybaeum, already referred to. Look for an exceptional mosaic. Visiting times are 9 a.m. to noon and 2 p.m. to one hour before sunset daily.

Nearby you can visit the **Church of San Giovanni,** with a grotto where the Cumaean Sibyl is reputed to have proclaimed her oracles, turning the site into a water-cult shrine.

Seeking to offset the high price of Spanish and Portuguese wines, such English families as Woodhouse and Ingham helped to launch the popularity of marsala wine with British tastes, including Lord Nelson. The companies of Woodhouse and Ingham joined forces with a Sicilian, Florio, when they merged under his name in 1929. Cinzano now owns the winery.

The visiting hours for the **Florio Winery,** via Vincenzo Florio 1, on the lungomare Mediterraneo (tel. 951-122), are Monday through Friday from 10:30 a.m. to noon and 3:30 p.m. to closing time. You can also make purchases of marsala wine here, including brandy. A curiosity is marsala all'uovo (with egg), which has the texture of a zabaglione.

The winery is reached by heading out the coastal road south, overlooking the sea. It's best if you speak Italian, but even if you don't you'll surely understand the automatic bottling process. Certainly the sampling of the wine is a universal language. You're also shown barrels stacked endlessly where the wine is aged, some bottles for as long as five years.

WHERE TO STAY

Accommodations are very limited, and many visitors stop off only for the day. However, if you should decide to stay over, you'll find suitable accommodations at the **Hotel President,** via Nino Bixio 1, 91025 Marsala (tel. 0923/999-333). A prominent sign indicates its position on a busy street running through town. Its functional beige façade faces a semi-enclosed parking area. Inside, the glistening lobby has floors of polished granite, a comfortable American corner bar, and a pleasantly modern restaurant. The tastefully decorated bedrooms cost 55,000 lire ($41.75) daily in a single, from 85,000 lire ($64.50) in a double, breakfast not included. Each unit contains a phone, TV, radio, private bath, and frigo-bar.

Motel Agip, via Mazara 14, 91025 Marsala (tel. 0923/999-166), a member of the nationwide chain, offers convenient, clean, and modern lodgings in a format many business travelers have begun to appreciate as one of the most trouble-free motel check-ins in Italy. Each room is tastefully but simply furnished, containing private bath and several useful features. In addition, the motel has plenty of parking space. Its 41 rooms rent for 42,000 lire ($32) daily in a single, 65,000 lire ($49.50) in a double. The restaurant is considered one of the best in the region, attracting both visitors and locals. They serve a mixed fish fry, a purée of rice with seafood, and a wide array of marinated meat and fish dishes. A full meal will cost from 26,000 lire ($19.75).

WHERE TO DINE

With windows opening onto the vineyards that grow the grapes to produce marsala, **Da Zio Ciccio,** lungomare Mediterraneo 211 (tel. 981-962), lies about half a mile from the Florio Winery. Many executives from the wine company headquarters dine here for lunch, enjoying the outstanding array of antipasti and the specialties of the house, which include large crayfish and an assortment of other seafood. The rustic decor is filled with the scents from the grill, where a variety of fish is cooked to flaky perfection. Diners equally enjoy the "cuscus" Marsala style, as well as the panoramic sea view. The restaurant is open from 12:30 to 3 p.m. and 8 to 10 p.m. every day (closed Monday during the winter). The charge for a complete meal is from 40,000 lire ($30.50) per person.

6. Selinunte

One of the lost cities of ancient Sicily, Selinunte traces its history to the 7th century B.C. when immigrants from Megara Hyblaea (Syracuse) set out to build a new colony. They succeeded, erecting a city of power and prestige adorned with many temples. But that was like calling attention to a good thing. As earlier mentioned, much of Selinunte's fate was tied up with seemingly endless conflicts with the Elymi people of Segesta. Siding with Selinunte's rival, Hannibal virtually leveled the city in 409 B.C. Despite an attempt, the city was never to recover its former glory, and fell into ultimate decay.

Today it is an archeological garden, its temples in scattered ruins, the mellowed stone, the color of honey, littering the ground as if an earthquake had struck (as one did in ancient times). From 9 a.m. to dusk daily, you can walk through the monument zone, exploring such relics as the remains of the Acropolis, the heart of old Selinunte. Parts of it have been partially excavated and reconstructed, as much as is possible with the bits and fragments remaining. Admission is 2,000 lire ($1.50).

The temples, in varying states of preservation, are designated by alphabetical lettering. Temple E, in the Doric style, contains fragments of an inner temple. Standing on its ruins before the sun goes down, you can look across the water that washes up again on the shores of Africa, from which the Carthaginian fleet emerged to destroy the city. The temples are dedicated to such mythological figures as Apollo and Hera (Juno). Most of them date from the 6th and 5th centuries B.C. Temple G, in scattered ruins, was one of the largest erected in Sicily, and was built in the Doric style.

On the southern coast of Sicily, Selinunte lies 76 miles below Palermo, 70 miles* west of Agrigento.

The telephone area code for Selinunte is 0924.

FOOD AND LODGING AT MARINELLA

The little seafront town of Marinella lies only a mile from Selinunte, reached by going along a winding country road lined in part with stone walls. In town you'll find the **Hotel Alceste,** via Alceste 23, 91020 Marinella di Selinunte (tel. 0924/46-184). After they erected the concrete walls of this hotel, the builders painted it a shade of sienna and filled its three-sided courtyard with dining tables and plants. This seasonal hotel is within a 15-minute walk of the ruins. The 26 simple bedrooms rent for 35,000 lire ($26.50) daily in a single, 55,000 lire ($41.75) in a double; or guests can stay here on full-board terms of 58,000 lire ($44) to 64,000 lire ($48.75) per person daily. Most visitors, however, stop only for a meal, enjoying a regional dinner costing 20,000 lire ($15.25) to 32,000 lire ($24.25). Open March to November.

7. Agrigento

Greek colonists from Gela (Caltanissetta) named it Akragas when they established a beachhead here in the 6th century B.C. In time their settlement grew to become one of the most prosperous cities in Magna Graecia (Greater Greece). A great deal of that growth is attributed to the despot Phalarís, who ruled from 571 to 555 B.C. and is said to have roasted his victims inside a brazen bull, eventually meeting the same fate himself.

Empedocles, the Greek philosopher and politician (also credited by some as the founder of medicine in Italy), was the most famous son of Akragas, born around 490 B.C. He formulated the four-elements theory (earth, fire, water, and air), modified by the agents love and strife. In modern times the town produced Luigi Pirandello, the playwright (*Six Characters in Search of an Author*), who won the Nobel Prize in 1934.

Like nearby Selinunte, the city was attacked by war-waging Carthaginians, the first assault in 406 B.C. In the 3rd century B.C. the Carthaginians and Romans played Russian roulette with the city until it finally succumbed to Roman domination by 210 B.C. The city was then known as Agrigentium.

The modern part of the present town (in 1927 the name was changed from Girgenti to Agrigento) occupies a hill site. The narrow streets—casbah-like—date back to the influence of the conquering Saracens. Heavy Allied bombing in World War II necessitated much rebuilding.

Below the town stretch the long reaches of "La Valle dei Templi," containing some of the greatest Greek ruins in the world.

The telephone area code for Agrigento is 0922.

THE VALLEY OF THE TEMPLES

Writers are fond of suggesting that Greek ruins be viewed either at dawn or sunset. Indeed, their mysterious aura is heightened then. But for details you can search them out under the bright cobalt-blue Sicilian sky. The backdrop for the temples is idyllic, especially in spring when the striking almond trees blossom into pink. Riding out the strada Panoramica, you'll first approach (on your left):

The **Temple of Juno** (Giunone): With many of its Doric columns restored, this temple was erected sometime in the mid-5th century B.C., at the peak of a construction boom that skipped across the celestial globe honoring the deities. As you climb the blocks, note the remains of a cistern as well as a sacrificial altar in front. There are good views of the entire valley from the perch here.

The **Temple of Concord,** next, ranks along with the Temple of Hephaistos (the "Theseum") in Athens as the best-preserved Greek temple in the world. Flanked by 13 columns on its side, along with six in front and six in back, the temple was built in the peripteral hexastyle. You'll see the clearest example in Sicily of what an inner temple was like. In the late 6th century A.D. the pagan structure was transformed into a Christian church, which may have saved it for posterity, although today it has been stripped down to its classical purity.

The **Temple of Hercules** is the most ancient, dating from the 6th century B.C. Badly ruined (only eight pillars are standing), it once ranked in size with the Temple of Zeus. At one time the temple sheltered a celebrated statue of Hercules. The infamous Gaius Verres, the Roman magistrate who became an especially bad governor of Sicily, attempted to steal the image as part of his temple-looting tear on the island.

The **Temple of Jupiter** (Zeus) was the largest in the valley, similar in some respects to the Temple of Apollo at Selinunte. In front of the structure was a large altar. The giant on the ground was one of several telamones (atlases) used to support the edifice.

The so-called **Temple of Dioscuri,** with four Doric columns intact, is a "pasticcio"—that is, it is composed of fragments from different buildings. At various times it has been designated as a temple honoring Castor and Pollux, the twim sons of Leda and deities of seafarers; and Demeter (Ceres), the goddess of marriage and of the fertile earth; and Persephone, the daughter of Zeus who became the symbol of spring.

The temples can usually be visited daily from 9 a.m. till one hour before sunset.

The **National Archeological Museum** stands near the Church of Saint Nicholas, on contrada San Nicola, and is open daily except Monday from 9 a.m. to 1:30 p.m., charging no admission. It is also open on Tuesday, Wednesday, Thursday, and Friday from 3 to 5 p.m. Its single most important exhibit is a head of the god Telamon from the Temple of Jupiter. The collection of Greek vases is also impressive. Many of the artifacts on display were dug up when Agrigento was excavated. For information, telephone 29-008.

HOTELS IN AGRIGENTO

Only a fair lot is offered, but they are compensatingly inexpensive, the best choices falling in the medium-priced range:

Hotel Villa Athena, ai Templi, 92100 Agrigento (tel. 0922/596-288), an 18th-century former private villa set in the Valley of the Temples less than two miles from town, rises from the Sicilian landscape. The grounds around it have been planted with fruit trees that bloom in January. During the day, guests sit on the paved courtyard, enjoying a drink and the fresh breezes. At night from one of the villa's windows, a view of the floodlit temples, a string of Doric ruins, can be seen. A twin-bedded room with private bath rents for 120,000 lire ($91.25) daily; a single 85,000 lire ($64.50). In a setting of gardenia bushes and flowers, a swimming pool has been installed. The dining room is in a separate building, serving both regional specialties and international dishes. In summer, it is wise to make reservations about two weeks in advance.

Jolly Hotel dei Templi, Parco Angeli, Viallagio Mosè SS 115, 92100 Agrigento (tel. 0922/606-144), in a commercial section, is a modern structure, boasting a swimming pool. Accommodations are air-conditioned and have a balcony and frigobar. In a double with bath, the rent is from 160,000 lire ($122) daily. A single with bath costs from 100,000 lire ($76). A buffet breakfast is included. The well-furnished lodgings come complete with radio and television as well. On the premises are a bar and a restaurant where meals cost from 35,000 lire ($26.50).

Hotel Tre Torri, strada Statale 115, 92100 Agrigento (tel. 0922/606-975), on the eastern approach to Agrigento, lies near the better-known Jolly Hotel in an unattractive commercial district. Yet some consider it the best hotel in town. Sheltered behind a mock-medieval façade of white stucco, chiseled stone blocks, false crenellations, and crisscrossed iron balconies, the hotel is a favorite with the Italian business traveler. A swimming pool within the small, terraced garden is visible from a restaurant. There's also a bar, sometimes with live piano music, plus an indoor pool, a sauna, and a disco. The simple but comfortable bedrooms rent for 46,000 lire ($35) daily in a single, 75,000 lire ($57) a double.

WHERE TO DINE

For a Sicilian meal, **Trattoria Del Vigneto,** via Cavalieri Magazzeni 11 (tel. 414-319), is a fine place to go after a visit to the Valley of the Temples, which is just a short distance away. Menu items include a mixed Sicilian grill, loaded with many kinds of meat, along with lamb cutlets and a flavor-packed beefsteak laced with cheese and local herbs. The welcome is sincere, and the cost of the meal, served from 12:30 to 3 p.m. and 8 to 10 p.m., will range from 25,000 lire ($19) to 35,000 lire ($26.50). Closed Tuesday and in October.

Le Caprice, strada Panoramica dei Templi 51 (tel. 26-469), is a well-directed restaurant with a loyal clientele who return for moments of celebration as well as for everyday fun. Specialties of the house include an antipasto buffet, a mixed fish fry from the gulf along with rolled pieces of veal in a savory sauce. Full meals cost 32,000 lire ($24.25) to 45,000 lire ($34.25). The restaurant is closed in July as well as on Friday from September to June. Otherwise, it's open daily from 12:30 to 3 p.m. and 8 to 10 p.m.

Taverna Mose, contrada Mosè (tel. 26-778). On Sunday afternoon this might be so crowded with everyone and his or her extended families that you'll have problems getting a seat. The rest of the week, however, a meal here can be pleasant, especially since many of the well-prepared Sicilian specialties sound like excerpts from the world's great literature. You might, for example, try the scaloppine alla Pirandello or rigatoni Moses style. You might also enjoy the mixed grill Sicilian style, eggplant with fresh basil, and penne Norma. The restaurant is about 1½ miles outside town on the road to the Valley of the Temples. It is open daily except Monday and in August, charging 30,000 lire ($22.75) to 40,000 lire ($30.50) for a complete meal, served from 12:30 to 3:30 p.m. and 7:30 to 10:15 p.m.

Fifty-four miles south from Catania you'll reach—

8. Syracuse (Siracusa)

Of all the Greek cities of antiquity that flourished on the coast of Sicily, Siracusa was the most important, a formidable competitor of Athens in the West. In the heyday of its power, it dared take on Carthage, even Rome. At one time its wealth and size were so great as to be unmatched by any other city in Europe.

On a site on the Ionian Sea, colonizers from Corinth founded the city about 735 B.C. Much of its history was to be linked to the despots, beginning in 485 B.C. with Gelon, the "tyrant" of Gela who subdued the Carthaginians at Himera. Siracusa came under attack from Athens in 415 B.C., but the main Athenian fleet was destroyed and the soldiers on the mainland captured. They were herded into the Latoma di Cappuccini at the piazza Cappuccini, a stone quarry. The "jail," from which there was no escape, was particularly horrid, as the defeated soldiers weren't given food and were packed together like cattle and allowed to die slowly.

Dionysius I was one of the greatest despots, reigning over the city at the time of its particular glory in the 4th century B.C., when it extended its influence as a sea power. But in 212 B.C. the city fell to the Romans who, under Marcellus, sacked it of its riches and art. Incidentally, in this rape Siracusa lost its most famous son, the Greek physicist and mathematician Archimedes, who was slain in his study by a Roman soldier.

The telephone area code for Syracuse is 0931.

THE SIGHTS

West of the modern town (take viale Rizzo) is the archeological garden, peppered with the three most important sightseeing attractions.

The archeological park, charging 2,000 lire ($1.50) for admission, is open daily from 9 a.m. to two hours before sunset all year (from 9 a.m. to 1 p.m. on Sunday). Closed April 25, May 1, August 15, Christmas, and New Year's Day.

Greek Theater

On Temenite Hill, this was one of the great theaters of the classical period. Hewn from rocks during the reign of Hieron I in the 5th century B.C., the ancient seats have been largely eaten away by time. You can, however, still stand on the remnants of the stone stage where plays by Euripides were presented. In the time of Hieron II in the 3rd century B.C.—a "term" that lasted through a golden jubilee— the theater was much restored. In spring the Italian Institute of Ancient Drama presents classical plays, works by Euripides, Aeschylus, and Sophocles. In other words, the show hasn't changed in 2,000 years.

Roman Amphitheater

This was erected at the time of Augustus. It ranks among the top five amphitheaters left by the Romans in Italy. Like the Greek theater, part of it was carved from rock. Unlike the Greek theater and its classical plays, the Roman amphitheater tended toward more "gutsy" fare. Gladiators—prisoners of war and exotic blacks from Africa—faced each other with tridents and daggers, or naked slaves would be whipped into the center of a to-the-death battle between wild beasts. Either way the victim lost. If this combatant, man or beast, didn't do him in, the crowd would often scream for the ringmaster to slice his throat. The amphitheater is near the entrance to the park, but it can also be viewed in its entirety from a belvedere on the panoramic road.

Latomia del Paradiso

The most famous of the ancient quarries, this was one of four or five *latomies* from which stones were hauled to erect the great monuments of Siracusa in her day of glory. On seeing one of the caves, Michelangelo de Caravaggio is reputed to have dubbed it "The Ear of Dionysius," because of its unusual shape like that of a human ear. But what an ear. It's nearly 200 feet long. You can enter the inner chamber of the grotto where the tearing of paper sounds like a gunshot. It is said that the despot Dionysius used to force his prisoners into the "ear" at night, where he was able to hear every word they said. But this story, widely reported, is dismissed by some scholars as fanciful. Nearby is the "Grotta dei Cordari," where ropemakers plied their ancient craft. The profession is still demonstrated today, but only for the benefit of visitors.

National Archeological Museum

In one of the best-arranged archeological museums in Sicily, the **Museo Archeologico Nazionale,** viale Teocrito, you can survey the Greek, Roman, and Early Christian epochs in sculpture and fragments of archeological remains. The museum also has a rich coin collection. Of the statues here (and there are several excellent ones), the best known is the headless *Venus Anadyomene* (arising from the sea). This work of art dates from the Hellenistic period in the 2nd century B.C. One of the earliest-known works is of an earth mother suckling two babes, from the 6th century B.C. Admission is 2,000 lire ($1.50). Hours are 9 a.m. to 2 p.m. daily except Monday. Last admission is at 1 p.m. Not in the monumental park but nearby are the:

Catacombs of St. John (Giovanni)

These honeycombed tunnels upon tunnels of empty coffers evoke the catacombs along the Appian Way in Rome. The early Christian burial grounds may be visited daily except Monday from 9:30 a.m. to 12:30 p.m. and 3:30 to 5:30 p.m. for an admission of 1,000 lire (75¢). Winter morning hours are the same, but afternoon visits are possible from 3 to 5 p.m. The world down below is approached from the Chiesa di San Giovanni, from the 3rd century A.D., and the present building is of a much later date. The crypt of St. Marcianus lies under what was reportedly the first cathedral erected in Sicily. The catacombs are at the end of viale San Giovanni.

THE ISLAND OF ORTYGIA

Its beauties praised by Pindar, the island, reached by crossing the Ponte Nuova, was the heart of Siracusa, having been founded by the Greek colonists from Corinth. In Greek mythology, it is said to have been ruled by Calypso, daughter of Atlas, the sea nymph who detained Ulysses (Odysseus) for seven years on the island.

Heading out the Foro Italico, you'll come to the **Fountain of Arethusa,** also famous in mythology. Alpheius, the river god, son of Oceanus, is said to have fallen in love with the sea nymph Arethusa. The nymph turned into this spring or fountain, but Alpheius became a river and "mingled" with his love. According to legend, the spring ran red when bulls were sacrificed at Olympus.

At the piazza del Duomo, the **Cathedral of Syracuse,** with a baroque façade, was built over the ruins of the Temple of Minerva, and employs the same Doric columns. The temple was erected after Gelon the Tyrant defeated the Carthaginians at Himera in the 5th century B.C. The Christians converted it into a basilica in the 7th century A.D.

The **Palazzo Bellomo,** fronting via Capodieci, off Foro Vittorio Emanuele II, dates from the 13th century, with many alterations, and is today the home of the **Museo Nazionale.** Not only is the palace fascinating, with its many arches, doors, and stairs, but it has a fine collection of paintings. The most notable is an *Annunciation* by Antonello da Messina from 1474. There is also a noteworthy collection of antiques, porcelain, and paintings. It is open daily except Monday from 9 a.m. to 2 p.m. (closes at 1 p.m. on Sunday), charging an admission of 2,000 lire ($1.50).

HOTELS IN SYRACUSE

The supply is limited, but most adequate and generally inexpensive.

The First-Class Range

The best place to stay is the **Jolly,** corso Gelone 43, 96100 Siracusa (tel. 0931/ 64-744), a member of a chain that is the Holiday Inn of Italy. You get no surprises here—clean, modern, functional rooms, short on soul but good on comfort. Rented out are 100 bedrooms, ranging in price from 115,000 lire ($87.50) daily in a single, 160,000 lire ($122) in a double. The hotel also has a restaurant, offering lunch or dinner for 40,000 lire ($30.50) and up.

The Medium-Priced and Budget Range

Hotel Bellavista, via Diodoro Siculo 4, 96100 Siracusa (tel. 0931/36-912), is hidden on a lane in a quiet residential section, surrounded by flowering trees and vines. Family owned and run, the hotel has an annex in the garden for overflow guests. The main lounge has a sense of space, with leather chairs and semitropical plants. The bedrooms are informal and comfortable, often furnished with traditional pieces. Most of the rooms have their own sea-view balcony, and all of them have either private bath or shower. The rate for a single room is 56,000 lire ($42.50) daily, and a double rents for 90,000 lire ($68.50).

Panorama, via Necropoli Grotticelle 33, 96100 Siracusa (tel. 0931/32-122), near the entrance to the city, on a rise of Temenite Hill, is a bandbox-modern, 51-bedroom hotel, built on a busy street, about five minutes from the Greek Theater or Roman Amphitheater. It is not a motel, but does provide parking space. Inside, a contemporary accommodation awaits you. The bedrooms are pleasant, and up-to-date with comfortable but utilitarian pieces. All the rooms have either a private bath or shower, and singles go for 38,000 lire ($29) daily; doubles, for 57,000 lire ($43.25). On the premises is a hotel dining room serving only a continental breakfast (not included in the room prices).

Motel Agip, viale Teracati 30-32, 96100 Siracusa (tel. 0931/66-944), has 76 rooms, each of which is comfortably furnished and well maintained, and contains several streamlined modern comforts. Singles cost from 52,000 lire ($39.50) daily; doubles 82,000 lire ($62.25). The restaurant is often visited by residents of Syracuse who consider the generous portions and flavorful specialties worth the trip. Menu items include a wide array of Sicilian and international dishes, including pastas, stuffed veal, tournedos American style, and a changing variety of fish. Full meals cost from 30,000 lire ($22.75). Open every day, the establishment lies near the archeological zone.

DINING IN SYRACUSE

Despite its understated decor, **Arlecchino,** via dei Tolomei 5 (tel. 66-386), is considered by some gourmets as the best restaurant in town. Many specialties emerge from this fragrant kitchen. These include a wide array of homemade pastas, a cheese-laden crespelline of the house, pasta with sardines, spiedini with shrimp, and a selection of pungent beef, fish, and veal dishes. Full meals range from 30,000 lire ($22.75) to 42,000 lire ($32) and are served from 12:30 to 3 p.m. and 8 to 10 p.m. It is closed on Sunday and in August.

Darsena da Ianuzzo, riva Garibaldi 6 (tel. 66-104), might not be all that much different from dozens of other seafood restaurants in town, except that the food here seems to be exceptionally good and the welcome warm. Specialties include fresh shellfish, spaghetti with clams, a wide collection of fresh grilled and baked fish, and the ever-present fish soup. A full meal, served from 12:30 to 3 p.m. and 8 to 10 p.m., ranges from 32,000 lire ($24.25) to 45,000 lire ($34.25). Closed Wednesday.

Ristorante Jonico a Rutta e Ciauli, riviera Dionisio il Grande 194 (tel. 65-540), is one of the best restaurants on the island for serving the typical cuisine and local wines of Sicily. Pasqualino Giudice is your charming host, and he offers a veranda and garden setting right on the sea, with a panoramic view (the location is about 100 yards from the Latomia dei Cappuccini). The decoration is in the typical Sicilian style. The antipasti array alone is dazzling. Superb homemade pasta dishes are served (ask one of the English-speaking waiters to explain some of the many variations or else settle for spaghetti with caviar). One of the most interesting fish dishes I recently sampled was spada à pizzaiola (a swordfish in a savory, garlic-flavored sauce). Meat specialties include polpettone (rolled meat) alla siracusana, and a delectable stew made of various fish. The dessert specialty is a cassatine siciliane. Expect to pay from 38,000 lire ($29) to 50,000 lire ($38). The restaurant, open from 12:30 to 3 p.m. and 8 to 10 p.m., is closed on Tuesday and from September 8 to 16.

Ristorante Rossini, via Malta 37 (tel. 24-317), is partially owned and operated by one of the region's most famous chefs, Pasqualino Guidice, who is also the guiding hand behind the just-recommended Jonico a Rutta e Ciauli. This home-like and comfortable enclave of regional gastronomy offers meals to 50 fortunate diners a night. The cost is from 35,000 lire ($26.50) and hours are 12:30 to 3:30 p.m. and 8 to 10 p.m. daily except Tuesday. You might begin with a selection from the amply stocked buffet table of antipasti, then select one of many main dishes, including a mousse of fish with fresh shrimp, perhaps a shellfish risotto with roast peppers and tomato purée. A twice-roasted swordfish is also a specialty. For food of this area, this place deserves a visit.

Ristorante Bandiera-da Lino, via Eritrea 2 (tel. 68-546), is ideal for those who want to dine at an old taverna, found near the entrance to the bridge leading to the Città Vecchia (old town). Restored, it is a mellow building, close to the fishing boats. It has a certain charm, and the cuisine is dedicated to the best of Sicilian dishes. A reliable dish is the zuppa di pesce (fish soup). An alternative choice is the zuppa di cozze, a plate brimming with fresh mussels in a savory marinade. Among the *asciutte,* the Sicilian cannelloni is good. The meat dishes feature a number of choices from the kitchens of Latium, Tuscany, and Emilia-Romagna. A complete meal, served from 12:30 to 3 p.m. and 8 to 10 p.m., will cost 28,000 lire ($21.25) to 40,000 lire ($30.50). The restaurant is closed Wednesday and from mid-September to October 10.

North from Syracuse for 37 miles or south from Taormina for 32 miles will deliver you to—

---

9. Catania

Ranking in growth next to Palermo, the second city of Sicily is a suitable stopover base if you're planning a jaunt up Mount Etna. Largely industrial (sulfur factories), the important port opens onto the Ionian Sea. In 1692 an earthquake virtually leveled the city, and Etna has rained lava on it on many occasions—so its history is fraught with natural disasters.

Somehow Catania has learned to live with Etna, but her presence is everywhere. For example, in certain parts of the city you'll find hardened remains of lava flows, all a sickly purple color. Grottoes in weird shapes, almost fantasy-like, line the shores and boulder-like islands rise from the water.

The present look of Catania, earning for it the title of "the baroque city," stems from the last earthquake. Splitting the city is **via Etnea,** flanked with 18th-century palazzi. The locals are fond of strolling through the **Bellini Garden,** named to honor Vicenzo Bellini, the young (dead at 32) composer of such operas as *Norma* and *La Sonnambula,* who was born in Catania in 1801.

The **piazza del Duomo** is also of interest, owing much of its look to Vaccarini, who designed the cathedral façade, the city hall, and the "Elephant Fountain" in the center. The elephant, made of lava, supports an obelisk from the East. The **Cathedral of Catania,** in which the body of Bellini was interred after its 40-year "exile" in Paris, was created by Roger I in the late 11th century, but had to be reconstructed after the earthquake.

Catania also possesses the remains of a **Greek theater** and a **Roman amphitheater,** the latter dating from around the 2nd century A.D. Both may be visited in summer from 9 a.m. to 1 p.m. and 3:30 p.m. till sunset; closed Monday.

Catania's telephone area code is 095, the same as that of Cannizzaro.

HOTELS

Accommodations in town are mediocre for the most part. Motorists may want to stay outside Catania at the seafront town of Cannizzaro, which has the most desirable hotels in the area. The distance is only 4½ miles north of Catania. I'll preview the best accommodations there before returning to Catania for those who want to stay in the traffic-clogged heart of the action.

Deluxe Choices at Cannizzaro

Catania Sheraton Hotel, via Antonello da Messina 45, 95020 Cannizzaro (tel. 095/271-557), is one of the most modern and professionally run hotels in Sicily, eager to cater to the needs of both the business traveler and the resort vacationer. Set across the road from a rocky beach, the hotel is ringed with a series of platforms, containing a glamorous collection of boutiques. Designed by a Swiss architect in 1983, its concrete and brick Le Corbusier–style façade is accented with jutting parapets and wing-shaped projections. Inside, a pebble-bottomed reflecting pool mirrors the windowed elevators as they glide along the side of a greenhouse-like atrium. The hotel's saltwater swimming pool with its adjacent bar is set into a terrace used in summer by clients of the excellent in-house restaurant, Il Timo (see "Dining in Catania"). The three-sided lobby bar is sometimes the most magnetic place along the coast. Upstairs, the 166 balconied bedrooms each contain all the modern electronic accessories you'd expect from Sheraton, as well as beautifully finished trim of lacquered birchwood. Rooms that face the sea are blue, while a handful fronting the mountains are beige. With breakfast included, singles cost 130,000 lire ($98.75) daily; doubles 192,000 lire ($146). Use of the tennis court is free, and motorists will appreciate the underground parking garage.

Hotel Baia Verde, via Angelo Musco 8-10, 95020 Cannizzaro (tel. 0951/419-522), lies only four miles from Catania and compares with a Hollywood-style deluxe residence. It's angle-shaped to provide a certain privacy for the balconies of each room. The well-furnished doubles or singles are reached from outside corridors. The furnishings are first class, the lobby being especially treated in modern, with a mixture of leather and wood. All 127 accommodations contain private bath, and the charge for a single is 145,000 lire ($110) daily; a double, 220,000 lire ($167). Full board is 178,000 lire ($135) to 225,000 lire ($171) per person. The hotel stands right above the sea and has a swimming pool for those who don't want to chance their luck on the rocks. In the restaurant, prices for a complete luncheon or dinner are 50,000 lire ($38) to 70,000 lire ($53.25).

First Class in Catania

Hotel Excelsior, piazza G. Verga, 95129 Catania (tel. 0951/325-733), is a businessperson's hotel. Opening onto a modern square, it is built with a façade of arcaded balconies branching off from the bedrooms, and each of these 161 rooms has either a private bath or shower. The hotel charges 120,000 lire ($91.25) daily in a single, 190,000 lire ($144) for a double, inclusive. All are air-conditioned, a life-saver in Catania, one of the hottest cities of Europe. The roof garden with its covered pergola is pleasant, and the bar with its terrazzo serves the purpose.

The Medium-Priced Range

Central Palace, via Etnea 218, 95131 Catania (tel. 0951/325-344), is not quite as big as the Excelsior, but it provides the same first-class style with more classic furniture. There's a definite touch of the modern about it. All its rooms have private bath and toilet, phone, and air conditioning. Most of them are quiet, on the inside hanging garden. With a continental breakfast included, singles cost 30,000 lire ($98.75) daily; doubles, 200,000 lire ($152). In the historic center, the hotel stands near the public garden and other interesting points.

Jolly Hotel Trinacria, piazza Trento 13, 95129 Catania (tel. 0951/316-993), is a chain hotel right in the heart of the city, a concoction of moderno splashed with color. Ideal for professional travelers, it is compact, comfortable, and offers fair service. Each room, public or private, is functional, but there the aesthetic story ends. Still, all 159 of the well-furnished rooms (lift-top mirror for dressing table) have private baths (showers and bidet). The charge in a single is 125,000 lire ($95) daily, 160,000 lire ($122) for a double. All bedrooms have air conditioning. The hotel also has a good restaurant. In honor of Bellini's composition, the spaghetti is "alla Norma."

The Budget Range

The **Hotel Moderno,** via Alessi 9, 95131 Catania (tel. 0951/325-309), is a preferred choice in Catania for those wanting to save money. Only a short walk from the piazza del Duomo, it stands at the end of a dead-end street, so the rooms tend to be quiet, a rare condition in noisy Catania. If your room has been renovated, chances are you'll find it pleasantly furnished and agreeable. Doubles with shower bath cost 83,000 lire ($63) daily. Singles go for 50,000 lire ($38). Only breakfast is served.

Motel Agip, via Messina 626, 95126 Catania (tel. 095/494-003), at km. 92 on S.S. 114 Orientale Sicula, at Ognina, 2½ miles from Catania, is a gap filler for those who don't want to press on to Taormina for the night. It's a tidy, compact, modern little motel. Owned by the gas company and bearing the familiar (throughout Italy) sign of a fire-breathing, six-legged beast, it offers a comfortable night's rest in a bedroom that is well- furnished and outfitted with a private bath and the routine amenities. The rate in a single room is 50,000 lire ($38) daily, 85,000 lire ($64.50) for a double, inclusive. Try to avoid the front rooms because of the heavy traffic passing by.

DINING IN CATANIA

A good choice is **La Siciliana di la Rose,** viale Marco Polo 52A (tel. 376-400). Several rooms, some in the garden, give this restaurant a hearty atmosphere, or else an intimate one. It depends on your mood. The inner rooms are more folkloric than the outer ones. In the garden you can select from fresh fish displayed in a cold glass freezer. The menu is written in Sicilian, which is not quite Italian, but the attentive waiters will help you translate it into English. The choice of platters is not wide, but copious enough. The average meal with wine will cost 30,000 lire ($22.75) to 42,000 lire ($32). The cooking is excellent. Most recently I enjoyed a typical Sicilian plate of antipasti called rigatoni maritata, large noodles cooked in a vine-ripened tomato sauce, with mushrooms and little bits of meat, a meal in itself. Fish plates are priced by weight. Try the local wine, but be careful, as it's quite strong. It has a taste similar to certain California wines. Hours are 12:30 to 3 p.m. and 8 to 10 p.m.; closed Sunday night, all day Monday, and from July 15 to July 31.

Il Timo, in the Catania Sheraton Hotel, via Antonello da Messina 45 (tel. 271-557), at Cannizzaro, is one of the best restaurants along the eastern coast of Sicily.

It's one floor above street level in this deluxe hotel, whose designers incorporated a wide staircase leading from the restaurant down to the elegant shopping mall below. Within a big-windowed decor of plants and soft piano music, you can enjoy sophisticated dishes. Your meal might include one of five kinds of risotto, a macaroni dish "embellished with fruits of the sea and mountain," pasta with flap mushrooms, fresh peas, madeira, and cream, or else tortelloni with truffles. There is a tempting array of grilled meats and a chef's special, filetto in thyme sauce. If you order fish, the maître d' will escort you to the most lavish seafood display in town, where he'll help you make a selection. A fixed-price menu costs 40,000 lire ($30.50), an à la carte dinner going for 60,000 lire ($45.50). Reservations are necessary, and before or after dinner you might enjoy a drink in the Melograno bar downstairs. Food is served daily from 12:30 to 2:30 p.m. and 8 to 11 p.m.

In the suburb of Ognina, 2½ miles from the center of town, the **Costa Azzura,** via De Cristofaro 4 (tel. 494-920), one block from the Motel Agip, provided me with my finest meal on my latest stopover in Catania. It is worth the drive from town. The food is considerably above the average one finds in Sicilian cities. Since Catania is a seaport, it is only natural that seafood be a specialty. The menu presents an array of fish dishes, including risotto alla pescatora and pesce all'acqua di mare. For a pasta to begin with, request rigatoni Costa Azzura. Among the local wines, I recommend the pale-straw-yellow Etna, which has a fresh and persistent bouquet. Villagrande is also a good choice. Expect to pay from 45,000 lire ($34.25) for a complete meal. It is open from noon to 3:30 p.m. and 8:30 to 11:30 p.m.; closed Monday and for part of August.

Il Commercio, via Francesco Riso 8-10 (tel. 447-289), is a good bet for a well-prepared Sicilian meal, served with aplomb and grace and seasoned with interesting flavorings. Fish and pasta are the specialties, items that it would be a good idea to order with one of the local Sicilian wines. Full meals range from 22,000 lire ($16.75) to 35,000 lire ($26.50). The restaurant, open from 12:30 to 3:30 p.m. and 7:30 to 11 p.m., is closed on Saturday.

Pagano, via De Roberto 37 (tel. 322-720), in the heart of the city, is considered the best restaurant in its price category, offering well-prepared meals for 23,000 lire ($17.50). Menu items include fresh pasta and peas, fish from the nearby sea, and an array of salads made with fresh ingredients. Depending on what you order, other à la carte specialties might run the tab up to 33,000 lire ($25). The restaurant is closed on Saturday and in August. Otherwise, hours are 12:30 to 3 p.m. and 7:30 to 10:30 p.m.

MOUNT ETNA

Looming menacingly over the coast of eastern Sicily, Mount Etna is the highest and largest active volcano in Europe. The peak changes in size over the years, but is currently listed somewhere in the neighborhood of 10,800 feet. Etna has been active in modern times (in 1928 the little village of Mascali was buried under its lava), and eruptions in 1971 rekindled the fears of Sicilians.

Etna has figured in history and in Greek mythology. Empedocles, the 5th-century B.C. Greek philosopher, is said to have jumped into its crater as a sign that he was being delivered directly to Mount Olympus to take his seat among the gods. It was under Etna that Zeus crushed the multiheaded, viper-riddled dragon Typhoeus, thereby securing domination over Olympus. Hephaestus, the god of fire and blacksmiths, was believed to have made his headquarters in Etna, aided by the single-eyed Cyclopes.

The Greeks warned that whenever Typhoeus tried to break out of his "jail," lava erupted and earthquakes cracked the land. Granted that, the monster must have nearly escaped on March 11, 1669, the date of one of the most violent eruptions recorded, destroying Catania about 17 miles away.

By road the approach from below is idyllic, past orange and lemon trees, as well as the vineyards from which both a red and a white wine known as Etna are made. As you near Rifugio Sapienza, the landscape becomes more rugged and bleak. Check with the tourist office, Ente Provinciale per il Turismo, at largo Paisiello 5 (tel. 095/317-720), in Catania, about the most convenient means of transportation for viewing Etna. These change, depending on conditions at the time of your visit. It is possible, for example, to take a bus departing at 8 a.m. from in front of the Stazione Centrale in Catania, taking you to Sapienza. There you can usually share the cost of a Jeep or minibus which will take you within a half hour's walk of the top. The grounds around the station evoke the setting for a science-fiction film of Earth people landing on Mars.

Because of Etna's more than 3½ miles of ski tracks and snow-covered slopes at 8,700 feet above sea level, it is frequented by skiers in winter. But even in July and August the weather will be cold, so dress accordingly.

10. Piazza Armerina

This hill town, 52 miles inland from Catania, is not a square, as its name suggests. In the Erei mountains, it is known for its baroque **duomo** or cathedral that has a wooden crucifix dating from 1485. The town also has many other baroque buildings, but is visited chiefly by those desiring to explore **Villa Romana del Casale,** a Roman villa renowned for its magnificent mosaics, lying 5½ miles to the south of Piazza Armerina on the road to Mazzarino. Dating from the 3rd or 4th century B.C., it is attributed to Maximianus Herculeus, co-emperor with Diocletian, and is open daily from 9 a.m. to 1 p.m. and 4 to 7:30 p.m. charging 2,000 lire ($1.50) for admission. In winter the morning hours are the same, but in the afternoon it opens from 2 p.m. until sunset.

These polychrome mosaics feature such themes as ten maidens in "bikinis," bathers, Roman circus sports, sea myths, a massage parlor, hunting, exotic beasts, and the "Labors of Hercules." To reach the villa, you'll need either a car or a taxi.

The telephone area code for Piazza Armerina is 0935.

FOOD AND LODGING
You can spend the night at the medium-priced **Hotel Selene,** via Generale Gaeta 30, 94015 Piazza Armerina (tel. 0935/682-254). It is the best hotel here and is rated first class by the government. Furnishings are adequate, as is the food. Singles go for 29,000 lire ($22) daily. The most expensive doubles cost 45,500 lire ($34.25). Meals are served in an air-conditioned restaurant, and drinks are available on the terrace. Expect to spend 30,000 lire ($123) for a complete luncheon or dinner, including local wine.

Da Totò Centrale, via Mazzini 29 (tel. 680-153), lies among a collection of other restaurants in a lively part of town whose noises might be augmented by the many Vespas that plague Sicily in summer. The food here is somewhat better than that of its neighbors, and might include on any given day an array of rich pastas, savory meats, and fish dishes that come from local seas. Full meals range from 18,000 lire ($13.75). The restaurant, serving lunch only, from noon to 3:30 p.m., is closed Saturday and from mid-December to mid-January.

11. Taormina

Runaway bougainvillea, silvery olive branches, a cerulean sky, cactuses adorning the hills like modern sculpture, pastel plastered walls, garden terraces of geraniums, trees laden with oranges and lemons, ancient ruins—all that and more is Taormina, Sicily's most desirable oasis.

Dating from the 4th century B.C., Taormina hugs close to the edge of a cliff overlooking the Ionian Sea. Writers for English Sunday supplements rave of its unspoiled charms and enchantment. The sea, even the railroad track, lie down below, connected by bus routes. Looming in the background is Mount Etna, the active volcano. Noted for its mild climate, the town enjoys a year-round season.

The **Greek and Roman theater** is the most visited monument, offering a view of rare beauty of Mount Etna and the seacoast. On the slope of Mount Tauro, the Greeks at an unrecorded time hewed the theater out of rock, but the Romans remodeled and modified it greatly for their amusement. The conquering Arabs, who seemed intent on devastating the town in the 10th century, slashed away at it. On the premises is an antiquarium, containing not only artifacts from the classical period but early Christian ones as well. The theater is open Monday through Saturday from 9 a.m. to 1 p.m. and 4 to 7 p.m., and on Sunday from 9 a.m. to noon and 4 to 6 p.m. Admission is 2,000 lire ($1.50).

The other thing to do in Taormina is to walk through the **Giardino Pubblico,** a flower-filled garden overlooking the sea, a choice spot for views as well as a place to relax. At a bar in the park, you can order alcoholic drinks.

The Taormina telephone area code is 0942.

HOTELS IN TAORMINA

The best in Sicily—in fact, the finest in southern Italy after you head south of Amalfi. All price levels and accommodations are offered, from sumptuous suites to army cots. Expect to be required to take half board in season.

A Deluxe Choice

San Domenico Palace, piazza San Domenico 5, 98039 Taormina (tel. 0942/ 23-701), is one of the great old hotels of Europe, converted from a 14th-century Dominican monastery, complete with cloisters. Overhauled, it almost begrudgingly boasts air conditioning and a flower-edged swimming pool. Its position is legend to discriminating travelers—high up from the sea coast, on several different levels surrounded by terraced gardens of almond, orange, and lemon trees. In the 19th century it blossomed as a hotel, with no expense spared, and was a favorite of the elite: kings, artists, writers, statesmen.

The large medieval courtyard is planted with semitropical trees and flowers. The encircling enclosed loggia, the old vaulted-ceilinged cloister, is decorated with potted palms and ecclesiastical furnishings (high-backed carved choir stalls, wooden angels and cherubs, religioso paintings in oil). Off the loggia are great refectory halls turned into sumptuously furnished lounges. While antiques are everywhere, the atmosphere is not museum-like, but gracious, with traditional upholstered chairs and sofas. Ornate ceilings climb high, and arched windows look out onto the view. Dining in the main hall is an event. The cuisine is supervised by a masterful chef. The bedrooms, opening off the cloister, would surely impress a cardinal. One-of-a-kind furniture has been utilized, including elaborate carved beds, gilt, Chinese red, provincial pieces, Turkish rugs, Venetian chairs and dressers. Behind the scenes are many amenities, including a private bath in all rooms. But staying here is expensive: from 250,000 lire ($190) daily in a single, from 425,000 lire ($323) in a double. The full-board rate ranges from 300,000 lire ($228) to 330,000 lire ($251) per person. These tariffs include service, I.V.A., the local tax, air conditioning, and swimming pool facilities. The hotel is open all year.

The First-Class Range

Jolly Hotel Diodoro, via Bagnoli Croce 75, 98039 Taormina (tel. 0942/23-312), is one of the most luxurious of the first-class hotels. Actually it was built and designed privately, and then taken over by the Jolly chain, which is as if one of the Jolly boys had suddenly married a lovely princess and brought her into the fold. The design of everything—the public lounges, the bedrooms—is well coordinated, on a high taste level. The dining room, with tall windows on three sides, is projected toward the sea and Mount Etna. If there's sun in Taormina, you'll find it here. The outdoor swimming pool is also a sun-trap; you can bathe, swim, and enjoy the view of mountains, trees, and flowers. The bedrooms are tasteful and comfortable, with well-designed furniture and the latest gadgets. The 103 rooms have private bath or shower, and many are angled toward the sea, with wide-open windows. The bed-and-breakfast rate in a single room is 120,000 lire ($91.25) daily, 180,000 lire ($137) in a double.

Excelsior Palace, via Toselli 6, 98039 Taormina (tel. 0942/23-975), seems like a Moorish palace, lost on the end ridge of the mountain fringe of Taormina. As foreboding as a fortress on two sides, the severity dissolves inside into style and comfort. The gardens at the back have terraces of scented semitropical flowers, date palms, yucca, and geraniums. The view of Etna and the seacoast below is of a rare enchantment. Renovated successfully, the hotel is managed so that superior facilities and service await all guests. The air-conditioned bedrooms have plenty of space and are decorated in a traditional manner. A single with bath rents for 96,000 lire ($73) daily and a double with bath for 160,000 lire ($122). You can swim at the hotel's seaside annex, and the kitchen staff will pack you a picnic lunch. The hotel is only open from mid-March to October.

Hotel Monte Tauro, via Madonna delle Grazie, 98039 Taormina (tel. 0942/24-402). Engineering skills and tons of poured concrete went into the construction of this dramatic hotel built into the side of a scrub-covered hill rising high above the sea, within view of the coastline. Each bedroom has a circular balcony, often festooned with flowers. The social center is the many-angled swimming pool, whose cantilevered platform is ringed with a poolside bar, dozens of plants, and comfortable deck chairs. The velvet-covered chairs of the modern, tile-floored interior are upholstered in the same blues, grays, and violets of the sunny bedrooms where Mondrian-style rectangles and stripes decorate the bedspreads and accessories. With half board, singles cost 100,000 lire ($76) to 130,000 lire ($98.75) daily, and doubles go for 114,000 lire ($86.75) per person.

Bristol Park Hotel, via Bagnoli Croce 92, 98039 Taormina (tel. 0942/23-006), is one of the all-out comfort hotels built high on the cliffside at the edge of Taormina. Close to the public gardens of Duca di Cesarò, it offers a spectacular view of the coastline and Mount Etna from most of its private sun balconies. The interior decor is amusing: tufted satin, plush, and ornate. In contrast, the bedrooms are traditional, with private bath, direct-dial phone, radio, and air conditioning. The hotel, open only from March to October, charges from 70,000 lire ($53.25) daily in a single, the cost rising to 140,000 lire ($107) in a double. Full board ranges in price from 150,000 lire ($114) per person up to 180,000 lire ($137). Meals, ordered separately, begin at 40,000 lire ($30.50). The dining room, with arched windows framing the view, offers international meals, with an occasional Sicilian dish. There's a private beach with free deck chairs and parasols, plus bus service to the beach from June 1 to September 30. The hotel also has a swimming pool, and there's a private garage.

Medium-Priced Hotels

Villa Fiorita, via Pirandello 39, 98039 Taormina (tel. 0942/24-122), one of the most charming hotels in its category, stretches toward the town's Greek theater from its position beside the road leading up to the top. Designed in 1976, its imaginative decor includes a handful of ceramic stoves, which the owner delights in collecting. A well-maintained garden is bordered by an empty but ancient Greek tomb whose stone walls have been classified as a national treasure. Bedrooms are arranged in a step-like labyrinth of corridors and stairwells, some of which bend to correspond to the rocky slope on which the hotel was built. Each unit contains some kind of antique, as well as a tile bath, air conditioning, phone, TV, radio, refrigerator, and usually a flowery private terrace. A double or single rents for 75,000 lire ($57) daily.

A swimming pool is set into an upper terrace. There's also a bar, a gymnasium, and a sauna on the premises. The tone is elegant, cordial, and alluring.

Villa Belvedere, via Bagnoli Croce 79, 98039 Taormina (tel. 0942/23-791), is a gracious old villa bathed in Roman gold near the Giardino Pubblico. In its garden is a heated swimming pool. From the cliffside terrace in the rear—a social center for guests—is *that* view: the clear blue sky, the gentle Ionian Sea, the cypress-studded hillside, and menacing Mount Etna looking as if she's about to blow her top—the same view, incidentally, enjoyed by clients at the more expensive first-class hotels nearby. The formal entrance is enhanced by potted plants and wall-covering vines, and the interior living rooms of this generations-old, family-run establishment would captivate Elizabeth Barrett Browning. The bedrooms have been restored, and all have private bath. Standard singles go for 63,000 lire ($48) daily; singles with air conditioning cost 68,000 lire ($51.75). Doubles rent for 110,000 lire ($83.50) to 120,000 lire ($91.25), the latter for air-conditioned rooms. All tariffs include a continental breakfast. The villa is open from March to October.

Palazzo Santa Caterina, via Bagnoli Croci 128, 98039 Taormina (tel. 0942/23-428), opened in 1975, and standing near the Greek and Roman theater, enjoys a convenient and tranquil position. The landscape has been enhanced with vegetation, and guests stroll about enjoying the scenery. Inside, a decorator has made a statement with bold fabrics. Everything is beautifully maintained and run, and you're made to feel at home. Only 22 rooms are offered, renting for 31,000 lire ($23.50) to 42,000 lire ($32) daily in a single, 54,000 lire ($41) to 65,000 lire ($49.50) in a double. All units contain private bath, mini-bar, adjustable air conditioning, and have a terrace. The view from many of the windows is stunning.

Villa Paradiso, via Roma 6, 98039 Taormina (tel. 0942/23-922), is a charming five-story hotel at one end of the main street of town, in the vicinity of the Greek theater and overlooking the public gardens and tennis courts. The creation of Signor Salvatore Martorana, it is a moderately priced center for those who want to live well. He loves his establishment, and that attitude is reflected in the personal manner in which the living room is furnished, with antiques and reproductions. Each of the 33 bedrooms is individually decorated, containing a balcony and private bath or shower. In high season, half board is from 99,000 lire ($75.25) per person daily, inclusive. Guests spend many sunny hours on the rooftop solarium, or in the informal drinking bar and lounge where wallflowers are rare. It's air-conditioned throughout. There's also a television room for guests, plus two elevators. In summer, prices include transportation to and from the Paradise Beach Club in Letojanni, use of sun umbrellas, deck chairs, and showers, plus changing cabins, swimming pool, hydromassage, and garden. The beach is private, and guests can play tennis free year round. The hotel is closed from November to December 20.

The Budget Range

Villa Nettuno, via Luigi Pirandello 33, 98039 Taormina (tel. 0942/23-797). What's probably my favorite budget-priced accommodation in town is in a geranium-colored villa with Renaissance-style stone trim. Visitors are obliged to climb several flights of steps after leaving the traffic of the main street leading into town. They pass beneath an archway whose keystone is carved with a grotesque stone face. The villa was acquired by the Sciglio family in 1887 and converted into a pensione by the warm-hearted but highly discerning Maria Sciglio in 1953. Guests enjoy breakfast in a garden with hibiscus and night-blooming jasmine. The dining room is like the rococo living quarters of an elegant Sicilian family. Each of the 13 attractive, well-scrubbed bedrooms contains its own modernized bath and panoramic terrace (all but two of the terraces look out to sea). Bed and breakfast costs from 25,000 lire ($19) per person daily.

La Campanella, via Circonvaliazione 3, 98039 Taormina (tel. 0942/23-381), offers an environment rich in the aesthetics of gardening, painting, and hospitality. It sits at the top of a seemingly endless flight of stairs, which begin at a sharp curve of the main road leading into town. You climb past terracotta pots and dangling ten-drils of a terraced garden, eventually arriving at the house. The owners maintain 12 clean and uncluttered bedrooms, each with its own bath. With breakfast included, singles rent for 35,000 lire ($26.50) daily and doubles go for 62,000 lire ($47).

Hotel Elios, via Bagnoli Croci 98, 98039 Taormina (tel. 0942/23-431), is built into the side of its more glamorous neighbor, the Bristol Park. Its white stucco façade juts above a narrow street a short distance below the commercial center of town, just opposite the entrance to the public gardens. The simple bedrooms are clean but offer no frills, each with a private bath and conservative furniture. Singles cost 30,000 lire ($22.75) daily; doubles, 52,000 lire ($39.50). One of the most sweeping views of Mount Etna stretches far away to the distance, a view amplified from a position on the rooftop terrace where members of the Bambara family set out iron tables and chairs.

Pensione Svizzera, via Pirandello 26, 98039 Taormina (tel. 0942/23-790), is a pleasant place to stay about an eighth of a mile from the center of town. The pen-sione is owned and operated by Antonino Vinciguerra, and his German-born wife, both of whom speak English. They charge 25,000 lire ($19) per person per day based on double occupancy. Singles pay 4,000 lire ($3.05) per day extra. An English breakfast is included in the rates. Try to get a room that overlooks the sea and Isola Bella. The funicular going down to the beach at Mazzaro is a little over 100 yards from the pensione, as is the bus terminal.

DINING IN TAORMINA

Opened in 1974, **Ristorante La Griglia,** corso Umberto 54 (tel. 23-980), is the best in town. The vestibule that funnels visitors from the main street of the old city into the interior contains a bubbling aquarium and a menagerie of carved stone lions. The masses of plants inside almost conceal the terracotta floors and big-windowed views over the feathery trees of a garden. Your meal might include a selec-tion from the antipasti display, Sicilian cannelloni, a mixed grill of meat, Venetian-style liver, Sicilian macaroni, and an involtini of spaghetti and eggplant. Full meals, served from 12:30 to 3 p.m. and 7:30 to 11 p.m. daily except Tuesday, cost 32,000 lire ($24.25) to 50,000 lire ($38).

Giova Rosy Senior, corso Umberto 38 (tel. 24-411), a rustically old-fashioned place, serves a variety of local specialties, including, for example, an array of linguine, risotto dishes, and a spiedini with shrimp and lobster dosed with a gener-ous shot of vodka. You might also enjoy Sicilian antipasti or eggplant with ricotta. You'll enjoy a view of the ancient theater, while giving your order to a member of the staff. Full meals range from 35,000 lire ($26.50) to 52,000 lire ($39.50) and are available from 12:30 to 3 p.m. and 8 to 10:30 p.m. The restaurant is closed Monday and from January to mid-February.

Ristorante Luraleo, via Bagnoli Croce 27 (tel. 24-279), is defended by a hand-ful of the city residents as being the best eating establishment in town, one that is ea-ger to offer excellent value for an attractive price. Many diners prefer the flowering ter-race, whose pastel tablecloths are shaded by the vine-covered arbor overhead. Of course, if you prefer to dine indoors, there's a not-very-large country-rustic dining room with tile accents, flowers, evening candlelight, racks of wine bottles, and a richly laden antipasti table. The grilled fish is good here, as are the pastas, regional dishes, and herb-flavored steak. Risotto with salmon and prosciutto is a specialty, as is the house tortellini and involtini siciliana. Full meals, including wine and all the extras, can come to around 45,000 lire ($34.25) per person, but many manage for much less. Hours are daily except Tuesday from 12:30 to 2 p.m. and 7:30 to 11 p.m.

Ristorante Angelo a Mare–Il Delfino, via Nazionale (tel. 23-004), at Mazzarò, about two miles from Taormina, offers a flowering terrace with a view over the bay. Both the decor and the menu items are inspired by the sea, and carefully supervised by the chef and owner, Aurelio Cingari. Mussels are a specialty, as well as house-style steak, along with involtini of fish, cannelloni, and risotto marinara. The restaurant is open from noon to 3 p.m. and 7 p.m. to midnight mid-March to October, charging 35,000 lire ($26.50) to 45,000 lire ($34.25) for a complete meal.

Ristorante Da Lorenzo, via Michele Amari 4, (tel. 23-480). Lorenzo Maffei is the owner of this clean and bright restaurant on a quiet street near the San Domenico landmark hotel. From 12:30 to 3 p.m. and 8 to 10 p.m., every day except Tuesday, you can enjoy meals which might include a fresh selection of antipasti, macaroni Norma (with eggplant), scallopine mozzarella, grilled swordfish, filet of beef with gorgonzola, and bean soup. Some of the oil paintings which decorate the white walls add an extra aesthetic to your dinner. Full meals cost from 30,000 lire ($22.75).

Ristorante U' Bossu, via Bagnoli Croci 50, (tel. 23-311). Vines are entwined around the façade of this small and crowded restaurant in a quiet part of town. Amid a pleasing decor of fresh flowers, wagon-wheel chandeliers, prominently displayed wine bottles, and burnished wooden panels, you can enjoy a meal pungent with all the aromas of a herb garden. Specialties include an antipasti from the buffet, pasta with sardines, homemade ravioli, grilled shrimp, fish soup, and grilled swordfish. Full meals, served from 12:30 to 3 p.m. and 7:30 to 10 p.m. daily except Monday, cost from 30,000 lire ($22.75).

Ciclope, corso Umberto (tel. 23-263), is one of the best of the low-priced trattorie of Taormina. Set back from the main street, it opens onto the pint-sized piazzetta Salvatore Leone. In summer, try for an outside table if you'd like both your food and yourself inspected by the passing parade. Meals are fairly simple but the ingredients are fresh, the dishes well prepared. Try, for example, fish soup or Sicilian squid. If that doesn't interest you, then go for the entrecôte Ciclope, or perhaps the grilled shrimp. Most diners begin their meal, costing from 30,000 lire ($22.75), with a selection from the antipasti di mare, a savory collection of seafood hors d'oeuvres. The restaurant, open from 12:30 to 3 p.m. and 7:30 to 10 p.m., is closed on Wednesday and for most of January.

BARS AND NIGHTLIFE

A popular spot is **Caffè Wunderbar,** piazza IX Aprile, corso Umberto (tel. 625-302). During the years he came to Taormina, this was a favorite watering hole of Tennessee Williams and his companion, Frank Merlo. It's in two areas of the most delightful square in town. The outdoor section is perched as close as is safely possible to the edge of the cliff beneath a vine-entwined arbor. I prefer one of the Victorian armchairs of the elegant interior where an impressionistic pair of sculpted figures fill symmetrical wall niches beneath chandeliers. There's also a well-stocked bar, as well as a piano bar. An espresso costs 2,800 lire ($2.20), and a cappuccino, 3,500 lire ($2.65), if you sit. Hours are 8:30 a.m. to 2:30 a.m. daily except Tuesday.

Waikiki, via San Pancrazio 5 (Porta Messina) (tel. 625-430). A gridwork of illuminated lattices stretches above the glossy dance floor of this underground disco, the only such club in the historic center of Taormina. Your first drink, including your entrance fee, costs 10,000 lire ($7.60). The club is open from 10 p.m. to 3:30 a.m. nightly.

MAZZARÒ

If you arrive in Taormina in summer, you may prefer to stay at Mazzarò, which is about three miles from the heart of the more famous resort (same telephone area code). This is the major beach of Taormina, and has some fine hotels, as reflected by those previewed below.

Mazzarò Sea Palace, 98030 Mazzarò (tel. 0942/24-004), is the only deluxe hotel in this little satellite resort of Taormina. It opens onto what is said to be the most beautiful bay in Sicily. Its modern design was completed in the early 1970s, and graced with enough big windows to let in cascades of light, as well as offer views of the coastline. Candlelight dinners are served beside the pool and a variety of folkloric shows presented for the entertainment of many guests, who are picked up at the airport in the hotel limousine. The food is served on fine china and crystal, and guests are pampered by the staff. The restaurant is named after the bougainvillea that grows in profusion in Sicily. The piano bar is a popular nighttime rendezvous point. There is also a private beach for guests. The hotel accepts clients only from April to October, offering a choice of 81 well-furnished rooms, opening for the most part onto beautiful views. It is customary to stay here on the half-board plan, costing from 225,000 lire ($171) per person daily.

Grande Albergo Capo Taormina, 98039 Mazzarò (tel. 0942/24-000), is a world unto itself, nestled atop a rugged cape projecting into the Ionian Sea. It was designed by one of Italy's most famous architects, Minoletti. There are five floors on five wide sun terraces, plus a saltwater swimming pool at the edge of the cape. Elevators take you through 150 feet of solid rock to the beach below. Bedrooms are handsomely furnished and well proportioned, with wide glass doors opening onto private sun terraces. The highest tariffs are charged from July 16 to September 15 and from April 1 to July 15. Half-board rates at those times go for 175,000 lire ($133) per person daily, based on double occupancy. Singles pay a daily supplement of 30,000 lire ($22.75). Otherwise, singles cost 131,000 lire ($99.50) and doubles run 202,400 lire ($154). You can coddle yourself in the air-conditioned rooms, enjoying a frigo-bar, plus an adjoining tile bath. There are two bars—one intimate, the other more expansive with an orchestra for dancing. The lobby blends the cultures of Rome, Carthage, and Greece, and an open atrium reaches skyward through the center. The food is lavishly presented, and is effectively enhanced by Sicilian wines. The hotel operates only from April to October.

Villa Sant'Andrea, 98030 Mazzarò (tel. 0942/23-125), stands at the base of the mountain, directly on the sea, where you can swim off its own private beach. A villa was converted into a first-class hotel. A cable car, just outside the front gates of the hotel, will whisk you to the heart of Taormina. The villa receives guests all year round. You'll feel like part of a house party. Rooms have informality, a home-like prettiness, with a winning dining terrace where you can enjoy good food. Accommodations are air-conditioned as well, with either a private bath or shower. For full board, including the price of your room, you pay 205,000 lire ($156) per person daily.

AN EXCURSION TO CASTEL MOLA

Once this little hamlet, three miles northwest of Taormina, rivaled the resort itself in importance. But it long ago retired to a happy slumber. Castel Mola is reached only from Taormina. Many visitors walk the entire goat-climbing distance, enjoying spectacular sea views and making a day of it.

Castle walls surround Castel Mola, and all the medieval fortification commands today is a view of the coast, Taormina, and formidable Etna, that repository of a thousand fearsome myths. (On my most recent visit, a guide explained that it was once called Mungibeddu by the Arabs, the name suggesting "unbanked fires and split-second fits of passion.")

Even if it weren't for that view, it would be worth coming to Castel Mola to enjoy the superb food at **Il Faro,** contrada Petralia (via Rotabile Castel Mola) (tel. 28-193). The proprietor, an older man, is handsome and charming, and inquiring if everything is pleasing. You'll see him going between the dining terrace and the inside room, filling glasses of wine, whatever. At his ristorante/bar, homemade Sicilian cookery is the specialty of the kitchen, and it's done with consummate skill. The food seems to reflect the rugged character of the people who inhabited this part of Sicily. Aromatic sauces cover the pastas; the stews are complicated, and the grills those of fruits of the sea. Of course, everyone overindulges in the wine, which makes it pretty hard to get back to Taormina without assistance. Etna has both red and white wines. Expect to spend 20,000 lire ($15.25) to 30,000 lire ($22.75) per person for a complete meal, including wine. Never make the excursion on Wednesday when Il Faro is closed. Other days, hours are 12:30 to 3 p.m. and 7:30 to 10 p.m.

12. The Aeolian Islands

The Greeks who came this way in the 6th century B.C. believed that the Aeolian, or Lipari, Islands were the home of Aeolus, god of the winds. Volcanic activity on these islands has been reported since ancient times. In Messina province, the islands cluster into a Y shape, the northern tip formed by **Stromboli**, with **Vulcano** at the southern tip. Both these islands have volcanic activity, the crater at Stromboli being the most spectacular. The largest island in the archipelago is **Lipari**, which produces a malmsey-type wine.

For the reader willing to make the journey, the islands form one of the most exciting itineraries in southern Italy. After the peak of the summer season is over, you'll have the Aeolians almost to yourself, except for the local people.

The best way to reach these islands is by a surface-skimming hydrofoil departing from Milazzo, about 20 miles west of Messina. There is also regular ferry service to the islands. Ferry schedules change rapidly, depending on the season, so you must check locally about actual departure times. By ferry, Vulcano is reached in only 1½ hours, Lipari in 2 hours. A ferry to Stromboli means that you must first go to Lipari and make connections from there. It is also possible to take hydrofoil (*aliscafi*) service from Naples. The hydrofoil is more expensive than the ferry, but much quicker.

The telephone area code for these islands is 090.

LIPARI

This is the chief town of the chain, with an important Aeolian archeological museum, **Museo Archeologico Eoliano,** housed in the former bishop's palace. The museum is open daily from 9 a.m. to 2 p.m. (from 9 a.m. to 1 p.m. on Sunday). Formed of volcanic rock, the town is framed by two beaches, Marina Lunga, which is the port, and Marina Corta.

The town is dominated by the castle on the site that was the seat of prehistoric settlements from the Neolithic to the Bronze Age and the acropolis of the Greek and Roman towns. The encircling wall of the castle is of the Spanish period (16th century), but it encloses the ruins of the Greek and Norman fortifications.

Food and Lodging

Lipari has lately seen some hotel building. The best place to stay is **Carasco,** Porto delle Genti, 98055 Lipari (tel. 090/981-1605), built directly on the beach with views of the sea and coast. Eighty-nine attractively furnished rooms are rented. Half board costs 75,000 lire ($57) to 130,000 lire ($98.75) per person daily. The hotel has a salt-water swimming pool and a nightly piano bar. Guests are received from April to the end of September.

Gattopardo Park Hotel, via Marconi (tel. 090/981-1035), has a main building constructed in the 19th century. It is nowadays surrounded by bungalows shaped in the typically Aeolian style in the midst of a large park. Open all year, the hotel is an inviting selection with well-kept bedrooms. Singles rent for 48,000 lire ($36.50) daily, and doubles cost 85,000 lire ($64.50). Guests select a seat on the terrace for dining, and the cuisine consists of typically Aeolian and Sicilian dishes, among others. The staff is always at hand to help guests organize trips by motorboat to the other islands of the archipelago. The tranquil hotel lies about a five-minute walk from a private beach. It is one of the best run in the archipelago and well recommended for an offbeat holiday.

Residence Mendolita, via G. Rizzo, 98055 Lipari (tel. 090/981-1002), is owned and run by Bernardi Antonio, who also operates Filippino's in the piazza Municipio, where you can inquire about bookings. The distance is about five minutes from the beach of Portinente. Attracting sun lovers, the apartments are equipped with the needed comforts. Prices range from 20,000 lire ($15.25) per person daily in low season to a maximum of 35,000 lire ($26.50) in high season. It's possible to stay here on the half-board plan, taking your meals at Filippino's from the à la carte menu. If that arrangement pleases you, the cost is from 45,000 lire ($34.25) per person daily in low season to 68,000 lire ($51.75) in high. It is advisable to reserve early.

Hotel Oriente, via G. Marconi 35, 98055 Lipari (tel. 090/981-1493), is a small, pleasantly decorated, recently renovated hotel about a one-minute walk from the town's main street. Edoardo Bongiorno, who speaks fluent English, goes out of his way to make his guests feel welcome and comfortable. Readers Gerald and Paulyne Lafrance of Sherbrooke, Québec, report that they found the garden in the back of the hotel a particularly delightful place to relax and enjoy drinks from the little hotel bar. The well-furnished bedrooms, all with bath or shower and phone, rent for 48,000 lire ($36.50) to 70,000 lire ($53.25) daily in a double, including breakfast.

The best restaurant on the island, and it's surprisingly good in such a remote place, is **Filippino,** piazza Municipio (tel. 981-1002), where Signor Bernardi Antonio will welcome you and feed you well, at a cost ranging from 35,000 lire ($26.50) per meal. His specialty is zuppa di pesce alla pescatora, a fisherman's fish stew that is excellent. To begin your meal, try his risotto with crayfish or squid. I also suggest maccheroni alla Filippino (freshly made pasta with eggplant, tomato, mozzarella cheese, and a dry ricotta sauce). Another delightful dish is bocconcini di pesce spada (swordfish). Local wines to ask for include Bianco Salina and Rapitala. The restaurant, open from 12:30 to 3 p.m. and 7:30 to 10 p.m., is closed Monday from October to May, and for most of November.

E Pulera, via Stradale Diana 51 (tel. 981-1158). Italian pergolas can be one of the most charming elements in a Mediterranean garden. The flowering lawn of this establishment contains an ornate version, a place where you'll probably want to linger. Aside from that, the specialties include an array of homemade pastas and a rich assortment of seafood antipasti (often laden with basil and garlic), along with a selection of fresh fish and succulent roast lamb. Perhaps you'll be in the mood for an involtini of eggplant. Full meals cost 35,000 lire ($26.50) to 45,000 lire ($34.25), served on tables tiled with pictures of the Aeolian Islands in ceramics. The establishment is open from June to October, in the evening only, from 7:30 p.m. to 2 a.m. It is advisable to make reservations, as the space is limited.

STROMBOLI

Stromboli is the most distant of the Aeolian Islands, about 50 miles north of the coastal town of Milazzo. If you've heard of it, you probably only associate it with the Ingrid Bergman movie made there during that so-called scandalous period in her life.

Throughout the year, hydrofoils run daily from Milazzo to the major islands in the Aeolians, turning around at Stromboli.

Your first impression as you approach the island is that it is simply a huge black rock jutting out into the sea. The 3,000-foot cone silhouetted against the sky is the only active volcano in the Aeolians, but its activity is more like that of a wheezing old codger than an explosive juvenile. In the late-afternoon sun, the volcanic rock reflects its orange-and-red highlights, giving the approaching visitor an exciting, almost Fourth-of-July display.

As you near the "lee" side—the part of the island away from the volcano activity—you'll see the tiny houses standing out in their glaring whiteness against the hillside. The volcanic soil is rich, and bougainvillea, geraniums, petunias, roses, and fig trees grow in profusion.

The real experience in Stromboli is outside. Activities on the island are limited to hiking, swimming, fishing, boating—and eating. You can dine, perhaps, on the terrace of a hotel, overlooking the deep blue of the Tyrrhenian Sea, with the black backdrop of the Stromboli volcano behind you. The food is always good and plentiful—freshly caught fish and local vegetables make up a great part of the diet.

If you want to get a closer look at the volcano during your stay, you can take a motor launch—the hotels usually have boats available (for a fee to be negotiated)—around the island. Fortunately, Stromboli pours its molten rock down the side opposite the inhabited portion, and it's exciting to watch the lava as it hisses into the sea. The more energetic may prefer to hike up the hillside. Guides are available for the three-hour trek.

Swimming in Stromboli is a rare pleasure. Scuba-diving is especially popular, since the waters are uncommonly calm and crystal clear. Fishing is an alternative sport, and spearfishing in scuba gear can be a rewarding experience—especially if you take your catch back to your hotel for dinner.

No cars are allowed on Stromboli—only bicycles, mopeds, and three-wheel vehicles, used by locals for transporting goods and guests.

Food and Lodging

If you're staying over, you'll have a choice of only a few hotels, really provincial inns with basic plumbing and simple but clean rooms.

La Sciara Residence, à Piscita, 98050 Stromboli (tel. 090/986-004), is the largest hotel on the island, offering 70 bedrooms. It also enjoys the most scenic position. The hotel, painted a glistening white in the often-fierce Stromboli sun, is vaguely Moroccan. Furnished with antiques in Mediterranean elegance, it stands in the middle of a park which embraces 12,000 square yards as it extends to the sea. Bedrooms have a private bath or shower, phone, and a sea terrace. Depending on the season, the cost of full board ranges from 130,000 lire ($98.75) to 160,000 lire ($122) daily. The Sicilian cooking in the hotel's restaurant is good, and you can quench your thirst at an American bar. Facilities include a saltwater swimming pool and a tennis court. Guests are received from April to mid-October.

La Sirenetta–Park Hotel, Ficogrande, 98050 Stromboli (tel. 090/986-025), has an intriguing address—"by the big fig tree." It stands side by side on the hillside with another hotel, at the center of the island, 20 yards from the sea. After a total restoration, it was upgraded to second class, with a total of 43 rooms, all equipped with private bath, shower, and phone. Each unit has a private terrace as well, and guests can enjoy the swimming pool, a solarium, two bars, and good Sicilian cookery. There's also a common room where guests can play cards or watch TV. In 1948 the hotel was the first to open, its inauguration coinciding with the filming of Rossellini's movie *Stromboli.* Now it is one of the best and most comfortable hotels in the islands. English is spoken. A guest can stay here on a full-board arrangement for 120,000 lire ($114) per person daily. A lunch or dinner, if ordered separately, will cost from 35,000 lire ($26.50). Children in the same room with their parents get a 20% reduction until they are 10 years old. Guests are accepted from April to October 20.

Villaggio Stromboli, Ficogrande, 98050 Stromboli (tel. 090/986-018), is set in a landscape of volcanic rocks and vegetation-rich gardens. It opens onto the seaside, and there is direct access to the beach. A third-class hotel, it offers 30 rooms, and each unit comes equipped with a private bath or shower. A single room rents for 50,000 lire ($38) daily, and a double goes for 70,000 lire ($53.25). An ideal place for a quiet holiday, the modest hotel has a bar as well as public lounges and reading rooms. Both classic Italian cookery and Sicilian specialties are offered in the hotel's restaurant except from November to mid-March when it's closed. Guests can relax in the sun on one of the hotel's large terraces, or ask the staff to arrange for underwater sports or excursions to the mountains and to the other islands of the archipelago.

VULCANO

According to mythology, this was the actual home of the god of the winds, Aeolus, mentioned earlier. The island is wild and desolate, attracting only the most adventurous to its rugged, rocky shores. Vulcano is the crater of a volcano that last saw action in 1890. Prehistoric sites have been discovered on the island, but the major interest is in looking at the volcanic formations, the sulfur vapors, and the hot mud flows. Instead of potentially dangerous climbing, I suggest that you negotiate with one of the local fishermen, arranging for a tour around Vulcano by boat. It's much easier that way.

Food and Lodging

Eolian Hotel, Porto Ponente, 98050 Vulcano (tel. 090/985-2152), is composed of a series of whitewashed terraces sloping gently down to the shore of a scenic bay studded with rocky vantage points. Set against dry cliffs, the hotel includes a verdant core surrounded by low-lying walls pierced with arches and wrought-iron accents. The restaurant has tables set on a tile surface open on two sides to the ocean breezes. The accommodations are attractive, simple, and graced with French doors and balconies for an aura of indoor-outdoor living. Each unit has a private bath and phone. There is no swimming pool; however, a few steps away guests enjoy the black sands of a beach. A handful of sulfurous fumaroles are near the hotel, some on the land and some in the open sea. They tend to raise the temperature of the water substantially. Rates, with full board included, range from 120,000 lire ($91.25) per person daily. The hotel is open from mid-May to September.

It's also possible to stay at **Garden Vulcano,** Porto Ponente, 98050 Vulcano (tel. 090/985-2069), which has just 30 rooms, renting them for 60,000 lire ($45.50) daily in a single, 100,000 lire ($76) in a double. The hotel, open from April to October, also has a restaurant, serving a complete dinner for 30,000 lire ($22.75).

The best restaurant on the island is **Lanterna Blu,** via Lentia (tel. 985-2287), which has a good assortment of well-prepared fish dishes, among other tempting selections. A complete meal costs from 35,000 lire ($26.25). The restaurant is open daily from 12:30 to 3 p.m. and 7:30 to 10 p.m. from May to October only.

SOUTHERN ITALY—APULIA

Known to the Italians as "La Puglia," the district of Apulia encompasses the southeasternmost section of Italy, the heel of the geographic boot. It is the country's gateway to the Orient, but more specifically, for most North Americans, the gateway to Greece from the port of Brindisi. Through it marched the Crusaders, and even earlier, the Romans, on their way to the possessions in the East.

For most foreigners, it is a little-known but fascinating region of Italy, embracing some of its most poverty-stricken areas and some of its most interesting sections (see the Trulli District). Many signs of improved living conditions are in the air, however.

The land is rich in archeological discoveries and some of its cities were shining sapphires in the crown of Magna Graecia (Greater Greece). The Ionian and Adriatic Seas wash up upon its shores, which have seen the arrival of cross-currents of civilizations and of the armies of tribes and countries seeking to conquer this access route to Rome. The Goths, Germanic hordes, Byzantines, Spanish, and French sought to possess it. Saracen pirates and Turks came to see what riches they might find.

Apulia offers the beauty of marine grottoes and caverns as well as turquoise seas and sandy beaches. Forests, wind-twisted pines, huge old carob trees, junipers, sage and rosemary grow near the sea, while orchards, vineyards, fields of grain, and vegetable gardens grow inland. Flocks of sheep and goats dot the landscape.

1. The Abruzzi

Although Abruzzo is the central region of peninsular Italy, it is considered a southern kingdom. It lies between the central Apennine chain and the Adriatic Sea, and can easily be reached from Rome on the Rome-L'Aquila–Adriatic Sea motorway. This mountainous agricultural land is symbolized by the goatskin-jacketed shepherd.

L'AQUILA

In the Aterno Valley, the capital, L'Aquila, is the best base for exploring the area, an artistic and cultural center, as well as a resort in both summer and winter.

Its **Basilica of San Bernardino** is from the 15th century. The harmonious façade—the most distinguishing feature of this magnificent building—was the work of Cola d'Amatrice. The interior is roofed by a polychrome ceiling carved from wood in the baroque style. In the right aisle is a chapel containing the mausoleum of St. Bernardino of Siena who died at L'Aquila.

The second major sight is the **castle** (tel. 64-043), an imposing example of 16th-century military art erected by the Spanish governors. Its galleries contain the National Museum of Abruzzo, with exhibitions of Roman archeological findings, plus an outstanding collection of medieval art. Hours are 9 a.m. to 1 p.m. daily. Admission is 3,000 lire ($2.30).

The **Basilica of Santa Maria di Collemaggio** is a masterpiece of Abruzzi Romanesque-Gothic art, and it's considered one of the most beautiful of the late-medieval churches of Italy. It is characterized by a façade of white and pink stone, as well as three rose windows and three portals.

Finally, the **Fountain of 99 Spouts** is connected to the legend of L'Aquila, which claims that the town was created by a miracle, with 99 quarters surrounding 99 castles, 99 churches, and 99 fountains. The fountain is said to date from the 13th century, but it was subsequently remodeled. At the time of its construction, it was one of the largest and most beautiful of the fountains of Italy.

The telephone area code for L'Aquila is 0862.

Where to Stay

Hotel Duca degli Abruzzi, viale Giovanni XXIII no. 10, 67100 L'Aquila (tel. 0862/28-341), is the most impressive hotel in L'Aquila, overlooking the city. A first-class choice, it offers bedrooms that are spacious and cheered by the use of bright colors. Many are individually decorated and often architecturally interesting. Singles range in price from 65,000 lire ($49.50) daily; doubles, 94,000 lire ($71.50). There are many public lounges as well, with comfortable overscale chairs. The best feature of the hotel is its panoramic restaurant, "Il Tetto," which is air-conditioned, offering a typical Abruzzese cuisine as well as international dishes. A typical lunch, not including wine, but with the view thrown in free, goes for 25,000 lire ($19) to 35,000 lire ($26.50).

Where to Dine

Tre Marie, via Tre Marie 3 (tel. 209-11), is the domain of the Scipioni family, who have decorated the tavern in the *caratteristico* style of Abruzzo. It offers the finest food in the entire province, and many Roman gourmets drive out just for lunch or dinner. The owner, Paolo Scipioni, proudly displays a painting depicting the Tre Marie, three legendary ladies, Cleofe, Maddalena, and Vergine. The ceiling is decoratively studded with handmade and locally painted dishes. Even your service plates are handmade, each one different. The setting is winning, and Tre Marie has been around long enough to gather a patina.

The food coming out of the kitchen is superb, featuring specialties of the region. The cuisine is rich and healthy, but doesn't betray the ingredients that have brought fame to this mountain gastronomy. For an appetizer, I suggest the local prosciutto e salame, lean and tasty ham. Worthy of praise are the pasta dishes, none more notable than maccheroni alla chitarra. This macaroni dish is so named because it is cut on a special utensil of beechwood and steel springs made by artisans. The pasta is dressed in a ragoût. For a main meat dish, I suggest involtini Tre Marie, a rolled-meat choice in a piquant sauce. Two recommendable vegetable courses are fagioli al pomodoro (beans and tomatoes) and lenticchie (lentils) alla paesana. The dessert specialty is dolce Tre Marie all'ananas. For the wine, I suggest vino rosé paesano bottiglia. For a complete meal, served from 12:30 to 3 p.m. and 7:30 to 10 p.m., expect to spend 35,000 lire ($26.50) to 45,000 lire ($34.25). Closed Sunday night and Monday.

---

2. Taranto

A seaport 44 miles west of Brindisi, 331 miles south of Rome, Taranto lent its name to both the tarantula (which haunts the hinterlands) and the tarantella, a dance that was supposed to free the victim from the spider's sting. Now a tarantella is the most popular folk dance of southern Italy, characterized by hops and foot tapping.

Taranto is reached by autostrada from Rome: head first for Naples, then cut east toward Bari and continue south until you eventually reach Taranto. The city is on the Naples-Brindisi rail connection, and traveling time from Naples is about 6 hours (another 2½ hours if you're coming from Rome). Trains arrive in the north of the city, the port area.

Taranto's telephone area code is 099.

THE SIGHTS

For the best view of the city, walk along the waterfront promenade, the **lungomare Vittorio Emanuele.** The heart of the old town, **Città Vecchia,** lies on an island, separating the Mare Piccolo from the Mare Grande. The modern city, or **Città Moderna,** lies to the north of lungomare Vittorio Emanuele.

On the Ionian Sea, Taranto is one of Italy's most important naval bases. As such, it was the first to be hit by Allied bombs in 1940. The British occupied it in the autumn of 1943.

Earlier, in 927, the Saracens swept over the city and leveled it. But before that time it was the most prestigious city of Magna Graecia, having been established by colonists as early as the 8th century B.C. The evidence of that former glory rests today in the—

National Museum

At corso Umberto 41, the **Museo Nazionale di Taranto** (tel. 22-112) offers an extensive assemblage of figured terracottas, Grecian vases, goldware, classical sculpture, coins, and Roman mosaics in all the glittering array of Magna Graecian art. You'll find Cupid, Aphrodite, a sleeping Hercules, and all the gang. Galleries exhibit important finds from the excavated necropolis at Taranto, dating from the 6th to the 2nd century B.C. Some of the pottery, originating at Corinth in the 7th and 6th centuries B.C., is among the most exceptional in the world. The designs of many of the Greek vases and terracottas would be considered sophisticated by today's standards (Picasso must have been inspired by some of the women). In Sala XII is enough jewelry to make Tiffany blush. The corridors contain figurines expertly arranged.

The museum is open from mid-June to mid-October Tuesday through Saturday from 9 a.m. to 2 p.m. and 3:30 to 7 p.m.; on Sunday and Monday, it is open only from 9 a.m. to 2 p.m. In winter hours are curtailed: it is open daily from 9 a.m. to 2 p.m. (closes at 1 p.m. on Sunday). Admission is 3,000 lire ($2.30).

HOTELS IN TARANTO

The choice is limited. Budget accommodations, in fact, may be impossible to obtain. Even if you obtain a room in a third- or fourth-class hotel, especially those around the waterfront, you may wish you hadn't. Many of these hotels are unsafe.

Proceed with caution in Taranto. Make sure you have a reservation before contemplating Taranto for an overnight stay.

The First-Class Range

Hotel Delfino, viale Virgilio 66, 74100 Taranto (tel. 099/32-05), stands on the waterfront, much like a beach club, with a swimming pool and garden overlooking the sea. It, along with the Palace (see below), is the best place to stay in Taranto. The magnet is the tile sundeck, with its garden furniture and potted semitropical plants. There's a cozy country-style drinking lounge and bar, with ladderback chairs and wood paneling. The dining room serves excellent fish dishes (try Taranto oysters) in an attractive setting of paneled pillars and sea-view windows. A typical double room offers tile floors, wood-grained built-in furniture, and armchairs in front of the view window and balcony. Each bedroom has its own bath, and the single rooms maintain the same comfort level. The 198-room hotel charges 90,000 lire ($68.50) daily in a single, 132,000 lire ($100) in a double, including air conditioning, service, and taxes.

Hotel Palace, viale Virgilio 10, 74100 Taranto (tel. 099/94-771), is preferred by many visitors over the Delfino. A first-class hotel, it lies at the eastern end of the lungomare Vittorio Emanuele III, opening onto the Mare Grande. The hotel offers 73 attractively furnished rooms, each with private shower (no tub), phone, and other thoughtful amenities. Rates in a single begin at 90,000 lire ($68.50) daily, 131,000 lire ($99.50) in a double. The appointments are contemporary in tasteful tones, and the Palace operates both a restaurant, bar, and café.

Park Hotel Mar Grande, viale Virgilio 90, 74100 Taranto (tel. 099/330-861), is even larger than the Palace, with which it competes. Its location, although on the same street, is much farther from the center. Most of its 93 well-furnished bedrooms open onto sea views. Furnishings are tasteful, and the rooms offer comfort, convenience, and cleanliness. Rates are 83,000 lire ($63) daily in a single, 125,000 lire ($95) in a double, most reasonable considering what you get. In summer, one of the hotel's most popular features is an outdoor swimming pool, and there is a year-round restaurant serving meals daily except Tuesday, costing from 35,000 lire ($26.50).

The Medium-Priced Range

Hotel Plaza, via d'Aquino 46, 74100 Taranto (tel. 099/91-925), is my choice for those who want some style with their comforts. This modern 112-bedroom establishment opens onto a pleasant main square, with each chamber possessing its own balcony. Inside, it's a forest of shiny marble, with classic furnishings, a haven for those wanting a dignified background and contemporary amenities. The bedrooms are well maintained, with coordinated furnishings and fabrics. Air conditioning, phone, and private bath with shower and bidet complete the picture. Singles cost 66,000 lire ($50.25) daily. A double with shower or bath goes for 85,000 lire ($64.50).

Hotel President, via Campania 136, 74100 Taranto (tel. 099/32-07), is a suitable choice and a good bargain in its middle-bracket price range. Modern and functional, it lies outside the center, offering 115 bedrooms with bath and TV at a cost of 62,500 lire ($47.50) daily in a single, 88,300 lire ($67) in a double. The hotel doesn't have a restaurant, but does offer breakfast.

The Budget Range

If you can get in, the **Hotel La Spezia,** via La Spezia 23, 74100 Taranto (tel. 099/337-950), is about the only acceptable budget accommodation in Taranto. And it's no prize winner, but it does offer 28 adequately furnished rooms, each with private bath. The cost is 42,000 lire ($32) daily in a single, 70,000 lire ($53.25) in a double. The hotel has no restaurant, but does serve a continental breakfast, which is included in the rates.

RESTAURANTS IN TARANTO

The leading restaurant of Taranto, **Al Gambero,** vico del Ponte 4, (tel. 411-190), is devoted, of course, to the world of fish dishes (Taranto is famous for its oysters and black mussels). It overlooks the bobbing boats in the harbor and the fish market of the old city. Diners have a choice of al fresco tables or the inside rooms of this big, two-story restaurant. The decor is enlivened by a collection of contemporary paintings. Two specialties make excellent beginnings. One is antipasti frutti di mare; the other, spaghetti al Gambero. Expect to pay 30,000 lire ($22.75) to 43,000 lire ($32.75) for a complete meal, including the local wine. Closed Monday and in November, but open otherwise from 12:30 to 3 p.m. and 7:30 to 10:30 p.m.

Nuova Lampara, viale Junio 198 (tel. 531-051). In clement weather, you might select a seat on the panoramic veranda where your view of the sea will be balanced by the visual display of the well-stocked antipasti table. In its center, a splashing fountain adds a grace note to one of the most elegant and spacious restaurants in town. House specialties include pappardelle with lobster, macaroni with mussels, seafood-flavored risotto, and spaghetti marinara. Fish comes in many concoctions, followed by a homemade dessert, which a French citizen might consider an exalted version of a millefeuille. Full meals, costing 30,000 lire ($22.75) to 50,000 lire ($38), are served from 12:30 to 3 p.m. and 7:30 to 10 p.m. daily except Monday. The restaurant lies outside the center in the satellite community of San Vito.

All'Assassino, lungomare Vittorio Emanuele II no. 29 (tel. 92-041), offers a panoramic view over the water and a wide range of Italian dishes, emphasizing regional specialties. The house spaghetti and the spaghetti marinara are good menu choices. Closed Sunday, the establishment charges 35,000 lire ($26.50) for a full meal served from 12:30 to 3 p.m. and 7:30 to 10 p.m.

---

3. Brindisi

The Italian word *brindisi* has entered the language of the world as a toast in 19th-century operas, such as Verdi's *La Traviata*. It is, of course, a major seaport on the Adriatic, used in ancient times as well as now as a gateway to Greece and such other points east as Israel and Turkey.

Known to the Romans as Brundisium, it was the terminus of the Appian Way, a fact noted at the harbor by a commemorative column crowned with carvings of the deities. Many famous Romans passed through here: Augustus and Marc Anthony to make peace, Cicero to write of it, and Virgil to die in 19 B.C. As an important seaport, it figured in many of the historical movements of Europe, such as the Crusades. In more recent times, it was a strategic Adriatic port in both world wars, falling to the Allies in the wake of the late-summer invasion in 1943.

Incidentally, some Brindisi food specialties that I've chosen not to recommend include gnummarieddi (goat entrails in envelopes, spit cooked) and stacchiodde (pig ears covered with tomato sauce).

Brindisi's telephone area code is 0831.

HOTELS

With a small courtyard, the **Internazionale,** lungomare Regina Margherita 26, 72100 Brindisi (tel. 0831/23-475), is like a modest palace, on the harbor in view of the departing and arriving vessels. It has been updated, yet still attracts those who favor an old-fashioned ambience. The entrance lobby has a vaulted ceiling and arches dividing it into various areas. In spite of the architecture, the furnishings are modern. The larger bedrooms have ornate paneled doors and marble fireplaces, but the furnishings are a mishmash. However, there is plenty of comfort. In rooms with private bath, the single rate is 67,000 lire ($51) daily, 100,000 lire ($76) in a double. The restaurant provides modest fish dishes. The Internazionale is only 400 yards from the main pier for car-ferries to Greece, and is 300 yards from the Maritime Station Building where liners dock en route to Mediterranean ports, Africa, India, and the Far East.

Hotel Majestic, corso Umberto I, no. 151, 72100 Brindisi (tel. 0831/222-941), is another first-class hotel in Brindisi, a total contrast to the antiquated Internazionale. It's so modern, in fact, that it tends to be a bit sterile. The popular chain hotel is right on the station plaza. Between boats it provides comfort. There is a good-size restaurant and grill on the premises, plus a lounge. Bedrooms contain private baths, satellite TVs, taped music, frigo-bars, phones, and air conditioning. In high season, singles cost 82,000 lire ($62.25) daily, and doubles go for 130,000 lire ($98.75), these tariffs including a buffet breakfast, service, and taxes.

Hotel Mediterraneo, viale Aldo Moro 70, 72100 Brindisi (tel. 0831/82-811), just outside the center, is considered "third best" in Brindisi. Modern, fairly comfortable, it offers 68 presentable rooms, each with bath, at a rate of 73,000 lire ($55.50) daily in a single, 105,000 lire ($87.50) in a double. The hotel also has a good restaurant, serving tasty seafood and other dishes daily, with meals costing from 25,000 lire ($19).

Hotel L'Approdo, via dei Mare 54, 72100 Brindisi (tel. 0831/529-667), is in the center of the city, a short walk from the sea. The hotel rents 23 rooms, all with shower and toilet. Prices for the adequately furnished units are 56,800 lire ($43.25) daily in a single, 79,500 lire ($60.50) in a double. The hotel has a restaurant, where a meal costs about 20,000 lire ($15.25). This is a good place to stay if you're waiting to catch the ferryboat to Greece.

DINING IN BRINDISI

The number-one choice is **La Lanterna,** via Tarantini 14-18 (tel. 24-950), whose walls were originally built as an inn in the 1400s. Set near the piazza Vittorio, near the center of town, it lies within a few paces of its own elegant garden. Along with a well-chosen collection of wines, it specializes in seafood. It also features a long array of different pastas in savory sauces. The risotto with seafood enjoys success, as does the crayfish in orange sauce. The kitchen also turns out a number of cream-based soups, some of which are laced with cognac. Full meals cost 40,000 lire ($30.75) to 50,000 lire ($38), and service is daily except Sunday from 12:30 to 2:30 p.m. and 8 to 11:30 p.m.

In the heart of the oldest part of the city lies **La Nassa,** via Colonne 51 (tel. 26-005). This restaurant is housed between the masonry walls of what used to be the stables for a 17th-century palazzo. Menu specialties change frequently, but you're likely to find exotic forms of pasta, as well as a well-prepared variety of fish (the mixed grill is very tasty), along with meats, fresh vegetables, and desserts. Full meals, served from 12:30 to 3 p.m. and 7:30 to 10 p.m. every day except Monday, range upward from 35,000 lire ($26.50). The location is near the southern terminus of the Appian Way, in the vicinity of the ancient Roman column.

Osteria Penny, piazza Eugelberto Dionisi 5-6 (tel. 223-013), is a pleasant restaurant filling the space between walls of an 18th-century palazzo. Under a stone ceiling, clients enjoy all the fruits of the labor of the owner. Menu specialties include fish of almost every description—grilled, baked, or steamed—along with several kinds of pungent pasta, many flavored with seafood. Serving from 12:30 to 3 p.m. and 7:30 to 10 p.m., it is closed Sunday night, all day Monday, and from mid-August to early September. The establishment charges from 38,000 lire ($29) for a meal.

Forty miles northwest of Brindisi is the heart of the—

4. Trulli District

The center of the area is the little village of **Alberobello,** a colony of beehive houses called *trullo*. What is a *trullo*? Unique in Europe, the houses are white-washed and characterized by their conical roofs of soil-colored stones. Often a house will have more than one of these small cupolas, even a second story, most often reached by a ladder and used for sleeping.

The narrow cobbled streets of what must be Italy's most fantastic village take you past *trullo* after *trullo*. The total effect is one of unreality, a feeling enhanced by the strange markings on the roofs, symbols whose meaning is lost to history. You can walk through the heart of the harmonious little settlement, perhaps even take a peek inside one or two if an invitation is forthcoming. The denizens of the town aren't averse to earning extra lire, even if it means having a stranger poking around inside their casa.

The telephone area code for the Trulli District is 080.

WHERE TO STAY

In what is almost a village unto itself, **Dei Trulli,** via Cadore 28, 70011 Alberobello (tel. 080/721-130), offers visitors unique living in one-of-a-kind beehive houses. Modern plumbing and appropriate furnishings have been installed in each *trullo,* affording guests an opportunity to go native. You sleep in a bungalow that may have one, two, even three cones—circular buildings wedged together in the Siamese fashion. One will be your entry way with bath, another the bedroom, and a third the sitting and dining rooms with a brick fireplace. All double rooms contain private bath, and couples pay from 115,000 lire ($87.50) per person nightly for half board. The cuisine is interesting, especially a regional veal stew called la pignata. It's served in individual ceramic pots. The restaurant also serves an intriguing red Primotivo wine from Turi.

Astoria, viale Bari 11, 70011 Alberobello (tel. 080/721-190), is an intimate second-class hotel run in a personal way. In a village dedicated almost totally to the *trulli,* it is a contemporary place at which to stay. Four floors high, the building contains two elevators. The tone here is oriented toward functional design and decor. The lobby is tasteful, with marble floors, wall panels, and a bar area of wood, brass, and wrought iron. The bedrooms, each with its own bath, are furnished in a utilitarian manner, with matching wood pieces and combination chests of drawers with lift-top mirrors that convert to dressing tables. The rate for a single room is from 45,000 lire ($34.25) daily, from 63,000 lire ($48) in a double. The fresh and airy dining room offers good home-cooking, including the wines of Apulia. Meals cost from 30,000 lire ($22.75).

WHERE TO DINE

A peaceful place, **Cucina dei Trulli,** piazza San Ferdinando 31 (tel. 721-179), is housed in an old building with a rounded ceiling, white walls, and many regional artifacts. The local cookery offers a different specialty every day, although calves' liver and grilled fish are always available. Cheese and desserts are from the region and homemade. A carafe of the red or white house wine is a good accompaniment to your meal. The restaurant offers inexpensive meals for 20,000 lire ($15.25) from noon to 2:30 p.m. and 7:30 to 9 p.m. It is closed on Tuesday (except in summer).

Il Poeta Contadino, via Indipendenza 21 (tel. 721-917). The cuisine at this bucolic restaurant enjoys a good local reputation. The decor is rustic, and the owner performs a certain poetry all his own with such regional specialties as fava beans with chicory, fire-cooked spiedini, grilled fish, a wide range of antipasti, and homemade desserts. The most popular first course is the tris di assaggini, which consists of three types of pasta. Full meals, which are served from noon to 2:30 p.m. and 7:30 to 9 p.m. every day except Friday, cost 22,000 lire ($16.75)to 32,000 lire ($24.25). Closed from mid-January to mid-February.

Trullo d'Oro, via Cavallotti 29 (tel. 721-8209), is one of the area's finest restaurants. With a rustic decor, it offers an array of southern cookery that usually pleases its foreign guests, most of whom are bound for Greece. For a final "taste of Italy," diners might begin with spaghetti with arugala and follow with roast lamb and a selection of vegetables accented with pine nuts. The baby lamb is roasted and basted on a grill. Many southern desserts, such as ricotta cooked with marmalade, are also offered. Meals are served daily except Monday from noon to 3 p.m. and 8 to 11 p.m., costing 20,000 lire ($15.25) to 35,000 lire ($26.50).

---

5. Bari

This is the teeming seaport along Italy's Adriatic coastline, often called the country's "doorway to the Orient." It was through here that Crusaders passed on their way to the Holy Land. The capital of Apulia, Bari is a crowded mass of people. One part is modern (that is, from the 19th century), and the other section, called Vecchia Bari, is ancient, dating from Byzantine times, although its present look is medieval.

If you decide to explore the old city—and it's worth a visit—be prepared to get lost in its maze of narrow streets, filled with shops, old women in black, and hordes of children, many of whom bathe in public fountains. Many locals will tell you that Vecchia Bari is "completely safe." Yet every season there are many incidents reported of mugging and purse snatching. Cars are often broken into. So take care.

To reach the old city, if you arrive at the Stazione Centrale, opposite the piazza Aldo Moro, head north to the piazza Umberto and continue along one of several streets, perhaps via Andrea da Bari, until you come to it. Another important square, piazza Garibaldi, at the southwestern corner of Città Vecchia, is a heart-beat center. From here you can head east along the corso Vittorio Emanuele to Porto Vecchio or "old port." A pedestrians-only thoroughfare, via Sparano is the main shopping street of Bari. Finally, you may want to either drive or walk along one of the most scenic streets of Bari, the **lungomare Nazario Sauro,** running along the Porto Vecchio, with distant views of the Adriatric.

Bari lies 281 miles east of Rome, and, like Brindisi, has become an increasingly popular embarkation point for ferries plying their way across the Adriatric to Yugoslavia or to Greece (summer only). The city, an eight-hour train ride from Rome, is also linked by autostrada (head first for Naples, then cut east). The fastest way to get there is to take an ATI plane, landing at Aeroporto Bari-Palese, five miles from the heart of the city.

Bari is the center of a famous trade fair, Fiera del Levante, held in September of every year. If you're planning to visit at that time, make sure you have nailed down a hotel reservation.

The telephone area code for Bari is 080.

THE SIGHTS

The city's most famous attraction is the **Basilica of San Nicola,** dedicated to Bari's patron saint (who later became Santa Claus). It is said that, in 1087, 62 Barese sailors returned home with the saint's bones stolen from Mira in Asia Minor (now part of Turkey). The saint was known for his kindness to children, and later he became the patron saint of children. His bones still rest in an underground basilica in this church, which was built in the Apulian-Romanesque style, incorporating parts of a palace once occupied by Byzantine rulers. The saint is said to have raised three children from the dead after a butcher had sliced them up and preserved their bodies in brine. The church was begun in 1087 and completed in 1197. In the upper part of the basilica, you can see a white-marble throne, supported by small figures, and this is the chief treasure of the church, other than the bones of Santa Claus. The feast of St. Nicholas is still celebrated in Bari every May 8.

The **Cathedral of Bari** (duomo) is also constructed in the Apulian-Romanesque style. It is primarily from the 12th century, but it has been rebuilt and "restored" many times. Its bell tower has a squat top. Note the big rose window imbedded in the façade and "protected" by monsters and grotesques. The interior is rather austere.

The **Castello Svevo** (Swabian Castle) (tel. 214-361), near the cathedral, was the host to Queen Isabella of Spain who held court here in the 16th century. It had been rebuilt in 1233 by Frederick II. You can go inside a harmonious courtyard, passing under a Gothic portal and an atrium with columns. It is open daily from 9 a.m. to 1:30 p.m. and 3:30 to 7 p.m. (on Sunday from 9 a.m. to 1:30 p.m.). Parts of it are likely to be closed as archeologists dig from Roman ruins on the site. Admission is 2,000 lire ($1.50).

There is also an **archeological museum** in the Palazzo dell'Ateneo, at the piazza Umberto I (tel. 521-1559), which is open daily except Sunday from 8:30 a.m. to 1:30 p.m. Admission is free. It displays Greek and Roman artifacts found in excavations in Bari province. In fact it has the most complete collection of Apulian archeological material in Italy. The exhibits are rich in ancient vases, including Corinthian ones from the 6th century B.C. that were brought in from Greece. There is also a remarkable collection of bronzes, along with carved amber, jewelry, a small assemblage of sculpture, and some fine numismatic exhibits.

HOTELS IN BARI

The traveler on a strict budget will not do well in Bari. Some of the once-acceptable *pensioni,* which some 20 years ago were among the bargain accommodations along the Adriatic, have been taken over by the government to provide shelter for the homeless. If at all possible, try to seek medium-priced or first-class lodgings when you visit this fascinating but often difficult city.

Palace Hotel, via Lombardi 13, 70122 Bari (tel. 080/216-551), considered the best hotel in Bari, is a modern building with severe exterior lines, rounded corner balconies, and a setting near the castle on an inner-city street. This is the best-equipped hotel in town, outfitted with air conditioning, plants, modern furniture, and more than 200 rooms, each with private bath, TV, radio, phone, and frigo-bar. There's a popular piano bar on the premises, as well as a well-recommended restaurant, which charges from 45,000 lire ($34.25) for a full meal. Rooms, well furnished and maintained, cost 175,000 lire ($133) daily in a single, 275,000 lire ($209) in a double. The hotel is open all year, although the restaurant closes Saturday night, all day Sunday, and in August.

Grand Hotel Ambasciatori, via Omodeo 51, 70125 Bari (tel. 080/410-077), is a comfortable first-class facility on the outskirts of the city. It is the only hotel in Italy with its own roof heliport. The soundproof, air-conditioned hostelry has a heated, roof swimming pool, American bars, private gardens, panoramic elevators, and a cinema. It also has a garage, which comes in handy, as it's unwise to leave cars unguarded on the street at night. The 177 rooms are attractively furnished and well kept, each with bath or shower, phone, color TV, and frigo-bar. They range in price from 120,000 lire ($114) daily for a single to 220,000 lire ($167) for a double. The hotel also operates a well-appointed restaurant, La Mongolfiera, serving both classic Italian dishes and occasional specialties of Puglia.

Hotel Executive Business, corso Vittorio Emanuele 201, 70122 Bari (tel. 080/216-810), is the finest middle-bracket hotel in Bari, but it's got only 21 rooms, so reservations are important. Right off the piazza Garibaldi, it lies on one of the main thoroughfares of Bari, at the doorway to Città Vecchia. Rooms are well conceived and comfortable; beds fold into the walls during the day, allowing more room for living. There is no restaurant, but breakfast is served. Singles rent for 98,000 lire ($74.50) daily, doubles 165,000 lire ($125).

Hotel Boston, via Piccinni 155, 70122 Bari (tel. 080/216-633), is a modern hotel near the center of town, the port, and the railway station. A member of the Best Western chain, it is one of the best of the middle-bracket hotels in town. Its 72 rooms cost 80,000 lire ($60.75) daily in a single, 120,000 lire ($91.25) in a double.

WHERE TO DINE

Reputedly serving the best food in Bari, **Ristorante Vecchia Bari,** via Dante Alighieri 47 (tel. 521-6496), is a Puglia restaurant directed by members of the Lagrasta family. The decor is strictly regional, while menu items include a wide range of spicy meats, fish, pastas, and seasonal vegetables, which might be accompanied by a regional wine. From 12:30 to 3 p.m. and 7:30 to 10 p.m., the restaurant serves full meals costing 40,000 lire ($30.50) to 55,000 lire ($41.75). Closed Friday, Sunday night, and most of August.

La Pignata, via Melo 9 (tel. 232-481), is considered one of the finest restaurants in the south of Italy. The owners toil in the kitchens and dining room, offering a warm welcome, old-world manners, and a style of cookery adhering to the ancient traditions of Pugliese cuisine. Specialties include a wide range of antipasti, several kinds of homemade pasta, salads, fish and meat dishes, along with regional desserts. Full meals, which are served from 12:30 to 3 p.m. and 7:30 to 10 p.m. daily except Wednesday and in August, cost 35,000 lire ($29) to 68,000 lire ($51.75).

La Panca da Nanuccio, piazza Massari 8, (tel. 216-096), offers a rustic yet elegant decor in a building near the historic center of town. Your meal, served from 12:30 to 3 p.m. and 7:30 to 10 p.m., might include anyone of several regional specialties. The antipasti are a visual as well as a gastronomic treat, and might be followed by one of the establishment's rich pastas and then a mixed grill of meat or fish. Closed Wednesday and in August, the establishment charges 28,000 lire ($21.25) to 42,000 lire ($32) for a full meal.

Ai Due Ghiottoni, via Putignani 11 (tel. 232-240), is a well-decorated restaurant a short distance from the Petruzzelli Theater in the commercial center of town. The cuisine includes international and northern Italian specialties as well as those from Puglia. Try a fava bean purée with chicory leaves, roast beef English style, or wide noodles with rabbit sauce, perhaps the house risotto with spinach. If you're in the mood for a particular type of Adriatic fish, it is probably available, and will be cooked as you like it. Full meals, served from 12:30 to 3 p.m. and 7:30 to 10 p.m. every day but Sunday and in August, cost 35,000 lire ($26.50) to 50,000 lire ($38). Translated, the name of the restaurant means "two gluttons."

---

6. The Spur of Italy

Called the Gargano, the mountainous wooded promontory is the Spur of Italy. It's best seen in the autumn when you can enjoy the colors of the Umbrian Forest. Featuring such trees as maple, ash, cedar, and chestnut, it's quite a sight. The world here has a timeless quality. Unspoiled salt lake areas are found at Lesina and Varano. Bathing and water sports are prevalent because of the mild climate and calm sea. The coast is a series of cliffs, rocks, caves, islets, and beaches. In addition to nature's wild and varied landscape, the promontory is rich in historic interest, showing off monuments that are Byzantine, Romanesque, Norman, and medieval.

It will take about seven hours to drive all around the Gargano (longer with stopovers, of course), staying on Rte. 89. I consider this sometimes-difficult route among the most scenically rewarding in Italy. In ancient times the peninsula was an island, until the sediment from a river eventually formed a "bridge" linking it to the mainland of Italy.

For some, the gateway will be—

FOGGIA

Many motorists seek lodgings here and use bustling Foggia as a base for exploring Gargano. Certainly there is little about Foggia itself that would make one want to linger. Allied bombers virtually destroyed it in World War II. However, it has a hotel with a superb restaurant worth seeking out.

Foggia's telephone area code is 0881.

Grand Hotel Cicolella, vial XXIV Maggio 60, 71100 Foggia (tel. 0881/38-90), is not only the leading hotel in Foggia, but offers the most outstanding cuisine in the area. This Victorian-era building is richly embellished. The interior, however, has been modernized into a streamlined format of good taste and pleasant accommodations. Each of the rooms contains a private bath or shower and much modern comfort. Singles range from 90,000 lire ($68.50) daily; doubles, 175,000 lire ($133).

The hotel is open all year, although the in-house restaurant is closed Saturday, Sunday, and for part of August. The rest of the week it's so popular that getting a seat on holidays is almost impossible. It's said that this place has the best roast lamb in town, along with a superb collection of Italian cheese, flavor some carpaccio, and a wide and well-prepared array of regional recipes and creations of the chef. Full meals cost 35,000 lire ($26.50) to 60,000 lire ($45.50).

MANFREDONIA

If you approach Gargano from the south, your first stop, perhaps at lunchtime, might well be at Manfredonia, a small port known for its castle. In the heyday of the Crusades, this was a bustling port town, with knights and pilgrims leaving for the Levant.

Two miles outside of town is **Santa Maria di Siponto,** or St. Mary's of Siponte, a church in a setting of pine woods. This church stands on the site of what was the old city of Siponte. It is in the Romanesque style, showing both Tuscan and Arabic influences. An earthquake and a plague caused the ancient city to be abandoned.

The telephone area code for Manfredonia is 0884.

Ristorante al Porto da Michele, piazza della Libertà 3 (tel. 218-000), near the center of town, at the port, is known for its fresh fish served in several appetizing ways. In summer a specialty is agostinelle (minnow-size red mullets), cooked within seconds in a deep-fried pot. Other choices include fish soup, a warm seafood salad, linguine with clams, and mixed fish or meat grills. Full meals, served from noon to 3:30 p.m. and 7 to 10 p.m., cost from 35,000 lire ($26.50). Closed Wednesday.

MONTE SANT'ANGELO

Motorists will find the principal town in the interior, Monte Sant'Angelo, in the great Umbrian Forest, to be a good starting point for a tour. From here you can venture into a landscape of limes, laurels, towering yews, along with such animal life as foxes and gazelles. Narrow passageways, streets that are virtually stairways, and little houses washed a gleaming white, characterize the town. The site of the town, standing on a spur, is most interesting, commanding great views. Before leaving the town, you may want to visit the **Sanctuary of San Michele,** in the Romanesque-Gothic style. The campanile is octagonal, dating from the last years of the 13th century. The sanctuary commemorates the legend of St. Michael, who is said to have left his red cloak after he appeared to some shepherds in a grotto in A.D. 490. You can also visit the grotto in which the saint is alleged to have appeared. To enter from the church, go through some bronze doors, made in Constantinople in the 11th century.

Opposite the campanile, you can also visit the **Tomba di Rotari** (tomb of

Rotharis). The tomb is said to hold the bones of the king of the Lombards, Rotharis, although it is in fact a baptistery dating from as early as the 12th century.

If you continue east along the coast, you can stop off at **Mattinata,** rising above the plain and planted with olive trees.

VIESTE

From here, you can drive to the farthest point along the coast, Vieste, a distance of 111 miles from Bari, 62 miles from Foggia. At Vieste, rooted firmly in the sea, stands a legendary monolith. The rock is linked to the woeful tale of Vesta, a beautiful girl supposedly held prisoner on the stone by jealous sirens. Many grottoes, such as Grotta Campana, along the coast can be explored by boat, leaving in summer at 8:30 a.m.

Vieste, on the far eastern shore of the Gargano, has in recent years blossomed as a summer resort. If you're just passing through, take time out to walk through its charming medieval quarter, with its whitewashed houses built on terraces. Vieste is also a good center for exploring the excellent beaches along the southern Gargano shoreline.

While in the area, consider taking a ferry (which has regular departures from Rodi Garganico in the north) to the jewel-like cluster of the **Isole Tremiti** or Tremiti islands, lying about seven miles off the shore. These islands have lovely reefs, gin-clear waters, and towering limestone peaks. Many old monasteries were also built in the Tremiti. Make reservations at **Gargano Viaggi,** piazza Roma 7 (tel. 78-501) in Vieste. These boats get crowded in the peak weeks of summer.

You'll arrive at **San Nicola,** one of the major islands, where you can explore the castle from the 15th century (it's not much of a sight, but the view is spectacular). You might also want to visit the Church of Santa Maria, which grew out of a 9th-century abbey but it has seen much rebuilding over the years.

It's also possible to take a boat to the island of **San Domino** to visit its grottoes. This is the largest island of the Tremitis, with a rock-strewn shoreline.

Vieste's telephone area code is 0884.

Where to Stay and Dine at Vieste

The best place to stay in the "Spur of Italy" is the **Pizzomunno Palace Hotel,** 71019 Vieste (tel. 0884/78-741), a modern structure in the Mediterranean style of architecture, surrounded by a large park. The most contemporary equipment went into this hotel, making it an appealing choice for a resort holiday. The hotel stands by the sea, with a well-cared-for private beach. Facilities include two swimming pools, three tennis courts, a sauna, and a massage room, as well as courses in swimming, windsurfing, sub-aqua, waterskiing, and sailing. Sailboats may be rented, as can canoes and beach rafts. The staff maintains an active sports program, including lessons in archery and horseback riding. In the evening, guests gather around the piano bar, later enjoying the cinema and disco. The restaurant serves well-prepared food, both regional dishes and international specialties. Rooms are handsome and breezy, containing private shower and bath, phone, air conditioning, and a balcony with panoramic terrace. Full board is required, costing 120,000 lire ($91.25) to 250,000 lire ($190) per person daily, depending on the season. The hotel is open from Easter to mid-October.

San Michele, vial XXIV Maggio 74 (tel. 78143). The stones that built this seaside house have by now been almost impregnated with the aroma of the cookery of many generations. Today the owners prepare time-honored regional recipes using the best of local vegetables, meats, and seafoods. You might begin with a flavorful and nutritious vegetable antipasti, then follow with a homemade pasta or fava-bean minestrone. Main courses include selections from the day's catch or perhaps a flavorful slice of veal marsala. With a ruby-colored bottle of the local wine, a full meal will come to around 40,000 lire ($30.50). The restaurant, open from noon to 6 p.m. and 7 p.m. to midnight, is closed on Thursday and in February.

SARDINIA

"**U**nconquered Sardinia" was what D. H. Lawrence called it. But that is no longer the case. Once overrun with bandits and malaria, Sardinia, if predictions hold true, will one day be flooded with visitors. Aga Khan's Costa Smeralda, the so-called Emerald Coast in the northeast, has already experienced that phenomenon.

Of course, away from the deluxe hotels and chic discos of the Emerald Coast, the land of the banditti, the family clan, and the vendetta is still pretty much what it has always been in the hinterlands. Some of the Sards still follow a lifestyle not far removed from the days of feudalistic Europe.

Its proud people reflect the heritage of an ancient civilization. They knew many invaders, including the Carthaginians, the Phoenicians, the Byzantine knights, the Saracens, the Pisans, the Genoese, and the Spaniards who ruled them for four centuries. The Sards are considered among the proudest and hardest working of all Italians.

Encircled by miles of silver-white sandy beaches, rocky coasts, bays, and gulfs, Sardinia is also an island of mountains and hills. Among Mediterranean islands it is second in size, bowing only to Sicily. It's a rocky, gnarled land of primordial beauty, some of it little changed since biblical days. In the interior are sand-colored villages where many Sards live in poverty. Scattered throughout the island are the ruins of thousands of tower-like *nuraghi*—homes of Sardinia's former inhabitants. They have been called "ponderous labyrinths."

GETTING THERE

The major car-ferry route to Sardinia (mainly in the summer months) is from Civitavecchia on the Italian mainland, which is 50 miles north of Rome, to Olbia on the east coast of Sardinia, site of the chic resorts of the Emerald Coast and Porto Rotondo. The crossing takes seven hours. Service is also available from Genoa and Livorno, but the car-ferry from Civitavecchia is the shortest route. There is also service from Civitavecchia to the Sardinian capital, Cagliari, that trip taking 14 hours.

Many lines operate these vessels, the biggest of which is **Tirrenia**. For tickets, inquire at the Tirrenia office in Civitavecchia at the Stazione Marittima (tel. 0766/ 28-801). In July and August it's necessary to book space well in advance of departure. Strikes have been frequent, and many summer visitors have been severely detained.

Sardinia also maintains air links with the Italian mainland. **Alisarda,** 07026 Olbia (tel. 0789/69-400), the Sardinian airline, operates direct flights from all major Italian cities as well as other European airports. Using jet planes, year-round daily flights link Olbia/Costa Smeralda airport with Milan, Rome, Pisa, and Bologna. In summer, there are flights from Turin, Genoa, Verona, Venice, Paris, Nice, Geneva, Zurich, Frankfurt, and Munich. Other flights connect Milan, Bologna, and Pisa to Cagliari, as well as linking Bologna and Catania in Sicily.

1. Cagliari

The capital of Sardinia, Cagliari is on the southern part of the island, and is surrounded by sea and hills. **Alitalia** will easily fly you there from either Milan or Rome. Well known to the Greeks and the Romans, its appearance is modern, except for the old medieval quarter, which occupies a long narrow hill running north and south.

For one of the best views, head for the large terrace at the south of the hill, the **passeggiata Umberto I.** From here you can see the harbor, the lagoon, and the lower city.

The telephone area code for Cagliari is 070.

THE SIGHTS

Constructed in the Pisan style, the **cathedral** contains some of the city's most important works of art. Built in the 13th century, it is a combination of the Romanesque and Gothic. Its most prized possession is its collection of pulpits by Maestro Guglielmo (these once stood in Il Duomo at Pisa). The 18th-century baroque tomb of Martin II of Aragon is impressive, as are the tombs of the princes of the House of Savoy. Yet another important work of art is a triptych by Gerard David, the Flemish artist.

Another church that merits a visit is **San Saturnino,** built in the style of a Greek cross and tracing its history back to the 5th century.

Actually, the greatest treasures are in the **Museo Archeologico** (National Archeological Museum), near the Torre di San Pancrazio. It is open daily from 9 a.m. to 2 p.m., and also from 3:30 to 6 p.m. on Wednesday, Friday, and Saturday. Admission is 3,000 lire ($2.30).

Massive monuments left over from medieval days include the **Torre dell'Elefante** from 1307 and the **Torre di San Pancrazio** from 1305.

North of the town is a **Roman amphitheater,** the largest such ruin in Sardinia, its impressive cellars carved out of a rock. In summer, opera is performed in front of an international crowd.

Its beach of **Poetto** stretches for some six miles, from the Margine Rosso (Red Bluff) to Sella del Diavolo (the Devil's Saddle). The beach is easily reached by public transportation from Cagliari.

The most popular excursion in the environs of Cagliari, at least for history buffs, is to the ruins of the old city of **Nora,** founded by the Phoenicians before falling to the Carthaginians and later the Romans. On a narrow peninsula at Cape Pula, the site is about 21 miles southwest from Cagliari. Ruins include a Roman theater of the Republican era (in fairly good condition), the temple of Tanit, and outlines of roads. You'll also see the 11th-century Church of Sant'Efisio and a watchtower of the 16th century. The ruins are open in summer daily from 9:30 a.m. to sunset. Admission is 4,000 lire ($3.05).

WHERE TO STAY

Long the dowager queen of Cagliari hotels, the **Regina Margherita,** viale Regina Margherita 44, 09124 Cagliari (tel. 070/670-342), has had its tiara restored. Today it is the only four-star hotel in Cagliari, restored after years of decline and then eventual closure. In the center of Cagliari, it is halfway between terrazza Umberto and the porto (in fact, the best rooms overlook the water). The rooms come in many sizes and shapes, as befits an old grand hotel. The single rate is 145,000 lire ($110) daily, while doubles cost from 175,000 lire ($133)—relatively moderate tariffs for such a well-rated establishment—Full board going from 210,000 lire ($160) per person daily. The Regina Margherita has one of the finest kitchens in Cagliari, and many locals prefer to dine here on "that special occasion." You can enjoy Sardinian and international specialties with them at a cost ranging from 35,000 lire ($26.50) to 60,000 lire ($45.50) per meal.

Right on the sea, the **Hotel Mediterraneo,** lungomare Cristoforo Colombo, 09125 Cagliari (tel. 070/301-271), is very central and enjoys a quiet position. It is the second leading hotel in the city, having been inaugurated in 1965. The location overlooks the Golfo degli Angeli. Each of the well-furnished accommodations contains private bath or shower, balcony, radio, and the usual modern comforts. Singles cost 175,000 lire ($133) daily; doubles, 200,000 lire ($152). In addition, the restaurant in the hotel offers a variety of national and international dishes, an average meal costing 40,000 lire ($30.50) to 65,000 lire ($49.50). The Mediterraneo receives guests all year.

Moderno, via Roma 159, 09124 Cagliari (tel. 070/653-971), is aptly named. It lies right north of the piazza Matteotti, near the air terminal and the inner port, a most convenient location. Popular with business travelers in Cagliari, it is suitable for an overnight stopover. It rents 93 functional rooms, each with private bath but few frills. The cost is 65,000 lire ($49.50) daily in a single, 90,000 lire ($68.50) in a double. The hotel has no restaurant but serves breakfast.

Less expensive, **Motel Agip,** Circonvallazione Nuova, 09134 Pirri (Cagliari) (tel. 070/521-373), stands near the airport and is connected to Cagliari by a ring road (head in the direction of Pirri). A worthy candidate, clean, functional, and well run, the motel—part of a popular Italian chain—rents 57 bedrooms, each with private bath. The cost is 48,000 lire ($36.50) daily in a single, 70,000 lire ($53.25) in a double. The beds are good, rooms are air-conditioned, and there is ample parking space. The restaurant serves many regional dishes such as malloreddus, frattau bread, and porceddu, along with a good selection of Sardinian wines.

WHERE TO DINE

The finest food in Cagliari is served at **Dal Corsaro,** viale Regina Margherita 28 (tel. 664-318). It's under the direction of the Deidda family, who see to it that the quality of the produce and its preparation are first-rate. The cuisine stands side by side with the fine wines of Sardinia, helping to give the island a reputation as one of Italy's leading gastronomical regions. To begin your meal, I suggest an order of malloreddus, little dumplings of corn flour flavored with saffron. They are served with a sprinkling of grated goat cheese, known as pecorino. If you want to continue sampling local dishes, ask for salsiccia brasata (a form of dry Sardinian sausage). Fresh seafood comes in infinite varieties, including lobster, clams, prawns, and "sea dates" (a type of mussels). If you see butariga on the menu, sample it. This is old dialect for Sardinian caviar, and it's superb. It's often grated into a simple spaghetti with butter. You might finish with sea bass (locally called spiggola) prepared with green olives in Vernaccia, a regional white wine. With your meal, try a thin, crisp Sardinian bread known as "sheet music" or carta da musica. Expect to pay 45,000 lire ($34.25) to 60,000 lire ($45.50) for a complete meal, including wine, served from 12:30 to 3 p.m. and 7:30 to 9:30 p.m. daily except Tuesday.

Ottagono, viale Poetto (tel. 372-879), is one of the best-known restaurants in the environs, lying 5½ miles southeast of Cagliari at Poetto. This is the kind of place local residents go for moments of family or business celebrations. Since expeditions into the local markets are so frequent, the ingredients are usually the freshest available. The cuisine reflects centuries of Sardinian cookery at its most pure. The Angelo family are the owners, supervising the service in the dining room and on the outdoor terrace where a view of the sea is only the first of many pleasures. Your meal might begin with a selection from the well-stocked antipasti table, followed by one of many shrimp dishes, including one with risotto, a mixed seafood fry (which includes anemone), grilled lobster, a savory house spaghetti with salmon and bottarga (a form of local caviar), and dozens of other varieties of seafood, beautifully prepared and elegantly presented. Full meals, served from noon to 3 p.m. and 8 to 11:30 p.m. every day except Tuesday and for part of October, begin at 60,000 lire ($45.50).

Antica Hostaria, via Cavour 60 (tel. 665-870). Part of the fun of this harborside restaurant will be the portside terrain you'll have to navigate to get there. The interior is elegant, the service correct, and the meal inspired by a host of seafood delicacies so abundant in nearby waters. Menu items include several burridas (that's a stew), with just about every kind of fish or shellfish imaginable, served with a zesty flavoring, along with a sampling of recipes that formally originated centuries ago. Full meals, served from 12:30 to 3 p.m. and 7:30 to 9:30 p.m. every day but Sunday, range from 35,000 lire ($26.50) to 50,000 lire ($38).

La Pineta, via della Pineta 108 (tel. 303-313), is a ristorante pizzeria, among the best in the capital. As an appetizer, prosciutto is featured, usually in three different ways. The chef offers three specialties: spiedino (brochette) alla Pineta, medaglioni di filetto allo spiedo (also on a brochette), and saltimbocca della casa, a variation of the popular Roman dish. Also preferred, if ordered first, is an antipasto di mare, with an assortment of sea fruits. The food is most acceptable, as is the service. Expect to spend 25,000 lire ($19) to 38,000 lire ($29) for a meal. Open from 12:30 to 3 p.m. and 7:30 to 10 p.m., it's closed Monday and in September.

Italia, via Sardegna 30 (tel. 657-987), is a modern, bustling ristorante rosticceria. I always go here for one dish—and is it ever good! It's called porchetto allo spiedo. This most typical dish of Sardinia is suckling pig, spit-roasted and highly spiced. Also good is a brochette of mixed meat (carne mista), as are the fish dishes. For a minestre, I recommend malloreddus. This dish, described earlier, is made of corn flour and saffron, then covered with a sprinkling of grated goat cheese. Depending on your selection of dishes, a complete meal will cost from 35,000 lire ($26.50). Hanging from the ceiling of this contemporary restaurant is a two-story-high cluster of spindle lights, illuminating the main dining rooms and the wooden mezzanine. It's a harmonious balance of stark white and wood tones. Open from 12:30 to 3 p.m. and 7:30 to 10 p.m., it's closed Sunday and mid-December to mid-January.

RESORTS IN THE ENVIRONS

If you're on vacation, it's far better to anchor in at **Santa Margherita di Pula,** 25 miles south of Cagliari on the southwest shore of the Gulf of Angels, 4 miles southwest of the town of Pula. You can then visit the capital for half-day shopping jaunts and sightseeing excursions. The pine woods skirt the coast, and fine sandy beaches and cliffs extend for five miles.

Is Morus Hotel, Santa Margherita di Pula, 09010 Pula (tel. 070/921-424), is a self-contained holiday world set in wooded coastal land, near a sandy beach. Lofty, pine-covered mountains drop to gardens overlooking the sea. Tree-shaded lawns are rimmed with bergamot and wild juniper hedging, while many flowers and shrubs blossom on the grounds and around a Moorish fountain. The terraced arcades are part of the white buildings of Moorish architecture. Inside, the decor is in blue and white with terracotta tiles, rush mats, and fabrics locally produced, all set off with bouquets of fresh flowers. The accommodations, 85 in all, are superb, with charming decorations, each unit being different. Guests are accepted here on the full-board plan, which ranges in price from 260,000 lire ($198) to 300,000 lire ($228) per person daily. The hotel is closed from mid-October to mid-April.

The Is Morus Golf Course is just ten minutes from the hotel, from which free shuttle service is provided to the clubhouse. At the golf course, facilities include a swimming pool, restaurant, bar, sauna, and disco. Experts have called this course one of the most beautiful and challenging in Europe and among the first 20 in the world.

Grand Hotel Capo Boi, at Capo Boi, 09049 Villasimius (tel. 070/791-225), 32 miles to the east of Cagliari, is set between a spine of rock-covered hills and the waters of the Gulf of Carbonara. Its focal point is a white-walled hotel whose three separate wings meet in a central hub like a giant airplane propeller. The pointed arches that fill the comfortable, pristine bedrooms with sun overlook conifers and vistas of mountains, capes, and sea. Guests who prefer not to swim off the crescent-shaped beach can use the pool, whose sides curve inward like the edges of an enormous hourglass. Each of the hotel's 180 bedrooms has its own phone and air conditioning, and most of them offer a private balcony or terrace. There are also town-house villas whose tile roofs stretch up the side of a nearby hill. Each of these contains two double rooms, two single rooms, two baths, a living room, veranda, air conditioning, and phone. Additional accommodations are available in what the management calls "the New Residence." This contains one- or two-bedroom apartments whose balconies zigzag in and out from an ochre-faced building containing them. Full board ranges from 150,000 lire ($114) to 220,000 lire ($167) daily per person. Guests find a wide range of water sports, bars, tennis courts, a disco, a beachside restaurant serving Sardinian specialties, and nighttime entertainment. Many conferences also take place here. The hotel is open from mid-May to September.

2. Alghero

On the northwest coast 142 miles from Cagliari, this former Aragonese fishing port is considered Sardinia's most beautiful town. Because of its heavy Catalán influence, it's been called "Little Barcelona." Encircled by ancient ramparts, it is built on a rocky ledge above the sea. Flowers and palms grow in profusion, the setting crowned by the campanile of the duomo in the Catalán Gothic style.

Best for exploring is the Città Vecchia, or old town, somewhat Moorish in flavor. Two miles north of the town are excellent bathing beaches.

The Alghero telephone area code is 079.

WHERE TO STAY

The leading hotel, **Villa Las Tronas,** lungomare Valencia 1, 07041 Alghero (tel. 079/975-390), was once the residence of the remnants of the Italian royal family, who used it for their holidays in Sardinia. Each room has a view of the sea and the bay, the latter considered by many the most beautiful in the Mediterranean. Surrounded by cultivated gardens, it stands near craggy rocks and tiny beaches. The architectural lushness of the villa has been retained, including the paneled silk walls, the parquet floors, the large gilt mirrors, the sconces, and the baroque furniture. The contemporary dining room has a baby-pink and sky-blue color scheme. Best of all are the 19th-century chairs and the view of the sea. Bedrooms are simpler and harmoniously decorated. Each contains a private bath. It's customary to take full board in high season: 150,000 lire ($114) per person daily. If there is no room at the main hotel, guests are housed in the annex where full board costs 120,000 lire ($91.25) per person. The hotel is open all year.

Hotel Calabona, at Calabona, 07041 Alghero (tel. 079/975-728), is close to a seacoast whose rocky edges blend into a desirable beach. There's a swimming pool, as well as a solarium and the possibility for several land and water sports. Open April to October, the hotel contains 113 well-furnished bedrooms. Singles cost from 56,000 lire ($42.50) daily; doubles, 70,000 lire ($53.25). Full board goes for 77,000 lire ($58.50) per person daily.

La Margherita, via Sassari 70, 07041 Alghero (tel. 079/976-417), is a modest centrally located hotel with an attractive stone-arched façade studded with balconies. Best of all is a rooftop terrace where you can order refreshments while scanning other rooftops and the bay. The lobby and lounge are serviceable and clean. The bedrooms are simplified in a home-like modern, each with central heating and private bath. Half board is 62,000 lire ($47) per person daily in high season, including tax.

WHERE TO DINE

Moreno Cecchini, the gregarious owner of **La Lepanto,** via Carlo Alberto 135 (tel. 979-116), has spread the world of Sardinian cookery as far as the United States, where he has taught a thing or two to restaurateurs about antipasti and Mediterranean seafood. His establishment is by now almost always associated with Alghero by the hundreds of people who pass through every month, usually stopping for a meal of the specialties he prepares so well. These include ricotta ravioli in walnut sauce, a local form of risotto with seafood, a wide range of seafood-studded pastas, and many kinds of grilled, baked, or steamed fish. However, lobster is king here. Try, for example, lobster algharese cooked with lemon and orange, among other ingredients; or lobster Catalán, with eggs, olive oil, and lemon. Full meals, served from noon to 2:30 p.m. and 8 to 11:30 p.m., cost 35,000 lire ($26.50) and up, although if you order one of the more exotic shellfish dishes, it could cost more. Closed Sunday night and all day Monday.

Ristorante Dieci Metri, vicolo Adami 37 (tel. 979-023). As its name implies, this pleasant establishment lies only about ten yards from something. In this case, it's the main square of town. Recommended specialties include mixed seafood antipasti, ricotta-stuffed ravioli with walnut sauce, ravioli stuffed with a purée of fish, sea polyps "devil's style," clams with basil, and risotto marinara. A few of the after-dinner drinks are made with local herbs and flowers. They are not only unusual, but very potent. Full meals cost 25,000 lire ($19) to 38,000 lire ($29). During the off-season (from September to June), the restaurant is open from noon to 2:30 p.m. and 8 to 11 p.m. daily except Wednesday; closed from January 10 to the end of February.

Ai Tuguri, via Maiorca 57 (tel. 976-772), is one of the most authentically provincial restaurants in town, housed in a 15th-century building whose massive walls almost echo with time and memories. The location, a short distance from the Tower of Sulis, attracts a regular crowd of locals into its ground-floor bar, while the upper floors are dedicated to fine recipes, many of them originating in the interior of Sardinia.

These would include savory and pungent lamb dishes, usually cooked with large amounts of wine, as well as spiedini and a wide array of meats, which are often prepared with onion, herbs, and crispy pieces of lard. Other dishes include a savory mussel soup, seafood antipasti, a mixed grill of fish, and lobster when available. Reservations are appreciated, and full meals cost a reasonable 35,000 lire ($26.50) per person. The restaurant is open from 12:15 to 3 p.m. and 8 to 11 p.m. daily except Sunday; closed all of November.

UNDERSEA CAVES

A major excursion can be made by land or sea to the **Grotto di Nettuno,** at Cape Caccia, which is one of the most stunning undersea caves in the Mediterranean, lying seven miles west of Alghero. If you go by land, you'll follow along the Escala del Cabirol or "stairway of goats." A wealth of stalactities lines the walls of the enclosures of the caves. For 5,000 lire ($3.80), you can visit the cave daily: from 8 a.m. to 7 p.m. mid-April to September; from 9 a.m. to 2 p.m. off-season. It's also possible to go by boat from Alghero from the last two weeks in April until around the middle of October between 9 a.m. and 3 p.m. (in the peak summer months, between 10 a.m. and 4 p.m.). Boats depart from the Bastione della Madalena in Alghero; the round-trip ticket costs 10,000 lire ($7.60) and the trip takes about three hours.

The location of the caves is in the vicinity of **Porto Conte,** the ancient Portus Nympharum or "port of nymphs." For either a meal or a resort room, you'll find one of the finest hotels in west Sardinia here.

Food and Lodging at Porte Conte

El Faro, Porte Conte, 07041 Alghero (tel. 079/942-010), enjoys a tranquil location. It's a contemporary first-class hotel positioned at the end of a rocky promontory. Filled with attractive summer furnishings, it contains a panoramic restaurant with a terrace. There is a rocky bathing beach, although a semi-covered swimming pool is on the premises. The El Faro offers 92 balconied bedrooms, each with air conditioning, private bath, frigo-bar, and phone. Open April to October, the hotel charges 90,000 lire ($68.50) to 180,000 lire ($137) per person for full board. Meals in the restaurant cost 45,000 lire ($34.25) for nonresidents. Hotel facilities include a disco, hairdresser, sauna, and tennis courts.

---

3. Palau and La Maddalena

Palau is a small port town in the far northern reaches of Sardinia, lying 25 miles north of Olbia. It can also be easily visited from one of the resorts along the Emerald Coast. Palau is of little interest, but it is an embarkation point for visitors wishing to take one of the frequent boats running to the **Archipelago della Maddalena,** which consists of 14 islands and islets, most of which are still in a wild state. Boats leave daily in season about every 15 minutes. There is no Sunday service between October and April. For tickets and information, apply to **Agenzia D'Oriano,** piazza del Molo 2 (tel. 0789/709-270), in Palau.

The largest island in the chain is **La Maddalena,** a favorite seaside resort. It has a port that was once heavily fortified, as it commanded the Strait of Bonifacio between Sardinia and Corsica. A 4½-mile-long panoramic road encircles the island, making for a most scenic drive, with spectacular views of the sea.

From La Maddalena, you can cross a causeway to the island of **Caprera** ("goat island"), which is a land mass of about 16 square miles. Here you'll find the former house and **tomb of Garibaldi,** the Italian patriot, soldier, revolutionary, and political leader. The house, built by Garibaldi, contains his personal souvenirs, documents, and some weapons. He died on the island in 1882, and his tomb is nearby in an olive grove in a site much visited by patriotic Italians. The house is open daily except Monday from 9 a.m. to 1 p.m. and 3 to 5 p.m. (from 9 a.m. to 1 p.m. on Sunday). Admission is free.

From La Maddalena, you can take a boat west to **Santa Teresa Gallura,** 36 miles from Olbia, and have lunch there. If you wish, you can go by boat across the Straits of Bonifacio to the southern tip of Corsica, landing at Bonifacio. Santa Teresa Gallura is a lovely old hill town with a bustling square clustered around a church.

DINING AT PALAU

A good choice is **Da Franco,** via Capo d'Orso 1 (tel. 0789/709-558). Its pasta specialty is tagliatelle Franco, and the chef is also known for his grilled fish and meats and Sardinian specialties. At Da Franco, a guest can order Leslie Caron's favorite dessert, sedaba (that is, freshly made cheese packed between two thin pasta pancakes that are deep-fried in oil and offered with honey that has been aromatically heated). The restaurant, open from 12:30 to 3 p.m. and 7:30 to 10 p.m., is closed on Monday from October to May and also in December. It charges 45,000 lire ($34.25) to 70,000 lire ($53.25) for a complete meal.

FOOD AND LODGING AT LA MADDALENA

Perched up high, **Nido d'Aguila,** 07024 La Maddalena (tel. 0789/722-130), is on a rocky cliff whose base seems to plunge into the foaming sea below. To get there, you follow a winding coastal road about 1½ miles west of town. The 44 simply furnished bedrooms are clean and comfortable, usually with panoramic views of the coastline and sea. Singles cost 65,000 lire ($49.50) daily; doubles, 100,000 lire ($76).

La Grotta, via Prìncipe di Napoli 3 (tel. 0789/737-228), is the oldest restaurant on the island, and it's long been considered one of the best. Family run, it has an informal decor influenced by the sea. The flavorful cuisine includes many varieties of fish caught in Sardinian waters, which often mingle with fresh tomatoes, garlic, and mozzarella in nutritiously tempting combinations. If in doubt, try the mixed seafood salad, spaghetti with clams, and a mixed fish fry. Full meals begin at 35,000 lire ($26.60), and are served from 12:30 to 2:30 p.m. and 7:30 to 9:30 p.m. daily (closed Sunday in off-season). In summer the establishment is open daily.

DINING AT SANTA TERESA GALLURA

For a homemade pasta—raviolialla Brancaccio—and roast suckling pig, **try Canne al Vento-da Brancaccio,** via Nazionale 23, Santa Teresa Gallura, 07028 Sassari (tel. 0789/754-219), which is a trattoria, part of a 23-room inn. If you want to stay over, you'll find the rooms clean and simply furnished. Certainly the price is right: full board for only 60,000 lire ($45.50) per person daily. Mainly guests come here for the food. The fish stew (zuppa di pesce) is outstanding. An exceptional set meal is offered for 30,000 lire ($22.75). If you order à la carte, count on spending 40,000 lire ($30.50). The restaurant is open from noon to 2:30 p.m. and 7:30 to 10 p.m.; closed Saturday off-season and from October to December.

---

4. Costa Smeralda

The owners of motor yachts nod to each other at the harbor at Porto Cervo. The white sands attract some of the best-looking bodies in Europe. The Costa Smeralda, or the Emerald Coast, in northeast Sardinia is a luxurious vacation haven "ruled" by his highness, the Aga Khan. The spiritual leader of some 15 million Ismaili Muslims arrived in 1961, and the coast hasn't been the same since.

Along with the Costa Smeralda Consortium, he transformed some 25,000 acres of savage coastal land into luxury villas, deluxe hotels, and marinas. Some of the excesses, such as high-rise buildings, that tended to mar the Italian Riviera have been outlawed. Buildings were commissioned to architects who were instructed to make them seem like part of the landscape. The Costa Smeralda has one of the most beautiful golf courses in the world, the Pevero Golf Club designed by Robert Trent Jones. The harsh natural beauty of the terrain was, of course, taken into consideration at this 18-hole, par-72 course near Porto Cervo.

The telephone area code for this district is 0789.

DELUXE LIVING

Built irregularly and low in earth tones, **Cala di Volpe,** Cala di Volpe, 07020 Porto Cervo (tel. 0789/96-083), looks like a Moorish-African village sprawling on a low sand bar. It's purposely deceiving. In fact, some have labeled it "Mediterranean village kitsch." The tile roofs, the patina of the white walls, and the flowers and plants on the patios and terraces look as if they've always been there. Irwin Shaw, the bestselling novelist, once called it "for the spoiled darlings of our age." These have included everybody from Linda Evans to Gregory Peck. Its French architect, Jacques Couëlle, labeled the result an "operetta." He was perhaps referring to the deliberate campaign to give the resort immediate rustico. Each air-conditioned bedroom has a balcony with a view of the sea. Your bedroom may have rough plastered walls, perhaps in butter-yellow, with reproductions of Italian antiques. The high season lasts from June 20 to September 15, and during this period half board is 408,000 lire ($310) per person daily. At other times, tariffs drop to 283,000 lire ($215) per person. The hotel is open only from mid-May to September. The public facilities include a saltwater swimming pool, a grill room, a nightclub, a piano bar, tennis courts, a private beach, and barbecue. Three hundred yards away is the 18-hole Robert Trent Jones championship golf course referred to earlier. Take along your choicest resort attire. There are facilities for waterskiing and boat rentals.

Pitrizza, Arzachena–Liscia di Vacca, 07020 Porto Cervo (tel. 0789/91-500), is another skillful re-creation of a group of six villas, inspired by Sardinian architecture. Native stone was used, and inside typical handcrafts were employed effectively. In fact, the interior bursts with contemporary taste and conveniences. The villas are clustered around a main clubhouse, which has a cozy and rustic drinking bar and lounge, plus an informal living and dining room. From the clubhouse an extensive terrace opens onto the sea. The swimming pool is sumptuous. Beachboys, lavish buffets, multilingual waiters, fleets of boats—hardly the comforts of home. Enjoying this luxury has been everybody from Elie Rothschild to Sam Spiegel. The hotel is open from May 15 to September 30, charging its highest rates from June 20 to September 15. At that time full board is 430,000 lire ($327) per person daily. In the low season, you can stay here on a half-board arrangement, costing from 293,000 lire ($223) per person daily.

Hotel Romazzino, Arzachena-Romazzino, 07020 Porto Cervo (tel. 0789/96-020), is a first-class resort, about a 20-minute drive from Porto Cervo, directly on the bay with its own sandy beach. It attracts the bikinied, bejeweled, and Bulgaried. The establishment, whose name is Sardinian dialect for Rosemary, is designed to simulate a village and has sprawling bedroom wings on flowered terraces. It's like an octopus with many arms. Each bedroom contains a private sea-view balcony as well. The accommodations are handsomely furnished, often with ornate brass beds, reproductions of antiques, parquet floors, and private lounge areas. In high season, half board is offered for 398,000 lire ($303) per person daily, dropping to 268,000 lire ($204) per person. The cuisine is a combination of Sardinian and international, emphasizing regional pasta dishes. In the evening, guests dance in the piano bar. Guests are offered beachside meals at a barbecue and pizza stand, as well as in the main dining room. The hotel has a beautiful natural-rock swimming pool for those who don't want to go to the beach. The hotel's season lasts from mid-May to mid-October.

Hotel Cervo, 07020 Porto Cervo (tel. 0789-92-003), is a yacht-owner's paradise. Near the center of town, it was built right at the edge of the harbor. It, too, is an idealized version of a Sardinian village. Life here is lush, pampered, and chic. Rooms are built in a hacienda style, opening onto flower gardens, vine-covered vista arbors, and sunpocket rustic patios. You'll probably join other guests for apéritifs in the main patio with its wicker chairs or in the informal, bamboo-sheltered luncheon area. Another social center is around the free-form swimming pool, with its adjoining refreshment and luncheon terrace. A cluster of tennis courts, even an indoor pool and barbecue, round out the facilities. The interior lounges and dining room are well designed and handsomely furnished. The hotel is open from April to October, charging its highest tariffs from June 20 to September 15. The half-board rate in a double in high season costs from 260,000 lire ($198) per person daily. However, off-season this drops to 165,000 lire ($125) per person in a double.

LESS-EXPENSIVE LODGINGS

Lying outside town, **Le Ginestre,** 07020 Porto Cervo (tel. 0789/92-030), is like a reproduction of a country tavern-farmhouse with Mediterranean vegetation.

It opened in 1974. Each of the 85 handsomely furnished and air-conditioned bedrooms and suites contains a private bath, phone, and TV. Half board costs from 120,000 lire ($91.25) per person daily in low season, rising to 222,000 lire ($169) per person in high season. The restaurant offers good food, with meals beginning at 56,000 lire ($42.50). The hotel, open from April to the end of September, has an American bar with a panoramic terrace, as well as two swimming pools and a tennis court.

Hotel Nibaru, Cala di Volpe, 07020 Porto Cervo (tel. 0789/96-038), is a comfortable, medium-size hotel set amid a grove of trees within sight of the sea and a swimming pool. Each of the 45 bedrooms contains its own shower and phone. Singles without breakfast cost from 100,000 lire ($76) daily; doubles, from 150,000 lire ($114). The social center is the bar area, where the staff knows how to mix American-style drinks. There is no restaurant.

Balocco, Liscia di Vacca, 07020 Porto Cervo (tel. 0789/91-555). There is no restaurant inside this Mediterranean bed-and-breakfast establishment, but many clients appreciate that freedom so they can select their restaurant elsewhere. The 28 bedrooms contain a modern bath, air conditioning, phone, and radio, and many offer wide views over the sea and port. Viewed as a well-managed property by local residents, the hotel offers good service. Accommodations cost from 100,000 lire ($76) daily in a single, 160,000 lire ($122) in a double. Open April to mid-October.

DINING AT PORTO CERVO

At a harborside tavern, **Il Pescatore,** Sul Molo Vecchio (tel. 92-296), you can enjoy candlelit meals, which sometimes extend out onto the flower-dotted terrace. The music comes from a discreet pianist "on loan" from Costa Smeralda Hotels, which manage the place. The marine-inspired specialties include arrays of fresh antipasti, a version of fish soup, a fisherman's salad of marinated sea bass and herbs, and a platter of mixed grilled fish or lobster, along with a more limited selection of meats. Full meals cost 50,000 lire ($38) to 75,000 lire ($57) (dinner only), served from 8 to 11:30 p.m. daily. Closed from mid-October to early May.

---

5. Olbia

Chances are your first introduction to Sardinia might be the dreary port city of Olbia in the northeastern part of the island, especially if you're heading north for one of the resorts along the Emerald Coast. This is a busy, bustling place, filled with souvenir vendors, and it's the terminus of the Civitavecchia steamship lines from the mainland of Italy. My advice is to make your way through this place with haste, so that you can begin to experience the real charms of Sardinia, which are not found here.

If you've been unable to obtain lodgings at the Emerald Coast (most likely in high season unless you made reservations way in advance), don't despair. In the **environs of Olbia** are some of the more reasonably priced accommodations, but also some of the most glamorous hotels in Sardinia. However, it must be pointed out that Sardinian hotel builders, with an eye on all the windfall profits garnered by the Emerald Coast, are definitely aiming nearly all their hotel development at an upmarket crowd.

Your best bet for accommodations on a resort level are at Porto Rotondo, 9½ miles north of Olbia, and at Baia di Marinella, eight miles northeast of Olbia.

LODGING AT PORTO ROTONDO

Some people consider this spot even chicer than the Emerald Coast. A so-called real estate resort, it dates back to the late 1960s as a tourist development, but its port was probably used by the Romans (ancient columns have been excavated nearby).

Porto Rotondo's telephone area code is 0789.

Sporting Hotel, 07020 Porto Rotondo (tel. 0789/34-005), sits on a promontory bathed by the waters of the open sea on one side and overlooking the marina and the village of Porto Rotondo on the other. Amid the Mediterranean maquis, its architecture blends with the environment. This is the kind of place where country rustic furniture, most tasteful, and a jaunty air combine with a setting much like a private village. It is surely one of the most sophisticated summer hangouts in Sardinia. The views from its terraces encompass the coastline, the port, and many of the buildings. Acquired by Aga Khan's Costa Smeralda Hotels, the establishment offers substantial levels of comfort and many marine sports. A saltwater swimming pool is set in the garden. The rambling wings contain 27 accommodations, all with balconies and sea views. Half board costs 330,000 lire ($251) per person daily in high season, lowered to 210,000 lire ($160) per person in low season. Its restaurant offers al fresco dining on a panoramic terraced, a club-like character, and a menu including everything from Scottish salmon to lobster. Other specialties are a vodka-laced rigatoni "Bloody Mary" and a beef-stuffed ravioli with an eggplant-flavored sauce. There is always a good choice of grilled meat or fish. Full meals cost from 90,000 lire ($68.50). Both the restaurant and hotel are closed from the end of September until mid-April.

Hotel San Marco, piazzetta San Marco, 07020 Porto Rotondo (tel. 0789/35-018), lies close to the center of everything, yet provides a tranquil retreat thanks to its surrounding walls, peaceful garden, and gracious management. The 27 bedrooms are tastefully and beautifully kept, costing 88,000 lire ($67) to 120,000 lire ($91.25) daily in a single, 130,000 lire ($98.75) to 200,000 lire ($152) in a double, with breakfast included. There's no restaurant, but dining facilities are available at the port. The hotel is open from April to September.

LODGING AT BAIA DI MARINELLA

Occupying an isolated position, the **Hotel Abi d'Oru,** 07026 Olbia (tel. 789/32-001), stands at one of the most beautiful curves of the bay. The broad expanses of glass that the architects designed as part of this conservative building encompass the glittering waters for miles in either direction. Most of the accommodations are in the main hotel, but a few of the rentable villas are scattered throughout a park. Regardless of location, each of the 59 accommodations has a private terrace, air conditioning, private bath, and comfortable furnishings. The charge for full board is 115,000 lire ($87.50) per person daily in low season, rising to 235,000 lire ($179) in high season. The hotel, open from mid-May until the end of September, offers a full array of water sports as well as tennis, along with bar facilities and a terraced restaurant.

6. Nuoro and Dorgali

Most visitors confine their look at Sardinia to the coastline. However, those seeking a closer look, and who are especially interested in local life and handcrafts, may want to dip into one of the cities of the interior. Two of the more interesting ones are Nuoro and Dorgali. Both can be reached in a day's drive from the resorts along the coast of northeastern Sardinia, but it would be a very long day, and you wouldn't get to see very much. Dorgali, for example, lies 72 miles south from Olbia, 21 miles east from Nuoro. Better yet, it would be preferable to arrange an overnight stopover in one of these towns, where the prices are remarkably different from those charged along the Costa Smeralda.

The telephone area code for Nuoro and Dorgali is 0784.

NUORO

Many visitors travel to this provincial inland city on a shopping expedition, as it charges far less for the same handcrafts (made locally) that are sold at inflated prices in the boutiques of Costa Smeralda. People look for good buys in carpets, rush baskets, terracotta items, woodcarvings, floral and damasked tapestries, lace from Bosa, ceramics, decorated leatherwork, and earrings in filigree covered with pearls and garnets in the shape of mulberries.

The 1926 Nobel Prize winner, Grazia Deledda, was born in Nuoro in 1893, and her memory is still venerated by the local people who keep her house in San Pietro as a monument. The town is beautifully situated on a hillside at the foot of Monte Ortobene. The best time to visit is August 29 of every year, during the Feast of the Redeemer, when the townspeople turn out in their regional costumes, each a painstaking handmade work.

Folkloric customs and traditions, or so it is said, are respected more in Nuoro than in any other provincial city in Sardinia. Nuoro has, of course, gone modern as well, and there is a curious blend of the old and new. For example, you'll see a late-model car going down the same street as a horse-drawn cart with a man in regional dress. The best repository of Sardinian handcrafts and traditions is the **Museum of Costumes and Popular Traditions,** via A. Mereu 56, which is open from 9:30 a.m. to 1 p.m. daily except Monday (also in the afternoon from 3:30 to 7 p.m. except Monday and Thursday). Admission is free. The museum is housed in more than a dozen restored dwellings once inhabited by peasants.

I'd skip the unimpressive neoclassical duomo from the 19th century and head instead on an excursion to **Monte Ortobene,** six miles from town. From its summit at 3,135 feet, a panoramic vista unfolds.

Food and Lodging

Hotel Grazia Deledda, via Lamarmora 175, 08100 Nuoro (tel. 0784/31-257). Named after the most famous daughter of Nuoro, the Nobel Prize winner, this traditional hotel lies near the train station. Considered the best place to stay in town, it contains 72 comfortably furnished bedrooms, each with private bath, phone, and air conditioning. Singles cost 45,000 lire ($34.25) daily; doubles, 80,000 lire ($60.75). Full board is offered at 90,000 lire ($68.50) per person. On the premises is a bar and a restaurant known for good food.

Motel Agip, viale Trieste 44, 08100 Nuoro (tel. 0784/34-071), offers 51 simply furnished, functional, clean, and comfortable rooms in a neighborhood just outside the central commercial district of town. Singles cost 42,000 lire ($32) daily; doubles, 56,000 lire ($42.50). This nationwide motel chain is known for the quality of its food, attracting motorists throughout Italy. In Nuoro, the chef specializes in regional Sardinian dishes, among other selections, with meals costing 28,000 lire ($21.25). No food is served on Saturday night and Sunday, however.

DORGALI

Against a dolomite landscape, Dorgali lies in an area that has long fascinated archeologists interested in Nuragic ruins. This was an ancient and flourishing civilization, its peoples believed to have settled the island between 5000 and 1800 B.C. But much about them remains a mystery; however, they left about 7,000 megalithic towers and ruins on the island, and both their civilization and construction are unique to Sardinia. The Nuragic village of **Serra Orrios** lies about four miles from Dorgali on the Nuoro road, and can be explored during the day by interested parties.

Save some time for Dorgali itself, at least to go shopping in its local shops where you can purchase leatherwork and filigree. Some patterns are based on prehistoric Nuragic art. The town is also known for its wine and local costumes. On the slopes of Monte Bardia, it was once a Saracen colony, and many of its people, of farming stock, still pursue a living from agriculture.

For a six-mile trek east toward the sea, you can go through a tunnel under Monte Bardia, which opens onto a panoramic vista of the coast and the small port of Cala Gonone. From there to the port, you face a series of hairpin curves. If you survive, you'll arrive at **Cala Gonone,** where boats leave in summer on expeditions to underwater caves and grottoes, which stud the coastline. Departures are several times daily, the trip lasting 2½ hours and costing 8,000 lire ($6.10) per passenger. The most famous cave is the **Grotto del Bue Marino** (Cave of the Sea Oxen), which is the last refuge of the Mediterranean monk seal, a survior of the Ice Age. However, these rare animals come out mainly at night, so you may not spot one. Seeing the cave with its three miles of galleries is worth the trip. South of the grotto, and only reached by boat, is the best beach in the area, **Cala Luna,** with its white sands and clear waters shaded by immense grottoes.

Food and Lodging at Dorgali

Il Querceto, via Lamarmora 4, 08022 Dorgali (tel. 0784/96-509), is attractive not only to visitors wanting views of the mountain but also to visit Gala Gonone, five miles away. Surrounded by greenery, the hotel offers 20 large, well-furnished bedrooms, each with a private bath. In high season (July 1 to mid-September), singles cost 32,500 lire ($24.75) daily; doubles 45,000 lire ($34.25). Full board is offered for 70,000 lire ($53.25) per person. The hotel has a tennis court, an amusement park for children, private parking, a bar, and a restaurant known for its typical Sardinian dishes and good regional cooking. Lunch or dinner costs from 25,000 lire ($19), if you're just stopping by. Open April to October.

Food and Lodging at Cala Gonone

L'Oasi, Cala Gonone, 08022 Dorgali (tel. 0784/93-140), is the most desirable place to stay in the area, lying 5½ miles east of Dorgali, just previewed, at the departure point for boat trips to underwater caves and grottoes. This hotel, open Easter to September only, is known for its flower garden and terrace opening onto a view of the coast and the sea. It rents 27 well-furnished bedrooms, costing from 50,000 lire ($38) daily in a double. However, most guests book in here on full-board terms, ranging in price from 60,000 lire ($45.50) to 70,000 lire ($53.25) per person daily —very reasonable. The hotel serves good food, usually with plenty of fresh fish, depending on the catch of the day. Because of the beauty of the place, many prospective clients try to visit for a meal, but you must be a registered guest to enjoy its regional cuisine.

Hotel Miramare, piazza Giardini 12, Cala Gonone, 08022 Dorgali (tel. 0784/93-140). From their perch in the flowering garden, guests can admire the vista of the crashing waves. This airy and sunny hotel is raised above sea level, thanks to the rocky and sun-drenched terrain around it. The 37 simply furnished bedrooms offer a sea view, TV, phone, frigo-bar, and private bath. Full board, depending on the season, ranges from 70,000 lire ($53.25) to 80,000 lire ($60.75) per person daily. Nonresidents can drop in for well-prepared meals, costing 25,000 lire ($19) to 35,000 lire ($26.50). Open April to mid-October.

INDEX

Note: Individual sights and attractions beginning with common words such as **"Museum," "Church,"** or **"Piazza"** have been listed in this index under the next significant word (e.g., **"Piazza** Barberini" can be found under "Barberini, **Piazza").**

NOW, SAVE MONEY ON ALL YOUR TRAVELS!
Join Frommer's™ Dollarwise® Travel Club

Saving money while traveling is never a simple matter, which is why, over 29 years ago, the **Dollarwise Travel Club** was formed. Actually, the idea came from readers of the Frommer publications who felt that such an organization could bring financial benefits, continuing travel information, and a sense of community to value-conscious travelers all over the world.

In keeping with the money-saving concept, the annual membership fee is low—$18 (U.S. residents) or $20 U.S. (Canadian, Mexican, and other foreign residents)—and is immediately exceeded by the value of your benefits which include:

1. The latest edition of any TWO of the books listed on the following pages.
2. A copy of any one Frommer City Guide.
3. An annual subscription to an 8-page quarterly newspaper, *The Dollarwise Traveler*, which keeps you up-to-date on fast-breaking developments in good-value travel in all parts of the world—bringing you the kind of information you'd have to pay over $35 a year to obtain elsewhere. This consumer-conscious publication also includes the following columns:
    Hospitality Exchange—members all over the world who are willing to provide hospitality to other members as they pass through their home cities.
    Share-a-Trip—requests from members for travel companions who can share costs and help avoid the burdensome single supplement.
    Readers Ask . . . Readers Reply—travel questions from members to which other members reply with authentic firsthand information.
4. Your personal membership card, which entitles you to purchase through the club all Frommer publications for a third to a half off their regular retail prices during the term of your membership.

So why not join this hardy band of international Dollarwise travelers now and participate in its exchange of information and hospitality? Simply send $18 (U.S. residents) or $20 U.S. (Canadian, Mexican, and other foreign residents) along with your name and address to: Frommer's Dollarwise Travel Club, Inc., 15 Columbus Circle, New York, NY 10023. Remember to specify which *two* of the books in section (1) and which *one* in section (2) above you wish to receive in your initial package of member's benefits. Or tear out the next page, check off your choices, and send the page to us with your membership fee.

FROMMER BOOKS
PRENTICE HALL TRAVEL
15 COLUMBUS CIRCLE
NEW YORK, NY 10023

Date_____

Friends:
Please send me the books checked below:

FROMMER™ GUIDES

(Guides to sightseeing and tourist accommodations and facilities from budget to deluxe, with emphasis on the medium-priced.)

☐ Alaska	$14.95	☐ Japan & Hong Kong	$13.95
☐ Australia	$14.95	☐ Mid-Atlantic States	$14.95
☐ Austria & Hungary	$14.95	☐ New England	$14.95
☐ Belgium, Holland & Luxembourg	$14.95	☐ New York State	$14.95
☐ Bermuda & The Bahamas	$14.95	☐ Northwest	$14.95
☐ Brazil	$14.95	☐ Portugal, Madeira & the Azores	$13.95
☐ Canada	$14.95	☐ Skiing Europe	$14.95
☐ Caribbean	$14.95	☐ Skiing USA—East	$13.95
☐ Cruises (incl. Alaska, Carib, Mex, Hawaii,		☐ Skiing USA—West	$13.95
Panama, Canada & US)	$14.95	☐ South Pacific	$14.95
☐ California & Las Vegas	$14.95	☐ Southeast Asia	$14.95
☐ England & Scotland	$14.95	☐ Southern Atlantic States	$14.95
☐ Egypt	$13.95	☐ Southwest	$14.95
☐ Florida	$14.95	☐ Switzerland & Liechtenstein	$14.95
☐ France	$14.95	☐ Texas	$13.95
☐ Germany	$14.95	☐ USA	$15.95
☐ Italy	$14.95		

FROMMER $-A-DAY® GUIDES

(In-depth guides to sightseeing and low-cost tourist accommodations and facilities.)

☐ Europe on $40 a Day	$15.95	☐ New York on $60 a Day	$13.95
☐ Australia on $30 a Day	$12.95	☐ New Zealand on $40 a Day	$13.95
☐ Eastern Europe on $25 a Day	$13.95	☐ Scandinavia on $60 a Day	$13.95
☐ England on $50 a Day	$13.95	☐ Scotland & Wales on $40 a Day	$13.95
☐ Greece on $30 a Day	$13.95	☐ South America on $35 a Day	$13.95
☐ Hawaii on $60 a Day	$13.95	☐ Spain & Morocco on $40 a Day	$13.95
☐ India on $25 a Day	$12.95	☐ Turkey on $30 a Day	$13.95
☐ Ireland on $35 a Day	$13.95	☐ Washington, D.C. & Historic Va. on	
☐ Israel on $40 a Day	$13.95	$40 a Day	$13.95
☐ Mexico on $35 a Day	$13.95		

FROMMER TOURING GUIDES

(Color illustrated guides that include walking tours, cultural & historic sites, and other vital travel information.)

☐ Australia	$9.95	☐ Paris	$8.95
☐ Egypt	$8.95	☐ Scotland	$9.95
☐ Florence	$8.95	☐ Thailand	$9.95
☐ London	$8.95	☐ Venice	$8.95

TURN PAGE FOR ADDITONAL BOOKS AND ORDER FORM.

A

FROMMER CITY GUIDES

(Pocket-size guides to sightseeing and tourist accommodations and facilities in all price ranges.)

☐ Amsterdam/Holland	.$5.95	☐ Minneapolis/St. Paul	.$5.95
☐ Athens	.$5.95	☐ Montréal/Québec City	.$5.95
☐ Atlantic City/Cape May	.$5.95	☐ New Orleans	.$5.95
☐ Belgium	.$5.95	☐ New York	.$5.95
☐ Boston	.$5.95	☐ Orlando/Disney World/EPCOT	.$5.95
☐ Cancún/Cozumel/Yucatán	.$5.95	☐ Paris	.$5.95
☐ Chicago	.$5.95	☐ Philadelphia	.$5.95
☐ Dublin/Ireland	.$5.95	☐ Rio	.$5.95
☐ Hawaii	.$5.95	☐ Rome	.$5.95
☐ Las Vegas	.$5.95	☐ San Francisco	.$5.95
☐ Lisbon/Madrid/Costa del Sol	.$5.95	☐ Santa Fe/Taos/Albuquerque	.$5.95
☐ London	.$5.95	☐ Sydney	.$5.95
☐ Los Angeles	.$5.95	☐ Washington, D.C.	.$5.95
☐ Mexico City/Acapulco	.$5.95		

SPECIAL EDITIONS

☐ A Shopper's Guide to the Caribbean	.$12.95	☐ Manhattan's Outdoor Sculpture	.$15.95
☐ Beat the High Cost of Travel	.$6.95	☐ Motorist's Phrase Book (Fr/Ger/Sp)	.$4.95
☐ Bed & Breakfast—N. America	.$11.95	☐ Paris Rendez-Vous	.$10.95
☐ California with Kids	.$14.95	☐ Swap and Go (Home Exchanging)	.$10.95
☐ Caribbean Hideaways	.$14.95	☐ The Candy Apple (NY with Kids)	.$12.95
☐ Guide to Honeymoon Destinations		☐ Travel Diary and Record Book	.$5.95
(US, Canada, Mexico & Carib)	.$12.95		

☐ Where to Stay USA (Lodging from $3 to $30 a night) $10.95

☐ Marilyn Wood's Wonderful Weekends (NY, Conn, Mass, RI, Vt, NH, NJ, Del,Pa) $11.95

☐ The New World of Travel (Annual sourcebook by Arthur Frommer previewing: new travel trends, new modes of travel, and the latest cost-cutting strategies for savvy travelers.) $14.95

SERIOUS SHOPPER'S GUIDES

(Illustrated guides listing hundreds of stores, conveniently organized alphabetically by category.)

☐ Italy	.$15.95	☐ Los Angeles	.$14.95
☐ London	.$15.95	☐ Paris	.$15.95

GAULT MILLAU

(The only guides that distinguish the truly superlative from the merely overrated.)

☐ The Best of Chicago	.$15.95	☐ The Best of Los Angeles	.$14.95
☐ The Best of France	.$16.95	☐ The Best of New England	.$15.95
☐ The Best of Hong Kong	.$16.95	☐ The Best of New York	.$14.95
☐ The Best of Italy	.$16.95	☐ The Best of San Francisco	.$14.95

☐ The Best of Washington, D.C. $14.95

ORDER NOW!

In U.S. include $2 shipping UPS for 1st book; $1 ea. add'l book. Outside U.S. $3 and $1, respectively.

Allow four to six weeks for delivery in U.S., longer outside U.S.

Enclosed is my check or money order for $_____

NAME _____

ADDRESS _____

CITY _____ STATE _____ ZIP _____

A